The Epic of
Latin America

The Epic of
Latin America

FOURTH EDITION

JOHN A. CROW

University of California Press, Berkeley, Los Angeles, London

UNIVERSITY OF CALIFORNIA PRESS
BERKELEY AND LOS ANGELES, CALIFORNIA
UNIVERSITY OF CALIFORNIA PRESS, LTD.
LONDON, ENGLAND
COPYRIGHT © 1946, 1971, 1980, 1992 BY JOHN A. CROW
PRINTED IN THE UNITED STATES OF AMERICA

4   5   6   7   8   9

Library of Congress Cataloging-in-Publication Data

Crow, John Armstrong
The epic of Latin America / John A. Crow
4th ed., expanded and updated.
p   cm.
Includes bibliographical references and index.
ISBN 0-520-078683 (cloth: alk. paper)
ISBN 0-520-077237 (pbk.: alk. paper)
1. Latin America—History.   I. Title.
F1410.C8   1992

980—dc20   91-34446
                                                CIP

TO MY FATHER'S BROTHER, AND MY FRIEND,

Randolph Fairfax Crow

Contents

Preface to the Fourth Edition

This revised and updated edition of *The Epic of Latin America* covers the history of that area from the earliest beginnings. Important recent events that have altered the perspective in our hemisphere are given particular attention. Long-standing inequities south of the border point to a coming explosion in Latin America, but few people in the United States are aware of this, and there is a strong feeling in the southern republics that our government, with one eye across the Atlantic, and the other across the Pacific, has come to regard Latin America merely as its troublesome back yard. Millions of dollars in U.S. aid sent to this region have been used to entrench military establishments and political bureaucrats while economies and hopes for the future deteriorated at a frightening pace.

During the past decade U.S. ventures in Central America have aroused widespread resentment seriously damaging our national image, and relations between the two Americas are now at a crucial turning point. The problems of the present will not be solved by applying equations that might have worked fifteen or twenty years ago. Given impetus by the upheavals that have already taken place in Europe, radical changes are being demanded in Latin America, and our hemisphere is now sitting on a time bomb of threatening proportions. If those who hold power make peaceful revolution impossible, violent revolution will become inevitable.

The date of this book's fourth edition, 1992, marks the culmination of five centuries of Latin American history. The discovery of America in 1492 was one of the most pivotal events in the history of mankind. Within a single generation the entire focus of man's thinking was changed as millions of people and millions of square miles of new territories were added to the Western World. Human beings will not again experience such an exciting penetration of the unknown until that problematic day when cosmonauts traverse the galaxies and set foot on another inhabited planet.

The early years of conquest and consolidation in Latin America were filled with marvelous exploits, epic in scope. Since then this region has gone through three centuries of colonial rule followed by two centuries of struggling nationalism. These five hundred years in the history of our neighbors were never closely followed in the United States, and to the people of this country Latin American countries became a big blur, all alike, and all dominated by unfriendly, undemocratic, and unprogressive governments. Recent events have done little to change this point of view, and conditions today, unsettled everywhere, call urgently for understanding and attention.

Latin America represents a potential market of more than half a billion people. The population of Brazil alone equals that of the United Kingdom, France, and Italy combined. Our nearest neighbor, Mexico, now has a population approaching one hundred million, and its phenomenal growth continues unabated. Spanish speaking persons in the United States total more than twenty million, and the number is increasing rapidly every year. The nations of Latin America share this hemisphere with us, and their problems are inescapably our problems as well. We are bound together not only by geography but by a common destiny and a common dream.

Latin America today finds itself on the brink of bankruptcy and revolution. The promising growth of ten years ago has gone into a sharp decline: There is extensive and galloping inflation; an enormous foreign debt of more than 400 billion dollars (that will never be repaid) hangs like a deadweight over staggering economies; an explosive population growth has produced added millions for whom there are no jobs and insufficient food. Political instability everywhere obstructs the path of progress; there is a rapidly expanding underground economy of vast proportions; a strong populist movement with leftist leanings presses for drastic social and political reform; big state capitalism is deliberately being replaced by private enterprise; an oppressive bureaucracy thrives both in government and in business. Many countries have a gigantic drug problem; a deeply rooted military establishment holds the key to political power in most republics; and an unhealthy urban growth has sapped the energy of the thinly populated and impoverished countryside.

The cultural achievements of the Latin American nations have always been ahead of their erratic political and economic development. This century has seen a burgeoning of the arts, especially in literature, with its five Nobel Laureates. Also, both music and painting have produced many internationally acclaimed artists. These cultural figures are well known and highly regarded in the United States. There is throughout Latin America, however, a widespread envy and distrust of the United States. This is coupled with a general unwillingness on the part of their own ruling class to guarantee basic human rights and economic justice to the masses. These masses look with longing and hope to the United States as the land of promise.

It will be no easy task for the two Americas to work out an ongoing and productive partnership. The sad fact is that we do not really know one another. I hope that *The Epic of Latin America* may help all Americans to understand better our southern neighbors and the lands they occupy, one of the most important, most misunderstood, and most neglected regions of the world. The future of this hemisphere, now hanging in a precarious imbalance, depends on cooperation, understanding, and mutual respect.

Los Angeles, 1992   John A. Crow

Prologue

By that dark miracle of fate or chance which sometimes alters the destiny of men and of nations, one year in the history of the Iberian Peninsula and of the world saw the fulfillment of events and promises which eight centuries had held in the shaping. The year was 1492. The events and promises were manifold. In 1492 Columbus, searching for the spice lands of the East, dropped anchor off one of the islands of the Antilles and spread before Europe America's virgin wealth. In 1492 Ferdinand and Isabella, after a ten-year siege of Moorish Granada, accepted the surrender of the city and saw King Boabdil "heave the last sigh of the Moor" and depart weeping from the land his people had so long considered theirs. In 1492, after the fires of the Inquisition had already consumed thousands of suspected Jews, the race was expelled in a body from the territory of Spain. In 1492 Antonio de Nebrija, a Spanish writer and scholar, published the first grammar of a Romance tongue, and in his introduction pointed out that language was the ideal weapon of empire. In 1492 a Spanish pope was appointed to occupy the Holy See at Rome. New World horizon, reconquest of old dominion, new "purity" of race, flowering of the national cultures, supremacy of the national religion—such was the significance of 1492 in the history of the Iberian Peninsula.

In both Portugal and Spain the individual rose to exalted heights. It has been said that during the Middle Ages the universe was centered on God, while during the Renaissance it became centered on man. But in Iberia, where the Renaissance was but a projection and a prolongation of the Middle Ages, the axis was inseparably "God and man." The individual who had been submerged in the mass until 1492 now became a symbol of the mass, and as a spark carries flame he carried the mass spirit with him wherever he went, into whatever he did, until the fires he had kindled burned deep in the wilderness of the New World he had set out to conquer and to save; and some of them are burning yet.

When Spain and Portugal came to the New World they brought with them an entirely new fabric of life which was imposed on a great raw continent. New social, economic, cultural, and religious values were transplanted intact and established amidst indigenous semi-civilization or carried into the wilderness. Neither the conquest, nor the colonial regimes following it, nor the motivating forces which brought them about can be understood without some knowledge of what Iberian civilization itself had come to be and why.

As Europe emerged from the chaos and barbarism of the Dark Ages, fifth to eleventh centuries, a new Christian civilization and art were taking shape, dominated by the Church of Rome. With the dawn of the eleventh century, the wealth and power of monastic orders began to express themselves in the building of great abbey-churches and monasteries as well as in the copying of manuscripts and in the study and teaching of the narrow scholasticism of the Church. Architecture which had been Romanesque in character—crude, massive, and powerful—now became in the Gothic, lofty, light, refined in detail, with delicate ribbed vaults, pointed arches, floral carvings, and stained-glass windows. Religion was centered again on the God of Beauty. Europe's magnificent Gothic cathedrals, sometimes two or three centuries in the building, were the cultural mass expression of the late Middle Ages. With the advent of the Renaissance and the revival of enthusiasm for classical and pagan Greece and Rome, a cleavage sprang up in many of the countries in Europe. But in Spain and Portugal this did not occur. In these two countries the Renaissance and the Middle Ages were fused. Their peoples found nothing incompatible between the Old and the New, and under their daily mead of warfare against the Moslems there was no time for the conflicts of art.

War and religion were the controlling forces of the medieval Christian world; the feudal regime and the Roman Church were the means of expression. In Spain and Portugal, where Europe's only large religious minority (the Moors) then existed, these two medieval forces were blended into one which was *religious war*.

During the Middle Ages obedience to the universal authority of the Church had been the rule of life, but the pagan spirit of the Renaissance glorified the individual, and the individual became absolute. Spain and Portugal found a way to fuse these feelings also. While other countries were content to establish themselves under Protestant or mixed Catholic and Protestant regimes which would grow toward religious liberalism, the Iberian countries created the Church-State type of authoritarian absolutism in which government and religious doctrine became inseparable.[1] Other countries made of religion a national expression, but Spain and Portugal maintained unbroken their belief in the holy internationalism of the Catholic Church. This idea was carried to the New World in the last great crusade. Add to this religious conception of the Middle Ages the trade spirit and lust for gold and capital of a later date, and the Hispanic colonization of America begins to assume those epic proportions of body, mind, and spirit which swept everything, or nearly everything, before it.

At no other time in their history could Spain and Portugal have achieved success on such a grand world-wide scale. In the tenth century or in the twentieth they would have been equally impotent, equally lacking in the drive and vision which must precede all great revolutionary achievements. But at the beginning of the sixteenth century, which marked the tag end of the Middle Ages and opened the door leading to the modern era, they alone of all nations stood on the threshold ready to undertake the impossible. They were not the most populous countries of Europe, nor the wealthiest, nor the most powerful, but they had developed to the highest peak their will to victory and to expansion. After eight centuries of battling for the faith, it is little wonder that, when the final triumph came, a halt could not be called at the borders of the peninsula.

Iberian civilization has never been characterized by orderly growth or progress, but has always expressed itself best in intermittent spiritual convulsions sandwiched in between long periods of relative inactivity. The greatest convulsion in the history of the world was the discovery of America and the consequent fight against every obstacle of nature and man to secure this conquest. Every nation has its day in the sun, and when that day corresponds with a period of unlimited opportunity, the main stream of history lunges forward with the speed of a catapult. Spain and Portugal knew how to take advantage of that moment.

When these two nations came to America they gave of themselves completely. Their practice of racial fusion, their rigorous persecution of all minority thinking, their transcendent ability as warriors, navigators, and explorers, alongside their miserable records as statesmen and economists, all of these things they brought to the New World. With cross, sword, and racial amalgamation, they forced them upon a not too readily receptive continent inhabited by millions of primitive Indians. Their conquest of America was but a parallel and prolongation of their conquest of the Moors. Every institution and every aspect of the national psychology developed during the long Moorish wars later became a part of their colonial policy.

The glorification of the soldier led to incipient militarisms. The propagation and defense of the faith meant national intolerance of minority attitudes of whatever nature. Carried over into political and social thinking, this was bound to result in the general acceptance of authoritarian rule. The weakening of economic institutions, the fusion of Church and State, the exaltation of personal rule and the disrespect for impersonal law, the disdain which every conquering soldier feels for manual labor, the psychology of the aristocrat and the exploiter, these characteristics of Latin-

American life have their roots deep in the Iberian past, and that past must be made clear before we proceed farther with our history.

Portugal reached her maturity before Spain, and before Spain she became a great maritime nation. By 1250 the last Moors had been thrown from her soil and by 1418 her navigators had reached out into the dark Atlantic and colonized Madeira. By the middle of the century she had occupied the Azores and her sea captains were wending their way southward along the African coast. With the discovery of America in 1492, Spain got the jump on her smaller neighbor and the tables were reversed. Portugal did not give up, and six years later her most intrepid explorer, Vasco da Gama, sailed all the way around Africa and found the long-sought sea route to India and the Spice Islands of the East. For a while both countries of the peninsula rode together on the crest of their maritime prosperity, then Portugal began to lose distance. Her smaller size and smaller resources were beginning to tell.

It is no easy task to bring out the similarities and differences between Spain and Portugal. They were born of the same Mother Iberia, were reared in the same house, and shared the same violent destiny. Rome overcame them both and added Hispania to her empire. The Moors invaded them both and for several centuries her caliphs held sway on the peninsula. Portugal first found strength to push out the invader; in 1140 she became an independent nation. But Portugal did not fight the Moslem alone; located as she was on the southwestern extremity of the European continent, she became a stopping-off place for crusaders from all northern Europe on their way to Jerusalem. In 1147 thirteen thousand of them from Flanders, Lorraine, Aquitaine, and England dropped the anchors of their two hundred ships in Portuguese waters and joined their banners with hers, inflicting a disastrous defeat on the Moors and recapturing Lisbon for the Portuguese. Then for four centuries Portugal stood alone with her glory. Gradually she pushed her dominion southward into Africa and grew rich with its commerce. Portuguese ships took down holds full of red caps, hawks' bells, beads, and other cheap jewelry, and "deckloads of horses for which the native chiefs paid extravagant prices."[2] Many were the imports which her captains brought back with them, bags of pepper, elephant tusks, gold dust, and Negro slaves. Lisbon became the slave-trading center of western Europe. Already cosmopolitan, she now became the crossroads of the continent. All the Mediterranean languages were heard in her streets, and men from every seagoing nation crowded her ships and quays.

The two heroes of this great Portuguese expansion were King John I and his son Prince Henry the Navigator. John the Great, as he was called, was the first king of the house of Aviz under which Portugal for two hundred years enjoyed the highest prosperity and power, and his own reign,

1385–1433, was one of the most glorious in Portuguese history. He consolidated the independence of his country by defeating the Spaniards; married the daughter of John of Gaunt, and thus commenced the long friendship between Portugal and England; took the strategic North African port of Ceuta from the Moors; reformed the administration of his kingdom; and fostered the maritime zeal of his many sons, Prince Henry in particular (1394–1460).

After fighting with extraordinary heroism at Ceuta, Prince Henry withdrew from the Portuguese court and established himself at Sagres, the extreme point of land in Europe facing southwest into the great sea of darkness. Here he constructed an observatory and school for navigation and a naval arsenal (1416) which served as a base for further explorations. He was Grand Master of the Portuguese Order of Christ, and most of the money for his undertakings came from his religious tithes. With "the garb of a monk and the soul of a sailor," Prince Henry lived in a tower of his observatory surrounded by charts and instruments high above "the wind-blown cliffs of Sagres." Here he took up his ceaseless vigil, hoping someday to conquer the great Atlantic into which he stared from paneless windows of intricate Moorish design, while into his face blew the cold, salty winds of unknown distances.[3]

Navigation was not easy in those days, for only the crudest instruments had been devised. Among these the magnetic compass borrowed from the Vikings was the most important. There was also a wooden astrolabe which served as a clumsy makeshift for the sextant in calculating latitude. The problem of longitude was not yet solved. A rope was flung astern to indicate the ship's leeway. There was no log to measure a day's run, nor any chronometer. The ship's progress was estimated by several modes of dead reckoning. One way, in a calm sea, was to spit over the bow and calculate the rate by timing its speed in passing this comparatively fixed point. Sailing on the dark waters was at best no job to be envied, and for especially dangerous trips peasants who knew little or nothing about manning a ship were sometimes pressed into service. The story goes that some were so ignorant they didn't know left hand from right, let alone larboard and starboard. One captain devised the scheme of tying a huge bunch of onions on one side of the ship and a bunch of garlic on the other. The pilot would then shout to the helmsman an unmistakable "Turn toward the onions!" or "Swing toward the garlic!"

Every year from his base at Sagres, Prince Henry sent out two or three caravels, and in 1418 one of his navigators rediscovered the Madeira Islands and added them to the Portuguese dominions. After that every year, for twelve years, his ships returned or were lost on the seas. Sea captains and sailors began to dodge the prince and came to dread the very mention of desolate Sagres. Prince Henry received both their failures and their fears with patient good grace and rewarded those who had served him well.

Finally, in 1432, one expedition discovered the Azores, where no human being had ever lived before; and in 1434 another captain sailed southward beyond Cape Bojador on the great African bulge. Eight years later a slave-trading post was established on the Guinea coast even farther to the south, and ships now began to return with lucrative cargoes of gold and Negro slaves. Portugal was at last finding the profit of listening to a man of vision. Wealth poured into her coffers, and Guinea became known as the Gold Coast of Africa. The Portuguese had no intention of letting other European nations in on their private preserve and maintained the greatest secrecy about their voyages, the source of their wealth, and the manner in which it was obtained. Portugal realized that she was a small country and that this was the only sure way of protecting herself from the rapacious sea hawks of her larger rivals. Every foreign ship caught in these north-western African waters was at once sent to the bottom.

In 1488—twenty-eight years after Prince Henry's death—Bartholomew Dias rounded the Cape of Good Hope. Following his path in 1498, Vasco da Gama found the sea route to India and ushered in the golden age of Portuguese empire.

Why was it considered so important to find this water route to the Spice Islands of the Indies? Prince Henry spent his life in an effort to reach them; Columbus died believing he had found them; Vasco da Gama knew beyond question that his twenty-three-thousand-eight-hundred-mile, two-year trip had taken him to India and back. The answer is simple. Spices and silks were the greatest luxuries in Europe at that time. In England a pound of cloves was worth two cows. All viands of the well to do were touched up with some favorite flavor. Sugar had not yet come to occupy its place at the head of the list, and spices afforded the only break in the monotonous European winter diet of coarse bread and imperfectly preserved meats. The phrase, "it has no spice," became indicative of lowly living, and with the lack of refrigeration, spices were also widely used as preservatives. Pepper, ginger root, cloves, nutmeg, and cinnamon bark were all costly, rare items which had to be imported, and the demand was always greater than the supply. Before Vasco da Gama found the water route to India these commodities were purchased by Italian merchants from Mohammedan traders, and both groups exacted the last ounce of profit. The precious cargoes were first shipped from India to the Gulf of Suez, thence on a ten-day trip overland to Cairo by camel caravan, next from Cairo to Rosetta down the Nile, and finally to Alexandria. Here a galley from Venice or Genoa would pick them up and transport them to Europe to be sold. After all these exchanges, tolls, and voyages, it is little wonder that prices were exorbitant. Yet so addicted had become the European palate, that spices not only paid for gold cuspidors used by the betel chewers of Calcutta but helped to build the palaces and to paint the pictures which still make Italy the mother of art.

When the first Portuguese set foot in Calcutta, a native indignantly exclaimed, "The hell with you! What brought you here?" And Gama's man retorted with equal vigor: "Christianity and spices!" It was this wealth plus the flicker of the last crusade which inspired Portugal to become mistress of the Eastern Sea. When the news of Gama's discovery reached Venice a chronicler wrote: "The whole city felt it greatly and remained stupefied, and the wisest held it as the worst news that had ever arrived."[3]

Once and for all Gama had killed the wealth for Venice, Genoa, Milan, and Egypt and for all the Mohammedan entrepreneurs. He rang up the curtain on a new trade which was to radiate from Lisbon, Cádiz, Seville, and finally from Bristol, Antwerp, and Amsterdam. The wealth which had fostered science and art in the Italian city-states shifted to Portugal, the Netherlands, France, Spain, and England, whose people created new art forms and new ideals of which America is the inheritor.[3]

The year 1474 marks the beginning of our story across Portugal's eastern border, for in that year Castile and Aragon were united and the nation we know as Spain was born. Her period in the embryo had come close to eight centuries. When the Moslems invaded the peninsula in 711, they overwhelmed all of it except a small corner in the northwest. From this refuge in the province of Asturias the reconquest of Iberian territory for Spain and Portugal and for the Holy Catholic Church began. For more than seven hundred years it had proceeded in long, separated waves across the peninsula. Along the border lay the frontiers of Christendom; back of them were the thinly organized, mutually distrustful, many-times subdivided petty kingdoms of the Cross. Two feelings alone spread over this weak fabric the invisible thread of unity which later made the Spanish nation: (1) a love of the land once theirs and now lost to the invader, which heightened to fever pitch the nationalistic urge for expansion; (2) a belief in their Church as the true and only religion, and a faith in their arms as the weapon of God's wrath turned against the foul infidel under its shadow. Despite all outward and visible signs of division these intangibles of nationhood became stronger with each passing century.

Spanish character was fashioned anew under the long arm of this crusade. The Church promised heaven for those who fell in battle, and the spoils of war always enriched the victorious soldier. Men came to die and live for this ideal of the "Christian Soldier." Who would soil his hands with menial labor when marching off to war offered a greater and far nobler reward? Individual prowess and faith became keystones of the new Spanish nation.

Spain emerged slowly from the Middle Ages, and it was not until 1469 that the promise of final victory appeared. Isabella, daughter of John II, whose reign had ushered Castile under the "Portico of the Renaissance," looked over the profligate degeneracy of her country and shuddered. Even among the clergy were many who had absorbed some of the Moorish sensuality and were living in open concubinage. The Castilian court was beset with dissension, greed, and rivalries which threatened to overwhelm the kingdom. Eight centuries of reconquest and growing strength which had united one after the other of several petty kingdoms under the Castilian monarch were on the verge of a collapse. Within her borders Isabella saw no hope of regeneration, and when she turned her blue eyes with their faraway stare to the east, they came to rest on the figure of Ferdinand, then Prince of Aragon, second in importance only to Castile itself. Under the shadow of profligacy and with the same keen will which characterized all her actions, Isabella undertook to marry Ferdinand and to strengthen her degenerating kingdom. At the time he was seventeen and she was only sixteen. Ferdinand's odyssey to meet his bride is highly col-ored in Spanish tradition. Disguised as a shepherd and accompanied by two or three trusted friends, he traveled to Valladolid, where Isabella awaited him. There they discussed the purpose of their union: together they would pursue the war against the Moslem; together as co-rulers—he supreme in Aragon, she in Castile—they would reign over the new Spanish nation. The marriage took place in 1469; five years later Castile and Aragon were formally welded into a single nation with the Catholic sovereigns in dual control. With the passage of time this co-power became more and more centralized, and after Isabella's death it fell completely into the hands of Ferdinand.

The struggle for union was not the only problem besetting the Spanish sovereigns. Darkly outlined on the horizon rose the power of the nobles, the power of the commons, and the power of the Church. How were these to be subordinated to the authority of the throne? Which could be utilized as the natural allies of royalty and which were the enemies? Under the Spanish system the parliament, called the Cortes, was composed of nobles and representatives from the towns. Noblemen were exempt from taxation and were characteristically taken up with feuds and grievances among themselves which they tried to settle by force of arms. As a consequence they were little inclined to participate fully in parliamentary action. They were powerful, but their strength was divided; and this, added to their natural disinclination to associate with commoners or to discuss politics with a sovereign to whom they professed a reluctant loyalty, made possible their subordination to the princely authority. Division and subtle piece-meal attacks upon their privileges eventually turned them into mere shadows around the throne.

In the towns or municipalities, on the other hand, there had grown up a tradition of representative government which was the natural enemy of the nobleman. Certain democratic rights had been won during the wars against the Moors when each town was a fortress and every man had to bear arms. In the frontier territory, where towns were frequently besieged and isolated, strong measures of self-government and self-dependence were necessities of life. By the same token the inhabitants of many of these towns, while still under the heavy yoke of a seignorial regime, came to look on the sovereign as their natural ally and protector. Economically their greatest compensation was communal ownership or utilization of certain near-by lands, consisting of agricultural terrain, woodland, pasture, and the uncultivated public *ejido*, used for a variety of purposes. These lands made up the village commons and were inalienable. Approximately 12,500 towns and villages participated in this form of public ownership which saved them from landless serfdom. Although their economic situation was sometimes miserable, the inhabitants of these towns had achieved a feeling of free men and of democracy unknown anywhere else in the world at that time outside of England. Occasionally, with the aid of the Church and the Crown, they were able to organize a real war against the nobles. Personal servitude disappeared from Spain and England long before it had in the rest of Europe, but personal or civil liberty reached the peninsula much later.[4]

Eleven years after the marriage of Ferdinand and Isabella some coordination of elements favorable to the throne was accomplished in the Cortes of Toledo (1480). The Catholic sovereigns "put the nobles out of the council and substituted lawyers educated in the Romanist conception of law, favorable to the princely authority, and anxious to curb the power of the undisciplined aristocracy. Henceforth the council, once composed of military leaders and nobles, became civil and bourgeois, active and youthful." A Spanish proverb states the new focus of Iberian life: "Who loses the morning, loses the afternoon; who loses youthfulness, loses life."[4]

Thus strengthened and rejuvenated, the Spanish state began the war of annihilation against the infidel which constituted the greatest minority of opposition in its midst. Already pushed far to the south, the Moors still occupied the fertile kingdom of Granada, rich out of all proportion to its size. The conquest of this land was to be no futile crusade to rescue Jerusalem from the Saracen; it was the final battle to make Europe and Spanish soil forever safe for the religion of Christ. It represented the culmination of a struggle which had been going on for eight long and inconclusive centuries. It was a war for "living room" as well as a war for the faith, for so long as the vine-clad hills and valleys of Granada belonged to the Moors, Spanish hegemony could not grow unchallenged. It was the embodiment of that aspiration toward imperium with its two poles of spiritual and physical strength so often glorified in the literature of the Renaissance. It was the struggle of emerging nationalism to end once and for all the checkered and petty politics of the Middle Ages. It was, above all, a psychological war which would focus upon the enemy the attention of a hitherto divided and mutually distrustful nobility and give common purpose to an otherwise disunited people. While this war was being waged against the Moors absolute unity on the home front was essential. Whatever opposition, division, dissatisfaction, or criticism still survived must be overcome or stifled. And it was on this point that Spain under Ferdinand and Isabella made the same foul decision as Germany under Hitler. She began officially to persecute her minority groups, particularly the Jews, and established the Inquisition for the specific purpose of rooting out all non-conformists.

This was not a sudden decision by any means, nor was it the first time that the Inquisition had blackened the pages of history. The tribunal was organized in 1233 under Pope Gregory IX and was active in ferreting out the heresies of the Albigenses in southern France and those of the Waldensians in northern Italy. It was also adopted by England and Germany and entered Aragon in 1242. But the "iniquitous Spanish Inquisition" did not begin until Isabella asked Pope Sixtus IV to permit its introduction into Castile. The Pontiff issued a bull of authorization in 1478; in 1480 four inquisitors were appointed. In 1481 they began work in earnest with an edict "requiring all persons to aid in apprehending and accusing all such as they might know or suspect to be guilty of heresy."[5] In that same year an estimated two thousand persons were burned alive by the Holy Tribunal. In 1483 Tomás de Torquemada, whose nefarious name has gone down in history, was appointed Inquisitor General in Castile and Aragon.

Spain had not always been an intolerant country. Under the Visigoths, Moors, and throughout most of the Middle Ages, Spanish Jews had been an accepted and integral part of the national life. Alfonso the Wise and many other famous kings surrounded themselves with Jewish scholars. Hebrew was taught in the universities. Jewish literature and philosophy flourished as never before in history, reaching a peak with Moses ben Maimonides of Córdoba in the twelfth century. But as the national character became sharpened in its reconquest for the faith, tolerance gave way to bigotry and bigotry to fanaticism and persecution. Under Henry II Jews were prohibited from giving their children Christian names, and under Isabella's father, John II, they were prohibited from associating with Christians and from following certain professions. Their residence was restricted to certain districts of cities; they were not allowed to wear luxurious or showy clothes, and were frequently forced to bear a distinguishing emblem on their garments. These were but official recognitions of a popular feeling; the real virus ran deep in the blood. As early as 1391 popular sentiment against the Jew, encouraged by those who owed them money and fanned by many fanatical priests, broke into the' open with violent mass assaults on Jewish homes in Aragon and Castile. Confronted with conversion or annihilation, Jews accepted Christianity in droves. In later years many distinguished converts rose to high fortune, married into noble families, occupied positions of trust and prominence, and even achieved distinction within the Church itself. But these "new Christians" were allowed only a brief respite, for by the time Ferdinand and Isabella got their policy of government well established, certain elements of the popular fancy were again hot on the heels of scandalous "apostates returning to wallow in the ancient mire of Judaism." Even their conversion had not been accepted. Guilds refused to teach their crafts to converts, and several universities refused to grant them degrees. Jewish blood, no matter how diluted, began to be considered a stigma.

Ferdinand, the realist, was easy to convince. He looked with covetous eyes on Jewish wealth which the inquisitors would confiscate. Isabella, for many years loath to take any such drastic action, was finally forced to it by the importunities of her husband and of the priests in whom she most trusted, particularly Torquemada, her private confessor.

There were many in Spain who did not take the Inquisition without protest. At first popular opposition to the Holy Tribunal was as strong as support of it. Many clerics condemned inquisitorial abuses and defended the converted Moor or Jew. Pope Paul III in 1535 and 1537 voiced a similar feeling. In both Castile and Aragon there were untold thousands of ordinary citizens who resisted co-operation. After Isabella's death the Cortes of Castile made a strong official protest. All this was too little or too late, and so came to no avail. It was the brave voice of Spanish minorities shouting in the wilderness, for while opposition to the new authority was scattered and ineffectual, support of it was concentrated and powerful. After eighteen years under Torquemada's efficient ministry the Spanish Inquisition had become an essential instrument of state policy.

The power of the throne was not lessened but extended by the establishment of this Holy Office. Through it centralized authority, which reached its peak under Philip II in the latter half of the sixteenth century, pressed into the very thoughts of the Spanish mind, molding it to a pattern. Spanish sovereigns would brook no interference from the Pontiff which might dilute their own religious authority. Even mild Isabella challenged Pope Sixtus in order to strengthen her control over the church offices. In 1482, after the Pontiff had unwisely lifted his own nephew over the Queen's choice for a Spanish bishopric, the Catholic Sovereigns promptly broke off relations with the Holy See, withdrew all their subjects from the papal dominions, and threatened to call a general European council to inquire into the state of the Church's health, which was admittedly none too savory at that time. The Pope, apprehensive at this prospect, countered with the conciliatory offer of affirming all nominations of the sovereigns to the higher church offices in Castile. Prescott in his *Ferdinand and Isabella* states that the papal mission which was sent to Spain was promptly thrown out of the country. Only after the envoy offered to come alone, waiving all immunities, did the Spanish sovereigns finally consent to receive him.

With this character, then, Spain emerged from the Middle Ages into her new birth as a modern state. The modernity was merely a political illusion, for it embraced only the infancy of progress and not the growth. Spanish society remained feudalistic to the core and the rest of the edifice was raised on that feudal frame. Yet its colors were nationalistic, totalitarian, and later imperialistic to an extent not conceived of since the days of the Roman Empire. To this was added the zeal of religion which spread its imprint over every characteristic of the Spanish state.

Why did Spain alone among modern nations embody most completely these attributes of authoritarian rule? It was because she alone found a way to fuse within herself the Catholic unity of the Middle Ages with the social, economic, and political unity of the Renaissance. In Spain there was no cleavage between the old and the new. Both were found compatible and were fused into one. The Gothic architecture of the Middle Ages was blended with elements of the new style of the Renaissance in the Spanish plateresque. Among the literatures of western Europe that of Spain was the first to become national and realistic, the last to become romantic. In Spain appeared the first grammar of a Romance language, and in Spain there never arose a single Protestant church.

The symbol of Ferdinand of Aragon, epitome of the soldier's strength, was wedded to that of Isabella of Castile, who embodied the whole nation's faith. Under this fusion there was no loophole of weakness save a growing resistance to change which later became the Spaniards' Achilles' heel.

When Isabella died, in 1504, Ferdinand became regent for their daughter Juana in the kingdom of Castile. He added Navarre to his realm and completed the unification of Spain. Then for twelve more years he ruled alone, the most powerful king in Christendom; always engaged in some enterprise, always dividing and deceiving his enemies, always successful in conquest. He was the embodiment of the new Spanish Church-State and an example before his people. It is little wonder that Machiavelli should have chosen him as the prototype of what the ideal prince should be:

"We have in our own day Ferdinand, King of Aragon, at present King of Spain. He may almost be termed a new prince, because from a weak king he has become for fame and glory the first king in Christendom, and if you regard his actions you will find them all very great and some of them extraordinary. At the beginning of his reign he assailed Granada, and that enterprise was the foundation of his state. At first he did it leisurely and without fear of being interfered with; he kept the minds of the barons of Castile occupied in this enterprise, so that thinking only of that war they did not think of making innovations, and he thus acquired reputation and power over them without their being aware of it. He was able with the money of the Church and the people to maintain his armies, and by that long war lay the foundation of his military power, which afterwards has made him famous. Besides this, to be able to undertake greater enterprises, and always under the pretext of religion, he had recourse to a pious cruelty, driving out the Moors from his kingdom and despoiling them. No more admirable or rare example can be found. He also attacked under the same pretext Africa, undertook his Italian enterprise, and has lately attacked France; so that he has continually contrived great things, which have kept his subjects' minds uncertain and astonished, and occupied in watching their result.

"And these actions have arisen one out of the other, so that they have left no time for men to settle down and act against him."[6]

Had Machiavelli lived to see the heyday of Charles V and Philip II in the sixteenth century he would probably have risen to heights of admiration verging on frenzy.

In both Spain and Portugal the methods to attain statehood—and along with it a "plenitude of imperium" or the governing power—had been essentially the same: to break the political power of the nobles, to make the Church an instrument of political policy, to purge racial minorities, to subordinate every element in the nation to the sovereign will. There was this difference: Portugal was more cosmopolitan, softer, more malleable than Spain. In proportion to her size she had absorbed more than Spain, and in proportion to her size she was able to conquer and to govern more.

Support of the people, lesser allies of the kingly authority, had enabled the throne in both countries to subdue the nobles and to dominate the Church; for the people, as always, held the balance of power. But they had neither the education, the experience, nor indeed the inclination properly to read the scales where their weight was so important, and consequently the common citizen was victimized longer in Spain and Portugal than in any other of the great European nations.

Another strong factor conspired to maintain this state of economic subserviency which replaced personal serfdom. It was the Spanish-Portuguese custom and law of primogeniture, the *Mayorazgo*, by which the eldest son of the family inherited totally and unalienably the father's estate. Economically the patrimony of landownership became as absolute as the prestige of lineage itself. This custom which was legally inaugurated in the thirteenth century meant that although the seignorial regime might be shorn of its political power, as indeed was the case, a new and even stronger economic power would appear in its stead. The noble might disappear, but the landlord would live on forever. The transference of this system to America, where there were vast areas of land at the disposal of the early conquistadores, meant that the fiefs of the Middle Ages, powerful and large as some of them were, would pale into insignificance beside the huge grants made in the New World. Inevitably this gave to the economy only two great classes, landlords and day laborers. The Indian obviously would be the laborer. No large middle class, no backbone of the small farmer, no development of industry or industrial workers would for centuries be able to challenge the absolute power of landownership concentrated in the hands of a few families. This is one of the main differences between the history of Latin America and that of the United States.

Every characteristic of Spanish and Portuguese society was transferred to the New World. The warrior psychology of the home countries found new fields in America. The victorious soldier soon became the exploiter. The Inquisition, which had begun as a religious instrument of faith purification, became an instrument of state policy. Eight centuries of religious wars against the Moslems plus inquisitorial Catholic thinking led directly to intolerance in political and economic expression. Feudalism in the Old World meant feudalism in the New. The one great ever-present and sometimes overwhelming obstacle was the tremendous preponderance of Indian blood and the powerful roots of the Indian's folk culture which reached broad and deep in the American earth. Into this immense red man's world was poured the fertile seed of Iberian life.

The Epic of
Latin America

1
THE MAYAS: "GREEKS OF THE NEW WORLD"

Even in the beginning America was a land of promise. According to Greek legend, the souls of dead heroes took up their abode on the "Blessed Islands" of the western sea. These were the Elysian fields where mortals became gods in a newer and better life. In other ancient chronicles it was said that beyond the sea of darkness, which was the unknown Atlantic, lay the lost continent of Atlantis. Solon had spoken of it; Strabo mentioned it in his famous geography, and Plato was convinced that a great civilization had flourished there until it was destroyed by a tremendous quake and swallowed into the sea. Atlantis came to mean Utopia, and Francis Bacon entitled his essay on the ideal state "The New Atlantis." Many maps of the Middle Ages show other sections of the Western world: Antilia, Saint Brendan's Isles, Brazil, and the Island of the Seven Cities. Whether or not the ancients had in some devious way actually heard of America may never be removed from the realm of legend, nor may we ever know whether a great culture did exist on some now lost continent or island, with those who survived its destruction moving westward to the mainland, there to begin life anew.

Far more likely, however, is the archaeological view that man first came to American shores in successive waves across the Bering Strait from Asia. Perhaps to these early Asiatics were added a few Polynesians who arrived in their dugouts from the far reaches of the southern Pacific. In any case, the American red man fifteen or twenty thousand years ago began to chart his own destiny, upward and alone, completely isolated from progress in other parts of the world.

During the first centuries of the Christian Era relatively high types of primitive civilization were reached in at least three widely separated regions. The Teotihuacán culture, noted for its great pyramids, arose in the Central Valley of Mexico. At more or less the same time Central America and the Andean area were producing very distinct cultures of their own.

The former was the early Maya culture of Central America; the latter, the Tiahuanacan, or even more vaguely termed "pre-Inca" culture of the Andes. As our archaeological investigations of the early Mayas and pre-Incas have touched only the high spots, so to speak, the origin of both remains much of a mystery. After thousands of years of snail-like progress through the vast level of that early archaeological period known as the Archaic, they finally appear on the horizon of history. Until recently we knew of very few beginnings, few halfway points, few connecting links to trace the development of these peoples. Due to the paucity of historical data they seemed almost to emerge as Athena from the mind of Zeus, near the zenith of their perfection. Their decline and fall were almost as mysterious. At an early date in the history of our era they dropped suddenly from their lofty heights and their cultures disappeared from the historic scene, swallowed up, overwhelmed, or absorbed by those which followed them.

At any rate, when the Spaniards arrived in Central America, Mexico, and Peru, the Teotihuacán, Maya and pre-Inca cultures were already dead. Their great centers, long since abandoned, were overgrown with forest and weeds. Many of their finest temples were masses of fallen stones, crumbled masonry, accumulated silt, and gaping holes where the woodwork had rotted away. In Mexico the Aztecs, whom the Spaniards encountered, had appropriated many of the achievements of their predecessors. In the Andean highlands the vast empire of the Incas had rolled like a juggernaut over all previous civilizations, and some of their most imposing monuments were constructed on bases found in the regions they had overrun. As for the Maya, Teotihuacán and pre-Inca peoples, they had either reverted to a state of semi-savagery or had been absorbed in the main currents of their conquerors' way of life.

But this is getting far ahead of our story. All of these Indian civilizations made contributions that were fundamental to the regimes which overpowered them, and these in turn were the foundations upon which the Spaniards had to build. The Indian background of Latin America is fundamental in history. In many regions Spaniards and Indians mingled and their cultures became one. In Mexico, Guatemala, Colombia, Ecuador, Peru, Bolivia, and Chile, Indian blood is still strong, and in all these countries except Chile there are today far more mestizos and Indians than pure whites. The greatest contemporary Mexican and Peruvian art is shot through with indigenous themes, colors, and rhythms. Except for the small upper class, evidences of Indian thinking and custom are apparent in every expression of life. There can be no understanding of these countries without a clear knowledge of their native past, its greatness and its decay.

The history of Indian America must be approached from a point of view essentially different from that employed in studying the development of western European civilization. In America there are almost no ancient records to guide us; there was never any contact with other civilizations outside the hemisphere, and consequently no exchange or analogies with nations whose history we know. Individuals do not stand out in Indian America, for few individuals are known, and many of these are lost in the mist of fable. We are not even certain where the red man came from, or how, or when. Such progress as we can trace is in terms of the culture substance of entire peoples. Unstudied and unrecorded, it moved ponderously forward in the folk arts and crafts of regions and of centuries. "We should realize that the earth must be our archive, the shovel our reading glass, and that nature, eternally destroying to create anew, has scattered our materials over mountain, plain, and forest" from Alaska to the southernmost sea.[7]

The archaeologist works mainly with broken things, with objects which have been wrought by human hands and shaped with a loving heart. If he is successful and makes a real "find," these objects are rescued and preserved for all to see. But the mind and heart "that reached beyond the requirements of utility and created a lovely thing . . . that endowed a Parthenon with the transcendent grace that has survived through destructive ages—that is the ultimate subject of the archaeologist's quest. Ancient monuments fascinate because of their builders, and builders are interesting for what they wrought under the urge of creative mind. Who? When? Whither? are the questions with which the archaeologist challenges the refuse heaps, the scattered shards, the broken shafts, to tell of the builders who came and lived and went their way into the templed past. Only as they are reflections of minds and spirits are ruins of importance. . . .

"At first, the archaeologist views a succession of tragic pageantries. Broken columns mean broken states. The wreckage of cities denotes the destruction of community aspirations. Ruins of house mounds tell of hallowed home life ending in sorrow. Fragments of pottery, basketry, fabrics, wearing apparel, bits of modeling, faded touches of color, record the agelong striving after perfection. Shattered temples, shrines, sanctuaries, holy places, reveal the yearning of the human spirit to find, to unite with, the Divine. By way of ritual, rhythm, song, and symbol, man approaches the deific presence. But all this goes the way of his material creations. . . .

"It is a mystifying thing that man, creator of all the beautiful and majestic cultural products of his world, should at the same time be the most brutal destroyer. Let a people create palaces of beauty, cities of delight, a cultural world which would seem to be the supreme objective of human effort, and another people must do its fiendish best to blast it from the earth. Let life become tranquil, happy, abundant in all that is desirable in existence, man rises up to crush it into poverty and utter annihilation. . . . 'They left a desert and they called it peace. . . .' Man does not hesitate to put out the torch that has lighted humanity for a thousand years."[8]

Many a superb marble from the Acropolis has gone into the lime pits of Athens; many a stone column fashioned with years of love by some unknown Maya sculptor has been hammered into bits to fence in a Central American pigsty; many a fine Inca wall has been wrenched from its perfection stone by stone to go into the house or barn of some inhabitant of post-conquest Peru. The monolithic stones of ancient Bolivian Tiahuanaco, considered by some to be the greatest monument in all America, were for years consistently ground into rubble for railroad ballast that La Paz might have an outlet to the sea.

But the Earth Mother, which was soil and seed to send man's striving up toward the stars, now with a marvelous persistence covers the scene of his ruin and his decline with friendly fingers of wind, rain, and sand, making her own dark womb into which are poured his highest creations, his highest reaching. "Over the ruins of cities, winds pile the friendly soil. Rains undercut the foundations of walls and columns so that they may fall and be concealed from vandals. . . . Nature is relentless in her protective work. She will convert fertile lands into desert wastes, cultivate valleys into impenetrable jungles, to the end that man's spiritual past may be saved for the life of the future."[8]

The job of the archaeologist is to re-create these things. He cannot depend on what historians have said. They do not agree. In America he cannot even go to what the Indian himself has written, for he has written almost nothing. No Inca, Maya, or Aztec ever wrote a complete sentence, or even made a start toward inscribing a chronological history of his people. Tradition fades into legend, legend into religion, religion into art. Back of all these is the psychology and growth of the people. That part of their history which cannot be falsified must be uncovered and restored to life. To the archaeologist "no idle fancy is the concept of the Earth Mother."

Early Spanish writers who witnessed the scenes of the conquest and the downfall of the Aztecs and Incas wrote of them in terms with which they were personally familiar, and in so doing drew out of focus the perspective of ancient Indian life. They used the words "empire," "civilization," and "culture" in a European sense, because that was the only way in which they felt able to describe this spectacular new world so completely different from anything they had seen before. The sincere historian berates "this handing on of a picture that every archaeologist knows to be misleading. . . ."

"As a matter of fact they saw no *civilization* at all—only barbaric culture, expressed in the riot of color derived from tropical birds, insects, flowers—a region where plant and animal life furnished gorgeous costumes for brilliant pageantry. In the Old World this meant royalty, wealth possible only to kings, power possessed only by emperors who exacted tribute and homage from subject peoples. In the New World it meant the ordinary life of all the people, tribe, or community, born into a world of color, reared in a perpetual round of invocation of deific powers to whom all this ceremony must be pleasing, all this splendor of ornament acceptable, because they were givers of it to man."[8]

When we use these terms of our own civilization—there are no others— the primitive earthiness of the American red man who never learned to read or write must be constantly borne in mind. While our civilization was developing its techniques of use and progress, the Indian was interested only in beautifying what he had. No man ever lived closer to the earth. He accepted life as he found it, and his unity with it was almost complete. Every force of nature was a part of his experience and of his religion and art. There were no higher techniques, no drives or urge to progress to separate him from what he knew and accepted. A wonderful plastic sense was innate in *all* of his people, and all of his people had a hand in creating and enjoying their art. It was as much a part of their daily lives as the impersonal drinking glass is a part of ours. We put use first; he never thought of use as separated from beauty. It is this complete integration of life which was then and is now the Indian's greatest strength. He carried it through countless ages alone, then when the Spaniards tried to break it down he reached up and drowned the white man in his sea of blood. The mestizo of today can never get away from being a descendant of the Indian who came to these unknown shores from some far place so many eons ago to blend himself completely with the great American earth.

Whatever his origin, the red man probably reached the great central valley of Mexico about eight or nine thousand years before the birth of Christ, and soon afterward began his migration toward the south, which ultimately peopled the distant region of the Andes. These early Indians were primitive and nomadic savages, wanderers across the face of the earth with no fixed homes or nation. No broader social conception than that of the tribe had entered their thinking, and whatever arts they had were crude refinements that grew naturally out of the daily necessities of their lives. When they had cleared one district of its fruit, its fish, or its game, they moved on to another. Their society was an endless cycle of hunting, gathering, and moving, which prevented the development of any permanent populated centers, and thus made impossible the sustained effort upon which civilization depends.

Then there occurred a fortuitous circumstance that altered the whole course of the Indian's life: the discovery of corn. No one knows exactly how this grain was first produced. Some say that it was domesticated from a wild variety of maize, others that it represented a hybrid between some unknown plant and the Mexican wild grass called teosinte, which will readily cross with corn, the pollen of either plant fertilizing the other.[9] In any case, corn or maize gave to the American red man his first chance to produce a quantity of food sufficient for his needs instead of his having to forage for it like a wild beast, and frequently on a day-to-day basis only one jump ahead of starvation. It enabled him to put an end to his nomadic life and settle down to an agricultural existence.

This experience was not new on the stage of history, for the civilizations of Asia had built their staff of life on rice and those of Europe were nurtured on wheat, just as the Indian cultures of America came to rest on corn. When the red man settled down in a fixed region to cultivate this new food, he at once changed the tenor of his life and began that long ascent which finally produced the great indigenous cultures of Mexico, Central America, and Peru. It is no wonder that corn entered so deeply into his art, into his religion, and into his thinking. There were corn myths, corn rites, corn goddesses, corn dances, corn prayers and songs, and ears of corn wrought in stone, gold, or silver as art motifs in many widely separated regions. Corn raised the Indian out of a state of complete savagery to the level of a great folk culture. It lifted him bodily from the unknown extent of the Archaic. It was more than a food to him, more even than the symbol of his religion; it was a way of life.[45]

One of the earlier tribes which made the most of this new agricultural existence was the Maya. When the Mayas first enter the currents of history we find them living in the lowlands on the Gulf coast plain of Mexico. Their land was extremely fertile, and when corn was put into cultivation there it was fruitful beyond their fondest hopes. Greater stores of food than had ever before seemed possible were rapidly accumulated, and the tribes of the Mayas prospered mightily. At about the time of the birth of Christ they pushed inland to the region of northern Central America, and finding this land good, established themselves there, principally in the Guatemalan lowlands. It was here that the first great Indian culture arose.

Once established on fertile soil and with sufficient knowledge of cultivation to attain a measure of productive stability, the Mayas soon found themselves in possession of the prerequisites of cultural development: they had stores of food which relieved them of the necessity of constant moving and impermanent thinking, and in between crops they enjoyed a certain amount of leisure time which they could devote to purely aesthetic expression. As in the case of many other early civilizations their religion and art were fused into one. This gave to their culture a refinement and beauty not achieved by any other indigenous American group. On the other hand, by concentrating on the spiritual, the refined, and the purely aesthetic, they paid little attention to the material techniques of supporting life.[7] Unlike the Incas of Peru, they built no great stone cities, no vast systems of irrigation, and their society was not blended into a strong social whole. Their people lived in the bush around their great religious centers in flimsy houses of reeds and mud. Only when some outstanding ceremony brought them all together did these centers teem with a large population. On those occasions the people who had come forth from the bush to raise the great stone structures as symbols of their mass expression then came forth again to worship and thus to reaffirm their single destiny. As one of the finest of modern archaeologists points out, this was somewhat the same situation that prevailed in the Middle Ages when so many poverty-stricken towns of individually wretched humans toiled together to construct the magnificent Gothic cathedrals that loomed massively from the misery of ordinary daily life as symbols of the mass aspiration and the mass expression of glory and of art. The same thing had also happened in many Asiatic civilizations, whose wondrous carved architecture has survived by many centuries the miserable dwelling places scattered over the surrounding countryside.[7] This is not to say that Maya temples and religion stood on a pinnacle above and beyond the common people, for rather the opposite was true. The Mayas poured themselves into this, their supreme art, with the whole of their bodies, their minds, and their devotion.

Before his home had become fixed on expansive and fertile land the Indian had been content to let time flow by, measureless and unlimited, without beginning or end. The single day or at best such general terms as the "hot" season, the "cold," the "dry," or the "rainy" season were his only conceptions in indicating the passing days. Now, however, with crops to be sowed, cultivated, harvested, and stored, some more accurate measurement of time became a necessity. How many moons did the long rains last which gave their waters to the famished earth? How many crops could be planted and gathered while the bright evening star showed itself in the sky? How many suns long were the hot days of summer? When the Maya set himself to pondering over these things he became more acutely conscious of time, and eventually the result was a calendar. By correlating the shorter cycles of the moon with the longer ones of the sun and of Venus, he arrived at a year of eighteen months of twenty days each, plus five "unlucky" days, making a total of three hundred and sixty-five. He also used a shorter and purely arbitrary or symbolic religious calendar of only two hundred and sixty days. Astronomical observatories were constructed in which Maya scientists could tell exactly when the sun had reached the equinoxes (March 21 and September 22) and the solstices (June 21 and December 21). In the light of these observations and of others made by studying the phases of Venus, Lord "Big Eye" of the heavens, such corrections as were necessary were made from time to time. In order not to throw our own seasons out of focus we insert an extra day in our calendar every four years, February 29. In their computations the Mayas did the same thing, adding an extra day to each fourth year, and over longer periods twenty-five extra days to each one hundred and four years. One archaeologist who has devoted his life to the study of Maya lore states that this calendar was so exact that no confusion could exist between any two days within a period of more than three hundred and seventy-four thousand years. It was more accurate than the finest measurement of time known in the days of Greece or Rome, and was superior to any calendar used during the Christian Era until Pope Gregory's modifications were incorporated in 1582.[11]

The Mayas attained these results by a careful study of the heavenly bodies; this in the course of time naturally led their scientists to become excellent astronomers and mathematicians, and also exerted a strong influence on their architecture and art. Every eighteen hundred days, or about every five years, chronological monuments or stone columns called stelae were erected on which the date, certain astronomical positions, and other still undeciphered information were recorded. The Mayas knew the courses of the principal stars and planets and were able to predict eclipses with great accuracy. Their stelae were often magnificently carved and thus represent art as well as scientific and historic expression. Perhaps when all of the recorded dates are found they will help to place many other early American cultures with which this race came in contact. According to some archaeologists, the dates of many Maya cities are already more accurately known than those of ancient Babylonia, Greece, or even imperial Rome.[11] But the specialists do not all agree as to just how the Maya calendar should be correlated with Christian dates. Consequently, while the sequence of events and even the amount of time elapsing between any two events are unquestioned, the concurrent Christian year varies according to which correlation one wishes to accept.[7] Further investigations will no doubt clarify this point.

The supreme expression of Maya culture, however, was not their calendar but a highly refined system of sculptured hieroglyphics. The loving care which was lavished on the execution of some of these complex symbols turned them into veritable artistic motifs. Other native races did borrow and even simplify many of their characters, but the Maya glyphs still stand as the only native American writing comparable to the graphic systems of Egypt, China, or Babylonia.[11] In addition to being inscribed on the chronological stone stelae these hieroglyphics were written on long strips of maguey (century plant) fiber which could be folded like Japanese screens and were thus easier to handle than the scrolls of the ancients. The figures were beautifully illuminated and were written on both sides of the sheet. "The paper was given a smooth surface by a coating of fine lime and the drawings were made in black and in various colors."[12] Deerskin and bark also sometimes took the place of the maguey strips. Although the Mayas were said to have had "many books upon civil and religious history, and upon rites, magic, and medicine," only three of their manuscripts or codices have survived.[12] Even these are incomplete and exist only in facsimile. Their subject matter seems limited to the calendar, numbers, and religious ceremonies.

Maya glyphs are of especial interest to students of languages because they are the only written characters ever found which represent a transition stage between a purely "pictorial" written language and one based on "sound" or phonetic symbols. In the "pictorial" language only concrete objects whose pictures might be drawn or represented could be expressed. A man, for example, would always have to be some kind of figure or character resembling a man. This limited expression, for feelings, actions, descriptions, and abstract ideas could be rendered only in the crudest fashion. Whatever could not be drawn could not be said in writing. However, in the "sound" or phonetic language toward which the Maya system was evolving at the time of the downfall of Maya civilization, the characters stand for sounds of words and make no attempt to present the idea in a pictorial manner. This increased manyfold the power of expression. It meant that the gap between a purely primitive or visual type of culture and the abstract refinements of higher civilization was rapidly being closed. But at this stage of their development the Mayas, divided by civil rivalries and strife, fell before the onslaught of the fierce Toltec warriors from the Mexican plateau. After a relatively brief period of fusion and cultural renascence, many of their great centers, for reasons as yet imperfectly understood, were abandoned to the tropical jungles and the shifting sands.

The Maya system of writing consisted of about four hundred simple characters and two hundred compound characters, something like 10 per cent of them being phonetic symbols. Almost none of the abstract characters have yet been deciphered, and only about half of the pictorial ones, mainly those dealing with chronology. Consequently, up to the present moment archaeologists, with considerable intelligent guesswork, are able to figure out only the general drift of Maya writing without being able to translate any of the details or shades of meaning. Another difficulty encountered in translating the Maya glyphs is that they are so interwoven with decorative motifs that it is often impossible to tell where the writing stops and the decoration begins. This is especially true of inscriptions on stone, for the sculptors apparently thought that all blank spaces were unsightly and often filled these in completely, sometimes using glyph-like characters to do so. No key to the Maya hieroglyphics has ever been found, nor has any tablet or stone like the Rosetta stone with parallel versions of the Maya and some other more readily translatable language ever been discovered. Only a single authority, the Spanish bishop, Diego de Landa, studied and recorded these Maya glyphs soon after the conquest. The bishop drew up what he thought was a complete alphabet, but what he actually compiled was an ambiguous hodgepodge of characters. When Landa asked the natives of Yucatan to give him the symbol for a certain sound or letter, they would do so, but these symbols apparently stood for many other things as well, so the resultant alphabet is not at all basic. Furthermore, this same bishop's fanaticism was the cause of the destruction of many invaluable Maya manuscripts which he is said to have gathered and burned as the evil documents of an idolatrous people. He did his work with the thoroughness of a good inquisitor, for only three incomplete Maya codices have survived. At the same time it must be said in Landa's favor that had his compilation not been made, much that we do know of ancient Maya glyphs and history would lie beyond an impenetrable veil.

A considerable remainder of our knowledge of these people has been obtained from the *Books of Chilam Balam*, purportedly written by a Maya priest of Yucatan, and from the *Popul Vuh*, a legendary and mythical history in the Quiché language of Guatemala. Both of these books were written after the conquest by native scribes who had learned the Spanish language and alphabet. These scribes, however, did not write in Spanish but simply used the Spanish script in order to reproduce as phonetically as possible their own native idioms, the *Chilam Balam* being in Maya, and the *Popul Vuh* in Quiché. The stories contain some fragmentary history, but are occupied mainly with popular myths. The *Popul Vuh* tells of the giant-killing and other exploits of a pair of "Hero Twins," and the *Books of Chilam Balam* "go somewhat into family history" and prophesy that "at the end of the thirteenth age [around 1500] white men would arrive in Yucatan." The first shipwrecked Spaniards set foot on those shores in 1511. Neither book goes very "far toward relieving the confusion that beclouds the Maya world."[13]

Maya mathematicians kept pace with the scribes and astronomers, and their calculations, while not exactly like our own, were extremely accurate. They knew the use of the zero symbol, the basis of modern mathematics, and in their higher numbers used a vigesimal instead of a decimal system. All numerical systems have been based in some way on the digits of the hands, or the feet, or both, for it is natural that man should begin his efforts to count in this manner. The Arabs who first gave us our own zero and decimals went by tens, while the Mayas proceeded by twenties. Their multiplication was also on a vigesimal basis. For example, our number twenty-seven signifies two times ten plus seven. In the Maya system a similar two-numbered figure would be two times twenty plus seven. When proper correlations are made this method works out as satisfactorily as our own.

Just as we begin our era with the birth of Christ, the chronology of the Mayas began with a definite date which happens to go back many centuries earlier. One specialist says that in terms of our calendar this date would be August 11, 3114 B.C., the significance of which is lost to us. The earliest certain dates which have been discovered on carved monuments go back to the beginning of the Christian Era. A date that correlates with 31 B.C., found on a broken stela south of Vera Cruz (Tres Zapotes) is accepted by many archaeologists, while another broken stela from El Baul in western Guatemala may bear the date A.D. 36. Carbon 14 and other calculations place the dates of several Maya substructures earlier than either of these.[180]

The earliest or Archaic Era of Maya history, or about the first nine hundred years, which stretched between 600 B.C. and A.D. 300, was the formative period and included the early migration of the race into the Guatemalan lowlands. The original habitat was possibly along the eastern Mexican coast. During this period the Mayas worked out the laborious beginnings of their calendar, their system of writing, the basis of their architecture, and an incipient art. The following six hundred years, A.D. 300 to A.D. 900, saw the formation of the so-called Classic Period which reached its zenith during the last three centuries of that span and found expression in the marvelous stelae, pyramids, and temples spread over northern Guatemala and other neighboring regions. During this period there began a gradual extension of the Maya frontier toward Yucatan, and by the end of the Classic Period these new colonies were firmly established and populated. At about this time the movement eastward seems to turn into a full mass migration, almost a flight away from the Central American centers toward the new land to the east.

Throughout the following half a century, more or less, there is a break in Maya history, and all chronology seems to disappear. This hiatus lasted until nearly A.D. 1000, when architecture and art in a new style began to appear. Perhaps pestilence, war, the wearing out of the soil, or the necessity for more "living room" caused this decline of the old Maya centers and the period of black regression which followed. In any case, it appears that during the prolonged transition period the Mayas were struggling to survive and to re-establish themselves after whatever holocaust it was that had wiped their old centers from the map. A people fighting for its life is hardly in any frame of mind and certainly does not have the time to think in terms of art or even to record the happenings of its day. Consequently, these years constitute the "Dark Ages" of Maya history. Once they were concluded, however, there is a great renaissance, and the flowering of a new culture seems to take up where the old had left off so many generations previously. Although the style was somewhat different and more modern, many fundamentals were essentially the same, except that the new Maya art embodied strong Toltec influences.

This new Maya-Toltec culture was centered in the Mexican peninsula of Yucatan and passes through three frequently intermingling phases. The first hundred years (A.D. 900 to A.D. 1000) represent an intermediate stage during which the new beginnings were consolidated. The years A.D. 1000 to A.D. 1200 show the resurgent art at its height, and the last two centuries (A.D. 1200 to A.D. 1400) represent a decline of the Maya-Toltec culture. The best-known center of this culture was Chichén Itzá, dedicated to the

God of the Plumed Serpent, called Kukulkan by the Mayas and Quetzal-coatl by the Toltecs and Aztecs. This city had been founded many centuries previously, possibly as early as A.D. 450, but it had not been continuously inhabited. The Chichén Itzá that we see today is mainly Maya-Toltec in its architecture. Around A.D. 1200 the city was abandoned after its defeat by the walled town of Mayapan whose rulers controlled most of Yucatan until 1441. The period 1200–1441 was one of disintegration. Pilgrimages were still made to Chichén Itzá, but its heyday was past. Mayapan, Tulum, and Izamal were the principal centers of this final stage. Magnificent as it is, Chichén Itzá never equaled the pure Maya art of the Classic Period.

Among the outstanding creations of this period were many magnificent pyramid-temples decorated with delicate stone carvings. These were always built on a height facing a great plaza and were situated in the center of thickly populated districts. They served as the Maya "civic centers," but as the higher expressions of these people were mostly of a religious rather than of a social or political nature, they reflected these sentiments. The façades of many of the temples were covered with brilliant frescoes in red, white, green, blue, and yellow. The sculptured figures were also highly painted, but little of their polychrome has survived exposure to the elements. As the years passed and one type of carving succeeded another, Maya sculptors dug deeper and deeper into the face of the stones on which they were working, and some examples of their handiwork stand out in such bold relief that it seems almost as if they are of separate and superimposed blocks, which is not the case. How these sculptors were able to fashion such perfect figures with the crude stone tools at their disposal passes understanding. One archaeologist who was working in the field recently gave a group of the natives a set of primitive stone tools and set them to carving a huge block. After a week of laborious effort they had been unable to make the slightest impression on their subject.[14] One possible conjecture to be drawn from all this is that there were Maya iron tools fashioned out of meteoric fragments which have since rusted away. Such implements have been located in the United States even among more primitive races, but not a single one has ever been discovered in Mexico or Central America. There is no reason to believe that iron was ever reduced from ore which does occur in great abundance in some of these regions.

Besides this highly wrought sculpturing the Mayas incorporated in some of their temples the finest wood carving in America, perhaps the finest of the ancient world. Most of these pieces have rotted away in the humid atmosphere of the tropics, but several altars and lintels of steel-hard sapote wood have been preserved. One such altarpiece, which is now in the museum at Basel, Switzerland, is a "richly costumed" representation of Kukulkan, God of the Feathered Serpent, surrounded by exquisitely wrought carvings of interwoven faces and hieroglyphics. This famous piece came from the ruins at Tikal, Guatemala, and "is a master work of the highest order, unsurpassed by any piece of wood sculpture in the old world. The design is exceptionally elaborate even for Maya art. The subject is a richly costumed personage holding a standard or baton in his right hand, his face framed in the open mouth of a grotesque monster. He is enclosed beneath the arched body of a feathered serpent of extraordinary design, the head appearing at the left. Perched on the serpent arch above is the figure of a mythical bird monster. . . . The central design is surrounded by hieroglyphic inscriptions among which are exquisitely carved portrait faces. It is said that a companion piece to this remarkable work of ancient American art was lost in the jungle in the process of transportation from Tikal to the seaboard."[13]

The earliest complete structure indicating Maya lines which has been discovered is a beautiful pyramid of silvery white, obviously part of an astronomical observatory which was uncovered in the jungles of Guatemala at a place called Uaxactún.* This pyramid is ascended by a series of stairways "flanked with pairs of great grotesque stucco masks, each eight feet square. The upper ones represent enormous human faces with slit-like eyes, large bulbous noses, filed teeth, and lolling tongues. The lower masks seem to be highly conventionalized serpent heads."[9] These are the words of its discoverer and excavator, Dr. S. G. Morley. He goes on to say that the construction in its entirety is "unquestionably one of the most magnificent examples of aboriginal American architecture extant—a silvery white, stucco covered pyramid of exquisite proportions and perfect outline."

This large pyramid faced a line of three smaller ones, the four of them so arranged that the Maya astronomer-observer placed on the main structure would see the sun rise from directly behind the other three at the exact periods of the equinoxes and solstices. The earliest date recorded in glyphs at Uaxactún is A.D. 328, but the glowing stucco substructure of the main pyramid goes back to the first century. Maya astronomical lore dates from an even earlier epoch, circa 300 B.C.[179]

The Mayas rarely constructed buildings of more than a single story, so in order to give an appearance of great height they usually erected their temples on mounds of earth or rubble, sometimes naturally and sometimes artificially formed. The outside surfaces were always coated with stucco or stones and mortar in such a manner that the entire mound seemed to be an integral part of the building raised on its summit. Temples having the appearance of several stories in height were in reality separate structures placed one behind the other, each being erected on a mound higher than the one in front of it. The total effect was that of a rising-staircase construction majestic in its sweep. Usually the temples surmounting these terraces were crowned by combs or slender flying façades that resembled the crests

* Pronounced *Wah-shock-toon.*

of ancient warriors' helmets. No indigenous American race ever learned the use of the true arch, the basis of European architecture; consequently Maya interiors and ceilings were of necessity very narrow and low unless the roof was constructed of light materials, such as thatch or wood. Sufficient support for heavier roofings was a constant vexation, and in many Maya buildings there are evidences of columns reinforced from time to time in order to prevent a total collapse. Whenever an interior was made larger it was generally at the expense of safety, but the term "larger" is purely relative, for all rooms were small and dingy. Not knowing the laws of architectural support, the Mayas had to rely on massiveness of walls instead of on arches, and as a result the proportion of wall space to actual room space was sometimes nearly forty to one.

Stucco was used to a considerable extent in most of these structures, and in the later years of the Yucatan or new culture period round columns with square capitals borrowed from the Toltecs of the Mexican plateau were frequently employed. Many of these embodied the stylized motif of the feathered serpent, some entire columns being representations of that sacred bird-reptile with ends of a heavy tail and jaws, both foreshortened, touching the roof and base respectively.

Three great ceremonial centers of the Classic Period are Tikal, Guatemala, a few miles from Uaxactún, and Palenque and Bonampak in southern Mexico. At Tikal the oldest date recorded in stone is A.D. 292, but other evidence indicates that the Mayas were building here five centuries earlier. Among Tikal's many tall pyramids is the highest in Mayaland soaring to 229 feet. Palenque reached its peak after Tikal, around A.D. 700. "All great Maya ruins are touched by magic, but Palenque more than most . . . for me it is second only to the Parthenon in terms of unadulterated beauty," writes Katherine Kuh. The scene suggests a poetic Chinese painting in which the luxuriant rain forest is blended with a fairy-tale architecture. Bonampak, hidden in the jungle until its discovery in 1946, is the site of the best Maya murals (c. A.D. 800), whole walls of glowing priestly figures.

Another famous cluster of ruins, which represents the Maya Renaissance in Yucatan, is at Uxmal, a few miles west of Merida. Uxmal rose in importance after the old classic centers in Guatemala and Chiapas, Mexico, were abandoned, around A.D. 900. One group in the concentrated complex of buildings at Uxmal suggests a cloister, and so was called the Nunnery Quadrangle. Another of the many beautifully decorated buildings at Uxmal is the Governor's Palace, a purely arbitrary name, which is three hundred and fifty feet long, with a mosaic façade composed of thousands of pieces of stone. Another structure, called the House of the Pigeons, is surmounted by a roof comb fifteen feet high and two hundred feet long. The faces of this crest, writes the archaeologist E. L. Hewett, are a mass of interwoven "mosaic masks, roof-comb ornament, open tracery suggesting latticework in stone—a wealth of geometric decoration, rivaling Mitla in design, and surpassing it in the variety of its patterns."[13] The walls of these structures are massive in the extreme, and their "small, dark interiors were places of mystery to the populace, cells for the priests for secret ritual, affording the seclusion that was necessary for maintaining the pall of superstition over the people."[13]

Besides these six centers there are at least a dozen or two more whose surfaces have barely been scratched. No attempt has been made to clear away the surrounding growth and rubble and to restore them to their former glory. Archaeologists frequently visit these places and cut down some of the rankest plants, but within a few months after they have departed the tropical jungles have again closed over shattered walls with discouraging rapidity. Groups of these ruins cover Yucatan, the northern Central American lowlands, sections of southern Mexico, and parts of the Guatemalan highlands. In this last region is located the famous city of Utatlan, sacked by Pedro de Alvarado, one of Cortés's lieutenants, which some authorities consider as being in the same category with the Aztec capital of Tenochtitlán (Mexico City) and the great Inca center of Cuzco. It does seem likely that after the decline of the new Maya culture on the peninsula of Yucatan, probably due to a combination of civil wars, conquests by outsiders, a loss of all feeling of union or pride in race, and perhaps the inroads of tropical fevers, many of the remaining Mayas trekked back to the interior Guatemalan highlands where the climate was cooler and more healthful and the means of defending themselves were afforded by Nature herself. Thousands of descendants of the older race still live in this region as well as in Yucatan. Some archaeologists believe that this highland region was the cradle of their culture, and that after expanding eastward and meeting a slow defeat they returned to their native mountains like homing pigeons. It is true that many, many thousands of the Indian inhabitants of present-day Guatemala still speak Maya dialects, still fashion beautiful pottery in the old designs, and still weave by hand some of the finest fabrics in all America. It is also possible that among them other old traditions of their race may survive, and that there still may be alive a few to whom have been handed down the secrets of Maya history, mythology, and art, who perhaps may even possess the knowledge to read, to write, and to interpret the ancient inscriptions of their ancestors. If such persons do exist they hold the key that will unlock many a fascinating chapter of now-hidden Maya lore.

In the meantime, whatever conclusions the specialists may reach about this gifted race must rest on an imperfect knowledge of their written language and on a detailed examination of the ruins and relics which have survived the jungles and the centuries. Even in this regard their work of interpretation will be limited until a greater proportion of the principal archaeological sites have been carefully excavated. So far only a single great center, that located at Chichén Itzá in Yucatan, comes within this category. Here is located by far the largest Maya ceremonial center in Mexico, and one of the greatest of pre-conquest America.

For over three hundred years, from the eleventh to the fourteenth century, Chichén Itzá was the Mecca of the Maya world. During the early part of that period the site was overrun by the Toltecs, whose own superb culture mingled with that of the vanquished to produce the last great flowering of these two civilizations. Primitive roads or paths stretched from the metropolis in all directions, and pilgrimages were often made there from more distant parts of the peninsula.

Chichén Itzá was the sacred center of the God of the Plumed or Feathered Serpent whose imposing temple lifted itself gracefully for more than a hundred feet above the level of the plain at its base. More imposing still was the Temple of the Warriors with its brilliant feathered-serpent columns. There was also a magnificent colonnade four hundred and sixty-five feet long, a huge plaza or Court of the Thousand Columns, a circular astronomical observatory, and many other notable buildings. The sides of the North Colonnade of the Court of the Thousand Columns "are beautifully sculptured and painted with a procession of warriors, the eyes of which are made of inlays of white shell, with pupils of some vegetable pitch mixed with charcoal to make them black. The cornice of the dais is composed of intertwining rattlesnakes decorated with plumes."[9]

The Mayas' interest in sports, probably taken over from earlier Mexican Indian cultures as a ritualistic expression, is shown in a large ball court where a kind of basketball was played. The ball used was made of hardened rubber, not known then outside of North America, and the purpose of the game was to knock this through the massive stone ring in one of the side walls of the court, hitting it with any part of the body. The game or ceremony, for it was both a recreation and a ritual, was also popular throughout Aztec and Toltec territory, and similar but smaller courts have been found in the southwestern United States. The ball employed was the first instance of rubber being used in the history of the world.

All of the Maya structures which have survived are public or religious in nature. Not a single ordinary home, shop, or store has been discovered. Apparently the general populace lived in inferior adobe or thatched houses at a much lower standard than that indicated by their religious monuments. Maya society was probably the old story of a small warrior or priestly caste holding sway over the masses of the people. They produced a great folk art and a beautiful religious architecture, but their daily living was on a more primitive scale than was the case in Europe at that time, or even hundreds of years earlier. They had no domesticated animals except dogs and fowls, and they had no knowledge of the wheel, the basis of transportation, nor of the arch, the basis of advanced architectural design. Their civilization was unique and wonderful but apparently not tough enough to strike progressively forward.

In the middle of the fifteenth century Chichén Itzá itself was abandoned to the forest. When the Spaniards arrived, the once-powerful Confederation of the Great Snake had already split up into small factions or "city-states" which were easily conquered. Without benefit of the white man's powerful arms or greed the most promising of all American civilizations had by itself twice reached upward through the laborious years, and twice had fallen back into darkness and decay. The story of the first cycle is not so well known, but that of the second shows the barbaric pomp and splendor of a heroic race dissipated under the all-too-well-known clashes of human violence and strife and the eternal desire for governing power. The civilization of the Mayas did not fall before that of a stronger or superior tribe, but because it was unable to hold itself together and face the enemy united. The seeds of disintegration were borne in its own body and were already thickly sown.

The Mayas gave to the New World its earliest and in many ways its greatest indigenous culture. When one calls them to mind there is a strong tendency to overemphasize their magnificent religious architecture, the most finely balanced of this hemisphere. Elaborate stonework, sculpture, brilliant frescoes, and a perfect sense of symmetry have made these monuments stand out above all else that the Mayas have left behind. But Maya artists also produced many finely wrought objects of jade, beautifully carved wood, and magnificent featherwork. Their polychrome pottery and textiles are surpassed only by the finest Peruvian pieces. Maya achievements in all of these arts plus their sense of architectural design, their written language which was just approaching the border of literary expression, their outstanding knowledge of mathematics and of astronomy have caused more than one archaeologist to refer to them as "the Greeks of the New World." In point of chronology, influence, and the strength of their creative talents they fully deserve such a title. At the same time, no amount of archaeological glamor should blind us to the fact that they were many centuries behind the ancient Greeks in the sum total of their accomplishments.

Nearly every artistic expression of these people sprang from a common religious sentiment. "The serpent motif controlled the character of Mayan art and was of first importance in all subsequent arts in Central America and Mexico," states the authority H. J. Spinden. The representation was not a realistic one, but on the graceful contours of stylized serpent bodies were added plumes of the beautiful quetzal bird, jaguars' teeth, designs, ornaments, and headdresses of various kinds used by the Maya priests, scrolls, and other sinuous details, all blended together with perfect symmetry in which artistic creation and fine workmanship vied with each other in intricacy of conception and execution. Variants of this Maya serpent motif later became an integral part of Toltec and Aztec architecture and art.

The Maya Empire, if it may be termed that, has often been called the Confederation of the Great Snake because of the emphasis which these people placed on their religion. Religion was the focus around which their emotional and artistic temperaments revolved, and it was part and parcel of their daily lives. It took the place of a widespread economic and political organization and was the very root and flower of Maya society. Much as the Roman Catholic Church served as the great unifying factor of dozens of kingdoms throughout the Middle Ages, so did Maya religion act as a bond which held together the many otherwise loosely united tribes in a great confederation. Similarly, just as the early European monasteries were the nuclei and repositories of Western culture during chaotic post-Roman and feudal times, so did the Maya priests create and preserve the finest flower of their own civilization in beautiful temples to their primitive gods. And these same priests who looked upward into the heavens, learning the laws of time and space, easily became the masters of man's destiny.

Since the Maya civilization was agricultural at its base, the religion which it produced was bound to be an earthy one, close to those manifestations of nature that most affected the daily lives of the people. Thus it came about that their four great "Gods of the Forest," symbolizing the four cardinal points of the universe, also represented the powers of "rain," "thunder," "lightning," and "hail." The principle of fruitfulness was at the bottom of them all, for on this all life depended. The planet Venus, bright morning and evening star, was Lord "Big Eye" of the heavens on which many of the calendar calculations were based—calculations that made an agricultural civilization sufficiently stable to give zeal and nourishment to a growing art. Venus was also god of the chosen few, the priests and astronomers who plotted the ways of the heavenly bodies and kept close account of the seasons.[14]

The Rain or Water God, Chac-Mool, was the deity on whom crops and consequently lives most directly depended, and was the only divinity to whom human sacrifices were offered. These offerings were usually Maya virgins, chosen for their beauty, who were cast into the Sacred Well at Chichén Itzá in order to appease Chac-Mool and beseech him to send his children rain. If the virgin cast into the well did not drown within a short period of time, she was hoisted out again and saved, for this was taken to be an expression of the god's will. The girl was then questioned as to what the Rain God had whispered to her down there below about the possibilities for rain. These sacrifices were rather infrequent among the Mayas, whose religion never approached the violence and bloodletting of the Aztecs. The Sacred Well at Chichén Itzá has recently been carefully dragged for contents, and many priceless relics have been drawn from its forbidding depths.

In addition to these gods there were many others, but two of these were outstanding. One was called "the Invisible and Supreme God of Gods," and he was worshiped by all the Maya tribes. The other was Kukulkan, the Feathered Serpent, patron deity of Chichén Itzá, who was also the famous Quetzalcoatl of the Toltecs and Aztecs. The latter name is the better known of the two, but the meanings are identical. The quetzal is a bird of lovely plumage native to this tropical region, and coatl means serpent, so the combination signifies the "quetzal bird-serpent."

In symbolic representations this god appears as a snake which has feathers or plumes instead of scales. Kukulkan, or Quetzalcoatl, was God of the Sky and Thunder, and it was he who was believed to have lived among the Mayas in human form in order to teach them the arts of civilization. There are many different versions of his life on earth, and these are doubly confusing because of the fact that there did actually exist a ruler who lived at Chichén Itzá during the twelfth century bearing this name. One archaeological authority cites the specific date of his death as A.D. 1208.[15]

Just how Kukulkan (or Quetzalcoatl) came to the city and got to be ruler of its people is not positively known. From all accounts he seems to be a Toltec by birth and not a Maya. One story tells us that he was a warrior captured by the Mayas who was thrown into the Sacred Well as a sacrifice to Chac-Mool. He did not drown, was hauled out, and saved, and later, through his great talents and personality, was elevated to chieftain. After his death, according to this version, he was deified as the Feathered Serpent. Just where the life of this ruler and culture hero ends and that of the deity begins will probably never be determined, nor indeed is it positively known that the man came first and the god later, for it might have been the other way around. The hero could easily have been endowed with both the name and attributes of an already recognized deity. In any event, a ruler and teacher known as Kukulkan or Quetzalcoatl may indeed have lived among the Mayas. Perhaps he was a highly regarded priest in the priestly succession. His life on earth certainly added greatly to the stature of the god and to the strength of his religion. Symbolically, of course the "plumed serpent" god represented the deific union of the "earth force" and "sky force" in one divinity.

In many of the versions which have come down to us this great hero is described as being unusually blond, and at his death he promised to return someday to his people and lead them from bondage. He was not only considered by all the Mayas to be the bringer of their arts and their laws, but had the reputation of being a firm and excellent governor. He established the city of Mayapan and united Church and State under his own strong central authority. Perhaps that is where the mythological character steps in. During his reign Chichén Itzá and the surrounding Maya centers of Yucatan reached the height of their magnificence. Feathered-serpent columns were added to Maya architecture, and the arts, astronomy, science, religion, together with this new architecture, all flourished in this Yucatecan reflowering of Maya civilization.

The manner of Kukulkan's end is also clouded in legend. One story says that he did not die but "disappeared" from the earth. Another states that he was consumed by divine fire. But before his final departure, in whatever form, he was supposed to have prophesied that in the year *Ce Acatl* of the thirteenth age pale-faced men from across the sea would overcome his people. Kukulkan promised that he himself would someday follow them in order to restore the old Maya religion and way of life.

Many of the details of variations of the story were obviously added by way of further color after the hero's death, the godly attributes gradually becoming more and more highly exaggerated, his human life less and less accurately remembered in its realistic details. Such is the inevitable course of all primitive religions, for the belief of man will surely fill in whatever is lacking in order to fashion the gods of his predilection. Superstition, ignorance, and mass folk worship are the soil in which hero myths come best to fruit. The symbol of Kukulkan's return from beyond the great waters of a raft of coiled serpents may no longer be a religion, but it is still an attitude of mind among millions of today's oppressed Indians in Mexico and Central America.

With Kukulkan ended the final upsurge of the Mayas who came and disappeared from the known currents of history, leaving only their ruins, their undeciphered hieroglyphics, their graves, and their legends. Historians do not know to the fullest extent just what befell them. But this much seems certain: that among fiercer nations they had become too soft, too peaceful, too unsuspecting, yet at the same time too violent and acrimonious among themselves, and that as a consequence of this their civilization was obliterated. In certain regions of the old Maya confederation the folk arts and traditions of these people are still alive, but centuries have passed without the construction of a single great stone edifice. The descendants of the Mayas now speak in a minor key; there is among them no mass sentiment, no supreme and uplifting art, no proud consciousness of power or race through which they might again learn to speak the great language.

The following table and that at the end of Chapter 3 give an approximate chronology. Calculating dates by using the Carbon 14 process, which measures age by the amount of carbon lost by a once living organism cannot fix a date exactly, the percentage of possible error being 100 to 200 years. Maya calendar dates can now be read easily enough, but the difficulty lies in correlating these dates with the Christian calendar. Our table follows the Goodman-Martínez-Thompson correlations accepted by most authorities (1968 revision made by editors of *The National Geographic* aided by Mexican specialists). Spinden puts all dates given below 260 years earlier.[180]

CHRONOLOGY OF MAYA CULTURE

Formative Period (Archaic or Pre-classic)   600 B.C.–A.D. 300
  Centers in Guatemala and Honduras:
Uaxactún, Tikal, Copan, etc.

Classic Period   A.D. 300–A.D. 900
  Early classic flowering at Tikal,
Uaxactún, Copan, Peten
  Late classic peak at Palenque,
Bonampak, in southern Mexico

Post-classic Period   A.D. 900–A.D. 1441
  Uxmal and Chichén Itzá in
Yucatan, Maya-Toltec fusion
After A.D. 1200 rapid decline

2

THE INCAS: CHILDREN OF THE SUN

South America is a continent which, like some fearful or infuriated beast, has arched its back in an attitude of challenge throughout the ages. Here on these frowning highlands life has gone on, changed only superficially, with the passing centuries. The population of this entire Andean region today is still predominantly Indian. Some of these red men inhabit tiny hamlets off the beaten track of civilization and have almost no part in the national life; but the majority are no longer pure Indians—they have entered into the Hispanic-American social structure, their blood has been fused with that of their former conquerors, and their voice is Spanish. Nevertheless, the visitor feels at once that he is in a "red man's country" when he enters the Andean highlands. Quito, La Paz, Cuzco, Sucre, and many other cities, despite all that the Spaniards have done to them, still seem more Indian than Spanish. The farther one draws away from this central nucleus of the old "Inca Empire," the more mestizo becomes the population, and finally, along the very perimeter, white blood asserts its dominance.

The Indian heritage is nowhere completely dead among these people. In the communal life of their mountain clans or *ayllus*, in their strong democratic regionalism and indigenous folk arts, in the Indianist attitudes everywhere present among the mestizo population, in their constantly evolving hybrid culture, the native background is everywhere the base.

It was in this same Andean region that the Incas of pre-conquest days developed the second of those primitive Indian civilizations which "arose and ran toward the sun." These people constituted the largest and most closely integrated native culture group on the American continents at the time of the arrival of the white man. Their chieftain was known as "the Inca," which means "great ruler" or "lord," and by analogy the plural of that term was also applied to his subjects. Inca territory covered the mountainous heart of South America from northern Ecuador to the middle of Chile, from the Pacific coast to the foothills of the Brazilian jungles. It embraced most of the present-day countries of Peru, Ecuador, Bolivia, and the northern parts of Argentina and Chile. Probably best known for their massive stone structures, without counterpart in the New World, the Incas also developed a superlative system of agriculture, many fine arts and crafts, and a social organization unequaled among primitive American peoples.

The more romantic-minded historians go so far as to state that in this vast territory there was no poverty, no unemployment, almost no crime, and that co-operative enterprise rather than competition was the mainspring of all work and living. If this is painting the picture too brightly, it is still difficult to understand how a relatively small tribe of highland Indians, with almost every obstacle of nature and man set against them, evolved from their early barbaric beginnings to the highly integrated society which the conquistadores encountered. Deep gorges, gigantic snow-capped ranges, barren and unfriendly soil, all worked against political unity and economic development. Yet in both these spheres the Incas achieved results that were remarkable. As one writer has pointed out, in the land of these people everything was inferior except man.

Unlike the civilization of the Mayas, which was dead long before Cortés and his men touched the shores of Yucatan, Inca culture was still flourishing when Pizarro invaded the country and many Spanish soldiers lived to see the glory that was Peru. Several Spanish chroniclers and one famous son of an Inca princess (his father was a Spanish conquistador) have left fascinating books on Inca history and life which can be correlated and compared, one with the other, until the salient facts are brought out. However, these historians, who were trained to interpret things with European eyes, obviously could not "see or think Indian." They threw a veil of exaggeration and romance over their subject which has falsified it to this day.

Recent archaeological research with the excavation of several hitherto unknown Inca and pre-Inca monuments, some of them entire towns in a marvelous state of preservation, has given us a less distorted picture of ancient Andean life. Archaeology is a science which sprang into being only within the past century, and the man with the spade who has brought back to life that which cannot be falsified—the actual remains and decorative motifs of Inca life—has debunked the old "empire builders" who wrongly saw in the world's largest and finest social integration of primitive folk culture the royalty, courts, and empire of their untutored imaginations. When such terms as these are employed, the reader must bear in mind that the Incas were Indians whose notions of rank and statehood were not at all like those of the European, but sprang out of a tribal and folk culture which lived next to the soil and never knew any other race or nationalism than its own.

The Incas were the culmination of the many diverse cultures of the Andean Indian groups which had preceded them. The earliest of these, known as the Chavín culture of the eastern slope of the northern Peruvian Highlands, began around 1000 B.C. and endured for 500 years. These people not only paralleled in time the Olmec culture of the Mexican east coast, but also worshiped the same man-jaguar god. The jaguar, apparently, represented to both peoples the fierce, wild strength of the earth, and so came to be in his deific union as man-jaguar the divinity who was both the creative force and the destroyer. The man-jaguar was the vital regenerative power, to which man could pray and beseech redress. He was also the destroyer, if things went wrong. By analogy he suggests the Dionysus of the ancient Greeks. The Chavin peoples built large ceremonial centers in the northern Peruvian Highlands. One large stone building, known as El Castillo, was nearly 250 feet square. Around 500 B.C. the Chavin culture faded from history.

From 100 B.C. to A.D. 200 the Paracas culture of the south coast of Peru produced its exquisite textiles of glowing colors and its impressive funeral offerings of gold ornaments, clothes, weapons, food, and pottery. The Nazca culture of this same region later mingled with and replaced that of the Paracas people. The period of the Nazca flowering was A.D. 200 to A.D. 600. The Nazca artists continued the weaving of textiles in the Paracas tradition, and also carved out grand designs on the near-by desert plateaus above their irrigated crop lands. They, too, molded exquisite pottery.

The Mochica culture of the northern Peruvian coast was contemporaneous with that of the Nazcas. The Mochicas spread out of several contiguous valleys. The name is from the Moche river near today's Trujillo. The Mochicas constructed large stone pyramids and produced strikingly realistic portrait vases which would be the envy of any modern artist. Their great temple to the Sun covered eight acres. The Mochicas maintained their dominance in this area for about three centuries, between A.D. 200 to A.D. 600.

At the time of their decline there arose near the shores of Lake Titicaca in Bolivia the Tiahuanaco culture, which became the first more or less universal culture of the Andean area, and its religion became the universal church of the Andean Indians of all the surrounding regions. The Tiahuanaco culture lasted from A.D. 600 to A.D. 1000, when it began to merge with that of the Incas.

The immediate predecessors of the Incas, however, were the Chimu tribes who occupied a narrow strip of land which extended for almost 600 miles along the northern coastland of Peru. The Chimus constructed massive fortifications in order to defend themselves against the advancing Incas, but were unable to stem the tide. Their period was between A.D. 1000 and A.D. 1200, when the Incas took over.

All of these preceding cultures contributed much to that of the Incas, but among them only the Tiahuanacans, whose great ceremonial center was in Bolivia, were endowed with the gift of organization and politico-religious control which later made the Incas unique in their part of the world. The ancient ruins of Tiahuanaco still stand as a mute and impressive testimony of their power and dominion. No visitor to Bolivia should leave without seeing them.

The railroad track out of La Paz westward passes directly through these ancient ruins, many of whose stones were torn from their places and ground into gravel for grading the roadbed. The Bolivian government has recently made possible extensive excavations in this area. The Bolivian archaeologist Carlos Ponce Sanjines has uncovered and restored the tremendously impressive sunken temple at Tiahuanaco where an extraordinary race existed many years before the Incas. In this temple great sculptured heads jut from walls of precisely cut stone blocks of enormous size.

The architecture of these people was more massive than that of the Incas, and the Spanish priest Acosta, who visited the scene shortly after the Spanish conquest, found one stone that measured thirty-eight by eighteen by six feet. There were many others almost as large. Some of these colossal stones were lifted and fitted into doorways; other entrances were cut out of a solid piece, and many of them were carved in bold relief. The massive retaining walls of Tiahuanaco, lifted upward by some incomprehensible prodigy of effort and held in place with the aid of metal clamps, formed one of the most gigantic monuments of all time. The Tiahuanacans, like the other American races, never knew the use of the wheel and must have depended almost entirely on human labor to drag these great blocks from the quarries to the final building sites. They probably utilized a combination of crude fiber ropes with which they bound and pulled the stones forward while levers were inserted under them from behind to apply force from that direction, and logs or cylindrical rocks over which they might roll were placed underneath. Time was of no concern to the leaders of these people. Whether it took five or fifty years to transport a great building stone was of only the slightest concern. Human labor, too, was a factor which they might extend, stretch, and multiply almost indefinitely. Ten or twenty thousand strong pairs of arms and legs stretched out over a period of one- or twoscore years is the rough equivalent of any machine devised by the ingenious brain of man.

The territory of the Tiahuanacans covered most of the central Andean highlands. These people organized government, agriculture, and conquest on a scale vaster than the grandest dreams of all who had preceded them on the American scene, and if the achievements of their architects and engineers are often confused with those of the Incas, it is because the latter took up where the Tiahuanacans left off, and on the bases of this earlier race constructed many of their great temples and fortresses. From

this point forward we shall make no attempt to distinguish between Incas
and pre-Incas, whose civilizations were thus blended to produce so many
of those megalithic remains which are the constant wonder of generations
that followed.

The exact date at which the Incas appeared in the central Andes is un-
known, but it was approximately four centuries before the coming of the
Spaniards, or about A.D. 1100. Probably originating somewhere in the region of Lake Titicaca, they established their first permanent center in the
Peruvian valley of Cuzco, eleven thousand feet above the level of the sea.
Here they found one of the loveliest and most fertile regions in all the
Andes. From the foot of a snowy peak the river descends through "groves
of fine trees alive with singing birds" and across the valley that increases
in fertility and beauty as it flows along. Between the mighty stone fortresses of Pisac and Ollantaytambo lies a part of the vale reminiscent of
our own Yosemite, with sheer cliffs rising abruptly on one side and snow-
capped mountain peaks towering above the other. "In the valley are raised
splendid crops of maize, unequaled elsewhere, grown on terraces arranged
in patterns," and the gardens are filled with tropical fruits. Clinging vines
of passionflowers embrace the trees and add their deep green background
to the flitting of brilliant wings. The altitude is too high and rare for the
white man to find entirely comfortable, but to the Indian of the Andes,
who could not endure life at sea level, Cuzco Valley was the enchanted
Eden of his desire. There in the center of this beautiful vale the Incas
raised—on the megalithic remains of those who had gone before—their
own great center. Even today the archaeologist looks at the city with its
old stone walls still serving as the foundation of many a Spanish structure
lifted upon them and speaks the whole truth when he says: "There is only
one Cuzco in the wide world."

Cuzco was the capital city of the Incas. It was also the Mecca of their
religion. From here they expanded in successive waves of conquest: north,
south, east, and west, until their dominions embraced the half million or so
square miles and the five or six millions of inhabitants encountered by the
Spaniards at the time of their conquest.

Just as we have our story of Adam and Eve, there were several legends
about the origin of the Inca people. One of the most current is the story
of the Golden Wedge, according to which the Sun, wearied of the crude,
barbaric ways of the uncivilized Indians, sent two of his children, a son
and a daughter, to lift them from their primitive life. Placed on earth near
the banks of Lake Titicaca, these two children of the Sun were given a
golden wedge which they were to carry with them wherever they wandered; and on the spot where this wedge sank without effort into the
ground and disappeared they were told to found their mother city. When
the divine pair reached the vicinity of Cuzco, their talisman slid into the
earth and vanished from sight. Then the son traveled toward the north

and his sister toward the south, telling all the Indians they encountered about their divine mission. Gathering many followers about them, they finally returned to Cuzco (which means "center" or "navel"), where they founded their new kingdom. The son taught the men the masculine arts, and his royal sister instructed the women in the finer accomplishments of the feminine world. From this pair all succeeding Incas of "royal" blood were said to have descended, and it was the custom of many of their rulers, if not of all of them, to marry their eldest sister in order to keep pure the divine pedigree of the Sun Father.[16] However, the Incas also indulged in polygamy to a liberal extent, and the offspring from these extramarital unions were said in some cases to number one, two, or even three hundred! Those who were descendants in the male line were all considered to belong to the Inca ruling caste, though not necessarily to the "royal" family itself. In time this caste came to assume over the conquered tribes of the territory much the same position as Roman citizens held over their subject peoples.

This whole legend of the Golden Wedge was obviously devised at a date subsequent to the time of its supposed occurrence in order "to gratify the vanity of Peruvian Monarchs and to give additional sanction to their authority by deriving it from celestial origin."

Consequently, Inca religion and state were one. The ruler could not only say of himself, "I am the State," but could add as well, "I am a son of the God of my people, and the Supreme Pontiff of His religion." Nowhere else in the world, except perhaps in pre-Westernized Japan, where the Son of Heaven was both Emperor and God, was such sweeping authority delegated to a single individual. When the imperial *llautu* or band with its distinctive red fringe was first placed on the Inca's head he became in essence the source from which all blessings flowed. The proudest chieftain, on entering the Inca's presence, had to appear barefoot and with a "light burden on his shoulders in token of homage." As the outstanding insigne of their rank all Inca chiefs had pierced ear lobes in which they wore large golden disks. With time their ears became so distended that they almost touched the shoulders, and for this reason the Spaniards referred to them as *los orejones*, the "ones with the lopped ears."

On the other side of the picture and resting on the absolute power of the ruler, as any law rests ultimately on faith or force, there existed throughout the vast Inca dominions a closely knit tribal structure under which every worker's job was assured for him and a worker was assured for every job. Beginning with communal agriculture and division of land, this doctrine of enforced co-operation gradually permeated the whole fabric of living and thought among the Inca people. The system was not born suddenly but was the result of hundreds of years of evolution.

The basis of Inca society was the community or clan, called the *ayllu*. In pre-Inca days these ayllus controlled every public act, owned all the land, and provided the community or tribal government. Tribes were made up of clans or communities of various sizes and were democratically run by their councils of elders. The ownership of land was communal; work was communal; government was communal. Each ayllu was fraternally bound together in the belief that all its members descended from a common ancestor. This kinship was often fictitious, but it was strongly maintained by tradition and kept the common spirit alive. Sometimes a confederation of several ayllus would band together for a common purpose and establish a larger organization. This is exactly what the Inca "empire" was in its initial stages. As time passed and the central authority increased, ownership of lands became theoretically vested in the Inca, but actually the ayllu remained (and in many regions still remains) as the backbone of the structure.

Under this system private ownership of land as we know it did not exist. Each Indian family did hold a small plot on which the house was erected and a few plants could be grown. But as the family grew, new divisions were made, each son receiving a like share from the community or from the Inca. These family plots could not be sold or accumulated, nor was their ownership a matter of prestige. Land existed for the use of all alike and was not a commodity. Aside from these small family plots the community or ayllu itself owned its commons. Work on them was performed co-operatively.

The Incas centralized this communal system and brought into being two other landowners. Under them lands were divided three ways: one part belonging to the Sun, a second part to the Inca and his family, and the third part to the communities or ayllus. The head of a family was allowed one *tupu* (about two acres) for each male in the household and a half tupu for each female. A checkup on this division was made every year, followed by the necessary adjustments. Guano droppings and dead fish heads were used for fertilizer. The plow was a one-pronged wooden spade driven into the earth by foot from a crossbar near its point. Most of the work was done collectively, and it was the enforced duty of all able-bodied farmers to share in the labor.

First the lands belonging to the Sun were cultivated; then those of the widows and orphans, the old and the infirm; next the land of the people in general was worked, and last of all that of the Inca. Only in tilling the people's land was a certain amount of leeway granted, and even then every man was expected to aid his neighbor and many crops were sown and harvested in common. In all other cases there was a strict direction of co-operative effort. When any section of land which belonged to the Sun, the Inca, or to those unable to work was to be cultivated, criers perched on the summit of neighborhood towers blasted away on shell trumpets to attract general attention and, that obtained, shouted "on such and such a date all workers will turn out to till the fields." Workers already knew from their foremen to which particular plot they should proceed. One regional chieftain who forewent the ordained order of tilling and had a relative's plot cultivated before that of the widows, the old, and the infirm was summarily executed on a gallows erected on the land where the crime had been committed.

When the turn for working the lands of the Incas came, it was a time for great rejoicing. Every able-bodied person in the district—man, woman, or child—arose at daybreak. They all put on their gayest attire and then proceeded to work as if to some great jubilee. In the fields they "went through the labors of the day with the same joyous spirit, chanting their popular ballads which commemorated the heroic deeds of the Incas, regulating their movements by the measure of the chant, and all mingling in the chorus."[17]

Other types of work were carried out under a similar pattern. Principal among these was the shearing of the great flocks of llamas and alpacas which belonged almost exclusively to the Sun and to the Incas. These Peruvian animals, which bear some kinship to both the sheep and the camel families, were scattered over the mountains under the care of shepherds, who drove them from pasture to pasture according to the season and attended to their care and feeding. They were sheared by all the workers of the district in common, and their wool was collected and placed in the central storehouses, from which it was later dealt out to various families as necessity demanded. The women then set themselves to the task of weaving it into cloth, covers, and articles of clothing. After this job was finished they were all required to weave for the Inca. Even though these tasks were performed inside the home, governmental inspectors appeared at unexpected intervals and checked up to see that there were no shirkers and to make certain that the quality of the weave was up to par. In every village there were two or three silos or warehouses—one to take care of the lean years of the town, the other belonging to the Sun or to the Inca. Along the highways, located at intervals of ten to twelve miles, there were others to take care of traveling military groups. The products of all community labor were sent to these commissaries: food, wool, clothing, arms, and footwear. The contents were built up over a long period of time and were sufficient to take care of the population of the district for several years.

Paternalistic rule did not destroy artistic expression among the Incas; and in weaving especially they produced fabrics which have never been equaled before or since. Both in the fineness of the weave and in the designs incorporated, the best Peruvian pieces are not primitive, they are superlative. The natives of Peru "discovered and made use of almost every known technique of weaving," and they developed the art itself "to a point unequaled by man in the whole course of human history."[7] Their pottery, too, was perhaps the finest and most varied in the Americas, oftentimes being fashioned in the form of well-delineated human heads, bodies, animals of various kinds, and with a richness of design that was almost limitless.

The construction of temples, royal buildings, roads, bridges, aqueducts, fortresses, agricultural terraces, and all similar labor for the public welfare, was performed by the community working together. A few artisans were instructed in metalwork, especially that of gold, silver, and copper, and the secrets of the trade were passed down from father to son. Work was found for everyone in the Inca territory, even for the children, and as sloth was a crime against the state, it was punishable by law. Nor was a man permitted to alter the nature of his work or his station in life. Both were fixed from birth, and a sense of nearly absolute security walked hand in hand with a giant leveling process. This was probably one of the reasons why the Incas never developed more than the crudest system of writing —that most fundamental of all products of the civilized imagination.

The only records left by these people were in the form of knotted strings of different colors known as *quipus*. The Incas had no hieroglyphics, no alphabet, and only a very limited scope in their quipu vocabulary. Abstract ideas, narration, or description of almost any kind could not be properly recorded. The principal use of the quipus was for the purpose of accounting and for keeping statistics. How many pounds of wool were in the central storehouse? How many persons were born or died in a given year? How many workers were engaged in such and such an engineering project? Records such as these were easy to keep on the knotted strings, but beyond this it was difficult to go.*

The quipu itself was a cord about two and a half feet in length on which other strings were tied and left dangling like an irregular fringe. A proper reading depended on both the number and the color of the knots to be deciphered. For example, gold was represented by the color yellow, white indicated silver, red meant soldiers, et cetera. A few abstract meanings were also possible; for example, red for war and white for peace. Since the range of available colors was extremely limited, one color often had more than one meaning, and it was then up to the highly trained keeper of the strings to remember which color referred to which meaning.

There were several of these keepers in each town, the number varying from four to thirty, depending on the size of the place and the importance of the records. By dividing up their work, an incredible number of records could be kept accurately. Accounts of vital statistics, population, tributes, crops, important dates, military figures, and innumerable other records could be entrusted to the keepers of these quipus. As a certain

* In August, 1970, a German cryptographer of Tübingen University, Thomas S. Barthel, reported in *Times* that the Incas did have a primitive script of geometric designs (*tocapus*) woven into fabrics or painted on vases. He also claimed to have deciphered 25 of the more than 400 symbols. Many other scholars were skeptical.

amount of memorization was implicit to the process, some history could also be recorded by a slight extension of the quipu meanings. For example, let us take our own dates of July 4 or February 22. Such dates as these would immediately call to mind the history surrounding them. In a similar manner more abstract messages might be preserved and the number five, let us say, could, in a certain case, evoke the commandment of that number, a certain important message or deed in the life of the fifth Inca, or some analogous tradition of the people. In this way much heroic history was passed on from generation to generation, but unfortunately, when the last keepers of the strings died, it was impossible for anyone else to decipher the knotted strings which they had left behind, and a great deal of this valuable information was lost. Many Indians of the Andean highlands still keep their records on these knotted strings. For example, a shepherd looking after a herd of sheep or llamas of mixed ownership will record those belonging to the proprietor in red knots, those which belong to him in white knots, and those of the priest in yellow knots. In order to arrive at these calculations, he generally first places stones on the ground and, after satisfying himself that the details are correct, will record them in final form in his knots, which show not only the proportion of the herd belonging to each owner, but also the number of ewes, lambs, and rams.

Among the most interesting ceremonies of the Incas was that of their collective weddings. Always careful to make every provision for maximum control and maximum production from the ground up, the Incas did not encourage individual marriages with their consequent waste of time and effort, not to mention the great surplus of bachelors and old maids invariably left over. Consequently, once each year or two all girls who had reached the age of eighteen and all men who had become twenty-four since the last collective ceremony were gathered into the main plaza of each town and there made man and wife by a minister of the Inca who passed among them, joining their hands and pronouncing the necessary words. Not all individual choice was taken away, for more often than not lovers managed to stand opposite each other and were united in these marriages. Those unfortunates who had made no choice were lined up face to face along with the others and wedded whether they liked it or not. There was also a limitation placed on the choice that one might make. No inhabitant of one community was permitted to marry a person who lived in another, nor were the newlyweds allowed to change the site of their residence without special permission. This made it easier to keep a close check on them and to circumvent the loss of time involved in the movement of workers from place to place. Every able-bodied person had to be continuously employed every waking moment, in order to make the Inca system work under the primitive conditions surrounding it.

In their religion the Incas were primarily worshipers of the Sun. There were other gods, too, among them a "Supreme Maker of the Universe" called Pachacamac, the unknown god who had never manifested himself before his people. This god, however, rarely entered into the thoughts or lives of either priests or people, among whom the Sun was generally regarded as the Almighty. Lesser deities were the Moon, who was said to be the wife of the Sun, and hence mother of the Inca race; the Rainbow, standard of all Inca armies; Venus, Thunder, and Lightning.

The Incas built temples only to the Sun, the Supreme Father of their daily worship. Their sacrifices consisted mainly of young llamas or alpacas, rabbits, birds, and the different fruits of the harvest. Though denied by some historians, it seems conclusive that there were also occasional sacrifices of human beings. When the Inca himself died, or, as he put it, "went to rest with his father the Sun," some of his attendants and favorite concubines were usually immolated on his tomb.

The Incas believed in the resurrection of the body, but apparently differentiated between body and soul, calling the former while it was alive "animated earth." There was a place in their religion for both heaven and hell, heaven being a state of blessed peace and rest, and hell, which was placed at the earth's core, was known as the "devil's house."

Besides the priests of their religion, with the Inca himself as their head, there were many hundreds of "Virgins of the Sun." These virgins, all of whom were of noble Inca blood, lived a cloistered life in quarters reserved for them and outside of which they never ventured. In Cuzco alone there were approximately fifteen hundred of them. Their mission in life was to guard the sacred fire obtained at the ceremony of Raymi, when all inhabitants of the land turned out to greet the rising Sun. Aside from their religious duties their principal occupation was to weave decorations for the temples and wearing apparel for the Inca and his family of the finest alpaca wool. The buildings in which they lived were called "Houses of the Chosen," for all virgins were selected on a basis of both birth and beauty. If one of these virgins was unfaithful to her vow of chastity she was buried alive, her lover was strangled, and the place of his residence was "razed to the ground and sowed with stones as if to efface every memory of his existence." On the other hand, the most beautiful of the young girls were selected from these cloisters to become mistresses of the Inca and were sent to fill his many retreats in different parts of the country. This was one origin of those often-told legends of the Amazons, because many savage Indian tribes either saw or heard of these virginal centers, and then proceeded to fabricate stories about whole countries run by women. The Spaniards took them at their word and sought for the nation of the Amazons but never found it.

The greatest religious celebration of the Incas was the Festival of Raymi, held at the season of the summer solstice when the Sun, having reached "the southern extremity of his course, retraced his path as if to gladden the hearts of his chosen people." As the appointed day drew near, nobles and pilgrims from all parts of the kingdom poured into Cuzco to be present at the sacred ceremony. Following a rigid three-day fast, all those within the capital city put on their finest garments and gathered at dawn in the central square to greet the rising Sun. Brilliant canopies of richest wool and lovely featherwork were borne over the heads of Inca chiefs. It seemed as if over the teeming masses of his worshipers lay the endless mantle of a barbaric god. When the rays of the rising Sun appeared over the eastern horizon, a great shout arose from the multitude, which swelled into a crescendo of dissonance as musicians burst forth on their primitive instruments, playing louder and louder as their deity arose in the heavens. This joyous celebration was followed by a more restrained devotion, and finally the sacred fire was kindled by means of a concave mirror focused on dry cotton. As a part of the Sun Father's body, this was entrusted to the Virgins of the Sun for safe-keeping until the year was out.

Any blasphemy against the Inca religion was punishable by death, and the Emperor along with his priests and people generally accorded the Sun the profoundest veneration. There were occasions, however, when an astute mind did call into question the verity of this omnipotence. The Inca historian, Garcilaso, tells the following story about Huayna Capac, greatest of all Inca conquerors:

One day this ruler, who happened to be in the presence of his high priest, stared directly into the rays of the Sun, and the priest had to remind him that this was not permitted by their religion. Huayna Capac then turned to the priest and said:

"I should like to ask you two questions about what you have just said to me. First of all, I am your king and pontiff: now is there any amongst you who would dare to command me to rise and undertake a long journey?"

The priest answered that this would be unthinkable, and the Inca then continued:

"And would any of my chieftains, no matter what his power or worldly estate, refuse to obey me if I should command him to travel to far away Chile?"

The priest responded that no chieftain would dare disobey such a command.

"Then," said the Inca, "I tell you that this our Father the Sun must have a greater master than he who thus commands him to journey across the sky day after day with never a respite, for if he were the Supreme Lord, he would surely sometime cease traveling and rest a moment, even though there were no necessity for it."[16]

In their temples to the Sun, the Incas placed the most lavish decorations of gold, silver, and precious stones. All mines belonged to the Inca, and consequently every bit of this great wealth flowed into his hands. Gold was never used for coin, nor did it have any actual cash value. It was esteemed for its beauty alone and was used extensively for ornament. It was, moreover, a sacred metal, for the Incas spoke of it as being "the tears wept by the Sun." Copper and bronze were the utilitarian metals of the Incas, and as such were turned into heads for war clubs, utensils of various kinds, tools, and other useful items.

In the great Temple of the Sun in Cuzco there was a display of barbaric wealth such as had never been seen before in the world. The four interior walls of the building were covered with roughly hammered paper-thin sheets of gold, and over the main altar was a huge golden figure of the Sun studded crudely with precious stones. The figure represented a massive round face with flaming rays emanating from it in every direction. When the Sun struck this image it shone brilliantly, and its reflected sheen cast a golden light through the great hall of the temple. On each side of the Sun were the embalmed bodies of dead Inca rulers resting on golden chairs, and according to many who saw them, with a marvelous appearance of life.

There was also a huge silver room in the temple dedicated to the Moon, and here were laid out the mummies of Inca wives. Other rooms were consecrated to Venus, Page of the Sun, to the gods of Thunder and Lightning, and to the Rainbow "emanation of their glorious deity," which was painted on the wall in all its glorious colors. The banner of the Rainbow was the standard of all Inca armies, and they carried it and their religion over all the vast lands they conquered.

The Temple of the Sun and several smaller chapels were surrounded by a great stone wall of magnificent workmanship, the top of which was covered with a cornice or crest of gold a yard wide that gave the building the appearance of wearing a golden crown. Inside the temple there were also decorations of gold and silver flowers, plants, and animals of exquisite workmanship.

When the Spaniards sacked Cuzco, they tore from the temple all the rich decorations that remained, and after dividing them by lot, melted most of the treasure down in the form of gold (bullion) bars and shipped it back to Spain. Only the one fifth reserved for the King was kept in its original form.

Cuzco with its temple was not alone among the mighty monuments of Inca architecture. There are many other ruins on an even greater scale, with Inca stonework often superimposed on even more ancient remains. At the north of the city, situated on a hill seven hundred and sixty feet above it, lies the colossal fortress of Sacsahuaman, its protective walls rising in three successive terraces above the valley below. The first wall, constructed of gigantic blue-gray stones, is half a mile long, and was once twenty-five to thirty feet high. One of its stones measures twenty-six by fourteen by twelve feet. Thirty-five feet back of this rampart is another wall eighteen feet high, and eighteen feet behind this is still a third, fourteen feet in height. The cyclopean masonry of this fortress is unique in the world.

If mighty Sacsahuaman were not enough to defend Cuzco from the hordes which might have looked greedily on its fertile vale from the open passes to the north, there were three more mammoth fortresses guarding its approaches: Pisac, Ollantaytambo, and Machu Picchu, each of them a memorable architectural monument in its own right. The last is also the best-preserved Inca town-citadel discovered thus far. Undoubtedly others still lie unexcavated, awaiting the hand of the archaeologist to give them new life. These three megalithic fortresses were not originally conceived by the Incas, but by their predecessors, those unknown builders whose mighty work is easily distinguishable from the finely dressed, more precisely dimensioned, overlaying stonework of the Incas themselves. The Incas took what they found and built upon it, incorporating the whole into a series of structures as unified in their completed forms as was the closely knit culture substance of their social order.

Ollantaytambo, set on a spur of rock and guarding its own beautiful valley, extends in massive terraces along the mountainside, its great blocks "shaped and polished and set so perfectly in the walls that the joints are hardly discernible. . . ." Many of its stones are "twelve to twenty feet in length, one-third as wide and one-fourth as thick."[8] The legend of the young warrior Ollantay and his beloved Cusi Coyllur (Joyful Star), daughter of the Inca whom he won after ten years of war and tribulations, hovers about these impregnable walls with its aura of romance.

But it is Machu Picchu, last of the four fortresses, holding the entrance to Inca-land from the jungles below, that most captivates the imagination of the visitor today. It is at a much lower level than Cuzco, at an altitude of about six thousand feet, which in the tropics means a riot of color bursting from the earth against a background of deep green creepers, trees, and moss. Here is an entire town preserved in an almost perfect state just as it appeared in the days when the soldiers of the Incas were garrisoned there. Even some of the thatched roofs have been replaced so that the buildings may be used as residences for the caretakers.

Machu Picchu is the most Inca-looking of all the forts. Its stones are more regularly proportioned, and many thousands of them are as perfectly rectangular in form as if they had been precisely sawed to fit into place. Amidst its wonderful stone walls, stairways, towers, and aqueducts, Machu Picchu, in a setting of wild red orchids and huge yellow lilies, looks down from dizzy heights on the Urubamba canyon which winds its way hundreds of feet below. No ordinary Indian host could have gotten by the ramparts of Machu Picchu and its companion fortresses of Ollantaytambo, Pisac, and Sacsahuaman. Each fort could have garrisoned hundreds, perhaps thousands, of warriors. There were storage facilities for food which would have lasted several years, aqueducts which made the water supply inviolate, and the mammoth stone construction which would have rendered any attack by blowguns, arrows, and Indian maces ridiculous. The Incas reigned supreme and uncontested in their sacred valley until the coming of the white man, who brought new weapons and a new manner of dealing out death.

The Incas used no mortar to hold their stones together, but balanced and fitted them into each other so perfectly that their structures were nearly imperishable under the ravages of time. The blade of a knife could not be inserted between the stones of the finest Inca work, and their smooth surfaces have puzzled many archaeologists, who could find no way to explain such precision cutting with primitive instruments. Recent investigation in the field by Dr. and Mrs. H. S. Tschopik, who lived in Peru for many years doing research for the Peabody Museum, shows that the Incas frequently sawed these stones into shape with saws made of extremely hard reeds of the Andean region, on which teeth of naturally formed silicon had accumulated. These reeds were split in two long pieces throughout their length, and each half became a saw. Sand and water were then placed on the stone to be cut, in order to increase the effectiveness of the abrasive, and the sawing began. The life of such a saw was probably not very long, but the supply was well-nigh inexhaustible. The discovery of several stones only partially cut through, as well as considerable piles of stone dust around cutting sites, plus the finding of the saw reeds themselves takes this explanation out of the realm of conjecture and places it among accepted archaeological facts.

The quarries from which most of the stone for Cuzco was taken are located at a distance of about twenty-two miles from the city. They are of trachytic and basaltic rock and cover an area of more than half a square mile. Stone chippings litter the precincts, and scattered here and there are blocks of various sizes in all stages of preparation, from the most rudely hewn to the most finely polished. There are rough stone huts for the quarrymen, and a larger hut with a wall around it for the foreman. Everything seems to indicate that the quarries were in full operation when their work was suddenly interrupted, and that at the time of the conquest the Incas were still enlarging and beautifying their capital.

Stones were quarried by excavating under them where possible, then a groove was cut in the upper surface where a fracture was desired. In this groove were bored oblong holes to quite a depth, and wooden wedges were driven in. Water was then poured into the groove and consequent swelling broke off the rock. The device is ancient and probably goes back as far as the art of stone cutting itself.[18] The block was next roughly shaped by hard stone hammers or axes, then its exposed surfaces could be more carefully wrought by chisels of bronze and its connecting surfaces sawed evenly with silicon-covered reeds. Finally the stones were dragged to the scene of construction on rollers by fiber ropes and sheer man power just as in pre-Inca days.

Despite its gigantic conception, Inca architecture was in many ways extremely rude. Ceilings were supported by beams laid across the walls and tied in place. No nails were used. The roofs were of thatch, sometimes piled up five or six feet thick, and were subject to constant repair. Even the Temple of the Sun was no exception. Doorways were closed only with strips of leather or hide, and the few small, high windows let in just enough light to keep the interior in a sort of semi-gloom. At that high altitude, however, this was much to be preferred to the chilly air which would otherwise have made the buildings untenable.

There seemed to be no such thing as a continuous building with one room running into the next or opening into a connecting hall, but only separate rooms, sometimes opening into an interior court with no roof. The "palaces" of the Inca, scattered in different places over a large territory, were constructed along massive, low-flung lines with little attempt at exterior elegance. Inside, however, they displayed a richness that many a European noble would have envied. Plaques of gold and silver studded the sides of the rooms, and lovely ornaments of the same metals were placed in specially covered niches in the walls. The finest Peruvian woolens, of so soft a texture as to suggest eider down, and all containing beautiful designs and colors of fast vegetable dyes, filled the rooms as rugs, covers, and draperies. Piled high, they also served as beds.

Dwellings of the ordinary citizen did not, of course, belong in the same class. In fact, a vast proportion of the houses were constructed of wood and thatch, or of adobe bricks made of earth and straw, and most of them contained only a single room. There was little comfort in these houses, as comfort was a luxury reserved for the mighty. They opened into narrow but long and teeming streets, on which brilliantly dressed Indians, in whose garments a deep red predominated, mingled with llamas of fleecy white, brown, or black wool peacefully bearing their burdens. The yellow thatched roofs of buildings brightened considerably the cold gray of heavy-set stone or adobe walls. On the whole, it was a scene suggesting security, contentment, and pride of race, which, if left to seek its destiny through the passing years, might well have produced a civilization comparable with the ancient world civilizations.

In their domestication of the llama and the alpaca, the Incas obtained not only beasts of burden, but animals producing a fine wool without which life on an extensive scale in those high altitudes would have been impossible. No other American civilization had such domesticated animals. There were four different kinds of these mountain sheep-camels in the Andean region: two of them existing in a wild state, the guanaco and the vicuña, and two of them in domesticated breeds obtained from these wild animals, the llama and the alpaca. Numerous flocks of the latter grazed throughout Inca territory just as they do to this day, and there were even more extensive herds of wild guanacos and vicuñas which roamed over the frozen ranges without shepherds or folds.

These herds were rigorously protected by the central government. A rich store of fine wool was obtained from them. Once a year there was organized a great hunt in which these animals were rounded up and sheared. On the date set, a huge number of men, sometimes several thousand, formed a cordon around the district which was to be hunted. These men were equipped with poles and spears, and to the accompaniment of shouts and beatings in the bush they scared up all manner of wild game and sent it scurrying toward the center of an ever-narrowing circle. When the hunt ended, all the timid deer, guanacos, and vicuñas were concentrated in a central valley with no way of escape. The male deer were slaughtered, their meat dried and preserved, and their hides made into Peruvian leather. The wild sheep were caught and sheared and then set free again to resume their life on the solitary mountains. Wool thus collected was stored in the central warehouses; as necessity demanded, the coarser guanaco wool was doled out to the people, while the silky fleece of the relatively few vicuñas was reserved for the ruling Inca and his chieftains.

The best known of these four kinds of Peruvian sheep is, of course, the llama. To this day it is the Andean beast of burden par excellence, the producer of wool for clothing and covers, the maker of fuel dung for the family hearth—in a word, the friend and provider of many a poor Indian household. The llama is the largest of the four above-mentioned varieties, and will sometimes carry a load of more than a hundred pounds. But under an overload, no matter how slight, it will often plop to the ground on its belly and refuse to budge even after the excess has been removed. Sometimes the Indian can start it up by calmly collecting a number of small stones and pitching these at its nose one by one until the animal finally gets tired of the play and rises to its feet.

The cost and care of maintaining these animals are almost nil, for they subsist on the scanty foliage of the mountain shrubs and grasses, and such is the structure of their stomachs that they can go for several weeks without drinking any water. The llama has a soft hoof from which emanates a sharp claw, enabling it to travel over the rocks and ice without slipping. It never has to be shod. Flocks of several hundreds of these animals can be seen plodding up and down the mountain paths, moving in perfect order under the direction of their Indian herder, who sometimes with a shout and sometimes with a stone cast from his sling will quickly bring stragglers back into file.

In addition to this pastoral side of life, the Incas carried out many marvelous engineering projects. Arable land was so scarce that reclamation had to be undertaken on a vast scale. Valleys were leveled off and freed of stones; the courses of streams and rivers were straightened out by means of newly formed channels of masonry, and, finally, slopes of the mountains themselves were fashioned into thousands of terraces held in place by supporting stone walls behind which tons of fine alluvial soil were placed. Irrigation was made possible by long aqueducts, in some places tunneled through solid rock, which brought water from remote distances and conveyed it along the summits, above the line of rain-loosened earth and washouts. On this reclaimed land, crops of potatoes, which Peru gave to the world, and many varieties of corn, as well as coca, quinoa or Peruvian rice, tomatoes, and other native plants were cultivated. In order to terrace and reclaim a single acre of this barren mountain land, it was often necessary to move by hand some five million pounds of earth. Despite this difficulty, the terraced farms of the Incas covered an extent of territory many times greater than that which is in actual cultivation today. Hundreds of mountainsides which are now overgrown with underbrush and weeds show in their ruined terraces the indelible imprint of these staircase farms of the ancients.[19]

In road and bridge building, also, Inca engineers achieved results which are amazing. Two long roadways linked the northern and southern portion of the empire, one passing through the desert along the coast, the other traversing the forbidding crags and ravines of the high sierra. Each road was from fifteen hundred to two thousand miles in length, and while they were mere footpaths throughout most of their extent, for no wheel ever turned upon them, they did embody many impressive engineering feats. A few ravines over which these roads had to pass were filled in with masonry; but streams, rivers, and the highest drops were crossed by suspension bridges whose giant fiber cables, often as thick as a man's body, were firmly secured to stone buttresses on the opposite banks. From these main cables dangled smaller ones, to the bottoms of which the foot passageway was fixed. Sometimes a bridge would dip toward the center and sway crazily over its abyss, but construction was good and the purpose was amply served. Many similar bridges are still in use in the high Andean sierra today.

On their highways the Incas maintained a regular post service of human runners, four or five of whom were stationed in huts at intervals of a mile or so along the road. These messengers or *chasquis* were especially trained for their jobs, and as the distance assigned to each man was short, messages and small parcels could be carried many miles in a single day. Fresh fish and choice tropical fruits were frequently brought from considerable distances over the mountains to Cuzco as special delicacies for the Inca's table.

In astronomy the Incas were behind the Mayas. They had a calendar of twelve lunar months which fell short of the solar year, but they made corrections from time to time by taking observations of the sun on cylindrical columns erected in the vicinity of Cuzco. In this way they were able to determine the exact days of the solstices. Equinoxes were ascertained by means of a single pillar in the center of a circle drawn in the Temple of Cuzco. When there was an almost complete absence of shadow under the noonday sun they knew that the equinox had arrived and said that "the god sat with all his light upon the column." Other observations were taken at Quito, which is situated almost exactly on the equator.

While the Incas were behind the Mayas in astronomy, they were far ahead of any other American race in their development of medicine, especially surgery. The difficult operation of trepanning, that is, drilling a hole directly through the human skull, was frequently performed with success. Some skulls have been found with several of these holes in them, their edges showing an extent of healing which makes it certain that the patient survived. These operations were probably made necessary because so many of the wounds suffered in battle were delivered by instruments which either crushed or pierced the skull. Trepanning was then resorted to in an effort to relieve the pressure and open and clear the spot of possible irritation. Sometimes the brain itself had to be pushed back inside the skull and held there by carefully placed shells or silver braces. Strong antiseptics of native herbs were applied to the incision to prevent the start or spread of infection.

Among the intangibles of Inca achievement, but perhaps the most important element of all, because without it the entire fabric would have collapsed, was the social and economic organization of their society and the method by which the system was superimposed on the less civilized tribes over which their dominions spread. Peace to the Incas, hence the possibility for social and economic progress, was always a relative quantity, and as such was accepted by them. On the frontiers of their territory existed a state of perpetual war, or at least of eternal vigilance, while within the heart of that great circuit life pursued a more or less tranquil course, undisturbed by the frontier conflicts which were adding constantly to the empire. In order that this state of internal peace might exist in the very shadow of war, it was necessary to devise an ethics of conquest which would quickly incorporate into the social and economic body the people vanquished by Inca arms. In the first place, the Inca was always careful to keep his enemies divided and to attack them one at a time, so that victory was almost a foregone conclusion. Yet he never pushed an advantage to an extremity, was always open to negotiations, suppressed depredations on the part of his soldiers with ruthless vigor, and took the attitude that the enemy must be spared in so far as possible, "else it will be our loss, for everything that belongs to him now will soon be ours."

When the victory was won, the first thing the Incas did was to substitute their religion for that of the vanquished. Idols of the conquered people were transported to Cuzco, and their priests were commanded immediately to worship the Sun. When they saw that their own gods were powerless, resistance was seldom offered. This was the surest way of touching all the people and giving to the newly incorporated tribe a feeling of belonging to the new society—a feeling the Incas did everything in their power to quicken.

Immediately after hostilities had ceased, the fallen chief and his family were taken to Cuzco, where they were treated with every courtesy, taught the Quechua language of the conquerors, and indoctrinated into the Inca way of life. When the period of indoctrination was over, the chief was permitted to return home and resume his position under the Inca eye, but his eldest son had to remain behind as hostage. The Quechua language, which these families learned at court, became a sort of second idiom employed by persons of most consequence throughout the territory.

All the old laws and customs of the incorporated districts which were not at variance with those of the Incas were at once reproclaimed by the Emperor himself and backed up with every moral and physical force to make them effective. The new subjects were made citizens of the empire with the same security and rights as those enjoyed by their conquerors.

A careful quipu account was taken of the population and every detail of its worldly goods and domain: fields tilled and fallow, mines, salt deposits, lakes, rivers, fruit trees, herds, and so on. In this way a proper division of the land and its wealth according to the Inca social system was arrived at. If there was any disposition on the part of the inhabitants to be rebellious, the Inca did not hesitate to transfer whole districts of many thousands to other parts of the empire where they would be surrounded by loyal followers who would soon break or absorb their rebellious spirit. Through a combination of all these means of government—religion, language, old chieftains, customs and laws, the granting of citizenship rights, moderation accompanied by a vigorous suppression of disloyalty—new additions to the territory were soon indistinguishable from the oldest provinces.

What was it that made this system work? Here was a land of several millions of primitive people, poor from an economic standpoint, spread over an area far greater than that occupied by most European nations, and with every physical and linguistic disadvantage between them and the proper functioning of their system; yet despite these obstacles they achieved a sort of agrarian communism which was stable, self-sufficient, and slowly progressive over several hundreds of years. Life for the average Indian was undoubtedly on a very primitive scale. Yet all who were able to work did work; no sickness went uncared for, few crimes were committed, no aged or infirm lacked the necessities of life; and co-operation for the public welfare, rather than competition for profit, was the mainspring of Inca economy. These are achievements which any civilized nation of today might well envy. But what was the price that was paid to obtain them?

The answer is simple and obvious: It was at a sacrifice of human and individual rights as we have come to know them. It was a sort of caste system into which one was born and in which one died without power to alter one's station; it was a delegation of governing power from the many to the few; a changeless sequence of slowly passing days wherein mind, risk, and initiative were sacrificed for economic security and order.

It was no hit-or-miss proposition with the Incas. They knew what they were about, and they knew how to obtain it. A detailed recitation of their basic checks and balances sounds like a "regimentation" such as we have never dreamed of. Their system began and ended with ceaseless vigilance and law. The entire population was divided into groups of tens—one squad leader and nine subordinates. Five of these groups of ten were under the direction of an even higher commander. A group of one hundred had another superior; five hundred still another; and the highest officer of all was placed over a thousand. The Incas did not go beyond this division, as they thought no one man was capable of looking after more than a thousand subordinates. Over and above this regime, which was deeply rooted in the tribal society of Indian life, stood the ruling Inca, who gradually drew more and more power into his own hands.

The squad leaders, on whom the immediate responsibility for government lay, had a manifold task to perform: first, they were to serve as their group's representative before the government. In that capacity they requested seed to sow, wool for clothes, tools or materials to repair or to construct a home, or any other necessity provided by the government. Their second duty was to supervise the work of the squad members for which they were held responsible. The leader's third duty was to give reports on vital statistics and the state and division of lands and herds in each province so that a proper adjustment might be arrived at and provisions made available for all. The squad leader's final duty was to denounce any crime committed by a subordinate. If there was even so much as a single day's delay in doing this, the leader himself had to assume the burden of the crime in addition to bearing the guilt of his own neglect. "Consequently," writes the Inca historian, Garcilaso, "there were no criminals, vagabonds, nor idlers, for the accuser was always at hand and punishment was swift and vigorous, generally being the death penalty, no matter how slight the crime, because it was said that they were not meting out punishment to fit the crime, but were calling the criminal to account for having broken the law and the Inca's personal commandments."[16] Immediate and harsh punishment was like jerking up weeds before they could bear seed.

There were, of course, a few minor transgressions punishable not by death, but by flogging, exile, or public humiliation. Even so, the Inca penal system sounds at first hearing unduly harsh, but the resultant facts attested by many Spaniards who have no reason for misrepresentation clearly prove its efficacy. Many common crimes, such as stealing, were practically unheard of among the Incas. Houses were left open day and night without the slightest fear of thieves. The white man's avarice and looting thoroughly disgusted these primitive Indians, but they soon found it impossible to exist and not fight back in kind.

Under Inca rule, children as well as adults were promptly punished by the state for any breach of the law, and the father, who was held accountable, received a like punishment. In order that governors in whose hand the law was placed and judges who passed sentence might not relax their vigilance, the Inca had numerous "observers" directly responsible to him whose duty it was to circulate around the various precincts and keep a constant check. Any infraction in these quarters met with a doubly harsh sentence, for the Inca thought it was a greater crime for one held up as a superior and chosen to enforce the law to be guilty of breaking it than it was in the case of an ordinary citizen. The results of observations taken by these "secret police" were so highly effective that Inca law and public action became one.

A generation before the Spaniards arrived the "Inca Empire" was in its golden age. Huayna Capac, father of the ruler whom Pizarro captured and executed, had carried the banner of the Rainbow over the northern kingdom of Ecuador which he added to his own territory. He fell in love with the daughter of the chief of Quito, and by her had an illegitimate son. The Inca remained for several years in the north and this boy grew up in his father's company and won a warm place in his heart. He was named Atahualpa, the "well-beloved." The legitimate heir, Huáscar, had remained behind in Cuzco, forsaken by his father's affection.

When the old ruler died he divided his land among these two sons, and thus, after reaching a summit, there began a decline in the Inca Empire. Civil war broke out between the two brothers who certainly had no love for each other; and just as the white-winged vessels of the Spaniards touched the shores of Peru, Atahualpa was victorious in battle and made Huáscar his captive.

What might have been the course of events had Pizarro never arrived on the scene no one can say, but in the light of what happened it is certain that the land of the Incas, despite the rigorous efficiency of its government, was always an empire and never a nation. A sense of both loyalty and unity did undoubtedly exist, but coexistent with them was an enforced dependence which stifled initiative at its source. Held together tightly by its ruling caste, when that caste became divided the whole structure, lacking a foundation, fell to pieces. The path of Inca conquests had not been marked by diminution of the central authority but by the increase of it. Bad under any system, this highly integrated social scheme was fatal for the primitive Incas who came to depend upon it so entirely. There had never been any attempt to educate the people toward more self-government, nor to stimulate initiative, imagination, or progress in individual thinking, and hence defeat, complete and diastrous, sealed the doom of more than fifteen centuries of flowering Andean life.

By striking down the Inca himself, the fountainhead of their whole society, Pizarro at a single stroke destroyed the foundation and symbol of Andean unity. In later years archaeologist after archaeologist has come to work and live among the ruined Inca cities, each murmuring in his heart that in the space of a few brief months a great race was crucified, its culture substance of more than a thousand years tumbled in the dust by right of conquest.

3

THE TOLTEC-AZTEC CULTURE

Around 1000 B.C. there arose in the hot, fertile area of the Mexican Gulf Coast south of Vera Cruz the Olmec civilization, which many archaeologists believe later branched out to produce the other great classic civilizations of Middle America: Maya, Teotihuacán, Totonac, and Zapotec (Monte Albán and Mitla). The principal divinity of the Olmecs was the man-jaguar god which also headed the pantheon of the Chavín culture in Peru. The Olmecs fashioned colossal stone heads, weighing up to eighteen tons. Ten of these have been found in the area of La Venta, so the Olmec culture is also known by that name. An Olmec date on Stela "C" at Tres Zapotes in Maya-type numerals reads 31 B.C.[181]

North of Vera Cruz near Papantla between A.D. 600–1200 emerged the "El Tajín civilization" of the Totonacs. Their beautiful pyramid at El Tajín is 190 feet high, and from it jut 365 hollow stone niches, one for each day of the year. The style is firm, clean, classic. Nearby are seven spacious ball courts. Midway in time between this El Tajín civilization and that of the Olmecs is the magnificent Teotihuacán civilization of the Valley of Mexico, which surpasses both of them. The Teotihuacán culture is the most remarkable manifestation of the plateau people. It began around 300 B.C., and by the time of the Christian Era in Europe Teotihuacán had become the greatest religious and cultural center in the Indian world. These people were governed by a rigid theocracy, and worshiped Quetzalcoatl, the plumed serpent. Around A.D. 100 they completed the great pyramids at San Juan Teotihuacán, only a few miles from Mexico City.

A large population was clustered around but not actually in the ceremonial center at Teotihuacán. In addition to its pyramid-temples the center also contained many large stone buildings, called by the archaeologists "palaces," with clay roofs held up by wooden beams. These buildings had numerous rooms and invariably surrounded a patio. In many instances the walls were decorated with glowing frescoes showing processions of priestly figures, allegorical animals, and gods in colors of bright blue, red, yellow, and green. These frescoes recall the Panathenaeic frieze of the Parthenon with its sculptured procession carved under the guiding hand of the incomparable Phidias. The influence of the people of Teotihuacán extended throughout Middle America. Their religion and arts permeated the fabric of early Indian life for a thousand years.

Around A.D. 700 the great center fell, perhaps overwhelmed by a massive wave of barbarians from the north. These were the Chichimecs who belonged to the same racial and linguistic group as the later Toltecs and Aztecs. The Valley of Mexico then sank into a Dark Age which lasted for over two centuries. Toward the end of this period, c. A.D. 900, a second massive wave of Chichimecs, the Toltecs, swooped down from the north and subjugated the Valley of Mexico. Around A.D. 950 they established their own great center at Tula, fifty miles north of present-day Mexico City.

When the Toltecs arrived they occupied the whole area around Teotihuacán, and until recent investigations at Tula it was widely believed that they had built the great pyramids. Toltec culture picked up the fragments of that of Teotihuacán but its ethos was quite different. Toltec influence was also felt at Mitla, where there was a Zapotec-Mixtec Renaissance around A.D. 1000. Last of all, during the thirteenth century, the Aztecs came down from the north and merged with the Toltecs. Such is the complex and fascinating story of the early centuries in the Valley of Mexico.

Two very early Mexican pyramids exceed in area and mass Egypt's largest ones. They are not as high and the large stone block construction of the Egyptians was not used in Mexico. The Pyramid of the Sun at Teotihuacán has been inaccurately restored, while the one at Cholula has a Spanish church on its summit and is so overrun with weeds and rubble that it now resembles a rocky hill more than a pyramid. The Cholula culture outlasted that of Teotihuacán and the great pyramid there, the last of many successive stages of rebuilding, probably dates from the eighth century A.D. There are five miles of tunnels inside.

In construction these pyramids were generally built much like those of the Mayas. They were larger in size but not so highly finished. There was a heart of earth and rubble, over this a layer of stones or slabs, and then there was a final surface of stucco painted a red ocher. They had stairways, terraces, and a considerable amount of sculpturing. Their summits were always truncated and not pointed, for it was here that the temple was erected overlooking all the other buildings on the level terrain at its base. The Pyramid of the Sun at Teotihuacán is about two hundred feet high excluding its temple, which has almost completely disappeared.

The awe in which tradition holds these ancient builders affects the modern visitor to Teotihuacán. "Here in the valley which bears its name, a vast area, three and a half miles long and nearly two miles wide, was given over to clusters of imposing buildings. The whole zone was paved with a plaster floor, not once but many times. This was no residential city but a great ceremonial center given over to temples and houses for the people engaged in religious activity. There is little trace of the humble refuse of communal life. Teotihuacán is an impressive monument to the toll which men exact from themselves for their salvation."[7]

There is, near the Pyramid of the Sun, a temple to Quetzalcoatl, the principal motif of which is a series of unlovely feathered-serpent heads in stone projecting from the front wall. The sculpturing is not nearly so refined as the best Maya work, but suggests barbaric power and splendor on a vast scale. These serpents "were originally painted and some still glare at the lookers through eyes of burnished obsidian. Along the façade the serpent heads alternate with those of a strange being, who may be Tlaloc, the Rain God. On the wall behind them the undulating bodies of the snakes are carved in low relief, and sea shells, all Caribbean varieties, are used to fill the spaces left by the curves of the bodies. The effect is massive and awesome."[7]

Among the smaller artistic findings at the same place were many lovely vases, painted in soft greens, pinks, and yellows, greatly superior to any examples of pottery which have come down from the long stretch of the Archaic. The Teotihuacán craftsmen developed a combination of three-colored pottery with a lost color process resulting in a highly characteristic four-color polychrome. This later gave way to "simple lustrous wares of black and brown or vases and large jars painted in red and yellow. A flourishing trade sprang up in the importation of a thin orange ware that attains at times an almost eggshell delicacy."[7]

The classical period of Teotihuacán represented a long epoch of cultural unity in the Valley of Mexico and the surrounding regions. The disintegration of this culture, around A.D. 700, was followed by a period of darkness which lasted until the Toltecs arrived on the scene two centuries later. History now dawns in the Valley of Mexico, a militaristic regime replaces theocratic rule, and the Toltecs slowly absorb all they are able from those who have gone before. However, there is an actual regression in nearly all of the arts.

The Toltec center at Tula, established c. A.D. 950, does not in any way suggest the refined artistry of Teotihuacán, but is characterized by a vigorous and savage strength. The Toltecs were great warriors; the cult of blood and fierceness guided their lives and even permeated their architecture. They continued the worship of the plumed serpent god, and established a tribute state which imposed its will by force on all neighboring tribes, much as the Aztecs did later on.

When Toltec power was broken c. A.D. 1160 and their great center at

Tula was overrun by northern tribes, the culture level of the people on the Mexican plateau again began a descent. The Toltecs did not suddenly disappear from the pages of history, nor was there any sudden mass migration. Many thousands remained in their homeland, fusing their blood, their religion, and some of their arts with those of their conquerors. For two or three hundred years longer it was considered a distinction to have Toltec blood, and members of the other tribes continued to regard them as "a sort of nobility." But all the while Toltec culture was on the wane, and when the Aztecs arrived (c. 1200) it remained merely as a base on which this final and warlike civilization of blood-letting warriors was superimposed.

Around A.D. 950 bands of Toltecs migrated to Guatemala and also to Yucatan, where they occupied Chichén Itzá, one of the great Maya centers recently weakened by civil war. They brought along with them their worship of Quetzalcoatl, their feathered-serpent art motifs and other designs, their rubber-ball game, and their human sacrifices. Here in Yucatan the Toltec-Maya culture blended to produce its last upward surge on the North American continent before the arrival of the white man.

To recapitulate, the Teotihuacán people, emerging from the shadows of time at the beginning of the Christian Era, developed the highest culture ever achieved on the Mexican plateau. They were unquestionably the greatest builders ever to inhabit that region, and while their history is largely the product of intelligent guesswork, their archaeological remains show them to have been an important part of every cultural expression in Mexico for over a thousand years. Some authorities seem to believe that these people originated the "great mother-culture from which the Maya germed." Others reverse the process. Certainly there was a time of close association and fusion between the two. In brief, the early culture history of this area recapitulates, unifies, and raises to a peak the efforts of all the Middle American tribes of the dark Archaic. When the Toltecs later arrived in the Valley of Mexico they built upon this base, but never equaled those who had preceded them.

The Aztecs, like the Toltecs, were only one of many tribes belonging to the Nahua group. They occupied the center of the stage on the Mexican plateau for about one hundred and fifty years before the conquest, and it was their "empire" under Montezuma which Cortés overcame. The Aztec tribe, in other words, was the strongest power in this region, forcing its will on most of the tribes surrounding it, but the territory from which obedience and tribute were exacted did not constitute a nation in either the economic, cultural, or political sense.

According to legend, the Aztecs, or "Crane People," left their homes in Aztlan, sometimes referred to as the "Seven Caves" or "The Place of Reeds," in about our year 1168. However, this date "is arbitrary and possibly represents the date of the invention of the calendar system in vogue in central Mexico." The Aztecs slowly wandered southward toward the central valley of Mexico, making several long stops on the way. They reached their final destination in the vicinity of Lake Texcoco about 1325, and established themselves there on two marshy islands, where for several years they lived a miserable existence among the reeds. This year 1325 is given as the date of the founding of their capital, Tenochtitlán, or, as it is known today, Mexico City.

In the Mendoza Codex, which traces sketchily the years of their legendary existence between 1168 and 1325, the story is told that when the Aztecs reached the banks of Lake Texcoco they saw in the middle of the marsh a great rock on which was growing an immense tunal bush. An eagle had made its home there, and scattered about were the bones and plumes of the birds it had devoured. The Aztecs saw that the land was fertile and decided to settle there, the presence of a permanent water supply probably being the main reason. They called their settlement Tenochtitlán, which means "tunal growing upon a rock."

In other stories of the founding of this city it is stated that when the Aztecs arrived they saw in the middle of the lake, perched on a cactus, an eagle with a serpent in its mouth and, considering this a good augury, decided to establish themselves in the same place. This phase of the legend is preserved in the Mexican flag and seal of today.

"The valley of Mexico was a superb place to live at that time. Seven thousand feet above sea level, high mountain chains walled in a fertile valley in which lay a great salt lake, Texcoco, fed at the south by two sweet water lagoons, at the northwest by two more, and at the northeast by a sluggish stream, the Acolman River, which drains the fertile valley of Teotihuacán. The lakes were shallow and their marshy shores, thick with reeds, attracted a teeming abundance of wild fowl. On the wooded mountain slopes deer abounded. During the rainy season thick alluvial deposits, ideal for primitive agriculture, were washed down along the lake shore."[7]

Shortly after their arrival the Aztecs entered into an alliance with two other tribes of the region and grew rapidly in power and influence. About a century after the founding of their capital they had become the most powerful tribe on the Mexican plateau. When the Spaniards encountered them they had reached a level of culture slightly below that of the inhabitants of England under King Alfred. Their religion and manner of writing were considerably more primitive than those of the Anglo-Saxons.

Under their system of government the Aztecs permitted elections of a sort, but the candidates always had to belong to a "fixed aristocracy." Except for a few priests all men were warriors. The choicest place in heaven was reserved for those who died in battle, for they entered directly "into the presence of the Sun." Some archaeologists have drawn a parallel between the Aztecs and the Romans, both warring nations, and between the Mayas and Greeks, both primarily creators.

Since war was a way of life for the Aztecs it is natural that violence, oppression, and bloodshed should have become characteristics of their government. Most of their laws were harsh, and death was the most frequent penalty. A heavy tribute was exacted from those whom they had conquered, and in order to curb rebellion, a regime of cruelty and terror was imposed. Aztec tax collectors circulated among the subject tribes in order to enforce prompt payment, and those who had been captured in battle were either sold into slavery or sacrificed on the altar. A deep and bitter hatred of the Aztecs smoldered among the vanquished peoples of Mexico and became one of the principal reasons for the success of the Spaniards.

Among their deities was an insubstantial "Supreme Cause of All," but he received only lip service, whereas their Sun, War, and Air gods, and many others, drank human blood with a thirst that was insatiable.

The legend of the birth of the War God, Huitzilopochtli, or Hummingbird Wizard, "tutelary deity" of the country, is typical of Aztec religious thinking. His mother was a pious widow who, while at the temple one day, noticed a ball of brilliantly colored feathers floating in the air. She grasped the bundle and placed it under her bosom and a short while later noticed that she had become pregnant. Her children soon learned of this and decided to kill her in order to wipe out the family disgrace, but when they attacked her the War God emerged fully grown and carrying a spear and shield. He wore a headdress of green hummingbird feathers, and on his left leg was a guard of the same material. The angry god immediately slew his brothers and sisters and took the name "Hummingbird Wizard." The woman who had given him birth became a goddess also, known as the "Earth Mother," and is generally represented as a horrible-looking death's-head with clawed hands and feet, wearing a skirt of rattlesnakes.

The number of Aztec deities was so great that the different attributes and provinces of each become confusing and repetitious. One god, Quetzalcoatl, stood out among the others because of his mild nature and the prophecy he had uttered about the coming of strange blond men in winged ships from across the sea, but he was not at all the principal god of the Aztecs. The bloodthirsty Sun and War gods occupied that place. Some said that Quetzalcoatl had angered one of the more powerful deities and had been driven from the land; others, that he had departed of his own accord, being consumed by a pillar of fire. According to still other beliefs, he had been to Yucatan, where he learned the arts of civilization, and had then returned to Mexico City to teach them to his people. Many priests used the name "Quetzalcoatl," and the confusion became so great that it is impossible to separate fact from fantasy in the story of this deity's life. All versions agree that he had said white men would come to the shores of

Mexico in the year *Ce Acatl* of the Aztec calendar, which would be near our year 1519, when Cortés landed at Vera Cruz.*

The Aztec calendar bore a great resemblance to the Maya and consisted of a year of eighteen months of twenty days each, plus five "unlucky days." This was the same arrangement as that made by both the Mayas and the Egyptians. When these five "unlucky days" fell at the end of a fifty-two-year cycle, which under their system might be compared to our century, the Aztecs lived through them in utter terror of a great catastrophe which would destroy the human race.

According to their traditions, four such catastrophes had already taken place at the close of similar cycles, and in order to reduce in so far as possible the likelihood of the fifth, they spent these five-day periods in a state of prayerful religious frenzy. They destroyed their household gods and many other furnishings, tore their clothes to shreds, and did not rekindle the holy fires in the temples.

During the final hours a great procession of priests marched to a high mountain a few miles outside the city, taking with them an exceptionally noble victim for the sacrifice. There they waited, expectantly watching the heavens. When at last the constellation of the Pleiades appeared, thus signifying the end of the cycle, a great shout arose and a new holy fire was kindled on the breast of the victim.

Aztec months were divided into four weeks of five days each, and on the last day of each week a huge market or fair was held in the village square. The calendar actually began with the year 1091, shortly after the Aztecs' mass migration from their original homes in the north. It was accurate over a period of about five hundred years. Their addition of twenty-five extra days each hundred and four years prevented the accumulation of a superfluous day until more than five centuries had passed. The knowledge of astronomy which the Aztecs possessed was far out of proportion to their knowledge of other sciences and obviously came to them from the Mayas, whose calculations were even more accurate.

The Aztec Calendar Stone, which has been preserved and is on display in Mexico City, is one of the greatest archaeological items of an ancient American people. It is a huge piece of black porphyry weighing about twenty tons. The sculptured surface, a great disk about twelve feet in diameter, is intact. It represents the Sun and contains much information about the Aztec culture and a mythical history of the world with its four great cycles of creation and catastrophes. It was placed in front of the Temple of the Sun and probably served as an altar on which human sacrifices were made. The Archbishop of Mexico City had it buried about 1560, fearing that its presence might revive the old pagan religion of the Indians, and it was not rediscovered until about 1790. It was then built into the

* The Spaniards first touched the shores of Mexico in 1511.

façade of the cathedral on the main square and was not removed until 1885, when it was taken to the museum.[12]

Aztec hieroglyphics represent "picture writing" at a lower stage than that of the Mayas. They were generally inscribed on scrolls of maguey fiber, which could be folded up into a compact bundle resembling a book. Sometimes they were also drawn on cloth or skins. Everything expressed had to be pictured and, as a consequence, Aztec manuscripts are full of tiny ant-like humans plodding all over the place, representing different actions. The human form was not very carefully sketched or the time taken would have been out of all proportion to the value of the writing.

The grotesque disproportion of most of the figures with their large heads set upon small misshapen bodies shows little skill in composition. Emphasis was always placed on that part of the figure indicating the action, and colors were frequently used to express or heighten certain meanings. There were a few symbolical characters; for example, the serpent which seems to indicate "time" or the "universe" as the scarab in ancient Egypt.

This form of writing was adequate for their needs, and all laws, tributes, legends, rituals, and chronology were recorded in such a manner. Oral tradition frequently helped to fill out the meaning. The Aztecs had many trained scribes who could quickly read or write these glyphs, and a great many manuscripts (some say hundreds) had accumulated by the time of the conquest. The majority of these were destroyed by the Spaniards, who considered them the inventions of heretics.

However, the story that the first bishop of Mexico, Juan Zumárraga, collected and burned all the national archives and literary products of Texcoco, the intellectual capital of the country, has not been borne out by historic research. Indeed, there is no writer of those days who mentions the marvelous library of Texcoco. It seems to be an invention of later historians, mainly Robertson and Prescott.

A total of three or four dozen Aztec manuscripts have survived, and Aztec picture writing has been satisfactorily deciphered by scholars, but many of the details dependent on oral tradition will never be fully interpreted. The Aztec glyphs are hardly comparable to the much more refined characters of the Mayas, who preceded them by over a thousand years. The Mayas and Egyptians came at the top of the scale of hieroglyphic writing, the Aztecs at the bottom.

The arts and crafts of the Aztecs were of a higher nature. There were beautiful dyed cloths of cotton and rabbit hair, pottery as lovely as any to come out of the New World, and ornaments of gold- and silverwork which the Spaniards claimed were not equaled in their own country at the time. The Aztecs delighted especially in their brilliant cloaks and draperies made of feathers of tropical birds pasted onto a webbing of cotton. The highest-valued object of all among them was jade, which was regarded as being worth much more than gold. Many of their finest pieces of jewelry were fashioned of this precious stone. Not having the potter's wheel, the Aztecs, like many other American races, made their ceramics by adding successive strips of clay which they then fashioned and molded with the fingers until the desired shape was obtained. Rhythm, form, and color were innate to this primitive process.

When Cortés and his men landed at Vera Cruz, Montezuma sent them an array of gifts which was fully representative of Aztec art at its best. One of the soldiers, Bernal Díaz, states that there were shields and helmets encrusted with plates of gold, collars and bracelets of the same metal, robes of cloth as fine as silk, "interwoven with featherwork that rivals the finest painting," birds and animals cast in gold and silver, crests of feathers fastened together with threads of silver and gold and decorated with pearls and other precious stones, and more than thirty loads of beautiful cotton cloth. The two items which excited the most attention were two huge plates of gold and silver respectively, "as large as carriage wheels." The one of gold represented the Sun and was "richly carved with plants and animals." Its value was placed at over sixty thousand dollars. The workmanship on both pieces was later examined by experts in Spain and the consensus was one of unbounded admiration.

Another art which the Aztecs carried to a high development was that of mosaics. Not only did they fashion lovely feather mosaics, but they also fabricated elaborate designs of small stones of different colors and shells of various kinds. This mosaic work was carried into architectural design with "a veneer of cut stone being applied to the rubble of a platform or building. The temples of Mitla, Oaxaca, influenced by the same Mixteca-Puebla culture to which the Aztec civilization owed so much, are masterpieces of this technique, for individual blocks have their surfaces carved to fit together in an intricate geometric design."[7]

The Aztecs never knew the use of iron, but they fashioned tools and instruments of copper, and with the aid of a siliceous dust they were able to cut the hardest precious stones with this material. Knives, swords, and jewelry were also made of black obsidian, a pliable volcanic stone which abounded in the vicinity. As in the case of nearly all primitive civilizations, the secrets of the various arts and crafts ran in families, being passed down from father to son.

Aztec agriculture, although not at so high a level as that of the Incas, was carried on extensively and has given the world some of its best-known foods. Indian corn or maize was the staple crop, but there were also cacao beans from which chocolate was made, wild bananas and many other tropical fruits, beans, and the indispensable cactus known as the maguey. The pulp and fiber contained in the broad spearlike leaves of this plant were made into a paste from which were rolled sheets of paper, while the juicy residue was fermented and became the famous alcoholic drink called pulque. This beverage had a certain nutritive value and to some extent made up for the lack of fresh vegetables in the diet of the Mexican Indians. The roots of the maguey also made a nutritious food; thread, cord, and even cloth sandals for the poor were fashioned of the long, stringlike fibers; pins and needles were made from the sharp thorns at the ends of the leaves, while the leaves themselves furnished thatch for walls and roofs. The omnipresent picture which we have seen of the Mexican Indian sleeping under the broad leaves of this plant is more than a symbol of a mere siesta; it indicates the line of least resistance in Mexican life and at least two thousand years of living next to the indispensable maguey.

The basic food in the daily diet of the Aztecs "was the tortilla, a flat cake of unleavened corn meal which measured a good foot in diameter, to judge from the size of the clay griddles used in cooking them, in contrast to the modern tortilla, which varies between four and six inches. At three the child received half a tortilla a day; at four or five his ration was doubled; from six to twelve a tortilla and a half were prescribed, and at thirteen the allotment was two. Supplemented by beans and game, this diet was filling and nutritious."[7]

The basis of Aztec agriculture, as in the case of the Mayas, Incas, Toltecs, and indeed all Indian tribes, was the communal ownership of productive land. The high council of the tribes divided it among the *calpullis* or clans, and the clan chieftains redistributed it among their heads of families. This was as close as the Aztecs came to owning land privately. Other plots were reserved for the upkeep of the priests, the chief, and, if necessary, for paying tributes or taxes, and these were all cultivated in common. If any landholder permitted his plot to go two years without cultivation it reverted to the clan.

This communal land tradition, uprooted by the Spanish conquest and destroyed still further by hacienda confiscations under the dictatorship of Porfirio Díaz, was revived by the Mexican Government during the past few years. Many millions of acres have been redistributed to landless communities in *ejidos* or "village commons."

The ejido or calpulli system of common ownership, similar to the Inca ayllu, was present not only among the pre-conquest Indian communities of America, but had its close counterpart in Spain also. The Spanish term ejido, generally used today to designate the village commons of Mexico, had its origin in a similar arrangement current in many hundreds of old Spanish villages, where certain tracts reserved for the common use were owned by the entire community. The word "ejido" (from the Latin *exitus*) means "on the way out," because these lands were generally located on the outskirts of the village. In Mexico the ejido includes all of the communal lands, while in Spain it was only a limited part of these lands, specifically a small, well-defined area used as the village pound, the public threshing and winnowing floor, and the community rubbish heap and slaughter pen.[129]

Neither the Aztecs nor any other Indian tribe ever bought or sold land or raised crops for a commercial profit. For the red man the soil existed only in order to meet the necessities of life, and production, not profit, was the basis of his economy. This meant a relatively low standard of living, but it also usually meant security unless the earth itself rebelled or the forces of nature undid the work of man. Unemployment was certainly never a problem in the Indian communities of early America.

In the vicinity of Mexico City, where good land was at a premium because of the dense population, agriculture was so intensively organized that fertile soil was scraped up from the lake bottoms and placed on floating rafts of reeds and fibrous roots firmly tied together and allowed to float over the lake surfaces. These "floating gardens" or chinampas were sometimes large enough to hold a hut and a caretaker, who used a long pole to change the position of his little agricultural domain. The so-called "floating gardens of Xochimilco" today (which float no longer) are derived from these artificially made plots of the Aztecs.

In the communal life of these people there was no place for the thief or idler, and as government was organized on a tribal or clan basis the divisions were so small that there was almost no chance of getting away with anything. For stealing and other anti-social crimes a person would often suffer the punishment of enforced slavery. Extremely poor or landless folk (usually those who refused to do their share) frequently sold their children or even themselves into slavery in order to achieve the means of livelihood. A slave could own other slaves, but his children were always born free.

There was no single currency in the days of the Aztecs, but fine pieces of tin stamped with a "T," quills of gold dust, pieces of copper, and bags of cacao beans served as money. Tribute was frequently paid in cacao beans, and the chocolate made from them furnished the luxury drink of the Mexican capital. The town of Tabasco alone was said to have sent Montezuma two thousand *xaquipiles* each year as its tribute; one xaquipil was about eighty thousand grains of cacao, hence the Tabasco contribution would be one hundred and sixty million grains—probably reckoned by measurement and not by count. The Aztec ruler and his chieftains consumed all this chocolate, for the cacao from Tabasco was the finest in Mexico. Many hundreds of cups per day were served in the rooms of Montezuma's palace. Cortés adopted chocolate as a regular part of his men's diet. When he sent sample beans to Charles V he wrote, "One cup of this rich drink gives a man enough strength to march all day." Oviedo reported that a native prostitute charged ten beans, the price of a rabbit.

The Aztecs frequently held banquets, and sometimes when there was an excess of pulque and food these turned into saturnalian revelries. On special occasions the particular delicacy of a slaughtered slave or the remains of a captive who had been sacrificed to the gods garnished the table. Sometimes after a battle, when there was a plethora of human flesh on the field, the soldiers stuffed themselves until they were hardly able to walk.

Every fifth day a huge market or fair was held in the large plaza of Mexico City which occupied several square blocks. In the absence of more permanent stores, stalls were set up where the goods were displayed and sold. Every type of ware had its special section in the market place, and the Spaniards were amazed at the quality and quantity of goods as well as the size of the teeming crowds which thronged to the plaza. Cortés states that sixty thousand people gathered there, and the lowest estimate given by any writer is forty thousand to fifty thousand; but these figures, like all estimates by most early chroniclers, were undoubtedly erroneous. The same error was probably made in estimating the population of Mexico City itself. The lowest figure given was sixty thousand houses, some of which were occupied by several families—an estimated total of at least three hundred thousand inhabitants, which seems entirely too high.

Nonetheless, the Aztec capital, Tenochtitlán, was by far the largest center in Mexico. It resembled the great capital of an empire, and as such the Spanish conquerors saw and regarded it. Actually it was a "city-state" organized and run on a strictly tribal basis. In its social, political, and economic make-up it consisted of twenty tribes which were banded together by a common interest and which usually fought as a single unit.

A considerable amount of democracy prevailed in the tribal governments, but the higher up in the scale the chieftains rose, the less democratic became the manner of selection. These twenty tribes, however, had all worked together to construct a magnificent center, and when the Spaniards first saw it they thought that it was "like the enchantments they tell of in the legend of Amadís."[20]

As the city was situated on marshy ground which was frequently flooded, canals crisscrossed it in every direction. Three long dikes or causeways connected the town with the firmer land surrounding it. Canoes were paddled in and out among the canals and over the surface of Lake Texcoco in great numbers. A large aqueduct with two earthen tubes about the size of a man's body brought drinking water from Chapultepec and emptied it into fountains and reservoirs in different parts of the city. The waters of the lake itself were too briny and probably too dirty for drinking purposes.

The streets were narrow, and a vast proportion of the houses were of reeds and mud, but a few of the better dwellings belonging to the chiefs were made of red stone.

All the houses were low-lying and had flat roofs. Flowers were planted in between the houses, in patios, and on the roofs. Nearly all dwellings were built around a patio, and when new rooms were needed they were simply added to the rambling structure somewhere, and, if necessary, other patios were incorporated. Montezuma's "palace" was an extensive building of this kind made of red stone with ceilings of cedar and other aromatic woods; on its walls were animal skins, richly stained cotton fabrics, and gorgeous draperies of featherwork. Outside the palace was a large aviary and gardens of flowers and medicinal plants. A second dwelling of the monarch was located on Chapultepec Hill, where the royal grounds were shaded by huge cypresses, some of them more than fifty feet in circumference.

Montezuma lived in the midst of a barbaric pageantry which dazzled many of the Spaniards. Prescott says that the semi-civilization of which he was the highest symbol did not equal that of the polished Arabs and Persians but belonged in the category of the Tartar races who found much pleasure in making a show for substance and in hedging "around the throne itself with a barren and burdensome ceremonial, the counterfeit of real majesty."21

In this great Aztec center of many thousands of inhabitants "the problem of sanitation must have been serious, but boats were tied up at strategic points for public use, and when filled, their contents were sold to fertilize the fields. Pottery vessels were kept in the houses to preserve urine, which the Aztecs used as a mordant in dyeing cloth. Hence sunlight and these simple methods for getting fresh water and disposing of offal kept down the pestilence that beset the city in Spanish times when the ancient methods of sanitation were abandoned."7

The use of human residue to fertilize the fields is still so common in many Indianist regions of Latin America that the outsider dare not eat uncooked vegetables or drink unboiled water even in some of the larger cities.

Occupying the place of greatest prominence in the Aztec capital was the great pyramid-temple, or teocalli, and its related buildings all surrounded by a high wall decorated with serpents. The construction was recent, dating from 1487, and was the outstanding architectural achievement of the Aztecs. The temple itself topped a large stucco-covered pyramid about three hundred feet square at the base and probably one hundred feet in height. On the summit was an extensive level area where the sanctuaries were located and the sacrifices were made. In one of these stood the hideous statue of the War God with hummingbird feathers on his left leg and with a chain of gold and silver hearts around his neck. The forms of priests flitted about in the dark background, their robes stained with blood, and the entire gloomy precincts gave off a horrible stench of human gore. There were many other teocallis scattered about the city which seemed to raise themselves far above the level of the everyday dwellings.

All Toltec and Aztec pyramid-temples were constructed so as to maintain the greatest illusion of mass and height. Even when they were not actually high, their series of several terraces, receding harmoniously at different levels from the great masses of which they were a part, were arranged so as to suggest a majestic sweep toward the sky. As their summits could not be seen by those standing at the base, and were lost in the sky above, the sense of infinite height was overpowering.

"The great gods lived in the sky, so that their shrines and images were very naturally lifted above the level of worldly affairs. The climate contributed indirectly to the conversion of religious requirement into an impressive art form. It was not necessary to house the congregation or protect it from the weather. The altar or shrine alone needed to be elevated, and the worshipers stood in the plaza below. Thus the temple capped the substructure and was the culmination of a harmonious series of ascending planes, calculated to increase the illusion of height by emphasizing the effects of mechanical perspective."[7]

When a great religious procession ascended the stairs of a temple the effect must have been stupendous, for the spectators below were "conscious only of the massive ascent disappearing into space." This monumental quality of Aztec religious architecture was reproduced on a minor scale in their sculpture. "The smallest piece has the same dignity that attends the most massive temple carvings," the same sense of proportion embodied in the great temples themselves.[7]

The Aztec religion and that of the surrounding tribes was built on the basis of human sacrifices. One of the reasons for the constant warfare of these people was to obtain victims for their gods. This was why many tribes were allowed to live in the vicinity unsubjected. It made waging war easier and provided the simplest method of taking captives. Before the sacrifice the victim was not cruelly treated, but if he seemed sullen or fearful priests attempted to instill in him the proper spirit of willingness and ecstasy for one who was soon to meet his god. Usually this was not necessary, for human sacrifices were common throughout Mexico and the captive died bravely, just as he had seen others die in his own homeland.

Sometimes he was regarded as an incarnation of the god himself, and as such was worshiped and treated royally until the day of his enforced demise. When that day arrived, however, there was no drawing back. He was stretched out on the altar with priests holding his arms, legs, and head. Another priest clothed in scarlet then drove a sharp knife of obsidian into his chest, ripped out the heart, raised it toward the sun, and finally threw it at the feet of the deity to whom that particular sanctuary was dedicated.

The Spaniards estimated that several hundreds of such victims were slaughtered each year, and two of Cortés's men claimed to have counted one hundred and thirty-six thousand human skulls strung out on poles in a single building. Even if these figures were reduced to one tenth, the killing was still terrific.

It is easy to understand why a primitive people, steeped in the traditions of war and depending on warfare for dominance among their neighbors, should have developed such a bloody religion. Killing and death were glories beyond all others which this world could offer, and very naturally a human life constituted the most acceptable gift that might be offered to a god.

The great temple of Mexico City was located on the same site as the present main square of the town, and its base has been used for the support of some of the modern buildings on that plaza. A large section of stonework, probably belonging to another of the constructions in the great temple enclosure, has recently been excavated in a vacant lot near by, but the time may never come when the entire religious center of Aztec life will be uncovered. Who knows what untold treasure of Mexican antiquities lies buried under the capital's present-day *zócalo* and the public buildings surrounding it? The building of the recently inaugurated subway system in Mexico City has unearthed tons of priceless antiquities, but countless tons will remain buried forever beneath the teeming streets and great modern edifices.

In the Aztec society, as in many other primitive warring nations where men are scarce and women relatively plentiful, polygamy was the rule rather than the exception. The first wife was the "mistress of the house," but concubines were perfectly legitimate. The poor man had recourse to prostitution. There were occasional divorces, and a man could "cast out his wife if she were sterile, or subject to prolonged ill-temper, or neglected the household duty." Girls had to be chaste and wives had to be faithful, but a man's relations were illicit only when they involved a married woman. Our Western civilization was not alone in inventing the double standard.

In the society of the Aztecs "freedom of thought, individual liberty, personal fortunes, were non-existent, but people lived according to a code that had worked well and continuously for centuries. An Aztec would have been horrified at the naked isolation of an individual's life in our Western world."[7]

It was not only in his strong sense of community and religion that the Aztec felt fulfillment. In his daily life his arts and crafts probably served that purpose better than any other expression. "Craftsmanship," says the archaeologist, "allows an exercise of the creative impulse, satisfying the individual through his domination of the raw material. In our modern mechanized age, most of us suffer from the lack of opportunity to create, since almost everything we use comes machine-made, and not even the skilled mechanic feels that his ingenuity and craftsmanship alone have produced a useful and attractive object.

"The ordinary modern floats like Mohammed's coffin, without contact with the earth on which he lives or the universe of which he is an infinitesimal part. The Aztec, however, lived in the most intimate contact with nature in its finite and infinite manifestations. Because his conscious being was set in terms of the group mind, he seldom felt that sensation common to the Western intellect, of having cut himself from the tree of natural existence with the saw of his own reason."[7]

There were also other senses of fulfillment which the Aztec craftsman felt. Such prestige as there was in his society, and it was a society where rank rather than caste was the measuring rod, could be attained through his own effort. If he was an enterprising man, he had a good house, beautiful articles for daily use, fine clothing, neat and well-tilled fields, while the unsuccessful man "had a small and miserable equipment." His rise to chieftainship or priesthood was also largely dependent on his own initiative. Among the Indians a man did not obtain, or at least could not hold for long, a position which he was unable to defend either by his strength or his ability.

Under the Aztec system, education was in the hands of the older and more respected members of the tribe, or under priests and priestesses who took those to be instructed under their wing in order to inculcate the beliefs, disciplines, arts, and crafts proper to their state. Priests and warriors formed a sort of nobility and fashioned their country's religion, its traditions, its government, and its social codes. They built the temples, wrote and enforced the laws, exacted the tributes, carried out the sacrifices, and ruled the nation. Constituting a small minority perched on top of the large population, theirs was the power and glory and the pompous certainty of all ruling classes.

While the majority of the inhabitants lived in houses of reeds and mud, the priests and warriors alone attained that modicum of leisure on which the higher intellectual life depends. They did not know how to use it. In the brief two hundred years of their supremacy they copied much but created little, and stalked about killing and mumbling the superstitious ritual around which their lives and ceremonies were centered. Yet with their help the untutored masses slowly developed a culture-substance made up of arts and crafts which remains alive to this day. These things grew out of the necessities of their lives and a deep innate feeling for plastic expression. Even this folk culture, however, the Aztecs did not create. It was appropriated from their more illustrious predecessors, the Toltecs, who lurked in the shadows of time till they emerged with sudden glory from the unknown that bore them.

How did these American cultures compare with each other? Which was the most advanced? Which was the lowest in the scale? No positive answers can be given to these questions, but a few valid comparisons can be drawn. The Olmecs of Mexico and the Chavín culture of Peru came first, emerging from the long sleep of the Archaic about 1000 years B.C. They were separated by hundreds of miles and it is not known what connections, if any, there were between them, but they worshiped the same man-jaguar god, which indicates a common origin or a strange and fortuitous coincidence. The Teotihuacános, early in the Christian Era, were the greatest builders of Middle America. The Valley of Mexico was their home.

The Mayas, whose early history paralleled that of Teotihuacán, developed the most refined of all the American Indian cultures. They excelled in painting, wood carving, sculpture, finely balanced architecture, and in hieroglyphic writing. They were also supreme as astronomers and mathematicians, and their calendar was the most accurate in the world at that time. Their culture stressed artistic expression and scientific thinking, but produced no great social organism or techniques of supporting life.

The people of Tiahuanoco near Lake Titicaca in Bolivia were the grandest builders on the American scene and in their constructions used stones weighing many tons. The Incas who followed them appropriated many of these buildings to their own use and frequently laid their smaller and better proportioned stonework on top of pre-Inca bases.

The Incas were the greatest all-around engineers among the native Americans, and their immense fortress cities, terraced farms, and aqueducts are still wonders to behold. Their unadorned architecture was stronger, more imposing than that of the Mayas, and their agricultural economy, social organism, and imperial conception of the state were more highly developed than those of any other Indian group. In the materials of living they certainly deserve first place. The Peruvians were also outstanding as doctors and surgeons, and produced the finest weaving and pottery in the hemisphere. However, their crude quipu record of knotted strings, their closest approach to a written language, was a paltry invention beside the beautiful wrought glyphs of the Mayas. And even the Inca buildings, magnificent as their stonework was, seem cold and primitive when compared with the refined, graceful, and highly sculptured creations of Maya architects or the exquisite frescoes of the people of Teotihuacán.

The Toltecs cannot be appraised accurately because they represent a connecting link between the Mayas, the builders of Teotihuacán, and the Aztecs. They absorbed much from the Teotihuacán culture and ultimately merged first with the Mayas and then with the Aztecs. However, Toltec culture does not represent the high water mark of Indian history in Mexico, nor does that of the Aztecs, who, despite all their barbaric splendor, constituted a regression and not an advance in Mexican civilization.

How did all these indigenous American civilizations compare in development with the highest achievements of the ancient Mediterranean world? Many writers, overwhelmed with an excessive zeal in their subject —and this is understandable in those who have dedicated their lives to unraveling history or to delving in archaeological research—lead us to believe that the New World civilizations were fully equal to those of the Old, and in many ways their superior. This is obviously not so. Years of nonrecognition followed by popular exaggerations have built up this "believe-it-or-not" approach which has drawn out of focus the real values of ancient American life.

Very little of this was conscious or willful. The two histories of Mexico and Peru which we would want to preserve, if all others were lost, were written by persons who could hardly have eliminated these misrepresentations had they been aware of them. The historian of Peru (Garcilaso de la Vega) was the son of an Inca princess and a Spanish conquistador who wrote about his mother's people during the latter part of his life, long after he had left Peru and was living in Spain. How could he have kept from glorifying his vanquished race?

The historian of the Aztecs (Bernal Díaz del Castillo) was a captain in the group that Cortés led to victory in Mexico who wrote down his recollections of the Mexican Empire and its downfall when he was an old man living in Guatemala many years later. Age must surely have spread about the scenes of his youth and the days of his glory an aura not entirely justified by the facts.

Such exaggerations have frequently been repeated by more recent authorities. Typical of this attitude are descriptions of Inca aqueducts or the Inca roads, only paths along most of their extent, as equal to anything in the same line ever constructed by the Romans. Similar accounts of Inca or Maya temples bring into our minds pictures of the incomparable buildings of the Greeks. This is very far from the truth. There never existed in ancient America any building comparable to the Parthenon or dozens of other Greek temples constructed many centuries before Christ; any statues even remotely showing the artistry of the Venus de Milo or the Winged Victory of Samothrace; any theaters like the Colosseum; any aqueduct like that of Segovia; nor any written language which should be mentioned in the same breath with Greek or Latin. About 400 B.C. Aristophanes, Plato, and Aristotle were writing in a language as fine as any today, while in America at that time there was no writing of any kind, not even the crudest hieroglyphics.

As a closer basis of comparison one might choose the civilization of ancient Egypt of 1000 or 2000 years B.C. Although this comparison is general rather than specific, the great American cultures of A.D. 500 to A.D. 1500 were at about the same level as that developed in Egypt nearly three thousand years before them. On the other hand, it is quite true that American culture had reached a relatively high state when some of our northern European ancestors were still living in caves. The most noteworthy single consideration in regard to ancient America is that its progress was attained alone, cut off from all such currents as frequently played across the European stage, enriching many nations, lifting the artistic expression, and heightening the thoughts of man.

In American cultures the folk was always supreme. There were no great individual artists in any field, but in all fields art itself was great. It was primitive art only in the sense that it was an expression of pure feeling untrammeled by the weight or rules of consciously attained technique. Form, design, beauty, and color occupied a place in everyone's daily life. They were not set apart on a pedestal reserved for the rich or the mighty. Consequently, they spoke from the heart and not from the mind, and in so speaking will remain forever beautiful.

There is no need to glamorize the fantastic pageant of early American life by further analogies with the incomparable civilizations of Greece or Rome. Such parallels are altogether misleading. The native achievements in folk culture which survived even the holocaust of the conquest and four hundred years of oppression, poverty, and neglect have added to our world an infusion of new loveliness and strength which can stand proudly alone on the stage of history. In that world to the south of us these values still pursue their inexorable way, and any attempt to understand Latin-American life must begin with a knowledge of the essential folk nature of society in that region before the conquest. It is upon this base that so many of the southern countries have raised the superstructure of Hispanic civilization.

CHRONOLOGY OF MEXICAN CULTURES

Oaxaca Area	Central Mexico	Mexican Gulf Coast
500 B.C. Danzante sculpture, Monte Albán	600 B.C. — A.D. 700 Teotihuacán culture	1000 B.C. Olmecs, colossal stone heads
A.D. 500 Zapotecs, Monte Albán	A.D. 1000 Toltecs reach peak	A.D. 800 El Tajín pyramid, Totonacs
A.D. 1100 Zapotec-Mixtec, Monte Albán and Mitla	A.D. 1300–1518 Aztec Period	A.D. 1400–1518 Cempoala

The chronology of the Maya culture is traced in the table at the end of Chapter 1. Many of its finest monuments are found in the southern Mexican state of Chiapas and in Yucatan.

4

THE NEW WORLD MEETS
THE OLD WORLD'S CROSS AND SWORD

During the course of the fifteenth century Portugal was the most forward-looking country in Europe. The Turks had closed the Eastern land passage to India, and such trade with the Orient as remained resulted in prices so exorbitant that only the most wealthy were able to buy. The Italian city-states floundered on the verge of complete bankruptcy. Their great commerce of the Middle Ages was at an end; that of the modern epoch had already begun in the little land's-end country of Portugal. Her caravels took up where those of Venice and Genoa had left off, and each year sailed farther and farther southward and westward into the Arab's "green sea of gloom." Navigators, sailors, geographers, and cartographers from all the Mediterranean world, thrown out of jobs at home, were drawn to Lisbon, mistress of the unknown waters. Among them was Columbus, a native of Genoa, who had come to Portugal in 1470. He made his living by sailing under the Portuguese flag, or while on shore by drawing and selling charts and maps. One of his voyages had taken him to Iceland, the Ultima Thule of the ancients.

Columbus, like every other navigator and adventurer of his age, had heard tales of the marvelous riches of the Orient. Every world traveler from Herodotus to Marco Polo had spoken of them. The Irish St. Brendan of the sixth century was believed to have traveled to a group of islands in the center of the Atlantic which bore his name. As recent as Prince Henry's day a Portuguese ship was said to have reached the mythical island of Antilia, and of course the legend of fabled Atlantis still lived in the minds of men. Many maps of the times showed rough outlines of these and other mysterious islands in the great Green Sea. Columbus also owned a copy of Marco Polo's journal and had read and reread such descriptions as this: "The King of the great island of Japan has a mighty palace, all roofed with finest gold, just as our churches are roofed with lead . . . the floors of the halls and many chambers are paved with golden plates, each two fingers thick. There are pearls in greatest abundance. . . ."[2] Columbus, of course, thought he was going straight to this land. It was the first dream of El Dorado.

But aside from these accounts Columbus had further and more specific reasons for wanting to make his voyage to the East by sailing directly westward. Out beyond the Azores a Portuguese pilot had picked up "a piece of wood, ingeniously wrought, but not with iron," and Columbus's brother-in-law had found a similar piece on Porto Santo, as well as large canes of a kind unknown in Europe or Africa. On the westernmost island of the Azores then known there was a huge "natural rock statue of a horseman pointing westward" which Columbus saw and took as meant for him.[2]

Columbus believed that the nearest point of land which he would touch after sailing from the Canaries was Cipangu, or Japan, and according to his calculations it was only 2400 miles westward. The actual air-line distance is 10,600 miles. Logic thus proves that those of Columbus's day who said that sailing into the west in order to reach the East was foolhardy and impractical were far more right than he. With the small ships and scant provisions of water and food carried in those days such a voyage would have been more than a perilous adventure. When Columbus presented his proposition to King John II of Portugal the royal mathematical experts turned it down with excellent practical judgment, stating that "it would be necessary to sail at least ten thousand nautical miles due west before reaching . . . the eastern fringe of the unknown world." On the other hand, Columbus "*knew* he could make it and the figures had to fit."[2]

There was never any question about the world being a sphere. Every European university of that time so taught geography, and seamen knew from practical experience that the surface of the globe was curved. Columbus did not have to convince anybody of this.

After he was turned down by the Portuguese in 1485 Columbus went to Spain and there laid his plan before Ferdinand and Isabella. It was the worst possible moment he could have chosen. Spain was in the midst of a war of annihilation against the Moors and all her resources were necessary for the campaign. In spite of this Columbus was not definitely refused—his proposition was merely pigeonholed for future consideration. As a matter of fact, that consideration began almost immediately, but it was seven years before anything came of it. During all this time Columbus was well treated by the Catholic Sovereigns and lived mostly at their expense. Finally, in 1492, with the victorious conclusion of the Moorish war, a definite decision was reached. It was a resounding "no." Columbus, who had come to Granada lighthearted and full of hope, took his departure from that city in deepest dejection. As a last resort he planned to present his scheme in France, for the French King had written him a letter expressing some encouragement. But he had hardly gone four miles when Isabella, after listening to zealous last-minute recapitulations of his arguments by ardent supporters he had in court, changed her mind, sent to call him back, and unequivocally endorsed the whole project.

A few weeks later, on August 3, 1492, Columbus sailed from the little town of Palos with his three ships. Jewish refugees had flocked to the larger ports of Seville and Cádiz in such numbers that it was thought unwise to depart from either of them.

The *Niña* and the *Pinta* were vessels about seventy-five feet long, twenty-five feet wide, and of about sixty tons carrying capacity; the *Santa María* was somewhat larger and could carry approximately one hundred tons. The total complement of men on the three ships was about ninety. There were no soldiers on this trip and no priests. Columbus wanted every man to be a sailor. The voyage was broken at the Canary Islands, and then finally, on September 6, the little fleet took leave of the Old World and headed into the west. The story of that voyage is too well known to need repeating here. The men were soon grumbling, and the admiral kept a fake log of the trip with shorter distances than they actually traveled in order to allay their fears. Nevertheless, the grumbling continued, and on October 10 flared into near mutiny.

Columbus promised to turn back if land was not sighted in three more days. The very next day the *Niña* picked a land flower out of the sea, and the *Pinta* dragged in "a cane, a stick, a piece of board, a land plant," and a piece of carved wood. Complaints ceased immediately and hearts began to beat faster. The admiral decided to sail all night long, and ordered all hands to keep a close lookout. That night, at 10:00 P.M., Columbus thought he saw a light in the west which resembled "a little wax candle rising and falling," but it was probably only his overwrought imagination, for they were still thirty-five miles off shore.

At 2:00 A.M. the lookout on the *Pinta's* forecastle saw "something like a white sand cliff gleaming in the moonlight on the western horizon, then another, and a dark line of land connecting them." He shouted at the top of his lungs, "*¡Tierra, tierra!*" America had been discovered.[2] Columbus thought at that time, and persisted in believing to his dying day, that he had reached one of the islands of Asia where he would find the great wealth described by Marco Polo and other ancient world travelers.

What the Spaniards had found was something very different: a land of naked Indians, brilliantly colored parrots flying through the trees, some strange quadrupeds, and endless miles of virgin soil. Yet there was no cause for disillusionment—quite the contrary, everything fed the flames of fancy. Every tree was strange; such red men had never been seen before by European eyes, and, most wonderful of all, some of the primitive but gentle savages wore little pieces of gold hanging from their noses. Gold in small quantities was also found in some of the river beds. Columbus assembled a collection of these things, including a few Indians, and took them back to Spain with him.

Bad weather during the last part of the trip forced Columbus to put in at Lisbon, and after dispatching a messenger to the Spanish sovereigns he awaited with some trepidation his interview with the King of Portugal. When John II of that country heard the tidings of the discovery from the admiral himself he was eaten up with envy and remorse. He was courteous enough but decided later to make it appear as if the expedition had been poaching on his private grounds off the west coast of Africa. In the meantime Columbus's messenger had reached Ferdinand and Isabella, and they were overjoyed at the good news. Columbus was ordered to report to them in person with all possible speed and to begin planning immediately to undertake a second and more elaborate voyage to the New World.

On reaching the court, then being held in Barcelona, he was wined and dined by the highest Spanish society, and when the King appeared in public, Columbus was always at his side. Together they discussed the geographical side of the discovery, and then the Catholic Sovereigns went to the Pontiff for approval, for technically he held the right to divide and assign all unchristian lands as he saw fit.

The newly elected Pope, Alexander VI, who was a Spanish Borgia, proclaimed in a bull (1493) that all lands discovered west of a line one hundred leagues beyond the Azores belonged to Spain, and a second bull added that "all islands and mainlands whatsoever found and to be found . . . in sailing or traveling toward the west or south" should also belong to Spain.

John II of Portugal now became really worried. His long-dreamed-of sea route to India was as good as dead just as he seemed on the verge of finding it. The Portuguese King saw that it was useless to try to do business with the Spanish Pope, so he appealed directly to Ferdinand and Isabella. They were unprepared to challenge John II's excellent navy, and in 1494 the Treaty of Tordesillas was negotiated in which the line of demarcation was moved to the meridian three hundred and seventy leagues west of the Azores. This not only gave Portugal plenty of room to breathe in; it pushed the dividing line so far to the west that a great part of the soon-to-be-discovered Brazilian bulge was included in Portuguese territory. The strong hold which Portugal thus obtained on the New World she never relinquished, but, on the contrary, expanded at every possible opportunity.

The discovery of America represents the greatest revolution ever effected in the history of mankind. It shifted completely the center of gravity of the known world, turned the eyes of civilization from the crusades of the East toward the conquest of the West, marked the end of the Middle Ages and the beginning of the modern era, and above all altered and broadened the entire nature of man's thinking. It was the end of the dark, the mystical, the inward life; the start of a forward motion which has not yet been arrested. The influx of gold and silver from the New World altered the value of money, created a new rich class, gave birth to capitalism itself. Men of action and enterprise replaced men of birth as leaders in deed and thought.

America was at first an illusion, later a hope, and when the great cities of gold did not materialize, the experience of the conquistadores (worth more than gold itself) made possible the creation of new empires beyond the sea. These men turned their gaze from the classic truths of antiquity toward the future and its promise of a fuller and richer life.[22]

The island of Santo Domingo, which was one of those visited by Columbus on his first voyage, was the earliest portion of American soil colonized by the Spaniards. At this time the home government, in contrast to its later colonial tyrannies, encouraged immigration with an extremely liberal policy. Settlers were to enjoy many privileges: free passage, exemption from taxes, ownership of such lands as they should cultivate for four years, and a supply of stock and grain from the Royal Treasury. There was to be no duty on imports or exports. The only illiberal provision was that converted Jews, Moors, and all foreigners except Catholic Christians were prohibited even from visiting the New World.

In 1501 the Spanish monarchs received from the Pope the right to collect the ecclesiastical tithes in America, and in 1508 Pope Julius II granted Ferdinand the "right of royal patronage"—a measure which later had far-reaching consequences when the great American mainlands were conquered. This right meant that the King could nominate, and thus actually appoint, all higher dignitaries of the Church in the New World. It prohibited the circulation of any papal bull in America without the Crown's consent, and made it mandatory for all priests who wished to enter the new lands to obtain the royal permission. No church, convent, or religious hospital could be constructed without an order from the monarch. The King was to receive one ninth of the ecclesiastical tithes for his own use, and a considerable part of the royal income was from the sale of indulgences, which everyone bought. Thus from the very beginning the Pope himself made the colonial Church a subordinate ally of absolutism and royalty.

Another noteworthy point of early colonial policy was that private persons were allowed to go to the New World in order to undertake the conquest and colonization of a certain region at their own expense. They automatically became governors and masters of the lands and peoples thus conquered. This system had been widely used during the Moorish wars and was especially acceptable to the adventuresome spirit of the Spaniards. A proverb of the day expresses the feeling well: "He who never ventures forth will never cross the sea." These private conquistadores were given the name of *adelantados*, which means "leaders." Left almost entirely to their own resources, unhampered by royal restrictions, they accomplished truly incredible things.

The keynote of this first century in America was action—action more dynamic and on a vaster scale than anything ever attempted before in the history of the world. By 1540, in a brief span of less than fifty years, Spain had conquered and was governing territories many times the size of the mother country. Portugal had laid a firm hold on Brazil, which alone is considerably larger than the United States.

Cortés, with a force never exceeding fifteen hundred Spaniards, had defeated tens of thousands of Aztec warriors and had taken their capital by siege and storm. Pizarro, with less than four hundred soldiers, had marched straight into the heart of the Inca Empire, where he seized the Inca ruler and subdued his country of several millions. Quesada, with only one hundred and sixty-six men, finally crossed the five-hundred-mile belt of swamps and wild mountainous terrain between the sea and Bogotá, where he defeated the native Chibchas and founded the present capital of Colombia. Orellana crossed the Andes from Peru, built a few makeshift boats, and traveled three thousand miles down the Amazon to the Atlantic coast of Brazil. Cabeza de Vaca tramped across ten thousand miles of the United States and a great part of Mexico and then proceeded to South America, where he made another thousand-mile trek across the Brazilian jungles to Paraguay.

Religion either accompanied or followed hot on the heels of conquest. When Balboa crossed the Isthmus of Panama and discovered and took possession of the Pacific Ocean in the name of the Spanish sovereign, a young priest who was a member of the expedition rushed into the waves with a crucifix, shouting, "I take possession of this ocean in the name of Jesus Christ."[23]

Neither the enormity of distances, geographical barriers, hardships, disease, nor the opposition of native warriors could deter these men of action from the swift completion of their tasks. The accumulated strength of centuries was their reserve, and it was not spent until almost the entire face of the American continents was marked with their paths, their bones, their towns, and their missions.

While other European nations made of the Renaissance an epoch of the arts, literature, painting, sculpture, and building—all exaltations of the new pagan spirit—the Iberian Peninsula made of it an epoch of religion and conquest, of prolonging the Middle Ages and of the super-heroism of the conquistador—their own highest achievement. These conquerors came from the lower classes. There was not a really noble family among them. They belonged to the people, and, representing the character of the people, they became like them: great and heroic, oftentimes zealous, cruel, greedy, bigoted, and ignorant, but always great and heroic.

It is fortunate that Spain and Portugal undertook the conquest at this time. No other countries were then ready for such an enterprise. A certain state of mind must precede a successful imperialism, and that state existed nowhere in Europe outside of Spain and Portugal. Luther, Calvin, and other Protestant leaders might spring up in other parts of Europe to disrupt the unity and authority of the state, but not on the Iberian Peninsula. Here the state had long since seized on the Church as its tool and weapon and would not relinquish it. Uniformity was not forced on the Spaniards and Portuguese. Centuries of warfare against the Moors had made it an integral part of their being, an expression of the collective will. Hence their forces alone were immediately prepared to undertake the conquest in which a unified home front was of the first importance.

Whenever warfare breaks out on a great scale, there is always a cross and sword, a reason for fighting, and a means of achieving victory. Unless victory becomes a religion, defeat in the long run is inevitable even if the campaign is won. To the realistic inhabitants of the peninsula these were no theoretic symbols. Throughout the many centuries of Moorish wars the "Christian soldier" had been a part of their daily living. And just as the soldier carried his physical strength into the field of religion, so did the priest take his onto the field of battle. He frequently went among the enemy, flailing about with a spiked mace, and, as the proverb succinctly states: "A Dios rogando, y con la maza dando [Praying for God's grace, and thumping with his mace]." But the conquest of America had more than one god; it created its own holy trinity: glory, gold, and Gospel. No more inspiring banner has ever waved in the heart of a soldier.

5

THE HALLS OF MONTEZUMA

About the year 1555 a retired soldier of nearly seventy, who was living at ease on his estate in Guatemala, got hold of a book called *Chronicle of the Conquest of New Spain*. The author was a certain López de Gómara who had for years been the private chaplain of Cortés after the conquistador had returned to the peninsula from his conquest of Mexico to spend his final days.

Gómara had gotten straight from that source all the details for his history, but being under a sense of obligation to the famous captain, he had not always written up his facts in the proper perspective. In every chapter, on nearly every page, it was "Cortés this" and "Cortés that," the captain made such and such a decision, won such and such a victory, defeated this tribe or the other, and finally overcame the empire of Montezuma.

When the old soldier who was living in Guatemala read these things his blood fairly boiled. He, Bernal Díaz del Castillo, had been on an expedition to Yucatan even before Cortés; later he cast in his lot with that captain, fought with him bravely through the entire Mexican campaign, took part in one hundred and nineteen battles, and was wounded several times. He had risen from the ranks to be one of the most trusted lieutenants of the conqueror of Mexico. He knew as well as anyone what the life of the common soldier had been throughout this conquest, and he knew to what extent the victory had depended on co-operative effort in battle and in camp, in decisions reached, and in policies carried out. Nobody admired Cortés more than he did, but he was incensed that justice had not been done to the private soldier. Although he himself had never been a writer, he determined to compile what he called the *True History of the Conquest of New Spain*.

The old man's memory was prodigious. He remembered not only the name of every man in the campaign, but the name and the exact coloring of every horse, and the minutest details of battles or descriptions of land-scapes, cities, or Indians. Not only was his memory good, but his style was earnest, straightforward, vivid. What it lacked in polish it more than made up in bluntness and vigor. The only points on which this soldier chronicler was not entirely accurate were his statistics and his tendency to exaggerate the initiative of the men and to minimize the rare alchemy of Cortés's discipline and leadership over as odd an assortment of ruffians as ever made up an army. Except for these extremely minor faults Bernal Díaz was the greatest historian of those epic days. His work did not appear in print until 1632, nearly half a century after his death.

Every historian of Mexico or Latin America who wrote in later years was indebted to the *True History* of Bernal Díaz. The Englishman, William Robertson, who published the first great *History of America* in 1776, relied on him heavily, as did William H. Prescott in his equally famous *Conquest of Mexico*, which appeared in 1843. So also did H. H. Bancroft, Antonio Solís, and all the other historians of Mexico.

The old soldier who remembered so much and forgot almost nothing was the epitome of all that was best in Spain when Spain was the greatest of all nations. When he speaks of his companions who had fallen, or who had been captured and sacrificed to the gods and devoured by the Mexicans, he is always careful to point out that "they died in the service of God and his Majesty, and to give light to those who sat in darkness, and also to acquire that wealth which most men covet."[20] That, in a nutshell, is the whole of the conquest.

Bernal Díaz was also characteristic of the fortitude which enabled the outnumbered Spaniards time after time to endure fruitless toil and death for final victory. So long had the old chronicler slept in the open fields with his weapons at his side that in his old age he wrote, "Since the conquest . . . I have never been able to lie down undressed, or even on a bed; yet I sleep as soundly as if I were on softest down. . . . Another thing I must add is that I cannot sleep long in the night without getting up to look at the heavens and the stars, and stay awhile in the open air. . . ."

Neither was this stout chronicler any shrinking violet when it came to praising his own part in the conquest. He had written his *True History* for the express purpose of lauding the role of the common soldier, and he had begun as a common soldier. In his closing pages, after expressing his admiration for Cortés, he adds: "A part of the honor also falls to me, for I was one of the most forward in every battle by his side." Then a little farther on he remarks: "The fact is I do not praise myself so much as I ought."

The two lawyers to whom Bernal Díaz had first shown his manuscript for criticism pointed out that it might have sounded better had he not mentioned himself and his comrades so often and in such glowing terms, and the old veteran, both hurt and nettled by this reaction, pointed out: ". . . and if we did not speak well of ourselves, who would? Who else witnessed our exploits and our battles—unless, indeed, the clouds in the sky, and the birds that were flying over our heads?"

Bernal Díaz was as dynamic and straightforward as the times which gave him birth, and as uncompromising in his convictions. Multiplied by a few hundred of the same power, such men as he were able to achieve what to more relaxed minds would have appeared unreasonable and impossible. But one thing remains to be added. Even such men as they, without the stern genius of leadership to stay their differences and their passions and to direct in a single straight line their divided efforts, would at best have won a few flashing victories on the road to ignominious disaster. The power which held them together, gave them confidence, welded them into a swift-striking unit hardened under the fire of discipline was that of the conquistador, and among the conquistadores none was greater than the conqueror of Mexico, Hernán Cortés.

Cortés was born in southern Spain in 1485 into a family which, although poor as church mice, laid claims to belonging to the lesser hidalgo nobility. Cortés was sent to the democratic university of Salamanca for an education, but after two years he came back home and devoted himself to the more enjoyable pursuit of a Lothario. At the age of seventeen, lured by exaggerated tales of wealth and adventure from the New World, he decided to enlist in an expedition to those regions. As a popular song of those days put it:

> "A la guerra me lleva
> Mi necesidad;
> Si tuviera dineros
> No fuera en verdad."*

Shortly before his scheduled departure, while attempting to scale a high and not too strongly built wall in order to proceed undetected to his mistress's bedroom, the stonework suddenly gave way and the young swain fell flat on his face with a heavy pile of rocks on top of him. The severe bruises he received made it necessary to give up all plans of joining the expedition. A couple of years later, in 1504, he did reach America, and with much reluctance became one of the colonists on Santo Domingo. "I don't intend to stay on this island or any other island of the New World very long," he said. "I came to get gold, not to till the soil like a peasant."

The city of Santo Domingo at that time was the capital of the Spanish new world. There was no town in Spain more beautiful or better constructed, unless it was the noble city of Barcelona. It boasted of fine churches, beautiful gardens, wide, well-kept streets, many stone houses, and several schools. Santo Domingo was also the "Falcon's Nest" from which much of the rest of America was conquered. During the first years

---

* My necessity drives me to war; if I had money I'd surely not go.

of the sixteenth century it was the head and nutritive mother of those vast new realms.

Somewhat reluctantly Cortés settled down there with a grant of land and Indians and gradually became one of the most popular young men on the island. His pursuit of women continued, and he fought several duels. After seven years of plantation life he took part in the conquest of Cuba and won great favor with the leader of the expedition, who later became governor of that island. This friendship had its ups and downs, and the young man was twice thrown in prison for minor offenses. However, the governor's anger did not last long and Cortés soon settled down again to a rural existence. He also worked some gold mines which had fallen to his share as one of the original conquerors of Cuba. Before long he became both prominent and wealthy.

In the meantime, reports of a rich empire on the mainland kept reaching the island, and finally a ship returned from Yucatan loaded with a valuable cargo of gold and silver. The governor immediately laid plans for a more formidable expedition, and Cortés managed to worm his way in as captain-general. The fact that his considerable wealth was invested in the enterprise certainly had something to do with the choice. Nevertheless, at the last moment the governor began to reconsider his appointment, and it came to the ears of Cortés that he was about to be replaced. With the same lack of hesitancy which characterized all his decisions, Cortés ordered the fleet to prepare to sail immediately. All night the ships were loaded with final provisions and early the next day the expedition departed for Yucatan. Cortés was thirty-three; the year was 1518. Reinforcements were taken on at Havana, and when the convoy reached the shores of Mexico it numbered one hundred and ten sailors, five hundred and fifty-three soldiers, sixteen horses, and a couple of hundred Indian islanders, who had come along to do the menial chores.

At his first stop on an island off Yucatan, Cortés demanded that the natives be converted to Christianity. Some incomprehensible explanations of the faith were delivered by a Spanish father, but the poor Indians still insisted that their own gods were good enough for them. Cortés then ordered his men to ascend the pyramid-like temple and roll the native idols unceremoniously to the ground. The Indians broke out in desolate lamentations, but, seeing that their gods were powerless to protect themselves, humbly accepted the religion of the Spaniards.

Just as the Spanish ships were about to shove off from this island an Indian canoe was seen racing across the waters toward them. A sunburned, almost naked man leaped from it and asked in Spanish if he was among Christians. When informed that he was, the poor fellow fell to his knees and thanked God for his deliverance. He turned out to be Jerónimo de Aguilar, one of the men who had survived a shipwreck on the Mexican coast eight years previously, and who had since risen to a place of prominence in an Indian community where he resided. He was anxious to join Cortés, and his knowledge of the Maya language proved invaluable in later contacts with the natives.

On reaching the coast proper, Cortés had the fleet drop anchor in the mouth of a river where the gold previously sent to Cuba had been obtained. It was the country of the Tabascans, and this time the inhabitants were not friendly. Neighboring tribes had been twitting them about their former meek reception of the foreigners, and on the morning after the arrival armed warriors lined the banks of the stream in considerable numbers. The Spaniards forced a landing against strong resistance, and the natives retreated, abandoning their crude barricades and the city which lay beyond them.

The next day they came back again, and a full-fledged battle took place. Spanish horses and guns finally overcame the Indians after the fiercest fighting. On tendering their submission, the Tabascans brought along many propitiatory gifts, including twenty female slaves, for the Spanish soldiers. Again Cortés insisted on conversion before taking his departure, and the natives, after their decisive defeat in the field, submitted in a perfunctory fashion. A solemn mass was celebrated by Father Olmedo, and one of the witnesses wrote that on hearing the soldiers chant, many of the natives, unused to such harmonies, burst into tears.

The victory at Tabasco was not important because of the size of the Indian forces engaged, but its effect on neighboring tribes, heightened considerably by exaggerated accounts of weapons of fire and thunder and charging centaurs, was extremely great.

In an entirely different direction it bore results which were equally far-reaching. Among the twenty women slaves given to the Spaniards was one young girl who knew both the Maya and Aztec languages. When Cortés invaded Aztec territory, she turned what was said by the natives into Maya, and Aguilar translated this into Spanish. Soon this roundabout method of interpreting was unnecessary, for to the Mexican girl, Malinche, Spanish became the language of love and Cortés her idol. Companion, interpreter, adviser, mistress, and nurse, she stuck loyally with the Spaniards through good times and bad and, whenever the occasion afforded, did everything in her power to mitigate the conquest of her people. Malinche was the only person in Mexico loved equally by both sides, and to both sides equally indispensable.

After their conquest of the Tabascans, the Spanish forces pushed on down the coast and finally dropped anchor off the shores of Vera Cruz. The chief of that district, who was a tributary of Montezuma, received Cortés well and presented him with "ten loads of fine cottons, several mantles of that curious feather work whose rich and delicate dyes might vie with the most beautiful painting, and a wicker basket filled with ornaments of wrought gold." Cortés accepted these gifts graciously and then presented those which he wished taken to Montezuma: a richly carved armchair, several bracelets, collars, and other ornaments of cut glass, and a crimson cap decorated with a gold medallion.

A Mexican chief suggested that a gilt helmet worn by one of the soldiers be added to the list, and this was promptly done, Cortés expressing the hope that it might be returned filled with gold dust so that he could compare it with that of his own country. According to the historian Gómara, Cortés told the chief "that the Spaniards were afflicted with a disease of the heart for which gold was a specific remedy." And the old Captain Bernal Díaz, who was moved to write his own version of the same scene fifty-odd years later, agrees in this instance that his leader "contrived to make his need of gold very clear to the governor."

After seven or eight days the royal couriers returned from the Mexican capital with gifts from Montezuma. These included a wide variety of articles of precious stones and metals and the famous gold and silver disks as large as carriage wheels, ornamented with carved plants and animals of beautiful workmanship. People who saw these plates later in Spain were deeply impressed with their value and the artistry with which they had been executed. The soldier's helmet was also returned filled with gold dust and nuggets. "And this," wrote one of the old Spanish historians, "cost Montezuma his life."

The emissaries from Mexico courteously informed Cortés that Montezuma regarded them as friends, but considered the journey overland to his capital too dangerous for them to undertake and urged them to return to their own country. This last statement showed clearly just how the land lay. The messengers were sent back with a stronger request for an interview, and they returned as quickly with a still more cogent prohibition against further advance toward the great central city.

Shortly afterward five chiefs belonging to the powerful Totonac tribe visited the Spanish camp. They invited Cortés to their village and informed him that all was not well with the Aztec Empire, that they themselves were unwilling tributaries of the great chief Montezuma, and that many other tribes were in the same situation. Cortés promised to repay their visit soon and thanked them graciously. This was the first time that he had received news of internal dissensions in Mexico, and he knew now that a way was open for the conquest of the country.

In the meantime, some of the soldiers in camp, particularly those who were close partisans of the governor whom Cortés had eluded, were chafing at the bit and expressed their intention of returning to Cuba. When their grievances were brought into the open, Cortés, instead of becoming angered, announced that they would all board their ships immediately and set sail the following day. This took the wind out of the opposition's arguments and there arose a great hue and cry in camp, the gist of which was that to leave the country while so much wealth was at their very finger tips would be madness. Cortés listened unmoved.

Finally, at their repeated insistence, he gravely addressed the soldiers, reminding them that his entire worldly possessions were invested in the expedition, and that he naturally was averse to giving it up, but that if his men wished to do so, he would not stand in their way. If, on the other hand, they wanted to remain in Mexico and establish a permanent colony in the name of the Spanish King, he would also acquiesce in that. Of course this was the alternative accepted, and on the following day papers were drawn up for the legalization of the colony. Cortés appointed the members of the new municipal government and they decided to name the town *la Villa Rica de Vera Cruz*, or "the Rich Town of the True Cross," later shortened to Vera Cruz.

After the final documents were duly notarized and signed, Cortés presented himself before the new council and tendered his resignation. A civil government had replaced the military, and they, not he, were now the supreme authority. With that alacrity and heroic gesture which have been characteristic of Latin-American politics throughout the years, the municipality promptly re-elected him with greatly increased powers. The soldiers who remained refractory were soon brought into line with golden promises, and, when necessary, with gold itself. Cortés now felt himself free of all ties that bound him to the authority of the governor of Cuba.

A few days later the Spaniards visited the capital of the Totonacs, Cempoala. Some of the cavalry who rode on ahead rushed back with the news that the houses of that city were all covered with burnished silver. The rest of the troops quickened their march, but, upon reaching the town, saw that the reported "silver" was only smooth-surfaced stucco which had gleamed under the rays of the sun, and more so under the heated imaginations of the credulous cavalrymen. While the Spaniards were in Cempoala, the hated Aztec tax collectors arrived, and a shudder of apprehension ran through the town's inhabitants. Cortés demanded that all tribute be refused and that the Aztec representatives be seized and imprisoned. There was a great show of hesitancy, but he strongly repeated the command and was finally obeyed. A few hours later he managed quietly to set the captives free, but not before apologizing for the Totonacs' violence and expressing his own high regard and friendship for Montezuma.

The affairs of business having been satisfactorily dispatched, the next step was the conversion of the Totonacs. When they received Father Olmedo's apostolic harangue untouched, fifty soldiers leaped up the stairs of the pyramid and threw the monstrous blood-spattered idols to the ground. The Totonacs broke into a long wail but submitted to conversion without resistance. The foul temple was then thoroughly scrubbed and an altar with a cross was placed on its summit decorated with garlands of roses.

Cortés learned from the Totonacs that at the head of the list of those tribes which hated the Aztecs were the fierce warriors of Tlaxcala. They had maintained their independence in a valley not far from the Mexican capital despite repeated and violent assaults made by Montezuma's soldiers. The captain decided to travel to Mexico through this valley. Reinforced with over thirteen hundred Indian allies and one thousand porters, the Spaniards took leave of Cempoala and started the long ascent which led to the tablelands of the central plateau. The captain's last act while still on the coast was to destroy his entire fleet except for a single vessel. In order to make the destruction more plausible false reports as to the unseaworthiness of the ships were drawn up. Some of the soldiers raised a row, but when Cortés blandly told them to board the remaining ship and sail for Cuba not a soldier moved. With every man of a single mind the little caravan headed toward the interior.

First they crossed a stretch of swampy land in which even their horses got mired down "clear to the belly." The heat at times was almost unbearable, for the soldiers always traveled and slept in full armor. After leaving this region they came to a drier and less torrid district where "grew many fields of native grapes under sunny skies." After this they entered mountainous territory and had to go through a pass which Cortés wrote "is so high and rough that there is not in all Spain one so difficult to get through." They finally reached a cold upland region where icy winds, hail, and rains drenched them for hours on end. They were now at an altitude of about seven thousand feet. There was little food and no relief from the cold. The tropical Indians died like flies of exposure, but the Spaniards, "with their clothes and armor as their only protection from the elements, endured everything with stoic Iberian adaptability."[24]

When the Tlaxcalans heard of their approach, a war council was called and they decided to fight. Had not the Spaniards desecrated temples throughout the country? And didn't they seem to be friends with Montezuma, their own mortal enemy? With such arguments before them the Tlaxcalans concluded that resistance was the only honorable course.

In the one great battle which Cortés fought with these people he learned a new respect for Indian valor. They massed their warriors before him on a great plain until the whole horizon seemed a sea of barbaric colors. Cortés estimated their number at one hundred thousand, and Bernal Díaz says forty thousand. The exact figure was probably much less, but there is no doubt they far outnumbered the Spaniards.

These fierce mountain warriors threw themselves on the white man with reckless abandon. Neither gunfire nor cavalry charges could stay them. They grabbed at the lances of the horsemen, chopped at the animals' legs and necks, and hurled a multitude of arrows and spears upon them. One horse and rider were dragged to the ground and the poor animal was pierced through with several swords. The horseman was rescued, but his steed was carved into pieces which were later sent all over the country to prove that the feared centaur was not immortal.

However, the natives' very recklessness, together with a lack of sufficient organization to utilize their greatly superior force, was their undoing. In the pell-mell rushes of their army only the foremost troops were engaged, and the constant pressure from those behind served only to encumber those who were forward. In this way, when their charge was completed and the Spanish finally managed to overcome the leading contingents, their fight became disorganized, and this disorganization was carried back to the milling thousands behind them. A near stampede turned into inevitable retreat, and that into victory for the Spaniards.

The Tlaxcalans did not submit after this defeat but decided to attack again at night. This time, however, the Spaniards were waiting for them and held their fire until the Indians had drawn near, then they let go with all they had. Cannons, rifles, and cavalry, all at once swept the field before them, and the battle was quickly won. A peace was agreed upon, and from this time on the Tlaxcalans were Cortés's loyal allies. They did not desert him even on that disastrous retreat from the Mexican capital during the *noche triste* (sad night) when he lost more than half his army.

The Spaniards rested in Tlaxcala and repaired the many wounds of these fierce encounters. Then with six thousand new allies added to his force, Cortés advanced toward the Mexican capital. His road led through the populous city of Cholula, where Quetzalcoatl was said to have remained twenty years, teaching the arts of civilization before his departure for the coast. The city was pre-Toltec in origin and contained a great pyramid which occupied more ground space than any in Egypt. It was about one hundred and seventy-five feet high, with a base covering forty-four acres, and had a huge level platform on its summit, about an acre in extent, where stood a temple and a statue of the God of the Plumed Serpent.

The Tlaxcalans were not at all pleased to visit Cholula, whose tardy and more or less forced invitation was distrusted, and on reaching the city their uneasiness continued to grow. Vague rumors of a conspiracy against the Spaniards seemed to be floating on the air. Malinche, Cortés's mistress, was urged to spend a few days in the house of a native chief, whose wife by devious means intimated that she might thus save her life. The Mexican girl promptly accepted the invitation and expressed strong resentment at the treatment she had been receiving from the Spaniards. This quickly won the Cholulans' confidence, and all the details of the conspiracy were revealed. Malinche at once relayed them to her master.

Cortés made plans to teach the Cholulans a lesson so cruel they would never forget it. On the pretext of needing a great number of porters, he succeeded in gathering all the chiefs into the main plaza, where his men suddenly attacked them from all sides until not one remained alive. Streets were then swept by artillery and horsemen and the houses were looted and burned. When order was restored, no one in Cholula dared challenge Spanish authority. Montezuma had apparently been at the bottom of the whole thing, but when his ambassadors were accused of this they placed the whole blame on the Cholulans. Cortés, who was anxious to remain on good terms with the Aztec ruler, said that he would not believe so base an act could possibly have been instigated by his friend.

The march toward Mexico City was continued through snow and chilling blasts from the mountains. Finally, on a wintry day toward the end of October 1519, they realized that the end of their journey was in sight. On rounding the last mountainous turn which stood between them and the Mexican capital, a panorama of great loveliness suddenly appeared below. The valley was covered with green fields, lakes, canals, and sprinkled with villages and towns which shone brightly under the clear air of those high regions. Forests of giant cedars extended down the mountainsides and brilliant flowers colored the valley.

A few days later they approached the queen city of Anáhuac, above which loomed the enormous mass of the great pyramid-temple. The red stone houses belonging to the Aztec chieftains stood out in bold relief against the gray-white adobe walls of the poorer dwellings around them. Over the waters of Lake Texcoco swarmed hundreds of canoes ferrying supplies to the city which lay on an island in its center.

Bernal Díaz wrote: "Gazing on such wonderful sights, we did not know what to say or whether what appeared before us was real, for on one side on the land there were great cities and in the lake, ever so many more, the lake itself was crowded with canoes and in the causeways were many bridges at intervals, and in front of us stood the great city of Tenochtitlán, and we—we did not even number four hundred soldiers."[20]

On hearing the news of their approach, Montezuma shuddered with apprehension. Were these the blond men of destiny which the Aztec gods had said would someday come to rule his land? The great chieftain prayed, but his prayers were unanswered, and when the Spaniards arrived he resignedly went out to receive them. A great multitude had assembled and lined the streets in every direction. This meeting of the two great leaders was a barbaric spectacle beyond description. Montezuma, wearing a beautiful feather headdress, was carried in his litter toward the Spaniards. Above his head attendants held a canopy of green feathers, adorned with gold, silver, and jade. He wore a blue mantle, richly embossed with gold threads, and before him a path was swept and tapestries spread, lest the noble feet be soiled by contact with the earth. "Cortés dismounted from his horse and advanced toward the great chieftain. And then for the first time they looked into each other's eyes." Two different worlds met in that gaze. Behind each man was a world of human spirit which had lived and grown for centuries, separated by differences greater than those of blood or language, "living, thinking, hoping, spinning its destiny out in time and space with the threads of individual lives and deaths so utterly distinct in their conceptions that it was almost as if they had been born on different planets. Yet, no matter how different they might be in form and color, the animal bodies of both races soon sought each other out with the eagerness of fertile love, as bodies of the same species have always done since the beginning of history."[24]

The white men were graciously received and ushered into the city. They were amazed at its size and at the dress of its inhabitants, so much superior to that which they had seen among the natives of the lowlands. Spacious quarters were provided for them in the residence of one of the previous Aztec rulers. Later on, when Cortés had an opportunity to talk to Montezuma in private, the latter laughingly turned to him, saying:

"You have probably been told that I was a god, and dwelt in palaces of gold and silver. But you see it is false. My houses, though large, are of stone and wood like those of others. And as to my body, you see it is flesh and bone like yours. It is true that I have lands, gold and silver. But your sovereign beyond the water is, I know, the rightful lord of all. I rule in his name. You, Malinche,* are his ambassador. You and your companions will share these things with me now."[21]

Lavish gifts were distributed among the Spanish soldiers, and each man received at least two heavy collars of gold for his share. With these presents, Montezuma unknowingly fed the flames of Spanish greed and made his downfall a certainty. A second error had followed the first, which was to receive Cortés as a friend. On that fatal day the doom of Aztec civilization was sealed. Montezuma had yielded and let the hawk into his house. There was no turning back now. Before the entrance into Mexico City, Montezuma had held the initiative, that most priceless of all weapons, but he had been afraid to use it. After the entry it was Cortés who seized the initiative, and, like the great conquistador he was, never let it slip from his grasp. The Aztec ruler was undone by his superstitions and his fears, for even the gods had told him that conquering blond men would come from beyond the sea.

"On that historic day," writes a Spanish historian, "the valiant sanguinary and warrior race which had lived in constant familiarity with blood and death, gave itself into the hands of a mere handful of foreigners who were violently to uproot its natural evolution. How many times have we been told that the victory of Cortés was due to the superiority of his armies, to his gunpowder, and to his horses! Now we know that this explanation does not correspond with the facts. Now we know that at the very first encounter, the Indians nearly decapitated the horse of the soldier Morón with the single blow of an obsidian sword, and certainly the Mexicans were not going to be frightened by mere noise all their lives. The

* This was the name of Cortés's Indian mistress, but the natives often used the same name to designate the captain himself.

real reason of the Mexican defeat was that their faith succumbed before a firmer faith. That man who bowed before Montezuma with smiling eyes and gracious gesture, was the epitome of the Christian religion . . . behind that singular figure his troops were the vanguard of the great European advance toward the broader knowledge of man and of this planet, the forerunners in action of the great adventure of the Renaissance, the true apostles of that Renaissance in the land of the infidels."[24]

The darker side of the picture was not long in appearing. A few days after the entry into Tenochtitlán, Cortés and some of the Spaniards asked Montezuma to let them ascend the stairways of the main temple, and after a consultation with the priests their request was granted. They entered the temple enclosure and finally reached the great pyramid itself, which they slowly climbed. On its summit were three sanctuaries: one dedicated to the God of War, another to the Creator of the World, and the last to the Supreme Being.

The War God was a monstrosity of ugliness, and his sanctuary was thick with the stench of human flesh and blood. In a platter before this statue lay three human hearts, still warm. Priests wearing blood-spattered garments and with clotted hair moved about in the darkness like apparitions out of a nightmare. The Spaniards hurried back into the open air, and Cortés at once tried his hand at converting Montezuma to the milder Christian religion. His suggestion was not well received. The captain looked down upon the vast and populous city spread out below him and decided not to press the point.

Things continued in this state for several days, and the soldiers began to fret under inactivity. The conquest of Mexico and all its immeasurable wealth seemed farther away than ever. At any time they might be attacked or besieged by the Aztecs and made to pay the supreme penalty for their folly. Spanish morale was getting low under this undeclared war of nerves. Cortés, with his usual directness, decided to take the bull by the horns. Using the excuse of an Indian attack against forces he had left on the coast, the captain accused Montezuma of instigating it, and demanded that he accompany the Spaniards back to their quarters as a hostage. The chief was thunderstruck. He paled and then flushed with indignation. Cortés then threw all courtesy aside and said that it would be either his life or his person. Montezuma finally acquiesced, and then, in order to save face, very greatly weakened his own position and strengthened that of the Spaniards by telling his people that he was accompanying them as a guest and of his own free will. The puppet regime of the imprisoned "emperor" was off to a good start. The Spaniards paid him every courtesy as a sop for his loss of freedom.

When about six weeks had passed news reached the capital that a considerable force of Spaniards had landed on the coast. Cortés, certain that these were troops sent by the governor of Cuba to replace his own authority, decided to go to meet them. Alvarado was left behind with a small garrison to await his return. The new fleet consisted of eighteen vessels and nine hundred men under the command of Pánfilo de Narváez. On the way down Cortés learned that these men were divided in their opinion, some anxious to back their commander against him, and others just as anxious to leave Narváez and join his ranks. After both gold and persuasion had done their part, Cortés slipped up on Narváez in the middle of the night, defeated his soldiers, and took him prisoner. The rank and file were quickly brought over to his side, and with forces thus augmented he returned to the capital, where pandemonium had already broken out.

Alvarado, a fine soldier but a hotheaded, cruel, and greedy leader, had allowed about six hundred of the Aztec chiefs to enter the temple enclosure in order to take part in a religious celebration. There he attacked and annihilated them, letting his soldiers loot their dead bodies. He excused this massacre by stating that a conspiracy had been detected among them. Later reports did not bear him out. At any rate, the Mexicans were now up in arms and the Spanish garrison was under siege in its own quarters. Cortés managed to reach them in time and believed that with his greatly increased force he would be able to restore order without difficulty. He was greatly deceived. The entire Indian population was in a state of insurrection which at any moment might burst into a conflagration. Montezuma was finally persuaded to address his people in order to ask them to return quietly to their homes. He showed little understanding of their feelings. Although his first words were received with respectful silence, his remarks about friendship with the Spaniards were greeted with jeers and missiles. One large stone hit him squarely on the head and knocked him down, badly wounded and unconscious. According to Spanish reports, he died several days later after tearing off every bandage that was placed on his head. According to the Aztec version of the story, he was strangled by the Spaniards.

In the meantime the Spaniards were furiously assaulted. They retaliated with a strong counterattack which drove the Aztecs back and then stormed the great temple, tore down the idols, and occupied its strategic summit. At this point Cortés tried to quiet the population but was heard with derision. The Indians shouted that he would never leave Tenochtitlán alive if it took a thousand Indian lives for that of a single Spaniard. All bridges across the canals were already destroyed and the foreigners were caught like rats in a trap with no means of escape.

The only possible recourse was to beat a path through the midst of their assailants, and this was what Cortés attempted to do. His attack began at midnight, but the Aztec warriors were not caught unawares. They blocked his path by the thousands. Slowly the Spanish forces advanced along the shortest causeway, dogged at every step by furious attacks, and their heads showered with stones, arrows, and spears thrown from the roofs of the highest houses. Many Spaniards, weighted down with their booty, fell into canals and were drowned; others were taken as prisoners and later served as sacrifices to the gods, but the retreat continued. The unbridged gaps across the causeway were filled in with stones and rubble, and finally the defeated remnants of a once-proud Spanish army emerged on the plains beyond the city. They had lost all their cannons, had even thrown away their muskets in order to flee faster; most of their horses were dead, and not a man had escaped unwounded. Four hundred and fifty Spaniards were slain in that one night alone. This is the famous *noche triste,* or "sad night," when Cortés was supposed to have stopped under a tree to weep over the misfortunes of his soldiers. The tree is still shown to tourists in Mexico City, but it is very doubtful whether Cortés had time to indulge in any weeping, even had he been so inclined.

They at last reached the open plains and were heading rapidly for Tlaxcala, but were not yet free of the Aztecs, who kept close on their heels, constantly taunting them with the words "not a Spaniard will leave this valley alive." On the seventh day, as they neared one of the passes through the mountains, the attack began in force. Surrounded by a vastly superior number, without firearms of any kind and with only a few horses, the exhausted and wounded warriors of Spain here rose to their greatest heights. Some measure of their valor was communicated to their faithful Tlaxcalan allies, for all fought with the courage of lions.

The Spaniards formed a compact square which threw off every charge the enemy could hurl against it. Their cavalry, in groups of three and four, charged among the Aztecs recklessly, spreading death in their wake. But the Indians now knew how to handle the situation—they re-formed their ranks and counterattacked with new fury. Many hours passed. A hot sun was burning in the sky. The Spanish forces were reaching the point of complete exhaustion, whereas new Aztec warriors constantly replaced those who grew tired or were wounded.

Seeing that the day was lost unless some miracle turned the tide, Cortés stopped fighting long enough to single out the principal Aztec leader. He was a young chief borne in a litter over which waved a crest of plumes, and to whose back was attached a golden net that served as the Aztec banner. Calling on his best horsemen to follow him, the Spanish captain charged like a thunderbolt through the Indian army toward this personage. With the fury of desperation they speared him from his litter, tore the golden banner from his back, and destroyed his supporters. Cortés grabbed the bloody banner, and again they charged into the fight, but now the spirit of the Indians was gone, and, seeing their chieftain slain, they broke ranks and fled from the field. The most decisive battle in the history of Mexico was ended.

From this time forward, though the perils they faced continued for nine months, Cortés and his troops held the upper hand in Mexico. They retired to Tlaxcala to lick their wounds, picked up considerable reinforcements which from time to time had landed on the coast, renewed their supply of ammunition and their spirits, and continued the conquest of the country. They did not yet dare to make a direct assault on its capital, but with a war of attrition—attacking first one town and then another, keeping the enemy forces always divided and their own intact—they gradually wore the Aztecs down to such a point that finally a siege of the capital became possible.

In order to make the siege absolutely airtight, Cortés had his men construct thirteen brigantines which were then carried across sixty miles of mountainous terrain and placed on the lake. The Spaniards next occupied all three causeways leading out of the city and began a slow day-by-day advance along these, methodically destroying every building between them and the center of town. In order to have more room for cavalry maneuvering, they filled in the canals with rubble. Every day that passed saw them nearer their objective, and every day found the inhabitants of the city more closely crowded and with fewer provisions. Gradually the Aztecs were reduced to a pitiful plight—disease and famine weakened them beyond hope of victory.

After several weeks, with seven eighths of their capital destroyed, a final valiant assault of the Spaniards slaughtered most of those who had survived. Their resistance was stubborn until the last, and they never surrendered. The atmosphere was so foul that big torches had to be carried to clear the air before the advance could continue. In desperation, the young chieftain, Cuautemoc, whose statue now stands on the Paseo de la Reforma in Mexico City with a raised lance in his hand, tried to escape in a native canoe but was overtaken and captured. Resistance was at an end. Tenochtitlán had ceased to exist (August 13, 1521).

The siege had lasted for seventy-five days amid almost hourly scenes of bloodshed. The Spaniards lost about a hundred men, or approximately one tenth of their total number, but their allies and the Aztecs had perished by the thousands. Famine, smallpox, and other diseases wiped out tremendous numbers of the besieged. "Peace being proclaimed the surviving Aztecs began to crawl forth from their pest-holes and seek the fields adjacent, now lustrous green under the refreshing rains, filing in long processions over the causeway, while the very sun struck black on their pinched features and plague-stricken forms."[25]

Although the battle was over, the Spaniards still had before them the business of collecting what they thought was a proper indemnity. Some of the Aztec treasure had already come into their hands, but not enough. They believed their enemies had hidden it, and, in order to find out, put Cuautemoc and several other chieftains to the torture. Their feet were slowly roasted before a fire and then anointed with oil so that they would not char and could be hurt again. One of the chiefs whose stamina was not so great as that of the others turned to Cuautemoc with pleading eyes. The last of the Aztec rulers was then supposed to have said, "Do you think I am on any bed of roses?" The story is in character and has been seized upon by poets to this day as a symbol.

At any rate, the Spaniards found but little treasure as a result of this deed which has blackened their names throughout history. For years it caused the Mexican people to despise the very name of Cortés, but recently in some quarters there has been a marked change in their attitude. A contemporary Mexican historian, José Vasconcelos, who takes a strongly pro-Cortés stand and looks down his nose at the bloody and barbaric culture of the Aztecs, writes of this incident:

"The myth of Cuautemoc was invented by Prescott and other North American historians and is defended by all the indirect agents of protestantism who wish to erase every trace of Spain in America. If in Mexico we deny our Spanish heritage, we shall be left like the negro under the dubious godfathership of a Lincoln who only for political reasons abolished slavery, or worse yet, a step-father like Washington who kept negro slaves despite his liberating zeal. The sentimentalism which surrounds Cuautemoc is like that expressed today by those unconsciously influenced by British imperialism in favor of the Negus of Abyssinia. . . . Cortés on the other hand, the most human of the conquistadores, the most self-denying, is spiritually joined with the vanquished Indians when he forced them to the faith, and his action leaves us the legacy of a real nation."[26]

Salvador de Madariaga, the contemporary Spanish biographer of Cortés, praises the great conquistador unreservedly: "How could he ever have guessed that the day would come when they would even have to conceal his ashes, buried in Mexico at his own express wish, from the fury of the masses whose nation he had founded, who rose in destructive fury against the very man to whose vision they owed their country? How could he have foreseen that the Mexico created by him would some day erect a statue of Cuautemoc, not to honor Cuautemoc, but to insult *him*; that a painter of that race, for which he had done so much to ennoble and set free from their horrible practices, would one day adorn the walls of his palace in Cuernavaca with slanderous scenes of the conquest, about which even the said painter is innocent, since they burst forth out of the unfathomable abyss of racial feelings?"[24]

These statements neither add to nor subtract from the facts of the case, but they do help to bring into proper focus the conquest of Mexico and the Spanish regime in that country which has unjustly been characterized by such a recent writer as Stuart Chase as "four centuries or more of cringing abjection in a land where once civilized men walked free, fearless, and masters of their destiny."[27]

Cortés did not stop and rest after the conquest of Mexico City. He subdued the country for many hundreds of miles in every direction, and his exploring expeditions covered much of modern Mexico and a considerable part of Central America. He was confirmed by the Spanish King as captain-general and continued in this capacity for several years. His subordinates made many later marches into Central America; and Alvarado, one of his best lieutenants, was the conqueror of Guatemala. The captain-general himself lived for several years on his estate at Cuernavaca, but after being shoved into a subordinate position by the King's governors he later returned to Spain and died there in 1547, an embittered man, at the age of sixty-three.

It is difficult to recapitulate an epic achievement of such scope as the conquest of Mexico, but a few things do stand out as characteristic of the age and as indicative of that which was to follow. Cortés himself was undoubtedly the greatest military leader and one of the greatest builders and statesmen of those epic days. He also represented most completely that fusion of soldier and Christian which had enabled his country to achieve its incredible strength. These same feelings he inspired in his troops to a degree not touched by any other conquistador. Under his leadership a band of restive vagabonds and adventurers was molded into a unified, hard-hitting army. There was not a single soldier among them who did not respect his leader. Not only that, Cortés's achievements in political maneuvering rivaled those of King Ferdinand himself, and, considering that he was dealing with tribes of barbarians whose degree of civilization was so utterly different from his own, this conquistador attains a greatness unequaled in Spanish colonial history.

After the epoch of warfare was closed he took up the tasks of reconstruction and government with equal skill. Colonists, seeds, plants, and cattle were brought to Mexico, and a policy of justice and conciliation soon re-established the native population under the rule of their tribal chieftains.

Cortés was by character neither a sadist nor a destroyer, as many have described him. He was simply an imperialist in a world whose highest ideals were conquest and conversion. When he destroyed, it was in order that his own conception might prevail, and his conception was always based on constructive discipline, not aimless destruction. When compared with most of the other conquerors of his day, of whatever nationality, his moderation becomes obvious. The exigencies of war forced him to destroy the capital city of the Aztecs, but when that won him the campaign, he proceeded at once with the work of reconstruction, reconciliation, and justice. Thousands of Indian friends and allies whom he had rescued from Aztec tyranny regarded him as their savior. If the later course of events shows no progress during many a decade of Mexican history to follow, that is another matter.

With great pride Cortés wrote to the Emperor in 1524 that Mexico City had been rebuilt and was populated with thirty thousand families all living as orderly as before. "Moreover," he continued, "I have granted them such liberties and immunities that they would increase greatly. They live quite as they please, and many artisans make a living among the Spaniards, such as carpenters, masons, stone-cutters, silver smiths and the like. . . ." Then he goes on to stress the point that new plants and seeds must be imported in order to increase the health and productive capacity of the people, and he assures the Emperor that if these could be obtained in sufficient quantity from Spain "the ability of the natives in cultivating the soil and in making plantations is such that they would surely produce an abundance, and great profit would accrue to the Imperial Government of Your Highness." He closes, begging the Emperor that "no ship be allowed to sail without bringing a certain number of plants which would favor the increase and prosperity of the country."[10]

We should mention here that American foods, such as corn, beans, potatoes, and many others hitherto unknown in Europe, soon doubled the food supply available to the ordinary man in the Old World and did much to prevent the recurrence of the great famines of an earlier epoch.

From an entirely different angle, Cortés's relationship with Malinche gives us an insight into the new Mexico which was to rise out of the ruins of the old. This affair is symbolic of all that the conquest came to mean for the native races. For several years the captain and his mistress were inseparable, and when Cortés was addressed by Montezuma, the Aztec ruler always referred to him, too, as Malinche. The union of these two seemed to form a new oneness, and from its dual blood stream there emerged a mestizo son, Don Martín.

This young man rose to a high political station in Mexico but got mixed up in a plot to make his half brother, Cortés's legitimate son, king of the country. The legitimate son, also named Martín, made good his escape and left his mestizo partisan to take the consequences. The first Martín was then tortured shamefully in an attempt to make him reveal the names of his co-conspirators, but he never did. He died a poor and broken man. The analogy may be carried even further. After five or six years Cortés wearied of his native Malinche, who had accompanied him on every campaign, and gave her to one of his Spanish companions-at-arms in marriage.

The Mexican girl at this point suddenly drops out of the pages of history to assume that blurred and shapeless anonymity of which the exploited Indian is the inheritor. If Cortés ever really loved his Malinche, and he probably did, he put use above love and remained with her only so long as that utility endured. No more complete symbol of the native races can be found. Malinche's requital, although she probably never thought of requital, is that of her people, whose blood has almost blotted out the pale face of the Spanish conqueror.

A reflection on the literal interpretation which circumstances often caused the Spaniards to place on their religious creed is suggested by the treatment meted out to the many native women who were given to them from time to time by the Indians. These women were first baptized; then, after purification, the soldiers at once proceeded to use them so long as it suited their fancies. In this way the mestizo population, often not knowing its father's face, sprang into being from the very first moment the Spaniards set foot on American soil.

What were the rewards of the conquest in the terms of gold and silver won by Cortés and his men? One of the lowest estimates is that while they were guests in the capital before general warfare had broken out Montezuma gave them a total of over five million dollars' worth of precious metal. They later collected more, but nearly all of it was thrown away during the disastrous night retreat along the causeway.

After the conquest was concluded, Cortés, with his eye now on encouraging the colonization, kept up the lure of easy wealth by sending back to Spain for exhibit many imposing articles of gold and silver. Among these was a large cannon made entirely of these two metals, worth around three hundred thousand dollars.

Perhaps the greatest of all results of the conquest of Mexico is that it served as an example of what a few brave men could do. With this triumph before the eyes of Spain's young and adventurous soldiers, nothing seemed beyond their grasp, no victory too difficult to achieve, no hardship too great to be endured. Cortés not only symbolized the best of his stout race, he left those who followed him a higher mark to emulate than they had ever known before, and Mexico, or "New Spain" as they called it, became the brightest jewel in the diadem of the colonial empire. For many years it was Spain's greatest source of wealth, her best-governed and most populous colony—her grandest achievement.

Pedro de Alvarado, one of the lieutenants who accompanied Cortés, later became a conquistador in his own name. This impetuous young leader of unknown parentage had needlessly brought the Aztec capital down on his men during Cortés's absence. His light blond hair and fair complexion caused the Mexicans to give him the sobriquet of "*el Tonatiuh* [the Sun God]." After the conquest of Mexico, Alvarado led about four hundred men southward into the jungles of Guatemala, where there were said to be great cities decorated with gold and silver. The legend of long-abandoned Maya centers still persisted in the memory of many Indians. Alvarado never found the gold he was seeking, but the wealthiest Guatemalan city, Utatlan, he sacked without compassion, burning the houses, attacking the women, despoiling the people. The countryside all around was then scourged with fire and sword and hundreds of miserable captives were brought in and branded to serve as slaves on Alvarado's land in 1524.

Three years later the conqueror of Guatemala went to Spain, where he made a good marriage, became an *adelantado*, and was made governor of

Guatemala. In 1534, not content with his Central American conquests, Alvarado assembled a large group of soldiers and sailors and sailed for Peru, hoping to reach Quito, the great northern center of Inca territory, before Pizarro. One of the latter's lieutenants, Belalcázar, had arrived there first, and both he and Alvarado were bitterly disappointed to find no gold.

Pizarro was anxious to get rid of this hornet who would probably plague him out of half his booty if he remained in Peru, so he offered Alvarado more than one hundred thousand dollars for his provisions and equipment; and the Sun God returned to Guatemala, though many of his men remained behind. He established several towns in Honduras, Salvador, and Guatemala, and fitted out a fleet to search for the Spice Islands of the East, which were now thought to lie westward across the southern Pacific. In these small "homemade" ships tremendous voyages were carried out, and after Alvarado's death one of the ships did reach the East Indies, while another touched the coast of California.

In June 1541 Alvarado was hurriedly called to the aid of a Spanish garrison in southern Mexico, and, while leading an assault on a fortified hill in the province of Jalisco, his men were driven back and a frightened horse ran into him and then rolled over his body. When they picked him up with the blood coming out of his mouth and asked him where it hurt him most, Alvarado answered them, saying, "In the soul; take me where I can cure it with penitence and resignation." He lived a few days longer, but Alvarado knew at that moment that his life was at an end. An unfriendly critic of this conqueror's life summarized it by saying that every plan he made was begun with impetuosity, continued with cruelty, and ended in disaster.

The same black fate pursued Alvarado's wife after his death. On hearing of her husband's accident, this high-born lady, Doña Beatriz de la Cueva, burst into loud recriminations and blasphemy against all the powers of heaven. When her companions suggested that a greater calamity might have befallen her, she shouted back, "There could be no greater catastrophe than losing my master."

Alvarado had proclaimed her his complete heir, so she became one of the first women in the New World to hold a high political office. One of her first acts as governor of Guatemala was to have the entire gubernatorial mansion painted black inside and out. She signed all her decrees "Beatriz, the ill-fated (la sin ventura)." The natives were awed by her blasphemies and excessive show of grief, and expected dreadful consequences. These soon began to materialize.

In the same year her husband died a cloudburst and flood, combined with an earthquake, swept over the capital of Guatemala. For three days the waters rushed through the streets, destroying buildings, uprooting trees, devastating everything. Beatriz and her maids fled to the near-by chapel. Just as the "ill-fated" woman reached the altar and threw herself down before the cross the entire chapel was engulfed in the flood and swept away.

The survivors set themselves to the tragic task of burying the dead, but when they came to the body of Doña Beatriz, they angrily demanded that her bones be thrown to the dogs or into the current of the river. The bishop finally persuaded them to permit her to have a Christian burial.

A fate similar to that suffered by Alvarado and Beatriz seems to have pursued Guatemala City itself, which has had to be rebuilt many times and even moved from one site to another because of violent quakes which on several occasions have left it in ruins.

6

PIZARRO'S EXPLOITS
IN THE "EMPIRE OF THE SUN"

The second great conquistador was Francisco Pizarro, illegitimate offspring of a Spanish colonel and a peasant woman. He became one of
Spain's wealthiest sons before his death and was made a marquis, but he
never learned how to sign his name. Unlike Cortés, he was not a great
statesman and leader as well as a soldier. To the end of his life he was
much prouder of his title of marquis than he was of his conquest of Peru,
not realizing that there were many marquises, whereas there was only one
Pizarro. This attitude was typical of his peasant upbringing.

Pizarro was born about 1475, but the exact date is unknown, as neither
parent was anxious to commemorate the event. At an early age the young
child was left to shift for himself, and the story goes that while he was still
a baby his mother abandoned him on the streets where a sow wet-nursed
him. Later he became a swineherd, one of the most despised of all occupations. When he was sixteen or seventeen years old one of the pigs he
was watching got away, and the boy was so afraid to face his employer
that he fled the country and next showed up fighting in the wars in Italy.

Marvelous reports from the New World soon reached his ears, and in
1510 we find him on the island of Santo Domingo ready to take part in
the expedition of Ojeda to the mainland of Venezuela. The colony they
established was attacked by disease and famine, and after many of the
men had died it was abandoned. Pizarro then joined Balboa in his epic
march across the mountains of Panama and was one of the first to view
the Pacific Ocean. Balboa had heard from the natives that somewhere bordering that southern sea there was a great Indian empire where gold was
as common as iron in Spain. He never found it. However, out of sheer
jealousy for his successes the governor of the isthmus had him beheaded

on some trumped-up charge of treason, and this brought to an untimely close one of the most brilliant careers among the conquistadores.

Pizarro, who had distinguished himself by his stoic resolve on many expeditions, left Panama in 1524 to go in search of this golden land. He was then an old soldier of fifty. He had only a single ship and about one hundred men. His companion, Almagro, was to follow with another vessel as soon as possible. The season was not propitious for sailing, and storms, wind, and incessant rains buffeted them about, and their provisions were soon exhausted.

Finally they came ashore at a point many thousands of miles north of the place they were actually seeking and commenced their explorations. The land was soggy, for the rains had never ceased. Insects attacked them in droves, and their only food consisted of wild berries and a few shellfish. Those who did not starve to death on this diet were soon reduced by famine and poisonous foods to a pitiful state. No signs of any great wealth were found, and when Pizarro was finally forced to return, more than twenty of his men left their bones behind.

However, a few paltry articles of gold had been collected; enough, he thought, to warrant another and larger expedition. His friend, Almagro, who had followed the same course down the coast without ever meeting him, also brought back a few articles of the precious metal.

The second time the expedition was planned more deliberately. A famous three-way contract was drawn up in which a priest, Fernando de Luque, was to furnish the money, Pizarro and Almagro the leadership and brawn. Never had a stranger trio gotten together on any proposition. Pizarro and Almagro were both illiterate foundlings who had little to recommend them except brute strength and energy. Luque was not only a priest and schoolmaster but a well-educated man of substance. He did not actually finance the expedition himself but acted for a fourth and silent partner, Gaspar de Espinosa, a wealthy judge of Panama.

Luque was to look after the legal and financial side of the scheme; Pizarro was to lead the expedition, and Almagro was to be chief liaison and supply officer. There was to be a three-way split in the profits. With much religious fanfare to seal the bargain the trio split a holy wafer three ways, and then carved up and divided the unknown empire with all its imaginary wealth and inhabitants as if it were already within their grasp. The contract stated that religion was the primary object of their conquest, but it was obvious that gold overshadowed every other purpose.

The two ships sailed south again in 1526, and, with better weather on this occasion, reached as far south as Ecuador. Here they saw evidences of a much higher level of life than any before encountered: settlements were more numerous, fields were more widely cultivated, and several beautiful woolen pieces and articles of gold were collected. Two of the natives were taken aboard by the Spaniards so that they could be taught the language and later serve as interpreters. But the land of gold and great cities did not appear. Provisions soon dwindled, disease and famine broke out again, and it was decided to send back to replenish the supply.

When the rank and file heard this they burst out in bitter recriminations and demanded to return to Panama rather than to be left to die like famished dogs on such barren shores. Knowing that only complete bankruptcy, disgrace, and defeat faced him in Panama if he turned back now, Pizarro rose to the occasion. With a heroic gesture he took out his sword and drew a line on the earth running east and west. Pointing to it, he said:

"Friends, comrades! On this side are toil, hunger, nakedness, drenching rains and storm, desertion and death; on the other side, ease and pleasure. There lies Peru with its riches; here, Panama in its poverty. Let each man choose his own destiny. For my part, I go to the south."

Saying this, he stepped across the line. Only thirteen of the men followed him. Knight-errantry, which believed in the triumph of its own destiny against whatever odds, had spoken out in the voice of a swineherd.

The little handful of fourteen men waited for seven months before help arrived. When it came in the form of a single small vessel, they sailed southward for three or four weeks and finally arrived at the town of Tumbez, one of the northern outposts of Inca territory. Here they found food in abundance, saw well-constructed houses, a temple and fortress made of hewn stone, several of the strange humped llamas of which they had heard so much, and, best of all, they noticed that many of the natives wore ornaments of gold and silver. On leaving Tumbez they sailed as far south as the present site of Trujillo, Peru, stopping at several towns en route and assembling quite a collection of native articles. The purpose of their expedition was now amply supported with evidence, and, realizing that such a few men could accomplish nothing against so vast a dominion, they then turned about and headed back for Panama.

The backers were by this time practically bankrupt. They had already faced prolonged delay and ridicule, and although they accepted the latest report with great hope and interest, it was impossible for them to raise further funds. There was only one recourse left open. Pizarro would have to go to Spain to seek royal aid for the project. Perhaps with the few valuable objects which he was able to display and with the conquest of Mexico still much in the royal eye, he and his men might in this way be able to carry on.

The old soldier had a dignity and sincerity about him which impressed the court, and on July 6, 1529, his hopes were realized. An agreement was signed making Pizarro governor, captain-general, and adelantado over all the regions he was about to add to the territory of the Crown. Titles were distributed liberally among the members of the expedition and some financial help was extended. Almagro, however, came out on the short end of the deal, for Pizarro was clearly granted supreme honors and supreme command. This caused a feud to spring up between the two which inter-mittently smoldered, burst into a blaze, was extinguished, and then burst out again, until eventually it led to the violent death of both men.

According to the agreement the Crown had signed, the expedition was not to leave Spain until at least one hundred and fifty men had joined it. Pizarro found it hard to get half this number and, even with the aid of Cortés, the best he could do was to raise the total to about one hundred and twenty-five. Finally, he slipped away in one ship, leaving one of his brothers behind to convince the authorities that the required number had been raised. The ruse worked, and shortly afterward the two ships were heading toward the isthmus.

Early in January 1531 three ships and one hundred and eighty-three men, thirty-seven of them provided with horses, left the harbor of Panama to embark on their conquest of Peru, the population of which at that time numbered five or six millions. They disembarked on the northern coast of the country and after some weeks of diligent prospecting sent the ships, well loaded with gold, back for reinforcements. Then began their march across the country in a southeastern direction toward the encampment of the Incas. Before leaving the coastal region, Pizarro was joined by more than one hundred men, several of them mounted, among whom was Her-nando de Soto, who later gained fame through his explorations in the Mississippi Valley in the United States.

Peru at this moment was just emerging from a bloody civil war in which the favorite but illegitimate Atahualpa had defeated his brother, Huáscar, legitimate claimant to the throne. Their father, the last great Inca ruler, had unwisely divided his territory between them when he died, giving Atahualpa the kingdom of Quito, and Huáscar that of Cuzco. The latter was to exercise a certain over-all authority in both sections. However, war soon broke out. Huáscar was defeated and captured and Atahualpa got it all. When Pizarro arrived he was still in the field, encamped in the vicinity of Cajamarca, several miles north of Cuzco.

Almost at a snail's pace, the little band of Spaniards picked their way from the lower coastal region into mountainous territory. As they gained altitude, the air grew cooler, then harsh and chilly. Rain- and snowstorms lashed at them frequently, and the nights were intensely cold. Both horses and men suffered greatly from exposure. At every stop they paused long enough to proclaim publicly that they came as emissaries of the Holy Fa-ther in Rome and of the great Spanish sovereign. They demanded that the natives swear fealty to both, and taking the whole thing in a light vein, for they hardly understood the consequences, the poor Indians gladly com-plied, and their compliance was duly attested by a notary.

Pizarro sent couriers ahead to inform the Inca that he and his men had come to the country as friends and were anxious to aid him in battle. They also informed him, none too advisedly, that they represented the true faith to which they were anxious to convert his people. Atahualpa did not warmly encourage either prospect, but he made no attempt to stop them, which at this point would certainly have been easy, due to the topography of the country.

From time to time, as they advanced along narrow ledges, hundreds of feet above almost bottomless chasms, the Spaniards went through passes where a small group of resolute warriors could have held back an army. Perched on the mountainside high above these ledges or sometimes blocking the narrowest passes were strong fortresses fashioned out of huge boulders. Other strong points were cut out of living rock. Again and again the invaders gazed up at these forts with a shudder of apprehension, but they were all unmanned.

Pizarro slowed down his pace, hoping that reinforcements would arrive, but none came. He finally reached a broad, swift river, and his fear of attack was now so great that he would not cross until one of his brothers had slipped over the stream during the night and established a bridgehead on the opposite bank. Only a few natives had been encountered and they all fled at the sight of the Spaniards, but one of them was overtaken and captured. When the prisoner refused to divulge any information about Atahualpa, he was put to the torture and finally stated that the Inca was decoying the white men into the valley of Cajamarca, where he could easily cut off their retreat, surround, and annihilate them. Other reports made by peasants along the road did not bear out this information or even the location of the Inca's camp.

At this point Pizarro sent another courier ahead to tell Atahualpa that he would soon arrive, and also to keep a careful lookout for any evidences of an ambush or other military preparations which might be aimed at his men. Before this messenger had returned, a representative of the Inca visited the Spanish encampment to find out the date of their arrival, and, so Pizarro thought, to spy on them. This Indian brought gifts of llamas and drank fermented native *chicha* out of a golden goblet which he had brought along especially for his use. He assured the Spaniards that Atahualpa was expecting them and would receive them well.

While this man was in camp, Pizarro's own courier returned and, the moment he laid eyes on the Inca, lunged toward him in a fury. He had been thrown out of Atahualpa's camp and had barely escaped with his life. Cajamarca was completely deserted, but an Inca army of tremendous size was encamped three or four miles on the other side of the town. There were answers made to all these things, but they were not wholly convincing. Pizarro's courier had carried no credentials, and as he was a native, the Incas probably thought he was lying when he claimed to be an envoy of the white men. The Inca was at the moment observing a religious fast and could not be disturbed. Cajamarca had been emptied of its inhabitants so that the Spaniards would have comfortable quarters to stay in.

Pizarro had no alternative but to appear to believe these answers, so he released the Inca representative and continued his march.

When they crossed the last mountain barrier before the valley of Cajamarca, the panorama that met their eyes caused the deepest amazement and concern in every Spaniard's heart. The valley floor was crisscrossed by irrigation canals, aqueducts, and green hedges that marked off the fields, all of which seemed to be intensely cultivated. The city itself lay in the center of the valley, its white houses and yellow thatched roofs standing out in contrast with the deep green around them. On the farther side of the town was the Inca encampment, its pavilions extending for several miles along the slope like a great field of cotton hemmed in by the towering peaks behind it. Pizarro drew his men up in battle formation and entered the deserted town on November 15, 1532.

Cajamarca means "the place of ice," but the day the Spaniards arrived the sun was shining brightly. Then suddenly, as often occurs in the tropical uplands, great black clouds gathered and it began to rain and hail. Chilled to the bone, the troops scattered and took refuge in the stone buildings around the square. When the cloudburst had ceased, De Soto and fifteen horsemen were detached and sent to the Inca camp to announce Pizarro's arrival.

They were immediately ushered into Atahualpa's presence and had no difficulty in distinguishing him from his retinue because of the scarlet fringed headband or llautu. It was about eight inches wide and pressed down tightly over his forehead. His face was expressionless and he made no move to greet them. The Spaniards gave some account of themselves and the country they represented, but to all this the Inca answered nothing. His eyes remained on the ground and his face did not even express comprehension when the words were interpreted for him, but one of his chieftains responded a brief "it is well."

Pizarro's brother, now somewhat nettled, asked Atahualpa to speak for himself, and this brought a reply from the Inca that he was fasting, but that he would visit the Spaniards in Cajamarca the following day. In order to get some kind of reaction and also to display his horsemanship, for the horses were the only thing in which Atahualpa had shown the slightest interest, De Soto suddenly applied his spurs and charged across the field. Wheeling around a few times, he headed toward the royal personage at full speed, barely bringing his charger to a halt at the Inca's knee. Several of the Incas drew back in terror, but Atahualpa did not budge an inch or change his expression in the slightest.

Fermented chicha was then served in large golden vases by members of the harem, and the Spaniards returned to their quarters. No matter what they said to each other by way of encouragement, their spirits were dejected, and their companions in Cajamarca soon caught their mood. That night the fires lighted in the Peruvian camp sparkled in the darkness "as thick as the stars of heaven."

Pizarro did not grow uneasy but promptly called a meeting of his officers and placed all the possible moves before them. Retreat or battle were both manifestly impossible at this stage of the game. They would be annihilated in either instance. Further peace was equally dangerous, for it would only place this small band entirely in Atahualpa's power. But there was one way still open: to receive the Inca in a friendly manner and then suddenly to fall upon him and seize him as hostage before he had any chance to escape or fight. The example of Cortés was evidently operating in Pizarro's mind. His officers agreed, and plans were carefully laid for the surprise attack. Most of the men were to remain hidden until a given signal, then all would rush out at once and overpower the Inca. Horses were to be kept mounted, ready to dash from their quarters without an instant's delay. Atahualpa would be completely surrounded and there would be no chance of his getting away. The troops received this decision with mortal fear, says one of the chroniclers who was present, but at that late hour there was no turning back.

The next morning the Spaniards performed a mass and all joined in the chant which begins: "Arise, O Lord, in thy wrath and judge thine own cause!" The words of the hate-filled prayer continued with its prophetic symbols: "This is the corrupt land where Kings have become prostituted and the people drunk with fornication; the Devil stands upon their altars and with his evil light, hides the true God. The dragon will march against you spewing blasphemies from its mouth. . . . Then you shall hear the sound of harps and behold the new Jerusalem with its walls of jasper, its palaces of shining gold, its streets paved with precious stones and its gates of pearl."[155] Upon conclusion of the chant, every man was dispatched to his post with a final warning not to let the Inca escape. By this time the Spaniards were so stricken with terror that many of the men were unable to hold their water.[28]

At noon the Indians broke camp and started slowly toward Cajamarca. About half a mile outside the town they halted and began to settle down again for the night. Atahualpa sent word that he would not be able to visit them until the following day. Pizarro, who knew that the temper of his men was already at the breaking point, sent back the message that everything had been prepared for the reception of his great red brother that night, and that he was counting on the Inca's sharing his repast. Atahualpa changed his mind and said he would come ahead with only a few warriors, all unarmed.

As the procession of natives entered the main square, the Dominican priest, Valverde, advanced to receive them with a crucifix in one hand and a breviary or Bible in the other. He halted before the Inca and began to explain his mission and that of his countrymen, which was to convert the

Indians to the true faith. He then expounded this briefly, touching on the Holy Trinity, the crucifixion, the resurrection, and the manner in which the popes of Rome came to be God's representatives on earth, and the kings of Spain the representatives of the Pope in America. From this it followed that Charles V was the divinely chosen master of the Inca Empire.

When this harangue was interpreted, Atahualpa became indignant and said that he would be no man's tributary, and that the god which he worshiped, the Sun, could never be killed by his own children. Then he demanded to know by what authority the priest had spoken, and when Valverde pointed to the book in his hand, the Inca took it, and after turning a few pages with a puzzled expression on his face, suddenly threw it to the ground, exclaiming: "Tell your comrades that they shall give an account of their doings in my land. I shall not go from here until they have made me full satisfaction for all the wrongs they have committed."[17]

The priest, incensed at this attitude, rushed to Pizarro and said: "Let's not waste any more time. Attack at once! I absolve you!" The captain waved a white scarf in the air, a prearranged shot was fired, and the Spaniards rushed from their places of concealment. Taken completely unaware, the Indians fell over each other in a mad scramble; horsemen ground many of them down and closed in on the Inca from all sides. Little resistance was offered, because the natives, as Atahualpa had said, were unarmed and helpless before the onslaught. In half an hour the plaza was running with blood and hundreds of corpses littered the ground. Many brave natives grabbed the horses' legs in a futile attempt to impede their advance, but finally the royal litter was reached and the Inca himself was almost knocked to the ground. Pizarro hastened to seize him and received the only wound suffered by the Spaniards that day, when one of his own men inadvertently struck his hand. With their leader overcome, the natives soon lost heart and fled wildly from the town.

On the following morning Pizarro sent soldiers to the deserted Inca camp, where they picked up a vast fortune in gold goblets and plates. Several hundred native women who had accompanied the Inca army as official concubines were permitted to come over to the Spanish camp, where they "accepted the advances of the Christians."[28]

Atahualpa had not spent many days in the Spanish camp before he saw that the principal concern of their lives seemed to be gold. With this in mind, he told Pizarro that if they would promise to set him free, he would fill the room in which they were standing with articles of gold up to a point on the wall as high as he could reach. The room measured about twenty-two by seventeen feet, so the amount promised was truly incredible. The Inca would also twice fill a smaller neighboring room with silver. As the Spaniards had collected relatively small amounts of these valuable metals up to this moment, Pizarro agreed, and the contract was properly notarized and signed. The Inca immediately dispatched messengers to all corners of the territory, and gold soon began to accumulate under the greedy eyes of the Spaniards. Before long, more than two hundred loads of golden vases, golden ears of corn, and delicately wrought dishes decorated with animals and birds had been placed in the room. Then the pace of collection began to slow down somewhat.

When about eight or nine million dollars' worth had been accumulated, the soldiers could not stand the strain any longer and insisted that the articles be melted down into bars and divided at once. Only the royal fifth was preserved in its original form so that the King might see some of the examples of the marvelous native workmanship. The amounts received were gratifying, but each man felt his appetite whetted for more, and as reports continued to come in that native priests were concealing many golden objects in their temples, the Spaniards became anxious to go on to Cuzco before it was too late. Almagro, Pizarro's partner and companion, had recently joined them with considerable reinforcements, and these men who had received only a small share of the ransom were insistent in their demands to continue the march.

They were also beginning to consider the presence of Atahualpa in their camp as a hindrance. The Inca's regal bearing irritated them, and vague rumors of a rebellion plotted by him clinched the hatred and suspicion in their own minds. The person most responsible for these rumors was Pizarro's principal interpreter, Felipillo, who had a deep personal grudge against the Inca because the latter had demanded his death when he was found consorting with one of the ladies of the royal harem. After that, Felipillo colored everything he was supposed to be interpreting so that it soon looked black for the Inca.

Atahualpa denied all these allegations vigorously, and pointed out that he would surely be the first to suffer if any rebellion took place. He asked Pizarro to send envoys out into the country and even to Cuzco in order to ascertain the truth. This was done on a limited basis, and no evidence of an uprising of any kind was brought in. The Spaniards were received everywhere in the friendliest manner. But a large portion of Pizarro's men had already made up their minds and stubbornly called for the Inca's execution.

Pizarro finally yielded to the extent of bringing Atahualpa to trial before a military court, in that way washing his hands of the whole business. The charges against the Inca were numerous and many of them were ridiculous: usurping the throne of his brother, squandering the royal revenues since the arrival of the Spaniards, following a religion of idolatry, having too many wives, and plotting against his jailers. He was found guilty and condemned to die at the stake, but through the efforts of the priest, Valverde, his sentence was later lightened to death by strangulation as a reward for his renunciation of his faith and acceptance of baptism.

The execution took place at once, and the Indians who had been assembled in the square huddled there "as if they were drunk" while Atahualpa's body was rent with its final agonies. One of the native women voiced the cry of her race when she said, "On that fatal day, darkness fell at noon."[28] A puppet Inca was immediately selected, and in a great ceremony was crowned with the imperial crimson.

Without its leader, who was both absolute god and ruler to his people, the Inca dominions fell apart with a rapidity which proved the instability of even that primitive system of centralized authority. The more recently conquered territories immediately revolted and claimed their independence, and the heart of the empire stood helpless, as if suddenly struck by palsy in every member.

Pizarro and his men advanced on the Peruvian capital, which they finally entered November 15, 1533. Like Mexico City, the town was located in a valley surrounded by towering peaks. Most of its houses were of adobe and straw, but the public buildings were of finely hewn stone, and the Temple of the Sun was a marvel to behold. The Spaniards did not find as much gold as they had expected, but several hundred thousand dollars' worth was accumulated and melted down into ingots for easier distribution. The natives, who had observed the foreigners' greed for this metal, now came to covet it for themselves, and all over the country golden articles were taken and hidden from the prying eyes of the white men.

In the meantime, Pizarro's first puppet had died and a second one was quickly put in his place. The Spanish garrison was now increased in size by the addition of several men who had come down with Alvarado from Guatemala. Pizarro himself left for the coast where on January 6, 1535, he founded Lima as the city of his government. In his absence the garrison became unruly and, following the example of Alvarado's men, took to lording it over the natives as if they were less than beasts. Houses were entered at will, articles stolen, and women violated on such a scale that finally the puppet Inca was no longer able to endure it.

He escaped and placed himself at the head of a quickly mustered but numerous army which then methodically surrounded and laid siege to Cuzco. Showers of arrows dipped in burning pitch were shot onto the thatched roofs and most of the buildings were soon gutted by the flames. All over the country similar uprisings took place as if by preconceived plan, and many isolated groups of Spaniards or persons living on their recently acquired estates were captured and slain. But after five months the garrison in Cuzco was still holding out, and the native hosts, seeing their planting season was about to pass them by, gradually melted away and left the remains of their capital in foreign hands.

At this point Pizarro's companion, Almagro, returned from Chile, where he had been prospecting for gold, and at the head of a sizable army took over Cuzco for himself, imprisoning those of the garrison who showed a mind to contest his will. He believed that the city was well within the grant which the Crown had given him and saw no reason to let others enjoy it further. A few weeks later he unwisely agreed to negotiate the whole affair with Pizarro, but at the first opportunity the latter threw the agreement out of the window and had Almagro captured, tried, and beheaded for treason.

This action was not long in bringing about further violent repercussions. The country divided into two camps, those who supported Pizarro and those who for one reason or another hated him and were partisans of the faction now headed by Almagro's mestizo son. One of the principal bones of contention was the unbridled favoritism being exercised by the old marquis's secretary. Since Pizarro was unable to read or write he was forced to depend to a large extent on a subordinate who could, and gradually he allowed more and more power to fall into his secretary's hands. This power was used most unscrupulously, and Pizarro's regime became one of insolent sycophants and favorites. To make matters worse, many of the governor's supporters went out of their way to insult and browbeat young Almagro's men, and finally the latter, seeing no possible redress except through violence, decided on assassination.

The governor was forewarned of their plot in many different ways. When he appeared on the streets, all conversation suddenly ceased. Indian women informed their white paramours of what was in the wind, and some of these brought the word to Pizarro, who dismissed the information as "Indian gossip."

One night the heavily cloaked figure of a priest suddenly appeared at a house where the marquis was having dinner and whispered that the date for his assassination had been set for the following Sunday. Pizarro seemed inclined to believe that the informer had merely been after a tip and refused to take the news seriously. His friends did persuade him not to attend mass that Sunday, and some halfhearted directions for the arrest of a few suspects were given. They were never carried out.

When that Sunday morning arrived, June 26, 1541, twenty or more men assembled in Almagro's house and then proceeded openly to the palace of the governor. As they passed down the streets several people murmured: "They are going to kill the marquis." But this was all; no one made a move to stop them. Pizarro had inspired no great love in his subjects.

The old man was at home, chatting with a group of friends whom he had invited to the noon meal, when the assassins suddenly smashed through the strong street door, which had been left unbolted. A page rushed in, shouting: "Arm yourselves! They are coming to kill my master!" Only half a dozen of the governor's guests stood by him; the rest climbed out of the windows and disappeared. Pizarro called to one of his intimates to bolt the outer door to the large room in which they were gathered, but this man indiscreetly held it ajar and attempted to parley with the assassin. He was pierced with a sword and the door was hurled open.

Pizarro partially armed himself but did not have time to buckle on his helmet before the conspirators were upon him. The old conquistador defended himself bravely and for a time held them at bay. His two pages were struck down at his side, but he continued fighting. He ran his sword through two of the opposition and gravely wounded another. No one dared to close in with the old tiger. Finally the assassins pushed one of their own number violently against Pizarro, and while he was off balance another lunged at his unprotected throat, catching it squarely on the point of his sword.

The marquis fell to the floor mortally wounded. He raised himself long enough to trace the sign of the cross on the floor, probably in his own blood, and to mutter the word "Jesus!" Then as he bent forward to kiss the the spot another sword found his vitals and left him dead. Still flaunting their weapons, the assassins rushed back into the street, shouting: "The tyrant is dead! The laws are restored!"

Pizarro was not so great a man as Cortés, but he overcame an even richer empire, and in many ways his story is more heroic. He was a man of about fifty when he led his first group of adventurers down the South American coast. The following eighteen years of his life were a battle all the way against disheartening odds. But never for a single moment did Pizarro falter. His peasant mother had given him a brute strength which stayed with him until the day of his death. Both his parents had given him courage. He lacked the instinct of reconciliation which characterized Cortés, and never inspired much admiration in his men. His inability to arouse the religious fire in his followers' hearts was one cause of this, his own coarse ways was another, and his illiteracy was probably a third.

Garcilaso tells the story that one day a Spanish soldier who was guarding Atahualpa wrote the word "God" on the earth and, after telling the Inca what it meant, asked several other Spaniards to read it. Later on it happened that Pizarro came on the scene and Atahualpa asked him to read the word. When the old captain was unable to do so he fell immediately in the Inca's estimation, for to the Indian ruler a leader of men was one who was superior to his followers in every way.

Pizarro's conquest was characterized by more plain cruelty and butchery than was that of Cortés, and it never had the redeeming grace of being so complete a crusade to replace a barbarous religion with a more merciful and superior one. Pizarro was after loot, and in its pursuit he was inflexible. He was not the judge of human nature that Cortés was, nor did he possess that rare ability to pacify aroused tempers, to allay suspicions, and to smell out treachery. Both Pizarro and Cortés were builders, but while Pizarro constructed only an outward and visible structure of Peruvian life in the city of Lima, Cortés built with a more far-reaching hand and laid out the basic foundations for the Mexican state and the Mexican people. Cortés was well loved by many Indians; Pizarro had few real friends even among the Spaniards.

There is much similarity in one main chapter which stands out in the lives of each: Cortés and his imprisonment of Montezuma, and Pizarro's capture and execution of Atahualpa. Cortés saw, and Pizarro was astute enough to follow him in the belief, that *power* was the immediate and indispensable prerequisite of any hope which the Spaniards might have of winning a victory against such tremendous odds. They had to achieve that power over their enemies in any way they could, and since a battle to the death would have meant annihilation for them under these circumstances, they resorted to trickery and ensnared the Indian rulers into their hands.

Cortés and Pizarro both went straight to the heart of Indian sovereignty, risked their own lives in doing so, and once they had their hands on Montezuma and Atahualpa, the conquest was as good as decided. The symbols of unity and leadership were then destroyed, but before this destruction they were used and perverted to the invaders' own ends.

Cortés and Pizarro became immensely wealthy in gold, land, and Indians as a result of their conquests. Pizarro and his descendants received a grant of twenty thousand natives "in service," which meant in a state of perpetual vassalage. Cortés owned an estate of twenty-two towns and twenty-five thousand square miles inhabited by twenty-three thousand "heads of families." However, both men died under unenviable circumstances, their estates were taken over by the Crown, and no power was left in the hands of their heirs. In a word, they each performed the work of soldiers but were not allowed to enjoy the fruits of their victories. The politicians then gained control.

When Francisco Pizarro himself died by the sword it was the opening scene in the first great Latin-American revolution. After the assassination, old Almagro's son assumed power in Peru, but opposition sprang up almost immediately. The onus of personal rule, that plague which was to tear Latin America apart for centuries, soon brought about a counter-revolution, and Peru's first civil war was on. Those who supported the King met the Almagro forces in a pitched battle and defeated them. The young leader himself escaped temporarily but later was apprehended and publicly beheaded on the same spot where his father had been executed before him.

In the meantime a third figure had been watching these proceedings with an eagle eye. It was Gonzalo Pizarro, brother to the marquis, who had been on a two-year trip of exploration in the upper Amazon region when Francisco Pizarro met his death by assassination. That trip alone would have been enough to assure Gonzalo, who was another bastard son of Colonel Pizarro, of his niche in the hall of fame. He had left his governorship in Quito with about three hundred and forty soldiers and a supply train of four thousand Indians. One of his captains, Orellana, had improvised some boats and had sailed all the way to the mouth of the Amazon. Gonzalo himself, after two and a half years in the tropical jungles, stumbled back into Quito in 1542 with eighty emaciated companions at his heels. Not one of the four thousand Indians remained. Gonzalo found most of his power gone and his brother assassinated. He retired for a time to his large estate in southern Peru (Bolivia), where his income "was greater than that of the Archbishop of Toledo and the Count of Benavente."[29]

Not long after this, however, a personal representative of the King arrived in Lima to proclaim the famous "New Laws of the Indies for the Good Treatment and Preservation of the Indians." They are often referred to simply as the "New Laws of 1542," and signified in a word that the landowners' power over the Indians was to be strictly limited, that the natives were to be considered as "free men." As if this were not bad enough, when the "New Laws" were proclaimed in Peru it was learned that every Spaniard who was guilty of having taken any part in the civil disturbances of Francisco Pizarro and the younger Almagro was to have his allotments of lands and Indians confiscated. This meant practically every white man in Peru.

Gonzalo Pizarro found himself at the head of a large number of violently protesting landowners. Several months later, when they saw that persuasion was of no avail, they took to arms and determined to maintain their "rights" by force. Gonzalo and his troops marched from Bolivia down to Lima, gathering strength as they moved. The Supreme Court of the capital finally invited the second Pizarro to assume control over its government. The Viceroy had been forced to leave the city six months previously by an irate populace, but a few weeks later he showed up in Quito where he was now busy assembling an army "to defend the interests of the King." Gonzalo was no man to wait for someone to attack him. He led his force over the incredibly difficult terrain between Lima and Quito, lured the Viceroy into a trap, defeated his troops, and killed him with a shower of bullets. After a few more maneuvers by land and by sea Pizarro's power extended all the way to Panama, and he was ruler over a far greater territory than most European kings.

The Emperor Charles dispatched a priest, armed with absolute powers, to deal with the rebellion. Gonzalo by this time had gotten a taste of power and was unwilling to relinquish it. Some of his closest friends urged him to crown himself King of Peru. One of his political advisers, Zepeda, railed against Charles V, saying that every monarch was a descendant of tyrants, and that all nobility began with Cain, while the common people were the offspring of Abel. This was clearly proved, he said, by the insignia and coats of arms which the royal and noble authority displayed: dragons, serpents, flames, swords, decapitated heads, and other like symbols. Pizarro's band eventually declared their independence of the King, burned the royal standard, and raised their own revolutionary banner.[30]

They did not raise it for long. The minister plenipotentiary of the King was discreet enough to move slowly, passing out pardons with a lavish hand as he advanced. He had already suspended the despised "New Laws." People flocked to his support and began to desert the revolutionists. Gonzalo, after marching all over the country in a vain attempt to strengthen his hand, finally came face to face with his adversary before the city of Cuzco. When the two forces met, many of Pizarro's soldiers deliberately passed over to the other side; among these was Captain Garcilaso de la Vega, father of the famous mestizo historian of Peru. There was no great battle. In the end Gonzalo turned his lance on his own men before he was caught and carried into the enemy camp as a prisoner. On the following day he was executed as a traitor to the King. Of the five Pizarro "brothers of doom" who had set out from Spain for the conquest of Peru eighteen years previously, but one now remained alive and he was in a Spanish prison.

7

THE CONQUEST OF CHILE

It was Pedro de Valdivia, one of Pizarro's stoutest captains, who left the relative ease of life in Peru to embark on the hazardous conquest of the poor and savage wilderness which was the province of Chile. In the first letter which he wrote to the King, Valdivia said: "I only desire to discover and colonize lands for your Majesty, so that my memory will endure in fame. . . ."[31] No gold, no slaves, no great glory, not even the intrinsic wealth of fertile land drew this conquistador and his small band into the narrow swordlike land which has since become one of Latin America's greatest countries. All reports on Chile were blacker than night. Pizarro's old partner, Almagro, had been there in 1535 with five hundred Spaniards and fifteen thousand natives; he had returned a year or two later with empty hands after having spent five hundred thousand gold *pesos* on the expedition. His advice was that the place should be "shunned like a plague." All of his men told Valdivia that he was crazy to spend his substance on so perilous a project. Nevertheless, the conqueror of Chile maintained his zeal, borrowed funds to add to his own small capital, aroused the instinct for adventure in one hundred and fifty soldiers, and set out for the unpromising land.

This was something new in the Spanish conquest of America. Soldiers were going to a country where they would have to turn settlers and work for a living. Probably this thought did not enter their minds, but in the end it determined the fundamental character of the Chilean nation.

Valdivia and his small troop left Peru in January 1540. They carried a variety of seeds to plant, and were accompanied by a drove of swine, several brood mares, and about one thousand Indians. Among the members of the expedition was a single woman, Inés de Suárez, Valdivia's inseparable mistress, who was as hardy as any man.

It took them eleven months to cross the high mountain barrier and to

traverse the desolate thousand-mile expanse of the Atacama Desert, where
even today the land is so ugly and devoid of vegetation that it seems as if
some violent claw had raked away every growing thing. Valdivia found
that the natives fled at his approach and hid their food, for Almagro had
treated them mercilessly. Consequently, it was necessary to make them all
kinds of promises before something resembling friendly relations was established.

After a year of being on the march the Spaniards reached the beautiful
central valley of Chile, where four out of every five Chileans live today,
and there, on February 12, 1541, was founded the city of Santiago. The
valley itself, which constitutes the heart of the country, was covered with
flowers and green grass, and made a very favorable impression on the men.
It is well described by Valdivia in the first letter he sent back to the King
four years later. "This land is such," he wrote, "that there is none better in
the world for living in and settling down; this I say because it is very flat,
very healthy and very pleasant; it has four months of winter, not more, and
in them, it is only when the moon is at the quarter that it rains a day or
two; on all the other days, the sun is so fine that there is no need to draw
near the fire. The summer is so temperate with such delightful breezes that
a man can be out in the sun all day long without annoyance. It is the most
abounding land in pastures and fields, and for yielding every kind of livestock and plant imaginable; much timber and very fine for houses; endless
wood for use in them."[31]

The town was laid out in the center of the valley and, with the aid of
the Indians, several poor houses of wood and thatch were constructed.
They were hardly better than the miserable native huts. Surrounding lands
were distributed among the soldiers, a fort was erected, the fields were
plowed and planted, and the pigs and chickens were cared for as if they had
been made of gold. Valdivia himself designed the church.

The colony went forward at a snail's pace, and, though the country was
fertile and beautiful, the men became restive in their desire for quicker rewards, and in their relations with the Indians they became more and more
demanding. When it was learned that there was some gold to be found in
the vicinity of Valparaiso, they forced the natives to wash and dig in water
up to their knees day and night. The friendliness which had been so carefully built up over a long period of months was thus swiftly brought to an
end by greed—the prevailing vice of the conquistador everywhere. The
Spanish poet, Alonso de Ercilla, who was in Chile shortly afterward, and
whose famous epic La Araucana describes the entire conquest of the country, sums up the guilt of his companions-at-arms in these words:

> Oh cureless malady! Oh fatal pest!
>   Embraced with ardor and with pride caressed;
> Thou common vice, thou most contagious ill,
>   Bane of the mind, and frenzy of the will!

Thou foe to private and to public health;
Thou dropsy of the soul, that thirsts for wealth,
Insatiate Avarice!—'tis from thee we trace
The various misery of our mortal race.[32]

The whole poem was a spirited invective against the greed of his countrymen by one who saw them on the scene and knew them well. Under these circumstances the natives rose up while Valdivia was away in the south and assaulted the town of Santiago, practically blotting it off the map. The buildings were burned to the ground, the surrounding fields were laid waste, and the animals were killed. While the fight was in progress Inés de Suárez fought with the rest of the garrison and encouraged them with her daring. At her suggestion several captive chieftains who were prisoners in the fort were beheaded and their heads thrown out among the assailants. The Spanish cavalry then rushed forth from its untenable position, and with the sure knowledge that they would either win or die on the spot, finally managed to drive the Indians away. Valdivia returned in time to consolidate the victory, if mere survival can be termed victory.

There was not a post left standing in the town, and the men had nothing left but their arms, their horses, and the rags they had worn in the fight, a little maize, two handfuls of wheat, two little sows and a boar, and one cock and hen. Undaunted, they rebuilt the place at once, this time of fireproof adobe. War horses were used to plow the fields, and rations were cut to the bone. Everybody dug, plowed, and planted with hardly a moment's rest. The Spaniards dared not stray far from the town and, as Valdivia wrote later, "went about like phantoms . . . and at whatever time the Indians came to assail us, for they knew all about night attacks, they found us awake, and, if need be, upon our horses. . . ."[31]

Not long afterward it was decided to send what pitifully small amount of gold they had collected back to Peru, along with an urgent request for more supplies and colonists. In order to make their small wealth as impressive as possible, the spurs, saddle ornaments, sword hilts, and even the glasses from which the six messengers drank were fashioned of the precious metal. Only a single man of this expedition ever reached Peru, and two years passed before meager reinforcements were sent. The colonists were forced to keep at their agricultural labors with every ounce of strength in order to eke out a bare subsistence.

By 1545 things had improved somewhat. Valdivia reported that there were eight thousand swine, as many chickens "as blades of grass," a great amount of corn, and that the season would see harvested ten to twelve thousand *fanegas* of wheat. The Indians were temporarily quiet, and crops had been exceptionally good. Valdivia, however, had irritated many of the settlers by permitting his mistress to act as a sort of sub-governor and by forcing them to go to her for favors. Another cause of discontent was the scarcity of Indian workers. The two hundred Spaniards then in Chile were hardly able to keep their lands cultivated; some had allotments of only thirty Indians, and hardly any had more than a hundred. These natives were not good laborers, and the colonists complained that they were not sufficiently numerous to maintain a man decently. What really brought forth these complaints was the knowledge that in Peru many soldiers lorded it over two thousand or more vassals. Valdivia reduced the number of estates and gave more Indians to fewer landholders. This was not a satisfactory solution. A third cause for disgruntled tempers was Valdivia's peremptory way of forcing the settlers to contribute large portions of their golden treasure every time a ship was sent to Peru. These contributions were either made graciously, or, as the governor said, he would "take their gold and their hides too."[33]

The most exasperating thing of all, however, was the lack of news from Peru. Messengers had been sent on two occasions and so far nothing had been heard from them. What had actually happened was that the rebellious Gonzalo Pizarro was then in control of Peru and they were unable either to obtain supplies or to return quickly. One messenger had died in Peru, and another had joined up with Pizarro, finally persuading him to prepare an expedition to send against Chile.

Valdivia was unaware of these events, but his temper grew worse daily. He got into the habit of associating only with a very small group of intimates, and was unapproachable by the rest. The whole town went about in a perennial bad humor. When at last a messenger did arrive from Peru with the startling news of Pizarro's rebellion, Valdivia's frame of mind sank to its lowest depth. Then one day the little group of intimates which met at his house stayed considerably longer than usual, and immediately afterward the governor seemed to be in his usual good spirits again. He came out of his retirement and made a point of speaking to those whom he had slighted, encouraging them to hold on for a little while longer, as he was certain things would soon improve.

"I've been much too self-centered," he said abruptly one afternoon, "and I am sorry that I have sometimes abused my authority. I intend to leave my own bones in this land, but as God is my witness, I am not going to force any of you to do likewise."[33]

Those who heard these remarks hardly knew how to take them and assured Valdivia that they had all been under exceptional tension. But three days later they realized what he had meant when the secretary read a special proclamation from the atrium of the church. It reversed an old rule of the governor's and stated simply that all who wished to leave the country might do so on the next ship which would be sailing in a few days.

About twenty of the wealthiest citizens declared their intention of leaving, and then proceeded about the business of liquidating their estates.

Valdivia himself bought quite a few things at ridiculously low prices. When all their property had been converted into gold they set out for the seacoast, which was a three-day journey to the west. Valdivia accompanied them with the intention of looking over the port of Valparaiso and bidding them a good voyage.

The passengers boarded the ship, which was already in the harbor, and placed their golden treasure in the purser's care. Valdivia then asked them all to join him in a farewell feast on shore, and they gathered under the branches of a large tree to share their last meal together. While the feast was at its height and everybody was engaged in conversation, the governor slipped away and walked rapidly down to the beach, where a rowboat was waiting for him. He had nearly reached it when one of the diners spied him and shouted at the top of his lungs: "The governor's clearing out!"

They all dashed pell-mell for the shore, where the boat was still stuck in the sand. Valdivia and the boatman made a tremendous effort to release it and just did get away in time. One of the diners grabbed the gunwales, but the boatman cracked him over the head with an oar and sent him hurtling into the water. Then pandemonium broke loose on land. Some of those who had been rooked began to curse, others threw themselves down on the sand and went through ludicrous contortions of pain, still others wept and wailed as if their hearts would break. One poor fellow grabbed his trumpet and commenced to play a popular tune over and over again, then in an attack of fury smashed the instrument against a rock, yelling that since all his life's earnings were gone he might as well have absolutely nothing left. The substitute governor whom Valdivia had left in charge was forced to execute one man who became violent. Another went out of his mind and never recovered.[33]

Valdivia had no intention of fleecing these men permanently; they were all to be repaid from his own mines and estate, but in the meantime his colony was in peril and in order to ensure its success he had collected their entire private fortune which he intended to place at the disposal of the King's forces in Peru. When he did arrive there with his ten traveling companions, they were as welcome "as if they had been eight hundred men," and Valdivia himself was made commander of the army that faced and defeated Gonzalo Pizarro, thus restoring order in the viceroyalty of Peru. By this time the gold episode had caught up with him, and a searching inquiry was made into the whole affair before he was confirmed as governor of Chile. One condition of that final confirmation was that he sever relations with his mistress, who was either to return to Spain or to get married. She chose the latter course, but could not marry the governor, who already had a wife in Spain.

When Valdivia returned to Chile he was able to bring along a large quantity of provisions and equipment and about two hundred men. The town council, or *cabildo*, of Santiago did not receive them at all warmly.

That democratic body had been greatly irked by the governor's high-handed departure, and although it was unwilling to rebel openly against his authority, especially in the face of two hundred new soldiers, it did insist in no uncertain terms that Valdivia take an oath "as a man, as a gentleman, and as governor," that he would "govern in peace and justice, respect all liberties, privileges, exemptions, and *gracias* which the sovereign grants to those persons who discover, conquer, and people new territories. . . ." Even this oath was not sufficient. He was asked to place his hand on the cross and swear, "in the name of God and the Virgin Mary, rigidly to fulfill all that he had promised."[34] Such were the beginnings of democratic government in Chile. The Spanish colonial administration, both because of the remoteness and poverty of the country, was less eager to assert itself in this region, and the hardy colonists were better able to devise their own system of governmental controls.

It is to Valdivia's eternal credit that he constructed more out of less material than any other Spanish conquistador. Half a dozen Chilean towns owe their founding to him, and toward the end of his brief rule he even sent an expedition across the Andes to establish centers in Argentina. They were all of the hedgehog variety—mere strong points in a great wilderness of Indian territory—but the Spanish soldiers defended them firmly and little by little extended their dominion over all but the southernmost part of the country, where the "Indian frontier" remained until the late nineteenth century.

In his relations with the natives Valdivia was not so constructive. After overcoming their initial fears and receiving their help in erecting his capital, he turned on them and forced them to perform all kinds of labor to which they were unaccustomed. Those who refused were severely punished or slain. As Ercilla wrote:

> The Indians first, by novelty dismayed,
> As Gods revered us, and as Gods obeyed;
> But when they found we were of woman born,
> Their homage turned to enmity and scorn.[32]

Their first rebellion against the treatment meted out to them was their assault on Santiago in the very year of its founding, but the three-centuries-long conflict between these fierce Araucanian warriors and the Spaniards did not begin in earnest until Valdivia returned from Peru in 1549. He pushed the war bravely into Indian territory and established a series of outposts in southern Chile. Finally there was a bloody battle at the town of Concepción in which the governor took four hundred prisoners. Before setting them free he had the nose and right hand of each one cut off as a lesson to their companions. He did not know the Araucanian psychology very well, for from that time forward the Chilean natives swore a war of extermination against the invaders, and one leader after another arose to lead them in battles which Ercilla has related with such verve in his great epic.

The Araucanians were by all odds the fiercest fighters Spain ever faced in the New World. In many ways they were more primitive and barbaric than the Indians of other regions, but to them war and patriotism were a religion which no number of devastating defeats could ever shatter. Their fierce love of freedom, their innate democratic instincts, their strong, lithe bodies and stubborn temperament all find reflection in the Chilean masses of today.

Shortly after Valdivia's victory at Concepción there occurred one of those instances which often affects the destiny of a nation and provides a national hero. One of Valdivia's grooms, an Araucanian captive named Lautaro, escaped from the Spaniards after serving about a year, and rejoined his people. During his captivity Lautaro had learned a great deal about Spanish methods of fighting, and this knowledge, coupled with his strong personal leadership and an uncanny ability to find his enemies' weak spots, soon made him a leading general among the natives. His strategy was so successful that Valdivia himself decided to take the field against him. When the two met, the first wave of advancing Indians was quickly dispersed by a cavalry charge, and Valdivia thought that the day was won. It was only the beginning. Ercilla described the encounter as follows:

> The steady pikemen of the savage band,
> Waiting our hasty charge, in order stand;
> But when the advancing Spaniard aimed his stroke,
> Their ranks, to form a hollow square, they broke;
> An easy passage to our troop they leave,
> And deep within their lines their foes receive;
> Their files resuming then the ground they gave,
> Bury the Christians in that closing grave.[32]

When one of these Indian squares had exhausted itself in fighting against the superior arms of the Spaniards, its place was promptly taken by another. With methodical regularity wave after wave of them formed and met the Spanish attack. Valdivia could see the very troops which had been driven off being rallied, rested, encouraged, and re-formed by his opponent. Not a second's respite was allowed the Spaniards, and after several hours of fighting, in which most of them had already fallen, the remainder were completely exhausted.

The governor called his captains around him and shouted, "What shall we do, gentlemen?" And one of the captains answered, "What can your excellency expect us to do but die fighting!" Most of them did exactly that, but a few of them were taken alive by the Indians, and among them Valdivia. He promised a great reward for his freedom, but was ridiculed for his pains. He and his companions then awaited their doom with stoic resolution. No Spaniard witnessed the execution, so all firsthand reports of it came from the Indians themselves. These versions all agree that Valdivia was slain by a blow on the head with a war club. Tortures preceding the execution were not mentioned in the earliest reports, but at a later date Spanish historians of Chile embroidered the tale with detailed accounts of the scene in which the natives were supposed to have cut off their captives' arms while they were still alive, and, after roasting them slightly, to have eaten them before their owners' eyes.

Another story stated that when the Araucanians had Valdivia firmly trussed up they shouted to him, "You wanted gold, didn't you? Well, here it is!" and then they poured bowlfuls of the molten metal down his throat. These versions are replete with a poetic justice which smacks too much of the Spanish rather than the Indian psychology.

At any rate, Valdivia died in 1553 at the age of fifty-three, after almost thirteen years of rule in Chile, to which country he bequeathed in a remarkable degree his "fierce tenacity of purpose and shrewd common sense." He did not have the heroic qualities of Cortés or Pizarro, but in the long run his drive and single-mindedness went just as far, if not farther, toward the final molding of his colony.

Lautaro also defeated Valdivia's successor, set fire to the city of Concepción, and chased the Spanish forces back toward Santiago. He kept good discipline in his camp, forced his men to plant sufficient food grain for their needs, and continued to improve the quality and training of his troops. The great advantages formerly enjoyed by the Spanish cavalry he turned to his own benefit by digging pits in front of where they were likely to charge, and covering these over with branches and leaves. One night, however, after he had met and driven back some Spanish forces in what he believed was a decisive engagement, Lautaro slept too easily, and the Indian camp was taken by a surprise attack in which the young chieftain lost his life.

There was still another and even more famous leader, named Caupolicán, to take his place. The contest in which this gigantic warrior was selected as chief is one of the best-known traditions of the country. The aspirants for leadership all shouldered in turn a great log, and the one who was able to hold it aloft for the longest time was to be chosen. Caupolicán not only won the contest by bearing the log for thirty-six hours, but at its conclusion he made a tremendous leap and threw it away as if it were a mere sprig.

For many months thereafter he led his troops successfully in battle, but finally was betrayed and handed over to the Spaniards, who condemned him to death. With Valdivia's fate before them, it was decided that he should be executed by being forced to sit on a sharp stake protruding from the center of a raised platform where all the soldiers could observe it. According to the story, Caupolicán kicked his executioner off the platform and quickly sat down on the stake without so much as a sign of discomfort.

It is fitting that Lautaro, Caupolicán, and the conquest of the Arauca-nian Indians should be immortalized in one of the finest pieces of Chilean literature and America's greatest epic poem, *La Araucana*, written by the Spaniard Ercilla, who took part in the campaign. Coming from the enemy camp, this tribute is as notable for its poetic generosity as it is for its high literary value. Yet it was unfortunate that this great American Iliad should have entered so completely into the minds of Chileans of all classes, caus-ing many of them to accept it as gospel. The poor Araucanians were thus clothed in a knightly and romantic light which blinded the nation to a great segment of the population as it really was. Nevertheless, all Chile respected its great Indian heroes, and during the struggle for independence many years later the patriots often called themselves the "sons of Caupoli-cán," and the first warship in the Chilean navy was named the *Lautaro*.

The conquest of Chile cost Spain more in time and money and gave her less in return than any other territory taken for the Crown. The governor himself expended more than three hundred thousand ducats (much of it borrowed) in the conquest and was never able to pay it back. He stated in one of his letters to the King that each soldier in Chile cost him a thou-sand pesos a year. "I have spent it all," he reported, "for the good of the land and the soldiers who have defended it, since I cannot give them what is just and what they deserve—full freedom."[31]

He did his best to give a favorable report on the country, but despite this praise he had to point out that "all flee from this land, while to other new territories many go, owing to the good report of them." Yet settlers such as Valdivia did come to Chile, and as the years passed their numbers slowly grew. In 1552 there were about one thousand Spaniards living in six cities. Some had brought Indians with them from Peru, and their settle-ments covered over one thousand miles of conquered territory. It was a small number for so great an extent of land, but, what was more impor-tant, their spirit was that of true pioneers. They came with the full knowl-edge that their lives and their fortunes were to be molded out of the earth's neglected soil by their own efforts. This gave to their society a strength, a unity, and ultimately a freedom not yet achieved in either Mexico or Peru.

8

COLOMBIA YIELDS TO
THE "KNIGHT OF EL DORADO"

The last great knight of El Dorado, and in many ways the most heroic, because he endured the most for the longest time, was an Andalusian named Gonzalo Jiménez de Quesada, the exploring, prospecting conquistador of Colombia, then known as New Granada. Quesada did not begin his career as a man at arms but as a lawyer; however, before he died he had gained renown as a conquistador, leader, captain, and statesman, and his name had become a legend. It is Quesada who best typifies the illusion which drove humble men to become great in those epic days. It is Quesada who, following the examples of Cortés and Pizarro, made the most grandiose start, lived with illusion the longest, and came to the most miserable end of all the conquistadores. And it is perfectly evident that what drove him to greatness never existed at all outside of his own imagination.

Through him we are led to understand why even material gold was a disaster for Spain, just as the failure to find the gold of El Dorado was a disaster from which Quesada himself never recovered. When madness runs in the lifeblood of a nation it makes little difference whether the goals are real or illusive, so long as they are believed. But perhaps after that, lacking the substance of truth to stand upon, they are bound to lack strength and to topple. This is the story of what wealth meant to those Iberians who did not know how to use it. And it suggests the epilogue, with which the drama has not yet been concluded, wherein the stoic grandeur of the parents, worth more than gold itself, has remained alive, growing, and with promise, in the children.

It is a striking commentary on Western civilization that while most of Europe was under the impulse of youth and youthful kings, the conquest of the New World was carried out by middle-aged men. Columbus was forty-one in 1492; Pizarro was fifty-six when he captured Atahualpa; and

Cortés was thirty-four when he first entered Mexico City. Valdivia was forty when he led his first expedition to Chile; Quesada was thirty-six when he began the conquest of New Granada and seventy when he led his last band into the wilderness. But Charles V was only sixteen when he became King of Spain and nineteen when elected Emperor of Germany. Henry was crowned King of England at eighteen and Francis was twenty-one when he ascended the throne of France.[35]

It seemed almost as if Europe were getting tired of herself; as if, when the house became too confining, it was the older men who left home, unable to stand the same routine any longer. And it was the incredible endurance of this older dream, far stronger than any bright rose flush of youth, which was able to face disaster as well as success without losing the belief in victory. Most wars may be won or lost by younger men, but this was not an ordinary war in any sense of the term, and younger men did not fight or win it. Perhaps they would never have survived the things which older men did, or perhaps, if they had, the New World of the south would have been vastly different. As it was, older men came and conquered and, together with their dream, brought a too faithful replica of their Old World life, which even in the exaltation of victory they were unable to alter.

When the expedition to Colombia was being organized, Jiménez de Quesada did not stand too well with the people at home because he had just lost an important law case, one in which his mother's family had a considerable financial stake. Then, as the old chronicler Oviedo tells us, the wealthy organizer of the expedition appeared in town "with a drummer on the one hand and a friar or two who later joined him under the pretext of converting the Indians on the other, and they went about promising riches and turning the heads of ignorant people."[35] The defeated lawyer, Quesada, saw them and signed up as chief magistrate and second in command.

It was not an ordinary expedition. The commander, then governor of the Canary Islands, had bought the governorship of Colombia for a tidy sum, and with an equally tidy sum he had equipped several ships and assembled over a thousand adventurers to accompany him. Nor did the governor have cause to believe he was after any will-o'-the-wisp. Columbus, on his third voyage in 1498, had touched on the Spanish Main, and when he saw the pearls that were to be gathered there, he had told his men unequivocally, "You are in the richest land that there is in the world, and Glory be to God that we have found it." From that time on, the waters which lapped the northern coast of Colombia and Venezuela came to be known as the "Sea of Pearls."

The year after Columbus's third voyage several conquistadores had gathered large quantities of pearls off this rich coast, and the following year, 1500, a colony was established near Venezuela for the specific purpose of obtaining them. At first it flourished, and the King's fifth was rarely under fifteen thousand ducats, or about thirty-five thousand dollars. But then the pearls began to give out, water was lacking on the island, slave-gathering expeditions aroused the savage cannibalistic natives, and the place was abandoned. Coche Island and the Island of Margarita, or "Pearl Island," had already outdistanced it in productivity. Here the Spaniards forced the Indians to endure a rigorous training and to live on half rations so that they could stand the pressure under water and hold their breath for long periods of time. Many of them burst their eardrums and blood vessels, but the pearl fishing never ceased.

As a result of stories which came back from the Pearl Coast the Germans got interested in Venezuela, and in 1528 Charles V gave two of them who were representatives of his banker the right "to discover, conquer, and populate" that territory.[36] They were to get 4 per cent on the returns of their conquest and were exempt from paying many taxes. As if these reports, magnified a dozen times, were not enough, a sailor who had just returned from Colombia had visited the governor and told him of the fabulous riches in both gold and pearls which were to be found there. For further proof, Montezuma's treasure stood as a living testimony before the timid eyes of all the doubting Thomases.

When Charles V granted the governorship of Colombia, or New Granada, he made it clear that he "wanted these discoveries made without men dead, or Indians robbed, or slaves taken. The Indians were not to be ordered to work in the mines against their will."[35] Many good priests, especially Las Casas, had railed at the unchristian iniquities of the conquistadores and the enslavement of the natives, so this time there was to be none of them. Christianity was to be spread, but it must be done properly. Whenever the explorers came in sight of the Indians a priest was "to read two or three times in a high and intelligible voice" a sort of specially prepared catechism in which they were to be asked if they believed in the Father, the Son, and the Holy Trinity, and if they were willing to surrender themselves to the religion of Christ.

The explorers accepted all this as a matter of course but, as one distinguished Colombian historian says, with plenty of mental reservations: "To hell with this idea of converting the Indians and going easy with them! On the other side of the Atlantic there was only one sure thing—booty in the form of slaves and gold."[35]

It took the expedition two months to reach the small coastal settlement of Santa Marta, where the governor was going to set himself up and which would be the base for future operations. After their eight weeks at sea the men all craned their necks for this first glimpse of the New World which was to make them so gloriously wealthy. The town had been founded ten years previously, and they all expected to find a neat and thriving settlement fully characteristic of the tales of wealth which had come to their ears in faraway Spain.

What they actually did find was a stinking conglomeration of hovels and filthy, disease-ridden colonists, who went about like a band of gypsies, dressed in skins or roughly woven and padded cotton clothes made by the Indians. They slept in rude hammocks, had dirty Indian women as mistresses, and lived in the crudest huts covered with fern leaves as a protection against the tropical rains. They had no gardens, "nor was any land plowed up for crops. Their clothes and food were pried out of the Indians, for they did nothing for themselves." The shock of that first encounter was deep, and the newly arrived women were especially disgusted by the sordid scenes before them. It certainly made a disheartening contrast to the "brilliant cavaliers, all dressed in silks with velvet cloaks and shining arms, gilt morrions and waving plumes," who disembarked on the beach with their handful of finely dressed ladies.[37]

The contrast is worth remembering, for on one side stood illusion fresh from the Old World, while on the other was the naked reality of life in the tropics. But sometimes there is an illusion that never wholly dies, that drives a man or a nation until its dying day, then passes the belief on to others that follow. Finally, when the illusion itself fades away, its place is already taken by an accomplished fact, and the framework for a new realism is laid. In such stuff as this did all the great conquistadores believe, and among them was Jiménez de Quesada, who stood that day on the squalid beach of Santa Marta and saw before him the degeneration of life in the tropics and refused to believe it. He would fashion for himself the kind of reality in which he trusted and would someday found his own colony more suited to his fancy. When, like Don Quixote, he died in a wretched state after his last great defeat, the way had already been cleared for others. The groundwork was accomplished and the ideal had been made immortal.

The colonists' first shudder of apprehension soon passed away, and the new arrivals with their bright coats of mail had many a good laugh at the bulging cotton-padded clothes worn by the old-timers. In a few days, they thought, with a little hard work they would quickly put the place in order and then they would look for gold. It was not long before they were laughing out of the other side of their mouths. Food became scarce, and even what provisions they had began to deteriorate. Tropical fevers smote down the strongest and left them alternately burning with fever or shivering giddily. The hammer blows of dysentery hit at their bowels, and there was no relief from them. Outside of town, in the tangled forests, flitted naked cannibalistic Indians with poisoned arrows, waiting for a feast of human flesh. The time came when bells were tolling all day long to announce the dead, and as many as twenty corpses were thrown into a common grave at one time and covered with a thin layer of sod.[35] The governor stared defeat in the face, and, as the Spaniards say, "took heart out of the guts of his adversity." Perhaps to the south—far across the swamps, the jungle, and the mountains—he would find that El Dorado which had once run so warmly in his blood, and it would save him.

The first thing was to choose a leader, and as there were many fine soldiers in the group who had already fought in Venezuela, Mexico, and Peru, that matter should have been easy. But Don Pedro's choice "fell on none of his tried captains, for without hesitation he named Quesada general of the expedition, having found out that he was born to be a leader, although not bred to arms. His choice was justified as the young general proved himself valiant in action, patient in hardships to an incredible degree, tactful in council, and in difficulties that at once beset his path, staunch and as true as steel."[37] The expedition left Santa Marta with great fanfare, and hope beat fast in every heart. Only the padded armor of horses and soldiers added an incongruous note to the gay procession. When Quesada set out, he hadn't the slightest idea that two other expeditions were also on their way to the Colombian uplands: one from Coro, Venezuela, under a German; the other from Quito, Ecuador, under Belalcázar, one of Pizarro's men. These three groups were later to meet on the site of present-day Bogotá under circumstances which read like a fairy tale.

Quesada had nearly eight hundred men under him when he left Santa Marta. They were divided into two groups. One of these, led by the captain himself, was to hack its way through the jungle to the Magdalena River. It consisted of about five hundred Spaniards and several hundred Indians. The other group was to sail along the coast to the river's mouth, turn up it and join their companions who had come by land. Then together they would swing upstream to the magic mountain barrier. No matter what happened there would be no turning back.

It was truly a pilgrimage of courage. The rains, the mud, the marshlands, and the forests extended for five hundred miles before the expedition would reach the cool savannahs of Bogotá with only one hundred and sixty-six living skeletons out of the original eight hundred soldiers. No journey was ever harder. Every inch of the way it was a battle of man against insects, wild beasts, disease, starvation, and climate. Sometimes they inched along in mud or water up to their waists. Sometimes, machete in hand, they slashed a path through the tangled underbrush, trees, and creepers. Sometimes poisoned arrows sent them writhing into eternity or bloated their bodies with a torment which was worse than death. Many nights they slept with the rain beating upon their exhausted bodies until they were half drowned, and frequently they were forced to climb trees and get what rest they could while strapped to the branches. Ticks, bats, and galling itch, voracious serpents, alligators, and tropical fevers attacked them constantly, and famine soon wasted their bodies. One night, while the camp was sunk in the sleep of exhaustion, a jaguar pulled a soldier out of his hammock and carried him away to be devoured. The noise of the rain and the exhausted condition of the men prevented them from hearing his cries, although they were probably too weakened to be of much help anyway.

There came a time when they fell ravenously on snakes, lizards, frogs, and finally even boiled and ate the leather torn from their harnesses and the scabbards from their swords. The hardships faced by Cortés and Pizarro in the relatively open country which they had to cross could not compare with those of Quesada and his soldiers. Not only did the fauna and monstrous vegetation of tropical America harry them constantly, but also hunger and disease, the handmaidens of death, were ever present. Once, when they were so weak from want of food that they could hardly walk, "they found an Indian dog or two and boiled them whole, not stopping even to take off the skins, and it was as if they had been lambs. . . ."

Quesada had to be on the lookout to prevent the men from eating their horses, but whenever one of these animals died they fell upon it like famished coyotes and had a great banquet. Men slunk together in furtive groups which eyed each other with the animal fear of being devoured, for it was whispered that some of their companions had been roasted and eaten. "Every night the river carried off a corpse or two or three, cast into the water to prevent alarming the timid and arouse the incipient cannibalism of the most unscrupulous."[38] Before many weeks had passed six hundred had left their bones to mark the path over which the famished pilgrimage had passed, and the men verged on mutiny. But Quesada kept his eyes fixed toward the south, and with the priest at his side he pointed to the distant mountains and said that he would continue.

Finally the pitiful remnants of the once-gallant procession, eaten by disease and hunger, hobbling on canes, arrived at the foothills, and with a desperate effort ascended the flank of the high sierras. What lost world lay before them now five hundred miles from the sea? Quesada's wish was father to the thought, and he told his soldiers that they were about to reach their heart's desire—the land of gold and emeralds, and of beautiful white salt that filled the core of numberless mountains. They had come to a new way of life, he said, and they would need a captain-general with greater authority to lead them. Remembering Cortés, he resigned and called for an election. Quesada was elected captain-general, and threw off the last link that held him to the governor.

Two chieftains ruled the savannahs of Colombia. They called themselves the *Zipa* and the *Zaque*. The Zipa, so the Spaniards heard, traveled over his dominions in a litter plated with gold. His name was Bogotá. The Zaque lived behind a circular palisade over which hung sheets of gold that tinkled in the breeze like a sounding of biblical cymbals. There was also a great Temple of the Sun over which gold sheets were strung and whose floors inside were covered with carpets made of golden threads. And somewhere farther away there lived still another king who anointed himself with turpentine, dipped his body in heavy gold dust, and as part of a great religious ceremony plunged into the lake while his priests "offered their gods golden idols and emeralds by the handful."[35] This was the true, the ultimate, the authentic El Dorado. Twice again a Quesada was to seek it, and twice again he would fail to find it.

The native villages on the savannah were certainly not strewn with gold, but from a distance they were imposing with their rectilinear streets or paths, with their high triple stockades around all the main dwellings, which made them resemble primitive walled fortresses. Everything was of wood and painted in the brightest colors. At the intersection of every street stood high poles daubed with a red varnish and topped with a sort of sail-like contrivance. These marked the houses of the chiefs.

It was a land of laborers and farmers where cotton, potatoes, yucca roots, and corn grew in the fields, and where well-made cloth was much in evidence around the houses. A closer inspection revealed the extremely crude workmanship of the buildings, which were not nearly so large or carefully constructed as they at first appeared. Nevertheless, their high encircling stockades still gave them considerable prominence. The plateau Indians were mostly Chibchas, stocky in build, with round flattish faces and very small eyes. They had a more Mongoloid cast to their features than most American Indians.

The savannah itself was the most beautiful thing of all. Its deep fertile land spread for miles in every direction. Only on the east, in the direction of Venezuela, did mountain peaks tower above the plain. The Spaniards felt certain that this was the promised land. They got themselves new clothes, ate plenty of good food, inhaled the pure cold air, and saw their bodies grow daily stronger. And the poet sang, "This is the good earth that puts an end to sorrow."

> Tierra buena, tierra buena
> Tierra que hará fin a nuestra pena.
> Tierra de oro, tierra bastecida
> Tierra para hacer perpetua casa.
> Tierra con abundancia de comida,
> Tierra de grandes pueblos, tierra rasa
> Tierra donde se ve gente vestida. . . .
> Tierra de bendición, clara y serena,
> Tierra que hará fin a nuestra pena.[39]

Once having reached the relative safety of these high ranges, the lawyer Quesada determined to control his men more rigorously. There was to be no robbing without his consent; no killing unless he gave the word. Once he had to execute a Spaniard for stealing an Indian's pack. But that was before the great quest began. The Indian chiefs all lied to Quesada's men, who wanted to despoil them, but the Spaniards stumbled on the emerald mines anyway and found the golden cymbals. Chiefs were imprisoned now, put to the torture, and treasures were taken. At last even the famed Temple of the Sun was discovered, and as the soldiers entered with torches blazing the reflection of a million golden fireflies gleamed in the forest. But fingers of flame reached for the dry wooden columns and suddenly the whole temple was a golden glow in the night. Many a precious nugget was lost in the ashes.

The Indians of that region told them that Chief Bogotá, who lived to the south, was the richest of them all, for all were his tributaries. Bogotá had sense enough to flee before these locusts arrived to eat up his gold as if it were grain. He hid himself in a cave in the mountains, and the Spaniards, who wanted very desperately to take him alive, killed him by accident. His successor, Sagipa, was appointed, and Quesada's men went after him like a pack of bloodhounds. One day a squad of soldiers cornered him and took him prisoner. Quesada spoke his honeyed best, and Sagipa promptly swore that he would send his couriers for Bogotá's treasure. They would bring huge piles of gold and handfuls of emeralds. Within forty days it would be piled up in a room next to his cell, but he must be allowed to proceed in his own fashion, without any snooping or interference. That was the Indian way.

Quesada agreed, and Sagipa's couriers, accompanied by a strong native bodyguard, soon began to arrive with bags on their shoulders. It was plainly gold that they brought, for Sagipa made certain that the guards saw it on the way in. They also heard the sweet clink of metal as the articles were emptied on the floor. But the chief kept everyone out of his treasure cell. After the forty days had passed Quesada entered the room and saw that the floor was immaculate. The couriers had brought in the gold and the Indian guards had divided it up and slipped it out again under their loose clothing. Sagipa had planned the whole joke, thinking he might be able to escape while it was going on, but the delay had not helped him, for he was still a prisoner. He now promised to lead the soldiers to the treasure personally, but on the way he tried to jump over a precipice and they slew him. It is said that his treasure still lies at the bottom of a lake—like that of the Aztecs, like that of the anointed King of El Dorado, like that which the Inca priests were supposed to have thrown into Lake Titicaca.

As the land had now been pillaged under the law, it was time to establish a colony so that the earth itself might properly belong to Quesada and his men, and to their master, the King. They chose a spot next to the towering peaks of the east, where the land was high and the rains would quickly run off, where the mountains would protect them from Venezuela and the jungles below. A fortress erected on such a site would be practically impregnable. The air was clearer in this locality, and there was stone for building, plenty of wood, and many miles of fertile and fruitful land extending toward the west.

On the day of the founding a large crowd gathered, scribes and notaries took their places, and an altar was set up for mass. Hundreds of Indians stood in the background watching the affair with blank expressions on their faces. Quesada rode carefully out into the center of the field, dismounted, and pulled up a tuft of grass. He then placed his right foot on the bare earth and said simply, "I take possession of this land in the name of the most sovereign emperor, Charles V." Then he remounted his horse and drew his sword, asking if there were any present who wanted to challenge the conquest. No one came forward, so Quesada sheathed his sword, and it was duly recorded that the Kingdom of New Granada should be added to the Spanish dominions. Twelve houses were constructed of adobe and thatch representing the twelve apostles, and a few of the Spaniards with their Indian women moved into permanent quarters. For many years there were no panes in the windows of the houses, and over the doorways were hung hides with the hair still on them. At first they called the settlement the New City of Granada, but later they changed it to Santa Fe de Bogotá, and now it is known simply as Bogotá. In regard to the actual construction of the town, one of Quesada's biographers states, "The huts were built of canes by the Indians of the place for by virtue of their conquest all the soldiers had become gentlemen, and no one cared overmuch to work."[37]

The construction was hardly begun when Quesada heard that two other expeditions, one from the east and one from the west, were advancing swiftly toward his chosen site in their own quest for El Dorado. From the west came Belalcázar, one of the captains of Pizarro who had mutinied against his leader and who had beaten Alvarado to the site of Quito, where they both futilely looked for gold. Belalcázar then went to the seacoast of Ecuador, founded Guayaquil, returned to Quito, and, accompanied by nearly all of his men and a huge retinue of pigs, headed northward into Colombia. There he also founded the city of Popayán in its beautiful valley which the chronicler tells us has the best grain, best sky, best land, best bread in America. It became the cradle of colonial culture in New Granada. Belalcázar was advancing toward Bogotá from Popayán.

From the east came an expedition under the leadership of another mutinous captain, Nicholas Federmann, a German, who had rebelled against another German named Hohermuth, into whose hands had been placed the governorship of Venezuela. These men had pushed their way into South America as agents of German bankers who had made loans to Charles V. The Spanish Emperor had given them the unexplored colonies of Venezuela as a sort of collateral.

The first of their governors and captains was a redheaded giant named Ehinger, who tramped hundreds of miles through Venezuela jungles in search of the gold of the Chibchas. A poisoned arrow caught him in the throat and sent him into eternity. Then came Sinserhoffer, who was content to sit in his gubernatorial chair near the relative safety of the coast. But the bankers were not playing this game for fun or safety; they wanted gold, and Ehinger's paltry sums had only whetted their appetites.

Sinserhoffer was replaced by a more daring man named Hohermuth, and leaving Federmann as his second-in-command on the coast, this governor headed in the general direction of Bogotá, thinking of El Dorado. Federmann soon became restive and started out on his own account. For over three years he had been hacking and pulling at the jungles, trying to find a passage through the mountain barrier, until now at last his way was clear to Bogotá.

It was an epic scene when the three captains met on the savannah of New Granada. Federmann, agent of the great bankers, came straggling along with his hens and his soldiers. His men were clothed in animal skins, for their own clothes had long since rotted or been torn away by the brambles. Their bones and flesh stuck out in red lumps and they could hardly walk upright. Belalcázar, founder of cities and former donkey boy in Spain, came in martially with his pigs and his troops and his ever-present silver service. His men were all sleek from the good food and fine airs of Popayán, and were dressed in showy scarlet.

Quesada awaited them stolidly and brushed up the appearance of his native "allies" so as to increase as much as he could the formidable array of his army. Federmann came in first, and his men were graciously given food. Belalcázar followed, and for some time Quesada's glib tongue kept him at arm's length. When it seemed that a conflict was only a matter of hours he persuaded them both to accompany him back to Spain, where they would place their claims for governorship in the hands of the sovereign. They did this, but not one of them got it. Belalcázar did become governor of Popayán, but he was later tried and condemned to death; an illness cheated the executioner. Federmann died a pauper in Spain; and Quesada, after nearly a dozen years of wandering disconsolately through the gaming halls of Europe, returned to New Granada in 1550.

He settled down, and for nearly twenty years lived the life of a prominent and respected colonist whose early exploits had earned for him the highest consideration of his townsmen. But Quesada was like Don Quixote—if his dream was gone there was nothing. In 1569, at the ripe age of seventy, he placed himself at the head of another mighty expedition composed of three hundred mounted soldiers, fifteen hundred Indians, eleven hundred horses and pack animals, six hundred head of cattle, eight hundred pigs, and a large number of Negro slaves. They were all going to the promised land: the sweet, mystical El Dorado, where life was a child's dream of heaven and gold was as common as leaves on trees or the quivering brilliance of butterfly wings over miasmic jungles. They went forth to the sound of bugles and drums, and with banners waving, all laughing and singing like school children on their way to a festival. How brief was the memory of disaster; how long was the illusion that drove men across dark and trackless jungles toward a golden tomorrow!

It was the same as thirty years before. Voices were soon stifled with hardship, disease, hunger, and death. Three years later Quesada and twenty-five friends turned back and retraced their steps to Bogotá. Accompanying them were four Indians out of an original fifteen hundred, eighteen horses out of more than a thousand. There were no pigs or cattle. Miserable, broken, old, bent double, and hopelessly in debt, the *adelantado*, Jiménez de Quesada, re-entered the city he had founded. When he laid his last hopes aside it was like Don Quixote come home to die.

But there was to be no rest for the "Knight of El Dorado." An Indian uprising cut short his desolate reveries, and the old conqueror once more picked up his sword and scabbard and ranged "through the burning lands of Mariquita . . . circling around his death." Sometimes he was so weak that he had to be carried in a litter, but whenever there was a battle, he would suddenly find strength to mount his horse and charge into the affray with his soldiers. He won a quick victory and returned to Bogotá in triumph. A few months later, afflicted with leprosy, overcome with despair at his debts, owing more than sixty thousand ducats, he was forced to seek a milder climate and died quietly in an insignificant village of New Granada.

9

CONQUEST OF THE RIVER PLATE

The section of South America comprising Argentina, Uruguay, and Paraguay is known in Spanish as the *Río de la Plata* region, or the region of the "River of Silver," which is more commonly called in English the River Plate. The conquest of this section of the New World by Spain was a slow and arduous process, much like that of the English settlements in the United States. There was no central Indian civilization, almost no gold or silver, and only the rudest attempts at agriculture. Every step of the way was contested by savage nomadic tribes who attacked the settlers violently, burning towns and massacring their inhabitants, then melting into the night. These Indians either lived in tents of reeds and grass or, in their more permanent settlements, in little round one-room huts of mud and wattles, with thatched roofs, and a narrow open door. Around the village was sometimes thrown a rough palisade.

Strange to say, the doorways of these primitive dwellings were in the form of a real arch rounded at the top. With the exception of a sort of bastard archway that the Indians of the Peruvian coast happened to hit upon a time or two, without realizing its significance, these slits in the rude Argentine houses were the only true arches ever known to primitive America. However, this hardly merits mention as an archaeological achievement, for the pampas Indians were at about the same stage of development as our North American tribes when the Pilgrims landed on Plymouth Rock. They numbered seven or eight hundred thousand but were split up into innumerable small tribes, most of which were constantly at war. Their social organization included a chieftain, but they paid little attention to his authority. Some of them wore a breechclout as their only article of apparel, occasionally adding a rough skin cloak when the weather was cold, but many went entirely naked. They were fierce warriors but rarely attacked in the open field, relying instead on surprise and stealth like many of their North American counterparts. Most of them were not particularly attached to any locality. In some quarters they received the Spaniards in a friendly fashion, but in others they deeply resented the intrusion. On the pampas especially a deadly enmity sprang up between the two races, the effects of which lasted until 1879, when the last bands of these savages were finally subdued.

The settlements in this land, such as they were, rarely contained more than a few houses and were generally along the banks of some river or stream in which fish abounded. There were no great native cities to be sacked, no treasures to be stolen, no storehouses of any kind, and very little food. Most of the land was a great prairie known as the Argentine pampas. For hundreds of miles it spread like a vast fan of grassland and sky from the seacoast to the Andes. It was a green ocean which often lapped high as a man's knee, even when he rode over it on horseback. One could never venture to cross it alone, for the man who lost his way here never returned but continued to wander until exhausted; "he lay down to leave his bones beside some stream, haunted by flamingos and Magellanic swans." The only safe way a European could traverse the region was by horse, and for want of a better hitching post the rope was generally thrown around several reeds of pampas grass and then drawn tight. An occasional gnarled tree called the *ombú* was one of the few trees native to the pampas, and wild life was scarce except for myriads of birds, considerable flocks of wild ostriches and deer, the ever-present burrowing rodent known as the *vizcacha*, and several species of armadillos. But there were great stretches where even a small force of men would have difficulty in finding sufficient food.

The first white man to set foot on this soil was a Spaniard, Juan Solís, and he was killed there after sailing his ships for several miles up the River Plate in 1516. The man who followed him, Sebastian Cabot, son of John Cabot, took the same course up the river and continued until he reached the neighborhood of the present city of Asunción, capital of Paraguay— a distance of nearly one thousand miles from the sea. This was in 1526. Cabot's passage was blocked at one point by about three hundred Indian canoes filled with warriors, but he drove his two ships into the midst of them and wedged his way through, slaying as he went. Soon afterward he reached the end of his journey and entered the land of the unwarlike Guaranís, who came down to the banks of the river in great numbers to greet him. They were unarmed, wore feathers in their hair, and had thin plates of silver hung from their necks. Such was the origin of the name Río de la Plata and perhaps also the name of Argentina itself.

Both names were misnomers, for all the silver the Guaranís had was from Peru. Cabot laid in a goodly supply of this metal in exchange for the usual mirrors, red cloth, and brass hawks' bells. He promptly sent this back to Spain and not long afterward returned himself. The King received him well and made him captain-general of the new territory, but just as he was about to set sail again three noblemen whom he had left marooned on an island showed up, and after their denunciations, the whole thing was called off. Cabot's title was annulled and he never returned to America.

Two years passed, and then one of the greatest expeditions ever to set out for America was prepared at the expense of Don Pedro de Mendoza, a nobleman at the Spanish court. The fleet consisted of eleven vessels, about twelve hundred men, and one hundred horses and mares which were later to become of much greater consequence in the history of Argentina than Mendoza himself. The expedition was extremely well outfitted, and among its members were several noblemen. They were not old-timers in Indian warfare, but many of them had distinguished themselves in the campaigns of Italy. Cabot's tales of the River of Silver, exaggerated by several retellings, were probably the principal cause of their wanting to share in the adventure. The fact that the leader was a wealthy noble seemed to clinch the argument of those who believed that all of America was a land of gold and silver. They reached the shores of the River Plate without incident, and in February 1536 founded on its southern bank what was later to become the great metropolis of Buenos Aires.

The width of the estuary at this point, for it is really the estuary of the rivers Paraná and Uruguay which is called the River Plate, is approximately twenty-eight miles. The distance from the Atlantic coast is about one hundred and seventy miles. Here the great hidalgos of Spain, several of them accompanied by their wives, disembarked and founded their settlement on the bank of the river which they thought practically flowed silver. It was certainly not a very prepossessing-looking spot, and the water was so shallow near the shore that the ships had to be anchored a mile or two out. The weather was hot and muggy, but according to the story, a fresh breeze sprang up at the moment of landing and the first man ashore remarked on what good airs (*buenos aires*) were those of this land. The capital is said to have taken its name from these words.

From this time on the story of Argentina was inseparably linked with the history of that colony. It was blotted out for nearly forty years, but many of its inhabitants reached safety upriver and came back later to found a second city on the ashes of the first and thus made certain of the growth of the Argentine nation. There was no outstanding conquistador of this region, for conquest and consolidation were synonymous here and extended over the lifetimes of many generations.

Don Pedro de Mendoza, regarded as the founder of the city, though his colony was abandoned, was not a great leader in any sense of the term and spent half of his time ill in bed. He suffered from a bad case of syphilis which bothered him constantly. Such was the legacy which this proud scion of Spanish nobility left in the River Plate. Yet Don Pedro's blood was most certainly not made of water. In spite of his constant pains and weakness he put his whole heart in his enterprise.

There were not any great campaigns in the River Plate, nor any chroniclers such as Bernal Díaz in Mexico, or the Inca Garcilaso in Peru, or Quesada, who cast his noble shadow over Colombia. The historian of the unceasing skirmishes of the River Plate was a humble German soldier named Ulrico Schmidl, who came over with Don Pedro and remained there for eighteen years, taking part in nearly every battle and writing down his memoirs in his native tongue after his return to Germany in 1553. Schmidl's gruff and straightforward narrative is the one indispensable document in the early history of this region.

From the very first the settlement of the River Plate country, embracing Argentina, Uruguay, Paraguay, and part of Bolivia, was the story of a collective and popular will, sometimes magnificent in its achievements, at other times exasperating in its blind or fearsome and stupid submission to demagogues, but at all times capable of a rebound, such as characterized the refounding of its metropolis, Buenos Aires, by the very people who had been driven from it thirty-nine years before. There is also a cosmopolitan note in the history of the River Plate which is not found anywhere else in Latin America, except in those two great sister nations which touch its borders: Chile and Brazil.

In Schmidl's chronicle we find the following description of the countryside and inhabitants around Buenos Aires and of the original settlement itself: "We found in this land a tribe of Indians known as the Querandís. There were about three thousand of them, men, women, and children, and they brought us fish and meat to eat. The women wore a single piece of cotton cloth. As for the tribe, it has no permanent settlement in the whole country; they wander over the earth in the same manner as the gypsies do in the German countries."[40]

He goes on to tell how, when they migrated inland during the summer, water often became so scarce that the Indians were forced to chew on wild roots or to drink the blood of animals they killed in order not to die of thirst. For two weeks after Mendoza's arrival the Indians shared their own scant provisions with the Spaniards, but on the fifteenth day they failed to show up, and it was soon learned that during the night they had broken camp and withdrawn several miles from the white settlement. The Spaniards had come to take their gifts of food for granted, had paid what and when they wished or not at all, and the natives had simply pulled out.

Don Pedro at once sent a deputy and a couple of bodyguards to find out what was wrong. Propositions and promises were used to no avail, and finally, in exasperation, the deputy let his anger get the better of him and threatened dire punishment. The natives may not have understood every word of the previous harangues, but they immediately caught the gist of this sudden change in manner and met it by falling on the three Spaniards, and after giving them a sound beating sent them fleeing back to their camp. Don Pedro promptly dispatched his brother with three hundred soldiers and thirty horsemen to teach the barbarians a lesson. He had certainly made an ill choice. The horses were still so weak from their cramped quarters and scant rations on the long ocean voyage that they were hardly able to make the distance. The Indians awaited the Spaniards in battle position on the farther side of a stream, about ten miles from Buenos Aires, and after a few had crossed they broke into a furious charge and drove them back into the water. There was a mad scramble along the slippery banks, and Indian arrows, lances, and large stones hurled from slings, or *bolas*, rained on the attacking force with unremitting fury. The Spaniards eventually did get out of the creek and slew hundreds of Indians on the other side, but when they turned around to head back to camp, their leader, Mendoza's brother, and about thirty other men lay dead on the field, and several horses had also been slain. It was a tremendous loss, and though the Indians had been driven off and all their provisions captured, a new weapon, the deadly accurate bolas, had been introduced in the war of conquest. Even in the hands of these savages it came close to equalizing the struggle. The Spaniards returned to camp with their meager loot and feeling much discomforted by their "Pyrrhic victory." The worst enemy had not yet been encountered. This was famine, and it was just around the corner.

The city was fortified with an adobe wall three feet thick, and a strong fortress was erected near one end of the settlement. The protecting wall had been hurriedly made of mud, without straw or proper hardening in the sun, and every time rain fell it nearly melted away. The colonists managed to scrape by for some time, but eventually food became so scarce that rations were reduced to an ounce and a half per person each day. In these desperate straits famished inhabitants repeated the experiences of Quesada's men and devoured rats, mice, snakes, lizards, even their shoes, and all available hides. Some gorged on the bodies of those who had died. The Indians attacked the town again and again with arrows to whose tips had been tied small bundles of ignited straw, and several times the place was nearly consumed in the flames. On more than one occasion the exhausted Spaniards escaped annihilation by sheer dint of courage.

Don Pedro's syphilis had now become extremely painful, and he appointed one of his men to take his place as captain-general. This man, Ayolas, constructed eight light vessels of shallow draught and sailed up the river with a large part of the remaining force. After defeating the Guaranís and making a treaty of friendship with them, Ayolas founded the town of Asunción, Paraguay, in 1537. In order to cement their new friendship the Guaranís gave the Spanish captain seven young Indian maidens and presented each soldier in his army with two, "and in this way," writes Schmidl, "we became friends." Not very long after this Ayolas was killed while away on an exploring expedition and a third man, Irala, was elected to the governorship. The Indians broke out into a revolt but were quickly subdued, and again the treaty of peace was backed up with gifts of Indian girls. This was becoming a habit. The Spaniards were already off to a rather prolific start. Such was the beginning of the Paraguayan race.

In the meantime, in 1537, Don Pedro de Mendoza had sailed for Spain and died en route. He had left a force behind him at Buenos Aires and promised to send aid. His last thoughts were for the colonists there, and in his will he begged that more men and provisions be sent from Spain in order to redeem his city from famine and the wilderness. But help did not arrive in sufficient quantity, so Buenos Aires was abandoned in 1541, and its settlers moved up the river to Asunción, which became the base for the reconquest of Argentina. Everything made of wood in Buenos Aires was taken out with the men, even a few wooden houses that had been erected, and nothing remained behind but several horses which had escaped and now roamed wild over the pampas. The Indians very quickly made use of some of these and soon became as expert horsemen as the Spaniards themselves.

Buenos Aires was now in ruins and its first two governors were dead. The third governor, Irala, who had been elected to the post temporarily by his own men, had gathered the remnants of the River Plate colonists into the interior. King Charles V then sent over a governor from Spain. This was Cabeza de Vaca, the same man who had been cast up on the Gulf coast of the United States many years before, and who, with three companions, one of them a Moroccan Negro, had tramped unarmed through wild Indian territory halfway across the continent and finally to Mexico City. The trip lasted eight years. Not only did Cabeza de Vaca arrive safely, but he was accompanied on a great part of his journey by several hundred adoring Indians who had been won to him by his fine character and his ability as a doctor. These savages had gradually grown in numbers until they formed a veritable army. When Cabeza de Vaca finally met a group of Spaniards in Mexico and understood that they wanted to enslave his Indian friends, he sent the latter home with such gifts as he could muster and earnestly begged them to continue leading upright lives.

This was the man who had been chosen by the King to become the governor of the River Plate. He understood Indian psychology and customs perhaps better than any Spaniard alive, and his own character was so patient and inspirational that some of the wildest tribes had become his devoted followers and friends. His secret was a simple one. He had felt only kindness in his heart and had been repaid in kind.

But Cabeza de Vaca was inexperienced as an administrator, and perhaps in his many years' close association with the natives he had forgotten a great deal about his fellow Spaniards. His expedition to the River Plate reached the coast of Brazil in 1541 and he decided to march overland to Asunción—a distance of eight hundred miles across the most difficult terrain. He made the trip in one hundred and twenty days and got across the wild Indian territory with a minimum of difficulty. When he reached Asunción he promptly appointed the acting governor, Irala, as his second-in-command, and after about a year at his post marched overland toward the west, hoping to blaze a land trail to Peru.

At one point on this journey his soldiers collected about a hundred native girls whom they said had been given to them by the chiefs of the district. Cabeza de Vaca insisted that they release the girls, and so spontaneous was the gratitude of the families concerned, it is supposed that the word "given" was a euphemism. The soldiers were infuriated, and Cabeza de Vaca wrote in his memoirs: ". . . from that time on, I was hated by most of them. . . ." Add to this his persistent refusal to allow his men to enslave or maltreat the Indians in any way, and the end of his story begins to loom before us. When he returned to Asunción after an unsuccessful trip and so racked with fever that he was hardly able to stand on his feet, the officials of the city, rabid partisans of Irala, threw him into jail on false charges and kept him there for ten months, until he was finally sent to Spain for trial. There he was exonerated completely.

It was clear that the principal charge against him was the unspoken and unspeakable one of having insisted on absolute justice in dealing with the Indians. Irala and his partisans were not essentially bad men, but they were interested primarily in Indian man power, with a little woman power thrown in, and not seeing any way to bring Cabeza de Vaca over to their side, used trumped-up charges to get rid of him for good. Irala took no active part in the rebellion against the governor and, playing the role of Pontius Pilate, pretended that his authority was thrust upon him by the inhabitants of the city.

The isolated colonists (since the Indians did not count) had decided to take the law into their own hands. It seemed to them a much easier way, and if it was not entirely right it was at least right for their purposes. Irala proved himself to be an extremely able administrator and lawgiver and he soon had things completely in hand. It was not long before he "proceeded to make new grants of land and Indians in order to exploit the first and secure the subjugation of the second. He assigned to the colonists about twenty-six thousand Indians." Perhaps in a case of this sort—perhaps in any conquest, imperialism, or aggrandizement—the effort which will produce material returns most quickly is the only possible one to expect. Obviously it would have meant nothing for Cabeza de Vaca to remain at his post unless he enjoyed sufficient authority to govern properly. He had "made himself a savior and was crucified, as runs the Spanish saw. He has no statue, either in South America or Spain, though he deserves one more than many a conquistador who, glorious in bronze, lords it in market place and square."[41]

Irala, on the other hand, soon entrenched himself firmly both in the government and in the hearts of his people. He deliberately kept at a minimum all communication with the seacoast and thus initiated Paraguayan isolationism. Yet there was a strong integrity to this man who at his death "carried the tears of Paraguay with him to the grave." He died almost a pauper, never having taken advantage of his position to gain wealth where power alone had sufficed.

For several years the colony of Asunción continued on its way under the benign climate of Paraguay. Sheep and goats were brought overland from Peru and the Portuguese brought cows from Brazil. A life of relative ease and pleasure was shaping up for the governing few. But a restless blood ran in the veins of these people and they were far from content to sit back bottled up in Asunción, situated on a navigable river but with no secure outlet to the sea. It was high time to think of refounding Buenos Aires. Cabeza de Vaca had attempted it in 1544, but nothing permanent had come of his endeavor.

In that same year the founder of today's Buenos Aires, then a young boy of fourteen, had arrived in Peru with his uncle. At the age of nineteen he had accompanied some Peruvian colonists to the northern Argentine province of Tucumán. In 1568 he established his residence at Asunción and rose quickly in the esteem of his fellow townsmen. This was Juan de Garay, a Biscayan by birth and one of the best-loved heroes of the River Plate. With nine Spaniards and seventy-five young men who were "natives of the land," Garay proceeded down the river, and at the halfway point between Asunción and the sea planted the colony of Santa Fe in 1573.

The preponderance of native-born colonists, all of whom were mestizos and who outnumbered the whites eight to one, proved how rapidly racemixing was already moving along in Argentina. Later it was to be the first Latin-American nation to absorb completely the native population. Garay had decided to found Buenos Aires by stages this time, and his colony at Santa Fe was the first step. Rapid communication upriver was to be assured, and there would be no repetition of the isolation or famines of an earlier date.

The city of Córdoba in central Argentina was founded in the same year by Peruvian colonists pushing down from the north, and the Spaniards now occupied a strategic square in the heart of the River Plate territory. From this time on it was only a question of time before the edges of that square would spread out in all directions, obeying always the maxim of the famous Argentine writer Alberdi who said, "To govern is to populate."

Seven years later Garay was ready to move down toward the coast. "He gathered more than sixty men with the necessary farm implements and munitions, one thousand horses and five hundred cows."[42] If man was the motive force in the colonization of the Argentine, his ambition, wealth, even his national history, were already linked with these quadrupeds, who felt so at home on the pampas and multiplied there in the greatest profusion, making secure the future food supply. They were the real lifeblood of the new Argentina. In 1580 Buenos Aires was founded again, and of its sixty-three inhabitants this time fifty-three were native-born mestizos.[42]

As in the case of the ancient Greek cities which faced the sea, the principal square was placed almost upon the banks of the river. Ordinances were drawn up distributing plots of land for houses inside the city and larger parcels outside the city for the Indians and for those settlers who wanted to establish ranches of beef cattle. The Argentine was now fully formed and ready to come forth from the fetal stage of the conquest onto the pampas which is its home.

10
BRAZIL: LAND OF NO LURE

The greatest poem in the Portuguese language and one of the world's finest epics is *The Lusiads* of Camoëns, whose majestic cantos have immortalized the "deeds without peer" of the sea captain, Vasco da Gama, who in 1498 rounded the Cape of Good Hope, found the sea route to India, gave Portugal a new empire, and clinched a monopoly on the lucrative spice trade with the Orient. It was a tremendous achievement, but not one which left the Portuguese free to rest on their laurels. The natives of India had not exactly greeted Gama with open arms, and other European powers might any day try to force their way in, so a large fleet was sent out to establish Portuguese rule there beyond any shadow of a doubt. There were thirteen ships bearing the red cross of Portugal on their sails, and about fifteen hundred men, all under the command of Captain Alvares Cabral.

Gama warned Cabral about getting caught in the doldrums off the African coast, so he sailed far to the west and unexpectedly (say some reports) landed on the coast of Brazil in 1500. Other historians claim that Cabral's "discovery" was the result of a carefully conceived and premeditated plan. They point out that Gama's pilot went along with this expedition, that the winds were reported as being extremely favorable, and that the captain must surely have known it would not be necessary to sail so far out of the way toward the west. Portugal in those days was the weakest of the maritime powers, with a total population of only a million and a half, and, as a consequence, she maintained the greatest possible secrecy about her plans and discoveries. No maps of new territories could be published and not even accounts of voyages were permitted. The Treaty of Tordesillas, which Portugal had the foresight to persuade Spain to accept in 1494, pushed Portugal's claims so far to the west that several years before Cabral's discovery she had a clear title to the great South American bulge which makes up a considerable part of Brazil. It is quite possible then that

Portugal knew about this region before 1500, had kept that knowledge a carefully guarded secret, and that Cabral's landing there was no accident.

The captain cruised along the coast for several miles until he found a bay that suited him. Then he and his men disembarked and claimed the country in the name of the King of Portugal. Carpenters made a huge wooden cross of native trees, and this was set up by the altar on which mass was celebrated and before which the claims of possession were recorded. Naked Indians mingled freely with the Portuguese soldiers and sailors in the most friendly fashion during the ten days the expedition remained ashore. The vessels were reloaded with fresh water, native fruits, and firewood, and all but one of them continued the voyage to India. This ship returned to Lisbon to give King Manuel an account of the discovery.

The King sent three ships to reconnoiter the coast line of the new land, and these met Cabral on his return journey. Together they sailed along the Brazilian coast and drew up charts of amazing accuracy. Logs from the coastal forest which contained a much-prized red dye "equal to that known in Europe as *Brazil*" were taken back to Portugal in some quantity, and the entire country soon came to be known by this name. The land was lovely beyond conception; Amerigo Vespucci, who touched its coast about that same time, exclaimed in admiration, "If there is a Paradise anywhere on earth, it cannot be very far from here."

With the rich spice empire of the East firmly in her hands, and with her extremely small population, Portugal was in no condition to undertake colonization of this vast new territory. But she did encourage its development in every way possible under the circumstances. In 1503 a converted Jew obtained a special grant to cut and export brazilwood, and during the years immediately following several other "new Christians" came to Brazil in order to escape the rigors of the Portuguese Inquisition. These early Jewish arrivals later became a mighty force in the development of Brazilian wealth and commerce. In 1521 a colonist planted some sugar cane in the province of Pernambuco and thus laid the basis of Brazilian economy for two hundred years to come. King Manuel helped things along by making over two hundred crimes punishable with exile; this killed two birds with one stone, cleaned out the Portuguese jails, and gave Brazil colonists.

Early Brazilian history is vague and nebulous. There were no great marches of conquistadores, no rich native cities to seek and plunder, and for over thirty years there were no fixed Portuguese centers. Brazil was strictly a business side line and nothing more for the moment—a mere stopping-off place on the voyage to India. When Portugal announced her claims to the new territory the royal letter sent to the court of Spain was careful to point out that Brazil was a country where there was "no gold or silver or any other precious metals." It was a land of no lure.

The picture changed slowly. Spices began to accumulate in Lisbon in such volume that by 1510 the profits were more than cut in half. And by

1520, with military trouble in India, Portugal began to borrow money right and left with disastrous consequences for both borrower and lenders. Yet the mirage of India still continued to shine, while Brazil was only a country of parrots, monkeys, and dyewood. Had not caravel after caravel entered Lisbon, packed to the gunwales with "costly woven goods, jewels, precious stones, and spices" brought from a land where wealthy rajahs and zamorins could duplicate their cargoes a million times over?

The little nation which had outdone herself was now caught between a deadly cross fire: her commerce with the East was sinking fast, and her small population and smaller national income made large-scale colonization of Brazil prohibitive. Would she let them both slip from her grasp? Her answer to the dilemma was as characteristic as it was intelligent. A perhaps unconscious, but certainly deliberate, self-ruin would slowly be imposed on the homeland in order that the child might live to outstrip its mother.

For at least half a century it was nip and tuck. A few temporary trading posts were set up on the Brazilian coast, mainly for the purpose of obtaining the valuable red dyewood, but French sea hawks swooped down on the ships in the middle of the ocean and returned to their ports with both cargo and crew. Other enterprising Frenchmen had the effrontery to establish a garrison and trading post of their own near Pernambuco, which was the center of the coastal bulge, and north of that Dutchmen were already beginning to move in by the dozens. Portuguese men-of-war went up and down the coast sinking these ships on all sides, but the cure was not permanent.

In 1531 the King decided that it was high time to put some order into this chaos, so a convoy bearing four hundred settlers was dispatched to Brazil under the leadership of Martim Afonso de Sousa, a nobleman in the court of King John III. Afonso de Sousa carried soldiers, cattle, seeds, agricultural implements, and was to have the trouble, honor, and duty of (1) cleaning out the French, (2) exploring the territory and making an accurate map of it, (3) founding permanent Portuguese settlements. The first two of these duties would show immediate results, but the fate of Brazil as a Portuguese colony would depend on how well the third was carried out. Afonso de Sousa decided to establish one colony in the north at Bahia as a protection against the French, and two in the south as centers from which expeditions might guard against Spanish encroachments in that direction. One of these bases was placed near the present coffee port of Santos, the other near the great inland metropolis of São Paulo. The captain made his selections well, for both regions were later to become great centers of colonial life. Bahia, with its huge plantations of sugar cane and tobacco, would come to resemble our own "Old South"; São Paulo, with its enterprising half-breeds, called mamelucos in Brazil, would more than once push expeditions into Spanish territory and spread panic as far as Buenos Aires. It was also to become a base for tremendous migrations westward—migrations in some ways similar to those of our early North American pioneers, which would win for Brazil the vast territories of the west in the Amazon Basin. Fortune came to Afonso de Sousa's aid both in the north and in the south in the guise of a couple of shipwrecked sailors. One of these was living with a chief's daughter and numerous offspring near Bahia, where he and his progeny were of great help to the colonists who settled there. Portugal had started early the surest means of conquest at her disposal—that of amalgamation with the natives.

The story of this shipwrecked Portuguese is a fascinating one. Diogo Alvarez was of noble birth, but he had set out, like many of his countrymen in those days, to seek his fortune in foreign lands. About the year 1505 his ship was wrecked on the shoals near the present city of Bahia, and Diogo, with eight of his companions, was cast up on the shore. The natives, who were cannibals, made quick use of some of his companions, and Alvarez, in order to protect himself and gain their good will, swam back to the wrecked vessel and brought in several items which he distributed among them as gifts.

He also got hold of a musket and some powder, and one day, when a sufficiently large crowd was assembled, shot down a bird before them. The natives shouted in great fear: "*Caramurú! Caramurú!*" which meant "man of fire." From that day forward "Caramurú" was the only name by which this man was known. He accompanied the men in battles and aided them in defeating all of their enemies, thus gaining favor with the chieftains. In order to show their appreciation, they signified that they would consider themselves honored if he would accept their daughters as his wives, and Caramurú gladly embraced polygamy.

A few years later a French vessel put into the harbor, and after helping to load her with brazilwood Caramurú and his favorite wife sailed for France. The French would not permit him to go to Lisbon, thinking that he would be of great use to them in their own scheme for Brazil. Nevertheless, Caramurú managed to communicate with the King of Portugal in writing, and urged him to colonize "the delightful province in which his own lot had been so strangely cast." A short time afterward he and his wife bribed a rich merchant to take them back to Brazil and to furnish them with some arms and ammunition as well as a supply of articles likely to appeal to the natives. In return they persuaded the natives of the region to help the Frenchman load two vessels with brazilwood.

For several years after that Caramurú remained unmolested with his wives, his friends, and his children, like some biblical patriarch of old. For nearly thirty years he was the only white colonist in the Bahia region, and, needless to say, when Afonso de Sousa cast anchor in the bay they were each glad to see the other. Caramurú's aid to the new arrivals was invaluable, and for many years he continued to serve as an intermediary between them and the Indians. The trading post they established was soon abandoned, but in 1549, when the city of Bahia was founded, the old "man of fire" was still there among his Indians.

When Afonso de Sousa reached the southern part of Brazil the story of old Caramurú was repeated, for here also lived a shipwrecked Portuguese with his tribe of native friends and half-breed children. The name of this man was João Ramalho, and it is one which bears remembering in Brazilian history, for Ramalho was literally "the father of São Paulo," throughout the years the nation's most aggressive city. Afonso de Sousa founded two settlements in the south, one on the coast near where Santos, the big coffee port, stands today, and one several miles inland near where Ramalho and his tribe were living. The early days of these settlers are almost as difficult to follow as were some of the later peregrinations of their restless descendants.

It was fully realized that Portugal was in no position to undertake the colonization of both the coast and interior of so vast a domain, and that if she made the attempt she would in all likelihood lose them both. Therefore, the coastal strip was decided upon, for it was rightly thought that if this were firmly occupied it would fence off the hinterland until the proper time for a migration westward.

An exception to this rule, of course, was the already flourishing settlement of Ramalho's half-breeds, whom Afonso de Sousa had found residing "in the fields of Piratininga," an inland mountain valley. The township which Afonso de Sousa founded in the district, after making an alliance with Ramalho's friends, did not last long, but Ramalho's own community near by continued to thrive from the earliest days.

The city "was by its situation almost cut off from any intercourse with other towns; it had little or no communication with Portugal, no trade for want of outlets, but it had every advantage of soil and climate. To such a place adventurers, deserters, and fugitives from justice would naturally resort. They consorted with Indian women, and the mixture of native blood, which everywhere in Brazil was very great, was perhaps greater here than in any other part. This mixture improved the race, for the European spirit of enterprise developed itself in constitutions adapted to the country. But the *mamelucos* (as these half-breeds were called) grew up without any restrictions of law or religion." As we shall see later, they pursued the Indian slave trade with indefatigable energy and combated the Jesuits at every possible turn.

Captain Afonso de Sousa also had the frontiers of Brazil marked off with several stone monuments placed at points where disputes were most likely to occur. One of these was set up about one hundred and fifty miles inside the present boundary line of Argentina, and all of Uruguay was claimed by Brazil. It is little wonder that Uruguay later became the battleground of these two behemoths of South America.

King John III now viewed the handiwork of his distinguished noble and found it good, but not nearly good enough. Of what use were two measly centers, separated by fifteen hundred miles, in covering half a continent? But with the recent numerous expenses in India, the Royal Treasury was bankrupt. The banking houses of Europe probably had plenty of money, but it was not for the King of Portugal. How, then, could he undertake further colonization of Brazil? For if he did not do so quickly, the prize would soon slip from his grasp.

The policy which had already worked in the Azores and Madeira, and which was essentially the same policy followed by Spain, seemed to be worth a trial: let individual noblemen bear the expense and give them in return permanent land grants and governorships. It would be difficult to turn down a chance to become an almost absolute sovereign over a great domain and to be able to pass that along to one's heirs indefinitely. Even the Spanish grants did not include quite so much scope, but then Spain had found gold, the magic element whose alchemy converts everything it touches into action and power.

In 1534 the King's plan was carried out, and captaincies were awarded to twelve outstanding Portuguese nobles. Beginning at the north and heading southward down the coast, parallel dividing lines were marked off every so many miles. There was to be no limit inland. A man could go as far toward the west as he was able, bearing in mind only the Tordesillas line, the ultimate western boundary of the country. Even that might be ignored, as it was ignored when the time was ripe, and Brazil took by default a huge territory the size of half the United States on the other side of that line in order to attain her present dimensions.

The twelve noblemen accepted this plan with much fanfare. Their captaincies on the Atlantic would measure on the average two hundred miles of coast line, each man getting a width commensurate with his services to the Crown and with his ability to expend wealth. In this way the King hoped that at least the outer crust of the colony would be made secure from Portugal's sniping enemies.

He did not know his nobles. And for the most part he selected men who were too old for the rigors of colonization. When the first enthusiasm had worn off, most of them left their colonists to their own resources. There was soon no law or order in the majority of the captaincies; the riff-raff among the settlers started squabbling; Indians rose up in some quarters and wiped out settlements; new colonists did not want to join hands with old criminals, and the whole setup fell apart, leaving the coast wide open to attack and the serious colonists all but forsaken in the wilderness. Of the twelve captaincies only two prospered—Pernambuco, with its sugar cane in the north, and São Vicente with its settlements of Santos and São Paulo in the south. People everywhere were anxious to get back to Portugal.

In 1548 one of their leaders wrote to the King: ". . . if Your Highness does not help us in a hurry before we lose our lives and estates, Your Highness will lose the country." The same man went on to say that only a strong central government equipped with sufficient military force to demand respect and obedience could save Brazil from certain disaster. The King realized the urgency of the situation, and the next year he drastically limited the powers of the captaincies and appointed Thomé de Sousa, a nobleman who had won great respect in both Africa and the East Indies, as governor-general of all Brazil. He founded a new town at Bahia, between Pernambuco and São Paulo, and made that his capital. With him the country clearly entered the period of colonial history.

Spain and Portugal had won the physical victory in their conquest of the New World in considerably less than a century. In many ways this exploit calls to mind the legendary battle of David and Goliath. David won because his ingenuity gave him a superior weapon. But the conquest of America was not so immediately decisive as that. In this case it was as if those Davids of Spain and Portugal, the conquistadores, had knocked their colossal opponent over and were now sitting on him, but there was still fight left in his huge body and he was still able to give his victors some bad moments.

It would be absurd to pick out a date, any date, and say that the conquest stopped there, and afterward began the period of consolidation and colonization. But it helps to understand the picture if certain general movements are made clear. Columbus landed on an island in the Antilles. He later touched the Atlantic coasts of Central America and the so-called Spanish Main, which is the northern coast of South America. With an amazing mixture of intuition and good luck the Spaniards plunged immediately into the search for the crossroads of the New World which was the Isthmus of Panama. A colony was placed there in 1508, and in 1513 Balboa discovered the Pacific Ocean, thus opening the way to Peru and Chile.

The big sweep of the conquest soon got under way with Cortés in Mexico in 1519–21, and then moved southward. When the gold of Montezuma was exhausted the greater gold of Atahualpa drew interest to the south. The torch of conquest burned brightly until the entire South American continent had been explored and conquered for the Iberian Peninsula. By 1540 Mexico, Central America, and the northern part of South America, Peru, Colombia, and Venezuela were firmly in Spanish hands. In 1549, when Portugal sent a governor-general for all Brazil, this territory also was given a fairly stable colonial government. But in Chile and Argentina, which made up the southern part of the continent, the battle was still going on with unabated fury. Buenos Aires was abandoned in 1541 and was not refounded until 1580; and Valdivia, governor of Chile, was defeated and killed by the Araucanians in 1553. We might say that the most violent stage of the conquest in that region had not ended until 1580, when the city of Buenos Aires was re-established near the mouth of the River Plate.

The conquest of Latin America was not merely the last crusade, it was the only successful crusade in history. Never before or since did glory, gold, and Gospel offer so great a prize, or, to put it more plainly, land, labor, and capital, plus the enslavement and conversion of some twenty million heathen. It is clear that of this Holy Trinity the principal god was "gold." Gold became both a religion and a fever for the conquistadores. On the altar of El Dorado were laid the hopes of every soldier; and more often than not he ended by forgetting every consideration of which decent human beings are capable. Only three golden treasures were actually found in the New World—in Mexico, in Peru, and in Colombia; but to these must be added the later discovery of huge silver mines in Bolivia and Mexico. However, in those early days every man believed that treasures beyond conception were just over the horizon. For years people continued to believe in these treasures, and for years they were sought. If they did not exist it would have been necessary to invent them in order that the conquest might be carried out.

Spanish and Portuguese imagination did, in fact, conjure up numberless legends of great wealth, each with its ever-increasing gloss of descriptive details. In Colombia and Venezuela it was the legend of El Dorado. In Argentina and Chile it was the "City of the Caesars," which lay somewhere in desolate Patagonia. In Brazil it was the civilization of the Amazons. In northern Mexico and southern United States it was the Seven Cities of Cibola. But there were dozens of others, all of them alike in their houses and streets of gold, one at least for every region. The more difficult the road to be traveled, the greater the reward at its end. El Dorado became the state of mind without which the conquest might have been delayed for a century.

It was this state of mind which molded early Latin-American society and economy. When a man did not find gold he looked around for a substitute. It was land. And land was no good without labor. So he took both land and Indians and worked them to death so that they might produce as much gold as he had failed to find. At least that was the psychology involved. No amount of Christian benevolence, no number of human statutes could change it. One historian remarks that "every step of the white man's progress in the New World may be said to have been on the corpse of a native." This, of course, was even truer of the United States than it was of Latin America, not because the English colonists killed more Indians, for they did not, but because they consistently refused to assimilate the Indians into their society. The story of John Rolfe and Pocahontas, which is almost unique among us, was repeated thousands of times in Latin America.

But cruelty among conquistadores or among settlers who "carry the torch of civilization" to a more defenseless or a more primitive people was never a monopoly of any nation, nor of any race or creed. In those days it was so general as to make any exception open to ridicule. The finest, most Christian character among the Spanish leaders was Cabeza de Vaca, and his regime was a complete fiasco. Then, as now, too much idealism in government did not seem to work out, not because of any intrinsic error, but because it was too rare and had insufficient backing ever to be given a fair trial.

Looking back over those first years of the sixteenth century, we see that there were really two different types of conquest which would lead necessarily to two kinds of colonial society. In Mexico and Peru, and to a lesser extent in Colombia, the battle was against centralized Indian organizations with well-established agricultural economies and social systems. Once the central power was overcome the whole social structure gave up and accepted defeat. In these countries the conquest was rapid. In the second place, the natives who lived under these systems were accustomed to paying tribute and to doing work for their superiors. They were used to obeying. When the conquest was over they merely changed masters and continued more or less the same way of life. Therefore, Mexico and Peru were better organized to support colonists than the other regions and would inevitably become great centers of Spain's colonial government. Mexico City and Lima would be the leading administrative cities and the greatest centers of culture and wealth. In the third place, both Mexico and Peru produced not only golden treasures, but later great mines of both silver and gold from which a constant stream of wealth flowed toward Europe. This meant that the Viceroy's courts in their two capitals became places where a strong aristocratic society sprang up. Government officials, ecclesiastical dignitaries, and wealthy colonists were all drawn there, and the cleavage between them and the masses of primitive laboring people grew broader and deeper. A sense of fissure would come to characterize those countries.

The other type of conquest was carried out in Argentina, Uruguay, and Chile, where there were no strongly organized central governments to challenge and overcome. The battle there was against dozens of primitive Indian tribes who kept up a constant guerrilla warfare for many years. They would be defeated time and time again, but they could not be either liquidated or assimilated quickly. In this way there grew up in those countries a feeling of the frontier which did not exist in either Mexico or Peru. In their long-extended struggle to maintain themselves against the Indians, colonists from the peninsula were knitted together with a feeling of unity, equality, and nationality which would more quickly form them into homogeneous nations. This homogeneity was helped along by another factor. Since men who came to the River Plate or to Chile knew that they would be exposed to the rigors of military life, they rarely brought women with them. Under such circumstances a family would be a hindrance. But when the occasion arose—and if it did not arise they went after it—these men mated with Indian girls, and a large mestizo class was quickly produced.

Another thing which made assimilation more complete here than in Mexico or Peru was the relatively smaller number of Indians encountered. Besides, there was little gold in these countries, and the higher dignitaries were not drawn to them. A living had to be made out of the soil, and it was a slow and arduous process. This made their society more democratic, kept the cleavage between classes at a minimum, and prevented the domination of traditional and reactionary elements.

In Brazil, as in the River Plate and Chile, there was no centralized empire, relatively few Indians, and during the early years little gold or silver. A frontier existed, but it was so vast that it could not serve as a great unifying factor except in one special sense. Brazil was almost surrounded by Spanish colonies, and where it touched them the nationalistic feeling was bound to become strong. In addition to this there were French, Dutch, and English colonies planted on what she considered her own soil in the north, and which still exist in a much diminished size in the three Guianas. Brazil was frequently forced to fight against them all, and these conflicts were sufficient to make Brazilians of all classes nationalistic minded, even if it could not mold them into a homogeneous people.

In Brazil, a colossus in her own right, things moved along more slowly than in most parts of Spanish America. Lack of gold made her society agricultural from the beginning. When her Indian servants did not make good workers, millions of Negro slaves were imported to cultivate her lands. They formed the backbone of her national economy. Finally her plantations, like ours, were destroyed and her slaves were set free. The climate, the nature of the country, and the Portuguese race slowly brought about a fusion with these new Brazilians. The story of Brazil was not heroic, but it was steadfast, always moving in the right direction, even when the colossal shadows of her forest obscured it.

11

IBERIANS AND INDIANS

Spain and Portugal faced tremendous disadvantages when they undertook the colonization which followed the period of conquest. They were thinly populated countries with no excess population to send overseas. They were poor and lacked an overflow of wealth or of the products of industry to help finance and strengthen the development of the new territories. They were unified in their outlook on religion and politics and had no refugee minorities who might serve as immigrants.

Portugal's population was about 1,500,000 in 1492, and Spain's was approximately 10,000,000. The Inquisition had liquidated religious dissenters, and the absolutist states had liquidated political minorities. As for the products of agriculture or industry, these had been gravely lowered by the wholesale exodus of the Jews and Moriscos, the most industrious element of the peninsular population. It was a well-known remark of Charles V, who had traveled frequently in both France and Spain, "that everything abounded in France, but that everything was wanting in Spain." This was long before the peninsula reached its economic bottom.

The measures taken to overcome these disadvantages determined the course of Latin-American history throughout the colonial period. In order to make up for their small number of emigrants both Spain and Portugal attempted from the very first moment to incorporate the natives into their colonial society. In place of religious minorities who might have become Pilgrim Fathers of the new territories, the Iberians sent crusading priests, who were the shock troops of this work of assimilation and who became a more powerful factor in shaping Latin-American character than was the Puritan influence in the United States. For the peninsula's lack of material wealth two solutions were found, both of them good on the surface, both of them inherently bad in the end. The first answer was: borrow funds from the international bankers of Europe and repay them with American gold and silver. The second was to establish a strict commercial monopoly over the colonies so that whatever profits came of that trade would go into peninsular coffers.

Unlike England in North America, Spain and Portugal never attempted to establish small, slow-growing colonies which would be left to develop and govern themselves much as they saw fit. What they undertook was an imperialistic conquest in the Roman sense: to impose their languages, their religion, their culture, their way of life on millions of colonial subjects of a different race and level of civilization. Thus while every step of these two nations in Latin America was toward assimilating and utilizing the native inhabitants, the policy of the English settlers in the thirteen colonies was to regard them as strangers, enemies, or friends, as the case might be, but never as an integral part of the same state and of the same society.

A more accurate comparison might be drawn between the Iberian conquest of Latin America and that of the English in India. In this Asiatic region a small white nucleus struggled to impose itself over a tremendous native population. The results of any such comparison redound to the greater glory of Spain and Portugal, not to their detriment.

What Rome had accomplished in several centuries these nations repeated in a matter of decades. They expended themselves completely in the conquest and colonization of the New World. They made a frontal attack on the ever-present, ever-important problem of race relationship.

Racially, the Indian was the dominant element in Latin-American colonial life, and in many regions he still is. This proves that the conquest of Spain and Portugal was in one way, at least, less rigorous than the Anglo-Saxon conquest of the United States. But the difference is not nearly so great as it appears on the surface. Estimates of the Indian population of America at the time of the discovery vary greatly, but a fairly satisfactory average can be struck. A German geographer, Karl Sapper, states that both Americas could have supported a maximum population of forty to fifty million natives in 1492. Dr. A. L. Kroeber, of the University of California, makes an estimate of only 8,400,000. The Spanish priest Las Casas stated that about 15,000,000 Indians had been killed by his countrymen in the New World up to the year 1541. Another priest says that the Franciscans baptized 43,000,000 Indians in Mexico alone, and a would-be historian writes that 6,000,000 people assembled to witness the dedication of the great temple in Mexico City in 1486.[13] These figures, of course, are utterly fantastic. Even when Bernal Díaz, Cortés's captain, speaks of four hundred Spanish soldiers defeating fifty to a hundred thousand Indian warriors, we have to take his calculations with a grain of salt. These early writers were not trained statisticians, and any figure above ten thousand was to them a matter of the rankest guesswork. They were anxious to magnify their deeds and add to their glory.

But there are fairly accurate means of getting a reliable estimate. Angel Rosenblatt made a special study of primitive conditions of life in America at that time, the productivity of the land, and the amount of territory occupied by the various Indian groups. Carefully collating these conclusions, he arrives at a total population of 13,385,000 for both Americas. His estimate for Canada and the United States is 1,000,000 natives, for Mexico 4,500,000, for Central America 800,000, and for South America 6,785,000, with the greatest concentration where it still remains, in the Andean region. This would give the Inca territory a population of approximately 4,000,000. A contemporary Spanish American historian, L. A. Sánchez, takes Rosenblatt's figures and works them upward to a total of 20,000,000. The actual figure, which will never be known exactly, probably lies somewhere between these two estimates. In Latin America, then, we find a total of approximately 15,000,000 Indians as compared with only 1,000,000 for both Canada and the United States. These Indians were largely concentrated in two regions, Mexico and the Andean highlands, whereas in the United States and Canada they were rather thinly spread over the whole territory. Moreover, in these two Latin-American regions the natives were already organized into productive economic units used to obeying a central authority, while in North America they were still tribal and nomadic savages. The Indians who made up the heart of the Spanish Empire could thus be more readily incorporated into colonial life, and in fact they became so immediately indispensable as workers that the colonization would probably have been impossible without them.

In order to bring these strange red men and women into their orbit of life the Spaniards used every trump in the pack: deception and outright violence, sex, strict economic direction, religion, social and political domination, and the intangible forces of cultural assimilation. The conquest itself corresponds to the period of deception and outright violence. This approach never disappeared completely, nor could it ever disappear, under the imperialistic concept, but it was opposed and gradually eaten away by the other means of relationship as the colonial period got under way.

In regard to sex relations between Spaniards and Indians, they began the very first day Columbus set foot on American soil. Some of his men took out after the naked island beauties, who found this game of catch-as-catch-can most appealing. Amerigo Vespucci's men in Brazil encountered the same pleasant acceptance of their long-starved caresses. This type of intercourse and all that it signifies became the most powerful instrument for the propagation of peninsular culture in the New World. Millions of mestizos and mulattoes were produced, and in the Spanish America of today there are at least thirty million mestizos, while in contemporary Brazil approximately one fourth of the population has some Negro blood. In the Brazilian backlands Indian blood is also an important racial element.

This mingling of the blood of two different races was nothing new to the inhabitants of the Iberian Peninsula, nor was it by any means a mere expression of physical lust on the part of Latin men, though the fact that few white women came to Latin America in the early years of colonization did add great impetus to sex relations between these men from overseas and native women. But as a well-known Spanish historian points out, miscegenation had been current on the peninsula long before the conquest. "Everyone knows that the Moslems arrived in Spain [and Portugal] without women, and that their preference for beautiful and blonde *Gallegas** led to the occupation of the throne of Córdoba by caliphs with blue eyes and fair hair."[4] This mixing went on for several centuries and was taken for granted in most of the peninsula. It did not result in a deterioration or degeneration of either race, but, on the contrary, the caliphate of Córdoba in southern Spain during the tenth century, which was the product of the best which each race had to offer, represented the world's highest scientific and cultural flowering at a period when the rest of Europe was under the shadow of its darkest ages. With this history and this achievement before them, white men from the peninsula could not possibly feel that there was anything degrading in sexual relations with native women or the production of mestizo children.

The Portuguese attitude was essentially the same as the Spanish. Mixing with the Indians went on from the very first, but sex relations with imported blacks were looked down on for a while because the Negro had constituted a special slave class since the days of Prince Henry the Navigator. The feeling was more economic than racial and it soon disappeared under the stresses of Brazilian life.

This miscegenation was part of the conquest, in the long run its most powerful part. Indian blood was soon absorbed completely in the islands of the Antilles. The soldiers of Cortés slept with their native women (always after having them baptized) and started the mestizo race of Mexico. Cortés himself had his Malinche who bore him a distinguished son. It was the same with the followers of Pizarro in Peru. Of Argentine women, one of the original conquerors wrote, "They are beautiful in their way, and very well know how to sin in the dark." The soldiers of Irala, conqueror of Paraguay, received three Indian women each.

In Colombia the native girls took to their blond overlords from the first, and many of them left native husbands in order to remain with fair lovers from beyond the sea. When Quesada returned to Bogotá, after an absence of eleven years in Europe, he found that almost all of his old friends "lived with Indian women on land grants."[35] Both the King and the Church attempted to make marriage a prerequisite to obtaining such grants, and the Church fully sanctioned taking Indian women as wives. But in those early days the Spaniards, although they consorted and lived

* The word *Gallegas* means "women of Galicia." Galicia is a province in northwestern Spain.

openly with native girls as common-law wives, did not see the necessity of marrying them, and Quesada informed the King that "where there are in my belief three hundred land grants, there are not a dozen married men."[35]

In Chile the Spaniards took Indian women so freely to bed that "mestizos greatly exceeded the Spaniards in number before the end of the first half century after the conquest."[43] In Brazil the mixing between Portuguese men and Indian girls started when those first shipwrecked sailors who were cast upon the Brazilian shores took native mistresses and begot a numerous mestizo progeny called mamelucos. These Brazilian mestizos, especially in the district around São Paulo, became the most dynamic element in early colonial life and were the primary factor in enslaving the pure natives of the interior.

In general, the mestizo race was the product of "intercourse of white men and Indian women outside the pale of matrimony."[42] Few mestizo children were born of white women and Indian men. Besides the scarcity of white women in the colonies, and the ability of men to procreate so many more offspring than women, there was an economic reason for this. Children whose fathers were white acquired some of their sires' privileges and were exempt from paying tribute.

At first these mestizo offspring remained with their mothers, who gave them what little instruction they received and whose psychological attitude they absorbed. Therefore, for a few generations they appeared to be more like Indians than like Spaniards or Portuguese. It was this very fact which made them such an invaluable element in the spread of peninsular culture, for it goes without saying that, like all hybrid races, they wanted desperately to achieve the economic and social dimensions of their more favored blood. In their efforts to achieve this they became a perfect bridge between the two races, constantly representing the one before the other. Only in these regions where miscegenation was consummated to the fullest, completely wiping out both racial extremes, did the mestizo cease to be a bridge and become the mainland. But even as a bridge his importance was fundamental.

The Crown and Church both supported this race-mixing on a moral basis, that is, they encouraged and protected marriages between whites and Indians. An early law stated explicitly the state's wish "that Indian men and women should enjoy complete freedom to marry whomsoever they might desire, either aborigines or Spaniards, and that no impediment should be put in their way." It was in spite of this legal encouragement that most of the unions between natives and whites were out of wedlock. But, legitimate or illegitimate, the mestizo class soon came to form the majority of the population in the vicinity of nearly all civilized centers. Before two centuries had passed a well-known historian wrote: "It is chiefly by this mixed race, whose frame is remarkably robust and hardy, that the mechanic arts are carried on in the Spanish settlements, and other active functions in society are discharged, which the two higher classes of society, from pride or from indolence, disdain to exercise."[42]

It is impossible to overemphasize the difference between the Mediterranean attitude toward race and sex and that of Anglo-Saxon North America, for it is one of the two or three basic fissures which exist in this hemisphere. The Puritan, obsessed with sex, had illicit relations with women of a different class or race, but they were always clandestine, and if children were born he refused to recognize them and forced them outside the pale of organized society. So strong was this standard that even his consorts' own people generally followed him in this ostracism. In the warmer Latin regions, where for centuries miscegenation had been the rule rather than the exception, the men of better classes consorted openly with women of a different color, and they were tender to their children and generally took them to heart. It was the difference between a Puritan world, which places an act before a belief, a world in which the obsession of physical sin is paramount, and a warmer Mediterranean world, in which belief itself is paramount, and sin may always be overlooked and forgiven as a weakness of the flesh so long as the mind remains orthodox. Both worlds were equally intolerant, but in very different ways. The Puritan was intolerant of what he thought was an expression of his weakness, so his society became strong in muscle, bone, and fiber, but lacking in strong spiritual direction, hence it resulted in an inevitable fissure between the races.

On the other hand, the Latin was intolerant of a different thinking, and so his cultural and spiritual expressions have a mestizo unity and strength which in the very midst of poverty and illiteracy are often amazing, and his race problems were on the whole quickly moved toward a solution. But his religious, political, and economic structure was lamentably lacking in that willing tolerance to coexist with a different belief. An authoritarian society was the inevitable result. Both worlds have gradually grown away from their intolerant bases. The descendants of the Puritan now receive sex with a semi-scientific wisdom and ridicule the callow obsessions of their tight-lipped ancestors, while the hybrid descendants of the Latins have turned away from their Church in droves, rightly or wrongly identifying it with political reaction, bigotry, and economic oppression.

The different thinking and feeling embodied in this attitude toward sex and race have made the history of North and South America follow divergent paths which with time have grown even farther apart. These attitudes may not be the bases of our national lives, but they are certainly the bases of our cultural differences which will continue to remain at opposite poles until a greater tolerance or broader education brings them slowly together.

Back of this slow-moving force of miscegenation there existed in Latin America an even greater immediate force of economic necessity. The Spaniards and Portuguese had not occupied any tiny strip of territory like ours on the Atlantic, where a small coastal nucleus would gradually gather strength and expand until it finally embraced the breadth of a continent. By 1607, the date of our first permanent settlement at Jamestown, Virginia, they had already pushed themselves over an area many times as large as the entire United States of today. There were well over two hundred Latin-American towns in that territory. From the first it was obvious that if their dominion was to be maintained it had to be done with the help of the Indian. Any other attempt at a solution would have been foredoomed to failure.

12

THE DIVISION OF LANDS AND LABOR

For ten years after Columbus made his first landing in the West Indies there existed a state of near chaos on the island of Santo Domingo. The greed and violence of the early settlers had turned a gentle and peaceful population into bitter enemies. A regular civil war was being waged between colonists and natives, while famine and epidemics turned the whole colony into a miserable warren to which few Spaniards wanted to emigrate. In order to provide colonists, convicts under sentence of death were shipped to the island and, after two years of service, their crimes were automatically forgiven. The insular government was corrupt and inefficient, the natives intermittently fought and fled, and the colonists practically starved to death. Finally, in 1502, an old warrior monk named Ovando, who had formerly governed conquered Granada, was sent to restore productivity and order. With him began the economic organization of Spain's overseas dominions. A famous North American historian, Bourne, calls Ovando "a man of scrupulous integrity, of just and inflexible firmness in regard to the Spaniards; but implacable in unleashing horrible blows on the Indians when he was convinced, or even when he suspected that they were planning to rebel against his authority."[44] Ovando did his work so thoroughly that within a single year the island was again on a paying basis. A few years later, despite the terrible mortality among the natives, it had become a flourishing colony.

Ovando's expedition consisted of twenty-five hundred men, among whom was Bartolomé de las Casas, later to become the famous "Apostle of the Indies" and defender of the Indians. Ovando's orders from the Catholic Sovereigns were as follows: to be friendly with the natives, to convert them to Christianity and give them religious instruction, to collect tribute from them but to see that they were paid for their work, to prohibit their enslavement, to regard them as subjects of the Crown. It did not take Ovando long to see that if these orders were carried out the Spaniards on the island would find neither workers to serve them nor souls to save. In the first place, the natives were not used to steady labor; in the second, they had no idea of value, and the matter of receiving payment did not at all entice them; in the third, they had already been so badly treated by the Spaniards that if it were left up to them they would simply take to the woods and have no dealings whatsoever with the white intruders. Ovando reported to the home government that either the island would have to be abandoned or some way must be found "to force the Indians to work" in return for their instruction and their salvation, and incidentally so that they would produce enough to pay their tribute and keep the Spaniards provided with food.

In 1503 the Spanish Sovereigns gave Ovando authority to gather the natives into villages, if necessary by force, where they could be supervised by a protector. These villages were called "reductions." The Indians were to be given lands in the vicinity of their villages; there was to be a school in each where they were to receive instruction in the Catholic religion, the Spanish language, and in the elementary arts of civilization. Oppression on the part of their chieftains was prohibited, and their primitive idolatrous ceremonies were suppressed. In order that they might be more easily formed into productive economic units the natives "could be obliged to work in the construction of buildings, in gathering gold or tilling the soil," but in each instance they were to receive the salary which the governor indicated. The chiefs of the reductions had to furnish a certain definite number of workers for these purposes, but it was clearly stated that their labor was to be performed "as free men and not as serfs." Their Spanish protector or "trustee" had the duty of carrying out all of these orders, and in return for his management the Indians were made to pay him a small tax or tribute. Other groups of natives were obliged to cultivate the lands of the King, and their tribute went directly to him.

This was the beginning of the trusteeship, or *encomienda*, system in the Spanish New World. It went back to the Middle Ages, when peasants living in certain neighborhoods often "commended" themselves to the lord of the manor, rendering him specified personal services in return for his protection. In the New World whenever an allotment of Indians was commended to an *encomendero*, or trustee, the commitment usually ran something like this: "To you, John Doe, are commended such and such a number of Indians under chief so and so, in order that you may employ them on your lands or in your mines, and it is your duty to instruct them in the Spanish language and our Holy Catholic faith."[44] The encomenderos were supposed to be high-minded and God-fearing men who had rendered some service to the Crown.[45] However, they were usually noted for their military skill rather than for their culture or administrative talent.

The granting of an encomienda did not include ownership of the land itself. It gave the encomendero the right to collect tribute and to demand certain services of the inhabitants. It was a feudal fief. However, the soldier class also received grants of land, and so their encomienda privileges frequently filled out the pattern of lord and vassal, and in the minds of many historians the union of the two became inseparable.

On the island of Santo Domingo and throughout the Antilles, where the natives had never before done any steady work, the encomienda system was an unmitigated disaster. The lure of gold, untrained and recalcitrant workers, and Spanish cupidity all combined to bring about the rapid liquidation of the native islanders. Those who would not work were forced to do so or hunted down by packs of bloodhounds and slain. The population of Santo Domingo in 1492 had been at least one hundred thousand; by 1508 an estimated forty thousand Indians had been killed or had died of disease, and by 1548 no more than five thousand remained alive.

This lesson was not without its long-range advantages. Several Dominican priests who were on the island had observed the process of annihilation with horror and drew up a strong case against it. Bartolomé de las Casas was at their head. The Crown issued new altruistic laws in 1512, but so far as Santo Domingo was concerned it was too late and their effect was almost nil.

A few years later Cortés conquered Mexico, and his soldiers, who did not find as much gold as they would have liked, demanded as a substitution encomiendas of Indians who would pay them tribute. Against the King's orders, and contrary to the best judgment of Cortés, they were paid off in this manner. Not to be outshone by any of his men, Cortés then took the biggest encomienda of all for himself. The Spanish Crown was forced to recognize an accomplished fact.

There was no repetition of the tragedy of the Antilles. The natives of Mexico were "a hardy agrarian people, long inured to the exacting labors of the field and to the primitive feudalism of the native overlords."[45] They merely accepted a change of masters. The Spaniards began to realize that the greatest of all spoils in the New World was Indian labor, for with it everything else was obtainable, and without it everything would be lacking. The encomienda system spread to Peru, to Chile, to Argentina. The fate of the Indian was sealed. Indian labor and tribute, which first had been granted as privileges, now came to be demanded as rights. They were regarded with the same possessive spirit as private property and, as such, would be defended to the last drop of blood by those who profited from them.

In regard to the number of encomenderos and tribute-paying Indians we have some fairly accurate figures drawn up by an investigator named López de Velasco in 1574. In that year he estimated that out of about thirty-two thousand Spanish families in the New World, four thousand of them held encomiendas. A total of 1,500,000 Indians were paying tribute at that time, some of them to these encomenderos, others directly to the Crown. The latter group was increasing steadily at the expense of the former. Counting the priests and soldiers, there were an estimated one hundred and sixty thousand Spaniards in America at that time, and approximately five million Indians were regarded as "civilized," that is, as having been brought into the orbit of Spanish colonial life. This number included Indian children as well as adults.

The tribute which the natives were to pay was either to be in kind: corn, wheat, chickens, et cetera, or it might be in gold or silver. At first it was only two or three pesos a year, but later the amount increased three- or fourfold. Only males between the ages of eighteen and fifty were legally obliged to make this payment. It was against the law to sell wine in the native reductions, and Indians were not allowed to possess firearms or to ride a horse. Immediate authority over them was to be exercised by their own chieftains under the encomendero's direction.

The system did not sound bad on paper. Many priests supported it as being the only possible means of incorporating the natives into the white man's society. The fact was that large land grants had already been parceled out among the soldier-colonists, and land without labor did not mean prosperity but bankruptcy. The Indian immediately became the most indispensable element in agriculture, in domestic service, in mining, and in cattle raising. "He had to do everything, closely watched by his master."[43]

According to the law, encomiendas were to be granted for two generations, that is, to the original encomendero and his heir. However, this restriction was frequently overlooked if the heir rendered some service to the state. Otherwise the encomienda reverted to the Crown. As the grants were usually made to soldiers, the principal significance of the system was that the soldier class became also a class of feudal lords. These men were nearly always holders of land grants as well, who naturally carried the methods of warfare into the era of peace, ruling far too often by fear and force. In many regions Indian workers were directed by foremen armed with whips. Describing conditions in Chile, a historian of that country writes: "Neither women nor children nor the aged were exempt. All were obliged to devote their personal service to their masters. . . . At the least sign of languishing the lash fell on their shoulders. . . ."[43] The writer adds that thousands of Indians were transferred from their homes in the south to the northern regions, and each of them "had one foot cut off a little above the toe joints in order to make them incapable of flight."[43] In Argentina, Peru, and Mexico conditions were not so drastic, but they were bad enough. The Indian bore an uncomfortably close resemblance to the serf of the Middle Ages.

It was in view of these excesses that a group of priests who had seen the mutilation of the natives in Antilles rose up to defend them before the Crown. There were other defenders in the New World itself. Even in faraway Chile one priest was driven from his pulpit because he denounced the enslavement of the natives. In Mexico, Bishop Zumárraga stirred up a hornets' nest when he insisted on certain measures of elementary justice. But the man whose name has come down to us as the great defender of the Indians was the Dominican, Bartolomé de las Casas. Supported by a strong group who believed in his principles, but opposed by other priests who defended the *status quo*, Las Casas gave his entire life to the unfortunate Indian. It was largely as the result of his efforts that it became the established policy of the Crown to stand between the native and his rapacious overlord, affording such protection as was possible.

Las Casas had come over to Santo Domingo in 1502 with Ovando and had settled down on the island with a grant of land and an allotment of Indians like the other colonists. Later, when he became convinced that the encomienda system was morally wrong, he willingly gave up his estate and in 1510 became the first priest ordained in the New World. He soon found that many other priests and nearly all landowners formed a strong numerical majority against him when he spoke of protective legislation. They did not want any laws which would seriously interfere with the new gold mine of human labor to which they had so quickly become accustomed, and his steps in defense of the Indians were blocked at every turn.

Finally Las Casas appeared before the King himself, and his plea was so eloquent that new laws were passed (1542) which stated that encomenderos could not demand personal services of Indians, but only tribute. The King and Las Casas were attempting in this way to suppress the encomiendas, but the colonists rose up in wars against them and refused to obey the new statutes. Personal representatives sent by the Crown to enforce these regulations in Mexico found that they were hitting their heads against a stone wall. The majority of the priests joined heartily in the general rebellion and cried that if the throne took from them the means they had been employing for their support, they would abandon the Church.

The same thing happened in Colombia or New Granada. The Viceroy of Peru, however, tried to enforce these regulations, and the encomenderos, headed by Gonzalo Pizarro, rebelled, organized a larger army than the Viceroy himself could muster, met the latter in a pitched battle, and riddled him with bullets. They then cut off his head and displayed it on top of a pole in the central plaza of Quito, near which city the battle had taken place. Only after a severe struggle was Gonzalo himself defeated and executed. A similar rebellion occurred in Central America. The Crown acted quickly to suppress these revolts, but as promptly revised the New Laws in favor of the encomenderos. It was not enough to suit the feudal lords. Again a rebellion broke out in Peru only ten years after the last one. This time the encomenderos raised the cry of "liberty," which clearly meant "liberty" to do as they pleased with the Indians. Again they were defeated and their leader executed. In spite of this ways were always found to pervert the law, and although the condition of the Indian was somewhat ameliorated by the government and by the Church, he continued in a state of servitude. Nevertheless, the New Laws were not entirely ineffective. They resulted in the liberation of thousands of Indian slaves, sixty thousand being freed in Mexico alone, and they put the encomenderos on notice that their privileges were under scrutiny. For a time it looked as if the Crown really meant business, but in the long run the victory turned out to be a hollow one, for enforcement of any law which was against the interest of the landed aristocracy was impossible.

Throughout all these squabbles Las Casas was the true "Defender of the Indians." He even went so far as to tell the Emperor that if the natives were entrusted to the Spaniards in any way, "no matter how many laws, statutes, or penalties are imposed, your Majesty will see that it is the same as if it were decreed that America be made a desert." It was natural for the good priest to be regarded as a "troublemaker" by the majority of the Spanish colonists during his own lifetime. Yet in spite of the success which rewarded his first efforts of kindness and gentleness among the natives, and the statutory improvements which his pleas caused to be passed, Las Casas was guilty of two mistakes which in some measure detract from his blasting indictment of Spanish cruelties and of the encomienda system. His first mistake was to suggest that Negro slaves and Spanish peasants be brought to America in greater numbers to do the type of work for which the natives were not fitted, mainly agriculture and mining. Negro slavery had been taken so for granted that Las Casas thought of it by second nature. Thousands of black-skins were actually imported into the Caribbean area. Later in life, "with deep regret and humiliation," Las Casas confessed that he had made a very grave error in suggesting this measure because "the same law applied equally to the Negro as to the Indian." So far as bringing Spanish peasants to America to till the soil was concerned, there were none among them who wanted to come to the New World to carry on the old way of life.

The second error of Las Casas was the glibness with which he produced huge figures of slaughtered natives—estimates which at best could have been only the rankest guesses, and which in fact were oftentimes so exaggerated as to be absolutely ludicrous. His essay, *The Destruction of the Indies* where these figures are stated, was finished in 1542 and published in 1552. It was almost immediately translated into all of the principal languages of Europe. In this work Las Casas claimed that the Spaniards had killed about twelve million Indians since the conquest, not counting those slain in the struggle itself. The grand total up to 1541 was fifteen to twenty million dead Indians—somewhat more than the total native population of both Americas at that time from Alaska to Patagonia. Four million were killed in Mexico alone, Las Casas said, during the twelve years after the invasion by Cortés. His exaggerations favored the natives in still another way, for he stated that while no Spaniards had estimated the number of yearly sacrifices among the Aztecs at less than twenty thousand, "this is the estimate of brigands, who wish to find an apology for their own atrocities, and the real number was not above fifty!" Other persons who were on the scene and knew that this figure was ridiculous did not hesitate to say so. Las Casas even went so far as to rebut his own reporting. In his *History of the Indies,* one of the fundamental works to come out of those early days, he wrote that a Spanish soldier killed ten thousand Indians with his lance in one hour, that is, one hundred and sixty-seven Indians a minute, or three a second—quite a record even for a modern machine gun. His calculations are more reasonable and agree with other fair-minded estimates when he speaks of those slain on the island of Santo Domingo, where he had an opportunity to observe the liquidation of the natives at first hand. In the long run, most of his fine efforts, even when embodied in royal statutes, ran against the grain of his times and came to nothing. Las Casas himself was offered the wealthy bishopric of Cuzco as a reward for his labors, but he refused to take it and continued his work among the poor natives of Central America. He returned to Spain in his seventies and died there at the age of ninety-two, after having ameliorated, as much as any one man possibly could, the harsh excesses of his countrymen in the New World.

Unfortunately, Father Las Casas was an exceptional individual who did not believe in imperialism, yet lived in an age when nearly everyone else did. Like most of the world's great humanitarians, he was crucified by the "compact majority" of his fellow men. The idea back of the encomienda system, which he and a good many other priests unsuccessfully opposed, was to establish a workable and stable economy—one which would utilize the huge native population, gradually incorporating a larger and larger proportion into the new society. This was undoubtedly one way of solving the problem. It did not work out in the islands of the Antilles because the natives were simply not used to hard labor and were quickly killed off. In Mexico and Peru, where they were already organized into fairly well-disciplined productive units, the encomienda at least served its purpose. In some parts of Mexico it was probably better than the tyranny of Aztec slavery, tributes, taxes, and human sacrifices which preceded it. It was also humanely superior to the war of annihilation which the North American colonists waged against the Indians in the United States, a war which is still glorified in American textbooks and histories as being forced on the white man by the violent savagery of the native population. William Penn, who tried a different method in his colony of Pennsylvania, found that brotherly love would work even among savages. A somewhat similar method was to be given a widespread trial a little later in Latin America in the mission settlements, but in the beginning the encomienda embraced both civil and religious authority, and the encomendero was the original lay missionary in the New World.

The essay which Las Casas published in 1552, however, was seized upon by Englishmen and Hollanders, the other two great imperialists of those days, who of necessity were then playing second fiddle to Spain, as expressing the very epitome of Spanish cruelty in the New World, a cruelty, they shouted, which was characteristic of the Inquisition, of Spanish character itself, of the "papists" in general, but of course not of themselves. William the Silent of Orange and Henry VIII had already broken the back of international Catholicism in their countries and had established national churches in its stead. All Protestants viewed Catholicism askance, but those of England and Holland, with organized state support, spat vituperation on the papacy and the kings of Spain. Economic rivalry and the envy felt for the more immediately successful Spanish imperialism gave to their campaign of mudslinging a tinge of out-and-out propaganda. The Spaniards have a word for it—one which has burned deeply into the flesh of their people. They called it "the black legend," the legend of blackmail and lies which was based on the assumption that everything Catholic and Spanish was bigoted, bestial, degenerate, and inquisitorial, while everything Protestant was in protection of the broader way of life, and such slips as did occasionally occur were intrinsic to the process, but not to the warmer ideal embodied therein. This heritage has been passed down to us by Protestant historians of those bigoted days, and in many quarters is still taken at face value.

One incident in regard to the publication and reception of Las Casas's essay on the oppression of the Indians will show how this propaganda worked. The exact title of the book in Spanish was *Very Brief Account of the Destruction of the Indies*. When it was translated into English the title became: *Bartolomé de Las Casas; The Tears of the Indians, being a true account of the cruel massacres and slaughter of about twenty millions of innocent people*, London, 1556. It became one of the most widely read books of the times, and was considered as one of unquestioned authority, for a bishop had written it indicting his own people. Forty-two foreign editions of the work appeared during the next century—an incredible number for that illiterate epoch. Many of these were decorated with illustrations of dogs running down and eating Indians, and of cruelties of all sorts inflicted upon the non-resistant natives. The whole upshot of this early but very effective polemic and propaganda was to leave the people in general with the idea that any means which England or Holland took to counter these cruelties would have a thorough justification.

Las Casas and his supporters could not kill the encomienda system, but they did undermine it. The Indians were given official protectors; special investigators were sometimes sent to examine into cases of flagrant injustice; even the Viceroy and Supreme Court sometimes acted against the encomenderos and in favor of the natives. Representatives of the Crown and many of the clergy, especially those who resided in the Indian villages, defended their charges vigorously. The whole trouble was that things had a way of slipping back to economic rock bottom. The colonists demanded Indian labor, and neither the King nor anybody else could prevent their getting it. Before long a considerable proportion of crown officials and of the clergy gave up trying and stuck their hands in the grab bag along with everybody else.

Between 1542 and 1600 the Crown made several attempts to abolish the enforced labor of encomienda Indians. Almost no headway could be made in Chile, Argentina, and Paraguay, where money was scarce and labor was poor. In Mexico and Peru, however, the measure was carried out pretty generally. Indians were to pay tribute only, and when they worked they were to receive wages. Unfortunately, for the second time this approach failed to work just as it had in Santo Domingo many years previously. Well-meaning officials found themselves right back where they had started. The Indians simply did not want to work for wages; they had no conception of money, no idea of property, no desire to accumulate, no acquisitive instinct. And the work had to be done or the colonial economy would come to a standstill. The system of *allotting* natives to certain tasks was begun. Under this system a specified proportion of Indians was assigned to agricultural labor, to mining, to building, and so forth. They had to work a specified length of time out of the year and were to be paid certain set wages, which were generally a microscopic ten to twenty cents a day. In order to obtain such workers the employer had to appear before the authorities and state his case. If it was decided that the work he wanted performed was "for the good of the commonwealth" (and it was generally so decided) he was allotted his quota of Indians. The clergy as well as the colonists and the government officials were eligible to obtain labor in this manner.

By the end of the sixteenth century—that is, around the year 1600—the number of private encomiendas had already decreased considerably in the two most thickly populated regions of Mexico and Peru. Many of them had lapsed to the Crown, and those which remained had become merely sources of "pensions" for a few privileged aristocrats. The encomienda in these colonies was no longer a labor system, that phase of it having been replaced by the allotment, or *repartimiento*, idea. However, the encomienda was not formally abolished until 1720.

In the meantime another and much more iniquitous system had sprung up. Many owners of large land grants had in one way or another pushed the native inhabitants off onto poorer and less productive soil. Unable to make a living on these poorer lands, much less pay their tributes from them, considerable numbers of Indians drifted to the large estates as workers. Sometimes, for reasons of economic security, they gave up trying to cultivate their own lands. In order to make a good thing stick, the land-owners then lent their charges money or goods, and so long as these debts were unpaid the workers were not allowed to leave the estate. This was the so-called debt-peonage system which was the origin of the great haciendas. Thus when compulsory labor was abolished by law it had little effect on the actual state of the Indian, who was no longer a free man.

The whole process was a vicious circle which first made the Indian a slave, then a vassal, then a peon. The names were different, but the ex-ploitation was identical. Progress toward a wage-paying economy was being made all the time, but at a snail's pace. At the end of the colonial epoch (1803) Baron Humboldt made much of the fact that for thirty or forty years previously all miners in Mexico had been paid wages and could work, quit their jobs, or change their employers as they might wish. This was one of the few cases of a real wage-paid laboring group in Latin America before the era of independence. Everywhere else the landed gentry had wiped out "labor agitation" with a stern hand and always found some way to enthrall their workers. The only refuge of the Indian was to enter a mission or, if he was fortunate enough to live off the beaten track, to con-tinue his old communal life without benefit of civilization. Both were stopgaps on the road to ultimate assimilation. Race-mixing afforded his only true haven, for by losing himself in the mestizo stream he became a part of the civilized community of his white overlords. The position of the pure Indian was not permanently improved to any considerable degree throughout the colonial epoch.

The division of colonial society into the two extremes of landlords and day laborers was now becoming clearer with each passing year. One group had property, the other did not. One group worked, the other did not. One group enjoyed economic and social privileges, the other did not. The old curse of Spain's own agricultural economy: the *latifundia*, or huge estate, had been transported to the New World with a vengeance. Once started on its path of concentration of landownership in a few favored hands, it moved with a startling rapidity. Every phase of American life was on a magnified scale, and landowning was the biggest business of all. Another old Spanish legal custom, the *mayorazgo*, gave it a boost all along the way; that is, the custom of entailing estates or of making ownership of them *inalienable*. In other words, such land could not be sold, for it represented the very heart of family name and privilege.

As soon as the colonist acquired a fortune, writes one authority, "he would seek a title of nobility and with his title would go the estate, which must then remain undivided. Distinguished services to the crown were also rewarded by the bestowal of a title, accompanied by the creation of a *mayorazgo*, and often by a large grant of land or of tribute villages. It was this custom of forming *mayorazgos*, a custom which prevailed until the era of independence, that was largely responsible for the preservation of large estates in Mexico. Aggregation was constantly going on; division of property was almost impossible."[129]

The mayorazgo was not merely a symbol, it was the proof and the life of the gentleman's honor and the gentleman's income. Each inalienable estate was passed down from father to oldest son, never divided up among the several children, but, on the contrary, always becoming larger and larger, snuffing out small farmer and middle class alike and exaggerating the economic extremes that already existed. One great abiding and mammoth difference between the United States and the Latin-American nations is that most of the land in this country was not settled until *after* independence from England. The true pioneer and small farmer then came into his own. But in Latin America a great proportion of the best land was doled out and formed into huge estates during the colonial epoch. When independence finally came it faced the accomplished fact of concentrated landownership, which nothing less than a complete economic revolution could alter. Latin America was not prepared to undertake any such revolution at that time; independence alone had to be enough.

13

THE EMPIRE CONSOLIDATED

As soon as the period of conquest was terminated in a given region the King replaced the conquistador's martial law with a civil government appointed directly by the Crown. The monarch knew that a victorious general did not make an obedient subaltern. For the first few years this civil government consisted of a tribunal called an *Audiencia*. The term itself, derived from the Latin *audire* (to hear), came to embrace the broader meaning of Supreme Court with special executive functions. The members of the Audiencia were called *oidores*, or hearers.

The first Audiencia appointed to rule in Mexico (1528) was made up of as unscrupulous a band of ruffians as ever sat in judgment anywhere in the New World. Prodded on by the example of their chairman, who wanted to carve out a little kingdom of his own, the oidores of this tribunal cast aside all sense of duty to Emperor, God, and fellow man. They strengthened their hands for evil "by usurping the functions of the ordinary ministers of justice, and in order to conceal their iniquities, suppressing all letters that contained complaints of their conduct."[25] One historian refers to this period as the "gangster interlude" of early Mexican history.

The Bishop of Mexico, Juan de Zumárraga, tried unavailingly to remedy the disastrous and arbitrary rule of these men. Finally he drew up a document which indicted them in detail and managed to smuggle it out of the country in a hollow wooden image sent back to Spain as an example of native art. The gangster judges were then replaced by upright men of exceptional administrative ability.

However, government could not continue long under so many heads. The governing authority was divided, responsibility did not fall upon any one individual, and administration was made most difficult. The situation called for a responsible executive armed with full powers to deal with troublesome conditions as they arose. It was decided to select such an executive from the nobles at court, one "whose birth and position would insure his loyalty, and act as a safeguard against malfeasance."[25] The Emperor did not want any more of the conquistador type of ruler who would defy the central authority. He wanted a competent but obedient subordinate to "represent his royal person" in the New World. Above all he wanted a man who would not undertake to decide matters of great moment without first sending back home for the monarch's instructions.

Such was the origin of the viceroy system, and such was the character of the great majority of the men who became viceroys in the Spanish colonies during the sixteenth century. As time passed their caliber deteriorated and their corruption increased.

Throughout the first two colonial centuries there were only two viceroyalties in the Spanish New World: New Spain (Mexico) was organized on this basis in 1535, and Peru was placed in the same category in 1542. In the eighteenth century two more regions were raised to viceregal status: New Granada (Colombia) in 1718, and the River Plate (Buenos Aires) in 1776.

The Spanish colonies were regarded as being the personal property of the King, rather than as belonging to the nation as a whole. The Viceroy, therefore, was a sort of satrap or proconsul sent out to rule in the King's name and in his favor. He was the overseer of a huge kingdom and was armed with tremendous delegated authority. The term of office of the viceroys was deliberately limited (at first to three and later to five years) so that there would not spring up too great a desire for personal power. This perhaps did give the Crown a more complete control of the overseas dominions, but it also took away a great part of the urge to viceregal achievement. The King shortened or lengthened the number of years of a viceroy's appointment if it so suited his judgment.

The two great "kingdoms" of the Spanish New World, New Spain (Mexico) and Peru, were much larger then than now. New Spain included all of Central America and a great part of the western and southwestern United States; Peru included all of Spanish South America. The salary of the Viceroy of Mexico was 20,000 ducats (about $45,000) a year, and the Viceroy of Peru, considered to be even a higher post, received 30,000 ducats ($65,000). These figures show the ducat calculated in gold content only; in terms of purchasing power of most daily necessities the value would be considerably higher. The King had granted these fabulous incomes in order to discourage graft, but rare indeed was the viceroy who returned to Spain with only his savings in salary. Connivance and political corruption were taken for granted by most of them, and when the judicial review of the term in office came around as the Viceroy was ready to depart, he was in most cases able to buy off those who might be disposed to tell on him. The great financial abyss which separated the Viceroy from his humbler servants can be gathered from comparing the former's yearly income with the meager $300 a year paid the soldiers of his private guard. Their captain and commander received a mere $600.

To all intents and purposes a viceroy of the Spanish colonial empire was a king while he was in the New World. The only great limitation on his power was the time limit involved. He could be retired at any moment, and his term in office was never long enough for him to become completely entrenched. Yet "all other officers and subjects, ecclesiastical and secular, were ordered to respect and obey him as the representative of the king."[46] He was president or chief justice of the Supreme Court and commander in chief of the army. "In the exercise of his powers he maintained the state and dignity of royalty. His court was formed upon the model of that of Madrid, with horse and foot guards, a household regularly established, numerous attendants, and ensigns of power, displaying such pomp as hardly retained the appearance of delegated authority."[46]

The Spanish monarch, it is true, held a sword over his head, but it was too distant to be very effective. And his power was supposed to be diluted and checked by both the Audiencia and by the judicial review of his term held when he retired. "But any beneficial effect which this might have had in protecting the people was counteracted by the inordinate power of the viceroys, and their consequent means of influencing the *Audiencia*, and every other subordinate authority, civil, military, judicial, or ecclesiastical."[46] Occasionally one of these subordinate authorities did get out of hand, and there were several clashes, always over economic or jurisdictional issues, between the viceroys and the ecclesiastical dignitaries.

Theoretically, the viceroys were all personally appointed by the King and were responsible only to him. However, the Council of the Indies, which had been established in 1524, acted as a clearinghouse for their appointments and for all matters relating to them. This body of specialists in colonial affairs advised the King, received the viceregal reports from overseas, suggested courses of action, and frequently took the initiative in both legislative and executive matters. The viceroys and their subordinate governors or captains-general were watched over like hawks, and every possible safeguard was thrown around them to prevent the usurpation of authority. While in the colonies "they could not contract marriage . . . , nor be godfathers, nor receive gifts, nor assist at private celebrations, except in an official character." They were strictly prohibited from "having any private business whatever."[43]

These checks and balances were well intended, but it was difficult to keep them functioning smoothly. All of the strings went back to Madrid, where the King tried to hold them personally. Philip II, that stern and tireless zealot who worked in his office twelve to fifteen hours a day for over fifty years, did gather most of them into his own hands. Perhaps that was why he had better viceroys than any other ruler of the House of Hapsburg. But it was impossible even for Philip to oversee so many men and so many tasks without both his files and his minions sometimes getting the better of him. Graft and self-willed colonial governments thwarted many of his best-laid totalitarian schemes. The King never gave up. He pulled his strings like a master of marionettes and tried to keep every appointee bouncing about the great stage of the Spanish Empire responsive to his slightest whim. Yet the harder Philip worked the more he got behind. Finally, a tired and broken man, he retired to the great stone Escorial which he had constructed as a sepulcher for Spanish royalty, and there, from his bed, with painful open ulcers covering his body, he watched the rehearsal of his own funeral. It was a symbol of Spain's doom.

This was the man who consolidated, organized, and gave final form to Spanish colonial government. Several years before he came to the throne Philip was placed in charge of colonial affairs, and as "the chosen of God" he wanted America to bear the indelible stamp of his royal will. Not even a viceroy was to be trusted completely. It was the special duty of the ecclesiastical authorities and the members of the Audiencia "to watch the governors, take care of each other, and give an account to the King of what they observed and considered worthy of his knowledge."[43]

Other observers or examiners with high-sounding titles, such as royal investigators (pesquisadores), visitors (visitadores), and seers (veedores), were sent out by the King from time to time in order to make personal reports to him as to what was going wrong and who was to blame. And when the viceroy or governor retired from office he was subjected to a public hearing before a lawyer appointed by the King, who acted as a sort of one-man court before whom all who had grievances could air them. This review, or residencia, of his term in office could become a very onerous matter, but the viceroys usually were able to buy themselves free. One viceroy of Peru compared this review with "one of those little whirlwinds we see in the streets which only raise up a lot of dust and other needless filth and blow it in our faces."[44] Sometimes, if the Viceroy enjoyed sufficient favor back at court, he didn't have to face a residencia at all. Had it not been for the great distance separating the colonies from the homeland and for the poor system of communications in those days, it might be said that the kings of Spain had about as vigorous a spy system as any modern totalitarian government. By pulling a single one of his fingers the monarch could jerk any governor in America off his pedestal, slap him into prison, or send him to the gallows.

The result of all these snoopings was to prod the Viceroy into finding some way of getting around them. This gave rise to an unhealthy body politic which made effective and progressive rule next to impossible. Each unit often came to distrust every other unit, and the people themselves were given almost no opportunity for expression or for learning or expanding the machinery of self-government. Nothing comparable to the old New England "town meetings" existed in Latin America. The nearest approach to them was in the town councils, or *cabildos*, which were molded on the relatively democratic town councils of Spain before the time of Charles V. The conquistadores revived this old Spanish institution in the New World. The duty of the cabildo was to look after the public works, to exert a small judicial authority, and to express the general consensus on certain issues of municipal government.

In the beginning the cabildo was made up of members selected by the governor, and thus became a sort of colonial House of Lords. During the first colonial century these "men of property" were allowed a considerable autonomy in running their towns. When these appointees retired from office they were supposed to choose their successors, but sometimes the governor interfered. Later, in many regions, the offices were put up for sale at public auction, at first for a temporary period, and after 1606 for a lifetime. The incumbent could retire at will and appoint his successor or sell his place for whatever price he could get for it. These cabildos did occasionally challenge the governors, but they rarely succeeded in expressing the popular will except on matters of slight importance until near the end of the colonial period.

In the face of all these counterbalances, restrictions, and spyings it is a wonder that the Viceroy enjoyed any real power at all, yet he was in fact as well as in name the vice-king and, if he were a man of ability and drive, often came near to being a supreme dictator in his own region. Separated by distance and time from his monarch, and enjoying the nominal headship of both the civil and religious authorities under him, the Viceroy usually managed to keep the worst from happening to him. At the same time, by hook or crook, connivance and compromise, he was able generally to amass for himself quite a neat private fortune during the few brief years of his administration. This graft was accepted as a matter of course even by the King, who wanted to keep his colonial satraps so satisfied that they would have no desire to poach on his own royal income.

Furthermore, if the Viceroy was prohibited from marrying or socializing too much, there was always the possibility of a young and luscious concubine, and few viceroys turned that possibility down. When people began to whisper too loudly a succulent bribe passed out now and then among the less faithful, in the form of a government job, generally quieted things down. The wealth and territories under each viceroy were many times greater than those of most European monarchs, and even the many strings tied around the office were only placed there to prevent the usurpation of authority—an unlikely contingency which seldom arose, or at least which seldom ever got back to the ears of the King.

With the example of his monarch before him, and with his very appointment usually the result of some pull at court and rarely dependent on ability alone, the Viceroy swam with the current and with few exceptions set an example of stupid or at least of inept government, which kept his domains marking time throughout most of the colonial epoch. Under him the lesser cogs and puppets floated along in the same stream, disdaining the honest and just use of authority, intent only upon those abuses of power which would redound to their personal benefit. For nearly three centuries this was the symbol of government which the peoples of Latin America had before them.

During the sixteenth century less than half a dozen viceroys were outstanding. The best known among these were Antonio de Mendoza, first Spanish Viceroy in the New World, who ruled Mexico from 1535 to 1550, Francisco de Toledo, fifth Viceroy of Peru, and the two famous Luis de Velascos, father and son, both of whom achieved distinction in the administration of Mexico. These men left the imprint of their characters on the regions in which they ruled and made possible the organization of colossal new territories on a colonial basis which endured for two hundred and fifty years. Most of the viceroys who followed them were corrupt or colorless men who showed little disposition toward good government. The later Hapsburgs sought such figures deliberately in order to have governors who might not be likely to strike out on their own.

The epoch of viceroys and colonial courts began with Antonio de Mendoza, scion of one of the noblest Spanish families, who came to Mexico City in 1535 to rule in the name of the Emperor Charles. He was a man of integrity, well fitted to initiate the viceregal regime in the New World. "Austere of habit, and abstemious to a degree that was injurious to his health, he was ever faithful in the discharge of his duties, and none of his successors felt more keenly the responsibilities of a difficult and by no means enviable position."[25]

The country was in turmoil when Mendoza arrived. Cortés, Alvarado, and other encomenderos had already taken a strong stand against the official government, and the Indians were on the verge of open revolt. Little by little the new Viceroy put down his clamps, carefully playing each party against the other. When the Indians rebelled he took to the field in person and defeated them. The authority of Cortés he undermined piecemeal, never exposing his hand, and Alvarado was finally slain while fighting the Indians. The Viceroy appropriated his men and equipment, thus entrenching his own position.

In 1542, just as Mendoza was getting a grip on things, the famous New Laws, for the preservation of the Indians, were approved, and a couple of years later they were brought into the country by a special representative of the King, who was entrusted with announcing and enforcing them. The encomenderos got wind of what was in the offing and decided to go out and greet the royal visitor in heavy mourning. Mendoza dissuaded them, but he could not allay their fears. The visitor insisted on promulgating the New Laws, and civil war seemed imminent, but Bishop Zumárraga announced from the pulpit of the cathedral that these laws would not be enforced if it was determined that they "were opposed to the interests of the Spaniards." The Viceroy also refused to push the issue, and the royal visitor was left without a foot to stand on. "The settlers took hope not only from the address of the bishop but also from the knowledge that the clergy were holders of important *encomiendas,* and that their interests in them were likely to weaken their natural loyalty to the crown. The ecclesiastics were, with very few exceptions, in favor of continuing the system of *encomiendas* and opposed to the liberation of the Indians. With the church as an ally, the *encomenderos* had very good grounds for believing their cause was not hopeless."[46]

Their arguments were simple but effective: we fought and sweated blood in order to win these lands and encomiendas; they now constitute our estates and the productive power of the nation; take them away from us and the country as a whole will suffer even more than we. The Viceroy Mendoza saw the necessity of temporizing, spared Mexico a devastating civil war, and, by delaying action, cautiously led her into a regime of unity and order. He continued to hack away at the power of the encomenderos with telling but indirect blows. His personal generosity and lavish hospitality, however, won many of them over to his side. On one occasion he is said to have given a banquet for about five hundred guests at which the principal dish was "huge pastries filled with live quail and rabbits which afforded much merriment when these animals escaped." Such great gestures made Mendoza personally popular with all the ruling caste. On his retirement he confided to his successor that "the secret of good ruling was to do little, and to do that slowly."

Another custom adopted by Mendoza helped greatly to win the native population over to his side. This was to set aside one day each week to hear Indian grievances. Hundreds of Indians "took advantage of the privilege of seeing the viceroy in person, and he listened patiently to their harangues. There is no record of his having done anything spectacular about them, but the wisdom of the custom was manifest."[45] In fact, the practice became so well established that a few years after Mendoza's retirement it took up so much of the Viceroy's time that a General Indian Court, which endured for over two centuries, was set up to replace it.

When Mendoza left Mexico it was a well-organized colony, the last fierce vestige of Indian resistance had been put down, Cortés had returned to Spain in disgust and the great power of the conquistadores was broken, the territory had been carefully explored, the Philippine Islands had been added to the empire, rich mines of silver had been discovered and were already pouring out their wealth. The viceregal power now stood unquestionably supreme over all others. From a disorderly territory of squabbling and embittered factions a great colony had been molded. After his fifteen years' service in Mexico the King asked Mendoza to become Viceroy of Peru; he died only a few months after his arrival in that country.

His successor in Mexico, Luis de Velasco, occupied his post for nearly as long a time as Mendoza himself, and continued the early beginnings of good government. Under Velasco the modified New Laws were carried into effect, and thousands of Indian slaves were freed. The Viceroy appointed upright judges to assist him who were "as stern and incorruptible as himself." He sent forth many exploring expeditions, extended the authority of the central executive, and won not only the love of the Indians but the title of "The Emancipator," which was spontaneously accorded him. When Velasco died in office "very poor and in debt," the cathedral chapter of Mexico wrote to Philip II that his death was deeply mourned by all classes, "for he governed with such prudence and rectitude, doing wrong to none, that all looked up to him as a father."[45]

Twenty-six years later Velasco's son was appointed as the eighth Viceroy of Mexico; after that he was made Viceroy of Peru and then returned to Mexico to serve a second term. In every way he carried forward the fine traditions of his father.

In the meantime the viceroyalty of Peru had been rent asunder by the civil wars of the Almagros and Pizarros; its vast Indian population was restless under the yoke; its encomenderos, after having been twice defeated in the field, were still defying the central government; its Audiencia had usurped the Viceroy's executive power and was now making a mess of running the country. In 1569 Philip II sent Francisco de Toledo to Lima to occupy this difficult post.

No viceroy ever took his job more seriously, and few were as competent and hard-working as Toledo. First of all he landed about six hundred miles north of Lima and made the rest of the journey overland in order to inspect that part of his territory. It was a tedious and long-drawn-out trip, but when it was over Toledo entered Lima with no illusions about the work before him. Peru was a disorganized mass of regions and classes, set off one against the other, so that a general disrespect for law and order prevailed. Toledo plunged into his task almost as if the spirit of King Philip were standing over him.

In the first year he established the Inquisition. Then he started on a series of trips which eventually took him to all of the principal towns of the Andean region and through an infinite number of Indian villages. He made a careful study of Inca history and social organization, forced scattered villages to come together in larger nuclei, let them have their own native chiefs, and through these managed to bring most of the natives into the Spanish orbit of life. Toledo was certainly no paragon of virtue but, like Mendoza, he was one of the few truly great Spanish viceroys.

He broke the one-sided power of the encomenderos, made the Church subordinate to his authority, secularized and subsidized the university, deposed the Supreme Court from its high executive position to purely judicial supremacy, cleaned up the boisterous military elements which were disrupting the peace, supervised the construction of many public works from Potosí to Lima, infuriated the Spaniards by restoring to the Indians many of their old social customs and even some lands, and above all became inflexible in his enforcement of the law.

In his five years of travels and inspections over the most difficult terrain in America he ruined his health and on more than one occasion exposed his life and stirred up bitter enmity among many encomenderos and members of the clergy. But, unlike his predecessors, Toledo would under no circumstances compromise either with the law or with his duty. He was an imperialist pure and simple, as was nearly every other European of those days, but, among the few good and the many bad examples of that ubiquitous trend, he was one of the best. Unfortunately, most of his successors were not of the same breed.

One of the most noteworthy contributions ever made to American history was the series of careful studies on the Incas carried out under his stimulation. Of particular importance among these was a work entitled *Historia Indica* by a man named Pedro Sarmiento de Gamboa, who had lived in Peru for many years. When this study was completed, a group of outstanding Indians was assembled and each part of it was read to them in the native tongue. The Incas who had been chosen were all descendants of princes and were among the oldest and most trustworthy repositories of historic information then alive in Peru. Three carefully selected interpreters asked them all manner of questions, and unless there was unanimous agreement in the answers, every effort was made to get at the facts by strenuous cross-examination.

Toledo and Sarmiento, realizing that within a very few years all those who had lived under the Incas and knew their history would be dead, wanted to compile every possible bit of information still available on firsthand evidence or memory. The questions, discussions, and criticisms which followed the reading of the manuscript enabled the author to correct many errors and made it a truly invaluable work. This and other studies on the Incas compiled at that time exerted a great influence on the Viceroy's method of dealing with the natives, and also started one of the hottest battles ever waged in the field of Latin-American history.

The crux of the matter, and of Toledo's entire period of office, began with the rebellion of a group of Incas in 1571, under the leadership of Tupac Amaru, who was living secluded in the mountains and had been enthroned as their "rightful" lord. The Viceroy sent an ambassador to the Incas asking them to carry out their duties as vassals of the Spanish King. This emissary and a Spanish priest were both killed. A primitive expedition was then sent against Tupac Amaru and his little band of followers, and they were all either slain or captured without great difficulty.

Their leader was tried and condemned to death as a traitor; he was executed by being beheaded in the central plaza of Cuzco before a terrified group of Indians. His death had the desired effect, and there were no more serious rebellions on the part of the natives for over two hundred years. Many persons, however, both Spaniards and natives allied with them, considered it a great tactical error. Toledo disregarded these criticisms and methodically proceeded to do two things: (1) to uproot the last vestige of loyalty to the old regime, and (2) to adopt as his own policy toward the natives as many of the Inca social principles as he considered practical.

From this point on the word battle gathers momentum. Writing several years after Toledo's regime, the Inca historian, Garcilaso de la Vega, whose *Royal Commentaries* are the basic study on the social organization of his mother's people, referred to the execution of Tupac Amaru as cruel and unjust, called Toledo's Indian policy unreservedly iniquitous, and blackened the names of the Viceroy and his authors with diatribes which have resounded through the pages of history ever since. Garcilaso's conviction was that Toledo and those working for him wanted only to "anathematize the Inca dynasty in such a way that their fair name would perish," their "supposed" tyrannies become hateful to all, and the legitimate lordship of the King of Spain to their dominions thus be duly justified and recognized.[47]

Among the foreign authorities who have supported this thesis are Clements Markham and P. A. Means, both distinguished historians of ancient Peru. The recent studies of Means on Inca civilization and the fall of the Inca Empire are excellent and widely read interpretations. He divides the historians of Peru into two general classes, those who adopt the "anti-Inca" Toledo thesis, and those who follow the indigenist Garcilaso. It is natural that Means himself, as an Inca antiquarian, should be absorbed by this latter feeling.

On the other side of the fence stands the equally distinguished Spanish American historian, Roberto Levillier, whose biography of Francisco de Toledo is a fundamental and strongly pro-Spanish work. Levillier defends the Viceroy stoutly and after an exhaustive study of the letters and documents of the period concludes that his attitude was not only correct and just but the only alternative to relinquishing Spanish control over the Peruvian colony. After referring to the Norman heritage in England, the Arabic influence in Spain, and the Roman tradition present throughout much of Europe, he says: "Few nations exist whose history is not a superposition of races, languages, and cultures, resulting from invading currents momentarily triumphant, then assimilated. And the consequent fusion of bloods, languages, and customs composes in each nation after a few centuries an expression of human verity, a truism of blood and bone, one and indissoluble, which cannot be obliterated by blackening it or by stirring up hatreds in order to produce disaffections among the elements of which it is composed."[48]

As would be natural with such specialists, Means discounts the Viceroy's good work almost entirely, ridicules as mere propaganda the studies compiled while he was in office, and holds high the flaming torch of Inca civilization. Levillier, on the other hand, minimizes the desire, conscious or unconscious, of Toledo and Sarmiento to present the Incas in a bad light, and accepts the imperialism of the Spaniards with such unrestrained admiration that an improper perspective is given to those harrowing days. His work nonetheless is performing the indispensable function of bringing "indigenist" bibliophiles out of a dead dream into the cold world of social reality.

Levillier's characterization of the Viceroy and his work, though altogether too credulous, is clear-cut and excellent. "The government of the Viceroy Toledo was one of the most inspired and fruitful in the history of Peru and marks a transcendent turning point in its course. It is the step from chaos to a definite social and institutional structure destined to regulate in a humanitarian fashion the life together of Indians and Spaniards, to extend the evangelical labor of the priests, to establish the norms of work and to demand of the Supreme Courts, as well as of the *encomenderos* and the municipal governments, the observance of the laws, the respect for certain privileges of the communities, and the protection of the native. Those reforms were not all fulfilled in his time, but they start from there, and once the course was plotted, it was easier for his successors to hold the flock in line, because the habit of respecting the Royal Power already existed, if not through spontaneous discipline, at least through fear of sanctions."[48]

There is no question but that the Viceroy Francisco de Toledo was the "supreme organizer of Peru," as Levillier calls him in the subtitle of his biography, or that he "gave to the colonial government of Peru its final shape, which it preserved in the main for over two hundred years," as Means points out. But the "humanitarian" relationship between Indian and Spaniard which Levillier regards as a fact has been largely a fiction, as Peru's numberless and almost perennial dictatorships clearly attest. And Means is undoubtedly wrong when he leads one to believe that the Viceroy Toledo was primarily obsessed with a desire to anathematize the Incas.

In reflection on Toledo's period of rule one would think that he was exactly the type of man who would appeal to Philip II of Spain, but he was entirely too much like Philip for the Spanish King to appreciate him or even to be grateful for the sacrifice of his health and his life in the King's cause. When the Viceroy returned to Spain after thirteen years of absence, Philip, in whose breast the Inca rebellion and its swift suppression still rankled, said to him bluntly: "Go to your home, for I did not send you to

Peru to kill kings, but to be the servant of kings." The following year Toledo died under such circumstances of neglect and embitterment as pursue most leaders who follow a stern middle course for a long enough time,
satisfying no one and vexing nearly all. Only after he had long been dead
was justice done to his memory.

On the whole Philip II's viceroys who served in the last half of the sixteenth century were hard-working and reasonably competent men. There
was not another group like them until two hundred years later, during the
latter half of the last colonial century under the enlightened Bourbons. By
that time independence was near at hand and these men were powerless to
avert it.

A total of sixty-one viceroys were appointed to rule in Mexico or New
Spain, and Peru had thirty-eight. They might be called "limited monarchs,"
but their power was limited by the King, not by constitution. However,
even in those countries where no constitution exists, the will of public
opinion, blunted but nevertheless real, takes its place. This was the only
power in the New World which the Viceroy was unable to subdue. The
imponderable influence of basic social and economic forces time and again
obliged him to temporize even as the first great Viceroy, Antonio de Mendoza, had been forced to do. If the Crown persisted in sending over a law
which was contrary to the fundamental "interests" of the colonists, the
Viceroy would simply not enforce it. While an open challenge of the royal
authority was unthinkable, furtive disobedience mixed with an outward
show of respect became a widespread fact.

After a time this became an established practice of viceregal rule, and
was so generally recognized by all in the colonies that a special ceremony
was held to celebrate it. "When a royal statute considered to be contrary,
to the colonial interest arrived, the viceroy or the president of the Supreme
Court would read it solemnly, and then placing it over his head as a token
of submission and humbleness, would say in a loud voice: 'It shall be respected, but not enforced [*Se acata, pero no se cumple*].' This act satisfied
both the principle of submission to the king, and the necessity of realism
in colonial government. The common people referred to such royal statutes
as 'unconsecrated hosts.'

"Naturally, once such a back door was opened to tolerance, unscrupu-
lousness as well soon took advantage of it; and abuses could filter through
what should have remained only as an escape valve. This legal fiction had
repercussions which soon contaminated the legal spirit and was the means
by which the protective Indian laws and those aimed at abolishing the
abuses of the encomenderos and town councilmen became dead letters."[49]

The psychological significance of all this struck roots that ran deep into
the character of Latin-American political practice. Disrespect for the unifying principle of impersonal law became universal. It was a double-edged

ord which cut the props out from under progressive government in two
...ys: (1) individual interests were placed above both the central authority and national welfare, and (2) the only unifying factor in the body politic was the name of the King, which to most of the people was a mere
shadow. The first edge of this sword made impossible progressive self-
government, which depends on give as well as take; the other meant that,
once the kingly shadow had set, there would not even remain a figment of
unity, and chaos would be the inevitable result.

There always existed, of course, certain free social forces whose growth
would continue despite the fact that neither the soil in which they were
planted, the air they breathed, nor the food which they received gave them
more than a bare minimum of strength and nutriment. Latin-American
society was so organized that these forces, elsewhere generally among the
most progressive, were cut and starved from the first moment they sprouted
a bud. It could hardly be otherwise, for the peninsula itself, which was the
head of the entire colonial body, was rapidly sinking into a state of atrophy.

14

TRADE MONOPOLY AND PIRATES

The underlying idea back of Spanish regulations controlling trade with the colonies was to insure the greatest possible profits for the home country. Spain was like a prospector for gold who suddenly strikes it rich and then makes every effort to keep others away from his stake. In order to safeguard her colonial "gold mine" she established a commercial monopoly: only Spaniards could trade with the colonies, goods must be carried in Spanish ships, and finally, for protection, these ships must sail together in a convoy. The colonies were not only prohibited from trading with other European nations but were not allowed to trade among themselves. For many years goods sent from one colony to another had to go first to Spain and were transshipped from there.

On the surface it sounded like an airtight system. Every ounce of colonial gold and silver would reach Spain, and Spain, in turn, would furnish all the imports which the colonies needed. England, Holland, and France had all established similar monopolies. The main difference was that while these countries had strong productive industries which could supply the wants of their colonists at reasonable prices, Spain had a rapidly weakening industrial system, a declining navy, and a disintegrating merchant marine. Her commercial policy, therefore, was like a mother saying to her famished child: "Take no other milk but mine," when she had no milk to give.[22] Nevertheless, many millions of dollars in trade passed across the ocean before this truth became evident.

From its center at Seville the Spanish *Casa de Contratación*, or House of Trade, established in 1503, directed all this colonial commerce. It not only served as a clearinghouse through which all trade was channeled, but it had virtually dictatorial powers over all cargoes, customs, posts, permits, papers, and personnel having to do with ships sailing for or arriving from the New World. Each vessel carried an official scribe or notary whose duty it was to keep a complete record of everything that happened on the trip, and in each port the House of Trade had its official representatives to re-check the cargo and report on its disposal. It also had charge of emigration and of the exports of seeds, plants, and animals, and was a sort of general storehouse and market which provided these essentials of colonial life. It had the further responsibility of compiling and keeping a complete file on the economic geography of all sections of the New World. Every discov-erer, conquistador, or explorer was obliged to send in a report on the ter-rain, climate, peoples, and products of the regions which came under his inspection. The House maintained its own bureau of navigation, and among its first chief pilots were Amerigo Vespucci and Sebastian Cabot. Every employee of the organization was under severe restrictions and was not permitted to engage in trade or even to make recommendations touch-ing his field of activity.

In 1524, when the House of Trade found itself swamped with more work than it could possibly do, the Council of the Indies was established to direct the political, judicial, and military affairs of the colonies and to act as an advisory body in regard to all civil and ecclesiastical appoint-ments. These dual bureaucracies functioned side by side throughout the colonial period. While Philip II was King (1556–98) he tried to be a vir-tual one-man dictator of this council, and, living as he did among suffo-cating piles of papers, *el rey papelero*, or "the king of the endless files," nearly succeeded in his purpose.

At first single ships or small groups of vessels were permitted to carry on colonial trade, but they were restricted to sailing from the ports of Seville or Cádiz, and on their return all had to unload and pass inspection at Seville. When the wealth of incoming cargoes had increased to such an extent that those boats were attacked by corsairs or by Spain's enemies, they were forced to travel in convoy. This system lasted from 1561 to 1748, and two such convoys were supposed to leave Spain every year. However, their departure was frequently delayed for many months until a sufficient number had assembled, or because warships to escort them were not at the time available, or because the country was at war. Even when none of these conditions prevailed, Spain finally became so destitute of both goods and ships that sailings were irregular. On the average a fleet of from forty to seventy vessels left Spain about once in every year and a half, but the average is misleading because sometimes many years passed without a single sailing.

Their route was as follows: on leaving Seville or Cádiz they all headed for the city of Santo Domingo (Havana later became the port of arrival when the growth of that city had overshadowed the earlier splendor of Santo Domingo). There the fleet divided into two sections, one going to Vera Cruz, Mexico, the other to Cartagena in Colombia and thence to Portobello, Panama. The first section was to take care of all the Mexican and most of the Central American trade, while the second was supposed to do the same for the entire South American continent. After many years of this monopoly restrictions were relaxed, but the harm had already been done and contraband trade was widespread throughout the colonies. The whole Spanish commercial policy was medieval, with the fleets taking the place of the old caravans and the fairs being an almost exact replica of those of the Middle Ages.

The ships which went to Panama unloaded at Portobello, about twenty miles from present-day Colón, where a huge forty-day fair was held. Cartagena, on the northern coast of Colombia, was the port of entry for Venezuela, Colombia, and Ecuador. All the rest of South America was served through Portobello. The harbor here was discovered by Columbus, who gave it the name of *Puerto Bello*, or Fine Port, "because it is quite large, fair, inhabited and encompassed by a well-tilled country."[2] The Spaniards later selected this site, with its large and easily defended harbor, as the Atlantic terminus of their mule track across the Isthmus of Panama and as the central trade point for their colonies in the southern continent. The town had a vile climate and was normally a small, disease-ridden pesthole, but when the trade fairs were held it attracted hundreds of merchants from all sections of South America, and the population swelled many times over.

As soon as the first ships of the fleet had landed at Cartagena messengers were dispatched overland to the interior and to Peru to spread the news. Merchants immediately began to come in, and a large fleet of vessels with native goods sailed up from Callao, the port of Lima. The fleet from Spain then sailed up to Portobello and met the South American merchants who had landed on the other side of the Isthmus and crossed by mule caravan.

The little town of Portobello grew as if by magic. Rents and prices both were sky high. Small booths were rented for one thousand pesos or more and single houses for four thousand to six thousand pesos. Many merchants brought their own tents and set them up along a primitive-looking midway in order to display their wares. Transactions were carried on in the open air, and stalls were stuffed with all kinds of cloths, laces, shoes, hardware, wine, machinery, articles of apparel, notions, implements of many kinds, oil, slaves—in a word, every conceivable importation from the Old World.

Buyers from Peru and even faraway Argentina and Chile came with their mule trains to purchase and haul their stuff across Panama, where it was again placed on ships and carried down the western coast of South America. They brought native products to sell, such as sugar, cocoa, cotton, tobacco, hides, indigo, vanilla, pearls, gold, silver, copper, tin, salt, cochineal, and many others. Portobello for six weeks became "the most thriving town in the Americas," the "emporium of South American commerce, the Buenos Aires of the sixteenth and seventeenth centuries."

However, after the fairs were over, as suddenly as they had risen on the shore, tents and stalls were dismantled, merchants took their leave, and the town slipped back into its habitual sleepy routine. Sometimes an epidemic would break out while trade was in progress, and the merchants would then hasten their exchange and flee from the town. In the long intervals between visits made by the fleet all ports were officially put under lock and key and remained as dead as graveyards, while merchandise was gradually accumulated in the warehouses awaiting the arrival of another convoy.

Thomas Gage, an English priest, visited the fair in 1637 when the incoming fleet was small and when the sale of merchandise lasted only two weeks. Even under those conditions he reported that they charged him one hundred and twenty pesos (about $200) for a room "no bigger than a rathole." Prices of food also were ten to twenty times higher than anywhere else. The thing which most attracted Gage's attention was to see the mule trains come in loaded with silver ingots. In a single day he counted two hundred mules which were driven to the public market place where their precious loads were taken off and piled up like mounds of stones, apparently without any fear of thieves. The same traveler also mentioned that the merchants, soldiers, and seamen who gathered for the fairs often died like flies of tropical fevers and of dysentery "caused by the abuse of fruits and of the water which they drank."

Since Portobello represented such a great center of wealth it was inevitable that the English corsairs should be drawn there like a swarm of bees to a flower, and the place was often subject to attack. "Sir Francis Drake died on shipboard when about to attack it, in 1596. . . . In the eighteenth century, when the fairs ended [after 1737], the town dwindled away almost to nothing; but the remains of several forts that once protected it, and the vast ruined *dogana* or customhouse, testify to the former grandeur of Porto Bello."[2]

All in all the fairs were a fantastic sight, and the profits were something fantastic too. As Spain was unable to produce enough goods to supply her colonies, a great proportion of these was imported from England, France, and Holland, and Spanish merchants merely became agents for foreign concerns, many of which had branches in the peninsula. Although, according to monopolistic practice, only Spaniards were supposed to profit by the colonial trade, as early as 1505 the door was left open for foreign competition with the ruling that "foreigners resident in Spain may trade with the colonies provided they employ Spanish agents."[50]

At one time Holland alone was sending one hundred and fifty ships a year to unload Dutch goods in Spain. Since Englishmen and Flemings were among the best sailors of those days, many Spanish vessels counted

considerable numbers of each among their crews, and it was not long before England and Holland knew the waters about the Spanish colonies as
well as Spain herself. They also had friends in every port. The peninsula
had found a neat way of cutting its own throat. All foreign goods had to
be sent to the colonies on Spanish ships, and every foreign vessel which
entered an American harbor was liable to confiscation, but in the end it
was impossible to prevent even this infraction of the monopolistic law.

When merchandise had passed through all these hands, plus a long and
hazardous trip across the Atlantic, plus a dozen different kinds of taxes, it
was no wonder that the charges were exorbitant. The merchants of the
fleet, having no competition, agreed beforehand on prices which would
give them a return of two or three hundred per cent or even more on their
investment. It was the first large-scale application of the vicious trust or
cartel system against which the unorganized purchaser is powerless. Only
a still bigger cartel, which would at best remedy the situation temporarily,
or direct government action, could launch a frontal attack against such
an arrangement. Damaging blows could be dealt by contraband trade,
however, and these blows eventually (after two hundred years) destroyed
the monopoly.

As early as 1624 the royal inspector placed in Panama reported that legally
registered goods to the value of 1,446,346 pesos had passed through but
that an estimated 7,597,559 pesos' worth had been smuggled by without
paying any duty. Another authority estimated that for every 1000 tons of
merchandise which entered Peru through legitimate trade channels, 7500
tons came in via contraband. Perhaps the estimate is excessive, but beyond any doubt one half of all imports were smuggled in, and in some
years the percentage of contraband goods was as high as eighty or ninety
per cent. During most of the eighteenth century, after the backbone of
the monopoly had been pretty well broken, an average of only forty ships
a year came to America from Spain, but there were about three hundred
ships from other nations.

The fact that exorbitant prices were collected by the merchants of the
fleet at Portobello was not the half of it. This was only the beginning.
These same merchants banded together to buy native products at costs
which were ridiculously low. The same double-barreled punch which soon
laid low the Iberian Peninsula also kept the colonies in a state of relative
poverty for over two centuries. For example, says a historian of Chile, in
that country "a *fanega* [1.6 bushels of wheat] was worth two *pesos*, a cow
the same," and a sheep considerably less, but at the same time "a package
of paper cost more than one hundred *pesos*, a sword three hundred, and a
cloth cape not less than five hundred. Under such circumstances the colony
was condemned to poverty."[43]

It is easy to see that this practice would leave few people indeed in a
position to purchase European products, and few individual workers in

ny frame of mind to exert themselves in the production of native goods. But the effect went farther than that. It meant that those few who, through their wealth, were able to buy would become more and more demanding of the Indians under them in order that they themselves might continue to live in some luxury. This constant driving and milking away of every possible cent of profit resulted in an exploited laboring class which was rarely able to achieve more than a bare subsistence. Built upon this tradition, Latin America is still a land of poverty and riches where the middle class, our own great bulwark of democracy, is only in its infancy.

Under the monopoly Chile, Argentina, and Uruguay, which were the greatest distance from Portobello, had to pay considerably higher prices than Mexico or Peru, which were near the points of debarkation. Besides this, gold and silver were abundant in the latter countries, and numberless Indian workers were available to labor in mines and fields. Thus the aristocratic caste systems of Lima and Mexico City became firmly entrenched in their enjoyment of Old World luxuries and the Old World way of life. But when we trace the progress of goods to Argentina or Chile quite the reverse is true. Hardly anyone could afford to purchase legally imported goods in that part of the world.

The route to those more distant countries was as follows: on leaving Portobello merchandise had to be carried by mule train overland to the Pacific side of the Isthmus of Panama. Here it was loaded into ships again and sent down to Callao, the port for Lima, separated from the inland Peruvian capital by only a few miles. From Callao it was reshipped to Chile and Argentina. Frequently it was also resold by the Peruvian merchants, who generally brought it down from Panama. If the final destination was Chile it went by sea, but if bound for Argentina it was transported from Callao by mule train all the way over the Andes and across the continent, finally arriving at Buenos Aires or some other Argentine city.

An intermediate fair for Bolivian and Argentine merchants was held at Potosí, Bolivia, the great silver center which for many years was the most populous town in the entire Western Hemisphere, and here again further costs were tagged on. An Argentine historian says: "In Potosí, prices were four times as high as in Lima; while in Tucumán [northern Argentina] prices were twice as high as in Potosí."[42] In other words, by the time goods reached northern Argentina they cost eight times as much as they did in Lima and perhaps fifteen to twenty times as much as they had originally cost in Europe. This meant that the region of Argentina, Chile, and Uruguay came to depend almost exclusively on contraband trade, a fact which affected their whole society to its very core.

The Spanish mercantile policy also restricted the free exchange of products among the colonies themselves, and, in order to safeguard further the monopoly of the mother country, it was prohibited to produce goods in the New World which might compete with the same commodities shipped over from the peninsula. For example, grapes were not to be grown in the colonies and wine was not to be made there. However, as these restrictions were nonsensical and impossible to enforce they were gradually either lifted or disregarded until they became dead letters.

Fleets, trading companies, caravans, and monopolies were institutions which served well enough "for the beginnings of trade, and for the lower stages of civilization; but Spain tried to perpetuate them in her colonies." While other countries outstripped her in navigation, shipbuilding, and in the art of commerce, she doggedly persisted in the old manner of life. It was partly due to the psychology of the race which loved tradition and hated change; it was also a sort of religious reflex because Spain knew that a free importation of goods would also mean free entrance for Protestant and heretical ideas. This artificial adherence to the lower stages of economics meant that while the tiny island of Mauritius enjoyed a trade of 36,266 tons with England in a single year, the Spanish fleet, at its very height, never carried more than 27,500 tons, which represented the total *legal* trade of all Spanish America. It would not be fair to dismiss the subject at this point, however, without showing that the other maritime nations of Europe practically forced Spain to follow the tightrope path of monopoly and isolation.

The insignificant West Indies islands of Tortuga, San Cristóbal, and the larger ones of Jamaica and Santo Domingo play little part in contemporary Latin-American history. Yet at one time they were alive with nests of corsairs or buccaneers from England, France, and Holland who lay in wait at these central vantage points to pounce on the rich gold and silver fleets of Spain and Portugal. For nearly two hundred years the corsairs made life miserable for the Spanish galleons. They were one of the primary causes for the peninsula's poverty and decay after 1588, when British sea dogs swept the Invincible Armada from the coasts of England and delivered the deathblow to Spanish supremacy of the seas.

Francis Drake, born in 1540, led the way. He was a sort of pioneer or precursor, and was one of the principal reasons why Philip II finally assembled the Armada. In the 1560s Drake and his kinsman, John Hawkins, engaged in the slave trade with the West Indies. The Spaniards were angered at these intrusions on their colonies and attacked the English ships so vigorously that all were sunk except Drake's own vessel and one other. After taking a lesson in caution the hard way the Englishman came back with a vengeance. In 1569–70 he slipped into the Indies, spied on their ship movements and the size and location of their forts and garrisons, and in 1572, with only two vessels and seventy-four men, he headed for Panama. There he attacked and looted the trade center Nombre de Dios, port of arrival for Spanish ships in Panama before it was displaced by Portobello in 1584. After this successful venture he captured a ship in the harbor of Cartagena, then fell on Portobello, sacked it thoroughly, crossed the Isthmus, and seized three mule trains bearing thirty tons of silver. After his return to England with this loot Drake became a national hero and was made an admiral.

Soon afterward Queen Elizabeth secretly gave him permission to raid the Spanish colonies on the Pacific, but this was denied officially, for England and Spain were not then at war. Drake left England in 1577, with a Portuguese pilot, and was the first foreigner to sail through the Strait of Magellan. He had started out with five ships, but by this time four of them had already been lost, two in the River Plate, one in the stormy Patagonian seas, and the fourth, not being able to find the commander after the storm, had returned to England.

Drake continued up the west coast of South America in his flagship, the *Golden Hind*. His first stop was at the Chilean port of Valparaiso, then only a small village, which he attacked and plundered. He captured a ship which was standing in the harbor ready to sail for Peru and took its cargo of gold, hides, and tallow, then he thoroughly ransacked all the warehouses and put out to sea again. At Callao he made another attack, cut all the ships loose from their moorings, but did not feel strong enough to take a chance against the Spanish forces which he knew would be dispatched immediately from Lima.

From Peru he sailed northwest and, in his search for the northeastern passage back to England, went all the way up the west coast of the United States. Not finding this passage, he repaired and reprovisioned his ship in California and then sailed across the Pacific, visiting the Philippines and several other points in the Orient, and finally rounding the Cape of Good Hope. In 1580 he reached England safely after the second circumnavigation of the globe. The whole country went wild with celebration, and Queen Elizabeth, finding her official friendship for Spain unsuccessful anyway, came aboard the *Golden Hind* in person, knighted Drake, and received a treasure worth more than five million dollars.

Five years later, with a much larger fleet of nineteen vessels, the Englishman attacked Spain directly, plundered the port of Vigo and the town of Santiago, then, sailing for the New World again, he captured the cities of Santo Domingo and Cartagena and forced the Spaniards to pay a huge ransom for the deliverance of the latter city. Spain began to prepare her revenge on a grand scale, and, getting wind of it, Drake decided not to await the attack which was certain to come, but "to singe the beard of the Spanish king."

He entered the harbor of Cádiz with thirty English ships and destroyed the entire fleet which the Spaniards were assembling. This was in 1587, and in the following year, when Philip did send his huge Armada against England, Drake served as vice-admiral of the English fleet which, with considerable help from the stormy weather, dispersed the one hundred and thirty vessels which were the pride of the Spanish navy, and ended for all time Spanish dominion of the seas. Only about half of the ships of the Armada ever got back to the peninsula. The year after this Drake invaded Portugal and tried to capture Lisbon, but was forced to retire.

His last expedition, with John Hawkins, was in 1595, when he again appeared in the West Indies. This time the Spaniards were ready and drove him away. He sailed on to Panama, hoping to find the cities there less prepared to defend themselves, but died of dysentery off Portobello and his body was cast into the sea.

Drake was only the first of a long line of sea hawks called at various times corsairs, buccaneers, pirates, freebooters, or filibusters, and to the Spanish generally known as "those heretical dogs." Protestant England had come to despise the Spanish "papists" with a hatred that had begun as colonial rivalry, but when the differences of religion were added to the differences of politics and economy, the revulsion of these two nations toward each other became deep and irreconcilable. The likewise Protestant Dutch had their even more galling memories of Spanish supremacy. What, in the English, was mostly envy at Spanish wealth, power, and expansion, in the Dutch was an ingrained hatred for all friends or compatriots of the Duke of Alba and of Kings Charles and Philip, who had for so long occupied their land, terrorized and slaughtered their people. Finally, in 1581, the Low Countries declared their independence. Spain did not recognize this independence, however, and so a state of continual warfare and violence existed between these nations for over a century.

France, also, hated the peninsula with a vengeance. As Spain's nearest scourge and rival, she never lacked some motive to attack her neighbor. The French Huguenots—and there were plenty of these among the buccaneers—had a standing religious reason as well. The enmity of these three countries was heightened by the fact that ever since Balboa had taken possession of the Pacific in the name of the King of Spain, and even more so since Magellan had found a sea route into it while sailing under the Spanish flag, the Spanish Crown had closed that ocean "to navigation and to the commerce of all the countries of the world." The Spanish policy in this matter, as in the instance of their supposed commercial monopoly with their colonies, was simply a case of not wanting to let anybody else in on a good thing. Other countries followed the same identical principle, but Spain had got a head start and so was attacked, as the leader will always be attacked, by those who would like to take his place, or, failing in that, would at least enjoy seeing him toppled from his lofty seat. Even the Spanish policy in the Netherlands, cruel and oppressive as it assuredly was, did not surpass in iniquity that of the Dutch later in the East Indies, or that of the British in India.

Drake did not stand alone among the corsairs of the sixteenth century;

he was only the best known and a sort of justification for all the others. The French had begun their forays against the Spanish at about the same time, and several of their freebooters had looted settlements in the Hispanic New World, frequently putting all their prisoners to death. In 1625 a Frenchman and an Englishman colonized the little island of San Cristóbal near Santo Domingo. Several Frenchmen passed over to the larger island, and here they hunted down the wild cattle which had escaped from the Spaniards settled on the opposite extremity.

These men made a living by selling the hides of the animals they killed to Dutch smugglers, and they depended mostly on the beef for their subsistence. This they barbecued on spits or *boucans,* as did the natives. Hence the term "buccaneers." These buccaneers and others of the same breed established a firm hold on the western side of Santo Domingo and were able to challenge Spanish supremacy in the Indies. The present-day country of Haiti, in whose people the Negro element has almost blotted out the French, is the final result. French is still the official language of Haiti.

Perhaps the bloodiest pirate of all was the Frenchman known as L'Ollonais, or L'Olonnois, because of his birth in Sables d'Olonne. His real name was Jacques Jean David Nau. Beginning his activities as a buccaneer in 1650, this nefarious Frenchman coursed along Spanish American shores for over twenty years, tracing his path in fire and blood until his death at the hands of the Indians of Panama in 1671. L'Ollonais (called Olonés in Spanish) "began with a real hatred of Spain and ended with a strong love of cruelty. He pulled out tongues, and carved his prisoners to pieces with his sword. The Spanish men would far rather have met the devil in any form than L'Ollonais. The whisper of his name emptied the villages in his path of every living unit. It was said that the mice fled to the jungle when he came."[51]

He captured and sacked Maracaibo, Puerto Cabello, New Gibralter, and even penetrated the peninsula of Yucatan, put its wild inhabitants to the sword, left its towns a maze of rubble and embers. One day, with a whetstone in one hand and his sword in the other, he passed along a line of prisoners and is said to have cut off the heads of eighty-seven men with his own hand. Finally, his ship was wrecked on the coast of Panama and the natives who captured him gleefully tore off small pieces of his body while he was still alive and consumed them before his eyes. L'Ollonais and others of his breed were a constant menace to the wealthiest Spanish cities along the coasts of the Spanish Main.

The Dutch were not far behind. In the early 1600s they made life miserable for the Spanish and Portuguese trade fleets, and in 1624 they established themselves firmly in Brazil, capturing and occupying the cities of Bahia, Pernambuco, Olinda, and making a desperate attempt to colonize the entire northern Brazilian coast. They were finally driven out in 1654.

The English preserved a certain secrecy about their piratical expeditions and, unless a state of open warfare existed, officially washed their hands of them. The Dutch, whose independence had never been recognized, had no such reasons for concealment, and their rich merchants and commercial companies openly made their plans for looting and colonization. As Portugal was under Spanish rule from 1580 to 1640, and as the Portuguese colonies were not well defended at the time, these Dutchmen first fell on the Portuguese possessions in the Orient and, meeting with considerable success, then decided to attack Brazil. They also came to the United States, where their colony of New Amsterdam was founded under the noses of the English in 1614.

The English, for their part, went about singeing the beard of the Spanish King with organized persistence after the year 1655. In that year Jamaica fell into their hands, giving them a base from which to operate. Their original plans had been more ambitious still. Oliver Cromwell sent a flotilla of sixty vessels and ten thousand men into the Antilles under the command of Admiral Penn, the father of William, who later colonized Pennsylvania. It was the purpose of these forces to take over a large portion of the Spanish colonial empire. They attacked Santo Domingo but were decisively beaten off, then they proceeded on to Jamaica, which they occupied—that is, they occupied the shore line, for many Spaniards escaped into the interior. In order to get rid of them the newly arrived English offered the native buccaneers a set reward for the head of any Spaniard brought in to them, and in this fashion Jamaica soon came entirely under their control.

Only four years previously (1651) Cromwell had passed the famous Navigation Act, making the use of English ships a requirement for all British trade. This kept the British merchant marine built up to capacity at all times, and, now that it had a new center from which to operate, the attacks upon Spanish shipping became more frequent and more deadly.

Henry Morgan (1635–88), who came to Jamaica as a poor Welsh lad and who was forced to work in the tobacco fields under the lash, eventually rose to such a high place among the corsairs that he challenged even the position of Francis Drake. John Steinbeck gives a vivid if somewhat over-poetized account of his life in his novel *Cup of Gold*. In 1670 Morgan ravaged up and down the coasts of the Caribbean and took the town of Portobello. From here he sent the governor of Panama City a note saying that he would pay him a visit within the year. The governor sent him back a gold ring with a large emerald in it as a token of his admiration and begged him to desist. But Morgan had already decided on the destruction of Panama, the crossroads of America, the lovely rich *Copa de Oro*, or Cup of Gold, of the Spanish colonies.

When he arrived the governor faced him with vastly superior forces, but such was Morgan's reputation that the Spanish leaders were loath to attack. A large herd of wild bulls was driven onto the battlefield in front of the Spanish army and an attempt was made to stampede it over Morgan's men. The English remained calm and, firing at the animals as they advanced, turned them around into a stampede against their enemies. The Spanish cavalry, which was all neatly lined up in another quarter with sabers gleaming and held at just the proper angle, then charged bravely into the fray. Morgan had seen to it that a marsh lay between him and these horsemen, and in a moment they rode headlong into the morass and were but a jumble of writhing bodies. The defeat of the Spanish forces was catastrophic.

Morgan entered Panama and collected enough gold, silver, jewels, and fine laces to load a hundred and seventy-five mules. They were followed by six hundred prisoners. Behind them Panama was a shambles, and all that remained on the site where the proud city had once stood was the gutted tower of the cathedral which, with its tropical vines and crumbled masonry, is still a mecca for all tourists. About the only item of value to escape Morgan's greedy eye was the magnificent golden altar in the Church of San José, which was painted black by a monk. Although the pirates saw this altar they thought it was wooden and refused to cart it away.

After Henry Morgan had ransacked the Caribbean shores and obliterated Panama it would seem that few wealthy Spanish coastal cities could have remained. But there was still one great prize which had never been touched, and in 1683 a group of combined filibusters, mostly French and Dutch, delivered a devastating attack against it. This was the rich Mexican port of Vera Cruz.

The filibusters were distinguished from the other pirates in that they stole their own ships as they went along; the term itself is derived from a Dutch word meaning freebooter. In order to gain strength these men frequently brought together the oddest possible assortments of characters and nationalities. They often referred to themselves fraternally as "the brothers of the coast."

A large fleet of these pirates, numbering about fifteen hundred men, fell upon Vera Cruz, the port of entry for Spain's wealthiest colony. After occupying the town and locking the massed inhabitants up in the churches, where many suffocated or were trampled to death, they began to pile up their booty in the central plaza. There were twenty-five thousand pounds of wrought silver, enough silver coin to give each of the common soldiers six hundred pesos and the leaders many times that amount, then there were boxes of jewels, kegs of flour, packages of merchandise worth many thousands of dollars, fifteen hundred slaves, and many other items. When the fleet sailed Vera Cruz was picked as clean as a bone. Fourteen years later, in 1697, another group of filibusters captured the city of Cartagena, pride of Colombia, and escaped with ten million pesos, eighty pieces of artillery, and countless other articles of value.

There seemed to be no end to these men. Among the Englishmen alone, besides Drake, Morgan, Walter Raleigh, and John Hawkins, there were a score of others. Thomas Cavendish attacked the west coast of South America; Bartholomew Sharpe captured the Chilean city of La Serena and demanded a hundred thousand pesos for its deliverance; William Dampier abandoned one of his sailors named Alexander Selkirk on the island of Juan Fernández and gave us the story of *Robinson Crusoe*; John Oxenham received an undue recognition in Kingsley's novel *Westward Ho!*, and as late as 1740 Lord Anson established his headquarters on the same island and made it a center for forays against the coasts of Peru and Chile. The Dutchman, Pret Heyn, became famous when he captured an entire Spanish silver fleet on its voyage to Europe, and later took Bahia, the capital of Brazil. Spelberg made an almost successful attack on Lima, and Edward Mansveldt towered above the rest of the brotherhood in his dream of founding a regular pirate colony and nation on St. Catherine's Island. Men flocked to his banner, the colony was founded, and the dream seemed near realization, but Mansveldt's ship was wrecked near Havana and the Spaniards caught and strangled him.

No quarter was asked or given in most of these encounters, and many a Protestant pirate fed the flames of the colonial Inquisition, and many a Spaniard was shot, beheaded, or strung up in cold blood, and without any reason. One Spaniard who slew a group of prisoners is said to have left a sign on the scene which read: "Not because they are French, but because they are Lutherans." And when some Huguenots retaliated in a like manner they left a sign which read: "Not because they are Spaniards, but because they are traitors and murderers."

These pirates of the Spanish Main, of course, did not always come out on top. Spanish arms had their moments of triumph and glory. For instance, in 1741 the English Admiral Vernon (after whom George Washington named his mansion) attacked Cartagena with fifty-one men-of-war and over twenty-eight thousand men, but the city was in a state of complete readiness this time and its thick walls were manned with excellent troops under a capable general. The Spaniards had only three thousand men, but their position was well-nigh impregnable. Vernon, who had come with such superiority in man power, was so certain of success that he had already had medals struck in his honor on which appeared the figure of the Spanish governor in a kneeling position delivering his sword into the admiral's hands. The legend read: *The Spanish Pride Pulled Down by Admiral Vernon.* On the other side of the coin this sentence was finished with the words *who took Portobello with six ships only.* But Vernon had met a foe worthy of his steel at Cartagena, and after besieging the city for more than two months, and losing over eighteen hundred of his men, he retired from the scene. Vernon had stated as his reason for making the attack "the necessity of Great Britain undertaking the emancipation of the Spanish establishments in America, in order to open their markets to the merchants of London."[42]

As a rule, however, the hit-and-run tactics observed by the corsairs gave them the advantage, and especially so since they took great pains to swoop down on centers not expecting an attack or which were poorly defended. There was not a coastal fortress or city in the Spanish or Portuguese colonies which did not at one time or another feel the weight of their destructive blows. The lure of rich gold and silver fleets was one which never ended, and many an insignificant island off the Latin-American coasts is still said to conceal millions of dollars' worth of buried treasure. Although these corsairs alone did not break the back of Spain or Portugal, they were one of the strongest forces holding back the development of their colonies.

Exactly how much booty the pirates carried away can only be guessed at, and the number of ships which they captured is almost as indefinite. However, in the reign of Charles V a total of 2421 vessels left Spain for the New World and only 1748 returned. The difference of 673 was either taken by the corsairs or lost in storms. Then, even after the convoy system was established (1561), the Dutch alone captured around 550 Spanish ships within a period of only thirteen years, between 1623 and 1636. What the European wars had left undone these pirates accomplished thoroughly, that is, the utter destruction of Spanish sea power.

The Spaniards had their own names or distorted spellings for such sea devils as Drake and Hawkins. The first became *Draque,* pronounced *Drah'kheh,* and the second was *Aquines,* pronounced *Ah Kee' Nes.* Both of them and all the others were, of course, piratical dogs and infidels. But in England, we must remember, it was *Sir* Francis Drake, *Sir* John Hawkins, and *Sir* Henry Morgan. These men were not only performing an invaluable function in preserving British dominion of the seas, but the first two had fought well against the Armada whose defeat had given England her maritime supremacy. They were the true founders and epitome of the early traditions of the British navy, and their role in history can hardly be overestimated. They cleared the way for British expansion all over the world, and English imperialism in Asia, Africa, America, and on the islands of the seven seas would not have been possible without them.

What Spain might have achieved in the Hispanic New World, had she been permitted to pursue her policy to its conclusion, no one can guess. But such was the concourse of powers against her, and so great the appetite aroused by Spanish gold and silver, that hardly a moment passed when she was unmolested. Soon her grandeur had passed into defeat, and defeat into bitterness and then decay. No group or nation which has had defeat consistently shoved down its throat can for long maintain that rare combination of upward drive, flexibility, and disciplined leadership on which progress, national and international, must surely depend.

15

FLOWERING OF THE MISSIONS

The three most dynamic institutions in Spanish American colonial life were the township, the encomiendas, and the missions. The towns and encomiendas were closely linked together and really formed a single economic unit, for the majority of the encomenderos lived in towns and merely traveled over their fiefs from time to time on tours of inspection. The estates, with their allotments of Indians, were the main producers in the colonial economy, which was largely agricultural or mining. The towns themselves had few industries and produced little; they were the consumers, the trading, collecting, and distributing points rather than the creators of colonial wealth.

On the other hand, the religious missions in many instances were almost completely self-sufficient economic units. They were under the government of priests instead of civil authorities and were often kept isolated from the civil channels of colonial life. "The missions were born," says the distinguished Spanish historian, Fernando de los Ríos, "as a religious aspiration and as a protest against the covetousness of the conquistadores, against the exploitation of the Indians and against the *encomiendas*, though they were a specific and conventual form of *encomiendas*."[4] In other words, certain elements in the Church, seeing that it was impossible to defend the natives against the rapacity of the encomenderos, determined to undertake the work of assimilation directly and in their own way.

In general the mission settlements functioned more smoothly than the lay organizations and eventually came to represent such a strong, competitive, economic power that in some sections the lay authorities destroyed them. These missions existed all over Latin America, but they were particularly strong in the early centuries in northern Argentina, Paraguay, and in several parts of Brazil, where they were established and run by the well-organized and well-disciplined Jesuits. The Dominicans and

Franciscans also founded missions in many widely separated regions. But the mission "empire," as it has been called, was centered in the heart of South America in northern Argentina and Paraguay.

Beginning with Father Las Casas and continuing throughout the colonial period, there was a section of the Spanish and Portuguese clergy which took to heart the humane and merciful principles of Christianity so frequently thrown overboard when conquistadores, encomenderos, and the parish priests undertook the conversion and religious instruction of the natives. These parish priests were sometimes as fired with the zeal for gold as for salvation, and goodly numbers of them, freed of the more rigid controls which had been exercised over them in the peninsula, led scandalous and greedy lives. On the other hand, the regular clergy, members of orders and therefore under a sterner discipline, showed a much greater disposition to teach their religion by example, particularly during the first century after the conquest, before the new environment had broken down some of their ideals. When these high-minded men saw that all their efforts to ameliorate the exploitation of the Indians by statute had failed, they decided to tackle the problem personally. Deliberately isolating themselves from all the comforts and security of colonial civilization, many priests belonging to the Jesuit, Dominican, Franciscan, and other orders lived and died in the midst of their Indian flocks. Oftentimes the natives who lived in the wild regions into which they plunged were primitive savages who at first repaid kindness with violence. In spite of these setbacks the missionary work continued, and everywhere along the remote frontiers of civilization large native populations were assembled under the jurisdiction of these patient priests.

The first great flourishing of the mission idea was carried to fruition in Mexico in the first century (1520–1600). Thomas More's idealistic *Utopia*, published in 1516, served as a great spur to drive missionary thinkers forward in the establishment of their own social order. Their fundamental idea was "to restore society to its Christian bases, adopting as supreme guide the norms of natural rights."[4] In other words, what in More was a dream "in the Spanish [and Portuguese] monks were actions, and actions that they did not consider as social experiments, but that they performed convinced of their absolute value. They sought a social order without 'social sin,' and in order to achieve that . . . they entrusted direction not to the philosopher, as in Plato, but to the priest, converted particularly into supreme magistrate. They founded citizenship on active work for the community and made the basis of economic organization a public and functional conception of that economy."[4] Christ was their ideal in collective as well as individual life. Co-operation rather than competition was to be the keystone of their economy, and religious law the basis of their social and political structure.

At the very beginning of the conquest "the Dominican Pedro de Córdoba, hostile to the Laws of Burgos (1512–15) because although the laws modified the regime of the *encomenderos* they did not suppress it, expressed to Ferdinand V his adverse judgment. The King answered him: 'Take upon yourself then, Father, the charge of remedying them; you will do me a great service therein.' Henceforth Pedro de Córdoba became the propagandist in the New World for the plan of the mission."[4] Many others, among them Las Casas and Quiroga, were won over to his idea. Despite all these idealistic beginnings, several of the first missions were complete failures. The first one, founded by Las Casas on the coast of Venezuela in 1520, ended in its total destruction by the Indians. But the priests did not give up hope, and finally there was a noteworthy success.

The priest Vasco de Quiroga, who had arrived in Mexico in 1530 and later became Bishop of Michoacán, thought that Europe had fallen into sin, and "we must," he said, "raise the life of the Indians to a level of virtue and humanity superior to that of the European."[4] In 1531 he wrote to the Council of the Indies that he had determined to put his idea into effect by gathering the Indians into communities where they might live safely and prosper from the products of their co-operative labors and lead orderly and Christian lives. In a later statement he asserted that Thomas More had envisioned the republic from which he deduced his own, and that he was going to attempt to "restore the lost purity of the primitive Church."

In Patzcuaro he founded the Hospital de Santa Fe, which was also "a home for children, a school, and a lodging for a community that aspired to live a Christian life of perfection."[4] At its height the community contained approximately thirty thousand Indians. All land was communally owned, but each family enjoyed the use of a small plot for fruit trees, flowers, and vegetables. No land could be sold, but, if deserted, would revert to the community. The Indians were taught arts and crafts and more efficient methods of agriculture. Quiroga supervised the co-operative harvests and rigidly maintained a six-hour workday. His community was an outstanding success, and Quiroga himself is still venerated as a saint by the natives who live in this district, but when his inspirational directive power was taken away the Patzcuaro mission soon fell into decay.

It was in the following century that the mission idea reached its climax in the "Jesuit missions" of northern Argentina and Paraguay. Philip II gave his permission for the establishment of missions in this region in 1579, but several years passed before much headway was made in actual organization. It was a work which was bound to proceed slowly but which in the end, due to the unflagging and patient zeal of the Jesuit fathers, attained a unique success. The Guaraní Indians who lived in this territory, hemmed in on one side by Spanish settlements eager for their labor, and exposed on the other to frequent forays by Brazilian slave gatherers, were not long in choosing life in the missions under the gentle fathers of the Church.

During the first few years some Indians, unused to such discipline, ran away and filtered back into the forest, but the growing menace of expanding colonial civilization, plus the ever-present good will of the Jesuits, induced nearly all of them to return. After the first hundred years had passed —that is, by 1679—there were twenty-two missions in this area, with a total of 58,118 inhabitants. This semi-Arcadian, semi-communistic empire continued to grow and to prosper, and endured for nearly two centuries, until the Jesuits themselves were expelled from Spain and all Spanish dominions in 1767 by royal decree for reasons which had nothing to do with religion.

The beginnings of these unique communities go back to the year 1609, when a group of Jesuits selected about the wildest and most impenetrable part of South America for their missions and set out to establish themselves there. They were empowered to create and govern their own society without encroachments or interference from the civil authorities. The land they chose was one of riotous tropical swamp growth: thorny trees, pampas grass, the steel-hard quebracho tree, cane thickets forty feet tall, waters infested with alligators and electric eels. Periodically the region suffered deluges which left floods in their wake. No legends of gold or silver served as a lure to draw the good fathers into this virgin wilderness. Nor did the Guaraní Indians who lived there offer a particularly attractive medium for the work of discipline and salvation. They were largely nomads who used agriculture as a secondary means of subsistence, and their lives were spent wandering from one place to another in the trackless forest.

While the territory had these serious drawbacks, it also had the advantage of being far removed from the covetous eyes of Spanish settlers; and the slave-thirsty mamelucos of São Paulo, Brazil, were a good eight hundred miles distant. By 1619 one hundred and nineteen Jesuits had arrived in Guayra and Paraguay to take part in the building of these missions. They hoped that their work might proceed undisturbed, and that the special permission for self-government which they held from the King would at least protect them from other Spaniards. For several years their labors continued uninterrupted, and by 1630 several thousand Indians were living under them in half a dozen large missions. But the priests had failed to take into account the unworthy yet natural reactions of the society which surrounded them.

In the first place, they had made their purposes perfectly clear to all, and the Spanish colonists who looked on every Indian as a potential slave were rendered furious by the advent of the Jesuits, who treated them as men.[52] The fact that the missions were miles away in the jungle did not help the situation; in fact, this added distance caused all sorts of rumors to arise about fabulous mines whose locations the priests had long known and kept secret and whose wealth they now sought. In the second place, the half-breed Paulistas or mamelucos of Brazil watched proceedings like a "nest of hawks" and considered the neophytes as pigeons "fattening for their use."[52] The use was slavery, and the fattening was the rudimentary discipline and training which the Jesuits gave to their charges.

Attacks by the mamelucos began in 1629 and continued until 1631. They came with horses, guns, and bloodhounds, and against them the poor Indians, who were not allowed to possess firearms, could offer only the most futile resistance. One after another of their communities were destroyed, and the natives themselves were driven to the slave marts of São Paulo like so many cattle, hundreds of them dying en route. Two Jesuits once accompanied a caravan of fifteen thousand to the coast, going all the way on foot, confessing those who fell, and constantly, but in vain, beseeching their captors to release them.

By 1631 matters had become so desperate that either the missions had to be moved to another and more secure region or abandoned entirely. The zeal of the most faithful Indians was waning in the face of continued and devastating attacks by the Paulistas, and there were some among the natives who attributed everything to the "poison" of their having been baptized in the first place. However, about twelve thousand of the faithful were assembled and plans were made to move them in a mass into an even more isolated region down the Paraná River. They headed into the morass of the tropical forest with each man, woman, and child carrying all his worldly possessions on his back.

The growth was so thick that oftentimes a path had to be cut with machetes. The rains were falling day and night, and the earth was soggy and flooded as under the monsoons of Asia. A party of Spaniards got wind of their departure and swooped down behind them, hoping to capture a few stragglers as slaves. For five hundred miles the caravan pursued its course, and when, finally, the end was in sight, all who had not died were so ill and exhausted that hard work was out of the question.

In this state they settled down, and their first feeble efforts at agriculture did not half meet their needs. In a single community six hundred who had survived the horrible trek across the jungles died of famine. But better days were ahead of them; better locations for their settlements were found, and out of the money which the King of Spain had provided ten thousand head of cattle were purchased and life began anew. They remained in their new homeland for nearly one hundred and fifty years and, with their center in the town of Candelaria, eventually expanded into thirty permanent communities containing approximately one hundred and fifty thousand Indians.

During all these years Portugal and Spain formed a single kingdom (1580–1640). Philip II had made good his claims to the Portuguese throne by force, and the little kingdom did not regain its independence until 1640, when Spanish power was well on the decline. Consequently, the Spanish monarch was also ruler of Brazil, and the mamelucos of São Paulo, as well as the Jesuit mission Indians, were his subjects. He was much averse to taking too strong a stand against his largest colony. But after Portugal had won her independence it was a horse of another color, and then Philip IV granted the Jesuits' request to distribute firearms among the Indians. From a mere nonentity, which paid nominal taxes to the Crown, the missions had suddenly become the bulwark against Portuguese encroachment on Spanish territory, for they occupied the most strategic districts between the two colonial domains. From this time on, then, the mission Indians, under stern Jesuit discipline, became a considerable military force in the struggle between these two powers, and more than once their forces saved the day for the Spaniards. Had it not been for them, a great part of the countries of Uruguay, Paraguay, and Bolivia might now be Brazilian territory.

After the Jesuits had brought their Indians safely through that great exodus and away from the imminent dangers of slave-gathering expeditions, they set about the work of building new centers and training their charges in a very businesslike manner. Among the priests were many well-trained architects, agriculturalists, botanists, husbandmen, and technicians, as well as others who had made a careful study of social and economic organization. The program which they carried out was no hit-or-miss plan. Mission settlements were always built around the square, with the large church and central storehouses on one side and long dormitories for the natives on the other three sides. In the center was an extensive lawn of fine grass kept closely cropped by a herd of mission sheep. The churches were sometimes of stone and other times of native hardwoods and were always colored a deep red. The soil of these regions was generally of a rich and warm red color and, mixed with other earth of a yellow shade, was readily used for this coloring. This has led some writers to refer to the entire district as "the red land of the missions."

The churches were always imposing structures both in architecture and size, and it was generally conceded that Buenos Aires itself had none of such magnificence. They were always adorned with lofty bell towers and many fine items of statuary, altar carvings, et cetera, imported from Italy and Spain. Some of the native woods used in these buildings, especially that of the steel-hard quebracho tree, have survived over three hundred years of tropical dampness while the iron bolts and gratings have long since rusted away. The quebracho (meaning ax-breaker) is so heavy that it will sink if thrown into the water.

The churches had numerous windows, which were a necessity lest the stench of the unwashed congregation turn the preacher's stomach. Glass was unknown in this region until the middle of the eighteenth century, so generally paper or linen was used in its stead. Occasionally talc from Tucumán was employed, but it was expensive. There were also a few windows made of alabaster brought from Peru at great cost, and this substance was used for windows of southern exposure even after glass was introduced, because the latter material would not withstand the strong gales which blew from that direction. "The eggs of the Emu, or American ostrich, were sometimes used to hold holy water, sometimes placed as ornaments on the altar. The altars, which were usually five in number, were remarkable for their size and splendor: the only ambition of the Indians was to vie with each other in ornamenting their churches, which were therefore profusely enriched with pictures, sculpture, and gilding, and abundantly furnished with images. Pope Gregory the Great called these images the books of the poor."[53] Both the vestments worn by the priests and the church plate were noted for their richness.

The native dormitories were extremely long buildings (on the average of 30 × 150 feet) "of sun dried bricks or wattled canes." The usual method of construction was to form a framework of stakes and canes firmly planted in the ground and tied together with thongs of fiber or leather. Over this frame was then spread a plaster of mixed mud, straw, and cowhide. The roofs were at first of thatch or of shingles made of the caranday tree, and a strong waterproof compost was formed with clay and bullocks' blood. Later on many of the roofs were covered with tile. Each family had its own apartment, which was separated from the others by a lathe and plaster wall or partition. These so-called apartments were in reality only a single room about twenty-four feet square. There was one door and no windows to let in the light and let out the smoke. One veranda and one roof often served for more than one hundred families. Although there was the strictest instruction in sexual morality, when the two sexes were brought together in this intimate manner without sufficient separation or privacy, a certain amount of promiscuity was certain to result. The fathers fought against it in many ways but never with satisfactory results.

As a rule, each mission was under the direction of two priests who had the responsibility for its discipline, development, and welfare. They were aided by native "mayors" and "councilmen," through whom social pressure was generally exerted indirectly, the Indians always having the feeling that they were being ruled, tried, and punished by their own kind under stern but benevolent Jesuit leadership. There was no capital punishment, but lawbreakers were quickly sentenced, and punishment was swift and certain. The most frequent crime was drunkenness, and the most frequent punishment was a flogging with stiff leather thongs. Life imprisonment was meted out only in the most extreme cases.

The natives were never forced into these missions and were, in fact, free to leave and take up their semi-nomadic life at any time. That they did not do so, but continued to enter in increasing numbers, proves that they preferred this type of existence to the risks of the forest or of the rapacious slave gatherers. The Jesuits made their isolation more complete by digging ditches and throwing walls around each settlement and stationing a guard at every gate. As the guards were all Indians this measure was obviously one of self-preservation.

The Indians were generally married at an early age, the boys at about seventeen, the girls at fifteen. This was thought preferable to clandestine sexual relations, for even the Jesuits knew that continence in that environment would be impossible for these children of the earth. The sexes were separated from the earliest age and were never allowed to enter the church by the same door. Neither women nor girls were ever allowed to set foot in the houses of the Jesuits. A few children who showed evidences of possessing good voices were taught "reading, writing, and music and made choristers. There were usually about thirty in a reduction. Except for these choristers, only those children were taught how to read and write who were designed for public officers, servants of the church, or for medical practice." They were almost always chosen from the families of the chiefs, or caciques. There were a few Indians in every mission who knew Spanish, but Guaraní was the language in general use there, just as it was throughout most of Paraguay in those days.

There were workers of nearly every kind in the missions: carpenters, weavers, blacksmiths, turners, carvers, painters, and many others. Metal was brought from Buenos Aires at an enormous cost, having been imported there from Europe. There were among the finished artisans some who could cast bells and construct organs. The Guaranís seemed to possess the faculty of being able to reproduce anything, no matter how intricate, that was laid before them.

Many of the neophytes were stark naked when they first entered the reductions, but they quickly became fond of wearing clothes. The men ordinarily went draped in the poncho, a large blanket with a slit in the center through which the head was passed. This garment was of blue and red stripes. Only on days of great celebrations did they don Spanish clothes. The women wore a loose cotton cloak which covered the entire body except for the face, throat, and the feet, which were bare.

Money was not known in the reductions, and exchanges were made in kind. The representatives of the company in Buenos Aires took care of obtaining imported goods for such products as the Jesuits wanted to dispose of to an outside market. The tribute which the Indians paid as subjects of the King was a peso (a dollar or two) per year for each adult male; this was only a fifth or sixth of what natives on the encomiendas were made to pay.

Wild yerba mate, or native Paraguayan tea, was the first important export of the missions. The Indians went many miles to gather it, for the forests were not near by. Later on plantations were laid out in the mission vicinity. The tree whose leaves produce this drink or infusion resembles an orange tree in appearance, but in reality it is a type of holly. In those days some of the wild trees were so large in circumference that a man could not encircle them with his arms. Practically all of these have disappeared by now. The leaves were soft, and after the branches were slightly toasted over a pit they were placed on the ground and beaten with switches until all the leaves had dropped off. These were then dried and pulverized and the sticks were carefully picked out. The resultant green tea was ready for use, and if it was to be shipped outside the mission territory it was packed in large square leather trunks containing about one hundred and fifty pounds each.

Gathering wild mate was not dangerous except for the ticks which often caused serious sores and ulcers if neglected. After a day's work the men plunged into the nearest water and picked one another's bodies clean. The Indians pruned the trees of only a few branches, and so did not harm the vast forests where the mate grew, but when the Spaniards got into the territory in later years, "with the blind rapacity of men who seek only immediate gain," they cut the trees down and within a relatively short time left only fields of stumps where magnificent forests had grown before.

The mission economy was semi-communistic. Lands were owned by the community and work was often performed in common. Each family had a plot of its own, and there were also large areas cultivated for God, the produce of which was sent to the common storehouses. These fields were always tilled by the community as a whole. There were extensive fields of wheat and corn, tobacco, vegetables, sugar cane, and other agricultural products, and especially large areas were given to the cultivation of domesticated yerba mate. The Jesuits had carefully brought small yerba striplings from remote jungle districts and laid them out in plantations near their settlements. Tea made of these leaves is still by far the most popular drink among the poorer classes of Paraguay, southern Brazil, Argentina, Uruguay, and parts of Bolivia and Chile. It is the favored Gaucho beverage of the Argentine pampas, and still today, as in the times of the Jesuits, is the mainstay of the countryman's breakfast.

Other products of the missions were barrels of honey, hides, wools, native woods, cotton and linen cloth, and other articles and necessities of daily life. There were extensive fruit groves, especially of oranges, lemons, and limes, hundreds of which now grow in great wild thickets in the same region. Large herds of cattle, sometimes numbering over fifty thousand head, and many thousands of sheep and horses grazed over extensive pasture lands.

Inside the mission workshops were large looms on which weavers labored in common, and there were also mills for grinding corn and flour, "tanneries, tailors, hat makers, coopers, cordage makers, boat builders, cartwrights, joiners, and almost every industry useful and necessary to live. They also made arms and powders, musical instruments and had silversmiths, painters, turners, and printers to work their printing presses, for many books were printed at the missions and they produced manuscripts as finely executed as those made by the monks in European monasteries."[52]

Everything was the property of the community, and the community shared in every activity of labor, religion, or festivity that went on in its midst. The natives were about as self-sufficient economically as was possible under the conditions in which they lived. There were also hospitals and schools, but most of the teaching was in arts and crafts, and only a chosen few received technical training or what might be called instruction in reading, writing, and arithmetic.

All work was carried on with a note of gaiety, and when the season for cultivating the fields came around, "the Jesuits marshaled their neophytes to the sound of music," and, singing hymns, they all formed a body and marched to their labors behind the figure of a saint which was borne aloft at the head of the procession. As the group marched into the countryside it became smaller and smaller as Indians dropped off to work the various fields. At lunch they all gathered together again and enjoyed a two-hour rest during which more hymns were sung. Then they went back to the fields and worked until sundown. Finally they returned home again, all of them singing, and after a brief rest they assembled in the church to sing the "rosary." Then supper was served, and after that, as the sound of the Angelus struck on the tower of their church, they all retired.

Work on the looms was performed in much the same manner, and on rainy days the entire population carried a communal loom indoors. There were frequent festivals and dances with much tolling of bells and discharges of rockets and firearms. There were also many masses, confessions, and sermons. It is extremely doubtful if all the mysteries of the Holy Trinity, or the meaning of the creed, or even the significance of the sacraments were entirely understood, but at least a primitive type of Christianity was actually practiced by thousands of people.

The Jesuits, of course, as in all their efforts at teaching and preaching the Gospel, passed many anxious moments with their neophytes, especially in the early days of their labors. One father, in a letter to a friend, gives us an idea of what some of the worries of the priests must have been among the natives who were being thus lifted from their primitive state into a higher life which they often found so difficult to understand. The good father writes: "What really bothers a missionary most who doesn't understand the nature of these peoples, is to hear their confessions: for they become very confused depending as they do entirely on the manner in which one asks them the question, and it is a well known fact that they respond much less truthfully to the actual questions that are asked than to the tone and manner in which the words are expressed. For example, if I ask them: 'Have you committed such a sin?' They will answer 'yes,' even if they have not committed it. And if they are asked, 'Have you not committed such a sin?' they will say 'no,' even if they have been repeatedly guilty of it. Moreover, if later one asks them the same questions in another and round about way they will confess what they have already denied and will deny what they have already confessed.

"Another great difficulty occurs when one wants to get out of them the number of times they have committed the same sin. They are so ignorant that they don't even know how to count; even the most intelligent can't go above five, and many don't get beyond two. So if they want to explain the numbers three, four, or five, they will say 'two and one' times, or 'two times two and one'; or they will express number five by holding up the five fingers of the right hand; and if they want to count to ten they also hold up the fingers of the left hand. If the number they want is above ten they will plop down on the floor and successively grab the toes of each foot up to the number of twenty. Since their manner of explaining themselves is hardly fitting before the tribunal of penitence, the confessor must arm himself with limitless patience, and let them repeat the same sin as many times as they have been guilty of it."[54]

When they tried to carry the good work of conversion up into the Chaco region, where probably the wildest Indians of South America lived, the Jesuits ran into still further difficulties. They always took their linguistics seriously, and nearly all of the grammars and studies of the native languages were written originally by some priest. But in the Chaco, wrote one father, "the sounds produced by the Indians resembled nothing human, so do they sneeze, and stutter and cough." No wonder the Athanasian creed itself was puzzling to a neophyte.[52]

However, the Jesuits did not give up; they studied the languages assiduously for years. Even then they were stumped, for whenever they preached the Indians received their words with shouts of laughter. One priest attributed this laughter to "the presence of a mocking devil who possessed them." But this mocking devil, says an English writer, was probably only "a sense of humor, the possession of which, even amongst good Christians, has been known to give offence."[52]

The economic side of life in the missions had its spirit of lightheartedness, too, but here no levities were permitted. There was music, marching, pageantry, and fiestas, but the work had to be done, and no drones were allowed to thrive in the colonies. These were carefully separated from the rest and sent to work along with the children, in fields especially reserved for them, where they could be under the constant and close watch of several carefully trained guards or monitors.

Provisions and clothes were dealt out at the common storehouses or workshops at regular intervals, and each family received enough for its subsistence. In addition, vegetables were grown in family plots, and some of the Indians even had their own horses and cows, "but all the products were obliged to be disposed of to the Jesuits for the common good, and in exchange for them they gave knives, scissors, cloth, and looking glass, and other articles made in the outside world." An adequate supply of coarse clothes was never lacking, but the natives never became accustomed to wearing shoes. All produce over and above that actually needed for their primitive subsistence the Jesuits either kept in the storehouses or sold in the outside world in order to obtain the few articles which they had to import. Direct exchange of one commodity for another was also frequently resorted to, and cattle were exchanged for cotton, sugar for rice, wheat for pig iron and tools from Europe, et cetera. An English defender of the missions wrote that though the priests obviously "had the full disposition of all the money earned in commerce, and of the distribution of the goods, neither the money nor the goods were used for self-aggrandizement, but were laid out for the benefit of the community at large."[52]

This, at least, was the ideal, but as time passed it did seem as if the Jesuits either came to esteem the acquisition of worldly wealth for its own sake or because through it they enjoyed great economic and political power, or at least that they did not utilize such profits as they made in a manner to raise the standards of living and educational development of the natives who lived under their absolute tutelage.

The total income of the thirty missions has been put at anywhere from one hundred thousand to three million dollars a year net. One author, Blas Garay, states in his book *The Communism of the Missions* that the Jesuits took in a million dollars a year and laid out only a hundred thousand; their profits being nine hundred thousand dollars, or 900 per cent. Another writer, the famous Argentine poet and historian, Leopoldo Lugones, who was appointed by his government to make an extensive trip through the entire mission region, after giving many months of careful study to the "Jesuit Empire," as he called it, calculated that each Indian worker brought in about forty pesos a year, and on a basis of one hundred thousand able workers that would mean four million dollars annually. Lugones figured expenses at a million dollars a year and profits at three million dollars. Extending this over one hundred years, he arrived at a total net income of the amazing sum of three hundred million dollars. All this, says Lugones, went into Jesuit coffers, because the order had an absolute monopoly on trade in the region. Utilizing the figures in the inventory of 1767 (date of expulsion of the Jesuits), our own estimate would be less than either of these. Whatever the amount, it was certainly large enough to make Jesuit competition exasperating to lay producers whose taxes were higher, whose economic machine was less efficient, and whose marketing was undoubtedly more cumbersome.[172]

The whole mission region was a closely knit economic unit linked together with posts and roads which led spokewise from the central axis of Candelaria to all parts of the mission territory. About eighty postal centers, all equipped with messengers, guards, and horses, were maintained constantly in the upper reaches of the River Paraná. There was also a considerable flotilla of canoes and river boats which carried their products to points where they could be sold. At the time of the expulsion of the Jesuits in 1767 the mission territory was exporting thirty thousand green hides a year and six thousand cured ones, together with about eighty-five hundred pounds of horsehair, wood valued at about twenty-five thousand dollars annually, in the neighborhood of two hundred thousand pounds of yerba mate, and some seventy-five thousand pounds of tobacco. Their herds at this time as shown in the inventory then taken, contained a total of 719,-761 cattle, 44,183 oxen, 27,204 horses, and 138,827 sheep. Their cultivated fields and pasture lands spread over thousands of square miles of fertile territory.

Within two years after the expulsion of the Jesuits all this wealth, and all the years of labor which had gone into accumulating it, and practically every evidence of once cleared and cultivated fields had disappeared. The Indians filtered back into the forests; a few hundred head of cattle escaped with them and returned to a wild state in the heavily covered grassland regions where they remain until this day. Wild-orange groves sprang up in the thorny wilderness, and heavy tropical growth soon covered the deserted settlements, while the wet rot of that humid atmosphere soon gutted them of most of their thatch and woodwork and all of their interior decorations. Mortar and stones became loosened, and lianas ate their way through the holes and crevices of once towering and majestic churches, while hundreds of neatly kept dormitories fell into rubble and disappeared.

The end came unexpectedly, although many years of vicious rumors, highhanded politics, and even open rebellion had preceded it. Portugal and Spain had for many years been haggling and squabbling over the frontier which was to separate southern Brazil from northern Argentine territory. The colony or fortress of Sacramento (now the city of Colonia in Uruguay), located on the north side of the La Plata estuary, just opposite Buenos Aires, was the Sudetenland of these disputes. It occupied a most strategic position and changed hands several times with the fortunes of war. While under Portuguese control it was infested with smugglers from England, Holland, Brazil, and France, all bent on beating the Spanish monopoly and cheating the King of Spain out of part of his royal revenues. The mission Indians had several times sent down large forces to help defend or retake it for Spain and Argentina.

Finally, in 1750, statesmen of the two home countries signed a treaty acknowledging Spain's claim to the colony for good and giving Portugal in return the seven best missions along the upper Uruguay River. Without consulting them or taking their rights or feelings into consideration, the Jesuits and Indians were abruptly called upon to move out of the territory which they had occupied over one hundred years and to establish themselves elsewhere or come under Portuguese control. The Indians loved their lands and also knew only too well the characteristics of the mamelucos. When a commission arrived to take over the region and fix the new boundary a native delegation met it and refused point blank to budge an inch. That some of the Jesuit fathers had urged them on there is no doubt.

The resultant "war" lasted for nearly five years, but eventually the last mission was besieged and captured, for what could a few thousand primitive Indians accomplish against the combined forces of Portugal and Spain? Most of the natives fled into the forests. The so-called "Jesuit war" was hardly over when the King of Spain, Ferdinand VI, died and his son, Charles III, came to the throne. In the meantime Brazil seemed loath to give up the colony of Sacramento and the Jesuits had been working tirelessly to right the wrong done to them and their charges, so Charles III promptly annulled the treaty with Portugal and told them they could reoccupy their missions.

The few years which followed were only the calm before the storm. Spaniards living along the River Plate rose to a pitch of fury against the priests and Indians who had successfully challenged their arms. Other even deeper hatreds and greeds were eating at their vitals. The old story about tremendous Jesuit wealth and hidden gold mines was revived and set before the envious population all gilded anew. To many colonists the unpardonable sin of the Jesuits was their obstruction of that economic *sine qua non* of the Spanish settlements, Indian slavery, which they had thwarted at every turn among those who had wanted to carry off mission Indians.

Furthermore (complained the settlers), the priests had obstinately refused to let Spaniards even enter the mission territory, where they had made slaves of the Indians themselves and were keeping a good thing from their fellow countrymen. The Jesuits were obviously building up a state of their own, independent of either the King or the colonial authorities. Most unbearable of all, their economic competition was driving many a good colonist toward bankruptcy. This was the state of mind in America. In Spain similar accusations against Jesuit interference in economic and political affairs, and their acquisition of considerable wealth, were repeatedly made before the Spanish court. Charles III could finally stand it no longer. Internal peace would have to be restored somehow, and, faced with the problem of choosing between the Jesuit minority and the civil authorities at large, he threw his support behind the latter and in 1767 decreed the expulsion of all Jesuits from Spain and the Spanish dominions.

In many regions the expulsion was carried out before the priests knew what was happening to them and there was no immediate trouble. At a given hour in the dead of night authorities armed with the order arrived at all the places where Jesuits lived and served their summons. However, Governor Bucareli of the River Plate hesitated for nearly a year before venturing to enter the mission territory. When he did so the Jesuits came out to meet him calmly enough and handed over the keys to their settlements. Priests of other orders, who had had no training in missionary work, were sent out to replace them. These men not only did not know how to govern the Indians or how to direct their labors, but most of them at once

took Indian women as mistresses, a thing the Jesuits had never done, a
in that way and many others soon aroused a general feeling of revulsion
against themselves. The natives very soon began to return to their primitive
lives in the wilderness, and in a few years there was not a trace of the teeming mission life which, in a territory larger than France, had for nearly two
centuries proceeded with its Arcadian life. Even to this day, however, the
Jesuits are remembered with great love in those regions, and many a wild
Indian still goes through the ritual which his great-great-grandfather or
some even more remote ancestor had handed down before he died. Other
than this there is nothing save the ruined towers of churches which raise
their gutted spires to the blue heavens.

Why did two hundred years of this semi-communistic civilization leave
so few traces in the lives of thousands of people? This calls into question
the essential merit of the whole Jesuit-inspired system. The primitive Arcadian life pursued by these Guaraní Indians hardly progressed upward
during the entire two centuries. Their communities were productive; they
were thrifty, orderly; they were even comfortable and joyous, but these
things were like scaffoldings around a weak building. Some writers say—
partisans of the Jesuits, of course—that this was bound to be the case considering the ignorant semi-nomadic state of the Indians concerned, and
that it would not have been possible to form a better society on such a
base.

But the glaring fact is that this mission society disappeared almost overnight. If it was not static in theory, or even in fact, it was at least too static
for the milieu surrounding it. Economic greed of those on the outside was
not the only cause of the Jesuits' ultimate failure. Deeper than this by far
was the equally incontrovertible fact that the society outside, good, bad,
and indifferent—and mostly bad and indifferent if its morals were compared to those inside the missions—was one in which the Indian mingled
his seed and his blood with that of his conquerors and so, forming a new
race, could look to the future, if not to the present, for his redemption.
The society of the mestizo was bound to endure. On the other hand, the
Jesuit missions formed a static and medieval theocracy inside the liberal
and forward-looking empire of Charles III. The two were certain to collide
head on, and there was no possible compromise between them. The missions were an anomaly, perhaps a threat, and certainly a challenge to this
zealous Bourbon king who lived on the eve of the French Revolution and
who strove to divest the Church of its strong temporal powers as his relatives in France had done many years before him.

No civilization can live to itself for long, and those Jesuits who molded
for themselves and their Indians a retreat in the heart of South America
were like the isolationists of a later day who believed that their country
might go its own way undisturbed and unimpeded even though surrounded by an economy of chaos and a world at war. Nor can one civiliza-

tion ever be pulled up by the bootstraps of another. Creation and progress are not instilled by discipline imposed from above. Self-willed achievement and order must form the soil in which they may thrive. Without the slow growth of individual character, differences, dignity, and an almost religious respect for initiative, material advancement may appear to have gone far, but once the props are removed the entire edifice must topple.

However, if the Arcady of those one hundred and fifty thousand isolated Indians in the "Jesuit Empire" was one which was doomed to perish, the application of the mission thesis to frontier life elsewhere in Latin America performed a function that was prerequisite and indispensable to the spread of Hispanic culture over the vast territories and peoples under its dominion. In 1767 the Jesuits alone numbered 2260 in Latin America, and under their control were 717,000 Indians. Franciscans and Dominicans also had dozens of mission settlements along the frontiers of both continents. Slowly these missionaries of different religious orders moved forward along the entire perimeter of colonial civilization. From Sonora in northern Mexico they came to the southwestern United States and advanced into Texas, New Mexico, Arizona, and northward along the California coast.

They founded San Antonio, El Paso, Santa Fe, Tucson, San Diego, Los Angeles, Monterrey, San Francisco, and dozens of other settlements which are now modern cities. From coastal Peru they spread over the Andes, crossed the mountain barrier, and descended into the tropical jungles on the other side. In Brazil they fanned out both northward and southward along the coast and then headed into the interior. Wherever they were allowed to remain long enough unmolested by the insatiable slave gatherers they accomplished wonders. From central Chile they went down into Araucanian territory in the south and established the new faith and culture in the very midst of the enemy.

These missions were everywhere "frontiers against paganism," or, more bluntly speaking, Hispanic "cells" in unfriendly territory. Out of these "cells" individual circuit-riding friars went on muleback to even more remote villages for occasional visits to preach the law and the Gospel. The missions later followed them as the hand follows the finger, and later still came the straggling hordes of lay colonists, until finally the old frontier was absorbed entirely and a new one had been extended beyond it. Sometimes the mission priests went accompanied by military guards, and garrisons were established to protect them from the natives, but this was the exception. On the other hand, the Indians themselves did enjoy a considerable amount of protection inside the mission settlements and frequently made up their own garrisons to fend off their more savage brothers.

The missions may be divided into three general periods: first, during the sixteenth century, under Dominican leadership (Las Casas, Pedro de Córdoba, and Vasco de Quiroga), they got under way in Mexico; second, during the seventeenth century the Jesuits established their powerful series of missions in the heart of South America, the greatest concentration being in Paraguay; third, during the eighteenth and final colonial century Fray Junípero Serra and his Franciscan followers built their beautiful chain of mission settlements along the coast of California.[4] In all of these regions the organization was similar.

The extreme regimentation of mission life, the strongly paternalistic controls of the religious fathers, who directed everything and provided everything, the very techniques of civilized society which they so carefully taught left no room for the development of the individual as a human being. The mission Indian became a contented automaton going through the motions of life, isolated from all the free social forces which mold human character, protected from every inimical influence of the outer world, of which he was certain someday to become a part. To put it plainly, he was for nearly two centuries treated like a mere child who was never permitted to grow up. There is no question but that the protection he received gave him a considerable measure of happiness, but it also made him face with helplessness, embitterment, fear, and trembling the day of his inevitable release into that maelstrom outside.

Of outstanding importance in the formation of Latin-American economy was the lack of a sense of property which these missions emphasized in their workers, but without emphasizing equally the dynamic and creative side of co-operative enterprise. The Indian in America did not view things in terms of private ownership, and the missionaries took advantage of this community spirit to erect their own theocratic and paternalistic structures. In the end, when the native was forced out into civilized society where private ownership was the veritable goal of life, he was completely at a loss as to how to defend himself and what little community property he did share. As a result he came near to losing it all.

The missions were a religious version of what the encomienda should be. That is what their founders intended. They were also a fundamental form of frontier garrisons and work centers, resting on faith and supported if necessary by force, until such time as their work was accomplished and the Hispanic "wave of the future" should engulf them. Their founders did not anticipate this. Nevertheless, their mission settlements not only performed an indispensable function as part of the advancing frontier, but they gave to that frontier, and hence to the peoples left in its wake, a strongly militant politico-religious cast, especially in education, which survives to a marked degree even in the most advanced nations of Latin America today.

Iberian culture, which came to America during the conquest in the form of the priest and soldier, grew roots and expanded in the two powerful institutions which followed them: the mission and the encomienda. They both issued from the same source, but the mission put religion first and depended mainly on persuasion, while the encomienda put labor first and depended mainly on force. The mission flourished along the colonial frontier; the encomienda became strong behind it. The mission preached race separation and attempted a utopia on the borders of a society which had little respect for impersonal justice or law, but by teaching and training the natives in some of the techniques of that society, it unwittingly shoved them toward the miscegenation to follow.

The encomienda was a halfway step between the mission and the town which became one great bed where natives and whites lay down together until their children eventually displaced them. This lay society of towns, estates, and encomiendas took up where the mission left off and carried forward the essential work of assimilation. The mission continued as a buffer as long as there was a frontier, but the expulsion of the Jesuits in 1767 dealt it a staggering blow. Although these religious and civil institutions hated and despised one another and squabbled, fought, and heaped vituperation on one another's heads, as social forces they went hand in hand, preparing the ground and planting the seeds of Iberian culture which gave to the American world a new population, a new religion, a new language, and a new outlook on life.

16

THE CHURCH AS
INQUISITOR AND MORAL CENSOR

The mission was probably the greatest institution established by the Church in the New World, and the activities of the clergy touched every walk of life. They were the teachers, architects, engineers, moral censors, writers, and scientists of the colonial period. Many leading priests who occupied high church office were later made viceroys by the King. The idea of separating the Church from the state did not even occur to the Spaniards or Portuguese of those days, in whose eyes only one true Church existed on earth. It was unthinkable for a man to entertain "heretical," that is, non-Catholic, ideas. Worse than that, it was a matter for the Inquisition.

The very mention of this name sends shudders down many a spine. The untold thousands who died in the flames in Spain and Portugal (their numbers doubtless exaggerated by Protestant writers) immediately come to mind. That other churches in those days were committing the same foul crime against the principles of humanity and tolerance is too often forgotten. But, whatever its nature on the Iberian Peninsula, the Inquisition in the colonies was a relatively mild affair.

Its purpose, of course, was to maintain the purity of the faith, to serve as the moral and spiritual censor, to judge, pass sentence, and punish crimes against religion. During the first few years of the colonial period the bishops and archbishops were permitted to carry out what little work of an inquisitorial nature arose in the colonies. There was not much because each immigrant was carefully scrutinized and given a religious bill of health before he left the home country. Sometimes priests came aboard a parting ship to make a final check. A man could be a syphilitic or a criminal and still remain aboard, but if there was the slightest doubt as to the orthodoxy of his faith he was thrown off. Thus very few cases which might later call for inquisitorial investigation ever reached America.

In regard to the Indians there was a considerable display of religious tolerance and the Inquisition was never allowed to touch them. It was considered that since the natives had had no previous opportunity to know the true faith they should not be held so strictly accountable for their mistakes. These slips were not sins but errors, and corrections, but not inquisitorial penalties, should be administered. For many years after the conquest, in fact, there was a difference of opinion among the Spaniards as to whether the Indian, with his limited mind and soul, was worthy of sharing in all the sacred rites of the Church. Discussion on this point became so bitter that in 1537 Pope Paul III issued a special bull stating that the native Americans were henceforth to be considered by all as rational human beings capable of receiving the holy sacraments the same as any white man.

In view of these considerations, the Inquisition was not brought to America immediately after the conquest, but when the population commenced to grow rapidly and some churchmen abused their religious powers by taking on unauthorized inquisitorial functions, the Holy Tribunal was set up. Philip II, in 1569, established central offices in Mexico City and Lima, and the organization began its work in the following year. "Its establishment," remarks one Latin-American writer, "coincided with the strongest effort made by the King to direct the civil, military, and economic life of his overseas dominions within the bounds of a certain definite channel,"[49] a channel whose flow he could control by sitting personally on the floodgates of central authority.

The Inquisition in America never attained the widespread violence which characterized it in Spain. The total number of those it condemned to die was approximately one hundred persons during the two and a half centuries of its existence. Probably another one hundred died in its prisons before final sentence was passed on them. This would result in an average of less than a single death a year out of many millions of inhabitants. Nevertheless, when a man was called before the Inquisitors of the Holy Office he had every reason to shake in his boots whether he was guilty or not. The accused never knew who had denounced him or what witnesses would be called before the tribunal to testify in his case. Sometimes he was not even told what his alleged transgression had been, but was merely asked to search his memory for it, and then recant.

"On his first appearance he was flattered with a pardon, in order to make him confess his crime, and afterward if this method failed, he was subjected to atrocious torture. If no success was gained by any of these methods of forcing a confession from the accused, he was declared acquitted; but a suspicion of guilt always hung over him."[43]

In extreme cases, when a person was being tried for heresy, if he died in prison because of illness or torture before the trial was concluded, "then he was buried secretly and the process was continued. If nothing was finally proved against him, absolution was read to his effigy and the site of his grave was told to the family. But if on the other hand he was found guilty, his body was dug up and burned, and his ashes were thrown to the winds."[43] He was also burned in effigy in an *auto de fe* before the crowds who had gathered to observe the punishments meted out to other live sinners who had survived their trials.

In these latter cases if the guilty party was a condemned heretic he was advised "to reconcile himself to the Catholic faith. If he did this, he was hanged and his body was burned. If he did not, he was burned alive."[43] This burning was carried out with solemn auto de fe or "manifestation of the faith," and could take place only in Mexico City or Lima. People often gathered from miles around to be present at these horrible spectacles. There was a great procession "to the sound of trumpet and drum" which filed slowly to the *quemadero*, or stake, where the execution was carried out. Some spectators looked on with sadistic pleasure, but others came to fear and despise the very words "auto" or "inquisitor."

Heresy was the only crime for which death was the penalty. Most of the heretics were accused of Jewish or Protestant practices, beliefs, or statements, but there were also many among them who had made heretical statements about the Catholic faith. Typical of the former were a few Jewish converts who had somehow managed to get into the New World and had been suspected of practicing their old religion in private, and also a few English sea dogs or pirates who had been captured while raiding coastal cities. Among the "old Christians" themselves a few were executed who had denied the truth of Catholic dogma. One Spaniard claimed that he was Jesus Christ in person; another, who wrote religious books "containing erroneous doctrine," was strangled and his body burned with his books hanging around his neck; a third poor fellow, who confessed that he was an agnostic, but who admitted that he was both ignorant and half-witted, was also found guilty, as was a fourth who was accused of a pact with the devil. This last man "gave signs of insanity, but on examination by physicians was pronounced sane. Under severe torture he remained perfectly quiescent and insensible to pain, which could only be explained by diabolical aid, so he was shaved all over and inspected carefully for charms or for the devil's mark, but in vain. A second torture was endured with the same indifference and he was condemned to relaxation as an apostate heretic. On the night before the *auto* he said to the confessor who endeavored to convert him, 'There is no God, nor hell, nor glory; it is all a lie; there is birth and death and that is all.' During the *auto* he manifested no emotion and was burned alive as an impenitent."[55]

When the Inquisition was temporarily abolished in 1813, the inhabitants of Lima stormed and sacked the Holy Chamber in that city with a fury reminiscent of the Bastille. One of the articles found there was a figure of a crucified Christ in natural size with the head attached in such a manner that it could be moved by means of cords held by someone behind the scenes. If this head was moved up and down after a trial it meant that the accused had been found guilty, and vice versa.

The colonial Inquisition probably tried a maximum of six to seven thousand cases, most of these being persons who were accused of religious or sexual offenses of a relatively minor nature. The vast majority of these trials took place in the sixteenth and seventeenth centuries, that is, before the advent of the French Bourbons to the Spanish throne. Inquisitorial interference in matters which in no way related to religion was a frequent cause of disturbance to the civil authorities, for even the Viceroy was subordinate to the inquisitor, and by 1696 these "arbitrary extensions of inquisitorial jurisdiction over matters wholly foreign to the objects of its institution" had become so disruptive an influence that the Council of the Indies "addressed a formal remonstrance to Charles II, recapitulating a long array of abuses and violences . . . and the Council supplicated the King, if not for the total extinction of the tribunal, at least for the dismissal of the officials."[55] Final dissolution of the Inquisition, however, did not take place until the year 1820. Its temporary suppression in 1813 lasted only a single year, or until the liberal Spanish Government was ousted and replaced by the absolutist Ferdinand VII.

Typical as it was of religious fanaticism and blight, the cruel and ignorant zeal from which the Inquisition sprang was not at all a Spanish monopoly. Such practices were characteristic of the world in general at that period. In the United States at Salem, Massachusetts, in the year 1692, nineteen women were tried and found guilty of practicing witchcraft and were hanged in a great ceremony. In England hundreds of Catholics lost their lives by burning or by decapitation after licentious Henry VIII had seceded from the jurisdiction of the Pope and from the Catholic Church in order to establish his own national religion, which then blessed the bigamies that the Pope had refused to sanction. The treatment of natives in India by the English at a much later date, and the lynching of dozens of persons, many of them innocent, in the United States within our own short memory, the persecution of the Jews by the Nazis in Germany and Poland—all these things go to prove that while we have a historic duty to know the truth about the Spanish Inquisition, we have no reason to feel self-righteous about it.

Aside from its religious dictatorship, the colonial Inquisition exercised a strict censorship over all books and works of art in the colonies. In this less spectacular sphere its work sank far deeper roots. Inquisitors closely supervised all presses and publications and frequently entered bookshops and private libraries in order to make a search for heretical writings. Most of the books printed in the colonies in the early years were of a religious nature. Importations of books and art objects were carefully examined before being allowed admittance. Such works as Milton's *Paradise Lost*, Robertson's famous *History of America*, or the writings of Voltaire and Rousseau were considered to be thoroughly heretical. At first religious heresy was the main consideration of the inquisitors, but during the eighteenth century an expression of democratic ideas became equally detestable in their eyes. A total of over five thousand authors appeared on the Index of blacklisted books in the eighteenth century. As the years passed this censorship was gradually relaxed and special permission for reading and possessing books on the prohibited list was more easily obtained. However, the long-standing and bigoted censorship of thought, supported always by the Church and the central government as a regular policy for perhaps a longer period of time than had ever occurred anywhere before in history, not only cast its blight on early colonial culture, literature, and art, but impeded trade, held back political and economic progress, molded with intolerant fingers the very way of life among the Latin-American peoples.

The Catholic Church, as has been pointed out by many of her unorthodox children like George Santayana, was always a very human institution in regard to the foibles and emotions of the animal man. Only in matters of religious dogma was it absolutely intransigent. To sin was human, and was an understandable human weakness, but to disbelieve was a crime against the Church and God. It might almost be said that North American Protestants, particularly those with puritanical tendencies, turned this statement the other way around.

One of the consequences of this was that morality in the Spanish and Portuguese colonies, particularly sexual morality, was generally rather lax even among the priests. Careful supervision of their daily lives was manifestly impossible, and many of them took advantage of this situation to indulge "the lusts of the flesh." This is brought out repeatedly in the many efforts made by the better-disciplined clergy to wipe out such laxity on the part of their undisciplined brothers. Official reports sent back to Spain and Portugal from time to time show how widespread this immorality had become. The Jesuits in Brazil fought a losing battle against it from the very first and complained without avail to the authorities back in the peninsula; the Archbishop of Mexico, in 1575, sent a report to Philip II in which he spoke of the immoral practices of many individuals among his clergy; Father Angel de Valencia and other Franciscans went so far as to state that "most of the clergy who come over here to America" were guilty of "dissoluteness and breaking of their vows, which is a great pity"; and in Chile there were so many scandals of priests who made gifts of considerable parts of their estates to their illegitimate daughters, either as dowries or as legacies after their death, that the King had to pass a special statute forbidding it. The leading Spanish historian of today, Rafael Altamira, sums up the situation by stating that the great distances which separated priests from their supervising authorities made this looseness possible, and that "the trials before the colonial Inquisition, contemporary chronicles, the archives of the courts and of the government, all abound in documents which reveal the exceeding frequency of that immorality."

Some of these priests lived in open concubinage, as did many high government officials. The Viceroy Amat of Peru flaunted his mistress, the famous Perricholi, before the public, in theaters, and on the streets daily. However, it was immorality within the Church which had the greatest effect on the people at large, leading many of them to feel a disrespect for the clergy in general. Long after the Council of Trent and other reform movements had put the lives of Spanish and Portuguese priests living in the peninsula under rigorous discipline, licentiousness continued on a large scale in the colonies. It never embraced a majority of the clergy, but did infect a sufficiently numerous minority to become one of the leading influences in arousing a feeling against the Church, just as a similar widespread immorality had previously been one of the principal causes for the Protestant reformation in Europe.

Although Government and Church both fought against sexual laxities with vigorous laws, the higher officials did not always practice these moral principles in their own lives. Kings Charles V and Philip II both had several illegitimate children, and Philip IV sired thirty-two known bastards. Many of the earlier popes were guilty of similar transgressions of the moral law. Caesar Borgia, who was made a Spanish cardinal at the age of seventeen, was an illegitimate offspring of Pope Alexander VI, and Lucrezia Borgia was his daughter. Pope Alexander was a native Spaniard who occupied the Holy See during the reign of Ferdinand and Isabella. It so happened that the New World crusade was carried out while Catholicism was at its lowest moral ebb, and this laxity, once planted in America, grew to such proportions that it was nearly impossible to root it out. It was a rank weed in an all too friendly soil.

Nor was sexual license the only clerical offense against recognized social propriety. There were violent jurisdictional disputes between different religious orders and between orders in general and the lay clergy. In Chile the Franciscans set fire to an Augustinian convent; in Mexico a widespread riot broke out in 1569 when a group of secular clergy attempted to stop a Franciscan procession; later a bitter dispute between Bishop Palafox and the Jesuits again rent the Mexican Church asunder. When the bishop attempted to replace the members of religious orders with secular priests in the country's schools the Jesuits ran him out of Mexico.

These disputes, however, were mild if compared with those which raged between civil and ecclesiastical authorities. Religion was never the issue in such cases, but it was frequently dragged in by the heels and was invariably the loser, no matter who won. The Church, both in the mother countries and in the colonies, enjoyed a vast amount of economic wealth and power which was bound to conflict with the civil economy.

Subordinate only to the Crown, the ecclesiastical dignitaries in some regions became the supreme law not only in matters of faith but in matters which did not pertain to religion at all. This was especially true in those sections of the empire where viceroys did not reside. "When anyone," says a famous historian of Chile, "whoever he might be, even the governor himself, resisted the mandates of the bishop, the latter fulminated his excommunication against him—a weapon stronger than a whole army, because it left the rebel outside the church and isolated from society. This was the principal element that gave the ecclesiastical authority predominance over the political."[43]

For example, the encomenderos of Chile paid their parish priests certain set sums. Once, upon their petition, a governor of the country reduced these payments by ordinance. The Bishop of Santiago "required the revocation of the ordinance under penalty of excommunication," and the governor had to give way.[43]

Another example of ecclesiastical interference in temporal matters is the following: Sometimes even the church inquisitors, contrary to the law, received their allotments of lands and Indians, and in Mexico in 1666 they threatened the Viceroy Mancera and the officials of the Treasury with excommunication if they refused to furnish, on terms proposed by themselves, the quicksilver which was needed in working their mines in Zacatecas.

In dozens of similar instances which in no way affected religious belief or church doctrines, the ecclesiastical authorities used their religious power for political or economic purposes. In that manner they frequently disqualified and discredited their religious authority as well in the minds of many intelligent people.

17

GOLD AND SILVER IN FOREIGN COFFERS

From the earliest years of the conquest almost to the end of the colonial period Spain was intent on building up in her American dependencies a mining economy. There was, of course, agricultural development, cattle raising, some manufacturing, and monopolistic trade, but the foundation of the structure was mining. Although a mining economy affords the greatest immediate returns, in the long run, when unsupported by a well-rounded development of other activities, it is by far the most costly to maintain.

During the first century (between 1492 and 1600) approximately two billion pesos' worth of gold and silver was shipped from the colonies to the mother country. This was at least three times the entire European supply of these metals before the discovery of America. Alexander von Humboldt estimated the total production of gold and silver in the Spanish New World from 1492 to 1800 at six billion dollars. At the close of the colonial period the annual output was about forty million pesos, or ten times the known production of all the rest of the world.

Because of the enormous influx of gold and silver from the colonies, the Spaniards at home became unwilling to work hard to accumulate a competence, but would far rather by hook or crook get their share of the incoming wealth. As a consequence they permitted their industrial enterprises and even their agriculture to deteriorate to such an extent that the peninsula was soon unable to supply either herself or her colonies with the goods needed for subsistence. Not manufacturing these goods, Spain was forced to import them and pay for them with the treasure coming out of the New World.

As is always the case where there is a plethora of money and a scarcity of goods, prices mounted sky high. To cap the climax the King always had a war waging, and by the end of the sixteenth century, despite its great income, the nation was close to bankruptcy. Sometimes in a single year Philip II spent more than five years' income. Funds were borrowed right and left from the international bankers (at 18 per cent interest), and Spain became merely a funnel through which the wealth of the New World flowed into foreign coffers.

Between 1550 and 1600 conditions inside Spain became so miserable that hundreds of thieves, sharpers, and beggars walked the peninsular streets. The Spanish picaresque novels give a full account of them. They were the people who had missed their chance in the general scramble, "the conquistadores out of date, the gold-seekers gone to seed." The demoralization of the social and economic order was now almost complete. "The fortunate adventurers who came back from the New World were as great a terror to public morals through their extravagance and recklessness, as the unsuccessful through their destitution and despair."[56] Productive labor of all kinds was neglected under the influence of the Midas dream. Villages and towns fell into ruin, and vast treeless wastes appeared, covered with weeds and briars, where cultivated fields or forests had been before. The poverty was so widespread that there were scarcely any marriages.

In all this drab picture there were only two havens, the one illusory or limited, the other unlimited and real. They were the Church and America. In order to find security, countless thousands sought entrance into the Church and thus decreased even further the rachitic productive power of the peninsular economy. This solution was at best a stopgap, for the Church obviously could not support the great droves who asked admittance. An estimated 1,141,000 persons held religious office of some kind in the Spanish Empire of the seventeenth century. Another 447,000 held government jobs.

But there was America. And for Spaniards, too, America was "the land of opportunity." By the end of Philip II's reign it became "the refuge and haven of all the poor devils of Spain, the sanctuary of the bankrupt, the safe-conduct of murderers, the escape of all gamblers, the promised land for women of free virtue, and lure and disillusionment of the many and the incomparable remedy of the few." These are the words in which Cervantes describes the feeling of one of his characters who went to the New World after losing nearly all his worldly possessions in the Old, and twenty years later returned with a great fortune. "The poverty of some, the greed of others, and the madness of all" caused a great exodus from the stricken peninsula to this land of the freer life. Those who had hesitated before pulled up their anchors now and set forth for the new horizon, for even if disillusionment should finally stare them in the face, it was better than to sit and to wait for the certain rot and the final curtain of their fates and their fortunes in a nation which had already drained itself to perdition.

When these emigrants arrived in the New World they naturally tended to think in terms of gold and slaves. Agriculture, industry, cattle raising, all kinds of productive enterprise had to take a second place. As Adam Smith pointed out many years ago, slave labor is in the long run the dearest of all, for whatever work the slave does beyond that which is necessary to purchase his own maintenance can be squeezed out of him by violence only, and not by any interest of his own. On such a base as this the economic foundation of Latin America was raised.

Nevertheless, these people had to eat, to clothe themselves, to live. A minimum of agricultural development, manufacturing, and cattle raising was carried out. Many and easily procured workers made possible large incomes for the few, despite the poverty of the masses. The importation of new plants and animals broadened the agrarian base. By the year 1800 the value of the agricultural and cattle products of Mexico totaled thirty million pesos annually, and her mine products amounted to twenty-three million. Cattle multiplied rapidly on the warm pasture lands, and as early as 1625 one Mexican rancher was said to have owned forty thousand head. The story was even more striking in Argentina, where there were forty-two million cattle and horses by the eighteenth century. In both regions cattle sold for about two pesos a head.

The element in early Spanish colonial life which came closest to industrial organization was the *obraje*, or "workshop." It was a kind of community workshop and reformatory where much of the labor was performed by debtors or minor criminals. They slept on a hard board at night, with their feet sometimes firmly chained to it so that escape was impossible. Here coarse woolen cloth was woven for the colonial population, and in view of Spain's inability to supply woven goods in sufficient quantity these workshops performed an indispensable function. They were usually situated on the banks of a stream whose water power could be used for some of their operations. The workers were supposed to put in ten or eleven hours a day but, unless they fell in the convict category, were granted Sundays off. In most cases they were paid some wages. Debts were counted against earnings, however, and sometimes the worker received nothing at all. In 1609 a royal statute demanded that payment of salaries "be made daily, or at least every Sunday, in actual silver and delivered directly into the worker's hands." Both women and children worked in these centers, although it was prohibited to employ a child of less than ten years of age. The obraje represented the start of manufacturing in Latin America and was no better and no worse than similar small workshops elsewhere in the world at that time. By the end of the colonial period some regions had large and flourishing looms, but in most places they were definitely a combination of sweatshop and chain gang. The traveler, Concolorcorvo, describes the obrajes of Peru in a rather favorable light, but Baron Humboldt, who found so many things to praise in Mexico, was shocked by the horrible conditions he found in the workshops there, the half-naked and filthy workers, the indiscriminate mixing of criminals and honest day laborers, and the merciless floggings dealt out to those who broke the slightest rule. The weaving and dyeing were both extremely poor, and the whole setup was one to turn the stomach of any real humanitarian.

There were a few other small factories or workshops in which the labor contained no criminal elements and was better treated, but the total of manufactured goods produced in the colonies was extremely small. Spain's monopolistic laws directed against every product which might offer competition with her own, plus the native disinclination to take part in manufacturing activities, kept this industry in the pygmy stage throughout the colonial period. In the wealthiest colony, Mexico, the annual value of manufactured products during the eighteenth century was only about seven million pesos, or slightly less than one peso per inhabitant. Agricultural and cattle products came to more than four times this amount, and gold and silver to more than three times as much.

There are no complete figures on the commerce of the colonies, but in the year 1747, out of a total of approximately thirty-eight million pesos' worth of exports, thirty-four million pesos of that amount was in gold and silver. This does not include smuggled goods. By the end of the century, with the gradual lifting of trade barriers, the above total was nearly quadrupled.

One Latin-American writer has compared the commercial monopoly and tax policy adopted by Spain to the workings of a huge elephant trunk which sucked all the wealth out of America and then squirted it in the general direction of itself, but hit mainly all the bystanders—in this case the other European nations. The figure has its merits. The King, of course, was the main part of that snout. He got in on the ground floor and was to receive as his share of the loot collected by his conquistadores the "royal fifth." This continued as the royal fifth of all gold, silver, and precious stones taken from American mines. Finally, when this extremely large tax made further production of some of these things economically impossible, the amount was reduced to one tenth and, a few years before the struggle for independence, to one twentieth. The King also owned completely many of the richest mines, and he rented or sold the right to operate these at a great profit. He was also to receive one half of all treasures found in Indian graves or temples, and such was the legend of buried wealth in the Americas that, for centuries after the conquest, every stranger who appeared in one of Latin America's more isolated regions was immediately suspected of seeking for these *tapadas* (buried treasures), and a crowd of natives invariably shadowed his heels to see what might be uncovered.

At the base of the colonial tax structure was the *alcabala*, which was a general tax on the sale or exchange of any article. It was more than a sales tax, for even gifts were subject to it; only belongings of the clergy were exempt. The alcabala had been in force on the peninsula for many years in varying forms, and was transferred to the New World when the royal purse began to run short. Beginning in 1574, at 2 per cent on every transaction, it was later raised to 4 per cent, and finally became 6 per cent.

Another tax which hit everybody, rich and poor alike, was the ecclesiastical tithe or *diezmo*. This was supposed to pay the way of the Church, but was levied by the state on all agricultural, cattle, sheep, garden, or fruit products, and on all domestic fowls. Pope Alexander VI, in 1501, had given his faithful subrulers, the monarchs of Spain, the right to collect this tax with the understanding that it was to be devoted to the Church. They were empowered to retain a small portion for the Royal Treasury.

A still further tax, which hit all of the natives, and hence for several years the majority of the population, was an out-and-out tribute which each Indian had to pay either to the King or to his feudal master, the encomendero. At first, of course, the Indians were unable to pay this tribute in coin, and so it was delivered in kind, that is, in wheat, corn, fowl, fish, et cetera. Later on many of them made their payments in silver coin.

There was also a customs duty, or *almojarifazgo*, which was as heavy a tax as the word signifying it. This duty was levied on all goods exported or imported. It was 10 per cent in Spain and 5 per cent in the colonies. Then there was a tax to pay the expenses of the warships which accompanied the merchant fleets, another tax for the Admiral of the Indies, another still which was a sort of seaman's labor-union dues that went to the central office of that organization in Seville. The clergy did not escape untouched either, for they had to pay a direct tax to the King equal to one month's income. This income tax was payable every year and was called the "ecclesiastical allowance." There were dozens of other minor taxes such as we have today, fines, fees, stamp taxes, property taxes, tolls, and so on.

The Crown also received half of the first year's income of every civil or ecclesiastical royal officer, whatever it could collect for the sale of public offices, and a considerable return from the royal monopolies, or *estancos*, state-run commissaries, from which many essentials of daily life, such as salt, gunpowder, quicksilver, lead, tin, tobacco, and many other commodities had to be purchased. The total income from these taxes, as we have already seen, was never enough to meet the needs of a monarch almost constantly at war, whose nation was rapidly becoming depopulated and whose industries were prostrate. Consequently, he often authorized the viceroys or governors to contract loans in his name, and then rarely, if ever, felt any responsibility to repay them. At other times he took possession of all the gold (or silver) that any of the merchant fleets brought from America to Spain, and gave a receipt in his name in favor of the persons despoiled. His needs were such that there is no record of his ever returning these sums, though frequently they were the aid which settlers in the New World were sending back to their destitute families.

As to the total receipts which the Royal Treasury obtained from these many taxes, some fabulous estimates have been made, but the Argentine historian, Ricardo Levene, one of the most painstaking interpreters of Latin-American history, placed the annual average at approximately nine million pesos. "The viceroyalty of New Spain," writes Levene, "produced a net income of from five to six million *pesos*; Peru, 1,000,000; Buenos Aires, from 600,000 to 700,000; New Granada, from 400,000 to 500,000; and the remaining colonies scarcely produced what was needed to cover the expenses of administration."[42] The above figures refer to the annual *average*; the amounts taken in during certain periods were somewhat higher. Mexico, for example, jumped from a total gross revenue of about six million pesos in 1750 to twelve million in 1775, and to over twenty million in 1802. Considerably more than half these amounts was net.

The constant mention of the word peso in reference to the financial setup in the colonies makes some explanation of that word necessary. In the first place, actual money in coin form was scarce in the New World. There were few mints, and those which existed often lowered the value of their output by a rascally practice of including much less of the noble metal than was called for by law. In the second place, there were never enough of these coins to go around anyway. A substitute was adopted of simply using bits of raw silver, silver being much more common than gold, of a specific *weight* or *peso*.

These bits of silver took the place of coined money for a long time, and later, when coins were actually available, the word still continued in use. But such were the fluctuations in the economies of the different regions that the value of the peso soon varied considerably from country to country. At the present moment, for example, the Colombian peso is worth about sixty cents in United States money, whereas the Chilean peso is valued at only a little more than three cents. The value of the peso in colonial times is equally hard to determine. However, a few definite examples of its purchasing power can be called to mind. In the early days of Argentina it bought two bushels of wheat, or one goat, but a horseshoe cost a peso and a half, because iron was scarce. A yard of linen cost one third of a peso. In Paraguay twenty-five pounds of yerba mate, the native green tea, could be bought for two pesos. In Peru a pound of bread cost only one real or one eighth of a peso.

Throughout the River Plate territory—that is, in Argentina, Paraguay, and Uruguay—the peso was worth one fourth less than it was in the other colonial dominions. The King of Spain had by specific decree declared that it was to contain one fourth less silver. But the purchasing power of the peso was sometimes exactly the same, for in Chile a blacksmith was obliged by law to make a pair of horseshoes for three pesos, the same identical price for them in Argentina. A Chilean doctor collected a fee of one peso for a call during the night, and a little more than half that for a call during the day. A tailor had to make a suit of clothes for thirteen pesos. The *cabildo* decided on what would be a fair price for every article, and these price lists had to be posted in plain view in all the shops. The price ceilings of the Office of Price Administration in the United States are hardly innovations.

In some sections, as in Argentina, where coin was always scarce, actual commodities were often used as a means of exchange, especially wool, tallow, sheep, tobacco, yerba mate, horseshoes, wedges of iron, and goats. Imported goods naturally brought exorbitant prices in these remote regions. We have already mentioned that a package of paper cost one hundred pesos in Chile, a sword three hundred, and a cape around five hundred, while a cow or two bushels of wheat were worth only two pesos. In Argentina a pound of spices brought thirty pesos, a bottle of oil an equal sum, one of wine twenty-five pesos, a yard of velvet fifty pesos. These prices were those collected in Buenos Aires, the highest consumers' market in Latin America.

In an attempt to arrive at a satisfactory conclusion on the purchasing power of the peso in colonial days, all one can do is to make a guess, because if it is in terms of native products the purchasing power will seem extremely high, whereas if it is in terms of imported goods the value will appear to be unreasonably low. Probably as good an estimate as any would be to say that in most of the larger centers the colonial peso was worth from one to three dollars in United States currency as applied to native products, and only five to ten cents as applied to most imports on which duty had been paid. However, we must remember that cheaper contraband goods flooded all markets and supplied most imported goods after the first few years of monopoly.

In those years of the sixteenth century when discovery, conquest, looting, conversion, and colonization went hand in hand, a world revolution was taking place without the knowledge of its participants. The addition of America to total world wealth was at the core of it. New lands and new peoples represented incalculable sources of income which would enter the stream of Western civilization. Through a lack of foresight on the part of Spain and Portugal, and because of the nature and traditions of the peninsular inhabitants, feudalism would be perpetuated in the New World. But capitalism and industrialism would be born in the Old. The increase and accumulation of wealth, new markets, an expanded horizon which would send trading ships over the seven seas, the will to imperialism, the industrial revolution, an exalted interest in scientific progress, all of these things began their great forward march on the American base.

In his work on *Kapital* Karl Marx writes: "The discovery of gold and silver in America, the extirpation, enslavement and entombment in mines of the aboriginal population, the beginning of the conquest and looting of the East Indies, the turning of Africa into a warren for the commercial hunting of black-skins, signalized the rosy dawn of the era of capitalist production. These idyllic proceedings are the chief momenta of primitive accumulation. On their heels treads the commercial war of the European nations, with the globe for a theatre. It begins with the revolt of the Netherlands from Spain . . ."

Adam Smith, father of modern economy, in his *Wealth of Nations,** amplifies the picture in these words: "The discovery of America, and that of a passage to the East Indies by the Cape of Good Hope, are the two greatest and most important events in the history of mankind. Their consequences have already been very great: but, in the short period of between two and three centuries which has elapsed since these discoveries were made, it is impossible that the whole extent of their consequences can have been seen. What benefits, or what misfortunes to mankind may hereafter result from those great events, no human wisdom can foresee. By uniting, in some measure, the most distant parts of the world, by enabling them to relieve one another's wants, to increase one another's enjoyments, and to encourage one another's industry, their general tendency would seem to be beneficial. To the natives, however, both of the East and West Indies, all the commercial benefits which can have resulted from these events have been sunk and lost in the dreadful misfortunes which they have occasioned. These misfortunes, however, seem to have arisen rather from accident than from anything in the nature of those events themselves. At the particular time when these discoveries were made, the superiority of force happened to be so great on the side of the Europeans, that they were enabled to commit with impunity every sort of injustice in those remote countries. Hereafter, perhaps the natives of those countries may grow stronger, or those of Europe may grow weaker, and the inhabitants of all the different quarters of the world may arrive at that equality of courage and force which, by inspiring mutual fear, can alone overawe the injustice of independent nations into some sort of respect for the rights of one another. But nothing seems more likely to establish this equality of force than that mutual communication of knowledge and all sorts of improvements which an extensive commerce from all countries to all countries naturally, or rather necessarily, carries along with it."

The discoverers, Spain and Portugal, were in a position to carry out the conquest of much of the American territory, but in this new economy of the industrialists, of the middle class, of the workers, of the shopkeepers handling the new goods, they were quickly forced to take secondary roles. Their own intransigence, hatred of manual labor, and showy wastefulness were as much the causes as anything else.

* This work was first published in the year 1776.

There were also certain intangible values which were sliding off the impervious core of the peninsula like water off a duck's back, for the Spaniard was certain that his own values were superior to all others. Speaking of Spain alone—but the words are equally applicable to Portugal—a Latin-American historian remarks that her people endured with derision "the constant shock suffered by a nation which still lived in the Middle Ages, and yet was battered night and morning by the ardent wave of the Renaissance which reached it from Italy, by the biting wave of the Reformation which came to it from Germany, by the ironic and subtle wave of Humanism which flowed from the Low Countries. All Europe was in the grip of a feverish desire to change its values, to revise its intellectual life, and only Spain with Charles V—who retired to pray in the midst of his victories and was to end his life in a monastery—Spain with its Catholic King, its mad queen, remained silent and alone, tightening the screws of the Inquisition."[35]

From the earliest days there were essential differences between the conquest and colonization of Latin America, on the one hand, and of Anglo-Saxon America, on the other. Our forefathers came to this continent seeking religious and political liberty, and as settlers willing to till the soil. A desire for personal liberty, a willingness to endure hard labor, and the absence of gold or Indian slaves molded them quickly into an aggressive and forward-moving nation. From the very beginning they came with their wives and maintained the race. The Spaniards, and later the Portuguese, came to Latin America without women, in a crusade of conversion, and in search of gold and slaves. They found all that they were seeking and so for more than three centuries perpetuated and intensified the economy of exploitation, which is the economy of oppression, scarcity, poverty, and improvidence.

Many other things served to accentuate the picture. The Hispanic colonies were taxed heavily to support their home countries and their State-Church. The North American colonies were not, but on the contrary England spent more in protecting them from attack than she ever got out of them in monetary return. In the second place, Spain and Portugal were not able to supply the wants of their colonies because (1) their own industries were stricken, (2) they did not have enough ships to carry these goods across, (3) what ships they did have were often attacked and captured by the superior navies of their enemies, (4) what goods did arrive sold at exorbitant prices. The inevitable result of these conditions was contraband trade on a huge scale which little by little destroyed the close link which had at first existed between the mother countries and their children. Economic motives in history determine the course pursued by a nation more frequently than do factors of political belief or affinity, religion, or even blood relationship.

18
THE BRAZILIAN COLOSSUS
BEGINS TO MOVE FORWARD

Of the four or five geographic divisions into which all Latin America falls, about which her history has centered and will surely in the future continue to revolve, Brazil is by far the largest, the most populous, potentially the wealthiest, the most powerful, and the most conglomerate in her racial fusion. Throughout her history she has been like a giant dinosaur, a colossus in her own right, large and powerful-looking, yet except for her great size almost defenseless. So far her size has been defense enough. She awaits immigration and industrialization on a vast scale to achieve her destiny.

Brazil's history has been a succession of economic errors compounded on a slow-moving cosmopolitan base which has felt its way forward with a methodical sureness unique in Latin America. For fifty years she was the neglected colony while Portugal continued to waste her strength in India, until the lucrative spice trade brought only wars, debts, and bankruptcy. The growing challenge of Spain's dominions around Brazilian territory was perhaps the goad which first served to awaken Portuguese interest in the sleeping behemoth. In 1549 the first governor of Brazil was sent over from Portugal. He was Thomé de Sousa and established his center and capital city at Bahia, at the midway point along the Atlantic coast of the territory. His instructions were to absorb the twelve disintegrating captaincies and bring them together under a single government.

Thomé de Sousa, like so many other noteworthy Europeans of his time, was a bastard, but he was also of noble birth and his temper "had been tried and approved in the African and Indian wars." His expedition was made up of about a thousand colonists and soldiers, among whom were four hundred *degredados*, or men banished from Portugal for some minor criminal activity. Their colony, Bahia, was to be a strong military fortress which could protect the Brazilian coast both from the Indian forays organized in the interior and foreign encroachments from without. Strangely enough the city's coat of arms was made up of a white dove with three olive leaves in her beak, on a background of green. Among the colonists were six Jesuits, the first to set foot in Brazil. One of them was Father Nóbrega, who later distinguished himself in the service of the natives.

The old Portuguese sailor, Caramurú, who had been shipwrecked on the Brazilian coast many years previously, was settled in the Bahia region with his wives, children, and friends, and when Sousa's men landed, there were hundreds of Indians and half-breeds on the shore to greet them and help unload the ships. The new governor freely distributed gifts among them, and the discipline which he imposed on his men soon made them all good friends. The Indians gladly aided in the work of construction, and within four months "a hundred houses were built and sugar plantations were laid out in the vicinity." Bahia was located near the site of an older abandoned trading post, and the materials left behind by this earlier establishment aided the new colonists in building their own town. Besides the hundred houses there was also a cathedral, a school for the Jesuits, a large residence for the governor, and a customhouse.

The buildings had hardly been erected when an Indian slew a Portuguese a few miles from the city. Sousa demanded that the native be turned over to him for trial and punishment; fortunately even the Indians admitted that he had been to blame and handed him over. The governor had this poor wretch tied to the mouth of a cannon and blew him to pieces before an assembled multitude. One historian remarks, "No mode of execution devised can be more humane to the sufferer, nor more dreadful to the beholders." At any rate, the execution had the desired effect, and from that time on the colonists were not molested by the neighboring Indians.

Further supplies were brought in the following year, and the year after that the Queen of Portugal sent over a number of "female orphans of noble family, who had been educated in the Convent of Orphans; they were to be given in marriage to officers," and were distributed along with the Negro slaves, the cattle, and the brood mares which the Crown had sent over to improve the settlement. Supplies and reinforcements continued to arrive in the following years, and the colony prospered. The governor visited other settlements along the coast from time to time and strengthened them considerably. He soon brought an administration of justice to their former state of chaotic demoralization and lawlessness. Sousa saw so many Indians in the coastal regions that he remarked, "Even if hundreds were killed daily for market there would be no end of them." Little did he know what was about to happen.

The six Jesuit fathers who had come with the colonists immediately set themselves up as protectors of the Indians, and no obstacle or hardship was too severe for them to endure in defense of their principles. Fathers Nóbrega and Anchieta, both of whom became great heroes in the civilization of the natives, roamed up and down the coast, gathering them into villages, giving them some elementary instruction, and holding off the slave gatherers. Their most difficult task at first was to stop the cannibalistic orgies which were the natives' greatest pleasure. At times they were obliged to slip the bodies of the slain away at night and bury them secretly in order to prevent these gorgings on human flesh. One priest found a most effective preventive by baring himself from the waist up and then marching through the streets of the guilty village, flogging himself until the blood came, and crying out all the while that he was but trying to avert the terrible punishment which God would otherwise inflict upon the sinful natives. They could not bear this gory sight and repented of their wrongdoing, swearing never to repeat it, but the custom was so deeply ingrained that they still carried it out in secret. On one occasion, when an old native who had recently been converted became ill, the good fathers trying to cure her were horrified when she confided that the only thing which might possibly restore her health would be to eat again her favorite dish and to pick the meat off the tender hand of a young baby.

Another difficulty that the Jesuits frequently encountered was in getting the natives to accept baptism. The haste with which priests baptized the dying and those who were ill gave the Indians the idea that it was the baptismal water itself which carried the pestilence, and they fled from it in terror. Sometimes when a Jesuit appeared in a particularly remote district he would find the whole tribe sprinkling burnt salt and pepper on the ground over which he was to pass in order to fumigate it and drive away the devils under his control. In order to overcome this difficulty some of the Jesuits would wet their sleeves and manage to squeeze out a drop or two of water where a surreptitious baptism had to be performed.

Still other difficulties faced the good fathers in the sins of their own countrymen. Concubinage and slavery had become synonymous with New World freedom to most of the settlers, and it was impossible to stamp out these two practices. While the Jesuits refused to confess those who indulged in either sin, there were generally other priests in the neighborhood who were not so scrupulous. Nóbrega stated that no devil had persecuted him and his brethren so greatly as some of the Portuguese priests who "openly maintained that it was lawful to enslave the natives because they were beasts, and then lawful to use the women as concubines because they were slaves." Another point of bitterness between the Jesuits and other priests was that the former would at any time give their blessing or say mass gratuitously, whereas the latter far too often seemed to be out for whatever they could collect.

In spite of all these obstacles the Jesuits continued to make considerable headway. They had the backing of the government of Thomé de Sousa, and later of that of his successor, Mem de Sá, who took over the governorship from 1558 to 1572. One of Mem de Sá's first acts was to order all Indians who had been enslaved to be set at liberty. When one powerful colonist refused to obey, the governor commanded that his house be surrounded and leveled to the ground if he did not immediately give in. This and other similar measures of summary justice were partially or temporarily effective, but nothing could obliterate either Indian slavery or widespread concubinage. As soon as official vigilance was relaxed for an instant, the colonists broke loose again like a taut rubber band rebounding from a sudden release.

Little by little, however, the natives were gathered into villages along the coast and in time became at least semi-civilized. There were some schools in which classes were held in reading, writing, arithmetic, and religious education. Most of the pupils were either orphans sent over from Portugal or native boys of Indian or mestizo blood. Father Nóbrega saw that a few were especially trained for the choir, and when they paraded through the villages in their impressive vestments, singing strange hymns, the other natives were deeply affected, for music fascinated them all. At other times, however, the Jesuits had to resort to more unorthodox measures. The first priest who learned the native Tupi language, for example, found that an ordinary delivery of his sermons left his hearers completely cold, so he incorporated a few of the tricks adopted by the Indian orators, and while delivering his message ran among his auditors, stamping his feet, clapping his hands, singing and shouting the mysteries of the faith in all the tones and with all the barbaric gesticulations which the native orators had found so effective.

In the year 1554 Father Nóbrega established on the plateau of Piratininga a Jesuit school which was to become more famous than any other in Brazil. The Society had received many orphan boys from Portugal to instruct and train, and their native pupils had also increased considerably in numbers. Up to this time they had done their teaching in a school on the southern coast, but that location was not well chosen and it was decided to move farther inland. The spot selected was about thirty-five miles from the sea and about forty-five from São Vicente, or Santos. It was on the high mountain barrier which extends along the Brazilian coast. "The way was by a steep and difficult ascent, broken with shelves of level ground, and continuing for about 25 miles, then a track of beautiful country appeared in that temperate region of the air. Here were lakes, rivers, and springs, with rocks and mountains still rising above, and the earth as fertile as a rich soil and the happiest of all climates could render it. The best fruits of Europe thrive there, the grape, the apple, the peach, fig, cherry, mulberry, melon, and the woods abound with game."

Nóbrega sent thirteen Jesuits to establish this new mission colony and to look after the converts who were already living in the vicinity. The above pleasant description did not wholly fit the locality at that time, for it was midwinter and cold mountain winds pierced the thinly clad bodies of the priests who had been accustomed to living in the lowlands.

The life which these early "crusaders of the jungles" led among the natives was a constant round of hardships with few ameliorating moments. Yet time after time they would deliberately leave the civilized centers and push into the wilderness among the most savage tribes in order to carry on their work. They never were able to develop anything comparable to the Arcadian "empire" of their Spanish brothers in the northern River Plate region, but their missions eventually embraced the wildest districts of Brazil. After fifty years—that is, by the year 1600—they had incorporated most of the coastal Indians into their missions. Father Anchieta, who took up the work where Father Nóbrega had left off, once wrote to Loyola, founder of the Jesuit Order, about his labors in the district of São Paulo in these words: "Here we are, sometimes more than twenty of us in a little hut of wicker work and mud, roofed with straw, fourteen paces long and ten wide. This is the school, this is the infirmary, dormitory, refectory, kitchen, and store-room. Yet we covet not the more spacious dwellings which our brethren inhabit in other parts, for our Lord Jesus Christ was in a straiter place than this when it was his pleasure to be born among beasts in a manger, and in a far straiter place when he deigned to die for us upon the cross."

Besides the confined quarters in which Anchieta and his subordinates lived, they had to endure all the rigors of a cold winter without heavy clothing, nearly smoked themselves out of the place every time they built a fire, and depended entirely on the generosity of the natives for food. The usual staple was manioc flour, made of the root of that plant, with perhaps an occasional fish from the stream. Their beds were primitive hammocks; they had no cover at night, and after their shoes wore out they were forced to go barefooted or make themselves rude native sandals. Over the door of their hut was hung a mat through which both the cold and rain forced an entrance; and leaves were their only plates and only stationery. There were no textbooks, but Father Anchieta made up his lessons as he went along and wrote each one on a separate leaf. In this way also he composed a grammar and a vocabulary of the Tupi language. At other spare moments he turned all the popular songs which he and his friends could remember into proper hymns, and did the same with all the native ballads. He was not only preacher and missionary, but teacher, physician, manual-labor instructor, song master, barber, general director, and executive of the motley group under him.

The mestizo mamelucos who lived in the neighborhood of the São Paulo mission resented his intrusion bitterly because it interfered with their slave gathering, and a standing conflict arose between the two groups. The mamelucos continued their forays on the side and went to great lengths to turn the natives away from the Jesuits, especially by calling them cowards, an insult the Indian could hardly bear, and saying that the Christian neophytes sought baptism and took refuge under the folds of the fathers' robes in order to escape a more masculine battle-testing in the open field confronted by their enemies. A large group of neighboring Indians, thus aroused, finally were persuaded to attack the mission outright, but the converts beat them off and gave them a sound drubbing into the bargain.

In these primitive circumstances the Jesuits became the earliest great civilizers and colonizers of Brazil, for, like their Spanish counterparts in other regions of Latin America, they were the true pioneers, those who took all the risks with no prospects of material gain in order to open the way toward fitting the natives into the European pattern of life. It is sad to reflect upon the fact that all this martyrdom was spent in kneading the Indian clay, so to speak, and molding it into more civilized bread which the greedy European and the still greedier mestizos were to snatch from their hands and consume in their very presence before many years had passed.

While the Jesuits were carrying out their work of conversion and education, the more materialistic settlers proceeded faster and faster along the path of exploitation. For the first thirty or forty years they had given themselves mainly over to the cutting and shipping of brazilwood. The word "brazil" is supposed to be derived from the Portuguese or Spanish word *braza*, meaning "live coal." A much-sought-after dye was called "brazil" by analogy, and the same name was given to a large legendary island which appeared on many maps of the Middle Ages about halfway between Europe and America. Chaucer mentions the dye "brazil" in his Nun's Priest's Tale, but an even earlier mention of it had been pointed out by Muratori as occurring in a treaty between the people of Bologna and Ferrara. The tree itself was about the size of a large oak, with widely spreading branches. The wood was extremely hard and could not have been cut or loaded on the early ships in very great quantities without the help of the natives, who in those days were paid attractive wages of looking glasses, beads, hawks' bells, red caps, and other flashy trinkets appealing to the savage eye. No horse or ox power was available in the territory for several years.

Both French and Portuguese traders carried away considerable cargoes of this valuable wood before colonies had been permanently established. One of the old Tupi Indians who had watched the French load several ships with it was said to have remarked: "How is it that you come so far to fetch wood? Have you none for burning in your own country?" The French trader assured him that it was not for burning but for dyeing, just as the native himself dyed his cottons and feathers. Then the Indian wanted to know why so much of it was needed, and the Frenchman, in order to astonish him, said that in his country people were so wealthy that any ordinary citizen possessed more looking glasses, knives, scissors, and red cloth than the total quantity of those items which had been brought over to Brazil, and that as a consequence a vast amount of red dye was necessary. He added that all the wood which he carried away was sold to a single merchant. The Indian then wanted to know if that merchant never died, and on being assured that he was mortal like all men, the next question was as to who inherited the red dye money when he was gone. When told that his children or heirs received it, the old Tupi answered that the whole affair was utterly beyond his understanding: "For why should you endure all the hardships which you tell us of in crossing the sea to get these things for your children or your relations who shall come after you? The same earth which supports you, would it not support them also? We too have our children and our kin, and we love them, as you see, with an exceeding love, but we know that as this earth supports us, it will in a like manner support them when we are gone, and with this we are contented." The French trader to whom these thoughts had been expressed put them down in his memoirs as being fully characteristic of the higher native intelligence and outlook on life.[53]

Soon other days than these came to the natives of Brazil. White men arrived in ever-increasing numbers, and with greater and greater greed. Their ships were a chain of insatiable maws which sailed into the wild coves of the Indian's territory, disgorged their men, who hacked through the soundless forest with the harsh destructive noise of a new way of life, stuffed the holds of their vessels, and sailed away again. Time after time they came, always with the same desire, and distributing their gifts with rapidly growing ill will. The Indian, who hardly knew what was happening to him, gave his labor more and more reluctantly, and then only by force.

During the first hundred years of its colonization (1500–1600) Brazil was settled only along the thin shell of its coast. In the following century much of its great interior territory was to be explored from this perimeter. The slave gatherers of São Paulo would lunge westward from the south, and the plantation owners of the north, with their Negro slaves, would also move westward and southward into the interior. Before this migration could begin, however, the perimeter itself had to be made secure, and that alone was a colossal task. Obviously, the Portuguese could not do this by themselves, but with the enforced aid of Indian and Negro slaves they were finally able to achieve it.

Brazil was necessarily an agricultural and cattle-raising colony, for no mines of gold, silver, or precious stones had yet appeared on her vast horizon. Much of the land was covered with giant forests, and the Portuguese were not numerous enough to clear and to cultivate their farms, or fazendas. "From such an economic necessity," writes a Brazilian historian, "did slavery arise."[57] He was not entirely mistaken, but everything in history of which later generations are ashamed has been explained away in terms of this same "economic necessity." Man generally seems to believe that he can move forward more rapidly through ill means than good.

As the supply of native labor was nearly inexhaustible, that source was tapped first. In some quarters, especially in the south where there was a large mestizo class, this worked out satisfactorily. But in general the Indian turned out to be a poor risk. He was a semi-nomad and apparently incapable of learning new techniques or of prolonged and dependable effort. Moreover, he died quickly under the lash, frequently committed suicide, and kept trying to flee back into the forest. The Negro made a much better slave. In the first place, he had already reached a much higher level than the Brazilian Indian, who "was still in the neolithic period and had barely reached the stage of fetishism."[57] The Negro "knew how to work metals," was higher in the scale of religion and architecture, possessed a more enduring physique, and, best of all, when he was imported into the colony did not dare to escape into the wild interior. According to most anthropologists, the Negro of the Sudan was the first man in history to learn the secret of smelting iron. As a slave he very quickly acquired the white man's skills and was soon an indispensable element of colonial life. Under the direction of his master he became the very backbone of Brazilian development. This was especially true in the northern equatorial regions, where the climate was much like that of his native Africa, and where he was imported in greatest numbers.

This section of Brazil known as "the Northeast" begins at Bahia and extends northward through the state of Pernambuco, which is the point nearest Africa. It is the great Brazilian bulge. Here there developed a type of agricultural life which has been called "the sugar-cane civilization"; for just as cotton was the basis of our plantation life in the Old South, sugar cane was its foundation in the Brazilian northeast. The first cane was brought in about 1521, and when Afonso de Sousa made his explorations and laid out the twelve captaincies in the 1530s, he also brought sugar cane and other Portuguese plants and seeds along with him.

The colony of Pernambuco was the first to prosper. Its cities of Olinda and Recife (also called Pernambuco) soon became agricultural centers of considerable wealth. In the meantime the capital of Bahia had been founded in 1549, and it was mainly into this city that the "floating coffins" which arrived from Africa unloaded their black cargo of human flesh. Frequently 30 to 40 per cent of the slaves died en route. A loss of 20 per cent was considered to be extremely favorable to the slave dealer. Importation of Negroes began before the mid-century, but did not become a large-scale industry until Bahia was founded. At first only two or three thousand Negroes a year were imported, but this number grew steadily, and by 1600 it had at least doubled. When the first census of the slave population was taken at the beginning of the nineteenth century it was estimated that a total of approximately five million Negroes had been imported into Brazil.

The Negro made it possible to establish the famous "Big House," or

Casa Grande, of Brazilian plantation life. He also had his own less pretentious quarters known as the *senzala.* These two extremes in the society of
those early years had their roots in the great fields of sugar cane which
flourished with a minimum of care in those lush tropical regions. The cane
itself could not be shipped to Europe, so there was a third cog in the plantation wheel called the "shop," or the *engenho,* which in this case had the
specific meaning of "sugar mill." Only the wealthier settlers were able to
afford the outlay necessary to construct one of these engenhos. In the beginning it was a crude refinery where the cane was ground by hand in a
large wooden vat over which the grinding machinery was placed. The
grinders were attached to a long wooden handle which stuck out from
them parallel to the floor. A Negro slave held this handle and walked
round and round the vat, mashing the juice out of the cane as he did so.
The process of evaporation in large flat pans was also carried out by slaves
who held these pans over the fire by their long handles.

These "shops" also later produced rum, and for this purpose copper
tubing, water power, plus a considerable number of slaves, were necessary
to make the engenho a profitable enterprise. Sugar in the early days was
almost worth its weight in gold, and the kings of Europe frequently exchanged boxes of sweets which were considered to be the supreme gift.
Consequently, the capital required to establish an engenho could be invested with the certainty of a large return. A good-sized engenho employed from fifty to one hundred slaves and cost about ten thousand
cruzados ($5000), including the capital invested in the slaves who were
essential for its operation.

Sugar cane, of course, was not the only product of these colonies, although it constituted the basis of their wealth. Cattle raising was widespread, and in many sections cotton was grown and woven into fabric.
There were also sheep, pigs, poultry, and most of the basic plant and vegetable foods known at that time in Portugal. Both the cows and horses
multiplied prodigiously on the grasslands around Bahia, and orange and
lemon trees brought over from the home country soon produced an abundance of those fruits which the fertile soil and climate enlarged considerably beyond the ordinary size hitherto known. Tea was found to grow
wild around Bahia, and coffee beans were brought from Portugal and
planted there. This was at a time when the rest of Europe had hardly
heard of that beverage, but the Portuguese had probably become acquainted with it through their contact with the Orient. Melons and grapevines were also planted, but they were attacked and destroyed by vicious
colonies of ants. So great were the depredations caused by this omnipresent insect that some of the settlers facetiously referred to it as the King
of Brazil. In some regions, at a certain season of the year, ants would
swarm into the towns in such numbers that the people had to quit their
houses temporarily while they passed through. This visit, however, was

not altogether harmful, for they cleaned every crevice in the place of scorpions, centipedes, spiders, and other annoying tropical pests.

By the year 1581 the "sugar aristocracy" was well established in the northeastern region of fertile tropical land. The total civilized population of Brazil in that year was estimated by one of the earliest chroniclers at fifty-seven thousand persons, of whom some twenty thousand were whites, eighteen thousand civilized Indians, fourteen thousand Negro slaves, and perhaps five to ten thousand mamelucos or mestizos. Living beyond the Portuguese coastal perimeter were possibly five hundred thousand Indian savages. The most thriving cities were Bahia, Recife, and Olinda, twin city of the latter. These cities contained many fine mansions in which the "sugar barons" lived their lives of relative luxury and ease. They wore fine imported clothes; their wives displayed many jewels, and in their comfortable well-furnished homes these colonial families practiced all the refined customs of the Old World.

Bahia, the capital, was the center of officialdom, education, and religious life. A rich agricultural district of neatly cultivated fields radiated from the town for ten or fifteen miles into the interior. The city itself had a population of eight hundred Portuguese families, and the state could count about two thousand. Five hundred mounted soldiers and two thousand infantry were held in readiness to defend the colony. The cathedral was an imposing building, but its interior lacked the brilliant adornments so dear to the heart of the Latin worshiper of those early days. There was a total of sixty-two churches in the state of Bahia. There were also three monasteries and three colleges for the Jesuits. In these colleges the Jesuits could train neophytes to carry on their good work, and the sons of the wealthy attended school there. The range of subjects taught was not particularly wide: reading, writing, arithmetic, morals, philosophy, and theology made up the list. The teachers and preachers in these schools and churches received salaries of between thirty to forty dollars a year.

In the Bahia district there were twenty-one large engenhos using water power, and thirty-six without it. Fifteen of the latter used oxen to move their grinders. There were also eight molasses factories, all doing a fine business. A considerable quantity of their products went to Portugal every year; in 1581 alone 3,840,000 pounds of sugar were exported. About a million dollars' worth of Portuguese imports were purchased annually. Some of the wealthier citizens had numerous horses and as many as forty to fifty brood mares in their herds, and cattle were extremely abundant. Ginger had been brought in from the Island of St. Thomas and had thrived to such an extent that over one hundred thousand pounds a year were produced. But before long the cultivation of ginger was completely prohibited because it interfered with imports from India.

As long as the sugarworks remained near the coast the principal diet consumed by their operators was beef, occasional vegetables, many native fruits, and especially "crabs, sharks, and a fish called the *chareo*; the roe of this latter is salted, pressed, and dried as a sort of caviar, in which state it is much esteemed. Oil was extracted in considerable quantities from shark-liver. Whales were not uncommon; and ambergris was frequently cast up." This was a much-prized waxy substance left by the sperm whale, and thought to be the highly digested food of that animal for some morbid biological reason spewed out from time to time. Birds were always ravenous for this stuff and after a storm often gobbled it all up before the natives could reach the shores to gather it. One colonist received a dowry of one hundred pounds of ambergris with his wife.

"There were over one hundred persons in Bahia whose income was from three to five thousand dollars, and whose property was from twenty to sixty thousand. Their wives would wear nothing but silk. The people were generally characterized by extravagance in their apparel; even men of inferior rank walked the street in breeches of satin damask. Their wives wore shirtwaists and skirts of the same material, and were trinketed with gold. Their houses were as prodigiously ornamented as themselves. There were some settlers who possessed silver and gold to the amount of two and three thousand dollars. The market at Bahia was never without bread made of Portuguese flour, and varieties of good wine from Madeira and the Canaries."[53]

This early writer was at pains to mention "Portuguese flour" because the ordinary flour used in Brazil was of manioc. The tuber of this plant, which looks something like a sweet potato, was the principal food of the natives of nearly all the tropical regions of America. In many localities it is deadly poisonous if eaten raw but, on drying out or boiling, becomes perfectly edible and can be fashioned into a variety of dishes. Tapioca is made from it at the present time, the word itself being of Brazilian origin. The Brazilian Indian usually prepared manioc by scraping the root to a fine pulp with sharp oyster shells or stones. Then it was rubbed with a large stone until absolutely dry and finally eaten as a porridge or made into bread. The juice was boiled and fermented into a strongly alcoholic beverage, and a syrup was also made by the addition of honey or sugar. Early Portuguese colonists made some improvements in the method of preparation, but continued to use manioc flour and juices in various recipes. Portuguese flour was a distinct luxury.

The town of Olinda in Pernambuco was almost as flourishing as Bahia. It had not yet reached the heyday of its "sugar-cane civilization," but it was a town of nearly seven hundred families and fifty engenhos, which were not in the town proper but were located at various points in the vicinity. Each of these had twenty to thirty residents. As this region had been settled before Bahia, the Indians had been pushed farther into the interior. In fact, they had abandoned coastal Pernambuco entirely, and their nearest villages were more than two hundred and fifty miles westward.

The founder of the colony, Duarte Coelho, had expended many thousands of dollars on this captaincy, and his men had waged war against the natives for five successive years when they first arrived. It was the only successful captaincy in the north, just as São Paulo (then called São Vicente) had been the only successful one in the south, and it had never ceased moving forward. Consequently, when Bahia was founded in 1549, Pernambuco was already a well-developed and flourishing region. Coelho's work had been done so well that special privileges were granted to settlers living in his state when the royal governor was sent over by the King to establish centralized control. In the 1580s Coelho's son was receiving a yearly income of more than ten thousand dollars from his fisheries and sugarworks.

In the south the state then known as São Vicente, now called São Paulo, was also progressing, but its inhabitants did not live in any such splendor as those of the northeast. It was cool enough in this region for wheat and barley to grow, but the colonists produced only small crops of these grains and lived mainly on native foods. A few vineyards had been planted near the town of São Paulo, and marmalade was made both here and on the coast and sent to the other Brazilian colonies. The place was free of ant swarms, and an early chronicler (1582), after praising the vineyards and fruit trees of the district, added, "There is another better fruit, which is gold and silver, if the mines were searched for." A hundred years later that prophecy was to come true with a vengeance.

The early settlers in Brazil suffered from a multitude of tropical insects and diseases which made even the lives of the most prosperous families anything but a bed of roses. Perhaps the most widespread pest was the *chigua*, or chigger (jigger), whose name has come to us in English in much the original form. However, the Brazilian chigger was not only larger than our own but considerably more potent. It got under the nails of the hands and feet, attacked the joints, and infested the whole body with little inflamed sores which, in that tropical climate, frequently turned into larger cankers and resulted in the loss of a foot; this member, being closest to the ground, was especially susceptible to attack. The native treatment, later adopted by the Portuguese, was to anoint the inflamed parts with a thick red oil made from a native fruit called the *couroq*. One of the French doctors carried twelve large jars of this oil back with him, and "as many more of human grease, which he had collected when the Brazilians were broiling their prisoners." This grease also was supposed to have its curative value for many ailments.

The mingling of the three races, white, Indian, and Negro, as the early writer Piso points out, "produced new diseases, or at least new constitutions, by which old diseases were so modified that the skilfullest physicians were puzzled by new symptoms." Among the lower classes a serious ailment of the liver was endemic. One of the symptoms was an insatiable craving for food, yet in spite of the vast quantities the sufferers consumed they became as cadaverous-looking as mummies. Diseases of the eyes often resulting in blindness were also frequent, and the usual remedy was a bit of white lead in human milk!

Another affliction was called simply the *ar*, or "air," because the Portuguese believed that the "bad airs" of the country caused it. The sufferer was overwhelmed with a tremendous sense of weight and listlessness which became a sort of prolonged semi-stupor. The cure for this was to place the patient on a bed of hot horse dung sprinkled with a touch of frankincense and myrrh. Powdered horse excrement taken in any liquid was also the favorite cure for smallpox. There were numerous other diseases and other remedies too painful to relate.

Among the decent medicines were many of native origin, and some of these concoctions of antiseptic and astringent herbs produced almost miraculous cures. A number of our own most common medicines are of South American Indian origin. Quinine was used for years by the Indian to combat malaria before he revealed his secret to the white man; coca leaves, of which cocaine is a derivative, are still widely grown in Latin America as a stimulant; oil of *copahú*, a powerful astringent, is common among the Brazilian natives, and they also have an effective remedy for dysentery called *puchurim*. Rotenone, the active ingredient of most of our insecticides and plant sprays, is also a Brazilian product. It was formerly used by the Indians to stun the fish in ponds and streams so that they might be more easily caught. Curare, the poison with which blowgun arrows were tipped, has been of great value in the treatment of spastic paralysis in American hospitals.[58]

During the first few decades the Portuguese women lost two out of three children before the age of five. This mortality was drastically reduced when they were finally persuaded by the native women, but only after prolonged obstinacy, that they had kept their babies much too warmly clothed, and had in that manner opened the way for chronic colds and other respiratory diseases. As soon as they took off these heavy swaddling clothes with which they had thought to protect their infants from the "bad airs," and followed the native custom of dressing them lightly and giving them frequent cold baths, the rate of illness was more than cut in half.

According to the Jesuits who had come over to Brazil in order to give their lives in the conversion and education of the natives, the worst diseases which the white settlers suffered were not of a physical but of a moral nature. Their greed expressed itself in inhuman exploitation of the Indians, and their lust found an outlet in promiscuous sexual intercourse with as many native women as they were able to seduce. With all the Old World barriers removed, profligacy became so general that it was truly one of the characteristics of the epoch.

The fault, of course, did not lie entirely with the Portuguese men, as even the priests recognized. So few white women had come to Brazil in the first decades that no other relationship was possible. The Jesuit Nóbrega, first of a long line of great civilizers, had written to the King, insisting that more women be shipped from Portugal. He began by asking that as many orphans as possible be sent, "for they will all find husbands here." It was a foregone conclusion that men of good family would never allow their womenfolk to head for Brazil to marry into that hodgepodge of licentiousness, no matter how anxious they were to get them off their hands. So, when relatively few orphans arrived, Nóbrega asked that all the fallen women and streetwalkers of Lisbon be assembled and exported to the colony for a new start in life. Even these would find husbands in Brazil, he said.

One of the results of these early days of promiscuousness was that syphilis soon infected such a large proportion of the population that it became endemic in many parts of Brazil. Some reports have it that this disease in time assumed a milder form there than in any other region of the world. Many known cases have been cured by attacks of malaria fever, which apparently burned out the venereal germs and enabled the patient to recover.

Brazil's troubles were not all internal by any means. The French established a colony and fortress at Rio de Janeiro, and later the Dutch occupied most of the principal Brazilian cities of the central coast regions and the northeast, and the English ensconced themselves at the mouth of the Amazon. Long before any of these things occurred, however, the settlers and mamelucos of southern Brazil had encountered their first Spanish rivals in the province of Paraguay. Brazilian slave gatherers had pounced down on the peaceful Guaranís under Irala in Paraguay, and that governor had protected his Indian allies as best he could by driving the invaders out and founding a settlement above the great falls of the Iguazú.

From this time up to the final establishment of Buenos Aires, the colonists of Paraguay and those of southern Brazil were in constant contact and in frequent conflict (1552–80). Since the mouth of the Paraná River was so far removed from Asunción and held no settlement, the land route across Brazil to the sea near Santos was often followed. Cabeza de Vaca had come to Asunción along that path. This manner of contact between the two civilizations accentuated the high feeling already existent along the border. In 1580, however, Buenos Aires gave the Spaniards a direct outlet to the sea, and in that same year Portugal came under the rule of Spain. The pressure was for a time considerably relieved.

The Spanish Jesuits then entered the region of the headwaters of the Paraná and began to found their missions among the Guaranís. These were so successful that the slave gatherers of São Paulo, who followed mainly the allegiance of economic interest, could not resist the temptation to raid them. Brazilian and Argentine tempers again flared. The Jesuits yielded and moved farther southward, where their famous "communistic empire" was developed. It was the only section of the interior which was being developed, for the colonists around Asunción had long since performed their function of refounding Buenos Aires and giving Argentina an outlet to the sea. Then they had sunk back into their proverbial isolation or "independence" which, with the passing years, became a stupor of inertia. Both Brazil and Argentina were content to let well enough alone, and this backward and iniquitous buffer has remained between them ever since as a sore tribute to their blind solution of a problem. The border conflict between Brazil and Argentina now moved down to the more progressive region of Uruguay near the mouth of the Paraná.

In the meantime, throughout Brazil "a race of men was growing up, fierce indeed and intractable, but who acquired from the mixture of native blood, a constitutional and indefatigable activity. While the Spaniards on the Paraguay remained where Irala left them, . . . neglected the discoveries which the first conquerors had made, . . . suffered the paths which they had opened to be overgrown, . . . and almost laid aside the manners and even the language of Spain, the Brazilians continued for two centuries to explore the country; months and years would these persevering adventurers continue among the woods and mountains, hunting slaves, or seeking for gold and jewels after the reports of the natives; and ultimately they succeeded in securing for themselves and for the House of Braganza, the richest mines, and the largest portion of South America, the finest region of the whole habitable earth."[53]

19
STRUGGLE OVER
POSSESSION OF THE BEHEMOTH

The greatest anomalies in South America are the three Guianas, which occupy the northeastern fringe of the continent between Brazil and Venezuela. The population is largely East Indian and black. Formerly European colonies known as British, Dutch, and French Guiana respectively, these dwarfed colonies recently became; (1) the Marxist republic of Guyana (1970), scene of the infamous Jonestown mass-murder suicides; (2) the Dutch-speaking republic of Suriname (1975); and (3) French Guyana, since 1946 a department of metropolitan France. The Guiana colonies were formed when Britain, Holland, and France each attempted the conquest of Brazil, and failed. A Guiana apiece helped to buy them off. The United States permitted these colonies to remain despite its Monroe Doctrine, and Brazil herself, after repeatedly trying to extend her territory, finally decided to call it quits and let well enough alone.

The French came to Brazil first and, seeking as ever for something of charm and beauty, headed straight for Rio de Janeiro, the most magnificent natural setting in the world. The place was uninhabited then, and so without interference the Frenchmen erected a wooden fort on an island in the bay. The year was 1555. Although there were only eighty of the French, they calculated that they were worth at least eight hundred Portuguese and very quickly considered the whole territory as good as their own. It was given the name of France Antarctique, a phrase in no way indicative of the weather of that tropical region. They made friends with the natives, who had no reason to love the Portuguese, and, with an eye to the future, began to instruct these savages in the use of arms.

France was in such straits at home that little was done to aid the colonists, else they might easily have made the place impregnable. Before many months had passed the Portuguese attacked vigorously, drove them off their island onto the mainland, where for several years the Frenchmen, with the aid of their native allies, put up a stiff resistance. It was not until 1565, ten years after their arrival, that they were finally defeated and expelled. Although others of their countrymen returned several times after this and caused much trouble along the coast, they did not again threaten the safety of Brazil. In 1567 the Portuguese themselves founded the city of Rio de Janeiro in order to strengthen their position at that midway point between Bahia and São Paulo.

Historically, the most important occurrence during the French occupation was the outbreak of a deadly epidemic of smallpox which wiped out more than half the natives of the state of Bahia. This disease, together with the slave drivers and the influence of profligate living, soon did away with most of the Indian population along the Brazilian coast.

The Dutch who followed the French were a more stubborn lot. They did not come merely to take on loads of brazilwood or to swagger among the natives at some uncolonized point. In 1621 the West India Company was chartered for the express purpose of making conquests in Brazil, of carrying on a lucrative slave trade from Africa, and of establishing an illegitimate commerce with the Spanish colonies on a broad base. The company was well financed and was expected to provide its own army and navy. Until 1648 Holland and Spain were officially at war, and the company was entrusted with the main responsibility of carrying the fight to the enemy. It was but one of several similar organizations of those days which received from their governments the right to monopolize the commerce with newly discovered regions of the globe in the East and in the West. (Spain and Portugal formed a single country in 1580–1640.)

The first such companies were established to trade with the Orient, and the most important of these were the so-called East India companies of the British, Dutch, and French, chartered in the years 1600, 1602, and 1664 respectively. The Dutch secured a firm foothold on the East Indies, and the English, after being pushed out of that region, moved to the mainland of India. The history of colonial India was synonymous with that of the British East India Company. With the attractive profits which had been obtained in the East before them, the Dutch in 1621 also decided to try the same scheme in Africa and Brazil. The ease with which the Portuguese had been pushed around in Asia helped to confirm their judgment.

Holland at that time was the only country in Europe where the Jew enjoyed anything approaching liberty, and so the Jews of Brazil, now under strict Spanish dominion, were only too glad to furnish whatever information the company might request about that colony. Preparations were undertaken with a thoroughness that left no room for doubt. A great fleet was carefully outfitted, and several hundred well-equipped soldiers formed part of the contingent which sailed straight into the harbor of the capital city Bahia and took it by storm (1623).

The Portuguese colonists, accustomed to the raids of piratical bands, promptly took to the woods with as many valuables as could be carried. They expected the Dutch to pick the city clean and then sail away, but instead the newcomers established themselves securely in the houses and strong points and made ready their defense. When informed of this, the escaped colonists were distraught. They had not been prepared for a prolonged life in the wilds, and many of them had already sickened and died. They rallied sufficient strength to attack the city, but were beaten off.

In the meantime, the loss of Bahia had sent a shudder throughout the colossal territory of Brazil which had reverberated even in the remote and sickly court of Philip IV of Spain. A huge armada, the largest ever dispatched to the New World, was sent to teach the Hollanders a lesson. The latter had already received considerable reinforcements from their home country, and many converted Portuguese Jews, Negro slaves, and even a few of the Portuguese colonists had come over to their side.

When the Spanish squadron struck it met powerful resistance and was forced into a state of siege which, however, could only lead to the ultimate starving out of the Dutch. Their numerous English and French mercenaries soon realized this and mutinied; then the Spanish-Portuguese forces captured the city.

The court of Spain seemed to believe that this would end all Dutch attempts on their colony, but it was only the beginning. In 1629 the West India Company prepared an even greater expedition against Olinda and the wealthy state of Pernambuco. Their financial adviser had estimated that a total of one hundred and fifty shiploads of sugar might be freighted annually from this captaincy. This time, in order to conceal their plans, the Dutch fleet was assembled in small units at several different ports. They made up a grand squadron of more than fifty vessels.

The Spaniards and Portuguese, on getting wind of this expedition, expended most of their efforts in fortifying Bahia. As a result Olinda and all the other cities of Pernambuco fell into Dutch hands like ripe fruit dropping off a tree. When it became apparent that the town of Recife, which was only four miles from Olinda, could no longer be held, the Portuguese commander gave the order to set fire to everything in the place. Thirty ships were consumed in the blaze, along with many thousands of casks of sugar, and other valuable merchandise. The loss in this town alone reached the sum of nearly five million dollars.

Pernambuco was the region of greatest wealth in Brazil at that time. The best brazilwood grew in that colony, and the largest plantations and sugarworks were established there. "In the four years from 1620 to 1624, it appeared by the books of the Custom House that not fewer than fifteen thousand four hundred thirty slaves had been imported from Angola (only one of the African points) into this Captaincy. Many of the *engenhos*, indeed, were as large as villages of no inconsiderable size. The Dutch said that Pernambuco was esteemed the Paradise of Brazil; and that it was itself as good as a kingdom. This Paradise, which abounded with slaves, sugar, and tobacco, they were resolved to make their own. They were now in possession of the port and the capital; and so sure were they of making the conquest, and so determined upon retaining what they should win, that a civil establishment for the administration of the conquered colonies had been sent out with the expedition."

It was not long before the Dutch commenced to branch out in both directions up and down the coast. The Portuguese fought them at every turn, and for a time the conflict raged without any definite decision. A mulatto traitor named Calabar, who has come down in Brazilian history with a reputation somewhat akin to that of Benedict Arnold in the United States, finally turned the tide in favor of the Hollanders. He knew every foot of the land, the disposition of the Portuguese forces, and time after time led his new masters to them over circuitous paths for surprise attacks. Calabar was also a keen-witted fellow whose judgment frequently saved the day for the Dutch, and in the end the Portuguese were completely defeated.

Not only was Pernambuco lost, but five other provinces covering the entire Brazilian bulge had been captured, and there seemed to be little chance that any of them would ever be retaken. Count Mauritz of Nassau was charged with their administration, and despite the devastation of many square miles of fields and cities he soon restored orderly productivity. A force of 6180 men was at his disposal, plus about one thousand Indian allies. The town of Recife again flourished, and, out of one hundred twenty-one sugarworks in that province, eighty-seven were soon back in production.

Count Mauritz was also indirectly responsible for some of the most unusual painting to come out of colonial Latin America. He brought to Brazil two Dutch artists of considerable ability, Albert van Eckhout, a pupil of Rembrandt, and Franz Janszoon Post. Eckhout has left several interesting canvases of the inhabitants of the Brazilian northeast, including one striking oil painting of a cannibalistic Tupi lady with a basket thrown over her shoulder from which a dismembered human foot protrudes. Post painted with almost scientific accuracy the details of plantation life in the same region. Buildings and landscape were his usual subjects, and nearly all of his paintings had a background of luminous blue vapors against which was silhouetted the lush tropical growth of Pernambuco province.[170]

The orderly spirit of the Dutch was soon everywhere in evidence: streets were kept clean, many new and neat houses were constructed, public works were the special concern of the government, and a regime of liberal laws was offered to all who were willing to accept the new rule. Count Mauritz began to build himself a great palace and an entirely new city for his government. A large island was cleared, and to the amazement of the Brazilians, seven hundred full-grown cocoa trees were dug up and transplanted there. Orange, citron, pomegranate, and many native trees were also transferred to the palace grounds "in their full growth and beauty." A long bridge laid on piles and costing over $100,000 was raised to connect the island with the mainland.

While these plans were being carried out the Portuguese and all who had refused to co-operate with the Dutch were gradually, and for the first time, being made to think, feel, and act as Brazilians. In those days there were no newspapers and public opinion was expressed and directed from the pulpit. The good fathers of Brazil, more than any other group, saw and breathed living fire as long as the heretical Hollanders remained on the sacred soil of their land. Raising this cry before their congregations, they started a campaign for liberation such as those dark days had seldom seen.

Father Vieira of Bahia was in the vanguard of the procession. He never delivered a sermon without fulminating against the miserable Brazilians who had let such things come to pass, against the Portuguese who had deserted their richest colonies in their hour of need, and against the Dutch who had taken them. "Brazil," he said, "has had many opportunities for recovery; many times we have had the remedy, as it were, in our hands; but we came always a day too late. And how can a man lay hold of Occasion, who always attempts to seize her where she is bald?" He said that Brazil, like Lazarus, was dead, but that the Christ whom he promised could raise her from the grave. He would be the Moses to lead his people out of their slavery. No help could be counted on from Portugal, for the saying, "Brazil gives, Portugal takes," was too well known to them all to need further comment. They must take matters into their own hands.

While such sermons as these were being preached over the length and breadth of that part of Brazil which remained in Portuguese hands, Portugal rebelled against Spanish rule and began the long war of her own liberation. It was now unthinkable that she could or would furnish any aid to her colony. In that same year, 1640, Brazil drew herself together and lashed out at the Dutch. No quarter was asked and none was given. It was a warfare of annihilation which was to last fourteen terrible years before the foreigners from across the seas were forced from their final strongholds at Olinda and Recife.

Out of this war a new Brazil was born. She, whose frontier had been so vast that it had little meaning, had found something on which to focus her energies, something which would keep her people united, and forge their loyalty in fire, and give them strength and victory. In this war many Negroes and mulattoes fought alongside whites, and regiments of "men of color" frequently distinguished themselves in battle. They doubtless fought because they were forced to do so, but a few of them had probably found out that Dutch "liberty" did not extend to the black man, and that slavery under the Portuguese was about the same as lip freedom among the race-proud merchants of the Netherlands. In compensation for these loyal services the "man of color" now received an actual social status. He still continued to be a slave, but he was also a human being worthy of admiration and consideration. And his women were also human beings, made the more desirable because of the distinguished and long-suffering valor of their race.

One noteworthy exception arose. The Negro was far too much of a human being to let these chaotic days slip by, with their precious opportunities for wholesale escape, without some of his people taking advantage of them. No sooner had the Dutch wars broken out than several large groups took to the woods, hoping that their numbers would protect them. Now that they had learned the ways of the Indian and knew the country this proved to be the case, and from time to time other groups of slaves joined them. This amorphous black mass flowed over the land until it struck a large extent of wild country covered with palm trees, and here it settled down to a forest existence. By 1630 the escaped slaves numbered nearly ten thousand. A king was chosen and the Negroes called themselves "The Confederacy of Palmares," or "The Palm Confederacy." More romantic-minded historians have referred to it as "The Negro Republic" of Palmares.

By whatever name it is known, after the last Dutch were expelled from Pernambuco province in 1654, these escaped slaves began to represent a distinct threat to the government and security of the Portuguese colonists. They were attacked several times, but always defended themselves resolutely, and the attacking forces were obliged to withdraw. Finally, when the "Confederacy" had swelled to approximately twenty-five thousand members, the governor of the state hired as bloody a slave gatherer as ever roamed the forests of Brazil to exterminate them. Money and firearms were expended in considerable quantities, and a regular army of several thousand besiegers was assembled. After many months of gory fighting in the palm forests the remnants of the Negro confederacy were encircled, and as the noose was drawn tighter around them, they all fled to the highest mountain stronghold in the vicinity and there made a last stand (1695). At this point legend takes over and tells us that a few dozens of miserable black skeletons, wasted by famine and disease, hurled themselves in a body over the precipice rather than surrender. "It was a Negro Troy," writes a Brazilian historian, "and its history was a true Iliad."

In summary, when the Dutch took last leave of the inhospitable shores of Brazil they left behind a warmer regard for the loyal man of color, an amorphous Negro "kingdom" which for nearly half a century disturbed the peace of Pernambuco, more efficient methods of sugar refining and neater towns, and above all they had aroused in the country a new unified feeling which made the inhabitants of the great land all Brazilians.

Although warfare between the Dutch and Brazilians ended in 1654, it was not until 1661 that final peace was made. Portugal promised to pay an indemnity, or rather a bribe, of four million dollars "in money, sugar, tobacco, and salt, as might be most convenient to her, in sixteen annual installments." Holland was to give up all claims to the six provinces which she had held for a generation. It is doubtful if she would have signed the agreement at all, however, had not both England and France sided against her. They wanted Portugal left free to fight Spain.

The West India Company, rather than the Dutch state, which had had complete charge of the Brazilian venture, thus came out of the bargain a big winner. It had expended about twenty million dollars on the conquest, but had made back an estimated eighty-five million dollars besides what it now expected to get from Portugal. After the defeat in Brazil its area of activity in South America was narrowed down to the territory north of this country, which was then known as Dutch Guiana.

The last of the three European nations to attempt to gain a foothold in Brazil was England. The way was prepared by several corsairs, among whom Cavendish and Lancaster were the most notable. The first of these men plundered several regions along the coast and in 1592 burned the town of São Vicente, while the second captured and sacked both Olinda and Recife. However, neither made any effort to colonize the territory. A few years later, after Walter Raleigh had thrown a romantic glow over the northern part of South America with his search for El Dorado, it was decided to establish a settlement near the mouth of the Amazon River. Raleigh's first voyage had been made in 1595, and through him the northern regions became known in Europe. He described Guiana as a "country that hath yet her maidenhead, never sacked, turned nor wrought. The face of the earth hath not been torn, nor the virtue and salt of the soil spent by manurance, the graves have not been opened for gold, the mines not broken with sledges."

In those days it was believed that the Orinoco and the Amazon ran together in the interior of the continent, thus making a great island of the land between them, and to this island the name Guiana was given. A tributary of the Amazon does in fact touch the Orinoco, but it is so many miles from the coast and the rivers are so small at the point of contact that the original conception is hardly borne out. However, by setting themselves up at the mouth of the Amazon, the English thought to have a fine waterway through the entire region, and in 1630 an advance group constructed a fort there. Shortly afterward five hundred settlers followed, but in the meantime the Portuguese had wiped out the fort, and when the newcomers arrived they were driven away. Perhaps this fortuitous circumstance changed the ownership of all northern Brazil.

The trio of invaders, French, Dutch, and British, all came to Brazil hoping that it might be the highroad to great mines of gold and silver. If no considerable wealth was to be found inside Brazil itself, at least the country would make a base from which to operate against Spanish Potosí and Peru. It was a great victory for the Brazilians to force these nations to be content with an inconsequential slice of the Guianas. As late as 1665 they all still claimed the whole country between the Orinoco and Amazon rivers, but they had nothing to show for it, except a few paltry settlements along the Guiana coast. They squabbled over these constantly, and were an ever-present thorn in Brazil's flesh until a few years ago when definitive boundaries were traced.

At present the three Guianas look about as one would expect of a three-hundred-year-old dream long since putrefied with the dry rot of the tropics. Yet in the old days their truly magnificent scenery had given birth to more than one magnificent illusion. Stories of gold and diamond washes bearing the wealth of Midas somewhere in the wild interior floated about the coast, intriguing adventurers. Perhaps a second Kimberley will yet reveal its secret to one of these ranging prospectors. The early history of this region is also linked inseparably with that of the United States. Even the Pilgrim Fathers, writes an English historian, "thought of coming to Guiana before they decided upon the bleaker shores of New England, and it was often compared with Virginia as a field for settlements. A little later comparisons were made between it and the New Netherlands [or New York], when the advantages of a warm climate and two or three crops a year were proven to the satisfaction of the writers on the matter. Even when, after the Dutch wars [1667] Surinam [a part of British Guiana] was virtually exchanged for New York, few Dutchmen felt aggrieved and some Englishmen were hardly prepared to agree to the transfer."

The Guianas have another claim on the white man's history in the New World: it was there that he treated other white men who were his prisoners with the most abominable cruelties, and it was there also that the native Indian received a fairer deal than perhaps anywhere else in either America. The penal colony of France on Devil's Island near Cayenne, where Dreyfus was unjustly imprisoned for so many years, represents the white man's stigma, and British and Dutch Guiana represent his greatest tolerance.

The Dutch, who were the first traders in these parts, made pacts with the natives to which they adhered rigidly, and when the British arrived later they followed suit. As a consequence the Indian in the colonies of these two provinces has enjoyed privileges which his brothers in other parts never attained. The Indian's lands—good lands and not waste corners—have been assigned to him in perpetuity. He pays no taxes and may ride free on any public conveyance, railway, or boat. Trade with the natives is under the strict supervision of the government, and "the prices of forest products, the wages of Indians, the rations they must be given when employed are all fixed by law and are enforced." The red man is allowed to gather and sell these forest products "wherever and whenever he chooses." He is legally regarded as "the true owner of the land."[59]

This treatment was not exactly the outgrowth of humane considerations, but was rather the result of necessity, for the Guiana native was so elusive and dangerous an adversary that settlements could not have been maintained without his co-operation. He does have one quality which has always ingratiated him to the white man, a generosity which seems to be limitless. The traveler in a wild region has but to admire a carved war club or headdress of an Indian and it will be presented to him forthwith. Native women have also been known to strip themselves naked and hand over a dress which some untutored missionary had admired.

The three Guianas today are Latin American only in geography. English is the language of independent Guyana, a Marxist state, which has a total population of about 800,000. In the Republic of Suriname the official language is Dutch, although English is widely spoken, and "negro English" is a kind of *lingua franca* understood by all. When Suriname received its independence in 1975 nearly one third of its population returned to Holland. The total number of inhabitants is less than 400,000. French Guyana, or Guyane, has only 60,000 inhabitants, mostly black. There are some excellent new hotels, and tourism is being encouraged. The entire area is very backward, and all three Guyanas have a very low standard of living. Brazil and Venezuela are eyeing this territory covetously, and the boundaries are in some places still in dispute.

20
AFTER THE BANNER INTO THE "SERTÃO"

In 1554, when Father Anchieta and his Jesuit companions huddled together in their miserable little room on the coastal plateau of southern Brazil and established the township of São Paulo, they had no thought of starting the most aggressive community and the most spirited people of that country's vast domain. As the cold winter winds beat into their crowded hut, they kept their minds on God and on the teaching and defense of the Indians. A few miles away from their missions dwelt another and more numerous group, made up of the half-breed descendants and friends of one João Ramalho, whose plural wives and family had been encountered many years previously by Afonso de Sousa.

This band of mamelucos had been confirmed in possession of their lands, and watched the Jesuits' entry into their territory with great misgiving. The Jesuits, on their part, sought no connection with Ramalho's tribe; "they could no more convert those half-breeds than they could make the hardy impenitents on the coast give up stealing Indians."[60] The precarious truce between the two elements was never long in balance, for the mamelucos, driven by greed and glory, seemed always to hold the initiative which lies with those who are meanly obsessed. Sometimes superstition rather than religion got the better of them and they sought the fathers' forgiveness, but generally they were out on some rampage, disturbing the far corners of Brazilian life, and taking an especial pleasure in upsetting the best-laid plans of the Jesuits by setting fire to their missions and capturing their Indians for slaves. The coastal regions were soon so depopulated of natives that the mamelucos forsook this region and struck out into the interior and virgin land.

These mamelucos were also called Paulistas or Paulists because of the city from which they came. São Paulo was not located on the coast like all the other Brazilian colonies, but was on a high mountain barrier at an altitude of two thousand feet and less than fifty miles from the sea. The distance was not great, but it was over severe country which measured the difference between isolation and a European orientation toward life. No pirates could attack this city, and it was free of the influx of ideas and merchandise brought by incoming ships. A strong feeling of regional pride grew up which more than once asserted itself in peculiar ways.

For example, in 1640, when Portugal freed herself from the yoke of Spain, the Paulists decided to declare their own independence of Portugal and choose their own king. The man they picked out, an illustrious citizen named Amador Bueno, was threatened with death if he did not accept the crown. The people began to shout on the streets, "Long live Amador Bueno, our King!" and to this Bueno responded, "Long live John IV, our King and Lord for whom I would give my life!" After saying these words he had to take refuge in a monastery to keep from being slain on the spot. Finally the priests and Bueno together persuaded the latter's partisans that a throne would do them no good and they gave up the idea.

Not only was the early Paulist a proud and self-centered rascal, but he knew from the beginning that he could not depend on anyone but himself for a living, and the Jesuit fathers in his vicinity, with their preachments against slavery, had only made that living harder to obtain. Therefore, they were his deadly economic competitors who must be destroyed. He also felt, as a mestizo, that he was as good as most white men and far better than any Indian. The surest way to prove this was to serve the whites for profit by asserting his dominance over the native and over his native land. This feeling was the psychological pole around which all the Paulist's activities revolved. His strong body and keen mind, half Catholic and half savage, gave him a definite advantage in his struggle with the Indians and in his conquest of the interior.

In the beginning the Paulist depended mainly on deception rather than violence to round up his prospective slaves. Small Paulista bands would travel into the hinterland and, speaking in the native language, would tell of the marvelous life led by those who had gone to the coast. Hundreds of natives were taken in by these blandishments and walked into the slave trap like sheep to the slaughter. Once on the coast, there was no possible chance of escape. The Paulists, naturally, had to travel farther and farther afield on their hunts. In the meantime the Jesuit missions of Paraguay and Argentina were being built up and priests were warning Indians against these slave gatherers. The latter now organized themselves into well-disciplined bands under a chosen leader and went about their work in a businesslike manner.

They always traveled with a banner, or *bandeira*, at their head, and so the group was known by that name, while its individual members were called *bandeirantes*, or "followers of the banner." These bandeiras continued for nearly two centuries, plunging across mountain and plain into the farthest reaches of their sprawling country, and when the last one was carried out around 1750 they had tripled Brazilian territory. With diminishing zeal Spain still pressed her claims to this region which had been given her by the Treaty of Tordesillas. But in the Treaty of Madrid (1750) she was forced to yield by default, for the bandeirantes had already explored and populated the most strategic parts of the entire western hinterland.

Enslavement of the natives was at first the principal motive of the bandeirantes, and they undertook it with a sort of fierce delight. Sometimes they would disguise themselves as Jesuits, and numbers of them even practiced singing mass in order to lure the neophytes out of their folds or fields. More often they depended on surprise attacks and outright violence. The general procedure was to surround a settlement or large tribal dwelling house and order the Indians to come out, all the while regaling them with fair promises. If this had no effect the house or houses were set afire, and the Indians forced into the open, where they were quickly captured. Then they were placed in a large pen out in the open, where they remained night and day until the allotment had increased to a sufficient size to justify a trip back to the coast. Sometimes the natives would remain in the open in this manner for several weeks or months before the return march began, and as they were accustomed to sleeping in closed huts with a fire constantly going near by, hundreds of them died of exposure. Rarely did more than half the captives ever reach the coastal settlements to be sold as slaves.

For a time, however, their original numbers seemed to be almost limitless. In a single swoop on the missions in Paraguay the Paulists once captured fifteen thousand slaves and drove them to the coast. Their hunts for human merchandise became more and more brutal as time passed, and naked Indian men, women, and children, all tied to long poles to keep them from escaping, were herded along jungle paths like cattle. Those who sickened or died were left by the wayside.

Even though the natives did not make particularly good slaves, and died like flies under the lash or in confinement, yet the terrible slave gathering continued because the bandeirantes could sell an Indian slave profitably for from thirty to forty dollars while an imported Negro brought a minimum of one hundred to one hundred and fifty dollars, and in some cases their price went as high as five hundred dollars each.

But slavery was only the beginning of bandeira history. We have already seen how the Paulists attacked and destroyed the Spanish missions in Paraguay and drove the Jesuits with their Indians many miles farther south. They also cleared the southern province of Rio Grande do Sul of Spanish settlers and took possession of it in the name of Portugal. They even pushed on across Uruguay and founded the town of Colonia do Sacramento on the other side of the river from Buenos Aires. At this point they kept up the fight with the Argentines for many years. The glory which they had won in these campaigns, plus the fact that the Indians were receding before them, left the bandeirantes with their zeal undiminished but pointing now in other directions besides those of slave hunting and border warfare.

Just as our pioneers traveled westward for many different reasons—the Mormons for religious freedom, the forty-niners for California gold, Lewis and Clark for exploration, and countless thousands in order to establish new homes in the wilderness—so also did the bandeirantes, for a variety of reasons, now begin to roam the length and breadth of Brazil. So few people could not populate the whole of that wild interior, but many of them did remain to found settlements in the states of Minas, Mato Grosso, and Goyaz. Others, "returning after years of absence, found their wives married to other men, while many heroes brought back from the hinterland or *sertão* children whom they had not taken in."[60]

The Paulist "was compelled by his habitat to be a *bandeirante*," says a Brazilian writer, and "the conquest of the interior was written in his destiny." A man who had not taken part in at least one bandeira came to be regarded much as would a draft-dodger in any country during a great war for survival. Some men made twenty to twenty-five such journeys, and of course many of those who started out never returned.

The discipline under which these bands operated was rigorously maintained. A leader was chosen to whom all swore obedience, and his word was absolute law. The entire bandeira heard mass before leaving, and "the leader confessed and made his will, invariably including the phrase: 'setting out to war and being mortal and not knowing what the Lord our God will do with me . . .' A priest accompanied each *bandeira*, not only to shrive the dying and bury the dead, but by way of easing the conscience of the band regarding their mission and reconciling it with the Divine Mercy."[60]

The bandeira was always a strictly private enterprise, and in this differed from the state-organized expeditions which occasionally penetrated the interior. Each man paid for his own equipment, and all went prepared to spend many months or even years in the wilderness. When they departed the towns were left deserted, except for the oldest and most infirm men, and the women and children. After passing the mountain barrier they usually followed the course of some river across the sertão. The Paraná and Paraguay led them toward Paraguay and Argentina; the São Francisco, Brazil's second largest waterway, took them northward, and other rivers flowed westward along the tilt of the hinterland.

Sometimes the band would consist of only a hundred or two members, but there were frequently two or three thousand. They were a sort of mission in reverse, and their marching song was a backhanded version of "Onward, Christian Soldiers." Not only was their way contested by obstacles of nature and wild Indians, but miles of foodless land often lay between them and their goal. On these occasions they would leave well provided with seeds and would halt in green valleys to plant and to gather the fruited grain before moving on. Sometimes several years would pass before they again headed homeward. All of the rivers were highways to adventure which led them to Paraguay, Bolivia, Argentina, and even to the doors of Peru.

"The *bandeira* in its greatest phase was a traveling city, a commune . . ."[60] Held together by one common desire, its members surged over the silent land, withstanding hunger, fatigue, disease, and death, and facing with stoic equanimity the crosses of those who had gone before. They ascended unknown mountains, passed trackless forests, traveled over boundless plains with only a sea compass and the stars of night to guide them. Along the outward limits of their trajectory, wherever they encountered Spanish colonists, they stopped and created a stronghold. To them alone is due the credit of making Brazil the largest nation in the hemisphere. One of them, Antonio Raposo Tavares, became a legendary hero when it was reported that he had traversed the entire continent in a northwesterly direction, "entered Peru, scaled the Andes, crossed to the Pacific and waded into those waters sword in hand; returning he discovered the headwaters of the Amazon, sailed down it, and when at last after years of travel he came back to São Paulo no one recognized him."[60]

In the 1660s the Portuguese government, which had for many years been receiving nebulous news about great deposits of gold and silver in the interior, offered special rewards to discoverers of mines, and the bandeirante, who by that time had driven into the remote jungles all surviving wild Indians, now let his zeal for slave hunting give way to a greed for mineral wealth. A different set of values arose, and when finally gold was found it was a bandeirante who carried the news to Rio and another bandeirante who brought it to Bahia. In the rush which followed, the mameluco and his Indians were pitted against the Portuguese, the mulatto, and the Negro, and the latter won out. The age of great scope in which the bandeira had risen to glory was now displaced by one of assiduous and confined effort in which the mameluco was a misfit. The Negro, directed by the white man, rose to pre-eminence in Brazil.

A Brazilian historian, in summarizing the two centuries of bandeira dominance, divides them into two main periods: from 1580 to 1670, when slave hunts were the primary motive, and from 1670 to 1750, when prospecting for mineral wealth furnished the essential drive. Soon after this the bandeirante as such disappeared, but he had already turned his main efforts to cattle raising or agriculture, and many of his descendants to this day continue to lead their hard lives on the great interior sertão. The epic days were gone, but the backwoods farmer, or *sertanista*, now began to build up a legend all his own.

In the meantime, the city of São Paulo, removed from the coast and piratical attacks, left to its own resources, and relatively free of Negro slaves, continued in the same aggressive mold which its earliest settlers had outlined. It was the first region in the country where Brazilian blood, in this case half Portuguese, half Indian, asserted its dominance. Therefore, it was a region where the fabric of unity was not disturbed by a great mingling of the races. It was also the section of most fertile agricultural lands, of most temperate climate, of greatest appeal to the European immigrant. Here the European would feel at home, and when, years later, he began to come in great numbers, São Paulo recaptured out of its past some of that epic spirit which again placed it in the vanguard of the Brazilian procession, this time as a modern agricultural and industrial power.

21

THE FEUDAL PATTERN
OF COLONIAL SOCIETY

Spain and Portugal brought over to the New World a society that was essentially feudalistic. It was arranged in clearly defined layers or castes, which often overlapped but never merged into a strong homogeneous social structure throughout the colonial era. At the bottom was the vassal Indian; over him was the feudal landlord, or encomendero, and over the feudal lord was the government official, representing the King. Strung out among these three economic classes was the clergy, some identified with one group, some with another. Speaking purely in social terms, the historian must point out that the Church never did support any one group to the exclusion of the others.

This society was regulated in such a manner that it afforded the least possible opportunity for economic growth, and a minimum of those elements which contribute toward social progress or the free development of democratic ideas. For many years every law, every governmental action, was directed to the end of greater concentration of power in the hands of the Crown. The social classes were balanced one against the other in such a way that each one's striving was offset by another's privilege, and each one's privileges were carefully weighed in order to leave the balance of power in the hands of the King and his officials. It was a perfect setup for a benevolent or paternalistic despotism which might easily have emerged into social democracy in action. But the kings of Spain and Portugal, in addition to being noted neither for their benevolence nor their progressive paternalism, soon lost the initiative and saw the whole squirming fabric slip from their grasp. In compensation it must be said that never in the world's history were so many cards of social forces so chaotically stacked; never had the tasks of conquest, distance, race, geography, religion, government, and economics been presented to an imperial power on so grand a scale. The little chance that remained of attaining a brilliant success, had the entire energies of the peninsula been directed toward the colonization of America, was wasted in warfare and in an economic policy which resulted in complete disaster for the homelands.

In spite of all these things, the imperialism which was carried out has no parallel in the world's history. Never before had so great an area or so many diverse peoples been absorbed into the cultural consciousness of a superior power. Never before had the problems of race confronted a nation on such a scale, and never before or since have they been moved toward a solution with less racial bitterness.

The fundamental weakness of Spain and Portugal as colonial powers, and the ascension of British imperialism over them, lay in the backward and feudalistic nature of the former countries' political and social institutions, in their static economy, in their religious intolerance, in their general unwillingness to swim with the current of social change, but most of all in the vastness of the problem which they undertook to handle. While Britain was content to colonize a little territory at a time, and to consolidate that thoroughly before moving on, Spain and Portugal attempted to possess, colonize, and to govern twenty times the amount and all at once.

A comparison of the thirteen colonies of the United States in 1776 and the immense colonies of Spain and Portugal a century or more earlier will make the picture clear. It is a wonder that this imperialism has survived at all, and it could not possibly have survived had not the cultural and social forces which were operating there been imbued with the conviction that they were performing a mission or taking part in a crusade. This feeling too was essentially feudalistic.

The society of colonial Latin America, then, was organized on the following feudal pattern: first, natives of the Iberian Peninsula who held the supreme governing power. In the early decades these were the conquistadores, and in the following decades they were the viceroys, the higher government officials, the chiefs of the military, the ecclesiastical dignitaries, many big merchants and seekers of fortune in the New World. "The relations which this social group enjoyed at court, the authority and power they held in their hands, the ostentation displayed by them in clothes and customs—more in keeping with European usage—were motives that led them to disdain those who did not belong to their class. In every case, as they enjoyed public authority, they constituted the privileged, dominating element of the colony."[43]

Second were those persons of Spanish and Portuguese extraction born in America, called the Creoles. In the beginning they were of pure peninsular blood, but in time some native admixture was absorbed. For many years this class was made up largely of descendants of conquistadores. They did not hold the governing authority after the conquest proper, but they did enjoy "the stable wealth of the country," the lands, Indian labor, the wealth of the mines, the products of such industries as existed, and later the leadership of the merchant class. They formed a clear-cut landed aristocracy of feudal lords. Their political influence was wielded in the town councils, or cabildos, which they tried to convert into a sort of colonial House of Lords. Some of these Creoles acquired titles of nobility, and most of them entailed their landed possessions; that is, they followed the peninsular practice of the *mayorazgo*, making ownership of their estates inalienable, passing them down intact to the eldest son of the family, throughout succeeding generations.

The Creole class was very proud of its part in the colonial economy, felt that its members alone were true Americans, and was aggrieved that the Crown should have placed the governing power in any other hands. From the very first these American-born landowners deeply resented the intrusion of peninsular natives into their midst as political overlords. The rivalry of these two groups burst into flames several times before the conquest was ended, and set the pace for many a Latin-American revolution to follow.

Third in the social scale came the mestizos (in Brazil called mamelucos), who of course existed in no considerable numbers until a few decades after the conquest. For many years they were an orphan caste, denied the love of both races, but always struggling hard to swim in the current of white supremacy. Eventually they were successful and formed a bridge between the two extremes.

Fourth in line, and near the tail end of the procession, stood the Indian native, upon whom all the other classes came to rest. He was the true vassal and tributary, the tiller of the soil and menial laborer, and as indispensable as the land itself. There was no doubt about his being one of the spoils of the conquest, and it was the battle waged over his prostrate body which determined Latin America's political system as it existed throughout the colonial period, and as it continues to exist in some regions of Latin America today. The only difference is that in colonial days government officials and landed gentry were on opposite sides of the fence, whereas today they stand united.

These two groups, landed gentry and government officials, during the colonial period held viewpoints which were basically incompatible. Each of them wanted to possess and enjoy the spoils of the conquest; each of them wanted the economic and the governing power. Consequently, they often came to blows. Many compromises had to be made, but in the end the greater resources of the Crown assured the dominance of the kingly authority. Thus throughout the three colonial centuries the landed gentry had over their heads the superior power of the government officials. The King realized how important it was to retain the loyalty of these officials, and he saw to it that all important offices fell into the hands of persons from the peninsula whom he thought he could trust. Persons born in

Canadian Frontier

CLAIMED BY SPAIN

San Francisco
1776

Santa Fe
1605

San Diego
1769

Tucson
1700

Boston 1630
New York 1626
Philadelphia
1682

Guadalajara
1530

San Antonio
1716

SPANISH

Charleston 1670
Savannah 1733
St Augustine
1565

Vera Cruz
1519

Mexico City 1325
1521

FLORIDA

ATLANTIC

OCEAN

Barranquilla 1629

Cartagena
1533

Caracas
1567

Buenaventura
Cali 1535

Bogota
1538

Quito 1534

Guayaquil
1535, 1537

Pará 1616

PACIFIC

Lima
1535

OCEAN

Arequipa
1540

Pernambuco
1536, 1561

Bahia
1549

Córdoba
1573

São Paulo
1532

Rio de Janeiro
1567

Santiago
1541

Concepción
1550

Valdivia
1552

Buenos Aires
1536, 1580

Comparison of the
frontiers of the Eng-
lish and Hispanic col-
onies in the year 1776.
Frontiers extend to
shaded areas.

America were for that reason alone excluded from such positions. Both classes were of white blood, but they were competitors all the way along the line. The colonial-born Creoles thus began to develop a strong independent and definitely *American* feeling.

Under all of these classes, at the very bottom of the colonial ladder, was the Negro slave. The red man enjoyed at least a semblance of legal protection, whereas the Negro had only such immunities as his master felt disposed to grant. He could be sold at will to the highest bidder, and even his life was often subject to the caprices of his white owner. Almost immediately he plunged into the current of race-mixing in order to blot out or lighten the blackness of his skin.

In Brazil both the Indian and the Negro were used as outright slaves; there was no encomienda, or trusteeship, of Indians. However, the number of Indians was relatively so small and their caliber and stamina as workers so low that they were soon replaced almost entirely by Negroes. It was not necessary to import many blacks into the Spanish colonies except where the Indian had been killed off or where he was a poor worker. Consequently, we find the greatest concentration of African blood in the islands of the Antilles and along the northern coast of South America, where the native suffered death rather than servitude. In the larger centers Negro slaves were considered as a distinct evidence of luxury and belonged only to the wealthier classes. Several thousands were imported into Argentina, especially Córdoba, and Lima was for many years flooded with them. Chile also received ten to fifteen thousand and Mexico a few hundreds. In all of these latter countries the Negro has now almost completely disappeared, absorbed long since into the life stream of the people.

Miscegenation on a broad social base and on a narrower economic one was silently solving the problem of race. The social class to which a man belonged came to be reckoned by his "degree of whiteness," and that in turn became both officially and socially a matter of his economic status. In the last century of the colonial period, "driven by the needs of its treasury," the Spanish Government "went so far as to sell certificates of white blood—the famous *cédulas de gracias al sacar*—the cost of which naturally increased in proportion to the doubtfulness of the color of the aspirant . . ."[61]

The name given to the certificate meant literally "decree of thanks for getting out of . . ."; the remainder of the phrase being an implicit "out of the colored ranks." However, the very officiousness with which the government granted these decrees for a stipulated sum greatly irritated the proud American-born Creole class of Spanish blood. They already resented bitterly the fact that all lucrative and influential government positions went to those who had been born in Spain, and now they came to resent almost as bitterly this purchased intrusion into their sacrosanct social sphere. The eighteenth century, which marked the end of the colonial epoch, also saw the birth of a strong surge of race prejudice which hitherto had not existed. It became so strong in some circles that unless a person's mother was actually in Spain when conception took place there was difficulty getting into the ranks of the elite four hundred. Only the violence of revolutionary days was finally able to reduce this feeling to a minimum.

In the Church quite a few persons of mixed blood rose to positions of some prominence, and there were occasional pure Indians and Negroes who achieved distinction. The general principle of democracy within Christianity, however, was conspicuous by its absence, since nearly all of the higher offices were reserved for those of Spanish or Portuguese blood. In the social and political fields some Indians and numerous white-skinned mestizos and mulattoes were admitted to the lesser nobility, or at least into the social circle among which the members of this class moved, "but the army, which is the symbol of effective dominion, never failed to be European in its command, if not in its rank and file . . ."

In Brazil, where the mulattoes especially had distinguished themselves in the wars against the Dutch, they were allowed to form private regiments "in which they could rise to the post of captain. A parallel for such a situation might be found at the present time," says a Brazilian writer, "in the conditions existing in Hindustan." This same writer, Oliveira Lima, who is one of Brazil's most distinguished sons, adds that "the genealogical tree of many families of distinction has been jealously guarded from contact with all strains of inferior blood," and that "the whites of the colonies maintained and defended their titles and rights to certain posts and functions, which had been reserved to them by . . . their respective mother countries."[61] The writer was speaking to a North American audience when he made that statement, else he would certainly have deleted the phrase "inferior blood." Such a feeling is implicit in certain circles of Brazilian society, but it is not expressed in public.

The society which nurtured these seeds of one caste rule was, as we have said, essentially feudalistic. But it was not a static feudalism any more than any society is static, and different tendencies can be traced in each century of its growth. During the period of conquest and consolidation (1492–1600) it reached the peak of its dynamic force. The aggressive white was struggling to assert his dominance in every sphere. He was constantly on the go, ever vigilant and quick-acting, willing to try all kinds of schemes in order to see his dominance prevail. This society was truly a revolutionary one, because one means of living which had been followed for thousands of years was being supplanted by another which was totally different. Obviously, small Spain and Portugal could not superimpose their culture and their systems on the entire raw continent without compromises. The compromises which were reached are the pith of Latin-American character and history.

In that first century it seemed that the white man would win out completely. His conquerors, his soldiers, his church, his government, his culture in general were full of explosive power. But America's wealth corrupted them all and divided them against themselves. America's immense geography and primitive millions stretched to the breaking point the expansive quotient of their will. Gold, isolation, and a preponderance of native blood led to two centuries of political stagnation and social cleavages which have not yet been erased.

The second colonial century—generally speaking, the 1600s—saw a new focus brought into Latin-American life. Expansion slowed down and was followed by consolidation. Centers of security, of Indian labor, of wealth, of university cloisters and colonial courts now stood like tiny but brilliant European islands in a sea of red faces. Such centers were Mexico City, Bogotá, Quito, Lima, Potosí, all raised Atlas-fashion upon the back of the Indian. The produce of the American earth flowed into them as the surrounding country was exploited.

Immigrants also poured into these nuclei of European life, and the process of city against country, of Europe against America, of civilization against barbarism became intensified. But while it was a process, it rarely became a conflict: the seventeenth century was one of drowsy monotony in which two social currents, separated by a world of time, of feeling, and of blood, existed placidly side by side, their fever and combative energies spent. Year after year passed by and no change was evident on the riftless surface of this white-Indian New World. The seventeenth century was thus one of restorative sleep, broken only by an occasional dream of old glories or by some brief and fretful nightmare prophetic of things to come.

The third and final colonial century, beginning with the advent of the French Bourbons to the throne of Spain in 1700, injected a new spirit into the pallid Spanish Empire. As that century advanced, French liberalism came more and more into the ascendant, government was more efficient, the empty hull of a nation which the last Hapsburg had left drained came slowly back to life again. With the reign of Charles III (1759–88) Spain showed promise of once more attaining a considerable stature. The Inquisition spluttered and faded away; restrictions on commerce were gradually lifted; viceroys were men of higher caliber; the refined and broadening spirit of French manners and thought permeated the Spanish New World. From utter nothingness Spain moved to a position of influence and power.

Culturally, the advance was much slower. The old flash was gone and the body was feeble. French culture, then leading the world, was almost blinding in its brilliance. Voltaire, Rousseau, Montesquieu, Diderot, and dozens of others led the vanguard of an intellectual army which stunned Spain into mental inertia. Ever suspicious, she shied away from these liberals, yet what culture she had became a pale reflection of that of her northern neighbor. Her colonies followed suit. The North American and

ι revolutions brought reaction to a head, and for the first time the
ιle of despotism was openly challenged by leaders in both Spain and
ιιc colonies.

The triad of these three colonial centuries, moving ponderously forward from action, to reaction, to French liberalism in a minor key, characterized the Hispanic New World. The sixteenth century's finest sprinter
had undertaken a long-distance race and had lost—to England, to geography, to time, to the native red man, to her own fast pace.

However, beginning in the century of conquest and continuing throughout the colonial epoch, the final pace-setter of that long-distance marathon
was not the Spaniard, nor religion, nor gold, nor geography, nor anything
else whose lines can be clearly seen and traced by white men who have
knowledge of these things. The pace-setter was the Indian, the veritable
sea of Indian blood into which those Spanish soldiers and priests had so
rashly plunged. No man, no nation could move fast for long across that
myriad-faced sea. In the end there was only one solution possible: assimilation. The rate of assimilation was extremely slow in Mexico, Peru, and
the other most populous Indian countries, where the triumphant mestizo
did not emerge until long after independence. We cannot be sure that his
day has yet arrived. In Paraguay, where the blood became almost totally
mestizo during the colonial period, the great preponderance of Indian over
white practically obliterated the white. In Chile, Argentina, and Uruguay,
Spanish America's most advanced nations, large-scale European immigration ultimately absorbed, and in some regions obliterated, the Indian in a
great white stream. This did not occur until the late nineteenth century.
More than anything else the emergence of Spanish American nationalities
has depended on the solution of a racial problem, which immediately became also an economic and cultural issue.

Back of this strong caste system, which was economic and not racial
in its expression, lay the deeply imbedded unwillingness of the pure Spaniard or Portuguese to take part in manual labor. Long accustomed to the
life of soldier-conqueror who forced others to perform these ignoble tasks,
when he came to America he measured a man's worth in gold and slaves,
for they alone had the power of turning a peasant into an aristocrat. And a
man became an aristocrat in order not to have to work with his hands.

In the second place, to have performed labor in the presence of the very
Indians whom he had conquered would have been a degradation that no
Iberian could endure. So deeply ingrained was this sentiment that Charles
III, in the latter part of the eighteenth century, promulgated a special
decree which stated that a man might engage in mechanical or agricultural
labor without losing social caste. Yet the same feeling still continues so
strong in the Latin American of today that a majority of the upper class
would never carry a bundle in public. This inordinate pride, perhaps as

much as any other characteristic, made the Iberians great soldiers, great crusaders, great explorers, and at the same time miserably incompetent in economic organization or political co-operation. Where idleness is a virtue, exploitation is inevitable and good government is impossible.

22

LIFE IN THE COLONIAL TOWNS

Society as a whole throughout the first century after the conquest was that of a frontier pervaded with an atmosphere of chaos. Its extreme poles of whites, on the one hand, and Indians or Negroes, on the other, were clearly visible in the maelstrom, but all social classes were in a state of revolutionary flux. The free interplay of strong social forces, which no political regime can ever entirely direct or overcome, was causing the fringe of each class to merge into that of every other. The resultant collision of these forces seeking a common level resembled the desperate struggles of a suddenly mounted wild stallion twisting and turning in every direction, running and leaping here and there, then finally taking out across the fields with at least a semblance of agreement between rider and steed.

In many regions Latin America's frontier did not exist in space, but it was present everywhere as a race relationship moving forward in time. The element here was not occupation of the land, but assimilation. That borderland was clearest in the first colonial century, and these years defined all those which were to follow. Peninsular blood, government, culture, and religion took the place of pioneers; the Indian, and, later, the Negro in some sections, represented the territory to be assimilated. The forces of assimilation were centered in towns, missions, or fortresses, any nucleus where peninsular elements were strong. Their weapons were soldiers, priests, and miscegenation. The fact that schools had to fight against such tremendous odds along this cultural frontier was the greatest intrinsic weakness of Latin America's colonial and republican years. An ignorant and disorganized majority is the diet on which dictatorship most easily thrives.

In this society the town was paramount, for every directing force emanated from the town. It was the anchor point of European culture in a primitive wilderness. There were probably 200 of these towns in 1575, and perhaps 250 by 1600. Spanish towns were not at all hit-or-miss propositions, but were officially founded by groups of settlers from Spain and enjoyed many special privileges. A few were badly located in order to be near mines, or because they were mere way stations to other and larger centers. But most of the Spanish towns were placed at the best possible geographic points, in fertile valleys, on good harbors, or at strategic locations which would insure the best defense against the Indians. A few important Spanish centers were built on the ruins of large native cities: Mexico City, Cuzco, Quito, Bogotá. Others were started from scratch: Lima, Santiago, Buenos Aires.

The founders of all new towns, says one writer, after choosing the general region of their new settlement, always decided what the best spot would be by scrutinizing the color and complexion of the natives and selecting the most healthful place to live. They always tried to find a place where the sky was "clear and benign, the air pure and mild, without great variations of weather, neither where there is an excess of heat or an excess of cold, but if a choice must be made between the two cold would be preferable." As a result of these considerations there is not today in all Latin America a large city with the abominable extremes of weather so generally encountered in the United States and elsewhere in the world.

The center of the town was always the plaza or main square on which all public buildings were erected: the church, the city hall or municipal building where the civic council (cabildo) met, the King's building, or *casa real*, where the representatives of the Crown gathered, and also several stores of traders and merchants. If the town was located on the seacoast the plaza fronted the water instead of being placed in the center of the settlement. Each town had its village commons for the grazing of cattle and oxen, and the remainder of the surrounding land belonging to the township was distributed among the citizens for cultivation. If it was allowed to remain fallow for an extended period it reverted to the township and was reassigned.

"As in the New England towns, the land was divided among the colonists in proportion to their merits, capacity or number of family dependents." The average small farmer, for example, received a dwelling lot inside the town limits about fifty by one hundred feet in size, and "outside the building area he received enough to sow ten thousand pounds [one hundred *quintales*] of wheat or barley, and ten of corn. He was also given a measured plot of ground for a garden and an orchard," besides the right to pasture ten sows, five mares, one hundred sheep, and twenty goats. A settler who had been a soldier received more space than an ordinary civilian, and a mounted soldier was allotted four or five times as much, for his services in the conquest had been truly invaluable and placed him automatically among the lesser lights of the new landed aristocracy.[62]

The town dominated completely the country around it. It was the center of governing power, the military headquarters from which soldiers were dispatched, the seat of the Church from whose bosom the missions were established. The encomendero lived in the town or very near it, and the "civilized" (meaning incorporated) Indian lived either in its vicinity or in a mission, established by priests, whose directors lived there.

For a time there was almost no country life except that of unsubjugated savages, because the town was essential as a protection. It was a strong point as well as a place of culture and residence. Life there was much like living in a combination armed camp and mining town. A large proportion of the population was always either just preparing to leave for some other place or had just arrived. Hodgepodge crowds of every conceivable type milled about the streets. Prospectors were getting ready to go in search of mines; soldiers were receiving their equipment and last instructions for the campaign; missionaries were preparing to depart silently into the wilderness, or perhaps some government or church official was about to arrive and the inhabitants had turned out in a mass to greet him. The general feeling was that of living along the borders of a great unknown, that the town was merely a center from which the true promised land was soon to be reached. Moral and legal restraints were thrown to the winds. The streets and central plaza were a bedlam of noise, animals, processions, drunken brawls, murders, whores, Negroes, primitive Indians, priests, showily dressed officials, and general filth.

"The whole system established by the mother country," says one writer, "seemed calculated for men who kept moving and must shortly return to their native land. The colonists did not appear to be inspired by any distinct purpose. Their first forms of production and labor, just like their local ordinances of trade and industry, left the impression that they dwelt in encampments rather than in cities and that, instead of living in families, they always lived in campaigns, fighting at the same time against nature and man. Their necessities were not yet more than those of soldiers."[43]

If the purpose of these people did not seem clear it was because the premise did not need to be stated. Glory, gold, and Gospel soon merged into the necessity for economic dominance, and that in turn gave way to a cultural frontier. The result, inevitably, was a fusion of civilization and barbarism. In the populated centers it was not long before some measure of stability had been reached, and the characteristics of different types of towns began to appear. While the typical frontier settlements of Chile and Argentina continued as armed camps, Mexico City and Lima, heads of the two great viceroyalties into which all Spanish America had been divided, and which were the earliest centers of colonial wealth, became the show places of the Spanish New World. Bahia, capital of Brazil, with its several hundred naked slaves walking the streets, could not hold a candle to them. And no wonder, for the accumulated treasure of two great Indian civilizations was poured into these capital cities, and still more was found in the rich mines of Mexico and Peru. It, too, flowed toward these most secure centers of the dominant race.

Back in the hinterland, far off the beaten track and almost completely separated from civilized centers, were the Indian villages. They were still organized on a communal basis, were incomparably cleaner than the mestizo towns, and pursued their isolated way like small truncated parts of a once-great body. If they had any contact at all with Hispanic civilization it was through the priest and the tribute collector. If christianized, their religion was shot through with elements of their primitive and idolatrous past.

A little closer to the governing centers were other Indian towns, but these were organized on a Spanish basis as an integral part of colonial life. Slowly but surely the search for more land, gold, and silver pushed spearheads into the dark interior. Occasionally at the site of a rich mine a large Spanish-Indian-Negro city would spring up almost overnight as a symbol of the mestizo future toward which all towns were pointed. In the early mining economy such places became the backbone not only of Mexico and Peru but of Spain itself.

The silver mountain at Potosí in the Bolivian province of Peru was such a place. Silver was discovered there in 1545 when an Indian herder chasing a llama up the slope grabbed at a shrub in order to keep from falling, inadvertently pulled up the whole plant, and disclosed at its roots a great vein of that precious metal. The first mine in the province of Zacatecas, Mexico, was discovered in 1548, and two military colonies were immediately planted there in order to defend it from the Indians. By the end of the sixteenth century—that is, within a period of about fifty years—mines found in the Spanish colonies had produced "at least three times as much gold and silver as had been current in Europe at the beginning of the century." The phrase *vale un Potosí* (it's worth a Potosí), came to indicate that a thing was priceless.

Lima and Mexico City basked in the gleam of pieces of eight. Two billion dollars of them were coined by a single Mexican mint. Potosí, Zacatecas, and other mining camps "were rugged, full-blooded, and wide open. Wealth poured forth tumultuously, like a cloudburst, and flowed through the skyland places like a swollen river." Potosí grew to be the largest town in all Latin America and maintained that position for over a hundred years, yet it always resembled a rich mining camp rather than a great city. Its story is typical of a whole era.

The legend was that even the great Inca, Huayna Capac, father of Atahualpa, had once camped in the vicinity and had suspected the wealth that lay in the bosom of this fabulous mountain. However, when he set Indians to digging they suddenly heard a great noise in the bowels of the earth and a mysterious voice warned them: "Take no silver from this hill which is destined for other owners." The Indians took no silver, and Huayna Capac passed on to Cuzco. Under the Incas, of course, all precious metals belonged to the Sun or to the ruling caste and had no purchasing power, being "wrought into plants, trees, animals, and flowers, which were used to adorn the temples . . . There was thus no temptation to steal them, no object in possessing them, and no incentive to search for them."[63] So the great hill lay unmolested until the Spaniards came.

The herder who discovered its wealth was a native in the service of a Spaniard named Villaroel. Most chroniclers say that he pulled up a shrub and disclosed a rich vein, but there are variations to the story. One version has it that he built a fire while camping near by and the heat caused "little streams of pure silver" to trace a patchwork on the ground. Other versions say that the animal was a goat or a deer instead of a llama. In any case, it is clear that an Indian discovered the silver and that a Spaniard cheated him of his find. When the natives of the neighborhood heard that one of their own was being defrauded they banded together, armed themselves, and attempted to take possession of at least a small portion of the claim. They were met by the Spaniards with organized gunfire and dispersed, leaving fifty of their dead upon the field. After that there was no question as to who the owners were.

When Charles V was informed of the discovery he seemed to sense its importance at once. He gave the city the title of *Villa Imperial de Potosí*, Imperial City, and granted it a coat of arms with the great hill itself in the center. For further decoration the crest carried the imprint of the imperial crown, and the columns of Hercules from which our dollar sign is said to be derived. It contained this legend: "I am the rich Potosí; of the world I am the treasure; I am the king of mountains, and I am the envy of kings." Little did Charles know what that mountain of silver would in the end do to his empire, gutting it of fiber and lifeblood, leaving only a skeleton of mock grandeur to strum its everlasting praise.

When the first vein of silver was discovered Potosí was a cold, barren, and deserted region. It was on the altiplano of Peru, situated at an uncomfortable altitude of over two miles above the sea. But no sooner had the secret of discovery leaked out than a great rush began and people of all classes and descriptions poured in from neighboring towns and villages. Within a few years over forty thousand Spaniards had flocked to the silver mountain, bringing along with them six thousand Negro and mulatto slaves and more than sixty-five thousand Indians. By 1580 the population of Potosí was 120,000, and a few years later it reached a peak of 160,000, which was maintained for several decades. It was far larger and richer than any other city in the Western Hemisphere.

As always, the Indian was forced to do nearly all the labor, and the white man reaped nearly all the profit. The *mita* system was established, by which the natives, who were gathered into 139 native villages in the suburbs, were forced to work in the mines for a few months and then were supposed to receive a few months off. But mining was carried on under such dangerous and miserable conditions that four out of five Indians died in the first year of their employment. Great wealth, however, continued to accumulate in the hands of a few. In 1580 the fortunes of Potosí's elite ranged from a minimum of around $300,000 to a maximum of $6,000,000. A certain General Pereyra bestowed a dowry of $2,300,000 on his daughter Plácida when she got married, and General Mejía gave his a cool million. A woman named Catalina Argandona made a fat profit of $800,000 from her vineyards which kept the menfolk in drink.

Social living and dress were in keeping with the wild fortunes of these newly rich. "The ladies of Potosí had jewels and dresses for each *fiesta* which were worth from twelve to fourteen thousand dollars; one lady spent five hundred dollars merely for pearls to adorn her overshoes. The *mestizas* wore sandals and belts of silk and gold, with pearls and rubies, skirts and jackets of fine cloth, and other rich jewels."[63] The town boasted fourteen big dancing schools, thirty-six gambling houses, and a single theater "to which the price of admission ranged from forty to fifty dollars."

All popular celebrations were on a similar scale. In 1556 the city spent eight million dollars on a twenty-four-day extravaganza inspired by the accession of Philip II to the throne of Spain. There were magnificent bullfights, carnivals, masked balls, banquets, free liquors of every imaginable nature for everyone, jousts and tourneys in extravagant dress, dramatic representations, and a general saturnalian revel such as the New World had never seen before. A few years later three million dollars were spent on a waterworks for the town, and hundreds of thousands were expended on elaborate funeral services for Charles V and Philip II. When Philip III died, a six-million-dollar series of services were held for him. Everything the townsmen touched was carried out on a grand scale.

Yet while the streets of Potosí practically flowed silver, the physical make-up of the city and the society which inhabited it were anything but refined. Armed soldiers, miners, and government officials roamed the streets ready to fight at the drop of a hat. Duels were of daily occurrence. Oftentimes the adversaries were dressed in robes of scarlet so that when the blood spurted they would not see it and be afraid, and the observers thus be cheated of a show. The narrow winding streets of the town were always flooded with crowds "on foot, on horseback, in carriages, and in litters, as if going on a pilgrimage." Every class and every color brushed shoulders, and women of loose life walked around at their leisure, exhibiting the finery of their apparel with the shrill gay cries of freedom unknown to the more respectable feminine class. Every time the town council met its members attended fully armed and wearing coats of mail, and the meetings more often than not ended in a free-for-all.

Potosí was a barren, unproductive community, but everything could be imported and the cost did not matter. Shops displayed wares which could not be found elsewhere in America at that time, and wealthy merchants flocked to the emporium from all quarters with costly items. On one occasion the royal judge and treasurer raised the sales tax from 2 to 6 per cent, and the merchants raised a howl of protest. The official persisted in his decree, and the merchants went to him in a body and said: "We are disposed to give twelve millions which we have in clothing and money in order to have the pleasure of taking the life of your honor with a thousand stabs." The royal judge assembled a considerable force of bodyguards and proceeded to the houses of some merchants with the intention of imprisoning them. An organized band was awaiting him and the two groups collided head on. In the general pandemonium and hand-to-hand fight which ensued the merchants were victorious and, grabbing the judge, dragged him to the main plaza, tearing off his breeches on the way, and there made ready to pummel and stab him to death. Some priests arrived in the nick of time and saved his life. A few of the merchants later retired from the vicinity in order to escape punishment. The only safe places in town were the churches and monasteries, and many hundreds of thousands of dollars in money and jewels were deposited in them for safekeeping.

As the city had been built on the spur of the moment, piling itself along the mountainside in a jumble of streets and buildings, it was not until the Viceroy Toledo came there from Lima in 1572 that there was even a central plaza. That official cleared off a place for the square, widened, straightened, and cleaned the streets, and put some semblance of order into the miserable-looking town. He also had a city hall, a prison, and a mint constructed, and attempted to relieve the oppressive measures under which the Indians labored.

But Potosí never became a really civilized community. As the source of South America's greatest wealth for so many years, it felt free of the social or legal restrictions imposed on more normal and ordinary societies. Many comforts were also lacking. The houses had no heat except that of small circular braziers which were placed in the center of a room while the whole household crowded around to absorb some of the warmth of the tiny smoldering embers inside. This method of heating was current throughout Latin America, but in cold Potosí it seemed utterly ridiculous. Llama dung had to be used for fuel as it was the only thing obtainable. Sometimes the snow would fill the streets to a height of several feet and make them impassable. Once, in 1557, the entire region was blanketed with a snowfall which lasted for seven days and nights, and each dwelling became an isolated cell. For weeks no one was able to venture out upon the streets, and many died of grippe and pneumonia before enough of the snow had melted to bring the town back to life again.

The mercury process of amalgamation, which made the extraction of silver from its ore easier and more profitable, was discovered by a Mexican miner in 1556, but it did not reach Potosí until the visit of the Viceroy Toledo sixteen years later. These shots of mercury were obtained from a near-by mine of quicksilver, and their frequent injections kept Potosí alive for over two centuries. Throughout nearly all of those years a sort of medieval anarchy permeated the air of the place, with the froth of lavish display drowning out the sharp hurt cry of the dispossessed and the exploited. The poor herder who had enjoyed the misfortune of uncorking the mountain which held that apparently inexhaustible silver stream disappeared into the shadows along with his legend.

Even the great hill of Potosí, however, was not limitless, and as the decades dragged by its core was eaten out and hollowed by the ravenous claws of the slave-driving mineowners. The town suffered its first major setback in 1626, seventy years after its birth, as the result of a devastating flood, and never completely recovered. The flood was not due to heavy rains but to the breaking of a dam above the city. As steam power was not known in those days, water power was used almost exclusively whenever a greater force than could be mustered by men or horses was needed. The engineers at Potosí had constructed thirty small reservoirs whose water turned the wheels of 132 ore crushers.

On a cold Sunday afternoon in the year 1626 one of the largest dams suddenly broke and unleashed an avalanche of water upon the town. The flood destroyed all but a dozen of the ore-crushing mills; many hundreds of people lost their lives, and more than a thousand buildings were torn from their moorings and swept away in rubble. Some began to speak of divine retribution, and after the holocaust mining zeal was never again as strong as it had been previously. Superstition, a growing lack of high-grade ore, the difficulty of obtaining food, and an abominably cold and inhospitable climate sent the Imperial City slowly downhill. The mines of Mexico had by this time already taken pre-eminence over those of Peru.

A Dutch trader who visited Potosí in 1659 left one of the best descriptions of the place that has come down to us. He described it as being a city of four thousand well-constructed stone houses, many of them having several stories. The churches were all solidly built and richly adorned with silver, tapestries, and other ornaments. The Indians, who lived in less pretentious dwellings in the neighborhood, numbered about ten thousand. There were also a few foreigners, mostly Dutch, Irish, Genoese, and French. Many of these claimed to be from the Basque provinces of Spain. The considerable number of mestizos were "lazy, inclined to be quarrelsome, and so nearly all of them wore three or four rough leather jackets, one on top of the other as a protection against sword stabs." The Indians were not allowed to carry arms of any kind, nor were they permitted to wear Spanish clothes. They all went barefooted and barelegged. The Ne-

groes and mulattoes, as they were entirely in the white man's service, could
wear his type of clothing and were also allowed to go armed.[64]

Almost everybody in town, even those in government positions, carried
on some kind of commerce. "There were some who had fortunes of two,
three, and four million crowns; and many of them were worth three or
four hundred thousand crowns." The wealthy people owned priceless silver
and gold services, and eating from plates valued at many hundreds of dollars was a common occurrence. Even the poorer inhabitants made a point
of wearing showy clothes. The women were kept closely secluded and almost never left the house except to attend mass. Many of them were addicted to the coca-chewing habit and "sometimes became so excited that
they hardly knew what they were doing with themselves." The coca plant,
which was cultivated by the Incas and is still widely grown in the Andean
region, takes the place of tobacco among the natives. Its leaves contain a
certain amount of cocaine, and when a wad of these is placed in the hollow of the cheek, sometimes with a bit of lime added, it forms a veritable
cud which will last for several hours and give the chewer a sense of great
exhilaration. Until very recently workers in these high altitudes were always allotted a portion of coca leaves for everyday use. The drug kept
them from feeling cold, tired, or even hungry, and increased the amount
of work they could turn out. On the other hand, it was often taken in
excessive amounts and ate up a man's reserve energies so that by the time
he was thirty he resembled a wizened octogenarian. Although still widely
used, coca leaves are legally prohibited in many regions at the present
time.

Speaking of the mines, this Dutch traveler wrote that the King did not
have any of them worked directly on his own account "but left them to
the persons who had made the discovery, and who remained as their owners after the councilman had visited and legally recorded them in his
books." The King always was due his royal fifth and thought that this
means of encouraging private initiative would increase his receipts, which
it probably did, in spite of the fact that great quantities of silver were
mined without any legal report being rendered or any fifth being paid to
the Crown.

When the councilman recorded a mining claim he very carefully described the surface of the ground where the prospector was permitted to
begin digging. But there was no limitation as to what course the tunnel
should follow once the miner got well under the surface. He was allowed
to keep after his vein of ore, no matter in which direction it might turn,
and consequently after a few years the interior of the great hill was gutted
with subterranean twistings and turnings which often met and crossed
and wound about in the cold darkness like a nightmare of hell. Many a
bloody encounter took place when two such tunnels met head on, or when
one miner dug in the side of another's burrow in order to get across it.

The King limited the number of natives who might be forced to do duty on any single claim, and thus saw to it that there were always enough to go around. Work underground could proceed only so fast anyhow, and this measure prevented idling at any time. The native chieftains were obliged to provide the number of workers demanded of them, and these were to be kept ready at a moment's notice. If an order went out for them, and they were not available, the chief was forced to pay the authorities double the amount which the workers would have received in wages. In the year 1659 there were only about twenty-three hundred Indians working in the mines at any given moment. When they were brought to the scene they were placed inside a high stockade at the foot of the mountain, where the councilman distributed them among the mineowners. "After six days of labor they were returned to this stockade where the councilman checked over them again in order to verify the wages they were to receive and in order to find out how many of them had died, so that he might oblige their chieftains to make up the deficit." Respiratory diseases took a huge toll among them despite their being physically adapted to the rarefied atmosphere. Coca leaves were chewed regularly while at work, and if nausea set in, a heavy dose of yerba mate was given in order to make the worker vomit and clear his stomach.

In 1659 there were still over a hundred ore mills in the neighborhood, and the mercury process of separating silver was going at full blast. However, the total quantity being produced was nothing like what it had been a century previously. Later on a special school of metallurgy was established near by in order to study more improved methods of extracting the metal. But the town had already passed its zenith, and even improved or stronger doses of quicksilver were no longer effective. Worn out and gradually deserted, the houses and streets took on the look of a cemetery. By 1825 the great center of 160,000 had dwindled to a filthy village of about one twentieth that size. Today it is one of the most backward communities in all Latin America.

Among the other large centers of Spanish America, Lima and Mexico City stood at the opposite pole from Potosí. Viceroys, archbishops, magnificent churches, universities, and a crust of colonial nobility gave them an air of refinement which was utterly lacking in the mining metropolis on the bleak Bolivian plateau. When a silver king became sufficiently wealthy or sufficiently weary of living on the lunatic fringe of that or some other mining town, he would invariably gravitate toward one of the great viceregal capitals. Titles of nobility were on sale for a moderate consideration, so newly dubbed counts and marquises were all over the streets, having their ears pleasantly tickled by obsequious lackeys. The viceregal social whirl was like the cape-and-sword dramas of romantic Spain re-enacted on a large scale. Ricardo Palma, Lima's greatest writer, in his famous *Peruvian*

Traditions gives an earthy picture of this bawdy and colorful society which seemed to live suspended on heroic dreams. The crudities of Potosí were carefully polished off, but seductions, masked encounters, duels, bribes, vengeances, even religious miracles, were all thrown in against the magnificent backdrop of viceroys and colonial courts.

In the early seventeenth century Lima had between thirty and forty thousand inhabitants, about one third of whom were Spaniards or their white Creole descendants. Another third of the population was predominantly black, emanating from the imported Negro slaves, and the final third was predominantly Indian. Race-mixing had already made considerable headway against the barriers of color, but mostly among the lower economic groups. The proud Spaniards and Creoles held their noses high, guarded their pedigrees with far more zeal than their virginity, and strutted peacock-like through the narrow streets of colonial Lima with a more aristocratic disdain than was evident anywhere else in the hemisphere. As the wealth of Potosí began to pour into the city it became opulent and magnificent in the very middle of the period of decay of the Spanish monarchy. The small factories or workshops of the sierra, called obrajes, also added to Lima's wealth, as did the monopoly of the fairs at Portobello, where Peruvian merchants went to purchase goods for distribution throughout their own country, and what is now Chile, Bolivia, Paraguay, and Argentina, all of which then formed part of the great viceroyalty of Peru.

Everything centered in Lima, from the government offices to the personnel of the university with its Latinistic culture, its students of theology, and the mass of religious establishments which, together with the viceregal salons, were the nucleus of social existence. The city also shone through the luxury of the higher castes: in the fineries of their dress, the rich manner of their living, their many servants, silver table services, and showy furnishings. Religion flourished within Lima's cloistered walls, and there were in the capital alone twenty-six convents of friars and twelve nunneries besides the other church establishments. To these came children of many principal families, some moved by religious impulses, others motivated by a desire to occupy preferred positions at court or in society when they came out. Priests were the counselors of governmental and judicial authorities, of families, and were the teachers in the universities and colleges which they maintained. There were also a considerable number of Portuguese Jews in Lima, who had somehow slipped into the city by way of Brazil or some other circuitous route, and much of the banking was in their hands.

Over a thousand carriages promenaded through the streets of the city, the bright liveries of their drivers and footmen and the shiny encrustations of their gold- and silverwork gleaming out as fit frames for the lovely faces of the *limeñas* on parade. It was about their only diversion except attending some fiesta or other. The city was on a smaller scale than the capital of Mexico; as it had been raised on unpopulated land it was more purely Spanish in feeling, prouder, more profoundly aristocratic. Of all the cities of the Spanish New World it still retains a greater proportion of that colonial color and charm than any other.

Mexico City was in some ways a fairly close replica of Lima, but was much larger, wealthier, more obviously raised upon the shoulders of the Indians who plodded its streets by the thousands. Many of the Indian's foods and ways were everywhere evident. The day was begun with thin and foaming chocolate flavored with vanilla, followed a little later by a more substantial breakfast. With the heavy noon meal hot tortillas were eaten instead of bread. Wine was served after the midday repast, and then came the siesta period which in both Mexico City and Lima is still religiously observed, all shops closing during part of the afternoon. At night there was the *tertulia,* or social gathering, which lasted from about six until nine, and after that dinner was served. The principal sport at these tertulias was voluble conversation, but games of forfeit, singing, and dancing were also enjoyed.

"The afternoon drive was a favorite feature, which gave the best opportunity for a display of apparel and jewelry. Hundreds of the heavy, springless coaches of the period, covered and embellished with designs, rolled slowly down the avenue, drawn by four horses or mules, and with servants dressed in livery. Within were women in evening dress, without veil or head-covering, exchanging glances and greetings with passing acquaintances. Between the lines of carriages were prancing steeds, their riders being seated in saddles stamped, gilded, or embossed in gold or silver. The leather or fur covering of the horse was embellished like the saddle, and fringed with dangling pieces of precious metal which jingled at every step." The rider, or *charro,* wore a "broad-brimmed hat, edged with gold or silver lace, fur-trimmed and embroidered jacket, silver buttoned pantaloons, and leather leggings, with immense silver spurs and inlaid whip."[25] Frequently this equipment, of which he was inordinately proud, formed his only worldly wealth, and his parade along the alameda was the height of his glory.

Thomas Gage, a renegade English Dominican who was in Mexico City around the year 1625, describes the city as having a population of between thirty-five and forty thousand Spaniards and two or three times that many Indians. There were practically no Negroes. At least fifteen thousand coaches circulated on the streets of the Mexican capital, which were lined with fine shops, especially those of the goldsmiths. Both sexes were "excessive in their apparel," and precious stones and silks imported at great expense in galleons from the Orient were commonplace. Many gentlemen wore "a hatband and rose made of diamonds, and a hatband of pearls is common in a tradesman." There were about fifty religious establishments in the city, which Gage calls "the fairest that ever my eyes beheld, the roof and beams being in many of them all daubed with gold, and many altars with sundry marble pillars, and others with brazilwood stays standing one above another, with tabernacles for several saints richly wrought with golden colors, so that a hundred thousand dollars is a common price of many of them."

Here also was being raised the great Mexican cathedral, largest in the New World, and many houses of the aristocrats took on an air of elegance and refinement which was seldom seen in the peninsula. In both Mexico City and Lima special laws were passed against wearing too richly decorated clothes. Yet the legend that a nation may attain power, wealth, and advancement through the acquisition of precious metals became almost universal. The story of the old country was being repeated in New Spain, and in all the new Spains where mines poured forth the glistening torrent of fool's gold and silver. Those other accouterments of civilization—civil liberties, honest government, an educated electorate, tolerance, and diligent labor—were not much in evidence. Beggars infested the streets of even the wealthiest cities, sticking out their filthy and diseased paws at every encounter to receive the largess of some member of the ruling caste. Like Spain, both Mexico and Peru were great kingdoms, and silver was enthroned in the highest chair.

Some of the stories of the newly rich were epic. For example, that of the French boy, De la Borde, who came to New Spain at the age of fifteen in order to seek his fortune.* With nothing in his favor except a willingness to work hard he wound up in the vicinity of Taxco and engaged in silver mining. Before long he had become the wealthiest man of the district. His generosity was noteworthy, as were his magnificent gifts to the Church. He used to say: "God gives to Borda, Borda gives to God." This, however, did not prevent his worldly pomp from asserting itself, and on one occasion when he was holding a fiesta in honor of some friends, Borda had the walk over which they were to pass covered with sheets of pure silver. On nearing the end of his life he tired of these things and determined to erect a cathedral so fine that it would forever be a monument to his memory. The famous baroque cathedral of Taxco was the result.

Another wealthy Mexican mineowner invited the King of Spain to visit his "palace" and promised that if he would come the entire road between Vera Cruz and Mexico City, over which the monarch would have to pass, would be covered with silver. Still another silver king paid 800,000 pesos in taxes (well over $1,000,000), and many of the newly rich purchased titles of nobility. The old cry "pieces of eight" (eight reales to a peso) was the symbol of an epoch.

The mansions in which these wealthy people lived were in keeping with the vast incomes they received. They were jealously enclosed and guarded,

* In Mexico De la Borde is known by the Spanish version of his name, Borda.

but interior patios furnished a flowering retreat from the ugliness outside. The inside of the houses themselves was "enriched and made lovely with carved furniture, with gilded and brightly colored leather work, with tiles and pottery and silks brought from the Orient; and throughout the spacious rooms there shone the moonlight gleam of silver mirrors, silver brasiers with their glow of hot charcoal, silver dishes on the dining table, reflected in the soft rays of candles held in silver sconces. . . . The age of silver had, too, its comforts, and added to comfort its charm and splendor."[169] But it is well never to forget that these were the exceptions, and not the rule, in that age of silver which was raised upon the poverty of an exploited people.

Civil life in the early colonial towns, although constantly under the aegis of the Church, was itself a vigorous social force. The urban population was divided into three classes: encomenderos, indwellers, and transients. The first two were actual settlers; the last group was made up of soldiers. There were also the specially privileged groups of government officials and clergy. The encomenderos were the wealthiest class, the indwellers, or *moradores*, were artisans and traders. The first were also overlords of Indians, while the latter were not.

An idea of the proportionate distribution of population in a typical town can be gathered from the following: in 1569 Lima had thirty-two encomenderos and twenty-five hundred indwellers; Cuzco, in the heart of the Indian district, had eighty encomenderos and five hundred indwellers; Quito's population included fifty encomenderos and two hundred and fifty indwellers; La Paz had thirty and two hundred respectively. These encomenderos probably had from one hundred to several hundreds of Indians paying them tribute. Tucumán, Argentina, in 1583 had twenty-five encomenderos and three thousand Indians; Córdoba, forty encomenderos and twelve thousand Indians; Santiago del Estero, forty-eight encomenderos and also about twelve thousand Indians. Most of these Indians did not live inside the towns but in villages near by. In 1574 the total number of Spaniards in America was 160,000; of these four thousand were encomenderos. Approximately 1,500,000 adult Indians paid tribute either to these encomenderos or to the Crown.

A considerable proportion of the encomenderos held land grants as well as their encomienda privilege to collect and use Indian tribute. Other favored colonists were given land grants but not encomiendas of Indians. The number of large landholders around the year 1600 would thus be approximately four to five thousand. This number did not increase greatly with the passing years, but the amount of land held did increase considerably. Although the encomienda was suppressed in 1720, the large landholder lived on. As the strongest economic power in colonial life he came to resent bitterly government interference, in this case represented by the

ll governing caste of peninsular officials. The towns thus became strong
ters of political and economic disunion at the same time that they
were equally strong centers of cultural and racial fusion. Latin America,
from its inception as a group of colonies, was torn asunder by these two
forces operating simultaneously and pulling in opposite directions, the
one toward division, the other toward homogeneity.

This process was the exact opposite of that which was evolving in the
English colonies of North America, where political union was to come
first and cultural maturity much later. The issue of race, which many years
ago reached solution in Latin America, has not yet been squarely faced in
the United States. The reason for this essential difference between the
two Americas is not at all complicated: the English settler came to North
America for political, religious, and economic freedom, and as he always
put those things first he first attained them.

The Latin, on the other hand, emigrated as a fortune seeker and as a
spiritual crusader. As he made these things his primary goal, he also first
attained them. His ready acquisition of gold, silver, land, and labor kept
him in a state of political and economic backwardness, but his burning
conviction as a crusader made his mission successful. The history of his
people, who had in their homeland already absorbed so many races, is part
of the explanation for his success in this sphere in America, and the cultural influence of his powerful church fills out the picture.

City life in those days was, of course, far removed from the amenities
which we of the present so often take for granted. In many towns the
sewer ran down the middle of the street, and it was an old peninsular
custom to throw all the slop out the front door, the only legal order being
that the thrower must give fair warning with the shout of "¡Agua va!" the
equivalent of "Here she comes!" Those who failed to dodge quickly enough
were justifiable targets.

In contrast to the magnificent religious establishments and the houses
of the wealthy, most of the ordinary dwellings "presented a poverty-
stricken appearance. The low buildings had walls of adobe or plastered
mud, and roofs of tile or straw—one to three rooms at the most."[43] They
were ill lighted, smelly, and meagerly furnished, seldom containing more
than rude benches, tables, and perhaps a wooden chair. The floor was uncovered earth or brick, and the walls were slaked with a coat of lime. An
animal skin or a straw mat was the bed, and, if the place was large enough
to have a patio, the chickens and pigs were generally found there.

In Buenos Aires the streets were unpaved and during the rainy season
became so deeply mired that it was impossible for even a cart to pass
through. Usually one or two main thoroughfares and the main plaza were
covered with cobblestones. "At night there was no traffic through the un-
lighted streets after a certain hour. At the stroke of curfew, given by a
bell or drum, everyone had to go home. The curfew sounded at dusk for

Indians and Negroes and one or two hours later for the rest, according to whether it was winter or summer."[43]

The outside of all except the very finest buildings was extremely plain; the windows were usually covered with an iron grating, and there were occasional small projecting balconies underneath. When the baroque style of architecture became almost universally popular much stone lacework and many incrustations adorned the churches and public buildings. In a few centers there was a notable fusion of Andalusian Spanish elements with certain motifs of native inspiration.

Even in the largest cities public sanitation was almost nonexistent. As late as 1796 one of the members of the Board of Regents of the University of Mexico protested vigorously "that the populace should be prevented from relieving themselves with complete abandon in the Zócalo, the central plaza."[65] In other towns the situation was equally bad. Signs written on the walls of churches and other public buildings reading *Se prohibe hacer aguas mayores o menores* (It is prohibited to do either the big or the small wetness here) had little effect on the population. No wonder old Captain Bernal Díaz, who entered Mexico City with Cortés, was so deeply impressed with the cleanliness of the streets of that Indian town down which he said he could walk for many blocks without stepping in anything. Such conditions certainly did not prevail in Spain at that time. A very considerable proportion of the blame for this filth, then, lay with the Spaniards and not with the natives. The Indians who lived in contact with Spanish civilization became dirty because of the disintegration of the moral fiber of their people under the heel of the white man's rule. A vanquished race always tends to pick up the vices of its conqueror.

Epidemics of smallpox and other virulent diseases broke out with alarming frequency in nearly all regions. One Peruvian author states that at least every four years his country was visited with a terrible epidemic of "small-pox, measles, syphilis, typhoid fever, itch, dysentery, diphtheria, bubonic plague, yellow fever, rabies . . ." and that an average of two hundred thousand lives were lost "at each blow." In Mexico smallpox killed nearly half the population in the first century. The epidemic of 1555 followed by the disastrous run of 1576 was said to have wiped out nearly two million persons.[65] The total Indian population of Peru decreased from about five million in 1530 to a mere six hundred thousand in 1796. The white man's diseases were a far more terrible scourge than even his guns or his lash.

In dress the better classes followed the lead of the peninsula, the men wearing a broad-brimmed hat, a waistcoat, knee breeches, silk or wool stockings, frilled collars and cuffs, and, if they could afford it, a large Spanish cape. The women usually went about in the typical saya, a long single-pieced dress which was gathered in at the waist with colored ribbons, thus fitting closely over the breasts, and reaching almost to the ground. Many of the wealthier class wore hooped overskirts, embroidered ruffs and collars, and the Spanish mantilla was invariably used in place of a hat.

There was little free social intercourse between the sexes, the women being zealously guarded within their homes, and going out only to attend church or to be present at some special fiesta, where they were closely chaperoned. Marriages were generally arranged by the parents, and sometimes the girl would hardly know or perhaps never have seen the man to whom she was promised. Such love-making as went on outside the social pale was conducted either at church or near its portals, where the gallant frequently awaited his truelove, or else in the dark of night with a good strong barred window between the girl inside and the swain without, who stood hidden in the shadows, whispering his passion and sometimes trying to get at her through the grating. This gave rise to the Spanish idiom which refers to that particular kind of love-making: it is called "eating the iron."

The men, of course, had a much freer time of it, and a woman's honor was considered to be fair game. It is no wonder that the women were so carefully protected by their menfolk behind a stretch of ironwork. Seduction was the greatest masculine amusement, but there were also bullfights, jousts, cockfights, and gambling with dice or cards. Dramatic representations outside of the churches were seen only in the largest centers, and then infrequently. They were usually a part of some bigger general celebration and were performed on a temporary stage in the central plaza.

Bullfights also took place on the main square where an arena had been cleared and stands set up for the spectacle. The men taking part in them were not professionals in the present-day sense but were distinguished citizens of the town who took this opportunity of exhibiting their skill and courage. The bullfight was nearly always a part of some religious holiday, and everybody in town turned out to see it. The bullfighters entered on horseback, displaying "the greatest luxury in their dress and trappings." Town buglers and musicians kept up a constant accompaniment while the fight was in progress, and, as is still the case on the peninsula and in many Latin-American countries today, a daring and skillful performance was wildly cheered while a poor or cowardly one was hooted and derided, with the spectators hurling a rain of cushions and other missiles into the ring. Another popular game was cane-tilting. In this, two horsemen bearing canes in the position of lances came at each other in a full charge, the point being to break one's cane on the opponent's breast while escaping untouched oneself.

The most lavish social events of all, however, were the public celebrations held at the inauguration of a viceroy or governor, or when some other outstanding official ceremony took place. When the first Viceroy, Antonio de Mendoza, came to Mexico in 1535 his trip from the coast was like a triumphal march. "Arches were erected along the way from Vera Cruz to Mexico City, and the inhabitants of the towns through which he passed came out in holiday attire to do him honor. His entrance to the capital was made the occasion of displaying all the magnificence which the city could lavish on a high state ceremony." Later on the expenses attending this display became so great that the King issued a decree limiting to eight thousand dollars the sum that might be expended for this purpose on any single occasion.

Francisco de Toledo, "the supreme organizer of Peru," met with a similar reception when he entered Lima as the fifth Viceroy in 1569. Although he had specifically requested that there be a minimum of ceremony, the townsmen seemed bent on outdoing themselves. The whole city donned its finest dress and formed a parade while every church bell and every musician in town sounded away until the populace was in a veritable state of ecstasy. Soldiers wore glittering uniforms of gold, black, and scarlet, and the women were covered with jewelry of gold and precious gems. Even this ostentation, however, could not blot out the miserable adobe houses of the majority, the waves of dust which arose from the streets, the filth and poverty of the Indians drinking *chicha* on every corner, and the rickety impermanence of movable wooden booths placed on the sidewalks. Ribbons, flags, and arches floated over the whole city, hiding its diseased body, but the Viceroy saw at once what he was up against. After parading around the central plaza his first act was to enter the cathedral, where he knelt down with the archbishop and prayed.

Other similar celebrations took place when a new king came to the throne of Spain. The royal banner would be carried through decorated streets with great pomp and solemnity. At regular intervals the procession would come to a halt and the Viceroy or some other official would shout the name of the new monarch and announce obedience to his power. At each stopping place coins would be tossed to the crowds, and there would be a mad scramble while the parade passed on. At night all the houses and streets would be gaily lighted and everyone would stroll about in finest attire. Such events were celebrated with a special mass in the cathedral, and there were also the usual bullfights, jousts, dances, drinking, and general hilarity.

The usual tenor of colonial life was so humdrum for the ordinary citizen that every possible opportunity was seized upon for some such celebration. The women, especially, looked forward to them for months in advance as there were no other outlets to their social urge. The government also took advantage of these occasions to impress on the populace the solemnity of its omnipotence and the splendor with which it ruled. Every political power was shown to stem straight from the personal rule of the Viceroy or of the King. In Bogotá in 1550, when the first Audiencia, or Supreme Court, was installed, the Royal Seal, a large silver disk on which was engraved the Spanish coat of arms, and which was considered "as a representation of the person of the king," was placed in a beautiful coffer and carried through the streets on a white horse under a panoply whose supporting poles were borne by the members of the town council. The judges of the Audiencia followed on horseback, and the seal was deposited with great solemnity in the court building. Above the door of that edifice was written the inscription: "This place abhors evil, loves peace, punishes crimes, conserves the law, honors virtue."

A similar ceremony took place in Chile on the eve and day of the Apostle Santiago (St. James), patron saint of the capital city. It was called "passing the banner," and consisted of a big parade on horseback of all the principal citizens, at whose head was carried the royal banner and coat of arms. As this procession passed by, shouts of "Long live the King" split the air, and when it reached the cathedral, the banner was deposited there overnight. The next day the same ceremony was repeated in the opposite direction and the banner was returned to the municipal building.

In places like Bogotá and Santiago, where there was no viceroy, such ceremonies kept the central power of that person and of the King constantly before the minds of the populace. It was all part of an attempt to teach people to obey the law, not to question or to change it. But since most of the important legal aspects of government were not known to them, the habit of personal rule was established. If a governor or viceroy was popular and said that he was properly interpreting the law, the people took him at his word. If he was generally disliked, however, and a popular archbishop or president of the Audiencia said that *he* was properly interpreting the law, then the populace followed him instead. The political custom became to obey the man, and not the statute; consequently there was only slight advance toward democratic government. The governing power became static and a matter of personalities rather than of intelligent analysis or criticism.

23

THE BEGINNINGS OF COLONIAL CULTURE

The first century was one in which the military spirit reigned supreme; society, culture, and the Church were all of a militant and expansive nature. The second century saw this military spirit give way to a more courtly system in which the old conquistadores became economic overlords, under the watchful eye of viceroys and other Spanish-born political officials. Conquest had given way to government, movement and expansion to retrenchment and consolidation, martial law to courtly custom and religious canons. The purely social or civil spirit, which must be born among the majority before any nation can enter the channel that leads toward tolerance and democracy, was still being held back by the stratification of the classes and the ignorance of the masses.

As the Chilean writer Galdames points out, the Spaniards of that period "were never friends of any but religious enlightenment, because they believed all study not entirely in accord with the precepts of the Church harmful for society."[43] It was also a belief generally held among the Spaniards of those days that it was dangerous to educate the lower classes because it might make them too astute or too ambitious, that it was wrong to educate women because it might corrupt their morals, and that it was especially important to supervise rigorously all institutions of learning for the colonists because "if instructed they might aspire to take part in the government or perhaps even desire to make themselves independent."[43]

Under such conceptions as these it was inevitable that education and culture would tend more toward indoctrination than in the direction of liberal teaching meant to furnish nourishment for the free growth of mind. The Church taught and society accepted the principle that since this life is a "dream . . . a shadow . . . a fiction . . . a frenetic illusion in which the greatest good is small," and that the real life was to come only after death, the primary purpose of man on this earth was to prepare himself for that which lay beyond. Religious teaching and practice were supposed to do that, and all things which obstructed this doctrine were considered inconsequential. One who can place himself in the position of a believer who accepted this implicitly begins to understand the overwhelming influence it had on every manifestation of life, and also, incidentally, the perhaps unconscious but nonetheless sweeping apology which in certain well-to-do hands it would make for poverty and wretchedness in this world.

The Church began its educational labors as soon as the conquest itself was over, and, branching out from the larger centers, Jesuits, Franciscans, and Dominicans established mission settlements in the back country and all along the Indian frontiers. The first large contingent of Franciscan friars arrived in Vera Cruz in 1524 and immediately set out to walk the two hundred and fifty miles which separate that port from Mexico City. As soon as Cortés heard of their decision he ordered that when they passed through a village the roads were to be swept clean before them, every available church bell should be rung, and all Spaniards whom they met must kneel down and kiss their hands and their habits. As the friars neared Mexico City the captain himself, accompanied by a large group of soldiers and many high-ranking native chieftains, went out to receive them. Cortés was the first who dismounted and tried to kneel before the leader of the group, but the friar took his hands and prevented it. He did, however, kiss the priest's robes with great reverence. The Indians were deeply impressed to see the Spaniards, whom they considered almost as gods, showing such humility before these unarmed, emaciated men in coarse and tattered robes. "And still more so," wrote Bernal Díaz, "when they noticed that even the great Cortés would never speak to one of the fathers without first taking off his hat and expressing in every manner the greatest respect and reverence." This attitude on the part of the Spaniards, the humility and selflessness of the priests themselves, and the fact that they had made the entire journey from the coast on foot caused the Indians everywhere to receive them with the best of will.

These friars and others like them immediately set to work organizing the Indian communities under their direction, in all cases using the native chiefs as their deputies. Churches and other religious buildings were constructed; schools were started, and, in order to sustain interest in the new religion, neophytes were divided into brotherhoods, each of which was responsible for the celebration of a certain fiesta or ceremony. To play a leading part in one of these celebrations was considered a great honor, and the Indians struggled manfully to win it. The disgrace and punishment of being left out of the cast was taken as the worst calamity. The plays themselves were like the church mysteries of the Middle Ages, except that the good friars often outdid themselves and wrote in parts for angels, devils, Julius Caesar, Cortés, Alexander the Great, or any other figure which struck their fancies with no regard for chronology. Battles in costume between the Christians and Moors were one of the stand-bys of these fiestas, and the dramatic representation of biblical stories made religion alive.[45] Even today in hundreds of the out-of-the-way districts of the Andes, Mexico, and other parts of Latin America, such celebrations survive as an integral part of the community life.

One of the most famous of these missionaries was the Fleming, Pedro de Gante, who had reached Mexico City in 1523 with two other Franciscans as a sort of vanguard of the larger group which entered the country a few months later. Gante, said to be an illegitimate half brother of Charles V, founded the first school on the continent, that of San Francisco de Mexico, in that same year. The friars who were to teach in this school, of course, did not know the native language when they arrived, but they began to learn it at once, and not by bookish study but by mingling with the natives, playing their games, taking part in their conversations, and becoming a part of their daily association. They referred to their experience as "becoming children again among those who were children."

Gante also paid the most careful attention to all of the ceremonies, costumes, and folk ballads of the natives, and subtly turned these to his own use by making changes here and there and applying them to the new religion. Within a few months his school had an enrollment of approximately a thousand students, many of them members of families of native chieftains, and the original curriculum of elementary instruction in religion and in reading and writing was amplified to include Latin, music, painting, and all the arts and crafts. The work in music was especially important, for the Mexican Indians, always a musically minded people, were taught how to make and play most of the Spanish instruments and how to enrich their own native melodies with the more intricate harmonies of European origin. This school of St. Francis in Mexico City under Pedro de Gante and his Franciscan brothers represented the first application of the principle of spiritual fusion which was to constitute the basis of the mestizo culture of the Hispanic New World.

Not many years had passed before other schools and colleges were established in Mexico and, later, in Peru. The Franciscans and Dominicans occupied the field at the beginning, but other orders soon followed. The Jesuits did not enter Mexico until 1572, and in that country they became identified with the select upper classes and were the outstanding teachers and scholars of the following centuries. The secular clergy—that is, members of no particular religious order—did not have a great part in the evangelism or education of those first hundred years.

Not only did members of religious orders monopolize these posts at first, but throughout the colonial epoch they furnished a vast majority of the higher church dignitaries. The reasons for this are clear: members of orders were better organized, were under a more rigorous discipline, had taken stricter vows, were in general better educated, and so constituted a sort of aristocracy among the clergy. They fought bitterly against yielding their places of leadership over the natives to secular priests, whom many of them considered as "hirelings," incapable of maintaining the high standards which they had set.[45] The orders, moreover, held certain special privileges or immunities granted by both the Pope and the King, which made them more or less free of state interference, leaving them to carry on their work according to their own ideas. The Jesuit missions in Paraguay, with their theoretic absolutism, were an extreme example of this. Naturally the government officials were anxious to replace as many as possible of these privileged friars with secular priests in order to assert their own complete dominance over the Church in their territories.

A strong rivalry between the secular clergy and the orders flared up and sometimes burst into riotous conflicts between the two groups, thus jeopardizing the whole colonial program. In 1640, Bishop Palafox was sent to Mexico as a royal "visitor," or special representative of the monarch, with explicit instructions to replace the friars with secular priests in a goodly proportion of the schools. The friars did not give up without a vigorous word war, and the learned Jesuits practically ran the bishop out of Mexico with the weight of their erudition. Nevertheless, secular priests had by then secured positions of considerable influence in the populous centers, and members of religious orders, finding themselves displaced there, headed toward the frontiers, where they carried on their work with tireless zeal throughout the remainder of the colonial period.

Some of these early clerics, having the "book burnings" and other worse inquisitorial abuses of the peninsula fresh in their memories, applied the same principle to native records, and thus perished many priceless and irreplaceable treasures. At the same time a great part of the information about native civilization which has been preserved is found in works compiled by these same men. They were on the scene early and recorded in great detail practically every phase of Indian life. A few statistical exaggerations and frequent outcroppings of pure superstition do not mar the immense intrinsic value of their works.

Las Casas has given us facts about the discovery and early conquest which can be found in no other documents; Father Sahagún left a careful study of the Aztecs of Mexico; Bishop Diego de Landa learned the Mayan tongue and left a fundamental work on that mysterious race; the Jesuit Acosta's history of the New World is an indispensable study; the Portuguese Jesuit Anchieta compiled a grammar of the native Indian Tupi language of Brazil; Bernabé Cobo studied carefully the customs and environment of Andean life, and there were dozens of others whose works are just as basic in the field of historic, linguistic, scientific, and cultural research. A great majority of them labored under conditions of tremendous hardship, and yet on the whole produced a set of studies which has never been equaled by any other conquering or colonizing nation.

Higher education was a little slower to gain headway in the New World, but there was a total of twenty-three universities in the Spanish colonies during the colonial period. Brazil did not have a single one. The first university was established in the city of Santo Domingo in 1538, but after a brief period of flourishing leadership it withered away. The whole island fell into neglect as the focus of colonial life gradually shifted from the Antilles to the mainland. The first permanent universities were those of Mexico City and Lima; both were chartered in 1551. The University of Mexico opened its doors in 1553, but the University of San Marcos (Lima) did not begin to function until at least twenty years later. Among the other higher institutions the best known were those of Córdoba (Argentina), Chuquisaca (now Sucre), Guatemala, Bogotá, Santiago, Quito, Havana, Cuzco, and Caracas.

They were all modeled after the medieval universities of Spain and were "the very warp and woof of the Church" in the Spanish New World. Without them a trained clergy, the "solid rock" upon which colonial culture rested, could not have survived.[65]

The Viceroy Toledo (1569–81) secularized the University of San Marcos and added to the curriculum a chair in the native Quechua language which was in general use throughout the territory of the Incas. He made a study of this tongue prerequisite for graduation. A few years later courses in native languages were also being offered at the University of Mexico. On the whole, however, the tenor of education given by these institutions of higher learning was of a scholastic and distinctly medieval flavor. Theology was the highest and best-paid chair, and the rest of the curriculum was made up of courses in sacred writings, canon law, classical authors, Latin, grammar, and, later on, medicine. The two pillars were theology and a select list of "non-heretical" classical authors.

Colonial universities were opened with solemn ceremonies in which Government and Church took an equal part, and the inaugural addresses were read in Latin. For two centuries all courses were given exclusively in that tongue. The atmosphere was that of a resurrected medievalism little touched by the intellectual advances of the Renaissance, and not in the slightest degree affected by the Humanistic or Protestant currents which had called into question so many of the formerly accepted truths by which men lived and died.

The colonial universities were not heavily endowed. They received some subsidies from the Royal Treasury, and the Universities of Mexico and Lima were given small endowments in the form of encomiendas. The university in Santiago, founded in 1743, was so poor for the first few years of its existence that honorary degrees were peddled and sold like any merchandise. The professors on the average received salaries of 150 to 200 pesos a year (a maximum of about $500). Teachers were not expected to devote their entire time to instruction and often held other positions as well. Most of them were clergymen, lawyers, or doctors. The same system prevails today in nearly all Latin-American universities; most of the professors are professional men who teach only a couple of classes on the side.

The rectors or presidents of the colonial universities enjoyed certain privileges which set them apart with an air of medieval importance. For example, the Negro lackeys of the rectors of the Universities of Lima and Mexico were allowed to wear side arms even in public. This was considered the highest possible honor and greatly chagrined the "viceroys, archbishops, and regents of the *audiencias,* who were themselves denied so Janizarian a privilege."[65] Occasionally, in order not to ruffle an unusually touchy viceroy, the archbishop persuaded the rector to forego the actual practice.

Student life was not at all a round of unbroken study, but was filled with nocturnal scandals, brawls, and occasional duels, which kept the university authorities constantly on the alert. Carrying weapons led to so much trouble that there was a special law prohibiting a student from attending class "equipped with either offensive or defensive arms." A student caught while so equipped "was denounced by the rector. The arms were sold, one-third going to the *bedel,* or whoever discovered and took them, and the other two thirds to the treasurer of the university. The offending scholar was then clapped in jail (as much a part of the university as the chemistry laboratory) for eight days. Whoever resisted or refused to surrender his arms lost all credits for an entire year."[65] In order to apprehend students red-handed, proctors often prowled about the streets at night or visited the night spots where clandestine visits were likely and there lay in waiting. The whole thing became a sort of sport of student versus recognized authority.

The bedeles, or monitors, were Jacks-of-all-trades about the university quarters. They were guards, messengers, janitors, and proctors. Few of them knew how to read or write, but they picked up a smattering of heavy erudition, and in many institutions learned enough Latin to sing out their announcements in that ancient tongue. They went about the corridors and classrooms with an air of great importance and often broke in on a lecture to place a pitcher of water on the professor's table or to perform some other errand. When the period for a class was just beginning they shouted a premonitory warning in the halls, and when it was concluded they stuck their heads inside the door of the classroom and called out in the language of Caesar that the time was up.

Each Wednesday and Saturday (and also for final examinations) the student had to "champion a thesis." A controversial passage was selected at random from St. Thomas Aquinas, Aristotle, or some other acceptable author, and the student was asked to defend his interpretation of it. If the professor did not feel like bothering with choosing a passage, a child of six or seven was requested to stick a knife between the pages of one of the erudite tomes and whatever page it hit was to furnish the topic for the "thesis."

The professor won his chair, or *cátedra*, in much the same manner. For each vacancy a contest called the *oposición* was held, and all those who aspired to the position were obliged to face each other in this "opposition." They could be interrupted by hecklers on any point, and in the end the man who showed the best grasp of the subject was selected. Most Latin-American universities of today still select their professors through similar competitive examinations.

The actual conferring of a degree was one of the most impressive acts in that age of pageantry. On the day preceding the final ceremony there was a parade led by a band in which kettledrums and oboes predominated. Behind the musicians marched the faculty dressed in their caps and gowns, then came the monitors also decked out in their finery and carrying the university maces, and at the rear were the candidate and his "godfather" or patron. On the day of the investiture itself there were even more imposing exercises. A temporary stand was erected in the cathedral or largest church in the city, and there, surrounded by "the royal, metropolitan, and family arms, was placed a table bearing the doctoral insignias, a book of the gospels, and urns for the fees." The candidate's patron or sponsor, usually a wealthy relative who was able to bear the expense of the ceremony, announced in hastily memorized Latin the title of his protégé's thesis. The candidate himself then came forward and defended it verbally until the rector had enough of it and called a halt. If the student was approved he then "knelt like the knights of old and, with his hands on the mass book, was dubbed doctor."[65]

His honors were now concluded, but his troubles were just begun. In some quarters he was expected to pay a set fee to every member of the university staff who had been present at the ceremony, and to present the members of the Board of Regents with such articles as "six fat hens, four pounds of cold viands, and a pair of gloves." At the heyday of the University of San Marcos in Lima he had to bear the expenses of a bullfight, and give a banquet for those who had attended his investiture. Sometimes the cost of a degree was as high as several thousand dollars. Expenditures were finally *lowered by law* to a maximum of fifteen hundred pesos, or approximately the amount that a professor would receive in seven years of teaching.

During the colonial period a total of approximately 150,000 degrees was granted. The University of Mexico alone granted nearly 40,000. The curriculum itself and manner of study had changed but little since the thirteenth century. Those subjects or ideas which did not "symbolize with revealed truths" were excluded. The more than five thousand books on the Inquisition's blacklist were not to be examined. Some of the more

foreign writers were studied, but interpretation of them was made
,form to a certain predestined pattern. All of this emphasis on mental
astics, which led in one predetermined direction, gave to the Latin-
American mind throughout the first two and a half centuries of the
colonial period a philosophical cast which it has not lost entirely to this
day. It became the custom of intellectuals to discuss theoretical points
with such fire that an observer would have thought their lives depended on
the outcome. All of this produced a very eloquent and oftentimes brilliant
verbosity which, for the most part, went around in an abstract circle. The
average North American's lack of interest in these "philosophical" matters
has caused many well-educated Latin Americans of today to regard him as
somewhat of an intellectual upstart, interested only in the material things
of life.

Had the culture of these university cloisters been more open-minded
and progressive it would have carried itself forward and perhaps might
have pulled the masses along with it. But the spirit was not at all progressive; it was as stale, narrow, and self-centered as it is possible for a culture
to be. The enthronement of doctrinal theology was symbolic of the cult of
memorization which held the boards in these centers of medieval erudition. Graduates of "stupendous rote memory" came forth from their hallowed doors, but they were not interested in social progress, and their
minds were cluttered with hundreds of memorized facts all neatly filed
away in the prison house of dead memories. The scholars themselves, whose
highly vaunted erudition was the pride and lifeblood of colonial university
life, lived isolated among dusty tomes behind an impervious wall of caste.
Their culture in many cases was indeed impressive; it was that of the grave-
yard. Half a dozen notable exceptions do not invalidate the rule.

It has often been pointed out that Latin-American culture is much
older and more widespread than that of the United States, and that there
were several universities in the Spanish colonies before our first one in
1636. Such a comparison is misleading, for there was no permanent
English settlement in North America until 1607. Harvard University was
founded twenty-nine years later. The University of Mexico was chartered
thirty years after Cortés captured Mexico City. In the second place, the
so-called culture of all those early colonial institutions was extremely
limited, to say the very least. It would be grossly unfair to make out a case
against the universities of either Latin or Anglo-Saxon America, for both
were under the bondage of a similar intellectual inquisition. Before the
American Revolution the following institutions of higher learning existed
in the territory of the United States: Harvard, Yale, Brown, Dartmouth,
King's College (which later became Columbia), Rutgers, Princeton, the
University of Pennsylvania, and William and Mary. An American historian,
after listing these nine names, tersely states: "These institutions devoted

themselves chiefly to the training of ministers." No nation had a corner on progressive education in those benighted days.

The following characterization, made by an Argentine historian of early Latin-American schools, hits the nail squarely on the head so far as that region of the world is concerned: "It has already been stated that the religious orders devoted themselves to the promotion of education. They were the teachers in the schools and the universities. Both in the organization and teaching plan these institutions were a faithful reflection of the Spanish schools and universities, that is, they were vitiated by verbosity and theology."[42]

Not until near the end of the colonial period did the universities of either the English or the Spanish colonies become centers for the dissemination of those new ideas of social freedom which erupted from France and spilled out over the entire world of thought. Portugal's offspring, Brazil, was no more open to the infiltration of foreign ideas than were the Spanish colonies, and there was not a single university in that country until after the colonial period. However, in both regions, and especially in the large Spanish centers, from about 1750 until the struggle for independence, liberal French and English writers became better known and, in the hands of upper-class Creole intellectuals, this knowledge was a strong weapon for republican ideals.

The "burning question of race feeling" never reached that degree of intensity in Latin America which has characterized it in the United States. Yet in the early years racial lines were rather clearly drawn, particularly in regard to Negroes, who constituted a distinct slave class. As miscegenation became more pronounced and mulatto children more numerous this prejudice diminished, and in Brazil after the Dutch wars it very perceptibly decreased. Numbers of mulatto boys of good family were sent to the famous Portuguese University of Coimbra to study. In the Spanish colonies there were social color laws directed against permitting mestizos, Indians, and Negroes from matriculating in the institutions of higher learning, but in many sections these were not enforced. Not until 1697 were "sons of Indian chiefs" excepted from this ban.

The University of Mexico was more broad-minded in this respect than the University of San Marcos in Lima. Mexico City had been built on the foundation of an older Indian capital and was from the earliest years a leading center of social, cultural, and racial fusion. The native or mestizo population always greatly outnumbered the whites, and in society, as well as in university life, barriers of race were kept at a minimum. Lima, on the other hand, was a Spanish city founded in 1535 as a stronghold from which Pizarro and his captains might rule Peru. Its native population was never comparable to that of Mexico City; the wall of caste was stronger there from the very beginning, and everything contributed toward intensifying this feeling. Lima and the Peruvian coastal area became an aristocratic "white man's world," whereas the mountain territory of the interior was "Indian country." Furthermore, Negro slaves were imported into Lima in large numbers in the colonial period, and this slave class reaffirmed the prejudices of race in the higher circles. A visitor who was in that city from 1740 to 1746 states that the population at that time was around fifty thousand, and of these there were "sixteen to eighteen thousand persons of Spanish extraction, a comparatively small number of Indians and half-breeds, the greater part of the population being Negroes and mulattoes."[60]

The decree that "no person of mixed or Indian blood might matriculate" in either the University or the Faculty of Medicine of the college of Los Reyes, the two institutions of higher learning in the opulent capital of Peru, were enforced rather rigidly. Social prestige and university life were closely associated in Lima, and the professorships were so sought after that they sometimes "produced genuine disturbances, giving rise to factions which did not hesitate to come to blows.

"If a *mestizo* of very light color succeeded in gaining entrance to these institutions of higher learning it was because of the difficulty in proving that he was not of pure blood. One of the Viceroys, the Count of Monclovia, who ruled from 1689 to 1705, went so far as to decree that in such cases, once the mixed blood had been proved, the degree given should be cancelled." There were numerous protests, and an appeal finally reached the Supreme Council of the Indies. Two royal decisions of 1752 and 1758 respectively upheld the Viceroy and banished from the liberal professions "all colonial subjects who were not direct descendants of Spaniards. These same decrees, however, excepted those who in 1697 had been declared free from mixed blood, of noble birth and qualified for the exercise of high offices, that is to say, the Indian *caciques* and their offspring.

"The Church was more liberal than the State, for it not only admitted into its association all new converts, but occasionally raised them to the priesthood, without making any distinction between the subject Indians and their chiefs. It is significant, however, that the Indians took but little advantage of these favors."[61] The prejudices which existed then, even in aristocratic Lima, were rather those of a small upper class which was in this manner attempting to safeguard its privileges against competition. The actual difference of race had little to do with the situation, and in Spain and Portugal, where the classes of color were not sufficiently numerous to present an economic threat to upper-class power, such prejudices were almost nonexistent. Eight centuries of miscegenation with the Moors had effectively absorbed it. Consequently, while the University of San Marcos was the center of racial separation, the vast majority of the people, to whom this institution was only a name, mingled and mixed their blood with that of the Indians and Negroes to such an extent that today it is difficult to find a person in Lima whose skin suggests a mulatto color, much less that of a pure Negro. The Indians, of course, were much too numerous to be absorbed in any such period of time, but in their case, too, there was a considerable lightening of the skin.

The primary bases on which education and culture fundamentally rest —elementary schools, printing presses, and newspapers—were few and far between in colonial Latin America. Such primary schools as existed were under the direction of priests, the Franciscans, Dominicans, and Jesuits being dominant in different regions. Many of these schools were integral parts of some mission, and nearly all others were regularly attached to some religious establishment. Not until the very close of the colonial period did the municipal town councils either subsidize or secularize education to any appreciable degree. It was the intention of these teachers to instruct the natives and also the children of colonists in reading, writing, and in religion, but such instruction did not embrace more than an infinitesimal proportion of the population as the high rates of colonial illiteracy bear testimony. The well-to-do families hired special tutors for their children, or at least for their sons. Daughters by and large were left to shift for themselves without much attempt at giving them an education. A Colombian writer points out that "rare indeed were the daughters of the aristocracy who knew how to read and write, and it goes without saying that the daughters of the common people lived in utter ignorance."

Books for use in the lower schools were at a great premium, and the system of education was directed more toward the same "cultural" fields which reached their apex in the colonial universities. "Each child read the books that he could bring from home: profane histories, the narratives of which neither they nor their teachers understood; books of chivalry or similar productions; and the most pious fathers gave their sons ascetic works to read which were products of an ill-digested piety or lives of saints which had been written by authors without judgment and were consequently laden with apocryphal passages and pretended miracles."[42]

The Indians, being at the bottom of the ladder, were infinitely worse off than the upper classes when it came to the ability to read or write. The vast majority of them were taught arts and crafts, for which they showed an especial inclination, but their religious and literate instruction was in most cases narrowed down to their memorizing in Spanish, Portuguese, or Latin a few set phrases, generally the catechism, whose meaning they did not understand. Even among those Indians who were under mission control for several generations—as, for example, the Guaranís in the Jesuit missions of Paraguay—there was not more than one in a hundred who could read or write.

These conditions prevailed throughout colonial days, and although the eighteenth century brought some improvement in general education, it hardly touched the broad illiterate base of Latin-American life. One of

Argentina's revolutionary heroes, Belgrano, on the eve of the struggle for independence in 1810, spoke the following words: "How can it be expected that men can love labor, that customs can be regulated, that there will be plenty of honorable citizens, that virtue will overcome vice, and that the government will receive the fruits of its cities, if there is no public instruction and if ignorance is handed down from generation to generation with greater and greater increments."[42]

It was in this field of elementary schools that the North American colonies were far ahead of Latin America and thus at an early date began to follow the different path which gave to our society a broader literate base. New England especially took the lead in popular education, and other sections of the country later followed her. As early as 1647 a Massachusetts law "required every town of fifty families to establish an elementary school where children could learn to read and write. The teachers were to be paid either by the parents or by public taxation. Every town of one hundred families was further required to set up a grammar school in which students might be prepared for college. This law became a model for similar legislation throughout the United States."[67]

The growth of the public-school system after independence has been one of the greatest factors in shaping the character of the United States as it is today, and while our colonial institutions of higher learning, much like those of Latin America, were mostly devoted to classical studies and the training of ministers, our elementary schools directed their efforts toward reading, writing, and arithmetic, the three basic mainstays of every literate man. Primary instruction in Latin America laid most of its stress on the elements of religion rather than on the elements of literacy, and university training throughout most of the colonial period only heightened this misconception of the cultured man. Of course the problems in the two regions were hardly comparable, for a world of difference lies between teaching a few thousands of English-speaking children to read and write their own language and Latin America's attempt to convert, instruct, and assimilate five or ten millions of primitive Indians into the main stream of an entirely different and foreign cultural system.

Printing presses existed in Latin America from an early date. Mexico had one in 1532, only ten years after the conquest, and another was set up in Peru in 1579. All presses were under the strict control of the Church and published mostly religious books. They were under the constant and vigilant supervision of the Inquisition. Most of the really valuable works written by colonial authors were sent back to Spain and Portugal for publication, where a much greater leeway was allowed. The Inquisition in America did not want to accept the responsibility in any but obviously "correct and proper" cases, and thus made difficult the printing of colonial books touched by creative or imaginative zeal. The great works which came out of that first century of conquest and consolidation were mostly wonderful compilations of fact. The Chilean epic, *La Araucana*, written by the Spaniard, Ercilla, is the only worthy exception.

Anything approaching free thought or a free literature in our sense of the term was always up against religious censorship, and of course writings which contained any expressions contrary to church doctrine could not be published at all. Obviously, too, works of fiction or those in which the free flights of fancy reigned were not likely to be printed on religious presses. Reading matter in the colonies was also carefully circumscribed, and as late as 1800 special permission had to be obtained from the Pope if one wanted to read such authors as Rousseau or Voltaire. The principal cause for the great dearth of worthy colonial literature, however, must be traced back to the nature of the society itself, and cannot be laid at the door of religious intolerance, which was only one among many stupefying influences.

24

COLONIAL BELLES-LETTRES

It is a fact frequently pointed out that the Golden Age of Portuguese and Spanish letters and arts was contemporaneous with the Inquisition and a period of rapid social deterioration. Portugal in the sixteenth and Spain in the sixteenth and seventeenth centuries attained the finest flower of their national cultures. The magnificent art of El Greco, Velázquez, Murillo, Ribera, and Zurbarán spread far into the otherwise decadent 1600s. Portraits which Velázquez made of the two stupid Spanish Philips (III and IV) have perpetuated the empty finery of their courts and their own bloodless, set, and prognathous jaws for the observation of posterity. The Inquisition was in full swing when Cervantes wrote his *Don Quixote*, as fanciful a work as ever existed, and the entire Golden Age of peninsular letters came during the years 1500–1650, when religious dogmatism was at its worst.

Spanish literature of those days boasted a group of playwrights and novelists who still challenge the world in the quantity and quality of their literary output. Lope de Vega, most prolific of all great writers, with his four hundred full-length plays and more than a thousand other pieces, was followed by the refined lyrical priest, Calderón de la Barca, later so greatly admired by Shelley, Archbishop Trench, and the famous Edward Fitzgerald, who translated several of his dramas into English. There were other dramatists almost as great, and in the field of novels of chivalry, of the picaresque, or romances of roguery the peninsula stood supreme. This literature was at the opposite pole from the refined sentiments and exquisite lines of Calderón, and filled out the picture of ordinary life with details which held nothing from the peering gaze. In this century also lived the philosophical essayist, Baltasar Gracián, whom Schopenhauer preferred to read above all other authors; and during the early 1600s the great Góngora, idol of every would-be Spanish American poet, wielded his prodigious pen.

Altogether it was as great a collection of cultured writers and artists as any nation has produced at any one time in the history of the world. Consequently, when people hear mention of the early dates of many Latin-American universities, or startling figures about poetic contests in the colonies in which hundreds of aspirants took part, the natural conclusion is to believe that all of the above-mentioned artistic values of the peninsula were simply transferred to the New World. Such a conclusion is superficial and without any basis in fact.

The peninsula had been building up for this last burgeoning of her culture for centuries, and so, even after the decay of her physical body, her spirit was able to carry on. The spiritual momentum of centuries is not stopped dead in its tracks by the frailties or diseases of its shell. And the peninsula at this time was rapidly becoming a shell out of which was being emptied a part of its immortal soul in a golden age of art and letters, and an even greater part of its physical body in emigration to the New World. It would be expecting far too much to look for an immediate rebirth of every value in this new environment. Every living thing wilts perceptibly when it is transplanted, and this transplantation of Iberian civilization to America was carried out under the most unfavorable conditions.

On the other hand, there were rich cultural values in the peninsula which were not literate or technical. That is, there was a deep undercurrent of folk art, as varied and wealthy as any in the world, which required no technique or training for its expression. People who could neither read nor write, and who had never thought of painting a picture, were a living part of this folk tradition; perhaps for that very reason they were more a part of it than could otherwise have been the case. It was a sort of literacy of the illiterate, a kind of feeling which has nothing to do with schools or with masters, and it pervaded the daily lives of all kinds and classes of people. It is significant that one of the foreign critics who lavished greatest praise on this folk expression of the peninsula was the philosopher, Hegel, who referred to the myriads of Spanish popular ballads as inimitable jewels among the world's great literary treasures. There was also a folk music which in extent and richness surpasses even that of Russia.

The illiterate *pueblo* of the peninsula, which had absorbed so many currents into its soul and body, had become in its own right a great creative artist. The reason this folk side of Hispanic life is so important is that nothing in history seems able to blot out the creative and artistic feelings which spring constantly and forever from the genius of a great people. These feelings were transferred intact from the mother countries to the New World. There they met another folk culture of almost equal value, and the two immediately began to blend into one, into the mestizo art which is today Latin America's very breath of life. Upon it, already, the great technical masters are beginning to build with their own broad strokes, just as they did previously in the Golden Age of the Iberian Peninsula. The great day of Latin-American culture is for the now and for the future. It does not lie in the dusty precincts of her wrongly hallowed colonial past.

This does not mean that a colonial culture did not exist. Latin Americans point to it with undeniable pride; people in this country mention it in a hushed breath, comparing it with our own unworthy one. Our admiration springs from sheer ignorance, theirs from the misplaced emphasis of an educational system which puts tradition above value. This double error contributes nothing to hemispheric understanding, and is a distortion of fact. We both have been guilty of emphasizing the culture which belongs to the upper classes, while all the time creative artistic feeling was truly alive only among the folk. There was no culture for the upper classes outside of the Church. All of it reflected the spirit of the times, but, only reflected; it did not lead or light.

The figures of this upper-class culture should be examined briefly, if only to take the wind from their sails, if only to point out how strong an element tradition is in Latin-American life. If only to pry down beneath the polished veneer in order to disclose where the real seeds have grown.

Colonial society of the dominant few, as might be expected, took up where peninsular society left off. Toward the end of the first century after the conquest—that is, around the year 1600—a change in the general perspective of life in the colonies became noticeable. Prior to that time every social institution partook of the epic nature of the conquest. No task was too great to be undertaken, no hardship too rigorous to be endured. Not only did dynamic conquistadores and proselyting friars perform miracles of achievement, they laid down the base and defined the social structure which was to be raised. When the century drew to a close it left a maze of overlapping institutions, race fusions, social classes, architecture, feelings, and thought, all hammered together onto a single frame. Generally speaking, this framework did not change greatly in succeeding years. But in the focus and in the flavor of life, in how men reacted to their environment, in what they said and in what they wrote, the change from a society dominated by action to one in which retrenchment and conservatism reigned supreme began to be clearly evident.

During the first century every man who lifted his pen had something new to say, and practically all who wrote were active priests or soldiers. Voyages of the discoverers, chronicles of conquest, histories of the native races, grammars of indigenous languages, studies on American geography, flora, fauna, and art, every step and sight of those first one hundred years was material for the hardy chroniclers. These men often wrote while on active campaigns, under primitive conditions which would have discouraged a less sturdy lot, and always while the zest of discovery and the thrill of achievement burned in their brains. They told in direct and straight language what they had done, and seen, and heard. When the second century dawned, and life became easier with the accumulation of wealth and all the things that money can buy, the old fires soon played out. Colonial literature, aping colonial society, went in for all the false amenities of life, became showy, long-winded, of vapid content and impossible tautological style.

It was the natural thing to expect. Cities were now firmly established in the wealthier colonies, and culture, which generally follows comfort where there is comfort to follow, migrated toward these new centers like moths to a light. Mexico City, Lima, and Quito led the procession in this new focus and parade of life. In them the viceregal courts, sumptuous religious establishments, and the society of the upper class entrenched their European culture and their class-conscious wealth deep in the fertile soil of Indian slavery and ignorance. Those colonists who said that they were American now did not identify themselves with the Indian majority; all they wanted was to get their own sharp fingers a little deeper into the pie.

The Viceroy was top mirror of this reflected glow. Like a pope of the Renaissance or a European monarch, he tried to be a "Sun-King" in his own small way, patron of the arts, leader of colonial society, and head star to a group of satellites who were to perpetuate his name forever. But the Hispanic colonies were not at all like the courts of Europe or the Italy of the Renaissance. Tradition was new in America, and a large slave caste was in process of being trained. Brilliance was mistaken for talent, form for the spirit of art. There was no breath of vision, little will to create, and such sparks of genius as flew from the ponderous social wheel were all but blotted out by the mediocrity which surrounded them. The Viceroy held his court; the intellectual elite met in his mansion at regular intervals, and every official or religious occasion was inspiration for a burst of similes and metaphors which titillated the viceregal ears with obsequious flattery. Literature and thought became superficial expressions of a stagnant and lopsided social system; it wore the tinseled trappings of the minority and ignored the rags and indigenous culture of the masses; it ate cake, danced, and played with metaphors, while the multitude sweated blood.

The Church, which in earlier days had made a cult of defending the Indians from the rapacity of the encomenderos, now, in its sumptuous centers, became wealthier, more mercenary, more upper-class-minded. Many monks and nuns had huge numbers of Indian servants; the higher church officers were mostly Spaniards, who naturally identified themselves with the Spanish and not with the Indian class. Rarely did a native Indian or even a Creole hold any religious or political office except the most menial. Many did enter the Church in order to find security. The whole organization of society in the seventeenth and early eighteenth centuries contributed to mental, spiritual, and literary stagnation. The vast majority of those who wrote were either sedate priests or untalented political parasites, as during the first century they had been dynamic conquistadores and proselyting friars, essentially men of action.

The Golden Age of Spanish literature, which reached its zenith in the seventeenth century, had no counterpart in the colonies. The one peninsular poet who was worshiped above all others was Góngora. His rare genius could not be duplicated, but his stylistic innovations were imitated by all the devotees of Mexico City, Quito, and Lima and kept colonial literature at a standstill for nearly two centuries. The rigid etiquette of the viceregal court furnished excellent soil in which every excess of language and ideas might grow to the absurdest proportions. The black pall of gongoristic law spread its wings over every expression in the colonies. Writers attempted to mold their language on Latinisms, to utilize Latin terms, to observe rules of Latin syntax, to supplant the usual meanings of words with entirely different connotations, to employ lavish metaphors, hyperboles, classical allusions and acrostics, which made their thoughts nearly impossible to decipher without the expenditure of much time and research. This crossword puzzle of language soon turned into a crossword puzzle of ideas, and then sometimes even the writer had trouble following the twistings of his creation.

Góngora in Spain was a poet's poet, a man of unquestioned genius and almost limitless culture, an initiator who enriched his language with the vast power, beauty, and scope of a mighty pen. His influence on style exceeded that of any other Spanish writer, but not one of his imitators even remotely approached the spirit of originality which characterized their idol. In fact, so strong and deeply embedded was this feeling of dependence in the colonies that long after Gongorism had ceased to exist in Spain it continued on its devious and ostentatious way in Spanish America. The colonial writers seemed content to live by reflected glory. They Italianized themselves when Spain became Italianized because of the Italian campaigns, aped Góngora during the epoch of that great peninsular master, became Frenchified and neoclassic when Philip V of Anjou accepted the Spanish throne at the beginning of the eighteenth century after the reign of degenerate Charles II. Form and show became the two pillars of colonial culture. The few things that were composed of a spontaneous desire to create circulated briefly in clandestine manuscripts, looked down on by literary formalists and university critics, frequently persecuted by the Inquisition, and nearly always denied the right to appear in print. It was for these reasons that Spanish American literature during the colonial period, despite its glorious tradition and great intrinsic promise, came to mature so little fruit.

On the other hand, its years were overflowing with a plethora of shriveled stuff which never became ripe, or which, if it did, passed quickly from that stage into plain rottenness. Every urban center held its poetic contests in which scores of verbal gymnasts vied with each other in obscure and high-flown verse. In a single one of these celebrations, held under the auspices of the University of Mexico in 1682 in honor of the Immaculate Conception, more than five hundred poems were submitted, of which sixty-eight received prizes. One of Mexico's savants, Sigüenza y Góngora, reviewed these outbursts of his country's muse in a book entitled the *Triumpho Parthénico*, or *Parthenical Triumph*.

This outstanding scholar, who through remote kinship happened to bear half of the name of the great Spaniard Góngora, was the leading luminary of his age. He was a specialist in physics, astronomy, mathematics, languages, philosophy, history, Indian antiquities, and he won a chair for himself in mathematics at the National University of Mexico through competitive examinations. He was, incidentally, also a literary critic and poet who contributed a prize piece to the above-mentioned *Triumpho Parthénico*. Unquestionably a man of tremendous knowledge and talents, he wasted his energies by turning in every possible direction, yet no matter which way he turned found himself circumscribed by the stale, prison-like medievalism that surrounded him. Toward the end of his life he wrote bitterly: "If there were only someone to pay for the printing of my books, I might bring out many other studies of interest which the love I feel for my country has stimulated me to compose . . ."[68] These unedited works to which he refers have not yet appeared in print. The great Mexican's fame reached Europe, for Louis XIV of France invited him to his court, where he would receive a large salary and pension, but Sigüenza y Góngora did not want to become involved with the "frivolous elegance" of that monarch. He did accept the title of "royal cosmographer" to Charles II of Spain.

The same stultified spirit permeated the atmosphere of Lima and Quito in the seventeenth century, although in elegance, gaiety, humor, and occasional delicate lyricism the Viceroy's entourage at Lima did sometimes, but not often, produce real poetry. In 1630 Father Juan de Ayllón initiated Gongorism in Peru with his model of unintelligible twaddle entitled *Poem to the Twenty-three Martyrs of Japan*. He was followed by other inferior Gongorists of the same ilk. It was in Lima also that the viceregal salons captured the imagination of the literary elite. On Monday nights bands of these colonial bards would gather in the Viceroy's drawing room and propound to each other riddles in verse, anagrams, acrostics, and other such poetic nonsense on puerile themes of absolutely no esthetic value.

However, Lima also had its counterpart of the Mexican savant, Sigüenza y Góngora. A man by the name of Peralta y Barnuevo (1663–1743), who was a professor of mathematics at the University of San Marcos, and later its president, distinguished himself as an engineer, cosmographer, astronomer, and as a student of navigation, metallurgy, and history. It is said that he was fluent in six languages and composed in all of them. In

1662 another Peruvian, who went by the nickname of The Birthmarked Fellow (*El Lunarejo*), because of two large blotches which he had on his face, produced one of the best analyses and defenses of Góngora extant. The style of this study is as clear as a mountain spring and anything but gongoristic in its language.

El Lunarejo was born in the Peruvian mountains, of Indian ancestry, and wrote as glibly in Quechua as in Spanish. He was the author of many poems, sacred pieces, and dramatic dialogues and is regarded by some critics as composer of the so-called Inca drama, *Ollantay*. He showed his talents at an early age, distinguished himself in his studies, graduated from the University of Cuzco, rose from his peasant environment and rags to become one of the most brilliant literary and religious lights of his country. He was also one of the leading priests of his day, and his oratory in the Church exceeded in eloquence that of all his contemporaries. In addition to all this he became a professor and finally president of the University of Cuzco.

These men are worthy of recognition only because they stand out among the great mass of worthlessness which characterized the turgid culture of the seventeenth and early eighteenth centuries. None of them produced a single work of great actual merit. Isolated completely from every current flowing in the outside world, save those which might slip in through the narrow doorway of the peninsula, and lacking the background which the home country possessed, colonial culture was lulled into a sleep of the dead by the heavy scholasticism and theology which were its greatest bulwarks. The universities, which by their very nature were dedicated mainly to the cultivation of select groups, harbored behind their almost impenetrable moats and walls "sanctuaries of Latin phrases which flowed ceaselessly over the warping-chain of dialectical concepts." Colonial courts, pulpits, and authors' minds all performed essentially the same dance to the great theological tune.

There were, nevertheless, one or two great stars in this galaxy of mediocrity, and first place in colonial letters indisputably goes to the Mexican nun, Juana Inés de la Cruz (1651–95). It is said that she commenced to study seriously at the age of three. Her mother was sending an older sister to a private school for instruction, and Juana went along, insisting that she also was supposed to receive instruction. It was probably only a natural childish reaction, but was entirely characteristic of this woman's later life. When Juana reached her teens she urged her mother repeatedly to permit her to put on the dress of a man and attend the university. Girls, of course, were not allowed, as education had "a pernicious influence on the feminine mind." Her wish was never fulfilled, but Juana did continue to study privately, despite the fact that a mother superior friend warned her that "too much study was a thing the Inquisition might want to look into." The young girl was frightened into obeying for a period of about three months, but then she decided that since God had made all things, including her mind, for a proper use, there was certainly no sin in attempting to learn everything within her power.

When she was about fifteen or sixteen the young girl's beauty and brilliance attracted the notice of the wife of the Viceroy Mancera, to whom she became a maid of honor in the viceregal palace. Here her keen mind and incredibly broad knowledge aroused such interest that the Viceroy decided to make a public exhibition of it. He gathered together the professors of the university, the outstanding theologians, philosophers, mathematicians, historians, poets, and all the other learned men in the capital, and before this group of some forty choice intellects the young girl of sixteen was cross-examined on all possible subjects. Speaking of the event later, the Viceroy stated that she brilliantly answered every query "like a royal galleon beating off the attacks of a bunch of rowboats."[68]

Exactly what happened after this is not known, but it is certain that Juana was assiduously courted by some of the males in the Viceroy's entourage, and perhaps one of them gained her love completely. Legend and not biographical fact, however, tells us that this lover died and that Juana, for that reason, determined to enter a convent. At any rate, just before reaching the age of seventeen the talented young girl became Sister Juana Inés de la Cruz. When asked for her own explanation of this act in later years she said, "There were so many things in the mundane world which were repugnant to me . . . marriage seemed to be a total negation . . . my one wish was to live alone that I might have absolute liberty to continue my studies . . ."

At any rate, there in the cloister, surrounded by her large library, her maps, musical instruments, and scientific apparatus, she lived out the rest of her life devoting herself to reading and writing. About five years before her death she wrote a very learned criticism of a sermon which had been delivered by the famous Brazilian Jesuit, Father Vieira, and it came to the attention of the Bishop of Puebla, Fernández de Santa Cruz. The bishop wrote to Sister Juana urging her to give up mundane studies and to devote her entire time to religious labors. His letter was signed with the pseudonym of *Sor* (Sister) Filotea. In the answer which Sor Juana sent him are contained nearly all of the known biographical details of her life. But the letter is much more than that; it is a beautiful essay in defense of womankind and of a woman's right to use her mind as she will. It is also, of course, an indictment of those narrow days in which any evidence of feminine initiative in thought or action was frowned upon by the majority of the elite. The bishop's criticism was not the only one which had come to her ears, and Sister Juana was taking advantage of this opportunity to justify her stand before them all.

Nevertheless, the words which Fernández de Santa Cruz had directed to her must have had their effect, for three years later Juana withdrew her attention entirely from profane things, sold the four thousand volumes of her library, together with all of the musical and scientific paraphernalia she possessed, gave the proceeds to charity, and then in her own blood wrote a general confession in two "protestations of faith." For the next two years she lived almost entirely secluded, reading only religious books. At the age of forty-four, when an epidemic of malignant fever broke out in the convent, she worked herself to the point of exhaustion, caught the malady herself, and died. Sister Juana has since been glorified in the literary traditions of her people as *La Décima Musa*, or The Tenth Muse.

The writings of this unique nun ran the gamut of colonial letters. She wrote much occasional verse, a considerable number of religious pieces both in poetry and prose, and in many instances the shroud of Góngora fell darkly on her pen. But in many other instances she escaped the prevailing gongoristic influences of the day and wrote as beautifully as the greatest Spanish masters. Strangely enough, it was her love poetry which caught the flame of spontaneity that no amount of formal tutoring had been able to destroy. It is odd enough for a nun to write love poetry at any time, but for one to compose it during the height of the Inquisition is indeed strange. Of course Sister Juana's love lyrics are hardly those of Edna St. Vincent Millay, whose lush, sensual metaphors stir the deep sexual fire in flesh and blood. But she represents the high flowering passion of Latin-American womanhood at its poetic best, and as a strong feminist defending her kind against the double standards of the man's world in which women must live, Sister Juana has no counterpart in Hispanic letters. Although her muse sings poignantly of love, on occasion the gentle nun handles irony and frivolous humor with telling effect. Her deepest tone, however, is not one of gaiety, satisfaction, or fulfillment, but of absence, separation, and loss. Sometimes in her religious poetry she also strikes a note of intense beauty and reminds one of some of the Church's mystic sinners in the presence of God's boundless love. Sister Juana was not only the greatest poet of colonial Latin America, but the greatest feminist. Yet her influence on colonial letters was negligible. Not even the strongest genius could swim against the heavy and deadening current of those gongoristic days.

Although the Mexican nun stood far above her contemporaries, there lived in Lima at this time one young writer who deserves a special mention, for, despite a scabrous and riotous life, he distinguished himself above all others in the colonial letters of Peru. His name was Juan del Valle y Caviedes (1653–94). Caviedes was born into a good family and received sufficient income from his father to enable him to lead the life of a sybarite, at least for a few years. He quickly picked up a bad case of syphilis and passed this on to his young wife, who later died partly because of it. After her death Caviedes abandoned all pretense at decent living and became the most licentious nonconformist in town. When his money was all gone, he joined the ranks of the pauper merchants and set up a squalid wooden stall in front of the Viceroy's palace.

Caviedes belongs at the opposite pole from Sor Juana, yet in the variety of his expression he rivaled even the Tenth Muse of Mexico. Most of his poems were shot through with bitter satire, and some of them are plain filthy in their humor, yet at times he wrote as fervid religious poems as ever came out of the colonial period, and some of his finer lyrics on nature and death are deeply moving. It is principally his biting satire, however, which has won for him an imperishable place in Peruvian letters. Doctors were his special targets, and every conceivable insult was hurled upon that hapless class, who, according to this poet, worked hand in hand with death in order to increase the business of the undertakers.

Caviedes also attacked social hypocrisies, the morality of women, and falsity of every colonial standard save that of religion. Whores and cuckolds strut through the pages of his verse in lines of shameless zest. Frequently he will go through some contortion of phrasing which is reminiscent of Góngora, but generally he sticks strictly to the super-mundane. Next to an exquisite lyric evoking some rare beauty of woman or nature will be placed a piece of startling and gleeful ribaldry. In some ways Caviedes is a rough mixture of St. Francis of Assisi, Sor Juana, and Rabelais. He never attains the stature of any one of this trio, but does struggle manfully in that general direction. Few of his poems appeared during the poet's life, and it was only at the turn of the twentieth century that some of them were collected and passed on to the public, which through them learned something of those loose colonial wits who lived beyond the pale of sacrosanct literary and social laws. He is an escape valve that breaks loose when the strings of the colonial corset are cut; he calls into question every conception of his day except that of religion, and he could not have done that and lived, even had he wanted to.

Far more symbolic of the general trend in colonial thinking than either Sor Juana or Caviedes was the Mexican Jesuit, Matías de Bocanegra, who was a child of the same century and who won undying fame among his contemporaries with his mediocre *Allegorical Song to Disillusionment*. In this poem a priest who subconsciously had become wearied of life inside the cloister is taking in the beauties of nature around him; his attention is caught by a linnet singing merrily in a tree. Suddenly the priest pauses in his thoughts and wonders if this gay and natural freedom is not, after all, that which the good Lord had meant for men to enjoy. His gaze shifts from the walls of his cloister to his own dark robes while the linnet continues to sing joyously. Again, suddenly, the priest's thoughts are interrupted when a hawk swoops down out of the sky and grasps the unsuspecting bird in its claws. A realization of the truth now runs through the priest in a great shudder, and with calmness again restored to his mind he slowly picks his spiritual way back within the walls of the cloister. Colo-

ıl letters, colonial thought, and far too much of the colonial conception
religion, social economy, and government followed in his wake.

The progress of society as a whole was now slowed down almost to a
standstill. This was especially true in the predominantly Indian regions of
Mexico, Central America, and the Andean highlands. A small white minority had imposed itself on a vast native population and was living at its
ease, but the whole setup was false and lacked the security which progress
demands until the mestizo class eventually became the most numerous
and acquired the reins of power. On the other hand, in Argentina, Chile,
Uruguay, and Brazil, the state of initial flux was still maintained. There
was little or no colonial "culture" in these raw countries, while the frontier continued to be a dominant factor in the national life. Therefore, they
did not sink into that state of oppressive desuetude which nearly ruined
the Indian regions, but rather kept their society and their concepts elastic
so that in the end they were able to achieve both political and cultural
unity long before the neighboring states.

The complacent hauteur of the propertied Spanish minority in the rich
Indian sectors was a principal cause of their inertia. A class which has enjoyed many years of uninterrupted rule can rarely, if ever, conceive of a
day when that rule might be brought to an end, by whatever means. In
1862 a well-known Peruvian historian, writing at a time when his own
country was undergoing a change of presidents on the average of once
yearly, and when the native majority had advanced little if any since the
days of the Viceroy Toledo, makes this oversanguine evaluation of colonial
society: "The slight cohesion of its heterogeneous elements, although encouraged by private interests and preoccupations or by other moral and
political causes, became a coalescent whole through the welding of the
races in feelings, ideas, and blood. National fusion was slowly carried
forward by the mutual attraction between the passionate heart of the
Spanish race and the tender submission of the natives, by the community
of labors, dangers, and pleasures, and above all by the supreme force of
religious beliefs. Religion which was one in its dogmas, brotherly in its
teachings, and with a cult that absorbed both the souls of the rulers and
of the serfs, created a common outlook making even those who least participated in its fruits profoundly interested in keeping alive and protecting
the new nationality . . .

"Almost all of the influences exerted on Peruvian society under the
colonial regime impeded rapid progress, either because improved means
were not at hand, or because the desire for bettering the situation was
deadened. But Providence, which directs all things for the welfare of humankind, made this very slowness a strong contribution to the more normal and more solid formation of the new nationality. The past was being
transformed without losing its value; antagonistic elements were being

drawn together; the population was growing deep roots in the soil; its future was less dazzling but it was more solid. Political bodies, like living beings and crystals, only acquire a perfect state when they are formed under the natural conditions of space, time, and repose."[69]

This estimate, which is philosophically so sound, was erroneous basically in its perspective, for the middle ground, which tended toward drawing the two extremes together, was of far less actuality than the ever-widening breach or abyss which tended to push them farther and farther apart. This fundamentally wrong perspective, so characteristic of the upper-class attitude toward life, has meant the perpetuation of colonial feudalism to a greater or less degree in all of the Indian regions of Latin America to the present day. The problem unquestionably was vastly more difficult than it was in Argentina, Chile, Uruguay, and Brazil, where the native races were inferior in numbers. But it was also tackled with far less zeal. Gold and serfs corrupt the hardiest of men, and even religion is polluted by an easy life.

25

ARCHITECTURE AND THE FINE ARTS

Throughout these trying years the Church represented culture and art. Small men gave to it of their labor; mighty men made it gifts of great riches, oftentimes to receive such favors as they thought could be purchased with money. The Middle Ages arose again in a great flowering of religious architecture which symbolized the lives and the aspirations of all the people. Their search for beauty in this ugly world was more acute, more far-reaching than that of the Englishmen in the north, whose first thought was of the earth and of their families, and whose churches were seldom more than drafty structures of wood, made deliberately austere and unlovely. Hundreds of beautiful monasteries, cathedrals, missions, and nunneries dotted the fertile landscape of Latin America from California to the south. Little wonder that the people around them should have come to live culturally through the mother church which, willingly or not, afforded such a retreat from reality.

Not every builder of this magnificent church architecture labored of his own free will, although later all undoubtedly took pride in the results. Hundreds of Indians carried out construction work under the direction of priests in order to raise sumptuous edifices, frequently out of all proportion to the economic status of the communities which they were to serve. In 1531 the Queen herself severely reprimanded the Dominican friars for having erected one such building, and in 1556 the Archbishop Alonso de Montúfar, who was also a Dominican, bitterly criticized the friars in a letter to the Council of the Indies in these words: "The excessive costs and expenditures and personal services, and the sumptuous and superfluous works which the friars are erecting in the Indian villages at the Indians' expense, should be remedied. With respect to the monasteries, in some places they are so grandiose that although they are designed to accommodate not more than two or three friars, they would more than suffice for

Valladolid . . . It is nothing for a friar to begin a new work costing fifty to sixty thousand dollars . . . and bring Indians to work on it in gangs of five hundred, six hundred, or a thousand, from a distance of fifteen to twenty miles, without paying them any wages, or even giving them a crust of bread . . ."[45]

The archbishop goes on to say that the cost of the magnificent ornaments which adorn these buildings was met by heavy assessments, which the native chieftains were only too willing to levy in order that they might stick their own hands into the community moneybag and take out their share. Only occasionally did the Indians themselves rebel against this type of labor, for, in the first place, the priests were their protectors against the great landowner, and, in the second, they could actually enjoy and in a way possess the final fruits of their labors. They felt an intense loyalty to the order with which they were identified, and were anxious to make their church larger and more beautiful than any other in the neighborhood. In spite of this, and in spite of the fact that these buildings represent a cultural and esthetic heritage whose value is truly inestimable, their very sumptuousness came to stand as a symbol of that part of the religious and economic system which placed form and number before content and development.

"By 1596, according to Father Mendieta, there were churches in the four hundred convent towns of New Spain, and an equal number in the secular parishes, not counting the thousands of chapels in the smaller villages, the so-called *pueblos de visita*, served by the circuit-riding priests and friars." The idea of the religious architects, of course, was not original with them; it was a tradition of the period: "the more beautiful the church the greater glory to God."[45]

The glory of God was indeed infinite to those whose minds and hands and hearts raised these lovely architectural gems across the great Latin-American earth. Before the decline in religious enthusiasm began, Mexico alone boasted of ten thousand churches, monasteries, and convents. In other regions the number was proportionate. Everywhere the beauty, size, and richness of this religious architecture and the fineness of its execution loomed above the poverty-stricken and slovenly adobe houses around them just as they had once before in Europe in the Middle Ages. Where the Indians themselves had been great builders before the Iberians arrived, the priests found willing and trained technicians to aid them, and churches rose from the fertile ground in endless flower. The golden glories of Quito, the priceless shrines of Peru, the delicate cloisters of Mexico, all blended with the earth and with the folk who made them, as if they had been planned in the mind of Providence since the beginning of time.

That was not all. "Architecture was mother to painting as to sculpture and even to music; churches were not only art galleries but academies as well."[70] On the outside were magnificent façades fashioned with loving care, and inside were gilded ceilings and altars covered with gold leaf, exquisitely wrought pulpits, choir stalls, confessionals, and sculptured figures in richly adorned polychrome. Everything that post-conquest Spanish, mestizo, and even Indian art could offer was gathered into the bodies of these graceful buildings. It was also in that proportion: creatively Spain gave most; the mestizo came next; the Indian entered least into this supreme art of the colonial epoch.

Nevertheless, it was in its architecture as well as in its religion that the Church gave voice to the inarticulate feeling of the Indian and mestizo for something higher than a dog's existence on earth. Rich and beautiful buildings not only expressed the artistic sense but were a material answer to the longing of these masses for some share in the economic wealth of the society of which they formed so large a part. To them the Church was the symbol, the only symbol, of hope realized on earth and promised in the world to come. Here were the fine things of life in a form they could touch. These wonderful buildings belonged to *them*, for they had made them. To many a worshiper the Church was the only protection, the only security. Miserable Indians, stinking and in tatters, could enter the portals of these houses of God and, for a brief moment, become one with their masters. It was a kind of freedom, specious but comforting. The priest would say that they became primarily one with the infinite. Perhaps the Indian thought of this also; perhaps he did not. The anchor he tied to seems of a more earthy nature. Undoubtedly during those early years after the conquest, when a new religion had just replaced his old one, he was more pagan than Christian in his thinking. Surreptitiously he kept his "idols behind altars" and worshiped the new God along with the old. As the centuries passed the Indian became more of a Catholic and the white man less.

Both in its architecture and in its religion the Church was a symbol of fusion. When the principal pyramid-temple of the Aztecs was leveled in Mexico City, the Cathedral of Mexico, largest in this hemisphere, was raised on its base. When the great mass of Acolman was constructed a few miles away only a brief while after the conquest, Indian workers decorated it with native designs, animals, plants, and rhythmic motifs. When the marvelous Temple to the Sun at Cuzco was destroyed a large Spanish church was at once constructed upon its truncated walls. The massive, close-fitting, rounded precision of its unsurpassed Inca stonework still contrasts sharply with the thinner, more delicate, more temporary quality of the structure lifted upon it. In the church of San Lorenzo at Potosí, "side by side with God and the Virgin the Indian artists carved the Sun and the Moon, the two principal divinities of the Incas, and instead of angels there appeared sirens playing the *charango*, a native instrument made of an armadillo shell." There were many other motifs showing the flora and fauna of the New World: "macaws, monkeys, toucans, humming

birds, chinchillas, and especially pumas. On the bases of the columns decorating the Cathedral of Puno there are two magnificently sculptured jaguars. At Arequipa, the gargoyles of nearly all the houses are stylized
puma heads through whose mouths the water pours off the roofs. In the
church of Santo Domingo at La Paz, on each side of the great window
lighting the choir appear two huge toucans." There were also ears of corn,
pineapples, cherimoyas, and cactus flowers. The favorite motifs were
"either corn or the cantuta flower, which was a sacred emblem of the
Incas." The cantuta is a pendulous bell-shaped flower of extreme loveliness. Numberless saints and angels were given the Indian features of the
artist who made them, and the figures of native dancing girls adorn many
a religious building of the high Andes.[168]

These indigenous themes were most pronounced where the Spanish
overlordship was weakest and Indian art strongest. In South America they
reached as far north as Quito, but had little importance there. They did
not reach Lima at all, where the Spanish overlord raised his viceregal capital on a site where no native town had stood. The style which arose from
this Hispano-Indian fusion may truly be called American or Creole. "It
made its appearance timidly during the first two hundred years, then, at
the beginning of the 18th century, burst forth so vigorously and so undis-
guisedly that from then on it can be classified as an independent style."[168]

Some of these mestizo elements even reached back to Spain and were
incorporated in such buildings as the Carthusian Monastery of Granada.
Despite these fragmentary details, church architecture was mostly Spanish (or Portuguese); it was never Indian. Delicate fingers of the baroque
and plateresque stretched themselves over the Indian's world, accepting
all that he had to offer and giving him the white man's God: more powerful, more merciful, more beautiful than his own.

Wherever the Indian was transformed into a mestizo he accepted this
change completely. Where his blood remained pure he accepted it with
reservations. Race-mixing absorbed him more surely than did religion. Yet
the Church was always a refuge and a protection, a surcease from toil.
The human body can stand just so many days of labor "from sun to sun";
then it has to stop. The Indian is like all other men in that. The Church,
with its services and its religious fiestas, afforded him that repose, that
escape from an unkind and ugly life. In many regions the fiesta became in
itself a work of art. Architecture in movement, saints and virgins walking
the streets with Everyman. At the same time perhaps it is no mere coincidence that on these occasions the Indian so often got dead drunk and
fell in a heap. Sleep was a more curative medicine than the anguish of
his brightest dream.

Was the price of these lovely churches too high? This is no question
with a ready answer. But it is well never to forget that more and more
wealth poured into the coffers of the mother church. From the mines,

ı the fields, in ownership of land itself, and of course in productive
ır, perhaps as much as half the total wealth of all Latin America entered the hands of the Church. It was not by any means unproductive.
Missions and church estates were often more efficient economic units than
the best which the laymen could offer. But the churches themselves which
so obsess the landscape with their beautiful lines and their beautiful light:
what justification for fifty to sixty fine buildings in a town of twenty thousand? What justification in the Archbishop of Mexico's receiving an income of 130,000 pesos a year, the equivalent in purchasing power to about
$250,000, and many times the salary of the Viceroy? What justification for
such pomp and splendor in these lands of economic blight? One might
say that if the Church dares point with pride to its achievements in religion or art, he who speaks in its defense should lower his head and admit
freely, and without reservation, that its outlook on economic justice was
sadly wanting. A glorious art does not blot out the anguish of a miserable
people. The saving of a soul does not lessen the blame of contributing to
the hurt of its body.

How did the white man, with his superior intelligence, enter into this
picture of religion? As in the Old World, perhaps as all over the world, he
and his womenfolk—especially his womenfolk—let practice and form too
frequently blur the significance of deep religious faith and action. The
difference was that with these people the form, being traditional, was
more extensive and more obvious. It was the accumulation of centuries.

But the Latin white man did believe, does still believe, that his value
comes from within, from his Church, from his family, from his culture,
and from his nation, and not so much from his own achievements. His
Church, with its unbroken tradition from the distant past, undoubtedly
stood and stands in many Latin-American minds as the strongest symbol
of that outlook and that heritage. Even when a man is a free thinker himself he often feels a gladness in knowing that his wife, his sisters, and his
children carry on that tradition. It gives him a feeling of security. It is
the conservative instinct in part, and in part it is the pride which he has in
his culture, which is also conservative. Any writer who attempts to diminish the power of the Catholic Church in Latin America outside the realm
of pure religion is guilty of the grossest error.

In the United States we hold to another belief: that a man is worthy
only of that which he achieves through his own efforts. Our world is strong,
new, and in some ways incredibly rough and undeniably ugly. As the Latin
sees us, the technical achievements of our civilization stand on a base
which is raw and unpleasant. We appear immature and material. This is a
fundamental fissure between us which the hemisphere must face squarely
both now and in the future.

Under the protective wings of the colonial Church there were also arts
other than architectural expression. Painting, music, sculpture, and litera-

ture all flourished in a reflected glow. Only in exceptional instances did any one of them reach the level of greatness during the colonial period. Culture, we know, has a habit of following money as well as tradition and population. And the Church was not only banker but by far the wealthiest institution during the formative centuries of Latin-American life. Leisure and money are the prerequisites to a flourishing art.

In painting no truly great name stands out. There was a School of Quito, a School of Cuzco, a painter or two of some note in Bogotá, Mexico City, and Lima, and a handful of Dutch artists in colonial Brazil. Of all these perhaps Miguel de Santiago, dean of the School of Quito, is the best known, though not necessarily the best painter. He and all the rest were imitators, not creators. The Spanish and Italian masters, above all Ribera, Zurbarán, Morales, and Murillo, exerted an all-consuming influence over colonial painting. The canvases themselves were stiff, decorative, hieratic. Hung on the dark walls of churches, their young virgins or somber saints were lost in the semi-gloom of great buildings. The better artists of the School of Quito struggled against this overwhelming shadow, but with only occasional success. One of the earliest fine works of Ecuadorian art is a canvas which represents the portraits of the first three Negroes who came out of the northwest territory to be baptized in the capital, in 1598. This canvas is now in Madrid. It is a moving work, finely executed, from whatever standpoint one might wish to consider it. The painter of this, piece, a mestizo named Adrián Sánchez Galque, was the first of a long line of Quito artists. Galque was the teacher of Miguel de Santiago, and Santiago in his turn taught Goríbar. These three men constituted "the glorious trinity" of colonial Ecuadorian painting.

There is a story about Miguel de Santiago which shows how he, too, fought to preserve his individuality in the hieratic river which swallowed colonial art. The artist had set his heart on painting with life-like emotion and realism the agony of Christ on the cross. Model after model posed for him without Santiago's ever being able to catch the anguished expression for which he sought. He persuaded, exhorted, threatened his models, all to no avail. One day in desperation he grabbed a spear and slew the model before him, and with that dying man's tortured face impressed on his memory, drew the picture of which he had dreamed. As a result of this slaying the legend tells us that the artist was forced to spend the remainder of his life inside an Augustinian convent.[177]

In the eighteenth century Quito turned toward sculpture for expression, and this art flourished in the works of Manuel Chili, better known as *Caspicara*, Bernardo de Legarda, and Zangurina. The statuettes and figurines of these men were first covered with gold or silver, and then painted. This gave the garments of the statue a scintillating richness, for no matter what colors might be painted over the precious metal, the gold or silver always shone through. In order to give a greater appearance of life to some of the larger statues actual human hair, fingernails, and eyelashes were frequently affixed.

Today in Quito one can best observe the first fruits of painting in colonial America. The whole town is a city of churches, each vying with the others in profuse loveliness. Quito has changed least of any of the large colonial capitals. Some exuberant writers have called it an architectural gem which should be preserved intact forever. In block after block crowds of Indians in tatters press into the aisles of gorgeous churches to kneel humbly before altars as shining and rich as any in the Old World. Few if any of them notice the dark canvases strung along the walls. Overhead in places the roof often leaks and rain has seeped through to dim the luster of many of the finest pieces of the School of Quito. Fortunately, by way of recompense, Ecuador today has more worthy painters per square mile than any country in Latin America. They are young strong men whose every stroke brushes away some lingering gossamer of the unpalatable past. Crying out for recognition beyond the limits of their little land, they must feel some bitterness in the recollection that within a single decade of the eighteenth century 266 large boxes of paintings and sculpture were shipped from the port of Guayaquil.

Quito was in colonial days, and is now, a center of wood carving and of sculpture. Beautiful polychrome statues still adorn many of the religious buildings, some of them not only in color but in brilliant clothes as well. Bogotá also has its plethora of virginal statues dressed or painted in delicate pastel shades, which stand out strongly against the somber walls of the gray city's places of worship.

Cuzco, heart of the old Inca culture, set off in its mountain valley far removed from the sea, boasted of a more Indianized or mestizo style, but even here the main rhythm, color, technique, and inspiration were clearly Spanish. By and large painting was an art mastered only by the white Creole aristocracy during the three colonial centuries. It existed as an imitation of European models and stood apart from the earthy folk in the midst of whom it blossomed as an imitation flower stands apart from the rose on the vine. By the close of the eighteenth century, lacking a true source of nutriment, it faded and collapsed almost completely.

In colonial sculpture few individual figures stand out, but two of these are truly outstanding. The Ecuadorian, Caspicara, left a treasure house of lovely miniatures, statuettes, and wood carvings, and the greatest of all colonial artists, who was one of the most gifted creators of this hemisphere at any time, was the Brazilian mulatto, Antonio Francisco Lisboa (1730–1814), generally known as *Aleijadinho*, the little cripple. The art of Aleijadinho expressed the agony of Christianity, had about it a strong and tragic Old Testament monumentality. In the mellow mountain villages of Minas Geraes, not far distant from Rio de Janeiro, he chiseled his series of Apostles, figures of a "tortured, naïve grandeur," with something of

Michelangelo about them, something of El Greco's saints, but mostly nothing but Aleijadinho.

"He was a dark, yellow man with a heavy head on his short thick body, and a delicate face. A bitter man. Bastard son of Dom Manoel Francisco da Costa Lisboa and an African slave called Isabel, he took the double curse of his race and his birth, bitterly."[71] When he was born the culture of Brazil's northeastern bulge, Pernambuco, and of Bahia to the south, had already begun to decline. The art of Minas, which had suddenly burgeoned forth in response to the precious mines of gold discovered only a few decades previously, was now at its height, but it was more Portuguese rococo than Brazilian. Aleijadinho learned all that he could from the artists of Minas while he was still a very young man. Then he turned away from them, as Waldo Frank says, arrogant and successful, despising the current art of his land and its leaders.

"God loved him with an especial love; therefore chastened him. At forty-five, God made him a leper." The body of Aleijadinho began to fall apart; his soul was transformed with living fire. "His toes rotted and fell off; he could not walk, he had to crawl on his knees. Also his fingers, in long ruthless paralysis, decayed. And his eyelids became flame. His teeth fell out; his mouth was a hideous forever gaping grimace. So sinister and fierce was his look that those who saw him in the streets fled in terror."[71]

His ugliness became almost a legend, and, as God's recompense, the fame of his art spread throughout the province. Aleijadinho had nothing to live for but his work. He passed his hours in a sacred and creative frenzy. Sometimes inside and sometimes outside the church on which he was working he would set up his tent, and throughout the long hours of day and night fashion his anguished Apostles.

When his strength became less "he bought a slave, named Januario, to help him in his work. Januario, in horror at sight of his new master, tried to kill himself. *Aleijadinho* drew the knife from the slave's breast; healed him, taught him. Taught him to help and to love him."[71]

When his fingers were no more than stumps he began his great work. He strapped mallet and pincer to his hands and hacked away at the formless soapstone of his native Brazil. He lived in constant pain, wore a huge hat to hide the scar that was his face, threw stones at the curious who tried to see what was going on inside his tent. At night he "crawled home to his bed."

For eighty-three years this disintegrating body was held together by the sacred fire of its holy dedication. Aleijadinho worked on many churches in Minas, but his story is connected especially with the towns of Ouro Preto and Congonhas do Campo. There, in both wood and stone, he revealed himself as the most original genius produced by the three colonial centuries of Latin-American history. He also created churches which are "transfigurations of Portugal's melodious stone into a clumsier, earthier, more spiritual beauty." But it was in face, figure, and posture that he attained the supreme anguish, the supreme love and tenderness, his own soul's dedication.

There were no other truly great artists in colonial days. But art itself was becoming great, flowing, growing in the mestizo stream. Music was the first art to become fully mestizo in character and feeling, and it was obvious that this had to be the case. In music two great folk feelings came together, blended, were reborn in one.

The native Indians had few instruments. They used only the primitive five-tone scale. On Aztec *huehuetl* or *teponaztli* and other crude drums, flutes, timbrels, rattles, and trumpets made of shells, bones, clay, and stone, the natives of Mexico marked out the rhythms of their religious songs and dances. The Indians of the Andes everywhere used a primitive pipe made of reeds of varying length tied together with fiber. A small flute called the *quena* was also widely employed in that region. To round out the Andean "orchestra" there were whistling pots, gourds filled with pebbles or seeds, trumpets of many different styles. There may have been a musical bow fashioned after the hunter's bow, but this is most doubtful. There is no proof of there being any stringed instrument in America before the conquest.

It is easy to see what limitations such instruments imposed. Indigenous music was not full and rich with polyphony, harmony, and strings which swelled out the orchestral voice. It did not even have a system of notation. But it was rhythmic, direct, reiterative, almost hypnotic in its effect. As in every true folk art, the music and dances of the American natives embraced all of the people who were at the same time creators and interpreters. No one was left out; no one was mere critic or listener; no one was a technical interpreter of some strange composer's score. Music to the Indian was a state of exaltation, a state of life. Even when a lone lover played the flute or Panpipes for his lady the whole folk called out in his melody.

Garcilaso tells the story of an Indian girl who, in the middle of the night, left her home and went to join her lover who was calling her on his reed flute. A Spaniard met her in the dark street and tried to persuade her to return home, and she explained: "Señor, let me go where I must go; that flute calls me with such passion and tenderness that it forces me to obey; let me go, señor, for I cannot restrain myself. Love calls to me in that player's voice making me his wife and him my man."

Music exerted a real hypnotic power on the native Indian. It was never a side show on life but part of the great emotions: religion and love; voice of the great language, that of the heart. Its repetition of the same notes over and over again would probably drive the white man into a frenzy of nerves, but to the Indian it evoked the single emotion which it was intended to express directly, completely. And there was no escape from its spell.

As to styles of native music, these varied greatly. The Aymará of Bolivia, where today the primitive melodies are perhaps preserved most nearly intact, had songs which were vigorous, rude, incisive, broken with sudden sharp wails which frequently left those who played and sang in tears. The melodies of the Quechuas of the Peruvian sierra were more refined, less suddenly rending, more resigned to fate. Oftentimes the two were fused, just as the Incas blended their Quechua race with that of the surrounding Indians. The Aztecs had a music of more percussion, of rawer and more martial tonology. It drummed into the ear with a persistence that obliterated the individual, caught him up in the lap of his people.

Almost immediately after the conquest this native folk music was altered by contact with the deeper, richer Iberian scale and more intricate system of harmonics. During the years of conflict with the Spaniards the bodies of the two races clashed; even the spirits were set one against the other, but the folk arts, especially music, became merely two voices speaking together, and the result was a greatly enriched fusion.

Even in Garcilaso's day Spanish musicians and priests had introduced European instruments into the sierras of Peru. With those instruments came the European scale. This blended with the five-tone scale of the natives and produced the so-called mestizo scale which the D'Harcourts have studied and reproduced extensively. Spanish strings—guitars, harps, and violins—broadened the scope of indigenous musical expression. Before many years had passed there was hardly a hamlet within reach of civilization without its stringed instrument. Sometimes when the real thing could not be procured a native substitute was fashioned. The well-known *charango* of Bolivia, a sort of mandolin made with the shell of an armadillo as the sounding box, is an example of this. The sense of harmony widened and music became a mestizo art, the first real mestizo art in America. It is still one of the richest and least-known heritages of the fused Spanish-Indian culture of the colonial period, one on which the contemporary masters are only now beginning to create extensively.

It is interesting to note that while this fusion was taking place in the folk music of the two races, art music, that which was composed and interpreted for Spanish purposes, if not for Spanish audiences, was limited almost exclusively to church music and had practically no indigenous elements in it. The music of many cathedrals—for example, that of the Cathedral of Mexico—rivaled the church music of many European cities, but it was not American in character, although it was supposedly American in function. Its purpose was to bring the two races together in a common religion, but the religion was clearly to be that of the conqueror, and not a trace of that of the vanquished was desired.

Thus while church music represented the ideal of religious absorption, folk music represented the actuality of racial fusion. The one was never carried to its final conclusion; the other was a reality from the very first decade of the conquest. Two races, separated by a world of tradition and a world of feeling, are always brought together most immediately, with slighter evidence of conflict, with more absolute blending, in their folk arts than in any other expression. This is a proof that while the veneer and manners of life vary from time to time and from region to region, the essential human aspirations and emotions express the same love, the same longing.

26

REBELLION OF THE BEAST BELOW

The greater part of the colonial period is often regarded as one of restorative sleep following that burst and blaze of action known as the conquest. To be sure there was no great war in the Spanish New World throughout the three colonial centuries. Despite the forays of pirates and the rebellions of Indians, the American colonies enjoyed more peace during those years than they ever did afterward. Nevertheless, the economic situation was so oppressive and inequitable that it would have been a miracle for no sore to have broken out on this riftless glimmer of dead gray. Furthermore, the cleavage of class against class, of one privileged group against another, of those who governed against those who owned land, of ecclesiastical against state authorities, became more sharply drawn as each of these groups jockeyed for a better position or fought to maintain the position which it already enjoyed. Such outbreaks as did occur were generally given the Spanish name of *tumultos*, "tumults," a term of disparagement employed by the classes of property to dismiss the rumblings of the beast below them. Such an attitude is often a blind and fatal error.

It is noteworthy that the tumults of most consequence took place in Mexico, which later turned out to be a country with an exceptionally strong social consciousness, perhaps the strongest social consciousness in all Latin America. During the colonial period the over-all power of the King was able to restore order after each tumult, but not before the deep scars and seams in the national life had been momentarily revealed. One of the deepest was between Church and State.

The great riot which took place in Mexico City in 1624 is a perfect example of how this expressed itself. The archbishop, Pérez de la Serna, had a private slaughterhouse in the archepiscopal palace, and when the Viceroy asked him to close it because it was against the law, Serna became infuriated and headed a strong political attack against the government. In the meantime, one of the archbishop's friends, a well-known food profiteer, who had been tried and found guilty of running a grain trust, was fined, and the police were sent to take him into custody. His crime was one of the most serious against the people and against the state, because Mexico lived then, as she does now, on the staple corn, and by hoarding the stocks of this commodity the entire populace was made to suffer the hardships of hunger and high prices.

The Viceroy was entirely within his rights in ordering the arrest of the guilty party, Pérez de Varaiz, but when the police went to his house he and several of his servants, all armed, drove them bodily from the precincts and Varaiz himself fled to the Dominican convent for sanctuary. The Viceroy apparently did not dare to violate this holy building, but he did throw an armed guard around it. The archbishop, who had stoutly defended his friend, the food profiteer, visited him daily at the convent, made plans for his escape, and continued his attacks on the government "with incandescent adjectives." He claimed that this violation of the right of sanctuary by the Viceroy's guards was a direct threat to his religious authority, and when the government refused to release its prisoner and arrested one of the archbishop's notaries, the latter excommunicated the Viceroy, the trial judges, and the soldiers of the guard.

The Viceroy appealed to the apostolic judge, who ordered the archbishop to withdraw his excommunications. The archbishop "not only refused; he locked up every church in the capital and laid the whole city under an interdict."[45] Anathema was called out from the pulpit; all services and sacraments were suspended, and the bells of the churches and convents began to toll day and night, in a ceaseless and frightful clamor as for the dead. The ignorant people began to mill about in the streets in a state of semi-terror. They saw the awe-inspiring spectacle of a long file of priests marching through the city, carrying lighted candles and intoning incomprehensible phrases in Latin while, at the head of the procession, went a large cross all draped in black. At the houses of each excommunicate was affixed one of the Church's papers casting him outside of the religious pale. No person was to speak to or have any kind of association with these religious criminals. The populace observed this frightful spectacle and thought that every one of them was bound straight for the eternal fires and brimstone of hell. Not a moment's surcease was allowed, for the slow and awful tolling of the bells continued unbroken through all hours of the day and night.

The apostolic judge, now driven to rigorous action, made the archbishop lift the interdict, and he himself suspended the excommunications. The archbishop did not take this lying down but marched to the office of the Supreme Court with a mob at his heels; the court ordered him to sign a judicial warrant and he refused. He was then requested to leave, and again he refused, breaking out into loud and belligerent complaints against the authorities, his remarks frequently punctuated by shouts of encouragement from the mob at his heels. As a result of all this the archbishop was arrested, fined heavily, and officially banished from the colony. However, when he had been escorted a few miles from the city he excommunicated the entire government and "blasted the city with a new interdict."

The bells again began to toll and the ignorant populace arose in a body to defend the integrity of the Church. As the cathedral was in the process of construction there was a large supply of loose stones near by, and when these gave out the mob took to tearing up the paving stones of the square, showering them on the viceregal palace. They were led by a priest on horseback and entered the fray with shouts of "Long live Christ! Long live the King! Death to the heretic!" In front of one of the doors of the cathedral, and seated in a chair placed on top of a large table, was another priest with a mass book in his hand, "absolving of blame and penance all those who took part in the assault on the palace."

The attack continued throughout that day, and on the day following the mob stormed into the palace, set fire to one wing of it, and opened the jail. The Viceroy's guard fired on them several times and many were killed. Finally, when it became obvious that the mob was going to have its way, the Viceroy, who was now in a furious rage and wanted to dash out into the midst of that howling band, sword in hand, was persuaded by calmer minds to blacken his face, put on some tattered clothes, and escape through the besiegers to the Franciscan convent. When the archbishop received the news of this turn of events, he somehow persuaded his guards to set him free and "made his triumphant entrance into the city at night accompanied by more than four thousand men on foot and on horseback, many of them holding aloft lighted torches so that it seemed in the midst of day."[72]

The King immediately sent a royal visitor or investigator, armed with special powers, to ascertain the facts and issue an official report. There is no reason to suspect this report of being biased, because the clergy were dependent upon the King for their positions and there could never be any question of a rift between them and the Crown. Nevertheless, the visitor's report stated that the great riot of 1624 had clearly brought out three facts: "first, the conspiracy was organized, directed, and led by the clergy, that is to say, by the class believed at court to be the principal and most firm support of the government of the mother country; second, if the matter were followed through it would be found that all, or almost all, of the population were accomplices; third, the hatred of the dominion by the mother country, and especially by the Spaniards who came to establish themselves in Mexico City, is deeply rooted in all classes of society, and was one of the principal means used to incite the masses to action."[45]

Four lay leaders of the mob were executed and five priests were sentenced to the galleys. The Viceroy was completely exonerated.

All considerations of blame aside, the main point of this early tumult was that bishops and archbishops frequently made the grave error of utilizing religious authority for economic or political ends, and that they permitted and abetted the ignorant populace to rise violently against the established government. This rebelliousness did not assert itself against the faraway King because ecclesiastical appointments were made by the Crown. Once that distant king symbol was removed the Church-State conflict would inevitably become intensified.

In early colonial years the weight of church authority rested mainly on the use of the power of excommunication; later on sheer economic wealth became a tremendous political influence. It cannot be emphasized too strongly, however, that in no case of a dispute between the Church and civil government was religious belief itself an issue. The conflict between these two parties invariably revolved around how much jurisdiction the temporal authorities should exercise over the clergy and religious property or income, and how much secular power or immunity the Church should enjoy. The second fundamental point to be remembered is that these conflicts were always between two subordinate parties, both of which were clearly under the headship of the Crown. In the last analysis, then, it was the State and not the Church which held the upper hand. But it was not the State in any democratic sense of the term; it was rather the person of the King, who was utilizing both ecclesiastical and civil authority as the two pillars of his dominion. When a difference of opinion between either of these subordinate parties occurred, the King, not the Pope, was final arbiter, and when there was a difference of opinion between either party and the Crown itself, the latter asserted its dominance immediately.

The King, in a word, was the ultimate ecclesiastical, civil, judicial, and executive authority in the colonies and in the mother country. When he ordered several thousands of strongly organized Jesuits to abandon their homes, their estates, and their country, they left. The Supreme Pontiff supported him in this action and later dissolved the order completely. This does not mean that the King was immune to social suasion. He compromised with the civilian encomenderos when they battled against him, and he later permitted the Jesuits to reform and re-enter his dominions. Nevertheless, he was always the supreme power, and he delegated only a part of that power to the church and government officials under him who occupied their positions and ruled in his name.

Another important historical fact to bear in mind is that whenever a conflict between these two delegated powers took place it involved primarily only the upper economic stratum of society. The majority of the common people sometimes supported one group, sometimes the other, and oftentimes neither, but they were so bereft of political or economic

influence that they were seldom able to sway the scales permar
either direction.

On the other hand, the influence of the Church as an economic _
political factor did continue to grow throughout the colonial period. In
some regions it controlled more of the national wealth than the civil government and enjoyed almost, but not quite as much, political power. In
the first place, "the clergy was an economically privileged class from the
beginning. The members of it received large grants of land from the
crown. Many monasteries, cathedrals, and individual prelates were given
encomiendas . . ."[73] In addition to this source of income the Church
received its tithes, frequent "gifts and bequests of money and property;
parochial fees for marriages, funerals, baptism, confession, and for masses
both ordinary and requiem; special collections to honor some patron saint;
alms gathered by the monasteries; dowries given to convents of nuns, and
so forth . . ."[74] The first two of these items—tithes and gifts or bequests
—would naturally tend to enrich the Church more and more as time
passed and a greater proportion of colonial capital and income found its
way into ecclesiastical hands. Furthermore, it must not be forgotten that
"ecclesiastical capital was free from taxation—legally in the early days,
virtually always." This gave the Church "an economic advantage over the
richest of the *encomenderos,* who had to build their own houses and provide their own working capital . . ."[73]

When it was a matter of capital expenditure for the purpose of con-
structing churches, monasteries, and residences, the Royal Treasury furnished a portion of the funds, one third or one half, and the encomenderos,
other Spaniards, and Indians furnished the remainder. Indians always
performed the labor without remuneration as their part of the contribution; but, as a matter of fact, the entire burden ultimately came to rest on
their shoulders because their tributes to the Crown made the royal portion
possible, and their work for the encomenderos also enabled that class to
pay its quota. In this manner the Church became one of the principal
means through which the impoverishment of the native races continued
unabated, causing the fissure which divided the well-to-do from the poor
to become broader and deeper with the passage of time.

In spite of these accusations, which undoubtedly express the truth but
not the whole truth, there were always thousands of members of the clergy
who lived in dire poverty and self-sacrifice in order to devote their lives
and their labors to the betterment of the Indians' lot. The clergy who became wealthy usually lived in the larger populated centers, or not far distant, while most of those who continued to live in Christian dedication
were found in the wilderness or along the remote frontiers. Obviously the
wealthy class always stood in the political and economic limelight, and
this has caused posterity to judge the Church almost entirely in terms of
this relatively small group.

Such an interpretation is entirely understandable, indeed inevitable, because the self-sacrificing missionary fervor which characterized the first century of colonization was followed by two centuries during which increased wealth became so outstanding in some quarters that it blotted out all other considerations. Greater and greater numbers of adventurers and social parasites found their way into the ranks of the clergy in order to enjoy the honorable, and in their cases, the comfortable livelihood which the religious life afforded. As early as 1644 the town council of Mexico City sent an official report to Philip IV imploring him to send "no more monks, as more than six thousand were without employment, living on the fat of the land."[73]

By the end of the colonial period the Church and its well-to-do clergy owned an estimated one half of the total wealth in the countries of Mexico, Peru, Colombia, Ecuador, Paraguay, and almost that amount in all of the other Latin-American nations. A considerable proportion of the remainder was "controlled by the clergy through mortgages." After the expulsion of the Jesuits from Mexico in 1767 one hundred and twenty-eight of their large haciendas were offered for sale to the public. The fact that the control of this wealth and this influence was in the hands of relatively few members of the clergy is only a recognition of the historic fact of minority rule among the Latin-American peoples. It neither exonerates the Church economically, nor does it justify the vitriolic denunciations which have been heaped upon the heads of all the clergy by oftentimes intolerant civil authorities. On the other hand, it would be absurd to suppose that the ecclesiastical majority would align itself against its own leaders when the conflict became intense. Emotional factors, generously appealed to by both sides, turned a difference of opinion over secular power into a religious war which, on more than one occasion, has split Latin-American society wide open with a consequent loss of tolerance that education and patience alone will ever retrieve.

Church and State, however, were not always aligned against each other at the moments of greatest colonial stress. Their conflict was one between equals, each struggling to hold the upper hand. Throughout the colonial period the leaders of both groups belonged invariably to the same ruling class. Together they controlled all of the policies and owned all of the property in the countries in which they lived. When they were united, their power was absolute. When they were divided, the King served as a last court of appeal. The masses whose destiny lay in their hands, and over whose productive power they so often quarreled, formed a voiceless majority whose poverty, ignorance, and disorganization were never a threat to their authority. In those rare instances when a general upheaval against economic oppression flared, they patched up their differences and stood together to hold back the flood. Such an instance occurred in Mexico City in the year 1692. It was the second "great tumult" or riot to burst out of the oppressive and stagnant monotony of Mexican life within seventy-five years.

This time the trouble was not caused by any rift within the dominant caste, but was a spontaneous mass uprising against those who held the strings of political and economic power. It was blind, undirected, and gained nothing, but was indicative of a new trend. The government and the Church, representing property, were on one side, and on the other stood a howling, famished, and frenzied mob of the city's poor, who erupted like a volcano, throwing the streets of the town into wild disorder and causing fear to invade the heart of every propertied citizen. The earlier riot of 1624 had already defined the intransigent lines of a Church-State conflict which was later to tear Latin-American nationalism asunder, and this riot of 1692 completed the prophetic picture by giving a brief preview not only of the struggle for independence, but also of the Mexican Revolution of 1910–20, when the blind masses would rebel against all established authority, eager only to topple from their high places those who had become symbols of oppression.

The year 1691 had been one of continuous rains and floods. There was also an unusually cold spell in the month of August, and the grain crops began to suffer considerable damage. Dampness, fog, and cold weather spread over the central valley region, and even the ripening grain was attacked by a species of rust which destroyed the greater part of it. The government anticipated an extreme shortage and sent inspectors over the countryside to make a careful survey of the amount to be expected and to purchase, or, if necessary, to seize, all surpluses. The poorer classes were already suffering privations, and the whisper went about that these inspectors were buying up the entire harvest in order to increase the price. A seething discontent broke out on all sides, for no one seemed to credit the reports of a general crop failure.

When the government began to ration grain strictly in the capital, prohibiting its sale by private individuals and obliging purchasers to obtain it from the public granary, this discontent became a loud murmur of complaint against the government. The long waiting in lines before the granary increased the tempo of this grumbling. When the following spring arrived matters had become desperate. Not only was the scarcity in the capital more acute, but "the price of grain had increased so enormously that a load of wheat which usually sold for five dollars could not be purchased for less than twenty-four dollars."

The city at this time was divided into nine districts or wards, six of them inhabited entirely by Indians, each with its own governor. The total population was perhaps 140,000, but not more than a small proportion of that number were Spaniards. Consequently, when the disaffection spread it gradually embraced a vast majority of the town's inhabitants. Only the elite minority was more or less removed from complete dependence on wheat and corn. In the month of June, 1692, the supply of grain became so short that there was not always enough to take care of those at the end of the line. One day violent scuffling broke out for the first places, and while the disorder raged several helped themselves to as much as they could carry away. The government official in charge grabbed his whip and cane and rained a shower of blows on the heads of the women nearest him. There were, of course, no men in the waiting line. Incensed by this treatment, the crowd milled over to the archbishop's palace and then to the Viceroy's residence, demanding justice. The guards pushed them back, and finally the clamor died away. No men had yet joined the rioters, and the government seemed to believe that it had the situation under control.

On the following day the same scene was re-enacted, and this time one of the women at the head of the line was accidentally thrown to the ground and trampled on with serious results. The mob was now joined by several men, and the whole howling mass went again to the archbishop's palace, demanding to see him. When this was refused they commenced to curse that dignitary bitterly. Next they turned their attention to the Viceroy and were met by a few of the guards who charged into them, driving them back across the main plaza. However, by this time the mob had reached a considerable size and quickly re-formed, returning to the attack with a rain of sundry missiles and heavy stones. All available troops were now called up, but by the time they arrived on the scene the mob had increased to nearly ten thousand persons and it was impossible to deal with them. The doors of the government palace were closed, and this was done in such haste that two or three of the palace guard were locked outside. They were seized by the crowd and immediately torn to pieces. The entire mob now advanced to the assault, shouting: "Death to the Viceroy! Death to the cuckold Spaniards! Death to those who have all the corn and are killing us with hunger!" They broke into the pulque shops along the plaza and helped themselves to the fiery stuff in order to gain courage. As more pulque went down their famished gullets their temerity increased.

The archbishop, now thoroughly frightened, came out of his residence surrounded by several priests and holding aloft a large cross. The mob took one look in their direction and began to flail them with sticks and stones. One large rock hit the holy crucifix squarely and sent it toppling from the archbishop's hands. The representatives of the Church hurriedly withdrew. Things had reached such a point that the crowd would hold absolutely nothing sacred, not even that holiest emblem of Mother Church. The greatest of all stresses, continued hunger and poverty, were at last having their cumulative effect, and the result was a blind beating out against all recognized authority.

The soldiers fired on the mob a few times, but as their ammunition was soon exhausted this only had the effect of heightening the anger of those ten thousand howling demons of destruction. These latter, no longer fearing anyone, now determined to burn down the governmental palace. They went through the main square, ripping apart the rows of flimsy wooden and reed stalls in order to get firewood. This they placed in large heaps next to the government buildings and applied the torch. Within a few moments the heart of the city was a mass of flames.

"Then followed a scene which no pen can picture. Darkness was creeping over the city, and in the glare of the conflagration, the spacious plaza, thronged but a few hours before with the wealth and beauty of New Spain, appeared like a hall in Tophet. Filling the square and the adjacent streets, the maddened populace might be seen surging to and fro in dense masses like an angry sea, and above the roar of the flames arose hoarse shouts of exultation as the work of destruction went bravely on. From the palace corridors the archbishop and his attendants gazed in the silence of despair, while in its neighborhood groups of citizens watched in speechless terror the progress of the flames.

"Suddenly the cry was raised, 'To the stalls!' 'To the stalls!' and instantly the crowd surged in that direction, arming themselves with knives, machetes, and iron bars. And now the rabble became raving maniacs."[25] They broke into the small booths, robbing them of all their contents and setting fire to the remaining empty shells. The owners of these shops, not daring to interfere with the wholesale robbery, frequently were in the forefront of the mob, snatching up as much of their own merchandise as they could save. Others watched carefully which persons carried away their goods and later stealthily followed them and at a convenient moment knocked them in the head, taking the stuff away again.

All the near-by streets became a pandemonium of murderous roving bands mixed in bloody clashes, all grotesquely silhouetted against the lurid and ever-increasing flames. "Houses were broken open and plundered, and the torch applied to the dwellings of friend and foe alike, while rape and massacre spread almost unchecked throughout the city. Gradually the infuriated yells of the mob sank to a low murderous roar of voices, interrupted only by the crash of falling buildings."[25] The insurgents had by this time taken all they could carry and their drunkenness was wearing off. Bands of Spaniards who had bolted themselves inside their houses now sallied forth in armed groups and attacked the waning forces of the populace. By ten o'clock that night the great riot of 1692 had died out like a huge grass fire.

On the following day the sun rose on a mass of smoldering ruins and dead bodies in the heart of the Mexican capital. Along blood-spattered streets were scattered pieces of merchandise which had been dropped by overzealous robbers. Many buildings were completely destroyed or badly gutted, among them the viceregal palace, the halls of the Supreme Court, the prison, the mint, several government offices, the granary, and the city hall. This last building was burned to the ground, and in it perished many invaluable public archives. The damage caused went into several hundreds of thousands of dollars.

For a time the unorganized masses had had the entire city in their control, to do with as they might wish. But they had no plan, no purpose, no motive other than that of blind hatred and destruction. They had been driven to revolt by want of food and prolonged injustice and maltreatment, but held no program of their own to offer in place of the official repression. Without leadership the great tumult had come and gone spontaneously and ineffectively, leaving but little permanent imprint on the policy of the central government. Widespread ignorance and poverty continued unabated. It did show of what powerful stuff the revolt of the masses was made, and it proved that when property was threatened the Church must stand alongside the government in order to protect its own economic interests. It had burned out the heart of a great capital with prophetic fires, but it had taught the nation next to nothing. Over a hundred years would pass before another such tumult was to sweep across the face of this stagnant social order, disturbing the cold sleep of centuries.

27

CHILE EMERGES BEHIND
THE ARAUCANIAN FRONTIER

In history only those peoples who have been imbued with the same ideal, or who have fought together in unity against a common problem, have been able to achieve that degree of homogeneity in society and feeling which is the prerequisite to forming any great nation. Countries which face the greatest adversities during the first years of their national lives often attain maturity more rapidly than those where life is relatively easy and the means of subsistence plentiful. Adversity is a better start toward nationhood than abundance, for abundance separates people, whereas adversity forces them together. The existence of a large slave or serf class may also retard national consciousness, because the subject classes are bound to resent their chains, and the country is thus divided against itself. Many old aristocratic societies thrived despite their servile base, but in modern times this has become increasingly unlikely.

The existence of a moving frontier, the desire for a common destiny, the struggle against a common enemy, all of these are factors which contribute to the growth of a nation. Linguistic and racial unity accelerate the process of national development. War itself, if directed against an enemy without, and provided it does not exhaust the material and spiritual reserve of a people, can do much to bind a nation together. But while actual warfare is only a temporary cause of union, which often disrupts into the most violent cleavages once the outside pressure is relieved, the prolonged or ever-present threat of war can become a mighty influence in the achievement of permanent nationhood.

In Latin America the three A B C countries, Argentina, Brazil, and Chile, came nearest to fulfilling these conditions. In them the frontier was both a spiritual and a physical factor in the national life. Along it the threat of war and behind it the necessity for co-operative effort were strongly ıng influences, and the presence of an aspiration toward liberty and /idual freedom was also indisputable. There were, nonetheless, great ːrences which held these countries far behind the considerably younger ʋ͟ited States in attaining real nationhood. These differences were partly traditional, but they were mostly implicit in the processes of development which the three nations had to follow.

In the first place, their colonists did not come to the New World with a strong background of individual liberty and self-government, nor did they cross the ocean with any particular desire to create these conditions of society for themselves. In the second place, their frontiers existed mainly during colonial days, long before they dreamed of national freedom, whereas the expansion of our western frontier in the United States came after this country had won its independence from England and at a time when its expansion could contribute most to its dream of growth and unity. In the third place, the A B C countries fell into disruptive and often violent political divisions within themselves soon after independence was obtained, a condition which the United States barely avoided due to the straight thinking and vigorous action of a few outstanding men, who pulled together the weak props of our national frame with the bitterly disputed federal Constitution.

Each of these great Latin-American nations is completely different from the other, and these differences, upon which their national characters developed, were plainly delineated even as early as the period 1580–1640, when all three were under Spanish colonial rule. Chile, the smallest and poorest of the three, was the first to be firmly established. Its capital city, Santiago, was founded in 1541, eight years before Brazil's Bahia, and thirty-nine years before the permanent founding of Buenos Aires. The Chilean colony was a clear-cut projection of Peru and was bound indissolubly to that more populous and wealthier viceroyalty throughout the colonial regime. Its government was subordinate to that of Lima, and even its official expenses had to depend heavily on the appropriations which the Spanish monarch ordered Peru to furnish. The incessant drain of the Araucanian wars would have made the land untenable under any other conditions. In 1600 the King decreed that Lima should appropriate sixty thousand ducats to help defray the expenses of Chile's army; two years later this sum was raised to 140,000 ducats, and in 1606 it became 212,000 ducats, or approximately $500,000 annually. This subsidy continued throughout most of the colonial epoch.

In other words, Chile was a bad investment from the very beginning; she cost Spain far more than she ever gave in return. Yet, like many other investments which never seem to yield anything but which on the contrary constantly demand more funds in order to prevent complete liquidation, Chile held a certain fascination for the Spanish Government, which kept pouring money into her in the hope that someday, somehow, it would all be repaid with interest. This was indeed the case, but when that time came it was Chile herself, and not Spain, which reaped the benefits.

Perhaps the thing which contributed most to this fascination was the fact that from the year of Santiago's founding, and for well over two centuries thereafter, the Spaniards in Chile were never free of the threat of war along their southern frontier. This condition was in many ways a repetition of the experience from which Spain herself had just emerged in her many centuries of struggle against the Moslems. The unsubdued Araucanian Indians in southern Chile became a challenge to the national pride which the conquistadores and their descendants could not let go unanswered. Here again, as in the case of Spain, this unceasing struggle welded the inhabitants of the country into a mold perhaps stronger than that which held any other Latin-American colony. Disunion would have meant disaster; only through absolute unity of effort was survival possible.

Great stretches of Chilean land were inhospitable and poor. An immense northern desert over a thousand miles long separated the central valleys from Lima. Over its course the very earth seemed spewed up in barren and broken rocks which mocked the blue skies above it. Not a leaf, not a tree relieved the changeless sterility of that hideous expanse. No one then knew what wealth of nitrates was held in its unknown depths. The central valleys, it is true, were fertile and lovely, and the southland was a sort of American Switzerland of beautiful lakes, mountains, and forests where the Araucanian tribes were concealed. Even the central valleys, however, were not free of the threat of destruction.

When the city of Santiago was assaulted and burned in the very year of its founding, the Spaniards claimed the victory because they survived to tell of their fight. But their homes, their clothes, their precious store of food and farm animals were nearly all consumed in the ashes. For two years afterward the meager garrison of Santiago held body and soul together on a starvation diet, working, thinking, living only for the future.

The war against the Indians never ceased. There were periods of armed truce, during which both sides regrouped their forces; there was even one brief spell during which the colonists tried desperately to reach a *rapprochement* with the natives. But by and large, war or the threat of war was the daily bread on which many generations of Chileans lived. As one outstanding writer of the country points out, "the formation of Chilean nationality is the history of the Araucanian war." He does not even bother to pluralize the word; the conflict was omnipresent, unending.

In 1553 there was a great uprising in which the founder of the country, Valdivia himself, was slain; and in 1598, forty-five years later, there was an even greater eruption of the natives, lasting several years, in the course of which seven of Chile's cities were sacked and destroyed. The Spaniards who braved this incessant danger were miserably few. Valdivia brought only one hundred and fifty men into the country with him. During the next twenty-five years, or up to 1565, a total of only twenty-five hundred Spaniards entered the colony. This number continued to grow slowly, and by the turn of the century was increased to perhaps four or five thousand, all of whom had at one time or another fought along the Araucanian frontier.

A Chilean writer characterizes these days in the following words: "Chile in the sixteenth century offers the aspect of a widespread battlefield. Military camps and fortresses are its cities—the cities which the conquistador has founded—soldiers are their inhabitants and the laws of war, their law.

"In the other countries of America, during the period of conquest warfare went hand and hand with the itch for destruction. Here, quite the contrary. Our sixteenth century, besides being one of constant battles, was also constructive. These two characteristics—side by side—exemplify its nature. If in the fury of war it reached incredible proportions, incredible too was the laborious and constructive tenacity of those Spaniards who rebuilt the desolated land. Within a few decades where there had previously been only trees and bushes inhabited by savage tribes, there arose a political and administrative organization; there arose cities—twelve cities in all—there arose industries.

"The Spaniard who lived here, isolated and not provided with even the most indispensable necessities, was forced to struggle against both the keen fury of the Araucanians and against the greatest obstacles of a hostile nature: abrupt mountains, thick forests, sweeping and unfordable torrents where each step meant exposure to ambuscade and imminent death: 'Never before with such imposing obstacles,' sang the poet, 'did nature attempt to hold back the passage of man.' "[75]

Two or three thousand Spaniards were pitted against two or three hundred thousand Araucanian warriors, and there was never a single great campaign or battle whose issue would ensure defeat or victory. The men "only thought and lived for war." They had of necessity come without women, and of necessity their own labor behind the front was cut to a bare minimum. Natives were forced to perform the indispensable tasks of construction, agriculture, and gold washing. There were only two classes: masters and serfs. Even the governors of the colony during that first century were obliged to live in the southern city of Concepción in order to direct the endless military campaigns. A mere tenth of the white population lived in the capital, Santiago, which bore little resemblance to more opulent Lima, Quito, or Mexico City. "Under an intense blue sky set in a frame by the magnificent sierra surrounding it, the incipient city rose. Its appearance was sad and miserable: narrow streets, dusty in summer and impassable with mud in winter, low-lying houses of clay and adobe, whose meager and only half-furnished rooms were lighted at night by a tallow candle. During the day all activity centered around the main plaza, a mere corral, along whose sides the more important buildings of the town were located. Here also was held the primitive market where the first fruits of the soil were on sale."[75]

The soldiers' camps were always supplied with a few Indian women who performed more than the mere domestic duties. One chronicler states that in a single camp he counted seventy new babies born in a week. During many years of this first century the number of mestizo children far exceeded the total of white men in the entire colony.

Although there was a complete absence of colonial culture such as was arising in Lima, Quito, and Mexico City, Chile did give to Latin America its only truly literary production of the sixteenth century, Ercilla's epic *La Araucana*, which is the greatest historical poem in the Spanish language. Its author came to Lima in 1556 and then proceeded to Chile, where for several years he was engaged directly in the Araucanian war. "Now with his pen in hand, and now with his sword," this poem was composed and written. Never in the history of literature was an epic so completely fused with the experience of its author.

Not only did Ercilla compose a great part of *La Araucana* while in the midst of campaigns along the Indian frontier, but frequently, for lack of paper, he wrote verses on small strips of leather, the bark of trees, leaves, or any available material which would temporarily preserve his thought. The heroes of the poem are the Araucanian Indians—Lautaro, Caupolicán, Galvarino—not the Spanish conquerors, among whom Ercilla himself was numbered. This is a further proof of what has already been said about the similarity between the Spanish wars against the Moors and the Chilean campaign against the Araucanians; that is, despite the cruelties and bitterness of the struggle there was about it a prolonged epic spirit which caught the imagination of the Spaniards. Under such conditions the genius of Spain has always risen to supreme heights of liberality and glory.

No other poem of worth was produced in Chile throughout the remainder of the colonial epoch, or indeed, for that matter, during a century of independence. *La Araucana* was so sweeping in its power and scope, and in its influence on the literature which followed, that much of the remaining Chilean poetry was shot through with pale imitations of some phase or other of its unique nature.

As the sixteenth century drew to a close, Chile's formative period came to an end, and the country entered its adolescence, the "incongruous and tumultuous years" of the century following. No great wealth or easy living, no long peace, no inexhaustible source of well-trained serfs or servants mark this transition from a purely military regime to a society of civil and religious government such as had marked the transition in Peru, Ecuador, Mexico, Guatemala, and Colombia.

Chile's society continued to be military at its base. Warfare or the threat of war was to continue for many years along its southern perimeter, but at least some measure of security had been won for the central valleys. The governor could now move from Concepción in the south to Santiago, which was in the center of the country. Soldiers could return to this and other central towns while on leave from the frontier, or during the extended periods of armed truce. The military command of "Attention!" now gave place to the temporary order of "At ease!" Men began to flow back into the cities in search of relaxation. Society there would become more showy in its customs and in its trappings. Generations which had been bred on war would seek in the truces which were to follow the same reckless spirit of adventure in their pleasures. Authority had passed from the iron hands of military captains into the grasp of intriguing and disorderly political favorites. It was the century of the "great catastrophes and the great scandals"; all Chile was a nation of people who sought release from discipline.

In spite of this diminished strength in the discipline or moral fiber of the people, there was an increase in the material welfare of the country. The colonists had grown beyond the disheartening gold-washing stage and now turned their activities toward agriculture, cattle raising, and small industries. The Society of Jesuits was especially important in teaching improved methods for carrying out these various phases of economic development.

As in all Latin America, the Spaniards of Chile did not perform manual labor themselves when it was possible to avoid it. The Indians did all the hard work, but they were not the well-trained serfs of Mexico or Peru, and demanded constant overseeing. Relations between the two races improved little with the passing years; the Indians never attained the status of vassals; rather, they were regarded as enslaved, but constantly dangerous, enemies. Even the official government stand was strongly against them; so that there was great bitterness, sometimes flaring into open violence, between workers and their masters.

In 1606 a Spanish garrison in the south was almost wiped out by an unexpected Indian attack. Two years later Philip II decreed that henceforth all Araucanians captured in the war were condemned to perpetual slavery. This decree remained in force for the better part of sixty-five years—that is, up to 1674—and gave a new impetus to the Spaniards, for slaves could be sold at a profit, and so slave gathering was considered to be a far more masculine occupation than tilling the soil.

Yet the basis of Chilean life was from the very beginning agricultural. Agriculture and cattle raising were then, and still remain, the foundation upon which every other activity came to rest. During the first years of conquest this foundation had been somewhat insecure, but in the second colonial century it sank deep roots into the Chilean earth. The climate and soil of the south and central valleys were particularly adaptable for growing a great variety of crops, and the distance from large outside markets made a variety essential. This fact saved Chile from falling into the single-crop or single-product rut which nearly ruined Brazil on several occasions.

The Araucanians had cultivated a few primitive foods, such as potatoes, beans, corn, and vegetables. The Spaniards quickly enriched this native stock with wheat, grapevines, barley, flax, melons, citrus fruits, pears, peaches, olives, nut and cherry trees, and a variety of wild stock. In the year 1604 three large estates in the south, which were maintained for the explicit purpose of providing for the soldiers, produced a total harvest of 11,856 bushels of wheat, 800 bushels of barley, 350 bushels of potatoes, and on this land also grazed herds of 6000 head of cattle and about the same number of sheep. The yield of these three large estates was fair, but, since it provisioned a considerable proportion of the total population, was certainly not excessive, and shows the relative poverty of Chile as compared with almost any other Latin-American colony at that time.

A few primitive industries also sprang up for the manufacture of woven goods, leather, shoes, munitions, agricultural implements, tools, ship repairs, and pottery, but these barely took care of the needs of the inhabitants. Although individual incomes went up slightly, due to the general expansion, there was no considerable wealth in any one person's hands, and nearly all of the bigger merchants, whose business required a large capital, were those who came from Lima. This relative poverty of all alike was basic in fashioning Chilean character.

Further obvious proof of its extent was given in 1620, when certain public offices were offered for sale. Many of them were never occupied. Even in the eighteenth century, when the lifetime position of town councilman was offered for two thousand dollars, there was not enough ready money to fill the vacancies, and the minimum was then set at three hundred dollars, with the office open to auction, in the hope that it might bring in a higher return. The total revenues produced by the colony in 1788 was only $592,178 for a population of nearly half a million persons.

Throughout the seventeenth century this poverty continued to be general. It was not the resigned poverty of a nation of peasants but the rebellious poorness of a citizenry of soldiers. The soldier-citizen on leave from the wars and in search of a good time had little money to spend, and few things to do or places to see. It was inevitable that he would return to licentiousness on a grand scale. "This wave of unrestrained lechery swept into even the most illustrious homes and everyone seemed possessed by an evil and aggressive demon." Street brawls, duels, killings, feuds, and reprisals of all kinds blot the history of Chile during this century.

One notorious woman of those years, La Quintrala, member of a most distinguished family, poisoned her father, personally cut off the ear of one of her many lovers, had another murdered in her presence, caused many slaves and serfs to be mutilated or slain, and, using her political power, had several civil and religious authorities flogged when they dared to impugn her evil life. La Quintrala's desire to dazzle continued even beyond her death. Thousands of candles were kept burning in the hope that her dark soul would be saved from hell, and a hundred priests were well remunerated to intone masses for her deliverance. La Quintrala was certainly not the typical Chilean woman of the seventeenth century, but the virus that had contaminated her was present everywhere and manifested itself in a general debauchery of the entire social order. It was like the Borgia regime in Renaissance Italy, without the Borgia finery or finesse. Beginning at the top of the scale, the new type of "political favorite" governors fell in with the general spirit and "contributed to the licentiousness which sprouted up everywhere. In the domain of government and administration demoralization reached incredible heights. Frequent violent encounters between the executive power, the bishops, and the courts disorganized all public services. Magistrates prostituted justice, governors embezzled funds, and arbitrary taxes were levied on the prostrate population."[75]

Widespread banditry took possession of many roads and outlying districts, and a feeling of semi-anarchy pervaded the country. Inside the cities many women called "crazy with their bodies" walked the streets in search of masculine game or to meet a lover, and not all of them were out-and-out prostitutes. The people blithely referred to them as "those Portuguese women," but this was not stating the facts. When night fell whole droves of them would come out of their houses and go down to the stores under the pretext of buying what they needed. "The bishop finally ordered all stores closed by nine, under penalty of excommunication, but the evil did not cease, and 'houses of seclusion' had to be constructed in Santiago and other cities in order to teach these women Christian virtue, sewing, and other work which would give them an honorable interest in life."[75]

In spite of all these factors which seemed to be pulling society apart, there was always present a spine of unity which immediately came forward in the presence of the common enemies: poverty and the Araucanians. They prevented Chile's moral chaos from becoming a great disintegrating factor in the national life; it became on the contrary a means by which the pent-up emotion of battlefield and economic wretchedness found escape and brought society to a common level. Throughout these years the Jesuit Order was a strong moral force, eternally calling the country to account, but it was a voice crying in the wilderness. Even religion became a hyperbole. On church holidays and especially during Holy Week there were innumerable processions, sometimes two or three in a single day, in which the entire population turned out and took part as in an orgiastic carnival. The colony was going through its social orgasm and a new nation was being born.

The immense native masses of Chile were not successfully incorporated into this emergent state. Both as Christians and as laborers they had proved a poor investment, and by and large were treated more cruelly than in any other Spanish American country. The relentless bitterness of the Araucanian wars was one cause of this; landlords who had been soldiers were almost invariably filled with the spleen of vengeance. Another cause was the obstinate refusal of the Araucanians to work at forced labor. They had been brought up under a regime of savage individual freedom, and the conception of serfdom was not in their mentality. Like the natives of Brazil, countless thousands of them died in harness rather than perform tasks for their despised white masters.

There was only one saving grace in the relationship between the Chilean Indian and white man: it produced a large mestizo class whose dominance would eventually blot out the problem of race relations. The Chilean mestizo was hardy in the extreme, capable of quick learning and the greatest sustained effort, and possessed such strength and integrity that even in the face of a rigorous exploitation he was able to preserve his character.

Nevertheless, during the sixteenth century and on into the seventeenth, he was regarded by the white man as an outcast, and by the native as a renegade. Nowhere in Latin America was this feeling against the mestizo stronger. Despite Pope Gregory's decree in 1576 that the prelates of America "should forgive the mestizos the impediment of their origin in order that there might be more ministers who could teach, indoctrinate, and confess the Indians," Philip II in 1580 came out with a royal statute by which it was forbidden to confer orders on any person of mixed blood. For a time this statute was vigorously enforced, and it was reiterated in the royal decrees of 1594 and 1621. But the necessity for priests was so great and the available candidates so few that with time it came to be disregarded, like so many other royal statutes which were legislations against the reality of Latin-American life.

By another law it was forbidden to give the man of mixed blood any public office, even that of notary. The same thing happened in this case as in the former, yet the exceptions were relatively so few that a vast majority of mestizos remained distinctly beyond the social pale. In Chile, especially, Araucanian war enmity came to the fore and made the lines of cleavage clear. Consequently, the mestizo caste, by and large, for over a hundred and fifty years lived in a state of ostracism and unproductive idleness in which the very worst traits of both their white and Indian forebears were brought into action. It was not until the year 1703, after the French Bourbons had come to the throne of Spain, that the situation was remedied. In that year Philip V ordered his officials in Chile to "stimulate the mestizos into offering their services on a basis of contracts freely arrived at by both parties." By this time the mestizo caste had apparently achieved a distinct social status which differentiated it from the natives.

In recapitulation, the second colonial century in Chile added up as follows: there was a scandalous immorality in the governing classes, a sense of hyperbolic unrestraint in the soldier-citizenry, and a continued but diminishing cleavage between the races. These factors of disintegration were more than counterbalanced by other strongly unifying social forces: the wars against the Araucanians, a generally poor economic status which saw no sudden rising peaks of wealth, the rapid increase and growing dominance of the mestizo class in the productive economy, and a realization that the country's stability and wealth must rest essentially upon the land. These last two factors indicated that, while the extremes in Chile would not be nearly so great as in the less homogeneous countries of Mexico and Peru, the two-class society of landowners and peons did exist there also and would obstruct the path of economic progress.

With the birth of the eighteenth century the country's attention was fixed on its two greatest sources of wealth: land and labor. These were exploited in deadly earnest, and an extraordinary change came over Chilean life. Border warfare had finally assumed a secondary role in the national thinking, and there was no longer any place for the extravagances of the soldier on leave. As in the rest of Latin America, the eighteenth century in Chile was an epoch of progressive development. The material welfare of the country increased rapidly; public improvements were many; new cities were founded, and government was better. The degenerate officials of the seventeenth century, offspring of a degenerate Hapsburg despotism, were replaced with the more competent choices of the Bourbons. Two new poles around which life would revolve appeared in Santiago: the so-called Palace of the Mint (*Palacio de la Moneda*), and the Cathedral. There was also a police force, a customs organization, and a postal system, to exemplify the now well-established landed economy.

The amorphous mass of three different racial groups, hitherto all living at cross-purposes, at last fell into a settled society in which the mestizo was accepted (on the white man's terms), and the Araucanian almost disappeared from the national scene, so completely was he bottled up in his southern mountains and forests. In this century Chile began its life as a civilized country. The slow-moving and orderly spirit of colonial ceremony, religion, comfortable living, and political liberality pervaded the national life. It was the colonial century par excellence so far as Chile was concerned.

A strong religious flavor took the place of moral debauchery, and it was not the hyperbolic religion of the past century, but a comfortable and gentle religion which beckoned to many of the daughters and widows of fine families, who left their hearths in order to take the veil and to live in comfortably appointed cells. Many of them had mulatto maids to wait on them while living this secluded life. The clergy, especially the Jesuits, formed a strong moral and cultural nucleus around which society could develop, and even the menfolk during the first part of the century thought much of religion after their excesses of former decades. Reflecting the new security, fathers pointed with great pride to their daughters who had taken the veil and to their sons in the priesthood. But as the century advanced and French ideas flowed in, the younger generation of men gradually became freer in thought and drifted away from the gathering point of the Church in order to assemble around that of political liberty.[75]

During the first half of the century, when things were settling down into the general mold, with order, material prosperity, and colonial culture on the ascent, Chile in many ways resembled the Mexico or Peru of one hundred years earlier. The same air of charm existed for the upper classes, the same feeling of having at last achieved the victory and now being able to enjoy in security the fruits of their conquest. One or two fundamental differences, however, show how deceptive these surface appearances were.

Unlike the vast Indian population of Mexico and Peru, Chile's masses were mainly mestizos. Therefore, in the following years, no racial and cultural cleavages arose to tear apart the fabric of Chilean life. The mestizo was indeed forced into a state of economic servitude on the country's great landed estates where he took the place of the Indian, but he did not cease fighting for his political rights. In the second place, the ruling caste, which had already learned how to accept the freer mestizo in place of the enslaved Indian, would, at a later date, also be willing to accept a freer middle class in place of the exploited mestizo. In the third place, the mestizo himself, feeling that he really belonged in the main stream of his country's society, was ultimately able to achieve his rightful place in the national life.

Chile's total "civilized" population at this time (1700) was considerably less than half a million. So, in addition to being a "harmoniously concerted society, respectful of constituted authority," she was also small enough to be highly malleable in a social sense. When a strong current struck her it would not bounce off as it did in the case of ponderous Peru or sprawling Mexico, whose split populations were at least ten times as large. On Chile's small and plastic spirit an impression could easily be made, especially so since the country had just reached that point at which growth and nourishment might be most expected. Such currents as did strike her in the eighteenth century were of various natures.

First, there was the spirit of political liberalism which the Bourbons had brought into the peninsula and the Spanish colonies with the accession of Philip V to the throne of Spain in 1700. Second was an increasing wave of immigrants of fine stock who came to Chile, attracted by her progressive spirit, immigrants who knew that her long seacoast had placed her in contact with the ships, the peoples, the trade, and the trends of the seven seas. There were hard-working Basques by the thousands, a sprinkling of Irish, French, and English traders, Spaniards from many provinces who came, knowing that they would find no soft and easy life, but only a chance to achieve something through their own efforts. Chile was small

enough and far enough removed from the great centers of viceregal aristocracy and wealth not to be set in her ways, and these immigrants, with
their new blood, their new ideas, and their hard work, very quickly became
an organic part of her society, helping to brush away many of the lingering
gossamers of colonial thought.

One characteristic of the eighteenth century, however, was carried over
into the period of independence and has survived to this day. Its effects in
Chile were particularly strong. It was the deep admiration for French culture which arose at this time, and which has been widespread in Latin
America ever since. Obviously, French influence never supplanted the
Spanish tradition, which was basic, omnipresent, and of more enduring
root. But it did become almost a cult, and has remained so among the
minority intelligentsia of many countries today. The reasons for this are
both historic and psychological.

Historically, France in the eighteenth century was the leader of world
thought. Louis XIV, who reigned for the incredibly long span of seventy-
two years (1643–1715), was Europe's most famous, most powerful king.
His dream of dominating Western civilization was spent in a series of wars
which turned all his neighbors against him and finally exhausted the military resources of his country. Nevertheless, the following years saw the
greatest ascendancy of French culture. With Rousseau and Voltaire at
their head, French writers were perhaps the most powerful single influence
in bringing about the end of political despotism in France, Spain, and
eventually in the Spanish dependencies. The idea of Gallic cultural superiority, and the acceptance of French as the international language,
arose in that century and has not died yet in many parts of slow-moving
Latin America, although Germany's defeat of France in 1940 dealt it a
staggering blow.

Spain's contact with France in the early years of the eighteenth century
were especially close. Charles II of Spain, "bewitched and impotent," had
no direct heir. Germany, France, and England were all squabbling over
the Spanish crown before the King himself was dead. In this wrangle Louis
XIV obtained the support of the Pope, and so on his deathbed Charles II,
who hated the French, signed away his patrimony to Philip of Anjou,
grandson of the great French monarch. Then, overwhelmed with a sense
of disaster, the King of Spain fell back on his pillow, broke into tears, and
murmured: "I am already nothing." Almost immediately Germany and
England declared war on France and Spain, in an effort to enthrone an
Austrian prince, and the thirteen-year War of the Spanish Succession was
begun. It ended with the exhaustion of both sides. The Bourbons were
permitted to keep the Spanish throne, but there was never to be a union
between that country and France.

With the advent of Philip V to power in Spain, "there was inaugurated
in the New World an epoch which must be pointed out as the first breeze

of liberty that let itself be felt in the dominions hitherto under the iron grip of the empire on which the sun never set."[77] One hundred years later that same French liberalism fanned the flames that burst into the wars of independence.

Spain's Charles II left almost a vacuum when he died: an army consisting of one division, a bankrupt treasury, no fleet or merchant marine. During his entire reign (1665–1700) "the population of some six million souls dwelt in misery in a country without roads, without commerce, and without industries. The aristocracy was ignorant and haughty, the clergy fanatical, the King an idiot."[78]

Philip V and his able ministers began the work of reconstruction with energy. They reformed Spanish government, cut down bureaucracy, established the royal academies of language and history after French models. They cleaned up the colonial tax policy whose revenues had been leased to revenue farmers and whose proceeds "were consumed by swarms of office holders. Even positions so high as the viceroyalties, as well as lesser administrative places, had been sold to produce funds which had been wasted in bootless wars."[78] More efficient control and better administration now became the order of the day; both improved steadily as the century progressed. Life in the colonies was also visibly affected, and in the beginning with somewhat of a jolt.

When the War of the Spanish Succession began, Spain found herself under immediate blockade by the English and Dutch fleets. The few ships she was able to send to America were promptly chased down and captured. The treasures of Peru, so necessary for the prosecution of the war, might as well not have existed. In these desperate straits, and with her own coast line under constant peril of enemy attack, she was forced to follow the more southerly route around Cape Horn to the Pacific coast. Her vessels were not equal to the task. She threw open the gates to France, and for the first time in history her American colonies engaged legally in trade over a direct route carried on by the fleet of a foreign power. French vessels in considerable numbers sailed along the coasts of Chile and Peru laden with goods and protecting those shores from the depredations of the British and Dutch. Throughout the thirteen years of warfare this commerce continued. When news that the Peace of Utrecht had been signed reached Chile in 1713 there were in the harbor of one port alone, Penco, "not less than fifteen French vessels boasting a total of 250 cannons and with more than 2600 crew members aboard."

French commerce around Cape Horn had already transformed completely the condition of Chile, subjected formerly to the tyrannical manipulation of the merchants of Peru who controlled Chilean products. French vessels flooded the shops of Concepción, Santiago, and La Serena, with a multitude of articles hitherto unknown in the country, or at least so rare and so costly as to make their purchase all but impossible. Fine clothes,

laces, perfumes, jewelry, ribbons, mirrors, and sundry articles, adding to
the general amenity of life, entered Chilean ports in an ever-increasing
stream. Glass panes for windows for the first time became available in
any number. Comfort, refinement, and manners all took a spurt forward.
Many French sailors, "attracted by the benign climate and the beauty of
Chilean women, established their homes in the colony."[77]

Many books which would otherwise never have reached the country
were brought in on these French vessels and became the basis of education, thought, and culture in the larger centers, not only in Chile but
throughout the rest of South America. French scientists also visited the
colonies and gave a lift to the long-outmoded Spanish approach in many
fields. Some of them wrote invaluable books on the New World.

Most important of all was the fact that during these years it became
the fashion to admire French things, clothes, books, manners, ideas.
France had taken Spain's place as leader of the Latin world, and has not
relinquished it to this day. The Spanish dependencies, who had already
suffered much because of their mother country's backwardness and intolerance, naturally grasped with eager fingers at this new cult on their horizon. Its charm was overpowering.

The War of the Spanish Succession lasted thirteen years; at its conclusion many of the former restrictions on colonial trade were lifted. This
liberal policy grew broader as the century advanced, and by 1778 the last
of the Spanish fleets had sailed and the colonies were wide open to commerce with all friendly nations. The entire eighteenth century, therefore,
represents for Spanish America a new growth of body and spirit which
were inseparably bound up with the great French nation, whose Bourbons
sat on the throne of Spain and whose culture had furnished the food on
which these ideals came to fruit. So much for the historic reasons of the
"French cult" in Latin-American life.

There was a psychological reason as well. In those days of the eighteenth
century the mestizo was just beginning to come into his own. During the
nineteenth century he became predominant in many countries. Chile was
probably the first region where race-mixing almost obliterated the extremes
of red and white to produce a new and homogeneous mestizo race. French
influence in Chile has unquestionably been strong. The mestizo, of course,
followed his betters when he saw them swept away in admiration for
French culture. But there was a more fundamental reason than this. The
mestizo is forced toward snobbery wherever he is and of whatever blood.
He resents his white "superiors" and looks down upon his red or colored
"inferiors." He is obsessed with a desire to show off his superiority, whether
it is real or not. As intellectual values have always been highly regarded in
Latin America, the mestizo of those regions was anxious to display his intellectual endowments, his broad knowledge, his world vision. He could not
begin to read a page of German or of English; those languages were too

utterly foreign for his own make-up, his language, and his traditions. But French was sufficiently similar to Spanish for him to be able at least to read at it. He might understand only 75 per cent, or 50 per cent, or even less of what he read, but when he placed a French book under his arm he became immediately the admiration of his mestizo companions. That, in a nutshell, is the story of French influence in Latin America as seen by one of her most distinguished intellectual leaders. Generally speaking, this influence has always been a surface thing like manners, etiquette, or fashion. The "cult of France," beginning in the eighteenth century, became an intellectual and political fashion in Latin-American life. It is now rapidly being supplanted by the "cult of the United States."

"Let us turn our gaze backwards," writes a Chilean essayist in recapitulation. "The men dressed in iron of the sixteenth century—it must be remembered—gave birth to a generation of barbarians clothed in silks and laces, and perhaps this seemed natural to us; but when these barbarians clothed in laces and silks left behind a progeny of suave, affable, money-grasping men, with spiritual preoccupations, it doubtless appeared an incredible phenomenon."[75] When we add to these characteristics those of a growing social and political liberalism, the beginnings of a real national culture, and a strong cosmopolitan spirit, all shot through with the strongest possible practical sense, the country becomes an almost incomprehensible anomaly among the Hispanic nations. "The key, the true key to the problem, is concealed in a long ethnic and educational process, begun in the early colonial days but whose fruits we are only now able to comprehend."[76] Its result was a complete fusion of the races and the improvement of both in the mestizo stream.

It must be pointed out, however, that even in the progressive eighteenth century Chile was still far from being what one would call a modern or well-educated nation. However, she of all Latin-American nations had best caught the spirit of the times and was emerging into the light. Educational growth was intrinsic to the process. There was a much greater stress on primary schools than there had been previously, but this meant simply that instead of instruction being limited to large convents, it was now offered in each parish. The methods used were primitive, and there were few books. The Spanish equivalent of our "spare the rod and spoil the child" was the accepted motto of every teacher and went as follows: "*La letra con sangre entra,*" or "It takes blood to let the learning in." The town or municipal councils supported many of these schools, and they were free. A director general of the educational system supervised them all. Since Chile, like the rest of Latin America, was under a one-church regime, this supervision of course had little to do with the curriculum, which was permeated with indisputable religious dogma.

In summary, then, the eighteenth century in Chile was sober, well ordered, harmonious, but constantly growing. Perhaps among the eighteenth-century characteristics that of an intensely practical sense was the greatest common outgrowth of them all. The ethnic counterpart of this practical sense was the country's eagerness to receive hard-working immigrants, her consequent absorption of the Indian natives, and a noticeable lightening of the mestizo's skin. One distinguished Chilean sociologist states categorically: "The mestizo class, which as we have said constitutes the great majority of the Chilean people, is the most glorious fruit of Spanish colonization."[76]

Long before independence, in the year 1791, there was no such thing as seeing in Santiago an Indian wearing his national costume or speaking his native language. At that early date Chile had reached a degree of homogeneity in feeling which neither Mexico nor Peru has reached today. At about this same time, on the eve of the struggle for freedom, the population of the entire country, totaling perhaps half a million, was divided as follows: 300,000 mestizos, 15,000 peninsular-born Spaniards, 150,000 native-born whites or Creoles, a mere 3000 pure Indians, 20,000 Negroes and mulattoes, and perhaps 100 or so persons of admittedly foreign nationality. Many others had undoubtedly gained entrance into the country by claiming to be Basques. There still remained on Chilean soil something like 100,000 Araucanians living in isolation in their southern territories, but these took no part in the national life. A final peace settlement with them was not signed until 1882.

The practical Chilean spirit was not given to flights of poetry or fancy. The country was too poor to nourish a gongoristic literature or an expensive art. The people were too much concerned with work to indulge freely in the pastime of invention or speculation. Their development was toward a strong body which later would harbor the creative mind. When independence came they received it practically, because they were prepared for it, and they achieved political union because it was a natural outgrowth rather than because it was an ideal. They had come to know the scope of their own abilities through a century of war, followed by a century of excesses, and that in turn succeeded by a century of practical living. Their greatest colonial creation was not culture or art, but an enterprising state.

28

THE ARGENTINE PAMPAS:
CRADLE OF A GREAT PEOPLE

While Chilean character was being tempered in the crucible of poverty and war, across the Andean barrier another great Latin-American region, the Argentine, was following a somewhat similar course. But it was not to be for so long a time; this land was different. It was broader, richer, ten times as large, and its vast central pampas reached from the country's heart straight down to the sea. In the territory of the Argentine could be found all climates, all geographical contours, all products.

The northern Chaco was a subtropical paradise of towering forests. In their shadow once stood the missions of the "Jesuit Empire." East of the Chaco was Paraguay, the nuclear colony; then came mountain-studded Bolivia on its high plateau, and below Bolivia the northwestern mountains and hills of irrigated Tucumán. South of all these stretched the central pampas, bordered on the far west by the jagged peaks of the Andes, and on the far south by the bleak, arid, and ugly Patagonian steppes. To the east of the pampas lay Buenos Aires and the south Atlantic.

The Chaco forests are one of the natural wonderlands of the South American continent. Here grew myriads of trees whose dried leaves furnished the region's most popular brew, the green yerba mate tea. Many of the wild yerba trees were so large that a man could not reach around them with both arms. Here also thrived the iron-hard quebracho and lapacho, whose timber will sink if thrown into the water and which have the durability of steel. The quebracho, whose name means ax-breaker, often reaches a height of seventy to eighty feet, and besides furnishing a unique source of lumber it also yields large quantities of tannin, which is an essential ingredient for curing leather.

The lapacho, perhaps even more lasting as construction timber, was widely used in building many of the Jesuit missions of northern Argentina and Paraguay, and beams of this wood have survived the humid tropical weather for nearly three centuries, whereas the iron employed by the Jesuit architects has long since rusted away. Polished lapacho takes on the smooth brilliance of red marble and makes a truly beautiful decorative or support- ing wood. In the Chaco forests also abound stands of magnificent cedars, some of them attaining a height of one hundred and sixty feet, and big stretches of algarrobas, another fine timber, whose leaves and fruit are used for fattening cattle, while the beanlike pods can be turned into the native firewater called *chicha*.

The central part of Argentina is pampas. On the north it is bordered by the giant subtropical Chaco and the irrigated mountainous northwest around Tucumán, one of the earliest settled districts. On the west it runs gradually into the foothills of Córdoba and then into the vineyards of Mendoza, almost directly under the Andes. This region belonged to Chile for over two hundred years. Tucumán, Córdoba, and Buenos Aires form a triangle, the heart and base of which is the Argentine pampas. Begin- ning at Buenos Aires, this great fertile prairie, the largest on earth, extends westward for five hundred miles, and is another five hundred miles from north to south. All of the pampas is a wide level highway converging on the queen port of the Southern Hemisphere. There are fine rivers skirting its eastern limits which flow from north to south and empty into the River Plate estuary, thus linking the northern interior with Buenos Aires. The land is fertile beyond conception. To the man on horseback it is a sea of grass which, somewhere on the far horizon, curves downward to meet the sky.

Radiating from the towns and cities that lie upon its hard flat surface, the pampas is a gigantic green field, more overpowering in its immensity than any mountain. Nothing really stands out on the pampas; "there is no middle ground." In every direction it is a highway of escape from which no escape is possible. Under the wings of an air liner it strokes past like some forgotten agricultural utopia, all fair, all flat, all limitless, yet so su- premely satisfying to the weary eye that it suggests the somnolent soft murmur of a final dream. The pampas empties into nothing; all the rest of Argentina seems but to border upon and empty into the pampas. The green mountains of the south move northward and become pampas; the cold barren steppes of Patagonia join them and become pampas also.[71] Mendoza's vineyards, the rolling sugar fields of northern Tucumán, the giant forests of the Chaco, all empty into the pampas which reaches down to Buenos Aires and to the sea. Even today this great heart of the Argen- tine has reached only its primary stage of development and so, for the fu- ture, "constitutes a veritable granary of the world."

In colonial days this immense region of pampas and all the bordering lands to its north formed a single political union, which was known as the River Plate or the Viceroyalty of Buenos Aires. It included one fourth of

South America and was made up of Argentina proper, Paraguay, Bolivia or Upper Peru, and, after Montevideo was founded (1729), a considerable portion of Uruguay also. Until 1776, when the River Plate became a viceroyalty in its own right, the whole territory was subordinate to the government at Lima, which was the central point of control for all Spanish South America. A secondary control station was established at Charcas (also called Chuquisaca, La Plata, and finally Sucre) in the province of Bolivia or Upper Peru.

Although the Spaniards did not recognize it at the time, nor indeed at any period throughout the colonial epoch, the 250,000 or more square miles of unbroken Argentine pampas constituted their greatest potential source of wealth in the New World. But as Spain had no excess of population, her colonies were not established through any economic necessity, nor with the drive to produce for life. The central economic motif of her colonists was to acquire. In the presence of precious metals the acquisitive instinct became an obsession. Argentina was neglected in order to favor Bolivia and Peru.

Thus, in spite of all her natural advantages, which constituted the basis of a productive rather than a symbolic wealth, Argentina proper, the focusing point of the entire River Plate territory, was thinly settled in colonial days. When the struggle for independence began, half of the viceroyalty's total population of approximately 800,000 lived in the Bolivian sector near the great silver mines of Potosí.

Argentina and Uruguay together held hardly a fourth of the total inhabitants, and 50 per cent of these were Indians. This most fertile region of all Spanish America was deliberately restricted and neglected in order that the more immediate wealth from the mines of Bolivia and Peru might continue to flow toward the mother country. The great trade fleets, which sailed from Spain once every year or two, disgorged their wares at Portobello, Panama, while direct commerce between Buenos Aires and Spain was prohibited. Imports destined for Argentina had to be carried via a combination land and sea route to Portobello, then to Lima, then across the Andes, then all the way through Bolivia and Argentina until they reached their final destination.

One reason for these regulations was the Spanish desire to establish a commercial monopoly with her colonies, but there was another powerful reason also, and one which made much better sense. An astute Dutch trader who traveled overland from Buenos Aires to Bolivia and back again in the years 1658–59, sums up the situation as follows: "I must not omit the reason which the Spaniards have for not tolerating that silver from Bolivia and Peru be shipped down the River Plate, nor that ships be allowed to trade freely with that region. If they permitted free commerce with Europe in that direction where the country is good and fertile, the land abundant in fruits, the climate healthful, and there are easy means of transportation, the merchants who trade in Peru, Chile, and Bolivia would soon abandon the route of the galleons across the Atlantic, then down the Pacific, and finally across the entire continent, which is difficult and mean, and would follow forthwith the route of Buenos Aires. This infallibly would result in the abandonment of a greater part of the cities in those other regions, for in them the climate is bad and the necessities and comforts of life are not available in such great abundance."[64]

Such a willful restriction placed by the mother country on the very elements of natural growth—accessibility and the opportunity to trade—for over two centuries prevented Argentina from becoming the wealthy agricultural colony for which her gifts of climate, fertile land, easy transportation, access to the sea, and industrious population so plainly endowed her. This absurd policy was based on the presumption then current throughout the world that gold and silver were of more value than a well-developed agrarian economy. Precious metals add to the wealth of individuals because the individual can buy whatever he wants or needs with gold or money. But precious metals mean nothing to a nation except in a false and temporary sense, because when a nation's economy becomes centered around the acquisition of these metals, her productive capacity in agriculture and industry is consequently diminished, and finally the very necessities of life must be purchased in a foreign and exorbitant market. Furthermore, the greater her supply of gold and silver becomes, the higher the prices asked for these foreign goods, and eventually she reaches the point at which the cost of producing precious metals is beyond her means to afford.

The necessities of life are food, clothes, and shelter, and if men are unable to buy these things, money, gold, or silver are of no use to them. A mining economy unsupported by a well-rounded agrarian and industrial development is the most certain road to national ruin. By the time Spain realized this now obvious economic truism she was more than two centuries behind the rest of western Europe in development, her colonies had lagged accordingly, and no part of this once-great empire has yet been able to make up the deficit. In those colonial regions best fitted by nature for productivity and trade, this policy was bound to be most objectionable, for it placed an arbitrary limitation on both. Consequently, the history of Argentina is wrapped up in her struggle to throw off these unnatural restrictions.

Concomitant with this struggle were several other molding factors. First, the frontier continued to exist in Argentina for nearly three centuries, and, as in the cases of Chile and the United States, it was a tremendous influence in the development of national unity. Second, there was neither gold nor silver in Argentina proper, and her economy of necessity was agrarian, her workers agricultural laborers or herders rather than miners. This meant that once social stability was attained these essentials of life—

food, clothing, and shelter—would be more abundant and more easily acquired by the average individual in Argentina than elsewhere in Latin America. In the beginning the economic status of the country was unquestionably primitive, but it was also unquestionably laid on a broader base than that of Mexico, Peru, or Colombia.

Third, in spite of the fact that the threat of Indian raids continued to exist along the Argentine frontier for nearly three centuries, a few years after the firm establishment of Buenos Aires in 1580 thousands of natives had submitted to the conquest. These Indians worked on the lands of their masters and made good farm or ranch hands. They were not forced to undergo killing labor in mines. In many sections they thrived and their women entered freely into unions with Spaniards. They were nowhere so numerous as to make pure Indian blood racially dominant for long, nor were they universally such bitter fighters as the Araucanians, thus making almost impossible the relationship of employer and laborer. As a consequence Argentine society was less feudal than that of any other Latin-American region, and the basis for a democratic social structure was laid. All the fruitful elements of life and progress were there, both in the inhabitants and in the land itself.

Out of unions with the natives who submitted to the Spanish way of life a "new, strong, and beautiful" race quickly emerged, and after the River Plate region had been occupied for four decades the children of Spanish men and Indian women were considered as pure Spaniards and constituted the very lifeblood of the colony. At the same time the natives themselves, subjected to social servitude but not to enslavement, shared with their masters the advantages and the penuries of the new life, laboring for them and with them, but eating the same bread.[79] Native blood thus entered the Spanish stream in Argentina with infinitely greater ease than in Peru or Mexico, and the doctrine of racial hatred, which for so many years had held the mestizo apart from society as a whole in Chile, did not exist in the territory across the Andes. On the contrary, those Indians who had become a part of the Spanish colony were forced by the circumstances of frontier warfare to turn to their white masters for protection against the more savage tribes which would have slain them.

In the early colonial years "as the free bounty of nature and the fruits of labor were more or less the patrimony of the entire community, as civil life was uncomplicated and the clash of interests less harsh, as in reality there were neither poor nor rich, all being relatively poor, there resulted from all this a kind of equality or social equilibrium which held from the beginning the seeds of a free society.

"The geographic contours of the land contributed powerfully to these results. The immense and unbroken pampas gave its unity to the territory. The Plate Estuary centralized all communications. The naturally fertile pasture lands extended a helping hand to pastoral development. An extensive seacoast placed the region in contact with the rest of the world by means of river or maritime navigation. Its healthful and temperate climate made life more pleasant and work more productive. It was, in brief, a territory ideal for cattle-raising, well-constituted geographically to prosper through trade, and predestined to become populated through the acclimatization of all the races on earth."[79]

The progress of the Argentine commonwealth from a poor to a wealthy community did not follow a single course, for, while the misleading wealth of immense quantities of silver was making Potosí the most populous and richest city in both Americas, the colonization of Buenos Aires and the surrounding plains "was being born amidst hunger and misery, begging the earth for its sustenance, and strengthening itself on one hardship after another." Then finally, when the great horn of plenty which was the pampas began to pour out its riches into the port on the River Plate, Argentina commenced a long ascent which has not yet reached its peak, while the Bolivian and Paraguayan parts of its territory, isolated and abandoned, remained at a standstill for centuries and even today are the most backward communities of all South America. We have already traced the rise and fall of Potosí, of Bolivia. The story of Paraguay is not at all similar, but it leads to the same dead-end street.

Here was a region where life was too easy, the climate too conducive to indolence, and morality so loose that men and women seemed to exist for no other purpose than fornication. The immediate result of this was a prolific mestizo race, but with such a preponderance of Indian blood that instead of becoming more vigorous and more progressive as the years passed, it became more backward, tended to revert more and more toward the old ways of life, and the small Spanish stream was almost blotted out in the native flood which engulfed it. There has never been sufficient immigration into Paraguay or Bolivia to give either of these countries a new impetus forward, and until that day arrives they are doomed to sporadic moments of progress which bud precariously but seldom mature on the supine inertia of centuries.

Historically, however, the roles played by these two regions have been fundamental in the development of South America. Bolivia, the so-called "land of mines," was one of the strongest reasons for the existence of Peru, and this region was, after Mexico, Spain's most favored colonial possession. Paraguay possessed no wealth in metals but was the nucleus or strong point to which the exhausted colonists of Buenos Aires retreated when that city was abandoned, and was later the center from which the lower River Plate and the port were repopulated. While living in Asunción, Juan de Garay, later the founder of both Santa Fe, halfway down the river, and of Buenos Aires, near its mouth, had expressed the feeling "that we should open the gates into that region and that we should not be inclosed." However, the result was that these gates were soon thrown so wide and were so strategically placed that, before long, landlocked Paraguay was abandoned to its fate and the focus of colonization in the River Plate region passed into the hands of Buenos Aires.

In the meantime life pursued its seedy, pleasant, but inexorable way in the colony of Paraguay, where starlit skies looked down on so many torrid nights that sleeping indoors became impossible, and men and women alike laid their blankets along the streets and slept there together, indulging freely in all the promiscuous pleasures of love-making. It was a land in which the nights seemed made for sexual release; the days were entirely too hot for comfort or for extended labor, and the soil too fertile to make necessary much work for a living.

By the mid-century (1650) Paraguay's energy as a molding factor in River Plate life had already passed its peak and was on the rapid downgrade. "In this city of Asunción," writes a visitor to the capital at that time, "the native Indians as well as the Spaniards are obsequious to foreigners; they give themselves freely to the pleasures of the flesh, even the women. And since they have a great abundance of good things to eat and to drink, they indulge in promiscuity and indolence without bothering to trade with the outside world, nor to earn nor save money, which for this reason is very scarce amongst them. They seem completely contented with exchanging their own products for others which are more necessary or more useful."[64]

If racial amalgamation alone was the highest goal of the conquest, as some Latin-American historians seem to believe, "the mixing of Spaniards and natives was exemplary in Paraguay. Irala was the perfect colonizer who knew how to fuse an army of a few dozens of Spaniards with a populace of thousands upon thousands of Indians . . . Life in Asunción was compared with a Mohammedan paradise because each Spaniard had at his disposal a number of women ranging from five or ten to a hundred. Among them were mothers, daughters, and sisters, and all shared the marital pleasures of the conquistador who possessed them. The clergy shouted to high heaven; but the Spaniards sealed family alliances with the innumerable relatives of these Indian women and thus each white man was able to call himself the brother, uncle, or son-in-law of hundreds of Indians . . . Peace was assured and thanks to the immorality of the Spaniards the colonization was made safe from the assaults of the more savage tribes."[80]

So far so good. But a successful colonization does not merely rest on possessing the land or controlling the people; it rather depends on whether that land and those people can be revitalized and integrated in the direction of growth and progress. Despite the good beginnings of assimilation and the absence of strong racial or economic conflicts, this was obviously not the case in Paraguay.

Nevertheless, this landlocked region was the nerve center of colonization along the River Plate for half a century. Fortunately the degeneracy caused by its stagnation did not follow those colonists who left it for the broader and fresher currents which swept toward Buenos Aires from across the open sea. Never was the destiny of a great city more heavily insured by the privileges of geography than that of the Argentine metropolis. In time, when this insurance had been collected and the capital had grown out of all proportion to the population of the land around it, South America's proudest jewel would lie like a dead weight athwart the fertile pampas which was its home. This turn of events, however, did not come about until our own time, long after the heroic days of the growth of Argentine nationality.

The progress of Argentina from poverty to riches depended mainly on three factors: incorporation of the natives into the new social structure, immigration of Spaniards, trade. Given these three things, the colony was bound to grow and enrich itself rapidly. Its principal source of wealth, throughout the colonial period and far into the nineteenth century, was there for the taking and needed only a stable society to be converted into a profit. When the first settlement of Buenos Aires was abandoned in 1541 several horses and mares were left behind and escaped to the open country. These multiplied so rapidly on the succulent fodder of the pampas that when the city was refounded in 1580 they had already increased to many thousands. Friar Rivadeneyra, in a letter written to King Philip II in 1581, made the first mention of these wild horses, stating that there was "a tremendous number" of them. Garay himself, founder of the city, in that same year made a trip southward with thirty companions in search of the famous City of the Caesars, another one of those undying illusions of El Dorado. They did not discover the fabulous city, but did come across several herds of wild horses. One writer asserts categorically that by 1585 there were at least eighty thousand of them. Another author, who was on the scene in 1600, refers to the great herds as stretching over such vast expanses of territory that they resembled "huge tracts of tree-covered land."

The cattle industry had a similar beginning. Around 1552 the Portuguese brothers Goes brought seven cows and one bull over water and land to Paraguay, where they were worth their weight in gold. Later others were added to this stock pile, and they all multiplied prolifically. When Garay refounded Buenos Aires, less than thirty years after the first cattle had entered the River Plate district, he and his sixty-three colonists carried along with them one thousand horses and five hundred cows. Some of these in time also escaped to the pampas and added to the wild stock already living there in great herds. The first ship which sailed for Spain with news of the city's refounding carried a cargo of Argentine hides. Outside of the land itself, which was basic, cattle, horses, and mules constituted the true wealth of Argentina.

Such an assortment of wild stock, even though they numbered many thousands, was not alone sufficient guarantee of a healthy economy. In the first place, they gave the Indians of the pampas both an excellent source of food and clothing as well as a new means of attack. It was not long before these savages felt as much at home on horseback as a Spanish cavalryman, and this made their hit-and-run raids doubly dangerous. Each Spanish town became a stronghold, and life there was very similar to that of the early settlers along our own frontier.

Prior to the securing of a port (1580) the stream of colonization reached Argentina overland from the north and from the west. The northern currents came both from Peru (via Bolivia) and from Paraguay, the Peruvian stream flowing into northern and then central Argentina, whereas the Paraguayan colonists, as we have seen, came back down the river to found first Santa Fe and finally to re-establish Buenos Aires. A third movement entered the Argentine from Chile, coming across the mountains of the west.

In point of time the Peruvians arrived first and laid out a settlement called Barco, near present-day Tucumán, in 1550. Valdivia, governor of Chile, considered this trespassing on his grant and promptly sent an expedition to take it over. There was a clash between the two groups at Barco, and Valdivia's men won out, moving the entire settlement to another location not far away. This was Santiago del Estero (1553), which became the first permanent Argentine settlement. Five years later another expedition from Chile crossed the Andes and founded three more towns in the northern Argentine province of Tucumán, but only one of them, Londres, survived. The men from Chile were also responsible for Mendoza (1561), San Juan (1562), and San Luis (1596), all just across the Andes from Valdivia's domain. A few years later the King placed Tucumán definitely under the Viceroy at Lima, and then the Peruvian stream of colonization, which came via Bolivia or Upper Peru, again got on the move and established several towns. The first of these was Tucumán (1565) in the north. Then they reached far down into central Argentina to found Córdoba (1573) on the western fringe of the pampas. With these anchor points secure, the colonists from Peru laid out three other settlements in rapid succession, all of them in the north: Salta, La Rioja, and Jujuy.

In the very same year that Córdoba was founded by these Peruvian settlers, Garay and his mestizos from Asunción laid out their city of Santa Fe (1573) on the river halfway between Paraguay and the Atlantic. Seven years later Garay and another group of Spaniards and mestizos resettled Buenos Aires. This gave King Philip II a South American empire that stretched "from sea to sea."

The early days of all these towns were full of trial. There were no precious metals, no Indian cities, few cultivated fields. Over the surrounding country roamed indomitable tribes, dressed in rude animal skins, whose primitive diet consisted of corn and game. Like their brethren of North America, they were sometimes inclined to be peaceful and at other times swooped down on the Spanish settlements with fire and sword. When one of these raids occurred the friendly Indians who lived near the settlements would come rushing from the fields to seek shelter inside. The alarm bell then commenced its terrifying clang, and the men-at-arms leaped on their horses and dashed toward the main plaza, adjusting their armor and helmets as they went. The captain in charge hastily formed ranks and made ready to fight.

By this time the assailants would have run like an avalanche over whatever friendly Indians obstructed their path, and would be advancing upon the settlement like a whirlwind. The Spanish soldiers generally went out to meet them, seldom awaiting the attack inside the town. Under a rain of arrows, spears, and sometimes of deadly stones hurled from slings, all accompanied by shrill and savage shouts on the part of the attackers, the tiny garrison would stand its ground. Its infantry formed a compact square in order to break up the momentum of the onrushing mass, while the cavalry charged into their midst. Often these encounters went on for many hours at a time, yet when the first clash was over and the Indians withdrew it was only a beginning. With the full knowledge that further attacks were certain, the Spaniards often followed the enemy day and night, giving him no respite, hitting him here, striking him there, never affording him an opportunity to work up another psychological frenzy which seemed the necessary prelude to a full-scale assault.

"These fights went on at all hours, in the clearings of woods, in the middle of swamps, on rocky mesas, in shallow river beds, on the grass covered pampas, under a broiling sun, or during the darkness of the night. Finally, when human endurance could stand no more, the men would return, famished and starving, disfigured with powder burns, sweat and blood, and so exhausted that they were hardly able to lift hand or foot." Their women, who had been intermittently praying and weeping while they were away, came forth to greet them with shouts of welcome and triumph. After a brief rest the normal order of life would be resumed "with its mixture of privations and idleness, its minor squabbles over some Indian worker who had fled to another colonist's *encomienda*, over an Indian woman who was brutally desired, or over some legal question which exasperated spirits temporarily."[81]

Oftentimes the encomenderos would leave town in order to live on their fiefs among the Indians, allotted to them where they might enjoy a sort of small-scale omnipotence. This was strictly against the law, as it not only denuded the towns of their garrisons but frequently threw the Indian hamlets into disorder and even into moral chaos. Most encomenderos had a regularly established family in town and an irregular Indian harem somewhere out in the country among the natives. Tucumán was nearly obliterated on two or three occasions because its encomenderos were not present in sufficient numbers to defend it. Occasionally all of the forces available were insufficient to withstand the raids of the savages. "Town after town then fell in rapid succession, the friendly Indians were almost annihilated, garrisons were besieged, fields were laid waste but there was always a settlement or two which pushed back the barbarians and remained like an island in the midst of a furious sea as a monument to its own heroism. From these centers other towns would be raised to take the place of those that had been destroyed."[81]

Money was scarce in all parts of Argentina, and Indians usually received payment for their labor in cotton cloth. Wages for six days' work was a yard and a half of this cloth, valued at six reals, or about a dollar. Luxury in dress was rare indeed, but some of the women did bring costly clothes from Peru or purchased them through contraband. Means of communication were few and difficult, and the daily routine inside these small towns would have been of deadly monotony had it not been for the ever-present fear of an Indian raid.

Many Argentine encomenderos had only three or four Indians under them, but a few had four or five hundred. Some personally oversaw the cultivation of their lands, meted out just treatment to their charges, and did all that was in their power to help civilize them. Others were cruel to an extreme and when forced to return to their town left their fiefs in the hands of overseers, often mestizos, who were taught to abuse the natives pitilessly. Some overlords struggled to amass a few ducats so that they might be able to purchase one of the government positions with a title and be called "powerful sir" or "magnificent sir." All of the faults of Mexico, Peru, and Colombia were to be found in the Argentine also, but the scarcity of wealth kept corruption to a minimum, while the relationship between Spaniards and subjugated or friendly Indians was generally on a better basis here than in any other Latin-American country.

Women were almost one hundred per cent illiterate during the first years, and were uninformed in every way except in regard to domestic duties and religious practices. Almost invariably when a woman found it necessary to sign a legal paper she had to do so with a cross. Many governors did their best to find good mates for the daughters or widows of soldiers killed defending their towns, and sometimes a small encomienda with two or three Indians or some minor official position would take the place of the dowry which was the prerequisite to nearly every marriage. Irregularly established homes were also prosecuted by some governors who considered them a poor backbone for a stable society.

Intellectual life as it was carried on in the wealthier colonies was absolutely unknown in Argentina throughout the first century. Neither the atmosphere, nor the economy, nor the general tenor of living made it possible. Struggles between the civil and ecclesiastical authorities, the

arrival of a legal judgment from the Supreme Court or of some traveler
from Peru with news of Spain, Lima, or Sucre were ample themes for both
private and public conversations. The arrivals and departures of missionaries were events of transcendent importance in this dull life, and the
whole population usually turned out to welcome them or to bid them God-
speed. The visits of bishops or governors were also occasions for great
fiestas, but always the one imminent, crucial, inexhaustible, and ever-
present subject was the threat, immediate or distant, of the savage Indians, their campaigns, their assaults, their alliances, their truces, and
their warlike preparations, or perhaps some almost miraculous conversion
carried out among them by a Franciscan, Jesuit, or Mercedarian father,
renowned for his eloquence and for his valor, or else the return to his old
idolatrous religion of some famous native chieftain, or the exploits of some
intrepid soldier who dared pass alone through the regions inhabited by
these savage tribes.[81]

If the necessity for a lawsuit arose—and there were many of these due
to ambiguous property grants and ineffectual surveying—it was always
referred to the central court in Chuquisaca, Upper Peru, and the plaintiff
had to be present in person. Sometimes this entailed a trip of five hundred or even fifteen hundred miles, for Buenos Aires, too, was subject to
the legal jurisdiction of Chuquisaca. Spanish legal custom being what it
was, this usually meant a tedious wait of months, or in many cases of years,
before the case finally came up in court. In the meantime, the plaintiff's
funds were often exhausted, and he would return home in disgust without ever appearing before the judge, or, with his imagination inflamed,
would join the procession of those who went to seek their fortunes in
Potosí. If he was of an even more restless turn of mind he might wander
through Bolivia and Peru until he reached Lima, or else would head southward for Chile in order to take part in the Araucanian wars. "The three outstanding virtues of that early epoch were loyalty to the King, valor, and
the feeling of taking part in a religious crusade; the three greatest vices were
greed, sexual lust, and cruelty." Argentina, like the region of Chile across
the Andes, was a land being tempered by the suffering of privation and
war, the necessities of whose population had not yet evolved beyond those
of soldiers.

Six years after the permanent establishment of Buenos Aires the governor, Ramírez de Velasco, was sent to take over all this chaotic region of
interior and northern Argentina (1586). His governorship extended from
Upper Peru as far south as the city of Córdoba, situated in the central
Argentine foothills on the western edge of the pampas. There were five
towns in his jurisdiction at that time, populated with a total of only two
hundred encomenderos. Despite the abundance of cattle and the fertility
of the soil, poverty was general; the subject Indians frequently wearied of
their labor and fled to the open country, whence they pillaged the popu-

lated centers. Trade with Peru was slow and ineffective; travel was difficult because of the ever-present threat of ambush, and the towns themselves, as they appeared to Velasco when he finally reached them after his trip from Lima through "the four opulent cities of Peru," appeared little more than miserable agglomerations of adobe and wood buildings inhabited by concupiscent soldiers.

Previous governors had left the country in a turmoil, and the number of allotted Indians had been decreasing steadily in most sections. Velasco, who was a man in the stern conquistador tradition, immediately set about restoring order and brooked no halfway measures. He cleared the roads of pillaging bands by rounding up as many of the bandits as possible and having them all publicly executed. Then he went after more workers for his encomenderos. Regular Indian hunts were carried out on a small-scale bandeira fashion after the manner of Brazil; the war against recalcitrant tribes was pressed vigorously, and missionaries were employed to use every art of persuasion on those who showed the least inclination to enter peacefully into the Spanish scheme.

One day each week all encomienda Indians were ordered to come into town and work on municipal improvements. Immoral priests were summarily expelled from the domain, and with every promise of governmental assistance others were urged to take their places. The governor carried out these promises, but exceeded his own authority by establishing a sort of private inquisition to ferret out witch doctors in the Indian Pueblos under Christian jurisdiction. On one occasion he had a number of them burned alive. He also went after the immoral encomenderos and, invoking his power to distribute and in certain cases to take away lands, cleaned up many an irregular seraglio. These measures of purification did not last long.

Mills were constructed, irrigation ditches dug, and every effort was made to establish regular channels of trade. Imports from Spain were so exorbitantly priced that it was impossible to live with luxury in interior Argentina at that time, nor was this by any means Velasco's ideal. He wanted merely to establish a firm agricultural and livestock economy which would raise life to a stable and comfortable basis. Caught as he was between Buenos Aires and Potosí, without the advantages of either, this was the only course open to him.

In spite of these labors, or perhaps because of them, Velasco ran head on into Bishop Vitoria of Tucumán, a dictatorial prelate who seemed primarily interested in amassing a fortune as quickly as he could and then getting out of the country. The dispute between these two went on for some time and was the center of public attention throughout the country while it lasted. Hardly had Velasco arrived on the scene when the bishop wrote to the King in these terms: "Juan Ramírez de Velasco came to govern this country with such little talent for the office which your Majesty has entrusted to him that it is a pity to speak of it, for in fact I can state in all truth that he doesn't seem to be quite in his right senses."[81]

The governor sent a letter to the King at about the same time, stating: "In this city of Santiago del Estero is the cathedral which has as its bishop Father Francisco de Vitoria, of the Dominican Order, who is generally despised by everyone throughout the land."

The bishop then accused the governor of being so greedy that "he would eat up the profits of a thousand kingdoms." And Velasco came back at him with the accusation that "All the bishop's business seems to be in contracts and commercial deals from which he tries desperately to make a profit of a mere thousand per cent."

The bishop then wrote: "Because I corrected him he became my enemy and writes whatever comes into his head, also having the cheek to ask Your Majesty to make him perpetual governor of this territory in spite of the harm he has done. All he wants is to make these peaceful Indians slaves and to amass as much money as he can and establish large estates, and in this way he has gotten the whole country in a turmoil." The statement about Indian slaves might, at first reading, sound authentic, had not the bishop himself complained to the Supreme Court in Chuquisaca that he did not have enough Indians to perform his work and so had requested and received permission to import from Brazil one hundred and fifty Negro slaves for his own use. More than one hundred and twenty-five of these finally reached Tucumán.

The governor answered this charge with: "The lack of priests here is due to the treatment that the bishop gives them, for even the clergy are unable to stand him . . . He has excommunicated me twice because I ordered that no priest leave the city of Salta without permission." Salta at that time was merely a garrison rather than a town and, of all the establishments in Argentina, was the most frequently assaulted. It was surrounded by savage tribes and had to be maintained as a way station if travel through the district was to be carried on at all. Permissions for travel were necessary because people had to move in large escorted groups. The dispute involved here was not about the necessity of providing an escort, nor even about obtaining a permit; it was one of those jurisdictional questions as to whether the bishop or the governor should have control over issuing these permits when priests were concerned. Shortly after this last encounter the bishop, his pockets now well filled with ducats, was able to leave the province for good, and when the governor asked him to show his travel permit, he excommunicated him for the third time.

Of the five cities, or rather villages, which the Spaniards had established in this great interior territory of Argentina, none had as many as a hundred white inhabitants when Velasco became governor in 1586. However, these settlements were not isolated. They were all connected with a road called the "Peruvian Road," which was wide and fairly well marked. It required no special care, as most of the route was through flat or rolling country, although the rains sometimes turned it into a veritable lake. Velasco had inns put up in every town in order to encourage traveling. Goods were transported in huge *carretas*, two-wheeled carts with enormous wheels eight to ten feet in diameter, so that they would not get stuck in the mud. The town of Tucumán made a specialty of building them.

Along the road there would be an occasional Indian village of encomienda natives, but most of the distance was across uninhabited country. Not only were Indian ambushes a constant threat, but the tall grasses and occasional clumps of woods were infested with snakes and wild beasts. There were also great numbers of wild ostriches and deer. Traveling was generally by wagon train. Armed soldiers on horseback escorted the trains of enormous carretas loaded with the fruits of the soil and drawn by oxen. The Spanish inhabitants of the towns, nearly all of whom were men-at-arms, had the duty of accompanying merchants for long distances in order to protect the country's feeble economy. A caravan could tell when it was approaching an inhabited region because the fields there would be laid out in green and well-cultivated squares, small houses of laborers dotted the countryside, and flocks were scattered about, grazing in considerable numbers. Irrigation ditches in many sections were filled with flowing water as a protection against the frequent long, dry spells.

Prior to the coming of the Spaniards the natives had cultivated the land only in a few regions, and their primitive crops were limited to corn, quinoa, or wild rice, beans, and what wild fruits they could gather. The colonists who emigrated from Chile in 1556 brought with them seeds of many kinds—cotton, wheat, barley—and also cuttings from grapevines, and small fruit trees of several varieties. Within a few years the marvelous fertility of the soil had caused these to multiply in the greatest profusion. Indian raids, droughts, and swarms of locusts were the only drawbacks, and these were gradually controlled or overcome.

Ten years after Velasco's arrival he sent a report to the King (1596) in which mention was made of a total of 200,000 converted Indians, of whom 56,500 were allotted on encomiendas. The Indian men paid their tribute to encomenderos in personal services, while the women were generally required to spin one ounce of cotton per day as their share of the work. The three largest towns were the capital, Santiago del Estero, Córdoba, and Tucumán. Santiago, which was the most populous and wealthiest city, in the year 1583 was inhabited by only 48 encomenderos with approximately 12,000 Indians. By 1596 the number of Indians had gone down to 8000, and by 1607 they were still further reduced to 6729, distributed among 100 encomenderos. In 1583 Córdoba had 40 encomenderos and 12,000 Indians; by 1607 the number of encomenderos had grown to 60 and the Indians had decreased to 6103. Tucumán's encomenderos in 1583 had been 25 and her Indians 3000; by 1607 these numbers had become 32 and 1100 respectively.

The numbers of Indians allotted to each encomendero are also interesting. For example, in Córdoba, in 1607, one encomendero had 500 Indians under him, three had 200 each, five had as many as 100, and the remainder had on the average of between twelve and twenty, although some did have fewer than half a dozen. This was one of the most highly cultivated regions of the country; the Indians of the neighborhood were used to tilling the soil and made good farm laborers.

When the Spaniards arrived the natives lived in neat subterranean villages surrounded by cactus walls and carefully cultivated fields. Their clothes were of wool adorned with pretty designs and metallic spangles, and they carried a dagger hanging from the right wrist. Their houses were spacious, being large enough to hold "ten men mounted on horseback," and were dug out under the surface of the earth. Only the upper portion and roofs of the buildings were visible above the ground. The Indians themselves were described by one of the founders of the city as being "fine farmers, industrious, and sober in temper." They, together with the fertile and flourishing land on which they lived, were undoubtedly one of the primary causes for the growth of the town of Córdoba, which before long was to become the largest and wealthiest city of interior Argentina.

In the north conditions were not so favorable. The natives were much more primitive, and their only crops were a few scattered fields of corn. They wore ostrich feathers and animal skins, and the women sometimes dressed themselves in crude straw blankets. They did not make good workers, and fewer of them submitted to the Spanish regime. In 1589 the largest encomienda did not have as many as eighty Indians and the average was considerably below that of Córdoba. Nevertheless, the region prospered agriculturally and became a great sugar-producing center, as well as being the location of the factory which, in the early days, manufactured nearly all of the two-wheeled carretas used on the roads of Argentina.

This interior country between Córdoba, Tucumán, and the coast was the basis of the productive economy of all Argentina, while the port of Buenos Aires was the mouth of its funnel, the trade center and focus of its livelihood, the symbol of its wealth. As greater and greater quantities of produce flowed toward the queen city, bringing ever-larger returns, people and culture soon followed in their wake, and Buenos Aires in time attained a size and power entirely incommensurate with the national economy. A cleavage which split Argentina for many years then began to appear in the fabric of the nation. The seaboard and Buenos Aires stood on one side and the interior hinterland stood on the other. Each region was bitterly resentful and distrustful of the other, and each struggled to assume the leadership. Finally a measure of compromise was reached, but Buenos Aires continued and continues to exert an economic and psychological pressure on Argentina which has thrown out of perspective the entire social aspect of its people.

Obviously, a port alone, without a rich territory behind it, would be meaningless, and it is for this reason that the governor Velasco was so important in the history of his nation. He placed the productive economy of the land on a stable basis, gave it a system of communications and a system of laws, converted it from a hodgepodge of isolated and miserable way stations into an organized social force. The cabildos, or town councils, of Santiago del Estero and of Tucumán wrote to the King commending his "just and honest government." No force compelled them to do this; in fact, the cabildos were more often than not the harshest critics of their governors before the regal authority. But despite his inquisitorial bigotries so characteristic of the age, Velasco had indeed been a good executive. When he retired from the governorship he was not only completely bankrupt, not having received a cent for his services, but was unable to pay back the sums which had been advanced to him when he assumed office. In view of the promises of the country, he was expected to collect his salary out of the Royal Treasury at Potosí, but there had been so much red tape that he had never been able to do so. Consequently, when the government inspectors reviewed his term of office he was found guilty of not paying his debts and was condemned to prison. Velasco complained directly to the King and not only received a full pardon but was made governor of Buenos Aires. In the following year he died. His usefulness as organizer of the great hinterland and as a link between that region and the port of Buenos Aires had already been written, for better or worse, on the imperishable pages of Argentine history.

In the meantime, the city at the mouth of the funnel was also continuing its slow growth, despite the exasperating privations which must plague any incipient agrarian economy. Instead of attempting to ameliorate these conditions, the government of Spain seemed bent on accentuating them. Trade restrictions throttled every possibility of healthy progress. In 1594 the King decreed that no ship should go in or out of the River Plate, and the Bishop of Buenos Aires wrote, "If the port is closed up we will all soon be going naked or wearing animal skins." In 1599 one of the friars recorded that "there are not half a dozen citizens who have shoes to cover their feet, not a single one has socks of any kind, and only a handful can boast of owning a shirt."[82]

The city itself was a "mere bunch of huts . . . sleeping a siesta of the centuries." All buildings, religious, government, and private, were of "hardened mud and straw since no stones nor other permanent building materials were available." Immigrants who arrived there tried to get away as quickly as they could to some more promising locality. Buenos Aires was undoubtedly the most expensive city in all Latin America for imported goods, and its inhabitants were among the poorest. Ordinary cloth cost twenty to thirty dollars a yard; oil and wine brought a similar amount per jug, and in the earliest years iron was so scarce that it took six dollars to shoe a horse.

The monopolistic trade system was predicated on this false thesis: precious metals, gems, and pearls were more to be sought after than a stable agrarian economy. Consequently, every effort was turned toward their acquisition, and in order that they should not be shipped on several different routes, all open to piratical attacks, the route of the trade fleets was established by law. It just so happened that poor Buenos Aires was at the tail end of the line over land and over sea and had to suffer accordingly. The monopolistic principle resulted in high prices everywhere, but in those regions where there was gold, silver, gems, and pearls, and which were nearest Panama anyway, this meant only a relative hardship. Their wealthy classes merely paid the price. Even more distant Bolivia had its great mines at Potosí, so it, too, passed the buck. Buenos Aires, which had neither these sources of wealth nor a choice location close to Panama, got the buck, hair, hide, hoof, and all. She found it impossible to dispose legally of her large and bulky cargoes of hides, cereals, and grease, yet was obliged to make her purchases at Potosí, the highest market in South America, and at a distance of 1617 miles. Goods coming to Buenos Aires also had to be carried overland from Lima to Potosí, 1215 miles farther.

As one of Argentina's greatest historians and presidents points out, this policy "could only have been conceived by the imbecility of an absolute power, and supported by the inertia of an enslaved people." The whole thing wound up by "suppressing navigation, exaggerating the prices of European products and depressing those of American goods, making capital stagnate, discouraging work, provoking abuses, fomenting administrative corruption both at home and in the colonies, and creating sordid interests which thrived to the detriment of the community as a whole. Such a system inevitably embraced both the ruin of Spain and of America. Thus, before a century had passed, the population of Spain was reduced by half, her factories ruined, her merchant marine existed in name only, her capital had dwindled away, her commerce was carried on by foreigners through contraband, and all the gold and silver of the New World went everywhere except to Spain."[79]

Spain's fundamental error was not alone her overweening desire for precious metals. That desire was and is omnipresent in the psychology of people everywhere, and government policy could have altered it but little. The error lay rather in her obtuse restrictions on Argentina, a logical region to develop, and one which should have become, but never did, the granary and productive center of her colonial empire.

Buenos Aires, the focal point of this great potential storehouse, was situated on the biggest estuary in Latin America, near the mouth of one of the finest water systems in the world, one whose tributaries reached out across fertile interior lands like the fingers of some productive giant, and whose waters bathed immense regions of accessible plains over which transportation might be carried on with a minimum of difficulty. All of this territory had direct connections with Europe and was ideally situated. By the year 1600, however, Spain was under an absolutism so decadent that it had already lost its zest for life. Her ravenous jaw had bit off more than she could chew. Hers was by far the largest empire the world has ever seen. Her colonies were located in Africa, Asia, included a great portion of North America through Florida, the great Southwest, and California, and her King was also the supreme ruler of Portugal and of Brazil. Even though her fire was spent and her digestion overloaded, a modicum of tolerance in government and a small measure of progressive spirit in economics might have saved the day.

All that was needed in this vast empire was trade among its members, which would have meant growth. But Spain did not permit nature to take its course; she stifled natural law. There is no doubt that all this was done in good faith and sincerity, but the Inquisition was in her soul, in her body, and in her blood. It was this intolerance to growth and change which in the end spelled the doom of Spain as a great world power. Like every other empire in history, it finally encompassed its own destruction. It is a sufficient commentary on the depth of that error to point out that at present by far the most progressive countries of the former Spanish Empire are Argentina and Chile, its most restricted colonies; whereas among the most backward of modern nations are those which gave to Spain her wealth of gold, silver, and gems. Another and further proof of Spain's fundamental blindness is the fact that England, which in the year 1500 was a far smaller, less populous, and poorer nation, is even today able to boast of her headship in a mighty commonwealth of nations, and furthermore gave birth to the United States, one of the greatest of today's world powers. The English, despite their own tight-lipped bigotries, were willing and able to grow, whereas the Spaniards were not. Their psychology was that of the soldier: when strength failed there was no alternative but to dig a foxhole and crawl into it as the wave of battle passed them by.

Yet it was this same unwillingness to compromise which gave Chile and Argentina their start in the right direction. It forced their inhabitants to depend upon themselves for a living. An ever-present frontier and thousands of savage Indians completed the picture, bound their people together, and goaded them forward.

Spain, of course, was not completely adamant; not even the most absolute of tyrants can fail to take into account the sentiments of the majority of his subjects. Her concessions, however, were invariably too little and too late. Between 1541 and 1580, while Buenos Aires remained deserted, Argentine trade was, of course, virtually nonexistent. Beginning about

1580, a few single ships under special register or permit were allowed to enter the harbor of Buenos Aires. They could travel directly to Spain and, in certain cases, were allowed to trade with Brazil, then a part of the Spanish Empire. In 1595 one of the citizens was given the right to import six hundred Negroes a year for nine years, and the ships bringing in these slaves also carried a few clothes and provisions for them. It was forbidden "under penalty of death" to carry other goods; nevertheless this was done. Under the slave flag contraband merchants sneaked their way in, and thus began the illegal commerce which later was to become the most profitable industry of the country. The slaves themselves did not come in sufficient numbers to affect the economy or society profoundly; they went mostly to wealthy families where they worked as domestic servants. By 1776 there were one hundred and seventy-four free Negroes to one hundred slaves, and the proportion of blacks to whites was about one to five. They fought well in the war for independence.

Contraband trade continued to grow, and the King made a few small concessions to the colony. Each one of these brought a loud howl from the Peruvian merchants, who thus saw themselves cheated of just that many more customers. In 1622 certain imports were even permitted to pass through Argentina on their way to Peru, but an interior custom-house was set up at Córdoba where 50 per cent was added to their cost. When the expenses of the long overland trip were also tagged on, it is easy to see why this commerce remained at a minimum.

In the meantime, Holland and England were doing everything in their power to break in on the Spanish monopoly. In 1616 a Dutchman had discovered the route around Cape Horn, which was much safer than through the Strait of Magellan, and this opened up the entire region of the western South American coast, hitherto Spain's exclusive domain. These two great maritime nations were ready to take every advantage of the new opportunity thus placed before them. Like all the rest of western Europe, they were angered at the country which wanted to reserve for herself all this colonial wealth, and which was insistent that "the winds of the two great seas should blow only on her sails and that their waters should wet only the keels of her ships." In Holland there was both a psychology of freedom and a will to expand behind this imperialistic envy.

The little country at that time was not only the most liberal nation in Europe but the most aggressive and forward-looking as well. In 1625 Hugo Grotius, a Dutch jurist, published his famous work on international law, which has since become the starting point for any consideration of this field. In this book he proclaimed the freedom of the seas. It was no idle theory. Holland, between 1623 and 1636, launched more than eight hundred ships and during those same years forced more than five hundred and fifty Spanish vessels, loaded to the gunwales with New World gold and silver, to haul down their standards. She pushed her own colonial empire into New York, Dutch Guiana, occupied the six finest provinces of the Brazilian coast, and spread herself firmly in the Dutch Indies of the remote Pacific. For several years she possessed the strongest fleet in the world and her ships sailed the seas, trading wherever there was a market, legitimate or otherwise.

Anticipating what was bound to happen by nearly half a century, one of the great Spanish jurists, León Pinelo, in 1623 wrote, "Necessity has no law, and if license is denied them the colonies will go beyond the law, because they have a right to clothe themselves, to eat, to live!" Confronted by that necessity, abetted by a huge Dutch trade fleet and the proximity of Portuguese Brazil, which was an ideal center from which to carry on contraband commerce, the port of Buenos Aires commenced to take its first strong steps outside the monopolistic Spanish legal pale. What had begun as the tottering walk of a nation's infancy soon became the mad race of a vigorous child whose rebellious energy seemed boundless and free.

It was in the nature of things. When the Dutch traveler Acarette arrived in Buenos Aires in 1658 he saw in the harbor "twenty Dutch and two English ships loaded with hides, silver, and vicuña wool which they had received in exchange for their own merchandise." The port was already wide open, and smuggling was being carried on under the very noses and generally with the connivance of the Spanish officials. The ship on which Acarette himself arrived was one of the few which had obtained a special permit to enter Buenos Aires, so there was a great show of checking credentials. It carried a cargo of "silks, ribbons, thread, needles, swords, horseshoes and other articles of iron, tools, drugs, spices, a huge quantity of cotton cloth manufactured in Rouen, and many articles of wool."[64]

The traveler remained in the city several days preparatory to making his long overland trip to Potosí. He describes Buenos Aires as being a town of about four hundred houses and approximately fifteen hundred inhabitants. There was still constant danger from Indian raids, and, though they did not take place very often, the threat was always there. The governor kept twelve hundred horses in a neighboring field ready as mounts should the need arise. The houses in the town were made of adobe covered with a roofing of straw and reeds, and were all of a single story. Many of them were quite spacious, and nearly all had large patios. Behind them were orchards and gardens, where a profusion of fruit trees and vegetables grew. Fowls of many kinds also abounded, and people in general were living on a much higher scale than had been the case half a century earlier. The homes of the upper classes were adorned with many draperies, pictures, fine furniture, and other ornaments, and even those with moderate incomes owned silver services and had several servants, Indians, Negroes, mestizos, and mulattoes. "They employed these slaves," writes the traveler, "in domestic duties or to cultivate their fields, because they own large estates abundantly planted in grains; or to take care of their horses and mules which live entirely off the natural fodder of the pastures throughout the year; or perhaps to kill wild steers . . . The great wealth of these people is cattle which multiply so rapidly in this province that the countryside is almost completely covered with them. There are also innumerable sheep, horses, mules, donkeys, pigs, and deer, and if it were not for a great number of wild dogs which eat the young they would devastate the country."[64] This statement is doubtless somewhat of an exaggeration, as is the estimate that the twenty-two ships in the harbor were loaded with nearly three hundred thousand hides, but the fact becomes obvious that Buenos Aires was thriving by the middle of the seventeenth century. Compared with the miserable village of hovels of the year 1600, it was already a great commercial center. The cargoes of hides, which made up the principal commodity of the export trade, sold in Argentina for about a dollar each, but in the European market brought from five to six dollars. With the possibility of such fabulous profits in the offing nothing could have prevented the growth of contraband.

The traveler goes on to say that the majority of the cattlemen were extremely rich, "but among the merchants the most wealthy are those who trade in European goods; many of these have the reputation of possessing fortunes of $300,000 or more. Those who are worth less than $15,000 to $20,000 must be called small retailers, and there are perhaps two hundred families of them in the town." These all-too-specific estimates of Argentine fortunes must be taken with a grain of salt, for the traveler doubtless depended on hearsay, and the citizens of the great port have always been noted for their love of a bit of high color to adorn a tale. That some fortunes had been made in the Argentine as early as 1650, however, seems beyond any reasonable doubt. There were several foreigners in Buenos Aires, but all of these passed for Spaniards, "else they would not have been permitted to reside there, especially if they happened not to be Roman Catholics." The city also had a hospital to care for the poor, "but there were so few poor people in the vicinity that it was put to little use."[64]

The countryside west of Buenos Aires was spottily cultivated for about one hundred miles, and then there was a long stretch of several leagues covered with many kinds of wild fruit trees, especially wild peaches. Occasionally there would be a regular forest of these from ten to fifteen miles across. They produced excellent fruit which was eaten both in the ripe state and dried, and the tree itself was widely used for firewood in Buenos Aires and the surrounding districts. Within a very few years these wild peaches became almost extinct, and now the open country is as denuded as if it had never grown more than grass.

The city of Córdoba at that time, situated about five hundred miles west of Buenos Aires and on the other side of the pampas, was about the same size as the port itself, having a population of about fifteen hundred whites and forty-five hundred Indians, Negroes, and mestizos. Its trade was principally in mules, and between twenty and thirty thousand of these were sold to Peru each year. They brought five to six dollars apiece. The citizens of Córdoba also carried on quite an extensive business in pampas cattle, which they sold to people living in the mountainous regions of Bolivia who were always hard pressed for meat.

As early as 1609 the wild cattle on the pampas had become so numerous that the town council of Buenos Aires laid down the principle that, since they were all descended from escaped domesticated cattle, the owners of the latter should have first claim on them. Consequently, cattlemen of the city went before the courts to swear how many head had escaped, and they were then given the official right to ownership of a certain number of wild cattle. This right could be passed on to others through inheritance, donation, or sale, and continued until the eighteenth century. In many instances the ownership of land itself became confused with the right to take or slaughter cattle.

After Acarette had finished his round trip to Potosí, and the ship in which he held part interest had safely reached Europe again, he made an interesting review of the difficulties, expenses, and profits of the voyage. In the first place, the vessel had to remain in Buenos Aires for several months while the overland trip took place and the cargo was being collected. Sometimes it took as long as two years for a full load of hides to be gathered, because wild pampas cattle had to be hunted down for this purpose. Domesticated stock was not available in any considerable number until about 1725. Consequently, the rent of the boat and the wages of the seamen were always relatively high. The entire cost of this particular voyage to and from Europe had amounted to approximately $350,000. Of this total more than $2000 had been spent in Buenos Aires "in order to get into the city and as gifts to the officials, and it cost another $1000 to get out again." On the return to Spain there was a handout of more than $4000 "in order to keep from being searched and visited by the customs inspectors." In spite of these and many other expenses which made up the considerable total of $350,000, the Dutch trader estimated that profits of 250 per cent were made on the investment, certainly nothing to sneeze at. The ship was apparently a large one, for it carried seventy-six sailors and fifty passengers; the cost of a passage was about eight hundred dollars.

The seventeenth century saw the growth of Buenos Aires as a center of contraband trade, a growth which gradually swept all other considerations before it and became the very breath of life for the queen city of the Argentine. Only a few months after Acarette's trip several Dutch cargoes went through the customs openly (1660), and one of these, writes the Argentine historian, Bartolomé Mitre, was valued at more than $3,000,000. The credit of the new market was rapidly raised in the estimation of the outside world, and from this time on nothing could prevent a boom in the locally sanctified smuggling. The character of the new nation and of the turbulent and rebellious democracy in its economic order was plainly defined during these incipient years.

In the meantime, the River Plate's northern province of Paraguay, "isolated, reduced to its own resources, deprived of the revivifying currents of immigration and of the exchange of products, stagnated and ceased to be the center of a fruitful and growing civilization. In contact with the Portuguese of southern Brazil, the Paraguayans collided with them on the Upper Paraná and had to withdraw vanquished. Their province of Guayra was raided by the Brazilian-Portuguese frontiersmen of São Paulo, and three towns were wiped out for good. Simultaneous with this decadence another decomposing and sterile factor commenced to operate on Paraguayan society: the famous Jesuit missions, which constituted a theocratic empire, composed exclusively of Indians subject to a communistic regime and monastic discipline. The influence of these centers, which up to a certain point were favorable in the sense of forming a bulwark between Brazilian and Spanish territories, was in the end fatal for Paraguay. They stopped the impulse of European colonization, wherein lay the only possible seeds of growth, were an impediment to racial fusion which was the pacific means of conquest, and deliberately isolated the natives from all contact with European immigration. A great part of the country thus became occupied by an unconscious population and an artificial civilization."[79] The opportunity for growth or progress did not exist.

Fortunately for Argentina, in 1617 Paraguay became a separate political division and was no longer a drain on the scant resources of the port city and the interior plains. Even at this early date, which was several years before the Jesuit theocracy got fully under way, Buenos Aires had already become "the center of population for this vast southern region as well as its capital and its market."

However, the city was constantly under two disruptive influences: contraband trade, which fed its pocketbook well enough with the passage of time, but which also resulted in a great disrespect for established law, and the ever-present threat of Portuguese-Brazilian domination. These two factors were eventually fused into one because the Brazilians soon extended themselves southward to the very banks of the estuary opposite Buenos Aires, and, in 1680, founded a colony there which became the smuggling headquarters of the whole River Plate. A frontier conflict was certain to arise.

The Spanish-Portuguese boundary question had started with the famous Tordesillas line, which gave Portugal all territories to the east and Spain all territories to the west of a dividing line placed three hundred and seventy leagues west of the Azores. This division had been agreed upon only a few months after the discovery of America, while the Western Hemisphere was still thought to be Asia. That mistake alone had caused confusion, but the two countries had also neglected to state from which island in the Azores the three-hundred-and-seventy-league measurement was to begin. Spain claimed it should be an island in the center of the group; Portugal insisted that it should be the westernmost one. According to this latter interpretation, and perhaps with a little fudging on the part of Portuguese cartographers, Buenos Aires fell within her dominions. Since possession was nine tenths of anybody's law there was only the slightest chance of her ever occupying the city, so her Brazilian colonists did the next-best thing. They infiltrated into Buenos Aires in great numbers and moved southward from Rio and São Paulo until they had occupied a considerable part of present-day Uruguay. They had every intention of holding onto Uruguay permanently. As a matter of fact, in the year 1643, out of a total population of approximately fifteen hundred in Buenos Aires, three hundred and seventy were Portuguese. This was three years after Portugal had regained her independence from Spain. At the same time the Brazilian Paulistas were keeping up a constant pressure on the Spanish Jesuit mission territory and had driven several of these settlements a good many miles to the south.

Consequently, when the Portuguese colony of Sacramento was founded just across the river, the inhabitants of Buenos Aires very properly regarded it as a direct threat to their security and attacked forthwith. The Argentine governor Garro, aided by three thousand Indian soldiers from the Jesuit missions up the river, led the assault and took the town (1680). Portugal became incensed and threatened Spain, and that poor country, never at a lower ebb, yielded before her smaller adversary and made Garro give the place back again. For nearly a hundred years thereafter Sacramento was a thorn in the side of every governor of Buenos Aires, not only as a rival colony but as "the citadel of organized contraband." It was well fortified and menaced the navigation of both the rivers Paraná and Uruguay. "Slavers from England, Holland, and German ports crowded the harbor. Arms of all kinds were stored there, and were distributed to all adventurers who meditated assaults against the crown of Spain." Whenever contraband merchandise was denied an entrance into Buenos Aires directly, it went to Sacramento instead and was then sneaked in. On two or three occasions governors of the Argentine became furious and captured the citadel, but the home government seemed to suffer chronic cold feet and they always had to return it to Portugal. Finally they gave up in disgust and openly connived or took part in the lucrative contraband trade, but at the same time never ceased to covet the Portuguese stronghold. It is easy to see the importance of this city when we compare the Spanish and Portuguese fleets of those days. Spain, with fifty cities in her vast domain, sent an average of only six or eight ships per year, while Portugal, with only five cities in Brazil, sent over from one hundred and five to one hundred and twenty ships yearly. The lower duties paid on the Portuguese goods enabled merchants of that nation to undersell Spaniards and Creoles just across the river from their own market. This was adding insult to injury, and the only possible chance the Argentines had of evening the score was to destroy or take over the Portuguese citadel.

This prolonged struggle over Sacramento kept the two greatest regions of Latin America at each other's throats throughout the most crucial years of the colonial epoch, with first one and then the other holding the advantage. The Treaty of Utrecht (1713), which ended the War of the Spanish Succession, gave that citadel to Portugal. The movement of Portuguese and Brazilians into Uruguay then increased so rapidly that the inhabitants of Buenos Aires again arose in alarm. When Portugal occupied the beach at Montevideo, only a few miles from Sacramento, the governor of the River Plate assembled a small army and chased them out. Then, with the help of a thousand Indian workers from the Jesuit settlements, he constructed an Argentine fortress on the same site in the year 1726. Colonists were granted special immunities as an inducement to move across the river. In 1729 Montevideo was founded officially, and the two rival colonies then stared at each other over land as well as across the river.

In 1750 it was again agreed by treaty that Sacramento would be given to Spain permanently in exchange for seven of the best-developed Jesuit missions up the river. The Indians of this region rebelled against being turned over to their traditional enemies, the Brazilians, and flew to arms, fighting blindly against both Portugal and Spain. This was the so-called Guaraní or Jesuit War. The Indians lost; the missions were abandoned, and the Portuguese began to move in. The war had hardly ended when the new King of Spain, Charles III, hearing what a valuable region he had lost, decided that he wanted the territory back again, but by then the Indians had nearly all left anyhow, so it made little difference.

In 1762 Governor Cevallos of Buenos Aires, one of those dynamic leaders who has been called "the last flash of Spanish greatness in the New World," again attacked Sacramento, this time with an army of six thousand men. He took the place easily and was advancing rapidly into southern Brazil when the war was called off and he had to return the city to Portugal. The border question had by this time become one of paramount importance, and it was plain that Uruguay was the prize. The Argentines felt that their lives depended on control of the River Plate, and a Brazilian fortress across from their own capital seemed to them intolerable.

In 1776 the Argentine region was raised to the status of a viceroyalty, mainly in order that it might put an end, once and for all, to Portuguese expansion southward. For once Spain followed sensible geopolitics and placed under the new regime all regions which formed an integral part of its physical and economic domain. Bolivia and Paraguay, which flowed down into the pampas, became a part of it, and the rich province of Cuyo, under the shadow of the Andes, was taken from Chilean jurisdiction after two hundred years and added to the River Plate, where it had always logi-

cally belonged. Uruguay, with its havens of contraband, was also theoretically included, but as that region was then under Portuguese control
the decision meant that final ownership must be decided in the old way,
by force of arms. It was not long delayed.

The same Cevallos who had already taken Sacramento once was made
first Viceroy of the new River Plate domain, and at the head of "the largest
expedition that had come to South America during the colonial period"
(one hundred and sixteen vessels and ten thousand men), he again advanced into Brazilian territory. Cevallos not only captured the fortress but
was making ready to occupy Brazil's southernmost province, Rio Grande do
Sul, when peace was signed (1777). This time Spain got her hands firmly
on Sacramento, and her ownership of the then almost valueless mission
territory was also recognized. Brazil received great stretches of interior land
to the west of the Tordesillas line which her indomitable bandeirantes
had already explored and partially occupied. These regions make up the
heart of Brazil today. The contraband flag which had flown over Sacramento for one hundred years was finally lowered, and Argentina was left
in possession of Uruguay. She lost no time in settling it.

While this border rivalry was sharpening the feeling of nationality on
both the Spanish and the Portuguese side of the River Plate, Spain herself
was attempting to fight an even more deadly and insidious rival: the contraband trade. Buenos Aires was only one of many regions where smuggling had reared its ugly head in her dependencies. In fact, the eighteenth
century, in spite of the fairly liberal policies of the Bourbon kings, represents the enthronement of contraband over legal commerce. During the
War of the Spanish Succession (1701–13) French vessels had monopolized
it. A few of them were given special permission to trade with the Spanish
colonies, and dozens of others traded without permission. Then, when
peace was made in 1713, England secured the right to bring forty-eight
hundred Negro slaves into Spanish American ports annually for a period
of thirty years. She also was granted the right to send one ship a year duty
free to Portobello loaded with a maximum of five hundred tons of English
merchandise. The Spaniards should have known the English better; these
two concessions sealed the death warrant of Spain's commercial monopoly.

In the first place, using the slave trade as an argument, English merchants established themselves in several Spanish American ports. In the
River Plate they even received "vaguely bounded territory upon which to
establish plantations where their negroes could be employed." They
seemed to like the place, and several years later, at the beginning of the
nineteenth century, took over both Buenos Aires and Uruguay by force.
This has been fondly called "the purple land that England lost" and is
immortalized in the prose of that great writer and naturalist, W. H.
Hudson.

All of these English slave agents abetted smuggling, which rapidly became Latin America's chief industry. As for that single vessel which England was allowed to send duty free to Portobello, by 1736 it remained many months in front of the port "as a floating warehouse," loaded with many more tons of merchandise than it was supposed to carry. At the same time "at least forty English vessels of light draught were plying trade on the Atlantic seaboard of the Spanish colonies, in spite of protests."[78] In 1750 the slave agreement was terminated, but by that time the smuggling trade was firmly established. The period of the Seven Years' War (1756–63), known in the United States as the French and Indian War, "was a period of unprecedented contraband prosperity, which continued after peace was declared. During the latter half of the eighteenth century the Portuguese, the French, the Dutch, the English, and finally the Americans were all engaged in illicit commerce with the inhabitants of Spanish America, both on the Atlantic and on the Pacific coasts."[78]

The kings of Spain struggled against this in every possible way, but to little avail. In 1720 a program was devised whereby "registered ships" with special permits were allowed to sail directly to several American ports. The fleet system was now on its last legs. In 1735 it was suspended completely for South America, and in 1740 for Mexico. Fourteen years later it was reestablished for Mexico, but, strictly speaking, it was as good as dead. In 1778 fleets were abolished altogether. These measures, laudable as they were, had come at least a century too late. The risks, the profits, and the fever of contraband trade were now in the blood of Spaniards, Spanish Americans, and foreigners alike. Finally things reached such a pass that a mere one tenth of the colonial commerce was with Spain; nine tenths came in and went out via contraband.

But the "industry of contraband" cannot be laid entirely at the door of foreigners, however predatory these might be. "Smuggling on the grand scale which developed could not have been carried on had it not been welcomed by Spanish merchants and customs officials. Ecclesiastics, too, availed themselves of immunity from payment of import duties on goods for their own use, to bring in large quantities of merchandise which found its way into the markets. In most cases smuggling was permitted for simple commercial advantage, though actual necessity at times prompted it, especially in ports unfrequented by Spanish ships."[78]

Buenos Aires was the principal one of these ports. During the course of the eighteenth century it became the center and emporium of a great and rapidly expanding region of Spanish South America, and before long was the largest market on the continent. The district of the River Plate, Paraguay, Bolivia or Upper Peru, and Chile were all directly dependent on Buenos Aires, and even Lima soon fell into eclipse when contraband trade ran away with the purse. The Viceroy at the Peruvian capital protested vehemently, but his cries fell on deaf ears. "Buenos Aires," he said, "is the ruin of two commerces, the gate through which our wealth is slipping away, and the window through which Peru is being tossed to disaster." The two commerces were that of Peruvian silver, which flowed secretly through Buenos Aires to Brazil and Europe, and European goods, which followed the same route into South America. In the early days of smuggling the Argentines had tied their sacks of silver to the anchors of their ships, then lowered these into the water, not drawing them in again until the inspectors had passed the vessel. Now no such precautions were necessary. Everybody connived with the smuggler. Spain and Peru went down in the economic scale, and the River Plate went up.

Buenos Aires at this time was an enterprising and fast-growing town whose primary characteristic was a good business sense. Its inhabitants were not the proud and aloof aristocrats of Lima, nor the almost equally proud and aloof aristocrats of Mexico City. They were merchants, ranchers, and businessmen who devoted themselves to their homes and to their business and thus came to constitute the bourgeoisie in a society whose only aristocracy was the political oligarchy. These bourgeoisie were the "nice people" of the capital city and expanding market on the River Plate. They were the descendants and grandchildren of old functionaries and conquistadores, who cultivated their hereditary lands with Negro and Indian workers, and were always alive to get the best of a good business opportunity. European immigration had come in sufficient quantity to keep their blood stream in energetic and constant ascent. All of Argentina was an agricultural and pastoral community which supplied them with the means of trade. In the north, around Tucumán and Salta, they grew sugar cane and traded in mules. The biggest mule mart in the world was held in this region, with over seventy thousand animals sold each year. In the province of Cuyo, across from Chile, they raised grapes and manufactured wines, and in the province of Buenos Aires merchandising was their principal occupation, while cattle was their outstanding product. They were all an enterprising people who now stood on the threshold of their greatest opportunity.

In the year 1770 Buenos Aires had a population of 22,007 inhabitants, of whom 4163 were Negro and mulatto slaves. There were approximately the same number of Indians and mestizos in the town, and perhaps three times that number living in the surrounding territory near by. The total number of free Negroes and mulattoes was almost equal to that of the slaves. Many Creole "whites" must have had considerable Indian blood in their veins. The racial make-up of the city as a whole was as follows: One third of the inhabitants were predominantly white in blood; one third were predominantly Indian, and one third were predominantly black. In actuality, of course, the majority was already composed of various mixtures of these moving rapidly toward complete assimilation.

The whites held both the government and church offices as well as the principal control of business, but they readily blended their blood with that of the red and the black types around them. They were mostly Andalusians from southern Spain whose ancestors had lived among the Moors and were not so prone to racial discrimination as the more blue-blooded aristocrats of the older viceregal centers. Even the considerable number of Negroes were soon to disappear from the national scene, blotted out entirely by race-mixing and the rapid influx of Caucasian elements. As Negroes usually lived with families where treatment was good, "they did not spread hate, did not represent a great investment on which the nation's economy depended, and did not break the unity 'of our American type.'"

An astute Creole traveler who had been in Buenos Aires in both 1749 and again in 1771 noted the considerable increase in wealth and comfortable living which had taken place in the intervening years. The population of the city had also doubled within that brief period. He considered the women the loveliest of all Spanish America and remarked on their extremely simple manner of dress, which was almost severe beside that of Peru. Their principal garment was a flowing black dress with a hood which went over the head in place of a hat, leaving only the face bare.

There were no free public schools in the town at that time, and some of the inhabitants sent their children to Córdoba or to Santiago if they did not want them to attend an ecclesiastical school in Buenos Aires. Those who wanted a university education generally went to Chuquisaca, Bolivia, the next most important institution of higher education in South America after Lima itself. Others went to Santiago, Lima, and to Spain. Toward the end of the century the Creole class had grown considerably in intellectual prestige, and, living as they did at the door of the pampas, their bodily development had at least kept pace with their minds. Nearly all of them were fine horsemen. One day they would return from abroad after having imbibed liberal ideas, and then they would make up the leadership of the revolutionary struggle; after that they would be forced to give way to the tyrant folk of the pampas, each of whom wanted to be a king in his own domain.

In 1770 Buenos Aires was the fourth city in Spanish South America, coming after Lima, Cuzco, and Santiago. Neither the Argentine nor the Chilean capital could boast of the showy wealth or richly adorned churches which characterized the two Peruvian centers. Buenos Aires had only sixteen carriages as compared with the hundreds of Lima and Mexico City, yet there were many thriving merchants, and even on the out-of-the-way streets were numerous clothes shops, the total being at least four times that of Lima. The four largest stores in Buenos Aires, which supplied a great portion of the interior country, contained truly tremendous stocks of goods. "The people here hardly think about anything else but their business," wrote the traveler Concolorcorvo, "and everybody wants a good home and a house in the country for recreation. Meat is so abundant that when it is carted in quarters across the plaza, if a quarter happens to slip off, the driver never stops to pick it up even if someone tells him about it, and even a poor beggar on the street doesn't bother to carry it home with him."[83] The slaughterhouses gave away free meat nearly every day, because merely in order to get the hides they always killed a greater number of cattle than could possibly be consumed. Numerous fat dogs and rats infested homes and streets, for even the poorest houses were plentifully supplied with beef. Fruits, vegetables, fowls, and fish were also abundant, and in order to make a catch of the latter, the fisherman simply drove his cart into the water along the river's edge and let his team of oxen stand there up to its neck while he pulled in his catch.

The pampas Indians, still untamed, frequently went on the warpath in groups of about fifty, and were careful to attack only inferior forces. They placed single and unarmed spies along the roads, and these would try to take up with a band of travelers, saying that they were being chased by the savages. Then at the first opportunity the spy would escape and carry all his information with him. The system of forts was not well advanced in those days, but there was an occasional military establishment, sometimes consisting of only half a dozen soldiers living in covered wagons.

There were many fields of wheat and corn bordering the highroad between Buenos Aires and Córdoba, and enormous herds of cattle grazed on the pasture lands. The domesticated stock was always run into corrals at night so that they would not trample down the grain. These corrals had stockades made mostly of hides, the stakes being placed a hide's length apart, and the dried skin acting as sole fencing material in between. Boats made of blown-up hides were also used to take travelers across the river near Córdoba. Wood was obviously much scarcer than leather in this region. Our visitor of 1771, after commenting on the fine health of the cattlemen of this region, states categorically that two thirds of the deaths on the pampas were either from falls from horses or from gorings by angry bulls.

The town of Córdoba in the 1770s was not much of a city. Although the inhabitants made more than $600,000 a year on mules and hides, the religious establishments were poorly built and even more poorly kept. The town had grown little during the past hundred years, the visitor of 1771 giving it approximately the same population as had the Dutch trader of a century earlier, that is, from five to six hundred families, exclusive of the slaves. The nunnery of Santa Teresa alone owned three hundred Negroes of both sexes, and our visitor states that two thousand were being offered for sale while he passed through the city. They had brought an element of opulence and ease into the manner of living, and as the cost was only one or two hundred dollars each, slaves were owned by a considerable number of families. In the Treaty of Utrecht (1713) the English had acquired the right to import twelve hundred Negroes yearly into Buenos Aires, and they were now pretty well strung out all the way between that port and Lima.

The region of northern Argentina around Tucumán was "as lovely as it could be, and there the earth produces whatever fruits are planted at the cost of very little effort." But one bad characteristic had already appeared: every landowner had ten times as much land as he could possibly work, and most of it had to remain fallow. There was a crying need for aggressive farmer immigrants, both to till the soil more completely and to revitalize the spirit of these people who seemed to be permeated with the Paraguayan inertia or laziness. After describing the beauty and fruitfulness of the land Concolorcorvo says: "There is abundant wood here to build comfortable homes for the inhabitants of the two largest European kingdoms, and there is plenty of room for them all and fine lands for their subsistence. The only scarce things are stones and a sufficient number of ports and commercial centers to keep trade moving; but the greatest lack is that of settlers, for in all this great north and interior land [from Salta to Córdoba] there live only one hundred thousand persons according to the maximum estimates." Our traveler urges the "small and miserable workers" of Spain, Portugal, and France to leave their homes and come to this new Canaan.[83]

Tucumán was also still the center for the wagon, or *carreta*, manufacturing industry. These enormous two-wheeled carretas were made entirely of wood, without so much as a nail or single piece of iron reinforcing them. They were generally drawn by four oxen and could carry a total load of about two hundred *arrobas*—close to five thousand pounds. In addition to their pay load of one hundred and fifty arrobas there was always a huge jug of water, firewood for the driver to use at night, beams and planks to repair the cart in case of a breakdown, and the implements and supplies which the driver had to carry along with him in order to make his long cross-country trips.

In spite of this basis for a rich agricultural community, the Tucumán region was so thinly settled that "the inhabitants may be compared to Pharaoh's cows which were lean in the midst of plenty. Yet the leading citizens of the province, especially in Salta and Córdoba, have sizable incomes and take care of their children well, sending them off to school where they make outstanding students. All the rest of the inhabitants are people readily capable of civilization. The greater part of the women know the Quechua language in order to get along with their servants, but they also speak Spanish without the slightest hesitancy, a thing which I did not find to be the case in Mexico, nor much less so in the viceroyalty of Peru."

This statement gives an indication of the extent to which race-mixing had gone in both the Argentine and the Mexican Peruvian regions, the former being way ahead. It also shows that Concolorcorvo, as well as the inhabitants of the country, considered as Spanish, socially and in blood, innumerable women who must have been largely Indian in their racial make-up and even in their language. For example, when Concolorcorvo, who had traveled widely throughout Mexico, Argentina, and Peru, passed through the Bolivian region on this particular trip, he made a point of mentioning that "in Chuquisaca, Potosí, and Oruro, even the women speak Spanish very well in their public conversations and gatherings. In La Paz they speak it reasonably well in private conversation with men, but Aymará is heard almost exclusively along the streets. In Cuzco, Quechua is spoken, but the principal ladies know Spanish very well though they still have a deep passion for the native tongue which they learned from their mothers, nurses, and servants."

These statements prove that racial fusion in the Andean and Mexican regions had not gone nearly so far as it had in either Chile or Argentina, where Spanish was the exclusive language in every populated center. The linguistic unity of these two latter regions, plus their more complete racial homogeneity, obviously gave birth to that stronger homogeneous feeling which is the prerequisite to forming any great nation. Thus even Spanish absolutism had its good side, for it had rigorously restricted foreign immigration during those slow and formative years when one race was imposing its civilization upon another, and when finally the era of great expansion did arrive the Spanish base was so firm and deeply rooted that it could easily absorb and convert into its own channel the blood and linguistic streams of many different nationalities. At the same time, unfortunately, Argentine character was being fashioned and blended in the crucible of contraband. Its seeds of equality, which were undeniable, were fertilized by the soil of irregular wealth, and far too many of the citizens, their pockets well lined with these devious gains, would come to look upon democracy and license as being synonymous. It would take the Argentines a long, long time to unlearn this ill-taught lesson.

Spain's error did not lie in her adopting the mercantilist system of monopoly. Every nation of that day followed a similar course. It was a logical point of departure for building up a new economy. But while the other nations of the world grew in economic scope as the years passed, Spain alone remained playing with her dreams of the past, stubbornly refusing to change with the times. The obstinate, fanatical, and single-minded intensity of her religious dogmatism had again been carried into another sphere, the economic, and it had proved her undoing as well as Argentina's tribulation.

It was the Viceroy of the River Plate, Cevallos, who in 1777, on petition of the municipal cabildo of Buenos Aires, delivered an "immortal proclamation" declaring the free trade of his viceroyship with the peninsula and the other colonies, and the free entry of goods for Chile and Peru. "Like a swollen river breaking its dykes trade rushed forward seeking its level, spreading wealth and abundance in its path." The population of the province of Buenos Aires had been 37,000 before this new era of commerce was inaugurated; now, within twenty-two years, it tripled.

Another index to the rapid growth of Argentine income was the number of hides exported. Up to 1778 the annual exportation had been about one hundred and fifty thousand; after that date, with relatively free commerce inaugurated, the number jumped almost immediately to eight hundred thousand a year, "and after the peace of Paris in 1783 (which terminated the war with England), the number of hides annually exported aggregated one million four hundred thousand." That is, within the brief period of five years, income from the country's principal product had increased nearly tenfold. Customs receipts increased at an even more rapid rate. Before the opening of the port of Buenos Aires they had averaged about twenty thousand pesos a year; in 1778, when the gates were thrown open to foreign commerce, revenues jumped to about fifty-four thousand pesos, and between 1791–95 annual receipts were about four hundred thousand pesos, or twenty times the old figure.[42] Domestic commerce also grew apace. Great days for the Río de la Plata were at hand. The vineyards of Mendoza sold seventy-three hundred barrels of wine a year to interior markets; Tucumán expended huge quantities of cured hides and cloth; even Paraguay disposed of seventy thousand mule loads of yerba mate, tobacco, and native woods to Peru. Agriculture also commenced to expand rapidly, and a new process for salting meat was discovered which made it keep better and hence easier to export.[79]

In 1794 the ranchers of Buenos Aires and Montevideo drew up a report for the government in which it was stated that 450,000 head of cattle could be slaughtered, salted, and exported yearly by the new process. It would take 390 large vessels per year to carry this salted beef. Of course these optimistic results could not be attained because of lack of shipping space at that time, but the total commerce did increase so rapidly that the region of the River Plate quickly became the wealthiest of South America. The same ranchers and merchants who had drawn up this declaration about potential exports of salted beef also proposed the exportation of a great number of other commodities, such as cheese, mutton, tallow, butter, horsehair, hogs' bristles, and so forth. They wound up their report with the optimistic and flattering declaration that "this is the richest country in the world!"[42] A glimpse of the real Argentine character was beginning to appear across the horizon, with its greatest strength and its greatest weakness balanced precariously.

The strength appeared first, for the wealth of this fertile and productive land was real and not illusory. It was made up of products that one could eat and wear, not metal to spend. Its economy, rooted in reproductive labor, and its society, established in unity on a firm base, was rapidly moving toward a homogeneous whole. It was the robust nucleus of a future nation, a free association of ranchers and merchants with the agriculturalists in second line, all enjoying the gifts of a productive nature and remunerative work together with the equality that lends it dignity, making it a "democracy in fact organized on civil life." These words of the Argentine historian and president, Bartolomé Mitre, must not be taken to mean a democracy in the present-day conception of the term. He meant simply that, while Mexico and Peru were nations of masters and serfs, one half of whom were completely disinherited, Argentina did hold the seeds of a homogeneous society, one in which a relative democracy prevailed even at this early date, and one in which the bases of a future democracy might be laid once the disruptive influences were overcome in the psychology of the people. These influences were strong.

Yet the viceroyship of the River Plate was "an incoherent mass without intimate affinities . . . without that harmonious unity which is the result of the equilibrium of life. Buenos Aires was the soul and head of this shapeless body; but neither did its spirit penetrate the general mass, nor did its action make itself felt simultaneously in the extremities." The Paraguayan part of it had already atrophied; the Bolivian part was like Peru, half slave, half free; the Uruguayan section was a thinly settled territory of purple land on which the colossus of Brazil was continuing to cast covetous eyes. The portion of Argentina alone held the germ of a great nation. Even here, however, the "wilderness, isolation, scant population, lack of moral cohesion, corruption of customs in the general mass, the absence of any ideal, and above all the profound ignorance of the common people, were causes and effects that produced side by side the semi-barbarism of the interior beside the weak and sickly civilization of Buenos Aires and the coast . . . It had in its arm the strength that destroys, without holding in its head the ideal that builds, nor did it hold within itself the creative power to construct out of its own resources."[79]

Spain's unnatural system had effects which reached much farther than this. Contraband commerce had from the beginning received the support of an increasing number of people of all classes. In the eighteenth century it became an open and full-fledged industry with merchants, government officials, and ecclesiastics taking part in it or abetting it. The physically impossible economic laws of the central government were at first disregarded, then openly derided. Disrespect for impersonal law became almost universal. The ideal was to look out for oneself and let the devil take the hindmost. When independence came, this feeling of individual, region, or class welfare above community progress immediately asserted itself in the political as well as in the economic sphere. Each group demanded absolute sovereignty for itself, and no group would bow to a superior law of equitable justice for all. Each group sought the chimera of peace and independence at the same moment that it shouted: "Our interests must come first!" Each group was willing and anxious that some other group give up a measure of its individuality, profit, or power, without ever thinking to ask itself: "What is it that *I* must renounce that the welfare of all may survive?" Seeking escape from tyranny and war, all groups made further self-created war and tyranny inevitable, as if that brand would be any different. It was the age-old story of man from the beginning of time eager to sacrifice all when it comes to fighting for an ideal, loath to sacrifice anything in order that that ideal may live.

29

BRAZILIAN PLANTATION LIFE
YIELDS TO THE LURE OF GOLD

While the bandeirantes of São Paulo were driving their caravans over the forest land, denuding it of native inhabitants, the northern colony of Pernambuco, lying along the coast of the Brazilian bulge and generally known as the northeast, was slowly building up the country's firmest, richest, most aristocratic colonial civilization of the sixteenth and seventeenth centuries. Like the Greek and Roman societies of old, like the beginnings of nearly every civilization on the face of the globe, like that of the United States itself, it was a society based on the productive effort of a slave class which gave the ruling minority the leisure time so essential for the development of the arts of living and the full growth of the creative mind.

Here in Pernambuco, Portuguese influence was strongest in those early days. The blood which came to this region was Portugal's best; the land was fruitful, and the living good. It also got off to a better start than any other Brazilian colony. Its founder, Duarte Coelho, had poured his wealth, his influence, and his life into making it a going concern, from its settlement in 1535, a score of years before São Paulo was set up as a miserable hut of missionaries in a wilderness of barbaric Indians and violently suspicious half-breed mamelucos, who regarded one another's every movement with mutual distrust. Obviously São Paulo could not for many years become a truly civilized community. Pernambuco could and did, and so strong was the influence which its early culture exerted over the national life during the first two formative centuries that one might almost say had it not been for Pernambuco and its neighboring regions Brazil today would have neither the racial make-up, the social and economic complexities, nor the refined Portuguese cultural traditions which have made it so distinct from the other great Latin-American nations.

The Portuguese did not come to Brazil unprepared. When the economic and civil life of the colony was first organized in 1532 by Afonso de Sousa, Portugal already had behind her more than a hundred years of contact with the tropics, that master annihilator of racial barriers. She had learned first in Africa and then in India how to adapt herself to the tropical regions and their slower pace of life. Her centuries of contact with the African Moors in her own territory, and her long coast toward the open sea, had given her a cosmopolitan, psychological, and racial basis possessed at that time by no other European country. Consequently, when the Portuguese went to Brazil, they did not have to learn these things.

The history of Portugal's former conquests and the mistakes had also taught her much which was to make the colonization of Brazil more successful. Beginning like Spain with the illusion of an El Dorado, she had found her golden dream earlier, had seen its glittering brilliance frittered away, and then, unlearning that myth of easy wealth, had turned her efforts to the soil from which all riches flow.

This more realistic side of Portuguese exploration and conquest had paved the way for the colonization of Brazil even before that vast territory was discovered. In Africa, Portugal had engaged in the slave trade and had learned how to select and to manage the black worker. In the Azores and Cape Verde Islands she had planted communities of entire Portuguese families and had learned how to develop agricultural colonies. Also in India, in Africa, and in some of the islands of the south Pacific, she had learned the art of slow conquest and had established many a trading post and fortress where colonization was not possible. The sum total of these things gave Portugal, in spite of her small size, an immediate advantage over all other European countries in the colonization of the New World. All that was lacking now was the desire to take and to settle. This desire came in the 1530s, when India's trade declined and the wharves of Lisbon were glutted with unsold spices.

Portugal had better sense than to attempt the colonization of densely populated India, or of Africa, where she had so many footholds. East Indian or Negro blood would soon have engulfed and swallowed her best efforts. She turned to Brazil where the odds were not so strongly against her and where, when the Negro did indeed become a necessity, she could import and utilize him on her own terms. Both in the south and in the northeast of the new land her colonies were successful, but it was in the northeast that the basis for the development of an early colonial culture was laid. It was founded upon cultivation of the soil, was conditioned by the patriarchal stability of family life, the assurance of a working class through slavery, the union of the Portuguese men first with the Indian women, and later with the imported Negress or the mulatto.

Even with these advantages in their favor the colonists of Portugal might not have succeeded had they encountered gold or other precious metals.

As they did not find these things a real colonization was forced upon them. They made up for their lack of numbers by occupying vast spaces of territory and carrying to the limit promiscuous sex habits which resulted in impregnating native women by the hundreds. They then made it possible for the mestizo children to align themselves with the imported civilization of their fathers. Everything was conducive to rapid race-mixing. The naked native women did not take much urging to lie with a white; in fact, they often reversed the process and went to the man. The tropical climate, the absence of Portuguese women, the stimulation and ease of seduction provided by the Indian girls, all this made the atmosphere of early Brazilian life almost one of sexual intoxication. Yet to some parts of Brazil, particularly Pernambuco, these Portuguese men soon began to bring their wives and their families. A rigorous start, good government, and a strongly maintained complement of soldiers in that province had soon cleared the way for a measure of security in which family life might find friendly soil.

Gilberto Freyre, Brazil's finest sociological historian, states categorically, "From 1532 on, the Portuguese colonization of Brazil, like the English colonization of North America, and unlike the Spanish and French settlements in both Americas, is characterized by the almost exclusive dominance of the rural or semi-rural family. It is a dominance only challenged by the Church whose Jesuits were sometimes hostile to its familiar authority. The family, not the individual, nor the State, nor any commercial company, is from the sixteenth century the great colonizing factor in Brazil, the productive unit, the capital which clears the earth, establishes the *fazendas* or plantations, buys the slaves, oxen, tools and implements; it is the social force which expresses itself most strongly in politics, building itself up into the most powerful colonial aristocracy of America. Over it the King of Portugal, it might be said, reigns without governing. The aristocratic colonial senate, an expression of that family ascendence in political life, soon limits the power of the kings and later on also the peninsular imperialism or rather economic parasitism whose all absorbing tentacles the mother country attempts to extend over the colony.

"The earlier colonization by individuals—soldiers of fortune, adventurers, exiled criminals, converted Jews fleeing religious persecution, shipwrecked sailors, traders in slaves, parrots, and brazilwood—these left only impermanent traces on the great plastic economy of Brazil. They spread themselves out so much and came in such relatively few numbers that their irregular population never formed a true colonial system in either a political or economic sense."[84]

Yet all types of settlers became a part of the moving frontier which was the heartbeat of the great new country. On the physical basis of Brazil's fine waterways the Portuguese tendency to extend, rather than to condense itself, was prolonged. Colonists spilled all over the vast country, occupying immense territories, separated by incredible distances, surrounded by and immersed in forest, waters, and native or African blood. The big rivers were highways of the bandeirante and missionary; along the smaller ones were spread streams of agricultural and cattle life. Progress was slow, very slow. Brazil became then, and has remained ever since, a group of "islands of man in a great sea of forest."

The region of widest and most stable colonization was in the northeast, in Pernambuco and its neighboring provinces; the basic factors in that northeastern colonial culture were a patriarchal family regime, Indian and Negro slavery, both of these resting squarely on the cultivation of sugar cane. It was a type of plantation culture in many ways similar to that of our own Old South. Sugar cane was not the only product of the northeastern economy, nor indeed was the plantation system limited exclusively to Pernambuco and its vicinity. It also existed in the central part of Brazil around Bahia and Rio de Janeiro and in the south around São Paulo. But Pernambuco was its heart, and sugar cane was its body. That is why it was called the Sugar Cane Civilization. Compared with it, the vast semi-civilized regions colonized by the bandeirantes or taken over by the Jesuits were primitive in the extreme.

The nerve center of this sugar civilization was the Big House, the *Casa Grande*, and its supporting members were the *senzala*, or slave quarters, along with the sugarworks or refinery called the *engenho*. The owner of one of these centers and its surrounding lands was known as a *senhor de engenho*, master of the sugarworks. Some of the sugar barons owned regions which were far from small in size. One of them was larger than Portugal itself. Within his own territory the law of the senhor de engenho was final; he was absolute master of the land, the slaves, and the women who made up his plantation community.

The Big House itself, isolated from the coastal settlements which kept up the various phases of European life, drew into itself all of these manifold expressions and reproduced them within its own vast precincts. The Casa Grande was large, often ponderously large in size. Its style was one of massive but simple lines, and its walls, usually of adobe or of mixed stones and adobe, were very thick as a protection against the heat and the tropical rains, and against the depredations of savage Indians. It was not at all a replica of the old feudal houses of Portugal, but was the outgrowth of a new environment, new necessities of life, and a new conception of culture. It was the first truly Brazilian thing in the country. It represented "a whole economic, social, political, and cultural system." Nothing was lacking to make its authority, and that of its master, complete. Within the walls of the Big House was everything that was needful for life and death: the school, the nursery, the infirmary, the family chapel (which sometimes became quite a large church attached directly onto the house), the master's harem, the bank, and even the cemetery. The great structure was manor house, fortress, and church. Its religion was distinctly of a family nature, and the chaplain or priest in charge was subordinate to the paternal authority, as was everything else in the Big House. He was pontiff, governor, and judge all rolled into one. Both in an architectural, realistic, and symbolic sense, the Big House dominated the northeast. This patriarchal feudalism overcame the Church and its initial tendency to become a great landowner in its own right. "Once the Jesuit was overthrown the *senhor de engenho* dominated colonial life almost without interference. He was the true master of Brazil, more powerful than viceroys or bishops."[84]

In the early days it was necessary to maintain quite a sizable army on these isolated plantations, sometimes numbering hundreds. The soldiers were Indians or half-breeds who had been brought into the colonial orbit and formed a wall against the savages of the interior or the corsairs who swooped in from the coast. These private armies gave the master of the Big House the force to back up his right to rule as he saw fit, brooking no interference from either Church, King, or colonial officialdom. It was very unlike the Spanish American colonial system, in which the wealthy Creoles came near to being powerless politically under the viceregal authority and in their inept municipal councils.

"The truth is that around these *senhores de engenho* was created the most stable type of civilization in Hispanic America; and that type of civilization is exemplified by the heavy-set, horizontal architecture of the Big House. Enormous kitchens, vast dining halls, numerous rooms for children and guests, chapel, wings or apartments for the accommodation of married sons, isolated chambers in the central part of the house for the almost monastic seclusion of the unmarried daughters . . ." The massive architecture of the Casa Grande was rooted deeply in the soil, climate, and necessity of Brazilian life. It did not spring up suddenly on the colonial scene, but was a combination of the old Portuguese manor house, plus Moorish and Asiatic elements picked up in Europe, Africa, and India, raised upon an authentic Brazilian forest base.[84]

Pernambuco and its Casa Grande thus became the outstanding expression of a new type of cultural and social order. Here Portuguese colonial culture reached its finest flower under a kind of paternal despotism which enjoyed every social and governing power. The master of the plantation not only ran his estate to suit himself, he ran the colonial government also. The colonial senate was composed exclusively of members of his class, and all of the higher ranks in the army were likewise reserved for his confreres. On at least one occasion the planters violently expelled a governor sent to Brazil by the Portuguese King. His Majesty then named a new governor, who knew how to rule without crossing the colonial aristocrats.

What manner of men were these proud senhores de engenho? The best blood of Portugal ran in their veins, and when it came to marriage they tried to preserve it undiluted. If this meant intense inbreeding, so much the better. The offspring would be just that much more aristocratic. This at least was the espoused ideal of colonial life among these wealthy landowners. Yet being cosmopolitan by training and tradition, and lacking any rigid racial feelings, they were not exclusive, like the more narrow Englishmen of Puritan contours, nor were they impervious to change, like the Spaniard whose orthodoxy covered every breath of life. The Portuguese planter often followed a motto which ran something like this: "A white woman to marry, a mulatto to take to bed, a Negress to do the work."[84]

There was even room in Brazil for the "new Christians," or converted Jews, and there was room for foreigners too. Both groups came to the new land and took leading parts in the national life, sometimes blending their blood with that of the Portuguese. The pioneer who came from Portugal seldom held to inflexible principles, and displayed a power of adaptation and assimilation which set him apart from the other Europeans of his time. This was his greatest asset in making up for his lack of numbers. It was the only way in which he could spread himself over such a vast territory and not be swallowed up.

There was only one point on which the Brazilian plantation owner was inflexible: his attitude toward his own womankind. He believed in every freedom for himself and in none for the female members of his family. This was, of course, a pretty general characteristic in those days, but the Portuguese gentleman probably carried it farther than men of any other nationality. His Moorish background made him look upon polygamy, condemned by his Church, as the natural state of masculine existence. It likewise caused him to enforce the utter seclusion, bordering on imprisonment, of his women. These two principles went hand in hand in the rigorously maintained double standard of the Casa Grande.

Native influences helped to strengthen this sexual autocracy on the one hand and license on the other. Most of the tribes in the vicinity of Pernambuco believed that the mother's womb was but a sack into which the man's seed was deposited in the same manner in which a plant seed is deposited in the earth. The offspring, thus, was believed to be a miniature replica of the father, no matter whether it was a girl or a boy, with none of the mother's characteristics. This belief was so general among the servants and workers on Brazilian plantations that many native women felt honored to seek out white consorts; contrariwise all the slaves co-operated with the father of the household in preserving the seclusion and virginity of the female members of his own family, lest some monstrous and degrading offspring issue from her befouled womb.

The father on his part was not so indiscriminate in sex matters as at first might be supposed. He had the choice of his Indian and Negro slaves and selected the most beautiful and the most intelligent to share his bed. One of the aristocratic Albuquerques, for example, who was married to a blue-blooded Mello, "had as the flower of his plantation harem an Indian girl, the daughter of a brave Indian chief." He had many children by this Indian beauty, and nearly four centuries later a descendant of one of these became the first cardinal in Latin America. When the proportion of Indian women had dwindled and Negro slaves began to be imported in numbers, toward the close of the sixteenth century, some of the planters tried "to arrange that pretty girls should come." They sought for the most advanced groups among the African blacks, and consequently many Mohammedan Negroes, "who knew how to read and write in Arabic, were imported to Brazil."[85]

The society represented by the Casa Grande in the colonial northeast was a sort of one-man show. It was monoproductive and gave rise to an autocratic monoculture, but there was no "one-wife" business about it. Polygamy was the soil in which it thrived. The sexual preoccupations of its patriarchal master, so "unworthy of Christian monogamic gentlemen," and the love and care which the father frequently showed for his illegitimate children, sometimes sending them back to Portugal for an education, prevented a rapid deterioration of the race. The forest which was standing there ready to swallow up the colonists' best blood and efforts, and eager to turn them "native," did indeed produce a native race, but it was one which represented a great advance and not a regression to the Brazilian savage. The white man's language and culture somehow always managed to hold the upper hand.

The woman's place in this scheme of things was distinctly subordinate, but legitimate wives did exercise a great authority over their slaves, servants, and children. Under the pent-up dominion of their great houses some colonial ladies became sadistically inclined and tortured their slaves with real pleasure. A few even let overpowering jealousy of their husbands' concubines challenge his right to a polygamous existence. One colonial lady had her spouse's mulatto favorite slain and then served up her eyes in a dessert placed on the table before him. Another concubine was thrown into a caldron of boiling mash. However, such occurrences were extremely rare.

The Casa Grande was noted far and wide for its warm hospitality and was always open to the passing traveler. The "lady of the house" managed the guest's entertainment and planned her best meals and refreshments for his pleasure, but she was never seen by him. Her seclusion was typically that of a Moorish woman who does not unveil or display herself in public. She did not even find churchgoing to be the outlet which it was for the somewhat freer town lady, whose attendance at mass or other religious celebrations indulged both her religious and social instincts. Occasionally, in the cities there was even dancing inside the church itself, and in later years girls ate ices there and flirted with the boys.

Brazilian parties anywhere, however, were seldom attended by outsiders. Girls danced with their relatives and in-laws, and the marriage of close cousins was quite frequent. Inbreeding was the rule rather than the exception among the aristocratic families of colonial Brazil. Segregation made any other kind of union extremely difficult and was so severe that "as late as 1757, at a ball given by the governor of Rio de Janeiro to French naval officers, there was not a single woman present, only four men dressed as women, to dance with these foreign officers."[85]

The colonial wives did enjoy a certain amount of luxury in dress, though the general tenor of their lives was one of sufficiency and bare comfort rather than of pomp or excess. Many of them found their pride and joy in silks, velvets, laces, and jewels, at first imported from the Orient or from Portugal and later rendered more brilliant by Brazilian gold and diamonds. Some plantation owners spent great fortunes on such finery so that they might shine in the reflected glory of their wives and mistresses. When a wife owned an extremely large wardrobe of exquisite clothes she would frequently have her slaves wear the finest dresses and the jewels she herself could not put on, in order to make a big show. It was always more of a private showing than a public exhibition, however. Aside from these rather infrequent displays, the *senhora* of the Brazilian plantation undertook much the same household duties as our Southern ladies. She supervised and often took part in spinning, weaving, the making of soap and candles, the preparation of preserves and liqueurs, and many other essentials of the self-contained economy of her fazenda, or plantation.

In spite of all the safeguards placed around the colonial family life, some deterioration of the white race was noticeable, due to the climate, to the lack of any strong drive to work, and above all to a faulty diet. Fresh vegetables, milk, and fruits were scarce, and sweets were omnipresent. Dried foods, manioc, and sweets made up the backbone of the colonial menu, and their effect on the body was what might be expected. The women had bad teeth and many of them aged early and became fat. Their men did not object to this latter tendency, for they believed—as did the Moors—that the most beautiful woman was *gorda e bonita*, or "fat and pretty." While the women were undergoing these particular changes, their men were also subject to certain deleterious environmental influences. The institution of slavery was perhaps the strongest one of these. Under this institution it soon became the custom for the master of the plantation to do absolutely nothing that might be called work. Slaves were trained to perform or oversee even the most technical operations, and eventually the most intelligent also became overseers of entire plantations about whose operation they often knew more than the master himself. The senhores de engenho thus "were so given to the slave system that they could no longer provide for themselves. A biological differentiation of functions, as it were, had left them, like Darwin's slave-making ants, in a sort of parasitic relation to the subject race."[84] And while all this was going on, the Negro was gradually raising his cultural level and was at least holding onto, if not increasing, his bodily vigor with hard work and a less ruinous diet than that consumed by his white masters.

Although the plantation of colonial Brazil was one of extremes, the supreme contrast being that between master and slave, nearly every influence of native life tended to diminish the gap between the two poles, reducing them gradually to a level which was purely Brazilian. The process is by no means complete even yet, but it has traveled a long way since 1600. Besides the diminishing influence of sex, climate, diet, and slavery itself, there was another institution which had a powerful effect on Brazilian amalgamation: the aristocratic brotherhoods.

These brotherhoods, or *irmandades*, were semi-religious organizations which filled a place somewhat similar to that of our Masonic and other lodges. It was considered a great honor to belong to the more exclusive ones, and membership was tantamount to full social recognition by the blue-blooded sugar aristocracy. These exclusive brotherhoods at first were limited to white persons who could prove no "taint of Jewish or Negro blood" for a period of four generations of ancestors. "There were also brotherhoods of mulattoes, closed to the blacks. And there were brotherhoods of free blacks, closed to mulattoes and whites."[85] These of course were the lowest in the social scale, and their subordination to white supremacy was shown by the fact that the civil and ecclesiastical authorities required them to give the position of treasurer to a socially prominent white man.

Brotherhoods of all kinds and degrees were of tremendous importance in the development of colonial Brazil. "Much of the work that was done by the government or by the church authorities in Spanish America was done in Brazil by the religious brotherhoods: that is, by private enterprise and not by official initiative; by laymen, and not by bishops nor by the clergy."[85] They built hospitals, churches, asylums, orphanages, provided for their members in sickness, poverty, or old age, took care of funerals, burials, and masses for the departed souls. Since Brazilian social status was the principal measuring rod of economic, religious, and political influence, the brotherhoods also came to wield a considerable power in Church and Government. Their members frequently held the best positions in these spheres.

The most singular of all the influences exerted by the brotherhoods, however, was that they possessed the power to make a colored person white. If a mulatto with influential backing gained entrance into one of the exclusive groups he immediately became white "for all social purposes." A good many mulattoes who were not particularly dark anyway, and whose fathers had given them both love and an education, were thus incorporated into the socially elite of the land. A Brazilian mulatto became "one of the greatest poets and scholars in the Brazil of the first half of the nineteenth century. Another became one of the most distinguished newspapermen of that century."[85] The total upshot of all this was that race distinction was gradually narrowed down, but never completely erased, with the passage of the years. Lightness of skin, breeding, and intelligence, rather than absolute purity of pedigree, became the common denominator in Brazilian life. White superiority was not and is not displaced by mulatto or Negro blood, but a narrow door was opened through which a chosen few might at least ascend to the precincts of the self-elected.

The Casa Grande, which was the nerve center of the culture, economy, sociology, and ethnology of colonial Brazil, did not follow a channel apart from the national life; on the contrary, it was for a century and a half the strongest single factor in determining what that channel would be and in which direction it would flow. As an institution it occupied the apex of the triangle whose base was made up of the bandeirante and the missionary, and whose material was the Brazilian land; white, native, and Negro blood; and Portuguese culture.

Brazil did not have a great central plain to give it unity, like the Argentine pampas, yet the country did form a "natural geographical unity" not separated by great physical barriers. Its colossal rivers and forests, enclosed by the mountain ranges, jungles, and waterways which separated them from the Spanish possessions around their perimeter, gave the country a certain undeniable oneness despite its thin population and immense distances. The periodic isolation and mass movements of its inhabited centers kept up the actuality of a moving frontier.

Those who have written on the transcendent importance of "the moving frontier" in the national life of a country begin by stating that isolation of inhabited centers is the first step toward movement. These isolated centers are forced to depend on one another in times of stress; they seek each other out across the wilderness, and that seeking and that dependency, plus the final meeting, make up the first stage of a moving frontier. Afterward mass migrations can begin in earnest. When movement is opposed by distance, geography, and man, the frontier may be said to exist in every sense of the term, symbolic and real, giving its unity to the territory as both fact and spirit. In the last analysis, anyhow, the frontier is not a state of territory; it is a state of mind. This condition existed throughout the colonial period of Brazil, and it still exists today, for much of the country's vast interior remains practically uninhabited. There lives in the heart of every true Brazilian a burning desire to reach out and to enfold these interior lands.

It would seem that the Amazon, that "river sea," the greatest of all world waterways traversing a continent, might have been the unifying factor in colonial Brazil. It lies athwart the breast of the country like a giant flowing octopus holding all the green forest land in its liquid fingers. When the rains fall it turns central Brazil into an immense inland sea, flooding millions of acres of land every year. But the Amazon plunges directly into the dark interior; it was far too large, too long, led too quickly away from the Portuguese fringe along the coast to serve as a basis of unity in colonial life. The role of the Amazon in Brazil's development lies in the future, and not in the past.

However, there was another river which almost paralleled the lower coastal bulge, flowing northward and emptying into the Atlantic just halfway between the cities of Bahia and Pernambuco. This was the mighty São Francisco, often called "the cradle of Brazilian civilization." When the northern colonists were in trouble with the Dutch the Paulists came up from the south, following the course of the São Francisco, to give them aid. When the Negro slaves rebelled and formed their Palm Confederacy, more Paulists came northward and under the leadership of a ruthless bandeirante put down the rebellion and wiped out the insurgents. Other bandeirantes, bent on no particular purpose, followed the great river up through the provinces of Bahia and Pernambuco. Many of them stayed in the new country and established their homes. Jesuits also roamed all over the wilderness with the São Francisco as a sort of north star to guide their steps aright. These contacts kept alive the feeling of unity in colonial Brazil and prevented the growth of two completely distinct and separated regions. Thus the São Francisco, along which these early Brazilians streamed from south to north, was both key link and nerve center of the emerging nation.

No country can live for long on a single product, for the dazzling profits to be won even from such a relatively new commodity as sugar, are soon bound to attract competitors with newer methods and fresher blood, who will take the field and displace the original producer. Moreover, a monoculture based on a single product, particularly if resting on a large slave class as it did in Brazil, tends to cause a softening of the fiber of the ruling caste, and the early vigorous expansiveness of their civilization soon goes to seed. During the seventeenth century Brazil produced most of the world's sugar supply. The expulsion of the Dutch in 1655 marked the first great change in the upward trend of export of this commodity. Dutch planters took away with them their efficient methods, their practical knowledge, their capital, and their slaves. Many of them settled in the West Indies, where they again undertook sugar planting with marked success. Before long the more efficient refineries and better communications of that region were able to break in on the Brazilian export trade; eventually they displaced it almost completely. The rapid growth of the United States sugar market, next door to the West Indies plantations, was another cause of the Brazilian decline.

There was also still another and more dramatic cause for the decline of the Sugar Civilization: the discovery of gold. For more than one hundred and fifty years the great colony of Brazil had escaped the fever of this yellow metal and had plodded her mammoth way upward on the

shoulders of Indian and black man. A few nuggets of gold had been found
as early as 1600, but they had amounted to little. Sugar had become king.
Then suddenly, in the years 1693–94, came the big discovery. In the region
about two hundred miles northwest of Rio de Janeiro, and another two
hundred or so miles inland, were found the great gold deposits of the
province of Minas Geraes, whose name means General Mines, or perhaps
it would be better to say Mines Everywhere. This new and uninhabited
region was a good twelve hundred miles southwest of the city of Pernambuco, and its discovery upset completely the center of gravity of Brazilian
life. The refinements of the old Sugar Civilization were pushed into second place, and the more attractive lure of an arising Gold Civilization
occupied the national throne.

The effects were not immediate, because communications in those days
were in terms of months and years, not days. However, between the years
1694 and 1711, and especially during the last ten years of that period, the
first great gold rush in history got under way in Brazil. Men in every walk
of life grasped at this new illusion of El Dorado. Spain's unfortunate example meant nothing.

From faraway Portugal tales of the glittering wealth drew thousands of
prospectors, who swarmed to the colony. From Pernambuco came droves
of sugar planters with their slaves; from São Paulo to the south came the
mestizo bandeirantes, now with a new goal before their restless eyes; from
all of the coastal cities—Rio, Bahia, and many smaller settlements—there
came a horde of Brazilian prospectors, merchants, Portuguese Jews, all
following the lure of Minas Geraes, all infected with the fever of easy
wealth. The colonial economy was reduced to a state of near chaos.

Plantations, which had been centers of production and culture for over
a century, were abandoned or left in the hands of inefficient foremen,
while the owners and a goodly proportion of their slaves went hurtling
across the wilderness, or down the great São Francisco toward the delicious
alchemy of Minas. New towns sprang up as if by magic. Slaves began to
pour into near-by Rio and were hurried to the black-mouthed tunnels in
which the yellow metal lay. Bahia and Pernambuco yielded to the new
impulse, and Rio de Janeiro became Brazil's first city. The great colossus
shuddered throughout its members, and a sudden palsy struck one Casa
Grande after another in the deserted northeast. Food became so scarce
that the officials of that region, in fear of actual privation for their families,
passed many rigorous laws in an attempt to check the exodus. Free laborers
were frozen to their jobs. Heavy taxes were slapped onto immigration into
the mining areas. But the stampede continued. Local officials now barricaded the roads, forcibly turning back all those who were southward
bound. Their efforts were futile. No artificial barriers could stay men dazzled by the yellow glory. The wilderness itself became a highway to the
promised land of Minas Geraes. The province of Pernambuco languished

and the economic frontier of the colony was shifted twelve hundred miles southward. It now lay less than half that distance from São Paulo and nearer still to Rio.

In 1711, while the gold rush was still under way but before it had knocked the props from under the sugar barons of the north, a Brazilian author by the name of João Antonil published one of the most interesting books to come out of the colony. Its title was *The Culture and Opulence of Brazil as Revealed by Its Products and Its Mines*. The book was dedicated to the lords of the sugar mills and to the miners. It painted such a rosy picture of Brazilian wealth that the Portuguese Government became alarmed lest the report might again fire the imagination of some foreign nation and bring about a wholesale occupation of the richest part of the great colony. The entire edition was confiscated by decree and all but half a dozen copies of the work were burned. Although Antonil's words about the newly discovered gold mines were probably the main cause of this action, the book also gives an accurate picture of Brazilian production in other items as well. The total number of sugar mills at that time was 528, with a production of about 1,285,000 arrobas per year. There were lesser quantities of hides, tobacco, cattle, and other products. A main diet of gold and sweets was being offered to the colonial palate. In a few more years gold was to win the upper hand.

In the meantime people continued to pour into Minas Geraes. Twenty to thirty thousand Negro slaves a year were imported into Rio and Bahia. They did all the actual work of mining for their white masters, some of whom had several hundred black miners under them. One northerner brought three thousand to the gold fields with him. The town of Ouro Preto became Brazil's Potosí, and black men became ants who were forced to live under the earth, tunneling here, burrowing there, under the constant menace of cave-ins and exhaustion, forever shoveling out the rock and soil on which their owners became rich. The vicinity still shows five hundred mouths of tunnels which give the impression that some giant monster once stood over the place with a huge cannon pumping great balls of lead into the earth. Some of these tunnels go three thousand feet deep, twisting their way after an elusive vein. In the dark, narrow holes Negroes often stood only an arm's length apart, and when the one in front got a basketful of rocks or dirt he passed it to the one behind him and so on down the line, until it finally reached the open air, where it was washed for nuggets.

In the light of profits to be won, the number of slaves employed was of no consequence. Nor was it of any concern to their owners if they died like flies in the bowels of the earth, as many did. One man hauled away more than fifty arrobas of gold, well over a thousand pounds! The price that was paid for this wealth in terms of human suffering and lives was enormous. Lack of proper food, and continued work long after the resistance point had been reached, caused many epidemics to break out. Time after time the ranks of the workers were decimated. Agriculture in the province was almost nonexistent, and in the presence of a large, eager, and wealthy consumers' market, where the supplies were strictly limited, commodity prices often rose twenty-five to fifty times their normal value. For at least a decade life in the mine fields breathed haltingly between a pitiable ratlike existence, famine, disease, and death. But black men came out of the slave funnel in an endless stream, and the white men who were taking the big profits did not worry. Mule paths were finally opened up to Rio and Bahia, and supplies then got through a little easier, but prices were always exorbitant.

Portugal added to this state of affairs by passing a law prohibiting the establishment of any industry in the gold region which did not directly further the actual mining operations. She was out for all the gold she could get, and the devil take the consequences. Her Midas touch turned the economic crisis of Minas Geraes into an official and semi-permanent condition. Thus did the rickety economy of this potentially multi-product state begin to creak and groan, serving merely as a vehicle for the transference of the yellow metal to the home country or to wealthy Brazilians who promptly took it there to be spent.

The biggest profiteers of all were the merchants, who somehow managed to get their goods and slaves into the province, where they were sold at fabulous prices. This particular kind of gold mine, exorbitant profits, afforded a steadier source of wealth than the mines themselves, for the element of chance was reduced to a minimum. All that was necessary was to get the goods to their destination. There were always a plethora of purchasers, no matter what the price, and frequently buyers bid against each other, raising the final figure beyond the dreams of even the most covetous merchant. It was a land gone mad with the thirst for profits. The bubble grew and grew until all Brazil was infected with the same disease, or a sympathetic reaction.

In 1720 the province of Minas Geraes was made a captaincy in its own right, and its first governor, Antonio de Albuquerque, finally brought a measure of order into its rip-roaring, hell-raising mining camps. Work in the mines came under government supervision, and the Crown began to get its 20 per cent more regularly. Royal wealth increased rapidly and with it the royal power often exercised in the most arbitrary manner. Prospectors squirmed and turned more and more to contraband and to out-and-out stealing. "Drastic measures were adopted by the government to suppress smuggling and prevent the concealment of gold dust."[57] The miners of Minas Geraes under this rigorous repression commenced to feel a deep resentment against the Crown authorities such as had not existed anywhere in Brazil up to that time. It is no wonder that this region provided the first revolutionary martyr in the colony's struggle for independence.

The discovery of gold not only affected the economy, the frontier, and the temper of Brazilian life; it also made an indelible imprint on the ethnology of the people. In the great rushes toward Minas Geraes the Negro moved south, and there in the mine fields he was pitted against the Indian and the bandeirante who came up from São Paulo. The black man won out. The Indian could not endure mine labor and did not possess the necessary skill to make a good miner. Moreover, the Negro outnumbered him many times over. And last of all, the Paulist from the south, with his crude wash methods, could not compete for long against the Portuguese from the north, whose slaves had for so many years worked with sugar-mill machinery and who knew how to use water power to the best advantage. Rivalries between the two groups became fierce and sometimes flared into civil war. Mass killings fouled many a gold field with the red-black stains of human blood. The better organization of the northern Brazilians also helped them to win out, and eventually, under Governor Albuquerque, the recalcitrant bandeirantes were expelled from the province.

Dislodged from one hold, they streaked across the interior in search of another, and within a few years (1725) had discovered more great gold fields far to the west, in the provinces of Goyaz and Mato Grosso. Only four years later immense diamond deposits were also found in another section of Minas Geraes. The westward movement of the Brazilian population continued at a steady pace, and by 1750 the territory beyond the Tordesillas line, which theoretically belonged to Spain and was claimed as a part of the viceroyalty of Peru, was so completely occupied by these prospectors that it went to Portugal by default.

Although the economic crises of Minas Geraes repeated themselves in these more western provinces, the total effect of the gold and diamond rushes was to bring all the distant regions of Brazil into contact with each other, to add a new impetus to the colonial economy, to increase the Brazilian feeling of the population, to gain territory and to people it with settlers who would remain there as farmers and cattle raisers after the yellow lure was gone, and to bring into sharp focus the essential differences that existed, and still exist today in an altered form, between the northern and the southern regions of Brazil. These differences were later accentuated when the north, deprived of much of its lifeblood and much of its labor, neglected to encourage immigration, while the south, especially the province of São Paulo, opened its doors to European immigrants who soon took over the economic leadership of the nation.

Hundreds of millions of dollars in gold and diamonds poured out of the mines of Brazil. During colonial times more than $600,000,000 came from the gold mines, and the diamond mines yielded nearly three million carats. For the last fifty years of the colonial epoch diamonds were a royal monopoly. Gold fleets reminiscent of the heyday of the Spanish galleons carried much of this immense wealth back to Portugal. And with results which were almost identical. Dom João V, who sat upon the Portuguese throne from 1706 to 1750, outdid himself trying to ape Louis XIV. He kept a sumptuous court and at a cost of one hundred and twenty million *cruzados* built his own version of a Portuguese Versailles in the form of the huge, "barrack-like monastery of Mafra" a few miles north of Lisbon. John V spent all of his royal income lavishly, squandered great sums on favorites of both sexes, tried to dazzle his courtiers with his extravagance, played patron to the arts by directing a part of the golden stream into a number of buildings of "more than dubious taste," and throughout his disastrous reign was subservient to a backward church. The Portuguese administration during the rule of John V was, in the words of a Brazilian historian, "one of utter nullity."[57]

As in the case of Spain, the Portuguese colonial system, with the great apparent wealth of precious stones and gold within its grasp, became an enormous suction pump which drew the glittering resources of Brazil toward its own shores, and then proceeded to squirt them at its own and all the other European courts. For many years Brazil profited little from its gold or its diamonds. A tightening of the colonial noose with more stringent governmental regulations only irritated the tempers of the colonists and helped force them to band together. Portugal made a big splurge temporarily, but by 1777 she was again in debt to the extent of three million pounds sterling.

In the long run, however, the development of Minas Geraes and of the territories stretching westward from that province to Bolivia enriched the colony with a knowledge of itself. The bandeirante continued to exist as a prospector and explorer, but the day of his forays for human flesh was done, and his lawless voracity gave way to an epoch of relative order. Minas Geraes became the colony's most populous province, the heart of a new Brazil. There was a new flowering of colonial architecture in the churches, mansions, and municipal buildings of the mining region. Despite Portugal's greed her child became rich. Gold and diamonds spread an aura of luxury and of art over the green land of forests. Minas Geraes, "a golden heart encased in a shield of iron," was El Dorado incarnate.

The nearly inexhaustible deposits of iron ore in its mountains and valleys have scarcely been touched to this day because of inadequate fuel and transportation facilities. A single one of these deposits, the huge "iron mountain," rises over the landscape like some colossus of old. It is the largest deposit of iron in the world and contains from twelve to fifteen *billion* tons of high-grade ore that is about 65 per cent pure iron, far superior to that found in most parts of Europe, and about equal to the best Swedish grades. Much of Brazil's industrial future still lies in the undeveloped resources of Minas Geraes, where the frontier of a new economy is already beginning to shape up behind the long-passed physical frontier which the gold and diamond rushes of the 1700s so violently pushed across the vast expanse of that province into Goyaz and Mato Grosso. In those days the colony was forming itself into a nation; in these days the nation is shaping itself into an industrial power.

30

ABORTIVE REBELLIONS IN SOUTH AMERICA

In every expression of nature and man we find the principles of life and death operating simultaneously, the one signifying expansion and growth, the other leading to disintegration from which a new life principle may issue. These parallel expressions operate upon the human body and upon every creation of the mind of man. They are especially noticeable in social organisms and nations, where they become the veritable spinal cord of the historic structure. While one factor works toward holding the organism together in healthy union and growing strength, the other leads toward weakness, division, conflict, and disintegration. When the dream of unity or growth has been spread too thin it may sometimes be maintained for many centuries by sheer emotional or physical power and then suddenly collapse, just as a balloon collapses when it is blown too full. As Aristotle pointed out many centuries ago, no society has ever arisen which did not bear within itself the seeds of its own destruction.

The Spanish colonial empire endured for over three centuries. The principle of unity within that structure was represented by Spanish culture and the Catholic Church and by the practice of miscegenation, the one working on the mind or spirit, the other upon the body. The principle of division was represented by economic, political, social, and racial cleavages which not only led toward separation of the dependencies from the mother country but toward disunity within the dependencies themselves. For the first two hundred years Spanish imperialism acted as a strong force binding these extremes together. During the century of Bourbon rule, beginning in 1700 and lasting until the struggle for independence in the early 1800s, the principle of division was gaining fast.

The Bourbons instituted many colonial reforms, and their efficiency did much to improve the American social structure, but the forces of division were moving faster still. It is one of the saddest truths of history that political and social reforms never keep pace with majority feeling or economic progress. This is why England lost the thirteen colonies, and why Spain lost her American empire; it is the explanation of every depression, revolution, or war in the history of mankind. Individual man is still so far ahead of man collectively that sometimes the results are almost incredible in their unreasonable destructiveness. There is no point in blaming the destructiveness. Every sore or disease is caused by some infection in the body; it is not spontaneously generated. Let us examine briefly some of the cankers in the historic evolution of colonial Spanish America.

When Gonzalo Pizarro and other conquistadores rebelled against the King in Peru in 1544 they claimed that they were fighting for liberty and captured and beheaded the King's representative. Gonzalo Pizarro himself was in turn beheaded by the royal authority after his forces were defeated. In Mexico at about the same time the two sons of Cortés, one legitimate and the other born of the Indian Malinche, also headed a plot against the King, which had as its purpose to place the legitimate son on the throne of Mexico in his own right. The cause of these uprisings in both Mexico and Peru was simply a desire to possess the loot of the conquest, but demagogues in both instances brought up the name of the common people in order to gain popularity for their cause.

There were many other isolated revolts during the early colonial years, but none lasted long. The Paraguayans ran their own district as they saw fit from 1535 to 1560; the Contreras brothers rebelled in Nicaragua (1542); Alvaro de Oyón led a small revolution in Popayán, Colombia, in 1553; Aguirre lifted the banner of rebellion against the King in the upper Amazon territory and wrote diatribe after diatribe against Philip II (1580). These rebellions were all indicative of that fierce individualism of the Iberian character which, after being suppressed in the home country, broke out again in America, where the means of control were more dispersed. They did not signify a mass feeling any more than had the rebellions of Pizarro and the Cortés brothers, but, like them, they did point toward the future, indicating to some extent the nature the final struggle for independence would take.

By the eighteenth century things were ripe for manifestations on a broader scale. Society now was like a neatly piled pyramid, with the Spanish whites sitting on the apex, directing the whole show beneath. Also near the apex, but under the Spanish-born privileged caste, were the Creoles. These two groups vilified each other constantly, for each wanted to occupy the dominant position. The rest of the pyramid was made up of all the other classes in the colonial population: mestizos, Indians, Negroes, and various mixtures of these. A good many mestizos had slipped into the Creole class, where they helped stir up bitterness against the foreign white oppressors. Two Spanish scientists, Jorge Juan and Antonio Ulloa, who were sent to America in 1735 by the King, made a secret report to the Crown in which they said: "It is incredible that among peoples of the same nation and even of the same blood there should exist so much enmity, bitterness, and hatred, and that every large city and town should be a center of violent discord between Spaniards and creoles. . . . It is a common occurrence to hear people say that if they could tear out the Spanish blood which they have inherited from their fathers, they would gladly do so in order that it might not taint that which they have inherited from their mothers."[86]

The mestizos and Indians fanned the flames of this ethnic division and kept things stirred up politically during most of the eighteenth century. In 1711 the mestizos and mulattoes of Venezuela proclaimed a mulatto king of that country, and in 1733, and again in 1751, the Creoles rose in arms against the Caracas Company, which had been given an almost absolute monopoly on Venezuelan commerce. Both revolts were fruitless. In Cochabamba, Bolivia, in 1730 several hundred mestizos rebelled against unjust taxation and won for themselves the right to appoint Creoles to take the place of certain Spanish-born town officials. In 1765 the Creoles of Quito also rose in protest against the *alcabala*, or sale and transfer tax, and four hundred of them were slain before they emerged victorious against the Spaniards and obtained an amnesty. "But these outbreaks which were the forerunners of the real revolution that was developing in the general conditions and spirit of men were only superficially of a political character; they were economic and lacked a definite form or deliberate purpose inspired by the desire for liberty and independence." In other words, they came nearer to being tumults or riots than revolutions.

The first strong movement of a political nature to disrupt the principle of monarchical control by setting up the symbol of popular sovereignty occurred in Latin America's most backward region, Paraguay. The governor of that territory was opposed by certain elements in the *cabildo*, or town council, of Asunción, and a special judge-investigator was sent there to settle the affair (1721). This man, José de Antequera, was a Creole, who promptly took over the governorship and put himself on the side of the cabildo. The old governor was clapped into jail, but he escaped and managed to persuade the Viceroy to reinstate him. When this news reached Asunción, Antequera called the cabildo together and very solemnly asked them what was their will in the matter. He stood before them "with a serene countenance," and asked the clerk to read the Viceroy's order. After the reading Antequera offered to send in his resignation if the cabildo so desired, but if they considered such action inadvisable he would gladly continue in office. "He besought each one of them freely to express his opinion, without being restrained by private reasons, but considering solely the public weal, as fathers of the country."[42] The cabildo gave him a resounding vote of confidence and refused to receive the old governor. The Viceroy then made a new appointment, but by this time it was too late. Antequera, the perfect demagogue, had already promised the people a redress of their grievances and to carry out their long-standing desire to attack the Jesuit missions. Again he called the cabildo together and asked them to render a decision based solely on the public welfare. On this occasion they requested that he leave the chamber in order that the discussion might proceed unimpeded. Antequera did so and after a stormy session the open cabildo decided not to accept the new governor who was already approaching the city.

Further orders from the Viceroy were received, demanding Antequera's resignation, but he claimed that these were forgeries and disregarded them. He strengthened his position by executing his most violent opponents and by attacking the Jesuits, who had moved up so near to Asunción that the townsmen were glad of any excuse to drive them back. This fixing of the public attention on an enemy outside made Antequera an extremely popular leader, and he soon felt strong enough to challenge the Viceroy directly. "The people do not abdicate!" he shouted to his partisans, and when troops were sent against the town they were met and defeated. For five years Antequera was dictator and his party ran Paraguay as it saw fit, but finally he was captured and taken to Lima, where he was imprisoned and condemned to be executed (1731).

Antequera never for a moment backed down on his principles and while in prison made an ardent convert of a fellow prisoner, Fernando Mompó. This man later escaped from Lima and headed straight for Paraguay, where in the words of the Viceroy "he revived the flames already smothered in ashes." Mompó found a ready ground for his doctrines and, with the aid of Antequera's old friends, went about haranguing and organizing the commoners for a large-scale rebellion against the King. "The authority of the commune is superior to that of the King himself!" he said. Before long the whole ignorant countryside was inflamed with these words and other similar ones with which Mompó regaled their ears. The revolt of the *comuneros*, or commoners, of Paraguay, as the rebels now began to call themselves, was fast coming to a head.

The Jesuit Lozano, commenting adversely on these happenings, wrote: "It was a ludicrous thing to see and hear a peasant, who came casually to the city and happened to hear Mompó, leave the place full of amazement and on meeting another peasant on the road say to him, arching his eyebrows and displaying in his countenance all the astonishment that possessed his soul: 'Ah, brother, what great things I have heard from a learned man in the city concerning what the community can do. He says that we can do more than the king and at times even more than the Pope. Behold, brother, what we had, without being aware of it. In truth how well they concealed this blessing from us, and would not teach it to us, so that we might not know how easily the community may cease to obey the Viceroy.' The listener would make the sign of the cross; and indeed this was necessary lest the devil enter into one's soul with this doctrine."[42] But despite violent Jesuit opposition Mompó continued to gain converts, and when the new governor arrived from Lima the comuneros drove him out of town.

Mompó had by this time organized his militia and was ready to take over the entire government of Paraguay. The city cabildo was undecided as to just how it should act, and while its members were still deliberating the comuneros surrounded the hall and tore down the only staircase leading to the street. In the meantime Mompó's organized militiamen entered the city shouting at the tops of their lungs, "¡Muera el mal gobierno [Down with the foul government]!"

When this howling mob reached the municipal building the chief magistrate, throwing caution to the winds, went out on the balcony to make an attempt to restore order. There were many in the crowd who had picked up several of Mompó's learned phrases, and before the magistrate could speak one of them shouted: "Honorable sir! What does vox populi, vox Dei mean? Answer what you like, but understand that it means the voice of the commune!"[42]

Shortly after this incident Mompó was captured and executed (1732), but his partisans did not give up the struggle until 1735. An army of Guaraní Indians from the Jesuit missions finally defeated them and restored the King's authority. There was another outbreak in 1741 but, with considerable spilling of blood, it too was suppressed, and the comuneros of Paraguay then gave up the ghost. The first real attempt to establish an independent government in a Latin-American country had gone down in complete defeat, although for twenty years it had disturbed the peace of mind of the royal authorities. There is no point in trying to make the rebellion appear as a mass movement for freedom, for it was anything but that. Hatred of the Jesuit theocracy and fear that its more disciplined authority might engulf their own shaky government were the mainsprings that stirred up Paraguayan emotions and released the germ of discontent. Antequera brought this feeling to a head with the strength of his personality, and Mompó continued the rebellion after the former's execution. The importance of the movement is that it showed the extent to which the central authority had already deteriorated, and the latent possibilities for revolt which lay in the long-oppressed and ignorant masses. The commoners had not initiated the movement, but they had encouraged and applauded every snipe at the King and every mention of their own right to sovereignty. The political implications of this rebellion in Paraguay soon spread to the far corners of South America, and the two grand-scale uprisings of the latter part of the century found inspiration in the brave but abortive independence of the comuneros.

Not long after these revolts in Paraguay came the decree for the total expulsion of the Jesuit Order from Spain and the Spanish dominions (1767). Eight years previously a similar decree had been issued by Portugal.

Although specific reasons for the act were never given by the central government, the principal motives are not difficult to find. First, the Jesuit theocracy, with all its immunities and particularly because of its unity, efficiency, and strength alongside the sprawling and inefficient civil government, had become so powerful that the King and his advisers considered it a threat to their own authority. Second, the Jesuit economic organization, with its control of vast mission lands, Indian workers, and haciendas, represented a direct economic challenge to the lay producers. This competition might easily have redounded to the benefit of the whole colonial empire, but in the totalitarian state of Charles III there was no room for an economically and politically powerful group among the clergy. A third and more obvious reason was that the Crown expected to enrich itself with Jesuit property, just as Henry VIII had done in England when he nationalized the Church of England and took over all church lands and buildings. Spain and Portugal were making a similar if somewhat more limited move two hundred and fifty years later.

The expulsion had to be planned and carried out with great secrecy, for the Jesuits were deeply loved by the masses of the people, and an open move might well have led to widespread rebellions. The officers who were to inform the Jesuits of the decree suddenly appeared in the dead of night at the hundreds of places where the fathers lived and made known their purpose. The Jesuits accepted the order without resistance and were taken to central assembly points, where they were placed on board ships and sent back to Europe. Large numbers settled in Italy and in the Low Countries. Many died before reaching their final destinations.

The expulsion did not increase either the wealth or power of the central government except for a brief period, and so far as the colonies were concerned it left a cultural and economic gap which was impossible to fill. A great proportion of colonial schools and colleges had been under Jesuit control, and when the order was expelled many of these institutions died away, for there were not sufficient trained teachers to take the places of those who had left. The shaky educational system of the colonies suffered a crushing blow. In the second place, the Jesuit missionaries, who lived among the half-savage natives of many border regions, had for years kept these districts under control and had made them productive parts of the colonial economy. When their guardians were expelled the semi-wild Indians more frequently than not reverted to their primitive state of life, and in some cases (Sonora, Mexico, for example) they revolted against the central government and had to be put down by force. Last of all, the Jesuit missions and plantations were by and large models of considerable efficiency. "The wealth of the Jesuits," states a North American writer who is not overly friendly to the Church, "lay, in fact, not in the hoards of silver and gold which they were supposed to have hidden, but in their ability to make things grow."[45] When this production was suddenly subtracted from the colonial economy it was bound to hurt.

In some places public resentment against the expulsion burst into open violence, and the cry of "Death to the Spaniards!" was raised by Indian and mestizo mobs. In Mexico the royal investigator, José de Gálvez, descended on the rebellious areas with a regiment of troops and "dealt out summary justice in a way that would have shocked Philip II. Eighty-five men were hanged, seventy-three were lashed into bloody ribbons, six hundred and seventy-four were condemned to prison, and one hundred and seventeen were banished. All of the convicts were Indians or mestizos. It may not be a coincidence that the jacquerie of Miguel Hidalgo broke out in the same region forty-three years later."[45]

The total effect of the expulsion order was to remove from colonial society one of the strongest pillars of order and social control. With the Jesuits gone, the road of revolutionary violence was easier to follow. Resentment at their expulsion also left a large body of the colonial citizenry at odds with the totalitarian policy of the King.

The first large-scale attempt at rebellion, however, which took place in Peru in 1780, had nothing to do with the Jesuits. It was a clear-cut protest against economic and political oppression. Before it ended the whole viceroyalty was torn apart with a full-fledged civil war. Briefly, the background was as follows: The *encomienda* system had been abolished in 1720, but a majority of the Indians were still forced to work their "turn," or *mita*, at whatever tasks their masters assigned. Legally, the system had been established to provide labor for public works; actually, it was made to provide whatever kind of labor the land, factory, or mineowners wanted.

The two Spanish investigators, Juan and Ulloa, in their secret report to the King stated bluntly that the Indians were forced to work three hundred days out of the year at an average yearly salary of fourteen to eighteen pesos, approximately fourteen to eighteen dollars. From this salary was subtracted eight pesos personal tribute tax, which left ten pesos, and from this remainder was taken the cost of the Indian's clothes—two or three pesos more. In many cases the master also obliged his Indians to purchase meat and corn from him at prices he set, and sometimes he made small advances so that there would be something to give the Church; these sums frequently brought the total debt up to a figure greater than the total income, and the Indian was forced to continue working indefinitely. If he died while still owing money the son had to assume the obligation. This was the condition of about half the Indians in the Andean region in the eighteenth century; Juan and Ulloa's report referred to the years 1735-44.

There were several kinds of labor which the Indians were forced to perform: tilling the soil, mining, and work in the *obrajes*, or cloth factories, of the mountains. Farming was the least evil of the three, for the work at least was done in the open fields. Many of those who were called up for work in the mines never returned; many died before their stint was out, and on various pretexts others were detained and forced to make up the deficit. Those who came out of the mines alive and with bodies unimpaired considered themselves fortunate. As a consequence of all this, "when it was announced that workers were to be drafted for this kind of *mita* the Indians would abandon their wives and children and escape to the high sierra where they hid among the trees or in caves and ravines."[87]

The workshops also employed a certain allotment of workers doing forced labor, and in them the poor Indian carried out his task "tied to the lathe, while his body slowly lost its vigor in the exhausting and interminable operation assigned to him. His miserable daily wage served mostly to pay for food and clothes, and the rest remained in the hands of the master to pay the personal tribute tax, the debts which had accumulated, and so on.

"The priests, for their part, received or extorted by a thousand means the little that was left to the Indian, the principal means being collections for saints, masses for the dead, domestic and parochial work on certain set days, forced gifts, and so forth. The tithe collectors also appeared at the moment of harvest to collect the portion which was due them."[87]

The Indians who were not caught in this net of forced labor were exploited by their *corregidores*, or provincial governors, placed over them by the central authorities. Male Indians between the ages of eighteen and fifty were supposed to pay the tribute tax, but the corregidor collected from everybody and pocketed the surplus. He also enjoyed the exclusive right of selling goods to his charges and brought goods from Lima which he distributed among them, whether or not they were needed. Such items as silk stockings and shaving implements were often foisted off on the natives at exorbitant prices. "As a consequence, the Spaniard who came over from the home country burdened with heavy debts, in five years of exercising his power as corregidor would frequently amass sixty thousand pesos and many of them received more than two hundred thousand. The system of exploitation of the Indian, therefore, was iniquitous and overwhelming."[87]

Although the above conditions were widespread only in the Andean region—Peru, Ecuador, and Bolivia, where the Indian element made up nine tenths of the population—they existed in other regions on a smaller scale. It must not be forgotten that every Spanish American country on the eve of the struggle for independence (1800) was predominantly Indian or mestizo in blood.

There lived among the Indians of Peru a native leader who went by the name of José Gabriel Condorcanqui and claimed he was a direct descendant of the Inca rulers and of that famous Tupac Amaru, who had been beheaded by the Viceroy Toledo in the sixteenth century. This man had

been educated in Cuzco and Lima, and the Spanish authorities had honored him with the title Marquis of Oropesa. He was the chieftain of several
native villages and had done everything in his power to alleviate the
sufferings of his people, oftentimes paying their tribute for them and
always ready to defend them in court. However, the abuses continued,
and José Gabriel, the Indian marquis, only incurred the hatred of the corregidores without permanently benefiting the Indians.

He was a highly educated man and was an avid reader. His favorite
book was one which was then prohibited reading in Peru, the *Royal
Commentaries of the Incas,* by the son of an Inca princess and a Spanish
conquistador, Garcilaso de la Vega. The Spanish authorities were afraid
that Garcilaso's sympathetic story of the past grandeur of his people might
incite some of them to rebellion, and made it a crime to read this book.
José Gabriel read and reread the pages which sang the glories of his ancient
race, and his hatred for the oppressors became more intense. Sometimes
his reading would be interrupted by the passing of lines of miserable natives on their way to the workshops or mines to perform their endless
"turn" of labor.

Among the officials of the district who were most guilty of exceeding
the law in the extortions from the Indians was the corregidor, Arriaga.
The Indian leader had more than once remonstrated with him about these
injustices, always using the phrase "my Indians." His complaints had
fallen on deaf ears, and he had then done what he could with his own
money to relieve them of oppressive taxes and tributes. The relationship
existing between the corregidor and José Gabriel was anything but friendly
when one night they both were invited to a priest's home to a banquet.
Much wine was consumed and many toasts were drunk to the King of
Spain. The Indian marquis took part in these amenities, but the guests
could sense the air of almost electric hatred with which he and Arriàga
regarded each other.

When the feast was over José Gabriel and his friends took their leave
first. Shortly afterward the corregidor, with several of his drunken companions, followed. About halfway home the marquis and a band of Indians were lying in wait for them. Suddenly swishing out of the darkness
came a well-aimed lasso which deftly settled about the corregidor's head,
jerking him from his mount. He was carried as a prisoner to a neighboring village, where a violent multitude of Indians demanded his life. A platform was raised in the plaza of the town and "solemnly as would be proper
in a well constituted state the noose was placed about the governor's neck.
José Gabriel gave the order for the execution. Unfortunately, the mechanism failed to function. The state was not so well constituted after all."[88]
The rope suddenly snapped and the corregidor raced like a wild deer for
the sanctuary of a near-by church. The marquis was faster still and over-
took him. This time the hangman's rope performed its duty. Turning to-

ward his people, the Indian leader then publicly proclaimed a state of rebellion, took the name of Tupac Amaru, his predecessor, and announced the re-establishment of the Inca Empire with himself as its monarch.

The whole Peruvian countryside was now in a state of seething revolt. Tupac Amaru II soon gathered about him a motley army of considerable size. Indians deserted their work in mines, fields, and shops, and joined his banner. At the head of six thousand men he advanced against Cuzco, the old Inca capital. Only three hundred of his soldiers had rifles; the rest were armed with lances, Indian slings, spears, daggers, and various other implements. In the vicinity of Cuzco he was met by a well-organized force and defeated, but he escaped into the hills and a few weeks later appeared again, this time at the head of an army of twenty thousand men. The viceroys both at Lima and Buenos Aires became alarmed, and each of them assembled forces which advanced on Tupac Amaru from several directions. The Indians were defeated, but again their leader escaped and continued the fight until one of his subordinates treacherously delivered him and his entire family over to the Spanish authorities.

The royal investigator passed the sentence of death on Tupac Amaru and his leading supporters. The execution was to be public so that it would serve as a reminder to other possible rebels, and the manner of carrying it out was like something from the pages of the Dark Ages. First of all, Tupac Amaru was to witness the death of his wife, one of his sons, an uncle, his brother-in-law, and his captains. Two of them were to have their tongues cut out before execution. When all this had been done the hangman cut out Tupac Amaru's own tongue and then a horse was tied to each arm and leg and suddenly driven in different directions. The stout body of the Indian refused to be torn asunder and went through the most horrible agonies until it was finally decided to strike off his head.

Other portions of the sentence were "to have his body burnt on the heights of Picchu, and to have his head and arms and legs stuck on poles to be set up in the different towns that had been loyal to him; to have his houses demolished, their sites strewn with salt, his goods confiscated, his relatives declared infamous, and all documents relating to his descent burnt by the hangman. It was also provided that all Inca and cacique [chieftain] dresses should be prohibited, all pictures of the Incas destroyed, the presentation of Quichua dramas forbidden, the musical instruments of the Indians burned; all signs of mourning for the Incas, the use of all national costumes by the Indians, and the use of the Quichua language should be prohibited. This sentence in all its barbarity was carried out on the 18th of May, 1781."[89]

The effect of these cruelties was catastrophic and was the exact opposite of what the Spaniards had anticipated. The Indians of the mountain country rose in spontaneous masses and continued the war. They captured one Spanish town and beheaded every one of the inhabitants, and an army of several thousands besieged La Paz for one hundred and nine days before it was finally relieved by troops from Argentina. It was not until 1783, two years after the death of Tupac Amaru, that order was finally restored. The civil war had cost approximately eighty thousand lives, and the country was devastated. The Indians were again forced to bow under the heavy yoke of oppression, but this rebellion had put them in a frame of mind which they could not easily forget, and when, forty years later, Bolívar appeared on the scene, they cast in their lot with his, willing to give comfort and aid to anyone who was fighting the hated Spaniards.

Across the northern borders of Peru, in the viceroyalty of New Granada (Colombia), at about the same time as Tupac Amaru was leading his rebellion, there occurred another large-scale outbreak against the local authorities. This revolt, like that of the Indians in Peru, was in the nature of things as they existed in Colombia.

When the Viceroy Flórez came to this region in 1776 as the representative of Charles III, he was filled with liberal dreams of what wonders he would accomplish. His superior, the Viceroy Guirior, who was soon to leave Bogotá for Lima, came to meet him, and together they talked over the situation. Guirior, who was also of a liberal turn of mind, had already become pessimistic. He had tried his hand at opposing the "vested interests" of New Granada and had been defeated. Flórez refused to believe him. Shortly after their meeting Guirior left for Lima, where the Indians were already beginning to rise in isolated rebellions in different parts of the country, and Flórez proceeded to Bogotá.

We already know what happened in Peru. The Viceroy Guirior again tried the policy of justice and conciliation, but the "interests" would not heed him. He argued for a stricter application of the laws passed to protect the Indians, and for more clemency when a native was tried by a Spanish court. They laughed at his innocence. Wasn't an Indian always an Indian, a child, almost an animal, who had to be forced to obey and who could not possibly know what was best for him? Whenever an Indian dared to challenge a Spaniard, they said that punishment must be swift and rigorous. The Viceroy argued in vain; it took the death of eighty thousand Peruvians to prove him right. And by that time the "interests" had gotten rid of him anyway.

In Colombia it was the same. The Viceroy Flórez carefully surveyed the state of his dominion, and a scene of inert misery met his gaze. "This New Granada, which might have been one of the richest colonies, was standing still, there was no progress, it was a land with a curse on it. There was no money in the royal treasury. There was almost no naval defense. All trade was in the hands of smugglers. Education was in a state of complete atrophy. The poor were wandering through the streets of the towns and cities refusing to work, and besides, none among them were capable of exercising any trade. Production was almost nothing. . . ."[88]

Then there was that "damned *alcabala*," the omnipresent tax on the sale or transfer of every piece of goods or property. Tallow candles, eggs, soap, honey, and every other thing were subject to the alcabala when they went from one person to another. In order that nothing would be omitted there was even an alcabala "on the wind" in New Granada which the traveling salesmen with no permanent domicile had to pay. In order to complete the irony of the thing here were the exemptions: books in Latin, pictures, gold purchased by the mint, hats from the royal factory in Madrid![88]

But the alcabala, despite its having been raised recently to 6 per cent on every transfer, was not bringing in sufficient revenue. The royal investigator, Gutiérrez de Piñeres, decided to increase several other taxes and to levy a few new ones on his own account. He also raised the prices of articles sold in the government *estancos*, or commissaries, such as salt, tobacco, playing cards, and so on, on a monopolistic basis. The royal investigator, however, was not content to stop here. He slapped special taxes on industries which formerly had been free, nearly ruined the cotton region of the north by taxing cloth, and then levied a toll "on the roads down which travelers and merchants had to pass, furnished guides to show them the way, and return guides to lead them back again by still another tax collector."

War had broken out between Spain and England, and the Viceroy had left Bogotá for the coast, which he was attempting to put into a proper state of defense. Piñeres, whose principal mission as the King's special emissary in Colombia was to obtain revenues to carry on this war, remained in the capital in charge of the government. He was still far from satisfied with the yield of the taxes he had levied and proceeded next to divide the inhabitants into two classes, on each of which he placed a capital levy. The well to do were to pay two pesos, the poor people one. Added to all this, the government guards had been taking the law into their own hands and went about pillaging, stealing, and violating women in the knowledge that they could be tried only by their superior officers who did not seem to want to bother. The result of these intolerable conditions was a series of outbreaks in different parts of Colombia.

The rebels claimed that they were representing the towns or communes and so called themselves the comuneros, just as had the Paraguayans of fifty years earlier and the Spaniards who had risen against Charles V in 1520. Verses and diatribes against the authorities began to appear on the walls in many towns and anti-government leaflets were distributed on many streets. Anger was not directed at Spain, but at the local regime and collectors. It was not a movement for independence, but merely to abolish manifestly unjust taxes.

One day in the little town of Socorro, when a large part of the inhabitants were gathered at the market place, a woman by the name of Manuela Beltrán made a public issue of tearing down several of the government tax announcements and trampling on them. In no time at all she had the whole mob howling against the local authorities, and at their head she advanced on the municipal building demanding justice.

Similar uprisings took place in other villages of northern Colombia and within a few days several thousand rebels had gathered in Socorro to appoint their leaders and take more drastic action. The chieftain who was selected made it plain that he was leading no separatist movement, but merely a public revolt against known abuses. When the comunero forces had swelled to approximately twenty thousand they decided to march on Bogotá. They mixed shouts of "Hurrah for Socorro and down with the foul government!" with other shouts of "Hurrah for the King and down with the foul government!" The belief still persisted that the King was on their side, or at least would have been had he been properly informed of the situation. However, the things that they shouted about the taxes and those who were trying to collect them are unprintable.

The mob also had its lyric moments. Folk poetry is innate in both the Indian and the Spaniard, so as this multitude of mestizos and Indians advanced on Bogotá regular ballads were composed to commemorate the event. One of them told how each government authority in turn passed the buck to some other authority whenever a grievance came up. As a last resort the poor complaining Indian, oppressed by rich and poor alike, might appeal to the King of Spain and of the Indies, "but the King was far away."

> Acallen los atambores
> y vosotros sedme atentos
> que éste es el romance fiel
> que dicen los comuneros:
> El rico le tira al probe;
> al indio, que vale menos,
> ricos y probes le tiran
> a partirlo medio a medio.
> Presto le advierte el Fiscal
> que al Alcalde vay a luego;
> el Alcalde lo transporta
> sulcando valles y cerros
> para que al corregidor
> él le confiese sus duelos . . .
> Resta al indio querellante
> como su mero consuelo
> el Rey de España y las Indias
> ¡pero el Rey está muy lejos! . . .[88]

When this multitude of nearly twenty thousand Colombian Indians and mestizos reached the vicinity of Bogotá, the royal "visitor" or investigator who was still in charge of the government there began to shake in his boots. He and the city authorities assembled the one hundred available soldiers and sent them against the camp of the comuneros. When the troops saw what a host opposed them they quickly broke ranks and fled. As soon as the royal visitor received news of the outcome of this encounter he took to his heels and headed in the direction of the Magdalena River. There he got on a boat and did not stop until he reached Cartagena on the coast. Left without a leader, the city authorities appointed a couple of commissioners and the Archbishop Antonio Caballero y Góngora to represent them. These representatives advanced toward the camp of the insurgents to sue for peace.

The insurgent leader, Berbeo, in the name of the comuneros presented to them a set of "capitulations," or conditions under which the soldiers of his army would retire peacefully to their homes. Certain taxes were to be lowered immediately, and certain others were to be canceled altogether. Specific public positions which had formerly been reserved for the Spanish born were to be occupied by native Colombians. These conditions were to be sworn to by representatives of the Audiencia, or Supreme Court.

The capitulations were accepted by the government, and early in June of 1781 the solemn oath was taken in the ancient parochial church of Zipaquira. The story goes that the church was too small to hold more than a tiny minority of the comuneros and so the ceremony was repeated on the great plain near the town. An altar was raised and the mob of twenty thousand heard a solemn mass celebrated by the archbishop himself. When the Host was raised, the government commissioners on their part and the commoners on theirs swore with their hands on the Testament to observe the agreement. Soon afterward the mob dispersed, carrying away copies of the agreement which they held over their heads in token of obedience. The archbishop accompanied them back to their homes in the north preaching peace, quieting tempers, and assuring the inhabitants that their grievances would be redressed. The rude townsmen of the north country received him with affection and warmth. Out of their generous hearts they brought him gifts of firewood, food, special fruits of the season, and the finest chocolate obtainable in all Colombia. And when he passed down the streets they took his plump hand in theirs, respectfully bent their knees, and kissed his signet ring. Sometimes at night, under a clear tropical sky, bands of the faithful would gather in the streets to serenade the illustrious visitor. To the accompaniment of a primitive pipes of Pan, and holding aloft the image of their Virgin, they sang a song in which they asked divine blessing for their good shepherd and begged him to remain among them "even though it be but for a single year."

The archbishop liked this song so much that a group of women in town had it carefully written down for him and after decorating the sheet with all kinds of minute sketches presented it to His Grace, who was deeply touched by this demonstration of affection. The townsmen did not know that all the while their illustrious visitor was carrying on private meetings with the town authorities, helping them to organize a better militia so that if the *plebe*, or masses, rebelled again matters might be more quickly brought under control. The archbishop himself later referred to that first revolt of the commoners in these words: "It was a flock of mutinous folk stirred up by deception and false lures . . ."[88]

The government in Bogotá did not hold to its agreement with the commoners. The royal visitor, who had reached the safety of the coast, worked on the mind of the reluctant Viceroy and together they had refused to abide by the solemn oath taken by their representatives in the capital, and endorsed by the archbishop himself. The reasons they gave for their action were those which might have been expected from men whose power and property were menaced by an uncontrollable mob. "That which is demanded and won from the authorities with violence brings with it perpetual nullity and is in itself an open declaration of treachery."[88]

When this news reached the northern provinces another leader, Galán, arose to lead the comuneros in defense of their rights. This time the authorities were better prepared, and the masses who had just gone through one long and highly emotional outburst were incapable of another. Galán and his co-leaders were quickly captured and brought to Bogotá for trial. In January of 1782 four of them were executed, their bodies cut into four pieces, the trunks burned and thrown to the winds in ashes, the members displayed to teach the villagers a lesson, their heads stuck on poles for public exhibition. The judges further ordered that the victims' houses should be razed and sprinkled with salt and that their descendants should be declared infamous forever afterward. This horrible sentence was punctually executed.

"In such a manner," comments the leading history of Colombia, "did the revolt of the *comuneros* terminate. This movement merits the respect of posterity because its participants fought with disinterest and enthusiasm in defense of those rights of property which make men free."[90] As soon as the second uprising was stifled in blood the old taxes were again slapped on a helpless and poverty-stricken people.

Again, as in the case of Mexico almost a hundred years earlier, a mob had rebelled against the established authority when it could endure oppression no longer. Actual hunger, poverty, and privation had aroused a mass feeling which burst into a sudden and unexpected blaze. It came like a conflagration which gains silent headway as people lie in peaceful slumber on a cold, dark night. Again the men of power, the men of property, the men of breeding and birth found an ally in the Church, and the ignorant commoners who trusted both were defrauded by both of their mess of pottage. Such uprisings as these may well be called riots, blind and rabble-inspired protests against recognized authority, revolutions without ideology or program, and their excesses may easily be pointed out. With all that granted they still teach more to the historian than any number of soft-spoken phrases which have issued from the compromised pens of those who occupy the seats of the mighty, anxious to please all, pleasing none, but defending their own interests with a logic and eloquence which seduce the casual reader. Paraphrasing the words of those earlier comuneros of Paraguay when they shouted to the chief magistrate of Asunción, we may say: "Call such riots what you may, honorable sirs, they are the cry of the people against tyranny and economic oppression!" Before long, as we shall see, that small voice crying in the wilderness found its echo in a hundred thousand tongues of flame, and the dumb beast unleashed swept in a great fury of blood and destruction over the fair cities of more than one Latin-American country.

31

REVOLT OF THE CLASSES

At the close of the eighteenth century Latin America was still living in the shadow of the Middle Ages. The Inquisition was still alive; the feudal system of master and vassal was the core of economic life; political absolutism was the rule rather than the exception, despite the reforms of the Bourbon monarchs, and taxation had become so oppressive that large-scale revolts had broken out in several regions even when the chances of success were practically nil. Everywhere the economic situation of the immense majority of the people was one of unmitigated misery. In the viceroyalty of New Spain or Mexico, which then included Texas, New Mexico, Arizona, and California, the average yearly value of agricultural products during the latter years of the eighteenth century was forty million dollars, while manufactured goods represented about seven million dollars. If we place the value of all other products at fifty million dollars yearly, the total productive capacity of Spain's wealthiest and most populous colony would still be less than one hundred million dollars a year. Mexico at that time had a population of between five and six millions, or about half the total of all Spanish America. On a per capita basis her income thus meant approximately twenty dollars a year for each inhabitant, and when we consider that the wealthy minority must have averaged many times this amount we begin to get some conception of the very primitive level at which the majority lived. Yet with the single exception of the region of the River Plate the remainder of Spanish America had a still lower standard than Mexico.

This economic wretchedness, plus the merciless and systematic exploitation by taxation and an enforced vassalage of the lower classes, was what caused the rebellion of Tupac Amaru and his Indians and the revolt of the comuneros in New Granada. However, such wretchedness was not what caused the struggle for independence. It was one of many causes, but it came nearer the tail than the head of the list. The struggle for independence in the Spanish colonies was mainly the result of a long-drawn-out enmity between Spaniards and Creoles which gave wings to thinking and planning for freedom among the Creole class. Creoles conceived of independence; Creoles assumed the responsibility for leadership; Creoles laid down the revolutionary programs, led the revolutionary forces on the fields of battle, and established the regionalistic regimes which were to follow. Without some support from the lower classes of mestizos, Indians, Negroes, and mulattoes, their ranks would indeed have been too thin to be successful. But it is well to bear in mind that the immense majority of these masses held themselves apart from the struggle, were indifferent and even suspicious of its aims, and in many regions profited in name only when one set of leaders displaced another to become the wielders of power over their flimsy and oppressed society.

There is nothing unusual about this apathy on the part of the masses. It is extremely doubtful if there has ever been a real mass revolution in the history of the world. In his *History of the United States* Channing estimates that out of a total population of approximately three million in this country in 1776 only 1,200,000 may be considered as rebels. James Truslow Adams, in his *Epic of America*, recalls that John Adams had said that only a third of the people wanted a revolution. A much smaller minority than this carried out the French Revolution of 1789, and the incredibly small minority of approximately fifty thousand "Reds" out of Russia's one hundred and fifty million brought about communism in the Soviet Union.

The historic facts differed greatly in each case, but in each there were one or two fundamental similarities. First, political tyranny and economic oppression gave rise to widespread unrest. Out of unrest grew the hope and idea of revolt which resulted in the rise of intellectual leadership for the revolutionary cause. Second, a combination of internal and external circumstances so weakened the central government that the revolutionary ideal suddenly found itself face to face with a wonderful opportunity to seize the governing power, and did so in each case despite its lack of preparation for efficient, tolerant, or progressive rule. Every *successful* revolution seems to follow this general course.

The similarities between the North American and Spanish American emancipations are more than casual. Both were struggles against the mother country in Europe; both were undertaken when the mother country was otherwise engaged; both were fought against incredible odds, and the first helped to bring about the second as a natural sequence of world events. In fact, the famous Argentine historian and president, Bartolomé Mitre, wrote that the independence of the United States was the extraordinary event which contributed most to create that atmosphere and ideology of liberty in Spanish America which were to give the final deathblow to the ancient colonial system. It not only aroused the hitherto inert Creole class to an awareness of its situation and of its potential strength, but even gave the mother country a forewarning of the independence that was bound to come sooner or later to her own American colonies.

The Count of Aranda, one of the finest statesmen in the court of liberal and forward-looking Charles III of Spain, advised his sovereign in 1783 to anticipate this struggle by placing the colonies under three kings, one for Mexico and two for South America, yet reserving for himself the title of emperor. After commenting on the difficulty of ruling efficiently such vast dominions at such a great distance from the home country, Aranda prophetically comments on the recent birth of the United States: "We have just recognized a new power in a great region where there exists no other to challenge its growth. This federal republic was born a pigmy, but the day will come when it grows and becomes a giant and even a colossus in those regions. Within a few years we will regard the existence of this colossus with real sorrow."[30]

The Spanish monarch closed his eyes to this danger and to this good advice. He had actually aided the North Americans in their war against England and had recognized them as an independent nation. But he had done this in his own interest, not theirs, and he was unable to see what far-reaching effects the birth of democratic government in this one small corner of the American hemisphere would eventually have. Six years later, when the French Revolution of 1789 "illumined the conscience of man with its sudden and brilliant light, it made clear the abyss which he had dug out at the foot of his throne."[30]

By then it was too late. The North American revolution had universalized itself in France, and its principles stirred the minds of thinking men all over the civilized world. The social and political leadership of Europe was now at an end and that of the New World had begun. Absolutism had been brought from the Old World to America in the first current of expansion, but now the current was reversed and America was bringing to Europe its torch of democratic ideas. There would be reactions, retrenchments, backward steps, but the path of the future was now clearly marked, and, after France, the Latin-American nations were the first to follow.

Rousseau, Montesquieu, Voltaire, and other French writers now inspired with a new liberalism many illustrious Creoles both in America and in Europe, were those who could afford it so often went to study and to travel. Commenting on this change in his own mind, the Argentine revolutionary hero, Manuel Belgrano, wrote as follows: "As I was in Spain in 1789, and the French Revolution was then causing a change in ideas, and especially in the men of letters with whom I associated, the ideals of liberty, equality, security, and property took a firm hold on me, and I only saw tyrants in those who opposed man's enjoying, wherever he might be, those rights with which God and Nature endowed him. . . ."[79]

Wearied of European absolutism and of political discrimination against their own class, Belgrano and many other leading Creoles thus began to identify themselves with the new liberalism then being born in the world. Especially among intellectual groups in universities, Masonic lodges, among cliques and societies of thinkers and writers, these ideas became a tremendous force. Those who in their impressionable youth had seen the triumph of democratic ideas in North America and France were the mature leaders in the struggle for Spanish American liberty which was to follow.

The central Spanish authorities did everything in their power to discourage liberal thinking. They knew that the North American revolution had not only been avidly followed by the Creoles of Latin America, but that medallions commemorating it and inscribed with the words "American Liberty" were secretly collected and became extremely popular in the southern countries. The government at Madrid by royal decree made it a crime to possess such medallions and directed its representatives to "keep a most careful watch to see that they do not enter our colonies."

Utilizing the Inquisition as its instrument, the central authority also persecuted many who were accused of being guilty of "heretical ideas," meaning the ideas of democracy and freedom symbolized by the North American and French revolutions. In 1788 the Peruvian Olavide, who with the help of the Chilean Salas had organized in Madrid a Society of Citizens from American Cities and Towns, was condemned by the Inquisition and forced to perform an ignominious public penance. He had been found guilty of heretical beliefs and of having possessed in his private library the writings of Montesquieu, Rousseau, Voltaire, and Bayle. Two years later (1790), when the Argentine Belgrano decided to read these and other works which were on the prohibited list, he went straight to the Pope for permission. His Holiness, with a much greater show of tolerance than that shown by the inquisitors in Spanish America, granted him the right "to read any books whatever of condemned authors even though they be heretical, and exactly as they were originally written, provided that he does not let them pass to other hands."[79] The wealthy and cultured Belgrano, of course, was an exception. It was still considered too dangerous to permit the common reader to peruse authors who defended individual liberty or who attacked the authoritarian principles of absolute monarchy or of the Catholic Church.

This was not the only way the Spanish Government had of protecting itself. Charles IV declared war on France after the beheading of Louis XVI, and everything possible was done to bring into disrepute the ideals of the new French regime. In Lima, for example, in 1793 the Viceroy founded the *Gaceta de Lima* for the explicit purpose of giving the public an account of the horrible excesses of the French Revolution, and in other colonies similar attacks were leveled at the newly born democracies.

Despite all these restrictions the new ideas continued to spread and gain force among the Creole class. One of the first great leaders of the liberal movement in northern South America was a young Colombian intellectual of aristocratic birth named Antonio Nariño. Born in Bogotá in 1765, Nariño at an early age became a strong influence among the youths of the Colombian capital. In the extensive and cosmopolitan library of his finely furnished home there hung a large picture of Benjamin Franklin. The young progressives of the city frequently gathered there for secret political discussions. This same group also met in the home of a distinguished lady of the capital, and Nariño was always the one who spoke loudest and most eloquently for independence and liberty. In 1794 there came to his hands a copy of the *Declaration of the Rights of Man*, promulgated by the Constituent French Assembly, which Nariño translated into Spanish and on his own private press had several copies printed and distributed among his friends. Nariño looked upon this declaration as the embodiment of the ideals of a "regenerated society," and copies of his translation which found their way into the most distant South American capitals did much to stir up a similar feeling in other quarters of the continent.

The translator was denounced before the central government, and as many copies of his "seditious pamphlet" as could be located were burned by order of the Viceroy. Nariño himself and several others who were involved in the affair were banished from Spanish America. As leader of the group he was also condemned to ten years imprisonment in Africa; his goods were confiscated, his family proscribed and left destitute. He escaped from his guardians as the ship landed in Spain, however, and later went to France and England, where he continued to work for the revolution in South America. The authorities again caught up with him in Bogotá. This time he was imprisoned in Madrid, but somehow he managed to get away and return to Colombia, where he took part in the actual revolution. In 1824 he died "alone and persecuted by the ingratitude of his compatriots." After his death he became a great Colombian hero and his heart-rending words, "I have loved my country; only History will say what this love has been," are inscribed at the foot of his statue.

Nariño was "the most genuine representative of the progressive and self-denying youth" who prepared the ground for the battles to follow, and his life was a "symbol of the hazardous destiny which awaited the great artisans of the South American Revolution." However, he was caught in a crosscurrent and did not take his place at the forefront of the revolutionary movement.

The outstanding precursor and "morning star of the Spanish American Revolution" was the noble Venezuelan adventurer, Francisco Miranda.

This mystic and ambitious dreamer was born in Caracas in 1750 into the family of a prosperous merchant. At the age of seventeen he bought himself a captaincy in the Spanish army and fought first in Morocco, then in North America under Rochambeau and George Washington; later he traveled to Russia, where he became an intimate friend of Catherine the Great; finally he enlisted in the ranks of the French revolutionists, where he attained the rank of general. Napoleon referred to him as a "soul filled with sacred fire," and had his name inscribed on the Arc de Triomphe in Paris. From the time of the French Revolution to the day of his final defeat and imprisonment in 1808, Miranda worked tirelessly for the independence of Spanish America, passing from one European country to another in an effort to gain support for his plans. Two or three times he was on the verge of success in England, France, and also in the United States, but on each occasion circumstances altered the situation before much help was forthcoming and Miranda had to carry his hopes elsewhere. He spoke with persuasive eloquence and logic, and if the slightest interest was shown he was always ready with charts, maps, constitutions, and other documents in support of his scheme.

Miranda's first great attempt to gain the independence of South America came in 1806 and was carried out from the United States. He had already obtained from England a "firm promise of military aid" and actually carried in his pockets a subsidy of twelve thousand pounds sterling. Jefferson, then President of this country, and Madison, who was Secretary of State, were unwilling to co-operate with him, but Alexander Hamilton showed more enthusiasm and helped push his ideas along. Miranda persuaded about two hundred Americans to join his banners, and with this small force set out to free South America from the yoke of Spain. He did not think that there was anything ridiculous in undertaking the enterprise with such a puny force, because he had been thinking and breathing independence for so many years that, as one of his officers wrote, he was convinced "all he would have to do would be to appear off the coast of Venezuela for South America to cease to be a Spanish province." Volunteers, he thought, would immediately swell his ranks to a powerful army, and the forces of liberation would then be able to sweep on to a quick and decisive victory.

The Spaniards were forewarned, and when Miranda's ships appeared on the horizon two strongly armed naval vessels attacked them, captured his two escorts, and drove the ship carrying the leader himself away. He sailed to the West Indies for reinforcements and came back again a short time later. On this occasion he managed to land at Coro, Venezuela. The place was almost deserted, and after being ashore a few days Miranda saw that the inhabitants were not at all disposed to take part in his venture. "Not a single Venezuelan joined the ranks of the Precursor." A large Spanish force was advancing on the town, so without further waiting Miranda cast off again, discharged his crews in the United States, and returned to England.

He had been away from his home country too long to know what the state of opinion there was, and learned to his sorrow that the mass of Creole citizenry had not kept pace with his own fervent zeal for independence. But there was another reason as well: the Creoles who knew his story had come to regard him "as an instrument of the English cabinet" and in their hearts had disavowed him from the beginning. To many of them the tyranny of Spain had become galling, but the bare suspicion of a foreign domination was even worse. Intuitively they had hit the nail squarely on the head.

When Miranda arrived in England after his complete fiasco on the Venezuelan beaches, he immediately began to negotiate for further British aid in his project. England and Spain were then at war, and Sir Arthur Wellesley, who later became the Duke of Wellington, finally agreed to lead an expedition of ten thousand men. Plans had been made and the army was being assembled when Napoleon suddenly marched into Spain and placed his brother Joseph on the Spanish throne. Deserted by their own King, who became a prisoner in France, the Spanish people arose against the invaders and the whole peninsula was aflame with bands of patriots eager to fight the hated French. England took advantage of this opportunity to get in a strong underside blow against Napoleon, declared herself in sympathy with the insurgents, and Wellington was chosen to head the English army which was sent to aid them. After thus suddenly making an ally of her old enemy, England could hardly proceed with the plans to steal her colonies out from under her nose, and Miranda's project was abruptly called off. Wellington, who was delegated to break the news to him, made the following comment:

"I think I never had a more difficult business than when the government bade me tell Miranda that we would have nothing to do with his plan. I thought it best to walk out in the streets with him and tell him there, to prevent his bursting out. But even there he was so loud and angry, that I told him I would walk on a little that we might not attract the notice of everybody passing. When I joined him again he was cooler. He said: 'You are going over into Spain . . . you will be lost—nothing can save you; that, however, is your affair; but what grieves me is that there never was such an opportunity thrown away!'"

Nevertheless, Miranda continued to work at his task, and circumstances soon proved that times were about ripe for a change in colonial affairs. Two outstanding events caused this change in Creole thinking, and before long many Creoles who had hitherto shown timidity in backing the cause of independence began to come out openly in its favor. The first event was the invasion and capture of Buenos Aires by the English in 1806–07, and the second was the disastrous situation in Spain itself. These two circumstances jarred loose the firm grip which the mother country still had on her colonial possessions, and she was never again able to get them in so strong a grasp.

The English invasions of Argentina came in a very roundabout way. Sir Home Popham, commander of a British expedition to seize the Dutch colonies in South Africa, had often talked with Miranda and was anxious to invade Spanish America on his own account. After the successful conclusion of his campaign in Africa he and General Beresford, without orders from the British Government, sailed from the Cape of Good Hope with ten vessels and about sixteen hundred men, and on June 25, 1806, they entered Buenos Aires and "took possession of a city of fifty-five thousand souls." The Viceroy Sobremonte was caught completely by surprise and fled at the first sign of danger. The indignant populace later lampooned him with the following couplet:

> Al primer canonazo de los valientes
> disparó Sobremonte con los parientes!

> At the first gunshot and the soldiers' shout
> Sobremonte and his kin cleared out!

The Spanish forces in Buenos Aires were quickly overcome; the English were soon in complete control of the city, and with much fanfare the loot from the government treasury was sent back to London. In the meantime the commander of the Spanish fleet in the La Plata region, Santiago de Liniers, a Frenchman who had for many years been in the service of Spain, was making plans to retake the city. The governor of Montevideo furnished him with one thousand men, and his ranks were further swelled by a large contingent of valiant peasants. He attacked vigorously and after a bloody battle forced the English general to surrender. About five hundred men were killed in the engagement. The city now convoked an open cabildo, or town meeting, and, without awaiting instructions from Spain, forthwith deposed the old Viceroy and elevated Liniers to that position.

The government in England had by this time received news of the capture of Buenos Aires and promptly dispatched reinforcements to secure the occupation. General John Whitelocke soon arrived on the scene with twelve thousand men. He first took Montevideo and then proceeded to the attack on Buenos Aires. In the early stages the battle favored the British, but when they actually began to enter the city they were met by a furious house-to-house resistance which, within a few hours, had cost them three thousand men and had broken their morale completely. General Whitelocke surrendered, and the defeated remnants of his British army returned to England. A motley and badly trained citizen army of Creoles and peasants had met and won a decisive victory over a well-disciplined and vastly more numerous force. Whitelocke had fought well, but the resistance he met was overpowering. He himself later commented on his disaster by saying that "every male inhabitant, whether free or slave, fought with a resolution and perseverance which could not have been expected, even from the enthusiasm of religion and national prejudice, or the most inveterate and implacable hostility."[42]

The victory of the citizens of Buenos Aires over the English stirred the entire continent with a new awareness of its native strength. They had seen the North Americans, then the French revolutionists wage a successful fight against great odds, but neither of these foreign struggles gave them the confidence which came out of their own successful defense of Buenos Aires. On the other hand, the Viceroy at Lima had sent aid to the gallant city to the extent of seven hundred thousand pesos, and after this scare the Spanish authorities took an account of their situation and improved their military establishment. These results of the English invasions might possibly have offset each other had not conditions inside Spain thrown the balance completely over to the side of the Creoles, who were already beginning to look on independence with more than surreptitious eyes.

When Charles III died in 1788, at the age of seventy-two, he was succeeded by his son, Charles IV, and Spain suddenly plummeted from her brief flight of regeneration into a long slump of degeneracy. Lecherous Charles IV and his even more lecherous queen, Maria Luisa, made the Spanish court the center of such profligacy as had rarely been seen since the days of ancient Babylon. There seemed to be a tacit agreement between this royal pair that neither would ever interfere with the licentiousness of the other, that both would exalt the god Mammon and let the nation slip back into misery as fast as it could move. The painter Goya has caught the sensual and imbecilic features of this entire royal family in many of his canvases, and history abounds with so many verified proofs of their degeneracy that no argument on the point is ever made.

A sergeant in the royal guards by the name of Manuel Godoy caught the eye of the Queen and he was several times promoted until he became eventually Prime Minister of the realm. Godoy was the King's friend and adviser as well as the Queen's lover, and it is doubtful if the latter's children knew for certain which of the two was their father. Among these royal offspring was the heir apparent, who was later to rule as Ferdinand VII. His Queen mother had characterized him aptly by saying that he had a tiger's heart but a mule's head.

Ferdinand plotted to poison his father in order that he himself might enjoy the crown at an earlier age, but the King got wind of the plan and slapped his son into confinement, hoping to have him executed and thus get him out of the way for good. The Spanish populace heard of what was going on and took Ferdinand's side. To them the iniquities of Charles and his Queen were an old story, and the young prince offered the only hope for relief from their national indignity. Mobs commenced to gather in the streets of Madrid after the fashion of the French revolutionists, and on one occasion when the Prime Minister Godoy appeared in public he was met with a shower of bricks and chased back into the palace with the mob at his heels. Godoy rolled himself up under some old mats and rugs and was forced to remain there for thirty-six hours while the people ransacked the place. He finally escaped with his life, but, as a result of the uprisings, Charles IV was obliged to abdicate in favor of Ferdinand (1808). Spain had undergone twenty years of the most corrupt government in her long history, but worse things were to follow. It was at this point that Napoleon intervened and placed his brother Joseph on the Spanish throne.

This was one European crown which had practically fallen into the Emperor's lap. First Charles IV and then Ferdinand had written him urgent letters filled with the most fawning phrases, each begging that Spain's great friend and neighbor lend his support to their cause. Napoleon happened to be going to Bayonne in southern France at about this time and so wrote to both father and son that he would be glad to discuss matters with them there if it was convenient. Charles and Ferdinand raced for the frontier, and with a minimum of coaxing Napoleon suddenly found the whole royal Spanish family, plus the Prime Minister, in his power. They fought over their personal quarrels in his presence most disgracefully, and Napoleon, who had by this time reached a definite decision in the matter, stated that he was going to place his own brother Joseph on the Spanish throne. Both Charles and Ferdinand acquiesced, the latter somewhat unwillingly, and a group of influential Spaniards, wrongly called a junta or national committee, was assembled in Bayonne to sign the document.

Napoleon settled a large estate and a tidy sum on each member of the royal family, and for the next six years they were his "guests" in France. The only Spaniard to show the slightest intelligence throughout these discussions had been Godoy, the Prime Minister, who had urged both Charles and Ferdinand to flee to the American colonies and establish kingdoms there. Neither of them took well to this suggestion, much preferring the easy and sensual life which the French Emperor had promised them. So it was that in 1808 Joseph Bonaparte became King of Spain, and the colonies were left without a "legitimate" monarch. Both Creoles and Spaniards in America promptly rejected the French intruder.

This was only the beginning. Thousands of French troops had already been stationed in Spain to protect Napoleon's interests and to support King Joseph, for the mass of Spaniards still looked on Ferdinand as their ruler and felt certain that the Emperor's machinations were holding him in France. Despite these precautions there were spontaneous uprisings in Madrid and in several other cities, and large-scale guerrilla warfare soon got under way. A Central Junta took charge of national affairs, and there were also several regional juntas in different parts of the kingdom. The Central Council was finally forced to flee from Madrid and established

itself at Cádiz in southern Spain, where it continued to hold forth despite
the French occupation of the northern part of the peninsula. This body
had enjoyed popular support during its first few months, but it had become more reactionary, vacillating, and self-seeking every day and finally
went into complete disfavor. Early in 1810 it disbanded and appointed a
committee of five regents with despotic powers to carry on its will; this
regency ultimately gave way to the first representative Cortes, or parliament, which had met in Spain in three centuries. In the name of Ferdinand
VII this Cortes of Cádiz carried on as the government of the country for
over three years (1810–14).

Although bereft of much actual governing power, the ideological importance of these councils and this Cortes was transcendent. In 1808 the
Central Junta proclaimed that "the American provinces are not colonies,
but integral parts of the monarchy, equal in their rights to the divisions of
Spain herself." But in 1809, when they got down to practicalities, the rich
colonies of America were allowed only twelve representatives on this
council, while the peninsula had thirty-six. The patriots were greatly irritated by this attitude. In 1810 when things looked much blacker in
Spain and the French had occupied nearly the entire country, the Regency
sent this notice to the American colonies: "Your fate depends upon neither
ministers nor viceroys nor governors; it is in your own hands."

While these things were going on in Europe the Spanish colonies,
hardly knowing where their loyalty rightfully belonged, but at least agree-
ing that it was not due Joseph Bonaparte, did precisely the same thing
that the Spaniards themselves had done. They formed regional juntas, or
governing committees, to take control of their affairs until such time as
the situation in Europe cleared up. Some of these juntas were established
as early as 1809, but it was not until 1810 that they arose in every quarter as a protest against the Cortes of Cádiz. By this time, too, the movement for self-government had gathered considerable strength among the
Creole class, and they planned to ease their respective regions into independence by declaring themselves against the Supreme Junta in Spain
and in favor of Ferdinand. In fact, some of their own juntas were called
"Supreme Councils for the Conservation of the Rights of Ferdinand VII."
In reality, however, it was their firm purpose by this means "to push the
populace along the road to absolute autonomy."

There were other excellent reasons as well. In the first place, such actions would confuse and throw off balance the Spanish-born governing
class, in whose hands control of the colonies had hitherto been held. In
the second place, after control had been wrenched from them, the name of
the King would serve as a symbol around which the lower classes might
gather, for they had never regarded the monarch as responsible for the
injustices perpetrated upon them. This would further confuse and baffle
the enemy. In the third place, England was the one European nation from

which the Creoles might expect to receive aid, and at the time that country was an ally of Spain (and of Ferdinand) with her troops actually engaged in freeing peninsular territory of the invading French. Hence, England could not openly encourage colonial independence on the one hand, while her blood and money were being spent for Ferdinand on the other. As a matter of fact, in the River Plate region the English themselves suggested the alternative of backing the imprisoned King, which would permit them to strengthen the republican movement with aid apparently being sent there in the King's name. Once the Creoles were strong enough they would be able to come out openly for independence without further beating about the bush. England would profit by gaining a vast commercial if not colonial empire in return for the colonies she had just lost in North America.

These incipient moves in the direction of independence had been taken in the spring of 1810 first in Venezuela, then in Buenos Aires and New Granada, where regional juntas were proclaimed. Chile and Mexico, where civil wars had got under way, were soon to follow the same course. When the famous Cortes of Cádiz met later on in the same year (September) there was a brief period during which a *rapprochement* might have been made, because this Cortes was supposedly to be made up of representatives from the colonies as well as from Spain. However, under the chaotic conditions then existent in the peninsula, it was impossible to hold elections or even to select delegates from the interior and northern provinces then occupied by the French, and it was also considered to be inadvisable to delay the assembly until delegates from Spanish America might arrive. Representatives for these regions were to be chosen provisionally by and from natives of said regions then residing in Cádiz. The number of delegates thus chosen was twenty-three for Spain and thirty for the colonies out of a total of one hundred and seven. Consequently the assembly was made up largely of liberal city elements and was far more democratic-minded than any governing body ever seen in Spain before. There were many members of the Cortes who had vigorously defended equal rights for the citizens of Spanish America, but when they got down to cases and saw that the colonies with their fourteen to sixteen million inhabitants could easily outvote the peninsula with its ten million, and that many colonial voters would be mestizos, Indians, Negroes, and mulattoes, there was a change of heart and the colonies were allowed only thirty of the one hundred and seven delegates. This alienated the Spanish Americans completely.

The Cortes proceeded to draw up a liberal constitution for Spain in terms of the sovereignty of the people. The King was to hold his position under strict limitations of power. They announced that "the Spanish Union cannot be the patrimony of a person nor a family—that sovereignty resides essentially in the nation . . ." However, this move irritated the friends and partisans of Ferdinand, and even before the constitution was proclaimed (1812) they had taken a strong oppositional stand. The cleavage between so-called "liberals" and "serviles" became bitter. On the one hand, the radical, strongly anti-absolutist elements of Cádiz went about singing their revolutionary songs and insulting the royal family with its clerical backers in verses similar to these:

> Si los curas y frailes supieran
> La paliza que les vamos a dar,
> Se pondrían en coro gritando:
> ¡Libertad! ¡Libertad! ¡Libertad!
> . . . .
>
> Trágala, trágala, trágala,
> Cara de morrón;
> No queremos reina puta
> Ni queremos rey cabrón!

> If the priests and friars only knew
> What a drubbing we were going to give them
> They would form a huddle and begin shouting:
> Long live liberty, liberty, liberty!
> . . . .
>
> So swallow it, swallow it, swallow it,
> Old horse-faced reactionary;
> We want no whore for a Queen
> And no cuckold for our King!

But this was entirely too drastic a change from the old and hallowed traditions, and the mass of the people, shocked by such words and their accompanying actions, and goaded on by a majority of the clerics, turned gradually against the liberal Cádiz assembly, with its ideal of a constitutional monarchy, and threw their support behind Ferdinand as absolute king. England had given them a little pushing, for as soon as Joseph Bonaparte entered Spain and the anti-French uprisings broke out she sent several thousand English troops to the peninsula under command of the Iron Duke Wellington to help the Spaniards fight her number-one enemy, Napoleon. These troops plundered the country right and left, but with native support they finally chased Joseph across the Pyrenees. England spent more than five hundred million dollars and lost nearly fifty thousand soldiers in this successful attempt to save Spain for reaction and its imbecilic King. The fight was widely publicized as the struggle of the brave Spaniards for their freedom, but it was clear that the principal British object was to strike a hard blow at the French Emperor from his soft underside. Napoleon later admitted that the blow had been nearly fatal. Ferdinand, the golden opportunist, was practically pushed back upon his throne.

The English, however, were soon to get a taste of their own m/ for no sooner did Joseph cross the French frontier than Napoleo; nized Ferdinand as King of Spain and got from him a solemn ag to run the English out of the country. This part of the bargain was promptly carried out, for the Spaniards were by this time tired of having any foreigners on their native soil. Great Britain howled that while she had won all the victories, Napoleon had made a better deal with Ferdinand than could have been expected had the French won the Peninsular War.

While these events in Europe had the effect of weakening the control Spain exercised over her colonies and thus left the way wide open for a declaration of independence, the sentiment of nationality in Spanish America which had long been a vague aspiration now became a potent desire. Nurtured by the natural course of events and fertilized by foreign ideas, it first reached the universities and intellectual class and then gradually permeated the masses. By that time independence was already attained.

"From 1808 to 1825 all things conspired to help the cause of American liberty," states the Peruvian, García Calderón, "revolutions in Europe, ministers in England, the independence of the United States, the excesses of Spanish absolutism, the constitutional doctrines of Cádiz, the romantic faith of the liberators, the political ambition of the oligarchies, the ideas of Rousseau and the Encyclopedists, the decadence of Spain, and the hatred which all classes and castes in America entertained for the Inquisitors and the viceroys. So many forces united engendered a sorry and divided world. The genesis of the southern republics is rude and heroic as a *chanson de geste*. Then history degenerates until it becomes a comedy of mean and petty interests—a revolutionary orgy. Such was the evolution of South America during the nineteenth century."[92]

32

LIBERATOR OF THE NORTH

The scene of the wars of independence, fought spontaneously under regional and not centralized direction, covered all the immense territory of Spanish America. They represented several distinct stages, campaigns, and even ideologies. In length of time and in the scope of territory covered, these wars far transcended the North American Revolution and fall into three main theaters of action: Mexico, northern South America, and the River Plate. In Mexico there arose no single great leader, but rather a series of heroes. On the other hand, in South America each theater had its revolutionary giant: Bolívar in the north, and San Martín in the south. Bolívar began his campaign in Venezuela and advanced slowly toward Lima from that direction, while San Martín came up from Argentina in the south. Eventually they caught the Viceroy and his forces in a pincers and broke the back of Spanish rule in South America. But many years were to pass and thousands of lives were to be lost before that net result was finally achieved.

When the revolutions broke out in the year 1810 in every quarter of the colonies with the exception of Peru they appeared suddenly on the horizon of world history as if by spontaneous generation. The truth of the matter was far different. In many regions the masses were indifferent, and in others, vast sections supported the Spanish regime. Throughout most of its history the struggle for Spanish American independence was definitely a revolt of the classes, not of the masses. In general it was also considerably more liberal in its beginnings than it was when the final victory was won and the basis of the new regime was laid.

The antipathy that existed between the two dominant castes was the spark that lighted the magazine. In the words of a meticulous Spanish American historian, Bartolomé Mitre, "the Spaniards on their part helped exalt this state of exacerbation in spirits already predisposed in its favor.

They seemed persuaded that the vast territory and all the native
America were the fiefs and vassals of the metropolis in general and of (
and every one of those who had been born in the peninsula in particu
They considered themselves as natural born lords, as privileged beings
belonging to a superior race and caste, and they believed that as long as
there existed in Spain a shoemaker of Castile with his mule, that shoemaker and that mule enjoyed the right to govern all America."[30] These
are not the words of some flighty demagogue haranguing a street gathering,
but express the calm and considered judgment of one of Latin America's
finest writers, who later became one of Argentina's greatest presidents.
They were written many years after the events to which he refers.

Mitre goes on to show how the disgraceful spectacle of Spain forced
the disinherited Americans to strike out on their own: an absolute king
was the only point of contact, rather than of union, between the exploited
New World and the exploiting metropolis. The divorce of these two was
a fact which already existed in laws and in practices, and which penetrated
spontaneously into individual consciences. The mother country was not
and could never be for the Americans either a mother or a homeland: it
was a stepmother. Thus their instincts of independence took form; they
became charged with passion and were transformed into ideas, symptoms
of the times through which they were passing and a presage of times to
come. In this way did the moral rebellion take place inside consciences
before it became a tangible outward power.

The wars for independence lasted for a full fifteen years in some sections, and frequently went on simultaneously with civil or regional struggles which weakened the unity of the first burst of enthusiasm in 1810.
Long before the end was in sight it was evident what character the forthcoming republican governments in Spanish America would take. That
unity had been raised on two points only: hatred of the Spaniards, and a
sincere belief in the republican ideal. The first gave physical body to action which carried out a successful war against tremendous odds. The
second was not sufficiently impersonal in nature to inspire the victorious
revolutionary leaders to submerge personalities in a united effort toward
real democracy. Both Bolívar and San Martín saw that, in the light of
Spanish America's ignorant state and economic backwardness, a real democracy could not possibly function there. Both warned their followers
against it; both were talked down by the opposition, and both died abandoned and almost despised by the bulk of their countrymen. The George
Washington who arose out of war leadership to become the father of his
country in peace and to save it from division and chaos with the strength
of his personality and intelligence never had a real counterpart in Spanish
America. This was not because Bolívar or San Martín were lesser men. In
many ways they accomplished more than Washington, and against greater
odds. It was simply because in the nature of things, in the immense field

of action over which they operated, in the veritable vortex of races, geographical barriers, climates, and distances, not to mention the complete absence of any training in self-government, the task was beyond the ability of man to carry out.

Simón Bolívar, who liked to think of himself as the George Washington of Spanish America, was born in Caracas, Venezuela, in 1783. His parents were distinguished and wealthy Creoles of ancient lineage. Bolívar's father died when the son was only three years old, his mother when he was nine. His private tutor was a Venezuelan bibliophile who had become so immersed in the writings of Jean Jacques Rousseau that he seemed to be almost a caricature of that incongruous and visionary Frenchman. Bolívar imbibed these doctrines during his tender and growing youth and came to accept them as gospel. Although circumstances somewhat modified his opinions in later years, the root and flower of Rousseau's anti-traditionalism remained with the Liberator till the day of his death.

At the age of sixteen Bolívar left his native country for Spain, where he "frequented the lecherous court of Charles IV," and three years later, at the age of nineteen, he married a sweet and lovely girl who was the niece of the Marquis de Toro. Shortly afterward the couple returned to Venezuela and settled down to a brief but idyllic existence on Bolívar's beautiful estate. Before a year had passed the bride fell ill and died (1803). The young man sank into a state of romantic melancholia which he tried to relieve with omnivorous reading and feverish thoughts and plans as to how he would someday free his country from Spain. He sought further consolation in a trip to Paris, where he spent two or three years in riotous libertinism (1803–05), joined a French Masonic lodge, and discussed frequently with Baron Humboldt and other leading lights of the day "the glorious future of South America." He witnessed the coronation of Napoleon in the great ceremony at Notre Dame Cathedral, and, despite future tirades against the French despot, there entered his heart an envy tinged with admiration for the little Emperor which showed up on more than one occasion in his later life.

This second trip to Europe was "a parenthesis between two great passions," Bolívar's profound love for his wife now dead and his emerging zeal for Spanish American independence. Many years later he recalled the death of his wife and its effect on his life in these words: "I loved her deeply, and at her death made a vow never again to marry. I have kept that vow. If my wife had not died, I would not have made my second trip to Europe. It is probable that there would not have been born either at Caracas or at my hacienda at San Mateo the ideas which I acquired in my travels: in America I should not have gained the experience nor should I have made that study of the world, of men, and of affairs which has served me so well during the entire course of my political career. The death of my wife placed me at an early age on the road of politics; it caused me to follow the chariot of Mars instead of the plow of Ceres."[91]

In 1806 he made a pilgrimage through Italy, immersing himself in the ancient glories of Italian art, and before leaving he stood on sacred Monte Aventino in Rome and swore never to rest until he had "freed America from the tyrants' yoke." Then, by way of the United States, he returned to his native country, where he had a part in the revolution of 1810 in which the independent Supreme Junta of Venezuela was proclaimed "in order to safeguard the rights of Ferdinand VII."

This Junta "suppressed the odious Spanish taxes, prohibited the slave traffic, admitted many foreign goods into the country duty free, and addressed a circular to all of the colonial capitals urging them to follow its example." However, the position of the revolutionists was not at all secure because of their lack of both money and arms, and a committee of three was selected to go to England in order to request British aid. Bolívar was one of the members of this committee. Another member was Andrés Bello, the dean of Spanish American letters throughout the revolutionary epoch and for many years to follow. The committee was well received in London, but no actual aid was forthcoming. Finally, Britain did promise the delegates her "benevolent neutrality" in their struggle against Spain and also stated that she would do everything in her power to promote commercial relations between the Venezuelans and the English.

With this unsatisfactory conclusion of the first part of its mission, the committee proceeded to the second part, which was to persuade the old precursor, Miranda, then living in London, to return to Venezuela with them as head of the liberating movement. The committee of three already had its heart set on complete independence and knew that Miranda's experience would be valuable. The situation was becoming difficult in Venezuela, where three of the provinces had refused to separate from the Spanish regime, and the coast line had already been declared under a state of blockade by the Spanish Government. Miranda was won over to their cause, despite his former disastrous expedition, and when a British man-of-war dumped the whole plotting group, with the precursor at its head, back on Venezuelan soil, it was the same as an open declaration of war against Spain. Miranda's republicanism was so widely known that subterfuges were no longer of aid.

Miranda, Bolívar, and the other returned patriots were greeted with wild cheers in Caracas, and they proceeded immediately to form a "Patriotic Society" whose ideal was absolute independence. It was the story of France over again in miniature, with the ardent "Girondists" of Venezuela blasting away at tyranny and prodding the indifferent masses with the burning torch of liberty. Finally, a general congress was called and the president of that body solemnly announced that the moment had come "to speak of absolute independence." The issue was debated with fiery brilliance, but in the end the radical wing won out over the conservatives, and, on July 5, 1811, independence was proclaimed. A few days later Miranda's old colors were raised over the city and the symbol of liberty, equality, and fraternity was enthroned in the first Latin-American country. Opposition broke out almost immediately, but the Congress proceeded with its work of organizing the new regime and drafting a republican constitution. In December of that same year the document was announced in final form.

The Venezuelan constitution was based largely on that of the United States, with a few shadings from Rousseau's *Social Contract*. It made the country into a *federal* republic, with considerable leeway left for state sovereignty. Both Miranda and Bolívar had opposed this provision with the sure knowledge that only a strong centralized power could preserve unity in their backward country and hold down the egoistic local rivalries which would otherwise destroy it. In the words of a Spanish American historian, this constitution "consecrated all kinds of political liberties for a heterogeneous and unadaptable people who neither understood their meaning, nor was itself capable of practicing them." The final upshot of the whole thing was that the revolutionists split into two groups: the *centralists,* or *unitarians,* on the one hand, and the *federalists* on the other. The mistake which had nearly cost the United States its life as a nation was being repeated in a country ten times less capable of self-government, and the results were certain to bring disastrous civil war. The same error and the same bloodletting of civil strife were soon to spread their gory claws over the entire South American continent.

Before things reached this stage, however, there occurred a catastrophe which nearly gave the revolutionary movement its deathblow then and there. The work of the Congress, without popular support and lacking the enthusiastic backing even of its own members, was already in peril. The lower classes of mulattoes, Negroes, and mestizos, who made up the great bulk of the Venezuelan population, were definitely hostile to the new regime. Their hatred was directed toward the wealthy Creoles, who had always been their direct and most persistent exploiters. For them, antipathy toward the Spaniards was pushed into the background, for there were few contacts between the two groups. Furthermore, the sacred symbols of King and Church played up by the old regime were effective with the ignorant folk who preferred to keep a far from perfect system rather than plunge into a radical change which seemed intent on pulling them up by their roots. The short-range intuition of these people was uncanny.

With these obstacles in its path the constitutional government was not even able to preserve order, much less to guard the civil liberties of its constituents. Spanish forces were rapidly increasing in size and striking power as the opposition gathered strength for the counterattack, and one of their small "armies," aided by Venezuelan "traitors," was already making a victorious march along the coast. It was at this point that a great geographical disaster altered the course of events, sending the patriots headlong into defeat.

On March 26, 1812, an earthquake of cataclysmic proportions almost leveled several Venezuelan cities, including the capital, Caracas, and its port, La Guaira. Nearly twenty thousand victims were buried in the debris, among them the military garrisons of the two above-mentioned cities. The heavy but not too secure stonework of their military quarters had toppled over on them in one sudden smash, making rescue impossible. On the other hand, the principal centers of Spanish resistance, which were located farther to the west and away from the center of the shock, escaped with only minor damage. After the catastrophe a majority of the clergy, "urged on by the opportunistic Archbishop of Caracas, Coll y Prat, preached that this disaster was a proof of divine intervention; they evoked biblical memories, inveighed against 'the revolutionists who through their disavowal of Ferdinand VII, the anointed of the Lord,' had provoked that 'terrible wrath of heaven,' and they urged on the poor mobs crazed with fright the necessity of repentance and of begging forgiveness of 'the most virtuous of all monarchs.' "[93]

Nothing could now stop the whirlwind of reaction. The executive governing committee appointed by the Congress made a vain attempt to do so by appointing Miranda generalissimo and supreme dictator, "entrusting the salvation of the country to his hands." But Miranda's support was already undermined with bickering behind his back, lack of discipline within his ranks, the disastrous inflation of paper currency issued by the revolutionary government, and the actual spread of treachery among his partisans. Even Bolívar resented the appointment of Miranda to a position which he thought should be his, and unwillingly took command of the garrison at Puerto Cabello. The insurrection of the slaves and lower classes, now fanned to a flame by the royalists, spread like wildfire, and a reinforced Spanish army advanced upon the revolutionists. Miranda appointed French and English soldiers of fortune to his staff and thus completely alienated his Creole supporters. The royalists advanced on the city of Puerto Cabello, the strongest-fortified center in revolutionary hands, and Bolívar's forces stationed there were betrayed and defeated. Many of them passed over to the enemy, and Bolívar himself was forced to flee.

Miranda now saw that the situation was desperate and sent agents to negotiate with the royalist general. The revolutionists agreed to lay down their arms on condition that their persons be held inviolate and that a general amnesty be declared for their political offenses. These terms were accepted, but before final negotiations had been concluded Miranda abandoned his post and attempted to flee the country. This action was not due to cowardice or treachery to the revolutionary cause but simply to the old man's desire to retire, as he had already done once before, in order to continue the work of independence.

However, Bolívar was infuriated at what he considered an act of treachery and had Miranda captured and imprisoned. The old man at the time of his arrest cried out contemptuously: "A tumult! A tumult! Such men as you are capable only of tumults!" Bolívar promptly informed the Spanish general of what he had done, and as a reward for "services rendered the king" was given his passport. Miranda, on the other hand, was thrown into a dark dungeon. He was later taken back to Spain, where he remained in close confinement until his death four years later. Other patriots who had led the revolutionary movement were similarly punished, despite the solemn agreement to the contrary.

It is a sorry commentary on Bolívar's inflated egoism at this stage of his development that he then did precisely the same thing Miranda had in mind: fled the country and eventually wound up in New Granada, where he joined the revolutionary cause. He probably did believe that Miranda was guilty of treachery, but there seems no doubt of his biting jealousy of Miranda's superior position. He could not endure another outranking him, and this betrayal of his old friend insured his own unimpeded leadership in the campaigns to follow.

An Argentine historian who views Bolívar with a fairly objective eye characterizes him as being at this time "a young, ambitious, sensual, impulsive, and enthusiastic man. He had the dogmatism and infatuation peculiar to the Jacobins. His strange notions of morality and justice made him incapable of distinguishing between his personal ambitions and his patriotic fervor, and in his haughty spirit weakened with pride was lacking the counterweight of achievements to balance the weight of theoretic formulas." However, the young man was learning fast in the crucible of disappointment, and though some of this haughtiness was to remain with him until his death, there would in later years come to offset it a growth of rare genius and a mellowing of character, which together were to make Bolívar one of the truly great men of all time.

While the revolution was going on in Venezuela all the rest of Spanish America except Peru had joined the movement. Working inside the town councils, which they controlled, the Creoles established their own regional juntas on the following dates in the year 1810: in Caracas on April 19, in Buenos Aires on May 25, in Bogotá on July 20, in Quito on August 2, in Santiago on September 18. The revolution broke out in Mexico under the leadership of a priest, Miguel Hidalgo, on September 16 of the same year.

The revolution in South America, writes a Venezuelan author, "arose simultaneously in nearly all the provinces, was of a municipal and oligarchical character. The populace had nothing to do with it at the beginning. With its crass ignorance and abject fanaticism, as suited the policy of the conquistador, the people could not well be moved by ideas which found no place in their heads nor by sentiments of which they were totally ignorant. It was a minority, the superior class, which aspired to freedom."[94] The independence which they envisioned was a theoretical and idealistic one. In Bogotá, for example, where ideology has always been more important than possibility or cold fact, an emissary of the Venezuelan revolution had been received, and the two countries had enthusiastically joined in a federal union which they hoped would later become the basis of a great confederation of Spanish American nations.

This was the status of affairs when Bolívar entered Colombia late in the year 1812. The events of Venezuela were being repeated. The lower classes remained apathetic or pro-Spanish, and the Creole class, after making a grandiloquent announcement of its new social reforms, immediately fell into a state of division both as to leadership and political ideology. In Colombia there was a full-fledged civil war in progress between those who believed in a strongly centralized or *unitarian* government and those who supported a *federal* or strong states-rights regime. Bolívar and other refugee Venezuelans were received gladly and Bolívar himself was made a colonel in the insurgent unitarian army of Colombia, which then held the upper hand.

He immediately began to use his post as a center of propaganda in favor of freeing Venezuela again from the clutch of the Spaniards. In a fiery manifesto he pointed out that Colombia would certainly be overcome by royalist troops coming across the Venezuelan border unless this action was taken at once. In the same declaration he explained the causes of the Venezuelan failure: the untenable federal system, the earthquake, the fanaticism of the people for Church and King, the internal divisions among the Creole leaders. He also addressed communications of a similar nature to the outstanding citizens of Columbia and urged upon them the necessity of immediately freeing Venezuela from the Spanish yoke. His eloquence and logic won for him the admiration of many distinguished Colombians who began to exert their influence in favor of his scheme.

But Bolívar could not wait. He was already chafing under the bit of inactivity and resentful of holding a subordinate command. Disobeying the orders of his superior officer, who certainly would not have charged him with a mission that might make him famous, he took the small force under him and launched a campaign along the Magdalena River. His generalship was not exactly brilliant, but he moved across country swiftly and several times caught the enemy by surprise, winning several victories. His superior was infuriated and demanded a court-martial, but Bolívar had already been acclaimed a victorious hero and the charges were dismissed. Next he led his men by forced marches over the difficult country of the Magdalena basin, which had cost Quesada so many lives three centuries previously, and finally caught a large Spanish force in the town of Cúcuta. For four hours the battle raged to and fro without much advantage on either side, then Bolívar's men fixed bayonets and in a deadly charge broke the ranks of the royalists and drove them from the field. It was a great victory, and enemy supplies worth nearly a million dollars were abandoned in the town.

Bolívar was raised in rank to general and was made an honorary citizen of New Granada. He had not only established his reputation in the great neighboring country, but had learned from firsthand evidence that this province, and not Venezuela, must be the center of operations if all northern South America was ever to be free. It was the most populous and richest region of the Spanish Main; the only South American viceroy north of Lima had his court in Bogotá, and the land itself was the veritable granary and storehouse of the revolution, not only in food but also in men.

His project for freeing Venezuela was now approved, and with five hundred men and some of the finest Colombian officers under his command he left Cúcuta and headed in the direction of Caracas. It was the same terrain over which the Germans, Federmann, Hohermuth, and Ehinger, had passed so disastrously three centuries before. It took Federmann more than three years to get from the Venezuelan coast to Bogotá. Bolívar, fighting against both man and nature, crossed the same jungles, swamps, and enemy-ridden plains in less than three months. It was a procession of triumphs against great odds, unparalleled since the days of the conquistadores.

This time the Liberator found a Venezuela which was prostrate under extreme misery and oppression. The earthquake had been followed by a great famine, the famine by a deadly epidemic, and the epidemic by the Spaniards. All former revolutionists had been persecuted rigorously, and many of them had been executed. Some had been tortured cruelly and then been thrown naked into foul swamps, where they were left to die. Others had had their ears and the bottoms of their feet cut off. The agreement of amnesty which Miranda had accepted had never been held to for a single day; no Spaniard seemed to have the slightest intention of ever holding to it. The old conquistador purpose had been served: win any way you can—and the Spaniards had won. Bolívar's fighting blood was now up; on hearing of these things it reached the boiling point and he issued his famous proclamation of "war of extermination." "Spaniards, you will receive death at our hands! Americans, you will receive life!" Such was the gist of this document which Bolívar put into immediate effect. His first large batch of eight hundred royalist prisoners was executed in cold blood. The Liberator's terrible proclamation, followed by this merciless action, "jerked the populace out of its apathy and opened its eyes, teaching it that to be a Spaniard was one thing, and a very dangerous one, whereas to be an American was something quite different."[94]

Many former Spanish sympathizers now came over to the revolutionary cause, and the abyss between Spaniards and Americans grew wider and deeper. On the other hand, the royalists retaliated in kind, and the war turned into an inhuman and vengeful blood bath in which a man was slaughtered with no more compunction than if he were a cow or a sheep. These campaigns, writes a distinguished Latin American, "were the bloodiest ever known in the history of America. The civil war maddened men, made them glory in slaughtering each other in cold blood, ruined them utterly and left their descendants with the horrible nightmare of a memory which even today incapacitates them for the art of decent government."[95] The so-called patriots had shown themselves to be no better than their adversaries and "had proved that they were only capable of destroying their country, for on such ferocious principles republics cannot be founded."

Bolívar had not yet learned magnanimity of action. Exasperated by the cruelties of his Spanish adversaries, eager to free his native land, and, incidentally, to make a name for himself, he took the course of inhumanity and temporarily defeated his own purpose. There was something of the feudal crusader in his attitude at this time. He was still a young and almost unknown leader with a meager troop of five hundred soldiers at his back, yet he was challenging, "as if he had an army of five hundred thousand behind him," the power of a vast imperial regime which had already endured for over three centuries. His cry of "war to the death" cost his people thousands upon thousands of lives which might otherwise have been spared and the same results obtained.

His action at this stage of his career, when his reputation both as a leader and thinker was at stake, was in direct contrast to other actions of a later date, when fortune had smiled on him and he was the most powerful man in northern South America. In 1816 he abandoned the policy of annihilation which his enemies still continued to practice, and in 1820, when he was riding the crest of his power, he proclaimed these words to his men: "Soldiers! . . . Colombia awaits her freedom at your hands; but she expects more than this, and demands imperiously that in the midst of your victories you fulfill the duties of our holy war. . . . I am speaking to you, men, of humanity, of the compassion which you will feel for your most stubborn enemies. I can already read in your faces the joy with which liberty has inspired you and the sorrow which you must feel in a victory over your brothers.

"Soldiers! Put your own bodies between the vanquished and your victorious arms, and act as great in generosity as in valor. . . . The battle will be fought to disarm the adversary, not to destroy him. . . . Whoever breaks any of the rules of civilized warfare will be summarily executed. And even should our enemies be guilty of an infraction, we must still hold to the honorable course so that the glory of Colombia may not be stained with blood. . . ."

But this is looking into the future. Bolívar, in his first great Venezuelan campaign, held to no such lofty principles. He did see and utilize the powerful forces of propaganda and always mixed political ideals with military victories. He created the public manifesto and issued dozens of fiery proclamations stating the reasons for his actions, the ideals in which the revolutionists believed, the type of republic which they were giving their lives to create for others. He did not repeat stereotyped European phrases, but made his manifestoes a kind of national prose epic, couched in the language which his people could understand, urging, prodding, exhorting them to make his sacred cause their own. By constant repetition and expansion of his fundamental beliefs, he carried these to all the people who would hear him, and the words eventually made an impression on their minds. As victory is the strongest persuasion of all, when he was victorious he found followers massing around him, but when he was defeated they slunk away quickly into the night.

Bolívar had also learned one vital lesson from Napoleon: that there is nothing which so stimulates the masses as a triumphant spectacle. When he himself entered Caracas, after a brilliant campaign of less than three months, the streets were covered with flowers and palm fronds and Bolívar rode into the city in a great carriage "drawn by a bevy of beautiful maidens." When his companion-at-arms, the Colombian officer and hero, Girardot, was killed in action, the Liberator had his heart placed in an urn and carried solemnly from Valencia to Caracas, where it was deposited with great ceremony in the cathedral. All the way from Valencia the Roman-like procession over flowers and palm leaves was repeated again for the public stimulation.

There were some who ridiculed these theatrical displays, but Bolívar had a far keener insight into the popular fancy than they and understood that such things go to make up the myth of hero worship which moves ignorant people to die for a leader, even when his principles may perplex them. The ceremony of Girardot's heart "was the first urn of Bolívar's political pantheon," says a Spanish American writer. He was a leader who "could be defeated, but he could not be conquered." As a matter of fact, while in Caracas, Bolívar neglected to pursue a Spanish army which he might have destroyed, in order that he might remain in the city and receive with appropriate fanfare the title of Liberator which the town council wanted to bestow upon him. This might well be called vanity, and in a lesser man the characterization would stop there. But in Bolívar it was also an evidence in long-term vision which built up a cause desperately in need of popular support along with bolstering the general's own ego.

However, while the Liberator was engaged in these ceremonies the mulattoes and mestizos of the Venezuelan plains were assembling in vengeful bands against him. These half-savage *llaneros*, or plainsmen, despised the strutting Creole aristocrats of Caracas. They could not understand the theoretical idealism of the patriots, and liberty was a meaningless word to them, but, at the mention of pillage and butchery, they picked up their lances, mounted their horses, and were ready for the assault. The Spaniards were glad enough to lead them on. The war was now becoming a war of *caudillos*, or regional leaders, whose destructive fury was to wreak havoc throughout Spanish America for a century to follow. To the plainsman a horse and a good sharp lance were ideal weapons, but only another plainsman would know how to use them. Two savage leaders did arise to form these fearsome bands into something resembling an army, and then they moved against the city Creoles of Bolívar. With no knowledge of military strategy they at least knew the plains, which are half the year a desert and the other half a flooded sea, and they instinctively realized that mobility was the secret of success in such a country. They struck even harder and swifter blows than Bolívar, and his forces could not withstand them. Time and again these bloodthirsty, loot-seeking bands swooped down on the cities Bolívar had liberated, drawing ever nearer to the capital itself. As they advanced they not only increased in number and in fury, but their ideological zeal, such as it was, took on a deeper significance. Their leaders aroused in them primitive instincts "of low class against higher classes, of men of color against whites, of nomads of the plains against city dwellers, and they also created the cult of brute force as a symbol of the highest political capacity. Authority was command and not government, terror and not conformity."[95]

The final disaster was drawing near. Hordes of these llaneros were advancing on Caracas under Boves, their bloodiest caudillo. With five thousand horsemen and two thousand infantry this bloody ex-convict overcame the last revolutionary resistance before the Venezuelan capital, which Bolívar then hastily abandoned. Almost the entire city of forty thousand souls turned refugee in the face of occupation by these monsters of the plains and, in a mass migration, followed the revolutionary army. Hundreds of families died along the road of thirst, fatigue, disease, and hunger. When the plainsmen arrived the city was practically deserted. Only a few priests in their black robes were in evidence on the deadly silent and abandoned streets of the great capital. The pitiful remnants of a defeated patriot army, with Bolívar at their head, were already well on their way to Colombia.

The Liberator reached the city of Cartagena in September 1814 and found the country still in the throes of its civil war. A dictator had arisen in Bogotá which had then withdrawn from the confederation. Bolívar was placed at the head of an army which had the task of attacking the city and forcing it back into the union. He carried out this campaign brilliantly and then returned to the coast to continue the war there against the royalists, but he could not assemble sufficient troops for the purpose. The largest coastal city, Cartagena, was loath to furnish men to pursue the enemy, preferring to await attack behind the relative security of its thick walls. Meantime, Bolívar was strutting about the place, chasing women and showing off like a gamecock. Some of the people were beginning to be irritated by his attention to every detail except those of a military nature and by his knowledge of every conceivable subject except how to co-operate with the Colombians.

While all this was going on in America, Napoleon had been defeated in Europe and Ferdinand was back on the Spanish throne. Liberalism had quickly shot its bolt in Spain and absolutism was again enthroned in the person of as degraded a monarch as has ever sat upon the golden seat. Yet Ferdinand's entry into Spain had been that of a triumphant hero. He had returned by way of Valencia and, as the semi-liberal Cortes was still in control of the situation in Madrid, had tarried there for a whole month, not being able to make up his mind whether or not to become a constitutional monarch. Finally the people decided for him. The King was literally flooded with petitions beseeching him to annul all his former agreements as to limited power and to rule as his ancestors had ruled before him. The ignorant masses, the generals, the army, the majority of the clergy, all were of this mind. Whenever the King appeared in public a shout went up, "Down with the Cortes! Long live our absolute monarch!" Ferdinand eventually decided to march on Madrid. The Cortes sent out troops to oppose his advance, but they received him instead with a great shout of "Long live our absolute king!" The nation was so debased that it gladly riveted the chains which bound its once-noble spirit to this vilest of regal imbeciles.

One of Ferdinand's first acts had been to dispatch a large army to subdue the colonies. More than ten thousand soldiers, under a cruel and implacable general named Morillo, had suddenly appeared off the shores of Venezuela. The patriots were already having a hard time of it and might gladly have made a decent peace with the home country had Ferdinand been willing, but he demanded complete disarmament and promised them nothing. He thus lost irreparably the greatest empire in the history of the New World.

The new Spanish troops quickly subjugated the few patriots still hanging on in Venezuela and made ready to attack Colombia. Bolívar, unable to obtain troops and viewing the inevitable, left the country and took a boat for Jamaica (May 1815). The walled city of Cartagena, key bastion of the Colombian coast, prepared for the siege which was not long in coming. Morillo's troops surrounded the city on the land side without difficulty and cut off all communications by sea. Within a few weeks food began to run out in the besieged town and the inhabitants ate dogs, rats, and all obtainable leather. An epidemic of disease followed in the wake of the famine. The streets were filled with people hardly able to drag themselves forward. After one hundred and six days the Spaniards entered the desolate city, and not long afterward they succeeded in "pacifying" the entire country. The revolution in northern South America was over. On the whole continent there was only one region which still held out, and that was many hundreds of miles away in Argentina.

Bolívar, while he was in Kingston, Jamaica, wrote his famous "letter addressed to an English gentleman," supposedly the Duke of Manchester, governor of the island (September 6, 1815). In it the Liberator surveys the origin and course of the revolution, examines the latent possibilities of the different regions, discourses on political philosophy, and takes a keen look into the future of Spanish America. It is one of the great social documents of Latin-American history, and not only shows that Bolívar's belief in the revolution's ultimate triumph was unshaken, but that he foresaw the nature of things to come with an extraordinarily keen and brilliant mind. He hoped that this letter would make known the cause of his people and call forth sympathy in their favor.

Venezuela, he wrote, had lost one fourth of her inhabitants through war, hunger, epidemics, famine, and emigration. "Her tyrants now govern a desert, and oppress the sorrowful few who, having escaped death, carry on a precarious existence: some women, children, and old men make up those who remain." Colombia, the "heart of America," was struggling for its life, as was indomitable Chile. In the region of the River Plate liberty was still enthroned, but in Peru the Spaniards were firmly in the saddle. Mexico with its 7,800,000 inhabitants (half the total population of Spanish America) had also embraced the cause of independence and was fighting a war of extermination in order to be free. Sixteen million Spanish Americans were either defending their rights to liberty or were under the tyrant's yoke.[96]

"What a demented idea our enemy has," wrote the Liberator, "to think that she can reconquer America, without a navy, without funds, and almost without soldiers! For she scarcely has enough to keep her own people in a state of violently enforced servility and to defend herself from her neighbors. Nor can she maintain the exclusive trade of half the world without industries, without agriculture, without arts, without sciences, without a political program. Yet granted that this were possible, and even granting that the reconquest of America were made, the children of the present inhabitants within twenty years would again form the same patriotic ideals which are today being so bitterly contested."

Bolívar never for a moment lost his optimism in victory. But both he and his people had hoped for help and understanding from other nations, and these hopes were bitterly frustrated. "Not only the Europeans," he laments, "but even our brothers of the North have remained as unmoved spectators to this contest, which in its conception is the most just and in its results will be the most glorious and important of ancient or modern times.

"I consider the present state of America," he continues, "similar to that which prevailed after the downfall of the Roman Empire, with each dismemberment forming a political system, in conformity with its interests and situation or following the private ambition of some leader, family, or corporation: with this notable difference, that those dismemberments reestablished their old nationhoods with such changes as time and events demanded; while we, who are hardly what we were in other days, and who are neither Indians nor Europeans but a kind of hybrid species half way between the aborigines and the Spanish usurpers, find ourselves in the extraordinary and complicated situation of being American by birth and European in our titles and privileges, and we have to dispute these with the natives while we maintain ourselves against the invaders.

"Even the tyranny Spain imposed upon us," Bolívar wrote, "was not of a kind in which we ourselves took part. If we had only managed our domestic policy and our local administrations, we would know something about the course of public affairs and their mechanism." But Spaniards, not Creoles, always ruled the colonies, and they kept them in a state of perpetual infancy in regard to public intelligence. Then the Liberator goes on to point out that America was not prepared to pursue its own independent course separate from the metropolis when the break suddenly came, as the result of several fortuitous circumstances. Without previous knowledge and utterly without experience in self-government, Spanish Americans found themselves "thrust upon the world stage playing the eminent roles of legislators, magistrates, administrators of public funds, diplomats, generals, and all the other supreme and subaltern authorities which go to make up the hierarchy of State organization." Obviously the job was not performed with efficiency.

He then points out specific instances. In Venezuela events proved that truly representative or democratic institutions "are not adaptable to our character, customs, and present state of enlightenment." Both Venezuela and Colombia proved that a highly centralized form of government was essential, and that until Spanish Americans acquired "the talents and political virtues which distinguish our brothers of the North, entirely popular systems, far from favoring us, I fear will come to be our ruin." The situation of Spanish America was like that of a suddenly liberated Icarus, whose flight toward the sun of liberty soon melted his wings away and sent him plummeting into the sea.

Bolívar did not believe that Spanish America could hope to form one great nation. That would require the "faculties of a God and at least the lights and virtues of all men." Even were a single strong monarchy to hold together all the Spanish-speaking countries of America, it would be only a shapeless colossus, and a republic could not hold them together at all.

The solution was to look toward several smaller independent states. Bolívar mentions seventeen. "The distinctive mark of small republics," he says, "is permanence; that of large ones is varied but always tends toward empire." Rome was the only great republic to endure, and that was because, in the Roman Empire, only the capital was republican while the rest was not.

Then, with as brilliant a look into the future as has ever been penned, Bolívar took up these different regions one by one and forecast their probable destinies. Mexico would attempt to establish a representative republic with great powers vested in the hands of the central executive. But if the dominant party was the military or the aristocrats they would in all probability demand a monarchy, which might begin by being limited but would certainly end in absolutism. "Only a people as intelligently patriotic as the English are capable of preserving the spirit of liberty under the crown of a king." The Central American states, up to the northern frontier of Guatemala, would probably form a union of their own, and when traversed by canals might well become the crossroads of world commerce. "Perhaps only there," Bolívar adds as an afterthought of impassioned longing, "the capital of the world may someday be located!"

New Granada, he continues, would probably unite with Venezuela and take the name Colombia. Its good land and climate assured this region of a great future. The government of this country would be democratic, with a president elected at most *for life*, but never hereditary. Regional frictions, however, might destroy this great union and break it down into smaller federal states.

In Buenos Aires there would be a strong central government in which the military would have the control. Their constitution would probably degenerate into an oligarchy or, at best, into a more or less restricted single-class rule, whose exact denomination no one could foresee. Yet "it would be lamentable if such a thing were to occur, for the inhabitants of that nation are worthy of the most splendid traditions of glory.

"The region of Chile," Bolívar continues without having yet missed a point, "is called by the nature of its position, by the simple and virtuous customs of its inhabitants, by the example of its neighbors, the fierce republicans of Araucania, to enjoy the blessings which the just and benign laws of a true republic bestow. If there is a democratic nation in Spanish America which survives as such, I am inclined to believe that Chile will be that one. The spirit of liberty has never been extinguished there; the vices of Europe and Asia will arrive late or never to corrupt the habits of that distant end of the world. Its territory is limited; it will always be outside the orbit of infectious contact with the rest of men; it will not alter its laws, usages, or practices; it will preserve uniformity in political and religious opinions; in a word, Chile can remain free.

"Peru, on the other hand, embodies two elements inimical to any just and liberal regime: gold and slaves. The first corrupts everything; the second is corrupt in itself. The soul of the serf rarely aspires to a sane conception of liberty: it bursts out violently in tumults or remains with passive humility in its chains. Although these rules are applicable to all Spanish America, I believe that they apply with most reason to Lima. . . . I suppose that in Lima the wealthy class will not tolerate a democracy, nor the slaves and freed mulattoes an aristocracy. The first will prefer the tyranny of a single man in order to escape from the violence of popular persecutions and to establish a rule that will at least be pacific.

"From all of the above we may deduce the following conclusions: the American colonies which are now fighting to obtain their freedom will in the end achieve their object. Some will then in the natural course of events become federal or unitarian republics; monarchies will almost certainly be established in the larger regions; and some will be so wretched that they will devour their own resources either in this or in future revolutions. A great monarchy will be very difficult to consolidate; a great republic impossible."

Bolívar admits that it is a magnificent dream to wish to form a single great nation of the Spanish New World, with its single origin, language, religion, and traditional background, but "it is not possible because extremes of climate, geographic differences, opposed interests, and distinct characteristics divide our America." Obviously "we need more of a sense of union than we now feel in order to complete our work of regeneration. Yet even this division is not strange, for such is generally the characteristic path of civil wars waged between two parties: conservatives and liberal reformers. The first are usually the most numerous, because the power of custom produces the effect of obedience to established authority; the latter are always less numerous, although more vehement and more enlightened. In this manner, the physical mass is offset with a moral force, and the contest is prolonged, its results being very uncertain. Fortunately, among us the mass has followed the intellectual leadership."

In this last statement Bolívar's wish was father to the thought, and what he affirmed as a present fact was only a development of the future. However, he clearly saw the essential weakness of his people, and for the third time evoked the example of the United States, and predicted the Monroe Doctrine in these words: "As soon as we are strong, under the auspices of a liberal nation which lends us its protection, the world will see us cultivate with a single accord the virtues and talents which lead to glorious accomplishment; then we shall move majestically forward toward the great prosperity and development for which our Southern America is destined. . . ."

Such were the thoughts of Simón Bolívar in September of 1815, while he was on the island of Jamaica, a refugee from his own country, with division behind him and in front of him, twice defeated in battle, denied an army to prosecute the war, and with ten thousand Spanish soldiers on Colombian soil prepared to strike at the heart of the revolutionary movement in the north. Later, when the Spaniards were temporarily victorious, he rose to even greater heights. The aroused moral spirit which is the prerequisite to any large-scale historic action had found its body and its mouthpiece in the person of the Venezuelan Liberator. The mystic fire of this man's will to liberty, his unconquerable leadership in the field of thought and on the field of battle, the very fact that he, among all the generals of the Revolution, was not a professional soldier but only a soldier of liberty, these things and many others were bound to make Bolívar a symbol around which his people would gather and be converted and strike off the chains of three centuries. "Always great, he was greatest in adversity," wrote his aide-de-camp, General O'Leary. "His enemies had a saying that 'when vanquished Bolívar is more terrible than when he conquers.' "[91]

Unable to obtain support of his revolutionary plans in Jamaica, the Liberator went to Haiti. There he obtained aid from the president of that country, and from a wealthy merchant named Robert Sutherland, which permitted him to outfit seven schooners and about two hundred and fifty men. He led these back to the Island of Margarita off the coast of Venezuela in March of 1816. The enterprise was badly timed; Bolívar's military leadership was not the most brilliant, and after he had met with disastrous defeats on two or three occasions his Venezuelan co-leaders were on the point of executing him then and there. However, they allowed him to escape again to the West Indies, and a few weeks later, after they themselves had made a complete fiasco of every attempt to hold the revolutionary forces together, Bolívar was called back to lead them.

This time he did not attempt to strike at superior enemy forces, but took to the interior plains country, where he could build up his army. The same llaneros, or plainsmen, who had previously driven him out of Caracas were now being recruited for the army of independence, under the generalship of the "Lion of Apure," General Páez. Perhaps a few of the revolutionary ideas had simmered from the top downward into that hybrid peasant mass of savage horsemen, but in general they followed their chieftain, Páez, rather than any ideal of liberty or democracy.

In that same year (1816), when the black slaves were freed in the hope that they would join the revolutionary forces, they shied away suspiciously and gave even firmer support to the Spanish cause. "The people do not want to be freed," Bolívar wrote in 1816. And wherever there was a population of Indians these either remained apart from the struggle or else served either side indiscriminately, without any notion of what they were fighting for. Nevertheless, little by little Bolívar's star gained a more brilliant light, and after one or two outstanding victories it was clearly in the ascendant. Revolutionary ideals seemed to hover about his personality, and his fate partook always of the same destiny.

In 1817 President Monroe of the United States granted belligerent rights to the Venezuelan patriots, and American privateers aided them indirectly by sweeping the seas of Spanish ships. A far more substantial aid came from England. More than a million pounds sterling was contributed by British merchants, and a British Legion was formed and sent to take part in the fight. Between the years 1817–20 more than five thousand men sailed from English ports to enter the revolutionary army. "It almost seemed," said the Spanish commander in chief, Morillo, "that all the soldiers of England wanted to be transferred to the New World, and along with them all the wealth of English merchants." British liberals were also speaking loud and often for the Venezuelan cause, and Lord Byron, who later died in Greece while fighting for the freedom of that country, named his yacht the *Bolívar*. The name of the Liberator was beginning to resound all over the world where the cause of liberty was loved. Add to that the "British object" of making a good commercial deal with the new countries, the fact that the Spanish court seemed palsied and impotent, and Bolívar's own success in winning the support of the llaneros of Venezuela, and the basis for a more heartening turn of events begins to take shape.

Bolívar was not one to view this slight upswing in his favor with hesitation or caution. At once he determined to call a congress at the Venezuelan city of Angostura, to establish a constitutional regime, and then to take his small army across the Andes and drive the Spaniards out of New Granada. His final goal was to unite the two countries into a single independent state which would have sufficient strength to stand alone, if need be, against the Spaniards.

Before leaving on this memorable march, which was to result in his first permanent triumph, Bolívar delivered his famous address to the Congress assembled at Angostura (1819). It was the second outstanding social and political document to come from his political genius, and outlined the type of constitution and political organization which the Liberator believed would be best for his country at that time. Bolívar himself was lauded to the skies by the assembly, but most of his warnings went unheeded.

"Many ancient and modern nations," he said, "have thrown off the yoke of oppression; but rare indeed are those which have known how to enjoy a few precious moments of liberty. More often they have fallen back into their old political vices, for it is the people rather than governments which drag tyranny after them. The habit of domination makes them insensible to the advantages of national prosperity and honor, and they regard with indolence the glory of living in a regime of liberty under the tutelage of laws dictated by their own will. The experience of the world proclaims this frightful truth."[96]

Bolívar believed that only democracy was susceptible of absolute liberty, but the question in an incipient state was what kind of democracy could unite at one time power, prosperity, permanence, and liberty? Many Venezuelans, carried away with their great admiration for the Constitution of the United States, had attempted to model their own government on a similar base. The first Venezuelan constitution of 1811 had made that fatal error, and it had been proven impractical. The patriots had called their new country the United States of Venezuela, but this was merely a wish distorting historic facts. Bolívar thought that, if permanence was to be achieved, an ideal more in keeping with the nature and conditions of their own land and people must replace this theoretical utopia.

"The more I admire the excellence of the Federal Constitution of Venezuela," he said, "the more I am convinced of the impossibility of its application to our State. And it is a marvel to me that its model in the United States has operated so successfully and has not been upset when the first embarrassments or perils appeared. In spite of the fact that the North American people are a singular example of political virtues and moral enlightenment, in spite of the fact that freedom was their cradle, that liberty was the air they breathed, and the food they ate; in spite of the fact (I will go the whole limit) that in many respects this people is unique in the history of the human race, still do I repeat: it seems a marvel to me that a government so weak and complicated as the federal system should have endured under circumstances so difficult and delicate as those through which it has passed."

Never was Bolívar more right than when he spoke that last phrase. Cornwallis surrendered to Washington in 1781, but from that time until well after 1788 the United States was not a nation. It was a group of "sovereign states"; in other words, it was a hodgepodge of petty territories beset by all the greeds, jealousies, rivalries, and recriminations which so often follow on the heels of war, even when the symbol of unity has been victorious. Some states proclaimed sovereign constitutions and turned themselves into would-be nations. Each section interpreted the victory in terms of its own interest, hence the unity maintained during the fight quickly disintegrated. New York laid heavy tariffs on New Jersey farm products, vegetables, eggs, and New Jersey retaliated by taxing New York's lighthouse on Sandy Hook eighteen hundred dollars a year. The merchants of Connecticut, by written compact, boycotted New York City, while Maryland and Virginia carried on a regular cat-and-dog fight over control of the Potomac River. Pennsylvania and Connecticut fought over ownership of Wyoming Valley, which lay between the two, and when Pennsylvania won the court decision there were rumors that the citizens of the sovereign state of Connecticut were "pumping up a rebellion" inside the boundary of their neighboring state. The Pennsylvania militia then got busy and booted five hundred "alien Connecticut scum" out of house and home, killing several, burning homes, and causing the first heart-rending refugee stories of the new republic. The Constitutional Convention finally met in the year 1787 to draft a federal document by which all of the states would be bound. The opposition thrown in the way of this convention, the bitterness with which the new Constitution was combated by shortsighted regional interests, the emergence of Washington, Hamilton, Madison, and many others of our early leaders as great statesmen, who overcame all opposition by sheer dint of personal sincerity, brilliance, and indefatigable effort, these imponderables, which have never been equaled in the world before or since, justly caused the great Bolívar to pause and wonder when he faced the achievement of federal union in the United States.

The Liberator then proceeded to paraphrase Montesquieu's *Spirit of Laws*, emphasizing his point that laws must always be adapted to the people for whom they are made, that, for example, the English system would never in a thousand years work out in Spain, and that thus the Constitution of the United States would be, had indeed already proven to be, unworkable in Venezuela, where the circumstances demanded a more highly centralized authority. Yet Bolívar was insistent that "the government of Venezuela has been, is, and should be republican. The bases of the Venezuelan government should be the sovereignty of the people, the division of powers, civil liberty, the prohibition of slavery, the abolition of monarchy and of special privileges."

He proposed not only a more unitarian type of government, but made specific suggestions as to the organization of its Congress. He wanted a hereditary Senate or House of Lords selected by the Congress itself from among the "virtuous, prudent, and valiant" race of liberators. These men were to hold their power permanently and could pass it on to their descendants. This was the most certain way of assuring the continuance of the republic. The House of Representatives, on the other hand, would be chosen by popular election and would add the necessary element of renewal and change.

Bolívar was especially fond of his hereditary Senate, stating that in his opinion it would be "the base, the core, the soul of our Republic. When political tempests break out this body will fend off the sword thrusts of the central authority and repulse the waves of popular violence. . . . Let us confess it clearly: the majority of our people do not know their own interests, and constantly endeavor to assail them in the hands to which they have been entrusted: the individual fights against the mass, and the mass against authority. Consequently, it is necessary in all governments to have a neutral body which will stand on the side of the offended party and disarm the offender."

This might at first glance sound like out-and-out aristocratic thinking, but even in the United States we have found it necessary to put the same principle to work in our Supreme Court, whose members are appointed for life. No such body is ever entirely neutral, but it does give stability in periods of unrest, and does guard liberty in periods marked by an excess of executive zeal.

In addition to the three usual powers into which a government is divided—the legislative, executive, and judicial—Bolívar proposed for his own country a fourth, the "moral power," to purify the national mind, to provide for the education of children, to guard against corruption, ingratitude, coldness, and sloth in the country's service. Under a more modern guise this fourth department of the Liberator might have been called the Ministry of Education, the Ministry of Enlightenment, the Bureau of Propaganda, or the National Censorship, whichever way one wants to take it. Under proper leadership it might have become an indispensable part of Venezuelan government; under corrupt or dictatorial leadership it would have led to nothing but a subversion of the national interest and to the perpetuation of tyrannical power.

In so far as the central executive was concerned, Bolívar saw clearly the necessity of providing him with sufficient power to enforce the popular will. The executive must "repress the tendency of the people toward license and the inclination of the judges and administrators to abuse the laws." Otherwise the executive power "will inevitably become useless or be abused, which will be the death of government. In republics," he said, "the executive power should be the strongest, for all conspire against it; while in monarchies the legislative power should be supreme, for all conspire in favor of the monarch. Hence the necessity of giving a republican magistrate more authority than a constitutional prince." He knew the dangers of autocracy, but feared equally the "ferocious hydra of discordant anarchy." Disorder would inevitably lead to dictatorship, and dictatorship would mean the end of democratic government. At the same time "indefinite liberty, absolute democracy, are snares in which all republican hopes come to grief."

In these ways, then, did Bolívar attempt to make the government fit the people and the conditions under which they lived. He was not outlining any utopian ideal but was providing balances and counterbalances to guard against the latent barbarism of illiterate masses and the Caesarism of the ruling caste. "The most perfect system of government," he said, "is that which produces the greatest possible amount of happiness, the greatest amount of social security, and the greatest political stability." His address before the Congress of Angostura in 1819 proved him to be far ahead of his contemporaries in providing a secure base on which these goals might rest.

Before concluding his address the Liberator resigned the dictatorial powers which had been temporarily laid in his hands, and requested the Congress to take up where he left off. They promptly re-elected him president of the republic, declaring that he should still exercise absolute dictatorship in all provinces in the theater of war. A few weeks later Bolívar entrusted the government to the vice-president and, with five hundred English volunteers, left to resume his military command on the Venezuelan plains, where a large force of llaneros under General Páez was awaiting his return.

While the Congress proceeded with its work of drafting a suitable constitution the Liberator and his aides returned to a primitive army camp whose troops were to give that constitution a chance to live. Sitting on bleached cattle skulls, whose bodies had furnished meat for the soldiers, they perfected plans for carrying the war to the enemy. It was finally decided to strike swiftly across the mountain barrier at Bogotá as soon as the rains set in and made the plains impassable for the Spanish forces then quartered in Venezuela. In this manner the whole of New Granada might be freed before aid could arrive.

The army consisted of about twenty-one hundred men when it left Venezuela, and these were joined by about four hundred more under the great Colombian leader, Santander, at the foot of the Andes. These forces, covered only with their light uniforms, and frequently lashed by rain, sleet, and icy winds, picked their way through the rugged mountain passes more than 12,000 feet high. Many men died of exposure and nearly all those who survived were suffering from exhaustion or illness when they finally came out on the other side of the barrier, their uniforms in shreds, without a single horse, their supplies practically exhausted. Here they rested awhile, gathered a few horses, and recouped their strength. The terrible experience of that long march which they had shared in common had already welded them into a strongly knit unit whose morale was unconquerable. The British Legion, consisting mostly of soldiers under Colonel Rook, had won the hearts of the natives completely by the impassive manner in which they had withstood the hardships of that memorable march.

The Battle of Boyacá, which was to settle for all time the destiny of Colombia, began on August 7, 1819. Two thousand patriots faced a veteran army of three thousand royalist forces. The patriots attacked resolutely and, despite meeting furious fire, advanced steadily until they had their enemies nearly surrounded. Bolívar, mounted on a black charger and wearing a tattered and stained uniform, went from one part of the field to the other, giving the necessary orders. In the end, the forces of the King were defeated completely and attempted to flee, but at least sixteen hundred prisoners were taken, along with considerable supplies. The total number of dead hardly numbered one hundred and fifty, but the results of the battle were decisive, for the road to Bogotá now lay open. The days of New Granada were ended and the country of Colombia was born.

On receipt of news of the victory the Viceroy fled from the capital "so fast that he left behind him in the royal treasury more than half a million *pesos*, and in the royal storehouses everything necessary to arm and equip completely a numerous army." Three days later Bolívar entered Bogotá in a Roman triumph and was greeted by a frenzied population. He was led to the main square, where a young girl, whose father had died for the revolutionary cause, crowned him with a laurel wreath. The Liberator then placed the crown successively on the heads of his two principal generals and finally tossed it out among the soldiers, saying: "Those liberators are the ones who deserve the laurels."

The Colombian general, Santander, was appointed vice-president of the region of New Granada, and shortly afterward Bolívar returned to Venezuela. This time his march was one endless series of ovations. He finally presented himself before the Congress of Angostura and announced the accomplished independence and union of Venezuela and New Granada. The Congress named Bolívar provisional president of Greater Colombia, and it was decided that the capital of the newly formed nation was to be a completely new city which was to bear the name Bolívar. Not many months after this the last royalist forces in Venezuela were defeated by the Liberator and the northern part of South America was free.

In the month of May, 1821, the Congress of the new nation met in the Colombian town of Cúcuta to draft a constitution. This assembly, made up of both Venezuelans and Colombians, declared that their government "is and will forever be popular and representative." They repudiated Bolívar's idea of a hereditary Senate, but did accept his conception of a highly unified state. They also abolished the slave trade, established freedom of the press, did away with the Inquisition, and canceled the tribute of the Indians. The constitution which they finally proclaimed exemplified the highest ideals of Colombia's golden age, and, had it been followed, might have led her to become a great nation before many decades had passed. The president of that august assembly hit the nail squarely on the head when, in his report to the nation, he said: "United, you are invincible; disunion is the only enemy which you should fear. Obey the laws which are your work, for they have been adopted by your representatives; and respect the magistrates elected by your votes. Think only of Colombia!" Unfortunately, this was the one thing which the Colombians were unable to do for over a hundred years.

Bolívar attempted to resign before the Congress, but by this time his resignations and re-elections followed in such rapid sequence that one feels as if they verged on the theatrical. In his address to the president of the Congress the Liberator said: "I am the son of war, the man whom battles have elevated to the highest position. I wish to become a simple citizen in order to be free and in order that all may enjoy freedom. I prefer the title of citizen to the title of Liberator, for the latter emanates from war, whereas the former arises out of law. Change for me, Sir, all of my honors and dignities for that of citizen." The president of the Congress answered Bolívar in these words: "The Congress looks upon your excellency as the Father of the Country. Your excellency will always receive the unbounded praise of history and the benedictions of posterity. Your illus-

trious name will be pronounced in Colombia with pride and with veneration throughout the world." Bolívar was then re-elected president. He
had heard what he wanted to hear. Less than a week after occupying his
office he was on his way southward to carry the war against the remaining
Spanish forces in Quito, Ecuador.

33

REVOLUTION IN THE SOUTH

While Bolívar was leading his campaigns against the Spaniards in the north a similar struggle was going on in the southern part of the continent. It had started in Buenos Aires in the same year Venezuela made her own first move toward independence (1810), and from there it had spread to Chile, Uruguay, and Paraguay. Each of these regions felt strongly the sentiment of nationality and produced an outstanding leader to guide its people along the path of independence.

The leader in Argentina was Mariano Moreno, whose meteoric career had a profound influence on political action in the south. Moreno received his education at the University of Chuquisaca (Sucre), then the most liberal institution of higher learning in South America. He specialized in law and theology and took a degree in the latter field. While at the university he was thrown into contact with French and North American political ideas which were the invariable theme of every serious session among the student intellectuals. After graduation he became a legal counselor for the Audiencia at Buenos Aires and was in the city when it was taken over by the British. The successful battle waged against these foreign troops greatly increased his patriotic zeal and his belief in the feasibility of independence.

The economic situation of the viceroyalty was at this time very miserable, for after the brief period of free trade under the English the Spanish monopoly had been restored. Many citizens resented this and clamored that the restrictions be removed. In 1809 Moreno drew up his famous *Memorial* for a group of cattlemen and landowners, in which the deplorable state of the country was pointed out and liberty to trade freely with the English merchants was asked for. The *Memorial* was couched in purely economic terms, and Moreno, who had kept himself hidden in the background, was not even known as its author. But he was wise enough to know that once the profit instinct had been thoroughly aroused independence itself would be just around the corner. One year later the second step in this direction was taken with the organization of a regional junta to govern in the King's name, and here again Moreno was the man behind the scenes, the moving spirit who pushed his compatriots over the hump, giving them the necessary momentum to strike out on their own.

Across the mountain barrier of the Andes similar events were shaping up in Chile. The leader there was Bernardo O'Higgins, later to become the first president and great national hero of his country. Bernardo was the illegitimate son of an Irish merchant, Ambrosio O'Higgins, a distinguished citizen of the Spanish New World.

The elder O'Higgins had left his native land at an early age in order to seek his fortune in South America. He set up his stall in Lima in the shadow of the cathedral, but was unable to compete with the big merchants of that wealthy city. For ten years he engaged in carrying merchandise from Cádiz to Chile and Buenos Aires. At the age of forty-two he was hired to go to southern Chile as a surveyor and engineer (1762) to improve the fortifications along the Araucanian frontier. This work was carried out so satisfactorily that O'Higgins was made head of all the outposts and public works maintained in southern Chile. He built roads, surveyed and opened mines, constructed dikes and irrigation ditches, and took a strong stand in defense of the Indians. The King of Spain finally recognized his merit (with considerable persuasion on the part of some of O'Higgins's powerful friends), and made the Irish-born immigrant governor of Chile. This position was a steppingstone to the highest office in the Spanish New World, that of Viceroy of Peru.

While in southern Chile, O'Higgins had for a time been lodged in the home of a certain Captain Simón Riquelme and had fallen passionately in love with his eighteen-year-old daughter. He himself was then fifty-five. He seduced the daughter and, as a result of this intimacy, Bernardo O'Higgins, the future national hero of Chile, was born (1778). In order to protect his government position the elder O'Higgins tried in every possible manner to conceal his son's birth, but at the same time furnished ample funds for his maintenance and education. Bernardo attended the best schools in Chile, Peru, and finally England. While in the latter country he became a close friend of the Venezuelan revolutionary, Miranda, precursor of Spanish American independence, and was converted completely to the patriot cause. "The liberty of my country," he wrote to a friend many years later, "was the essential object of my thoughts and the first longing of my soul from the year 1798 when General Miranda inspired me with that ideal."

Shortly after this the story of Bernardo's connections with Miranda reached the ears of the King and further investigation brought out the manner of his birth. The Spanish court punished the elder O'Higgins by asking for his resignation from the viceroyship. Fortunately the old man died before the full disgrace of the situation had time to fall upon him.

As a result of his father's death Bernardo inherited a considerable estate in Chile, and in 1802 he returned to that country. From that time forward he worked tirelessly for Chilean independence. Being a master of both English and French, he read many "revolutionary" works in each language and interpreted them for his compatriots. Gradually many of the leading Creole intellectuals, both clerics and laymen, were brought over to his side. When the revolution broke out in Argentina it was greeted in Chile with widespread enthusiasm and a salvo of cannon was fired in celebration. A congress was convoked; O'Higgins was elected as one of the radical deputies, and later became leader of the radical party. When actual fighting broke out he was as brave on the field of battle as he had been imposing on the rostrum. However, the Spaniards proved too strong for the Chilean patriots, and after a crushing military defeat O'Higgins temporarily fled to Argentina to wait for a more favorable opening, which was not long in arriving.

The revolutionary leader in Uruguay, or, as it was then called, *la Banda Oriental* (the Eastern Bank of the River), was José Artigas, son of a well-known rancher of that region. He had been reared on the open plains, was strong of body and mind, and felt keenly the love of personal liberty. Legend has it that he was for a time a sort of cattle rustler, smuggler, and Robin Hood all in one. He was a fine horseman and was inseparable from his mount.

In 1797 Artigas enlisted in the Spanish forces stationed at Montevideo and rose to the rank of captain. He took part in the battle of Buenos Aires against the English, and also fought the British bravely at Montevideo. In 1811, after the revolution had broken out in Buenos Aires, he went to that city and was persuaded to start a similar movement in Uruguay.

Artigas then began to assemble his army of Gauchos and openly declared his allegiance to the government at Buenos Aires. The royalists in Montevideo marshaled their forces and prepared to march against him. Artigas received considerable reinforcements from Argentina and met the Spaniards with only slightly inferior numbers. Some of his men, however, were armed in the rudimentary Gaucho fashion with poles to which long knives had been attached. He won the victory, captured five hundred prisoners, converted most of them to his cause, and then in conjunction with a large contingent from Buenos Aires laid siege to Montevideo.

The Uruguayan patriots chose five delegates to represent them in the assembly at Buenos Aires and instructed them to demand a complete break from Spain and a strong measure of autonomy for their province. These delegates were not permitted to take their seats. This and other high-handed acts on the part of the Argentines caused Artigas to abandon the army before Montevideo and take to the interior, where he proclaimed himself "the Protector of Free Peoples." By 1815 he had brought all of Uruguay and the neighboring portion of Argentina under his control. A couple of years later the Portuguese came down from the north and captured Montevideo; from that time on the star of the Uruguayan national hero began to decline. In 1820 he was forced to retire from his country to Paraguay, where he spoke bitterly of the leaders at Buenos Aires who were attempting to make of their city "a new imperial Rome."

Paraguay itself had found a leader in the person of José Gaspar Rodríguez Francia, one of the strangest rulers ever to occupy the executive's seat in that strange land of perennial despots. When it was learned in Asunción that the citizens of Buenos Aires had proclaimed their regional junta, many leading citizens of Paraguay called for a similar course of action in their own country. Among these was Dr. Francia, who had received his degree in theology from the Argentine University of Córdoba. The story goes that Francia walked into the assembly which was to decide Paraguay's fate and placed two loaded pistols on the table. "These are the arguments I bring against the supremacy of Ferdinand VII," he said.

Shortly after, this Paraguayan assembly appointed two consuls, of whom Dr. Francia was one, to rule the country dictatorially. Before long Francia had made himself supreme dictator and instituted a reign of terror which lasted for twenty-five years. He became the first in Latin America's long series of regional tyrants.

Back of all these events in Chile, Paraguay, and Uruguay lay the revolution in Buenos Aires. The great port was the largest, wealthiest, most liberal city of the southern part of the continent, and the capital of the viceroyalty of La Plata. Buenos Aires furnished the initial spark without which the independence movement in these neighboring regions would have been delayed indefinitely. What took place in the Queen City of the Argentine, therefore, was of supreme importance throughout South America.

The revolution began in Buenos Aires on May 25, 1810, which has become Argentina's Fourth of July. The day was cold, drizzly, and the sky heavily overcast. In the municipal building the cabildo was meeting to decide what course the country should follow while most of Spain was occupied by the troops of Napoleon. Some citizens wanted the Viceroy to continue in power; some favored the cabildo itself; others wanted a revolutionary junta. As the day advanced an anxious crowd gathered in the plaza and demanded to know what was going on. Two young citizens, one a letter carrier named Domingo French, the other a clerk in the treasury named Antonio Luis Berutti, both members of the secret revolutionary society, circulated among the members of the crowd passing out white and blue ribbons. These were the colors of a famous regiment which had fought the English in Buenos Aires a few years previously. After this Berutti and French formed a delegation and entered the building where the cabildo was in session. They presented a petition signed by several distinguished citizens, clerics, and officers, requesting the appointment of a governing junta made up of certain persons whose names appeared thereon.

In the meantime, while the crowd assembled in the plaza continued to shout its demands at the cabildo, the sun suddenly broke through the overhanging clouds and clothed the scene in brilliant light. The people looked upward with one accord and took it as a favorable omen for their cause. That was the origin of the "sun of May" which has appeared in the center of the Argentine flag and on the Argentine coat of arms ever since. The members of the cabildo hesitated to approve the list of names they had received, but the pressure of the crowd outside finally forced them to do so. The junta thus composed purported to take office in the name of the King, but its action has appropriately been called by later writers "the mask of Ferdinand," for the idea of complete independence had already taken root in many Creole minds.

Mariano Moreno, who was the guiding genius of this May Revolution, was appointed as one of the secretaries of the junta specifically charged with matters of politics and war. He drafted many of that body's most important decrees and founded a weekly periodical known as *La Gaceta de Buenos Aires*, the country's first uncensored newspaper, to publicize throughout the country what the central government was doing. The junta dispatched messengers to the outermost cities of the viceroyalty, Asunción and Montevideo, inviting the people of Paraguay and Uruguay to make common cause with them. This was refused, and Buenos Aires then unsuccessfully attempted to force these cities in line.

Moreno continued his propaganda in favor of independence in several articles for the *Gaceta*; he also edited a Spanish translation of the *Social Contract* of Rousseau, which he said "placed in a clear light the rights of the people" and "taught them the true origin of their obligations, and showed them the corresponding obligations which the rulers contracted." Moreno omitted in the translation certain passages of Rousseau which he claimed had "got off the track and become involved in attacking religion." Unlike Bolívar, the little Argentine firebrand was a strong and orthodox defender of the Church.

Moreno was the author of the proclamation which declared the innate spirit of democracy and liberty of the Argentine people: "Any despot can force his subjects to chant hymns to liberty—mechanical hymns which accord with the chains and the oppression of the singers. If we desire that a people should be free, we should scrupulously observe the sacred dogma of equality. . . ."[91]

Like Bolívar, this Argentine patriot was a great admirer of the government of the United States and its first chief executive. In his "Plan of

Operations for the Provisional Government" he called upon Washington to give him aid: "Where are the rules which guided you in the construction of your great work, O noble and grand Washington? Your principles and your system would be sufficient to guide us: lend us your genius so that we may accomplish the results to which we aspire!"

Then he proceeded to outline the advantages and dangers of the plan which he had in mind: ". . . if intrigue, ambition, and egotism smother the spirit of patriotism; in a word, if the general welfare is subordinated to private interest, then the emancipation of a nation will produce all sorts of excesses, and will cause the upheaval of the social order. . . . Never will there be afforded to South America a better opportunity than the present for the establishment of a republic upon the basis of moderation and virtue. The dynasty of the Bourbons has been brought to the ground; none of its cowardly friends came in time to lend it a hand: all that is now necessary is to let it lie and forget it. . . . Why is liberty pictured to us as being blind and armed with a dagger? Because neither an aged state nor a province can be regenerated or purged of corrupt abuses without rivulets of blood being spilled. . . . Let us give a most solemn character to our new edifice, and look solely to our own land. When our constitution secures to every person the legitimate enjoyment of the rights of true liberty in practice and in tranquil possession, without the existence of abuses, then will an American state solve the true and great problem of the social contract."[91]

In spite of this plea, which was presented only three months after the May Revolution, Moreno and his "radical" ideas did not win out on the junta, and Argentine freedom from Spain was not declared until five years after his death (1816). One of the reasons for this was England's advice (through her ambassador at Rio de Janeiro) not to make a premature declaration of independence. Moreno was on his way to Great Britain to negotiate for further support of his cause when he died on board ship and was buried at sea. When the president of the government in Buenos Aires received the news he was said to have exclaimed: "It took a lot of water to put out so much fire!"

The May Revolution had been brilliantly planned and carried out with the participation of the people of Buenos Aires. It had not given Argentina her full independence, but it had placed her clearly on the right path. In the initial stages it had been consummated without violence, as if it were the logical and peaceful result of historic and social forces, but even before Moreno's death this creative unity had been disturbed and a cleavage which was to tear the country apart for many years to come had expressed itself in Argentine life. This clash was between the capital city of Buenos Aires and the hinterland of the viceroyalty.

The great capital city wanted to be dominant and liberal; the hinterland—Paraguay, Uruguay, and Bolivia—all feared the hegemony of Buenos

Aires, and struck out for themselves, arousing the people to support regional leaders of their own kind. When the Argentine army entered Paraguay in 1811, in order to force the inhabitants into their union, it was met by a suddenly aroused "bulk" of natives which not only stemmed its advance but smashed it to pieces. Paraguayan isolation had reasserted itself with a desire to be left "free" to establish its perpetual dictatorships. More or less the same thing happened in Montevideo, except that here opinion was divided and a strong leader (Artigas) arose who joined forces with the people of Buenos Aires until it became clear that his country was to be deprived of political representation. In Bolivia the Argentines met with a reception which, if less heroic than either that accorded them in Uruguay or Paraguay, was at least dramatic in its way, and characteristic of that pathetic region for many years to come.

It was about a year after the events of May 1810 in Buenos Aires that General Castelli entered Bolivia with his men to proclaim the revolution in that province. In order to make the proclamation as theatrical as possible he called for the people to assemble under the shadow of the ancient ruins of Tiahuanaco, that timeless monument of pre-Inca days. As far as the eye could see the high plateau was covered with Indians in bright ponchos who had come to hear what the man from the great city would have to say. He mounted the rostrum and began to speak. He spoke of the new equality which had been born in Buenos Aires, of the liberty which the Indians would now enjoy, of the benefits which full citizenship in the new state would mean for them; in a word, of everything which the fiery Moreno himself would have spoken had he been present. But Castelli's words were greeted with a profound silence. He had never encountered such a reception before. Everywhere he had gone the people had turned out to greet him with enthusiasm. His words had been received with eagerness and cheers. But these Bolivian Indians sat there listening to him without uttering a sound. In desperation the great hero asked his audience what they desired most to make them truly happy. Then in a tremendous chorus they shouted: "*Aguardiente, señor* [Brandy, señor]! . . ."

They were fatal words which embodied the ignominy of a downtrodden people.

In spite of the reception in Bolivia, Paraguay, and Uruguay, the Argentine revolution was the first clarion note of the independence movement in the southern part of the continent. It was the only region where a reactionary counterrevolution never succeeded in gaining the upper hand. The outlying provinces prevented the centralized leadership of Buenos Aires, but it was this leadership, without their support, which carried the war to the enemy and insured the independence of all.

The two successful revolutionary movements on the South American continent had begun in widely separated regions: the River Plate provinces in the south, and Venezuela in the north. Both were cattle countries; both were lands of great prairies and nomadic plainsmen, whose spirit of independence penetrated into the capital cities, but whose primitive barbarism was unwilling to submit to city domination. Both were countries where a wealthy group of liberal intellectuals began a work which only the plainsmen could finish. From the very moment of its inception both realized that they could not maintain themselves alone on a hostile Spanish-controlled continent. Consequently, while the revolution in Venezuela was moving westward and southward through New Granada, Ecuador, and finally into Peru, the revolution of Buenos Aires expanded westward across the Andes into Chile, and from there northward by sea to Lima, the seat of Spain's power, the age-old capital of viceroys and colonial courts, the symbol of peninsular domination for the whole continent.

In the north it was the figure of Simón Bolívar which stood out in the midst of the revolutionary furore, giving unity to the divided patriot ranks, arousing the lethargic, prodding the uninspired, always in the foreground leading and canalizing the course of historic events which was to make his region free. In the south there arose another and very different character who was to head the legions of the River Plate and Chile and carry them victoriously into the very mouth of the Spanish stronghold in Peru. This was José de San Martín, greatest national hero of Argentina.

San Martín was born in 1778 in the Indian settlement of Yapeyú on the banks of the Uruguay River. Yapeyú was one of the missions founded by the Jesuits, and San Martín's father was for a time its administrator. José's first playmates were the little Indian boys who lived in the settlement. A few years later the elder San Martín was transferred to Buenos Aires and, when his son was only seven years old, was assigned to a post in Spain. The boy attended an aristocratic school in Madrid and at the age of eleven requested that he be permitted to follow "the distinguished profession of arms." By the time he was fifteen he was already a veteran who had fought in campaigns against both the Moors and the French.

When Napoleon's troops invaded Spain, San Martín was a young officer of thirty stationed in Cádiz. There was a French squadron in the harbor which had been there ever since the English had defeated the French-Spanish naval forces in the victory of Trafalgar. The people of Cádiz, on learning of the French invasion, demanded an immediate attack on this squadron. When their demands went unheeded, a large mob gathered in front of the building where the commanding general was quartered and threatened him with violence. An officer tried to calm them, promising that the attack would be carried out at the earliest possible moment. The mob either did not understand or did not believe the officer and assaulted the building. Captain San Martín commanded its defense. He boarded up the doors and placed his small force at strategic points of vantage. The mob got hold of a small cannon and blew the door open, rushed into the building, and, after considerable fighting, overpowered the garrison. Their hatred was centered on the general. San Martín was not molested while they ransacked the place in search of their prey. Before long they located the poor fellow hiding on the roof of a neighboring house and barbarously slaughtered him.

This scene left a bitter memory in the mind of Captain San Martín. Although he had performed his duty bravely he must have felt that his honor as a soldier and as an officer had been compromised by a violent mob. Furthermore, he had witnessed a perfect example of mass action headed by emotional and unreasoning leadership, which wound up in the basest violence without gaining any of its ultimate objectives. The future liberator of half a continent came to hate disorder with every ounce of his being. He realized the tremendous implications of mass action which might so quickly get out of hand and destroy the best-laid plans of disciplined leadership. If this took place when the masses and their leaders were fighting for the same cause it was certain to end in tragedy for both. As a soldier, as a leader, and as a liberator, San Martín never forgot that lesson.

So far as his personal character was concerned San Martín was always a reserved and self-contained man, not at all the flashy demagogue who could capture the imagination of the masses. He was not brilliant either in the field or on the public rostrum, but was methodical, careful, clear-seeing, and persistent. In Cádiz he learned once and for all the unwisdom of a soldier's letting himself be taken unaware or drawn into a risky position by those who were not soldiers. Above all he believed in discipline, order, and an absolute integrity of purpose. He refused to take part in political bickerings or partisan arguments of any kind. Holding himself apart from these differences of opinion, he was a leader who fixed his eye on the ultimate goal and permitted nothing to swerve him from that objective. At the same time he realized his limitations completely, was a sincere advocate of personal liberty, and was willing to sacrifice even his honor as a soldier so that the ideal which guided his life, American independence, might be attained. This is how he won his greatest victory and left his memory to live for all time in the hearts of his people.

In 1810, when the May Revolution broke out in Buenos Aires, San Martín was a colonel in the Spanish army with twenty years of distinguished service behind him. On receiving news of what had happened he immediately consecrated himself to the cause of Spanish America. Many years later he wrote: "I heard of the revolution in South America; and—forsaking my fortune and my hopes—I desired only to sacrifice everything to promote the liberty of my native land." His first action was to leave Spain for England, where he was initiated into Miranda's revolutionary lodge; then he sailed for South America.

In March 1812 San Martín reached Buenos Aires, and a few days later he was appointed commander of a regiment of mounted grenadiers. From that time forward, until his departure for Europe in disgrace after independence was won, the fortunes of the provinces of the River Plate were bound up inseparably with those of their leader. The new commander immediately set himself to the task of organizing and training his troops, schooling them in the rigorous and exacting life of disciplined soldiers, and instilling into them a strong *esprit de corps* which was later to carry them to victory after victory against great odds.

In 1814 San Martín and his troops were sent to reinforce the patriot army, under Belgrano, operating in the northern province of Tucumán. This was the contingent which had been thrown out of Paraguay and which later had been soundly trounced by the royalist forces near Tucumán. He quickly reorganized the patriot forces there, stabilized the whole northern front, then requested a transfer to the city of Mendoza, which lies almost in the shadow of the Andes next door to Chile. The reason San Martín gave for wanting to make the transfer was that he needed to restore his health in the delightful climate of Mendoza. But back of this stood his unexpressed desire to form and lead an army across the mountains into Chile, defeat the royalists on his flank, and finally proceed to Peru. He wrote these ideas to a friend at the time of his transfer and concluded by saying: "You may be certain that the war will not be over until we capture Lima."

While San Martín's army was in training at Mendoza the provinces of La Plata assembled in a congress in the city of Tucumán. It was the winter of 1816. The purpose of this gathering was to determine what united action should be taken in the face of the perils which confronted the peoples of the River Plate.

34

ARGENTINA PARTS COMPANY WITH SPAIN

During the six years which had elapsed since the [1810] May Revolution in Buenos Aires the La Plata provinces had been passing through one turmoil after the other. There had been a dozen changes of government and a state of near chaos reigned throughout the country. The rivalry between Buenos Aires and the interior was daily growing more intense, with the interior provinces (the federalists) making stronger and stronger demands for complete self-government, and the citizens of Buenos Aires (the unitarians) equally belligerent in their belief that a strong central government (which they would be certain to control) offered the only possibility for a peaceful and progressive regime.

Most of the leading Creoles favored a constitutional monarchy. Some wanted to offer the throne to Princess Carlota, sister of Ferdinand VII; others were looking for a prince of some other country. Moreno, after sounding out Carlota in Brazil, had died en route to Europe, and four years later (in 1815) two more distinguished citizens of Buenos Aires, Belgrano and Rivadavia, were sent to Europe in search of an acceptable ruler. The search was unsuccessful, not because the delegates were unable to find a royal representative who satisfied them, but because no prince or princess was content to reign with such limited powers as the United Provinces were willing to delegate. Just three days before the open declaration of independence at Tucumán, Belgrano, back from Europe, urged as a last resort that the country place a member of the Inca dynasty on the throne. He thought that this would do more than anything else to incorporate the vast native population, still far exceeding the whites, into the new state. Most of the inhabitants of Peru were Indians, and more than 50 per cent of the population of La Plata were either Indians or mestizos.

San Martín endorsed the plan heartily. He lived in deadly fear that the federalist faction might win out, and to him that was the same as signing away any possibility of order. It would mean the certain destruction of Argentine unity, the dismemberment of the country into regional governments, and the emergence of a society dominated by the hydra-headed Gaucho tyrants of the interior plains. Six months before the Congress of Tucumán met San Martín had written to one of his friends in words reminiscent of those Bolívar addressed to the Congress of Angostura: "I feel as if I want to die every time I hear people speak of a federation. Would it not be far better to move the capital from Buenos Aires to some other place and thus silence the just complaints of the provinces? How could a federation possibly be established here? If a country like the United States with an established government, well populated, artistic, agricultural, and commercial had so many difficulties under a federal system during the last war with England, what would happen if the provinces of the River Plate became jealous of each other? You have but to consider the rivalries and clashing interests of the various regions to see that they would become a den of wild beasts of which the royalists would be the masters."[91]

The Congress of Tucumán was convoked early in 1816 when the country faced a perilous situation both within and without. The revolution in the north, under Bolívar, had been suppressed; Chile was again under Spanish control, and Ferdinand VII had been crowned the "absolute King" of Spain. The delegates had no exact idea as to what they wanted to do, as to how they should proceed about it, nor how influential their decision would be once it was reached. Many of the delegates were out-and-out monarchists; others did not even want to declare for independence; still others were for a republic. San Martín and Belgrano, the two outstanding figures in the country at that time, both strongly supported a declaration of independence, and both favored a restoration of the Inca dynasty. Invitations had been sent to Montevideo, Paraguay, and to Upper Peru (Bolivia) requesting that they send delegates to the convention, but none arrived from the first two regions, and only a handful from the last. It was clearly a congress representative of the region which is known today as Argentina. Out of a total of twenty-nine delegates, sixteen of them were clerics.

When the Congress assembled, points out the Argentine historian, Mitre, with considerable sarcasm, "the great majority of the delegates were opportunistic monarchists, and the best thing they could think of was to establish a fictitious kingdom, based on crowning a descendant of the Incas, which would unite the River Plate and Peru, making Cuzco the capital. Public sentiment received this chimerical project with general derision, for it was in the consciences of all that the innate idea of a republic resided in the things themselves, had been conceived along with the revolution, and was inseparable from the idea of independence."[30]

San Martín never attended the Congress, but through close friends who did, among them Belgrano, exerted his own powerful influence toward an immediate declaration of independence. A few days before final action was taken Belgrano rose in the assembly and, in a flaming speech which convinced the doubtful and strengthened the zeal of the rest, he persuaded that body to bring forth its famous statement of July 9, 1816: "We the representatives of the United Provinces of South America, assembled in a general congress, invoking the God who presides over the universe, in the name and by the authority of the people whom we represent, and proclaiming to heaven and to all nations and peoples of the earth the justice of our intentions, declare solemnly to the world that the unanimous wish of these provinces is to sever the oppressive bonds which connect them with the kings of Spain, to recover the rights of which they were deprived, and to assume the exalted position of a nation free and independent of Ferdinand VII, of his successors, and of the metropolis of Spain. . . ."[91]

The title of the new state, the United Provinces of South America, was certainly a misnomer, for Argentine unity was not to become a fact until 1853, after nearly forty years of anarchy, tyranny, and bloodshed. Yet the action of those delegates at Tucumán, taken at a time when all the rest of the continent had been recovered by Spain, and with only their own meager resources and the brave will of their supporters to back them, represents a turning point in South American history. The May Revolution had now been made the property of the whole nation, for it was the nation's will to be independent of Spain and to become a republic. Those who considered themselves the masters of the country's destiny at the Congress of Tucumán continued to strive for a monarchy for several months, but in the end republican ideals, voiced by the masses of the people, triumphed and gave rise to a republican government.

While his country was giving birth to a regime on paper, San Martín and his small but spirited army lay encamped under the vast silences of the Andes, preparing for the campaign to free Chile from the Spanish yoke and secure for it an opportunity to work out its destiny. When the general heard of the declaration of independence made by the Congress of Tucumán he called it a masterly stroke, and "he and his chief officers took a solemn oath to promote and defend the liberty and independence of the United Provinces of South America."

Even before the Congress of Tucumán had met San Martín had written to the government at Buenos Aires pleading the necessity of his project, and less than a month after independence was declared plans were under way to carry out his expedition. San Martín was made commander of the Army of the Andes; more troops and equipment were assembled, and the officers were carefully instructed in the enterprise. Spies were sent out to reconnoiter the mountain passes, and false information was constantly fed to the enemy encamped on the other side of the mountains in order to keep him in a state of constant confusion. On one occasion San Martín, with a great show of secrecy, assembled the leading members of an Indian tribe which lived in one of the Andean valleys, told them that he was coming to deliver them from the Spaniards, and after obtaining permission to pass through their territory sent them home again bound never to breathe a word about the agreement. With the certain knowledge that this information would get back to the enemy, he planned to guide his army through other passes and fall upon the Spaniards by surprise.

The director of the government at Buenos Aires, Pueyrredón, sent him supplies, money, and men, and with them official instructions, many of which San Martín himself had suggested. These instructions served as a sort of set of principles for the army of liberation. It was not "to plunder or oppress the people of Chile," and there was no design "to acquire control of the liberated territory." General San Martín was empowered to establish a provisional government in Chile, and the hope was expressed that Chilean delegates might be sent to Buenos Aires "in order that ultimately Spanish South America should constitute one nation."

The total number of soldiers in this Army of the Andes, including the refugee Chileans under Bernardo O'Higgins, did not reach six thousand. In the middle of the Argentine summer, January 18, 1817, the march started, its vanguard consisting of men supplied with carts, anchors, and cables to aid in dragging cannon over the icy crags and precipices of the Andes. Nothing had been left undone to secure the success of the project, yet the general himself had written to a friend that it was not the royalist soldiers which disturbed his sleep "but the passage of these immense mountains."

That march was one of the most epochal in history. Hannibal and Napoleon made history by taking their armies across the Alps through passes at a maximum height of eight thousand feet. San Martín and his army had to climb to nearly thirteen thousand feet—an elevation at which the air is so rarefied that man and beast both suffer from the dread *soroche*, or mountain sickness. Nausea, splitting headaches, and a terrible pounding of the heart all attack and weaken the system simultaneously. Nor was the route itself easy. It led for three hundred miles over as barren and frightening a country as exists in the world. With a hot sun during the day and bitter cold at night, men, animals, baggage, and equipment were guided around peaks, along narrow chasms, through defiles and winding mountain folds, until finally they emerged in the valley of Aconcagua, with the Chilean plains not far below them.

They had made the passage in twenty-one days—an average traveling rate of over fifteen miles a day. The Spaniards were not only taken completely by surprise, but before they could muster reinforcements San Martín attacked resolutely, and on February 12 defeated them decisively in the Battle of Chacabuco. Two days later the victorious patriots entered the city of Santiago.

This battle is memorable in Spanish American history for many reasons. First of all, it was the result of a carefully planned campaign, carried out by well-trained troops under brilliant leadership. In that year 1817, when things still looked so black for the cause of independence all over South America, it came as a burst of light, giving hope and renewed energy to many an irresolute patriot heart. In the second place, one emerging nation had crossed its own frontiers and come to the rescue of another, thus making the engagement the first evidence of passing from the defensive to the offensive for South American independence. In the third place, that passage of the Andes, with all the baggage, equipment, and supplies necessary to maintain an army for a month, took place two years before Bolívar's famous crossing of the Colombian Andes with his equally brilliant victory of Boyacá and triumphant entry into Bogotá. Although Bolívar was a man who needed no one to show him the way, this phenomenal feat of San Martín's undoubtedly gave him further courage to undertake his own campaign under even more unfavorable circumstances. Last of all, the victory broke the threat of the Spaniards on the Argentine flank, checked the arrival of new forces from Peru, gave the United Provinces time to breathe and to expand, without which, as a historian of the country states, "they might have smothered in the cradle." From that day forward the course of Spanish power in the New World was thrown more and more on the defensive, and the realization that it had already passed its zenith and was on the descent boded no good for the morale of those peninsular troops and leaders who commenced to see the handwriting on the wall.

The people of Chile not only acclaimed San Martín as a conquering hero but offered to make him governor of their country. Faithful to the star that guided his life, he refused the honor, saying that "his armies did not fight battles to conquer governments but to liberate peoples." General O'Higgins was then made director; that is, virtual dictator of Chile. San Martín already had his thoughts fixed on the distant goal of Lima, separated from Chile by fifteen hundred miles over land or sea.

In order to gain the support of his own country in this enterprise San Martín retraced his steps over the Andes, this time with only two companions, and a few days later had placed before Pueyrredón, the director of the government in Buenos Aires, his plans for assembling a navy and assaulting the Spaniards in their strongest citadel. As a result of these discussions a well-known merchant of Buenos Aires was sent to the United States to plead the cause of his government. This merchant was supplied with two hundred thousand pesos and carried with him a letter from San Martín to President Monroe which stated the urgent need of obtaining vessels to prosecute the war against Peru. Monroe referred the matter to his Secretary of State, John Quincy Adams, who was anxious to pursue a neutral policy toward Spain. He refused point-blank to recognize the United Provinces or to enter into any relations with them. When the agent continued his efforts to secure vessels he was arrested as a violator of the neutrality law. Nevertheless, he managed to purchase two ships and sent them to join the Chilean navy.

A little more than a year after San Martín's first victory over the Spanish forces in Chile, the royalists had re-formed their ranks and were again threatening to take over the country. They made some successful surprise attacks but in the end were defeated in the Battle of Maipú (1818), which practically eliminated Spanish power in southern South America. Plans now went forward for the amphibious attack on Peru. The Chileans gradually acquired several small men-of-war, and this squadron sent the patriots into a burst of enthusiasm when it captured a Spanish frigate off the Pacific coast. San Martín returned to Argentina for further funds and supplies, and a famous English officer, Lord Cochrane, who had been born and bred in the naval tradition, was persuaded to leave his own country, where he had fallen into disgrace, and throw in his lot with the Chilean revolutionists. With this daring and resourceful man in command of the new navy the flag of Chile was carried up and down the western coast for a distance of two thousand miles between the cities of Valdivia in southern Chile and Callao, the port of Lima. The Spaniards gave the name of *El Diablo* to this phantom of the sea who swooped down on them in such widely separated places.

While Lord Cochrane was carrying out these exploits conditions in Buenos Aires had gone from bad to worse. A few influential leaders still favored the establishment of a monarchy; some of the interior provinces were on the verge of war in order to ensure themselves regional sovereignty under a federation, and the Congress was putting the finishing touches on a unitarian constitution. When this document was promulgated all the latent spleen which had been gathering burst forth, and the way was prepared for anarchy. In June 1819 Pueyrredón, finding himself at the end of his term of office and seeing that it was impossible for him to control the situation longer, resigned from his post. Almost immediately the capital city found itself under threat of attack by the Gauchos of the pampas, who had risen to fight for their "federation" and autonomy.

San Martín was directed to bring his Army of the Andes back from Chile in order to defend Buenos Aires, but instead of obeying the general sent in his resignation as commander and refused to move from Chile, as it would have meant the abandonment of his enterprise. His resignation was then referred to his own troops, who promptly reappointed him as their leader. The whole procedure was carried out in direct defiance of the home government, and from that time on San Martín had calumny after calumny heaped on his head in Buenos Aires. True to his star under these attacks, but not entirely oblivious of them, he sent back to the United Provinces of the River Plate a proclamation in which he attempted to make his position clear. He said that it would be "the last response to my calumniators," and the gist of the document was that San Martín's constant and only thought had been for the freedom of his native land. "I can do no more than to risk my life and my honor for the sake of my country," he wrote, adding that if this merited him the hatred of the ungrateful it would not sway him from his appointed task. So while anarchy and civil war rent the government which had given him a start, San Martín dedicated himself to the higher task of making possible the freedom of all the South American states.

In the fall of 1820 eight Chilean warships and sixteen transports assembled in the harbor of Valparaiso. The soldiers numbered about four thousand, and there were supplies on board to last for six months. Approximately half the force was made up of San Martín's old Army of the Andes, while the others were Chileans. A considerable portion of the officers were European, mainly British. There were about sixteen hundred sailors and marines. Lord Cochrane had command of the fleet, which took leave of the friendly harbor with much fanfare. After they were out on the high seas he opened his sealed orders and read: "The object of this expedition is to free Peru from Spanish domination, to raise her to the rank of a free and sovereign power, and thus to complete the sublime task of establishing the independence of South America." It was also made perfectly clear that the over-all command was entrusted to Captain General José de San Martín. The Chilean dictator, O'Higgins, was largely responsible for these instructions, and he had even taken the precaution of providing San Martín with other secret orders authorizing him to utilize his absolute powers of command as he saw fit, even to the extent of replacing Lord Cochrane with some other officer should that be his best judgment.

O'Higgins was not interested in adding Peru to his own territory, nor in controlling its government. Like San Martín, he simply looked upon the old viceroyalty as being the head of the octopus which had its tentacles stretched over the whole continent, and he was determined to crush that head and thus destroy completely the power of those coils. He had a proclamation prepared for distribution among the Peruvians in which his own intentions and those of the liberating army were made crystal-clear: "You shall be free and independent; you shall form your government and your laws according to the spontaneous wish of your own representatives. The soldiers of the army of liberation, your brothers, will exert no influence, military or civil, direct or indirect, on your social system. Whenever it suits you, dismiss the army that comes to protect you. A military force should never occupy the territory of a free people unless invited by its legitimate magistrates."[91]

35

SAN MARTÍN: PROTECTOR OF PERU

While San Martín was winning his victories in the south the revolution was spreading in the north, and the spheres of royalist resistance were gradually being constricted. Only three Spanish forces remained at this time: a small and rapidly disintegrating contingent in Venezuela, another small nucleus in the city of Quito which was already completely isolated, and a third powerful army in Peru, under the command of the Viceroy of that colony. All the rest of the continent was under revolutionary control.

Quito thus was the logical meeting place for the two large patriot armies, Bolívar's from the north and San Martín's from the south. The two spearheads, now near ultimate victory, had commenced their unpropitious campaigns in Venezuela and in Buenos Aires respectively many years previously. Step by step they had been pushing closer together, despite many anxious moments. Bolívar had suffered several severe reverses and on two occasions had been forced to flee to the islands of the Antilles in order to save his life. Yet he had always triumphed over his adversities and had returned to the attack with renewed vigor. No matter what his condition, he had given the Spaniards no rest. He was always on the offensive, both militarily and politically, and that ceaseless pressure, plus the brilliance of its being applied at the right time and places, had finally won the independence of northern South America.

When the Liberator heard that San Martín and his army were nearly ready to advance on Peru from Valparaiso he wrote to the dictator of Chile: "A Colombian army is marching on Quito under orders to cooperate actively with the armies of Chile and Buenos Aires against Lima." One month after San Martín's expedition had got under way he announced through his Secretary of War: "The day of South American independence is drawing near. Peru is going to receive her liberty through the soldiers of Chile and Buenos Aires. The troops of Colombia will fulfill their duty by freeing Quito, and will then conclude their mission fighting in Peru for the Children of the Sun."

San Martín responded to these promises in a similar vein. So far the two great leaders of South American independence were seeing eye to eye. The sharp blade of glory and power and of a difference in political outlook had not yet come between them.

Before San Martín actually began the operation of landing his troops on Peruvian soil Lord Cochrane performed one of those heroic deeds which has made his name so widely admired in Latin-American history. In the harbor at Callao was a large Spanish man-of-war, the *Esmeralda*, which mounted forty-four cannon. It was fully manned by three hundred and twenty men and could easily have blasted to pieces any of the lighter Chilean vessels. Lord Cochrane determined to capture this ship from the Spaniards and add her to his own fleet. One night, after the Spaniards had been celebrating royally on board the *Esmeralda* for several hours, the English admiral led a group of rowboats to the attack. His men were all dressed in white so that they would not shoot each other. They were to board the vessel from both sides and overpower her crew. If this part of the plan worked out successfully they might then board the smaller Spanish merchantmen in the harbor and set fire to them.

Like a group of phantoms, the assailants cut across the waters of the bay. On the way in they passed two foreign frigates which were then visiting Lima, one British, the other belonging to the United States. Men from these ships, especially from the latter, immediately saw what was in the wind and in low voices wished Cochrane's men the best of luck. Many United States vessels visited Latin-American waters in those days, and, as one Argentine historian put it: "They were always messengers of friendship and fraternity which under their neutral flag studied the men and conditions of the nascent republics, encouraging them in their struggle and spreading even further amongst them the ideas of independence and liberty."

Cochrane's small flotilla continued its advance and was almost upon the *Esmeralda* before the Spaniards realized what was happening. Many of them were still suffering from the aftereffects of the banquet of the day before. Cochrane himself jumped out of the leading boat and climbed the cable to the *Esmeralda's* deck. The man on watch began to shout "*¡Alarma!*" at the top of his lungs, and, as soon as the Englishman's head and shoulders appeared over the railing, rushed upon him, giving him a terrible blow on the chest with the butt of his gun. Cochrane toppled over backward and fell into one of his own boats below. His back was painfully wrenched in the fall, but, oblivious to pain, he immediately leaped to his feet again and mounted the cable. This time his whole crew followed. They shot the sentinel, and Cochrane's voice rang out in a clear: "Up, my lads, she's ours!"

The boarding party made for the sails and took possession of them before the Spaniards had come out on deck in any number. After that a bitter fight ensued, and Cochrane himself was shot through the thigh. His second-in-command was also seriously wounded. Seeing that attacks on other vessels were out of the question, the patriots then turned the ship toward the open sea and took her back to their own squadron. The royalists had lost well over one hundred dead, and two hundred were made prisoners on board. The patriots lost eleven dead and thirty wounded, and had added a great prize to their small fleet. The prisoners they had taken later made it possible to effect an exchange, and two hundred Argentines and Chileans were released who had been rotting in the jails of Callao for months. This move also forced the Viceroy to recognize the patriots as belligerents, a thing which he had consistently refused to do up to that moment.

The royalists were nonplused at having lost so shamefully one of their finest warships from under the very shadow of the strongest land fortifications in Spanish America; they immediately began to look about for some pretext which might afford a loophole of escape. They hit upon blaming the neutrals in Callao Harbor, and especially the crew of the U.S.S. *Macedonia*, whose sympathy for the cause of Spanish American independence was beyond doubt. The report that these North Americans had a large part in the scheme was circulated around the town, and when a small launch was sent ashore to take on provisions its commanding officer and crew, all of whom were defenseless, were barbarously assaulted by an infuriated mob. None escaped alive. Commander Downes demanded from the Viceroy a proper reparation for this affront and at the same time wrote San Martín in the following words: "I congratulate Lord Cochrane on the capture of the *Esmeralda*. Never has so brilliant an exploit been carried out with more skill."

So far as the patriots were concerned the capture of this big Spanish warship even before they had set foot on Peruvian soil added considerably to their stature. The Spaniards were now thoroughly rattled; their defenses were weakened by not knowing where the next blow might fall; they doubtless estimated the revolutionary strength much higher than it actually was, and, worst of all, those citizens along the Peruvian coast, who were already somewhat inclined toward independence, now went the whole way and threw the weight of their opinion behind San Martín.

Lord Cochrane was for following up the victory with a direct all-out attack on Lima, but San Martín overrode him and the fleet sailed several miles north of Callao, preparatory to landing at an unexpected point, the little port of Huacho.

Leading contingents of San Martín's army began to disembark on September 8, 1820. They met surprisingly little resistance and were soon firmly established on shore. The Viceroy was not anxious to fight and, with an eye toward settling matters amicably, sent messengers requesting an interview. This interview and two or three subsequent ones were held, but nothing came of them. San Martín insisted that Peruvian independence be recognized before further negotiations were carried on, and the Viceroy was both unwilling and unauthorized to make such a concession. The suggestion was also made that some European prince be placed on the throne of Peru, perhaps a prince of Spain, and while the Viceroy seemed favorably inclined to this he did not consider either himself or San Martín endowed with sufficient power to make such an agreement.

All this time the liberating army had been encamped outside Lima, and although it caught and defeated one small royalist force, no decisive battle had yet taken place between the two opposing groups. San Martín continued to make it clear to the Peruvians that he was not bent on any conquest, and that the day they took over their own government and no longer needed his support his mission would be completed. This attitude stimulated the zeal for independence inside Lima, even among royalist ranks. Many soldiers deserted the banners of the Viceroy and came over to the side of the patriots. Gradually the whole country moved in the direction of independence. Some of San Martín's officers were anxious to march at once into Lima, but the general said that such a move would defeat his whole object. He wanted merely to give Peru an opportunity to achieve its own freedom, and if he advanced upon the capital before this feeling had asserted itself among the majority he would be denying his own principles. He wanted Lima to fall into his hands "like ripened grain," and was determined not to advance a single step ahead of public opinion. It was obvious that he would not have to wait long, because the desire for liberty, fanned by his presence and his proclamations, was growing apace.

On July 6, 1821, the royalists evacuated the city and retired to the Andes. Their position had become untenable. A deputation from the *cabildo* immediately invited San Martín to enter the capital, and six days later this entrance took place. Again the general reiterated that the reasons for his occupation were "to give the people the means of declaring themselves independent, and of establishing a suitable form of government." He wanted to see the country "managed by itself, and by itself alone." But the manner in which it was to be governed was not his concern at all.

San Martín would have to eat these words before he finally left Peru. It was his firm conviction that a republic could not possibly be maintained in such a country, and that the monarchical form of government was the only one which offered any hope of success. This conviction had been growing in his mind since the day he set foot on Argentine soil after his return from Spain. After the first unsuccessful negotiation with the Viceroy he announced publicly in *El Pacificador*, a small newssheet which was printed and distributed in his camp as a sort of bulletin, that he favored this form of government. The article was written by one of his close friends,

Monteagudo, but San Martín was back of it. This statement read in part: "Every literate man who knows his country and desires order will naturally prefer a monarchy to the continuation of disorder and confusion. It is indisputable that the enemies of the peace of the State will oppose this project."

In spite of this expression of his personal opinion San Martín had repeatedly promised Peru freedom to choose its own form of government, and now was the time when a beginning must be made. An open meeting of the town's best citizens was called and independence was declared. All of the city's notables assembled on a large platform raised in the center of the main plaza, and there before an immense multitude the ceremony was carried out. San Martín unfurled the flag which he himself had designed, and after the thunderous applause had quieted down he announced in a firm and sonorous voice: "From this moment Peru is free and independent, by the general wish of her people and by the justice of her cause, which God defends!" Then he saluted the flag three times and, waving it exultantly over his head, exclaimed: *"¡Viva la patria! ¡Viva la libertad! ¡Viva la independencia!* [Long live this country! Long live its liberty! Long live its independence!]" The people assembled in the plaza took up these words and shouted them in unison. Cannon boomed forth their salute, and silver medals were scattered in the square.

Less than a week after this solemn event San Martín proclaimed that all civil and military authority was vested in himself, in order "to advance the sacred cause of America and to promote the happiness of the Peruvian people." His title would be *Protector*. Oliver Cromwell in England had been the last person to use that title, and San Martín was at least like Cromwell in one thing: he wanted to save the country from corruption, disintegration, and disaster. He disclaimed any intention of keeping this power after independence was a fact. It was to be strictly a war measure to ensure orderly government until the royalists were finally defeated. He thought that any other procedure might imperil the independence of a continent.

San Martín has been bitterly criticized for this act in some quarters and has been praised for it in others. An English traveler, Captain Basil Hall, who was in Lima at that time, defends the general's action in these words: "It was more creditable to assume the full authority in a manly and open manner, than to mock the people with the semblance of a republic, and at the same time, to visit them with the reality of a despotism."[91] On the other hand, many of San Martín's officers, among them Lord Cochrane, and a considerable number of influential citizens of Lima who had been led to expect their own government became indignant at what they considered an arbitrary dictatorship. San Martín had both experience and logic on his side. He knew what had happened in his own country when they attempted to set up a constitutional government too early, and he had no desire to see that wrangling and strife repeated in Peru, where there was less likelihood of finding those elements of compromise, co-operation, and self-effacement on which a united government depends. From both the military and political point of view martial law was what the case demanded, and martial law was what he had declared. The country was not only fighting for its life, but the life of all South America depended on the outcome, and the enemy was stronger, not weaker, than the army which San Martín had under his command. Up to this point he had played his cards carefully and well and had caused the enemy to retire to the mountains, but he could have no assurance that they would not return to the attack at any moment. The slightest opening on his own part would be a deliberate lowering of his guard and an invitation to disaster.

Yet there is not the slightest doubt that from the moment of his protectorship San Martín's fortune began to decline. He did not possess Bolívar's ability as a politician or orator, nor was he a keen psychologist of mass nature. His was the cold and deliberate logic of the military genius, not the heart-warming persuasiveness of the political leader or statesman. He might have made the people themselves elevate him to the rank of Protector or dictator had he been able to manipulate the mass mind so that it followed his suggestion while thinking that the initiative was its own. Bolívar was a past master at this sort of thing. San Martín was not. He was out of his element. He was neither a man of government nor a capable administrator. Such things were antipathetic to him. Above everything else he wanted independence and, in order to achieve independence, it was essential to have order. He may or may not have had some personal ambition for power, but if he did, this was subordinate to his long-range ideal of independence as his later actions so conclusively proved. Nevertheless, he had made an error in judgment, a psychological blunder, one which the majority of the ruling caste took as a deliberate insult to its intelligence. As Mitre, one of his most admiring biographers, states, in that larger sphere of action "San Martín, the Protector of Peru, does not grow in character, and shows himself inferior to his mission."

The general also made other errors which turned people against him. An outstanding example was his unremitting persecution of the Spaniards, especially those he suspected of treasonable inclinations. He announced that he had spies in the homes of the most important citizens and that no treachery could possibly escape him. San Martín then went to the limits of confiscating Spanish property after he had pledged his word that he would respect it. Cochrane stated that the Protector had said he intended to "leave the Spaniards with nothing but a shirt on their backs."

Another result of these mild excesses was the bitter estrangement of some of the higher clergy. In general, the lower clergy throughout Peru had been strongly in favor of independence, especially the parish priests. But the higher church officials were not. San Martín's lofty and threatening attitude toward the class to which they belonged did not help matters any. "I know what goes on in the most private corners of your homes. Tremble if you abuse my indulgence," he declared in his proclamation against the Spaniards. The higher dignitaries, taking advantage of their position, frequently assumed the lead in a counterrevolution against the patriots. The Archbishop of Chuquisaca (Sucre) and the bishops of Trujillo, Cuzco, Maynas, Huamanga, and Arequipa were all prominent in the reaction.

The Archbishop of Lima, eighty-year-old Las Heras, a royalist at heart, found himself caught in the net of revolutionary activity and co-operated with San Martín in restoring order after the evacuation of the city by the Spaniards. Shortly afterward, however, he objected violently to the closing of the religious retreats for women which the general considered to be a necessary military measure in view of the ease with which plotting might be carried on there. San Martín abruptly informed him that the order was irrevocable, and Las Heras replied in an equally abrupt tone that only the decrees of the Almighty were irrevocable. The archbishop then requested a passport for Spain, and it was given to him along with an order to leave the country within twenty-four hours. On departing the archbishop wrote Lord Cochrane, who had befriended him in many ways, in these words: "On leaving this country I am convinced that its independence is forever sealed. I shall express this opinion to the Spanish government and to the Holy See. At the same time I shall do everything within my power to overcome their obstinacy, to maintain tranquillity and to second the expressed will of the inhabitants of the America which I esteem so highly." The archbishop left San Martín apparently in complete control of the situation, even of the Church.

But San Martín had already reached and passed his zenith, and his career, like that of a brilliant and falling star, was nearing its end. When the crucial moment arrived his genius and moral equilibrium were not equal to the new task of creative energy which the situation demanded. He was tired in spirit and body and that weariness began to overcome him.

He and Lord Cochrane quarreled bitterly over several matters: San Martín's arbitrary dictatorship, the payment of the sailors of the fleet, the right of Cochrane to give such orders as he saw fit to the vessels of the squadron. The personalities of the two men met in a deadlock. After a few stormy sessions the result was a complete rupture. Cochrane and his entire squadron abandoned Peru. In this altercation the two men outdid each other in name calling: to San Martín, Cochrane was "the most perverse man of earth, a pirate, a subverter of the public interest, a criminal dishonored by his very acts." To Cochrane, San Martín was "a bloody tyrant, an inept general, a hypocrite, thief, coward, deceiver, and deserter of his flag." He was a "new Icarus" whose wings would not support his lofty flight.

To make matters worse, San Martín at this time "was attacked by a mysterious malady which confined him to his bed, convinced him of the precarious state of his health, and made him desire private life." His administration of the government was necessarily neglected and many of his lieutenants ruled badly. A rift appeared even inside the army itself, and a goodly number of officers began to resent the austere and highhanded attitude of their commander. There was an abortive conspiracy against him, and the title "King José" circulated in more than a whisper among the disaffected.

All this time San Martín refused to engage the enemy forces, which sometimes maneuvered before Lima under his very nose. Although the relative size of the two forces made a battle between them idiotic from the patriot point of view, there were many who began to accuse the general of cowardice, and many others whispered that his days of drive and creative brilliance were past. The general was able to do little to counteract these rumors.

In so far as the permanent government of Peru was concerned he decided in favor of a monarchy and sent a secret mission to Europe by way of Chile in search of a suitable prince. In spite of what his detractors were saying he did not intend to entrench himself in power. He wrote a letter to O'Higgins in which his position was made clear: that the government to be adopted should be in line with the conditions of the people over which it was to rule, that he was "convinced of the impossibility of establishing republics in these countries," and that a monarchy was obviously the only way of avoiding the horrors of anarchy. He also tried to persuade O'Higgins to let the mission represent Chile as well as Peru, but the dictator of the former country replied that while a monarchy might be desirable in the old viceroyalty his own countrymen were definitely opposed to such a regime.

It was at this stage of his life, when everything was in the balance and nothing was certain, when Lord Cochrane had deserted him and Chile had refused its support, when he was ill in body and worn in spirit, when his dictatorship had become distasteful to a considerable portion of the Peruvians and to many of his own officers, that San Martín went north to the Ecuadorian port of Guayaquil to take part in his fateful and dramatic interview with the Liberator of the north, Simón Bolívar.

Every turn of events in the northern provinces had cast further glory on the Liberator. His general and dearest friend, Sucre, had just defeated the royalists near Quito on the slopes of Mount Pichincha, and now the region of Ecuador was free. It was somewhat of an irony that a numerous contingent from San Martín's army which had been sent to reinforce Sucre made this brilliant victory possible, and also contributed to the reverses which his own soldiers had met to the north of Peru. Bolívar himself had marched into Ecuador from Bogotá and was at the height of his power at the head of a triumphant army. The time had come for him to fulfill his promise of sending aid to the revolutionary army in Peru, in order that the last stronghold of royalist resistance on the continent might be liberated. It was primarily to discuss this matter that the two great men met in Guayaquil.

Bolívar had been keeping a wary eye on San Martín for some time past, and had watched with increasing apprehension the growth of his monarchical scheme for governing Peru. He had already made one strong attempt to nip this project in the bud. One of Bolívar's Colombian friends, who was a colonel in San Martín's army, was asked to make a strong effort to dissuade the Protector from following out his plan. In case he met with a rebuff he was to inform San Martín of Bolívar's conviction "that Colombia does not consent to a monarchy, it is against our institutions, it is against everything for which we have fought, it is against the vehement will of the people for their liberty."

Bolívar had already made up his mind that he and his nation must not yield to the general from the south. The two men not only represented different political conceptions but were the symbols of two great nations, each of which sought the leadership of a continent. Bolívar's attitude was clearly brought out in several of his actions prior to the Guayaquil meeting. On one occasion, while present at a banquet being given in his honor in Quito, and which was attended by all the higher officers in his army, Colombians, Peruvians, Argentines, and Chileans, the Liberator rose to his feet to give a toast. Intoxicated with both words and power, he forgot the cosmopolitan nature of the gathering and exclaimed: "The day will not be long delayed when I shall carry the triumphant banner of Colombia clear down to Argentine soil!" Five Argentine officers were present, and their leader, who was commander of the contingent which had fought under Sucre, asked for the floor "in order to rectify an error." In a voice whose tone of arrogance could not be missed he said: "The Argentine Republic is independent and free of Spanish domination, and has been so since the day it declared its emancipation, the 25th of May, 1810. In all their efforts to reconquer our soil the Spaniards have been defeated. Our national anthem consecrates our triumphs." A silence settled over the banquet and no further toasts were offered that night.

On another occasion the Liberator was seated next to an Argentine colonel, and, noticing the man's proud bearing, Bolívar asked: "Who are you?" The colonel answered: "Manuel Rojas." "What is your rank?" Rojas leaned over and showed the colonel's insigne on his shoulder. "What country are you from?" "I have the honor of being from Buenos Aires," responded Rojas. Bolívar, now clearly nettled, replied: "It is easy to tell that from the haughty air which you have assumed." The colonel retaliated: "It is the proper air for free men, sir." Both speakers, realizing that they had gone too far, lowered their heads, and an icy coldness swept from one end of the room to the other.

On the other hand, Bolívar undoubtedly felt a suppressed admiration for the Argentine troops which had come to Sucre's aid. Their discipline and bearing made them stand out among the no less brave but more loosely organized and trained soldiers of his own command. Bolívar began to wonder what it would mean if, under such men as these, the leadership of Buenos Aires was extended through Peru to the southern borders of his own beloved Colombia.

There was one step which he could take immediately, and he did not hesitate. The province of Guayaquil, Ecuador's Pacific coast region, had already declared its independence and was now being ruled by a local junta. This tremendously important province, with its port, might be permitted to remain independent, which did not fit in with Bolívar's political ideas, or it might become a part of Peru, which fitted in with them even less, or it might be added to the territory of Colombia, thus extending that country's southern boundary in a regular line from the Andes to the sea. Bolívar chose the last course and entered the city with a considerable army. When it seemed as if the citizens of the town were a little reluctant toward being incorporated in Greater Colombia, Bolívar made the decision for them and declared their province under Colombian rule. This was the situation when San Martín arrived from Lima.

36

THE TWO GENERALS MEET AT GUAYAQUIL

The actual meeting in Guayaquil was somewhat of a surprise for both men. San Martín expected to find Bolívar in Quito and had planned to join him there. Bolívar, on his part, had not thought that the Protector would arrive so soon. As a matter of fact, the Liberator was just signing a letter to San Martín when the sails of the vessel bearing the latter appeared over the horizon. In that letter appeared these significant words: ". . . you will surely not disappoint the eagerness which I feel for embracing on Colombian soil the first friend of my heart and of my country." San Martín had lost the first round of the conferences before they had begun. Guayaquil, which he had wanted to add to Peru in much the same way that Bolívar had incorporated it in Greater Colombia, was already "Colombian soil."

After being greeted by Bolívar's representatives on board ship, San Martín landed and, amid tumultuous demonstrations, proceeded to the mansion where the Liberator was awaiting him. They embraced warmly and arm in arm ascended the steps leading into the building. There the formal reception took place; the proper presentations and speeches were made, and during the ceremony a beautiful girl came forward to place a crown of laurel leaves embossed with gold on San Martín's head. The Liberator of the south, who had never liked such theatrical displays, was considerably embarrassed. After the reception was over the assemblage dispersed and the two generals were left alone. Their first conference (July 26) lasted for an hour and a half, and when it was concluded they both came forth looking extremely grave. They walked together to the stairway and took leave of each other in a friendly fashion, but with little warmth.

The two great leaders held two more conferences, one on that same day, July 26, and the last one on the following day, July 27, 1822. Many historians have stated that these meetings were "enveloped in a cloud of mystery," but this is only true to the extent that no unbiased observer was present. The matters that were discussed, the decisions reached, and the general attitude of both leaders have been made perfectly clear in the light of documents later made available. Among these documents are letters of both San Martín and Bolívar.

The main purpose of the meetings was to plan the final campaign against the Spaniards in Peru. San Martín was anxious to find out how many troops Bolívar was willing to furnish. Other matters discussed were the status of Guayaquil and the form of government for the liberated colonies. From the first moment it was evident that there was almost no chance of a warmhearted co-operation between the two men. When San Martín asked Bolívar point-blank for "the active and efficacious cooperation of all the forces of Colombia" in order to terminate the war in Peru, the Liberator began to hedge. He offered only 1,070 men, paying back to the letter San Martín's aid to Sucre. Even these troops were to serve under certain limitations. The reason Bolívar gave was that he did not have the authority to lead his army outside of Colombia. This was obviously an excuse, for his slightest suggestion would immediately have been approved by the Congress of that country. San Martín knew that these slight reinforcements would not be enough to insure the defeat of the Spaniards. Bolívar must have known it also.

The real question which had not yet been raised was: who was to command the army which was to conclude South American independence? San Martín naturally assumed that this responsibility and honor should fall to him. He had cleared Lima of royalist forces, had organized the Peruvian Government, and knew the character and disposition of the Spanish army in Peru. Yet when it became apparent that Bolívar was unwilling to yield on this point, San Martín humbly asked that he be permitted the honor of serving *under* the Liberator in the final battles. Bolívar was unwilling to accept this compromise. There is no doubt that the Liberator, "radiant in glory," wanted to win the final victory himself. But he also knew that the compromise suggested by San Martín was too precarious, that San Martín's men and officers would have resented it, that the entire war might yet be lost should a division occur between the two groups.

There was still another point on which Bolívar and San Martín were unable to agree. After the war in Peru was won, what kind of government should be established there? San Martín made clear his opinion that a democratic form of government was not suitable for Peru. Bolívar opposed this vigorously. He stated that it was impossible to move back the hands of the clock and that if a monarchy were set up in Peru it would only be destroyed later by the people of that country. "Once the idea of a republic has taken root," he said, "it cannot be extinguished."

It is impossible to say which of the leaders was right. Events soon proved that Peru was not ready for a republic and that her tyrant presidents were as bad as any monarch. Bolívar himself admitted as much later.

Yet it is true that wherever monarchies were established in Latin America they have fallen. Mexico's early Emperor Iturbide was promptly executed. The same fate befell the Emperor Maximilian, who was brought to Mexico from Austria in the 1860s. Brazil, on the other hand, enjoyed a long epoch of peace under her monarchical regime, but finally that, too, was toppled and replaced by a republic. Besides, conditions in Brazil and Spanish America were far from identical. Brazil had endured no long revolutionary war in the name of republican ideals. Bolívar told the Bolivians many years later: "There is no power more difficult to maintain than that of a new prince." He believed that without the two strong props of a great nobility and great prelates no monarchy could endure.

Those who might be inclined to favor San Martín's ideas can easily point out that neither could republics be raised upon the backward and miserable masses who made up the immense majority of the inhabitants of the new Spanish American states. Hindsight is much easier than foresight when one is analyzing a period in history.

Bolívar himself knew that his people were not ready for anything approaching an absolute democracy. He had stated pointedly many times that such an attempt would be merely a snare "in which all republican hopes come to grief." And as he advanced in years and experience the Liberator moved gradually toward placing more power in the hands of the chief executive, and finally, when he drew up a constitution for the state of Bolivia in 1826, it stated that the president was to be elected for life and would virtually hold in his hands alone the right to appoint his successor. Was there a difference between this and monarchy? It was certainly not a very great difference. Perhaps the very name "republic" was difference enough. This name was a symbol and not a reality, but it was at least a symbol which represented the aspirations of the immense majority of the people of the new states. So long as they held to it and exalted it they would progress toward a real democracy. Had they turned their backs on the ideal and denied it by adopting a monarchy and disparaging democratic aspirations, no one can tell what might have been the result. In any case, Spanish America was not able to govern itself properly for many years. Both San Martín and Bolívar knew that when they met in Guayaquil in 1822. Both were attempting to devise some means of avoiding the pitfalls of regression and anarchy. Both failed. And while it was Bolívar who happened to come out on top after those interviews, the triumph of San Martín could hardly have altered the course of South American government greatly. His experience in Peru had already proved that he was unable to function as a great administrator. Bolívar's prophetic words written in that same year characterize the situation completely: "We shall not see, nor the generation following us, the triumph of the America we are founding. I regard America as in the chrysalis. There will be a metamorphosis in the physical life of its inhabitants; there will finally be a new caste, of all the races, which will result in the homogeneity of the people." This was speaking in terms of centuries, not decades.

It was San Martín, however, and not Bolívar, who was willing to sacrifice every personal consideration—his power, his pride, his political convictions, his leadership and his glory, even "his military honor"—in order that the America he loved might not at the very beginning be rent with a division which might have jeopardized its emancipation.

When the two men met for the last time at a banquet given in San Martín's honor, Bolívar rose and offered the following toast: "To the two greatest men of South America: General San Martín and myself." To this San Martín responded: "For the speedy termination of the war, the organization of the different republics of the continent, and to the health of the liberator of Colombia."

After the banquet there was a dance and Bolívar entered into the spirit of the affair with alacrity. He was passionately fond of dancing, and, as the hours passed, his animation increased and his military dignity was soon forgotten. San Martín, preserving an expressionless exterior to cover up the bitterness which he must have felt inside, remained the cold spectator throughout. Finally, at about one in the morning, he called his aide-de-camp and said: "Let's leave now. I can't endure this noise any longer." Without anyone noticing it he was shown out through a back door, as he and Bolívar had previously agreed. The two leaders never saw each other again. Their last farewell had already been spoken.

San Martín went directly to his ship and an hour later was on his way to Peru. The following day he arose very early and remained preoccupied and silent throughout the morning. After lunch, while pacing the deck, he exclaimed: "The Liberator got the best of us!" And in a letter which he asked one of his generals to send to O'Higgins in Chile these words occurred: "The Liberator is not the man we thought him to be!" San Martín must have felt his defeat and disillusionment deeply, but in order that his personal feelings might not in any way interfere with the prosecution of the war he did not express them publicly. Both at Guayaquil and afterward the two generals preserved an outward attitude of harmony and were rarely known to make any mention of the famous meeting.

While San Martín was away from Lima his fellow countryman and right-hand man, Monteagudo, who held the portfolios of both War and Foreign Affairs in the Peruvian Government, had been the power behind the scene. San Martín had frequently fallen back on Monteagudo for aid and support when his own physical constitution was unable to endure any longer. Monteagudo was his friend, his most ardent supporter, his faithful servant. They both had little faith in the people's ability to govern themselves; both favored a strong centralized government, preferably a monarchy, for the new South American states. Like San Martín, Monteagudo was a native of Argentina who looked upon all of the continent as his country. Unlike San Martín, he was given to all kinds of excesses which shocked the Peruvians. He was a mulatto, dictatorial, violently anti-Spanish, and atheistic. The aristocrats of Lima soon had enough of him, and while San Martín was away they drove him from the city and exiled him permanently from the country, stating that if he ever set foot on Peruvian shores again he would be considered "outside the law." The citizens of Lima, who would not have dared to attack San Martín himself face to face, had chosen this way of taking out their bitterness on his friend and compatriot. When the Protector returned and found out what had occurred he at once realized to what extent feeling had risen against him.[173]

Shortly after his return he wrote to his friend, O'Higgins: "Believe me, my friend, I am tired of being called a tyrant, and of having it said in all quarters that I wish to become a king, an emperor . . ." He went on to say that his health was failing, that the climate did not agree with him, and that as he could no longer be of public use he wanted to retire from the scene. A month later, on September 20, 1822, he presented his *irrevocable* resignation to the Peruvian Congress. In his farewell address to the citizens of that country San Martín gave some of the reasons for his action. "My promises to the countries for which I have fought are fulfilled: to secure their independence, and to leave them to select their own governments. The presence of a fortunate soldier, however disinterested he may be, is dangerous to newly established states. Then, too, I am weary of hearing people say that I wish to make myself a monarch. Nevertheless, I shall always be ready to make the last sacrifice for the liberty of this country. . . ."[91]

A few days later he left Lima for Valparaiso. It was the first stage of a long journey which led ultimately to lifelong exile from his native land. San Martín's name was already forgotten in Chile, and the dictatorship of his friend, O'Higgins, was tottering on the verge of a collapse. The Protector crossed the Andes to his estate near Mendoza, where in happier days he had gathered and trained his army, and from there went on to Buenos Aires. Everywhere he was received with public derision or indifference. He no longer had even a fatherland. Toward the end of the year 1823, accompanied by the "daughter of his love," he departed from Buenos Aires for England, passing from that country to Brussels, where he remained until his child had completed her education. Five years later, "feeling again the necessity of breathing the air of his native land," he returned to Argentina, determined to spend the remainder of his days there in seclusion. The Argentine had just emerged triumphantly from a long war with Brazil, and on his arrival San Martín was greeted with these taunting words which appeared on a large sign hung over the city streets: "General San Martín has returned to his country after five years of absence; but only after learning that peace has been made with the Emperor of Brazil." The general remained on the same ship which had brought him over and returned to Europe to die.

As his Argentine biographer says, he might well have exclaimed as had Scipio two thousand years previously when insulted on the anniversary of one of his great victories: "It was on such a day as this that I saved Rome. Let us retire to the temple to pray to the tutelary Gods of our city that there may always be generals like me." He did not make this reply, nor did he have engraved on his sepulcher: "Ungrateful country, you will not have my bones." He returned to exile without recriminations and before his death spoke these words: "I want my heart to rest forever in Buenos Aires."

This deliberate renunciation of a successful general, who still disposed of considerable political power and a well-trained army, has been characterized in many different ways. San Martín's own words have frequently been taken at their face value: that he was tired of being called a tyrant, that he had performed his duty and now wanted Peru to form its own government, that his presence as a successful general was a peril to the state. If these had been the real reasons for his withdrawal "he would have been a coward and a deserter to his flag and to his principles who retired in the face of hard work and danger." San Martín was not that kind of leader. Perhaps he was merely covering up for the sake of appearances, or perhaps the bitterness of his defeat made him express sentiments which did not reveal the facts.

There was only one valid reason for his retirement. It was that the independence of South America might be secured. He could not achieve it alone, and his presence in Peru made it impossible for Bolívar to command the entire revolutionary army. The only way out was to eliminate himself completely. San Martín was willing to make even that sacrifice, and it is certainly one which is unparalleled in all the pages of history. He moved against his strong political convictions, against his dignity and honor as an individual, against his pride as a victorious soldier, in order that independence might be secured. He acted with the full knowledge that emancipation under these circumstances might not lead to the kind of society for which he had hoped, nor even to peace and stability, but he also knew that without independence as a basis his America would lack the very breath of life, and the entire continent might slip backward into the abysmal pit of centuries from which with his aid it had so painfully risen.

On seeing the way clear to enter Peru in undisputed command of the patriot army, Bolívar, just as San Martín had anticipated, made preparations for the attack. In the meetings at Guayaquil he had greatly underestimated the royalist strength in Peru, and in order to counterbalance this San Martín had told him both orally and in writing that the Spanish army consisted of approximately nineteen thousand veterans, whereas the patriots were less than half that number. Bolívar at last took these figures to heart and went about the task of readying his troops with grim determination. When their training was completed and supplies were gathered he led them across the Peruvian Andes along one of the highest and most difficult routes in the world. The temperature was rarely above zero, and ice frequently covered the narrow mountain paths and ledges over which the army had to pass, frequently in single file. Some of the men, exhausted and nearly frozen, began to drop out of formation. A few had to be shot as an example to the rest, for any large-scale desertion would not only have resulted in the certain death of the deserters but in the defeat of their comrades later. At night, when camp was pitched, there were often many soldiers still on the slopes. Buglers were posted at intervals to keep blowing so that they would not lose their way. At the rear of the army a herd of six thousand cattle was driven to furnish meat for the troops. After a month of the most arduous marching the expedition came out on the other side of the mountains.

On August 6, 1824, they met the royalists in the first great battle, Junín. This was one of the strangest engagements in history, for not a single shot was fired. Only the cavalry took part, and lances and sabers were the only weapons used. The infantry was present but merely witnessed the battle from the side lines. The whole encounter was like a great tourney of the Middle Ages and lasted only forty-five minutes. At the end of that time the royalist ranks broke and the patriots were masters of the field. The legend of the invincibility of the proud Spanish cavalry had been destroyed. The remnants of the royalist forces, however, managed to withdraw toward Cuzco, and it became obvious that they were not yet ready to give up the fight.

Bolívar placed the command of the army in the hands of General Sucre and left to gather reinforcements. The men needed a rest and were to remain in camp for a few weeks before risking any further engagements. Sucre made the mistake of spreading his forces out too thin in order to occupy more territory, and Bolívar had to warn him by letter that occupying territory would only hurt their cause, not help it, unless the ground they occupied was the very spot where they had smashed the last Spanish army. Sucre reassembled his forces, and just in time, for he soon received news that the enemy was advancing to attack him. He planned the battle carefully and on December 8 the armies met at Ayacucho. It was a much longer engagement than Junín, and when night fell neither side had gained the advantage. A truce was agreed upon and the officers of the opposing forces gathered around the campfires to chat before resuming battle on the following day.

The revolutionists were considerably outnumbered, but Sucre's brilliant plan for the battle was carried out to the letter and the Spaniards were crushed. The bulk of their army surrendered on the most generous terms, the main proviso being the unconditional recognition of Peruvian independence. The wars for emancipation in South America were at an end.

Shortly after the great victory at Ayacucho, Bolívar was received in Lima like a Roman hero and the Congress of Peru outdid itself in fawning before him. Of its own free will this group named him permanent dictator of the country. The Liberator now felt that the future of all America was in his hands. He feverishly drew up a constitution for the new state and it was adopted by acclamation. The document was strongly monocratic and sanctioned a president and vice-president for life. The president was considered to be above the law and inviolable; that is, not responsible for the acts of his government. He was a sort of superior untouchable, elevated above the ordinary citizens and representatives, who was in everything but name an absolute monarch.

When the southeastern region of the viceroyalty (Upper Peru) separated from the coastal section and adopted the name Bolivia in honor of its liberator, General Sucre became that country's first chief executive. He was sworn into office to uphold Bolívar's constitution, but soon found that it needed considerable changing. In addition to calling for a chief executive in perpetuity the document embodied the Liberator's ideal of a moral power, a group of censors who also held their positions for life. They were to guard the social conduct of the authorities and of the people, and were expected to add a fourth dimension to the three essential powers—legislative, executive, and judicial—already accepted throughout the democratic world as the basic triangle of checks and balances on which representative government depends. The constitution also called for a literacy test for voters, which automatically deprived over nine tenths of all Bolivians of their ballot. The country is still nearly 75 per cent illiterate.

Bolívar as a lawgiver had not plotted any course for a nation able to govern itself in a democratic manner. On the contrary, realizing the lack of training for self-government, he had drawn up a constitution which he believed would prepare the way for a more liberal regime at a later date. His idea never had a chance, for, after the first burst of enthusiasm, public support was entirely wanting. After a little more than a year in actual practice both Bolivia and Peru tossed the constitution aside for more democratic ideals and in so doing fell immediately into the hands of regional dictators. Sucre himself resigned after a few tumultuous months in office, during which he was severely wounded while suppressing an insurrection. He withdrew from public life and settled down near Quito. A couple of years later he was slain from ambush by a group of hired assassins for reasons which have never been entirely cleared up.

Bolívar, too, was now nearing the end of his road. After having promulgated his constitution he had traveled widely over both Bolivia and

Peru, helping to organize the government. He was everywhere regarded as the supreme authority so long as he was present. But the Liberator was anxious to get back to Greater Colombia, the nation which was always nearest his heart. These were the people who had started him on the path of continental leadership, had named him Liberator, and elected him president. He renounced the dictatorial power vested in him by the Peruvian Congress and returned to Bogotá.

The country had passed through many changes during his absence. Vice-President Santander, who had served as chief executive while Bolívar was on his military campaigns, was now the man of the hour to a large section of the citizenry in Colombia. He had displayed outstanding leadership and executive ability in enforcing the idealistic constitution of Cúcuta which reflected much of Bolívar's unitarian ideology, and at the same time had worked tirelessly to assemble and dispatch men, funds, and supplies to the Liberator. Popular acclaim had given Santander the title *el hombre de las leyes,* "the man of laws." He was said to have kept a sword on his desk and on top of that the constitution. This was a symbol of his attitude toward the governing power. General Páez, governor of the Venezuelan part of Greater Colombia, had done just the opposite.

The spirit that pervaded Colombia was one of the strongest idealism and an almost worshipful regard for law. Colombians felt so grateful to England for her aid in the campaigns that English customs were widely adopted. Even the English style of handwriting displaced the Spanish in the nation's schools and public offices. One of Bogotá's newspapers was published in both English and Spanish. The love of civic liberty was present everywhere, and Santander received most of the credit for making this spirit work.

It was a new experience for Bolívar to be in a country where he was not accorded the complete and undivided devotion of the citizenry. But that was incidental to the actual events which took place. One of the heroes of Venezuelan independence had been found guilty of assassinating a man in Colombia, and Santander, "the man of laws" or the "general of the quill pen," as his enemies called him, promptly called for a trial. When the Venezuelan leader was found guilty, he was executed. From that moment on the movement for Venezuelan separation from Greater Colombia grew by leaps and bounds. General Páez, who was a rough-and-ready soldier, used to running things to suit himself, became more and more arbitrary in his rule. When the Colombian Congress demanded his appearance he balked completely and revolts in support of him broke out in Venezuela.

In order to restore peace Bolívar made a trip from Bogotá to Caracas. The people went wild with enthusiasm; he and Páez embraced, and civil war was temporarily averted. However, all along the way Santander's enemies, especially those in Venezuela, poisoned the Liberator's ears against the vice-president. When Bolívar reached Caracas he wrote to Santander, saying that he wanted the break between them to be complete, that he never wanted to see his Colombian friend again. Santander answered in a deeply humble and respectful letter that this was the greatest hurt of his life.

Bolívar's partisans then began to insist that he assume the power of dictator in Colombia. A deep split in the country immediately came into the open. The friends of Bolívar stood together on one side, those of Santander on the other. After a stormy congressional session, in which no agreement could be reached, Bolívar became dictator. He was immediately regarded as a tyrant by many Colombians, and a group of students plotted to shoot him while he was out riding, but Santander was informed of the plot and stopped them. Later a group of intellectuals did make an attempt on Bolívar's life while he was with his favorite mistress, Mrs. Thorne (better known as Manuela Sáenz), and this lady saved his life by parleying with the assassins long enough to give her lover time to escape through a back window. Bolívar was forced to hide under a bridge, where he passed the night huddling in water up to his knees. Santander was believed to be implicated in this conspiracy and was brought to trial. The evidence against him would not have been accepted by any fair court, but feeling ran so high that he was found guilty and condemned to death. The sentence was commuted to exile for life.

Bolívar, now entrenched in absolute power in Colombia, found it necessary to declare war on Peru over a matter of war debts. The campaign was won, but the Liberator returned to Bogotá completely broken in health and spirit. He no longer had anything like the majority support of his people. His dictatorship had turned out to be worse than Santander's rigid observance of the laws, and his very name was intensely hated by the intelligentsia and young revolutionaries. Like San Martín in Lima, he felt himself at last in the unenviable position of being in power despite the will of the people. Realizing that an impasse had been reached, he took the same way out, resigned from office and retired to private life. Colombians, Venezuelans, and Ecuadorians all turned against him. It was officially proclaimed in Venezuela, his native land, that if he ever set foot on the soil of that country the lowest peasant had the right and duty to seize him and turn his person over to the government. It was at this same time that the Liberator received news of the assassination of his dearest friend, "the immaculate Sucre," and of the separation of Ecuador from Greater Colombia.

With a sharp cry of despair he exclaimed: "America is ungovernable." Then, characterizing conditions completely, he added these bitter words: "There is no faith in America, neither among men nor among nations; their treaties and constitutions are waste paper; their elections are combats; liberty is anarchy, and life is a torment." And in his last message to the Colombian Congress he declared: "Independence is the only blessing we have gained at the expense of all the rest."

Many years later one of his own countrymen wrote that these were the cries of a great man without a great people. During Bolívar's prime there had been unity wherever he had gone. In his last years there was not even unity while he was present. He planned to go into voluntary exile but was afflicted with a severe attack of pulmonary tuberculosis and was carried on a litter by a few of his comrades into the little town of Santa Marta, the very same spot from which three centuries earlier the Knight of El Dorado, Jiménez de Quesada, had set forth on his quest for the golden land.

Don Quixote had again come home to die, his illusions broken. The Liberator took leave of his countrymen in a moving proclamation which was read to several persons who were present in the sickroom. "I have been the victim of my persecutors who have taken me to the border of the grave. I forgive them. Colombians! my last prayers are for the happiness of my country. If my death contributes toward checking factional disputes and consolidating the union, I shall rest tranquilly in the tomb." A few days later the Liberator of half a continent was dead. There is a legend which tells of his sinking back on his pillow for the last time as he muttered these words: "The three biggest fools in history have been Christ, Don Quixote, and I. . . ."

The passing of the great man had no effect on the consolidation of his beloved Colombia. Ecuador had already declared her independence from the larger nation, and the ground was hardly pressed over the Liberator's grave when Venezuela, under General Páez, followed the same course. The natural strength and union of a single great nation was now divided into three parts, with three regional governments and three dictators to support.

Bolívar had foreseen the difficulties that would arise in governing the new Spanish American states. He had applied in vain all of his political genius toward finding a solution. It was like a man caught in quicksand near the shores of the sea who observes the rise of the ocean and foresees what will happen unless he is freed. No individual alone, no matter what his capacity, could stop the advance of that ocean tide. With help he might have been saved to lead others to erect a bulwark against the engulfing waves. Otherwise, he was powerless except so far as his ideals served as an inspiration to those who would follow.

On many occasions Bolívar had been offered a crown. Páez in Venezuela, Lamar in Peru, Flores in Ecuador, Urdaneta in Colombia, all held before him that enticing prize. During his last years England and France made strong insinuations in the same direction. Bolívar did not accept. Knowing profoundly the temperament of his people, he said: "The generals of the revolution and ambitious personages of every stamp could never tolerate a government which would deprive them of supreme power."

With that knowledge he had attempted to centralize the government as much as possible under a republican regime. In that way the break with the past would not be too abrupt. Nor would government depend on the participation of all of the masses who were incapable of self-government. Even in this instance the Liberator faced to an extent perhaps never repeated elsewhere in history "the impossible problem of making bricks without straw."

Bolívar was a great admirer of the government of the United States; he realized the necessity of some kind of Pan-American Union, and in 1826 convoked the famous Congress of Panama, which was in reality the first expression of hemispheric solidarity. Three years previously the United States, under President Monroe, had made a declaration of this attitude, but Spanish America had then been in the throes of war and could not express her feelings. The Liberator also had in the back of his mind the formation of a strong Latin-American bloc as a balance against the power of the United States. He even thought occasionally in terms of a Latin-American "Union Now," which would make of the southern countries a single strong confederation, "the mother of all republics, the greatest nation of the whole habitable earth." But this was a dream, an ideal, and a symbol; Bolívar knew better than to believe in its immediate achievement.

The United States delegate to this Congress died en route, and before the second appointee could get there the assembly had ended. The English representative was there throughout the sessions, and as a result the prestige of England was considerably increased in the southern countries, while that of the United States was somewhat diminished. So far as actual accomplishments were concerned the Congress achieved nothing except that it prepared the ground for hemispheric solidarity at a later date, and expressed the state of mind current in the newly emerged states: namely, that union would exist among them whenever there arose a common fear of any outside aggressor. Such quarrels as they might have would be settled strictly among themselves.

Bolívar realized that Latin America's greatest problem would be self-government. His own personality exemplified the conflict which was certain to take place once his leadership was removed: the struggle between Caesarism and republicanism, and the further he advanced in years the more he tended toward Caesarism. It was the necessity of conditions which surrounded him, the necessity of his race. Economic backwardness and illiteracy were the prime but not the sole causes of this incapacity of his people for self-government. By temperament the Spaniard had always been such a stubborn individualist that only under the strongest possible absolutism would he submit to government at all. He had never become amenable to the principles of order which characterized other European nations. A certain innate barbarism ran in his veins. As Bolívar had said, Spain ceased to be European by virtue of her Moorish blood. Another historian had remarked that "Africa begins at the Pyrenees." The Arabian chieftain and the petty kingdoms of the Middle Ages were both an integral part of the Iberian political heritage.

Even under these circumstances good government might have been possible, had other conditions been more favorable. Bolívar, in 1828, pointed out one of them in these words: "The difficulties that exist to make up a good Congress are great. Men of merit will not attend it, the roads are horrible, the distances immense. Only fools, demagogues, and charlatans take upon themselves the representation of the people. . . ." And a little later, when his own best attempts at governing Greater Colombia had failed, he concluded his prophecy by saying: "These nations will inexorably fall into the hands of the undisciplined multitude, later to drop without realizing it into the grasp of petty regional tyrants of every color and political hue."

Bolívar knew that he had failed to create a great American consciousness or a great American nationality. Before he died the seeds of anarchy, diminutive countries, frontier warfare, opposed and doctrinaire opinions split apart the structure of Spanish American life. But of the Liberator's work the essential element still remained: the independence of the new states and the republican principle as the standard for the new governments. Thus the evolution of these countries was the reflection of his thought. The personality and ideals of the Liberator hovered over them all, leading them gradually forward, and preventing disintegration.

Another comparison comes to mind here: Unlike the United States, Spanish America had not even had a unified command during the wars for independence. They had co-operated magnificently, yet there was no unifying symbol, like Washington, covering the entire continent. Argentina and Chile never venerated Bolívar; Colombia did not look up to San Martín; Mexico had her own revolutionary heroes, distinct from both of them. Despite all this, while the war lasted an incredible amount of unity had been achieved. It was a common fear more than a common ideal which engendered this union. When the enemy existed no longer there was no longer a prop to solidarity. Bolívar saw this well when he wrote to a friend: "I fear peace more than war, and this will give you some idea of all that I cannot put into words, of all that can never be said."

This is not to gainsay the tremendous achievement of the revolution itself, nor to minimize or belittle the sacrifices which the patriots made over a period four times as long as our own Revolutionary War, and under conditions which surely must have been much harder to endure. It is but to point out a fact: that the new nations of the south were still untrained in the social and political spheres when we ourselves (with the great help of England, who left her colonists much to their own resources) had developed a considerable skill in self-government. This was no difference of essential worth, but was one of age, of education, and of political institutions which had been handed down from ages past, ours growing all the while, theirs standing still. However, the differences of race and geography were so great that perhaps even this comparison gives an erroneous impression. In the United States a homogeneous population of less than three million, trained in the art of self-government, occupied the tiny coastal strip of the thirteen colonies. In Spanish America not more than that number of Creoles, and probably far less, occupied a vast area twenty times as large, inhabited by perhaps 12,000,000 Indians, mestizos, Negroes, and mulattoes, at all stages of economic and cultural development. That this society could possibly have emerged from the conflict and semi-unity of war into the real unity of peace is truly inconceivable.

After emancipation conditions were as follows: On top of the heap stood a triumphant army proud of its victories. At its head were ambitious military leaders, hardened by fifteen years of war, knowing no other law than that of the sword. Theirs had been the glory of achieving freedom, and they had made the most direct and most tangible sacrifices of life and limb during the conflict. When the war was ended theirs was also the position of greatest influence and power at the head of the new societies. Opposite them stood a civil party, largely forgotten during the war, which was now also aspiring to govern. The great masses of people first gave their allegiance to the military leaders, or *caudillos*, who had brought them victory, but when they finally learned that this would bring them only perpetual dictatorship they gradually switched their support to the civil authorities. Not until these last had a majority backing did a real democracy emerge. In other words, the history of Spanish America throughout the nineteenth century, and on into the twentieth, was the story of gradual progression from a military-dominated society to one in which the civil elements finally gained a tenuous control.

This was not the only cleavage which divided the new nations. The ten to fifteen millions who survived the wars for independence were spread out over an immense territory, larger than all Europe and, as we have already said, twenty times larger than the thirteen colonies. Distance alone, accentuated by the geographical divisions of the territory, made union well-nigh impossible. There were also racial and class differences, divided into castes before the revolution, and now politically, if not socially, thrown together in a great shuffle as a result of the revolutionary victory. Besides all this, the new states, ruined by war, without industries, with scarcely any agriculture, and with almost no training in self-government, were hardly beginning to convalesce after an illness of fifteen years. "With such elements as these and under such circumstances, let us not forget," points out a Venezuelan writer, "the new republics are going to be established."[94]

37

THE CRY FROM DOLORES

It was early Sunday morning, September 16, 1810, when the bell of the parish church in the little Mexican town of Dolores began to peal with an unusual persistence, bringing the alarmed parishioners from their homes. They hurried to the church, but even the first to arrive found that the priest, Miguel Hidalgo, and many of his closest friends were already there before them. It took only a glance to show that something tremendous was in the offing. The curate and his companions were talking in tones of suppressed excitement, and nearly all were armed with such weapons as they could find: swords, pistols, clubs, lances, stones, even farm implements. A few had brought their horses. Only half a dozen knew the truth: Hidalgo had been roused from his bed during the night and warned that his conspiracy against the Spanish regime had been discovered.

The church was soon overflowing and the white-haired father of his flock took his place in front of the assemblage. They were mostly poor Indians, who instinctively felt, but could not have understood fully, the consequences of what they were about to do.

Father Hidalgo, whom they revered, began to speak to them in impassioned tones. For seven years he had been their priest and protector. He had helped them build a community they had every right to be proud of. Together they had planted grapevines and mulberry trees, made wine and silk, and organized a community factory where leather goods and pottery were manufactured. When the Spanish officials had uprooted his trees because they offered competition with a peninsular monopoly he had protested vigorously but in vain. He had always been a defender of the forgotten and lowly man; the Spaniard had always been his oppressor. This was past history. There was now an intensity in his voice such as the congregation had never heard before. The priest was calling upon them to throw off the yoke of their tyrannical masters, to declare war on the hated *gachupines,* to take arms under his banner and destroy the despotism which had come to their beloved land from across the seas. The congregation was not long in catching the spirit of their leader. Soon they were interrupting him with shouts of their own: "Long live America! Death to the *gachupines!* Down with the foul government!"

A few days later that battle cry resounded throughout the far corners of New Spain, and the first strong mass sentiment of Mexican nationality was born. Hidalgo lost no time but marched at once against the Spaniards. His lowly rabble grew by leaps and bounds. Workers left their labors in factory and fields to join his banners. The mob swelled to a vast multitude which swarmed over farm and countryside like some fast-flowing acid denuding it of human flesh. One of the insurgents, perhaps Hidalgo himself, picked up a portrait of the Virgin of Guadalupe, patron saint of the Mexican Indians, and bore it aloft at the head of the procession. Without having proclaimed the independence of Mexico, they were marching off to war against the Spanish tyranny. The church which was the center of learning in Mexico and the bulwark of the old régime had also made available the social ideals which became the spark to set off the revolution. These ideals had come to Mexico by way of France.

The government was quickly informed of what was happening, and official couriers, many of them priests, rushed from town to town ahead of Hidalgo's mob, holding out their crucifixes, urging and begging the Indians not to enlist in the revolutionary army, and threatening all who did. It was of no avail. The die was cast. The *grito de Dolores,* that famous "cry from Dolores" to which Father Hidalgo had given voice, had taken wings before them and the officials found that they were too late. Mexico was already in a ferment of revolt.

In the cities the Spaniards began to shudder. To ease the tension the Viceroy decreed that Indians were no longer to pay tribute and even extended the decree to include loyal Negroes and mulattoes. All royalist soldiers were concentrated in strong points and kept on a constant alert. Meanwhile, Hidalgo's motley army continued its triumphant march across the Mexican countryside. Finally it neared the city of Guanajuato, "set in a beautiful valley amid mountains that contained rich silver mines."

Hidalgo called a halt and sent ahead a messenger bearing an ultimatum to the Spanish garrison. He boasted of his fifty thousand men, promised to treat the Spaniards humanely if they surrendered, but swore to destroy them if they insisted on resisting. They chose the latter course and the battle was joined.

The city's defense quickly collapsed before the onrush of that enthusiastic multitude, and those who escaped took refuge in the public granary, a large stone building which made an excellent fortress. All the treasure of the Spaniards had been placed there for safekeeping, and nearly every Spanish family in town was quartered inside. They defended the place with great bravery, but the assailants climbed up over the walls like ants, and those who fell were immediately replaced by others. In a short time the fight was over, the citadel was taken, and the plunder began.

Hidalgo was not the kind of man to sanction the sort of thing which then took place, but his voice had no effect on that undisciplined mob. The Mexican historian, Alamán, who witnessed the scene as a boy, described it graphically, and so horrible was the impression left on his mind that he summarized the whole revolution as "a monstrous union of religion with assassination and plunder." The royalist soldiers were massacred; their wives and daughters suffered insult and violation; their homes and shops were smashed; their merchandise, furniture, and even their clothes were strewn up and down the bloody streets of the fair city. Drunken Indians paraded about in a state of complete frenzy. After news of this blood bath got around no Spaniard and few of the higher-class Creoles would have anything to do with Hidalgo and his pillaging band.

The revolutionary leader had revealed both his strong and weak side in this first large-scale engagement. He was undoubtedly an inspired mouthpiece for the insurgent cause. He could arouse the downtrodden and marshal them into immediate action, despite all the perils involved. He was a perfect exponent of the revolutionary symbol who knew how to fuse religion, hatred of oppression, class bitterness, and the human desire for justice, power, and revenge into a moral weapon which came near to being enough to win victory for his cause. At the same time Hidalgo was utterly lacking in any knowledge of military strategy; he had only the smallest measure of control over his undisciplined troops, and even his ideas for the independence of his country were vague and nebulous. He had no program but revolution itself. He had no party but only a mob behind him.

It was at this stage that one of the militia officers among Hidalgo's followers urged him to retire to the mountains with several thousand of his men in order to improve their fighting ability and to bring them under better control. "In two months," said this officer, "I will return these men to you disciplined and serviceable; if such a step is not taken, you will be left alone in the first reverse which you suffer, for all your followers will fly away like doves."[91] Hidalgo did not follow this advice.

Meantime, the authorities in Mexico City were doing everything in their power to bring the revolution and its leader into disrepute. Even the Inquisition denounced him as "a partisan of French liberty, a libertine, a formal heretic, a Judaizer, a Lutheran, a Calvinist, a rebel, a schismatic, and a suspected atheist." It was not the first time he had been under the suspicion of that Holy Tribunal. In 1800, ten years previously, he had been accused of doubting the virginity of the Mother of Christ, of libertinism, of studying the Scriptures critically, of speaking insultingly of the popes, of taking part in social hilarities unbecoming his priestly office, and of fostering liberal French ideas. It was even said that his home was known to the townsfolk as "little France." On this occasion the curate was not actually tried and sentenced, although at least some of the accusations against him seemed beyond any doubt. He was known to have two illegitimate daughters, and several prohibited French books were in his library. He also doubtless espoused liberal French ideas. But either the Inquisition felt itself too weak to condemn so popular a priest, or else Hidalgo mended his ways, for no punishment was meted out to him on that occasion.

Things were different now. He had taken a rebellious stand against the central authorities and his soldiers were pillaging the country. Hidalgo was ordered to appear before the tribunal within thirty days, under pain of excommunication. He did not appear, of course, and was later excommunicated along with all of those who followed him. Hidalgo denied every one of the religious charges against him and announced before his followers: "My beloved citizens! You may be certain that if I had not undertaken to liberate our kingdom from the evils which oppress it and from the greater evils which threaten it, . . . never would I have been accused of heresy." He pointed out the inconsistencies of the charges against him, and his supporters were satisfied with his explanations.

The revolutionary horde, with the banner of the Indian Virgin at its head, continued its progress toward the stately capital. On October 30 they were only a few miles away. The army now numbered about eighty thousand and was far more numerous than any force the Spaniards could put in the field against it. In the first engagement Hidalgo's men forced the royalists to retreat and opened the road to the capital, but were unable to follow up their advantage. Hidalgo said it was because of lack of ammunition. A few days later the revolutionists encountered another Spanish force on its way back to the capital from an outlying district, and this time they suffered their first definite defeat. The Spanish artillery and better strategy wrought havoc in their pell-mell ranks. The insurgent army retired to Guadalajara, Mexico's second largest city. There Hidalgo made some attempt to organize his movement on a stable political and social basis. His ideas on independence and government were published in a small periodical, but they came too late to give much body to the revolutionary ideology.

Shortly afterward, only four months after the revolt had started, the decisive battle between the royalists and insurgents took place. The date was January 17, 1811. Hidalgo's force still outnumbered that of his enemies at least ten to one, and for a time it seemed that sheer weight of numbers would gain the victory. Just as the engagement reached its highest fury, however, a grass fire broke out in the insurgent ranks and threw them into disorder. The result was a complete triumph for the Spaniards.

Hidalgo's men now deserted him in droves. At the first great shock all enthusiasm had fled and there was nothing else to hold them together. Factional squabbles further split the patriot ranks. The curate himself was displaced as leader, his prestige considerably undermined by his defeat. A few days later the remnants of the revolutionary army were ambushed and its leaders captured.

All of them except Hidalgo were tried at once, and most of them were executed. The trial of the chief conspirator was a more lengthy process. He was accused of high treason against the government and of several crimes against the Church. He did not attempt to shift the blame on anyone else and rigorously denied that his religious ideas had been in any way heretical. However, he did break down to the point of complete remorse for the disaster and death which he had brought upon the Mexican people and beseeched forgiveness of the bishop, the Viceroy, and the Inquisition. His confession of guilt is one of the most heart-rending documents ever signed by a great leader:

"Who will give water for my brow and fountains of tears for my eyes? Would that I might shed from the pores of my body the blood which flows through my veins in order that I may mourn night and day for those Mexicans who have died, and that I may bless the never-ending mercy of the Lord? . . . The night of darkness which blinded me has been changed to luminous day; and in the midst of the prison which I have deserved, the evils which I have brought upon my country are so clear to me that sleep deserts my eyes and repentance prostrates me on my bed. . . . I exhale each moment a portion of my soul. . . .

"Ah, America! Ah, Americans, my compatriots! And ah, Europeans, my progenitors! Have pity, have pity on me! I see the destruction of the soil which I have wrought; the ruins of the fortunes which have been lost; the infinity of orphans I have made; the blood which in such abundance and temerity has been shed; and—this I cannot say without fainting—the multitude of souls which dwell in the abyss because they followed me. . . ."[45]

This confession was addressed "To All the World," and although some historians have questioned its authenticity there seems little reason for doubt. A few days later Hidalgo was executed by a firing squad while holding aloft the crucifix. His head was displayed in an iron cage before the public granary in Guanajuato, where his troops had committed their first bloody depredation. He died without having proclaimed the independence of Mexico.

The Mexican revolution was not dead, but it had been cut from the vine before it could bear fruit. Unlike the revolutionary movements in South America, it had had from the beginning definite mass attributes. Indians and mestizos almost exclusively made up the ranks of its army. Hidalgo himself, however, great as he had been as a leader and as a symbol of the revolutionary zeal, had offered his followers only a negation and not an affirmative creed. The greatest lesson taught by his failure was that the Mexican masses alone could not bring about a victory. Without leaders who understood the use of strategy and power, without a broader use of the Creole intelligence and experience, any revolt would be foredoomed to failure.

It fell to one of Hidalgo's friends and former pupils, José María Morelos, to give the revolution a program. Together these two comrades had dreamed of Mexican liberty, and together they had fought to attain it. Hidalgo had sent Morelos and a squad of soldiers on a mission, and that squad soon increased to hundreds of men. Morelos then began to operate between Acapulco and Mexico City and won some notable victories. He was a better commander than Hidalgo. He also realized the necessity of organizing the revolution on an affirmative political basis. The battle cry of Hidalgo's men never got beyond a savage: "Death to the Spaniards!" But Morelos promptly called together a congress and fostered the promulgation of the most revolutionary social program to come out of the Latin-American struggle for independence. He was a hundred years ahead of his time, and it was not until after the Mexican revolution of 1910 that the government actually put into practice the measures for which Morelos had fought.

This program briefly was as follows: equality of the races, only native Mexicans to hold offices, judicial torture to be abolished, no religion other than the Roman Catholic to be permitted, no special privileges for either clergy or Spaniards, confiscation of all large estates and their redistribution for the public welfare, the utilization of certain accumulated church funds for the same purpose, the suppression of onerous government monopolies and unfair taxes, the enforced productive labor of all adults able to work. This plan, announced in September 1813, was a rudimentary form of socialization for the country. On November 6 the same congress formally declared Mexico's independence from Spain.

Morelos attempted to make his congress an inseparable part of his revolutionary movement, and propaganda one of his strongest weapons. After the death of his fellow priest and leader he saw the inefficacy of waging war with an undisciplined mob and organized his army into smaller and better-trained units. Time after time his troops struck lightning blows at Spanish garrisons in the regions where he operated. Many towns came under his control, and the congress which he had organized then took over. Morelos himself always made a point of recognizing the superior authority of this body and never accepted any other title than that of "servant of the nation." However, he did not possess the genius of social and military leadership which would lead to a final triumph for his cause. His governmental mechanism was too cumbersome for rapid functioning, and Morelos was never able to win an all-out victory against the Spanish general, Calleja, who kept him under constant pressure, preventing a full marshaling of his power at any one given point.

It was while he was escorting this unwieldy legislative body across country that the general and his troops were surprised by the Spaniards and Morelos taken prisoner. Like Hidalgo, he was condemned to degradation and execution. His priestly garments were stripped from him and he was shot in the back by a firing squad. The social phase of the Mexican revolution for independence was buried with him.

Hidalgo, Morelos, and their lieutenants had kept Mexico in a state of war for six years. The country was now in a state of chaos. Productivity had gone down to an alarming extent. Bandits infested many outlying districts; class was set against class; independence had turned into disillusion; government was worse than it had ever been, and social conditions had deteriorated even more. Only the soldier with his plunder was better off than he had been before the war began. Mexico had had her first foretaste of many a revolution to follow, and it had been bitter gall to the palate.

Both Hidalgo and Morelos are now national heroes in Mexico, but they have never been accorded the almost unanimous acclaim given Washington in the United States, nor do they enjoy the widespread veneration which Colombia and Venezuela feel for Bolívar or Argentina for San Martín. Both of these crusading priests made the fatal error of dividing those whose union might have ensured their victory. They aroused the lowest masses to a pitch of frenzy against obvious economic oppression, but they alienated the Creole class. Hidalgo let his men get out of control, and Morelos attempted to make the movement for independence into a real mass uprising for a new social order. Many Mexican historians have condemned them both for the bloody excesses of their troops. The contemporary Mexican writer, José Vasconcelos, makes a point of the fact that the thinking portion of the nation, even those to whom independence was an ideal, followed neither Hidalgo nor Morelos. He goes so far as to make almost a racial issue of the revolutionary campaign, assuredly an exaggeration. "That insistent desire to kill *gachupines* and to recruit pure Indians and Negroes only to hurl them upon town after town to sack and to destroy, which is all that a leader without plan or vision is capable of, must indeed have seemed suspicious to every thinking person." It was, continues Vasconcelos, merely pitting the underdogs against the rest without sensible purpose or plan. In this he is wrong. Morelos did have a plan. But it was assuredly not one which would have suited the propertied Creoles. It came close to being the ideal of the proletarian revolution. In any event, it divided those who wanted independence, and as a result independence was lost.[26]

Hidalgo and Morelos both suffered the indignity of degradation and execution because their thinking was not sufficiently in tune with the conditions under which they lived. It is the fate of all revolutionists who do not have sufficient strategy or power to achieve final victory.

Hidalgo died before the firing squad on July 30, 1811, and Morelos followed him on December 22, 1815. All was certainly not quiet on the Mexican home front after their executions, but the Mexican revolution which stirred in terms of a new social order was clearly ended. It is well to remember that both the white-haired Creole "father of the Mexican revolution" and the little hard-muscled mestizo who stepped into his place when he was gone were earnest, hard-working parish priests. Both identified themselves completely with the lowly masses of the Mexican population. The Catholic hierarchy, working hand in glove with the elements of conservatism, promptly excommunicated Hidalgo and Morelos, along with all who followed them. The official voice of the Church had become the mouthpiece of reaction. The actual voice of the Church of small priests and ordinary religious parishioners had, without speaking in the name of hierarchical dogma, already died for the freedom of man.

Unfortunately, it was not enough. Mexican independence was not to be attained in any such popular manner. It took a wave of reaction and subtle strategy to affirm the independence movement and to give the new Mexican state its freedom from Spain.

In those years of transition Mexico showed her true colors of action and reaction, of social idealism and barbarism, of class consciousness and economic cleavages, which have never yet permitted her two extremes to meet. This division in the social structure of the nation was evident from the very first moment news was received that Ferdinand VII had been imprisoned in France and Joseph Bonaparte was on the Spanish throne. The new Mexico of "radicals" and "reactionaries" was born in that year, 1808. The liberal Viceroy immediately convoked a junta of the leading citizens in the Mexican capital, and together they issued a manifesto declaring they would rule in the name of the Spanish King until he was restored to his throne. The wealthy Spanish landowners interpreted this as a move toward independence and took immediate steps to thwart it. About a month later they deposed the Viceroy by force, clapped him into prison, and finally deported him to Spain. A reactionary Spanish officer was elevated to viceregal rank. The counterrevolution, if such it may be called, was successful, and all was safe for reaction in Mexico until Hidalgo and his swarm of Indians suddenly appeared on the horizon. The counterrevolution defeated them also.

The problem now was how to bring into a united front those conservative Creoles who did want independence and the lowly masses whose struggle for independence had already been defeated. Such a union might open the path to victory, yet only the direst extremity could effect this fusion of elements obviously in opposition to each other. That extremity was reached on the part of the insurgents when their two greatest leaders were captured and executed. The surviving members of their group must be the ones to give in if a compromise were to be reached. They were in no position to hold out for principles. Independence alone would have to be enough, and even that independence would be on Creole terms.

The strange union between these two groups was brought about by one of the shrewdest political go-betweens in Mexican history. His name was Agustín de Iturbide, later the "Emperor Iturbide" of Mexico. He was said to be of noble descent, and his father was a prosperous landowner. As a boy Iturbide had shown little inclination for educational pursuits and failed to complete his schooling because of "idle and vicious habits." He took up the life of a soldier at an early age and was a young lieutenant of twenty-seven when Hidalgo's revolt broke out in the village of Dolores. There had been some talk of his liberal ideas, and Hidalgo offered him the position of lieutenant-general in the revolutionary army. Iturbide's intuition told him which way the wind would blow, and he not only declined the offer but took up arms against what he called a "lawless band that was harassing the country."

A few years later Iturbide, who certainly had no reason to assume a self-righteous attitude in the matter, described his reactions to Hidalgo in these words: ". . . The word insurrection in that instance did not mean independence and equal liberty; its object was not to reclaim the rights of the nation, but to exterminate all Europeans, to destroy their possessions, and to trample on the laws of war, humanity, and religion."[91]

Lieutenant Iturbide distinguished himself in the campaign against the insurgents. He won several small-scale victories, captured a rebel stronghold, and took some important prisoners. He fought in a battle in which Morelos himself was defeated. As a reward for these services, "Colonel" Iturbide, for he had promptly risen in rank and stature, was made commander of the districts of Guanajuato and Michoacán. The citizens of those districts did not like their new military commander. He was arbitrary, dictatorial, cruel, and his personal habits were certainly not such as would make him a model for young children. As a result of repeated complaints he was removed from his command after a few months and was sent to Mexico City. His trial lagged and he was never either dismissed or reinstated.

Four years later (1820) revolution broke out in Spain again, and for the second time in a decade the Spanish liberals imposed a constitution on Ferdinand VII. Repercussions of the new liberal movement reached Mexico, and freedom of the press was declared in that colony. Those insurgents who took the oath to support the new constitution were to be pardoned. Privileges of the clergy were curbed.

As a result of these decrees ideological and factional differences again reared their ugly heads. The Viceroy became alarmed and looked about for a strong leader to place in command of his troops. First of all, the country must be pacified. The scattered bands of insurgents must be brought forcibly into the national fold. After that would be time enough to put down the ultra-conservatives. Iturbide was selected for this job of pacification.

There was only one real insurgent leader left in the field, a famous subordinate of Morelos whose name was Vicente Guerrero. Iturbide was delegated to subdue the forces of this man and restore order. He had a different scheme in mind. Instead of meeting Guerrero in battle, the new commander negotiated with him, and together they reached a compromise known as the Plan of Iguala. Mexico was declared to be a free and sovereign nation, absolutely independent of Spain. She was to be ruled by a monarch, but until such time as that ruler was chosen a junta would govern. This government would be supported by the army of the "three guarantees" which supported these principles: the Roman Catholic religion, Mexican independence, a *rapprochement* between Mexicans and Spaniards.

Iturbide had learned his lesson well from Hidalgo and Morelos. He appeased the clergy, appealed to the Spaniards, and deceived the Mexicans. The compact majority of the country's citizens was soon back of him. Iturbide entered the capital in triumph at the head of his troops. He had won his victory without fighting a battle, and Mexican independence was now a fact. Iturbide praised his bloodless revolution in these words: "Six months were sufficient to untwist the entangled knot which had bound the two worlds."

While these events were taking place Iturbide never separated himself for a moment from the political direction of the new nation. He was careful to hold in his hands both the main military and civil authority. The governing committee made him generalissimo of the army and gave him the title of Highness. From that it was but a step to Emperor.

According to Iturbide's report of the affair, this highest monarchical honor was thrust upon him by the grateful people of Mexico. With a proper show of reluctance, modesty, and hesitancy he was persuaded to accept the imperial scepter. The inhabitants of the capital unhitched the horses from his carriage and pulled him joyfully through the streets of the capital. Cheering thousands acclaimed Iturbide as the father of his country. With some coercion the Mexican Congress also voted to make him Emperor, and he was ostentatiously invested with that supreme title.

There were many Mexicans who did not take kindly to this turn of events. At first they had been caught by surprise and had not been able to act effectively; now they gradually marshaled their forces against Agustín I. His Majesty clapped several of them into prison, but the wave of opposition was too strong to be overcome in any such manner. Finally, when some of his most influential military supporters, among them General Santa Anna, joined the opposition, Iturbide abdicated and was forced to leave the country. A salary of twenty-five thousand pesos annually was settled on him, provided that he remained in Italy in exile.

The ex-Emperor did not stay abroad for long. After the Holy Alliance had sent French troops into Spain to break the back of the revolution there and to replace Ferdinand on his absolute throne, Iturbide became alarmed that the same powers might intervene in American affairs and bring Mexico again under Spanish control. He decided to return to his native country in order to offer his services in her defense. It is quite probable that he also had his eye on the throne. Misguided friends had assured him that he would be welcomed, and so, in July 1824, he landed on Mexican soil accompanied only by his family and half a dozen intimates. He tried to sound out the situation incognito but was quickly recognized and arrested. Unknown to him, the national Congress had recently decreed that if he ever appeared in Mexico he would be considered outside the law. On the basis of this decree Iturbide was summarily tried, found guilty, and executed.

In this way were Bolívar's prophetic words to San Martín fulfilled. The Liberator had said that it would be futile to establish monarchies in America, for the people would only rise and destroy them. The republican torch, once lighted, could never be extinguished.

Some historians have referred to Iturbide's "majestic role" in the liberation of Mexico. He had indeed shown an uncanny ability to unite "discordant and belligerent classes," and with little bloodshed had achieved the independence of the largest, most populous, and wealthiest Spanish colony. Yet Iturbide was not a man to be mentioned in the same breath with Bolívar or San Martín. He had a streak of luck and was astute enough to follow it up; but the sum total of his career adds up to good strategy, not greatness, to political acumen, not statesmanship.

With the strange pageant of Iturbide the history of New Spain came to an end, and that of Mexico, Central America, and the southwestern United States began. Under the Emperor's brief reign the Mexican Empire stretched all the way from Panama to the uppermost reaches of California, Arizona, New Mexico, and Texas. It was approximately twice the size of present-day Mexico.

The whole Central American region except Panama, which was then a part of Colombia, had been annexed by the Emperor. Some of the states were strongly opposed to the move but were unable to prevent it. After Iturbide's abdication in 1823 all of them separated from the larger nation and formed the Republic of Central America, made up of Guatemala, Honduras, Salvador, Costa Rica, and Nicaragua. This union lasted for about fifteen years and then began to split up into the five countries mentioned. On many occasions since that time talk of a Central American Union has been revived, but regional rivalries have always stood in the way of permanent federation.

The European Holy Alliance, made up of Prussia, Russia, Austria, and France, not only intervened in Spain in order to reseat the despicable

Ferdinand VII on his throne after the liberals had knocked him off, but that august body also sent a wave of fear through the entire American hemisphere and brought about the proclamation of a new kind of foreign policy by the United States. The situation was this: Spanish liberalism, for the second time in a decade, had demanded that Ferdinand VII accept a constitution limiting his power. In 1820 the King was forced to accede to this demand. Then the Holy Alliance, with Prince Metternich at its head, stepped into the picture. This group of absolutists had no faith in the common man, were convinced that he could never govern himself, and believed that only the chosen few who belonged to their caste knew what was good for the people in general. They hated and feared any movement that smacked of liberalism. The new constitutional regime in Spain was a specific example. Left to itself, such a movement might cross national frontiers and bring royalty into disrepute everywhere. The Holy Alliance decided to act, and French troops were sent into the peninsula to support Ferdinand. Thus bolstered by outside aid, he managed to get back on his throne. The next step was for the Alliance to begin thinking of helping the Spanish King reconquer his American colonies. The Pope himself had encouraged this by issuing an encyclical in which he condemned American emancipation.

In the year 1823 the Alliance actually planned an expedition for the purpose of overpowering Spanish America. San Martín had just withdrawn from Peru; Bolívar and Sucre had not yet won their final victories in the same country, and Iturbide had just been forced to abdicate in Mexico. An opening unquestionably existed. Spanish America was on the verge of independence, but she was also on the verge of revolutionary exhaustion.

Two things prevented the consummation of this plan. First was the attitude of Great Britain. Her merchants and ships now dominated the seas. Trade with an independent Spanish America, freed from the peninsular monopolies, would increase their markets by several millions. These merchants were in no frame of mind to see Ferdinand slam the door in their faces after they had already got their feet inside. Nevertheless, the government in England hesitated. More or less the same thing was happening in the United States. Many citizens and members of Congress wanted to support an independent Latin America, but they hesitated to come out openly against the might of Metternich and his associates. President Monroe had gone as far as he could in 1822, when he told Congress that, in view of the progress of the revolution in Spanish America, this country ought to recognize those regions which were already free. Later that same year Chile, La Plata (Argentina), Colombia, Mexico, and Peru were recognized as independent nations. Farther than that the United States was unwilling to go.

At this crucial moment there was a change of government in England. The new minister, George Canning, motivated both by political liberalism and by the commercial advantages in the offing, made it clear to the United States that the power of Great Britain's fleet stood ready to back up any declaration against the plans of the Holy Alliance which this government cared to make. With this trump up his sleeve President Monroe, after consulting with his Secretary of State, John Quincy Adams, and former presidents Jefferson and Madison, sent to Congress his famous message of December 1823, later known as the Monroe Doctrine.

This message launched the United States as a world power and put it forward as the defender of the American hemisphere against foreign encroachments. President Monroe made four main points in his message: first, the United States had no intention of interfering with European colonies already established in the New World; second, this country would consider any attempt on the part of the Allied Powers (the Holy Alliance) "to extend their system to any portion of this hemisphere" as dangerous to its own peace and safety; third, any attempt to control or regain colonies which had already declared their independence would be regarded as "an unfriendly disposition toward the United States"; fourth, the American continents were "henceforth not to be considered as subjects for future colonization by any European powers."

The text of this message was printed in all British newspapers with the obvious backing of the government. Prince Metternich was forced to give way, Latin America gained her independence, and the United States became the protector of all the southern countries and the final arbiter of their destinies. The last strong surge of absolutism and reaction had been repulsed in the Old World, while in the New the principle of republicanism became supreme. For the next century America, not Europe, would be the leader of political thought. However, without being "married to the British fleet," as Jefferson put it, the United States and the entire Western Hemisphere might have had a very different history.

Charles and Mary Beard make the following comment on President Monroe's famous message: "Coupled with Washington's Farewell Address to the nation, the Monroe Doctrine was long a main 'cornerstone' of American foreign policy. Thus the last, as well as the first, of the Presidents belonging to the Revolutionary generation fortified the independence of the United States and the security of the Republic."

The reception of the Monroe Doctrine in Latin America was universally favorable. In Argentina it was proclaimed that the United States had constituted herself the guardian of the hemisphere, and in Colombia Vice-President Santander declared that the stand taken was "an act worthy of the classic land of American liberty." Bolívar received news of the proclamation just before his last great battle, Junín, and was deeply impressed. He immediately understood that the United States and England stood together with him and his people against Spain and the Holy Alliance. They were the two nations that he most admired in all the world.

In 1826, when Bolívar called together his own Congress of Panama, it was in order to carry this plan to its logical conclusion. The idea was originally his. Bolívar had always thought in terms of a united America, especially a united Spanish America, and as early as 1813 had put his ideas into clear-cut words. President Monroe and England had seconded him in 1823; now it was his turn again. As we have already seen, his people did not respond. The Congress of Panama fell far below Bolívar's expectations. Yet it was not a complete failure, for it canalized and symbolized the ideal of American solidarity, which, time and again, was to rise phoenix-like from its ashes when faced with the common threat of outside aggression. On those occasions both Anglo-Saxon and Latin America would stand truly united. Bolívar's ideal, rather than President Monroe's, would be their motivation. The Liberator's belief was in a common destiny to be shared by all America; the President's message was of a single destiny to be presided over by the United States.

38
MEN OF DESTINY

After the wars of emancipation were over and the entire continent was free to pursue its course, it was indeed true, as Bolívar had said, that independence was the only boon which had been gained at the cost of all the rest. A great Argentine historian adds, "Even at this price freedom was an advance. Independence was the boon of boons because it was life, and the continuation of the colonial regime would have meant death by the slow process of decomposition. . . ." The United States at that time "was a sun without satellites which shone alone in its brilliance. The appearance of a group of new nations, which after the manner of new astral bodies arose from the nebulous colonies of the south, formed for the first time in the history of the world a planetary system in the political order, with natural laws, universal attractions, and democratic harmony. A whole continent with twenty-five million souls was conquered for the Republican way of life, and this continent, almost equal in extent to half the world, traversed by gigantic mountains and immense rivers, extended from pole to pole. It was bathed on the east and on the west by the greatest oceans of the planet, it possessed all natural riches and resources, and in its varied zones could be acclimated every race on earth. The hemisphere seemed almost to have been expressly formed by the Creator into this geographical unity for a new and colossal experiment in human society."[30]

These are the words of Bartolomé Mitre, one of Argentina's greatest presidents. They express the abiding reality of a Pan-American spirit which transcends the differences of heritage and race to seek union in that love of liberty which is the only union that this hemisphere can know.

Mitre, however, inspired by the past, was looking into the future. His words expressed a dream, not a fulfillment. The origin of the new republics was anything but harmonious, as Bolívar pointed out. When the Liberator retired from active life he left most of South America in the hands of a dynasty: his generals. They quarreled over the spoils of victory "as the generals of Alexander disputed, after his death, for the provinces of Europe, Asia, and Africa, the remains of the imperial feast. . . ." Bolívar's lieutenants dominated life in the southern continent for nearly half a century: Sucre and Santa Cruz in Bolivia, Flores in Ecuador, Páez in Venezuela, Santander in Colombia. These men, and others like them, were not satisfied to play subordinate roles. They had become used to power and were unwilling to relinquish it. They demanded autonomy in their own regions, were jealous of the encroachments of their former companions-at-arms, could not forget that they had been generals when the time came to put aside the sword and take up the pen and plowshare. Santander was the only exception in a generation of military tyrants. Their governments were neither orderly, efficient, nor free. In other parts of Spanish America similar despots arose: Rosas in Argentina, Iturbide and Santa Anna in Mexico, Francia in Paraguay. When these died there were always others ready to take their places.

For half a century in some regions and for more than a full century in others, the new republics wavered between anarchy and despotism. Everything except independence itself had to be improvised: statesmen, a civil spirit, governments, constitutions, customs, politics, population, and financial stability. Being men of brilliant minds, these inheritors of the mantle of Bolívar were able to make the new regimes sound perfect on paper; being men with no experience in government, they were not able to make them work out in practice. Like Alexander, when some problem of government or some opposing figure arose to challenge them, they laid hands on the sword again and hacked away as if problems and men were but knots in a Gordian chain.

These new leaders arose out of their past and out of their environments as a prolongation of all the oppression that had gone before. They were the conquistadores, reborn with a mestizo skin. To them war and tyranny were a natural means of expression. War was resorted to in order to gain freedom, in order to impose liberal ideas, to defend this institution and that, to attain certain economic ends, to hold or win territory, to impose an individual's will, to defeat an opponent, to keep the masses in subjection. The Creole, like the Spaniard before him, came to love war. "He will expose his life in order to win wealth at the cost of slight effort. In him vanity will be a goad to prod him into the fight."[94]

The dead imposed upon those who survived a way of living, a way of thought. Under the guise of republics autocracies were founded; masked behind such titles as Restorer of the Laws, Protector, or Regenerator, the President-autocrat replaced the Viceroy or vice-King. The essential conflicts which lay in the blood and the environment of these men could be overcome only by violence. Only through violence and tyranny was it possible to attain a modicum of peace. The new leaders were called *caudillos*, which meant heads or supervisors. They differed in every region, took on the character of their people, forced them into a form, gave them a nationality, wrenched them from the revolutionary womb into the hard air of independent life. Wherever they lived they were men of destiny. The history of Latin America for the past hundred years is largely the history of these representative men.

Every condition of their society seemed to favor the development of caudillo rule. Among the more important social elements were the mixture of races, the scarcity of population and of means of communication, the lack of essential liberty, and widespread ignorance. Each of these elements held back progress, divided the society that existed, made despotism the synonym for order.

Race mixtures, which in one way had been the peninsula's proudest achievement, were not without their weaknesses. "Each individual," writes a Venezuelan who knows his people well, "has special ideas depending on whether Caucasian, Indian, or African blood is dominant in him." Partly due to heritage, mostly to economic circumstances, these differences often spring into conflicts which are not easy to blot out. Sometimes the racial conflict takes place inside the individual himself, making him lack stability and leading to discord. Race-mixing rather than final amalgamation, which still has a long way to travel in most Latin-American countries, represents a transition stage, not a net result, and transitions are nearly always periods of dictatorship or discord.

The scarcity of population and lack of means of communication also aided the caudillo. Against a background of towering mountains, tremendous rivers, torrential rains, exuberant and nearly impenetrable jungles, and all the other barriers of communication, the people were forced to lead more or less isolated lives. The usual social intercourse and exchange of ideas which, even at that early time, were taken for granted in other parts of the world were limited in Latin America to a few great centers, to a few people, while the remainder of the population lived in the utmost isolation, ignorance, misery, and neglect. Among these far-separated and illiterate people what newspaper could have a wide circulation? How could it be possible under such conditions "to form the national conscience or to reveal at a given moment the true soul of the country"?

The final conclusion is inescapable: a limitation of the horizon, the triumph of the strongest, most astute, or most useful villager, whether it be the general, the landowner, the regional politician, or, as was usual, a combination of all three. These smaller despots paid homage to the larger men of destiny who were the caudillos of the emerging states. The feudal social structure of colonial Latin America was repeated with a vengeance. Everything favored the dominance of a small, literate, economic class over the vast majority, and of that small dominant class a few men who were willing to seize fortune became the representative leaders of their nations.

As for the lack of liberty and the widespread ignorance of the ɪ
hardly more than a mention need be made. Under colonial oppressiᴇ
the Inquisition freedom of the press and free speech had been unl
during the revolutionary years both suddenly emerged as from the tomb.
After independence was won the inevitable despots either curbed these
newly attained freedoms or turned them into "official loud-speakers" to
back up their own particular brand of despotism, always under the sub-
terfuge of reformation and order. The critical spirit was entombed for
a generation, and public opinion was struck with a palsy in every member.
What tribune would be listened to in such a society? What healthy democratic instincts could thrive on such sickly fare? Charlatans and demagogues were bound to spring to the fore and establish themselves in the
highest seat. The people at large learned only one thing, but they learned
that well: that the only defense against tyranny is war, though both are
symptoms of the same evil—the ignorance and economic wretchedness of
a divided people. Revolution became known as a way of life because it
was the only possible answer to the sterility of permanent despotism.

The caudillos, or men of destiny, who engineered this pageant of violence, fall clearly into two categories and periods: the bloody centaur,
or "man on horseback," dominated the first, the civil autocrat the second.
Immediately after the conclusion of the revolutionary wars, when anarchy
was rampant in every region, they pushed themselves into power by brute
force and kept themselves there by assassination and bribery. In order to
escape the maelstrom of blood and chaos the people were willing to accept anything that offered the chance for a little peace. The man of destiny
was the answer to their weary and ignorant prayer. Perhaps he was the
only possible answer. The city hated the country; the intellectuals despised the masses; the masses feared the liberalism of the intellectuals;
each class was suspicious of every other class, each region of every other
region, and the all-powerful landowner was determined not to lose his
land or his slaves under whatever government. The caudillo who came
to power in the midst of these struggles bludgeoned right and left, hitting
some right places along with many wrong ones, and so fashioned the rough
elements of a new nationality, audaciously forcing dissidents into a common mold.

As representatives of that first period of unadulterated fear and force
we have Rosas in Argentina, Francia in Paraguay, Páez in Venezuela,
Santa Anna in Mexico, Santa Cruz in Bolivia, and Flores in Ecuador.
These men stood for the mixed or American race as opposed to the pure
stream of Spanish-Creole blood. They stood for the masses as opposed to
the aristocrats. They stood for might as opposed to tolerant intelligence,
but what they themselves lacked in tolerance they more than made up in
astuteness. They stood for the wild interior of the new America instead of

for the literate seaboard with its face toward the European heritage and life. They carried the revolution to its logical conclusion, which was military tyranny. They stood against the intellectual oligarchy and exiled or slew their opposition without mercy. Yet, as they had to depend on a continuance of the old economy in order to maintain themselves in power, not one of them wrought any fundamental change in the economic life of his country. If they executed or exiled criminal or despotic landowners it was because those landowners had attempted to subvert their authority. They did not fight against the despotic principle of concentrated land-ownership itself. On the other hand, they rather envied the great land barons and so acquired or increased the extent of their own estates. As a sop to the people they imposed a measure of racial tolerance, built up the bulwark of national consciousness, reconstructed the shattered material plants of their states, improved the means of communication, production, and marketing, and to some extent civilized as well as unified their peoples. However, they were primarily consolidators and not builders, tyrants who gave peace, generals who became civil governors, despots who imposed their stamp, not liberals who led or persuaded. They were a stop-gap in the progress of Spanish America toward a real civil government.

Spanish America was now passing through her political Middle Ages. Each regional tyrant gathered all powers to himself, in some cases even the power of the Church, which he converted into a state church, subservient to his will. The phrase, "I am the state," was characteristic of an epoch. These caudillos had constitutions, but they either interpreted them to suit themselves or destroyed and remolded them according to their fancies. Among an illiterate people the written and impersonal word has little force or meaning. It is the mouthpiece alone which counts. Oftentimes these caudillos, whose authority rested in great measure on the support of the lower elements of the population, received from those elements an adoration which verged on frenzy. Just as the illiterate and fanatical Spanish majority had fawned before Ferdinand VII, begging him to be their absolute King, so did these Indian and mestizo American masses fawn before Páez, Rosas, Santa Cruz, and their like. Each miserable person of the adoring mob saw in the supreme caudillo a reflection of himself elevated to the highest seat.

Yet, as the Peruvian García Calderón points out, there was a gradual growth from the military to the industrial period, from an epoch of authority to an epoch of discussion, from the stamp of status to the civility of contract, from a "regime imposed by despotic governors to a flexible organization accepted by free wills."

The youngest portions of the Spanish colonial empire were the first to attain maturity as republican nations, whereas the oldest colonies remained for the longest time under despotic caudillo rule. Age did not lead to social or political stability. The conquest had struck first at the most densely populated, the best-organized, and the wealthiest region. In these regions there had arisen a caste of aristocrats and a caste of slaves. To bring these extremes together was impossible, and self-government was unthinkable. After freedom from Spanish rule despotism was for a long time the only practical means of government. In the category of despotic states fell Peru, Mexico, Bolivia, Ecuador, wherever the Indian population was thickest, wherever there were slaves or gold. Dictatorship and civil war alternated in these countries.

The last-conquered regions—Chile, Argentina, and Uruguay—emerged first into the period of civil government, and in that order. They were not immune to the disruptive poison which followed on the heels of the wars of independence, but with their more homogeneous populations, their relative absence of class conflicts, their strong agrarian economies and lack of corrupting gold and silver, they were sooner able to throw off the yoke of the tyrants and enter into the current of civilized life. Chile took this step in 1833; Argentina did the same after the fall of Rosas in 1852; Uruguay did not follow suit until the beginning of the twentieth century. Colombia, with many unique attributes of her own, cleared the same hurdle around 1900, and so did the little Central American republic of Costa Rica. Caudillism remained in force in the other nations until later, and in some of them it has not disappeared even yet. However, the day of the old tyrant is gone, and those who are today's dictators dare not revert to the medieval and machiavellian principles of their predecessors. That they have supported the backward and stultified economy of the great landowners and nullified civil liberties is crime enough.

The greatness of a democratic state depends on the greatness of its masses of little men who will always compose the majority of its citizens. In Latin America those little men were never able to organize themselves so that their voice could be heard or the pressure of their several wills be brought to bear on a given point for a long enough time at a given historic moment. Sporadic outbursts of the popular will did occur, and the courage of small heroic groups was often directed against tyranny, with no thought of self-preservation. But such were the elements of disunion—divided classes, immense distances, the abyss between culture and ignorance, the traditional disuse and distrust of impersonal law, and the general lack of organization in all quarters—that no great mass expression could prevail.

During the colonial period, through the well-known policy of "divide and conquer," then "keep divided and rule," a small minority was for three hundred years able to circumvent the will of the subordinate and uneducated majority. After independence another small minority, with a change of brass buttons and a little darkening of the skin, continued the process. The revolt of the classes had been consummated. Self-government may not depend entirely on education, but education is the ground in which

...acy thrives. Both education and self-government in colonial ...pendent Latin America were a chimera.

...he time independence was won the class that had least preparation ...democracy believed in it most, took literally its promised liberty, equal-...cy, fraternity: the *pueblo*, or masses. The class that preached democracy loudest did not believe in it at all: the caudillos. They used it as a smoke screen to get themselves into office and to maintain their power. The Church continued to preach democracy as a religious principle but did not carry it out as an economic creed or as a social expression. The small middle class often went whichever way the wind blew. They came to hate disorder more than dictatorship and were often apologists for tyranni-cal scoundrels so long as their own lives were moderately secure.

In spite of all these things it would be unfair to say that the masses of Latin-American people got the kind of government they deserved, for they never ceased to rebel against deception and tyranny. This was the funda-mental cause of so many revolutions in the nineteenth century. The peo-ple of a nation might win a victory, and often did so, but they could not win the peace until education, organization, and a measure of economic self-sufficiency gave them the means to govern.

Alfonso Reyes, dean of Mexican letters, explains why it took the newly freed countries of Latin America so long to become stabilized, and then he comments on Mexico in particular, but his remarks pertain to Latin America as a whole:

"Would you wean a baby on absinthe? Well, we must realize that the American republics were born under the inspiration of a political philoso-phy that is actually a political philosophy for adults only. From an absolute and theocratic monarchy, a central and unified government, which had always been the political system in Mexico, before and after the conquest, we passed on to the Rights of Man and the federal constitution. We lived for a long time as though caught by the tail and dragged about by the chariot of an ideal we could not attain. The people had not been educated to take part in democratic representation, our whole pattern of customs was alien to the workings of the federal machine, the Indian was unpre-pared to rub shoulders with the white landlord possessing haciendas and owning influence in the city . . .

"At any rate, the duel of liberal and conservatives gradually created a rhythm of ebb and flow that more and more resembled a heartbeat, a co-herent circulation, the respiration of a being already an individual, already in the process of organized growth. The face of a new people was being carved with knives. The scars were giving it character. And in this way the first half of the century was spent."[186]

39

BRAZIL ESCAPES THE CHAOS OF REVOLUTION

The only region of Latin America which escaped bloody revolution and the harrowing travail of rebirth as an independent nation was Brazil. This was partly due to events in Europe which caused the whole focus of Portuguese life to swing westward; it was also partly due to conditions inside the colony itself.

At the close of the last colonial century Brazil was one of Latin America's most backward regions. She had not a single university, and there were only two small printing presses in the entire land. Racial types of every color and degree made up her amorphous population. She had the largest slave class in America. Negroes outnumbered whites by approximately four to one. Her towns were small provincial gathering points, from which the wealth of her land and mines was funneled back to Portugal. Their population was by and large the most miserable urban mass in Latin America. Brazil's largest and most important city was Rio de Janeiro, with thirty thousand inhabitants, which made it about one third the size of Lima and about one fourth as large as Mexico City.

The wealth that existed during the great Sugar Civilization and the Gold Civilization which followed it had gone into the hands of a few aristocrats. In mansions and plantations, which were centers of luxury, this small minority lived somewhat apart from the main stream of national life. The distribution of the products of human labor among the various elements of Brazilian population was as inequitable as it was anywhere else in Latin America. In spite of the heroic excursions of the *bandeirantes*, who peopled the trackless interior *sertão*, Brazil was still no closely integrated colony, but only a fringe of civilized living along the rim of the sea.

This very backwardness, the lack of integration among the colonial parts, the great unknown of the Brazilian interior, the omnipresent race-mixing which characterized Brazilian peoples, the melting away of class cleavages under the pressure of that attitude and the tropical climate were all characteristics which operated against violent change.

Even so, the great land of river and forest was not completely immune to the revolutionary virus. In the province of Minas Geraes, where mines of gold and diamonds had drawn magnet-like into their clutches the agricultural population of other regions to the north and south, conditions were almost insufferable. This province had endured the worst despotism of the Portuguese Crown for the very reason that it had furnished the Crown with its greatest and most immediate wealth. The greedy court at Lisbon had come to depend on the gold and diamonds of Minas to take care of its mounting expenses. As the early outpouring of mineral wealth neared its point of exhaustion the governors of Minas, at the insistence of the Portuguese monarch, became more and more oppressive and exacting. It was impossible to believe that the Midas touch had simply died a natural death. Taxes were raised to the breaking point; the rich diamond mines were made a complete monopoly of the Portuguese Crown; roads between the interior and the coast were no longer to be used; cloth factories in the province were to be closed; back revenues due the Crown were to be paid immediately. In a word, everything was done to wring the last possible cent out of the population of Minas Geraes. Because of these conditions and because among the native miners of the province were many who had received a liberal education in Europe, there was a movement for independence in Minas in as early as 1789.

The French Revolution, which began in this same year, was not the clarion of these Brazilian revolutionaries. Their inspiration came mainly from the United States. One of their leaders met Jefferson when the latter was the American Minister in France and asked him to aid in freeing Brazil from Portugal. Jefferson voiced vague expressions of sympathy but refused to commit himself. The chief conspirator of the revolution, a man known as "Tiradentes," managed to get hold of a copy of the Constitution of the United States, which was on the prohibited reading list, and very laboriously translated it into Portuguese. This translation became his principal means of propagandizing for the republican cause.

The real name of Tiradentes was Joaquim José da Silva Xavier. He was called Tiradentes, which means "tooth puller," because one of his many occupations was that of dentistry. It didn't require much training or technique to be a dentist in those days. The tooth remained in the jaw until decay made the pain unbearable, then it was jerked out. Tiradentes was also a sort of *curandeiro*, or country doctor, a traveling merchant, a miner, and finally a lieutenant in the colonial militia. In this latter capacity he often had to travel between Minas and Rio de Janeiro, and on these trips he always carried his translation of the North American Constitution, which he pulled out and praised to the skies before all who expressed their dislike of Portuguese rule.

Tiradentes was not the best-known member of the conspiracy, nor was he the wealthiest or best-educated, but he was the most ardent exponent of republican ideals. He was the true apostle of liberty, who lived and breathed in the hope of someday being able to make his country a republic. The majority of the conspirators belonged to the intelligentsia of Minas; among them were several writers and poets and five illustrious members of the clergy. They were all well read in the liberal French tradition. The revolutionary program embraced the following points: declaration of independence and of a republic, abolition of slavery, the establishment of a university, the construction of factories of all kinds, hitherto prohibited by the Portuguese monopoly, throughout the length and breadth of the land. The flag of the new republic would bear this line of the Latin poet, Vergil: "Liberty, better late than never!"

Several meetings of the conspirators were held in the capital of Minas, and there was such openness to the discussions, especially on the part of Tiradentes, who made no bones about his beliefs, that the government soon found out what was going on. The Judas was a Portuguese who had attended the meetings as a fervent supporter of the revolutionary cause. He denounced the conspirators to the governor, and they were all apprehended and thrown into prison.

The trial dragged along for two years. During the trial Tiradentes attained a stature that he had never enjoyed as a conspirator. He not only spoke openly and freely of his ideas on liberty, but supported them with strong arguments and, under the most detailed cross-questioning, showed himself to be a lucid and noble spirit whose altruistic motives it was impossible to belittle. Before the trial was over he had won considerable sympathy for his beliefs. Tiradentes also announced firmly that he was the real originator of the conspiracy and that whatever blame there was must necessarily fall on him. Never for a moment could the prosecuting attorney break down either his nobility of purpose or his confession of guilt.

In the meantime, the Queen of Portugal had decided that only the leading conspirator should suffer the death penalty. This decision was passed on to Brazil, yet when the final sentence was read aloud to the prisoners it took an agonizing three hours for the reading, and eleven persons were condemned to death. After this psychological torture the sentence of ten of them was commuted, Tiradentes alone being considered "unworthy of royal pity."

He died in the typical Iberian manner, heroic to the last, and the executioner fulfilled his duty faithfully by placing the great man's head on a pole for public display as a lesson to other would-be revolutionaries. The name of Tiradentes was made anathema; his home was strewn with salt, and a shaft was raised in order to commemorate forever his vile treachery against the Queen.

The results of the conspiracy of Minas Geraes were both economic and political. In the first place, the home government moderated its oppressive taxes and abolished the hated salt monopoly. In the second place, Tiradentes died with such a halo of martyrdom around his head that the colonial authorities were forced by the popular will to be less arbitrary in their rule. Tiradentes was the noble precursor of the movement of 1821–22, when Brazil won her independence from Portugal almost without bloodshed and set up her own monarchy, and also of the year 1889, when, again without civil war, that monarchy was converted into a republic.

Shortly after the turn of the nineteenth century, in the year 1807, Brazil still stood isolated and neglected by her mother country and completely unaware that her history was to be changed almost overnight. Her total population was scarcely above 3,500,000, and of this number almost two million were Negroes, between four and five hundred thousand were Indians, six hundred thousand were of mixed blood, and the remainder, about 14 per cent, were classified as white. In a political sense the colony was under the complete domination of Portugal. Economically conditions were improving slowly but steadily. As a result of the French Revolution and of the Napoleonic Wars that followed it, the English fleet had thrown a blockade around the little Emperor's conquests in Europe and was undisputed ruler of the Atlantic. Portugal and England had been allies for many centuries, and this alliance was still unbroken despite the threats and conquests of Napoleon. Under the protection of His Majesty's ships the vessels of the Portuguese enjoyed freedom of the seas. Brazilian trade grew steadily and exports remained above imports, giving the colony a favorable balance which increased the value of her currency.

In Portugal things were not going so well. Napoleon had sent his troops into Spain, and Portugal knew that she, too, was threatened with invasion. Her Queen, Maria I, was hopelessly insane, and John VI, regent in behalf of his mother, hesitated until the last possible moment before making up his mind. Not until the army of General Junot was almost upon Lisbon did he decide to flee with his entire court and go to Brazil.

John VI was not well loved by his people, and he was married to an extremely unpopular Spanish princess named Carlota Joaquina, a sister of Ferdinand VII. This ugly, rawboned offspring of the Bourbon breed had more than her share of the Bourbon intelligence, but along with it she inherited the sensuality which seemed to characterize all the members of her family.

John VI and Carlota had never got along since the day they were married, she a child of fourteen and he a young man of twenty-three. After the ceremony was over John bent dutifully forward to kiss his bride but suddenly straightened up in obvious surprise and pain. His new spouse had sunk her teeth clear through his ear. It was an indication of things to come.

It was now the year 1807, and many years had elapsed since that scene had taken place. John and his Spanish wife no longer shared the same room and were never together except on the most important public occasions. They had fulfilled the duty of royalty and were now the parents of several children, but it was rumored that Carlota had become about as profligate as her mother in Madrid. As the Spaniards expressed it, she had "put the horns on her husband" more times than would be decent to count. The Portuguese knew her reputation well and despised her for dishonoring their country. This was the situation in the royal family as it made feverish preparations to leave Lisbon and head for the great colony beyond the sea in order to escape the wrath of Napoleon.

When the time to board ship arrived a driving rain was coming down. The boom of Junot's artillery could be heard in the distance and delay was no longer possible. Hundreds of people lined the streets of the capital to see the royal procession pass by. They did not observe the departure with any good grace. It seemed to them that the royal family was running out and leaving them to face the music. A few bystanders picked up stones and held them threateningly in their hands. They did not become incensed enough to throw them.

In the harbor lay a fleet of thirty-six vessels, which John VI had had the foresight to assemble and load for just such a contingency. He had hoped that he would never be forced to use them. The ships were stuffed with royal goods: archives, books, works of art, treasures of all kinds. They carried all the supplies of food which could be conscripted on such short notice. The supply of water was much less than comfort or even safety demanded. Apparently more courtiers than had been anticipated decided to sail at the last moment, and every ship was dangerously overloaded. The largest vessels, which had a normal capacity of two to three hundred passengers, carried over a thousand.

Under escort of a squadron of British men-of-war the royal fleet lifted anchor and turned toward the open sea. Fifteen thousand of Portugal's proudest aristocrats saw their beautiful city fade into the distance. It was a horrible trip from the beginning. In the last rush nearly all of the royal wardrobe had been left ashore, and the passengers had to wear the same clothes day and night. Aristocratic pride quickly melted away under attacks of dirt, vermin, reduced water rations, constant seasickness, and only a subsistence diet of food. At night the courtiers were packed into the holds where they would have some protection from the chilly outside air, and before long the stench of these crowded quarters became almost unbearable. The only bright side of the entire crossing was furnished by nine-year-old Pedro, son of the regent John VI and his estranged Spanish wife. The curiosity and liveliness of this boy, who was later to become the first

emperor of Brazil, helped to bring a little cheer into an otherwise dread-
fully long and gloomy voyage.

In January of 1808 Dom João's* vessel entered the harbor of Bahia,
and shortly afterward the remainder of the fleet arrived. When the townsmen learned the identity of their royal guests they turned out en masse
to welcome them. Never before in the history of America had a ruling
monarch left his own country to come to the Western Hemisphere.

But the royal visitors and their entourage could not disembark at once.
Nearly every one of them was ill or exhausted after the harrowing trip,
and without exception they were all disgustingly filthy. For the better
part of two months they had neither changed their clothes nor been able
to bathe. Every house in Bahia was ransacked for wearing apparel; every
old trunk and family chest was opened, and the choicest finery of the
colony was placed at the disposal of the new arrivals. After repeated
scrubbings and some good wholesome food the passengers at last felt able
to face the landing. Many of them wore breeches or dresses that were
either too loose or too tight, but on the whole they made a stately appearance and the reception went off well.

There were two notable exceptions. Carlota had had to have her head
shaved in order to get rid of the vermin. Besides this, she took an immediate dislike to the new country and, after one look at Bahia's provincial
streets and hybrid population, summarized her reaction in the words: "It's
no place for civilized people to live in!" A further note of discord was added
by the demented Queen Maria I of Portugal, John's mother. Ever since
she had heard that Napoleon's troops were advancing on Lisbon she had
been in mortal fear that they were coming for the express purpose of mur-
dering her. Now, on reaching Brazil, she must have thought that she was
already dead, for as the procession advanced slowly down the streets, with
the population respectfully kneeling when the royal carriage itself passed
by, the old Queen shrieked at the top of her lungs: "I'm going to hell!
I'm going to hell!"

But these were mere details which had no effect on the town's warm
hospitality. Somehow the Brazilians sensed that this dramatic and unexpected arrival of Portuguese royalty would raise their scattered and
neglected colony to the status of a great nation. As to new relationship between this country and Portugal, they had invented a special phrase for
it: "the Brazilian inversion." They meant that from this time forward
Brazil would be the metropolis, and Portugal the colony.

The elite newcomers did not remain in Bahia for more than a few weeks,
for the climate of that region was entirely too hot to suit them. Having
received favorable reports of the land farther south, they again boarded

* Portuguese form of John, pronounced Zhwã-o.

their ships and made the short voyage down the coast to Rio. When his vessel hove into the harbor of the Brazilian capital Dom João was hardly able to believe his eyes. Against a background of high green mountains and fringing a chain of semi-circular bays, where tropical waters lapped gently on clear white sands, lay the most fantastically beautiful city in the world.

Here again on closer inspection the backwardness of the place destroyed some of that first breathless impression. There was no sanitation; the streets were unpaved and deeply rutted; the public buildings were few and poor; the citizens by and large were shabbily dressed, and the whole aspect suggested a provincial life of drabness and boredom. Yet the reception accorded the regent and his courtiers was so sincere that it warmed the hearts of all of them. Homes were thrown open and family heirlooms hoarded for generations were dusted off and turned over to the Portuguese aristocrats.

The situation was one which brought out the best qualities of the hospitable and unaffected Brazilians and the worst qualities of the haughty Portuguese. In no time at all many of the latter were demanding as their due things that had been extended to them as favors and with considerable sacrifice on the part of the colonial population. Friction between the two groups, heightened by the necessity of their living in entirely too close communion with each other, rose rapidly. To add further fuel to the flames the Portuguese took on aloof or unpleasant airs, began to ridicule their country cousins, called them unpleasant nicknames, and made themselves generally disliked. Dom João's royal spouse, Carlota, with her open disdain of everything Brazilian, capped the climax.

John himself met the situation in a manner worthy of the best Braganza tradition. Despite his lethargic and indecisive nature he was kindly and well disposed toward everyone and went out of his way to show the people every courtesy and consideration. Best of all, he really seemed to like Brazil. The Brazilians reciprocated his affection in fullest measure and tried to overlook every other annoyance as a favor to their ruler.

When the fleet was unloaded and the royal treasures were taken ashore Rio de Janeiro at once became one of the best-endowed New World capitals in every branch of the fine arts. Dom João immediately established a library, an art museum, colleges, and other cultural institutions. He also set himself to the task of improving the economic status of the colony, which he had deplored from the day of his arrival, often remarking that he had never been properly informed of conditions as they existed. Although this could hardly have been the case, restrictive laws were now lifted or relaxed, and both trade and industry took a new lease on life. A bank was established to make credit transactions possible. On a limited scale public works were undertaken, sanitation was improved, and foreign specialists were brought into the country to improve various Brazilian industries. John soon realized that the gold and diamond mines which had kept his family in the lap of luxury for over a hundred years were well past their peak. He stopped trying to squeeze abnormal profits out of them and turned his attention in a more constructive direction. Industries, trade, and agriculture were all stimulated, and the whole sprawling colony began to hum. With the person of the sovereign on Brazilian soil the loosely knit provinces all found a central focus and moved clearly in the direction of nationhood. Compared with European standards, the progress achieved was modest, but by Brazilian standards it was a considerable step forward.

John has frequently been praised for what he did in Brazil, but the facts show that he had little choice in the matter. After all, if he had to reside in Brazil some face cleaning was imperative, for the conditions there were truly frightful. And then in the background of his every economic move stood the shadow of Great Britain dictating the policy he should pursue. With most of Portugal occupied by the French, and with Great Britain, Portugal's ally, in control of the Atlantic, it was natural that the colony should throw open her gates to British trade. At the behest of his benefactor John signed commercial agreements with the tight little island, which was never known to drop a trade advantage, and the new relationship was made official and incontrovertible.

Not all of this was accomplished in warmest friendship, for the British minister to Rio, Lord Strangford, made it clear that he held the big stick. Hesitant, trembling Dom João found himself forced to make a virtue of necessity before his own subjects when he signed away all kinds of special concessions to persuasive Albion.

The die was cast even before the Portuguese royal family had left Lisbon for Brazil. British men-of-war were not placed at the disposal of the Portuguese court from pure generosity. The understanding was that His Majesty's fleet would see John and his courtiers safely across the Atlantic in return for an inside track on Brazil's commerce, particularly her imports. The monopoly had formerly belonged to Portugal; now there was to be no Portugal for a while, so it would belong to England. John was glad enough to accept the conditions of this contract.

He was caught in a net which was not of his own creation. For years Portugal herself had been the economic vassal of Great Britain. Ever since the English crusaders helped the Portuguese to run the Moors out of their country in the thirteenth century, England had been driving a good commercial bargain. Between 1642 and 1661 treaties had been signed which practically gave her control of the Portuguese markets. In the 1700s these concessions became so valuable that "Portugal outrivaled France in the esteem of the British merchants and industrial class."[97] The little land's-end country on the Iberian Peninsula finally came to have only a secondary control over her own economic destiny.

In the meantime, the "Portuguese inversion" was gradually taking place;

that is, Brazil, the colony, was rapidly becoming more important than Portugal, the homeland. This meant that she was also more important to Great Britain, and, when the opportunity arose to transfer the old privileges and pre-eminence in Portugal to the colony, the British fleet was at hand to see that it would not be lost.

Between 1808 and 1821 British capital poured into Brazil, British firms were established, British ships controlled the incoming and outgoing commerce of the great colony. In 1810 the British minister, Lord Strangford, exceeded his fondest expectations in the trade treaty which he persuaded John to sign. No other nation was to enjoy the commercial privileges and low duties granted to Great Britain; British warships might enter any port in Brazil where they would be supplied with food; timber might be cut from the Brazilian forests in order to build these vessels; English Protestants might worship freely inside Brazil (this despite violent opposition on the part of the papal nuncio), provided that their churches, in order not to attract undue attention, had no steeples, did not ring a bell to announce services, and did not attempt to gain converts; last of all, British nationals in Brazil were to be tried only by magistrates especially appointed by His Majesty's government.

The agreement was undoubtedly one-sided, but it did furnish the Brazilians with cheaper European goods than they had ever known before. The worst part of the bargain was that England was not interested in Brazil's exports; she wanted primarily to maintain the supremacy of her own goods in Brazilian markets. The gradual realization of this fact among Brazilians, and the slap at national pride embodied in the article which made Englishmen immune to the ordinary procedures of Brazilian courts, aroused a growing resentment within the colony. Oliveira Martins, in his *History of Portugal*, states that "once more the dynasty sold the kingdom as Esau had sold his birthright; once more, the House of Braganza, to preserve its throne, sacrificed the nation."[97]

The agreement, as can easily be seen, was between the ruling Portuguese house and Great Britain, who promised never to recognize any other ruler of Portugal than a legitimate Braganza. Brazil was never of primary concern to Prince John. What he wanted was to preserve his home country at all cost, to assure himself of his throne in Lisbon, and in order to achieve those two purposes he was willing to restrict the future of Brazil's commerce, regardless of what the Brazilians thought of it. At the same time it is perfectly plain that he was not in a position to act otherwise.

The British side of the question was not without its arguments. There would have been no Portugal at all, and certainly no Portuguese Government, had not British troops, ships, and loans given them a new lease on life. In regard to the effect of the trade pact on Brazil a historian who had written an entire book on the British pre-eminence in that country writes as follows: "The influx of British capital and enterprise stimulated the economic growth of Brazil, even though it crushed the budding industries which had sprung up since 1808. Professional men, artisans, trained mechanics, capitalists, and traders, invited by the special privileges announced in the treaties, flocked to Brazil. In 1808 the colony was emancipated, economically, from the decadent mother country; in 1810 it acquired a rich step-mother."[97] In a word, from 1810 to about 1850 Brazil was a protectorate of Great Britain, and from 1850 to 1914 she was, economically speaking, an adopted daughter.

As early as 1812 Brazil imported more British goods than all Asia and more than four fifths of the total sent to South America. Even the miserably poor countrymen of the distant Brazilian hinterland got used to Manchester ginghams. Great Britain was naturally loath to give up these trade advantages. Her ministers stood over the political destinies of Brazil for some time to come in order to protect them, and it was not until the colony became a closely knit nation, sure of her own strength under Dom Pedro II (around the year 1850), that there was a slow turn in the other direction. In spite of everything Britain maintained her pre-eminence in supplying Brazilian markets for over a century. There was not a break in this economic relationship until World War I, when the United States for the first time came into the ascendancy.

While these things were taking place Princess Carlota was grinding her own political ax. She was much more astute than her slow-moving husband and always had some iron or other in the fire. Her principal desire was to restore the divine-right absolutism of her family, with a special eye on what she could do for the Princess Carlota. This was no farfetched dream, for with both her father, Carlos IV, and her brother, Ferdinand VII, prisoners of Napoleon, Carlota was the legal regent of Spain; therefore, she was a political entity of no mean proportions. There was not much she could do to further her cause in the peninsula itself, where Joseph Bonaparte reigned in Madrid and the Spanish liberals were trying to govern from Cádiz. Carlota was not popular in either of those quarters. On the other hand, there were many Spaniards and Creoles in Spanish America who looked upon her as the titular head of the peninsular government. Carlota drew up a proclamation, pointing out the logic of her claims, and dispatched it to the colonial capitals of Spanish America. The Creoles of Buenos Aires took to her suggestion warmly, and, under the leadership of Manuel Belgrano, there was a strong movement to offer her the crown of the United Provinces of the River Plate. However, it was on condition that Carlota would rule under a constitution, and, when it was learned that she would not budge an inch from her absolutist creed, the citizens of Buenos Aires began to waver in their zeal. Carlota once went so far as to steal the crown jewels of Portugal in order to bribe a couple of dubious delegates from the Argentine, but her husband caught her before the deal was concluded. The *coup de grâce* to this scheme was a British veto, voiced by Lord Strangford, which put an end to Carlota's pretensions in Argentina for good. The royalist-minded Creoles of Buenos Aires carried their search elsewhere without ever finding an acceptable candidate.

This episode did not end Carlota's absolutist machinations. She was eternally at work as the head of the reactionaries in Brazil in an attempt to strengthen her hand in that quarter. She undoubtedly possessed a keen political mind and was always a Spanish princess at heart. These two characteristics made her dangerous both to her husband and to England, neither of whom wanted to see a strong Spanish empire in South America.

Carlota's personal habits continued to be despicable. She forced all who met her on the streets of the capital to kneel as she passed, whipping all who failed to do so. On two occasions she created international incidents by setting her lackeys on the British and American ministers, both of whom she despised. Her sexual morals were equally deplorable, and her tongue was loud and filthy. Once when the lonely young wife of one of her paramours burst into the palace and attacked her in a violent tirade Carlota seemed for the moment taken aback, but she recovered quickly enough to swear vengeance, and a few days later the young wife was shot through the neck by a hired assassin. This created a furor in Rio, for the murdered lady belonged to a distinguished family and had a large number of friends. Dom João determined to put his Queen away in a convent, where she would not scandalize the city further. He made a brave but futile attempt to do so.

In 1816 Dom João made his own bid for imperialistic expansion by sending Brazilian troops down into Uruguay. Using border conditions as a pretext, he occupied Montevideo and later forcefully annexed the entire region to Brazil. It was his last great gesture in America. A few years later (1821) he was on the verge of losing both his Brazilian and Portuguese thrones. The Spanish American revolutions had caused an upsurge of the feeling for independence in Brazil, and in Portugal the aristocrats were all clamoring for his return. Napoleon had been defeated, and the little peninsular nation was struggling with a liberal Cortes. Although John now dreaded the thought of returning to that anarchical kingdom, both because of his love for Brazil and his terror of the long sea voyage, he nevertheless was persuaded to make that decision.

He left behind him a Brazil that might easily have gone the way of every one of the Spanish colonies. Liberals were demanding a constitution. There had already been a couple of abortive uprisings against the monarchy. Taxes had again become oppressive because the colony had to support both itself and an impoverished Portugal which had lost nearly half her inhabitants during the Napoleonic Wars. John VI, still well-meaning but exasperatingly slow to move, had lost much of his early popularity among the people. Nevertheless, it was reported that when the day of departure arrived he wept to leave the land which had won his heart. He called his son Pedro to him and advised him in these words: "If the worst comes to the worst and Brazil demands independence, proclaim it yourself and put the crown on your own head."

They were words well spoken, and Pedro was to have occasion to heed them before long. John VI, for his part, did not leave the country empty-handed. A few years previously he had emptied the treasury at Lisbon on fleeing to Brazil, and now he repeated the act on departing from Rio for Portugal. The colony, which had borne the expenses of keeping up the Portuguese Empire for several years, suddenly found itself left high and dry without a penny. It was the perfect setting for a strong flare-up against the mother country.

Pedro was not the kind of man to take the bull by the horns. He needed a strong staff to lean on, and also a sharp point to prod him forward. This is exactly what he found in the famous Brazilian scientist, José Bonifacio de Andrada, who was the real "father of his country's independence."

José Bonifacio was a man of nearly fifty-five when he became the leading power behind the scenes in Brazil. In his youth he had gone to Europe to study the natural sciences just before the outbreak of the French Revolution. He not only learned enough to win international distinction for himself in his field; he saw how a social order rebels, how it fights and conquers, when it has a strong purpose and audacious leadership. From that time forward José Bonifacio undoubtedly had in the back of his mind the liberation of Brazil.[98]

In the meantime, he became a distinguished mineralogist, one of the best-known men of science in Europe. Portuguese savants had him named professor at the ancient University of Coimbra, but when he went there to begin teaching he found that there was not even the pretense of a mineralogical collection, and only three students showed up for the course. José Bonifacio was completely disgusted. It was the same way with everything else in Portugal. He was given an important post with the government Department of Mines, but every time he made any suggestions for improvement his hands were tied by red tape and corruption. Portugal was in the throes of a moral as well as physical decline and was not interested in progress.

In 1819 José Bonifacio returned to Brazil with his plan for independence now well defined in his mind. He belonged to a wealthy and influential family, and with the aid of his two distinguished brothers soon had this plan persuasively presented to those who would grant him a hearing.

José Bonifacio had already seen the excesses of the French Revolution, and after returning to Brazil he also received firsthand news of the bloody struggle for independence in Spanish America. As a mature thinker and man of science he could not sanction these blood baths which seemed only to delay rather than to hasten the achievement of real liberty. José Bonifacio was a statesman and not a soldier. He knew that he was no Bolívar and shuddered every time someone mentioned Pedro's intense admiration for the great Liberator. There was only one sane course of action left open: to utilize Dom Pedro as the instrument for his scheme of national independence. The regent's character, conditions inside Brazil, the arrogant attitude of Portugal, and José Bonifacio's own keen intelligence, all fitted together to make this plan work out perfectly. Strangely enough it was in Brazil that the monarchical ideas of San Martín and the semimonarchical ideas of Bolívar were put into effect. Brazil was the only Latin-American nation to pass in relative peace into the era of independence, the only Latin-American country which continued to enjoy a long span of both peace and progress after that independence had been achieved.

Portugal herself furnished whatever momentum José Bonifacio and his friends might have lacked. Realizing the trend of sentiment in the colony, her Cortes demanded that Pedro return to Lisbon in order "to complete his education." It was a barefaced move to get him out of the country so that the patriots would not have a symbol around which to mass their forces. José Bonifacio persuaded the regent to "depend on the love and loyalty of *his* Brazilians who would never desert him." And Pedro publicly announced that he would remain. The Brazilian patriots enthusiastically proclaimed a national "I remain" day. José Bonifacio, by unanimous consent, was chosen to head the new semi-independent ministry.

A few months later, while Pedro was down in the southern part of the country to gain converts for his cause, he received further dictatorial instructions from Lisbon. To have accepted them would have meant an immediate return of Brazil to her subservient status as a colony. The prince, therefore, who at the moment happened to be near the Ypiranga River, decided to act at once. He tore the Portuguese colors from his uniform, brandished his sword, and shouted to his comrades in a loud voice: "It is high time! . . . Independence or death! I proclaim that we are now separated from Portugal!" These words became known as the "Cry of Ypiranga," Brazil's declaration of independence.

Dom Pedro was at this time twenty-five years old. He was of a generous, clever, and liberal character, but had received almost no formal education and had been reared in an atmosphere of servants and sycophants. He tried desperately to make a good constitutional monarch, but so entwined had he become in the coils of absolutism at home and among his toadies that he often inadvertently took the wrong step.

His wife, Dona Leopoldina of Austria, was more strongly liberal-minded than her husband and had added her influence unequivocally to the cause of Brazilian independence, thus gaining considerable admiration among the people. On the other hand, she was ugly, hefty, and Germanic, was more interested in botany than in things feminine, was the robust outdoor type who preferred to rough it rather than to put on delicate frills. She was certainly not Pedro's idea of a queenly wife. Yet she loved her husband devotedly, and always wore a miniature of him on her breast. She also showed a warm and unassuming interest in the welfare of her subjects. The Brazilians soon came to regard her more highly than her sensual husband, who seemed to have inherited the worst qualities of his harlot mother.

Dom Pedro was not finding it easy to govern Brazil. He professed liberalism in politics, but, being a Portuguese by birth, he appointed a great many peninsular-born to high governmental positions. The implication drawn was that his heart was more interested in Portugal than in Brazil. When, after considerable wrangling, a convention was called to draw up the promised Brazilian constitution, there was a clear-cut split among the delegates, the Brazilians forming one group and Portuguese the other. Among the Brazilian leaders were José Bonifacio and his two famous brothers, perhaps the most influential liberals in the country. They now stood with the opposition. Rather than attempt a compromise, the Emperor abruptly dissolved the assembly and sent the brothers into exile. It was unquestionably a blunder and turned away much liberal support which had formerly been given Dom Pedro. Nevertheless, a constitution was finally approved and signed and he began to reign as a limited monarch.

Other troubles arose almost immediately. There was a revolt in the region of Pernambuco and a republic was proclaimed, modeled after the United States. Government forces had to be sent to suppress it. Then the province of Uruguay declared its independence, and, with Argentine help, broke away from Brazil. The Emperor did his best to hold the Uruguayans in line, but to no avail. Argentina and Brazil, with considerable prodding on Britain's part, finally agreed to recognize the independent republic of Uruguay.

At about this same time the Emperor's father, King John VI, had died in Portugal, and Dom Pedro was at once proclaimed monarch of that country. News of this move was received with great apprehension in Brazil, for here was another opportunity to reduce the new nation to the status of a colony. Dom Pedro's personal wishes were to return to Lisbon, but he knew that such a move would cause the immediate loss of Brazil, so he abdicated the Portuguese throne in favor of his daughter, on condition that she marry his own brother. Such close intermarriages were nothing new in Portugal and were one of the main causes of the deterioration of the Braganza line.

While these things were going on Dom Pedro and his wife were proceeding methodically with their royal duty of having children. The first

two sons died, and the royal pair had four daughters before the birth of
the third son, named Pedro after his father, who was later to become the
most famous ruler of Brazil. The Queen made an excellent mother to them
all and did everything in her power to bring them up properly.

Dom Pedro loved his children also but, except for odd moments when
he procreated other offspring, was completely estranged from his wife. He
had become hopelessly infatuated with a voluptuous wench named
Domitila de Castro Canto e Mello, more commonly known as Domitila.
She became the Emperor's confidante as well as his mistress, and she was
frequently consulted on matters of state. The affair was carried on so
openly that it scandalized the whole court. Domitila gave birth to Dom
Pedro's daughter, and the monarch then made her First Lady of his
Queen's bedchamber and later elevated her to the rank of Marchioness
of Santos. The Empress bore these indignities in silence, but when her
husband was in the south, taking part in a war against Uruguay, she became gravely ill, suffered a miscarriage, and died of a resultant infection.
Her last hours of agony were rent with cries of despair and hatred for her
illicit rival.

The news spread rapidly, and sympathy rose to a high pitch for the unfortunate Queen. The Emperor became more unpopular than he had ever
been. For a time after his return from the war he continued to live openly
with his mistress, but finally the aristocrats at court, particularly José
Bonifacio, who had returned from exile, made a national issue of the relationship, and Domitila was banished from Rio. Shortly afterward, and
again for reasons of state, they insisted that Dom Pedro remarry. This
time there fell to his lot a lovely young princess of seventeen, Amelia de
Leuchtenberg of Bavaria. After seeing her some of the Emperor's fire for
Domitila went out. The personal side of palace life was again placed on
a dignified plane.

Many other events had taken place which disturbed the tranquillity of
the empire. The effects of Bolívar's victorious campaign of 1824 and the
resulting republicanism of all Spanish America began to have repercussions
in Brazil. Comparisons also must have been drawn between Pedro's military fiasco in Uruguay and Bolívar's triumphant campaigns. To make matters worse, the Emperor had now reached the point at which he distrusted
nearly all Brazilians, and a majority of the members of his cabinet were
always Portuguese. The Brazilians could not endure this situation for long.
The press, which had not existed in Brazil until Pedro's father John had
established it a few years previously, criticized the Emperor's policy with
great vigor. Nearly all the leading citizens of the country, and eventually
the army, opposed him. Dom Pedro was handed a strong complaint,
signed by several highly respected deputies, in which the appointment of
Brazilians to certain offices was demanded. The Emperor saw that the

game was up. He could either sign away his constitutional rights or abdicate his throne. Wearied of the whole chaotic mess, he seized a pen and wrote out his abdication, naming his five-year-old son as successor. Shortly after that, in the year 1831, he left for Portugal, where he died three years later.

40

THE DEMOCRATIC EMPEROR OF BRAZIL

When his father left Brazil for Portugal, Dom Pedro II was only five years old. He did not fully understand the cause of all the jubilation going on in front of the imperial palace, where a great crowd had gathered to shout: "*Viva Dom Pedro II!*" The waving of handkerchiefs and joyous cries must have had their effect, but perhaps only in accentuating the loneliness of the young heir. His mother had died when he was an infant, and they had taken him to the bier to kiss her cold hands. He probably did not remember the incident, but ever since had missed a mother's care. Now his father, whom he loved devotedly, was for some strange reason leaving him alone for the rest of his life. Only his tutor, José Bonifacio, appointed at his father's behest, mitigated the child's sense of loss. The old scientist and statesman, then sixty-eight, gathered little Pedro into his arms and exclaimed: "My emperor and my son!"[99]

There was to be a regency for several years, of course, for Pedro was not old enough to govern. But he was to be brought up in Brazil and trained rigorously for the position before him. His "foster mother," the only mother he ever knew, was Dona Marianna, a noble lady of forty-six who probably had the greatest influence on his early character. Pedro loved Dona Marianna throughout his life, calling her always "Dadama," a childish mispronunciation of the word *dama*, or lady. José Bonifacio was the boy's tutor for the first couple of years, then he was replaced by the deeply religious Marquis of Itanhaén. There was also a priest who served as his instructor in mathematics and in religion. Other teachers taught him literature, art, music, geography, rhetoric, and languages. Pedro II did his best to please them all.

He was a frail blond child who had inherited his father's physical weaknesses but much of his mother's character and appearance. He was serious-minded from the very first, an attentive and diligent student, and, before

many years had passed, became a man of broad education and lofty principles. His early bereavements made him philosophical toward life, and the
lack of parental love brought out strongly his romantic inclinations. Everything that his teachers said or did seemed calculated to increase his sense
of responsibility and dignity.

It was not an easy life. They got him up at seven in the morning for the
first few years, then at six, and nearly every hour of the day was accounted
for. He had play periods, but even they were supervised. At mealtime he
dined with persons of some note who were able to bring to the conversation a useful, informative, or scientific trend. The boy was encouraged
to ask questions about everything, and this was one characteristic which
stayed with him until the end of his life, sometimes to the great irritation
of his ministers. At night, after the boy was left alone to entertain himself
briefly as he wished, he frequently read Scott's novels, the tales of Jonathan
Swift, Froissart's *Chronicles*, and other romantic tales and stories.

His tutors emphasized the fact that they did not want him to waste his
time in needless religious discussions like the Emperor Justinian, or to
become a "political fanatic . . . completely absorbed by his own megalomania." They wanted him to "learn how to rule with justice, wisdom, and
virtue, having the interest of his subjects always at heart."[101]

To this end Dom Pedro from his earliest years was trained in the liberal
tradition of French political thought. The principles of civil and personal
liberty were instilled in his mind and heart. He was made to feel the deepest respect, almost an awe, for "constitutional government," and it was
drilled into him that those monarchs of history who overrode or annulled
their constitutions invariably ended as hated despots. It was a lesson
which Dom Pedro never forgot.

While the future Emperor of Brazil was growing up in this fashion, under the discipline of well-ordered minds, his country was anything but
orderly. There were four different regencies during the first nine years. In
some parts of the country republican sentiment was strong; in the south
there was a full-fledged civil war. Portuguese residents in all quarters were
frequently assaulted and pillaged by excited mobs. Brazilians had received
almost no training in self-government, were probably 90 per cent illiterate,
and were floundering around helplessly in this new-found freedom. While
there were loud cries for more or less autonomous governments in several
regions, there was little disposition for co-operative rule, even among the
country's elite in the capital city. It was becoming more and more apparent
that Brazil was inexorably following the course of the Spanish colonies, a
course which, if continued, was certain to end in wholesale bloodshed and
chaos.

All credit must be given on this point: the Brazilians saw conditions as
they were; they were not roseate idealists by any means, and, realizing
the peril, they found at least enough unity to proclaim Pedro Emperor

before he had come of age. The liberal party was in the vanguard of those who demanded his coronation immediately. They saw that it was the only way to save the country. The Emperor was then less than fifteen years old, but he was the one symbol around which all factions could gather, so, after consulting with his tutors, who unanimously advised acceptance as "a measure of public salvation," Dom Pedro II was crowned Emperor of Brazil.

His reign lasted from 1840 to 1889, a period of nearly fifty years. For the first decade of that time the Emperor's great sprawling colossus of a country bid fair to slip off the traces and join the Spanish American states in their wild gallop down the revolutionary highway. The high-spirited provinces of the south broke out in open rebellion, and in the northern region of Pernambuco there were also flurries of civil war. To make matters worse, Dom Pedro's ministers often got the better of their young and inexperienced ruler, yet remained at swords' points among themselves. In spite of all these obstacles, the Emperor slowly but surely tightened his grip on the reins; the ministers were brought into line, and by 1850 peace was restored throughout the vast territory.

It was then that the Emperor's progressive rule began to make headway. He labored tirelessly for the welfare of his nation with an energy, tolerance, sincerity, and enlightenment which have few counterparts in history. He won the respect and admiration of all classes of people both within and without his empire. Bartolomé Mitre, who was president of Argentina for a term during his neighbor's occupancy of the Brazilian throne, referred to him as Latin America's greatest democrat. And Victor Hugo, famous French poet and republican, whom Dom Pedro met on a visit to Paris, remarked:

"Fortunately, we have no monarch in Europe who resembles your Majesty."

"Why?" asked Dom Pedro.

"Because," replied the Frenchman, "then we should lose all interest in being republicans."[102]

Dom Pedro did not win such plaudits merely because he was a gracious monarch. He fought a hard battle all the way against backwardness, ignorance, and intolerance. In spite of Brazil's progress under the reigns of his grandfather John and his father Pedro, the country was still one of the most backward in Latin America. Poverty, illiteracy, and general filth were characteristics of everyday Brazilian life. The cities were almost without sanitation facilities, and nearly everywhere garbage was dumped into the middle of the street, where the buzzards swooped down to gobble it up. Brazil still had no university and very few schools of any kind.

Beggars infested the streets of every town asking for alms and on certain set days came by the business establishments in droves to get a weekly handout. Women lived almost as secluded as they would in a Moorish harem, rarely ever going out of their houses except to attend mass. Only one person out of seven was white; over one half of the country's seven million inhabitants were slaves, and every family except the very lowest owned at least one or two bondmen. Sometimes these were hired out by their owners, who then received their wages. Other slaves peddled wares in the streets and supported their masters in this fashion. Throughout Brazil "labor was considered degrading. To suggest that a youth of poor but respectable family learn a trade was an insult. Work, in the opinion of the proud Brazilian, was the function of the unfree."⁹⁹

On the other hand, the color line was never sharply drawn in Brazil; manumission of slaves was becoming more and more common, and the freed Negro had at least a competitor's chance at a decent job and whatever social position went along with it. The most successful Negroes became professional men, and many church choirs were composed entirely of blacks. Discrimination was far less than it has ever been in the United States.

The incomparable loveliness of the country itself and the warm tropical climate injected a spirit of ease and tolerance into Brazilian life which carried forward the best Portuguese traditions. Along the narrow streets or in patios rose flowering jacaranda trees or the splendid "golden rain" whose vivid yellow blossoms hung from the branches in long tapering racemes. Bougainvilleas and climbing vines of brilliant colors festooned the houses; orchids burst into flower as easily as weeds; gardens were filled with brilliant hummingbirds of a dozen different hues and with huge butterflies of iridescent blue which measured six inches across. Mango, papaya, banana, tamarind, cinnamon, and orange trees grew profusely in town or country orchard.

In all this tropical glory the people lived slowly. All Sundays and more than fifty other church holidays were set aside for relaxation and pleasure. At least one third of the time Brazil loafed through life. Pageants connected with the Church or with the monarchy enlivened the interest of all classes. The folk lived like a great tree, their roots deep in the earth. They grew invisibly, in silence, sad, happy, or indifferent, as the case might be, but with every emotion dipped into an unspeakable sorrow. They were a poor suffering people who ate badly, lived like animals, but had all of man's diseases.

At the beginning of Dom Pedro's reign the marshes around the capital were all left stagnant and bred millions of mosquitoes. Only a few had been cleaned up by the end of his reign, because it was not until a decade later that the truth was discovered about the mosquito. Malaria and later yellow fever were the scourges of Brazilian life. The Emperor and many nobles escaped the worst epidemics by passing the summers in Petropolis up in the Organ Mountains, not many miles removed from Rio. This lovely resort was above the worst fever belt. Typhus and smallpox, both diseases of filth, the first spread by fleas and the second by personal contact, also struck frequently at the country's population. The water supply of the capital, brought from the country over beautiful aqueducts and made available to the people through fountains in various parts of the city, was another source of contamination.

There was almost no manufacturing of any kind except of cloth, leather, and sugar products. Mining was still carried on, but on the whole the country lived off its raw materials: cattle, timber, grains, manioc, and coffee. Tropical fruits abounded, and the general favorite, the *mamão*, or papaya, was everybody's food. Roads were practically non-existent, and transportation was by heavy oxcarts, on muleback, or by ship. Larger vessels sailed up and down the coast and along the largest rivers, and smaller raft-like boats covered regions where the water was not so deep. The wealthier travelers were carried across country in hammocks to which long poles had been attached. For short distances or within cities sedan chairs "with carved and decorated tops and heavily embroidered curtains" were frequently used.

Brazil was still living under a plantation type of economy. Formerly sugar had ruled supreme; now there were other products, but the big landowner, the *fazendeiro*, was the only controlling element of both economic and political power during most of the nineteenth century, and "the land was the only source of wealth." When the court was moved from Lisbon to Rio de Janeiro the fazendeiros welcomed the King, Brazilianized the monarchy, protected themselves with a constitution, took the reins of congressional and ministerial power, and established an empire of plantation owners and slaves.

The fazendeiro was merely the owner of the old Casa Grande and sugar plantation with a few new crops. He ruled Brazil in much the same way, except that now his symbolic monarch was in Rio instead of in Lisbon. His plantation was huge, for land was almost limitless in Brazil, and each estate was an entire economy within itself. On his fazenda the big landowner had "meat, bread, wine, the cereals which furnish his sustenance; leather, wool or cotton to clothe him; peanut oil and wax to furnish him light; wood and tiles to protect him from the inclemencies of the weather; arms to defend himself." He lacked nothing. He could challenge the world.[100]

Before the Portuguese court was transplanted to Brazil the fazendeiro lived like a king on his own isolated estate. But when John VI came over from Lisbon with his thousands of courtiers, his fifty millions of dollars from the Portuguese treasury, his collections of books and objects of art, Rio de Janeiro suddenly became a focus which drew these wealthy landowning aristocrats toward an urban life. Here was a bigger splash than even they could make on the national scene. They could not afford to live isolated from this suddenly imported splendor. A new type of relationship between town and country rapidly arose.

Well educated, wealthy, and in many instances widely traveled, these landowners became more liberal-minded in their new urban surroundings. Foreign ideas reached them more rapidly from the Old World. The newly freed press stirred up and kept stimulated their intellectual curiosity. A frequent contact with other cultured minds took some of the ego out of their cosmos. The landed aristocrats flourished again under the regime of Dom Pedro II, but gradually they became "absentee landlords," withdrew farther and farther from their estates, came to look upon Paris as a second or even as a first home, and so neglected the soil which had given them birth. The old type of culture slowly but surely slipped into decay, and industrialization began its feeble forward march.

Nearly all of Brazil still lived within a few hundred miles of the coast. Back of this coastal rim lay the mysterious *sertão*, the country's hinterland, inhabited sparsely by those few descendants of *bandeirantes* who in former days had carried their banners across the trackless interior in search of slaves or gold. In these backlands life had hardly changed in three centuries. The people there still lived like Indians and followed an Indian economy. Once a week they came to the village market to sell or exchange the fruits of their labor and then filtered back into the dry cactus lands or into the forest.

When Dom Pedro was Emperor of Brazil there was almost no communication between the coast and the sertão. The folk who were rooted in the country's distant interior simply did not exist so far as the national economy was concerned. Yet they did exist in the national life. They had already created the legend of the bandeirantes and were themselves the legend of the sertão, that dark and mystical land which embodied all that lay beyond the known frontier. Their immense habitat, boundless and free, was a great shock absorber for the amorphous masses of the coastal fringe. Their existence told the people along the sea that a frontier must still be pushed across Brazil. It was not then a moving frontier, but it would soon begin to move, or rather to crawl, and with its westward plodding the nation's economy would begin to grow. The people of Brazil knew then, and they know now, that not until the whole of the sertão has been brought into the national orbit of life will Brazil be a truly unified and great nation in the modern sense of that term. Perhaps that day is not so many decades away.

In the nineteenth century the only link between the coast and the interior was the mule driver, or *tropeiro*, who took an occasional pack train of supplies into the sertão. There was no other way to get in or out of that territory. A fringe of tangled forest (or in the province of Ceará an expanse of arid desert) said loudly to the outsider: "Do not enter here." Not many wanted to enter there. The court was in Rio. The country was becoming more and more urban-minded. Yet everyone wanted an estate, a fazenda, for that was the surest way to gain a competence. The desire for ownership of land became "an epidemic, a mania."[100] The two poles of Brazilian life drew farther and farther apart; the cities became cosmopolitan; the hinterland continued to live in its own half-Catholic, half-savage way.

Even during the colonial epoch this loosely knit agricultural society was in many ways far more tolerant than was that of the other Latin-American nations. There was no economic competition; there was no reason for prejudices. The Brazilian Church was notably liberal in comparison with that of Spanish America. Even the Inquisition did not function effectively in Brazil. There was something in the size and nature of the land that made man's refined inhumanities look incredibly mean. Many churchmen were Masons, and members of the clergy were always in the forefront of advanced thinking. During Dom Pedro's reign Protestant churches were not only allowed in the country, but they often received subsidies in cash from the Royal Treasury. In 1846 the papal nuncio in Brazil furiously denounced marriages between Brazilian Catholics and Protestant immigrants, and stated that those who had been married by Protestant ministers "were living in concubinage, their marriages were void, and their children illegitimate." In answer, the whole country's press, conservative as well as liberal, rose in anger to denounce the nuncio.[144]

The culture of the upper classes reflected a strong French influence. France had for many years been the intellectual leader of the Latin world, and in the case of Portugal and Brazil this was doubly apparent. Their own Iberian culture, fine as it was, could not compare with that of neighboring Spain. But Spain was their historic rival and enemy. Consequently, they turned their gaze toward France for cultural leadership. In Brazil nearly every well-educated person knew French, and many books in that language were imported yearly. Dom Pedro II heightened the sway of French culture through his own profound admiration of it. Once when he was in Egypt visiting some ancient ruins at Karnak he expressed this feeling in his diary: "I climbed to the top of the Pylon and there I adored the Lord and Creator of all that is beautiful; and I thought of my two lands, Brazil and France; the one, the patria of my intelligence; the other, the patria of my heart."[99]

Almost immediately after his accession to the throne Dom Pedro was informed that he must marry, and his representatives set about finding him a royal wife. They finally decided on the Princess Thereza of Naples, daughter of Francis I of that state. The young man, who was then seventeen years old, awaited his bride with all the romantic illusions which the reading of Scott and Froissart had instilled in his heart. His bride was nearly four years his senior but had seemed pretty in her picture, and Dom

Pedro offered no objections to the match. When they first met on the ship which had brought her to Rio de Janeiro, the young prince saw that Thereza was short, ugly, ungraceful in her movements, and lame.

Dom Pedro was overwhelmed. Instead of embracing the princess he stared at her for a moment, swallowed hard, and turned his back. Then, after struggling manfully to control his emotions, he went through with the formal presentation. The poor princess, who had liked him at first sight, burst into tears. A few hours later, when Pedro was with his governess, he said to her bitterly: "They have deceived us, Dadama." He even seriously considered calling the whole thing off, but after consulting with his governess and tutors, who told him that such an action would bring about international complications, he finally consented to the marriage.

For many years he never loved his wife, and indeed at no moment did there ever exist between them that devoted passion of which Dom Pedro had dreamed. But as the years passed and he learned of Thereza's fine qualities, her selflessness and almost saintly character, her deep affection for him and for their children, then the Emperor did feel for her an affinity far deeper and more all-consuming than the first rose flush of love. Thereza never meddled in politics in any way, was a perfect mother, a warm, unpretentious, and lovable queen, and soon won for herself the devotion of her subjects.

Dom Pedro's first foreign trouble was with England. That country had been the most powerful influence in obtaining recognition of Brazilian independence, and Brazil had promised to reciprocate by ending the slave trade. Great Britain wanted this trade to stop for two reasons: partly because of altruistic motives, and partly because cheap slave labor anywhere was against her best commercial interests. The two countries signed an agreement by which the slave trade was to be abolished in the year 1830. But after this date there followed two decades of upset conditions inside Brazil, nine years of turbulent regency, and ten years of strife in the provinces. The Brazilian Government attempted to carry out the agreement but found that impossible.

There is no reason to doubt that majority British opinion detested the "inhuman slave traffic," and there are equally valid reasons for accusing British officialdom of strong economic motivations in its fight against slavery. The British West Indies had already broken Brazil's sugar monopoly, but in the early 1800s Brazilian production was again humming and was greater than it had been a hundred years previously. The increased demand for sugar all over the world and the addition of the United States to the world market were the two principal causes. The British official view of the situation was expressed as follows: "The establishment of an independent metropolitan government in Brazil would be ruinous to our Sugar Colonies and to the commercial interests dependent upon them, and" would also "prove a heavy financial incumbrance instead of an advantage to Great Britain, unless the renunciation of the African Slave Trade" were made "an article of any Treaty of Commerce and Alliance into which we may now enter with that power." Therefore, in order to keep Brazilian planters from obtaining the workers they would need if sugar production were expanded there, the official British stand was in favor of making recognition of an independent Brazil dependent upon the stopping of the slave trade.[97]

In 1845 Great Britain decided to take drastic action, and all ships caught on the high seas loaded with human cargo were summarily captured by His Majesty's fleet. Every trader found guilty of engaging in the traffic was treated as a pirate. To the Brazilians this came as a deliberate slap at their sovereignty and national pride. Feeling was strong inside Brazil for the abolition of the slave trade, but it did not, of course, acquiesce in any such act of violence on the part of Britain.

Dom Pedro protested violently, but it did him no good. His country was impotent. England not only held the whip hand; she decided to use it. For over a year British men-of-war entered Brazilian harbors, seized vessels which were being used in the slave trade, and carried off Brazilian citizens.

In the meantime, conditions inside Brazil had gradually become more settled, and in 1850 the government decided to pursue the only honorable and practical course still left open. Every energy was turned toward a strict enforcement of the anti-slave-trade law, which had been on the books since 1830. English intervention then came to an abrupt halt, and within a few years the traffic had ceased completely.

At about this same time relations between Brazil and the tyrant Rosas of Argentina had reached the breaking point. Rosas, aided by the party out of power in Uruguay, had besieged Montevideo for nine years in an effort to reduce that city. Dom Pedro had wished to aid the beleaguered Uruguayans and Argentine refugees caught in the siege, but conditions inside his own country had prevented it. After the middle of the century, however, peace had been restored throughout Brazil, and as a result of the country's helplessness in the face of British sea power a serious attempt had been made to improve the military establishment.

In the year 1852 an allied army of Brazilians, citizens of Montevideo, and anti-Rosas Argentines was assembled to take the field against the tyrant of La Plata. The governors of the Argentine provinces of Corrientes and Entre Ríos were on the allied side, and General Urquiza, governor of the latter province, was made commander in chief. This army, in which Bartolomé Mitre, Argentina's great historian and president, served as a subordinate officer, met and decisively defeated Rosas early in 1852. The tyrant fled the country and passed the remainder of his life in exile in England.

International relations in the River Plate region were for a time cordial, but Brazil had embarked on a course of intervention which was not to end for some years. As one historian put it, she tried to assume much the same role in that area as the United States had taken upon itself in the area of the Caribbean, and found it "to her interest" to preserve order in the bordering states. Such an attitude promptly won for her the disparaging title of "Minotaur of the South."

Uruguay was the territory over which most of the wrangles originated. Almost constant civil war had raged in that thinly populated region, several border skirmishes had taken place, and many of the Brazilian inhabitants had suffered losses of both life and property. Dom Pedro was unable to obtain any sort of satisfaction from distraught Uruguay, and at the insistence of Brazilian landowners and generals, he decided to send troops into the territory as a protection for his nationals.

They had reckoned without Francisco Solano López, dictator of Paraguay. That ruler, third in a series of absolute despots of the inland warrior state, had never regarded any of his neighbors with a friendly eye. The isolation of Paraguay was to him a crime for which his neighbors were responsible and for which they should be made to pay. López built up the best army in South America and then dared the Brazilians to invade the sovereign territory of his neighboring buffer state, Uruguay. When they did so he hit them with the full fury of his attack. Refused passage across Argentine territory, he attacked that nation also. The resultant war, which lasted for five years (1864–70), ended with the death of López and the practical extermination of the male inhabitants of Paraguay.

Brazil did not come out without her own deep scars. She lost fifty thousand men, spent millions of dollars from her poor treasury which ought to have been invested in building up the country, and finished the war with a military machine of such power that a couple of decades later it was to snatch the reins of control from the hands of the Emperor himself.

Dom Pedro had grown old during this war. At its beginning he was a young, fine-looking man with light brown hair and fresh features. When López was finally killed he was almost completely gray-haired and his face was wrinkled and worn with care despite the fact that he was only forty-four years old. He went to the battle front himself, encouraged his soldiers, insisted that all prisoners be treated humanely, and decreed that all slaves of the state who took an active part in the war would be freed. About six thousand Negroes won their freedom in this manner.

López once gave the Emperor a chance to reach a negotiated peace, but Dom Pedro regarded the tyrant of Paraguay as an insidious disturber of continental order and as a cruel and vengeful ruler who had committed the most barbarous atrocities. There was not the slightest doubt about the latter of these two accusations, but as to the first perhaps López was only partially to blame. In any event, when these two men and the forces they represented came to grips, one or the other of them had to be obliterated. Fortunately, it was López who was killed.

The Emperor did everything in his power to educate his people in the difficult art of self-government. It was a tremendous task. Nine tenths of the population was illiterate; local authorities were notably corrupt, and the party in power usually managed to win the elections in one way or another. Dom Pedro himself dissolved the chamber of deputies eleven times during his reign, and thus helped to prevent a complete monopoly of control. It was not until 1881, forty-one years after the Emperor's accession, that the situation was cleaned up sufficiently for the Brazilians to boast of having held an honest election. A bipartisan investigating and supervising committee, under direction of a scrupulously fair ministry, turned the trick.

Nevertheless, such electoral improvements were merely a stopgap. Too many diverse factors had to function perfectly for honest returns, and when any one of them got off balance the whole applecart was upset. Within a few years elections were again as corrupt and as turbulent as they had ever been. Dom Pedro realized that only an educated electorate could safeguard freedom at the polls, and his strongest efforts were made in that direction. The laws Brazil had passed guaranteeing an honest ballot were excellent, but Brazilian politicians were either unwilling or unable to enforce them, and the masses of the people showed neither the disposition nor the capacity to oblige them to do so.

Dom Pedro always regarded the throne as a moderating power, one which not only served as a buffer between the political extremes of the country, but which should at all times represent every class of citizen to the very smallest minority. Such an interpretation of his power often forced him to move slowly, whereas had he seized dictatorial control he might have carried out his ideas more rapidly. But he was wise enough to know that such rapid progress was always built on sand, and would collapse at the first stiff blow. In him the democrat always won over the dictator. Despotism was against all his training and conviction. It became almost a religion with Dom Pedro "to rule within the constitution."

Nor did the Emperor's zeal end there. Time and again he insisted on the appointment to high government office of persons who had attacked him bitterly. The only requisite for such appointments in Dom Pedro's eye was capability. He carried this same tolerance into all of his private dealings. On one occasion, when he was asked to select a tutor for his daughter's two sons, the Emperor chose Benjamin Constant, a brilliant teacher who was also widely known as a zealous republican. Constant did not want to accept the position. He mentioned his strongly anti-monarchical views and declared that he might not always be able to maintain a discreet silence when politics was discussed. The Emperor only laughed and said that perhaps he could make republicans of the princes. On another occasion, when a brilliant young man who was an atheist had won a seat on the faculty of the School of Law in Recife against the candidacy of the son of a well-known politician, Dom Pedro refused to disqualify him, saying: "All creeds must be admitted so long as they are sincere."[167] In his personal life the Emperor was equally tolerant. He permitted "criticism, insults, and even calumnies to run their course unchecked, and their authors suffered no penalties, however outrageous their attacks. He never defended himself."[57]

In referring to his own responsibilities as Emperor, Dom Pedro once said: "I have no rights; all I have is a power resulting from birth and chance; it is my duty to use it for the welfare, the progress, and the liberty of my people."[149] This was the primary desire which motivated his life.

After his visit to the United States he frequently remarked that he wished Brazil were able to institute the republican system of government at once. However, he felt that his country was not then sufficiently prepared to undertake self-government. When feeling against the monarchy became strong he seriously considered transferring the executive power to a tribunal resembling the United States Supreme Court. He believed that in this manner the transition to a republic might be more easily made.

It was probably in the field of education that the Emperor's influence was most strongly felt both within and outside of Brazil. He established colleges for special studies of all kinds, and many primary schools. Rio de Janeiro's primary schools numbered only sixteen in 1846; by the end of Dom Pedro's reign in 1889 the total had reached one hundred and eighteen. The Emperor frequently visited these educational institutions in all parts of his realm and did his utmost to keep them at the highest level of efficiency.

He also subsidized many talented young students, and had it not been for his interest many of Brazil's most distinguished men would never have had an opportunity for development. Gonçalves Dias, a mulatto, became the best-loved poet of the country as a protégé of Dom Pedro, who twice sent him to Europe at his own expense. Carlos Gomes, composer of the opera *Il Guarany*, rose to become Latin America's most distinguished composer under the same circumstances. His opera was produced in England and Italy and was well received in both countries. The great Italian composer Verdi said: "This young man has begun where I left off." After his fame had become world-wide Gomes once remarked: "If it had not been for the Emperor I wouldn't be Carlos Gomes."[147] Another young student, Pedro Americo, once attracted the Emperor's attention with his sketching, and after considerable training at royal expense became one of his country's finest painters. There were many others: the historian Varnhagen, the poet

Magalhães, the painter Meireles, the bibliophile and scientist Ramiz Galvão, all of whom became internationally known in their fields.

The Emperor's interest in things of the mind was not for superficial show. He had been an excellent student in his youth, and he continued to study seriously until the day of his death. His intellectual curiosity was insatiable, and his diligence was certainly unique among those who occupied similar positions of responsibility as heads of great states. Science, philosophy, literature, archaeology, natural history, and languages all interested Dom Pedro tremendously; throughout his life he studied in these fields and corresponded with world leaders in each of them.

The Emperor was able to read and write fourteen languages well and could speak eight or nine with a considerable degree of fluency. His friendship and correspondence with foreign scientists and writers—the Frenchman Gobineau, the Swiss-American Agassiz, the German archaeologist, Schliemann, the North American poets Longfellow and Whittier, and many other distinguished world figures—show Dom Pedro to have been a scholar of taste, whose knowledge was indeed exceptional. These friendships and this interest were not merely personal expressions on the Emperor's part, but reflected a serious desire to inform himself of the best thought in the world so that he might aid in passing it on to his people.

Dom Pedro felt a deep love for Brazil and was extremely anxious to contribute in every way to making his country better known in foreign countries, particularly among those whose own reputations were worldwide and whom he most respected. Whatever he could do to bring this about in his travels, writings, personal contacts, and frequently by aiding distinguished foreigners who were in financial need, the Emperor thought was eminently worth while. He never regarded himself as a mere individual in such instances, but knew that he stood before the citizens of other countries as the symbol of Brazil. He was a true patron of the arts and sciences, a liberal humanist of the Renaissance, reborn in Latin America's own dark and revolutionary Middle Ages.

As a man who loved science he was anxious to see scientific knowledge made available in Brazil. His pet organization was the Brazilian Institute of History and Geography whose meetings he attended religiously year after year, despite rain or storm, in order to stimulate with his presence the interest and enthusiasm of his fellow countrymen. This institute became the most distinguished organization of its kind in Latin America and was the central focus around which scientific life in Brazil revolved for many decades. Dom Pedro provided it with funds, an excellent library, and furnished quarters in the palace. He offered prizes for the best work in the different fields which the institute embraced, and subsidized the publication of worthy studies.

When foreign scientists, such as the American Louis Agassiz and his wife, came to Brazil, the Emperor personally went out of his way to aid and encourage them. He and Dr. and Mrs. Agassiz became close friends during the sojourn of the couple in Brazil. When the Emperor visited the United States, he also made it a point to meet our most famous intellectual leaders, and perhaps for that reason Boston was the city that pleased him most. In Europe he sought out distinguished scholars in many different fields, attended numerous lectures and meetings, contributed anonymously to learned journals, and observed everywhere that spirit of humility and inquiry on which all scientific progress depends. In all of these activities Dom Pedro maintained an attitude which proved him to be one of the most emancipated and enlightened liberals of his day.

The Emperor was particularly interested in Hebrew literature and culture, and counted among his close friends many distinguished Jews. He learned to read Hebrew fluently and while on his visits to the United States and Europe often attended services in synagogues and spoke with outstanding rabbis. Some people criticized his intimacy with Jewish scholars, but Dom Pedro disregarded the barbs entirely, thinking them unworthy of his anger. His attitude toward all races was the same. If a Negro or a mulatto in Brazil showed superior ability or intellectual capacity, the Emperor was the first to help him get a start in life, and if a black man rose to the top in any field some imperial honor would be waiting for him just as surely as it would be for any white man.[147] The Emperor was taking the plastic clay of the Brazilian nation as he found it and was molding its best qualities into a definite liberal form and spirit. During his reign the character of the country was permanently "set" in this tradition.

As is the case with all Latins, Dom Pedro did not find science to be a purely cold and rational branch of thought. To him it was bound up with human feelings and conceptions of life, and so became almost a philosophy of living. He often advised Brazilian youths to "observe much and theorize little"—a maxim which he himself tried to follow. At the same time he saw in science one of man's clearest approaches to the ultimate truths, and on one occasion, when he was discussing Darwin's theory (which he called "undeniable"), the Emperor said: ". . . the more I read the more I am convinced that all truth is one and that all science meets in the point of truth. Therefore, no obstacle should be put in the way of the development of any science."[164]

His attitude toward religion and the Church was of an equally broad and tolerant nature. Although he remained a good Catholic until his death, and attended mass regularly, he thought that a man's faith was strictly his own business and that the Church should be a purely religious institution. He befriended and even subsidized Protestant schools and missions in Brazil because he believed that they represented another attitude toward life which, after all, might teach his own people something, if only by competition. This was the Emperor's way of putting into actual practice the "freedom-of-worship" clause in his constitution.

Here again he was not entirely the individual, but a reflection of the liberalism of his people. Brazilian churchmen, by and large, were the most tolerant and most broad-minded of any in Latin America. Father Feijó, who served as one of the liberal regents when Dom Pedro was under age, and a great many other leading priests advocated marriage of the clergy and took a strong stand against papal interference.[144]

The only time the Emperor ever clashed with the Church was over a jurisdictional dispute. The Pope had come out with an encyclical denouncing Masons. Among the well-known Masons of Brazil were many churchmen. In nearly all countries Masonry had been a distinctly anticlerical organization, but it had never been so regarded in Brazil. The Pope's words fell like thunder on Dom Pedro's ears. Standing on his imperial rights, he refused to permit the encyclical to be published in Brazil. It was circulated surreptitiously, and two bishops came out strongly against the Masonic order, demanding that all *irmandades*, or brotherhoods, expel their Masonic members.

Many brotherhoods refused to expel Masons from their membership, and the bishop then placed the chapels and churches with which they were connected under an interdict. A second bishop, who lived in the same northern region, backed him up. The Emperor and nearly all of the liberals in the country regarded this as an interference with civil authority, for the brotherhoods were both civil and religious organizations. The two interfering bishops were tried for violation of the national constitution, found guilty, and sentenced to imprisonment for four years.

Pandemonium now broke out in many parts of Brazil. In those sections of the country from which the bishops had come ignorant country folk formed mobs, frequently under the leadership of priests, and shouting such words as: "Down with the Masons! Down with the government! Long live religion!" they sacked many buildings and wrecked a considerable amount of other property. Troops restored order, but the split in the country's thinking was deep. Finally, seeing that the cleavage was becoming an abyss, the Emperor pardoned the two bishops. A pro-clerical paper in Rio editorialized: "The sword of civil authority, brandished against the religious conscience which took refuge in the impenetrable sanctuary, at last recognizes its impotence."[99]

Dom Pedro had lost the encounter. Hundreds of the clergy who had hitherto supported the monarchy now turned against it. The liberals were furious that the Emperor had given in to the clerical element, and many of them, too, deserted the imperial standard. The necessity of ultimate separation of Church and State, a weakening of the monarchy, and a burst of rather un-Brazilian fanaticism were the net results of the Pope's encyclical in Brazil.

The Emperor made his extensive trip through the United States in the year 1876. He had many friends in this country, and there were so many things he wanted to see that he was on the go constantly from dawn till dark. Often up at five in the morning, he hurried from place to place, seeing the sights, visiting intellectuals, attending the meetings of learned societies, or perhaps rushing to catch a train from one part of the country to another. Dom Pedro covered at least nine thousand miles on the railways, and was in such widely separated places as New York, San Francisco, and New Orleans. One newspaper commented that he probably knew the United States better than most of the members of Congress.

The Emperor was an eager and enthusiastic visitor, and his North American biographer, M. W. Williams, calls him "probably the most popular foreigner that has ever been in the United States." His extreme interest in this country did not blind him to its shortcomings, and he was as frank with his criticism as with his praise. He found our "educational palaces," as he called them, worthy of admiration; American schools in all parts of the country impressed him greatly, and he learned much that he was able to take back to Brazil with him. The universities, particularly Harvard, with its marvelous buildings and laboratories, also evoked his warmest encomiums. The democracy of the American educational system, in which the children of both poor and rich families mingled together on the same intellectual footing, was also especially appealing to his heart.

On the other hand, Dom Pedro did not like many of our asylums and found the treatment meted out to the unfortunates and insane on a lower level than was the case in Brazil. He also found the American tendency to make a big splash sometimes incomprehensible. Megalomania, size purely for the sake of size, made no sense to him. Once when he was in St. Louis he saw a huge and very costly stone customhouse being erected on a mud foundation. He thought that the size and nature of the building were out of all proportion to its use and suggested that a cheaper iron building would have done just as well. The natives, with a typical American gleam in their eyes, told him that the people in this country built for posterity. The Emperor, with a gleam of his own, responded: "But an iron building would last 400 years, and you do not mean to tell me that there will be any customhouses in 400 years."[99]

Dom Pedro was able to joke about his own people also. He admired the American spirit of enterprise and constantly spoke of the tendency in his country to put off all work of an unpleasant nature so long as there was any possible loophole of escape. "It's too much bye and bye with us in Brazil," he said. On another occasion, when he was at the Philadelphia Centennial Exhibition in the Hall of Machinery, one of the items which attracted his attention was the Corliss engine. He inquired as to the number of revolutions per minute made by the engine, and when the answer came he puckered his lips and said: "That's better than our Latin American republics!"[102]

The Emperor reveled in the exhibition and went from booth to booth like a curious schoolboy. In one of the halls Alexander Graham Bell was demonstrating his new invention. Dom Pedro had already met the inventor in Boston, where he taught in a school for the deaf, so he greeted Bell cordially and asked him to show how his new contraption worked. Bell withdrew to a distance of five hundred feet and began to recite Hamlet's famous soliloquy. The Emperor listened in amazement for a few moments, then repeated the words "To be or not to be." A few months later, when the telephone had been somewhat improved, Dom Pedro was one of the first to order its installation in a foreign country.[102]

The Emperor enjoyed his visit to the United States tremendously. He dined with Longfellow, chatted at tea with Whittier, talked for hours about Shakespeare with the great actor John McCullough, attended a service at the Mormon tabernacle in Salt Lake City, walked over the campus at Vassar College and visited the observatory there, saw the fine Bancroft Latin-American library at Berkeley, was delighted when the Boston and Washington fire departments put on special alarms for his benefit. All in all it was a great trip which the Emperor would not have missed for the world.

Dom Pedro was much interested in European immigration and encouraged settlers to come to Brazil by extending state help. However, in the face of the greater appeal of the United States, which was in those days a wide-open "land of promise," he found it difficult to attract colonists. The California gold rush of the 1850s and other favorable reports sent back to the home countries from North America outdid anything Brazil could offer. Most colonists who came to the New World after the period of independence did not come primarily in search of greater freedom. Their main idea was to get rich as quickly as possible, and America was the place where money was said to grow on trees.

It was not easy to get rich in Brazil. The system of aristocrat and slave left little room for the hard-working immigrant of European stock. The big landowner was all too ready to grab the profits from whatever crops were harvested and sold, and he invariably pocketed the "unearned increment" in land values. The immigrant worker had a hard time making a living. Such, in general, were the reports which those who came to Brazil sent back to their friends and relatives in the Old World.

Nevertheless, there were state-promoted colonies in Brazil in the early part of the nineteenth century. The first one was established in 1812, and it was followed by three others between 1818 and 1825. By 1875 there was a total of fifty-two colonies, with a population of 48,483. The greater part of these were established after the mid-century, when conditions had become stable under Dom Pedro's rule.[98]

The earliest immigrants were from Switzerland and Germany, and among their many settlements was the model city of Petropolis in the mountains above Rio, one of the world's loveliest resorts. After 1850 the government turned its attention principally toward recruiting Portuguese and Italians. These two nationalities then predominated, followed closely by the Spaniards. Many German settlers found conditions inferior to those back home; especially in the south the land was so wild and sparsely populated that their colonies in many instances were unsuccessful. Sometimes they had to fight the Indians in order to keep their lands, and marketing facilities were practically non-existent. In 1859 the German Government, after receiving continued unfavorable reports, temporarily put a stop to immigration from Germany.

There were two factors which made the importation of immigrants imperative: the expanding coffee plantations in the south where labor was scarce, and the gradual emancipation of the Negro slaves, most of whom lived in the northern regions. As paid workers the Negroes did not always meet the needs of the planters; they wanted to enjoy their new-found freedom, and in the tropical north of Brazil they could at least make both ends meet without having to work as much or as hard as their employers might wish.

In the south the situation was far more critical. Coffee culture had got under way in the decade 1850–60 and was growing rapidly. There were few Negroes in that section of the country, and the coffee planters needed workers desperately. They went out of their way to entice foreign workers into the country. For a while the system was for agents to round up prospects in Europe and then help them embark for Brazil with their passages prepaid. However, the hitch was that the cost of the passage was a debt which the immigrant assumed, and he could not consider himself a free man until it had been paid back. In the beginning immigrant workers were not paid in wages at all, but share-cropped on a certain piece of land which they did not own. Some of them got out of debt in four or five years and were then able to start from scratch as free workers. It was quite a premium to pay for so small a privilege. Others worked ten or twelve years and found the original debt still hanging over their heads. The situation soon became intolerable. Colonies disintegrated completely, and new settlers refused to embark. The wage system then took the place of share cropping, and immigration picked up immediately. Later still, the government, province, or private party most directly interested furnished arriving colonists with money, seeds, implements, and land; then the influx began to grow by leaps and bounds.

Of the 48,483 settlers who had entered Brazil up to 1875, about 20,000 went to the southern state of Santa Catharina, and 10,000 to near-by Rio Grande do Sul. Their numbers were not large, but they indicated a new trend in Brazilian life. The great day of the sugar barons of the north was at an end. The old plantation society based on slave labor was also rapidly nearing its demise. A new king, coffee, had lifted his head. Coffee grew only in the south. Just as gold had done a century and a half previously, coffee now changed the focus of Brazilian life. The hitherto thinly inhabited regions of the south were to become the center of "modern" Brazil. It would be a Brazil whose society consisted of hundreds of thousands of European immigrants: Italians, Portuguese, Spaniards, Germans, all fused upon the old aggressive "Paulista" base. It would not be bound by the traditions of the past and would strike rapidly forward, soon leaving behind the once-fabulous regions of Sugar Civilization in the north.

From 1860 onward immigration was considerably increased through the systematized efforts of the coffee planters of the south, and most of the immigrants were from northern Italy. These Italians came with their families, worked on the coffee estates as wage earners, and did not become attached to any one piece of land. They fitted in with the economic attitude of the landowners and blended quickly with the natives, being Brazilianized by the second or third generation. Many of them later acquired considerable wealth, and the present city of São Paulo owes as much to them as to any other racial group.

The Germans settled in more clearly marked nuclei and strove to recreate in their new homeland the same surroundings to which they had become accustomed in the old. Their towns rose neat and clean in the wilderness, and their farms reflected the same efficient tendencies. However, they also created their own schools, kept alive much of their old culture, and in some regions formed a definite "bloc" in the population. Yet they all spoke Portuguese as well as German, and their contributions to Brazilian life were undoubtedly great.

Between 1870 and 1890 Poles and Russians joined the immigrant stream in large numbers and settled in the Paraná uplands or in small communities in the state of São Paulo. These people usually worked their fields and shared their crops on a co-operative basis as they had done in Europe. They took little part in the national life, were not easily assimilable, and a considerable proportion of them became dissatisfied in their new homes and demanded to be returned to Russia. The Brazilian authorities were glad to see them leave. Those who remained were almost all engaged in transportation of goods across the Paraná highlands, where their descendants still carry on the same work. The town of Nova Odessa (New Odessa) in the province of São Paulo is their largest remaining center, and many of the buildings in this settlement are distinctly Russian in style. These folk still cling to their old customs; each house has its large samovar, though the drink which is brewed is often yerba mate instead of tea.

When immigration began to be a national concern, toward the close of Dom Pedro's reign, the state set up special agencies to aid the incoming settler. Likely places along rivers or near railways were selected for the establishment of colonies, and lands in these regions were sold to immigrants on easy terms. The average plot was approximately one hundred acres in size, and the average length of time it took the colonists to complete their payments was about five years. In cases of poor crops or other extenuating circumstances the Brazilians in charge of the colony usually showed themselves to be generous and helpful in tiding over the new-comers. If the head of the family died before payments were completed, his widow and children were allowed either to remain or to return to Europe at state expense. Of the fifty-two colonies which existed in the year 1875, twelve of them were promoted by the central government, fif-teen by the provinces, and twenty-five by private parties or organizations which were directly interested in procuring more workers.[98]

Dom Pedro personally did all he could to foster immigration. He often visited the colonies on trips of inspection and wherever he found in-justice saw that it was righted. In one place bad land had been given to immigrants, and the Emperor had the Brazilian in charge severely punished. On many occasions he either gave or lent money from his royal purse in order to help needy settlers. The Emperor reported that in the next to last year of his reign (1888) more than 131,000 immigrants had entered Brazil.

When Dom Pedro came to the throne his country was a backward ag-gregation of states whose population scarcely totaled seven millions; when he was forced from power in 1889 it had grown to approximately sixteen millions. The Emperor had taken a series of cities and plantations and had molded them into a growing national entity which immigration helped to drive forward.

When it became evident that the Germanic and Russian groups did not mix with the natives so easily as people of Mediterranean stock, attention was turned to Italy and to other southern European countries. Some Bra-zilian sociologists of today speak and write considerably of a process of "lightening the skin." While this is by no means a national problem or even a national concern, a certain proportion of the population undoubt-edly looks toward the day when the Brazilian blacks will have been ab-sorbed completely. Many writers tend to minimize the length of time this will take. Two centuries would not seem too long a guess for such a proc-ess to be carried to its conclusion.

Brazilians still stress the necessity of obtaining immigrants from the Latin countries who will blend more readily into the national fabric. They regard with some uneasiness the large Germanic blocs whose Nordic and Protestant habits are often at such variance with their own. They want immigrants who will make their country into a homogeneous whole.

European immigration became more and more of an urgent necessity during the latter part of Dom Pedro's reign because of the increasing lack of agricultural workers due to the emancipation of large numbers of Negro slaves, a great proportion of whom migrated to the cities. Total emancipa-tion was one of the goals nearest the Emperor's heart, and in every conceivable way he helped to lead his countrymen toward its fulfillment.

Importing tens of thousands of white workers was only one of many measures which speeded up the process.

When Dom Pedro came to the throne in 1840 approximately half of Brazil's population of seven million were slaves. In that same year the Emperor voluntarily freed all the bondmen he had inherited. He would never confer any title on persons who dealt in the slave traffic, and as soon as order was restored inside his empire he rigorously went after these people and wiped out their business entirely. Many wealthy Brazilians freed their Negroes simply because they regarded it as the humane thing to do. The non-existence of slavery in the Spanish American republics also acted powerfully on their Portuguese pride. By 1865 the country was well on its way to complete emancipation, but the five-year war with Paraguay interrupted the movement. No chances could be taken with national unity while the nation was engaged in this violent struggle.

In the year following the war (1871) a law was passed which included the so-called "freeing of the womb." Children born of women who were slaves were thenceforward to be considered free. All bondmen belonging to the nation were also declared free, and a special fund was set up in order to help slaves buy their own freedom. The total number of slaves in Brazil in 1871 was about 1,700,000, or only 50 per cent of what it had been thirty years previously when Dom Pedro ascended the throne.

The law of 1871 is known as the Rio Branco law, because the conservative baron, Rio Branco, headed the ministry when it was passed. This distinguished Brazilian had opposed emancipation before the Paraguayan War, but after witnessing the freeing of the slaves in Asunción he came over to the abolitionists and threw his whole heart into the movement. The country went into a fever of exultation when Rio Branco pushed the law through. Spectators who were in the parliamentary chamber as the final vote was taken threw garlands of flowers over the representatives and cheered them lustily. The American minister, James Rudolph Partridge, who was also present, picked up some of the blossoms and remarked: "I shall send these flowers to my country to show how you achieve here by law what there cost so much blood."[99]

All Brazilian slaves were not yet liberated, but ultimate emancipation was now a certainty. Twelve years after the Rio Branco law three states, Ceará, Amazonas, and Maranhão, proclaimed the complete abolition of slavery within their borders. Poets in the empire sang poems to freedom, and abolition became the ideal of every region. Slaveowners throughout the country accelerated the process of voluntary manumission, and the army helped the movement along by asking to be relieved of the indignity of having to round up escaped bondmen.

In 1888, when the Emperor was on a visit to Europe, parliament met to consider full liberation of all remaining slaves. More than one million had been freed since the passage of the Rio Branco law, and only 600,000 still remained in servitude. Dom Pedro's daughter, Isabel, who was ruling in her father's absence, was in the forefront of the fight for abolition. She had always shared the Emperor's views in regard to this problem.

Dom Pedro himself was not immediately informed of what was taking place in Brazil, for at the time he was gravely ill in Milan. He had been chilled while sailing on Lake Como, pleurisy had developed, and the old man's condition was becoming steadily worse. His physicians had little hope for his recovery; as a last resort they gave him oxygen and, finally, the Archbishop of Milan was called to administer extreme unction. Dom Pedro's mind remained clear, but his voice was no more than a whisper. He was still in this crucial state when they told him that the national parliament had by law abolished slavery inside Brazil. The Emperor murmured: "Thank God!" Then, after asking the Empress to telegraph his blessings and congratulations to his daughter and to the nation, he breathed a bit more easily and whispered: "What a great people! What a great people!" From that moment his condition began to improve, and within two months he was restored to a fair enough state of health to be on the move again.[167]

While her father was gravely ill, the Princess Isabel, back in Brazil, was enjoying her new-won popularity and was elated at the fulfillment of her dream of complete emancipation. Her eyes sparkled when she saw the Prime Minister, Cotegipe, and exclaimed triumphantly: "Well, we won the fight!" The minister, a mulatto who had opposed immediate emancipation, responded seriously: "Yes, your Highness. You have won the fight and lost the throne."[71]

The situation had become more serious than anyone in the royal family could be brought to believe. Many elements in the Church were aligned against the Emperor because they considered him too liberal and had never forgiven his imprisonment of the two bishops, and many elements among the conservative party were likewise hostile because they regarded him as personally responsible for taking away their property in Negro workers. The 600,000 freed in the single year of 1888 represented an investment of at least $120,000,000. Both the conservative spirit and the conservative body were on the march against the liberal monarchy.

On the other hand, the "radical" intellectual elements in Brazilian life were coming to regard the old Emperor as too conservative. Even many who admired him thought that he had outlived his usefulness.

With Dom Pedro out of the country things began to move fast. "The crown was made the scapegoat for all sorts of national sins and shortcomings," writes one historian. "This was largely because it was an exotic, unique in the western hemisphere, where all other governments were nominally republics. Such shibboleths as 'liberty' and 'democracy' counted for more in the dictator-ridden Spanish-American states than did the enlightened rule of Dom Pedro in Brazil, for the whole American psychology was against monarchical rule, and the competition of the eighteen republics of the western hemisphere was hard for the Empire to withstand."[99]

Matters were not helped by the unpopularity of the Crown Princess Isabel's husband, a Frenchman who belonged to the house of Orleans. Rumors spread thick and fast that this man would be the real ruler of Brazil after Dom Pedro's death. Through him the country would be linked with affairs in France, where one of his kinsmen, Louis Philippe, for a time occupied the throne. Brazil wanted no more foreign entanglements, and, although the dangers were undoubtedly exaggerated, republican propaganda seized on this idea of the "French sovereign" and drove it home to the people.

Another cause for the increasing lack of support of the monarchy was the growth of positivism in Brazil, which tended to call into question every phase of the old order of life. The tolerant society of the empire was a fertile ground for the spread of this philosophy of life so well presented in the writings of the Frenchman, Auguste Comte. Comte and his followers believed that the "positive" sciences afforded the only true approach to truth, and in the positivist conception of life there was no place for the supernatural. Collective humanity replaced a spiritual God as the Supreme Being which should be worshiped. Comte himself initiated the science of sociology, which he considered superior to all others, and from this developed his "religion of mankind." Positivism invoked its own creed and saints—those who had helped humanity most in its forward march. In England and in Brazil the positivist philosophy made considerable headway, and in both countries temples were erected by the followers of the new faith. The positivist temple in Rio is still one of the places of greatest interest in the Brazilian capital.

The doctrine of Comte was carried to an absurd extreme in Brazil, where it took especially deep root among the military elements. Officers came to despise all parliamentary representatives and ministers because they had no "scientific" learning and no scientific basis for their conceptions of government. On the other hand, they themselves, being trained in mathematics and other positive sciences, thought they had a corner on both statesmanship and truth.

The intellectual leader of this group was Benjamin Constant, a professor of mathematics and physical sciences who had been selected by Dom Pedro as tutor for his grandsons. Constant was one of the country's most fiery republicans, and the cadets at the military academy accepted his word as gospel. This middle-aged bespectacled professor, more than anyone or anything else, was the immediate cause of bringing about the downfall of the monarchy in Brazil.

Constant found many supporters among the members of the military clique and among the intelligentsia, but he never had anything like a mass following. The Emperor's own tolerant attitude speeded up the movement considerably. He often spoke of republicanism as being the highest form of government and frequently referred to himself as the first republican of Brazil.[167]

Republican clubs began to spring up in several parts of the country as early as 1870. Inspired by the earlier example of the United States *Federalist*, they even published their own newspapers, and many articles which appeared in them were signed by such pseudonyms as Hamilton, Jefferson, and Madison. The freeing of the slaves brought disgruntled monarchists over to their ranks, and by 1889 there were two hundred and thirty-seven republican clubs in the empire. Most of these were in the provinces nearest the capital, thus their strength was fully concentrated for direct political action. Nevertheless, they were unable to elect a single representative until 1884, when three republican deputies were sent to the lower house.

Without the support of the military the republicans would have been powerless. Ever since the Paraguayan War the Brazilian army and navy had been building up for this bid to power. It was not that they were more enlightened, more liberal, or more social-minded than the imperial government; it was simply that they had learned the love of power during the war with Paraguay, and now, wanting more, longed for the day when they might enjoy a monopoly of the governing control. Just before the final revolution one of the generals, Floriano Peixoto, stated in a letter to one of his friends that what Brazil needed was a military dictatorship which would help "purge" the country of its corruption.

The immediate spur to revolutionary action was the rumor that the government intended to diminish the power of the military elements, probably by exiling some of the higher officials and by sending the soldiers, if necessary, to distant corners of the country where they would be unable to take concerted action. In its initial stage the revolution did not look toward the establishment of a republic; a change of ministry and the appointment of men more favorable to the military clique were all that was expected. The army leader, Deodoro da Fonseca, was deeply attached to Dom Pedro and felt that this step would be sufficient.

Benjamin Constant was of another mind. As the brains behind the move he saw that once the revolution was begun no army leader would be able to stop it. Dom Pedro, who had returned to Brazil shortly before the crisis was reached, tended to minimize the whole affair. He could not believe that any such drastic action would be taken by those whom he had so often befriended. He was in the mountain resort of Petropolis when the "revolution" was carried out.

The whole movement, in the best Brazilian tradition, was almost bloodless. One man was wounded in Rio de Janeiro; no one was killed. When the soldiers marched down the streets of the capital the spectators watched them with only slight interest. Most observers undoubtedly thought that they were on parade. Dom Pedro received news of what was happening but failed to make a countermove until it was already too late.

Once the army had taken control of the ministry and ousted those in power Constant let go with his final bolt. Unless a republic was proclaimed and the royal family exiled, the plotters might well pay for their action with their lives. The military leaders saw the logic of that advice and Brazil slipped quietly, almost reluctantly, one might say, into a republic.

Events had moved so fast that there was no opposition. Neither was there any popular support for the military and republican elements. The great masses of citizens who lived in the small towns and on the plantations of the country could not have acted effectively had they so desired. They were leaderless except for the Emperor himself, and Dom Pedro was an old and ill man who refused to believe what was happening under his very nose. After the coup he might have fought for his rights as monarch from exile, but the spirit was not in him. He would have been glad to assume the presidency, but was unwilling to spill the blood of his people in order to remain on the throne.

The republicans expected the worst, however, and herded the royal family together, held them incommunicado, and finally gave them only a few hours' notice to leave the country. The rapidity with which everything had taken place left them all stunned. A handful of military men, incited to action by an even smaller handful of zealous intellectuals, had suddenly seized the government and toppled from his throne a monarch who had ruled honestly and well for half a century. The civil elements, through their inactivity and lack of organization, had thrown the reins to the generals, and these, goaded on by the "radical" intellectuals, had turned Brazil into a republic. They also turned it into a military dictatorship. Then the people of Brazil, who had observed with no great emotion the change from empire to republic, did revolt and demand constitutional government.

The story of the royal family itself was a sad one. They were all escorted to the pier by an armed guard and placed on board a ship bound for Portugal. The Empress, before boarding the launch which was to carry her to the larger vessel, fell to her knees and silently kissed the soil of the land she had come to love so much. Dom Pedro protested continuously: "I am not a fugitive . . . They must have lost their senses . . . I will not embark at this hour of the night . . ." Nevertheless, he did embark and was carried to Europe.

One of the last official acts of the republicans before the ship set sail was for a representative of the new government to come aboard and hand Dom Pedro a document which promised him 5000 *contos* ($2,500,000).* As soon as he found out the contents the Emperor imperiously refused the offer. He lived meagerly throughout the rest of his life.

* The *conto* was then worth about $500.

Not long after their arrival in Portugal the old Empress died, and Dom Pedro gave voice to the deepest anguish. He had come almost to worship the saintly character of his wife and had hoped to precede her in death. He continued to follow events in Brazil with great interest and longed for the people to call him back again before he died. There was never any chance of this. Some of his closest friends did try to bolster his spirits by pointing out the dictatorial policies of the republicans and by praising his own progressive regime. One of them remarked that he alone of all South Americans could properly be compared with George Washington. Dom Pedro objected to the comparison, but the speaker continued by saying that Washington had enjoyed the apotheosis of success, while the Emperor's struggle against great odds had led to his individual misfortune.

Dom Pedro thought back over his own lone childhood and his final violent exile and murmured that there was some truth, at least, in that part of the statement. A short time later the military government in Brazil arbitrarily dissolved the Congress, and the last opportunity for Dom Pedro's return was at hand. His friends pleaded with him to take the step, but he put them off, saying that he was then too old and too infirm to do his country any good. A month later he suffered a severe chill and went to bed with a fever from which he never recovered. On December 5, 1891, two years after his banishment from Brazil, he died in a second-rate hotel in Paris.

Perhaps the most pungent statement the Emperor ever made was spoken when he was asked to issue a manifesto explaining his position in regard to the revolution in Brazil. He replied briefly: "Why should I? My life is my manifesto."[99]

It was a life of which any ruler might well be proud. Dom Pedro had taken an incohesive mass of lands and peoples and had molded them into Latin America's largest, most populous, most liberal, best-governed nation. He had remade the physical face of the inhabited regions. When he ascended the throne there were no railways in Brazil; when he went into exile there were more than 6000 miles. Steamboats, telegraphs, telephones, agricultural and industrial machines also helped to modernize and link together the new country. The name of Brazil was respected all over the world, and the name of its ruler was admired wherever men thought deeply and were free. Science and the arts had taken a great step forward in the days of the empire, and Brazil had won for herself an international place in those expressions of man.

From an economic standpoint there was even more marked progress. Exports had jumped from between fifteen and twenty thousand contos in the first years of the Emperor's reign to over 350,000 contos during the final period. Under the famous Mauá banking houses were established along the coast. Opened economically, Brazil became international-minded. Foreign loans were floated in London at 4 and 5 per cent, with no special guarantees, and with only ¼ per cent sinking fund. Brazil's credit was good. During the latter months of Dom Pedro's reign her currency was quoted above par.[57] Three or four million slaves had been freed with no shedding of blood, and a respect for civil liberties had been instilled into all kinds and classes of people.

Struggling as he did throughout his reign against extremes of poverty and wealth, against illiteracy, against the obstacles of a sparse population, thinly spread over immense distances and lacking racial homogeneity, against a complete lack of experience in self-government and an atmosphere made to order for political corruption, Brazil's democratic Emperor achieved all that could reasonably be expected of a human being. Brazil has not enjoyed as long an epoch of peace and progress at any time since Dom Pedro's exile, and few Latin-American nations can boast of such tolerance under any republican regime of the twentieth century. Dom Pedro II was undoubtedly an anomaly among monarchs, but his life was indeed a glowing manifesto of which all Brazilians today are justly proud.

41

PARAGUAY AS A SYMBOL
OF PERPETUAL DESPOTISM

When the revolutionary wars were ended there arose from the ashes of the old Spanish colonial empire several representative *caudillos,* regional tyrants, or "men of destiny," who symbolized the nascent nationalisms and left upon their nations the imprint of their personalities. In each new republic the law of the land was their law, its will their will, its personality their person. As a sculptor takes modeling clay in his hands and molds a form, watches it until it hardens, then guards his handiwork with every power at his disposal, so did these Spanish American despots take into their hands the running chaotic emotions of their countries and twist them into the shape of their own desires, which were a reflection of the desires of their people.

These men ruled because they loved power. Yet no despot can long remain in power when opposed by the majority of his subjects, and no nation can escape the blame of its tyrannies by saying that its people willed otherwise. For that reason alone, when these countries were thoroughly sickened by their tyrants, when they wearied of their cruelties and their gore, when they became ashamed of the captivity of their own spirits, then the tyrants fell. Until that time the caudillo was one with the majority of his people or personified the resignation with which they accepted tyranny.

The first period of despotic rule was the worst, for then the most despotism was necessary in order to impose any rule whatever. There is no point in examining all of these men, but the stories of those who cast dark shadows over their countries for half a century bear more than a brief mention. These men and their periods of dominance, although they were not actually chief executives during the entire time, were as follows:

Paraguay—Dr. José Gaspar Rodríguez Francia (1811–40)
Argentina—Juan Manuel de Rosas (1829–52)

Venezuela—José Antonio Páez (1830–48 and 1858–63)
Mexico—Antonio López de Santa Anna (1833–55)

The story of nascent Paraguay was the story of Dr. Francia. He was the man who took his degree in theology at the University of Córdoba, the man who later brought a brace of pistols to the council meeting which was to determine Paraguay's course of action in the face of Bonaparte's invasion of Spain. Dr. Francia and his pistols wanted independence. When independence was declared, Francia was elevated to the supreme power of the new republic; when he died, he was worshiped like a God of the Old Testament.

Francia's father was a Portuguese who had crossed over into Paraguay from Brazil. His mother was an unidentifiable native of the latter country. The son, born in 1766, was a tawny, righteous-minded boy whose quick wit and serious demeanor won the respect of his teachers. He studied for the priesthood but became a lawyer. He was not only thoroughly honest in his personal relationships but demanded honesty in others. A bribe offered even surreptitiously to Dr. Francia called for the punishment of him who had attempted in this manner to subvert the law. Such was the character of this neurotic and inscrutable Puritan whose slightest wish was fiat in isolated and unknown Paraguay.

In 1811, after the Paraguayans had established their first national government, Dr. Francia wanted to resign from the governing committee. He claimed that it was because he feared military dictatorship. He was an honest and upright lawyer, a doctor of theology, and the committee believed him. But they insisted that his experience was such and his probity so great that he was a necessary man. Dr. Francia again joined the governing council, and after his act enjoyed the unanimous esteem of his compatriots. Why fear so honorable a statesman?

The doctor also suggested a plan for permanent government. It was to elect two consuls, who in Roman style would hold the reins of power. It had worked before; it could work again. Pilot and co-pilot of the country's destinies would be like a pair of scales counterbalancing each other perfectly. Dr. Francia was selected as one of the consuls, and a man named Yegros was chosen as the other. They were to enjoy absolutely equal powers. Paraguay was not to become the pawn of a single man.

In order to add dignity and interest to the ceremony of investiture Francia suggested that one consul be called Caesar, the other Pompey. His compatriots thought it was a fine idea, and two chairs were prepared properly marked with the names of the two great Roman leaders. A dais was raised for the inauguration and the ceremony began. As the two consuls were to be equal in power, they had not decided which chair would be for which man. Nevertheless, Dr. Francia made an obvious dash for the seat marked Caesar.

It was a good beginning. A few months thereafter the pilot and co-pilot idea had proved that it was unworkable. It seemed that the counter-balances were too perfect; they stopped all government. Yet on every issue which came up the people sided with Dr. Francia. Finally it was decided to elevate him to the position of *first* consul for a term of one year. The Paraguayan Caesar had won his battle against Pompey. Francia governed the country well and won for himself the admiration of his fellow citizens. The decision was then reached—by plebiscite, say the Paraguayan historians—to elect him *for life* as Consul, Dictator, Father of his Country, and Pontiff. This was in 1816, and in that year Dr. Francia became *El Supremo*, His Supreme Highness.

He governed without a congress, without ministers, without tribunals of justice. There were no makeshifts of democratic government around the despot of Paraguay; he was avowedly, obviously, and absolutely El Supremo to his people. The nation in reality had no government; Francia was its providence, his wish the Mosaic law of his countrymen.

Dr. Francia saw clearly enough what was going on in the countries around him: anarchy, factional warfare, the destruction of every productive element. He did not propose to have any of these in Paraguay, even if he had to build a wall around his country in order to shut them out. The Creoles of Buenos Aires tried to get him to open the door, and he slammed it in their faces. Bolívar wrote to the doctor with no better results. So did Brazil. It was necessary to erect a *cordon sanitaire* around Paraguay in order to keep out the disease of anarchy.

Francia stretched his rod out over his country's foreign commerce, saying to it, "Cease!" And the ships lay high and dry on the banks of the Paraná. Not a vessel could move without his personal license. No traveler could enter or leave the country unless he willed it. If Dr. Francia did not like a visitor's papers, his talk, conduct, or even the cut of his face, it might be the worse for such a person![103] Forts were constructed at strategic intervals both as a protection against the Indians and the foreign Creoles. The isolation was complete.

Then Francia went to work with a vengeance. He made his people clear their land and plant crops. He told them what to plant and how much to plant. Anyone who disobeyed might easily pay with his life. He also made them breed cattle and establish primitive manufactures. He did not hesitate to seize the lands or wealth of the Church in order to build schools or barracks. He passed laws against superstitions and reduced the number of feast days. Religious processions were forbidden.

No priest dared interfere with the perpetual dictator of Paraguay. At the beginning of his reign, when the bishop of Asunción dared dispute his will, Francia declared him incompetent to hold office because of insanity and replaced him with a priest more amenable to his authority. When a distinguished foreign traveler asked him about his ideas on religion he said: "You can be anything you want to be in Paraguay: Protestant, Jew, Mohammedan, Catholic. Anything except an atheist."

"What do you think about the Pope?" inquired the foreign visitor.

"If the Pope himself came to Paraguay," answered Francia, "I might make him my collection boy."

The doctor was not an anti-Christ; he knew how to utilize religion to suit his own ends. He collected the church tithes and then used them as he saw fit. The priests in his churches preached sermons in praise of Dr. Francia, their country's greatest benefactor. He was Pope and Caesar all rolled into one.

His Supreme Highness did everything possible to heighten the sense of Paraguayan nationality, already among the strongest in Latin America. He hated the Spaniards and used this hatred of them to degrade the country's former rulers and to exalt himself. A law stated that no Spaniard might marry a Paraguayan lady of Spanish descent. The penalty was ten years' imprisonment and confiscation of all property. But Spaniards might, if they wished, "marry Indian women, mulattoes, and negresses."

Francia was a remarkably keen, able, and even gifted administrator. Under him Paraguay enjoyed more than a generation of peace while all the rest of the continent was passing through the flames of civil war. There was no great lunge forward in Paraguay, but the people produced the necessities of life. No one starved to death. No one became tremendously wealthy at the expense of others. No one enjoyed any power at all except El Supremo. Paraguay forgot the meaning of civil liberties.

The doctor utilized many foreign visitors, but he ran a strictly one-man show. He knew that no South American nation was in any condition to hurt him and that no European was in a position to do so. He was not always highhanded with his foreign guests, for on occasion El Supremo could be a most friendly and brilliant conversationalist. He was able to discourse on a wide variety of subjects and possessed a fine analytical mind. The one law which every foreigner had to observe rigidly was: no meddling in politics.

Sometimes the doctor even went farther than that. When the famous French scientist, Bonpland, who was a friend of Baron Humboldt, established a botanical farm in the Argentine province of Entre Ríos, Francia evinced great interest in his undertaking. Entre Ríos was just across the threshold from his own private domain. In fact, the doctor thought that he had as good a claim to the province as Artigas, the Uruguayan caudillo who had approved Bonpland's project for scientific farming. So while the Frenchman, with the aid of some four hundred Indians, cleared the land and planted his native tea bushes, Dr. Francia kept an eagle eye fixed on him. When it began to look as if Bonpland would meet with considerable success in his venture, possible enabling Uruguay or Argentina to produce more green tea than Paraguay, then the doctor's hardhearted, monopolistic sense commenced to work on him. Yerba mate was one of Paraguay's principal products; every inhabitant of the land drank it, and every native farmer had an interest in it. El Supremo simply got a regiment of horsemen together and sent them across the border after Bonpland. They tore up his tea plants, scattered his Indians, and took the scientist himself back with them into Paraguay. France protested vigorously. So did Baron Humboldt. Even Simón Bolívar spoke haughtily of a war to free the distinguished scientist. Dr. Francia was not interested in their protests. When he had got out of Bonpland all that he wanted to know, he offered to set him free again. The Frenchman had been well treated in Paraguay, and he refused to leave.

On the other hand, among the few Europeans who obtained official permission both to enter and to leave Paraguay, some later wrote of Francia's reign of terror with a "running shriek." That was what Thomas Carlyle, the English writer who dedicated an essay to El Supremo, called their high-pitched accusations. Carlyle's hero worship comes out in this essay on Francia, and the Paraguayan caudillo is made to stand forth almost a pagan deity.

No one ever accused the doctor of exploiting his subjects or of dishonest government. He was meticulously frugal and honest. All he wanted was a monopoly of control. In that he would brook no interference. "*Por Dios*," he said, "no one shall conspire against me; I will never allow it. The Career of Freedom, be it known to all men and gauchos, is not yet begun in this country; I am still only casting out the Seven Devils. . . . By the high God, if you aim at my life, I will bid you have a care of your own!"

Dr. Francia put that threat into effect whenever there was even a suspicion of anyone aiming at his authority or at his life. He kept a well-oiled gibbet and filthy prisons; the first knew its business well, and El Supremo's stinking dungeons were well stocked with those who had insinuated that something might be wrong in the Francia regime.

Every attempt to depose El Supremo was ruthlessly suppressed. Carlyle, arriving at his estimate after reading several works by foreigners who had been in Paraguay, states that "upwards of forty persons" were executed by Dr. Francia. A painstaking North American historian, W. S. Robertson, says that "thousands of Paraguayans were arbitrarily executed." The Peruvian writer, García Calderón, writes that "his punishments revealed an Oriental cruelty. In 1821 he executed the representatives of the Paraguayan nobility. He leveled his subjects, and governed without ministers, surrounded only by informers and praetorian guards."[92] Since no accurate records were kept, the number of those killed at Francia's order will probably never be known, but in any event he did not pick on well-loved citizens. The people stuck with him to the end.

The Paraguayans were already thoroughly trained in co-operative labor. The Jesuits had achieved their most remarkable success in that region. El

Supremo tried to call back into existence their paternalistic despotism with himself alone in the director's seat. Large estates were owned and operated by "the country." All crops, all cattle raising, and all commerce were also directly under "the country's government," and the country's government was Dr. Francia.

The doctor opened great fairs for the sale of merchandise. He cleaned up Asunción and facilitated domestic trade throughout the state. He forced all able-bodied citizens to work; like the Incas of old, he regarded sloth as an enemy of the state. He improved agriculture by inviting foreign scientists into the country, and had sense enough to see that his people followed their advice. Foreigners resident in Paraguay during his reign stated that "not two ears of corn, but two harvests of corn grew where only one had grown before."

Francia's Paraguay was a unique theocracy; it revived a kind of perverted Spanish medievalism in the New World as a national ideal and as a national expression. El Supremo "created a Church and a Fatherland," both of them in his own image. But his image was a reflection of that of Paraguay. He formed a "proud and warlike race."

As the years passed something began to happen to Dr. Francia. He was always nervous, high-strung, with an icy stare, and oftentimes attacked by imaginary and unreasoning fears. Gradually his neuroses warped his entire outlook on life. For every plot that he discovered El Supremo saw half a dozen more in his imagination. Asunción became a whispering gallery. Informers roamed the streets to report the idle gossip on the chance that they might catch something seditious. Slowly but surely fear closed its sharp fingers around the doctor's aging throat.

Historians, even physicians, have written on the pathologies of Dr. Francia and how through fear he was transformed into a bloody tyrant. Whatever the reason, his despotism did become tighter and tighter with the passing years. Uneasy, tormented, mystical, El Supremo began to live in an almost monastic isolation. Every wall, every building, every tree might hide an assassin. All structures which surrounded the government palace in which he had taken up residence were razed so that his retreat would be open on all sides. Even the orange grove was cut to the ground for fear of lurking shadows behind its thick dark leaves. Within this sanctum the old man lived out the last months of his life, his only intimates being a drunken mulatto barber and a vengeful secretary.

If the doctor stepped out into the street the cathedral bell would ring as a signal for all the inhabitants to scurry to their homes muttering, "El Supremo." Each night he slept in a different room so that no one would ever be certain as to where to find him. Finally, when he died, the people refused to believe it. Many thought it was but another of the doctor's eccentric traps to ensnare the unfaithful.

All the same the funeral oration was delivered in the Church of the

Incarnation in Asunción by one Father Manuel Pérez. His obituary was all a defense of the dead Francia. "Amid the convulsions of the revolution," declaimed the priest, "the Lord, looking down with pity on Paraguay, raised up Don José Gaspar Rodríguez Francia for its deliverance. *And when, in the words of my text, the children of Israel cried unto the Lord, the Lord raised up a deliverer to the children of Israel, who delivered them.*"

That Dr. Francia killed those who opposed him? "What is this," said the priest, "to the demon of Anarchy? . . . Life is sacred, but there is something more sacred still: woe to him who does not know that withal."

When Francia died the whole city of Asunción began to turn black. Out of the windows were thrown black streamers. The people put on their blackest garments. All conversation was hushed, and this blackness entered the hearts of the inhabitants. When the catafalque bearing El Supremo's body was pulled down the streets by its horses caparisoned in heavy mourning, the whole city was draped in a tyranny of black.

Afterward the citizens worshiped at Francia's tomb, some afraid that he might again awaken if they did not, others because they loved him. Like Irala of three centuries before, El Supremo carried the tears of Paraguay with him to the grave. Months later some unknown persons broke into Francia's tomb at night and scattered his bones. It did not matter. Perpetual dictatorship had been born, blessed, and was now confirmed in Paraguay.

42

THE SPIRIT OF ARGENTINE NATIONALITY

I. THE CITY: RIVADAVIA

While Paraguay was enjoying its iron peace under Dr. Francia, the United Provinces of La Plata were passing through a decade of anarchy which, with only one brief but brilliant interruption, lasted from 1820 to 1830. During "the terrible year 1820" almost complete chaos reigned throughout the region. Conditions improved somewhat after that, but not a great deal. The provinces were aligned against Buenos Aires, and the issue was still undecided. The Gaucho hinterland was unwilling to accept the domination of this new "imperial Rome," which, of necessity, was its outlet to the sea.

Between 1821 and 1827 the leading figure inside the great capital city was Bernardino Rivadavia, a gifted and idealistic statesman, who was a mulatto. He headed the faction which desired the unitarian form of government and the hegemony of Buenos Aires. His party finally triumphed, and from 1826 to 1827 Rivadavia was president of the United Provinces. It was at best an illusory victory, for the interior regions never accepted their subordinate position.

Nevertheless, Rivadavia went to work as if he had hope of forging a democratic utopia out of the inorganic and turbulent dominion of which he was president. In 1826 he promulgated an idealistic constitution which granted all political rights to a people who were then hardly able to understand and appreciate the rudimentary principles of co-operative government. He doubled the number of representatives of the people and renounced all the extraordinary powers of his high executive office, gladly submitting to the dominance of the legislative branch. He stood for the inviolability of person, property, conscience, and expression. He established schools, a university, a library, and technical training centers. He reorganized the economic and financial setup of the government, check-mated the Church as a political power, and became the first great civilizer of his nation. In later years his people came to regard him as a symbol of their cultural ideal. "Were popular myths to rise in spontaneous birth in Buenos Aires, before the evocative ocean, as in the Greek cities lovingly bathed by the Mediterranean, then Rivadavia would be the genius of Argentine culture, the patron of the city, the creator of its arts and its laws."[92]

His constitution was deeply impregnated with the social ideology of Rousseau and countenanced the leadership of the great port city over the interior dominions. Neither the demagogues nor the masses were yet prepared for the enlightened regime which Rivadavia designed for them. He stood almost alone against the avalanche, and, while his ideals persisted as a prophecy, his actual leadership as president was soon without material backing. One of the immediate causes of his ultimate resignation from office was the war with Brazil over the province of Uruguay.

The fate of this small state, just across the river from Buenos Aires, was always closely bound up with the destiny of Argentina herself. The caudillo, Artigas, leader of the Uruguayan Gauchos, is regarded as the founder of his country. In 1811, when Montevideo was still occupied by the Spaniards, Artigas sought Argentine help to free his land and incorporate it into the United Provinces of La Plata. Three years later, while Montevideo was still holding out under siege, the Assembly at Buenos Aires refused to seat the delegates from Uruguay who favored autonomy for their province and a complete break with Spain. Artigas and his followers then set out to establish the independent nation of Uruguay. The army of Buenos Aires took Montevideo, but the remainder of the country and a large section of northern Argentina came under the control of Artigas.

For six years this great Gaucho confederation struggled valiantly but unequally against the dominance of Spain, of Buenos Aires, and of Brazil. Finally, in the year 1820, the armies of Brazil overran his territory and Artigas fled to Paraguay, where the inscrutable Dr. Francia condescended to grant him sanctuary.

From 1820 to 1828 Uruguay, or *la Banda Oriental* (the Eastern Bank of the River) as it was then known, was an integral part of Brazil, first of the colony, then of the independent state. When conditions settled down somewhat in Buenos Aires, with the emergence of Rivadavia as constitutional strong man, that country refused to recognize Brazil's occupation of Uruguay. In 1825 the famous group of thirty-three Uruguayans, backed by promises of Argentine help, disembarked on the riverbank of their native land and began the reconquest of their country. They had soon gathered an army of two thousand patriots and won two notable victories over the Brazilians. Then they requested to be taken back into the Argentine confederation; this was granted in spite of the fact that it meant certain war against Brazil.

Brazil got the worst of the war from the beginning, and by 1827 was ready to negotiate for peace. A representative from Buenos Aires was sent to Rio, and peace was made. The Argentine delegate exceeded his authority in signing a treaty which gave Brazil virtual control over a semi-autonomous Uruguay, and Rivadavia, back in Buenos Aires, refused to accept it. The war continued. In 1828 there were other negotiations. The Uruguayans were still in favor of joining the La Plata provinces, but Brazil seemed loath to yield on this point. It would shut her best southern regions away from the fine waterway which marked the southern boundary of Uruguay. At this stage of the game Great Britain, anxious to trade with both Brazil and the Argentine, stepped in and whispered cogently about absolute independence for Uruguay. Thus in 1828 the republic of Uruguay was born as a pillow thrown between the two behemoths of South America, and in order to facilitate the peaceful trade of the entire eastern coast with Great Britain. Uruguay did not at that time want independence; it was thrust upon her. For the next seventy-five years her territory was the scene of almost constant civil strife, as one Gaucho band struggled against the other for control of the national government and the country's capital city, Montevideo.

When the first negotiations between Brazil and Buenos Aires were initiated in 1827, Rivadavia was president of the government in the latter region. As soon as it was learned what kind of treaty had been signed, Rivadavia was vigorously opposed by his own people. He disavowed the treaty in strong terms, but it was already too late. The idealistic "forger of Utopias" no longer had popular support. Seeing that it was impossible for him to govern his country, Rivadavia resigned from office in that same year. With him the pure ideal of Argentine democracy vanished for more than a generation. Out of the wild interior pampas was stretched a hand of steel which forced the nascent republic to bend before it. This was the hand of the tyrant Rosas.

No two men could be more different than Rivadavia and Rosas, the first idealistic, a believer in the French ideals of democratic government, a strong supporter of the arts and of civil liberties; the second a ruler raised to power by the apotheosis of brute force, a cunning and vengeful despot, a symbol of Gaucho barbarism which had come to fruition on the wide pampas. Nevertheless, it was the second who was more in tune with his times, who, indeed, embodied all the dominant characteristics of his epoch, and who thus became the elevated symbol of the masses and the rude fashioner of a primitive nation. Nowhere else in Latin America were the forces of liberty and despotism more sharply matched than in the Argentine; for many years in this region there would be no compromise; one must win out completely over the other and impose its will with violence.

The key to the struggle, and to the character of the people themselves, lay in the Gaucho herdsmen who led their semi-wild lives on the Argentine pampas. It was their strength which made Argentina a nation, their barbarism which made Rosas its dictator. Even today, when the name of Rosas himself is execrated, the work of the Gauchos who placed him in power, and finally overthrew him, is glorified in history, song, and story. Argentines of today boast of their Gaucho honor, their Gaucho sentiments, their Gaucho friendship, and their Gaucho nation. The glorification of a type has become a reflection of the feelings of a great people.

II. THE PAMPAS: THE GAUCHO

The Gaucho was the outgrowth of both tradition and environment. He came into being in a rudimentary form shortly after the first settlements had been made in Argentina, about the year 1600. Economically, he depended entirely on the wild cattle and horses of the pampas; spiritually, he was the re-creation of a Spanish cultural tradition on that pampas. He was a class, not a race, but generally the Gaucho was the offspring of a Spanish father and an Indian or mestizo mother. Occasionally, however, there were pure-white Gauchos and pure Negroes. Any person who left behind the accouterments and centers of civilized life in order to pursue his destiny on the great Argentine prairie became a Gaucho.

In the 1600s the Gaucho was in a purely formative state; in the two centuries following his character and type were definitely molded; and between about 1780 and 1850 he was in his glory. After that, the Gaucho class declined rapidly and finally disappeared, only to be remembered as a cultural heritage.

The Gaucho led a pastoral life, only one rung above the hunting-and-fishing stage, which is the most primitive in human development. His life was hard, but subsistence was easy on the Argentine pampas. A distinguished Spaniard, Felix de Azara, who was sent to the La Plata region at the end of the eighteenth century to survey the northern boundary, estimated that there were perhaps 42,000,000 wild horses and cattle on the pampas at that time. These quadrupeds did not belong to anyone; they constituted the public domain in Argentina as much as the land itself. The government made frequent attempts to place restrictions on the numbers which might be slaughtered, but there was no possible way to enforce these laws. A Gaucho felt as free to kill a steer or to take a wild horse as he did to fish in a stream.

The house in which the Gaucho lived was built of mud and covered with long yellow grass. It usually consisted of a single room, in which the entire family lived, children and parents all together. In the summer there were often fleas and other vermin, and the family moved outside to sleep on the ground. Even within the walls of their own dwelling there were only piles of skins for a bed and rude woolen ponchos or more skins for covers. The kitchen was in a shed removed a few yards from the house, and farther away still was a primitive corral, which was in the form of a circle about thirty yards in diameter, enclosed by a number of strong, rough posts stuck firmly in the ground. Hawks and vultures usually sat on the posts patiently waiting for their turn at the entrails of a slaughtered animal, or perhaps some cut which the Gaucho did not care to eat.

Breakfast consisted of a gourdful of hot yerba mate; every other meal was made up of unsalted meat, with perhaps a dish of sweetened corn mush as a dessert. Mate was drunk between meals at any time out of a gourd into which a straw was thrust. There was never any variation in the diet. Vegetables were impossible to obtain; the Gauchos did not grow fruits and did not want to take the trouble of obtaining milk. Supper was the main meal, and when it was served a great iron spit was brought into the hut and its point stuck into the ground. Then the family all gathered all around, seated on the dried skulls of horses or cattle, and with long knives cut off the portions which they wanted to eat. A feeble lamp fed by bullocks' tallow illuminated the room, and if the weather was cold there might be a fire of charcoal, or perhaps of the ignited carcass of a cow.[104]

Personal hygiene was certainly not the Gaucho's strongest point. Oftentimes his hair and beard would both be permitted to grow to their natural length, never trimmed or cut. This hirsute section of the anatomy would then become the harboring place for filth, for the Gaucho seldom bathed. This was not because his moral fiber or pride in body had degenerated so that he became dirty out of indolence. It was because water was frequently hard to obtain on the pampas, and what there was had to be used for other purposes than bathing. Since his own body must remain dirty, the Gaucho soon reached the point where he cared little for cleanliness in anything else around him.

Gaucho dress was distinct from that worn by any other group in America. A pair of loose, baggy trousers, black in color, held up with a sash and with a heavy sashlike flap hanging between the legs, made riding easier. Over the shoulder was slung a woolen poncho of sheep or vicuña hair. The Gaucho's boots were made of horse leather or of the hide of an entire calf's leg. Sometimes, if he was able to obtain them, he had silver decorations on his belt, sash, saddle, or bridle. His hat was a large black felt *chambergo*.

What the mines meant to Mexico and Peru, wild horses and cattle meant to the Gaucho. If he wanted food or a hide he took out after a steer on his horse and whacked at the tendons of a hind leg with a sharp crescent-shaped knife. After sufficient cows had fallen he dispatched them at his leisure, taking only the hide, the easily obtained tallow, and perhaps the tongue—one of his favorite cuts. The rest of the meat was abandoned to the buzzards and wild dogs. Legend even has it that a Gaucho sometimes killed a cow so that he could tie his horse to its horns on the treeless prairie.

Eighteen or twenty men could easily dispatch seven or eight hundred bulls and cows in a single hour.

The Gaucho created what one writer calls "an age of leather." His *bolas* were covered with it; his lasso was made of it; nearly every item of daily use was in some way connected with leather. A distinguished Uruguayan writer, Alberto Zum Felde, describing life in that region in the early 1700s, wrote as follows: "Houses were constructed of leather at the founding of Montevideo. Leather made the protective roofs, as in the tents of the Indians. Nails being scarce, wire unheard of, rope and cord undreamed of, moistened leather served their purposes; leather was used as cables, as chisels, in all manner of joining and riveting. Doors and beds were of leather; you can still see them in the country. Doors of houses, trunks, canisters, sacks, baskets were made of leather with the hair still on it. Similarly fences for the gardens, bottles for wine (the old wineskins), yawl sails, cranes, chairs, and of course all the harnesses and ornaments of horses."[71]

The Gaucho was nominally a Catholic, but actually he had no religion at all outside of a few rude superstitions. There were few churches on the isolated pampas, and the Gaucho lived alone, not in a town, not even in a hamlet. Frequently he took up with his woman, or *china*, without being married to her, sometimes by kidnaping and running off with her on his horse. Every woman who lived on the Gaucho-inhabited regions of the pampas had a family, whether married or not. An English traveler who was in Argentina in 1825 wrote that he once asked the mother of a beautiful child who the father was, and she responded with a bland: "*¿Quién sabe, señor* [Who knows, sir]?"[104]

When a visitor approached a Gaucho's hut, if the owner was about he would usually be at the door with his hands folded. At home he never worked, and gave the appearance of being incurably indolent. His house was in a constant state of disrepair, but he never bothered to fix it up. The corral stank of old wool, of bones, bullocks' blood, and of unwashed animals. The house smelled of unwashed humans.

The Gaucho was not lazy. He had simply adapted himself to a certain type of life and was following it out the best way he could. He had no acquisitive instinct; he was a man without wants. His mount was his one invariable love; he had no desire to make money or to alter his way of life. On the other hand, the Gaucho was tireless in breaking in horses, in any work on the range, and could go for days with little or no sleep. He worked hard at the essential job of subsistence, and disregarded all others.

A Gaucho's children began to ride when about four years old. Within a few months every son became a true centaur and remained one until the day of his death. When an outsider spoke to a Gaucho of the advantages and luxuries of civilization, the response, if any, would always be that there could be no such thing as civilization where people walked. The Gaucho was truly inseparable from his horse.

The Spanish visitor, Azara, gave one of the earliest and fullest descriptions of the character of the Gaucho. He was an individualist who never wanted to serve anyone, no matter of what degree, yet he was content to work in a gang of herders along with Negroes, Indians, or mulattoes, even if the foreman were a black man. He had no love for any special locality, but wandered from place to place on his horse, as it suited his fancy. When Gauchos gathered together in the small *pulperías*, or country stores, on the pampas, usually run by Basques, they would remain on horseback, "even though the conversation might last for several hours. When they go fishing they also remain mounted, even if manipulating a net. If they want to pull a bucket out of a well they will tie the rope to the saddle and make the horse pull it up. If they wish to mix a bit of mortar, even if it's no more than a hatful, they will make their horse walk over it again and again with its feet without ever dismounting. In fine, they do everything on horseback."[105]

They knew horses far better than most men know people. If a rancher happened to hire a Gaucho to look after two hundred or even more horses, with a single glance he would take them all in and would never let one escape. A handful of Gauchos could drive hundreds of animals across the pampas, or even through tree-covered land, at a fast pace without losing an animal. Gauchos would often ride half lying on their horses, as if mount and man were a single beast. Only the word "centaur" could describe them.

Azara wrote that in the more isolated districts, where the wild horses had been living without newer additions to their herds for a century or two, they had all turned feral, reverted to a single color, which was between bay and brown. But there were few such herds; most of them had horses of all colors, and the Gaucho always gave his horse a color name, referring to his steed as "my bay," "my sorrel," "my black and white." Many of the colors carried with them supposed characteristics; for example, the white or nutmeg-gray horse was conceded to be the best swimmer; the piebald was reckoned the most difficult to tame, especially if it had white eyes, and so on through the whole range of colors.

In the early days, when horses were scarce as gold in the territory of the River Plate, they brought phenomenally high prices. Irala bought one in Paraguay in 1551 for four thousand gold pesos, or close to fifteen thousand dollars. Just six years later, however, the same man had twenty-four horses in his possession, so they must have increased rapidly.

A century or two afterward, when wild herds covered the pampas almost like an endless forest, the price hit rock bottom. Both the Jesuit, Falkner (1744), and Azara (1790) mention the average cost of a good horse as being about two dollars on the pampas, and perhaps four or five in Paraguay. Mares brought only two *reales,* or one sixth as much as a good stallion. In the most isolated regions, where money and all other conveniences of civilization were hardly known, a good horse would be exchanged for a single steel needle.

The Gaucho who lived in this isolation was like his mount, sinewy, nimble on his feet, tireless. He was always hospitable to a visitor, and offered him the best his hut afforded. His voice was low and pleasing to the ear, his demeanor as proud as that of royalty. There was a deep vein of poetry in every Gaucho. He would fight at the drop of a hat, but was not vindictive. He knew that he was as good as any man, and better than most. His attitude toward life and death was completely fatalistic.

Of a Gaucho's manner of facing death, Azara wrote that he accepted it as naturally as he would accept any other everyday occurrence, with absolute indifference. Even when mortally and painfully wounded he would make no cry, but might perhaps remark in a matter-of-fact tone: "That man has put an end to me."

The Gaucho always had a sense of pride and honor, and a strong equalitarian instinct, which was sadly lacking in other parts of Latin America. "While the allotments, *encomiendas,* and mines of Mexico, Peru, and Bolivia, tended only to wipe out or enslave the Indians, corrupt the Church, and create an indolent and privileged class, the wild cattle-filled pampas gave rise to a caste of strong, arrogant, and fiercely individualistic men, with marked equalitarian tendencies. Boss, foreman, and herder all worked together on the same task with lasso, knife, and *bolas.*"[106] The arrogance of the Argentine was not baseless; it was an affirmative statement of confidence and faith in himself.

The pampas forged the Gaucho into its spiritual mold. One Latin-American writer states that as landscape the pampas is "the most transcendent cosmic phenomenon which we find in the western hemisphere. It fulfilled the triple historic role of affording the means of life, of serving as the mold in which that life was fashioned, and of furnishing a never-ending inspiration for the nation's poetry and art."[106] The pampas was unity, and it gave its unity to the Gaucho. That is, it made each Gaucho follow the same economy, have the same philosophy of life, and the same cultural outlook. Its dissolvent endlessness embraced all who came to its bosom, made them over again in its own image, sharpened their sensibilities, strengthened their bodies, heightened their pride. It gave to the Gaucho a telluric quality which is the mainspring of all great folk cultures. It fused and absorbed completely racial and traditional differences and re-created every Gaucho on an enduring *Spanish and American* base.

The Englishman, Captain Head, who was on the pampas in 1825, gives a beautiful description of the wind passing over the wild expanse of waving grass, colored yellow and brown, with no habitation or human being as far as the eye could see. The pampas itself, boundless and free, was made up of two infinities: grassland and sky. Then, suddenly, a Gaucho appeared in picturesque outline against the horizon, his scarlet poncho streaming horizontally behind him, his bolas flying around his head, his horse straining every nerve. In front of him, at first a mere speck in the distance, was the wild ostrich he was chasing, its neck stretched out as it fled over the ground in the most magnificent style. The distance between the two was gradually diminishing as they passed behind the earth's rim. Perhaps the Gaucho let go his sling into the blue and brought the great runner to earth. Such an ostrich chase was one of the greatest delights of the herdsmen of the pampas.

Against this background of pampas and sky, wide as an eagle's flight, isolated from the ordinary channels of human association, but eternally close to the earth and to the infinity above, the Gaucho was bound to find solace and enjoyment in poetry and song. "He was a poet by temperament and by necessity." His guitar, or some variant of it, was his constant companion. Whether in his own small hut, or in a pulpería, or in the open air on the range, or even in the kitchen of a large ranch house, the guitar was there to serve as his alter ego. It gave expression to every facet of his being and was the only instrument he ever played.

There were some Indian elements in the Gaucho's folk culture, especially in the north, and many songs existed in both Quechua and Spanish. The monotonous and sad *yaraví*, with all its elegiac feeling, was carried over into some of the Gaucho songs. But for the most part Gaucho tradition was Spanish, Andalusian Spanish, and the songs, popular ballads and *coplas*, and dances of southern Spain were at the root and trunk of his own expression, while the pampas itself was at the flower.

The Gaucho expressed himself equally well in all three mediums: poetry, music, and dance. Poetry was pure expression; music was sublimation; dance was projection. They were frequently all woven into a single fabric. Dances took place at fiestas on the range, in the pulperías, later at the larger ranches, and finally even in the public plazas of the small towns. Sometimes there would also be a poetic contest called a *payada*, or *contrapunto*. One Gaucho would ask another a question in verse; the second had to answer it in the same vein, and then the turns would be reversed. Questions and answers would continue, until one of the two had won the contest, either by giving a better response, or by asking a question that his opponent could not satisfactorily answer.

On other occasions the men and women who were dancing carried on a kind of poetic dialogue, or perhaps the guitarist would serve both as accompanist and singer, calling out verses to suit his fancy. Many of the coplas sung or spoken at such dances had an erotic tinge, while others were lamentations of love, sadness, separation, nostalgia, and loss. One of the most frequently sung types of songs was the *vidalitá*, which reflected strong Quechua influences. The one below tells of a love that has gone, leaving behind only little fragments of life suffused with absence and sorrow. The singer says that no bird now announces the dawn, for even the lark is weeping for his sweetheart who has departed.

> *No hay rancho en el monte*
> > *vidalitá*
> *que florida esté,*
> *todos son despojos*
> > *vidalitá*
> *desde que se fué.*
>
> *No hay ave que alegre*
> > *vidalitá*
> *anuncie la aurora,*
> *hasta la calandria*
> > *vidalitá*
> *por su ausencia llora.*
>
> *Palomita blanca*
> > *vidalitá*
> *pecho colorado,*
> *llévale un suspiro*
> > *vidalitá*
> *a mi bien amado.*[107]

Impassioned love also spoke out in many of the Gaucho's songs, as for example in the lines: "I cannot see how the red carnations live on the volcano of your breast, under the fire of your eyes." The Spanish version runs:

> *Como viven no sospecho*
> *Niña, los claveles rojos*
> *Sobre el volcán de tu pecho,*
> *Bajo el fuego de tus ojos.*[108]

The Gaucho who so often took his love where he could find it, and in his independence was afraid of marriage, suspected all women of infidelity and would often sing such words as these: "They advise me to marry; that's what they'll never see, for I'll never give money to the priest that another Gaucho may enjoy my wife."

> *Me aconsejan que me case,*
> *eso es lo que no han de ver,*
> *que yo dé plata al cura*
> *pa que otro tenga mujer.*[109]

After the May Revolution in Buenos Aires, and while the ideas of liberty and country were being repeated everywhere, the Gaucho also composed ballads of a semi-political nature. One of these sings that "joy and liberty belong to the sky, and the sky gives us peace and union. Long live our patria, our independence, and our new nation."

Cielito, cielito y más cielo
Cielito siempre cantad,
Que la alegría es del cielo,
Del cielo es la libertad.

¡Viva la Patria, patriotas!
Viva la Patria y la Unión;
Viva nuestra Independencia,
Viva la Nueva Nación.

Cielo, cielo y más cielo,
Cielito del corazón,
Que el cielo nos da la paz,
Y el cielo nos da la Unión.[106]

This union which the sky gave was indeed the only kind of union that the Gaucho knew; it was a cultural union, an affinity which one Gaucho felt for all other Gauchos, without its binding them together. The union was not political, not social. The Gaucho was not a co-operative being. His cultural horizon was the endless pampas and the limitless sky, but his social and political horizon was his tiny region or province. His definition of nationality or nationhood meant himself above all others.

The Gaucho followed his semi-nomadic existence in a region where there were no schools, no churches, no industry, and almost no commerce. All communication was by horse. Without his horse the Gaucho could not have lived a pastoral life on the pampas. Distances were too great; the Indians were too savage; the grass was too tall and thick for travel on foot to be feasible. He could not possibly have utilized the wild cattle which became the economic basis of his existence had the horse not been his constant partner in the enterprise. To the Gaucho, then, the horse meant more than his wife, his children, his religion. His horse was a necessity; the other elements of his life were all luxuries. As one of the best Argentine poets put it, when writing of the Gaucho's attitude toward his steed: "My horse was my life, my love, my only treasure."

Mi caballo era mi vida,
Mi bien, mi único tesoro.

The Gaucho, therefore, bore only a superficial resemblance to our own cowboy so far as his historic and cultural significance was concerned. The cowboy followed civilization; the Gaucho preceded it. The cowboy arose as the partner of capitalism; the Gaucho bitterly opposed it. In some ways the Gaucho was more like our trapper or pioneer, but even this resemblance is mostly on the surface.

The Gaucho developed his animal skills to a degree perhaps never equaled by any other group of men in the world. As a tracker or pathfinder his knowledge and intuitions were truly incredible. The tracker (*rastreador*) could glance at footprints which had been made two years previously, take up the trail, and find his man. He could glance at the tracks left by dozens of horses and recognize at once if the animal he sought was among them.

The pathfinder (*baquiano*) could find his way even on the darkest night by smelling the earth or chewing a root, thus learning what kind of earth was under him. He could tell at a glance from a distance of many miles the best place to ford a river, and could look at a cloud of dust on the horizon and state how many men or animals were approaching. He could tell where water was to be found, even if it were many miles ahead and he had never been in that part of the country before.

Other types of Gauchos were the *cantor*, or singer, who composed ballads about the pampas and its legends, and the *gaucho malo*, or outlaw, who was a refugee from justice because of some "killing of honor." These killings, which were duels of man against man over some real or imaginary insult, were called *desgracias*, which meant "misfortunes." The Gaucho who was guilty of such an alleged crime, which was no crime to him, was forever afterward beyond the pale of the law. The Gaucho outlaw, of course, was a fairly late type on the pampas, because before the epoch of independence law was practically non-existent there.[110]

For two and a half centuries the Gaucho kept up a constant running fight with the Indians who lived on the pampas. Although he was usually part Indian in blood he never thought of himself as being identified with the native race; he was far closer to the Spaniard. Yet he despised the city Spaniard, who represented for him the city government, the police force, and the rural judges who were constantly after him for some real or alleged theft or killing.

He was, therefore, a sort of in-between type who lived in a no-man's land between urban civilization and the complete savagery of the Indian territory. He was the Argentine frontier both in flesh and in spirit. What the missions had done for the frontiers of other regions he accomplished for Argentina; that is, the slow expansion of territory and peoples included in the new orbit of life. The farther the Gaucho moved away from the cities, the more able was urban and country life to extend itself behind him with some degree of safety.

Sometimes the Gaucho who lived on the outermost rim of civilization existed under the constant menace of Indian attack. A sudden raid, or *malón*, might swoop down on him at any moment. One way to protect himself was to dig a wide but shallow ditch around his hut. The Indian would not dismount to cross it even though it might be only two or three feet deep. This protection was so effective that in 1874 a bill was presented to the Argentine Parliament to dig a ditch one hundred leagues in length along the entire Indian frontier so that the Indian would be kept out entirely.[111]

The Gaucho's best defense was his own strength and courage. He would fight bravely against whatever odds. In times of Indian attacks, when the Indians were on the warpath, several Gauchos would assemble and drive them off. These fights were not on a large scale, but they were fierce and bloody.

Thus, when Argentine independence came, the Gaucho was perfect clay for caudillo rule. He glorified strength, courage, stoicism. He was a savage fighter with only a regional horizon. He was one of the greatest stoics in history. Like the Spanish-born Seneca, Spaniards have always been stoics. Those who have nothing else to glory in, glory in their hard lives. It is a proof of their fiber, a tribute to their race. The Gaucho best carried on this tradition in America.

Even a stoic admires others who possess to a greater degree than himself those animal skills which he has elevated to the level of moral virtues. Therefore, as one of the finest Argentine writers of those days said: "The Argentine *caudillo* was a Mahoma, who could if he so wished change even the dominant religion and forge a new one. He has all powers." He was the leader of a region who gathered his Gaucho hordes behind him as the Tartar hordes of another day assembled behind their primitive Asiatic chieftains. When the revolution broke out it meant for him only one thing: a chance to be free of everybody, Spaniard and Creoles alike. Independence was synonymous with complete individual liberty, with absolute regional autonomy. That was what the Gaucho caudillo always said to those who followed him.

There could be no real national feeling in a hinterland with such sparse population. The Gauchos were too few in number and they lived too far apart. Isolation was their reason for existence. "The evil which besets Argentina is the evil of extension," wrote an Argentine who lived in those days. "The wilderness surrounds it on all sides; it works its way into the country's heart: solitude, the uninhabited plains which stretch for endless miles without a human dwelling, are the boundaries between provinces. Immensity is everywhere; the immense prairie, the immense forests, the immense rivers, the horizon always uncertain, always blending with the earth in a dim distance which does not and cannot define where the world ends and the sky begins."[110]

Under this immensity the Gauchos huddled in regions, no man trusting those who came from beyond the horizon. Each region had its prophet and its tyrant. The regions sometimes came together in groups of three or four under a particularly gifted caudillo. All regions stood against and in contrast to the cities.

There were really two kinds of civilization on a single soil. One was just being born, or had just been born, on the open plains. It was unconscious of what was hanging over its head and imitated the popular effects of the Middle Ages. The other, which was found in the cities, was attempting to realize the consolidation of European civilization. It did not see or failed to notice what was lying at its very feet. "The one was Spanish, European, truly civilized; the other was barbarous, American, almost indigenous. The revolution was only going to force these two remotely akin ways of life into each other's presence; it would make them attack each other, and after years of strife one would absorb the other."[110] These words of Sarmiento, who later became president of Argentina, were written in the 1840s, while the process was still fluid. At that time it seemed as if one current might absorb the other, but in reality a mutual absorption was what took place. Out of that clash emerged a new Argentina.*

Sarmiento called it the clash between civilization and barbarism, and he longed for civilization, the civilization of the cities, to win out over the barbarism of the pampas. He hated the Gaucho, ennobled the literate men from the cities. In spite of all this his famous book has done more to give the Gaucho immortality than anything else ever written. It was the prose epic of his country's formative youth, a strong, uncouth, but vibrant and richly blooded masterpiece. Its only rival for first place in Argentine and Spanish American literature is the famous Gaucho epic poem *Martín Fierro*, by José Hernández, which re-creates in lines of stirring beauty the epitome and the swan song of that unfortunate class.

It is clear that when the wars broke out in the provinces the Gauchos would make up most of the armies. They were inimitable duelists. Give them a leader they admired and a little discipline and they made excellent soldiers. Güemes in the north held back the Spaniards with his Gauchos; San Martín took his Gauchos over into Chile and up to Peru and conquered; Artigas controlled all of Uruguay with his Gaucho partisans; Rosas rode into power at the head of a Gaucho army, and when he was defeated another Gaucho army was responsible for the victory. In 1879, when General Julio Roca overcame the last stand of the pampas Indians in the south, it was at the head of another Gaucho army. Gaucho blood ran red over the whole territory of Argentina.

What was happening back of all the fighting in the River Plate territory was this: in 1810 the cities declared war on their Spanish overlords. They won that fight, and independence was the reward of their victory. Even before victory was achieved the hinterland, under the caudillos, had declared its own war against the cities, in order to free themselves of urban political domination. They won their fight also, at least temporarily, and the reward of their victory was a federal rather than a unitarian form of government. However, as federalism proved unworkable their victory was in the end illusory; it led straight to dictatorship.

Further confusion was added to the picture because of the tremendous difference that existed between the Gaucho level of life and the level of

* Sarmiento's book is entitled *Facundo; Civilización y barbarie en la República Argentina,* 1845.

life in the cities. The urban centers fought for political democracy. Even those royalists of Buenos Aires, who favored a monarchy, wanted a constitutional monarchy which they believed would best insure this political democracy. On the other hand, the Gauchos had no conception of political democracy, at least they had no conception of such a thing on a national scale. It was simply beyond their knowledge. They did know and practice a far greater degree of *social* democracy among themselves than the city intellectuals who sprang largely from the better families. Not until these two distrustful and discordant conceptions were forced together could there emerge a national state.

43
JUAN MANUEL DE ROSAS: TYRANT OF THE ARGENTINE

Juan Manuel de Rosas, the despot who hammered these inorganic elements of civilization and barbarism into the shape of a nation, was not himself a Gaucho. He came of good stock, in fact belonged to one of the best families of the La Plata region. There might possibly have been a drop of Indian blood in his veins, but it did not show. Rosas was a blond with blue eyes and clear-cut Spanish features. His father had achieved only a mediocre success, first as a captain in the King's army, then as a rancher. His mother had plans for the son to work in a store in order to learn the business, but young Rosas rebelled. Then the mother, one of those dominating types who run their families with a strong hand, locked the boy up and put him on bread and water, announcing that he was to stay there until he had changed his mind. When night came the rebellious youngster took off all his clothes, piled them up carefully, scribbled on a piece of paper, "I'm leaving behind everything that doesn't belong to me," and escaped stark naked. He signed his name Juan Manuel Rosas. The family name was Rozas, spelled with the letter z, but young Rosas already despised everything Spanish and everything traditional. That adolescent act announced the man to come.[112]

He received help and some clothes from relatives, and was put to work in the open fields. Shortly thereafter, in 1815, when he was only twenty-two years old, Rosas established the first meat-salting plant in the province of Buenos Aires. His business was eminently successful; so much so, in fact, that the ranchers began to fear that the young fellow would make more out of salted beef than they could ever make from hides and tallow, and laws were passed putting an end to the business. Then Rosas bought a considerable extent of land and undertook a more typical rancher's life on his own estate.

He soon learned the one great essential of success on the wild and limit-less pampas: *to command.* In order to command his wild Gauchos, Rosas became one of them. He adopted the Gaucho language, the Gaucho dress and habits, and was able to best any one of his workers in breaking in broncos, in his skill with the rope or bolas, or in any show of brute strength. Under him worked as wild a band of Gauchos as had ever been assembled on the pampas. When they were first hired many of them were army de-serters and ex-convicts, with little desire to perform efficient labor as cow hands. Rosas soon changed that. He gave them good quarters, fair treat-ment, no more work than a man could reasonably be expected to perform, but he was uncompromising in what was demanded in return. Drunken-ness, idleness, or the slightest theft was punished with a rigor not always according to best traditions of civilization. Before long, however, Rosas's Gauchos came to respect and fear him, hence almost to love him, for to them strength and skill were the highest measuring rods for appraising a man's worth and character. The estate of Rosas became one of the best run and one of the most peaceful and productive on the entire pampas.

Rosas himself had none of the minor vices. He was frugal even in his sex life—a rare thing for a strong man in any Latin-American country. He drank seldom, and always in moderation. To him, as to many dictators cast in the same mold, minor weaknesses were a subtraction from efficiency, from the one great ideal, which was to command men. Therefore, they could not be permitted. Nothing besmirched the legend which Rosas, first as the boss of a troop of Gauchos, then as general and finally as dictator, began carefully to build up around himself.

With the arrival of the terrible year 1820, when chaos and civil war broke out everywhere in Argentina, Rosas threw his authority behind the prin-ciples of law and order. He headed a regiment of Gaucho *colorados,* or "reds," so known because of the deep red color of the uniforms they wore. Out of that morass of anarchy Rosas and his men emerged with colors fly-ing, not only because of their discipline in battle, which was admirable, but because of their discipline after battle, which was unique and incredible. The young Gaucho leader rapidly became a national figure.

A few years later, at the end of the war with Brazil, an incident occurred which opened the door for the entrance of Rosas into the political lime-light. The army, which had returned from its victorious campaign in Uru-guay under General Lavalle, revolted when it reached Buenos Aires; the intention of these troops was to place their general in control of the gov-ernment in the capital city. The actual head of the government, Dorrego, was backed by Rosas and other Gaucho leaders. Before they could get organized General Lavalle and his hard-hitting, mutinous army struck a severe blow, captured Dorrego, and executed him in cold blood. The duly-elected governor of the province of Buenos Aires was thus displaced by a mutinous general. This took place in 1828, and from that time forward co-operative or democratic government became impossible in the Argentine. The struggle moved into the unknown arena of opposing bands without principles where the supreme prize was power for the sake of power.

This was a game that Rosas played with consummate skill. First of all, he turned himself into the public avenger and, with the aid of other Gaucho leaders, met and defeated General Lavalle, who was forced into exile. The door was wide open for Rosas to become governor of Buenos Aires, and in 1829 the legislature elected him to that office. Strictly speaking, it was a victory of the interior provinces over the seaboard and Buenos Aires, of federalism over the unitarian ideal, but actually neither principles, regions, nor ideas counted any longer. The people were weary of bloodshed and unstable government, and the only man on the horizon who might give peace was Rosas. He would have come to power no matter what he represented.

Rosas was inaugurated amid the wildest enthusiasm; he was the savior of his country, the restorer of its laws. The citizens of Buenos Aires, grateful for being rescued from the abyss of utter lawlessness and destruction, decided to strike off a medal commemorating the event. Below the bust of Rosas were to be placed these words: "He cultivated the fields and defended the Fatherland." Rosas was touched by this show of affection, but refused the honor. Like Dr. Francia, he announced his hatred of all such trimmings which lead toward despotism. "This is not the first time," he said, "when prodigality in the distribution of honors has stimulated public men until they reached the level of tyrants."[42]

Before many months had passed the new governor was called upon to meet his first great test. The forces in favor of a unitarian regime had been gathering strength, and under the distinguished General La Paz were prepared to challenge the control of Rosas and others who espoused the federal ideal. The Gaucho federalists assembled their men as quickly as possible and went forth to meet the challenge. Their troops were not nearly so well trained as those under La Paz, and the outcome was unpredictable. On May 1, 1831, the two forces faced each other across the plain on which the future of the nation was to be decided. General La Paz, full of confidence, mounted his fastest horse and sallied out to reconnoiter the battlefield and to gather information as to the disposition of the federal troops. It was the greatest mistake he ever made. The Gauchos of Rosas caught a glimpse of him and were soon hot on his heels. The general's horse was faster than any of theirs, and for a moment it looked as if he might elude them. Then a Gaucho who was proud of his skill with the Argentine bolas whirled this weapon around his head and let go at the legs of La Paz's horse. Horse and rider fell in a scrambled heap. The Gauchos hurried to the scene and took captive the commander of the opposing army. After that the unitarian cause was hopeless. A well-aimed bolas had cleared the last great obstacle from the path of Rosas.

The popular governor served out the remainder of his three-year term to the great satisfaction of the citizens of Buenos Aires. That a Gaucho federalist should have come out of the hinterland to give them their first durable centralized government seemed in no way an anomaly. The immense majority were strong for a second term, but Rosas pointedly refused re-election. He was waiting for better times.

Another governor was inaugurated, and Rosas was placed in command of an army which was sent to subdue the natives along the Indian frontier. For a time he dropped from public sight, but reports of his hard life and victories continued to reach the capital with sufficient frequency to keep his name in the public mind. When, after an absence of several months, he returned to Buenos Aires, the populace received him as a national hero.

Rosas was clearly the strong man behind the scenes, and nearly every element contributed to raise his star to final ascendancy. Conditions were still turbulent in Buenos Aires and throughout the country. The old jealousies were rampant; there was no such thing as the supremacy of impersonal law. Every region was under a caudillo, and every caudillo was a law unto himself. Bloody regional wars had become the norm of everyday life. Fierce Gaucho herdsmen armed with lances, bolas, and knives, charged at each other like packs of tigers. All who were captured had their throats slit from ear to ear as if they were wild cattle. If a caudillo was taken, his head was cut off and displayed on a pole in the nearest town. In the face of this complete savagery the governor of Buenos Aires, finding himself powerless, resigned from office in 1834. The legislature promptly appointed Rosas to take his place, and the people hoped that he would again rescue them from anarchy. This time Rosas was playing for higher stakes. He refused even to consider the offer. The legislature urged that he accept it as a favor to his country. Again he refused. The same offer and same refusal were made twice more, and then another governor was named.

At this point the strongest caudillo of the interior, Facundo Quiroga, whose name has been emblazoned on the black pages of legend in the famous book of Sarmiento, was invited to Buenos Aires. It was hoped that he might be able to restore the authority of the capital city in the northern regions. Quiroga came, was feted, and departed on his mission. Many of his friends warned him to keep a careful lookout for the wiles of his enemies, but Quiroga paid no attention to them. On February 16, 1835, while in the province of Córdoba, a band of soldiers rode up and surrounded the carriage in which he was riding. Quiroga stuck his head out and demanded to know what was going on. A bullet which caught him squarely in the face was his answer.

The author of the assassination has never been clearly revealed, but there was only one man who profited from it. That man was Rosas. Quiroga was his only possible rival in the entire territory of the Argentine provinces.

Less than a month later political conditions had become so intolerable that the recently appointed governor of Buenos Aires resigned, stating as he did so that it was no longer possible for him to preserve order. This time the legislature went to Rosas and offered him what he had been waiting for: *la suma del poder*, the sum total of the governing power, with no strings attached. Rosas was now ready to accept, but before rendering his final decision he insisted that the people vote on the issue. The whole city turned out and flooded the urns with a "yes" vote which was almost unanimous. Fascinated by the symbol of this stalwart Gaucho leader, the public insisted that he rule over them with his rod of iron. And Rosas, for his part, on accepting the position and seeing the triumph of his federal cause, thought as follows: "Federation is a kind of providence for the masses, a tame and earthy god, a very Gaucho divinity which they seem to understand and are anxious to follow."

An Argentine historian, commenting on the rise of typical caudillos to power, states that they always went through three phases: fascination, force, peace. The last stage was *imposed* by the first two. Rosas had passed through the first stage with colors flying. He was ready for the second.

For the first five years—that is, up to 1840—Rosas did not greatly abuse his power. He consolidated his position, met and defeated those who challenged his authority, and purged only the leading figures who opposed him. From 1840 to 1852, the date of his downfall, he put into effect a "reign of terror" which was one of the bloodiest in the history of any American nation.

Throughout the entire period of the dictatorship the principal element in opposition to Rosas was the small intellectual minority composed of the literary lights of the new country. They were young men, imbued with the romantic ideals of liberty, equality, and fraternity, but they exercised little political power. They did organize themselves into a literary salon, which later became a political-action committee called the *Asociación de Mayo* (May Brotherhood), and through it sought to further the ideals of free government. They called on all patriots to cast aside party labels and join them. The leader of this group was Argentina's best-known romantic poet, Echeverría, who was also the first representative of the romantic movement in Spanish South America.

Echeverría had traveled widely in Europe, had been in France when romanticism was at its height, and, while there, had felt the sharpening of his own national poetic sensibilities. He was also an ardent admirer of Lord Byron, and made a special trip to England in order to become acquainted with the country which had given birth to this idol. Byron's identification with the liberal political movements in Europe undoubtedly had a great effect on the young and impressionable Argentine's mind. On his return to his native land, in the year 1830, Echeverría published some romantic verses which gained him great favor. In the foreword of one of his volumes he stated that poetry in the New World should "take on the true and original character of the physical nature which surrounds us, and should be a living picture of our customs and the highest expression of our dominant ideas and of the passions and sentiments which arise from the immediate clash of our social interests." Echeverría became known as "the poet of the pampas," and especially in his *La Cautiva* (The Captive) evokes the stirring landscape of that great solitude which characterizes the country and impinges on the very city of Buenos Aires.

Echeverría took advantage of his prestige as a poet to become leader of the anti-Rosas faction in a political sense; he was the principal organizer of the May Brotherhood. This was in 1837. Rosas did not lose any time in getting after him. Echeverría fled first to the country, then to Montevideo, where he became one of a large number of distinguished exiles.

Throughout Rosas's "reign of terror" the civil opposition of this small intellectual group continued to grow in scope. First one, then another of the young liberal writers fled from the wrath of the tyrant. They flooded Montevideo, Bolivia, Chile, even Brazil. They included two future presidents of the Argentine nation, two of the greatest men ever to hold that high office, Mitre and Sarmiento. Among them, also, were Alberdi, whose essays on government and economics were the basis for the future constitution of the republic; José Mármol, author of the best-known Argentine novel; Juan María Gutiérrez, Rivera Indarte, Juan Cruz Varela, López y Planes, and many other writers of note. These exiles formed a veritable Argentine Pleiad in their foreign habitats, and ranged the length and breadth of the continent, penning and voicing their diatribes against Rosas. In Montevideo they held literary gatherings, poetic contests, gave prizes to the best writer, and continued to keep alive the fires of hatred of the Rosas tyranny. When the day of liberation finally arrived they were in the forefront of the struggle, some of them on the field of battle. The pens which they wielded undoubtedly contributed a great deal to the downfall of the national despot.

These writers gloried in attacking Rosas with exaggerated anathema, casting verbal vitriol on his every act, good as well as bad. Echeverría himself wrote a prose sketch called *The Slaughter House* in which the symbol of Rosas's men as indiscriminate slaughterers of human beings or cattle is made crystal clear. In another work, *Socialist Dogma*, he defines his political ideals. The novelist and poet, José Mármol, wrote in exile his famous novel *Amalia*, a blood-and-thunder melodrama through whose pages runs the story of the hated tyrant. In the end its sympathetic hero and heroine are caught in a trap and murdered by the minions of Rosas. For further vilification of the dictator there are some choice paragraphs describing a scene in his private household when, in order to prove his sense of democracy, the tyrant forces his daughter to embrace and kiss a repulsive and filthy mulatto servant. There is no reason for the act in the story itself, and it certainly had no basis in fact. It is simply a clear-cut example of anti-

Rosas propaganda which did not hesitate even to play on the dynamite of racial feeling in order to gain its ends. The dictator himself and the members of his family are painted with broad, crude strokes as sadistic perverts whose greatest enjoyment seems to be in the suffering of others.

At one point in the novel Mármol summarizes briefly the reasons for the triumph of Rosas by having one of the sympathetic characters point out how few persons are willing to stick by their guns in time of stress. At first, he says, the anti-Rosas meetings were well attended, and the enthusiasm was great. Then gradually attendance fell off, people were afraid to come, suspicion sprang up among them, and finally opposition became a dead issue and flight remained as the only possible action. "This is the philosophy of the dictatorship of Rosas," writes Mármol. "Our habits of disunion, even in the highest and most cultivated brackets of society; our lack of co-operation in everything and for everything; our lives of uncompromising individualism; our apathy; our negligence; our egoism; our utter ignorance as to the importance of collective strength; all this is what enables Rosas to remain in power, without there being half a dozen men who will clasp each other's hands in order to defend themselves united."

The other famous anti-Rosas diatribe was the work entitled *Facundo; Civilization and Barbarism in the Argentine Republic*, by Domingo Faustino Sarmiento, who was later to become one of his nation's most loved presidents. In this book, which is both a sociological study of Argentine life in the first part of the nineteenth century and an attack on caudillo rule, Sarmiento presents the monsters of regional tyranny in terms which call to mind the worst phase of the old Spanish Inquisition. The author is a master of propaganda, and there has probably never appeared in the history of mankind a work which embodies both invective and literary value to the extent of Sarmiento's *Facundo*. There is little of unified study to the book; the author lunges forward, using his pen as lance or lancet, ripping off the diseased skin of his nation as he sees it from his exile in Chile. The resultant picture is gripping and horrible.

The two characters who stand out in the book are Facundo Quiroga, caudillo of the plains, who at one time had eight provinces under his thumb, and Rosas himself. Quiroga's atrocities are described in detail. From the very first moment when he strikes his teacher in the face and runs off from school, up to the time of his assassination from ambush, this primitive Gaucho leader stands as the symbol of the barbarism of the pampas which thrives on cruelties, murder, and the lust for power. His cry raised against the centralized ideal of Rivadavia is "Liberty or death!" But in actuality he is the enemy of all social discipline, bloodthirsty and terrible.

Rosas himself emerges as another Quiroga, polished up a bit for city consumption, but equally bloody and even more cunning. Sarmiento's entire work might be regarded as descriptive of the birth pangs of his nation, drawn out and perhaps exaggerated as to detail, but nevertheless of such a great sweep and strength that it has become the real *Iliad* of nascent Argentina.

Sarmiento tells us that the atrocities of Quiroga and Rosas did not spring from any perverted desire to see human beings suffer, nor was their blood-thirstiness a mere bestial diversion. When they killed, it was for a purpose. Necessarily, they had to execute those leaders who opposed them, and even their murders of apparently innocent persons had a clear-cut goal. The victims were carefully chosen, being "perhaps a blind man, a paralytic, or a poor nobody of a sexton. . . . The motive for these killings was none other than *to make of terror a system of government.*" It was a far more efficient system than that raised upon the shoulders of patriotism, love of country, or any other spontaneous sentiment.

Terror in the days of the French Revolution, continues Sarmiento, was an effect and not an instrument; Robespierre did not guillotine nobles and priests in order to create a reputation for himself nor to raise himself on the corpses which he piled up. Terror then was synonymous with the amputation of every aristocratic member of a gangrenous body politic. It was the only way to save the trunk and mind of the state and to cement the revolution. "Our names will be execrated by posterity," cried Danton, "but we shall have saved the Republic."

But terror in the Argentina of Rosas was "an invention of the government to stifle all conscience, to blot out every civilized feeling, and finally to force men to recognize as the thinking head the very foot which stood upon their gasping throats." It was concerted barbarism, pure and simple, revenging itself on an unorganized people whose superiority the savage caudillo despised and feared. It was the mad action of the Roman Emperor Caligula in modern garb, the atavism which seems to break out in the world somewhere or other once in every generation, throwing all the carefully laid plans and structures of civilization into a turmoil.

Sarmiento did not believe that the caudillo as a person was important, but as a symptom of a national disease he was all important. "When evil exists," he wrote, "it is because it is in the *condition of things,* and there only should one go to seek it out. When a single man comes to represent evil, and we cause that personification to disappear, it will only emerge again with another face. Caesar, assassinated, was reborn more terrible than ever in Octavius."[110]

Rosas was symptomatic of a turbulent, ignorant, and inorganic state. He was an astute demagogue who knew all the popular passions. He served these passions and then turned them to the service of his own personal ambition for power. He made himself the instrument of the people in order later to make the people his own instrument. With terror and violence as his two watchdogs he knew how to take advantage of all the trappings of dictatorial government.

In the heart of the republic the color red flowered everywhere. Red was the uniform of the soldier, red the banner of his armies, and red the national badge which signified membership in the right party. The primitive Gaucho loved this brilliant color, say some, because it reminded him of the dripping fresh blood of a newly killed steer, his height of enjoyment. Every good Rosas federalist wore a red ribbon as a symbol of his political beliefs, and woe to him or her who showed up in public without it. In reality those red badges were but outward and visible signs of the terror which gripped the hearts of the people. But not all of the people. Rosas befriended the lower classes, was adored by his Gauchos, and the Negroes were his faithful servants. Through these blacks he had a spy in nearly every household. Racial equality was enforced upon the citizens of Buenos Aires. Only to the thinking classes was the mention of his name a Damoclean sword, ready to drop upon them at any moment. With Rosas as leader, the common people took great delight in putting the city folk in their proper places.

For the furtherance of the tyrant's political ideal a secret society called the *Mazorca* was founded. Its job was to ferret out all who sympathized with the unitarian cause and turn them over to the government police. Many members of the Mazorca entered the anti-Rosas camp and, by speaking loudly against their chief, discovered secrets which they might not have learned in any other fashion. The name itself meant an "ear of corn," and to the members of the society this signified that they were all as closely united for the sacred cause as were the grains of corn on a single ear. To the unitarians the name came to signify gallows (*más horca*), for the pronunciation of the word in the Spanish American manner also gave it that meaning.

In addition to his society of spies, his Negro and mulatto partisans who worked as servants in the best homes, and his own army and police, Rosas also had prisons which were always kept full. They were places of horrible suffering. Inmates were not only chained up in veritable sewers of filth, but were half starved, fed on a diet of putrid meat, frequently tortured, and every day or so the guards would come around to carry off a couple to be executed. Packs of dogs, writes one who escaped from the Rosas tyranny, had the sole duty of cleaning these places; they howled through the corridors and in the yards, lapping up the blood of persons who had been tormented or slain. The corpses of those who had been executed or who had died were tossed into a cart, hauled away to a near-by field, and piled in a ditch with no marker to show where they were buried. Their families were not allowed even to mark with a cross the place of their interment, and wearing mourning for a person slain by the order of Rosas was a crime in itself. The same writer, whose pages furnish the details for the above description, makes the following list of the victims of Rosas's reign of terror:

Poisoned	4
Shot	1,393
Hanged	3,765
Assassinated	722
Killed in armed clashes	16,520
Total killed	22,404

Rivera Indarte, who drew up these figures, was one of those who was fortunate enough to escape to Montevideo. There is no way in the world of either proving or disproving his estimates; but even if submitted to a deduction of 50 per cent they would still be appalling, for the whole city of Buenos Aires had at that time a population of only 60,000. One person killed out of every three inhabitants (or one out of every six) would be a fair record even for a more up-to-date dictator.

Another characteristic of Rosas, which also applies to the more modern tyrant, was his manner of speech. "His style was rough and unequal, but he often made use of high-sounding polished clichés which had no real meaning. His speeches were never clear or straight to the point; they were diffuse, complicated with digressions and incidental phrases. His wordiness was obviously premeditated and aimed at confusing his interlocutor. It was, indeed, almost impossible to follow just what he had in mind. . . . Rosas would show himself in turn to be the consummate statesman, a very affable and sympathetic person, a fine dialectician, a vehement and impassioned orator. He was possessed in turn, and according to his mood, by raging anger, simplicity, or the utmost candor. He always spoke with the ulterior motive of intimidating, deceiving, or swaying his listener to accept his own point of view."[112]

Change the name Rosas to Hitler or Mussolini and the same sentences would equally apply. It was the dictator psychology at work, the pathological despot who, despite all his seemingly high-strung lack of direction, invariably heads toward a single goal. His concern is to divide his opponents, unite his followers, strike fear and misgiving into the skeptics, and maintain his power over the majority.

Rosas, more specifically, had cut out for himself the task of subduing the Gaucho barbarism of the pampas and of imposing his own brand of Gaucho barbarism on the city elite. He proclaimed the doctrine of regional autonomy and achieved power as the symbol of Argentine federalism. He would never permit the name "unitarian" to be mentioned in his presence without some derogatory adjective. The phrase must be "those savage bloodletting dogs of unitarians," or "those filthy unitarian swine," or "those bastardly unitarian destroyers of the fatherland." He wanted such adjectives repeated, he said, "to satiety, to boredom, to exhaustion." Yet in all this Rosas was not really pursuing his espoused federal ideal. He was merely utilizing an excellent psychological point to further his own demagogic sway. As one of his own countrymen wrote: "He called himself a federalist, and was a firm centralizer; he proclaimed the fatherland, and was a regional tyrant; he spoke of a Holy American Cause, when no one had the slightest designs against America." He changed his colors like a chameleon, and always managed to reflect the majority hue.

Rosas has at different times been called by Spanish American writers "the Machiavelli of the pampas," "the Argentine Nero," "the Louis XI of Argentine history." He was indeed a tyrant who suggests all these persons. Perhaps the Peruvian, García Calderón, hit the nail on the head when he wrote that idealistic Rivadavia was thesis, the powerful Gaucho despot Facundo antithesis, and Rosas synthesis.

Rosas governed by making use of the hatred of the masses for the classes and by getting the Church on his side. He invited the Jesuits back into the country, and they supported him ardently. Any authoritarianism under the Rosas regime was a prop for Rosas.

In spite of his personal tyrannies Rosas was a good administrator; he punished public dishonesty with great vigor. He got under way a large public-works program, gave the country an orderly and progressive economic policy, and never sought to enrich himself by exploiting others. When he entered upon his dictatorship, he was one of his nation's wealthiest men; when he was defeated and exiled, he was obviously poor. From an economic standpoint "his invulnerable dictatorship was based on material progress and fiscal order."

Whether Rosas's regime was "a necessary terror," as some Latin-American writers think, it would be hard to say. Argentina might have attained nationhood through anarchy just as well as through Rosas. Repeated defeats of the unitarian ideal might have led eventually to its triumph when the citizens wearied of chaos. But such considerations as these are based on pure suppositions; they are not history.

Although Rosas came to power merely as the governor of Buenos Aires, not as the head of all the Argentine provinces, he gradually extended his power throughout the entire territory. The murder of the "tiger of the pampas," Facundo Quiroga, in 1835, was his last big hurdle. Thenceforth he stood before the country as the champion of the federal ideal. Many thought that he would soon draw up a federal constitution which would allow the provinces the local autonomy for which they had so long fought against the centralizing folk of Buenos Aires. When Quiroga himself spoke in favor of a true federal organization, Rosas said to him, "A federal republic is a chimera and a disaster unless the federated states are well organized, well trained in self-government, and closely knit." After that, every time a federal constitution was mentioned, Rosas simply replied: "It is not yet time." And it was never time. Many years later, when he was in exile, one of his friends remarked to him: "It is a pity that we were never able to organize the country on a constitutional basis." Rosas promptly responded: "That was never my intention." With Caesar-like cunning he saw that so long as the provinces, federated in name only, were governed without a constitution, Buenos Aires would enjoy the supreme authority. But if a federation were constitutionally organized, the capital could easily be outvoted by the hinterland. Rosas might be able to control those votes, and he might not. He decided to take no chances.

The tyrant enjoyed his power for a total of twenty-three years, from 1829 to 1852, and his "sum total of power" for the last seventeen years of that period. Yet "invulnerable" as Rosas seemed to be while he was dictator, his authority was gradually being weakened. Almost from the very first moment the intellectuals saw through his demagogy. After opposing it without success they fled into exile, where distance, separation, and loss gave them more strength and a better perspective than they could ever have achieved otherwise. Persecution and exile also forced them to stand together, to learn co-operation the hard way, to recognize that unimportant differences must never be allowed to break down the essential and fundamental aspirations of a group. Exile welded them into a unity which they had not known before. It taught them to see their country as it really was, not as they wished it to be. When they returned, after being passed through this trying crucible, they were able to give Argentina its first truly democratic government.

Meanwhile, they not only improved their own position, but fought unceasingly against Rosas. Their campaign carried the infamy of his name from one end of the continent to the other. Even inside Buenos Aires their writings were known and were effective.

Among the Gauchos, too, the slow realization of what Rosas was doing began to take root. He had indeed imposed their barbarism and their feeling for federal autonomy on Buenos Aires, but it was only to feed back to them the sop of a federalism in name, not a real federation. The capital city remained the head of the body politic; it was everything and they were nothing. It squatted there near the mouth of the great river like some colossus of old, eternally on guard lest the pampas break through to the sea. This was no mere symbol; it was a deadly fact. All of their products had to pass through Buenos Aires, both going and coming, hence the will of the city meant life or death for the provinces. The Gauchos did not reason this out, but they knew it was so.

By mid-century Rosas was on his last legs. Even his stanchest supporters were wearying of their tyrant. General Urquiza, governor of the province of Entre Ríos, who had at first seconded every move of the dictator, now turned against him. The federation Rosas had promised was a farce; the man to whom the whole nation had given its unlimited confidence had proven unworthy of the trust. He had indeed saved the country from anarchy, but he had given it chains.

In 1851 Urquiza put his feelings into words and issued a formal pro-
nunciamento. After referring to Rosas as a man of sinister intentions who
had "elevated himself above the ruins of national dignity, shattering into
fragments the glorious heritage of our country," Urquiza called upon the
"confederated peoples" to rise with him against the tyrant and throw off
their yoke.

The response was instantaneous. The province of Entre Ríos, which
Urquiza governed, furnished over 10,000 men; Corrientes 5000 more; there
were over 4000 soldiers from Buenos Aires itself willing to do battle with
Rosas; Brazil sent over 4000 troops, and Uruguay furnished another 2000.
Urquiza's first military act was to raise the siege of Montevideo, around
which Rosas's men had been encamped for nearly ten years. The blockade
had never been 100 per cent effective, but it had been a sharp thorn in
the side of Uruguay, Brazil, and northern Argentina. Then the general
led his men toward Monte Caseros to face the army led by Rosas.

Mitre, who was commander of the artillery of Urquiza, later wrote that
the battle was won before it was fought. Sarmiento, penetrating beneath
the surface of the Rosas regime, wrote as follows: "Buenos Aires was not
defending tyranny, nor was it defending liberty in the battle of Monte
Caseros. It was defending a cause which was far older than the dictatorship of Rosas and which was to survive that dictatorship—the cause of the
monopoly of foreign trade and hence of the treasury of the entire nation
which the tyrant of Buenos Aires exploited, and which later his successors
in the local government also attempted to exploit."

That was hitting the nail on its head. Buenos Aires enjoyed a natural
monopoly of the country's commerce. Its geographic position made this
inevitable. Once the megalomania was begun it became well-nigh impossible to stop it. Argentina would have to struggle for years with this colossus sitting upon its windpipe.

As the two armies met on the field of Monte Caseros nobody fought
truly for Rosas. Even the Gauchos, who had once felt only limitless admiration for their leader, were now only half heartedly behind him. Ideas
clashed in this battle, not firearms or soldiers. The defenders of monopoly
knew that they were also the defenders of tyranny and had no stomach
for the fight. Money at the price of a despot's heel had undermined the
morale of even the meanest soldier. The allied army under Urquiza, supported by the zeal for freedom which lives in every man, and driven by
the certain knowledge that they must either conquer or die, made the decision inevitable.

Rosas was defeated; he wrote out his resignation, hurriedly returned to
Buenos Aires, boarded an English ship, and sailed for Southampton
(1852). While at sea he was asked by a curious Englishman if he did not
believe that some of his measures had been a bit too despotic. Rosas
snorted in reply: "It was all that those people deserved."

He and his daughter lived for many years in exile in England, and the tyrant himself did not die until the ripe old age of eighty-four.

General Urquiza convoked an assembly to draw up a constitution, and in 1853 the new document was promulgated. It was a compromise between the extreme unitarian and the extreme federalist viewpoints. This time it was Buenos Aires that rebelled, preventing complete union. The inhabitants of the capital were afraid to take an "equal" role in the national government, which would have meant that they could be outvoted and their economic interests jeopardized by the provinces. Urquiza defeated the army sent out against him, but could not capture the capital itself. For the following six years he was president of the interior provinces, while Buenos Aires remained independent. Argentina had in reality split up into two countries.

The hinterland, now unified and ripe for progress, began to move determinedly forward. It would have a long way to go before it could catch up with the wealthy capital. Nevertheless, Buenos Aires, feeling that it might ultimately be cut off from its source of wealth, observed this progress with fearsome misgiving. In 1859, and again in 1861, there were armed clashes between the capital and the provinces. In the first of these Buenos Aires was forced back into the federation, and in the second the federation was forced to observe a more conciliatory attitude toward the great port province. In that final battle General Mitre led the forces of the seaboard against those of the interior, and his victory cleared the way for a permanent settlement of the issue. In 1862 Mitre was elected president of a united Argentina, and in that year the nation began its forward march with all elements working together under his progressive and liberal leadership.

The political significance of the Rosas regime was that it pushed the country toward unity: by forcing unity and peace upon those who remained in the national territory, by sharpening the love of liberty and democratic unity of those who lived in exile, by giving the country an efficient government, by teaching all Argentines both within and without that despotism was a high price to pay for rescue from anarchy.

On the economic side of the ledger the account is not so easy to read. Rosas helped to mold a stronger national economy, but he was hardly conscious of what he was doing. His economic program was pump priming all the way, a stopgap at best, never a permanent or farseeing plan.

Behind all of his outward and visible improvements the real economic struggle was going on. Capitalism was slowly displacing a feudal pastoral society. Agriculture and huge cattle *estancias*, or ranches, were displacing the wild Gaucho. The frontier was fast moving toward its final liquidation.

The city was apparently on the march against the hinterland, but the two were really fusing into a national whole.

Perhaps the most important single element in this whole setup, at least from an immediate point of view, was the introduction of barbed wire. Rosas was in no way responsible for this, but it had a greater effect on Argentine economic life than anything else which took place throughout his dictatorship.

In 1845 an Englishman named Richard Newton brought the first barbed wire into the pampas. He had a difficult time finding posts to which to attach it, and sent to the northern Chaco regions for a goodly supply. Then began the fencing in of the Argentine prairie. The public domain of the nation was doomed to its death. So were the wild horses and cattle. So was the Gaucho.

This did not happen all at once, but from the day Newton built his first fence across the pampas it became clear that the old unbridled way of life was soon to be a memory.

Without barbed wire the transition of the pampas from a purely pastoral to a semi-agricultural region would have been delayed many years. Sufficient timber was not available on the pampas for the construction of hundreds of miles of fences, and extensive agriculture was impossible without fencing. Wild quadrupeds would trample down the freshly planted fields and ruin all prospects of a decent harvest.

With the aid of barbed wire agriculture quickly became an important industry. It brought with it new necessities which were to alter fundamentally the complexion of the national life. First of all, agricultural lands had to be made secure from Indian attack. Consequently, the frontier must be advanced, government forts must be established, and that line of defense must gradually become a line of offense, pushing the native savage farther and farther away from the planted fields. Second, agricultural laborers would be needed to till the newly secured soil. The Gaucho would never perform this work, so European immigrants became a necessity.

Under Rosas these two processes got off to a hesitant start. Barbed wire was imported in 1845. In 1850 a line of mud forts was established along the Indian frontier garrisoned by government soldiers, mostly conscripted Gauchos. The principal frontier was to the south of Buenos Aires, and step by step the savages were pushed in the direction of the arid wastelands of southern Patagonia. Argentina's southern expansion paralleled that of the United States westward toward the Pacific. Rosas merely began the process; not until the days of President Sarmiento (1868–74) did national expansion become a settled government policy.

Because of the dictatorship, immigration during the Rosas regime was held to a minimum. Nevertheless, the population of the country was increased by approximately 200,000 during the reign of the tyrant. The growth of Buenos Aires was proportionately much greater, jumping from about sixty to ninety thousand in the same period. By way of comparison the population of the United States grew from about five million in the year 1800 to nearly twenty-five million just after the half century.

In the ten years that passed between the final defeat of Rosas and the elevation of Mitre to the presidency of a united Argentina (1852–62), a primitive society of mutually distrustful provinces was groping its way forward toward political union and social democracy. Oftentimes within the same region the partisans of federalism and the partisans of a strong central government squared off against each other in opposite camps. Ideas, regions, and personalities were simmering noisily in the crucible of nationhood.

It would be many years before these antagonistic elements were finally blended into a single whole. Real Argentine unity belonged to another generation. Nevertheless, the intelligent people of the country, particularly those who had lived in exile and so viewed Argentine life in its stark perspectives, were beginning to realize just what problems confronted their nation.

Juan Bautista Alberdi, the country's greatest jurist, who was more responsible than anybody else for the constitutional organization of Argentina, wrote the following words in exile: "We are incapable of either perfect federation or of a perfect unitarian government, because we are poor, we are insufficiently educated, we are few. . . . Democracy itself fits in badly with our conditions, yet we live in it and are incapable of living without it. The same thing will happen with our federalism or general system of government; it will be incomplete, but at the same time it will be inevitable. . . . Unity, after all, is not the starting point but the goal of all governments; history proclaims this and reason proves that it is so."[113]

Alberdi then proceeded to lay down what he called his *Bases for the Political Organization of the Argentine Republic.* The book was written hurriedly in exile in Chile, but was the result of twenty years of political and economic thinking. It was first published in 1852, the very year of the defeat of Rosas, and became the basis of the Argentine constitution of 1853 which gave definitive political form to the nation.

The "bases" of Alberdi became the most outstanding study in Latin-American political philosophy. Its conclusions, while mainly pointed toward Argentina, were applicable then, and are still applicable to every country south of the United States. Not one of those nations carried out completely the thoughts of Alberdi, but Argentina followed him most closely and became the leading industrial and economic power of the southern continent.

Alberdi began with this premise: the first constitutions proclaimed by the Spanish American nations immediately after breaking away from their mother country met only a temporary necessity. That necessity was independence and republican government. All other considerations, wealth, material progress, commerce, population, industry, every economic interest, were mere accessories or secondary goals at that time.

"Those constitutions fulfilled their mission," wrote Alberdi. "The men who drew them up understood their epoch and knew how to serve it. . . . But the nations of Latin America now (of the 1850s) have other needs. The same approach can no longer apply. . . . What we must now do is to emancipate our countries from their miserable economic backwardness."

Speaking of Argentina specifically Alberdi said: "What name will you give to an immense territory of 200,000 square leagues and a population of only 800,000? An unpeopled wilderness. What name will you give to the constitution of that country? The constitution of a wilderness. . . . No matter what its nature may be the constitution of Argentina for many years to come will be but that of an unpeopled wilderness. . . ."

Then, driving home his main point, Alberdi wrote: "The only sensible constitution for a country in this condition is one which will make its wilderness disappear. . . . *In America to govern is to populate.*" Alberdi said that the United States had already shown the way and was the amazement and envy of the entire world. He further clarified his belief in these words: "To govern is to populate in the sense that to populate is to educate, to improve, to civilize, to enrich and make great, spontaneously and rapidly, as has happened in the United States." Therefore, he wanted the most civilized peoples of Europe to come to Argentine shores. The United States, he said, could "take an abject and servile immigrant and make a good free citizen of him by the simple and natural pressure of its freedom upon him."

In his unbounded admiration for the great northern democracy Alberdi wanted to see the English language taught in all Argentine schools: "The English language, the language of liberty, of industry, and of order, must be made more obligatory than Latin; no one should get a diploma or university degree without speaking and writing it. This change in itself would profoundly transform our youth. How can we follow the example of the civilization of the Anglo-Saxon race without knowing its language?"

Alberdi, unlike many of his compatriots, admired hard work more than high-sounding words and nimble sophistries. "A hard-working man is the most edifying catechism. . . . He can teach our people more than many books of philosophy." South America must make a *science* of population and material progress.

"Today we must strive for free immigration, liberty of commerce, railroads, the navigation of our rivers, the tilling of our soil, free enterprise, not instead of our initial principles of independence and democracy, but as essential means of assuring ourselves that these will cease being mere words and will become realities. . . . We must begin by building up our young national bodies. . . .

"In order to populate our lands two things are fundamental: to open the doors so that all may enter, and to assure the welfare of those who arrive; liberty at the gates and liberty within. . . . Otherwise the wilderness will be the victor and not the vanquished. . . .

"Our revolutionary wars sought to establish liberty from outside oppression . . . what we now need is liberty within. But as these two freedoms are not achieved by the same means, to seek liberty within through violence rather than through peace is like trying to force the earth to produce grain by constantly digging at it and shifting the soil, thus making the harvest impossible."

Alberdi speaks with deep feeling and resentment against the Latin-American despot. "Our leaders want both glory and liberty, and the two are contradictory. . . . As South America has contributed nothing to world civilization except its wars and the victory in its struggle for independence, the only glory which exists among us is martial glory, and our great men are all military heroes.

"Not a single invention like that of Franklin, like that of Fulton, like the telegraph, and many others which the civilized world owes to North America, has been contributed by our America of the south. Neither in physical sciences, nor in industrial progress, nor in a single branch of human knowledge, does the world at large recognize one Latin-American genius whom we might call universal."

Alberdi shows how futile military victory is unless followed by the civic intelligence which can mold the peace. Again he returns to the United States by way of contrast, and in the highest terms praises the "father of our republic."

"If it were for his military reputation alone Washington would be buried in universal oblivion. Spanish America has many more brilliant generals than Washington. His title to immortality resides in the admirable constitution which has made his nation the model of the world. . . . Rosas had in his hand an opportunity to achieve the same thing in Argentina, and his greatest crime is to have failed so miserably in that trust."

But the point to which Alberdi returns again and again is that Latin America must have immigrants by the hundreds of thousands—immigrants who will help civilize the wilderness by bringing in European civilization, immigrants who will cultivate the fields, man the hammers, erect the tenement of the national state, immigrants who have the desire to work and are capable of achieving practical liberty.

Alberdi then goes on to analyze point by point the bases on which a new Argentine constitution must be raised. He summarizes the factors working toward unity and a unitarian type of government, and also those which tended toward division and in favor of the federal ideal. These diverse factors, he said, must all be united in a single body just as the separate physical organs of an animate being all stand together, giving life and strength to the whole.

Alberdi believed that the constitution and statutes which helped most to encourage physical development and to lead toward practical democracy in action would best meet the necessities of his day. One should not expect it to meet those of yesterday or those of tomorrow. "No one can hope for a constitution to express the necessities of all times," he wrote. Laws are the mere scaffoldings around which the national edifice is raised.

The type of constitution which Argentina adopted, in many ways similar to that of the United States, but with considerably more power in the hands of the federal government, was the direct outgrowth of this remarkably penetrating study of Alberdi's. The proof of its validity was that it lasted for more than seventy-five years and was not drastically broken until the poison of caudillo rule erupted again in our own generation, just when we thought that Argentina had passed forever beyond this stage of willful and unreasoning infancy.

44

SARMIENTO: CIVILIAN PRESIDENT

Against the background of Spanish American revolutions, caudillos, and dictatorships during the nineteenth century, the figure of Domingo Faustino Sarmiento, "the schoolmaster president" of the Argentine Republic, looms like the great Colossus of Rhodes astride the formative years of his country. Sarmiento was elected president in 1868. Mitre had just completed his six-year term, which initiated an era of relative peace and the birth of modern Argentina. When elections were held Sarmiento was serving as minister of his country in the United States. He returned at once and against disheartening obstacles commenced Argentina's "most constructive presidency."[114]

Among a generation of military tyrants Sarmiento was a distinguished civilian president. He had been born into a poor family and had pushed his way to the top through sheer drive and ability. The family lived in San Juan in the shadow of the Andes, where Sarmiento's father owned a few cattle, and his mother did weaving in order to help support her numerous tribe. The boy possessed a voracious desire to embrace all knowledge and educated himself by reading everything in any language that he could get his hands on. At the age of five he was able to read clearly, and his fellow townsmen were so proud of the fact that they invited him from house to house in order to show him off. He reaped a great harvest of cakes, embraces, and encomiums which filled him with vanity. When he was of school age the community selected him to go to Buenos Aires on a government fellowship, but the local political bosses cheated him out of it and appointed instead the son of a more influential family.

When Sarmiento was sixteen he was imprisoned for complaining too loudly of the vicious caudillo government in his province. He was soon free again, but four years later, in 1831, at the age of twenty, he fled to Chile in order to escape the tyranny of Rosas. He carried along with him a heavy load of books and wrote on the rocks of the Andes as he passed by, "You can't kill ideas!"

In Chile he taught school, worked as a shopkeeper, clerk, and mine foreman. After a severe illness he returned to Argentina for a short time but was soon forced to leave again for Chile. By this time he was fully matured mentally and began to write for Chilean newspapers. In 1845 appeared his *Facundo; Civilization and Barbarism in the Argentine Republic*, a violent attack on Rosas, which also contained several fine chapters on the Gaucho. It was the most famous Latin-American book of its generation.

Sarmiento's reputation was now made, and he became a close friend of Manuel Montt, then Secretary of State in Chile, who became the next president of his country. Montt encouraged him, helped him gain admittance to the better society which up to then had shut Sarmiento out because of his poor background. In that same year (1845) Montt had him appointed on a special mission to study European and North American schools with a view to reorganizing the Chilean school system on a more modern basis. The trip lasted for three years—1845–48.

In 1847 Sarmiento came to the United States on his first visit. He was especially anxious to meet Horace Mann, who had done so much for public education in Massachusetts. Mr. and Mrs. Mann were extremely hospitable and he visited them in their home. Sarmiento was deeply impressed with the progress of education in New England and wrote a book reflecting his views entitled *The Schools, Basis of the Prosperity and of the Democracy of the United States*. In 1848 he returned to Chile and helped put his new ideas into effect.

A few years later, when the troops of General Urquiza met and defeated the forces of Rosas, Sarmiento served as a colonel in the victorious army. From that time forward his rise was steady but not rapid. He became director of the schools in Buenos Aires, and by 1860 there were more than 17,000 children in attendance in the capital city. He also served as a senator and later as Minister of the Interior. In 1865 President Mitre sent him to the United States as ambassador, and he remained there until three years later, when he was informed that he had been elected president of his country.

The conditions under which Sarmiento came to power would have floored a man less inured to the hard knocks of life. There were flurries of revolution, a terrible epidemic of yellow fever, two devastating floods, a violent opposition to his candidacy, a severe drought which killed more than 2,000,000 head of cattle, and the terrible war with Paraguay. In spite of all these things the president soon had a firm grip on the government and was pounding away at his task of educating and civilizing the nation. In 1869 he had the first careful Argentine census taken, which showed a total of only 1,830,000 inhabitants. He built railroads, founded schools, colleges, libraries, broke up vast tracts of land for small farmers, passed laws to help fence in the pampas and stamp out the wild Gaucho spirit, increased foreign trade, prosecuted to a successful conclusion the war with Paraguay, raised public buildings, and invited immigrants to enter Argentina.

When he took office there were about 30,000 children attending the national schools; six years later, when he retired, there were 100,000. In the first year of his presidency 34,000 immigrants entered the country; in the last, 80,000. The total for the six years of his term was 280,000. He founded more than one hundred popular libraries, in order to make books available to people who had never before had an opportunity to read. He governed firmly but democratically, and at the end of his term retired with the nation strongly organized on an orderly basis. In his last public message he boasted with robust enthusiasm: "During my term of office each inhabitant has doubled his standard of living, with doubled income, doubled intelligence, doubled activity."[114] It might be said that the three-fold motto of Sarmiento was "opportunity, education, work." He had carried it out with results which were truly amazing.

Sarmiento was that rare combination of the fervent idealist and reformer who keeps both feet on the gound, yet lets his ideals stand out conspicuously so that they may constantly be stimulating others. Once when he was addressing his Congress he made mention of some fantastic figures of possible Argentine wealth and railroad mileage in the distant future, a future toward which he said they must then start planning. When the congressmen heard his figures they burst out laughing. Sarmiento flashed back at them: "Have that laughter put into the record also, for it will later prove the short-sightedness of our honorable representatives!"

Sarmiento is generally regarded among Argentines as their greatest president, and perhaps also their greatest man of letters. A total of fifty-two volumes rolled from his pen, on all conceivable subjects. Education was his mania, but sociology, politics, history, and many other subjects help to fill out the generous tomes of which he is the author.

There is one phase of the great man's life over which many Argentines pass quickly—his almost boundless admiration for the United States. Sarmiento has often been accused of wanting to make his country into the United States of South America. He has often been called blind to the peril of Yankee imperialism. The contemporary Venezuelan, Blanco Fombona, one of the most zealous United States baiters, wrote of Sarmiento: "He did not understand the hatred of that race for ours. He did not realize that the problem of both Americas is reduced to this: a duel of races. . . . He died a fanatic Yankee admirer."[115]

Sarmiento admired most in the United States the love of liberty and law, the tremendous urge to growth, the mania for education, the enormous increase in the material well-being of the average citizen, and the strong aspiration toward a national art. He looked on the towering Washington Monument, constructed through popular subscription which even included the pennies of school children from all over the country, as a sort of symbol of this feeling. "In that monument," he wrote, "the thing characteristic of Yankee genius is the height, that is to say, the national feeling for surpassing in boldness the entire human species, all civilizations, and all ages." He did not believe that this nation was yet the equal of Europe artistically, but he was convinced that the cultural growth of the United States was on the verge of taking immense strides forward, as indeed proved to be the case.

Most of all, of course, Sarmiento admired the North American public schools, and he asked Dr. Goodfellow, a well-known missionary, to contract a number of normal-school teachers who would come to Argentina to establish similar teaching centers there. Under the terms of this agreement a total of sixty-three teachers arrived, and the Argentine educational system became one of the finest in Latin America.

Not in a single sentence did Sarmiento ever express a real fear of the United States. Yet the war with Mexico was taking place while he was in this country on his first visit, a war which resulted in a larger grab than all our other imperialistic manifestations combined. He was convinced that when it came to a showdown, any international showdown, the United States would always align herself on the side of justice. As one of his biographers wrote: "He advocated the adoption of the United States as a model; first, in its political constitution and laws; second, in its program of land distribution, immigration, and colonization; third, in its use of education as a basis for democracy and a safe freedom; fourth, in its stress on the value of easy communication—canals, railroads, mails—as a basis for prosperity."[115]

Sarmiento was never elected to a second term as president of his country, although his hat was in the ring in both 1880 and 1886. Metaphorically speaking, he was crucified by his countrymen, who were all too prone to point out something small that was wrong in something big that was right. All great humanitarians seem destined to suffer the same fate. Argentina's record on this score is particularly notable, for both San Martín and Sarmiento were used, then discarded, then almost forgotten, finally to be called back to mind and glorified after they were dead.

Sarmiento in many ways was the greatest practical genius Latin America has produced. His whole life was "the clamor of modern civilization against the old dusk of feudalism." He wanted to organize Argentina by civilizing it, to elevate his people by educating them. He was the prophet of the modern ideal, still unrealized in most regions of Latin America, but his voice was not mere sound in the wilderness. People listened even if they did not follow, and Sarmiento fulfilled a historic mission of the profoundest significance. He was a leader possessed of such genius and such will that his people sometimes called him mad, *el loco Sarmiento*. It was the greatest praise they could have given him, for his madness was almost divine, a veritable religion for the future.[116]

45

THE PARAGUAYAN WAR

It is a strange and ironic commentary on history that the only Spanish American nation to escape the holocaust of civil war was Paraguay, undoubtedly the most backward region. The scales are more than balanced, however, when the cost is made plain: perpetual despotism. To escape from war at the price of tyranny is no escape at all; it is signing the death warrant of one's own spirit.

Even so, Paraguay eluded civil war only to plunge headlong into the bloodiest international conflict in that part of the world in the nineteenth century. She came out of it a nation completely broken, her soil desolated, her male population obliterated, her cities in ruins, her body and mind destroyed.

After the ordeal of Dr. Francia one might expect a popular revulsion against dictatorship in Paraguay. No such thing happened. They tried a general council for a year, but it did not work. Nobody knew how to command; everyone knew how to obey. That was Francia's bequest. So in 1841, only a single year after the somber doctor's death, Paraguay again established dual "consuls." It was to be the old story all over again.

One of these consuls, Carlos Antonio López, came out on top and three years later managed to elevate himself to the so-called presidency. His dictatorship lasted until his death in 1862. During those eighteen years López tried to reverse the economic policy of Francia. The doctor had isolated Paraguay; his reign was one of retrenchment. López wanted to make a place for his country in the continental scheme of things. He encouraged foreign commerce, built up the army and navy, played in the game of foreign politics.

He also fixed things so that it would be easy for his son Francisco to succeed him. If the old man did not live long enough to achieve his program, perhaps his son would. Consequently Francisco Solano López was sent to Europe, where he could learn how things were done on a big scale. Formally he was a diplomatic representative of his country, but his father was also anxious for him to pick up as much culture as possible. Francisco did not overburden himself on that score. But he did pick up an Irish mistress who stuck with him for the rest of his life, always encouraging, prodding, aiding his dreams of grandeur.

Francisco was in Paris at the time. Elisa Lynch was an Irish girl who had been married to a French officer at the age of fifteen. When the Frenchman divorced her she took up with a titled Russian. Then the Crimean War broke out and Elisa again found herself abandoned. Her eye fell on López, who was making the rounds of the lesser diplomatic set in Paris dressed in a ludicrous bemedaled uniform which caused much mirth on the part of the more sophisticated Europeans. He seemed a little uncouth, but under the surface Elisa saw something that appealed to her.

López was furiously patriotic. He made no bones about being in line for his father's place when the old man passed on. He spoke in glowing terms of what he intended to do for Paraguay. Elisa Lynch liked to hear that kind of talk. She longed for an exciting life; perhaps her squat and uncouth Paraguayan lover was cut out to be the Napoleon of the New World.

With this idea in the minds of both, Francisco and his mistress returned to Asunción, just in time to be present at the death of the older López. Before his father's body was cold the son had carried out a coup and seized control of the government. It was what had been expected. Then he got down to the business of organization.

He had inherited a good military establishment, and immediately set out to strengthen it. Before many months his army and navy were the largest in South America. They were the pride and joy of the dictator and his mistress. Late in the year 1864 López had a chance to use them.

The Emperor of Brazil had protested that his citizens were being robbed and slain indiscriminately in Uruguay, where many thousands of them had settled. The latter country had been in an almost constant state of civil war ever since the defeat of the Gaucho caudillo, Artigas; law and order were non-existent. Unable to gain any satisfaction from the government in Montevideo, Dom Pedro decided to support the party out of power. His troops and the forces of these "outs" marched into Uruguay. President Mitre of Argentine looked on the move with favor.

President López of Paraguay did not. He stated that such an invasion of the sovereign soil of Uruguay was a threat to the security of his own country. What he said no longer mattered; the die was cast. López then countered by marching into Brazil, and thus began the Paraguayan War which tore up the heart of the South American continent for five long years.

López used little discretion in making his moves. He wanted to cross Argentine soil in order to get at his enemy, and when Mitre refused permission he marched into Argentina anyhow. The net result was that little Paraguay, with a population of slightly over a million, found herself at war with Brazil, Argentina, and Uruguay.

It was a preposterous situation. López should have been defeated "within three months," as Mitre had predicted. But the war dragged on and on. Paraguayans fought behind their leader as a single man. No quarter was asked; no quarter was given. Slowly the allied forces built up their power, and finally they outnumbered López by at least ten to one. There were costly victories for the allies, but López would not surrender. Humaitá, the South American Sebastopol, held out for eighteen months. It became legendary in song and story.

The army of López was crushed by the juggernaut opposing it. Elisa Lynch organized the women, taught them the use of arms, and led them into battle on horseback. The whole Paraguayan army was composed of squads of six, each one of which had orders to shoot any of the others who fled or wished to surrender. Soldiers who did surrender knew that their wives or sisters would be publicly flogged to death by López or his mistress. Excruciating sadistic cruelties were perpetrated by the dictator of Paraguay and Elisa Lynch. When this was thrown into López's face by foreigners in the capital he only answered: "Why should I let traitors die easily while all the true Paraguayans are dying the hard way?"

Fear was not the only motivation for that incredible spirit. Every Paraguayan felt a fanatical, almost mystical devotion for something he called Paraguay. Their leader was one of their own. Toward the end of the war López was driven into the hills, and reports came in that he had a mere hundred men left around him. In a great gesture the triumphant allied armies released ten thousand prisoners, most of them hobbling wounded men from hospitals, and the entire contingent, "with their bandages caked in mud," passed through the besieging lines and joined their fanatical leader.

Many times López was asked to surrender. He invariably answered: "You will win a victory only over the corpse of Paraguay." They were true words. After the capture of Asunción the noose was slowly tightened around the band of López. They were encircled in a swamp. When López saw that the final moment had come he led his pitiful remnants in one last charge, and his body, pierced by a dozen lances, fell to the ground spurting blood. The victorious allies then saw what was left of the famous soldiers of Paraguay: boys of eight and nine and old men of seventy. The war had ended. It had lasted from 1864 to 1870.

What to do with the corpse of Paraguay? The allies soon decided that by carving off large slices of the national territory. If they had not bickered among themselves they might have taken it all. In any case what remained was no nation, and has never become one. Against this destiny the Paraguayans have continued to fight. They are proud to be called "the fightingest nation in the hemisphere." They are not so proud of being also the most backward.

It could hardly be otherwise, for out of a population of approximately 1,337,000 when the war began, Paraguay had only 220,000 inhabitants when peace was made. Of this total there were only 28,746 males. The country has never recovered from this unparalleled desolation. Even today it has less population than in the year 1864, when hostilities started.

Some Spanish American historians have lavished great praise on López. One of them wrote that he "carved the foundations of a nation out of the jungles" and "defended with his life his native land against the imperialism of Brazil and Argentina." Others refer to the reign of López, saying that he led the country "through heroism to disintegration and disaster." Whatever attitude one may take, López was a fool to think that he could defeat the combined forces of the two greatest powers in Latin America. His claims to heroism are marred by only too-well-proven stories of sadism and execution. The squat and ruthless dictator destroyed the very seeds of life among his people.

A poet has put the dirge of Paraguay into these pathetic words: "Weep, weep, *urutaú* bird, in the branches of the *yatay* tree; there no longer exists a Paraguay, where I and you were born." It is the lament of a native girl who has lost parents, brothers, and sisters in the terrible war:

> Llora, llora, urutaú,
> en las ramas del yatay;
> ya no existe el Paraguay,
> donde nací como tú.
> Llora, llora, urutaú.

The same feeling was expressed in the fine painting, *La Paraguaya*, by Juan Manuel Blanes of Uruguay, who was perhaps the outstanding artist in Latin America during the nineteenth century. His canvas shows an Indian woman "standing in deep meditation upon a rocky battlefield strewn with corpses of the dead."[170]

46

VENEZUELA AND COLOMBIA
UNDER CAUDILLO RULE

The first South American countries to rebel against the domination of Spain were Venezuela and Argentina, both countries which lived primarily from the wild horses and cattle on their interior plains. Both developed fiercely individualistic pastoral societies. Both bore the strong yoke of regional caudillos. Both produced a primitive breed of men, called Gauchos in Argentina and *llaneros*, or plainsmen, in Venezuela, who understood only the rule of the mailed fist.

While Argentina's great pampas extended to the sea, thus making it a highway for the export of hides, tallow, and other produce of the interior, Venezuela's *llanos* were shut off from the Gulf of Mexico by a coastal range of mountains. The country's largest city, Caracas, is placed in a fold of these mountains. Geographic unity does not exist in Venezuela. A few mountain passes and the Orinoco River, which reaches into the heart of the llanos, are the only outlets of the interior plains.

There are also many other reasons for the superiority of the pampas over the llanos as a cattle-raising district. The climate of this part of Venezuela is tropical and infested with insects. Not a single city lies at the mouth of the huge Orinoco basin. Pasturage is poor and uncertain. Rains flood the entire prairie district during several months of the year and turn the pasture land into a great lake. The Venezuelan plainsman, unlike the Gaucho, had to be an excellent canoeist as well as a rider. It was the only way to get over the flooded prairie in the rainy season.

Every time the rains came many cattle perished, especially the young. Others took to the swells of land and, after the sparse grass was all eaten, starved to death. By and large the llanos constitute a region of vile living conditions with an impoverished population.

In spite of all these things the Venezuelan cattle industry grew. It began toward the middle of the sixteenth century at about the same time as it did in Argentina. By 1650 "herds of wild cattle numbering perhaps 140,-000 were reported as grazing on these plains."[148] In the year 1811, when Venezuela declared its independence of Spain, there were approximately 4,500,000 head of cattle on the llanos. (The pampas pastured seven or eight times as many.) But Venezuela was to be the hardest hit of any Latin-American country by the four horsemen of the Apocalypse: war, death, pestilence, and famine. The armies of Spain and of Bolívar ranged over her lands, searing them to the quick. Men and animals perished by the hundreds of thousands in that engulfing flame.

Bolívar estimated in 1815 that his country had lost one out of every four inhabitants; ten years later that figure could surely be doubled. Native historians estimate that their country lost more than 450,000 inhabitants out of a total population of about 950,000 during the struggle for independence. Venezuela was a desert. It had no industries, no population, no food, hardly any cattle. The 4,500,000 head which had roamed the prairie in 1811 had decreased to 256,000 by 1823. It was as if a human organism had lost nine tenths of its blood and through some miracle or chance was still alive. The country had to exist on hope alone.

The plainsmen who inhabited the savage llanos kept the nation alive. They eked out an existence which was hardly one step above a dog's life. Exporting cattle products meant nothing to them. Beef was their bread of life. Practically all of the herds were of scrub cattle which furnished little and poor meat. To a large extent the same conditions prevail today. Cattle raising in Venezuela continues as a way of life, not as a great industry. It has almost no agriculture to prop it up. The glitter of recently discovered oil fields has obliterated every desire to develop a well-rounded economy.

Back in the days of the struggle for independence there arose on the plains of Apure a leader who became one of the Liberator's right-hand men, José Antonio Páez. He had once advised Bolívar to proclaim himself king. Páez was reputed to be white in blood, but he was a llanero born and bred. His partisans, all plainsmen, called him the "Lion of Apure." As a boy he had been apprenticed to a cruel Negro who forced him to work like a slave. He fought bravely in the wars of independence, rose to the rank of general, and finally, in 1830, became the dictator of Venezuela when that country sloughed off from Greater Colombia to form its own national state.

Of all the Liberator's lieutenants Páez enjoyed power the longest, not withdrawing from the national scene until 1863. Like the Argentine Rosas, he was a man who was admired for his physical prowess and for his skill as a horseman. Unlike Rosas, he possessed an ingratiating personality which made all who knew him like him. He was no tyrant whose power was nourished on an ever-increasing diet of fear and blood.

Páez did not have to be a tyrant. There was little effective opposition to him in Venezuela. The country was hardly animate, and he stood there with his strong body and his strong fist to give it life. There was no great city in the entire nation, hardly any intellectual class. The fires of war had wiped out the last vestiges of that generation which gave rise to Miranda, the morning star of the revolution; to Simón Bolívar, the continent's greatest warrior and polemist; and to Andrés Bello, its most revered man of letters. Bello, realizing that mind cannot function in a vacuum, had gone to Chile, where he had become president of the national university and the nation's leading jurist, teacher, and writer.

Of the generation of liberators Páez alone remained, and Páez was Venezuela. The Spaniards had thought that Bolívar was the revolution incarnate, and he was. But as the Liberator neared the end of his life in the little Colombian town of Santa Marta, an exile from his native land, and overcome with the unspeakable despair which only those who have lived for others can feel, the llanero partisans of Venezuela's separation from Greater Colombia came before Páez and saluted him with these words:

"General, you are our country."[95]

That was the beginning of more than a hundred years of caudillo rule in Venezuela. The strong fist began to push the illiterate body. Venezuela's illiteracy rate is still probably in the neighborhood of 80 per cent. Where there was no education, self-government became impossible; the strong man was the only possible means of achieving that minimum of order without which life itself would become unbearable.

Venezuela, like Argentina, might have had its struggle between civilization and barbarism when Páez appeared on the horizon, except that little civilization was left there to fight. That being the case, when Páez came to power he could maintain himself without those excesses which Rosas employed in order to drown out opposition in Buenos Aires.

Nevertheless, Venezuela was not free of disorder. Men's wills can clash even when there is little clash of principles. Between 1830, the date of Páez's accession to power, and the dawn of the twentieth century, the country passed through more than fifty armed uprisings. One might use the term revolution to apply to these grapplings for power, but it would be an insult to the word.

During more than thirty of those years Páez was Venezuela's greatest figure. He was not always "president" of the country, but he was unquestionably its strong man. Every time the national government failed or faltered, Páez would come back to "save the country."

Páez reached an agreement with the landed oligarchy. He gave them order, the prerequisite for profit if not for progress, and they helped keep him in power. In fact, the lettered conservatives took quite a liking to uncouth Páez, and he to them. He had the support of the classes; they still controlled a great part of their country's wealth but were not popular with the masses. Páez and the oligarchy could do well together.

One historian goes so far as to say that Páez "allowed himself to be taken in by the landlords and wealthy inhabitants of the towns and by the literary ideologues whom he once detested. In the end he became the leader —or perhaps the tool—of a group who in Venezuela may be characterized as Conservatives, but who, if they had been found in Chile or Colombia, might have been called Moderates. The constitution which they drew up in 1830 was a compromise between the federal and the centralist types. . . ."[161]

But Páez was not anybody's subordinate. He governed in as constitutional and liberal a manner as possible under the circumstances. A specialist in Venezuelan history points out: "The rule of the Oligarchy under the notable instrument, the Constitution of 1830, is regarded by Venezuelan historians as a sort of golden era in their history, a period of the reign of the law, in contrast to the earlier and later dictatorships. It must be admitted, however, and is, that behind the constitutional order stood the military *caudillo*, Páez. Observance and applications of the law were possible only at his will and through his personal prestige."[162] In other words, Páez himself respected the law and more or less singlehandedly enforced it upon his people.

Páez as caudillo was not interested in his personal gain and governed the country well. He gave Venezuela material progress. He revoked the immunities of the Church, which was not as strong in Venezuela as elsewhere in Spanish America because of the few cities and the wild nature of the country. He supported education, suppressed monasteries, proclaimed freedom of the press, and expressed himself in favor of freedom of worship.

Under General Soublette, one of Páez's friends and minions, who was president between 1843–46, Venezuela enjoyed her best government and greatest respect for civil liberties during the first century of her independence. Under the rule of Páez and the moderate oligarchy, 1830–48, the power of the Church as an economic institution was completely broken, and its intellectual dominance was destroyed. This was not achieved through violent anti-clerical actions, but under process of law which the Venezuelan clergy respected. From that time forward there never existed in Venezuela the bitter conflict between Church and State which has characterized most of the other Latin-American nations.

Páez had a deeply ingrained sense of tolerance and fairness, a strong equalitarian instinct, and a great admiration for minds more cultivated than his own. He sent his son to the United States to be educated. He imposed his own crude brand of democracy on the city aristocrats. He permitted the publication of a violent anti-government paper called *El Venezolano,* in which day after day appeared attacks against Páez and his colleagues. The publisher of that paper, Antonio Leocadio Guzmán, became the founder of Venezuela's liberal party. He was also the father of her second famous dictator of the nineteenth century. Guzmán attempted to symbolize the struggle of the dispossessed, the black and the mulatto, the impoverished crowd against the landed aristocrats.

Despite the relative progress of Venezuela under Páez, there was ample soil in which such demagogy might take root. The president's *hato*, or cattle ranch, which exemplified the best conditions of living on the llanos at that time, gives some idea of how miserable the standard of the populace at large must have been. The house itself was only a barn with walls made of reeds and mud. There were no windows at all, and only two of the rooms had doors. The furniture consisted of the most primitive pieces, and the chairs were rude homemade ones with seats of bullocks' hide "from which the hair had never been removed, except by usage, which left bare patches on the untanned skin, as if they had the mange. Grass hammocks swinging from the walls were used either as beds at night or rocking chairs by day, the sitter with one leg dangling keeping them in perpetual motion with his foot." The shed-like dining room was open on two sides, and when it rained hides were stretched between the posts on which the roof was laid, to keep the weather out.[163]

Yet around this shanty grazed many hundreds of cattle. They were all wild, and none of the cows would submit to milking. Two or three tamed milk cows were acquired from a neighboring establishment. "Each morning, as in the Argentine, a bullock was run up from the rodeo as near as possible to the dwelling house, lassoed and slaughtered. The offal, left where the animal was butchered, was soon devoured by the troop of half wild dogs that on most ranches in South America get their living like a pack of wolves."[163]

Such was the home of the president of the republic. The ordinary llanero, who owned no property at all, lived at a much lower level and was ready fodder for the ranks of military chieftains who rose from time to time full of golden promises backed by the might of their roving bands.

Páez instituted a period of personal rule in Venezuela which was to endure for more than a century. In that nation the conflicts which sprang up were always between rival caudillos representing no particular ideology, rather than between parties which stood for a political philosophy. In this purely physical struggle ideas remained static, social progress hardly existed, but several extensive periods of "mechanical peace" under dictatorship made possible the greater wealth of the oligarchy while the country as a whole continued in grinding poverty.

In 1847 President Monagas, whom Páez had put into power, turned against the old llanero, picked up the torch of the "liberal" party in order to gain support for his cause, forcibly dissolved the Congress, and proclaimed himself dictator. Páez led a rebellion against Monagas, but his raw levies were defeated. Only the swiftness of his horse saved his life, and the Lion of Apure fled to Jamaica. In 1849 he returned to Venezuela and attempted another unsuccessful revolt. This time he was thrown into prison and condemned to death. He was heavily ironed and confined in a close cell with windows and door bolted. The stifling atmosphere forced him to lie on the floor with his nose near the doorway in order to keep from smothering or succumbing to the heat. His powerful constitution gave way under this treatment, and he nearly died before his sentence was commuted to exile and he was allowed to proceed to the United States.

When Páez reached the port of Cumaná to board his vessel it was discovered that there was not sufficient coal for her to put to sea. "The inhabitants, fearing a plot to make away with Páez at the last moment, flew to the timber yard and piled wood upon the steamer's deck. Then, finding it was insufficient, tore down the doors and windows of their houses, adding them to the pile."[163]

Páez was well received in the United States and praised by the press. New York became his home for several years. The tattered boy who had once been forced to wash a Negro soldier's feet had come a long way. With his headquarters in New York he traveled extensively, visiting both Mexico and Europe.

By 1858 Venezuela had tired of the dictatorship of Monagas and his brother and "by a decree of the National Convention, Páez was reinstated in his military rank and all his honors were returned to him." Finally he was invited home to rescue his country from anarchy. New York organized a military parade to bid him farewell, and in the midst of the celebration the horse that Páez rode slipped and fell upon him, badly mangling his leg. In spite of the ironic accident the old plainsman returned to Venezuela, where he was received with tremendous demonstrations of joy.

Páez was then over seventy and had lost contact with the situation in his country; nevertheless, from 1861 to 1863 he resumed the governing power. It was of no use. Although the people had received him with frenzied ovations, they would not unite to make his government successful. Confronted with what looked like permanent civil war, the old man again left his native land and departed for the United States. This time he came in poverty and barely managed to eke out an existence. In 1868, when he was seventy-eight, he obtained a position with a cattle company and went to Buenos Aires, where he paid a visit to General Urquiza's huge *estancia*. The Argentine Government heard of his dire financial straits and made him a brigadier general in the army.

An outbreak of yellow fever in the Argentine capital drove him back to the United States again, where he died in the year 1873, at the age of eighty-three. His son Ramón wrote a book in English entitled *Wild Scenes in South America; or, Life in the Llanos of Venezuela*, in which he gives much interesting information about his father, glorifying him of course. On the last page of his book the younger Páez quotes a sentence which Charles Darwin had written about Argentina after his visit there on the famous voyage of the *Beagle*. Ramón Páez applies the words to Venezuela: "That country will have to learn, like every other South American state, that a republic cannot succeed till it contains a body of men imbued with the principles of justice and honor."

Chaos reigned in Venezuela for some years after the departure of Páez until finally, in 1870, Antonio Guzmán Blanco came to power. He was the son of the man who had published the anti-Páez tirades in *El Venezolano*, thus bringing about the founding of an opposition party. Guzmán Blanco was the strongest power in his country for nineteen years, until 1889.

Apart from the lives of these two representative caudillos Venezuela had little order and no progress in the nineteenth century. Every time the pressure of the mailed fist was removed the country slumped back into a morass of violence. Between the year of Páez's final departure in 1863 and the dictatorship of Guzmán Blanco, which was firmly established in 1872, the cattle of the llanos, lifeblood of the Venezuelan people, had decreased from 6,000,000 to 3,500,000 head, or fewer than the country had at the beginning of its war for independence more than sixty years previously.

Guzmán Blanco, titular head of the liberal party, was an audacious and cunning leader, but he was not noted for his moral rectitude or his respect for the lives, liberty, or property of his fellow citizens. One caustic historian, referring to the dictator's love of high-flown diction, called him "a dictionary without definitions." The Colombian intellectual, Miguel Antonio Caro, said that "he worshiped the cult of falsehood." There were other even less complimentary characterizations.

Guzmán Blanco, and his father before him, had stood for the federal ideal and for what passed for liberalism in Venezuela. But such terms were almost meaningless to both men. Many years previously, when questioned about his federal principles, the elder Guzmán had answered: "I don't know where they got the idea that the people of Venezuela are in love with federation, when they don't even know what the word means. The thought came to me and to certain friends of mine and we said to ourselves: *Since every revolution needs a flag, and since the Convention of Valencia refused to baptize the Constitution with the federal name, let us invoke that idea.* But if our adversaries, señores, had said Federation, we would have shouted Centralization."[38]

To Guzmán Blanco, therefore, liberalism was merely a blind behind which he hid his nefarious actions and elevated himself to the supreme power. It was a means and not an end. It could be discarded as excess baggage when the road became rough.

The dictator found it hard sledding at first. He fought for two long years before his power was secure. Then by decapitating the generals who opposed him, by exiling those who had plotted against him, and by confiscating the goods of those who complained, he finally achieved order.

Guzmán Blanco, who had traveled widely in the United States, wanted to be a paternal civilian autocrat. He spoke incessantly of highways, railroads, bridges, telegraph lines, mail service, and so forth. Under his rule the cattle of the llanos increased to about 8,000,000 head, the highest figure ever reached. He cleaned up the country's tottering finances, borrowed funds from foreign countries, rigorously enforced the peace which all classes desired, and was given the pompous titles of "Regenerator of Venezuela" and "Illustrious American." Medals were struck off bearing his name; the ruling oligarchy looked upon him as a Messiah sent from heaven, and the masses outdid themselves in worship of their new caudillo.

Guzmán Blanco visited foreign countries in search of loans. He had a plan for organizing a great development company which would invest money and workers in Venezuela, accelerating the pace of her progress. He spoke eloquently of his mission, saying that, under him, Venezuela had "undertaken an infinite voyage towards an infinite future." The citizens demanded dictatorship, he said, in order to be spared the horrors of anarchy.

Proud of his reputation as the "Illustrious American," Guzmán Blanco required every book and every sheet of music published during his regime to bear a mention of his name. He longed to go down in history as a great civilizer and great educator.

A Spanish American historian, Carlos Pereyra, makes the following pointed comment: "Guzmán Blanco had the boastful slogan of wanting to see a school on every street . . . Spanish America has always responded to the fanatical cry for schools. There is hardly a caudillo who would not feel more flattered to preside at a distribution of scholastic medals than to enter a city victoriously. The unlettered caudillos want to be protectors of culture in order to cover their own uncouth personalities with the magnificence of altruism. The most despotic tyrants prepare for themselves a grateful posterity through the benefits which they scatter among schoolchildren."[38]

Guzmán Blanco's love for education did not prevent his own infantile paranoia. He was vindictive, arbitrary, and cruel in his dealings with others. He was pompous to a point of ridiculousness, and insufferably vain. On one occasion he posed as a model of St. Paul, wearing a purple toga. The artist who had caught his resemblance to that great prophet won Guzmán Blanco's undying favor. The dictator appears in the finished picture flanked by St. John and St. Mark. St. Luke and St. Matthew are in the background.

Guzmán Blanco did not have any very definite political ideas. He ruled to suit himself. He boasted of being able to say, "I am the state." Yet he was a true lover of his native land, a sincere exponent of material progress, with an abiding faith in the education of his people.

He attempted too much with too little, and, incidentally, was not above building up a neat little pile for himself on the side. If everything he had placed on the agenda and on the statute books had been put into effect Venezuela would indeed be a great nation today. But Guzmán Blanco wanted to eat his cake and have it too.

He failed to see what was as plain as the nose on his face: that if he was the state then the citizenry of Venezuela constituted no state, and after he had passed on into defeat or death they would be left again hanging over the abyss. When the people finally wearied of his fanfaronades and told him he was through, that was exactly what happened. Guzmán Blanco, who was in Paris at the time, regarded himself as a great martyr. He died in exile, never returning to his native land.

After the fall of Guzmán Blanco there was a decade of chaos followed by two more military caudillos. Between 1899 and 1908 the country was governed by Cipriano Castro, a lecherous and greedy cutthroat who bankrupted the state and quickly aroused the hatred of his people. He was followed by Juan Vicente Gómez, last of the "old-line" tyrants, who ran Venezuela like a private estate between 1908 and 1935.

At a time when most of the nations of Latin America were moving toward a period of democratic government Gómez was stringing up his political opponents on meathooks. He had the stinking dungeons of Díaz, the spying police force of Rosas, the unpitying cruelty of Machado. Every decent Venezuelan citizen who could possibly escape from the country did so.

Gómez soon began to enjoy the "delights of perpetuity." He prided himself especially on his extensive program of road building, his cancellation of the country's foreign debt, and the financial responsibility of his government. He thought he could hide the less savory aspects of his dictatorship behind the material progress achieved during his regime. "Such progress," writes the Peruvian historian Luis Alberto Sánchez, "is the cure-all of every dictatorship."

Oil was discovered in Venezuela just after World War I, and foreign companies invested approximately $400,000,000 in the country. Oftentimes the Gómez government received as much as $25,000,000 a year in taxes from these foreign oil companies. The per capita income of Venezuela became the highest in Latin America. The federal government received annually three or four times as much income as Colombia or Peru, far more populous neighboring states. When Gómez died in 1935 at the age of seventy-eight he was worth at least $30,000,000.

Throughout its history Venezuela has suffered the penalty of its geographic location. The rich and populous part of the country is a narrow strip fringing the sea. Here fertile slopes and valleys make life pleasant on a small scale, but access to the Gulf is only through mountain passes, and no rich hinterland lies behind the coastal fringe. Instead of becoming the outlet for a developed interior, the Venezuelan coastal territory is hardly able to feed itself. Under such conditions the sea is an illusion.[95]

It is an illusion not only in an economic sense, but also because the caudillo and his henchmen, entrenched along that littoral, have kept out ideas. Political and economic backwardness have made immigration difficult and enabled the native autarchy to sustain itself on the two columns of poverty and ignorance. As far back as 1830 a Venezuelan periodical, the *Semanario Político*, saw the necessity for immigration and urged the national Congress to adopt a policy which would promote it. The article continued: "If there is no immigration, there will be no population. Without population we can not have liberty, wealth, and general happiness. Without these benefits, we shall be less than we are today! Nothing!!!"[162]

The advice went unheeded, and while the population of Argentina was increasing fifteenfold, Venezuela's hardly tripled. The fateful words of Alberdi referring to the Argentine as a wilderness might be applied to Venezuela with a vengeance. For over a century the barbarism of the llanos won out over the finer instincts of Venezuelan life.

The high per capita income of Venezuela has meant little so far as the average citizen is concerned. Inequitable distribution and exorbitant prices on many necessities have kept all possible benefits from the people at large. A one-sided economy, resting first on cattle and later on oil, prevented the development of the nation's resources as a whole.

According to the logic of the situation, the rich agricultural region around the city of Valencia should have caused that city to outstrip Caracas as the largest center in the country. But neither agriculture, cattle, nor oil have been able to take away the primacy of the capital city. Back of them all the main business of Venezuela has always been politics, and the center of political activity, the goal of every leading politician and caudillo, has been Caracas. The stamp of political opportunism has left its ghastly mark on both the character and the face of the Venezuelan nation.

Across the Venezuelan frontier, in the country of Colombia, the process of history was somewhat different. This was the country where Bolívar had tarried the longest; it was where he ate his heart out, where he died. Colombia was also the birthplace of General Santander, the "man of laws." While Bolívar was covering himself with military glory backed by the soldiers of Colombia and envisioning brilliant utopias, Santander slaved away at the thankless task of providing troops, of governing a distraught nation at war, of enforcing the statutes, of striving through both precept and example to instill in the hearts of all Colombians a respect for impersonal law. "Our arms gave us independence," he said. "Laws will give us our liberty." Santander placed on Colombia the stamp of civil government which even today so clearly distinguishes it from the other Latin-American republics.[117]

Colombia has never had a single president assassinated in office. No other American republic, not even the United States, can boast of such a record. Yet in Colombia men fought just as frequently and as furiously as in any other Latin-American nation. The difference was this: in Colombia battles were waged for ideas, while in most of the rest of the southern republics they were clashes of caudillos. Personal autocrats did not stand out in Colombia. The country never had a real despot maintain himself in power. Several tried it; all of them failed. Bolívar, the greatest of them all, lasted only a few brief months. Colombia never paid its allegiance to the person of a leader, but only to a symbol. When a dictator became false to his trust, he was promptly displaced. A real militarism never took root in Colombia. As a famous couplet of the country puts it:

> En Colombia, que es la tierra
> de las cosas singulares,
> dan la paz los militares,
> y los civiles dan guerra.

> In Colombia, which is a land
> Of the most singular things,
> The soldiers bring peace
> And the civilians cause wars.

This humorous bit of verse hits the nail on the head. In Colombia the military never rebelled against the established constitutional government. Aware of their subordinate role under the civil authorities, Colombian soldiers stood behind the laws of the land until these were changed by the civilians themselves. These civilians, on the other hand, revolted frequently, not against, but in defense of, the law and the institutions. Colombian idealism was primitive and often savage in its manifestations, but it was not stagnant or stifling.[165]

The geographic nature of Colombia, which has so deeply affected the history of the country, is unique in South America. Approximately 98 per cent of the total population lives on one third of the national territory on the high savannas or in basins and valleys set among the mountains. Each isolated region has developed its own small metropolis and market. These centers of population are not connected with one another overland, and their only natural outlet to the sea is the Magdalena River. A few years ago a trip up this river to the capital, Bogotá, took at least two weeks. Air lines now cover the distance in two hours.

As a consequence of her geography Colombia has thus become "a country of cities." The capital has not been able to dominate the rest of the country as has been the case in most of the other Latin-American nations, draining away the national resources and leaving the hinterland anemic. The same geographic conditions have made for a more balanced economy. The country's fertile lands and varied climates—dependent largely on variations of altitude—have produced a great diversity of products within a minimum of territory. Few indeed are the inhabitants who have been unable to earn a living from Colombia's fruitful soil. A sparse population and restricted market have slowed down the pace of material development, but the rudiments of economic democracy plus the natural balancing off of several cities against one another prevented the rise of caudillo rule and brought about the early development of democratic institutions.

Within the security of its mountainous retreats the best of the old order persisted. Interest in culture and in law thrived there from the beginning. Those words attributed to Bolívar: "Venezuela is an armed camp, Colombia is a university, Ecuador is a convent," state the salient characteristics of three nations. It is no accident that Nariño, translator of *The Rights of Man*, Santander, the "man of laws," and Núñez, the Thinker of Cabrero, were all Colombians. The political leadership of the nation has always represented the highest intellectual values.

However, if Colombia prides herself on being university-like in character, it is well to remember that the higher institutions of learning embrace only the few even in the most advanced nations. Since the days of her independence Colombia has been governed by a small intellectual minority, and culture there has remained the patrimony of the chosen few. The idealism of some, the obstinacy of others, and the ignorance of the majority were thrown together violently in order to produce the imperfect fabric of a modern state. Everywhere the mountain of tradition obstructs the path of progress. The country's greatest poet, José Asunción Silva, committed suicide at the age of thirty-two because he could no longer endure the stifling atmosphere of fanatical Bogotá.[142]

Colombia has always been a forge for abstract ideas. Political dogmatism for years blighted the finest opportunities for tolerance, moderation, and enterprise. Men have preferred to die for principles rather than to make human compromises and live for progress.

"For more than a century," writes a keen Colombian analyst, "we lived under the constant shadow of theological disputes and fratricidal wars, forgetting almost completely the arduous task of physical, social, moral, and intellectual betterment of the great indigenous and mestizo masses which inhabit the territory of our nation."

General Holguín, in his book, *Desde Cerca* (A First Hand View), published in 1908, stated that his country passed through twenty-seven civil wars during the first century of its independence. In the conflict of 1879 there were 80,000 killed; in the war of 1899–1903 nearly 100,000 lives were lost. Under such conditions material progress was impossible, political idealism notwithstanding.

The country generated all types and shades of ideologies. Its citizens time after time "abandoned fortune and family, as in the great religious periods of history," to go on a crusade for their particular principle. Colombia tried unitarianism, federalism, liberalism, conservatism, idealism, then repeated the process. The lines of demarcation soon began to overlap, but two main trends stood out: one was Catholic and conservative; the other was liberal and democratic. Followers of the first party ruled the nation until the mid-century, then the liberals came to power and maintained themselves for more than three decades. Vigorous anti-church legislation was passed. The Jesuits, who had been invited back into the country by the conservatives, were again expelled and their properties taken over by the state. The conservatives rebelled unceasingly.

In Colombia the opposition party always had a chance. As early as 1837 Dr. Márquez was elected, despite the opposition of Santander. The stresses of public opinion did strange things to men's attitudes when they came to power. General Mosquera, who was elected as a conservative in 1845, turned liberal when he became convinced that the majority was headed in that direction. Rafael Núñez, who was elected as a liberal in 1880, took on a strong conservative tinge when the opposition seemed to be gathering heavy momentum for a campaign against him.

The same was true of Colombia's constitutions. They became liberal, conservative, unitarian, and federal in turn, depending on the sentiment of the people at the moment. The liberal constitution of 1853 gave the states so much autonomy that they governed themselves almost like separate nations. All the freedoms were proclaimed, and Church was separated from State. Yet under this enlightened national document several of the states were ruled under regional constitutions which were rigidly conservative. Colombia's leaders were a group of brilliant but fanatical statesmen who had not yet learned the art of co-operation. The nation was exhausting itself in the fever of endless political crusades.

During all this time there were only two major changes in the national perspective, one at the middle of the nineteenth century, the other toward its close. They came very near to making a complete circle. Speaking of the first, a well-known Spanish American historian wrote that with the victory of the Colombian liberals in 1849 "the triumph was not that of a single man, but of a new spirit." However, the country was not prepared for this step forward, and the advance could not be consolidated. "Negro slavery was abolished; but no thought was given to the economic serf, inferior to the slave. Navigation of the river was opened to all ships, as if a great fleet were lined up waiting for this permission to navigate. The death penalty was abolished for political crimes, but not on that account was there any less bloodshed in the country's civil wars. . . . Universal suffrage was established, but nobody voted. Public instruction was declared free and compulsory, as if the placing of such a law on the statute books would multiply the schools."[95]

It was the fundamental contradiction of Latin-American life, the difference between the wish and the reality, the insistence on theory rather than action and practice which has everywhere held back the path of progress. Colombians began to realize that there was something wrong with their liberalism, but not until three decades had passed did a man arise who was able to clarify the situation in terms everyone could understand.

In 1880 the nation's most admired president, Rafael Núñez, came to power as a liberal. He was violent and impassioned in his beliefs, and began immediately to campaign against the Church. "While many Colombians still lived on their knees before the Cross chanting puerile songs to the Virgin Mary, the Thinker of Cabrero [Núñez] espoused religious and philosophical skepticism and fought to acquire power and influence among the citizens. Elected as chief executive by the radical party, after assuming power he renounced his previous sentiments as a man and as a philosopher and carried out the greatest program of political and social change that has ever marked the history of our republic."[117]

Colombian writers point out that Núñez established a new compromise party, and refer to the work of his regime as a "historic necessity." In reality he had become a conservative, but the change was so deftly made that he gained rather than lost support. He applied the brakes to careening Colombian liberalism in order to avoid a national disaster.

When Núñez assumed office he was faced with a nation bordering on anarchy. He did away with the rampant federalism which divided the country against itself, and proclaimed a unitarian republic. He gave Colombia a new constitution which, he said, had been "born in the soul of the people." The nation's educational system returned to the principle of Christian teaching, "since this was the alma mater of world civilization."[174] Núñez negotiated a concordat with the Pope and, because of its stabilizing influence, placed Colombia again under the national tutelage of the Catholic Church. For fifteen years he sought to unite all classes, to put an end to political fanaticism, to bind up the wounds caused by regional jealousies, to impose his authoritarian but democratic will upon all parties.

Núñez not only permitted but encouraged the minorities to have a strong representation in Congress as a counterbalance to what he called "the myopia of party spirit." He was conciliatory but firm in his use of authority; he was not arbitrary, cruel, pompous, or self-seeking. Some of his radical colleagues called him a traitor to their cause, but Núñez thought that he had a higher principle than sterile partisanship. "Politics is indissolubly bound up with the economic problem," he said. And "in politics there are no absolute truths, and all things may be good or evil according to opportunity and extent."[92]

Núñez died in 1894, and soon thereafter the country again plunged into violent civil strife. It seemed for a time that all the work of this unique dictator had been plowing the sea. Colombia righted herself after that one bloody adventure in atavism and its government has remained stable to this day. The conservative temperament of Núñez was dominant in Colombia from the year 1886, when his new constitution was adopted, to 1930, when the liberals again came to power. In this latter year the conservatives, despite their forty-four years of uninterrupted rule, accepted their defeat at the polls and with a real democratic spirit all too rare in the Latin countries, peacefully handed over the reins of power to the opposition party.

47

THE ANDEAN REPUBLICS

I. BOLIVIA: A SICK PEOPLE

In the three Andean republics which formerly made up most of the Inca Empire, Ecuador, Peru, and Bolivia, caudillo rule became established as a way of life which is not yet dead. In those countries a small white and mestizo caste has struggled constantly to keep the native masses in subjugation. Up to the present moment, making only such concessions as were inescapable, this minority has been successful in maintaining its power.

After the wars of independence, Santa Cruz in Bolivia, Flores in Ecuador, and Castilla in Peru were the caudillos who placed their stamp on the servile populations of these republics. The first two were generals of Bolívar who seized the spoils which the Liberator had left behind. Santa Cruz became dictator of Bolivia in 1829; Flores caused Ecuador to separate from Greater Colombia in 1830, and Castilla came to power in Peru in 1845. Each of the three ruled with a hand of iron for more than a decade.

Santa Cruz, who had royal Indian blood in his veins, attempted to carry out the ideals of the Liberator. Bolivia was the brain child of Simón Bolívar; it bore his name; it was given life under his constitution; he was its first ruler. If the old classic myth were true, Bolivia sprang full grown and armed from the mind of the Liberator.

But myths do not always apply to nations, as Bolívar soon learned to his sorrow. His refined political philosophy, despite all its theoretical logic, was absolutely impractical in backward Bolivia. The Liberator attempted to organize and govern the country as if it were at least the semblance of a nation; and what he actually had under him was only an aggregation of castes and tribes with no more feeling of unity than so many bands of wild Indians. Under these conditions only two types of government were possible: regional or tribal rule, or absolute dictatorship. Bolívar first, then the immaculate Sucre, found this out and turned away from the theoretical republic in disgust and embitterment.

Santa Cruz was not so easily dismayed. It was his land; the Bolivians were his people. With the tenacity of his Indian forebears he commenced the task of reconstruction. He used his experience as a general to put down rebellions, gave peaceful despotism instead of anarchy, and inspired his followers with the ideals of the Liberator.

Under him the country made some material progress, but Santa Cruz was not satisfied with plodding forward. He took his army into Peru, defeated the forces of that country, and assumed the leadership of a vast confederation of the Andes. Chile and Argentina immediately felt the spur of fear at that unbalancing of power. There was a scramble to restore the situation as they wanted it. The confederation lasted from 1836 to 1839, when Santa Cruz was defeated in battle.

With the fall of the caudillo, Bolivia and Peru became, as one Latin-American historian put it, a "den of wild beasts." Ecuador was not far behind. Throughout most of the nineteenth century all of these Andean republics oscillated between civil war, anarchy, and caudillo rule. Some of the caudillos were vengeful tyrants; others were only civil autocrats. Self-government was unknown. Free elections did not take place anywhere. A leader imposed his will and the will of his class either by violence or through concerted minority effort. The masses lived apart from the main stream of the national political life. So far as the central governments were concerned, these masses hardly existed. By and large their condition had improved little if any since the days of the conquistadores. Theoretically they were free men living in free republics; actually they were deprived of every economic means of advancement, denied real participation in their own government, and afforded practically no opportunity for education or progress.

A contemporary Bolivian who has written a penetrating study of his nation calls it *Pueblo Enfermo*, or *A Sick People*. In its first century of independence, he says, Bolivia was governed by more than forty chief executives, nearly all of them tyrants. Six presidents were assassinated in office. There were approximately one hundred and eighty-seven armed uprisings, several of which were full-fledged civil wars. The only real law was the law of bullets and bayonets. Bolivia, like Paraguay, her next-door neighbor, has never known any form of government except dictatorship. "Heritage, laziness, poverty, barbarism, here in brief are the true and everlasting causes of the evil state of our countries, of their disorganization, of their corruption." So writes the author of *A Sick People*, Alcides Arguedas. In those rare instances when a good leader arose his corrupt colleagues vilified him, rebelled, and struck him down, and the people either followed suit or were apathetic. The greed and corruption of some and the goodness of others were all soon forgotten, and any demagogue who arose with golden promises was cheered with passion. "In Bolivia," wrote Arguedas, "they have no memory. And this desolate truth of a lack of memory, this terrible phrase which depicts such a frightful mental state, instead of disappearing with the birth of social justice, increases apace, each day more awful in its implication, up to this very present shameful hour of disaster in which everyone wishes to forget everything, even his own misery, even his own wounds . . ."[157]

One of the worst caudillos to rise from the miasma of Bolivian life was Mariano Melgarejo, an ignorant and drunken murderer given to the wildest sexual orgies, who ran the country from 1864–71. Melgarejo got into power by killing the country's dictator, Belzú, in the presidential palace. The shooting took place before a great crowd which had gathered in the plaza to see the meeting of the two rivals. When Belzú fell dead into the arms of one of his escort, Melgarejo strode to the window and exclaimed: "Belzú is dead. Now who are you shouting for?"

The mob, thus prompted, threw off its fear and gave a bestial cry: "Long live Melgarejo!"

It was the beginning of seven years of moral depravity such as even Bolivia had not seen before. Melgarejo was so devoid of any knowledge of history that "he insisted Napoleon was superior to Bonaparte and that Cicero was a second-rate general of antiquity."[155] He once shouted in public: "I'll rule in Bolivia as long as I feel like it, and anybody who tries to stop me will find himself strung up in the nearest plaza."

In order to increase his finances, Melgarejo permitted Chile to move her northern boundary up into Bolivian territory and ceded to citizens of that country the right to work the rich nitrate deposits on Bolivian soil. On another occasion, when his army was about to get out of hand because of irregular pay, he told his ministers that he wanted to declare war on Peru so that there would be a good excuse for levying extra taxes. Then he insisted that his ministers take a look at his bed to see how thrifty he had been with his previous income.

"A fine president I am!" he shouted. "I haven't even got any sheets. And I'm going to Peru to get me some!"

On a third occasion, when a speaker intimated before the Bolivian Congress that the country might enjoy a return to constitutional government, Melgarejo responded:

"I want the gentleman who has just spoken and all of the honorable deputies gathered here to know that I have put the Constitution of 1861, which was very good, in this pocket [pointing to his left trouser pocket] and that of 1868, which is even better in the opinion of these gentlemen, in this one [pointing to his right pocket] and that nobody is going to rule in Bolivia but me."[155]

There were better dictators in Bolivia than Melgarejo, but the main theme of the national history was that of a militaristic society which lives in a state of constant moral anarchy. Parliament and political parties were meaningless names. Sometimes the same men would call themselves conservatives, liberals, republicans, nationalists. Their curious gift was in generally being able to associate themselves with one of the groups heading toward power. Decent parties standing for definite principles were a psychological impossibility in Bolivia. The motto of those who achieved power was "let us govern with our own, and turn the robbers out." Arguedas, quoting the Argentine writer Alvarez, comments acidly: "Enough of small men making great phrases. We need decent, strong, and sensible men to produce good actions. Actions cannot be imported, while ideas can." Then he adds pessimistically: "To trust the individual by reason of the cause which he defends is like confiding one's money to a thief because he wears good clothes."

Revolution follows revolution. Improvisation is the law of government. Aptitude, specialization, training count for nothing. Experience and honesty are elusive quantities. Only dictatorial minds take the business of government seriously and the result is autocracy, not progress. Even in the twentieth century Bolivia's first good president, Ismael Montes, was forced into exile. Those who followed him in power whipped up a nationalistic fever against neighboring Paraguay over a boundary dispute in the Chaco, and thus entrenched their own party. The resultant war lasted from 1932–35 and was one of the bloodiest and most futile in Latin-American history.

Bolivia is a weak and disunited nation living without an outlet to the sea. Her people inhabit the bleak and high altiplano or live clustered on small isolated intermontane strips which lie athwart the great back of the Andes. The two thirds of the country which is lowland is not "effective national territory." The population is 55 per cent pure Indian and about 32 per cent mestizo. Poverty, malnutrition, and disease are chronic symptoms of Bolivian life. Fertile land is at a premium and linking roads are almost non-existent. In this weak and divided nation the civil authority lacks the force of concentrated public opinion to make those guarantees on which progress and democracy are dependent. Under these conditions, almost inevitably, the military will achieve the final power.

II. ECUADOR: A THEOCRACY

Peru and Ecuador were somewhat more fortunate than Bolivia and Paraguay. They front the sea and were more closely in contact with the outside world. Not only ships and goods might reach their shores, but also ideas. Nevertheless, until the dawn of our own generation the difference between the landlocked republics and the countries bordering the sea was one of degree and not of kind. The whole heart of the old Spanish viceroyalty of

Peru suffered chronically from hardening of the arteries. The only remedy was and is new blood or surgery.

The founder of Ecuador, General Juan José Flores, who was a Venezuelan by birth, came to power in 1830 and was the principal caudillo in that country for the next fifteen years. Under him Ecuador split away from Greater Colombia and established itself as an independent state. Flores grew more despotic as time passed and greatly favored foreigners and friends in handing out positions and power. When a more honorable president managed to squeeze himself into power the imported despot either made a deal with him or ousted him by force. However, Flores never achieved his ultimate goal, which was to crown himself king, and in 1845 the country got rid of him for good.

From 1845 to 1860 the "liberals" were in control of the government. Some Ecuadorian historians refer to this period as the "triumph of democracy," but, as in the case of the other Latin-American countries, a premature liberalism simply caused the government to disintegrate into anarchy. By 1860 conditions had become so bad that the little mountain state was on the point of falling apart into several petty regional divisions, each under its local despot. Then García Moreno, one of the most unusual rulers in Latin-American history, stepped into the picture.

Ecuador at that time (and the figures have not changed greatly since) had a population which was about 75 per cent pure Indian. Less than one person out of a dozen was Spanish, and the remainder were mestizos. Schools were practically non-existent, and the country was still almost as isolated as it had been under colonial rule. Its twin cities of Guayaquil, on the coast, and Quito, in the mountains, were separated by high sierras which made communication between them impossible in the winter and extremely tedious in summer. Although Quito was a city of churches, whose ornate façades and gilt altars suggested opulence, its inhabitants by and large lived in abject poverty. The total national population was calculated to be approximately 760,000 persons.

When the three states which had formerly made up Greater Colombia met to determine what proportion of the debt caused by the wars of independence each was to assume, 21¼ per cent fell to Ecuador, 28¼ per cent to Venezuela, and 50 per cent to Colombia. Ecuador's total came to only 22,000,000 pesos, but such was the wretched financial state of the country that a native historian writes: "This debt fell on us like a pestilence and has caused great evil even down to the present day, more than a century removed from the date when we assumed the burden."[118]

Added to this poverty was an ignorant and fanatical people, nearly half of whom could not speak Spanish, an isolated territory, and political cleavages which made impossible all hope of willing co-operation or compromise. The stage was all set for a dictator, and Gabriel García Moreno was the man of the hour.

He was born in the port city of Guayaquil in 1821, and showed an early inclination for serious study. His family was extremely conservative and religious, and much of the boy's early education was received at the hands of a priest. In the university he specialized in civil and canon law, but also took courses in the physical sciences, chemistry, and mathematics. Later he studied in Europe, and then for two years he was professor of chemistry at the University of Quito. Along with his strong scientific turn of mind went a religious instinct so profound and so orthodox that García Moreno considered everything else in life as subordinate or inconsequential.

In 1851, when the liberal government of General Urbina decided to expel the Jesuits from the republic, García Moreno served as their lawyer, and when the priests left, surrounded by troops, he arose from a sickbed to bid them farewell. Uncovering his head, he bowed before the superior and said: "Good-by, Father. Ten years from now we'll sing the *Te Deum* together in the cathedral!" It was like the oath of Bolívar uttered on the Sacred Mount at Rome.

The government did not like this attitude and formally exiled the troublesome professor. From the safe distance of Lima, García Moreno vilified his calumniators, as he called them, and shortly thereafter departed for France, where he remained for some time, studying, thinking, preparing himself for the inevitable day of his return. It became his obsession to learn how to govern righteously. He was unquestionably a man of considerable culture and stern moral character, and pursued his ideal with a tenacity seldom seen among the plethora of opportunistic caudillos.

García Moreno's first strong feeling in exile was undoubtedly a deep hatred for the liberal republic and everything it hoped to represent. Democracy and suffrage, he thought, were hollow words for Ecuador. His second feeling, built upon the first, was that despotism was the only possible kind of government for his country, and from this it was but a brief step to seeing himself in the role of despot.

In the meantime he went to mass daily, and spent many hours alone within the holy temples of Paris, meditating upon the destiny of his country. His spirit, he thought, became purified. He worshiped with the intensity of a martyr and believed with the strength of an inquisitor. Jehovah was the great life principle of the universe, and "the Catholic Church is the Empress of the world before which all kings as well as all peoples should bend in homage."[119]

Thus Paris became for the exiled Ecuadorian a sort of human wilderness where he spent his forty days and nights in penance, gathering belief and strength for the task before him. In Paris he saw clearly the conflict between the Christian and the anti-Christian ways of life, and so far as García Moreno was concerned the first only was real, the other a mere representation of the devil.

When he returned to Ecuador in 1856 the people greeted him with wild applause. Religious enthusiasm for his defense of the Church swept him into immediate popularity everywhere except among the liberals. He was made mayor of Quito, rector of the university, and senator. In the latter capacity he called for suppression of the Masonic Order, for honesty and morality in government, for a return to the true religion. The majority continued to applaud and approve his every utterance.

In 1860 García Moreno was made provisional president of Ecuador. Crowds of citizens gathered in the streets and shouted, "Death to the constitution! Long live religion!" It resembled the mobs in Spain forty-five years previously who had shouted, "Long live Ferdinand VII, our absolute King!" Ecuador was ready and willing clay in the hands of the zealous prophet.

In 1861 he was elected "constitutional president." However, the constitution under which the mystical ruler was to govern had a strong liberal tinge. Either the president or that document would have to retire, and the choice was not in doubt. García Moreno proceeded to draw up his "Catholic constitution," one of the most remarkable documents in modern history.

No one could be a citizen and not a member of the Catholic Church; the civil power was to be subordinate to the ecclesiastical, which had final control over everything; there was no such thing as freedom of conscience, for there was only one way of seeing the truth—the Catholic way. All other erroneous attitudes were to be vigorously combated by the state. García Moreno's constitution, in a word, was an open invitation to the Church to run Ecuador to suit itself, to make one immense monastery of the entire country.

But this was not enough. García Moreno also concluded a concordat with the Pope, who hesitated to accept such sweeping responsibility, and even the right of appointing ecclesiastical officers was yielded by the national government. A journal was published, called *The Republic of the Heart of Jesus*, and García Moreno in a formal ceremony dedicated his state to this same Sacred Heart. "The infiltration of evil doctrines in infancy and youth," he wrote, "are the most potent cause of the disorders and catastrophes of which society is the victim, in the same manner that miasmic poisons are the cause of terrible epidemics of disease. . . ."[119]

García Moreno was not one of the caudillos who simply utilized the Church as an instrument of achieving or maintaining power. His Catholicism was completely sincere; his state was completely theocratic. He attended mass daily, always dressed in black somber garments reminiscent of those of the clergy, and whenever there was a religious procession the president marched at the head carrying the banner of the Holy Virgin or of the Sacred Heart of Jesus. With bowed and somber head he resembled the herald of an implacable divinity standing guard over his people.

Whenever a priest came into the presence of García Moreno the presi-

dent uncovered his own head and begged the father not to do so. He wrote
to the Pope frequently, always in the most humble and supplicating tones,
"abjectly upon his knees," as one author put it.

García Calderón, the Peruvian essayist, called him "indefatigable, stoic,
just," and the Argentine, Bunge, wrote that he "had religion in his blood.
And mysticism, when it does reach the level of a great passion, is like all
passions, it never remains stationary, it either decreases or increases. . . .
For García Moreno religion was a passion which grew in a continuous
crescendo."

He took a hand in everything. Like Philip II, he attempted to oversee
every detail of his nation's life. Government, education, finances, the army,
civil and religious ceremonies, public works—he worked unceasingly on all
of them. There was not a moment when he was still. He personally observed workers construct buildings or roads, and oftentimes showed up at a
school to catechize the students and check up on their religious instruction. He also made a point of going by the penitentiary in order to exhort
criminals to a better way of life. This penitentiary was one of the dictator's
pet projects. It was an exact reproduction of one of the largest in the
United States, and at the time of its construction was reputed to be the
best of its kind in Latin America.

The private life of the president was held up before his people as exemplary, and he did everything in his power to make it so. His family went
over the rosary together every afternoon; the president himself went to
confession at least once a week, and articles appeared in the journal, *The
Republic of the Heart of Jesus*, in which it was stated that he rejoiced when
people censured his acts, that he never spoke in praise of himself, and that
in private he performed acts of humiliation, such as kissing the earth. García Moreno had few close friends and discreetly avoided even the most
innocent familiarities.

On the other hand, he smashed rebellions with a ruthless hand, and
either killed or drove into exile all who opposed him. His favorite motto
was "Liberty for all and for everything except for evil and evildoers." But
he backed this up with an intransigent interpretation of what was evil, and
with the corollary: "Only through the application of force may good be attained." Force, he said, must be put on the side of right, and to García
Moreno the "right" was to save human souls from hell. Thus either through
suasion or imposition the president took upon himself the task of national
salvation, for so long as a single Ecuadorian went unredeemed the whole
nation would have a blot on its record.

García Moreno was no mystical dreamer. His program was based on religious action and he accomplished many material things for Ecuador. The
president resembled one of the old Spanish mystics; he was a man to whom
the belief and the deed were inseparable. Like Ignatius Loyola, he wanted
to establish a society of Jesus on earth, but while Loyola's society was one

of picked souls, García Moreno's was to include all of the citizens of his nation. And the national body was not to be neglected.

García Moreno constructed Ecuador's best roads, her most notable public buildings, gave her the only halfway decent educational system she had had up to that time. He brought scholars from abroad, stimulated learning, enforced honesty and morality in government and in private life. He suppressed militarism and made civil law superior to the army. Under him government revenues more than doubled. He reformed the clergy, who had hitherto lived in circumstances which more than one author had called truly revolting. He imposed an austere and exacting standard of conduct upon a backward people.

García Moreno's crimes against personal liberty were numerous and frequent; like an inquisitor of old, he believed that he acted always for the good of the individual and for the good of his nation. He gave Ecuador the only unity she had known. Like Núñez of Colombia and Portales of Chile, he was guided by a conviction that "religion is the only national tradition in these democracies at the mercy of anarchy; it is the creative agent, the instrument of political unity." His personal and national ideal was expressed in the three words: "Virtue, faith, and order."

In spite of everything he accomplished García Moreno had his enemies, and among these was Ecuador's most brilliant writer, Juan Montalvo. Montalvo was the mouthpiece of the few liberals who opposed the somber theocracy and all that it stood for. In this young firebrand, who wrote with a pen dripping vitriol, García Moreno found a foeman worthy of his steel.

They began to tilt from a distance when Montalvo returned from Europe, where the national government had sent him to study. The new regime had just begun to get organized when Montalvo wrote the president a letter in which the following sentences occur: "You have shown yourself to be excessively violent, Señor García Moreno. Virtue lies in moderation and outside of it there is no felicity of any kind. How much more meritorious to dominate oneself than to dominate others! . . . Let me speak to you frankly: there are in you elements of the great hero and of . . . let us soften the word, of the tyrant. You have valor and audacity, but you lack political virtue. . . ."

After that fusillade these two great Ecuadorians squared off on opposite sides of the fence and fought out their epic battle to the bitter end. García Moreno, undeniably a man of genius, deported himself like a Hebrew prophet of old. The writer, who was a paladin of personal liberty, needed no other weapon than his terrible pen. "They were a pair of quixotic enemies and the victory would lie with the one who defended the most noble ideas."[120]

In 1866 Montalvo founded a journal called *The Cosmopolite* (*El Cosmopolita*), and his attacks began to bear viciously upon the ever more inflexible president. García Moreno dared to answer Montalvo with a couple of burlesque sonnets. It was the greatest mistake of his life. With that fuel added to the flames of his inspiration Montalvo literally tore the tyrant to pieces. Very shortly he wrote from the safety of exile. For seven years the combat continued. García Moreno held the power, but Montalvo was stabbing at him day after day with a ceaseless persistence and with increasing brilliance. The younger intellectual element came over to his side, some openly, most of them cautiously. Then in the year 1875 it happened.

García Moreno and his bodyguard had just come out of the cathedral in Quito and started down the elevated portico in front. A man named Rayo, who had formerly been a government official, approached them. Rayo was not on good terms with the president, but the latter did not have any cause to believe that his hatred reached the limits of treason. When the two men met Rayo began to speak to García Moreno in an excited manner. Farther down the street three other men, all strongly suspected of sympathizing with liberalism, were rapidly approaching. Suddenly and without warning Rayo slowed his pace for a second, raised his machete, and swung a powerful blow across the neck of the president. It made a deep gash, and García Moreno staggered. His cowardly bodyguard fled for reinforcements. In the meantime the other three men had approached and at least one of them fired into the still-staggering figure at point-blank range. García Moreno stumbled backward, lost his balance, and fell off the portico down to the street level ten feet below. The assassins hurried to the spot and found the dying man surrounded by a group of women. Rayo pushed them aside and finished his job with further blows of the machete. A priest reached the scene just in time to administer the last rites.[121]

When Juan Montalvo heard of the assassination from his exile in Colombia he shouted exultantly: "My pen killed him!"

At the time of his death in 1875 García Moreno had just been elected for a third term. Already he had placed the stamp of his personality and his philosophy on the nation, transforming it from a den of wild beasts into an ordered society. People in Ecuador today still feel passionately about him, either execrating his name or exalting him to the skies. There is no lukewarmness when mention is made of García Moreno. To conservatives he is the greatest man the country has ever produced and is a national martyr.

If there was an essential flaw in the ideology of García Moreno it was that he looked backward for his inspiration instead of forward. What he wished to see in Ecuador had been the ideal of the Middle Ages, the ideal of Ferdinand and Isabella, of Philip II, and of the Grand Inquisitor Torquemada. The mission settlements of Paraguay had practiced the theocratic ideal in the New World and had gone under. García Moreno strove to resurrect that same ecclesiastical past, and it was impossible. Despite all this, the unity, sincerity, and integrity of his work still stand out in that land of churches like scaffoldings which were raised to create a great building whose truncated walls now lie within them, broken off and uncompleted.

In the history of this austere theocrat can be seen one of the fundamental conflicts of Latin-American life. Everywhere the Church symbolizes the strongest surviving element of the colonial regime. Linked with the fortunes of large landholders who find in its conservatism a protection of tradition, and hence of the virtue of their property, the Church as a political and economic power has frequently stood on the opposite side of the fence from the secular liberalism of the past century of independence. In those nations where the Church allowed itself to become an obvious bulwark of the reactionary elements—Ecuador, Colombia, and Mexico—the clash between the two parties has been violent.

Following García Moreno in Ecuador, there was a long period of political anarchy out of which eventually arose the triumphant "liberalism" of the coast in the person of Eloy Alfaro, who became president in 1895. The old conflict between the coastal region and the sierra, between Guayaquil and Quito, between liberalism and tradition now resolved itself in favor of the former. Eloy Alfaro and Leonidas Plaza were the two outstanding presidents in the new perspective of the anti-clerical state. The country tottered along the path of economic improvement while absentee landlords ate up the profits of their great estates. When the witch-broom disease hit the cacao plantations in the 1920s the entire Ecuadorian economy collapsed, and from a hundred pulpits arose the cry: "God's retribution!"[121] The nation had compromised but had not yet solved its fundamental problems. Again she turned her back on the path of political order and fell into the hands of a military clique. Hardly recovered from this atavism, Ecuador was struck by the full fury of the world depression, and in 1931 another long-term despot found his way into the presidential palace.

III. PERU: SOCIETY OF SLAVE AND MASTER

Peru, proud center of Spanish viceregal rule for nearly three centuries, emerged from the struggle for independence in no better condition than Bolivia or Ecuador. Her indigenous masses, whose revolt under Tupac Amaru in 1780 had been smashed, continued to live, as it were, on the border of life. Her Lima aristocrats, accustomed to wealth and social prestige, had learned nothing from the mistakes of the colonial past. Her generals, like all generals who are not strictly subordinate to the civil authority, fought for power wherever and whenever their forces met.

When Bolívar had attempted to impose his unitarian constitution on both Peru and Bolivia, Peru threw it off and plunged instead into twenty years of civil war. The Bolivian caudillo, Santa Cruz, managed to break into the arena, and for a couple of years his Confederation of the Andes seemed to indicate a return to the Bolivarian ideal. But Santa Cruz was defeated by a combined army of Peruvians and Chileans and there was more civil war on the soil of the old viceroyalty.

Geographically, Peru is divided into three distinct sectors: the coastal desert, the mountains, the jungles. The last sector, which lies next door to Brazil, has never really entered into the national life. The early republic, therefore, was only seacoast and sierra. The seacoast was Lima; the sierra was synonymous with Indians. The aristocrats, nearly all the wealth, the governing power emanated from Lima. The whole back country was exploited in order that this "pearl of the Pacific" might shine a little more brilliantly against its setting of green mountains and red men.

Lima was the intellectual center of colonial days; the University of San Marcos was South America's oldest and finest. Many viceroys held literary salons in Lima, and poets sprang up there by the dozens. Lima was also the center of the South American Inquisition. Spanish colonial government was harbored there with its large officialdom, and to back up that officialdom there was an army.

Lima was a center of reaction throughout the struggle for independence. The new feeling which burst across the literate classes of Venezuela and Argentina made little imprint on Peru. Some abortive attempts were made to free the country from Spanish rule, but, compared with the heroic struggles being carried on elsewhere, they amounted to little. Peru seemed made up of two classes only: the minority, which was accustomed to rule, and the majority, which was accustomed to obey. Even the revolution did not upset that balance. When Lima was finally liberated it was San Martín who came all the way from Argentina to perform the mission. The remainder of the country was freed by Bolívar and Sucre, two more foreigners, who headed armies which were largely foreign in their composition and thus assured the independence of the continent.

Yet this society, while inert, was not stable. Once independence became a fact, the ruling caste began to fight over the governing power just as they did in every other Spanish American country outside of Dr. Francia's Paraguay. Aristocrats and generals alternated in the presidential chair, but for more than twenty years none of them remained there long enough to accomplish anything.

In 1845 Ramón Castilla, a mestizo, became the first real caudillo of the Peruvian state. He did not have much culture, but was astute by nature and an "autocrat by vocation." The primary aim of Castilla's government was to suppress anarchy, and in achieving that end the caudillo pushed the country along the path of stability and economic progress. For fifteen years he either ruled Peru or stood in the wings waiting for his cue in case there was trouble on the national stage. Castilla was no bloody tyrant like Rosas; he had no ideological program like García Moreno; he was simply a general who knew his people and was able to command enough of them to maintain himself in power. When he retired in 1862 he had given life to the nation.

After Castilla there were other leaders who carried forward the same tradition of order and material progress. Not one of them had a real social program. Even without it they still contrived to shove Peru far ahead of the other Andean republics.

The key to the situation was guano, a rich fertilizer made up of bird droppings, which is found in great quantities on islands off the Peruvian coast. Guano contains from 14 to 17 per cent nitrogen and was a godsend to the almost exhausted agricultural lands of northwestern Europe. Beginning about the year 1840, these deposits were exploited on a large scale by the Peruvian Government. At first the supply seemed inexhaustible, and the government profited greatly. In a single small area specialists estimated that there were approximately six million birds.

"Between 1840 and 1870 this industry gave the country an unparalleled boom. Shipments of guano from 1862 to 1873 averaged 467,000 tons per year." The income obtained "furnished capital for development of agricultural lands, and built highways and railroads that put Peru far ahead of other South American countries in this respect. The industry attracted world-wide attention. It brought to Peru large numbers of immigrants as laborers on the guano islands; the oriental and negro elements of the coastal desert population were introduced at this time. They have left an indelible stamp on this part of the republic."[166] The central government came to depend more and more on guano for a living. For many years, more than 75 per cent of the total federal income was from this one source. Peru became a nation dependent upon a single product; her national economic structure was held up by a single prop.

These bird droppings had another effect on the society of Peru. Out of their profits emerged a new business oligarchy, a plutocracy of wealth alone which challenged the old Peruvian families. It might have altered greatly the basis of economic life inside the nation, but the two minorities joined forces in order to keep the majority in servitude.

When other fertilizers appeared on the world market, especially nitrate from the desert provinces between Chile and Peru, the price of guano dropped from eighty to fifty dollars a ton. The birds which produced it had been killed by the hundreds of thousands; the richest deposits were rapidly exhausted, and after its brief boom the country went into a financial slump. In the 1890s the federal government placed the islands under rigid control, and the supply gradually began to build up again. At present, production averages about 90,000 tons a year, and the fertilizer sells for from thirty-five to fifty dollars a ton delivered at the Peruvian plantations. It enables planters of cotton and sugar cane to use the same land for the same crop year after year.

The temporary loss of guano income was a disaster for Peru, but it was nothing compared with the blow which struck her in the late nineteenth century. The cause was a dispute over the nitrate provinces around the Bolivian port of Antofagasta. Chile wanted these provinces; Peru and Bolivia stood together to keep them from her. The superior Chilean army came up and occupied them by force, and in the peace which followed Peru was also obliged to cede her southern territories of Tacna, Arica, and Tarapacá.

As a result of the war, which had dragged along for four years (1879–83) and ended only with the occupation of Lima and most of Peru by the victorious Chilean army, Peru was left desolate and bankrupt. Her transportation facilities had been destroyed; her guano exports had gone down to nothing, and the country wound up with a war debt of approximately $250,000,000 while her federal income was only $7,500,000 a year. For the following twenty years Peru marked time; again the disruptive fever of revolutionary violence tore apart the weak structure of her national life.

During these harrowing years there arose a brilliant leader who, before his death, became Peru's most distinguished writer. His name was Manuel González Prada. All of the social movements of a later date in Peru hark back to the little group of intellectuals which gathered around Don Manuel, and to the ideas which were hatched there and injected sharply into the body of a dying republic. The APRA Indianist party, which is still a tremendous power on the political horizon of South America, owes much of its ideology to González Prada, and the Marxist group of the little cripple, José Carlos Mariátegui, also found inspiration in the mordant essays of Don Manuel. Perhaps neither of their parties will ever really control Peru, but the ideology of social justice for which Gonzalez Prada fought is certain someday to win out over the small oligarchy which still rules the nation.

González Prada was born in Lima in 1848, the son of a wealthy, conservative, and distinguished family of pure Spanish blood. He was sent to Chile to the "English School" in Valparaiso, and then returned to his native land, where he was placed in a seminary in order to complete his education. He rebelled at once and fled from the place. His father refused to send him to Europe as he wished, so Manuel enrolled in the University of San Marcos in Lima, where he studied law. The verbose sophistries and mummified echoes which characterized those hollow but sacrosanct halls caught the young man in their net and he struggled to get free. He never ceased to rebel until the end of his life. Although the struggle was hopeless and the means which he used were not always the best, González Prada dedicated his life to the future, and his essential faith is still alive in the Peru of today.

No one has ever criticized his own culture or his own people with more biting satire than González Prada. Of Peru he wrote: "We have never initiated a reform, never announced a scientific truth, nor produced an immortal book. We do not have men but mere echoes of men, we do not express ideas but repetitions of decrepit and moth-eaten phrases."

He spoke of the Peruvian Congress as a great sewer where all the filth of the country was gathered. The country itself was like an immense boil, "press down anywhere and the pus comes out." The people who inhabited the land "know how to love with their bellies but not with their hearts." They still suffer the "nostalgia of slavery. Here their faces ask for blows, their buttocks demand kicks. . . . All suffer from the abuse of force, and those who possess least suffer most; thus the poor Indian is crucified between the cassock of the priest and the poncho of the strong man or soldier."

Peru, he knew, was fertile ground for a revolution. He hardly believed that it would come during his lifetime, and it did not. It has not come yet. But González Prada believed that the day would surely arrive when "the true popular revolution, so long dreamed of and longed for by all thinking men of Peru, would drown out the leeches and deposit on the impoverished soil of the nation its fruitful seed." When success did not greet the efforts of the small and thinking minority, they should not, he said, despair nor call the earth or its people infertile, but should rather attribute their failure to the paucity of seeds they had scattered. Even in such failures new seeds are sown, and when enough of them are accumulated they will suddenly burst forth in violent and lovely bloom.

González Prada was no communist. He often thought of himself as an anarchist. In actuality he was a man with no clearly defined social program; he was the blaster who clears the forest before the fields may be planted.

When the war with Chile broke out, González Prada was living in Lima, where his home had become a kind of intellectual center in which the restless young spirits of the country gathered. With Don Manuel at their head these young men fought bravely for social justice against the minions of dictatorship who controlled their government. The war interrupted all this. González Prada enlisted in the army and took part in the losing campaign. The Chileans won and occupied the Peruvian capital. As a protest against this profanation of his native soil González Prada shut himself up in his home and during nearly three years of foreign occupation refused to go out on the streets. Intellectuals still assembled in his drawing room and discussed the miserable situation of their country.

In 1888 González Prada's mother died. She had been an extremely religious woman, and in deference to her wishes he had not attacked the Church while she was alive. After her death he ripped off every restraint and vilified the Catholicism he had known in vitriolic language. He was never an atheist, as some of his enemies stated, but he did firmly believe that in Peru the Church "preached the Sermon on the Mount and practiced the morals of Judas." To him the economic power of the clergy and the economic power of the military were the two great diseases of the national life. Both bore down on the masses, crushing and exploiting them, so that they had moved steadily backward for nearly four hundred years. Until these two wheels of the juggernaut were destroyed there could be no real hope for progress in Peru.

González Prada helped to form a political party known as the National Union. It was a party of "propaganda and attack." After more than a decade of futile struggle, during which time both of his sons had died, González Prada and his wife left for Europe (1891). For the following seven years he lived mainly in Paris, where many of his writings first appeared in book form. In 1898 friends wrote that his party wanted him to run for the presidency and urged him to return. He reached Lima in May of that same year and was greeted by a huge mob and a large band of musicians who had come out to receive him.

The government reacted at once. "He was prohibited from speaking in public, and he spoke. The publication of any newspaper in which his articles appeared was forbidden, and he founded newspapers of his own and continued to write."[122] The government became so uneasy that it offered him all kinds of positions and compromises, but he would not yield on a single point. In 1901, three years after his return from voluntary exile, they forced him out of the country again. From public rostrum and pulpit his name was shouted as anathema. But González Prada was not gagged; he continued to write and to be read eagerly by intellectuals, workers, and Indians. Those who could not read listened to others who could. His ideas stirred up a ferment from one end of Peru to the other. The government was gradually forced to yield some ground in order to maintain itself.

In addition to his "prose thunderbolts" González Prada found time to write some of the finest poems to come out of South America, and made many translations from the German, French, and English languages. The sum total of his writing makes him certainly the outstanding author of his country.

In 1918, without having seen the realization of any of his social ideas, the great leader died suddenly of a heart attack, and Peruvian reactionaries began to breathe more easily. It was not for long; five years later the indigenist APRA party was founded, which twice captured the presidency of Peru, and twice was defrauded of placing its candidate in power. Finally, in 1982, APRA again won at the polls and took over the government.

González Prada kept up a running fight with the Peruvian dictators who ruled his country while he was alive: Piérola, Romaña, José Pardo, and all the rest. He knew that it would be impossible to raise a national edifice which would last until the weeds of absolutism had been cleared away. His best books, *Propaganda and Attack, Hours of Struggle, Free Pages,* all indicate the tenor of his approach. He was close to Marx in his economic interpretation of society, but he hated all regimentation, and when the Russian Revolution arrived he did not greet it with any enthusiasm. He despised his own aristocratic caste for the crimes it had committed and for the opportunities it had thrown away. He called on those who would listen—intellectuals, workers, Indians, all the abject masses of Peru—to take over and make over their nation.

In his preface to *Propaganda and Attack* he wrote: "The national writer faces an arduous task, for he is called upon to counteract the pernicious influence of public men. His work must be one of propaganda and attack. . . . The people must be shown the horror of their degradation and their misery; a good autopsy was never made without cutting apart the body, nor has any society been fully known until its skeleton was denuded of flesh. Why should we be frightened or scandalized . . . ? The hideous disease is not cured by hiding it under a white glove."

In another book he speaks of revolutions in these terms: "Revolutions come from above but are carried out from below. Their way lighted by the gleam on the surface, those who are oppressed in the depths see justice clearly and thrust forward to conquer it, without hesitating as to the means nor feeling fear as to the consequences. While the moderates and theoreticians imagine geometric evolutions or get all tangled up in the details of form, the multitude simplifies matters, taking them down from the nebulous heights and confining them to earthy practice. They follow the example of Alexander; they do not untie but cut the knot which binds them."

González Prada believed "that all liberty was born bathed in blood. . . . Rights and freedom are never granted; they must be taken. Those who command give only what they must, and nations which sleep trusting their rulers to arouse them with the gift of liberty are like fools who build a city in the midst of a desert hoping that a river will suddenly flow through its barren streets."

González Prada is of tremendous importance in the history of Peru, not only because of the unity and strength of his writings, but because they are as alive today as when written. Although he never governed Peru he was greater than any caudillo. He was clearly a man born before his epoch, but his was not a voice crying in the wilderness. The ruling caste of Peru heard and was forced to make concessions; the masses heard and were inspired to demand their rights. Nevertheless, the revolution of which he was the herald has not yet taken place. Every thinking citizen of the land realizes this, and the present is a time of tense and anxious waiting.

48

CHILE: DEMOCRACY OF THE OLIGARCHY

Of all the Spanish American republics Chile was the first to establish a stable government. Even Chile's early years, however, were as chaotic as those of any other nation. "The Dictator O'Higgins fell in 1823; a *junta* followed him, and after the junta four governors—ephemeral figures which a turbulent democracy set up and destroyed." Between 1827 and 1828 there were five revolutions. Federalists fought unitarians; liberals fought conservatives; the oligarchy sought to impose its will over the masses. The people did not hesitate to employ the dangerous expedient of military might in order to achieve their political ideals. Congresses became disruptive assemblies; demagogy was rampant; government was impossible.

In 1829 Diego Portales, a merchant, gathered the supreme power into his hand, suppressed anarchy, and began to govern the country like a businessman. In 1833 he proclaimed the constitution by which Chile was governed until 1925. San Martín and O'Higgins had freed Chile from Spain; Portales made it a nation.

Portales belonged to a wealthy and distinguished family of Santiago which had shown little interest in politics. The men of the family were all successful merchants. Portales himself took no part in the revolution against Spain, preferring not to risk his life for the dubious ideal of democracy. Instead he sipped his drinks in the cafés of Santiago and took up those affairs of the heart which became with him almost an obsession.

In 1822, when O'Higgins was still in power, he wrote to a friend: "Politics doesn't interest me, but as a good citizen I feel free to express my opinions and to censure the government. Democracy, which is so loudly proclaimed by the deluded, is an absurdity in our countries, flooded as they are with vices and with their citizens lacking all sense of civic virtue, the prerequisite to establishing a real Republic. But monarchy is not the American ideal either; if we get out of one terrible government just to jump headlong into another, what will we have gained? The Republican system is the one which we must adopt, but do you know how I interpret it for our countries? A strong central government whose representatives will be men of true virtue and patriotism, and who thus can direct the citizens along the path of order and progress."[123]

Portales, as these words reveal, despised factional political quarrels, but was not averse to taking a strong interest in the art of government. He wrote the above letter eight years before he came to power, and before chaotic conditions within his country had forced him to think of how his ideas might best be applied. He had expressed well the apology of all dictators and tyrants: relief from disorder, efficient government.

The fact that an executive holds dictatorial powers does not necessarily make him a tyrant. Many leading rulers of democratic states have held such powers during war. The crux of the matter depends on only one thing: do the people still hold the right, the strength, and the desire to take back that extraordinary power which they have granted when the emergency is past?

Portales was a dictator, but, compared with the other dictators of his day, he was hardly a tyrant. The people of Chile wanted him, needed him, and when he was killed his death was mourned as a national disaster. The only question in his case would be: Did he use his power always in the best interest of the majority? There is no surety that he did; nevertheless, he was the founder of the Chilean nation.

Two things brought Portales into the political field despite his own inclinations. First, the business firm of which he was a partner had undertaken to run the government's monopoly of tobacco and other articles; second, the upset conditions of the country made any peaceful business practically impossible. Caught in this cross fire, Portales was obliged to take an active part in government.

In 1827 Portales first began to feel his way into the arena. The conservative party, which he helped to reorganize, started publishing in that year a journal called *El Hambriento,* or *The Starveling.* Its main purpose was to attack the liberal idealists who had been battling over the control ever since independence was declared. These liberals called themselves the *pipiolos,* or "white beaks"; the party of Portales was known as the *pelucones,* or "old wigs."

Portales was not a particularly learned man, but he had a gift for satire in both prose and verse and contributed many scathing articles to *The Starveling.* The people at large saw in these writings, and in the man who penned them, the hope of their country which was then truly starving to death for want of normal progress because of perpetual disorder. Portales won for himself a "vociferous popularity."

In 1829 the conservatives, through a revolution, came to power. Portales, as one of the most renowned members of the party, was called to fill the posts of minister of the interior and foreign relations, and that of the war and navy. He thus held in his hands the two fundamental portfolios for absolute government, and the energy with which he attacked the tasks at hand showed that he meant not to let the opportunity slip by. From that year until his death in 1837 he was the real dictator of Chile, although he was never once president. In fact, as an astute businessman Portales eschewed the presidency, thinking that it would tie his hands with factional promises.

As dictator behind the scenes Portales brought the generals to heel, exiling those who were not amenable to the new government. For further security he organized a civil militia over which he placed officers whose loyalty was unquestioned. The worst phase of militarism was thus ended in Chile.

Portales ruled for the oligarchy of landowners, miners, and merchants, and governed autocratically. When the press became violent in its accusations, he muzzled the worst offenders, not by doing away with freedom of the press but by having judges or juries render suitable decisions in each case. He made Catholicism the state religion and excluded from public worship any other sect. Like Núñez in Colombia and García Moreno in Ecuador, he saw the benefits of having the stable influence of the Church on his side.

Portales had no fixed political opinions. He did not represent a party with an ideological program. He was a "man of facts" who governed according to what he thought were the necessities of the moment. He strove for peace and order; progress and perhaps greater freedom might naturally follow. They were not primary to Portales; to him these further evidences of advancement were the results of order, not the foundation.

In 1837, when Portales went to review a body of troops which was being made ready to take part in the war against the Confederation of the Andes under Santa Cruz, the officers in charge arrested him and placed him in chains. It was strictly a mutiny, without popular support or knowledge. The mutineers escorted their captive toward Valparaiso where they were challenged by a larger body of soldiers. Before the brief battle took place, Portales, still in chains, was forced to his knees and riddled with bullets. A few moments later the loyal soldiers overcame the mutineers, all of whom were hanged for their crime.

Personal animus of some kind must have been the motivation for the assassination of Portales. All historians agree that the people of Chile were beside themselves with grief. The assassins had no reason or program, and Portales at forty-four went to his grave a national martyr.

Chile, under Portales, had resolved her political problem "without dynasties and without a military dictatorship by means of a constitution which was monarchical in nature and republican in form. . . . A republic can have no other when it follows immediately upon a monarchy." These are the words of the Argentine jurist, Alberdi, written when he was living in Chile as an exile from Rosas. Alberdi continues: "The new regime must contain something of the old; a nation does not pass from youth to maturity in a single leap."

During the regime of this merchant dictator of Chile all business had improved, especially the business of the wealthy class. There was one industry which was particularly fortunate, and Portales had nothing to do with its development. That was mining.

In 1832, only three years after the autocracy was established, a Chilean donkey driver, Juan Godoy, gave the mining industry a great impetus. Godoy was a woodcutter who gathered the scanty brushwood of his region, loaded it on donkeys, and carried it to town to sell. He grew tired of his way of life and decided to abandon it. His idea was to chase the roving guanaco, the wild predecessor of the llama, and perhaps eke out an existence on the plains of Copiapó. On his first trip Godoy sat down to rest on a hard rock, and when he arose noticed that the seat of his trousers had polished the stone until it gleamed with a silvery light. Godoy returned home with samples of the rock and shared his discovery with an educated friend, who aided him to make the most of it. He had struck one of the richest silver mines in South America. Up to that time Chile had developed no great mining industry to supplement her agriculture and cattle raising, so Godoy's discovery helped considerably in rounding out the national economy.

Another thing which had a considerable influence on Chilean life during the dictatorship of Portales was the arrival, in 1829, of the Venezuelan, Andrés Bello, Spanish America's most revered man of letters. Bello was the kind of bibliophile who, in his boyish years, had saved his pennies in order to buy the best classical authors. In 1810, when the revolution broke out in Venezuela, he was sent to London along with Bolívar to procure funds for the patriot cause. They were unsuccessful; the revolution was temporarily suppressed, and Bello was left stranded in England without funds. In order to earn a living, he taught Spanish and tutored the children of Lord Hamilton. Later he published a journal called *Repertorio Americano* in which the new ideas of freedom were presented. Bello himself contributed poems written in a classic Latin style which are among the best of their kind in Spanish.

In one of them, *A Call to Poetry*, he asks culture to leave the Old World, where she had become a mere prostitute, and take up her abode in America, where the horizon was unlimited and men's minds were free. In another poem he sings the beauties, the fertility, the promise of the tropics, and puts into glowing words the best feelings of that new generation of patriots who struggled so valiantly against Spain.

In time Bello's name became widely known and deeply respected throughout America. For nearly two decades he was the intellectual leader of the patriots in exile. In 1829, through the intercession of Chilean friends, he was invited to take up his residence in that country as under-secretary for foreign affairs. This going beyond the bounds of narrow nationalism, to select a Venezuelan who had lived for twenty years in London as a representative of the government of Chile, is a proof of the spirit of tolerance which was alive in the little nation of Portales.

Bello came to Chile at the age of fifty and remained there for the rest of his life; he died at the age of eighty-four. During all that time he worked constantly to train the young minds of the new republic; no matter what his position, he was always primarily a teacher and a thinker. He had a chance to do "what Bentham always wanted to do: to civilize a people and legislate for them."[124] In 1842 he became the first president of the newly organized University of Chile.

Bello was not interested in politics, and, being a foreigner, he did not meddle at all in the fiery discussions of local affairs. But he gathered around him the finest young minds of Chile, and inspired them all with a love of liberty, the desire for a broad culture, and imparted to them some of his own wise and harmonious humanity and clear thinking. Although he was a conservative in his political views, Bello saw beyond the necessities of the moment and knew that only education could at last redeem Chile from its unenlightened and backward state. Two of the country's most brilliant thinkers and writers, Lastarria and Bilbao, reached mental maturity under the guidance of the old master. The fires of liberalism later caused these young men to grow away from Bello, but he was the teacher who revealed to them the path of knowledge.

Bello himself contributed to the cause of political liberalism through his presentation of the ideas of the English writers he had come to know so well while residing in London. James Mill and Bentham had made an especially deep impression on his mind. Bello also had a wide knowledge of international law, and in 1855, after laboring on the project for twenty years, he presented to the government of Chile a complete revision and codification of the national statutes. His recommendations were approved and went into effect two years later. Bello's code was the most scientific and carefully prepared national legislation established in any Latin-American nation up to that time and became a model for many other countries to follow.

To the readers of today Bello is undoubtedly stodgy, yet his influence on Latin-American education, thinking, and law was perhaps more profound than that of any other man of his generation. Like all good patriots, he loved Liberty, but he did not believe in rushing her off her feet. "Liberty does not stand alone," he wrote, "as some people think. It is allied with all national traits, and it improves them without changing their nature . . . it gives wings to the spirit of enterprise, wherever it meets it, and breathes breath into it where it does not exist. But liberty cannot work without the two great factors of all human work: nature and time. Administrative measures now retard the movement, now hasten it, without doubt. But it is necessary that we not exaggerate its power. There are moral obstacles that it cannot banish. There are natural accidents which it is impossible to change."[124]

Bello, who loved liberty with a warm but classic love, and the Argentines, Sarmiento and Alberdi, who clasped it tighter because of their hatred of the tyrant Rosas, along with the distinguished young Chileans, Lastarria and Bilbao, all lived under the conservative and autocratic regime which Diego Portales had imposed upon his nation. They were all, incidentally, great admirers of the United States, so much so at times that one feels a bit sheepish at the sacred fire of their idealization.

Portales himself, the merchant dictator, laid down for these and other classes of men the tight foundations upon which the Chilean state was raised. From 1829, the year of his accession to power, to 1891, when the so-called "parliamentary republic" was inaugurated, Chile did not depart greatly from this base. She was under the more or less inflexible and autocratic government of the ultra-conservatives. Nevertheless, her government was not hidebound; a "liberal" opposition was gradually growing throughout those six decades; the people were becoming more interested in participation in their destiny and more aware of the necessity for social and political change. All power, however, remained in the hands of the propertied oligarchy, and every change was effected by and through that wealthy minority which, through division within itself, gradually sprouted two wings, the reactionary and the "liberal."

This latter group struggled primarily to restrict the power of the executive and to liberalize the constitution, especially in its electoral and religious clauses. The most enlightened leaders of Chile, during the latter half of the nineteenth century, belonged to this liberal wing of the conservative party.

Throughout her formative years Chile reaped considerable advantage from living almost entirely in her central valley; she did not contain great unassimilated Indian masses; she was not a land divided against herself by mountain barriers or jungles. A mountain barrier did shut the country off from its great pampas neighbor, and a northern desert one thousand miles in extent protected it from Peru. Geographically, as well as ethnically, Chilean unity was favored. The country was not too close to her neighbors, but was in contact with the world through her hundreds of miles of coast line which faced the expanses of the Pacific.

Chile was an agricultural nation, and her landed oligarchy set up and maintained the Chilean state. The men who owned the land controlled the selection of presidents. Militarism was suppressed and there was a succession of civilian autocrats, at first conservative, then liberal. Both groups were strongly conservative in a social sense.

The ruling oligarchy, under pressure from its own "radical" wing, was willing to grant a small measure of *political* democracy to the Chilean people. Agricultural workers do not easily band into rebellious masses. As a consequence the country moved slowly forward, little by little learning the meaning of self-government within the framework of an aristocratic state.

Alberdi in 1852 pointed out that while Chile had escaped prolonged disorder, she had not escaped backwardness. "Her good fortune is negative . . . she lives in order, but without a population; she lives in peace, but she is stationary." His answer was immigrants, immigrants, immigrants. It was, is now, and will be for years to come the pith of the Latin-American problem. Vast lands without people are like machines without workers. They do not add up to production, nor to progress.

Toward the end of the nineteenth century Chile began to feel the urge to expand. Within fifty years her population had grown from less than a million to approximately 2,500,000. Her domestic situation was improving steadily, and her small central valley seemed too cramped a place for so enterprising a nation. She built up her army and prepared to extend herself. She was passing through the same stage the United States had experienced a few decades previously, while expanding southward and westward into Mexican territory.

Chile grew northward, and the reason was clear. In that remote desert region, beyond any possible boundary which Chile had hitherto claimed, lay the recently tapped mines of nitrate, one of the world's richest fertilizers. Chileans, Bolivians, and Peruvians all worked these deposits. Bolivia had her only narrow outlet to the Pacific across them. The Chileans worked the hardest and made the most profits. Bolivia, with long-standing prior claim to the regions, tried to make up the difference by slapping taxes on the export of nitrates. Chile tried to buy her off by promising to help her conquer the southernmost provinces of Peru, provided Bolivia would cede to Chile her own rich nitrate territory. Bolivia not only refused this proposal but made a secret alliance with Peru: if either country was attacked the other would come immediately to the rescue.

In 1879 Bolivia broke an agreement not to raise the tax on nitrate exports, and Chile sent her armed forces into the Bolivian port of Antofagasta. Peru fulfilled her part of the contract and came to the support of her ally. Although the population of Peru and Bolivia combined must have been at least double that of Chile, the two backward countries did not have a chance. The well-trained Chilean forces took all the territory in question, including the three southernmost provinces of Peru, Tacna, Arica, and Tarapacá. After that they landed a few miles south of Lima and swept on to the Peruvian capital, which was occupied for two years.

In the treaties made following the war Bolivia and Peru lost everything. Both of them continued to complain bitterly of this despoliation, and Peru finally got back the province of Tacna plus a settlement of six million dollars. Chile deigned to grant Bolivia the right to use a railway which ran through her former territory.

This War of the Pacific had repercussions which have not yet died away. Bolivia was left landlocked, isolated, and powerless, a country whose backwardness became a festering disease. Peru was put in a vengeful frame of mind which still smolders. But the military might of Chile placed that little country on the road to national prosperity. Those were the days when a nation could fight a war and at least temporarily win it, along with a few resounding financial rewards.

Between 1880 and 1890 the production of nitrate more than tripled, and within that same ten-year period Chilean national revenues jumped from fifteen million to sixty million pesos. Chile actually felt four times as rich as she had been before the war began. Manufacturing promptly doubled and continued to expand. A small working class began to spring up. The wages of a day laborer increased from half a peso to a full peso, and salaries in nearly all the urban centers also went up 100 per cent.

As a country Chile had progressed notably, and some individuals made fantastic profits. A native historian refers to this period as one of "wealth and splendor." But the masses of people with their few cents a day, whether doubled or not, still lived in squalor. Disease and incredible poverty were in evidence on nearly every Chilean street. With hesitant and halting hands the nation had barely touched its greatest national problem.

At the beginning of this period of prosperity Chile was ruled by one of her most striking presidents, José Manuel Balmaceda, 1886–91. Balmaceda employed the great wealth which had accrued to the country following the War of the Pacific in material enterprises. Schools, railways, public works of a dozen kinds brightened the national horizon. Balmaceda was "the master-builder among presidents." He was also last of that long line of personal autocrats who had ruled Chile since the days of Portales.

Chilean historians divide the development of republican Chile into three periods: the autocratic republic, 1829–61; the liberal republic, 1861–91; and the parliamentary republic, 1891 to the present. Up to the close of Balmaceda's term the president was supreme over both courts and Congress. He administered the country, managed the elections, chose his successor. The enlightened rule of a series of civil autocrats saved Chile from the disasters of caudillo tyranny.

In 1891 this situation reached an impasse. Balmaceda was confronted with a majority opposition in the Congress. That body refused to approve his cabinet or to sanction his budget. A bloody civil war broke out, and Balmaceda's party was defeated. The President himself took refuge in the Argentine legation while the mob looted Santiago. There he drew up a manifesto of his principles. In it he also pointed out that "all the founders of South American independence have died in dungeons, in prison cells, have been assassinated, or have perished in exile." Balmaceda himself might easily have escaped such a fate by fleeing, "but this expedient," he wrote, "would not be consistent with my antecedents, nor my pride as a Chilean and a gentleman." As a consequence of this feeling he dressed himself in severe black, lay upon his bed, and fired a revolver shot into his brain. With him passed away the epoch of personal rule in the national life, and government descended from its pedestal to become the patrimony of the people.

In the years that followed Chile fashioned herself into a modern nation. The nitrate deposits of the north gave her the easy wealth with which to maintain stable government. When that income failed after World War I the lower classes and workers asserted their dominance in the presidency of Alessandri Palma, humble descendant of an Italian immigrant, who was the outstanding leader of the 1920s and '30s. Political consciousness grew in all the urban centers; the masses there now read the newspapers; electoral democracy and such freedoms as those of speech, assembly, religion, and the press became assured. In spite of these advances, an ugly and dangerous chasm still separates the two extremes of Chilean life.

49

SANTA ANNA LOSES HALF OF MEXICO

The situation in Mexico after the war of independence was perhaps more fantastic than in any other Latin-American nation. First there was Augustin Iturbide I, proclaimed Emperor of Mexico in 1822. He was exiled in 1823. In 1824 he returned from exile and was captured and shot. During that same year a Mexican congress met and drafted an enlightened constitution, based in considerable measure on that of the United States. The constitution did not work. Elections were a farce. Those who were elected could not hold power unless they had force to back it up, and those who lost claimed they had been defeated by corruption and attempted to reverse the returns by violence.

On the horizon of these chaotic experiments in self-government arose the figure of one of the greatest charlatans in the history of this hemisphere, Antonio López de Santa Anna. Santa Anna was an opportunist first, last, and always. He fought in favor of any issue or party which afforded him an opening for self-aggrandizement, and frequently was on both sides of the same issue at different dates, if he made up his mind that the wind had changed.

Santa Anna accomplished nothing for Mexico except to consummate her national debasement, defile the honor of her government, rob and exploit her people, while he himself strutted across the stage like a magniloquent combination of bantam rooster and Lucifer, demanding applause from the victimized and ignorant masses beneath him. Four times the people of Mexico rebelled and threw him out. Four times they found themselves in a dilemma and restored him to power.

In order to keep up a front every time he lost a battle, Santa Anna would proclaim a victory and march down the streets of the capital with a frenzied mob at his heels. He possessed only a single outstanding quality of the many which characterized other Latin-American caudillos: cunning. Time and again he turned it to his own advantage through lies, trickery, blustering fanfaronade, or bribery.

After emerging from the morass to lead his nation to its lowest depths of degradation, it was inevitable that finally even the mob should weary of his antics and refuse to applaud when he put on his show. In 1855 Santa Anna was deposed and exiled for the last time. Years later, when he was permitted to return to Mexico City, an old and broken man, no one any longer called him to mind.

This pompous churl of a caudillo, who might well have been a figure lifted out of some comic opera had his consequences been less disastrous for his people, was born in the town of Jalapa, capital of the state of Vera Cruz, in 1794. His parents were both white Creoles, and his father ran a mortgage broker's business. Santa Anna was destined for a business career, but he preferred the army and entered it at an early age. His first years as an officer were undistinguished. In 1821, as commander of the garrison of Vera Cruz, he supported the campaign of Iturbide and helped make him Emperor. In 1823, realizing that His Majesty was not going to allow anyone else much room to shine in, Santa Anna took the opposite side and aided in overthrowing the empire. For a few years thereafter he lived in a sort of self-made glory, thinking of himself as the founder of the republic. He was much put out that the people at large had not recognized his services more fully. In 1828, when the conservatives won a bitter election, Santa Anna saw his chance. With his armed support the liberal candidate took objection to the results and forced himself into power. Santa Anna announced that he was saving the country from abuses worse than those of the Inquisition. Nevertheless, the government which he had backed lasted only a few months.

In the meantime Spanish forces had landed at Vera Cruz, believing that all they would have to do to reconquer Mexico for Spain would be to show themselves in the country. They seized the fortress of Tampico, but yellow fever soon swept through their ranks and laid them low. Santa Anna, who was on the scene, fought no real battle against the invaders, but when they withdrew he claimed a great victory. From then on he made himself known as the "hero of Tampico."

In 1832 he entered the city of Vera Cruz and pocketed about four hundred thousand pesos in customs duties, in order to finance his rebellion against the "reactionary government in Mexico City." That tidy sum did wonders for his cause, and in 1833 Santa Anna was elected president of the Mexican Republic. Up to this time he had been supporting the liberals. It was the liberal party which put him in power. But Santa Anna began to regret his choice even before the inaugural ceremony. The really big money, he now saw, was on the other side. When the inauguration was held the president decided not to show up for it. Instead, he pleaded illness and had his vice-president, Gómez Farías, assume office in his place. Santa Anna's keen political nose had told him what was in the offing.

The vice-president and his liberal supporters—Masons, intellectuals, and zealous patriots—began work in earnest. A series of far-reaching "radical" reforms was approved. Education was to be taken away from the Church and secularized; many ecclesiastical funds were to be taken over by the government; army officials and priests were to lose all special privileges; members of the clergy were to be permitted to break their vows; the large landowners were to pay more taxes and bend before impersonal law. . . .

Santa Anna heard of all this and made his own plans for the future of the country. As he had foreseen, the propertied classes became alarmed. Members of the clergy and wealthy Creoles formed a growing opposition whose cry was "Religion and Privileges." When the iron was hot Santa Anna struck. In the name of the "holy revolution" he entered the halls of Congress, disbanded that body, dismissed his vice-president, and proclaimed himself dictator of the country. Conservative churchmen and landowners applauded vigorously. The liberals were taken by surprise, and it was not until a quarter of a century later that they recovered from the blow.

Santa Anna made the mistake of allowing new elections to be held, and, although a strong conservative majority was sent to Congress, there were among them many competent and honorable men who looked unfavorably on this so-called Napoleon of the West. The president again retired in a great sulk and let his henchman rule, hoping that calamity would soon befall him. In the meantime, he himself, like a vulture, lay in wait at his country estate until such time as he might swoop down in triumph upon the capital.

The Texas-Mexican crisis cut short his reverie, and the general came back to lead the troops of his country across the Rio Grande. The background of this bitter conflict, which was the beginning of a dismemberment that cost Mexico nearly half her territory, went back to the early 1820s. An American Yankee named Moses Austin had obtained permission from the Mexican Government to establish a settlement of three hundred Anglo-Saxon families in the sparsely inhabited region of southern Texas. It was stipulated that the immigrants were all to be of the Roman Catholic faith and were to become Mexican citizens. In the decade following this agreement thousands of pioneers poured across the frontier into Mexican territory. Many of them entered Texas illegally, and hundreds lied about their religion in order to get cheap land. Others squatted on vast estates, to which they had no legal claim. By the year 1830 there were more than twenty thousand of these Americans in northern Mexico.

Before the election of Santa Anna to the presidency, in 1833, these settlers had enjoyed a considerable amount of regional sovereignty. Mexico was organized on a loose federal basis, and Texas, as one of the outlying districts, was left to govern itself much as it saw fit. There were few Mexican officials in Texas; the land was one of great distances, and there arose a wide-open pioneer society with its curious mixture of serious colonists, adventurers, escaped criminals, frontiersmen, soldiers, and so on.

In 1834 Santa Anna swept the liberal Mexican constitution of the previous ten years into the discard and began at once to clamp down on the Texans. Regional autonomy was curtailed; import duties were to be paid on goods brought in from the United States; titles to lands were to be scrutinized, and those illegally held were to be confiscated. These provisions in themselves were bad enough in the eyes of the Texans, but when Santa Anna's police force of soldier profiteers appeared on the scene, relations between the two races rapidly approached an impasse. Stephen Austin, son of Moses, traveled to Mexico City to plead for a more reasonable treatment. He was thrown into prison. Feeling on both sides rose to the boiling point.

At about this time there arrived in Texas one of Mexico's most distinguished liberal leaders and writers, Lorenzo de Zavala. He had been governor of the state of Mexico, was able to speak many languages fluently, had traveled widely in Europe, and was a supporter of the liberal and federal cause in Mexico. When Santa Anna usurped power Zavala had fled to Texas, where he immediately began to fan the flames of discontent and separatism. It was futile, he said, to expect fair treatment at the hands of the central Mexican government. Austin eventually got out of prison and came back with the same story. A small group of leading citizens gathered around these men and, after trying halfway measures of regional autonomy, finally declared their absolute independence of Mexico in 1836. The eloquent oratory of Zavala, who spoke English as well as Spanish, was a potent force in bringing about this declaration. When the new state was established he was elected its first vice-president.

No strong racial feeling existed in the Texas territory at that time. Zavala, a mestizo and a foreigner, was immediately given a high position in the new government although he represented a small minority group of the population. The manner in which Santa Anna carried the war to the Texans almost overnight changed the whole focus of race relations. Before long the very name Mexican was hated and despised in the Lone-Star State. Zavala himself suffered because of his nationality and was ousted from a position which he had filled with competence. Ignorant Anglo-Saxons of a later date turned their prejudices against all Mexicans with a venom which was unreasoning and despicable.

In 1835 Santa Anna sent Mexican troops into Texas to collect the import duties. There were several skirmishes. Then, in February 1836, the war began in earnest. A group of one hundred and fifty Texans was assembled in the Alamo of San Antonio enjoying a fiesta. Santa Anna was informed of the situation and decided to surround the place. He slowly moved his forces into position, leaving no possible avenues of escape, but he did not attack immediately. Reinforcements were on their way to his army and Santa Anna waited until they arrived. With a preponderance of about three thousand soldiers to less than two hundred he attacked the tiny fortress of the Alamo.

Inside that building were some of the most famous frontiersmen of the century. They had come to Texas from all over the nation. The fight they put up has gone down in history with a blaze of glory, and the cry, "Remember the Alamo!" became the call of death for many a Mexican soldier at a later engagement. For two weeks the battle dragged on. The garrison was whittled down until not a man was left unwounded. Finally the doors were smashed in and the Mexicans entered in a wild rush. Only a few men remained alive and most of them were hardly able to stand. They died fighting to the last man. Davy Crockett, Bowie, Travis, and many other great pioneers of those early days perished at the Alamo.

The Texas orator, Joseph Weldon Bailey, has spoken of that event with ringing eloquence. Writers, speakers, and poets have often repeated this famous epitaph of that heroic stand: "Thermopylae had her messenger of defeat. The Alamo had none!" The story is committed to memory in all Texas schools, and, unfortunately, lives only too vividly in the minds of many people who utilize it as food for the bitterest racial propaganda.

The story of Goliad is not quite so well known as that of the Alamo, but for the Texas rebels it was a more significant battle both as to its military and moral consequences. At the Alamo the soldiers fighting for the Lone-Star State did not even consider terms of surrender. But at Goliad, where about three hundred and fifty of them were surrounded, they did decide to give up a hopeless struggle after all their ammunition was exhausted. When Santa Anna heard of their surrender he immediately ordered the Mexican commander at Goliad to slaughter all prisoners. The unwounded were shot or struck down after they had been disarmed, and the wounded were slain in their beds. Only a couple of dozen managed to escape.

They carried the news to Sam Houston, leader of the Texas army. General Houston ordered a retreat before the superior forces of Santa Anna. The Mexicans continued their advance with almost no opposition; the Texans slowly added to their forces as they withdrew. On April 20, 1836, the two armies met and there was a brief engagement with little advantage to either side. The following morning Santa Anna was joined by about six hundred reinforcements, and now his troops numbered thirteen hundred to the eight hundred men under Houston. The Mexicans began to feel a little easier. The new arrivals had been marching all night and were dog tired. Copious amounts of food were served; the guard was set, and after a few camp chores were carried out the whole camp relaxed and drowsed away in a siesta.

Houston and his men, crouching and completely hidden by the tall grass, stealthily approached the camp. At about three in the afternoon they saw the somnolent camp spread out before them. Only a few Mexicans were visibly awake, and these were engaged in cooking. It was a hot spring day, and the long gray moss streaming down from the trees gave the place an aspect of almost deathly repose. The Texans hauled their two cannon into position and loaded them to the muzzles with shrapnel. At a given signal they let go with both pieces, let out a yell that could have been heard miles away, and charged over the breastworks in a body. Only a few soldiers opposed them.

Santa Anna leaped from bed and rushed out of his tent. When he realized what had happened he began to pace to and fro in wild anxiety, wringing his hands. It was reported that he shouted, "Somebody get me a horse!" In any case, someone did get him a mount, and he fled from the scene like a wild man.

The Texans fought like beasts, butchering their enemies by the dozens. In every Mexican uniform they saw a reminder of the Alamo and Goliad. A large body of Mexican troops was sealed off near a creek back of the camp and literally pushed into the water, where they were killed or drowned. Finally the human bridge of bodies was complete and a few escaped by walking over the corpses of their comrades.

For a long time the Mexican officers seemed to have lost all command of the situation, but at last one of them did gather a few terror-stricken soldiers about him and raise the white flag. The total casualties for each side were as follows: the Texans had three killed, and eighteen wounded; the Mexicans had lost four hundred killed, two hundred wounded, and seven hundred and thirty prisoners. Santa Anna was not among the prisoners, but the next day they found him hiding in the grass, disguised in the clothes of a laborer.

Many Texans wanted to shoot him at once, but Houston demurred. The most propitious terms for the Texans were drawn up and signed. The state was to have absolute independence. Santa Anna ordered his remaining troops, which were in the field under other generals, to withdraw to Mexico. He signed his orders: "Santa Anna, for God and Liberty!" Then he went to Washington, D.C., where he enjoyed himself seeing the sights before returning to Mexico.

When he did go back he found that the people everywhere despised him for his cowardice; it was widely whispered that he had given away Texas in order to save his own skin. His stock slumped to rock bottom.

A few months later he was given another chance. The French were claiming damages committed against some of their nationals, most of whom ran pastry shops, and the Mexican Government had not made a satisfactory settlement. Finally a French fleet bombarded the coast and captured Mexico's strongest fort. The so-called "Pastry War" had begun. Santa Anna rushed to the scene and took command. In one engagement his leg was smashed by a bullet and had to be amputated. The general came back into favor again, and this time his popularity lasted about five years. In 1844 he was overthrown again and exiled to Havana.

In the meantime relations between Mexico and the United States had been growing more and more tense. Many people in this country had become scornful of a neighboring nation which did not seem able to maintain internal order, much less a decent national government. Santa Anna, for his part, heightened the tension by letting slip remarks such as the one he made to the French Minister when the latter questioned him about the affair of Texas: "If the Americans do not beware," he said, "I shall march through their whole country and plant the Mexican flag in Washington."

This emotional animosity might not have gone beyond the verbal stage had there not been other and far more important factors involved. Two things stood out: first, Texas wanted to be taken into the Union; and second, the Union was going through a period of expansion and was beginning to look with greedy eyes not only at Texas but also at California and all the other Mexican territory of the great Southwest.

At first the issue was not clear-cut. Pro-slavery states were in favor of annexing Texas because it would swell their votes in Congress; anti-slavery states were strongly against it. The election of 1844 hinged largely on that one issue; the candidates were Polk and Henry Clay. Polk, who ran on a platform favoring annexation, won the presidency. Tyler, whom he was about to replace, took this as a confirmation of his own desire for annexation, and two days before retiring from office Texas was taken into the United States by a joint resolution of the Senate and the House of Representatives. The President knew that he would never be able to round up the necessary two-thirds vote of the Senate in order to draw up this agreement with the Texas Republic in the normal way.

The year was 1845. The Western frontier of the United States was expanding rapidly. Wagon trains of pioneers were pouring across the Mississippi and into the great Western plains beyond. It was the great tide of a nation expressing the American dream of that moment: toward the setting sun the fields were a little greener. From the Atlantic seaboard it had moved across the Alleghenies, from the Alleghenies into Tennessee, Kentucky, and into the South; from there it had reached the banks of the Mississippi, and, when the Mississippi had failed to stop it, the human flood had flowed still farther westward into Texas, into the Midwest, into Utah, and now its spearheads seemed headed for California.

By 1800 a million Americans lived west of the mountains; by 1820 the number had become two and a half millions; a decade later another million had been added. These "men of the Western Waters" rolled at an ever-increasing pace toward the fringe of the Pacific. The Louisiana Purchase, cessions from the Indians, the urge for Americans living on the Eastern seaboard to get out of the rut pushed the stream westward.[126]

In the early days of North American independence Spain still claimed all territory west of the Mississippi River. Mission settlements had been made in the region from Texas all the way across to California. Settlers, however, were few and far between. Mexico had not viewed unfavorably the entrance of the first Anglo-Saxons to these almost unpeopled territories.

Long before feeling between the two countries had reached the breaking point, North American settlers, merchants, trappers, and mechanics had begun to move into California. The sea route around Cape Horn to these Western shores brought many visitors and traders. In 1830 an overland trail was opened all the way to Los Angeles, and in the 1840s other colonists crossed the mountains into the Sacramento Valley. There was something alluring about this new "land of promise" whose very name had been taken from the old romances of chivalry. Its climate of eternal spring, cool summers and mild winters, its lovely missions set among the palm trees and roses, its vast estates on which lived some of the finest families of New Spain, all these acted as a magnet drawing the adventurous pioneer toward the greatest of all oceans. "By 1846," write Charles and Mary Beard, "at least one fifth of the people in the little town of San Francisco were citizens of the United States."

So it was that the United States had one eye on California and the other eye on Texas, and the eye on California was the greedier of the two. The Mexican Government had attempted to disavow the independence which Santa Anna had granted to Texas, and had even withdrawn its minister from Washington when that state was admitted to the Union. But these were futile moves, and all Mexicans knew it.

California was a different story. Some Mexican historians seem to believe that if their government had acted more wisely and accepted the independence of Texas with good grace, war with the United States might have been averted. Theoretically, perhaps, it might, but the results of the war would then simply have been attained through other means.

Every nation, every people, every century has its high tide of growth and expansion. Spain enjoyed hers in the sixteenth century. The United States did not reach her heyday until the 1800s. When that day did arrive the people were on the march streaming westward with an irresistible force. Nothing in the world could have stopped them.

The Spaniards of the sixteenth century used to say, "Glory, gold, and Gospel." Their mission, they believed, was only partially economic aggrandizement. But those North Americans of the 1800s did not even mince words to that extent; they called their expansion "Manifest Destiny." It was fated that this nation should gird the hemisphere "from sea to shining sea."

The North American historian, Woodward, in his excellent interpretation of our country's life, refers to Manifest Destiny as "an irresistible impulse in racial life." He goes on to say that perhaps some North Americans thought of "the white man's burden," his duty to help, by force if need be, his more unfortunate and incidentally weaker neighbor. "Provided, of course," Woodward adds, "that the weak and servile peoples possess fertile lands, mines, forests, or something of the kind. Otherwise the weaker races could shift for themselves."[125]

Such was the situation in 1845. But how to get California, which was the key to the whole idea of Manifest Destiny? The Beards, James Truslow Adams, Woodward, and nearly all North American historians agree that, consciously or unconsciously, the government of this country felt it would be necessary to force Mexico into declaring war.

In 1845 the American consul at Monterey, California, was informed that "whereas we could use no influence to cause California to revolt against Mexico, we would gladly receive her into the United States if she should do so of her own volition."[126] In 1846 a group of Americans in the Golden State did hoist the "bear flag," proclaiming their independence. They hauled it down again in a hurry, for the movement was a few months premature. In that same year the American naval commander in the Pacific region was ordered to seize San Francisco as soon as he heard that Mexico had opened hostilities. All of this before war began. No more flagrant breaches of international law or decency had ever occurred in the history of two neighboring nations.

Ulysses S. Grant, who took part in the war as a lieutenant, wrote in his memoirs many years later that he regarded the conflict "as one of the most unjust ever waged by a stronger against a weaker nation. . . . Even if the annexation itself (of Texas only) could be justified, the manner in which the subsequent war was forced on Mexico cannot."

The United States Government did try to buy California from Mexico, but no Mexican Government which even listened to such a proposition could have stayed in power for a moment. In 1846 General Zachary Taylor was ordered to occupy some disputed territory in the Texas region. "We were sent," wrote General Grant, "to provoke a fight, but it was essential that Mexico should commence it." There was a skirmish. Americans were killed. President Polk assured Congress in eloquent tones that American blood had been shed on American soil, and called for a declaration of war against Mexico.

The story of the war itself is unimportant. Taylor went down into Mexico via land, and General Winfield Scott, "Old Fuss and Feathers," landed at Vera Cruz and marched on Mexico City over land. After a brief but arduous campaign he took the capital. The last stand of the Mexicans was made at Chapultepec Castle, residence of the Mexican presidents. There a group of young cadets, mere boys in their early teens, put up a desperate fight. Finally, realizing that further resistance was hopeless, the few who remained alive wrapped their bodies in the flag of their nation and plunged to death over the precipice, shouting an exultant "Long live Mexico!" By 1848 the war was over and Mexico was forced to yield everything.

What the troops of Santa Anna had done in Texas the soldiers of the United States repeated in Mexico. Captain Kirby Smith, later a distinguished Confederate general, who took part in the Mexican War, spoke in tones of deepest shame and disgust of the raping of women and shooting of civilians in which the soldiers of this country took part. Grant, who was certainly no great humanitarian, hated the whole mess every minute he was in it, and felt a burning sense of guilt. After dwelling on how wicked and unreasonable he considered the war to be, he added: "I thought so at the time, when I was a youngster, only I had not the moral courage to resign."

In justice be it said that the people of the United States supported this war less than they have ever supported any campaign in their history. Some North American newspapers decried the conflict in terms which in other days would have bordered on treason. The famous New England writer, Thoreau, became so loud in his complaints that they sent him to jail. Nevertheless, the people by and large did believe in their Manifest Destiny, did want Texas and California, were imperialistic-minded both in fact and in principle.

Woodward, in his A New American History, mentions that "Abraham Lincoln, who was then a member of Congress, voted for a resolution which thanked the officers of the army and navy for their gallant conduct 'in a war unnecessarily and unconstitutionally begun by the President of the United States.'"

The war had a deadly effect on the Monroe Doctrine. Many Latin Americans had previously held their suspicions as to the real motive behind the famous Doctrine. Now they were convinced that these suspicions were correct. The whole thing was but a false front behind which the powerful nation of the North could keep other countries out of Latin America until the time was ripe for its own imperialistic expansion.

Mexico, of course, felt the first strong resentment, for the war burned like gall in her throat. The feeling was passed on to Central America, to the northern part of South America, and there for a time it came to a stop. The remainder of the great southern continent was too occupied with its own internal affairs to be so easily aroused by the distant United States. Nevertheless, the ball had started to roll, and before it stopped it would reach clear down to the arid steppes of Patagonia.

It was in the very year the war ended, 1848, that gold was discovered at Sutter's Mill in California and there began the greatest gold rush in history. Mexico was probably fortunate that she lost California before these forty-niners brought their wide-open, rip-roaring, hell-raising ways into the Far West.

Santa Anna, who was in exile at Havana when the war began, had persuaded the Americans to allow him to slip through their blockade and enter Mexico in order "to help with peace negotiations." He did just the opposite, however, and it was under his leadership that the biggest battles against the United States forces were fought. In the end his defeat was so disastrous that he wound up in exile again, this time in Venezuela.

It was not for long. The anarchy which had followed the war caused a great upswing of liberal thinking. Young intellectuals gathered together in an imposing array of talent and with a large mass following behind them. They voiced many anti-church, anti-conservative ideas which threw a mighty scare into the old-timers. As a last resort the latter all banded into a conservative front, and, unable to find a man in Mexico on whom they could agree, called Santa Anna back from his exile and again made him dictator of Mexico, 1853. Their idea was to use Santa Anna merely as a stopgap on the way to a permanent monarchy, with some European prince on the throne. But the crafty general knew how to manipulate human wills even better than they, and very shortly afterward had himself proclaimed His Most Supreme Highness. He was afraid to assume the title of Emperor because of what had happened to Iturbide.

In the following year, 1854, the liberals got their own counterrevolution under way. They declared themselves in favor of a brief liberal dictatorship to be followed by new elections and a new constitution. Slowly but surely strength began to mass behind them. In 1855 Santa Anna saw that he did not have a chance and commenced to slip funds out of the country. In August of that same year he fled to the coast, boarded a vessel, and returned to his Venezuelan estate.

When the Emperor Maximilian took over the government of Mexico, Santa Anna offered his services and actually got back into the country. He was promptly thrown out again. A couple of years later he repeated the venture, this time as a candidate opposing the Indian Juárez, who also threw him out. In 1874 he was finally allowed to return to Mexico City, but by that time Santa Anna was an old and almost penniless man. Nobody recognized him. No one paid any attention to him. Battles in which he had taken part were commemorated and he was not asked to be present. It was the greatest possible punishment which could have been imposed upon him. In 1876 he died in obscurity and poverty in the city down whose streets he had strutted for thirty of the sorriest years in the history of the Mexican nation.

50

BENITO JUÁREZ: INDIAN PRESIDENT

Among the Mexican liberals who fled the country during Santa Anna's last dictatorship there was one who was destined later to become "the Abraham Lincoln of his country." He was a pure-blooded Indian from Oaxaca named Benito Juárez. Born in an adobe mountain hut of the most humble parents, Juárez had not even learned the Spanish language until he was twelve years old. When he came to town his first work was as a domestic servant. In physical appearance the boy was small, but his shoulders were broad and muscular and above them rose a magnificent head with black burning eyes. He was a fine worker. His employer took a fancy to him and gave him an opportunity for an education. The bright Indian boy proved to be a serious-minded and excellent student.

At first the young Juárez had enrolled in courses which were preparatory for the priesthood, but later he changed his mind and specialized in law. After a few years of successful practice in that field, during which his integrity and absolute honesty became well known, he was elected governor of the state of Oaxaca. He set an example of just and efficient government which would be a tribute to any man. The bankrupt state treasury was left with a surplus, and Juárez endeared himself to the Indian population by receiving their complaints in person and by acting on them promptly. The governor also kept open house for the liberals of his state, and among those present at these sessions was a mestizo boy, Porfirio Díaz, who was completely converted to the cause. Díaz became a veritable apostle because of the ardent, democratic, heart-warming zeal of the great Indian governor.

When Santa Anna came to power in 1853 Juárez was imprisoned, but he escaped and went to New Orleans, where he supported himself for several months by working in a tobacco factory. Toward the end of the Santa Anna regime he returned to Mexico and was in the vanguard of the liberal triumph. In 1857, when the new liberal constitution was proclaimed and elections were held, Juárez was chosen for the double job of vice-president and chief justice of the Supreme Court. From that moment until his death in 1872 he was the leading man of his country.

The name given to the political movement which arose in Mexico after Santa Anna's flight, and which continued for a decade, was *la Reforma*, or the Reform. The most famous promenade in Mexico City, the Paseo de la Reforma, was named after it. Juárez and this reform movement were one. He was not the only reformist in Mexico; indeed at the beginning of the movement there was a galaxy of outstanding liberals on the horizon. Among them was the writer and orator, Ignacio Altamirano, who was a pure Indian like Juárez; then there was Lerdo de Tejada, a famous intellectual; Ignacio Ramírez, fine writer and fiery atheist; Melchor Ocampo, economist; Guillermo Prieto, the national poet; and many other names famous in Mexican intellectual history. There was also Porfirio Díaz, no intellectual, but a general who would eventually emerge with a star over his head. Behind all of these stood Juárez, the small, silent, inscrutable Indian from Oaxaca who was the guiding spirit of the Reform.

The reformation these liberals were anxious to put into effect was directed principally against the economic power of the Church, which at that time owned approximately half of all productive lands in Mexico. These lands were to be taken away and sold. Education was to be directed by the state. Cemeteries were secularized and placed under the Department of Public Health. Civil marriages were approved. Religious liberty was proclaimed. Special courts were abolished and priests or army officials were obliged to face ordinary civil trials like everybody else. In order to make these laws appear less anti-ecclesiastical it was proclaimed that no corporation, of whatever nature, might own lands. Unfortunately this was a grievous error, for the village commons, or *ejidos*, on which so many hundreds of thousands of Indians depended for their living, came under this category.

The reaction of the Church was immediate and drastic. It was announced that every person who swore to uphold the iniquitous constitution of 1857—and all government officers were compelled to do so—would be excommunicated. They would be forced to live outside the pale of society; no Catholic could speak with them or deal with them, and there would be no religious burial for them when they died. The Pope himself came out and condemned the constitution in the most vigorous terms. All churches were closed to liberals and their supporters.

Mexico was split wide open in two opposing camps which have remained alive to this day. The conservatives began a rebellion, occupied Mexico City by force, and proclaimed that a new constitution would be drawn up. The vacillating liberal president, a man named Comonfort, finally approved this action. Juárez fled from the capital, announcing that in view of Comonfort's unconstitutional position he had become president of Mexico. The liberals of the provinces rallied to his support, and for the next three years the War of the Reform, one of the bloodiest in Latin-American history, was carried the length and breadth of the land.

At the beginning the conservatives won all the battles. The best generals, church support, all vested interests, more available funds were on their side. But it did not take the liberals long to learn this new game. Their intellectuals and lawyers soon picked up enough of military science and tactics to make a creditable showing. Juárez established himself at Vera Cruz, a strong liberal center, where the peril of yellow fever made attack by soldiers from the highlands most unlikely.

The church hierarchy gave large funds to the conservatives, but Juárez had a strangle grip on the customs duties of Vera Cruz. Nevertheless, expenses ran far ahead of income, and very soon both sides found themselves unable to pay their troops. They fell upon the silver trains which British and French capitalists were trying to get across the country, and ransacked properties belonging to all foreigners.

In 1859 Juárez announced his Reform Laws, an even heavier blow to the Church than the constitution of two years previous. The Church was stripped of all property without compensation; priests and nuns were not permitted to appear publicly in vestments; all monasteries and nunneries were to be suppressed. Whenever a liberal army overran a town the first thing it did was to loot the church of every valuable item. Images were piled up and burned. Occasionally priests were shot. Some art treasures were destroyed, but sufficient funds were procured to assure the triumph of the liberal cause. The old order was peeled away clear down to its marrow.

In 1860 a victorious liberal army entered Mexico City, and shortly afterward Juárez followed it. Both conservatives and liberals lined the streets to cheer him, but the Indian leader did not come with any pompous display of triumph. He made no great speeches, no grandiloquent gestures. He sat there silently in his black clothes inside his black carriage as if he were a stone sphinx brooding over the tragedy which had befallen his nation.

When he had anything to say his words were brief and to the point. "Mexicans, I congratulate you on the re-establishment of peace and on the rich fruits of the victories achieved by our valiant hosts. . . . Thanks to you who have learnt to undertake and carry through the gigantic enterprise of democracy in Mexico, an armed oligarchy no longer exists in the land of Hidalgo and Morelos, nor that other more terrible oligarchy of the clergy which seemed to be unconquerable due to the influence of time, interests, and prestige."

Hopeful words which the great Indian would have to swallow when he went to his grave. His work would take time, much time. "The native race," he also said, "which is the most numerous of our Mexican society, is subject to an even blinder obedience than soldiers, because its obedience springs from the poverty that bends and overwhelms it before the will of its masters."

The War of the Reform was over, but Juárez had inherited a country in desolation, without funds, without unity, owing heavy debts to many foreign nations, with bitterness and hatred a disease in every province. The glorious movement, which had begun with the intention of making Mexico over in the form of a modern state, had thus far not even had a chance of working toward its goal.

Juárez now believed that he had that chance, though he presided over a nation in ruins. Some progress was made in breaking up the large holdings of the Church; a new attitude of religious tolerance was inaugurated; State and Church were separated, with the civil power clearly superior to the ecclesiastical. However, the ideal of the liberals, individual Mexican ownership of former church lands, hit a blank wall. Most Mexicans were unable to buy them. Only foreigners and wealthy native families profited greatly from these government sales. To make matters worse, the splitting up of the native commons had dealt the masses of Indians a blow which was already opening the way to the horrible landless peonage of a later date.

In brief, the Reform was unable to accomplish even a modicum of those things which all civilized countries were by that time taking for granted. It had neither ushered in an era of democracy nor of economic improvement. It was merely the first faltering step from a feudal to a bourgeois capitalist society, thus revealing that Mexico was centuries behind the rest of the world in its economic development. Racially, the mestizos were displacing the Creoles in the political life of the nation. A small middle class was beginning to spring up, but the immense majority of the Mexican people remained in miserable bondage.

Juárez not only had a poverty-stricken and divided Mexico to contend with, but he was no sooner ensconced in the presidency than England, France, and Spain all pounced on him, demanding reparations for the pillaging of properties belonging to their nationals. Juárez put them off, for the Mexican treasury was empty. A bare two years after the war, in 1862, the combined forces of the three above-mentioned nations landed on the eastern Mexican coast in order to collect their debts by force. Before long they were squabbling among themselves, and the English and Spaniards withdrew. They could not bring themselves to support the ulterior motive of the French, which was to establish a colony on Mexican soil.

Napoleon III, then Emperor of France, had dreams of grandeur. A great French colonial empire south of the United States appealed to his imperial imagination. The United States, then in the middle of its own Civil War, could not possibly interfere. Napoleon persuaded Maximilian of Austria, a Hapsburg, to accept the throne of the new dominion. Maximilian refused to do so unless the Mexican people in a plebiscite requested him to become their Emperor.

In the meantime, the French troops had proceeded inland and occupied Mexico City, despite a resounding defeat at Puebla on the fifth of May. The plebiscite was easily arranged and carried off to Napoleon's satisfaction. Maximilian did not inquire too carefully as to its nature, and accepted the subsequent offer of the Mexican crown.

The brief three-year reign of this pleasant and liberal Hapsburg in Mexico (1864–67) is really an unimportant interlude in the history of the country, as many historians have pointed out. But its romantic interest, the character of the Emperor himself, always trying to do right, wanting desperately to make himself loved by his people, hoping against hope that he might become the savior of the oppressed, have aroused a chord of responding sympathy in nearly every writer's heart.

The whole picture was pathetic. Maximilian did not have a chance from the very beginning. He came to Mexico in the belief that the great majority of the people wanted him. After he had arrived, conservative Mexicans and French generals lied to him constantly, telling him that Juárez had no real support among the people. They also lied to him as to the extent of his own popularity.

Maximilian was no fool, but he was a foreigner who did not speak Spanish, did not know the people of Mexico, could not possibly in so short a time grasp all the complexities of the national life. He governed to the best of his ability, but it was not good enough. On one occasion he promised Juárez a complete amnesty and offered to make him his prime minister if he would cease in his mad resistance. The offer, of course, was rejected. Juárez knew that if he could only prevent capture long enough national feeling was bound to assert itself and he would return to power. The French drove him clear to the Texas border, but despite every defeat he held on desperately.

Maximilian found himself in another line of fire which was of even greater immediate importance. With his keen mind he saw at once that the Church-State conflict in Mexico was not a religious but an economic one. He sided with the liberal party on many issues. He and his queen, Carlotta, both spoke in firmest tones to the papal nuncio who was sent over to size up the situation. They reiterated their conviction that the Church had got no more than it deserved.

The Abbé Testory, chaplain general of the French army, made the following statement: "When in 1856 the law for the sale of the Clergy's property was proclaimed, the amount of that property was already enormous. The fortune owned by the religious orders reached the sum of 200,000,000 pesos; the income from that property plus tithes, voluntary contributions, fees, the proceeds from dispensations, altar offerings, et cetera, gave the Clergy every year a revenue greater by far than that of the State itself. It is not then, to be wondered at, that the State looked upon this vast wealth as an obstacle in the path of public prosperity. . . . Consequently, we may assert without hesitation that the State was strictly within its rights when it expropriated the property of the Clergy on the ground of public welfare. . . ."

As a consequence of such statements as these many of the conservatives lost their zeal for the Emperor Maximilian. In the meantime, the inscrutable Juárez was rolling over the land in his black carriage, always one jump ahead of the French army, trying to hold the reins of his government together. When the Civil War ended in the United States his stock began to rise. An American army was sent to the Texas border. Many people in the United States began to clamor for driving the French out of Mexico. Ammunition and arms were made available to the forces of Juárez. This, in addition to loud rumblings of war in Europe, frightened Napoleon and he withdrew his army. Maximilian was left to face the music alone.

Slowly, like a snake creeping upon its prey, Juárez advanced into Mexico from the northern regions. He was informed that the Emperor himself was at Querétaro with all his troops. Juárez invested the town with superior forces. They infiltrated the city, and captured it without a real struggle; Maximilian, who had refused a chance to escape, was taken prisoner.

Juárez, implacable as a pagan god, decreed the death penalty, and despite a deluge of telegrams from half the ruling houses of the world, Maximilian was taken before a firing squad. He made a speech in Spanish before he died, and said that he had only wanted to help the Mexican people, whom he had come to love with a deep affection. He ended it by saying softly: "Viva Mexico!" The shots rang out, and he fell to the ground wounded; the firing squad came closer and killed him.

Mexico returned to its life under Juárez, who in that same year of 1867 was elected to his third term of office. There was small interest in the election; less than twenty thousand votes were cast in the entire country. For the following four years Juárez labored unceasingly. He put the physical body of the nation back into order again, aided industry and trade, established efficient and honest government, and kept pounding away at his one pet goal: education for the masses. Juárez probably did more for Mexican education during those last five years of his life than had been accomplished in the entire half century before him. When he died there were between seven and eight thousand schools in Mexico, and possibly as many as three hundred and fifty thousand school children.

In 1871 presidential elections were again due, and Juárez wanted to run for re-election. This time even his closest collaborators opposed him. General Porfirio Díaz was among them. Nevertheless, Juárez ran, and when no clear-cut majority was returned for any candidate Congress again chose its Indian leader. Díaz rebelled, but his rebellion was promptly smashed.

Juárez began his fourth term with his reform program just getting into high gear. Three months later he became ill suddenly while sitting at his desk; he died that night. The official report was that he had suffered a heart attack, but many people believed that he had been poisoned.

Actually, Juárez never had the opportunity to become the reformer he had hoped to be. Two bloody wars had interrupted his three terms of office. Mexico was still impoverished when he left her. But a start had been made; the road had been cut; the masses were given new hope. Through Juárez, the Indian in Mexico, as nowhere else in Latin America, began again to believe in himself as a human being with all the thoughts, feelings, and aspirations of which human beings are capable, with all the opportunities for self-progress society can afford.

51

PORFIRIO DÍAZ: BREAD OR THE CLUB

Juárez had left the door ajar for Indian Mexico; Porfirio Díaz then appeared on the threshold and made as if to open it wider. When the Indian started to enter his new mansion, the door was slammed on his fingers, mangling them terribly. During the long years of "peace" to follow, the memory of that pain endured. Finally a crippled hand, almost a claw, reached out from nowhere and destroyed the regime of Díaz.

The sequence of events was as follows: for four years after the death of Juárez the nation was under the rule of Lerdo de Tejada, a man of tremendous intellectual endowment, but lacking on every count of personal or executive leadership. In 1876, when Lerdo de Tejada announced that he intended to run for a second term, General Porfirio Díaz, fearing he would never hear his cue, let out the still-repeated cry of *¡Sufragio efectivo, no reelección!* (Fair balloting, no re-election!) He backed it up with enough bayonets to get himself into the presidential chair. From then on, until his resignation under duress in 1911, Díaz was the master of Mexico.

He was the greatest of all the Spanish American caudillos. No leader of a nation ever evoked warmer encomiums from his foreign contemporaries. Tolstoi referred to Díaz as "the solitary silhouette of a modern Cromwell." He "possessed the reconstructive force of the English Puritan without his fanaticism." Andrew Carnegie and Cecil Rhodes, unconsciously responding to Díaz the builder, no matter how or what he constructed, called him one of the world's chosen. Elihu Root, Secretary of State under President Theodore Roosevelt, visited Díaz in Mexico City and made himself somewhat ridiculous by lavishing praise on the Mexican Caesar. Root stated that of all the men then living, Díaz was the one most worth seeing, then he continued: "If I were a poet I would write eulogies. If I were a musician I would compose triumphal marches. If I were a Mexican I should feel that the steadfast loyalty of a lifetime could not be too much in return for the blessings that he had brought to my country. As I am neither a poet, musician nor Mexican, but only an American who loves justice and liberty and hopes to see their reign among mankind progress and strengthen and become perpetual, I look to Porfirio Díaz, the President of Mexico, as one of the great men to be held up for the hero-worship of mankind." This was the same Root who has often been regarded as a pioneer in the field of Pan-Americanism. Theodore Roosevelt and the German Kaiser also outdid themselves in admiring the perennial despot. American journalists painted his name in glowing adjectives without end. American capitalists with money to invest in a safe Mexico went them one better and poured good hard cash, to the tune of more than a billion dollars, into Díaz's Mexico.

But back of the great façade the building was weak—gorgeous stage decorations fronting a Greek tragedy—an architect without blueprints, a structure laid on shifting sand. Mexico was a beautiful bridge laid across a yawning volcano.

All through the Reform War (1857–60), all during the early regime of Juárez, throughout the war against Maximilian (1864–67), Porfirio Díaz was a stanch supporter of the liberal cause, the right-hand man of the Indian president. When everybody else deserted the ship he stuck by the little leader from Oaxaca. More than anyone else he helped to put him back in power. Up to 1867 Díaz was a great Mexican patriot; his actions, if not always of the most civilized caliber, were at least all for Mexico, not all for Díaz.

But Juárez in 1867 decided to run for a third term, and after that for a fourth. Díaz, seeing himself left out of the Apostolic succession, backed out on the president, branded him a "coward . . . surrounded by cringing parasites . . . a dictator of Machiavellian wiles. . . ." While he, Díaz, was the brother of all Mexicans and democracy personified before the people.

Nevertheless, he did not quite make it. Juárez smashed his rebellion; Lerdo de Tejada followed Juárez. Then, when Lerdo de Tejada decided to follow himself, Díaz became president of Mexico. He was a liberal utilizing the support of disgruntled conservatives in order to make himself dictator. Díaz was now only a caudillo, fighting not for ideas but for power. "He was no longer preoccupied with being a liberal or being a conservative; what he wanted was to get into the presidency. And he got in!" Not once, but seven times.

The first thing Díaz set out to establish was a Mexican peace, a good strong *paz porfiriana*, or Porfirian peace, of such scope and firmness that it would redeem the country in the eyes of the world for its sixty-five years of revolution and anarchy. After that he proceeded to his next point, which was: *Nada de política y mucha administración*—no politics and plenty of administration. This was the motto of the Díaz dictatorship. The phrase, "no politics," sounded fine to a Mexico surfeited with civil strife, but what it really meant was "no meddling." The second phrase, "plenty of administration," was a promise of efficient government; hence order, profits, progress.

Let us see how well Díaz carried out his program. Some of the figures are truly imposing. In 1876, when he first assumed office, the country had but 407 miles of railway; in 1911, when he retired, there were more than 15,000 miles. In 1884, when Díaz was elected for a second term, imports amounted to approximately 24,000,000 pesos and exports to 47,000,000 pesos. By 1910 imports had jumped to 195,000,000 pesos, or about *nine times* as much, and exports had leaped to the astounding total of 260,000,-000 pesos, or more than *five times* the 1884 figures. When Díaz first assumed office his country was bankrupt and in abysmal debt; at the end of his seventh term there was a surplus of 136,000,000 pesos in the national treasury. At the beginning of the Díaz regime there was only a single bank in Mexico with capital and assets totaling 2,500,000 pesos. By 1907 there were thirty-two banks whose total assets amounted to 764,000,000 pesos. Even Mexican schools had jumped from seven or eight thousand to more than twelve thousand during the regime of Díaz, and the number of school children had doubled.

There was also an intensive development of harbors, factories, mines, public works, and so on. The postal service, which had carried less than 5,000,000 pieces of mail in 1876, in 1910 was carrying nearly 200,000,000. Within the same period federal income had increased from only 19,776,638 pesos to approximately 100,000,000 pesos per year.[150]

All of the above figures were given by the Díaz government to the American journalist James Creelman, who wrote up the regime in terms of highest praise just as it was about to go into its final eclipse. The statistics cited are fairly accurate and seem to indicate that the nation had made great strides forward.

A few additional facts will help to put the situation into clearer perspective. Díaz had wanted to build the country up as quickly as possible, so he invited the investment of foreign capital. Mexicans had no money, and the doors were thrown open to those who had. North Americans alone invested more than one billion dollars in Mexican railways, mines, factories, et cetera, during the Díaz regime. Great Britain and France also poured many millions of dollars into the country. These foreigners were not putting their funds into Mexico in order to help the Mexicans; they were looking for a good business proposition. Financial indexes jumped three, four, five hundred per cent while Díaz was president. Mexican mines yielded a total of more than 160,000,000 pesos a year. The production of these mines was turned into cash which went into the pockets of foreigners. And Mexican foreign commerce produced the staggering total of

454,910,775 pesos in 1910. A great proportion of these trade profits also went into the pockets of foreigners.

Yet Díaz held back enough to give his country the appearance of prosperity. Mexico City became a show place of the hemisphere. Trains ran, factories hummed, buildings rose, harbors were dredged, bands played. There arose the legend of Díaz, the great builder, with peace and progress as the two watchdogs of his government. No wonder foreigners praised him so much. He was a comfortable neighbor. And for Wall Street he became the true "golden boy," a blessed angel in the guise of a mestizo president.

But if Díaz gave so much of the national profits to foreigners, how did he maintain his power among his own people? There was a neat phrase for it: *Pan o palo*—bread or the club. This meant that Díaz handed out to the Mexicans who might challenge him either a political plum to silence them, or, if that failed, a clubbing to teach them a lesson. As a further persuader he kept a large and dark prison filled with political opponents or journalists who had refused to stop criticizing his government. Their feet dangled in water and slime; they never saw the sun. Slowly they wasted to death or went crazy. It was not a wholesome thing to oppose Díaz.

There was always the efficient federal police to chase down "criminals." It was rumored in Mexico that Díaz hired the most successful Mexican bandits and guerrillas in his police force and paid them more than they could ever hope to obtain by robbery. Whether this is true or not, the police under Díaz were perhaps more efficient than they have ever been either before or since. If a railway track was sabotaged, if a telegraph line was cut, if a town was robbed, these federal police immediately swooped down on the place and their first act was to punish the local authority responsible for law enforcement in that region. Then they went after the criminal.

In spite of all these precautions violence did not come to an end in Mexico. A generation which had been nursed with a gun in one hand and a machete in the other did not easily take to peaceful ways. There were hundreds of assaults with deadly weapons yearly. In 1896, with Díaz firmly in control, the total of armed encounters was 11,692. They were not rebellions against the government, of course, but deeds of personal violence which were the escape valve of a suppressed people.

The lives and property of the "persons who counted" were secure. Díaz protected them with every ounce of his strength. Whenever a foreigner or a landowner appeared in court it was tacitly understood that the verdict was to be rendered in his favor. The Mexican Indian or peon came to have no rights before the law.

This was a far cry from the Díaz who had fought so valiantly for the liberal cause. It was a far cry from the president's first term, when he had made overtures of friendship in the direction of the masses. In those days he even gave some of the ejido lands back to the Indians. However, he also paid the soldiers promptly and well and became their idol. Then he began to appease the large landowners and the Church. Those portions of the constitution or the Reform Laws which struck hardest at their interests were allowed to remain dead letters. Before long the vast majority of the clergy and other vested conservatives were zealously supporting Díaz.

During his second term it became obvious who was to be the goat: the Mexican masses, mostly Indians, who made up 75 per cent of the country's population.

From them Díaz obtained the gifts with which he bought the support of the most important Mexican families, the highest army officials, the church hierarchy, the government representatives. These gifts were in the form of land. Land served even better than money, for it gave the recipient an hacienda, which was a whole way of life: income, servants, and all. Money might be thrown away and the receiver come back for more. But land, which was a proof of prestige, gentility, family, would not thus disappear.

Díaz created in Mexico a small class of landowners, or *hacendados*, and a huge class of landless serfs. Here is the way he went about it: in 1884 he began to distribute the public lands of the country; and in 1889 and 1890 he decreed that all village commons must be divided up and become the property of individuals or companies. Theoretically, the Indians had a right to obtain these divided lands at the same ridiculously low prices as anyone else. But they had no money, no conception of private property, and for centuries their lives had revolved around the co-operative ejido type of economy. The result was that even those Indians who did come into the possession of plots of their own very soon lost them through some kind of legal swindle. It was easy to get an Indian drunk and have him make an "X" on a paper, or else lend him an insignificant sum of money which, if not repaid by a certain date, meant the confiscation of his property.

By the end of the Díaz regime there were few ejidos left in the most thickly populated central region of Mexico. Approximately 95 per cent of all rural heads of families were landless in 1910. In the state of Chihuahua more than 30,000,000 acres were divided among seven recipients; in Durango two grantees received over 2,000,000 acres each; in Oaxaca four recipients divided 7,000,000 acres, and so on down the line. Díaz doled out a total of nearly 135,000,000 acres of public lands to private individuals, most of them political favorites or influential foreigners. This was 27 per cent of the total land of the Mexican nation and included practically all of its arable soil.[74]

Mexico emerged from the Díaz dictatorship with no public domain and with almost no village commons. It was as if both the physical and the spiritual heart of the country had been eaten out by a pernicious worm.

Slavery had been abolished in Mexico, but the peonage that replaced it was probably worse. These peons did receive wages, but at what a level! Between 1792 and 1908 the day's wage for an agricultural laborer varied between twenty-five and thirty-five *centavos,* in purchasing power the equivalent of about fifteen or twenty cents in American money. During the entire Díaz regime at least half of all Mexicans continued to receive about the same wages which their ancestors had earned before them for the past one hundred and fifty years. Furthermore, while wages had remained practically stationary, prices of the ordinary daily foods had increased considerably. The following table which gives the prices in pesos shows the increase of the most common items:

	1792	1891	1908
Corn per hectoliter	1.75	2.50	4.89
Flour per 100 kilos	2.71	10.87	21.89
Wheat per 100 kilos	1.80	5.09	10.17
Beans per 100 kilos	1.63	6.61	10.89
Chile per 100 kilos	26.08	27.13	57.94

That is, while wages remained at the same level the price of beans had jumped 565 per cent, the price of corn more than 175 per cent, wheat had gone up 465 per cent, flour 711 per cent, and the price of chile had more than doubled. Even a dish of chile and beans, or a Mexican tortilla, cost three to four times as much in labor during the dictatorship of Díaz as they had under the old Spanish regime. The standard of life had thus gone down to an insufferable level for the majority of the Mexican people. An average farm laborer of the same class in the United States at the time of Díaz received fourteen times as much in return for his labor as his Mexican counterpart.[74] It is now clear that the imposing statistics cited by Creelman were made possible only through the complete despoliation of the average Mexican citizen.

Most foreigners who visited Mexico saw only Mexico City and associated mainly with the hacendados. These big estate owners made out all right despite what was happening to the peon. Their great haciendas contained all the fine things of life: a beautiful home, imported furnishings, plenty of servants, horses, even Indian girls to seduce. They yielded a steady income. The owner could either remain on his estate and live like a lord, or he could travel about, boasting of his hacienda, his family, and his prestige. The big estate was therefore not only a whole economy but was the irrevocable stamp which marked the Mexican aristocracy.

These haciendas contained about half of Mexico's total population, and if the town laborers who came there to work are added to the resident peons, perhaps 75 per cent of all Mexicans were dependent upon the hacienda for a living. "The railroads carried coffee, sugar, and other products abroad, but the *hacienda* itself, a self-sufficient state, was no market. Its

simple tools were made on the premises; modern tools were not purchased—peons' sweat replaced steam; oxen were cheaper than tractors. The
hacendado, interested in social status, not great income, cultivated the
best lands cheaply, let the rest lie idle."[127]

It never occurred to the Mexican hacendado to employ more modern
methods of agriculture in order to increase his profits. This would have
meant a capital outlay at the start, and perhaps a transition period before
income made up the expenditure. No estate owner was willing to make
this change. Things were good enough as they stood. The Spaniard, or
mestizo, was never one to take the long-range economic view of things.
Economy to him was so closely interwoven with tradition that the two
had become inseparable. He was still a feudal lord, living on a feudal fief,
with a feudal mentality. The only difference between him and the Spanish
landlord of colonial days was that now he had pretty generally taken on a
mestizo skin.

Since the hacienda was no market it meant that Mexican purchasing
power was desperately low. Consequently the few manufactured things
that the hacendado needed were imported from abroad. The hacienda
economy could not possibly support large national industries. Mexico became more and more lopsided in its economic organization.

The Mexican peon who was the producer for this whole setup was no
better than a beast of burden "destitute of all illusion and of all hope." He
was kept constantly in debt to the hacendado and this made his servitude
inescapable. His master could flog him at will, could even kill him if he so
desired, and he had no standing before the courts. The brave work of
Juárez was all undone by Díaz, and Mexico returned to its feudal heritage.
Only another revolution could shake off the firm grip of this combined
hacendado-political control.

It was in the year 1908 that James Creelman published in *Pearson's
Magazine* his famous interview with President Díaz, "the greatest man on
the continent." In praising the Mexican dictator to the skies Creelman
overstepped the bounds of discretion and played up one point which Díaz
would certainly have preferred to suppress. The president had told Creelman how much the Mexican people loved him, and how he was in reality
no dictator but simply their repeated choice for the presidency. The job
had been "pressed upon him." Díaz even went so far as to say that he
would welcome an opposition party as a blessing to his country. In fact, he
said that he was ready to retire and wanted only to have Mexico select
some candidate worthy to succeed him.

These statements were played up in the Creelman reports and received
wide publicity in Mexico as well as in the United States. A cautious but
new breath entered the prostrate Mexican underground. Dark undercur-
rents rose to the top. A great landowner, Madero, stood forth to lead the
arising opposition. Díaz then tried to clamp the lid down, but it was al-

ready too late—far too late. The Mexican mass-man sprang from the earth and hurled himself into the greatest and bloodiest Latin-American revolution of the twentieth century.

A contemporary Mexican writer commented on Díaz in these words: "He made Mexico presentable before the world. He gave her a bath, for she stunk to high heaven with all the filth of her revolutions, and then he dressed her up in clean clothes in order to present her before the other civilized nations. On the other hand, if Don Porfirio was an admirable tamer of wild beasts, he completely lacked the spirit to give a soul to his work."[128]

The Mexican author has given Díaz exactly double his due. He did indeed put new clothes over his nation, but it was like dressing a man who has not bathed for six months in fine linen. And it was not a soul which Don Porfirio forgot to give Mexico; it was a *chance*. No leader can give a soul to his people; he can only help to create those conditions in which a national spirit may be formed through self-expression. In order to achieve that he must identify himself with the highest feelings of the majority.

Power itself, whether good or bad, always attracts the attention of the world when it is on a large enough scale. If it is power which means comfort and security for other nations, then it is praised highly. If it means profits also, the praise becomes fulsome so long as the profits continue. Later, the perspective begins to clear up. This is the story of the Díaz regime and the great panegyrics accorded it outside of Mexico. But when the lovely façade was finally torn away it disclosed an unmitigated and stinking shambles.

52

ARIEL AND CALIBAN

When the peoples of Latin America began their struggle for independence they found their strongest inspiration in the North American Revolution; when the newly freed nations drew up their constitutions it was always with the Constitution of the United States before them as an example. The great Liberator himself had referred to the northern republic as "a singular model of political virtues and moral enlightenment unique in the history of mankind."

Within a period of less than a century that almost boundless admiration turned to resentment and bitter hate. This change in sentiment marks one of the unhappiest chapters in the history of the American hemisphere. It was no sudden about-face, but the gradual result of many years of increasing tension in inter-American relations. To most Latin Americans the whole unpleasant story is summarized in the words "Monroe Doctrine."

In the year 1823 the Holy Alliance, composed of Russia, Prussia, Austria, and France, was threatening to aid Spain regain her American colonies. They were anxious to "put an end to representative government," for the growth of this new idea endangered the security of their own absolutist regimes. Great Britain offered to support the United States in a strong stand against any such meddling in American affairs.

President Monroe sought the advice of Thomas Jefferson before reaching a decision, and the answer which Jefferson gave is almost as famous as the Doctrine itself. From his retreat at Monticello the former President referred to the question as the most momentous which had arisen since that of independence itself. "That made us a nation, this sets our compass and points the course which we are to steer through the ocean of time opening on us. And never could we embark on it under circumstances more auspicious. Our first and fundamental maxim should be, never to entangle ourselves in the broils of Europe; our second, never to suffer Europe to intermeddle in cis-Atlantic affairs. America, North and South, has a set of interests distinct from those of Europe, and peculiarly her own. She should therefore have a system of her own, separate and apart from that of Europe. While the last is laboring to become the domicile of despotism, our endeavor should surely be, to make our hemisphere that of freedom. . . ."

Jefferson went on to say that one nation most of all could disturb his country in this endeavor and that nation had offered to lend aid in its accomplishment. "With her [Great Britain] on our side," he wrote, "we need not fear the whole world."

President Monroe and Secretary of State John Quincy Adams concurred in this opinion, and the Monroe Doctrine was proclaimed on December 2, 1823. Reaction in Latin America was immediately favorable. Bolívar himself, still in the midst of his last campaign against the Spaniards, Santander in Colombia, Rivadavia in Argentina, Victoria in Mexico —leaders of the emancipation movement everywhere received Monroe's words with sincerest gratitude.

Yet they were all realists and knew that the puny spear of the President of the United States, unsupported by the might of the British fleet, would have meant absolutely nothing. Against the combined might of the Holy Alliance it would have been powerless. So while their thanks were given to Monroe, their strongest hopes were turned in the direction of Great Britain, who had already aided their struggle against Spain with both funds and men, and who now guaranteed their independence.

In 1826, when Bolívar called together his Congress of Panama, the first "Pan-American" meeting, he was at first loath to invite the United States. He was at this time hoping for a great confederation of Spanish American states, and believed that the inclusion of the northern republic would compromise his confederation from the viewpoint of England, which was its natural protector. Nevertheless, Bolívar was persuaded by revolutionary leaders of Mexico and Colombia to extend an invitation to the United States, and he did so most graciously.

The United States Congress was not strongly in favor of participating in this meeting, but finally sent delegates with the understanding that they should not approve any measure which would limit the freedom of each state to act according to its own interests.* This was an absolute negation of Bolívar's ideal of New World co-operation. The Monroe Doctrine, therefore, was to become purely an instrument of national policy; it was not to be, and was never intended to be, a charter for concerted hemispheric action.

At first the nations of Latin America were not at all disturbed by these implications. Bolívar's Congress of Panama, despite its grandiose start, was

---

* Neither of the two delegates arrived; one died en route, and the other had not yet left the United States when news was received that the congress had adjourned.

a fiasco. The nations which attended failed to do anything about the resolutions passed. British prestige was raised because British delegates were present while representatives from the United States were conspicuous by their absence, but by and large the whole thing was soon forgotten, or at least thrown into the background, in the fury of protracted anarchy and civil strife within the Spanish American nations themselves.

These nations not only praised the Monroe Doctrine excessively during the first half of the nineteenth century; they also gave it a one-sided interpretation which most suited their own national interests. Almost immediately after its proclamation Colombia and La Plata (Argentina) called upon the United States for protection. The Argentines sought protection against Brazil, and reasoned as follows: The Emperor of Brazil is a descendant of the Hapsburgs; the Hapsburgs are a European dynasty; therefore, the Brazilian threat to the Argentine is a European threat to the hemisphere. There were many other appeals made by Latin-American nations calling on the Monroe Doctrine, all of them turned down by the United States in these early years.

Yet during this period there was no real threat to the security of the hemisphere. The Monroe Doctrine perhaps exerted some small influence toward this end, but infinitely more important was the situation of Great Britain, the strongest maritime power of the nineteenth century. That nation had made commitments which demanded her greatest energy in Europe, India, Australia, Canada, Africa; in a word, all over the world. Since she could not extend herself farther and take over the control of vast Latin-American regions, she had decided to support the United States so that no other European power might obtain a foothold in the New World. It was this attitude on the part of Great Britain, rather than the Monroe Doctrine, which prevented the infringement of American sovereignties during the first half of the nineteenth century.

With the rapid growth of the United States and the continued success of British imperialism it soon became evident that no other nations could challenge the combined might of the two English-speaking nations. So long as Britain was the more powerful of the two the relations between her and her former colony were warm and friendly, but when it became evident that the United States itself was Britain's greatest rival in the Western Hemisphere, this feeling cooled considerably, and toward the middle of the century relations reached a point of friction which almost led to war.

In the meantime, the nations of Latin America were seeing the structure of the hemispheric policy of the United States being built up by this country. The first action taken against a Latin-American power was in 1831 when, after a dispute over whale-fishing rights, Captain Silas Duncan took his United States warship *Lexington* into the port of Soledad on the Falkland Islands off the southern Argentine coast. Here his men landed, destroyed the artillery, blew up the powder, and carried off the sealskins and everything else they could lay hands on. The United States diplomatic representative in Buenos Aires had authorized this expedition and refused an apology after the depredation had been committed. Great Britain went even a step farther, and in 1833 occupied the Falkland Islands by force and, despite repeated Argentine protests, has not relinquished them to this day.

The American expedition had taken place while Rosas was in power and at a time when the American consulate in Buenos Aires was about the only place of refuge for those fleeing the wrath of the tyrant. Consequently, after those Argentine refugees had later taken over the government of their country on the defeat of Rosas, they did not look upon this intervention with any serious misgiving. Their hatred of the tyrant and gratitude for American protection blotted out all other considerations.

The second intervention of the United States began with the Texas-Mexican War, followed by the annexation of Texas and finally by the war with Mexico (1846–48). This conflict resulted in the loss to Mexico of the entire California territory, comprising the states of New Mexico, Arizona, California, and adjacent regions. Great Britain vigorously but ineffectually opposed both the annexation of Texas and of the California territory by the United States. She wanted no rival to break up her commercial supremacy in the southern regions.

Although the war with Mexico was the greatest outrage ever committed by the United States against a foreign power, it did not arouse widespread anxiety in Latin America. Only Mexico and the Caribbean area were noticeably affected. The countries farther to the south were too far removed from the scene of the conflict and were too engrossed in their own national struggles against tyranny to give much heed to this writing on the wall. Sarmiento and Mitre, both of whom later became presidents of Argentina, regarded the Mexican War as a mere boundary dispute without hemispheric significance. Sarmiento, who was in the United States while the fight was going on, expressed no preoccupation or concern over the fate of Mexico. Alberdi, who was writing his brilliant essays from exile in Chile, did not let the Mexican War in any way affect his praise and admiration for the United States. Neither did the distinguished Chilean writers, Lastarria and Bilbao, whose panegyrics of the northern republic continued unabated.

The Mexican War and the subsequent annexation to the United States of vast Mexican territories did prove that while Britain had guaranteed the inviolability of Latin-American states, she would not go to war against the United States to prevent that nation's encroachments. It further proved that the United States, rather than any European country, was from this point forward the real threat against the sovereignty of the southern countries. These things become clear when hindsight is applied to their interpretation, but they were not immediately clear to the nations of Latin America.

The Mexican War was followed by the struggle between the United States and Britain for control of Central America. The British had been established in Honduras as early as 1642. Up to the mid-century after independence they had done in this region pretty much as they liked. The Central American states were played off against each other, thus preventing any concerted action against British interests. The governments of these states sent several appeals to Washington, calling on the Monroe Doctrine for protection, but the United States was unwilling to take a stand until the discovery of gold in California (1848) forced the issue. It was not until then that Central America became very obviously the key to the Pacific.

At this point the American soldier of fortune, William Walker, burst into the picture. Walker held an M.D. degree from the University of Pennsylvania, but, tiring of medical practice, he abandoned his old life and migrated to California. From there he undertook a filibustering expedition to Mexico in 1853, and when that proved unsuccessful turned his attention to Nicaragua, where a civil war was raging between the "liberals" of the city of León and the "conservatives" of the city of Granada. The war was mainly over the issue as to which of the two cities should be the capital of Nicaragua. Walker and about fifty-five of his "colonists" landed on the Nicaraguan coast and offered their services to the liberals. These American soldiers of fortune grew in number until they reached several hundreds. The conservative party was defeated; a liberal was proclaimed president, and Walker was made commander in chief of the Nicaraguan army.

Things went well until the general began to interfere with the transit of Cornelius Vanderbilt's stagecoaches across the country. This line had been built up after the California gold rush of 1849 to meet the demand for a short cut to that state without the necessity of a long and hazardous trip overland. Vanderbilt's ships left New Orleans for a Nicaraguan port on the Gulf of Mexico, then a stage line picked up travelers and took them to Lake Nicaragua, a river boat carried them across this body of water, and another stage took them to the Pacific coast, where they re-embarked for San Francisco.

Walker and Vanderbilt quarreled over the taxes to be paid by this line, and the former tried to stop all passage across Nicaragua. Vanderbilt retaliated by financing Walker's enemies, and the upshot of the whole affair was the final defeat and capture of the filibuster, who was executed by his captors.

The government of the United States had blinked at Walker's piratical activities and had also coaxed on Cornelius Vanderbilt. Control of Central America was a necessary prerequisite to the development of the West, and private individuals could help bring this control about without too directly involving the national government. If they fought among themselves on foreign soil, that was a matter of small moment. They were mere way-clearers for the later period of economic expansion.

At the same time as Walker and Vanderbilt were fighting it out in Nicaragua, back in the United States there arose a strong interest in building a canal across some part of Central America. Long before any definite plans had been made Great Britain and the United States had clashed over this issue. A treaty, made in 1850, placing the potential canal under joint control of the two nations proved unsatisfactory; feeling quickly rose to fever pitch, and by 1855 war seemed most likely. However, public opinion in England opposed any armed conflict; Disraeli spoke effectively against it, saying that his country would profit commercially by American control of that region, and finally the British Government gave way. It was perhaps this yielding more than anything else which prevented war and left the United States supreme in the hemisphere.

The annexation of Texas, the successful war against Mexico and expansion to the Pacific, the discovery of California gold at Sutter's Mill, the exploits of Walker and Vanderbilt, and the final pre-eminence of the United States in Central America—all these things entered into the early imperialistic policy of the United States, creating the legend of adventure, romance, revolution, and wealth which the majority of the citizens of this country began to see in the "ungovernable revolution-ridden but picturesque states of the Caribbean where pickings were ripe for the taking."

Only the outbreak of the American Civil War in 1861 prevented an extension of the imperialistic policy at this time. Latin Americans generally, however, did not feel the imminence of any such expansion, nor did their leaders indicate awareness of it. During the war and the period of reconstruction to follow, Mitre and then Sarmiento were presidents of Argentina (1862–74), Dom Pedro II ruled in Brazil, and Juárez came to the top in Mexico. All of these rulers were friendly to the United States, and three of them had been in this country, the last as a political refugee. While Latin-American patience had been sorely tried by the recent expansion of the northern republic, wholesale interventions had not yet taken place; the early friendship for this country was revived; and the hemisphere was again placed on a footing of good fellowship.

This *rapprochement* was strengthened by the French invasion of Mexico, under Napoleon III, and the establishment of the brief Mexican Empire of Maximilian. The invasion itself had taken place while the United States was engaged in fratricidal war and was powerless to act. The nations of Latin America, thus finding themselves suddenly without even the ghost of a Monroe Doctrine to protect them, felt the deepest anxiety and, after the Civil War, looked hopefully toward the United States for support of Mexican sovereignty. These hopes were realized when President Lincoln dispatched a strong cable to the French Emperor.

This French intervention of Mexico was the only great breach of Latin-American sovereignty since independence had been won; it lasted five years. Most American textbooks on the subject give the impression that the threat of the United States to enforce the Monroe Doctrine was the primary cause of the French withdrawal which left Maximilian to his fate. Mexican texts give the contrary impression—that the long-suffering Mexican army under the Indian Juárez was the principal factor in the defeat of the foreign Emperor. While both of these statements have a grain of truth in them—the second considerably more than the first—the pith of the matter was that Bismarck had already started a war in Europe and the French Emperor called back most of the troops he had sent to Mexico because he needed them at home. It was certainly no great victory for the Monroe Doctrine.

During the course of the nineteenth century the Latin-American attitude toward the Monroe Doctrine had changed considerably. Time after time the southern republics had called upon it for protection, always in vain. Time after time their national territories had been violated without any show of concern in the United States. Britain had taken the Falkland Islands from Argentina in 1833, and there was no suggestion of a protest from our country. In 1835 Britain had also occupied a portion of the coast of Honduras, and there was no protest. In 1838 France had bombarded Vera Cruz in the so-called Pastry War and the United States had said nothing about the Monroe Doctrine. France, Spain, Germany, and Great Britain had intervened in Haiti in the years 1869, 1871, 1872, and 1877 respectively, again without protests from the United States. Italy had threatened Colombia; France had used force against Santo Domingo, and several European nations had intervened in Central America without having the Monroe Doctrine brought to bear against them. One author refers to these interventions as "violations wholesale," and points out ten major instances, and several more minor ones, when European force was applied to countries of this hemisphere without protest from the United States.[130]

There were only three instances when the Doctrine was strongly invoked: during the French invasion of Mexico under Maximilian, during the British Venezuelan boundary dispute in 1895, and when there was a combined German-English-Italian threat to intervene in Venezuela in 1902. In the first instance Bismarck unwittingly helped to make the Doctrine effective; in the second, Great Britain found herself forced to back down because of the Boer question in South Africa, and in the third, President Theodore Roosevelt wielded his big stick over the head of the German Kaiser, sending him a cable stating that unless the Germans got out of Venezuela within twenty-four hours, Dewey's fleet, which was already on its way south, would blast them to pieces. Great Britain refused to back up Germany and the Kaiser had to withdraw. This was perhaps the only instance in which the Monroe Doctrine had really proved to be a positive protection to the hemisphere.

Nevertheless, the very existence of such a doctrine, whether invoked or not, served as a strong discouraging factor to imperialistic-minded European nations. On only a single occasion had a European power attempted to take over the government of a nation in this hemisphere. Most Latin Americans willingly admit this much. But they follow up this admission by adding that the Monroe Doctrine gave them the kind of protection that a cat gives to a mouse when other cats are in the neighborhood. Europe was being kept out of Latin America so that the United States might swallow up the southern territories at her leisure.

By the end of the century this began to be clearly evident. In 1895, when Richard Olney, then United States Secretary of State, invoked the Monroe Doctrine in the dispute between Britain and Venezuela over the boundary of British Guiana, he stated flatly that his country was "sovereign on this continent, and its fiat is law upon the subjects to which it confines its interposition." This statement became known as "Olney's fiat" and aroused considerable antipathy in the southern countries.

Only three years later the United States declared war against Spain because of the alleged blowing up of the battleship *Maine* in Havana Harbor, and thus began the unhappy period of "interventions wholesale" which caused a rupture between Latin America and the United States that has not entirely healed to this day.

Trouble had been brewing in Cuba for a long time; that island and a few smaller surrounding islands in the West Indies group were Spain's last colonial possessions in the American hemisphere. Her treatment of the Cubans was anything but enlightened. José Martí, the Cuban patriot and martyr, who lived for many years in New York City writing and working constantly to stir up enthusiasm for the Cuban cause, did much to fan the flames of hatred of the Spanish regime and to evoke sympathy for the island patriots. Theodore Roosevelt, with his inveterate love of making a big splash regardless of the consequences, whooped up the war fever and personally trained his "Roughriders" to take part in the campaign. William Randolph Hearst went all out in drumming up support for the war against Spain. The citizens of the United States felt considerable sympathy for the Cuban people, but popular feeling alone would never have resulted in war had it not been goaded on by Hearst, Roosevelt, the sinking of the *Maine*, the speeches and writings of Martí, and by certain business interests. Senator Thurston of Nebraska, for example, spoke for these interests as follows: "War with Spain would increase the business and earnings of every American railroad, it would increase the output of every

American factory, it would stimulate every branch of industry and commerce."[125]

All of these people except Martí, who had been killed in the meantime while trying to free his native land, were extremely well pleased when the *Maine* blew up at Havana and war was declared. However, as it was the first conflict in which the United States had engaged with a European power for nearly a hundred years, the inhabitants of the Atlantic seaboard lived from day to day expecting to see the Spanish fleet suddenly appear offshore with cannon blazing. No such incident ever occurred, and the United States Navy soon defeated the Spaniards.

General William Shafter, who commanded the American ground forces at Santiago, Cuba, did not have quite so easy a time of it. Shafter was a whale of a man who weighed close to three hundred pounds. No one doubted his courage but his obesity made his active campaigning difficult. The tropical heat almost prostrated him, and he spent hours daily lying half naked in a hammock "with one soldier massaging his balloonlike torso, while another swept cooling breezes over him with a palm-leaf fan." When it became necessary for the general to move about he had his men tear loose a huge door on which he ensconced his immense hulk and was thus carried over the rough terrain.

It was probably the worst managed war in the history of the United States. Medical supplies were at the bottom of incoming cargo, and a great portion of them never got ashore at all. Disease was rife in the American ranks; men were issued thick woolen uniforms for wear in the tropical heat, fed rations of half-rotten "embalmed beef," and in the long run there were fourteen times as many deaths due to sickness as to actual combat. W. E. Woodward, in his *A New American History*, says that this foul beef aroused such howling criticism of the meat packers that it later led to government supervision of their industry.

Despite all this, the Americans were quickly victorious in both the West Indies and off the Philippine Islands. In this latter sector Admiral Dewey defeated the Spanish fleet with the loss of only a single man, who had died of heart failure due to the excitement. The entire war lasted less than four months and American dead did not total 6000.

Before and during the conflict opinion in Latin America had been divided as between those who were pro-Spanish and those who were pro-United States. But Spain's quick, disastrous, and inglorious defeat aroused a quiver of racial sympathy in her former colonies, and this was not long in being converted into the beginning of a very real fear of the great northern power. When it became clear that the United States had "liberated" Cuba and Puerto Rico merely to take them over herself, this fear became widespread and intense.

Latin Americans were especially galled by the difference between the word and the deed of the northern republic. When war was declared on

Spain, in April 1898, the war resolution had included these words: "The United States hereby disclaims any disposition or intention to exercise sovereignty, jurisdiction, or control over said island [Cuba] except for the pacification thereof, and asserts its determination, when that is accomplished, to leave the government and control of the island to its people."

Such was the word. The deed was quite different. United States military forces occupied Cuba and ran the government between 1898 and 1903, and, after their withdrawal in the latter year, there were three more armed interventions, the last ending in 1922. These three interventions, excluding the first which might be attributed to conditions following the war, resulted in the military occupation of Cuba by armed force of the United States for a period of about eight years. The Platt Amendment (1901) gave the United States complete control over the foreign policy of Cuba and also sanctioned her intervention at any time "to restore order." Cuba was forced to incorporate this amendment in her constitution, and it was not abrogated by the United States until 1934.

The epoch of large-scale capital investments in Latin America, which led to large-scale interventions, began after the Spanish-American War. The United States had by that time recovered sufficiently from the Civil War, and from the terrible reconstruction period which followed, to be on the alert for good investment opportunities wherever these might appear.

Between 1870 and 1900 more than ten million immigrants had entered the United States, and during the next twenty years more than twelve million others followed. Most of these immigrants were adults who had lived through their unproductive childhood years in Europe. Many thousands of them had received their education and training at European expense. They came to America in their prime and entered at once into the productive fabric of American life. The call of the West had left a vacuum on the Atlantic seaboard which had to be filled with imported workers, and these immigrants were brought in for that purpose. The population of the United States had increased from 38,500,000 in 1870 to 76,000,000 in 1900, then to more than 105,000,000 in 1920.

The epoch of westward expansion and the glittering frontier had been brought to a halt. Railways now spanned the continent and vast industries had sprung up. The earlier and cruder age of the Vanderbilts and the Goulds had given way to a more impersonal "age of dinosaurs," as James Truslow Adams calls it, in which immense industrial trusts practically took over the economic life of the nation. Andrew Carnegie, J. P. Morgan, and John D. Rockefeller built up their fortunes during this period. The main characteristic of this period was size itself—the immensity of the nation's industrial growth, productive power, organization, and wealth. A sort of impersonal economic law seemed to hold sway over all individual tastes and character. It bore the indelible stamp which marked the path of property everywhere. It cried out its goal of the almighty dollar, wealth for the sake of wealth, size for the sake of size, a new American nightmare of megalomania.

During this age of the dinosaurs, or "Empire Builders," the nation had become a great world power. The enterprises of these men had built up the West, had girded the continent with steel rails, had developed the great resources of a rapidly expanding economy. That economy might receive a slight setback when the most obvious of these opportunities had been taken advantage of, but it would not stop. It would simply look for other and more fertile fields for investment—fields where the return would continue to be fabulous. They found these fields in the undeveloped regions of Latin America.

Between 1900 and 1922 the national wealth of the United States jumped from approximately $88,000,000,000 to more than $320,000,000,000—an increase of 263 per cent. During the same period the population had risen from 76,000,000 to approximately 108,000,000, an increase of only 42 per cent. This meant that there was a tremendous increase in the standard of living inside the United States, and that the amount of fluid capital had increased so greatly that there was a surplus left over from home investment which was ready to be placed in foreign countries.

Other considerations, of course, entered into the picture. Certain essential raw products not obtainable within the continental United States, such as rubber, had to be procured elsewhere if the automobile industry was to be kept from stifling. Certain more or less luxury products, such as coffee, would be imported in tremendous volume in order to cater to the raised standard of living inside the United States. These were only incidental to the process of imperialistic expansion. The primary characteristic of that expansion was the investment of United States capital in foreign countries, especially the other American countries. We are not speaking now of trade but of the purchasing of titles to lands and mines, the construction and ownership of rail lines, factories, and refineries, the development under United States ownership of sugar plantations in Cuba, oil wells in Mexico and Venezuela, copper mines in Chile, and so on over the whole range of possible investment.

In the year 1900 total United States investments in Latin America were as follows: $50,000,000 in Cuba, $185,000,000 in Mexico, and only $55,000,000 in all the rest of Latin America. By 1911, year of the fall of Díaz, investments in Mexico alone had risen from $185,000,000 to more than one billion dollars. In that year a small moneyed group of American citizens actually owned more of Mexico's productive industry than did the entire Mexican population. In the year 1911 United States investments in Mexico totaled $1,058,000,000, while Mexican capital investments came to only $793,000,000.

More or less the same thing happened in Cuba. United States investments there jumped from a paltry $50,000,000 in 1900 to nearly a billion and a half by 1925. Again a small group of American investors actually controlled more Cuban industry than the entire population of that island. Total United States capital invested in Latin America increased from $290,000,000 in 1900 to approximately four billion dollars in 1924, according to figures of the United States Department of Commerce.

It was in order to protect these investments of a small minority that the government of the United States, utilizing the tax money from all of the people, intervened time after time in internal Latin-American affairs. Sometimes these interventions took place merely to preserve order so that property would not be destroyed and money lost. Sometimes they took the form of strong United States support of the man or party most favorable to North American interests.

Sometimes when Latin-American governments defaulted on repayment of loans made by private banks the United States Government occupied the country involved, took over the machinery of government, controlled both elections and customs in order to enforce the repayment of these loans.

With the prospect of the United States Navy and Marines to give them support in collecting, American banks sometimes pressed loans on Latin-American governments with every trick at their disposal. It has frequently been reported that Jorge Leguía, son of the dictator of Peru, was given more than $400,000 as his "take" for persuading his father's government to accept a big loan from a New York banking house.[154] There were numerous other such incidents.

In many parts of Latin America economic penetration and political interference became inseparable. Together they added up to Yankee imperialism on a wide scale; and for millions of citizens of the southern countries the United States became known as the Colossus of the North, ready to impose its will by force whenever the occasion arose.

A brief summary of the most important of these armed interventions will give some idea of their scope. From 1899 to 1933 Nicaragua was virtually a protectorate of the United States, and for more than twenty years of that time the country was under military occupation. Aid was given to a rebellion in Panama and that province was "taken" from Colombia in 1903. The Dominican Republic was under absolute United States control between 1905 and 1924 and was occupied by Marines for ten years; Haiti was under military occupation from 1915 to 1934; between 1907 and 1925 there were six armed interventions in Honduras; Mexico was invaded several times between 1846 and 1916, including the bombardment and occupation of Vera Cruz in 1914, and the punitive expedition of more than 10,000 men sent into Mexico under General Pershing, who chased Pancho Villa for several months across that country while World War I was raging in Europe. Many other Latin-American nations were coerced by only slightly less violent means. The Mexican writer Luis Quintanilla in his book, *A Latin American Speaks,* mentions a total of sixty United States interventions in fifty years.

Some of these armed interventions read like the farfetched melodramas of cheap adventure fiction, but there was nothing fictional in the impression which they made on the Latin-American mind. Take, for example, the case of Panama.

For some years the United States had been interested in building a canal across Central America. The French had started the construction of one across Panama in 1884, but after five years the construction company charged with the job had crashed, and work was called off. The chief engineer of the French company, Bunau-Varilla, acquired the rights and equipment of the bankrupt organization, hired a well-known New York attorney named Nelson Cromwell to help him, and tried to sell out to the government of the United States for a big price. He asked more than $100,-000,000, and the congressional committee investigating the matter estimated the company's assets as being worth approximately $40,000,000. Consequently they advised that the canal be dug across Nicaragua instead of across Panama. Bunau-Varilla, fearful of losing everything, sent Nicaraguan stamps bearing pictures of erupting volcanoes to every member of the Senate in an effort to defeat the new bill. Fortunately for the Frenchman, one of these volcanoes broke loose just before a decision was reached in the Senate, and the Nicaraguan project was defeated.

Colombia and the United States then became engaged in treaty discussions about a canal across Panama, which was then a part of Colombian territory. The Colombian Congress was unwilling to accept the sum which the United States had offered ($10,000,000 cash and a yearly rental fee of $250,000) and adjourned without having approved the treaty.

Bunau-Varilla, his attorney Cromwell, and one of their Panamanian friends, Manuel Amador, physician of the Panama Railway Company, then plotted a revolution for the independence of Panama. There had already been flurries of separatism in Panama, and the potential sum of $10,000,000 which might be snatched from under the very nose of Colombia made prospects look brighter for the "patriots." Panama was promised immediate recognition by the United States if a revolution did occur, not by the government of the United States, but by Cromwell, Bunau-Varilla, and Amador. However, to help matters along, a United States warship, the *Nashville,* was sent to the scene with instructions to prevent an armed conflict. Soldiers from the *Nashville,* following these instructions, refused to permit a body of Colombian troops which had been sent to quell the revolution to cross the isthmus. The revolution thus came off; the news was wired to Washington; the new government was recognized promptly, and negotiations were entered into with the independent state of Panama. Construction on the canal was soon under way.

Several years later, in 1911, Theodore Roosevelt, while speaking at the state university in Berkeley, California, used these words: "I took the Canal Zone and let the Congress debate, and while the debate goes on, the Canal does also."

Colombia did not let these words pass unnoticed, but renewed her efforts to obtain some compensation for the loss of Panama. Finally, in 1921, she was given $25,000,000, but this payment did not in any degree allay her bitterness toward the Colossus of the North.

Bunau-Varilla served as the first Panamanian minister to the United States; the New York attorney Cromwell received a check for $800,000 for his part in the affair, and Amador, the railroad physician, became the first president of Panama.[131]

The Panama Revolution took place in 1903, and the few friends the United States had left in Latin America after the occupation of Cuba were now convinced of the Yankee menace. There was a great wave of protest from all quarters. Elihu Root, Secretary of State under Theodore Roosevelt, made an eloquent attempt to still these Latin-American fears at the third Pan-American Congress held at Rio in 1906: "We wish for no victories but those of peace; for no territory except our own; for no sovereignty except the sovereignty over ourselves. We deem the independence and equal rights of the smallest and weakest member of the family of nations entitled to as much respect as those of greatest empire, and we deem the observance of that respect the chief guaranty of the weak against the strong. We neither claim nor desire any rights, or privileges, or powers that we do not freely concede to every American Republic."

All Latin America applauded these words, but again the deed and the statement differed. Haiti, the Dominican Republic, Nicaragua, Cuba, Honduras, and Mexico all soon felt the sharp claw of Yankee imperialism upon their backs. For many years the first four of these countries were under United States military dictatorship, with their customs and finances under the complete control of banking houses of this country, which thus assured themselves of profits through force. Their interest in placing such loans under armed protection is readily understandable, for the sums involved were often fifteen to twenty millions in a single instance. The interest on $20,000,000 for one year at 6 per cent amounts to $1,200,000—no mean profit even for a New York banking firm.

The story of Mexico was somewhat different; it revolved around the development of Mexican oil, an issue still alive in Pan-American relations. In 1900 Edward L. Doheny and other American oilmen purchased 280,000 acres of Mexican land for the sum of $325,000, or about $1.15 an acre. President Díaz had encouraged the investment of American capital in Mexico, and Doheny simply took a wildcatter's chance and struck it rich. Fabulous oil wells were found on his Mexican lands. A good well in California brings in 600 barrels a day; a single Mexican well produced 70,000 barrels a day at the beginning, and, under forcibly reduced flow, continued to produce 25,000 barrels a day for many years. Another well, the famous Blue Hill, or Cerro Azul, the largest oil well in the world, produced between 45,000 and 50,000 barrels a day, also for several years.[132]

Toward the end of the Díaz regime things began to look a little less favorable for the American oil interests. The Mexican dictator wanted to open the doors to British investments in the same field on terms which made them serious competitors. Before things had reached an impasse Díaz was ousted by Madero, who had many friends in the United States. Madero lasted less than two years and was followed by Victoriano Huerta, who took over the government by force. Huerta had the idealistic but incompetent Madero executed and then threw his body into the street in an effort to make it appear that his death had been an accident. Immediately on assuming power Huerta made it plain that he favored British financial interests, especially British investments in oil, and Great Britain recognized him at once, making him a large loan.

It was at about this time that Woodrow Wilson was inaugurated as President of the United States. President Taft, who was just going out of office, had taken no action at all in regard to Mexico, regarding the Huerta issue as too hot to handle in the last days of his administration. American financial interests were asking for intervention, or at least for a strong stand against Huerta. President Wilson made the latter course the settled policy of his government. He not only refused to recognize Mexico but gave as his reasons that Huerta had attained power by unconstitutional and violent means, had disbanded his Congress and imprisoned the Mexican deputies, had assassinated his predecessor, and was unable to restore order in Mexico. No mention was made of the fact that he was anti-United States in his economic leanings, a fact which had at least as much weight as any of the rest. The wife of our chargé d'affaires in Mexico City, Edith O'Shaughnessy, made the following ironic comment: "*Our* government gave warning that it would not consider concessions granted during the Huerta regime as binding on the *Mexicans*. It makes one rub one's eyes."[133]

This was the beginning of a new epoch in the relations between the United States and Latin America. First of all, the "moral" principle had been invoked; second, recognition was being withheld from a *de facto* Latin-American government as a measure of coercion against that government. President Wilson later clarified the issue when he stated in conversation that it was his intention "to teach these Latin-American republics to elect good men."

The general consensus of opinion at the time seemed to be that Huerta was not a "good man." Most of his own countrymen now admit that he was an inveterate drunkard, a murderer, a ruthless tyrant who had no respect for constitutional law, an upholder of the feudal policy of the Díaz regime. No sooner had he attained power than he filled the jails with political prisoners, having dozens of them shot. He surrounded the halls of Congress, declared that body dissolved, and imprisoned one hundred and ten Mexican deputies. Revolution broke out against Huerta almost immediately under Carranza, Obregón, Calles, Villa, and other leaders. Carranza was declared "commander of the constitutionalist forces," and Huerta proved unable to "pacify" the country, which was the principal purpose for which he had forced himself into power.

In spite of all these things, when President Wilson stated that revolution and assassination must come to an end in Latin America, and that he was going to teach those nations to elect good men, he overlooked the fact that no Mexican government had ever come to power since the days of independence except through violent or fraudulent means. He also neglected to apply his "moral" principle to Peru, very quickly recognized by this country, although its government under Benavides was fairly steeped in blood. Latin Americans very naturally questioned the validity of President Wilson's sense of objective morality.

The attitude of Great Britain throughout this episode, and the attitude of all the Mexicans who supported Huerta, was that if the United States had recognized the Huerta regime the revolutions could have been suppressed. Non-recognition lent powerful support to Huerta's enemies, encouraging them to open rebellion.

Up to this point, however, feeling in Latin America, and even in many parts of Mexico itself, was not strongly anti-United States, because, despite the apparent justice of recognizing whatever government is in power, it was widely agreed that Huerta would have been but another edition of the bloody and incorrigible Díaz.

President Wilson did not stop with non-recognition. Prodded on by American oil interests, he lifted the embargo which this country had placed on arms crossing the Texas-Mexican border, and thus enabled the revolutionists who controlled that area to obtain weapons and munitions. It was later brought out in a congressional investigation in Washington that Mr. Doheny had, through his representative, Felicitas Villareal, helped along the "constitutionalist" cause of Carranza with $100,000 in cash. Furthermore, the oil companies refused to pay taxes to Huerta, and furnished oil to the value of $685,000 to the revolutionary forces.[132]

President Wilson in the meantime referred to his policy as "watchful waiting," and made the following comment: "Little by little Huerta has been carefully isolated. By a little every day his power and prestige are crumbling, and the collapse is not far away. We shall not, I believe, be obliged to alter our policy of watchful waiting."

He was mistaken, for that policy was soon to be altered most violently. The fuse was lighted by the so-called "Tampico flag incident." A group of American soldiers had landed in a forbidden area in Tampico, were arrested by the Mexican authorities, held for half an hour, and then released. A formal apology was given to the American commander; the Mexican official who had ordered the arrest was punished, and a salute was ordered given the American flag. The American admiral demanded that the salute consist of twenty-one guns. The Mexicans balked at making such a tremendous concession, for a twenty-one-gun salute is given only after the gravest outrages, and Huerta, who had already tendered his personal apologies, along with those of the commandant, attempted to excuse his government from the indignity. The Americans were adamant. For further argument ten warships were promptly dispatched to Tampico with a regiment of Marines. Huerta now offered to place the matter before the Hague tribunal. When this offer brought a negative response he agreed to have the twenty-one-gun salute fired, provided the Americans fired their twenty-one-gun return volley at the same time. Otherwise, he said, he was afraid that the salute might not be returned at all and his government would thus be humiliated.

The argument was still going on when it was learned in Washington that a German vessel, the *Ypiranga*, was nearing Vera Cruz with a load of munitions for the Huerta government. The government of the United States, now determined to bring about the fall of Huerta, decided to block the arrival of this aid, and President Wilson wired the American forces to take Vera Cruz at once. Despite strong Mexican opposition, a landing was made, and after considerable fighting the city was captured. Seventeen American soldiers were killed; about two hundred Mexicans, among them several women and children, lost their lives in the storming of Vera Cruz. Even the rebellious constitutionalists under Carranza, obviously aided by the incident, strongly protested against this violation of Mexico's sovereignty.

The capture of Mexico's main port cut off a fourth of that country's imports and made the survival of the Huerta regime impossible. Mexico City was taken by the revolutionists; Carranza became president. He was promptly assassinated, and the revolution continued. By this time the United States had become involved in World War I, and Mexico became a secondary issue. Naturally feeling in that country continued to be bitterly anti-American; it was rumored that the place was infested with German spies, and many journalists even suggested that Germany had been invited to use Mexico as a base from which to invade the United States.

The effect of this outrage against Mexico was to make a great part of Spanish America suspicious of the United States throughout the period of World War I when co-operation was so badly needed. Brazil, which considered herself as standing apart from the bloc of Spanish-speaking nations of the south, was the only large Latin-American power to declare war on the side of the allies. There was considerable pro-allied feeling in many quarters, but the Vera Cruz incident stood out like a sore thumb, preventing the mobilization of anything approaching the spirit of continental solidarity.

After the war there were further interventions and the military occupation of several Caribbean regions continued. Nicaragua was the last of these storm centers. In 1928, at the peak of North American occupation, there was a total of 5,821 officers and men in that country. One hundred and thirty-five of them lost their lives while serving there, and the occupation cost the taxpayers of the United States $5,517,832, as testified by Major General B. H. Fuller before the House Appropriations Committee, February 9, 1931.

It has often been said that investment follows the flag, but in the case of United States imperialism in Latin America the process was generally reversed. Investments were first made and then the flag was sent to protect them for the small moneyed group in whose interest they were held. The American people at large neither profited from these investments nor had any interest in backing them up with the lives of their loved ones or with millions of their taxpayers' dollars. Nevertheless, in those days this was our national policy and it aroused widespread ill will in Latin America.

A few quotations from outstanding leaders and writers of Latin America during the past century will show more clearly than any further generalized comment the slow growth of this ill will toward the United States.

In 1819 Simón Bolívar expressed his opinion of the United States in these words: "Who can resist the love which so intelligent a government inspires . . . Who can resist the sway of that inspired nation which, with a skillful, active, and powerful hand, directs all of its energies always and everywhere toward social perfection, which is the true goal of human institutions?"

In 1824 Santander, the national hero of Colombia, said: "The action of President Monroe in making that proclamation is eminently just. It is an act worthy of the classic land of American liberty."

In 1852 Alberdi, whose writings formed the basis of the Argentine constitution, wrote: "The type who best represents the greatness of the United States is no military Napoleon; it is Washington, and Washington does not stand for military triumphs but for prosperity, growth, organization, peace. He is the hero of order within liberty *par excellence*." Alberdi then says that the English language is the language of liberty, industry, and order, and he calls upon his countrymen to "follow the example of the civilization of the Anglo-Saxon race."

In 1873 Juan Montalvo of Ecuador, after viewing our Civil War, commented as follows: "A nation so extravagant and fantastic as the United States of America, where the customs run contrary to the laws . . . where democracy reigns in institutions and aristocracy in the form of pride and scorn excludes from the common society those whose color is not light enough . . . this nation, I say, in the midst of its liberty, its liberalism, its progress, must inspire terror in the breast of South Americans."[124]

In 1891 José Martí, the apostle of Cuban independence, who lived in New York for many years and probably came to know the United States better than any other outstanding Latin-American writer, made this statement in an article appearing in a Mexican newspaper: "The scorn of our formidable neighbor, who does not know us, is the greatest danger of our America. The day of our meeting is near, and it is urgent that this neighbor come to understand us well so that she will not continue to feel scorn for us. Through ignorance and greed, perhaps, she might be brought to lay hands upon us."

José Enrique Rodó, of Uruguay, whose essay *Ariel* became a sort of Bible for Latin-American youth for more than a generation, wrote in that famous little book in 1900: "The mighty nation of the north is now carrying out a sort of moral conquest over us. Admiration for its greatness and its power is a feeling that is growing rapidly among our ruling classes, and perhaps even more among the multitude which is so easily impressed with success or victory. . . . Today the people of that nation aspire to the leadership of the world's civilization and look upon themselves as the precursors and originators of the culture of the future. The well-known phrase 'America can beat the world,' ironically quoted by Laboulaye, is the deep conviction of almost any virile westerner. . . . There is no point in trying to convince these people that the torch lighted on the shores of the Mediterranean more than three thousand years ago, which soared to glory in the culture of Athens, a work and tradition of which we Latin Americans form a part, adds up to a sum which cannot be equaled by any equation of Washington plus Edison. North Americans would almost be willing to rewrite the Book of Genesis in order to put themselves on the front page."

Rubén Darío, born in tiny Nicaragua, but Spanish America's greatest and most cosmopolitan poet, wrote this final paragraph in the introduction to his finest book, *Songs of Life and Hope*, which came out in 1905: "If in these verses there is a political feeling, it is because that feeling appears universally. And if you find lines to a certain well-known president, it is because they express the protest of an entire continent. Tomorrow we may all become Yankee Americans (indeed, that is our most likely destiny). At any rate, my own protest remains written on the wings of the immaculate swans, as illustrious as Jupiter."[134]

In 1911 García Calderón, one of Peru's best-known writers, wrote at the beginning of a chapter entitled "The North American Peril" these stinging words: "To save themselves from Yankee imperialism the Latin-American democracies would almost accept a German alliance, or the aid of Japanese arms. Everywhere the Americans of the North are feared. In the Antilles and in Central America hostility against the Anglo-Saxon invaders assumes the character of a Latin crusade."

In 1917, when the United States asked for hemispheric solidarity in the face of the German menace during World War I, Ismael Enrique Artigas of Colombia wrote: "Our pro-Ally sentiments are so well known that it might be believed that the attitude of this journal would be definitely in favor of the United States in its contention with Germany. But—higher than these opinions—first in our minds is love of our country. And that love will never allow us to forget the offenses which the Anglo-Saxon republic has committed against us. When that nation invokes the principles of international law to induce us to join her protest against Germany, she is engaged in a mockery. . . . With what authority, after events like those of November 3, 1903 [Artigas refers to Panama], can a nation speak in the name of international law?"

From the end of World War I up to the year 1933 Latin-American antipathy toward the United States was deep, bitter, and almost omnipresent. Blanco Fombona of Venezuela blasted away at the hated northern colossus and its rape of the Caribbean countries, summarizing hemispheric relations as a "duel between two races"; Vasconcelos of Mexico called Elihu Root's suave Pan-Americanism "more dangerous than the cannon of the old English pirates," and in his *History of Mexico* reiterated a dozen times that all Mexican governments between 1913 and 1930 had been mere bootlickers of the Embassy of the United States; Manuel Ugarte of Argentina made himself famous with an attack on Yankee imperialism which became the classic analysis.

In between these spurts of bitterness were sandwiched a few words of admiration for the material progress of the United States, and of respect for the achievement of individual liberty within that nation. Fear was often mingled with envy in these Latin-American attacks, and the envy always shone through.

Bad as the history of American imperialism is, the other side of the picture certainly does not deserve to escape the criticism which it justly merits. The North American viewpoint is presented cogently in Duncan Aikman's *The All-American Front*, "The highlight in the Latin-American reaction was not that they protested against the stronger neighbor's conduct and suspected his intentions. The key to the Latin mental process is that the spokesmen for the indignant republics recognized no imperfections or provocations in the conduct of their own governments, that they dramatized themselves as the victims of a wholesale outrage before the outrage itself had developed beyond a local basis, and shrieked against the imperialism of the 'New Rome' without making the slightest effort to arouse, or co-operate with, the vast, latent forces in the northern republic which were opposed to imperialism."[135]

As an example of his argument Aikman points to the case of Panama, which brought forth prolonged and unanimous howls of "wolf" from the nations of Latin America, every one of which regarded Colombia "simply as the victim of her idealistic patriotism." There was no slight suggestion that Colombia "might have been obstructing an international enterprise of vast economic benefit to all the twenty republics. . . ."

This is the strongest argument that can be adduced in favor of intervention; the reader must decide whether it is strong enough. Aikman does emphasize one point which Latin Americans have often overlooked: that there has existed at all times in the United States a powerful popular feeling against economic imperialism anywhere, that the masses of the citizens of the United States "look with acute disrelish on the idea of subjugating independent republics for the benefit of powerful oil, mining, power, and banking interests."

Latin-American writers and speakers, particularly those who visited the United States personally and then took a belligerent anti-North American stand (Martí, Ugarte, Vasconcelos, et al.), did not weaken their enemies but only alienated their friends within this country by the manner in which they expressed themselves. Too frequently they demanded respect for the sovereign integrity of governments which had neither a real sovereignty nor a real integrity. They minimized or failed to point out that in case after case the Latin-American governments involved were utterly irresponsible, that they defaulted their obligations with a recklessness which was inexcusable, that frequently within the countries violated there were strong native elements which favored intervention, that some governments called for such intervention without duress, that many Latin Americans were not (and are not) above requesting help from the United States, provided it favors their side. Aikman indirectly suggests that to point out this distortion of the perspective might be like "accusing a lady of losing her critical integrity while being ravished," and thus almost nullifies his entire argument.

Far more significant than the opinions of Aikman or of any other writer defending the North American point of view were those expressed by the Uruguayan Rodó, in the year 1900. Rodó's little book *Ariel* transcends the ordinary bounds of an essay on a foreign country. He expressed the sentiments of a whole people in making that famous comparison between materialistic "Caliban," the United States, and the far finer embodiment of all cultural values, or "Ariel," which the nations of Latin America were made to represent.

Rodó characterized the United States as a nation practically without a culture. He even referred to our educational system as a vast leveling process which lost in profundity what it gained in extension. North Americans acquired but did not create works of art; they had never felt the "divine frenzy of poem or picture." Their civilization, despite its material progress, suggested a vast emptiness. They formed an uncouth nation whose God was utilitarianism.

Rodó admired the spirit of liberty which reigned in the United States, and praised the North American's robust efficiency, inventiveness, his powerful desire for betterment, and his ennoblement of useful labor. He praised but minimized the redemption of human lives through a higher standard of living, and suggested, following Emerson, that a nation should be judged by its superior minority rather than by its masses.

Rodó's conclusion was that the hemisphere might best fulfill its destiny by combining the North American's liberty and material progress with the Latin American's hallowed cultural tradition and respect for genius. He admitted great admiration among many Latin Americans for the democratic civilization of the north, and warned against its encroachment on the higher cultural values so long exalted in the south. Only through fusion of the two could there be attained a real fulfillment.

Rodó made at least one fundamental error in his essay, which was to deny the existence of a powerful and creative culture in the United States. Unfortunately this error was magnified by many of Rodó's less well-informed readers, and it became the fashion in Latin America to remember only the writer's premise: Ariel and Caliban. This was the starting point, not the end of Rodó's own thinking.

Latin Americans exalted their culture to the skies and felt in this way a kind of superiority over the average citizen of the United States. Culture became a sort of "untouchable" value which lifted many a high-soaring spirit above such materialistic considerations as decent government, material progress, education for the masses, and so forth. There is no doubt that this attitude, not begun but canalized by Rodó, has done great damage to the Latin-American way of life. Strangest of all is the almost incredible fact that long after Latin Americans generally had passed beyond the Rodó stage of thinking, in the years following World War I, people in the United States began to pick up the already fallen torch of the Uruguayan essayist and to hoist it on high, shouting to the heavens the superiority of the Latin culture as compared with that of their own nation!

During the past fifty years Latin America has been brought into intimate contact with the culture of the United States. World War I shut off France as a place to which her students, thinkers, and artists might journey as they had for so many years previously. The only country that remained open to them was the United States. Our universities, libraries, and other cultural institutions began for the first time to attract large numbers of citizens from the southern countries. The movement was greatly intensified by the flowering of American literature, drama, and art during the past half-century. The best plays in New York were immediately translated into Spanish and put on in Latin America. Eugene O'Neill, Ernest Hemingway, John Steinbeck, John Dos Passos, William Faulkner, Tennessee Williams, Henry Miller, Edward Albee, Arthur Miller became as widely known in Latin America as any of the native authors.

The motion picture and radio broadcasting became further mouth-pieces for the great northern culture, and covered the continent all the way from the Rio Grande down to Tierra del Fuego. By the time World War II began, Latin Americans had completely reversed their estimate of the cultural life of the United States. The Department of State and the Co-ordinator of Inter-American Affairs helped the process along by bringing distinguished Latin Americans to this country and by sending distinguished North Americans south. They also established centers for the teaching of English in nearly all of the leading southern cities, assembled and dispatched libraries for these centers, gave funds for educational projects of many kinds, and kept men of high intellectual standing in Latin America as cultural attachés. The zeal to learn English and the enthusiasm for the culture of the United States became omnipresent.

This feeling reached such a peak that the national librarian of Colombia, one of the most outstanding intellectuals of his country, made a special plea for a "defense against the wave of foreign culture which is flowing in upon us." His words were directed to a special congressional committee, and among the thoughts expressed were the following: "It is necessary for us to realize that times oblige us to think about defending our own culture and our racial tradition. Let us welcome the wave of foreign culture which is moving toward us, forcing itself upon us, but unless we devise practical means to defend our own native and traditional culture, it will disappear under the avalanche from abroad. If things continue in the present vein, the coming generation will cease to believe in any other culture than that which expresses itself in English; the children who are now growing up will think that nothing of value exists, that no book is worth reading unless it is written in English. Our defense must consist not in closing our doors to this wave from abroad, but in intensifying our own Colombian, Spanish, Latin culture in the minds of the generation now maturing."[160]

Ariel and Caliban had at last met face to face, and the difference was not so great as had at first been assumed. Two ways of life exist side by side, and the stronger, better organized, more systematized of the two is asserting its dominance. The fine techniques of the north are overrunning the hesitant folk expression of the south. In this transition state Latin America feels momentarily weak and unsure of herself, and this coincides with the moment of greatest United States cultural strength.

In the mind of the south the danger of absorption, or obliteration, has begun to seem very real. The only possible answer is cross-fertilization, which must become a common responsibility.

Latin America's deepest pride is that she has something of great value to offer. She longs for a reciprocal process. The grave danger to the hemisphere is that this small voice may be crying in the wilderness.

53

THE TWENTIETH CENTURY:
DEEP WOMB, DARK FLOWER

Latin America's growth in the twentieth century rests upon roots which reach deep into the past, and those roots have just begun to put on the leaf and flower of modern life. Nowhere have the southern countries yet produced the mature fruits of democracy, industrialization, a superior standard of living, honest elections, educational systems of first rank, an enlightened public opinion. Despite the tremendous differences which exist between one region and another, everywhere the old semi-feudal, semi-colonial society persists. There are new names, new social battle-cries gauged for the best demagogic response; there is even a certain measure of political liberty granted by the paternalistic ruling classes. Yet the old relationship of master and vassal continues, sub-standards of living are the rule rather than the exception, the political outlook is highly unstable, economically the nations of Latin America still live chained to the soil which is the patrimony of the chosen few. This minority controls the destiny of Argentina, Brazil, Chile, the most advanced of the southern countries. There are bright spots which relieve the dark omnipresent shadow of the colonial past, and they are rapidly gaining in light, but so far their victory is nowhere secure. It is best to make these things perfectly clear before attempting any presentation of contemporary Latin-American life.

So many elements enter into the picture, so many countries, so many diverse geographic regions, climates, racial groups, customs, traditions, economic and cultural extremes, that no single perspective could possibly cover the entire scene. Argentina is as different from Paraguay, its next-door neighbor, as the United States is from Tibet or Afghanistan. Buenos Aires is as far ahead of Asunción as New York City is of Addis Ababa. Racially, Argentina, Peru, and Haiti are as different from each other as are England, India, and the African Congo. All of these ethnic, historic, and geographic differences, which have been presented in detail in previous chapters, must be borne in mind as an attempt is made to strike some kind of a balance in the interpretation.

One of the most interesting aspects of Latin American life in the final quarter of the nineteenth century is the reawakening of something approaching a common spirit. The Latin countries had felt this spirit during their struggle for independence, when soldiers from all regions had fought for the common cause. Disputes among the victors and social chaos, however, then all but blotted it out. The tenuous cultured unity of colonial days seemed to disappear along with the common political desire. For many years conditions continued to be such that only local feelings could thrive.

By the 1880s, however, economic stability was at least far enough advanced to permit the conception and growth of a broad esthetic movement. A strong reaction arose against the former regional views and drew the different nations together. In literature, where the process can be most easily studied, this gave rise to the school of "modernism" which produced the most famous group of writers in Latin-American history. Among them were Rodó of Uruguay, Rubén Darío of Nicaragua, José Martí of Cuba, Gutiérrez Nájera and Amado Nervo of Mexico, José Asunción Silva of Colombia, and many others. These writers transcended their national frontiers, became known throughout all the southern countries, wrote in a manner which minimized regional differences and made the most of cultural affinities. Through them, for the first time, Latin America entered into the currents of universal literature.

"While the *modernista* movement began and grew in Spanish America, a similar one began and developed, independently, in Brazilian poetry. It was less sudden and less revolutionary."[171] The swing away from it was also less abrupt. Machado de Assis, the greatest figure in nineteenth-century Brazilian literature, wrote much poetry which might be identified with the modernist creed, but his novels about life in Rio de Janeiro were realistic psychological studies with a middle-class milieu. No writer in Spanish America embraces as much and as varied territory as this great Brazilian.

Just after the turn of the century, in 1902, there appeared in Brazil two outstanding works which have marked out the lines literature in that country was to follow for the next several years. These were *Os Sertões*, by Euclides da Cunha, and *Canaan*, by Graça Aranha. In *Os Sertões*, Cunha tells the story of a "delirious rural mystic, Antonio Conselheiro, around whom a fanatic multitude gathered and settled down in the *sertão*." The government sent repeated military expeditions against him until finally the backlands prophet was destroyed. It is a somber story, "powerfully and brilliantly told"; the descriptions of the land itself and the human types which it produced have moved many critics to call this the finest book to come out of Brazil.[171] The novel *Canaan,* by Graça Aranha, presents the other pole of Brazilian life: immigration into the vast South American crucible and the racial aptitudes in this new habitat. These two famous prose works fall outside of the modernist torrent which still flooded Latin America at that time.

The modernists, both of Brazil and of Spanish America, found inspiration in the Iberian heritage, but it was their ever-present veneration of French literature which gave their cult a new focus, started them all off in the same general direction, and lifted their art from the regional pigeonholes into which it had fallen before that time.

Rubén Darío, generally conceded to be the greatest of all Latin-American poets, symbolized the new universality of this artistic feeling in both a physical and spiritual sense. Born in tiny Nicaragua of Spanish-Indian-Negro extraction, he traveled, lived, and wrote all over Spanish America and Europe: Central America, Chile, Argentina (where he resided many years), Spain, France, then back to America again. Coming from a small backward nation, which has never had any literature or distinct culture of its own, he became the leading literary figure of all Latin America, more admired in Buenos Aires than the best known of Argentine poets. Darío and his generation achieved in literature what the generation of liberators had achieved in the political sphere: a strong continental consciousness.

It is no mere coincidence that these modernist writers crystallized the Latin-American attitude toward the United States. Rodó, Darío, Martí, José Santos Chocano, all felt strongly a cultural bond which unified them in the face of the threat of the Colossus of the North. They wrote about the imperialistic ventures of this country in terms of bitterest protest. They marshaled all of the intelligentsia of their countries behind them. They created the myth of the superiority of the Latin culture over that of the United States.

Yet the attacks of these writers were not completely one-sided. Darío himself in 1906, only three years after the "rape" of Panama, wrote a poem dedicated to the Pan-American Congress being held in Rio de Janeiro that year. He called it *Salute to the Eagle,* and the entire poem is a beautiful call for the solidarity of the hemisphere. Darío even went so far as to ask the beneficent eagle to teach its secrets to the peoples of the south: "Glory, victory, work! Bring us the secrets of the labors of the North, and teach our children how to cease being rhetoric Latins, and help them to learn from the Yankee, constancy, vigor, character." The poet even excuses North American imperialism by attributing it to the "necessity of opening the great fruitful womb of the earth so that the flow of gold and the ripening of the grain might burst forth giving man the bread he needs to move his blood."

Many Latin-American critics have indicated that this particular poem of Darío, so different in its slant from most of his verses in which there is some reference to the United States, was written with tongue in cheek because it was more or less an official piece for the Pan-American Congress. In view of the integrity of Darío as a poet, this hardly seems likely; there was no reason for him to sell his soul so cheaply. Obviously he felt the things which he expressed in his *Salute to the Eagle*. He also felt his adverse criticisms of the United States. Every man, every writer has his different moods, his varying points of view, his changing perspective, his inconsistencies.

There were of course many other sides to "modernism" than its relatively few references to the United States. As an artistic movement it followed more or less the ivory-tower approach to life and sought to escape the unpleasant realities of its environment. It was a movement of escapism, a cult of "art for art's sake," and to this extent at least it carried on the torch of previous colonial literature which was marked by its zealous avoidance of anything approaching an interest in social betterment. The sweating masses of Latin America, the oppressed Indian, the denial of democratic government have no real place in the modernist creed.

Take, for example, the cases of Gutiérrez Nájera and Amado Nervo, two of the greatest Mexican writers of all time. Both lived in the Mexico of Porfirio Díaz. They not only managed to exist under the dictatorship, but prospered under it. The government subsidized them and helped them to live. There is no suggestion in the writings of either man that this status might have been even in the slightest degree distasteful to them. They were apart from and above such petty considerations as social welfare or governmental decency. In their ivory tower of art they created a beautiful world of their own, which most certainly was not the world of Latin-American life.

García Calderón, the Peruvian essayist, in commenting on Spanish American literature in general and on the modernist movement in particular, makes the following remarks: "He who knows [Latin] America only by its imperfect social framework, its civil wars, and its persistent barbarism sees only the outer tumult; there is a strange divorce between its turbulent politics and its refined art. If ever Taine's theory of the inevitable correspondence between art and its environment was at fault, it is in respect to these turbulent democracies which produce writers whose literary style is so precious, such refined poets and analysts."[92]

What García Calderón fails to mention is that this kind of art, lacking in essential direction, emphasizing the erroneous separation of the artist from life around him, far too often compromising with political tyranny in the name of an esthetic creed, also did irreparable harm to the growth of the Latin-American mental outlook and to the creation of an enlightened public opinion. Certainly all art does not have to convey a social message, but when an entire generation of writers becomes deliberately escapist, living behind a sort of "cultural façade," then the lesser folk who follow them are bound not only to fall into but to increase the same fundamental error. In so doing they deepen the fissure which has always divided the extremes of Latin-American life, preventing the emergence of a completely integrated society.

Rubén Darío, greatest of the modernists, realized this before he ceased to write. The high-water mark of Spanish American modernism is his *Prosas profanas,* which came out in the year 1896. By 1905 Darío's perspective had changed considerably. The Spanish-American War, North American imperialism in the Caribbean, the poet's own travels in Europe, and most of all the growing maturity of Darío himself were the causes of this change.

When the last great volume of Darío's verse came out in 1907 the poet began his introduction with these words: "The greatest praise recently lavished upon poetry and poets has been expressed in the Anglo-Saxon tongue by a man hitherto unsuspected of any particular affection for the nine muses. A North American. I refer to Theodore Roosevelt.

"The President of the Republic judges lyrical bards with a more enlightened will than the philosopher Plato. Not only does he crown the poet with roses; he sustains his usefulness to the state and asks for him public esteem and national recognition. Because of this you will understand that the terrible hunter is a man of excellent judgment."

Then Darío expounds his own poetic creed, which has taken an about-face from its early days of seeing in life imaginary swans and princesses, ivory towers, and blue lagoons. The work of the poet now, he says, is to build toward the future with all the inspiration which his muse's angel can bring to bear.

This last phase of the development of Darío's poetic personality has been referred to as New Worldism, an identity of the writer with the environment around him. However, as is usually the case in matters of artistic expression, the public in general did not for many years catch the new spirit of this final maturity. Instead, people continued to extol the seclusion of the modernist cloister, the art which stood above and apart from the mainsprings of everyday life. It was the perspective of Rodó's *Ariel* and of Darío's earlier verses which shaped the artistic outlook of a generation.

It has often been said that in Latin America more people read and love poetry than in the United States; that in Latin America this awareness of the higher flights of the best men's minds is keener than here; that there responsiveness is quicker, sensibilities finer. Undoubtedly there is much truth in these statements if one holds to the surface values alone. But when one penetrates the mystic veil and looks beneath for that constructive spirit of which Darío spoke, then a very different perspective begins to appear. The Latin-American "cultural façade," now outgrown in the robust contemporary literature of those countries, still holds the boards in the general attitude toward life. Culture exists for the few. This has been one of the basic characteristics of Latin-American educational systems since colonial days. That to educate the many is to blunt the sensibilities of the few was a point of view expressed by the great Rodó as late as 1900. Consequently it is with the greatest disillusionment that the traveler from an outside country notes inside Latin America the wide wall and deep moat which separate the masses from their intellectual leadership.

Poverty and political immaturity excuse many of these failings; they do not excuse the wanton disuse of many excellent educational means which already do exist. For example, the national libraries. In country after country of Latin America there are fine collections of books which have been accumulating for the past four and a half centuries. Some of these collections are extensive and priceless. At least one of them, the National Library of Colombia at Bogotá, is housed in a beautiful modern building which is the latest creation of architectural genius, up to date in its last detail. Here as in case after case, in country after country, the books are not even catalogued. The reader, if he encounters the volume for which he is seeking, is not permitted to take it out of the library at any time. Hundreds of thousands of fine books thus lie in dust, pointed to with great pride by the intelligentsia, completely set apart from public use, serving no purpose whatsoever save to whet the minds of the fortunate minority and to accentuate the cleavage which exists between that esteemed minority and an ignorant people.

This cultural façade of the contemporary scene, raised upon the thesis of minority rule, is inseparable from the economic conditions which give it nutriment and life. Among those conditions, the concentration of land-ownership is the most notable. Everywhere the huge estate monopolizes the glut of cheap labor and holds back the path of progress. They call it the *hacienda* in Mexico, the *fundo* in Chile, the *estancia* in Argentina, the *hato* in Venezuela, the *fazenda* in Brazil, but no matter what the name, it stands for a way of economic life which has been passed down from generation to generation, accentuating the extremes of poverty and wealth. The system is reinforced by the Iberian view of landownership as a proof of a man's belonging to the socially elite class. Economically, politically, socially, this has meant the survival of a semi-colonial agriculture as the spinal column of Latin-American life. The many "revolutions" which have taken place in these regions have been, with but two exceptions, revolts of the classes which left intact this basic structure of agricultural, and later, industrial control.

The same separation exists today between the great urban centers and the hinterlands as existed in 1845, when Sarmiento interpreted the life of his own country, Argentina, on the basis of that comparison. The city represents civilization; the hinterland, barbarism. Even the city is lifted upon that semi-feudal relation of landowner and peon which throughout history has been the dominant characteristic of the Latin economies.

In Mexico, Porfirio Díaz made the hacienda into an octopus which strangled all real national progress. In nearly all of the other southern countries the situation was analogous. Even Chile and Argentina, two of the most advanced regions, perpetuate today this same outmoded type of economy. At the present time it can be said that approximately 10 per cent of the people in Latin America own most of the productive land; the rest of the population is landless. This status within nations which are still predominantly agricultural means an impoverished majority working for pitifully low daily wages.

In Chile, where land is at a premium because of the immense northern desert, and the cold, generally neglected southernmost regions, 2.1 per cent of the estates, owned by a few hundred families, embodied 59.8 per cent of all farm land in 1988. One of these vast estates contained four hundred thousand acres. Some biased reports have made much of the paternalistic nature of a few of these great landowners who provided their tenants with schools, medical care, land for their own use, and loans. Such superficial bright spots are bound to appear in any large plantation economy and do not alter the essential outmoded nature of the setup, its relatively inefficient productivity, and the low standard of life enjoyed by the infinite majority of the tenants.

In Chile these tenants were known as *inquilinos*, and while they were not legally bound to the soil in any way and were not separated from their landlords by any difference of race as in the Indianist countries, most of them cultivated the same land in the same manner as their fathers did before them. If they were to leave the estate on which they were born, other landlords would not hire them. Their only possible refuge would be in one of Chile's half a dozen cities, where they might become factory workers or menial laborers.

Until the 1970s the inquilino lived in a mud hut with a thatched roof and a stone-hard adobe floor. Usually it contained but a single room. The tiny high windows let in only a bare minimum of light and fresh air. Children slept on filthy straw mats on the floor, completely free to observe their parents' intimacies. Running water and hygienic facilities were unknown; there was no heating. In order to keep smells and smoke out of the house, cooking was done outside, even in winter, usually under a low shed.

The walls were sometimes adorned with old pictures of saints, and there were a few rickety pieces of furniture. All water was taken from a neary-by irrigation ditch, whether for drinking or washing. The tenant usually had a few domestic animals around his place, especially chickens and pigs, and he had the right to plant his own crops on a small piece of land set aside for that purpose. His living standard was so low that until 1976 more than two hundred out of every thousand children born alive in Chile died within the first year of life. These are the people who voted in a Marxist government in 1970.

In Argentina the situation is somewhat better because of the greater extent of land, the more extensive industrialization, and the greater productivity of the fertile soil. Even here the size of the estate is immense. Twenty families or corporations own nearly 7,000,000 acres. Slightly more than 2000 families or corporations own approximately 135,000,000 acres. Recently a deputy protested in the Argentine Congress that less than 2000 persons in his country owned more land than the total area of all Italy, Belgium, Holland, and Denmark combined. Fifty of the wealthiest hold estates worth over $700,000,000.

This is in a country where land is eagerly sought after by enterprising European immigrants who make up the bulk of the tenants on these huge estates. Yet the large landowner in Argentina would no more think of subdividing his place and selling out to these people than a Southern plantation owner of the Old South would have considered moving out on his friends and turning his land over to his Negro slaves. Land is the measure of a man's pedigree even in advanced Argentina. The newly rich capitalist or industrialist is frowned upon by a large part of the best society, while the landowner, though rapidly losing out to that rising class, still regulates the social laws and formulates the policies of the Argentine Government. As this control has become increasingly difficult for him in recent years, he has increased in like measure the arbitrary fashion by which he maintains his supremacy in the national life.

In Brazil the fazenda differs somewhat from region to region. In the northern tropical sections it still has many of the characteristics of the old Big House of sugar-plantation days. Pernambuco and the north have many of these huge estates. Around the city of Bahia freed Negro slaves have set up numerous small farms which they cultivate with admirable efficiency. The slaves of this region came largely from the Sudan and seem to have been of more enterprising stock than those of the other sections of Brazil, where they have not done so well since emancipation.

The southern part of the country, in the state of São Paulo, is the expanding coffee-growing region. Here the plantations pay better wages and there is little absentee ownership, for the landlord stays on his place in order to oversee production. The high proportion of European immigrants induced to enter the country by grants of land have created a great number of small farms. In the cities they form the basis of a virile middle and working class. This is one of the four regions in South America where a real settlement expansion is taking place—that is, the frontier is being expanded without any consequent loss of population behind it. São Paulo is one of the richest regions of all Latin America; approximately half of Brazil's total production comes from that one region, and the state pays more than one half of the total federal taxes.

The over-all picture of the concentration of landownership in Latin America, however, is extremely dark. It has meant that economically the dead have imposed their traditions upon the living, that progress is an uphill fight against history all the way, that minority rule is the accepted principle of government, and that production rests upon an impoverished people with a substandard of living, with neither the lure of frontier expansion nor the certainty of democracy to save them.

Within Latin America there are considerable variations, for prosperous Argentina stands at the opposite extreme from poor Paraguay, and Indianist Mexico is far ahead of Indianist Bolivia. Nevertheless, the perspective as a whole is covered with the black shadow of economic misery. It is impossible to make an accurate comparison between the income of agricultural workers in any two regions because frequently a certain amount of food, housing, and land goes along with a low daily wage. However, it would certainly be safe to say that the Chilean rural laborer, despite the doglike conditions under which he lived, represented his class all over Latin America until the decade 1970−80. The unskilled urban worker's income can be more accurately computed in the different countries, and the comparison immediately shows to what a tremendous extent industrialization and a large market have raised the standard of living of this group in the United States.

In the year 1990 the average unskilled worker* in the United States earned approximately $4.00 an hour; in Buenos Aires he earned the equivalent of about $1.55 in United States currency; in Rio de Janeiro, $1.00; in Mexico City, only 60¢; and in Santiago, Chile, approximately $1.00 for an hour of work. In the more accurate terms of actual purchasing power per hours of labor, the disparity is not so great, but it is still immense. Taking as a unit a food basket made up of one dozen eggs, one quart of milk, and one pound each of beans, rice, bread, and meat, the table below shows how many hours and fractions of hours the unskilled worker in each of the above places would have to work in order to purchase such a food basket:

United States	1.50 hours
Argentina	3.10 hours
Brazil	4.90 hours
Mexico	8.00 hours
Chile	4.60 hours

* In 1990 the U.S. skilled worker earned more than $10.00 an hour.

A worker in the United States, thus, would have to put in considerably less than half as much time in order to be able to purchase the above food basket as in Argentina, and only one third as much work as a laborer in Chile.

The difference in clothing costs is even greater. An unskilled worker in the United States must put in 8.10 hours of labor to buy a pair of shoes, and 2.05 hours to purchase a cheap shirt. The Argentine worker would have to work twenty and five hours, respectively, for these articles, or about two and one half times as much.

In terms of manufactured items such as automobiles, electric refrigerators, sewing machines, washing machines, vacuum cleaners, et cetera, the differences would be even greater, for nearly all of these articles are imported into the Latin countries. If the worker in each country laid aside 10 per cent of his annual earnings in order to purchase the cheapest automobile, it would take him only five years to save the necessary amount in the United States, but fifty years in Argentina, eighty years in Uruguay, and approximately one hundred years in both Brazil and Chile. That is, a car costs a worker in this country only one tenth as much labor as it would cost an Argentine, and only one twentieth as much as it would cost a Chilean or a Brazilian in the same job.

Further comparisons only serve to emphasize the economic impoverishment of the Latin-American nations. Brazil, which is larger than the continental United States, has only one tenth as many miles of rail lines. In the United States there is one telephone to every two persons; in Argentina one to every fifteen; and in Mexico one to every fifty. The United States has one automobile to every two persons; Argentina one to every seventeen; Chile one to every forty, Mexico one to every thirty-three, Colombia one to seventy-one. The comparison would be more or less the same in modern gas or electric stoves, refrigerators, radios, or any of the other inventions which have added so much to the standard of living, freeing man of the drudgery of long and tedious hours, giving him in the mass for the first time in his long history sufficient leisure for the enjoyment of life. In order to place himself in the shoes of the average Latin-American worker, the average citizen of the United States would have to think of what would happen to his standard of living if his own salary were cut drastically into a fraction. If it were sliced in half he would still be a little above the Argentine level. If it were cut down to about one fifth of what he earns that would place him approximately on the level of the average worker of Mexico, Colombia, or Peru. Living under such conditions becomes a mere matter of eking out an existence, keeping flesh and bones together.

Graphically indicative of this low standard of living are the following facts compiled by well-known Latin-American authorities: infant mortality in the southern countries ranges from twice the United States percentage in Argentina to more than five times the United States percentage in Bolivia; in Chile more than half the children born alive die before their tenth year; the per capita consumption of milk in Chile is only one seventh that of the United States; in rural Colombia 50 per cent of the children drink no milk, 45 per cent eat no meat, and 75 per cent eat no eggs; 50 per cent of Brazil's industrial workers consume no milk, no fruit, no vegetables.

"We do nothing well," writes the Brazilian sociologist Afranio Peixoto, "because our people are living in a perpetual state of malnutrition." In 1969 the Brazilian Minister of Health pointed out to Nelson Rockefeller that the undernourishment of infants during the pre-natal period and first year of life often weakens the brain cells irreparably. Everywhere the productive working population is depleted by a high percentage of early deaths. In cosmopolitan Rio more than one half of the workingmen die before their fortieth year, and in Buenos Aires 45.7 per cent die before age fifty. It has been estimated that such deaths represent a loss of approximately $350,000,000 a month to Argentina in potential earnings. Malnutrition, inadequate housing, and a lack of sanitation have resulted in widespread disease. One writer estimates that at any given moment one half of Latin America's four hundred and fifty millions are ill. Except for those fortunate few who enjoy their privileged position Latin Americans generally are indeed "a sick people."

In the largest cities these conditions do not meet the eye. Every resource of the country has been centered there. The streets are crowded with automobiles; the hotels are modern; beautiful buildings rise in astonishing numbers on all sides; the stores are filled with a variety of goods. The hinterland of the country as a whole must foot the bill for these lovely cities, which are held up Atlas-fashion on the back of a miserably poor working class, and especially a supine agricultural class in region after region. Though Latin America itself is immensely rich in resources, the Latin Americans are poor. Outside of the most prosperous urban regions millions of them have not altered their standards of living in four hundred years.

This is the direct result of a historic development which has kept immigration at a low level, fostered agriculture as the principal means of production, perpetuated the concentration of landownership, and placed the control of industry and government in the hands of a favored few. The colonial economy and the colonial attitudes toward life are still deep-seated in the nations of the south and still hold back the ripe rich fruits of education and democracy. The present history of every Latin-American country is a fight to break away from these chains of the past. The future can only accentuate this process. The base upon which that future rests will be industrialization, division of lands, better government, a more equitable distribution of wealth, and a lower birth rate. When these processes have been effected there will be a great leap forward in the standard of life, a burst of democratic enthusiasm in government, a new birth of public enlightenment in the nations of the south. Until that higher peak is achieved, such measures as are taken to better conditions will be mere stop-gaps, subject to the variable whims of economic and political instability.

In this basic framework the problem of land distribution exploded seventy years ago giving rise to the first real Latin-American revolution since the struggle for independence. This was the Mexican Revolution of 1910–20. While other regions were pursuing a policy of dodge and delay, Mexico made a frontal assault on the land problem, liquidated the old ruling caste, confiscated their large estates, and began the redistribution of millions of acres to her landless masses.

Since the Mexicans were a poor and disunited people who knew almost nothing about self-government, material progress after the revolution was painfully slow. But in placing before the nation a new sense of values, in reawakening the spirit of the native races, in creating a new artistic perspective, and in spreading throughout the vast territory of Latin America the restless zeal for social revolt, the Mexican Revolution, with all its failings, represents an experience unique in the history of the southern republics.

Porfirio Díaz was the most direct cause of the Mexican Revolution. He had hogged the land for his political favorites and had turned the Mexican masses into serfs. Yet in spite of his tremendous power, his political efficiency, and the wealth at his disposal, Díaz was never able to blot out completely the biological instinct of self-preservation among the Mexican people. This instinct continued to express itself in a growing hunger for land, a hunger for bread, and a hunger for justice.[138]

Francisco Madero, a rich landowner of the north, began the revolution against Díaz. Don Porfirio had declared to the American journalist James Creelman that in his opinion Mexico was ready for democracy, and that he would welcome political opposition in the coming elections of 1910. He found such opposition in the candidacy of Francisco Madero. When the elections were held, of course Díaz was again declared president. Madero, by this time feeling the exhilaration of his own popularity, claimed that the counting had been fraudulent and rose up in arms against Mexico's perennial despot.

At first the Mexican Revolution had no program except the overthrow of Díaz. Madero himself thought purely in political terms. He did not realize that what the people wanted most of all was to raise their economic level from a state of complete hopelessness, degradation, and starvation. On one occasion a member of his opposition asked Madero why he did not distribute his own wealth among the poor folk of Mexico if he was so intensely interested in their welfare, and the leader replied: "The people are not asking for bread, they are asking for liberty."

Blinded by his vision of political democracy, Madero had missed his cue;

economically his regime soon proved a complete fiasco; he could not maintain order. When repeatedly informed that treason was being plotted against his government, Madero refused to take any steps against those responsible. He was no doubt a great idealist, a visionary. In Mexico many people still refer to him as the "Christ fool," thus indicating the strange character which Madero possessed. In any case he soon fell a victim to a more realistic demagogue, Victoriano Huerta.

The revolution continued. Madero had begun it but had never understood his mission. Neither he nor the other early revolutionary leaders had any idea of the scope of the movement they had initiated. They simply started a human ball rolling, and after that economic and social forces beyond their control took over and carried the rebellion much farther than they themselves would have liked.

In the beginning the revolution did not even have a real slogan, much less a program. Madero cried, "Effective suffrage and no re-election," but the unenlightened Mexican masses hardly cared about such abstract terms as these. They wanted land, bread, liberty. Since Madero's government had not given them these things, it was necessary to try again. The revolution burst out spontaneously in many different parts of Mexico. Villa led one group, Carranza led another, and in the region to the south of Mexico City there arose a third leader who, more than either of these, seemed to understand the real meaning behind the movement. His name was Zapata. As a young boy Zapata had scrubbed stables and curried horses for a wealthy Mexican landowner. He soon began to make comparisons between the treatment received by the horses and that meted out to the peons on the same estate. The comparison left a bitter taste in the mouth of Zapata. From that moment on the Indian boy consecrated himself to the ideal of the Mexican Revolution. His cry was: "Land and liberty!" A group of peons gathered around Zapata and blindly struck out for those ideals.

The revolution now began to take on some of the characteristics of a class struggle. The masses were fighting against the landowners, against the wealthy Church, against the political bosses, against all entrenched privilege. They erupted over the countryside like a human volcano. It was Hidalgo's mob of a hundred years previously multiplied by many thousands. The revolution became blind, vengeful, bloody, cruel, destructive, ugly. But it was almost a cosmic force, something which carried away the people of an entire country, obliterating the individual. "If you are in it," wrote one of the revolutionary soldiers, "you are no longer a man. You are a dry leaf caught in a whirlwind."

In a way this force resembled the process of birth on a vast scale. The pain was terrible, and the nation was not at all certain what it would bring forth. But the fetus was there, demanding to be born. Nothing could hold it back. The period of pregnancy was ended.

The revolutionary armies often shouted their slogan, "Land and liberty!" It was a fine battle cry, but it was no program. Before many months had passed there no longer seemed alive any desire except to destroy. One of the finest Mexican writers, Mariano Azuela, who went through the revolution as a doctor in the army of Villa, described the movement in acid terms in his novel *The Underdogs* (*Los de abajo*). There is hardly a word of moralization in this book. The author has become a photographic camera taking in the scene before him. Yet sensing the cosmic proportions of the force which has swept him off his feet, erasing all moral values, Azuela gives a deep reality to the revolution. It is a perverted reality, filled with the unlovely saga of man suddenly torn loose from all civilized restraints. In spite of everything some hope does shine through, if only in the caustic self-scrutiny of the author, and through him of the Mexican people.

One character in the novel looks out over a burning village, sees white streams of rifle smoke spiral upward toward a blue sky, watches a horde of ragged women dressed in black descend on the town to strip the bodies of the dead of their belongings. Objectively, like the eye of a distant god, he is conscious of the whole scene piled against the hills beyond and with a brilliant sun above. He has become almost a personification of natural law which he sees pursuing its inexorable course there before him. Yet his reaction clearly reveals the man within:

"How beautiful is the revolution! Even in its most barbarous aspect it is beautiful," Solís said with deep feeling. Then a vague melancholy seized him, and speaking low he added:

"A pity what remains to do won't be as beautiful! We must wait awhile, until there are no men left to fight on either side, until no sound of shot rings through the air save from the mob as carrion-like it falls upon the booty; we must wait until the psychology of our race, condensed into two words, shines clear and luminous as a drop of water: Robbery! Murder! What a colossal failure we would make of it, friend, if we, who offer our enthusiasm and lives to crush a wretched tyrant, became builders of a monstrous edifice holding one hundred or two hundred thousand monsters of exactly the same sort. People without ideals! A tyrant folk! Vain bloodshed!"

Then suddenly he thought that he saw what all of that dying meant. He sketched a vast gesture and was about to put this feeling into words for the first time when there was a sharp blow in his stomach. "As though his legs were putty, he rolled off the rock. His ears buzzed . . . Then darkness . . . silence . . . Eternity. . . ."[139]

But the revolution was more than death. It became a symbol. All Mexico was ripped away from its colonial past and there was a new beginning. The old symbols of power for more than four centuries had been destroyed. As the death of vegetation in a forest feeds the trees that grow, increasing their height and girth, the death of the revolution would bring to the people of Latin America more awareness of their social problems. It is a natural law which applies both to the life process and to history.

What the revolution did for Mexico in a measurable and material sense is not so difficult to evaluate. It gave rise to the constitution of 1917, which is an advanced social document. The Mexicans were promised their lands, their liberty. Article 27 of that constitution states that the federal government has the right to confiscate and distribute lands to the villages, after paying proper indemnification. It also proclaims that the subsoil belongs to the nation and that the nation's right to enjoy its products is inalienable. Other articles of the constitution guarantee civil liberties and embody much social legislation.

Between the year 1917 and the present time many of the aspirations expressed in the new Mexican constitution have been carried into effect. The process began on a large scale in 1920 when General Alvaro Obregón became president of Mexico. He cleared away the debris left by the revolution and undertook the task of reconstruction. Obregón started the redistribution of lands to the villages in the form of *ejidos,* or village commons. President Calles, who followed him, intensified the process. President Lázaro Cárdenas, who came still later, carried the land program to its peak. Under him more than 45,000,000 acres were given back to the native villages—a total considerably in excess of that distributed by all previous administrations. Under him also the foreign-owned oil wells were confiscated and became the property of the Mexican nation. The educational and health programs took on new zest and the country moved ponderously forward.

There is no doubt that widespread corruption and inefficiency continued. Four hundred years of servitude cannot be wiped out in a decade. The ejido in many instances took the place of the hacienda as a breeding place for exploitation. Politicians, bureaucrats, persons put in charge of managing these commons, a host of job seekers from the small towns and cities—all of these ate away the true purpose of the land program, which was to give a way of life back to those whose heritage had been stolen. In spite of all these things there was progress. The standard of living was slowly raised. Many ejidos became what their founders had hoped. Mexico did not even begin to approximate the high level of material existence in the United States, but for the first time she had a chance.

The revolution had given her that chance. One who dwells too much on the barbarous aspects of a revolution, any revolution, is very liable to lose the proper historic perspective. The French Revolution, the Russian Revolution, the Mexican Revolution were orgies in blood. It has been estimated that Mexico lost one million dead in the ten years of her devastating and cruel revolutionary conflicts. But to balance the picture properly it is necessary to ask the question: Did these deaths in the end add

up to a greater freedom for those who followed? Did they in any way increase the material benefits of the next generations?

In a sense which cannot be measured the Mexican Revolution also had
effects throughout Latin America which were far reaching. It was the first
case of an uprising of the submerged masses in general, the first time when
the struggle was not clearly between two antagonistic groups of the small
ruling class. If its results prove disillusioning in the end, it will nevertheless stand as the first great step of the Indian-mestizo millions toward a
new social consciousness. This is clearly seen in what the revolution did
to the feelings of the Indianist majority of the Mexican nation, and
through them for the red man everywhere in the southern countries.

Now for the first time in four centuries the man of Indian blood became,
through his own efforts, an equal instead of a slave. He would not suddenly be released from poverty, nor overnight become democratic, or free.
But that hard-won victory meant something very real to him in a spiritual
sense. Values which had been dormant for generations now came into the
foreground. A new realism was brought into being, and fused with it was
that indigenous folk feeling which generated the leading artistic current
in contemporary Latin-American life.

The novel of the Mexican Revolution, with *The Underdogs* as its finest
example, cleared away much of the purely aesthetic escapism which had
preceded it. Azuela became Spanish America's best-known novelist. The
clutterings of French-inspired modernism gave way to the single-purpose
intensity of a new indigenous outlook on life. The oppressed red man became the primary concern of writers and artists in all the Indianist countries.

The vast scope of this new feeling can best be appreciated when one
compares the great murals of Orozco, Rivera, Alfaro-Siqueiros, Guerrero
Galván, and all the other fine Mexican painters of murals with the stiff
work of the schools which preceded them. These men have enabled their
nation to take a world lead in that Renaissance of painting which has
flowered so widely and so intensely all over the globe during the past two
decades. In South America, in Europe, in the United States, artists have
looked to the Mexicans for inspiration and leadership in this field.

"The great mural painting was born with the Revolution," writes Jesús
Guerrero Galván, one of its best-known exponents. Then going on to describe in greater detail the work of José Clemente Orozco, greatest of the
painters of the revolution, he says: "The horrible is its chief strength, and,
though it may seem paradoxical, its chief beauty too. By means of the eye
it produces a trembling, a shudder. Instead of producing a pleasure for the
eye, as the scholastics understood aesthetic enjoyment, it gives a sensation
of anguish, horror, and desperation."

The Mexican Revolution thus became a spiritual and a visual thing for the people of Latin America. Those who had never before paused to consider what the unleashing of the mass man might mean were now forced to experience some measure of his cruel might. Despite all dictatorships and corruption and inefficiencies of government this fear brought about a more honest consideration of the Indianist masses of many countries. It is doubtful if this consideration went far enough, but at least it did begin. Through the example of the Mexican Revolution the backward Indianist nations became truly social as well as political minded.

The Mexican Revolution carried its experiences beyond the pale of mere destruction. It showed that what begins as a mob movement, blind and directionless with hate, may well end as an artistic Renaissance, with a new birth of awareness to life. When the fires of killing went out in Mexico they were rekindled into fires of creation. The novel of the Mexican Revolution, the great painting of the revolution, the birth of a new Mexican music, the emergence of a powerful Indianist-mestizo social force—these are the most significant contributions of that movement in terms of Latin-American and world history. They prove that even ugliness, anguish, and death need not be hopeless for humanity at large. Some spark always survives to relight the torch of progress.

No other Latin-American country has yet experienced a revolution like that which swept Mexico. Cuba has slipped by default into Fidel Castro's communistic arms, and Bolivia has made a dramatic attempt at deep-rooted social reform but has been unable to maintain a stable civilian government. The case of Peru, the South American country most like Mexico, offers the curious parallel of a strong revolutionary party which has never really taken control of the country. Under Augusto Leguía, a Díaz-like dictator who ruled Peru from 1919 to 1930, there arose a strong Indianist opposition called the APRA. The term is made up of the first letter of each word of *Alianza Popular Revolucionaria Americana,* or Popular Revolutionary Party of America. The ideals of this movement were essentially those of the Mexican Revolution softened by lofty spiritual values. APRA made a brave attempt to carry these ideals to all the southern countries. It also bears the ironic distinction of having twice won the presidency of Peru, each time being prevented by political fraud from placing its candidate in office. Not until its 1982 victory was APRA to govern Peru.

The principal organizer of this very indigenous-minded movement was an intellectual named Raúl Haya de la Torre. He had attended the University of Córdoba, Argentina, and was there in 1918 when the students revolted against the moth-eaten scholasticism and clericalism which still characterized that ancient institution. A few years later he went to Mexico and served as the private secretary of José Vasconcelos, one of the original Madero revolutionists.

Haya picked up the pro-Indian torch of González Prada, vitriolic essayist of an earlier date, and continued the work of the little cripple, José Carlos Mariátegui, organizer of Peru's small communist party. But Haya de la Torre differed fundamentally from either of these men. He was profoundly religious and had always believed that in order to attain permanent success his political and social program must be fused with deep spiritual values. Consequently he turned away from the violent anti-Catholic stand. of González Prada, and also from Mariátegui's primary concern for economic betterment. The Scripture was and is an integral part of Haya's social thinking.

Haya and the other intellectual Aprista leaders of Peru were men of such high caliber that little by little their concepts, despite the overwhelming illiteracy of the Peruvian masses, began to sift from the top downward until at last there was a widespread popular response. APRA became a kind of religion, "indigenous as the llama." Even the self-styled communist Mariátegui had made much of his belief that "myths are what have always moved men most in history."

It was necessary, therefore, to give the masses a myth, a faith to which they might cling in order to bring about their permanent redemption from misery. To Mariátegui that myth was communism. To others it was the Catholic Church. To Haya and his millions of followers it was the APRA party and program, inseparable from its religious values.

In 1923 Haya made his first large-scale demonstration against the despotism of Leguía. He was promptly exiled from Peru and for the following seven years traveled and studied in Mexico, Germany, England, Soviet Russia, and the United States. On one occasion he lectured at Harvard University in English. In 1930, when Leguía was forced out of power by Sánchez Cerro, Haya returned to Peru and the following year he ran for the presidency. All objective accounts indicate that he won the election hands down but that he was defrauded of a fair count by the incumbent, Sánchez Cerro.

An immense crowd of Apristas gathered in the bull ring at Lima, perhaps the largest gathering in the history of the country, and Haya was present to address them. From thousands of throats rose the shout, "On to the palace!" If Haya had spoken the word no one could have stopped them. The police were on their side. So was most of the army. The entire capital was in a ferment of pro-APRA zeal. But instead of leading his followers to the palace and to political victory, Haya rose and spoke soft words of peace. He refused to utilize the means of violence in order to attain his ideal of justice. Sánchez Cerro, the ruthless executioner, continued to preside in the governmental palace, and very soon Haya was rotting in prison. The great moment had come and gone; Haya had not taken the tide at the flood.

Yet APRA was not a failure because its ideals still live in the hearts of millions of Indians throughout the region of the Andes. The day has passed when the party had dozens of branches in the different countries of Latin America and bade fair to become the most powerful international force in the southern countries. But the wheel of fortune is certain to turn again toward most of the APRA program. The name may be changed, but the necessity is omnipresent.

It is fascinating to note that both APRA and the Mexican Revolution turned back toward the Indian past for inspiration. Certainly their creeds are broader than a mere wish for Aztec or Inca living, but it is the native agricultural collectivism, the village commons, the spirit of folk co-operation and folk art, the almost religious integration of life under the indigenous peoples which both movements espoused and which enabled them to incorporate the Indian majority into their folds. It was a freedom within tradition that they sought, not any foreign political importation. They did not aspire to restore a past way of life so much as to redeem fifty millions of living people in whose veins runs the blood of the native American.

APRA, like the Mexican Revolution, did not confine itself to the social sphere alone, but also gave birth to an intense artistic movement. Throughout the Andean region the intellectual and the folk arts began to fuse in a true mestizo expression. Painters, writers, and musicians turned to indigenous themes for inspiration. In Peru, José Sabogal and his many disciples initiated a school of painting of which any nation might well feel proud. Sabogal himself stated the new feeling clearly: "I love the plastic beauty of my country, and have faith in a great artistic flourishing of Peru which will justify the parallel paths that Mexico and Peru have trodden since the most remote times."[141]

An intense Indianist school of writing also arose in the Andean region. In this field as well as in painting Peru, Ecuador, and Bolivia blossomed forth with a literature as vital in purpose as it is fine in presentation. The famous Latin-American prize novel, *Broad and Alien Is the World*, a moving epic of life in the Andes, was written by Ciro Alegría, a member of the APRA party. Dozens of other writers and artists, many of them forced into exile by reactionary governments, carried forward the great tradition of the new mestizo art.

Since the beginning of the Mexican Revolution artistic values have been turned inside out in the nations of the south. Now nearly every page and every picture is shot through with the imminence of some social problem and warm with the smell of earth and of human suffering. No longer do the lofty flights into an ivory tower obscure the horizon of Latin America's finest artistic expression.

In spite of these things the forward march of material and social progress has been tortuously, painfully slow. A great abyss still stands between the hope and the deed. Mexico alone, one of the least prepared of the southern countries, has blown off the apex of her economic pyramid and undertaken on a broad base the redistribution of land. This is the bedrock upon which every economic activity in Latin America must rest for many years to come. Other nations better endowed for a successful solution of the problem—for example, Argentina and Chile—have sidestepped the issue, thus only delaying an inevitable crisis.

Latin America, shackled to its agricultural past, and incapable of creating large capital for industrialization, continues to export mainly raw materials in the old colonial pattern, exploited by the highly industrialized countries. This disequilibrium in the national economies has been further accentuated by dependence on one or two outstanding products. Brazil is a perfect example of this tendency. In colonial days her illusive prosperity rested on sugar; in the eighteenth century gold became king; and in the 1890s fabulous rubber profits captured the national imagination. Each product collapsed in turn and flattened out the primitive economic structure. At the present moment Brazil lives on her exports of coffee; at least this one product represents her margin between a measure of well-being and economic prostration. Nearly 70 per cent of the world's supply of coffee comes from Brazil, and a break in the international market means immediate disaster for millions of Brazilian citizens. In a like manner Cuba lives on sugar, Chile on copper and nitrates, Venezuela on oil, Honduras on bananas, Argentina and Uruguay on beef and grains, Bolivia on tin, and so on down the line. These are not the products of modern economies but of colonial territories, and until a greater diversity of products is built up hand in hand with a greater industrialization, these regions must remain primarily dependent on outside nations for their subsistence. In the 1980s, sad to say, cocaine surpassed all other exports in many countries.

Industrial progress has been held back by the same factors which have prevented a well-rounded agricultural development. The historic disdain of the proud Iberian to engage in manual labor has been perpetuated into the twentieth century. Small populations spread over immense distances and with only poor means of communication render most difficult the mechanics of modern civilization. A lack of immigrants and a lack of capital have further retarded industrial development. The first has meant a dearth of skilled workers and a lack of markets; the second has made impossible great native enterprises. This combination opened the doors to foreign investors who were interested primarily in profits and not in development. As in the colonial days, wealth which should have been reinvested or spent on the spot enriching native economies has been siphoning off into foreign coffers. It is lifeblood flowing away.

Nevertheless, the process of industrialization has been the most marked tendency in Latin-American life since the period of World War I. During the years 1914–18 the nations of the south, shut off from many of their foreign markets and unable to purchase the manufactured necessities of modern life, became for the first time acutely aware of this gap in their national economies. Industrial development took a great spurt forward, the standard of living rose, and in many regions this was followed by a growth of democracy in government.

Industrialization is not necessarily synonymous with democracy, but the industrial society provides a friendly soil for the genesis and growth of democratic ideas. Its effect upon the social and political outlook of a nation is certain to be profound. Industrial plants pay better wages than farms or cattle estates. Such plants attract workers from the country and bring them into expanding urban centers. Here these workers become more conscious of themselves as a class, are better able to organize in defense of their rights, learn how to wield political power, receive a better education, grow more democratic minded, and exert a greater influence on the national life than was possible under their former state as isolated tenant farmers, farm hands, or share croppers.

In the years following the outbreak of World War I the ideals of social justice thus began to bear fruit in many of the southern countries. Liberalism seemed to come of age in Argentina under Irigoyen; in Mexico the regime of President Obregón at last gave that battered country a democratic peace; in Chile, Alessandri became the idol of the working class, and in Uruguay, Batlle y Ordóñez and his successors established the framework of one of the most advanced social programs of any nation.

Industry and democracy in these regions put on a modern face behind which, unfortunately, the old body persisted. Great cities arose where previously only disjointed colonial towns had stood. Some of the larger industrial centers more than tripled their population within a few years. Skyscrapers began to rise up on suddenly widened streets. Buenos Aires, São Paulo, Rio de Janeiro, Mexico City, Santiago, Lima, Bogotá, Havana and Caracas are all examples of this phenomenal growth. In both a material and spiritual way they represent the new industrial outlook which is bound to mean so much in the future development of Latin America.

The three most industrialized areas in Latin America are the regions that envelop Buenos Aires, São Paulo, and Mexico City. The importance of these regions in the national life of their respective countries can readily be seen in the following facts. The state of São Paulo alone produces approximately one half of the total national income of Brazil and pays approximately one half of the federal taxes. Argentina, largely because of her even greater industrialization, has 58 per cent of all the railway mileage in South America, and more telephones than the combined total of the other eight Spanish-speaking countries of that continent.

It is clear, of course, that the few widely separated industrial centers which do exist mark only the beginning of an industrialized economy. Latin America has just recently passed from a purely agrarian state into the production of consumers' goods: textiles, shoes, processed foods, and so forth. The machine, especially the heavy machine which is one of the great roots of the power and wealth of the United States, has made only spotty headway in Latin America. Today the per capita output of work in the United States is approximately seven times that of Argentina and Chile and about twenty times that of Brazil and Peru. The average North American worker receives wages that are so much higher because he *produces* so much more than his Latin-American counterpart.

The process of industrial development in Latin America continued hand in hand with the growth of democratic government until the great depression of the 1930s. This economic debacle was followed by drastic changes in the political outlook everywhere. Liberal governments turned reactionary and reactionary governments became liberal. People rebelled against hard times, laid the blame on those in power, and demanded a change in government. The best change seemed to swing as far as possible to the opposite extreme.

Even Argentina, which up to this moment had been Latin America's most articulate democracy, reacted quickly to economic deterioration, and the "radical" government of Irigoyen was forced out of power by a revolutionary coup in 1930. Shortly afterward a similar change took place in democratic Uruguay, and in Brazil the revolution of Getulio Vargas placed Brazil's first long-term dictator in power. Trujillo took over in the Dominican Republic, and the Central American states (except Costa Rica) made a like return to despotic government. Uruguay was the only one of these countries to restore democratic principles after a brief flirtation with dictatorship. In Argentina and Brazil the growing restlessness of the working class under adverse economic conditions caused the strongest apprehension in conservative quarters. Before long this resulted in even further suppression of civil liberties.

Mexico, with her purely agrarian economy, escaped the worst phases of the depression and suffered no political change. Chile and Colombia, which were under rigidly conservative regimes when the depression struck, took the opposite course from Argentina and Brazil and put in more liberal, more democratic governments. Cuba finally got rid of her despot Machado; Leguía was forced out of power in Peru, and the tyrant Gómez died in Venezuela. All of these countries moved toward greater democracy in government while Argentina and Brazil were moving away.

It was during this same period that the United States under Franklin Roosevelt was trying to establish its Good-Neighbor Policy toward the nations of the south. Relations between Yankee and Latin America became more cordial than at any time for the past century. The President himself, Cordell Hull, and Sumner Welles all worked laboriously to establish the principles of friendship, trust, and the sovereign integrity of nations. The last Marines were withdrawn from the Caribbean area. Non-intervention became an established policy of the North American government. Reciprocal trade agreements were made between the United States and the other American republics. Sumner Welles, one of the men most responsible for these changes, publicly admitted and abjured the "bullying and domineering" attitude of the United States during the previous half century. It was a far cry from the dark days of Dollar Diplomacy.

The Good-Neighbor Policy paid for itself a hundred times over when the United States was drawn into World War II. The apathy and suspicion so hard to bear during World War I did not revive with this second holocaust. Only a few weeks after the attack on Pearl Harbor the foreign ministers of the American republics met at Rio de Janeiro and recommended that the nations of this hemisphere break off diplomatic relations with the Axis powers. The Mexican Foreign Minister, Ezéquiel Padilla, made an impassioned plea for support of the United States. "Let us dictate a new Magna Charta to the free American," he said. "Let us stand together as one solid block against those who would divide and conquer us." Before many weeks had passed the United States was granted strategic bases throughout the area of Latin America and the majority of the southern countries had joined her in the war against the Axis. Toward the end of hostilities in Europe the Act of Chapultepec, drawn up at Mexico City, further affirmed the solidarity of the hemisphere and its abiding intention to remain united during the postwar years.

54

THE POSTWAR YEARS
A COUNTRY BY COUNTRY SURVEY

MEXICO

What has been the tenuous order of these postwar years? Each country is still different, indeed unique, in the strange pattern of contemporary history, as was so in the past. But these differences are slowly disappearing, ironing themselves out in the fundamental crucible of our time wherein are being blended the demands of all peoples everywhere for food and liberty. Each country, each region, each people is stumbling toward this goal. Let us briefly retrace some of the steps, beginning with Mexico.

Once the Mexican Revolution of 1910–20 had toppled the old colonial society, control of the country was taken over by the new revolutionary order whose leaders were mainly a group of middle-class generals. Like all revolutions, however, that of Mexico began to become conservative as soon as it had achieved power. Those who now controlled the country suppressed those who felt that they were not moving fast enough as well as those who felt that they were wrong in trying to move at all. After a decade of revolution, followed by almost a decade of revolutionary government, the national situation had become critical. Three presidents had been assassinated, government and Church stood in violent opposition, the national economy was prostrate, the masses existed in a state of utter misery, and those who had made the revolution were on the verge of splintering into several small and individually weak political groups.

In 1929 the various factions assembled and produced what has been Mexico's unique contribution to twentieth-century Latin American political life, the Party of the Mexican Revolution. The new party embraced all the various tendencies within the Revolution, and with an amazing political acumen its organizers agreed to work out their differences *within the party.* This party has successfully governed the country ever since, and as soon as it began to function the presidency moved beyond the stage of caudillism and became an institution that would survive no matter who was chosen as president. The party itself has almost unlimited power. Its presidential candidates are invariably elected, it controls the national congress completely, and it runs the local and state governments almost without exception. The opposition parties have been allowed a few members in congress, and a few local officers, but they have no real voice in running the country. The government and national economy of Mexico and the Party of the Mexican Revolution are one.

The party has undergone several changes since its inception, and its changes in name indicate what this progression has been. In 1929 when it was first organized the name was *Partido Nacional Revolucionario* (PNR) (National Revolutionary Party). In 1938 as the Revolution became stabilized the name was changed to PRM, *Partido de la Revolución Mexicana*, Party of the Mexican Revolution. Again in 1946 when that stability was strong enough to be considered as an institution, the party was renamed PRI, *Partido Revolucionario Institucional*, the Institutional Revolutionary Party, the name it retains today. Mexico's progress from revolution to stability to institutionalization is thus clearly marked, and parallels the move from political left to right.

Throughout these years the party has controlled the government and national economy of Mexico. The outgoing President, with the concurrence of the other high party officials, has invariably chosen his successor. All discussion concerning this choice takes place in a closed session where everything, as they say in Mexico, is *tapado*, that is, under a tight lid. An open fight for the presidency could break the party into a dozen splinters, and that would be the end of tranquillity in Mexico. Many foreigners and many Mexicans have excoriated such election procedures, which are hardly in the best democratic tradition. Others have seen in Mexico's unique one-party system of government the one factor above all others which has saved the country from the political excesses and dictatorial military rule that have ravaged almost every other Latin American republic. Those who hold this view insist that discussion of the succession within the party gives Mexico as much democracy as its underdeveloped political institutions will permit.

Following a similar line of reasoning the party bigwigs say that to allow the opposition to capture the national government in Mexico would be tantamount to undoing the Revolution and to betraying the nearly one million dead who lost their lives in that upheaval. On the other hand, to deny the people of Mexico elections would be still worse, so a controlled opposition is permitted, and a harmless few opposition candidates are elected, occasionally even as state governors. This has worked well in Mexico for half a century, the PRI leaders say, so why change it? A look at the recent history of the rest of Latin America is their most convincing argument.

The Mexican government, however, does suffer from two very great weaknesses: an inefficient, numerous and ravenous bureaucracy, and the *mordida*, or "bite" (bribe), which far too many an official will accept, and without which the applicant or supplicant would have to wait an eternity to be served. One of Mexico's greatest writers, Octavio Paz, summarizes the situation in these words:

> For a long time now I have been at odds not only with the foreign policy of Mexico, but also with our domestic policy. I have thought in the past, and many others like me, that the present system would modify itself and that the progress of the Mexican Revolution would continue. In other words: that the country was able to undergo rigid self-criticism. But all of the really vital forces have been eliminated or absorbed by a rampant bureaucracy. The Party, revolutionary in its origin, has now been converted into a mere administrative machine, which constitutes from this day forward an obstacle to the modern development of Mexico.[182]

Mexico today is a country of over 80 million people. It is by far the most populous Spanish-speaking country of the world; its population is more than twice that of Spain and is equal to that of Argentina, Chile, Bolivia, Uruguay, Paraguay, and Venezuela combined.

Mexico's national product, however, is less than that of Canada which has only two fifths as many people. So far its political stability has amazed the Latin American world. Its population growth, 2.6 per cent annually, is one of the highest in the world. It is a spottily developed country with a semicapitalist economy, heavily dependent on the tourist trade and on foreign investments. Good planning has enabled Mexico to escape the single-product economies which have plagued so many other Latin American countries. This diversification has been carried out with both efficiency and wisdom. Yet at least 50 per cent of the Mexican population still lives close to the subsistence level, producing almost nothing beyond their immediate needs, buying almost nothing in the industrial market.

About one fourth of Mexico's population is illiterate, and at least one Mexican child out of five does not attend school. The country presents the anomalous picture of an old colonial economy existing side by side with a flourishing twentieth century capitalism. The Mexican Revolution has now been taken over by middle-of-the-roaders, and Mexico today stands at the crossroads. Her deprived 50 per cent have no faith in their government (less that 40 per cent of those eligible vote in the national elections), for the one-party system which runs the country is certain to win.

In spite of all these things since World War II Mexico has been Latin America's most stable country economically, and one of the most stable politically. During the decade 1960—70 industry and agriculture expanded faster than population, and Mexico began to produce almost all her prime necessities. Hundreds of United States companies established branch factories in the country, and Mexicans themselves invested their money at home. About 85 per cent of Mexican capital investments are self-generated.

With the aid of funds and scientists provided by the Rockefeller Foundation, Mexico was able to close the food gap by developing better and more blight resistant strains of wheat and corn. The new strains enabled Mexican farmers to increase yields two, three, and even four times as much on the same amount of land. Improvement in growing other farm products slowly changed the traditional diet of beans and corn to a more balanced regimen including meat, dairy products, and vegetables. There is very little land left to distribute in Mexico, but by learning how to use more efficiently the land that is cultivated Mexican farmers increased agricultural output in a spectacular way, and the entire country benefited.

Mexico stopped having to import wheat and corn, and each year of the period 1965—70 exported sizeable quantities of wheat and over half a million tons of corn. Venezuela, Colombia, Ecuador, and Chile sought Mexico's aid in solving their own agricultural problems. Mexican sugar production quadrupled, the cotton crop doubled, and for a few boom years industrial production grew at the rate of 7.5 per cent a year. Mexico City, whose metropolitan area today contains twenty million people, became one of the most beautiful and dynamic of world capitals. There is a new subway system, rolling on rubber wheels, to alleviate the intolerable traffic. A high-speed expressway rings the city. The water supply, alas, still leaves much to be desired.

A strong president and a military that is subordinate to the elected government were the essential factors in this noteworthy development. The Mexican presidency and the way it operates is baffling to the foreigner. The president theoretically represents only the executive power, while the legislative and the judicial power reside respectively in the national congress and in the courts. But in fact the president always has a firm grip on what is proposed, what is approved, and how the laws operate. Everything important begins and ends in the presidential palace that sits atop "grasshopper hill." The president's power of decision is crucial and almost omnipotent.

The legislature seldom initiates but invariably passes the pet bills of the chief executive. With more than eighty ministries, departments, and agencies under his direct control, the power of the president reaches into every niche and cranny of Mexican life from Indian affairs to the armed services and the oil industry. The president makes up the budget and decides how to spend the money. He has as much power as most Latin American dictators, but he has learned not to display it flagrantly or to use it unreasonably. The Mexican judiciary is overworked, underpaid and lacking in confidence; it is not at all a proper balance to the executive power, nor is it always a firm and stalwart protector of justice.

The president is not only the head of the nation in a symbolic and a political sense, he is also somewhat like a tribal chieftain who receives petitions and grievances as a court of final appeal. Each month he will receive directly, consider, and pass judgment on a hundred or more such appeals from individuals and from groups.[183]

With such power in his hands it is to be expected that the Mexican president should leave his personal mark on the country. Thus Lázaro Cárdenas (1934–40), called Tata (Daddy) Cárdenas by the masses who adored him, nationalized the oil industry, affirmed Mexico's control of her own natural resources, and distributed millions of acres of land to the peasants. Avila Camacho (1940–46) "shifted the country from Cárdenas' 'socialistic' agrarian leanings and began its transformation to an industrial nation."[183] He also saw that the co-operative ejidos were not by any means a utopian answer to the land problem, and stressed instead the small private farm.*

Miguel Alemán (1946–52), "the playboy President," built airports all over the country, most of which still bear his name, he encouraged the *Nacional Financiera* to help finance industry, which was his pet project, improved agricultural productivity, carried out two Mexican TVA-type projects, allowed United States investors to drill oil wells in Mexico again, and so increased oil output and, most impressive of all, put every ounce of his personal influence behind the construction of the magnificent new National University which has become a model for many others in the southern republics, a university, incidentally, which by 1980 enrolled 150,000 students, and is thus the biggest single-campus university in the world. Tuition is less than $50 a year.

Under the direction of the dynamic young architect Carlos Lazo, 150 architects, engineers, artists, nearly 100 contracting companies, and 10,000 laborers, the largest labor force ever assembled in Latin America for a single building project, drove themselves with real dedication until the campus was ready for occupancy three years later. Great relief frescoes and mosaic murals by Diego Rivera, Chávez Morado, Alfaro-Siqueiros, Juan O'Gorman, and Francisco Eppens decorate the impressive modern buildings. At first Mexican students were reluctant to go that far into the outskirts of town to attend the university, but now they are proud to do so.

President Alemán's private life, unfortunately, was not above reproach. His friendship with the motion picture actress, María Felix, was common knowledge, and when he left office he was a multimillionaire, hardly the result of scrimped savings from his modest salary as president. Even before leaving office he had become a big-time operator, with wide-scale interests in Mexican

---

*Over 200 million acres of land have been redistributed in Mexico since the Revolution, and this agrarian reform program has now reached a point of no return. Insufficient good land remains. From now on the problem of the poor rural population must be solved not only in the fields, with more scientific methods of cultivation, but also in the cities, by expanded industry and commerce. The ejido system has collapsed.

industry and real estate. Acapulco, that most un-Mexican of cities, attained international prominence under his hand. He invested in a hotel at the resort, anchored his yacht in the harbor, and on leaving public office, retired there to lead the life of a twentieth-century jet-set tycoon. A land boom hit the area and choice lots often jumped in value from 250 to 200,000 pesos in a few years. Acapulco soon became a tourist Mecca for North Americans in flight from the rigorous winters of the north and east, and a whole series of modern shops and plush hotels soon ringed the beaches and dotted the hills, which in the 1930s had marked off the precincts of a sleepy little town with its typical Indian market, its burning blue sky, its fleeces of lazy clouds.

Alemán's hand-picked successor, Adolfo Ruiz Cortines (1952–58), brought to the presidency an admirable probity. Not a colorful figure, Ruiz Cortines, found himself faced with an overextended public works program, an empty treasury, and a sudden lack of tourist business from the United States, because of the Korean War and its aftermath. American tourists had been dropping half a billion dollars a year into the till, and the shrinkage of this sum by 50 per cent was profoundly felt throughout Mexico. Tourism had become Mexico's third most important source of income, topped only by agriculture and industry.

The end of the Korean War in 1953 caused the prices of many essential materials to topple, and Mexico was faced with a growing foreign-trade deficit. Devaluation of the peso became mandatory. The rate was changed from 8.60 pesos to the dollar to 12.49, and the national currency was stabilized at the latter level. Mexicans tightened their belts and tourism began to pick up. The austerity program paid off, and before long the program of industrial expansion and public works was again under full swing. Ruiz Cortines not only put Mexico back on her feet, he gave her a new set of muscles.

When he retired from office in 1958 Ruiz Cortines made a report to the nation on his accomplishments. It was an astounding record. The colorless president through hard work, honesty, and goodwill had achieved the following benefits for his people:

During his six years in office Mexico had constructed 20,500 miles of highways.

Mexico's industrial productivity had increased by an amazing 40 per cent.

The country had placed under irrigation three million acres of desert land.

In 1952 Mexico had to import 439,000 tons of wheat; in 1958 she exported a surplus of 300,000 tons of wheat.

The Mexican Rural Social Welfare Program which began in 1953 with four centers in 1958 had over 4,000 centers providing aid for over six millions persons.

Mexico had constructed a new school for every single day of those six years of Ruiz Cortines' term in office.

Mexico had built a new hospital for every week of those same six years.

Mexico, in a word, was becoming educated, urbanized, industrialized at a rapid pace. The president's wishful statement: "It is imperative that the labor of our men and women, in the fields as well as in the cities, yield more . . . through incessant work, work without pause,'' had taken a big step toward its fulfillment.

Mexico's next president, Adolfo López Mateos (1958–64), son of a small-town dentist, received approximately 80 per cent of the votes in the elections that put him in office. He had shown competence as Minister of Labor in the government of Ruiz Cortines. Ironically, one of his first acts was to call in the army to crush a strike among the railway workers which paralyzed the country in 1959. He jailed recalcitrant leaders of the strike and kept them locked up for several months without due process of habeas corpus. Mexico's famous mural artist Alfaro Siqueiros, one of the nation's best-known Communists, was also thrown into jail for four years because he had violently insulted the government and the president.

López Mateos completed the nationalization of the Mexican electric power industry, and changed the focus of the land distribution program. He distributed the huge total of 25 million acres, but mostly to individual landowners rather than to the co-operative ejidos many of which had bogged down because of misuse of funds, improper management, improper methods of agriculture, and also because many individual farmers participating in them felt little incentive to put forth their best efforts. Perhaps López Mateos will be remembered by future generations mainly because it was during his presidency that the incomparable National Museum of Anthropology, occupying eleven parklike acres, was constructed. Brilliantly designed around an impressive six hundred-foot patio by architect Pedro Ramírez Vásquez, the grand sweep of this museum makes it unique in the world. There are outdoor exhibits of ancient Mexican stonework, including a small Maya temple, in its spacious grounds. The artists Chávez Morado and Rufino Tamayo have beautified the interior. Carved in stone on its wall are these lines from one of the "Songs of Huexotzingo," laments composed by the Aztecs after the fall of their capital to Cortes:

> *Is this all I will leave behind:*
> *Like a withering flower?*
> *No memory of me upon this earth?*
> *At least a flower . . . at least a song.*

Gustavo Díaz Ordaz, 1964–70, received almost 90 per cent of all votes cast. He epitomized Mexico's present middle-of-the-road government, a far cry from the violent leftism and anticlericalism that characterized the early years after the Revolution. But when his daughter got married Díaz Ordaz found it politically expedient not to enter the church, and his stand was duly approved by the Mexican press. It was a perfunctory gesture, because Díaz Ordaz is a practicing Catholic, but in public life the presidents of Mexico keep a judicious distance between them and the Church just as the presidents of the United States are expected to maintain a discreet closeness to some church by attending an occasional service. No strongly pro-Catholic candidate could be elected president of Mexico any more than could an avowed agnostic or atheist be elected president of the United States.

It was, of course, under Díaz Ordaz that the army was called in to suppress rather bloodily and indiscriminately the nine-week student strike of September and October 1968, which preceded the Olympic Games. Some 6,000 students had assembled in a Mexico City housing project plaza to march on the National Polytechnic Institute to protest army occupation of the campus. Troops moved in with tanks and machine guns and broke up the demonstration. The trigger-happy soldiers and police killed, according to official figures, about forty people, including many uninvolved residents, old folks, children. Unofficial estimates placed the toll of dead from five to ten times that figure.

But the Olympic Games went on as scheduled, the main streets of the capital were face-lifted, colorful billboards were raised to conceal the shacks behind them, and Mexicans cheered wildly when their athletes won gold medals in swimming and boxing. The University Stadium put up by Alemán and the nearby Aztec Stadium were the center of these activities and all participants agreed that Mexico put on a great show. The 1968 Olympics were seen live via television by more viewers than any other athletic event in history. The ancient Greeks could never have imagined what they were beginning in 776 B.C., when their heralds traveled throughout Hellas bearing garlands of flowers to summon their own finest athletes to the original Olympic Games. All wars ceased while Greeks from the various city-states assembled in fraternal competition and fraternal union.

The brilliant success of the Olympic Games did not take away the shock of those needless killings on Tlatelolco Plaza, for Mexicans believed they had moved beyond this kind of action. In the main they attributed it to an overreaction on the part of the armed forces, and to the government's dreadful fear that the strike might mar the Games and make Mexico look barbaric before the world. In any event, much soul searching has since gone on in the intellectual and political circles. A few comments on Mexican character, by Mexicans, will provide a better background for understanding this traumatic event.

Octavio Paz holds an honored position in contemporary Mexican culture and political life, not only because of his fine poetry and his penetrating essays collected in *The Labyrinth of Solitude*, but also because he has been one of the country's most distinguished public servants. He had been Mexican ambassador in India for six years when the deplorable explosion of October 2, 1968, took place. When Paz heard what had happened he resigned from his position and in an interview published in *Le Monde*, Paris, (November 13, 1968) he bitterly denounced the Mexican government and its trigger-happy armed forces.

In this interview he probes deeply into the reasons for such violence which has so frequently been a part of Mexican history, and he concludes that it comes mainly from the Aztec past of Mexico and not from the trauma caused by the Spanish conquest, as many have preferred to think. The Aztecs, he points out, made a ritual of the blood sacrifice.

It is no accident that in our great Anthropological Museums the center is always dedicated to the Aztec Hall, that is, to the oppressors of pre-Columbian America, those who terrorized the Mayas and the Zapotecs. It is not mere chance that the young Mexicans who were slain on the second of October fell on the ancient Plaza of Tlatelolco, where there used to rise an old Aztec temple in which human sacrifices were made. The death of these students was a ritual sacrifice, for there was no political reason to justify the action. The only possible cause was to terrorize the people.[182]

Then Paz goes on to say that in Mexico it is necessary above all else to exorcise violence, the Aztec heritage.

The great danger for our country consists in realizing literally its black myths instead of sublimating them. These black myths, in any case, took vengeance on us all in plain daylight the second of October in Tlatelolco.

José Vasconcelos, whom we have frequently quoted, suggests a similar origin of Mexico's psychological problems:

The so-called Latins, perhaps because they are not really Latins at all, but a conglomeration of types and races, persist in not taking the ethnic factor into account for their sexual relations. . . . The Spanish colonization created race-mixing: this defines its character, fixes its responsibility and determines its future.

He then refers to *nuestro mestizaje inconcluso*, "our inconclusive racial mixture," and a compatriot of his clarifies the statement by adding that "The two bloods we carry within us have not yet reached a state of peaceful blending; they find themselves in perpetual conflict."

The choices are limited. "Give a Mexican a free choice between justice, power, great intelligence, wealth or beauty, and he will invariably choose beauty," writes a perceptive Mexican essayist. Other Mexican writers put the desire for power in first place. Mexico's young and justly honored novelist, Juan Rulfo, in his novel *Pedro Páramo*, embodies in his main character the twin search for beauty and for power. Beauty is found briefly and lost, the quest for power replaces it but does not satisfy, so the result is violence, a destructive explosion of the self frustrated and fragmented by both of these polarities of contemporary Mexican life.

The novel oscillates between love and hate, hope and despair, fecundity and sterility in a world that is dead. The dialogue is mainly between two bodies which lie in nearby graves, and is a record of their memories. In this manner the author presents a timeless, changeless reality, the immutable world of man's anguish which suggests the Hispano-Jewish literary tradition in which nothing has value, and life is agony. *Pedro Páramo* adds to this tradition the wandering of lost souls like the legendary Mexican animas en pena, and so gives the whole novel a mythic Mexican flavor.

Pedro Páramo is also an excellent example of a nation and an individual in search of identity. The young Juan Preciado seeks for his father, Pedro Páramo, much as Telemachus sought for Odysseus in Homer centuries ago, and much as so many nameless thousands of Mexican sons search for the father they never knew hoping thus to find some kind of stability in a hostile environment. Juan Preciado, dead, also tries to reconstitute his life out of whispers, hearsay, idle conversation (*murmullos*), as Mexico has tried to reconstitute and rewin its past with its Revolution which brought about the attempted resurrection of past values. But that past is dead and cannot be regained. Juan cannot recapture his lost childhood, and Paradise always lies behind us, never ahead. Only an irreversible sterility permeates Mexican life today.

Sex permeates almost every episode in the novel, but it is a kind of wild and reckless blight which never reaches any real fulfillment. Guilt and violence walk hand in hand with the cult of death. The whole novel is a "homecoming" in reverse: man's (civilization's) return to the barren rock from which they both emerged. Rulfo synthesizes his and Mexico's anguish when he writes: "Why does the world press in on us from all sides, and break us into pieces, and water the ground with our blood? What have we done?"[215]

Samuel Ramos, in his *Profile of Man and Culture in Mexico*, probes more into sex and the concept of maleness as characteristic of Mexican culture. Ramos writes that the Mexican male sees in the phallus the idea of power. He is not interested in fertility like the ancient gods, but in domination, in being on top. He will say "A European has science, art, technical knowledge, and so on; we have none of these things here, but . . . *we are real males*." Beneath that exterior, however, the Mexican may be unsure even of this quality of maleness. Ramos continues:

> The most striking aspect of Mexican character is distrust. This attitude underlies all contact with men and things. It is present whether or not there is motivation for it. It is not a question of distrust on principle, because generally speaking the Mexican lacks principles. It is rather a matter of irrational distrust that emanates from the depths of his being. It is almost his primordial sense of life. Whether or not circumstances justify it, there is nothing in the universe which the Mexican does see and evaluate through his distrust. The Mexican does not distrust any man or woman in particular; he distrusts all men and all women. His distrust is not limited to the human race; it embraces all that exists and happens. If he is a businessman he doesn't believe in business; if he is a professional he doesn't believe in his profession; if he is a politician he doesn't believe in politics. It is the Mexican's view that ideas make no sense and he scornfully calls them "theories." He is the least idealistic person imaginable. He unreasonably negates everything, because he is negation personified.[184]

"What then does the Mexican live for?" Ramos points out that he does not have to think in order to live, and so his life becomes an unreflecting activity, entirely without plan. Mexicans are concerned only with immediate issues. A Mexican will work for today, and perhaps for tomorrow, but never for anything later on. As he so profoundly distrusts the present, he will not prepare for the future. He lives by instinct and by improvisation, so he is drifting constantly.

Juan Rulfo recapitulated the distrust syndrome of his countrymen when he scribbled on the back of a photograph that he gave to a friend:

> Quit being scared. . . . Nobody can frighten you any more. . . . Think pleasant things. . . . Because we are going to be buried . . . a long, long time. . . .

There is something terribly sad about all this. As if man's thoughts and actions were controlled by the constant presence of death. Another Mexican, the modernist poet Gutiérrez Nájera, who drank himself into an early grave (committing suicide in little fragments), made much the same statement almost a hundred years ago in his most celebrated allegory, *Rip-Rip*, which concludes with these words: "It is good to throw a lot of earth over our dead." Forgetfulness makes possible the continuance of life.

Mexico's most popular novelist, especially outside of the country, Carlos Fuentes, strikes the same vein in his novels. He appraises the Revolution as a cruel and empty dream. It is now a mere source of political power, says Fuentes, and he is obsessed with the ritual of blood sacrifice which has been such an integral part of Mexico in her history. Fuentes sees struggle, frustration, deception, violence, and savage ritual in the life of his people, and he concludes that Mexico is a country of slaves to a value system that is not really Mexican. The ritual now has little meaning, because it consists only of verbalization, not action. It is but sound and smoke, for "the defeated (the Indians) have been glorified and the dead are our heroes because they were sacrificed. In Mexico the only saving fate is sacrifice."[206] Justice is no longer a naïve concept, and gone are the days when Latin American authors and intellectuals can give simplistic solutions to very complex problems. In the past generation writers were Ministers without Portfolio, they expressed the national ideal as a kind of dream (Rómulo Gallegos in *Doña Bárbara*, Ricardo Güiraldes in *Don Segundo Sombra*, José Eustacio Rivera in *The Vortex*, etc.) The writers of today can only attempt to state, they cannot even begin to solve the problems which confront mankind.

Fuentes himself, in *The Death of Artemio Cruz*, has his protagonist slowly die as he painfully recalls his lost youth, lost love, lost ideals, lost destiny. He had become one with the new ruling caste, and every key decision in his life had pulled him in the wrong direction. In Artemio Cruz we see the tragedy of Mexico.

Oscar Lewis, in his *The Children of Sanchez*, recorded on tape in the midst of a poverty-stricken family in Mexico City's slums, took a neutral stand which pleased Fuentes, but which was an affront to many Mexicans. The Mexican Geographic and Statistical Society condemned the book as "obscene and slanderous," and demanded its suppression. Fuentes came to the rescue of Lewis and made a film version of the book. In defending it Fuentes said: "We have arrived finally at a moment in Mexico's history in which we must distinguish between two types of nationalism. One type is an affirmation of our human and economic direction, and the other is negative, neopatriotic, chauvinistic, and totally inefficacious because of its isolated, dehumanized and blind mystique.''

Lewis lets the members of the Sánchez family condemn Mexico's ruling party. ''Here the PRI runs everything,'' says one of the characters, ''so if there's another candidate they stick a machine gun in his face. So who won? Well, the PRI candidate. That's all there is to it.'' In another passage: ''There's nothing dirtier than politics. It's pretty rotten, and there's been a lot of blood-shed too, and who knows what else. How many people die so a man can get into power.'' And a third passage:

> That's why I don't worry myself about anything but my work. I don't know potatoes about politics. I read one or two paragraphs in the newspapers, but I don't take it seriously. A few days ago I read something in the news about the leftists. But I don't know what is the left and what is the right, or what is communism. I am interested in only one thing . . . to get money to cover my expenses and to see that my family is more or less well.[185]

In spite of these very bitter reactions of an ordinary Mexican citizen of the lower class, Mexico's progress from a feudal (at least a colonial) economy to a semicapitalist society has been phenomenal. The rapid growth of both the agricultural and industrial complex for the past three decades is not accident or coincidence. Mexico's emphasis on schools, given such a boost by the Revolution, has been paying off handsomely.

When José Vasconcelos, Minister of Education in the early 1920s, went all-out to develop a widespread small-town and rural public school system, he hit upon the very thing that the country needed most in order to enter into the industrialized and highly technical twentieth century. The hard work of the Mexican people achieved the rest. And the huge sums in dollars spent in Mexico by tourists from the United States greatly facilitated the process. It was this same Vasconcelos, incidentally, who turned the walls of Mexico's public build-ings over to that generation of mural artists and thus began along with schools Mexico's great surge forward in art. It was all the product of a nation searching for its identity.

Alfonso Reyes, the grand old man among Mexican writers, recognized the supreme importance of education in the postrevolutionary epoch. ''We thought getting rid of Porfirio Díaz would be the Revolution's main problem,'' he wrote, ''but that turned out to be easy. The Revolution triumphed in an instant.'' And then:

> The Revolution spent ten years searching for itself. Much of this was the dis-comfort of a man who wakes after a long sleep. Everything had to be set right, and it was natural to fall back on all the remedies known to political hope: formulas for workers' socialism and formulas for agrarian socialism, systems of corporations and of labor unions, prescriptions for the redistribution of the land, and for the regulation of labor in the cities. *And above all, schools, schools.* A grand crusade

for learning electrified the spirit of the people. Nothing to equal it has ever been seen in the Americas. It will be Mexico's highest honor in history.[186]

The cult of education replaced the cult of ignorance and of violence. It almost replaced as well the cult of the church itself. To be able to go to school became the first necessity of every Mexican child. It is a necessity that is not always fulfilled. In many rural areas schools are still lacking, although the government's educational program is its proudest achievement. In the cities there are simply not enough classrooms or teachers to take care of the great numbers of children whose families have poured in from the countryside.

The last time I was in Mexico City was in the month of January, and the schools were getting ready to open for the spring term. One night at about ten I was taking a walk; the streets were dim. Mexico does not believe in wasting electricity. The streets were also cold. A blast of chilled air swept down from the snow-covered mountains. It penetrated the skin like needles, hit the bones, chilled the marrow inside. On the sidewalk ahead a line had formed. There were perhaps forty or fifty people in the line, mothers and fathers, but mostly mothers. One lady had her baby in a brown *rebozo*, carried in front, in a big bulge over the stomach. Two of the men had old serapes flung around them, one gray, one brown. They were hooded figures, shrinking from the wind. No one in the line was heavily dressed, but it was not a poorly dressed crowd. I stopped to ask what was going on.

"The school, *señor*. It is the school," a fat, Indian-looking mother woman tells me. "The schools are all crowded and this is one of the worst."

"The very worst," affirms the man in the brown serape.

"They will not take in any more students after the classrooms are filled," his companion chimes in. "They will not take students if there are no seats."

"And if the children don't get into school they will be sitting in the streets," the first mother adds.

Several people in the line were now squatting down in little groups near the wall, one of those thick stucco-covered walls with broken bottles on top that line so many Mexican streets. One group hovered around a charcoal fire in an old iron brazier. Another group of four had made a fire of old kindling and scraps of branches in a worn-out washtub. Two other groups had tin buckets burning with low flames that reminded me of the California citrus smudge pots. Before long they had all settled down for the night, sprawled out in all kinds of positions, but mostly humped together, for greater warmth, and for the spark of contact.

"When does school start?" I asked.

"Day after tomorrow," the man in the brown serape said. "It's first come, first served, so we want to make sure that *our* children get enrolled."

He pulled out a cigarette and rubbed the back of his hand across the stubble on his face. He offered me a cigarette, and I refused. As we talked the crowd grew silent and began to sleep. Faces disappeared behind heavy serapes, *rebozos*, blankets. The fires burned dimly in the night.

These mothers and fathers would wait on the street, through the long cold of two plateau winter nights, huddled around makeshift fires, so that their children might enter school. The desire of these people to better themselves is so intense that it almost brings tears. The church was the heart of the old Mexican culture system; the school is the heart of the new.[217]

Mexican teachers frequently have sixty to sixty-five students in their classes. So great is the eagerness to learn that there is never any problem of maintaining order. However, many of the teachers themselves have scarcely been beyond the seventh or eighth grade. They do the best that they can teaching what they do know, which is far better than nothing. The most interesting part of my recent trip to Mexico was visiting the grade schools and actually sitting in the classrooms with the students while their lesson was in progress.

In one of the classrooms, after class was dismissed, I picked up some notebooks that belonged to first-grade pupils and began to thumb through them. The handwriting seemed exceptionally good, and I commented on this to the teacher. She informed me very frankly that her pupils had not written those paragraphs. The tablets had belonged first to the older brothers or sisters in the family and had been passed on so that these first-graders could make use of the few blank pages that remained in them.

"Our parents are always complaining about how much school supplies cost," the teacher explained. In a poverty area this is not hard to understand.

The government is making gargantuan efforts to provide more teachers and more schools. Special prefabricated schools are being sent to the country areas which can be assembled in forty-eight hours. The townsfolk work around the clock in shifts to get them ready. Everybody does what he can. At present 25 per cent of the national budget is spent on schools, while military expenditures are only 10 per cent. During the peak decade (1960–70) a new classroom was completed every two hours, twenty-four hours a day, every day of the year. Largely as a result of this emphasis on schools Mexico has become the radio, television, and motion-picture capital of Latin America, and of course her writers and musicians, as well as her painters, occupy the very front rank.*

If the Revolution has ceased to be a vital influence in social progress, it is still very much alive in all of the arts. After the revival of painting in the 1920s at the hands of Rivera, Orozco, and Alfaro Siqueiros, came the generation led by Tamayo. Rufino Tamayo, born in 1899, reflected the new designs and ventures of modern painting but never lost his Mexican touch. His colors are rich, refined, strong and logical; his forms are firm but fantastic; his modernism is nourished in the ancient Indian art.

Tamayo and Carlos Mérida inspired Ricardo Martínez, Juan Soriano, Pedro Coronel, and many other younger artists. José Luis Cuevas has gained dis-

---

* Mexican teachers are grossly underpaid, as are the professors at the National University where most full professors earn less than $10,000 a year. Consequently, almost all professors hold two or three outside jobs. Tuition at the university, however, is only a fraction of what U.S. students pay. More than 100,000 students are enrolled, but the dropout rate is nearly 50 per cent.

tinction by following the expressionistic line of Orozco, while González Camarena, Alfredo Zalce, and Raúl Anguiano are realists. Also outstanding among present-day artists are Rafael Coronel, Olga Costa, Leopoldo Méndez, Jesús Reyes, Gunther Guerzo, and Carrillo Gil, and among the sculptors are Carlos Bracho, Germán Cueto, Zúñiga, and Monasterio. Foreign artists who have become a part of the heritage of Mexico by adoption are Jean Charlot, Wolfgang Paalen, Pablo O'Higgins, Leonora Carrington, Alice Rahon, Remedios Varo, and Vlady.

All these fine painters and sculptors and many more besides have enabled Mexico to maintain the preeminent position she took in world art after the Revolution. If Alfonso Reyes were still alive he would be very proud of what is going on in Mexico today in the field of the arts. He might not be so proud to find that his country is still a "guided democracy" with a "guided economy."

Luis Echeverría Álvarez, a dynamic young lawyer, was president of Mexico during the period 1970–76. He took over a burgeoning economy and represented progressive business interests, but he spoke ardently and frequently of helping the country's poor masses. In 1973 he went on a world tour visiting Canada, Britain, Belgium, France, the Soviet Union, and China. He made a big splash by proclaiming friendship with both the Communist and the Western European powers. In that same year Mexico began to import corn, for she could no longer produce enough to feed her fast growing millions. Youthful guerrilla bands were springing up all over the country and defying authorities. They demanded revolutionary reforms and kidnapped many well-known citizens who were held for ransom. The government cracked down on them and liquidated their leaders without paying any attention to due process, but it was several years before "law and order" were firmly restored. In 1974 the national economy sputtered and faltered. Mexicans who had investment capital became jittery and sent $4 billion out of the country. Recession had struck the United States, the market for two-thirds of Mexico's exports, and there was a 23.3 per cent rise in the cost-price index, which weighed most heavily on the rural population.

The country was on the brink of the abyss when new oil fields were discovered in 1975, and Mexico felt a sudden surge of euphoria. But in 1976 the inflation rate hit 27 per cent, the price of oil plummeted, and the peso began its long and staggering decline, reaching 2,900 pesos to the dollar in 1990. Almost half of the country's labor force was unemployed. To find work thousands of Mexicans illegally crossed the border to enter the United States. The Mexican economy, which for twenty years had been growing at 6.5 per cent or higher a year, reversed this trend and continued to decline for the next decade. The population explosion was producing more mouths than the country could feed and more workers than there were jobs. The government attempted to slow population growth with a birth control campaign, but the results were only partially effective.

In the last months of his term Echeverría, anxious to leave office as a champion of the poor, announced the expropriation of 200,000 acres of land to be distributed among the peasants. The landowners and industrialists who were to be dispossessed protested, and there were strikes and threats of armed resistance when peasants occupied a portion of these lands. The next administration found the problem too hot to handle, and the whole program was canceled.

In 1976 Echeverría was followed in the presidency by José López Portillo, the former minister of finance. His father was one of Mexico's foremost authorities on oil and was the author of several books on the petroleum industry. López Portillo was Echeverría's hand-picked successor, and although he received over 80 per cent of the votes cast, scarcely 40 per cent of those eligible had voted. López and Echeverría had been close friends since high school, and both had won scholarships and had studied at the University of Chile, Santiago, in the 1940s.

López Portillo inherited a country in the midst of a severe depression. National productivity that year (1976) had grown only 1.7 per cent, and a 27 per cent inflation cruelly lowered purchasing power. The president instituted a rigorous austerity program, and attempted to curb Mexico's strangling bureaucracy and corrupt politicians. He had considerable success with the first campaign, but very little with the second. Meanwhile, the country's population continued to grow at an alarming rate. The annual increase had declined from 3.5 per cent to 2.6 per cent, but was still very simply overwhelming the economy. A lowered birth rate seemed an impossible dream.

The cult of *machismo* in Mexico and throughout Latin America is a strong psychological stimulus to this rampant population growth. Machismo is the double standard at its most extreme. It demands watchfulness of the men over the feminine members of the family at the same time that it exalts the men's need to affirm their masculinity and social prestige with the conquest of as many women as possible, and the production of a large number of children, both in and out of wedlock. A considerable proportion of Mexican (and Latin American) men maintain a mistress in a little *casita* apart from the official family, and there are often as many children in this second house as with the wife. In many countries the percentage of children born out of wedlock is extremely high. Official Mexican figures estimate illegitimate births at 25 per cent of the total, certainly a minimal figure. In the countries of Central America (with the exception of Costa Rica) illegitimacy rises to more than 60 per cent. The single mother, *la madre soltera*, and her brood of "fatherless" children, constitute a problem of national proportions in many countries. In Mexico her numbers are legion. Spain invented Don Juan in the seventeenth century, but Latin America has made him a universal hero.

In all but the most progressive Latin American countries machismo at the national level becomes a collective drive to create nations of great population. There is a widespread belief that the larger the population the greater the national weight on the international scene. Fast-growing Mexico and Brazil, the two most populous countries of Latin America, are patent examples of this dubious logic. Modern hygiene and medicine have wiped out many dread diseases of the past, and thus have contributed their part to today's population explosion that has become Latin America's and the world's number one problem.

Despite a rapidly expanding population, President López Portillo was able to bring Mexico's economy back to a healthy state through belt tightening and good planning. In 1979 the annual rate of growth for the national productivity was back at 7 per cent. It seemed possible that this very impressive rate of growth might continue or even be exceeded for the next ten years. One of the reasons for this optimism was the discovery of great new oil fields in the gulf coast area of the country, from Tampico to Villahermosa. Official Mexican figures indicate that these discoveries have increased the total oil reserves of the country from forty billion to perhaps one hundred billion barrels. This would place Mexico among the largest oil producing nations of the world, far ahead of Venezuela and very close to Saudi Arabia. Some North American experts, however, are wary of accepting these Mexican figures. They point out that much of the oil may not be recoverable. A large part of the recoverable deposits lies many miles under the earth, and much more is deep beneath the ocean floor. One derrick in the area is higher than the Empire State Building and cost $265 million. The cost of extracting oil in these fields may be ten to fifteen times as much as it is in Saudi Arabia. Furthermore, the Mexican figures refer to a total of hydrocarbons, that is, oil and gas lumped together. Petroleum reserves would be much less.

There are additional causes for doubt. Pemex, the national oil company of Mexico, is one of the most inefficient large companies in the world. It is literally shot through with nepotism and corruption. In the Villahermosa area a large number of employees who collect their checks without doing anything are called "aviators." They touch down long enough to collect their pay and immediately take off again. A nonproductive job of this kind may be bought outright from the Oil Workers Union for about $3,500 in kickbacks. [219] In a recent poll, when queried about the new oil discoveries, most Mexicans stated flatly that they would benefit only the rich, and not help Mexico's impoverished millions.

In the meantime, Villahermosa was booming. Its population more than doubled, and its hotels and streets were filled with oilmen from all over the world. Heavy trucks cut deep ruts in the primitive country roads, and dust and pollution ruined the surrounding farm and grasslands and befouled the water. A huge oil blowout gushing into the ocean paralyzed the fishing industry. This blowout, the biggest in history, damaged the beaches of Texas 600 miles away. Gas flares from some of the wells are so bright that a newspaper can be read at night 5 miles away. More than 100 million cubic feet of natural gas are being wasted daily, enough to heat and light a city the size of Denver for almost a week in winter.

Several U.S. companies were seriously interested in buying this gas, and had already accepted the Mexican-set rate of $2.60 per cubic ton. Mexico had begun construction of the 820-mile pipeline that would convey this gas to McAllen, Texas. But the U.S. government refused to approve the purchase, and Mexico was left holding the bag. The reason given was that gas was already being purchased from Canada for forty-four cents per 1,000 cubic feet. In any event, the deal fell through, and when President Carter visited Mexico in early 1979, President López Portillo gave him a very cold reception. López had put himself out on a limb by approving the deal from Mexico's end, because there was strong opposition inside the country from those who feared such a large sales commitment might put Mexico in a too dependent position vis-à-vis the United States. The amount of gas to be purchased was less than one half of one per cent of total U.S. consumption.

The oil and gas bonanza was Mexico's great chance to catch up with the economically healthy nations of the world. López Portillo and other Mexican politicians were saying this publicly, and were acutely aware of it privately. But they did not want oil to make the national economy lopsided, as in Venezuela, where this had created a consumer oriented society forced to import many necessities, including foodstuffs. Mexico made plans for a broadly based and self-sufficient program of development.

These plans did not come to pass. The best that can be said is that Mexico's so-called oil bonanza did give the country a breathing spell. For a few years it brought in $22 billion a year in gross receipts. Conversely, oil profits eased the pressure on Mexican industry to become more efficient in order to compete in foreign markets, and these profits also delayed long overdue tax reforms. The national oil company, Pemex, was notoriously inefficient, corrupt, and bureaucratic. One of Mexico's most urgent needs is to clean up this huge state oil monopoly, about which, J. Paul Getty once cynically remarked, "is the only oil company I have known that lost money." What happens to Pemex will almost certainly tell what will happen to Mexico.

In the 1990s Mexico's daily oil production may possibly reach a total of three to five million barrels daily. The 1980 total was less than two million barrels a day, with one half of this amount sold in the export market. The daily consumption of oil in the United States is about twenty million barrels. It is easy to see that Mexico's oil will not be the solution to the gasoline problem in the United States.

If Mexico fails to extract and sell this oil in a well-thought-out and regulated way, it will place a great burden on the national economy and social institutions. Mexico will have 135 million inhabitants by the year 2000, if the present rate of population growth continues. Mexico City will be the largest city in the world with more than 30 million people. It is a city of glaring extremes. Its plush Zona Rosa, a luxury shopping and hotel center in the heart of town, is a dramatic contrast to the stark satellite slum called Netzahualcoyotl ("Netza" to its 1,800,000 residents) where ugly miles of gray houses line streets devoid of trees or flowers, yet no one in Netza wants to return to the country.[220] Here at least they have found work and survive. Mexico must create 500,000 new jobs every year just in order to keep unemployment from increasing. There will be at least twice that many workers added to the job market every year, so without some effective measure of population control the future seems hopeless.

Mexico City, which has become a kind of Goliath's head, is growing at the phenomenal rate of 500,000 inhabitants a year. Two thirds of this is internal growth, the excess of births over deaths. One third consists of peasants lured in from the countryside where wages are about $219 a year. The city workers average $1,200 a year, but unemployment at any given moment is close to 40 per cent. Hundreds of thousands of workers hold no steady job, so are unemployed as much time as they are employed. The shantytowns that have mushroomed all over and around the city already represent a political, hygienic, and economic problem of mammoth proportions.

In recent years the inhabitants of these shantytowns, often called *colonias populares*, have organized themselves into effective political units. Their "squatters," called *posesionarios* in Spanish, settle on vacant plots of land and simply take possession. It is about twenty years since the first group of such families made their rickety homes on the dust-choked lakebed on the eastern edge of Mexico City. Since then dozens of similar squatter settlements have arisen around the perimeters of nearly all Mexican cities. One of the most dramatic stories can be told about the colonia called Campamento 2 de Octubre where 35,000 people from the countryside established themselves just outside the capital several years ago. This colonia was named for the 1968 second of October massacre that took place on Tlaltelolco Plaza of the Three Cultures just prior to the Olympic Games. This communistically inspired settlement organized consumer cooperatives, ran its own police force, and kept outside interference at a minimum. For a time the authorities in the capital were seriously worried.

President Echeverría took a hard line toward such colonias, but was unable to undermine their leadership. The central government, however, did not give up. The country's postrevolutionary rulers are very skillful in the way they combine brutal repression with calculated conciliation. They kept chipping away at the Campamento 2 de Octubre with mixtures of promises and repression until they had divided the squatters into two opposing camps, those who now favored the government (the PRI) and those who did not. Eventually the leaders were brought over to the government side, and the political threat posed by the colonia ceased to exist.

The other end of the spectrum is represented by the Maoist settlement of approximately 15,000 inhabitants on the outskirts of Monterrey, Mexico's great industrial city only 200 miles south of the Texas border. This colonia is called Tierra y Libertad, the phrase that Zapata used as his revolutionary cry over seventy years ago, Land and Liberty. In the center of this community the burned-out wreck of a police car is mounted on four brick pillars and bears the words "a trophy of the people." The car is surrounded by red flags and clenched-fist symbols. The police car is the relic of the last visit that the Monterrey police made to Tierra y Libertad. The squatters here run their own jails, factories, schools, and clinics. Alcohol, firearms, and prostitution are prohibited within the limits of the commune. The city authorities of conservative-minded Monterrey leave them alone. They even look the other way while the settlers take their electricity and water freely from the city supplies. The squatters hold no legal titles to their land, but they now form a tightly-knit and very militant minority opposition to the municipal and federal authorities. [221]

Monterrey's total population today is about two million, and there are about 300,000 squatters within the metropolitan area. These are organized in 50 colonias that cover the hillsides, the majority of which were organized and are subsidized by the government. This is the establishment's answer to the handful of communal colonias that ring the city of Monterrey, with which a continuing tug-of-war is in progress.

Monterrey is the heartbeat of Mexico's economy. "The people here are stingy, hardworking, and save their money. They are the Scots of Latin America." The wealthy industrialists of Monterrey have invested over $5 billion in plants and equipment. President López Portillo, shortly after taking office in 1976 in the midst of a severe recession, journeyed to Monterrey to ask the business leaders of that city to help the government restore economic order in the country. They decided to give him that aid. Today a modern sculpture at the center of the city celebrates this government-industry compact, which has been so eminently successful. In 1979 Monterrey's fourteen largest companies churned out over $4 billion worth of manufactured products: steel, cement, pipe, beer, copper wire, trucks, buses, containers, cigarettes, and a variety of processed foods. Many of the largest factories are run by the descendents of Isaac and Francisco Garza Sada, Sephardic Jews, who emigrated to Monterrey from Spain many years ago.

These factories provide their workers with subsidized apartments, free hospitals and clinics open twenty-four hours every day, and many other fringe benefits. Subsidized stores sell clothing, sporting goods, furniture, and appliances at a large discount. Grocery orders are delivered to the doors of each family at about 40 per cent off. The wages paid are high and retired workers collect good pensions, adjusted for inflation. This paternalistic system has worked well for many decades, and outside unions have been kept at an arm's distance.

The squatters in Tierra y Libertad, at the other extreme, live in cinder-block houses, not much larger than two parking spaces. Their houses are certainly not beautiful, but many of the families have grown gardens, put up fences, curtains, TV antennas, and street signs. Some have painted their dull block-made homes a bright pink or blue. There are public restrooms, a clinic visit costs 20 cents, and electricity and water, tapped from the municipal lines, are free.

In the Congressional elections of July 1979, Communists were allowed to vote for the first time in Mexican history. President López Portillo had appointed as his secretary of the interior Jesús Reyes Heroles, who was charged with the responsibility of revamping the country political system so that all opposition parties might be given a fairer participation in the government. Mexicans were eagerly awaiting these electoral reforms. But on May 17 Fidel Castro visited Mexico, the first time he had been in the country since the 1950s when he left Mexico to launch his revolution in Cuba. On the very day of Castro's visit the president fired three of his most powerful cabinet ministers, among them Reyes Heroles. The other two dismissed were Foreign Secretary Santiago Roel García, and Secretary of Planning and Budget Ricardo García Sainz. Herbert Castillo, leader of the Mexican Workers party, stated that the president "took advantage of Castro's visit to give an impression of a turn to the left, while the reality inside Mexico is a turn to the right." Mexicans were caught by surprise by these "resignations," and some referred to them as Mexico's "Wednesday massacre." The net result was that while oil and economic expansion were galloping along at a good pace Mexico's old political establishment was again in firm control.

One interesting sidelight on the firings was brought out when well-placed Mexican politicians commented on the dismissal of the foreign secretary, Roel García, who had recently visited detention camps in the United States where hundreds of illegal Mexican aliens were being held prior to deportation. Mexican politicians thought he should never have made this visit. One said: "He was giving legitimacy to a system of deportation that we should not even concede are legitimate."

There is no doubt that these illegal aliens constitute a problem for both the United States and Mexico. Mexico takes the view that crossing the border is the escape valve for her excess population. Mexicans do not believe that illegals displace American citizens in jobs because they invariably take menial work which Americans do not want. Americans dispute this claim, and are becoming fearful of the economic and social implications of so many illegals in their midst. The Los Angeles Times, in its issue of July 23, 1979, reported an alarming increase in hepatitis, malaria, tuberculosis, and intestinal parasites in this country, largely due to the influx of these and other immigrants. The United States government for its part is unable to control the situation and has adopted the chicano term for "illegal aliens" by referring to them as "undocumented workers."

The Los Angeles Times estimated that there were approximately one million illegal Mexican aliens in the city in 1979. Perhaps three to five times that number are in this country as a whole. It has been estimated that about a million cross the border each year, and at least half of these are eventually caught and deported. But many of those deported come right back again. I personally have talked to several who have admitted to four or five crossings. Many illegals remain only a few months and then return to Mexico with their savings. There is really no way of knowing how many are in this country at any given time.

To Mexicans the illegal alien problem has become a very emotional issue.

They point to the fact that one million Mexican workers made possible the stunning growth of the southwest United States by expanding and maintaining the railways between 1900 and 1930. No hue and cry was raised in this country at that time. Nor was there any strong dissent when the *bracero* farm workers were invited into the Southwest in the 1950s and 1960s to help harvest the crops. Mexicans also feel that Mexican workers in the United States have often not been treated fairly, but are forced to live under conditions that are far below standard. Thousands live in makeshift huts that are crowded, unhygienic, without adequate toilet or health care facilities. They work long hours and are poorly paid. When recently a many-mile-long steel link fence was proposed for a strategic section of the border with Mexico, that country reacted as if it were an insult to the national honor. To the Mexican government closing the border would be an act of economic aggression.

The strongly held beliefs about the illegal alien problem have not been carefully examined, and no solution is in sight. Former CIA Director William Colby stated that these "millions of illegal aliens are a greater threat to the United States than the Soviet Union." Those in this country who agree with Colby see the problem in similar exaggerated emotional terms. The bare statistical facts, however, are staggering. If Mexico's population continues to grow at anything like the present rate, a veritable tide of illegal aliens will enter the United States within the next few years which the U.S. Immigration Department will be powerless to control, much less to stop.

Miguel de la Madrid, who succeeded López Portillo as president in 1982, was less flamboyant in style and more realistic in viewing Mexico's economy than his two predecessors. But de la Madrid had inherited a problem of gigantic proportions. The previous administration, under a false state of euphoria caused by the oil bonanza, in 1981 alone borrowed $20 billion. In 1982 there was a drop in oil prices and Mexico suddenly faced her worst financial crisis in fifty years. Billions of dollars in capital fled to foreign banks, leaving the country without financial resources. This was followed by a serious "brain drain," as many well-trained professionals also left Mexico seeking a brighter future across the border. In August 1982, after an urgent appeal from the Mexican minister of finance, the United States bailed Mexico out financially by extending $1 billion as an advance payment on oil, but at less than the market price. An additional $3 billion in loans soon followed.[245]

Not long after this crisis, on September 19, 1985, the center of Mexico City was struck by an earthquake of 8.1 intensity which destroyed the center of the city, killing 10,000 to 20,000 people, leaving other thousands homeless, and causing over $5 billion in damages. The vaunted zeal and efficiency of the PRI were not evident in responding to the disaster. De la Madrid, once he became aware of the magnitude of the destruction, did appear personally on the scene and provided generous federal aid, but the real heroes of the catastrophe were the residents of the area who spontaneously organized themselves and worked around the clock. The men crawled into the rubble at great risk to their own lives and rescued many victims. They helped to clear the debris of fallen buildings, which included the capital's great medical center and hospital and the totally destroyed Hotel Regis, a famed landmark for many years in the center of the business district. The women organized themselves as self-appointed workers and nurses. They also demanded en masse that the government expropriate the affected terrain and construct new homes for those whose dwellings had been destroyed. Their demands were effective, and within two years 60,000 new dwellings were constructed for 350,000 people on 625 acres of expropriated land.

In late 1987, as de la Madrid's term neared an end, the president and the PRI, under mounting public pressure, selected six presidential candidates to speak on national television, thus giving the impression that there might be a real choice in the 1988 elections. This turned out to be window dressing, for soon afterward, de la Madrid, with strong PRI support, chose as his successor a close friend and former student, Carlos Salinas de Gortari, who was secretary of the budget and planning in his cabinet. Salinas has a Ph.D. in political economy from Harvard, and his selection as PRI candidate was tantamount to election. Once again the PRI had proved that it was the only game in town.

Under de la Madrid, Mexico expanded industrially, diversified its economy, and gradually became less dependent on oil. However, agriculture languished and the country did not and still does not produce enough food to feed its rapidly growing population. Between 1982–88 agriculture grew at only 1.28 per cent a year, as compared with the previous growth rate of 4.5 per cent annually. The Mexican farmer produces an average of only one fifth as much corn per acre as his U.S. counterpart. A few years ago there was a surplus of corn in Mexico, but since 1982 the country has had to import more than eight million tons of foodstuffs annually, including great amounts of corn. There is widespread malnutrition, hunger, and disease in the country. The death rate among children is astronomical. Water is polluted almost everywhere. Women wash their clothes, themselves, and their children in filthy ponds, rivers, and streams. Contaminated drinking water is the scourge of millions, and the visiting tourist has come to dread it as the main source of the *turista*. Mexicans themselves consume more carbonated soft drinks per capita than is the case in any other Latin American country. Coca-Cola, Pepsi-Cola, and other watersafe carbonated drinks are popular even in the remote country areas. Beer is also widely drunk, and Mexican beers are among the world's best. In a recent beer-drinking test held in Los Angeles, sixteen connoisseurs voted *Bohemia* number one and *Dos Equis* number three in quality out of the thirty-six beers assembled from all over the world.

Tourists drop $2 billion into Mexican coffers every year, and without this influx of foreign money the country would be in much worse financial shape.

Gringo visitors are now big business. * Unfortunately, most of these tourists get sick, some of them very ill. Often, even the most common precautions are not taken: the visitor should drink no local water, consume no ice, eat no salads or unpeeled fruits, and not drink the bottled water hotels often place in the room marked "purified." It is advisable not to drink any bottled water except the carbonated brands. There is a big profit made in refilling the well-known soft water bottles directly from the tap. Beer and soft drinks, hot coffee, tea, and soup, or properly boiled or treated water, are the only reliable liquids.

Montezuma's revenge, also often called the *turista*, is no joke. It is a violent form of diarrhea that dehydrates and weakens the victim frequently ruining the journey. Dr. B. H. Kean of Cornell University Medical School, who has spent twenty years studying the turista in Mexico, reports that more than 50 per cent of the Americans who visit that country come down with it. Mexico, of course, is not the only culprit. Any country where the water is polluted and unhygienic habits are ingrained will pass turista on to the visitor. Dr. Kean found that the turista bug is a minicholera. "The bacteria produces a toxin which attacks the cells and causes them to give off water."[235] Mexico City with its earthquake-damaged pipes is a high-risk area. Rural Mexico is even worse. Diarrheal diseases in their most lethal forms, such as typhoid fever and amoebic dysentery, rank together as the Number One killer in five Latin American countries.

Boiling water for a prolonged time is the best form of sterilization, and an immersion heater is the best gadget the traveler can pack into the suitcase. Water can also be purified by adding two to four drops of chlorine bleach, a sterotab tablet, or five to ten drops of tincture of iodine per quart of water half an hour before drinking. It is dangerous to eat raw vegetables, salads, shellfish, or partially cooked meats. Eat a hearty American breakfast of well-cooked foods. Stick to hot soups, well-cooked beef or chicken and rice the rest of the day. Do not vary the diet. Enterovioform, also called Mexaform and Entosan, is definitely not indicated. Lomotil slows the illness down but may make it last longer. Dozycycline or sulfasuxadine, which require a prescription, may prevent or cure turista, but they should not be taken frequently. The best preventive is precaution and moderation in drinking and eating.

The major health risk from turista is dehydration, so plenty of liquids should be consumed. Dehydration may cause severe weakness and is particularly hard on the elderly. It is advisable to replace the lost fluids by drinking an electrolyte solution along with plenty of pure water. This is also the principal therapy for cholera. The electrolyte solution is simply pure water to which has been added the minerals needed to replace those depleted by dehydration. Electrolyte pow-

---

* *Gringo* is derived from the Spanish word *griego, Greek,* and indicates any outsider or stranger, not necessarily a North American. In Argentina *gringo* refers to the Italian. The word has no connection with the song "Green grow the rushes." The story about its origin in that song is on the same level as the silly but widespread belief that Castilians use the *th* sound in their speech because a certain king of Spain lisped.

ders may be purchased in foil packets at the drugstore, or the traveler can prepare his own by using half a teaspoon of salt, half a teaspoon of sodium bicarbonate, one fourth teaspoon of potassium chloride (salt substitute), and four tablespoons of sugar. Add these ingredients to one liter of water, but do not leave the solution outside the refrigerator for later drinking because standing at room temperature promotes the growth of bacteria.

Mexico's foreign debt of $114 billion is a millstone around the country's neck. Thirty-seven cents out of every dollar in the federal budget ($1 billion a month) go to pay just the interest on this debt, and Mexico is pressing for some readjustment in the rate and manner of repayment. During the period 1982–86 profits from Mexican industry continued to decrease, and inflation rose to more than 100 per cent a year. De la Madrid proclaimed an austerity program, but this was like bleeding a corpse, and the peso plummeted. Devaluation of the currency made Mexico a bargain paradise for American tourists who came in droves literally saving the country from economic collapse. Nevertheless, in 1987 real per capita income in Mexico was 25 per cent less than in 1982, declining to the level of 1963. There is still at least 20 per cent unemployment, and another 30 per cent of the work force is underemployed.[247]

The de la Madrid administration worked hard to diversify the economy. One of its most notable achievements was promoting what the Mexicans call *maquiladoras,* assembly plants that receive primary materials or parts from the United States and process these into finished products which are then shipped back. These materials are imported into Mexico without being taxed, and when the resulting products are exported not even the value added is taxable. Most of the maquiladora workers are young women between the ages of 16 and 25, mostly nonunion, who receive an average salary of $23 a week. This setup makes the cost of the finished products cheaper. Sadly, most workers have poor living conditions, and many plants pollute the land with waste.

The maquiladoras put together a great variety of things: appliances of all kinds, stationery and office supplies, toys, sporting goods, shoes and other leather products, electrical materials and supplies, tools, food packing and canning, furniture, clothing and textiles, chemical products, and transportation equipment. Knowing a good thing when they see one, the Japanese have also gotten into the maquiladora field, and many major Japanese manufacturers are now operating plants in Mexico. Strengthened by this competition the maquiladora is a fast-growing industry. But the process does cost jobs in the United States, and American workers are howling. Approximately 500,000 Mexicans earn their living in these maquiladoras, which now bring into that country around one billion dollars annually.[248]

Confidence in the economy was gradually restored and native capital that had previously fled to foreign countries began to return. Within a five-year span more than $10 billion in foreign investments poured into the country, and by the end of 1987 Mexico had accumulated approximately $15 billion in capital reserves.[251] Suddenly there was more cash than the country knew what to do with.* The United States now offered to help Mexico with her foreign debt. Mexico will pay $2 billion cash for U.S. bonds that the United States guarantees to redeem for $10 billion in twenty years. Using this guaranteed $10 billion as collateral Mexico will then buy back outstanding loans from its creditor banks.[249] However, below the surface in Mexico there are still serious weaknesses: a low level of per capita productivity, the high level of the country's foreign debt, a bloated state bureaucracy, endemic corruption, uncontrollable inflation, and uncertain government direction. A total of 4,350,000 persons work for the federal and state governments, up 640,000 from 1982. Notwithstanding, one well-known economist, Professor Rudinger Dornbusch of MIT, made this prediction: "The prospects of Mexico's sustaining a real growth in its economy are, in the long run, the most brilliant in all of Latin America."

Better education and better training of the Mexican worker are essential if Mexico is to realize this goal. Per capita productivity is only one-seventh that of Canada, so there is still a long way to go. The government itself is a big question mark. Mexicans are the least taxed people among those of any of the industrially expanding Third World powers. In the countryside millions live and work under semifeudal conditions, barely eking out a living. Open and fair elections are still out of the question. The opposition knows just how far it can go, and if that point is passed opposing political leaders sometimes "disappear." The government refuses to discuss this issue, stating simply that human rights violations do not exist, but some reputable foreign investigators and reporters assert that Mexico is one of the worst human rights violators in the hemisphere. Widespread corruption is also a deeply rooted problem. It permeates the economy and the entire political system. Every Mexican president sticks his hand in the till and retires from office a wealthy man. Corruption in business is closely linked with corruption in government.

The presidents of Mexico not only enrich themselves while in office but many of them also engage in expensive liaisons with young women in show business. Frequently there are melodramatic twists in these relationships that provide an interesting sidelight on the Mexican presidency.

The much publicized affairs of Díaz Ordaz and López Portillo are typical. Irma Serrano, the tempestuous mistress of Díaz Ordaz, was a popular entertainer who had previously been linked with other well-known political figures. She was from Chiapas, the state that borders on Guatemala. In provincial Chiapas young girls were forced to wear uncomfortable chastity belts, and years later when Irma wrote her autobiography she gave it the title *Knotted Underwear*. As an eight-year-old she revealed her violent temperament by clubbing her grandfather while he was asleep, sending him to the hospital with a fractured skull. Later, in Mexico City, Irma became a highly touted singer and actress.[293]

---

* However, one Mexican newspaper, *El financiero* (February 22, 1988), estimated that $70 *billion* of Mexican capital was stashed away in foreign banks.

As the mistress of Díaz Ordaz she entered the profitable business world. Aside from receiving expensive jewelry, furs, and clothes, Irma was given two clothing plants in Puebla, a shoe factory, three brickmaking facilities, and several choice plots of real estate. Her affair with the president was kept quiet for a while, but eventually Díaz Ordaz's wife found out about it. In her fury she demanded that many of Irma's film, television, and recording contracts be canceled. Irma, to avenge herself, appeared unexpectedly at the presidential palace on Señora Díaz Ordaz's birthday accompanied by a mariachi band. She easily convinced the palace guard that she had come with the mariachis to give the president's wife a surprise birthday serenade. The president, caught entirely unaware, heard the music and came out to express his thanks, but as he began to speak Irma punched him in the face with all her might. His glasses went flying and the palace guards cocked their guns ready to shoot. The president stopped them and waved the intruders off. The onlookers were stunned, but the incident was covered up, and the president never saw Irma Serrano again.

The more openly acknowledged affair of López Portillo with Rosa Luz Alegría had no such melodramatic twist, but the president brazenly appointed her to the choice post of minister of tourism, where she basked in public view and raked in a fortune. The president also gave her a luxurious home in Acapulco worth several million dollars. Bribery and corruption permeated the presidency of López Portillo, and when he retired from office it was conservatively estimated that he had pocketed well over one billion dollars. But this was not the worst of it. Under him the police force of Mexico City was hardly distinguishable from a well-organized crime syndicate. Named chief of police was Arturo "El Negro" Durazo, who had previously been the chauffeur and bodyguard of the capital's most notorious gangster.[293] At the time of his appointment as chief of police he was under indictment for drug trafficking, but in his youth Durazo had been a school chum of the president who insisted on his appointment. Durazo weathered all opposition and became a multimillionaire before he was finally brought to trial. Meanwhile, the policemen of the capital gouged the citizens mercilessly. Mexican police may also be involved in the more recent kidnapping, torture, and killing of U.S. drug investigator Enrique Camarena in Guadalajara, which created an international incident and exacerbated considerably relations between our two countries.

Agriculture, once vigorous and the mainstay of Mexico, is now in decline and cannot feed the growing population. Big farmers have turned away from corn because they can make three or four times as much by growing and selling tomatoes, melons, strawberries, cucumbers, eggplant, peppers, and squash to the United States. Many U.S. growers say that they are being run out of business by lower Mexican prices, and by occasional episodes of dumping. Meanwhile millions of Mexicans go hungry. More than a billion dollars have been spent on rural development and agricultural reform, but there is no more land to distribute, and millions of rural families are still landless. Thousands of small farms are cultivated in the most primitive manner; they cannot feed those who till the soil. The modernization of agriculture must go hand in hand with increased industrialization. This two-pronged attack will alleviate, but it will not solve Mexico's difficulties. In spite of its rapidly growing industries Mexico is still very much a Third World country.

Industrialization has its own hazards which have already emerged. Lack of planning and the desire to make a quick dollar exacerbate the process. Mexico City now faces a very critical problem brought on by its industries and its riotous, mushrooming growth: pollution. The relatively small Valley of Mexico has a population of more than twenty million people living in one of the fastest growing, most crowded, and most polluted areas on earth. There are 35,000 industrial establishments, and over three million automobiles that belch 5.5 million tons of contaminants into the air every year. Added to this is the fecal dust of three million people who have no toilet facilities and ten million animals. This fecal dust quickly becomes airborne and is breathed in daily. In January, the most polluted month, schools are closed in order to protect the children. One medical researcher recently tested a sampling of newborn infants and found that 50 per cent had toxic levels of lead in their blood. Another study, made by the World Health Organization, found toxic concentrations of lead in the blood of 60 per cent of the fetuses tested. It is clear that the Mexican capital does not provide a healthful environment for its population or for its visitors, and conditions are getting worse every day.

The national elections of 1988 in Mexico were more tumultuous than usual. Candidates opposing Salinas and the PRI challenged the final tally. They shouted fraud and produced hard evidence of widespread dishonesty in the count. Nonetheless, Salinas was declared the official winner with 50.7 per cent of the vote, a bare majority of less than 1 per cent. Cuauhtémoc Cárdenas, son of the revered ex-president, Lázaro Cárdenas, was given 31 per cent of the total, and the conservative PAN candidate, Manuel Clouthier, the remainder. Tens of thousands of angry and disillusioned voters poured into the streets near the point of open rebellion, but Salinas played his hand cautiously and mollified the opposition by proclaiming publicly that the time had arrived when Mexico must become a pluralistic democracy instead of the one-party state that it had been for sixty years. Rigging the elections, he declared, would no longer be tolerated. Some credence can be given to his words for when the state of Baja California elected its new governor in August 1989, the opposition PAN candidate won handily, and for the first time in history PRI acknowledged defeat in an election of this magnitude.

More specific Mexican reactions to the presidential elections were reported in a poll taken by the Los Angeles Times in August 1989 in forty-two randomly selected villages and towns of Mexico. This poll indicated that 68 per cent of those contacted doubted that Salinas had won honestly, but 79 per cent expressed a favorable reaction to the president's actions during his early months in office. It is surprising that 47 per cent believed that there would be an armed revolution in Mexico within the next five years. Octavio Paz, one of the country's most respected writers, commented pointedly: "In one day, the Mexicans' secret and free vote ended the one-party system. The PRI's own candidate, Salinas de Gortari, recognized that shortly after the election. We are beginning to take our first steps on unfamiliar territory: the region of pluralistic parties." Paz then cautioned his readers against the dangers inherent in taking this step: political intolerance, splintering parties, impatience, violence, and the lack of absolutes to which Mexicans have become accustomed. In brief, Salinas now faces a situation similar to that of Gorbachev in Russia. He can either try to clamp down or to allow increasing political freedom. Whatever his course, Mexico's long sanctified one-party rule has neared its end. Salinas has announced that his primary goal is to establish Mexico a dynamic and democratic free market economy. This will be a tremendous undertaking.

Mexico's main problem is that there are too many Mexicans, and the certainty that tomorrow will produce additional millions. If no way is found to control this population explosion there will never be a solution to any of Mexico's basic problems. Spain, Italy, and France, all Catholic countries, have been able to stabilize their population, but in Mexico ignorance and a lack of family planning goals make this very difficult. The government, doctors, and even some of the clergy are cooperating to reduce the birth rate. The Simpson-Rodino bill, giving legal status to Mexicans in the United States since 1982, eased the pressure temporarily. In the long run, what happens to population will determine the future of Mexico, and will also affect directly the future of the United States.

Our two countries do not know each other very well, despite proximity. North American tourists by the millions visit Mexico every year because it is picturesque, near, and relatively cheap, but when they cross the border they enter a world that is more foreign than Europe. Their behavior as visitors frequently leaves much to be desired. And millions of Mexicans, who pour across the border as if it did not exist, demand legal status, driving tests, and voting instructions in Spanish, and bilingual education in the schools, not available to any other linguistic minority. Alan Riding, in his excellent book on Mexico, *Distant Neighbors*, hit the nail on the head when he wrote that in no other part of the world do two neighboring nations have such little understanding of each other.[245] Far more than by their differing levels of development, says Riding, the two countries are separated by language, religion, race, philosophy of life, and history. Porfirio Díaz put it even better perhaps when he said: "Poor Mexico, so far from God, and so close to the United States!"

CENTRAL AMERICA

Central America, which Simón Bolívar thought should have formed a single nation, is composed instead of six small countries that have sometimes erroneously and disparagingly been called "the banana republics." Guatemala is by far the most populous with approximately seven million inhabitants. Costa Rica is the only country with a homogeneous population, almost entirely white, and is the only country that has not had a turbulent political history. Costa Rica also claims the distinction of having no army, and its capital, San José, is one of Latin America's most cultured centers.

The annual rate of increase in population in Central America stands at 3.3 percent, at which rate within one hundred years Central America's present 23 million will have multiplied to an incredible 250 million inhabitants. Overcrowded El Salvador, with the greatest population density of any Latin American country except Haiti, now has 671 inhabitants per square mile (1990), and gives only the faintest inkling of what this future figure would mean.

During the 1960s Central America's dream of a common market with millions of potential customers appeared to become a reality. A good start was made: tariff barriers between the Central American states were virtually eliminated, and during the first decade trade increased tenfold. Essential industries were divided up among the six countries. Honduras, for example, got the sole right to manufacture plate glass. Industrial development at first prospered, agriculture improved, and the standard of living slowly increased.

New enterprises included plants to manufacture television sets, refrigerators, optical supplies, paints, furniture, and cement blocks. Poultry, cattle, and farm profits rose. Unfortunately, most of this progress was undone in the 1970s. Political turmoil reached a peak in Nicaragua, El Salvador, and Guatemala. Economic stability was shattered. Honduras withdrew from the market, Costa Rica threatened to do so, and the bright dream lost its glow. The countries of Central America again went their divided ways.[277]

GUATEMALA

Guatemala contains nearly one third of the total population of all Central America. It is a country where political rivalries have led to violent conflicts in recent years. Still primarily an Indian country, Guatemala has a large depressed mass of peasants and a small class of rich landlords who own the large coffee plantations. Many experts state that Guatemalan coffee is the finest in the world, and it is by far the country's outstanding export product, the banana trade having declined steadily in recent years. Guatemala also has vast forests of valuable hardwoods: mahogany, logwood, and cedar; and the tropical west coast, largely undeveloped, with a topsoil many feet thick, is an area of great agricultural potential.

The country's political history has been explosive. General Ubico was dictator between 1931–44. He was the last of the old line tyrants, a man who regarded the country as his private club. Ubico cooperated fully with the United States during World War II. He was followed by Juan José Arévalo, a teacher, who served out his stormy term as constitutional president and moved his country toward drastic educational, labor, and land reform. The constitution of 1945 permitted expropriation and proscribed the latifundio. In 1950 Arévalo was followed by Jacobo Arbenz, who increased the pace of these reforms.

> During an 18-month period under Arbenz, from January, 1953, to June, 1954, a million and a half acres of private land and 700,000 acres of government land were distributed to 125,000 peasants. This amounted to more than 26% of the total acreage organized into farms.[187]

Three things went wrong. Arbenz worked hand and glove with the Communists and caused a shudder of apprehension in conservative Guatemalan circles and in Washington. Second, the speed of the land distribution produced disorganization and anarchy in the countryside resulting in a drop in production. Third, the government expropriated 234,000 acres belonging to the United Fruit Company, which was offered $2.54 an acre for land that the company claimed was worth eight times as much.

Washington's alarm took the form of action, as the CIA openly supported the Guatemalan "rebels" who moved in on Arbenz from Honduras and Nicaragua. In 1954 the Arbenz government fell and was replaced by that of Colonel Castillo Armas, the rebel leader. From that moment to this anti-U.S. sentiment in Guatemala has remained at a high pitch. The United States had made a very poor choice. The Armas government was hopelessly corrupt and Armas himself was assassinated in 1957.

A well-known Uruguayan novelist, Eduardo Galeano, head of the University of Montevideo Press, gives the following details which explain the widespread Latin American resentment evoked by this episode:

> Castillo Armas, a graduate of the U.S. Command and General Staff College at Ft. Leavenworth, Kansas, invaded Guatemala with troops trained and paid by the United States. His invasion was supported by C-47 bombers piloted by the CIA. When he had taken over the country, Castillo Armas returned all expropriated uncultivated land to the big landlords and gave away millions of acres of the country to an international oil cartel. The Guatemalan Oil Act was written in English and sent to the Guatemalan Congress in that language to be passed. One congressman, who still had some sense of dignity left, requested that it be rendered into Spanish. Opposition newspapers that had operated freely under Arbenz were closed; democratic political leaders, students, and labor union officers were sentenced to death, prison, or exile. Finally Armas himself was assassinated. "It is a great loss to his own nation and for the whole free world," Eisenhower said. The forces of the Right and of the Guatemalan military have been in control of the country most of the time ever since.[188]

And Mexico's most noted historian, Daniel Cosío Villegas, commented as follows:

> If North American intervention made any sense at all, it was the necessarily violent act of tearing out Communism by the roots so it would not sprout again, either in Guatemala or anywhere else in Latin America. Well then, Communism has

shot up in Cuba and to such an extent as to make Guatemalan Communism look like child's play. . . . To my way of thinking the only solution is for the United States and Latin America to attempt a reconciliation at once, a course which may have the unexpected effect of laying the foundations for a new concept in American solidarity.[189]

Armas was followed by Miguel Idígoras Fuentes, who was ousted by a military coup in 1963. In 1966 Méndez Montenegro, dean of the law school of the University of Guatemala, was elected president, and the country was temporarily rescued from dictatorship. However, the rift between rightists and leftists increased in violence, the problem of land reform was pushed aside, and tensions rapidly mounted.

The assassination of the United States ambassador on the streets of the capital in August 1968, and the previous gunning down of two embassy attachés, initiated a new terrorist trend with international overtones. In 1970 the German ambassador was kidnapped and killed in cold blood. These assassinations were the work of the pro-Communist group known as the Rebel Armed Forces, a guerrilla group which the government has been unable to control. Throughout the 1970s there were other assassinations and kidnappings. The people of Guatemala, as a consequence of all this, are sharply divided among themselves: the un-Hispanized Indians constitute one large group, the urban workers another, the foreign investors and large landowners still a third. The country is not a cohesive whole, its very heart and culture are divided against themselves. One native writer states that his people are caught and crucified "between the Cross and old pagan sacrificial stone of the Indians." They have not yet found a way to set themselves free. The violence continues in Guatemala today. Rightists and leftists face a confrontation beyond the hope of compromise.

The tourist visiting the lovely capital, however, may not be conscious of any of this. He will see beautiful shops displaying expensive jewelry, silver pieces in exquisite Maya designs, watches, cameras, television sets, perfumes, and refrigerators, while along the streets parades a steady stream of American, Japanese, French, German, and British cars. The cafés, restaurants, and excellent hotels are full of well-dressed guests. Surely this seems to be the affluent society, but in actuality these fashionable streets cater to a mere two or three hundred thousand people out of Guatemala's ten million. And even among them almost everything is purchased on time. Signs in the show windows invariably indicate the payment per month, not the total price.

In the outlying countryside 80 per cent of the inhabitants do not buy or sell anything, and they can neither read nor write. They suffer from constant malnutrition; infant mortality among them is extremely high. They live from hand to mouth, scarcely aware of the proud Maya culture of their remote ancestors. Anything would be an improvement on the miserable conditions under which they have to exist. They are ready grist for any demagogue who will come and make them appealing promises.

Guatemala has produced two well-known writers in this century, Rafael Arévalo Martínez and Miguel Angel Asturias, both of whom have participated in their country's political life, but on opposite sides. Rafael Arévalo Martínez, born in 1884, was for twenty years the director of the national library in Guatemala. He is a distinguished poet and novelist and is also the author of the most famous short story to come out of Latin America in this century: "The Man Who Resembled a Horse." In the political sphere Arévalo Martínez was the representative of his country at the Organization of American States (Pan American Union) in Washington in 1946–47. He is among the very few Latin American writers and cultural leaders who have expressed unbounded praise for the United States.

At a time when so very few are still willing to voice such admiration it might help to balance the scales to quote his words:

> The generous people of the United States take the bread from their own mouths in order to give it to those who need food across the sea. And similarly in many other things. A high level of civic responsibility, the highest that humanity has ever known, sparks the people of the United States. This country deserves the first place in the world, and one must never despair for it. This noble nation loves justice above all things.
>
> In the United States is found every excellence. Not only does this country have the strongest boxer, the most beautiful woman and the richest millionaire, but it also has the most profound philosopher, the most notable scientist, the greatest artist, the most exalted mystic, and the finest writer. Every superiority has here its home.

The only Central American ever to win a Nobel Prize is Miguel Angel Asturias, Guatemala's famous novelist, who received the award in 1967. The best-known novel of Asturias is *El señor presidente*, published in 1946, although it was written much earlier. This novel tells the story of a typical Latin American dictator of the old school, a story with which Asturias was very familiar. The tyrant in his novel rules through carefully manipulated fear. There is something almost magical and uncanny about him. No one ever sees him or hears him. But he is omnipresent on every street and in every café or home as a foreboding presence. There is no news except what is printed in his official newspapers. He allows no opposition, and he rigorously exterminates his enemies. He becomes a myth in his own lifetime.

Asturias takes a cue from Sarmiento who presented the Argentine tyrant Rosas in a similar frame, with fear as his main support. But he also based much of the novel on the dictatorship of Guatemala's own tyrant, Estrada Cabrera, who ruled that country with a mailed fist during the first part of this century, 1898–1920. The dictatorship of Estrada Cabrera was also an invisible tyranny, with terror as its constant companion. Once entrenched in power Estrada Cabrera sought the support of the United States and thus facilitated the entrance of the United Fruit Company into that country. In 1906 this company began to buy large landholdings and to plant bananas along the tropical eastern coast initiating what Asturias calls the epoch of North American imperialism in Guatemala.

In 1917 a terrible earthquake hit Guatemala and the whole capital collapsed. People from all walks of life ran out into the streets with whatever they had on. Class distinctions temporarily disappeared, and some of the aura of fear also began to dissipate. Opposition to the tyrant mounted. Less than three years later Estrada Cabrera was declared unfit to rule and was placed in jail.

Asturias describes the setting:

> I was secretary of the court where he was prosecuted. I saw him almost daily in jail. And I realized that undoubtedly such men enjoy special powers of some sort. To the point that when he was behind bars people said: No, *that couldn't be Estrada Cabrera. The real Estrada Cabrera got away. This is some poor old man they've dumped in there.* In other words, the myth couldn't be in prison.[206]

The tyrant in Asturias's novel is exactly the same kind of figure. And the story is told in a very dramatic, poetic style packed with tense repression, internal conflict, terror, and the ominous shadow of the invisible tyrant. This is undoubtedly the book that won for its author the Nobel Prize. Later in his novelistic career Asturias wrote a series of novels called the United Fruit Trilogy, in which he excoriates the North American banana interests in Guatemala. But in these novels he allows anti-U.S. propaganda to overwhelm his novelistic sense, and his characters, especially the greedy North Americans, are flat and colorless puppets who are totally unconvincing.

Guatemala still lives in violence and in fear. Amnesty International, after a careful investigation, reported in December 1976 that since 1960 more than 20,000 persons had been tortured and executed or had simply "disappeared." Elections were held, but they were always rigged by the military. The economic condition of the masses showed little if any improvement. The capital was hit by another strong earthquake in February 1976, and 23,000 people were killed, while over a million were left homeless. The United States and the Bank for Economic Development made large loans immediately available, and a reconstruction boom began. The next few months brought a burst of prosperity as new buildings emerged to line the streets of the capital.

In size Guatemala is as large as Portugal and Israel combined. Slightly more than half the national territory is populated. Indians, who make up over 50 per cent of the population, live in the northern highlands, and the "ladino" or mestizo population is concentrated in the intermont basins around the capital in the southern highlands. The country is two thirds mountains, 60 per cent forested, and one sixth of the total population lives in Guatemala City, which is by far the largest city in Central America. Over 60 per cent of the inhabitants are illiterate, and over 60 per cent are born out of wedlock. There are really two Guatemalas, one made up of the European and U.S. oriented ladino population, the other consisting of primitive Indians, most of whom speak no Spanish.

The geographer, Preston James, writing in the 1940s, stated categorically "There is no agrarian problem in Guatemala." Perhaps he meant that there was plenty of land to go around in Guatemala, or that the agrarian problem had not yet reached the crucial point which caused the explosion of the Mexican Revolution. In any case, he was wrong. Approximately 2 per cent of the landowners own 70 per cent of the land, and the mass of rural inhabitants are barely able to subsist on the small plots they till. There is a small industrial base in Guatemala, but it comes nowhere near to being an effective counterpart of the distorted agriculture, much of which is controlled by foreigners.

The Indian majority in Guatemala is finally beginning to assert its rights and to demand a redress of grievances. There have been many years of tension, murders, and evictions in the isolated Indian highlands where many inhabitants are now asking for legal titles to the land they have held for generations. Having no such titles has left them open to exploitation on a wide scale. Oil was discovered here a decade ago and, as highways pushed into this remote territory, the government has given away or sold land titles to hundreds of outsiders—politicians, the rich, the military—who are always on the alert for a profitable investment.

Guatemala has had an almost uninterrupted history of military rule in this century. Finally, in 1986, in relatively free elections, Vinicio Cerezo became the first civilian president in twenty-five years. He faced a bankrupt treasury, an angry and frustrated military establishment and, among the masses, distrust, poverty, fear, and hostility. Cerezo asked for sacrifice, patience, and austerity from his countrymen. He announced that his economic policy would be patterned after that of democratic socialist Spain. His foreign policy of strict neutrality sought a negotiated settlement of the Nicaraguan conflict. He said that he would restore a respect for human rights in Guatemala, but he was not able to control the military whose spokesman brashly boasted: "We are not going to be put on trial! We were victorious! In Argentina there are witnesses, there are books, there are films, there is proof. Here in Guatemala there are no survivors."

In the summer of 1987, the presidents of the Central American countries, except for Panama, met in Guatemala City and endorsed the regional peace plan proposed by Oscar Arias, president of Costa Rica. This plan called for free elections, freedom of speech, and freedom of the press in Nicaragua, but it also recognized the validity of the Sandinista regime, which did not go down well in Washington. The United States immediately proposed a counterplan demanding the withdrawal of all Cuban and Soviet "advisors" from Nicaragua, and continued support of the Contras until this was achieved. In the meantime, Cerezo's administration, overburdened by debt and facing the permanent threat of an army that had lost the government but which did not resign itself to having lost its political power, struggled to survive against almost overwhelming odds.

Guatemala has not been in the news as frequently as Nicaragua, Panama, or El Salvador, but its problems are just as critical and, as the most populous

nation of Central America, it is certainly of key importance. Since the overthrow of Arbenz, engineered by the United States, Guatemala has been the
center of constant bloodshed, violence, and instability. An *Americas Watch*
report made in the late 1980s estimated that in the previous two decades there
had been 200,000 deaths and 40,000 disappearances, leaving 80,000 orphans
and one million displaced persons. Death squads and the army itself killed with
impunity, shamelessly and irrationally slaughtering people all over the country,
but primarily in outlying villages accused of harboring "insurgents," citizens
who oppose the government. The civil war continues relentlessly. The government, seeking a military solution to this problem, requested that the United
States send to Guatemala 20,000 M-16 rifles to help wipe out all rebellious
groups.

President Cerezo was not able to control either his army or the political opposition, but he did make an attempt to pacify the countryside by offering the
peasants homes in "model villages," along with supplies of food, clothes, medical aid, schools, jobs, and amnesty if they would come out of the hinterland
and settle in these government towns. A big catch in the offer was that the
men must join government patrols which would then go in pursuit of the insurgents. By and large, the president's program accomplished little in solving
Guatemala's fundamental problems: land reform, illiteracy, and a respect for
human rights. The peasants were not at all eager to settle in these government
model villages, under constant military scrutiny, far from their native dwelling
places. But in some regions of the hinterland conditions are so terrible that
thousands did indeed come forth in rags, their bodies emaciated by hunger and
disease, to accept the government's offer. However, the only long-range productive governmental action would be to grant a plot of land to each landless
family, and to make this possible the large estates of the wealthy landowners
would have to be confiscated and distributed. No Guatemalan government
since the time of Arbenz has been willing to tackle the problem of land distribution head-on, and until this is done the country wastes its energies with
perfunctory gestures of reform.

In the elections of October 1990 only 30 per cent of those eligible voted,
and no presidential candidate won a majority of the votes. This resulted in a
runoff between the two leading contenders, both right-wingers: Jorge Carpio
Nicolle, a mediocre, well-to-do, and very conservative newspaper owner "with
the charisma of a baked potato," and Jorge Serrano, chief advisor to former
dictator General Efrain Ríos Montt, noted for his repressive and bloody regime.
Serrano is a Stanford University engineering graduate, and a notable figure
in the burgeoning evangelical movement which now embraces 35 per cent
of the country's population. Serrano won and inherited a 30-year-old civil
war, a bankrupt treasury, a 60 per cent inflation, and an economy in which
barely 15 per cent of the people live above the poverty level. During Cerezo's
term in office basic food prices rose 61 per cent, crime in the streets grew at an
alarming rate, and human rights abuses became almost routine. Every single

month there were more than 100 extrajudicial "executions" in Guatemala. Neither of the above presidential candidates even mentioned the need to bring about a more equitable distribution of the country's wealth, and until this is done there can be no solution to Guatemala's fundamental problems. This country is a volcano waiting to erupt.

EL SALVADOR

The Indianist mestizo population of El Salvador, unlike that of Guatemala, is thoroughly Hispanized and integrated into the social and economic fabric of the state. The hard work of the Salvadoran people, both in industry and on the land, did create a dynamic economy. El Salvador's population is so over-crowded, however, that in recent years thousands of Salvadorans have crossed the border into much more thinly populated Honduras in search of a better future. These migrants sent back frequent complaints of ill treatment at the hands of Honduran hoodlums. Their homes and farms, they said, were not given any protection by the local police. Tensions began to build up, and after a soccer game in San Salvador which the Salvadorans won, tempers on both sides exploded. Latin Americans often go into a frenzy of insult-swapping at important soccer games, even well-educated spectators indulging in behavior that is perhaps without parallel in modern times. This particular game, of course, was not the cause of anything; it was simply the trigger that set off accumulated tensions.

A few days later, in July 1969, President Sánchez Hernández of Salvador, a graduate of the United States Armored School at Fort Knox, ordered his troops to invade Honduras. They met little resistance and plunged wildly ahead. The OAS immediately intervened to put a stop to this senseless war, and success was achieved mainly through the efforts of the organization's secretary general, Galo Plaza, the enlightened and persuasive ex-president of Ecuador. At one stage in the negotiations Galo Plaza locked the Salvadoran delegation in his office for two hours to prevent their changing their minds on an agreement they had just signed.

> The State Department, which had carefully kept its voice in the lowest possible register during the deliberations, stated after the diplomatic settlement "the inter-American system, in which we proudly participate, has met a major challenge."

At the turn of the century El Salvador was a progressive and prospering coun-try because of the profitable coffee trade. Coffee financed highways, rail lines, and new buildings. But coffee caused a distorted economy, and what was even worse, El Salvador's legendary "fourteen families" controlled and still control 85 per cent of the land. When the population was less and the national political conscience was not very sensitive, the country was economically well off, peace-ful, and coherent. During the years 1970–80 there was a drastic deterioration in economic conditions and an increasing demand for land reform.

In 1977 General Carlos Humberto Romero, candidate of the dominant party (PCN, National Conciliation Party), was victorious in the rigged presidential elections by a two-to-one margin. Church officials refused to attend his inauguration. The opposition candidate, Colonel Ernesto Claramount, cried fraud. He along with 2,000 of his followers barricaded themselves in a park and sought to challenge the results. They were dispersed by troops and Colonel Claramount was exiled to Costa Rica. This was the first stage in a period of terror that has increased almost daily.

At least three leftist groups began a widespread campaign of guerrilla activity aimed at disrupting the government. They kidnapped many prominent businessmen, most of them foreign nationals, and demanded a ransom. In this way they were able to accumulate $100 million that financed their continued activities. Many persons kidnapped were murdered in cold blood, and these included a former president of the country and a foreign minister. Japanese, Dutch, Swiss, English, and other foreign nationals were also killed. The highest ranking Swiss diplomat, Hugo Way, and the nation's major coffee exporter, Ernesto Liebes, the leading member of El Salvador's Jewish community, were both kidnapped and assassinated. Carlos A. Herrera, former mayor of the capital city of San Salvador, who was minister of education, was machine gunned to death.

Prominent businessmen went about in armored cars, wore bulletproof vests, and varied their routes and activities constantly. The leftist guerrillas occupied public buildings, churches, and schools, and once held several foreign diplomats hostage. In May 1979 they seized the embassies of Venezuela, Costa Rica, and France, demanding the release of five of their jailed members. The government, enraged, responded by declaring martial law. On May 8 the police fired into a crowd of demonstrators in front of the cathedral, killing twenty-four and wounding many others.

The economy continued to deteriorate, and the country, violently polarized, erupted in civil war, which has up to the present cost 60,000 dead. In the 1980s leftist groups that emerged in the 1970s joined hands in a well-organized Marxist Liberation Front, called the Frente Farabundo Martí, modeled after the Nicaraguan Sandinistas. The military government had lost all popular support and finally, in 1984, with great fanfare, elections were held. Despite wide scale intimidation voters turned out en masse, voting was open and fair, and there was a landslide majority for José Napoleón Duarte, a nonmilitary leader. As an eccentric young boy Duarte was often called "el loco." His father had won a big prize in the National Lottery, and with this money sent his son José to the United States to be educated at the University of Notre Dame. In his campaign Duarte had promised to restore human rights and to carry out fundamental land reform.

The new administration was violently opposed by the Marxist "rebels" who demanded rigorous agrarian reform, and the costly civil war consumed more than 20 per cent of the federal budget. Rightist death squads operated on a vigilante basis, assassinating outspoken opposition leaders, priests who defended the poor, and hundreds of innocent victims. To cap all the other terrible problems, in October 1986 the capital, San Salvador, was struck by a devastating earthquake that killed 3,000 people, left 100,000 wounded or homeless, and caused $1 billion in damages. This quake made the Legislative Palace unsafe, so the Congress was forced to meet in a parking garage.

The United States has poured more than $1.5 billion in economic aid into Salvador, and an additional $500 million in military aid. U.S. officers and advisors helped to train the Salvadoran army which had quadrupled in size since Duarte's election. There was an annual inflation rate of 70 per cent, miserable pay in the workplace, and an intolerably high unemployment rate of 40 per cent. Paying the soldiers became the first priority. In the cities and towns stores were well stocked with native and imported goods, but few could afford to buy them. The cost of living was up but income had gone down. A few were made rich while the masses lived in grinding poverty, with a general feeling of hopelessness and desperation.

During the final months of his term President Duarte suffered from terminal cancer. He had already lost all his popular appeal, for he had accomplished little or nothing while in office. Rightist death squads still operated freely. The army had its own death squads and was accused of killing six Jesuit priests in cold blood. The United States had been giving Salvador $1.5 million in aid every week since Duarte's election in 1984, all to no avail. The neglected streets of the capital resembled a battle zone. Corruption and incompetence in the government and in the economy were endemic. María Julia Hernández, director of the Office of Human Rights of the Catholic church in El Salvador, commented: "Please stop sending military aid to El Salvador. This is not aid; you are destroying us!" Elections, finally held in 1988, were perfunctory and unproductive. Before the voting took place the Salvadoran archbishop, Arturo Rivera Damas, said pointedly: "After the ballots are cast, the civil war will continue."

Alfredo Cristiani, candidate of the rightist party, Arena, was elected president. Cristiani, a wealthy coffee plantation owner, was educated at Georgetown University in the United States. The rebels of the National Liberation Front (FMLN) would make no truce on the new government's terms, and the civil war did indeed continue. Cristiani worked to bring about a compromise, but progress was painfully slow. Roberto D'Aubuisson, founder of Arena, a military officer of considerable charisma, probably held the trump card, and he favored a military solution to the country's deep-seated strife.

El Salvador is a prime example of what the U.S. foreign policy in Central America has produced. It is a country where human rights are officially respected under a democratically elected and strongly pro-United States government, but real justice is a joke, the welfare of the people has been neglected, financial corruption increases daily, land reform has barely scratched the surface, the economy is a shambles, the brutal civil war continues, and the future holds little promise of improvement in any of these areas.

COSTA RICA

The small Central American republic of Costa Rica is an anomaly among the countries of Latin America. It has the longest truly democratic tradition of any of the southern republics, the most equitable land distribution, and one of the most literate populations. Its schools and cultural institutions are among the best in Latin America. Its capital, San José, is one of the most attractive, and it has a very small minority of poor people. Costa Rican women have the reputation of being the most beautiful in Latin America. The population of the country is homogeneous; 90 per cent of the inhabitants in the area surrounding San José are pure white, and it is in this area that 70 per cent of the total population lives. There are almost no Indians, and the Negroes along the tropical coasts, who were brought in from Jamaica to cultivate the banana plantations, number less than 2 per cent of the total population.

Costa Rica is a small country, and it has one of the densest rural populations in Latin America. Furthermore, the central highland nucleus is one of the four areas in Latin America of continued population expansion outward without loss of population at the center. The altitude of this meseta is about 3,500 feet, and the climate is mild throughout the year.

The first settlers encountered belligerent natives, not advanced in agriculture, and there were no mines in the region. The Indians soon died off as a result of the white man's diseases, and the fifty-five original families were then forced to make a crucial decision that pointed out the future direction of the country. They decided to till their own farms, and to put aside the Hispanic ideal of a landed aristocracy. This was the basis for Costa Rica's later deeply rooted democratic tradition.

Costa Rica was the first Central American country to cultivate coffee, but not until 1825 did export shipments of this product begin. The government immediately saw the benefits of larger coffee exports, and offered free land to anyone who would plant coffee trees and cultivate the crop. By 1850 this program had resulted in large scale coffee sales to foreign countries, and Costa Rican coffee acquired the reputation of being among the world's finest. Banana plantations were established along the tropical Gulf coast after the turn of this century, and during the years 1909–14 Costa Rica was the biggest exporter of this product. The banana disease of the 1930s wiped out most of these trees and bananas were then planted along the Pacific coast.

Costa Rica has no real land problem. Eighty per cent of its arable land is distributed among small landholders. The country does not have a military tradition. The army was abolished in 1949, and a civil guard of 3,000, along with a rural constabulary of 2,500, took its place. The president of the country receives a very modest salary, as do the members of Congress. Being elected to office in Costa Rica does not result in windfall profits for the victor. Good roads radiate outward from the highland nucleus, making communications easy. Crime is low and there is a widespread feeling of tranquility and well-being.

Costa Ricans, democratic and liberal in sentiment, have sympathized with the struggles of the poor people of Nicaragua, Guatemala, El Salvador, and Honduras to achieve a better government and a better life. The explosion in Nicaragua in 1978–79 called for more than sympathy, and Costa Rica not only gave asylum but extended aid to the Sandinistas who eventually overthrew Somoza. At considerable cost and inconvenience to themselves, the Costa Ricans allowed the Sandinistas to freely cross their border and regroup for further assaults on the Somoza regime and his hated national guard.

Voices were raised, however, inside Costa Rica warning that the new government might turn out to be just as bad as the Somoza dictatorship. These same voices have expressed the view that Costa Rica had better watch its step lest it be drawn into the maelstrom. There is now real concern in San José about what is happening with such rapidity in the neighboring states, but so far this has not resulted in a wave of defensive conservatism inside Costa Rica.

Costa Rica has long been the exemplary democracy of Central America, and it also has the highest standard of living in the area. In all the main cities drinking water, milk, butter, ice cream, and cheese are safe. The country has one of the most beautiful tropical rain forests in this hemisphere, and a greater variety of birds and butterflies than the entire United States. The scenery is magnificent. San José, the charming capital, lies in a fertile valley that produces coffee, sugarcane, dairy products, cattle, and tropical fruits. Its streets are far safer than those of Dallas, Los Angeles, or New York.

The pleasant year-round climate and cheap, agreeable living conditions have attracted many foreigners who have brought both capital and expertise into this small, progressive country. The government makes it very attractive for retirees, granting them freedom from many taxes. They are also allowed to bring in their automobiles and household goods duty free. Approximately 15,000 Americans now live in Costa Rica, and many of them have become citizens. They have established paint and plastic factories, plants making vegetable oils, soups, soybean flour, adhesives, printing inks, and chemical products. Others among them own large, modern chicken and shrimp farms. Some of these enterprises have branches in Mexico, Brazil, and Argentina. Costa Rica also has a thriving cultural life, an excellent orchestra, an outstanding educational system, first rate newspapers. Its citizens have a warm feeling for the United States.

Costa Rica does not want to become a platform to attack any other Central American country; its strongest resolve is to maintain a status of active and permanent neutrality. However, as one president of the country stated, "Costa Rica is in the eye of the storm," where political events have tossed it. The national economy has suffered many reverses, and the government has been pressured to take sides. Falling coffee prices in 1981–82, and the expense of maintaining encampments to house and feed the 200,000 refugees who have arrived from the less stable neighboring states, have caused the worst depression in Costa Rica since 1929, and forced the country to default on its foreign debt. This precarious insolvency has led some foreign observers to fear that Costa Rica faces the risk of becoming a second Lebanon.

In the summer of 1987 Oscar Arias, president of Costa Rica, devised a plan for a negotiated settlement to the Nicaraguan and Salvadoran conflicts: a cease-fire, amnesty for all so-called rebel forces and political exiles, the withdrawal of foreign advisers and soldiers, immediate lifting of censorship within Nicaragua, and free elections to be held in 1988. In the meantime, there was to be no further support of the Contras and a respect for the existence of the present Nicaraguan government. This plan was given enthusiastic support by the presidents of five Central American countries, who are eager to resolve their own regional affairs and conflicts, and Arias was awarded the 1987 Nobel Peace Prize for his efforts. However, the United States immediately threw a wet blanket on the proposal, calling it too favorable to the Sandinistas. Costa Rica, which has always been a good friend to the United States, felt slighted and humiliated by this rebuff. But Washington continued to insist on seeking a military solution to this vexing Central American problem.[254]

The United States has sent more than one billion dollars to boost the economy of Costa Rica since 1982, making this country the largest per capita recipient of U.S. aid after Israel. This has helped keep Costa Rica off the rocks, just barely. Dependence on the one-crop coffee economy has been eased by the development of several new export products: pineapples, macadamia nuts, cut flowers, textiles, and packaging materials that now account for 50 per cent of the trade. The purchasing power of the ordinary Costa Rican citizen has, however, shrunk greatly, and there is much discontent. President Arias did a good job of providing new housing, having put up 20,000 new dwellings each year, but the people are not eating as well as before. Prices keep going up and salaries do not keep pace. There is only 5.5 per cent unemployment, one of the lowest rates in Latin America, but underemployment stands around 20 per cent.

Subsistence farmers are being driven from the land by the sudden switch to a cash-crop economy. Government subsidies have been lifted from traditional crops such as beans and rice, so now these staples have to be imported and many small farmers have been pushed into poverty. The minister of agriculture and the minister of planning both resigned, partly in protest against this policy. Arias is no hero to his own people, many of whom feel that he has spent too much time on the Central American peace process and not enough time on trying to solve his own country's critical domestic problems. In a demonstration held in San José, the capital, one large sign read: ARIAS, WHY PEACE WITH HUNGER? Tourism, up 40 per cent in the late 1980s, helped to keep Costa Rica afloat, but with the weak economy there was a clear swing toward the right. Unless Costa Rica can find a way to give its poor people back their purchasing power, all the other achievements of the Arias administration may soon be forgotten, and democracy itself imperiled.

The elections of February 1990 were an indication of the direction in which the nation was moving. The liberal Arias-backed presidential candidate, Carlos Manuel Castillo, an experienced but rather colorless economist, was pitted against the conservative, Rafael Angel Calderón, who had been defeated by Arias in the elections of 1986. At that time Calderón had expressed very hawkish feelings toward Nicaragua, and had even said he might send Costa Rican guardsmen to help the Contras in their fight against the Sandinistas. This endeared him to the Reagan administration and to the U.S. Republican party, which contributed heavily to his campaigns, both in 1986 and again in 1990. Noriega also contributed generously. In the 1990 elections, Calderón was the victor and became president. Aid in running his campaign was given by Roger Ailes, the Republican media consultant who had worked on George Bush's presidential campaign, and there is no doubt that Ailes's counsel and help were a strong factor in his defeat of Castillo.

Although Costa Rica has a small population, it takes great pride in its thriving culture. It is a highly literate country of well-educated people. One of the best newspapers to come out of any Latin American country is the famous *Repertorio Americano* of San José whose editor, García Monge, was for more than a generation the cultural leader of this part of the world. Costa Rica is also inordinately proud of its long musical tradition. It has had a national orchestra for many years, and in 1970 this group was reorganized and more adequately funded so that foreign musicians might be enticed to come to San José on two-year contracts. Chosen as the new conductor was a North American peace corps worker, Gerald Brown, who was a Julliard School graduate. When the new orchestra gave its first concert the following year, the entire audience rose and gave it a twenty-minute ovation.

In 1972 the country decided to establish a National Youth Orchestra, and as a beginning 6,000 youngsters converged on the National Theater for their auditions. One year later the Youth Symphony was playing the classical masters and giving concerts. It was invited to the United States and performed at the White House, at the United Nations Assembly, at the Kennedy Center in Washington, and in several other cities. The concert before the General Assembly of the United Nations was a huge success, and the then seventeen-year-old cellist Gustavo Monge expressed it well when he commented: "We knew the concert was being sent by satellite back to Costa Rica. We knew everyone in the country was bursting with pride. We knew we also represented a country that has no army, no weapons, no wars. It was our chance to prove to the U.N., to prove to the world, what such a nation can accomplish through disarmament. It was our moment, and we played with our souls."

NICARAGUA

Nicaragua is the largest and the most thinly populated of the Central American republics. It is approximately the size of the state of Iowa, and has a population of less than four million. One half of the country is forested, and there are great stands of mahogany, rosewood, and cedar. The economy is basically agricultural, but agriculture utilizes only 10 per cent of the land. The main products are cotton, meat, sugar, and coffee. Before the dramatic fall of Anastasio Somoza in July 1979, Nicaragua was probably best known in history as the birthplace of the great poet, Rubén Darío.

U.S. marines occupied the country twice: 1912–25, and again in 1927–32. During the second occupation the United States opposed Augusto Sandino, the revolutionary, and helped to install the first Somoza as president. U.S. marines also helped to train the national guard that secured Somoza's continuance. Once that was assured the marines withdrew. This Somoza (Anastasio) was the first of three Nicaraguan dictators belonging to the same family. They formed, as some have called it, the Somoza dynasty. For ten years the U.S. ambassador, Thomas Whelan (1951–61) affectionately referred to Somoza and his heirs as "my boys." The Canadian Latin American specialist, Gerald Clark, writes that "he was as much hated by Nicaraguans as the Somozas themselves."

Clark then goes on to add that while our attitude and our representatives have improved "Nicaraguans who have been attacked, beaten, arrested, and tortured by Somoza's *guardia*—and the victims include one third of all the lawyers—are quick to point out that these Somoza goon squads were prepared by American military men." Most of them spent training periods at Fort Gulick in the Panama Canal Zone, while many others were taken to the United States itself.

The last man of the Somoza dynasty, also named Anastasio Somoza, came to power in 1967. He was educated in the United States where he was graduated from West Point. He was given the nickname of "Tacho." He beefed up the national guard, bringing its total number to 15,000 soldiers, and he secured their loyalty by giving them high pay, good living conditions, and all kinds of fringe benefits. The commander of this guard was José Somoza, the president's brother, and the military school established in Nicaragua was placed under the command of his son, "Tachito," a graduate of Harvard.

Tacho's first term as president ended in 1972, and he was not supposed to succeed himself, but that same year the Constituent Assembly rewrote the constitution allowing the succession. One of the worst earthquakes in the country's history struck Managua, the capital, on December 23, 1972, destroying 90 per cent of its commercial establishments and 70 per cent of the homes. More than 6,000 people were killed, 20,000 were injured, and 300,000 were left homeless. With foreign aid the task of rebuilding began at once and reached a cost of $775 million.

When elections were held in 1974 Somoza was declared the winner by a 20-to-1 margin, but the elections were a farce because special laws disqualified most of his opponents. One of the president's first acts was to ask international banking interests to underwrite a $6 billion six-year plan for reconstruction. Things then began to improve, but much of the money found its way into Somoza's pockets.

Tacho was in control of everything. He very adroitly added to his already large holdings, and when he was deposed his personal fortune was estimated to be close to $300 million. He owned a large chunk of Nicaragua's richest arable land, and his eight cattle ranches, producing some of the best beef in Latin America, covered 1.5 million acres, about a third of all the cattle land in the country. His two meat packing plants, one in Condega near the Honduras border, and the other in Chontales, were modern and efficient operations, two of the best in Latin America. Each of them cost one million dollars to construct.

General Somoza also owned large tracts of land devoted to the cultivation of sugar and rice, and two major sugar refineries belonged to him. He was deeply involved in fishing; he owned a large tract of land in the heart of the capital city; he held an interest in a large hotel, in banks, airlines, newspapers, radio and television properties. He deposited sizeable sums of money in foreign banks.

Opposition to this Somoza began to grow as soon as he had taken office and revealed his hand: *no change*. Those in the opposition called themselves *Sandinistas*, after Augusto Sandino, a revolutionary leader of the 1930s. There were sporadic attempts at rebellion, and in 1978 the rebels captured most of the nation's congress and held them hostage until Somoza freed eighty-three political prisoners. This episode was followed by a full-scale civil war in which the masses of the people opposed Somoza's well-equipped guard. The guard waged a relentless campaign against the rebels, killing many innocent civilians in the various battles. Perhaps ten to fifteen thousand were slain, twice that number were left homeless, and many thousands escaped across the borders, most of them entering Honduras. Many towns and cities in Nicaragua were destroyed in the struggle. At least $300 million fled the country, and the national productivity declined 6 per cent. Unemployment reached over 30 per cent. With only the slightest abatement, the fight continued into 1979. The United States and the five Andean nations asked Somoza to resign, and finally toward the end of July the general left for Miami, Florida. Nicaragua was bankrupt and devastated. Objective observers placed the total killed at 40,000 and the total cost to Nicaragua at $3 billion.

The arrival of the new junta in Managua on July 20 was hailed by the largest mass gathering in Central American history. The London-based *Latin America: Political Report*, in the issue of July 27, 1979, began its article on the Sandinista victory with this assessment: *The overthrow of the Somoza dynasty is the most significant political event in Latin America since the Cuban Revolution 20 years ago.* The new government immediately nationalized all Somoza's holdings and also nationalized the banks.

The junta was made up of representatives of all the groups that had opposed Somoza. It included two priests and represented many shades of political opinion. However, several of the leftist leaning Sandinistas immediately left for Cuba to talk with Castro, and from that moment it was clear that the Marxist majority on the junta would regularly override the democratic minority, rendering their votes meaningless. This minority resigned, left the country, and with their supporters became the nucleus of the Contra resistance, which received immediate U.S. backing. Within Nicaragua a Marxist-oriented government completely controlled the country. The Contras had hoped they would be supported by the people of Nicaragua, but this did not happen, and their struggle became an almost exclusively military confrontation, which depended for its continuance on U.S. money and arms. The Iran-Contra scam, in which several million dollars were subversively "diverted" from Iran and Israel to the Contras, further poisoned this operation.

The Sandinistas had been very effective revolutionaries, but as economic and political managers they were a total disaster. By 1989 inflation had risen to more than 1000 per cent, and national productivity, which had gone down for years, stood at the 1955 level. The industrial sector was operating at 30 per cent capacity. The national currency, the córdoba, 70 to the U.S. dollar in 1979, was well over one million to the dollar in 1990. The cost of supporting a huge military force consumed 50 per cent of the federal budget. Prices soared while income fell. The average clerk, cashier, or white collar worker received between thirty and forty dollars a month. A thriving black market undermined confidence in the ability of the government to manage things.[252]

Under Sandinista rule Nicaragua became an economic basket case. Inflation soared to astronomical heights, finally reaching 30,000 per cent. Industries disintegrated, and under the socialist government even agriculture languished. A U.S. trade embargo stifled the import-export trade, and the expense of maintaining an army of 70,000 men drained the treasury. There was 35 per cent unemployment and people had pitifully little to eat. The U.S.-backed Contras continuously invaded and occupied parts of Nicaragua, causing widespread destruction in the countryside.[281]

For a time Soviet and Cuban aid kept the economy going, but eventually this became sporadic and ineffective. Out of sixty buses sent by the Soviets in 1986, only seventeen were still in operation in 1988. Nicaragua was no longer able to pay for Soviet oil. Heavily subsidized, but strictly rationed, gasoline sold in Managua for 14 cents a gallon. The people at large were not happy with these conditions, yet many still believed in their "revolution." As Daniel Ortega said: "If it were not for the ideological consciousness of the revolution, Reagan would have won this battle years ago."

When the Arias proposal for a negotiated settlement of the Nicaraguan conflict was made, Ortega accepted it. On October 1, 1987, he approved a cease-fire, lifted the censorship, and the opposition organs *La Prensa* and *Radio Católica* began to function again after fifteen months of silence. Ortega, however, refused to deal directly with the Contras. He took this stance, he said, "because the owner of the circus is Ronald Reagan. There is no reason to speak with the clowns." Later, he changed his mind and direct talks between the two groups began.

An unexpected sidelight on the Sandinista government was the defection on

October 25, 1987, of Major Roger Miranda, chief aide of Humberto Ortega, Nicaraguan minister of defense, President Daniel Ortega's brother. Miranda, a longtime dedicated Marxist, declared that he had become totally disillusioned with the government of his country which he said was oppressing and bleeding the people, building up for its leaders large foreign bank accounts, and giving massive military aid to antigovernment factions in Salvador, Guatemala, and Honduras in an attempt to Sovietize Central America. "The Sandinistas," he said, "have established a totalitarian, antidemocratic regime of terror. They have betrayed the revolution, destroyed the economy, and militarized all levels of society. They are a gang of dictators, thieves and murderers." Their public acceptance of the Arias Peace Plan, declared Miranda in Washington, was simply a ploy to get rid of the Contras so that they might proceed summarily, and without opposition, with their dictatorial regime and expansionist goals.

In March 1988 a cease-fire was agreed upon by both sides, but it was only temporarily successful. In February and again in August of 1989, the presidents of five Central American countries (excluding Panama), headed by Oscar Arias of Costa Rica, worked out a plan to end the stalemate. First of all, they called for the dissolution of the Contras and their return to Nicaragua with full amnesty or, if it was preferred, their resettlement in other neighboring countries. To the dismay of the Contras, who had not been consulted, this demobilization plan was promptly endorsed by Nicaragua's twenty anti-Sandinista parties. The United States had already cut off military aid to the Contras, so they were left stranded in Honduras as unwanted guests. They still made up a sizeable group of more than 10,000 soldiers, plus at least 30,000 to 40,000 family members, wives, children, and old folks.

These two meetings of the Central American presidents put great pressure on Ortega. He was urged to democratize his government and find a peaceful solution to the conflict. Ortega agreed to allow unrestricted freedom of the press and of speech and promised to hold elections ahead of schedule, in February 1990. In order to guarantee open and free voting, he also agreed to give the opposition equal radio and television time, and to allow dozens of objective foreign observers at the polls. These would come from the United Nations, the Organization of American States, and various other groups, including a sizeable representation from the United States. Former president Jimmy Carter would head this contingent. Official U.S. reception of the plan was far from enthusiastic. Many in Washington believed that Ortega would renege on his promise, that the elections would not be free, that observers would be harassed or kept away, that voters would be intimidated, or that there would be chicanery of some other kind. The Contras themselves viewed the agreement with great distrust and declared that they would not disband until after the elections.

In November 1989, President Bush attended a summit with the Latin American presidents in San José, Costa Rica, where final details of the electoral plan were worked out. Here President Bush pejoratively referred to Ortega as "this little man" whose presence at the gathering was like that of "an unwanted animal at a garden party." Although Ortega was generally disliked by those at the meeting, these uncalled-for remarks did not endear President Bush to any of them.

Plans for the elections were made and carefully implemented. Opposing Ortega as candidate for the presidency was Violeta Chamorro, editor of the newspaper *La Prensa*, widow of the assassinated Joaquín Chamorro, whose death had hastened the end of the Somoza regime. Joaquín had bitterly opposed Somoza in *La Prensa*, of which he was editor before his wife replaced him, and it was believed by many that Somoza was responsible for his death. Both he and Violeta had joined the Sandinistas in their campaign against Somoza, but Joaquín did not live to see their victory. When the Sandinistas took over the government, Violeta became a member of the ruling junta, but she was quickly disillusioned by its rigid Marxist orientation, its members' total disregard of minority opinions, and their close association with Cuba and with Russia. She soon withdrew from the junta and began to criticize Sandinista excesses in her newspaper, which was closed down on several occasions, once for a period of fifteen months. Violeta pointedly commented: "The Sandinistas are, without question, worse than Somoza ever was. They are a disaster. After ten years of their control, there is nothing to eat. I had hoped, oh, how I had hoped, that their revolution would be for the people. But it's all for themselves."[291]

In her bid for the presidency Violeta Chamorro was supported by a coalition of fourteen parties, representing all shades of opinion, which called themselves the National Opposition Union, or UNO. Chamorro had to campaign in a wheelchair because of an operation on her knee, the result of severe arthritis. She and Ortega ranged the countryside giving impassioned speeches. Ortega promised a continuance of Sandinista revolutionary reforms, while Chamorro promised freedom and bread.

As the campaign progressed many polls were taken, several of which followed the North American pattern, using all the North American expertise. Most of these polls indicated that Ortega would be the winner by a considerable margin. Only a single Costa Rican poll showed Chamorro as victor, but the same prediction was made by one astute Latin American observer, Carlos Montaner, in his column in *La Opinión*, the Spanish language newspaper published in Los Angeles. He predicted that Nicaraguans would vote with their stomachs, and that Chamorro would win in a landslide. Contrary to the expectations of most people, including Ortega himself, who had made plans for a great victory celebration, Montaner and the Costa Ricans were right. In a follow-up article Montaner wrote that Oscar Arias of Costa Rica, who with his dogged persistence had forced Ortega to hold elections, was the real generator of Chamorro's victory. The final tally, with 90 per cent of those eligible voting, gave Chamorro 55 per cent of the vote and Ortega 41 per cent. There is little doubt that this election will have profound repercussions in El Salvador and in Cuba.

Octavio Paz, Mexico's best-known essayist and poet, commented: "The Sandinista defeat, like the defeat of the Marxist left generally, is the defeat of fantasy. The communist remedy to social injustice proved worse than the malady. Now our challenge is to find the political imagination to address those injustices that have outlived their untenable solution."

Nicaragua, like all of Central America, is in desperate need of economic integration as well as social justice. The United States, for its part, which during the Reagan administration clamped a strangling trade embargo on Nicaragua and promoted a civil war resulting in hundreds of deaths, has the moral responsibility to help rebuild the devastated economy of this poor country. Real justice in Nicaragua is dependent on economic growth and a fair distribution of what is produced. Neither of these things can be achieved without political stability, which still has a precarious future. Chamorro's supporters might split into antagonistic groups, causing political unrest and making economic progress impossible. Ortega and his cohorts, who still control the army and the labor unions, are in a position to veto any program not to their liking. The new government will be sorely tested as it passes through the ordeals of transition toward openness and progress, but at least the basis has now been laid, and the momentum has swung, just as it has in Europe, toward the side of democracy and freedom. Unfortunately, also, in an undeveloped country like Nicaragua, this means that its pitfalls will outnumber its advances.

HONDURAS

Honduras is larger than any of the Central American countries except Nicaragua. Only the western half of the country is populated, and even the capital city, Tegucigalpa, has no railway. In fact, there are no railway lines in the region of largest population. The northern coastal area, tropical and humid, was planted in bananas in the early 1900s, and this fruit still provides half the country's exports. Former African slaves were brought into this region to take care of the banana plantations, and still make up most of the population. Elsewhere in the country most of the people are mestizos.

Half of Honduras is heavily forested, and a considerable portion is mountainous. Only a small part of the land is cultivated; there are no mines of importance, and there is very little industry. More than 60 per cent of all births are illegitimate, and half the children have no schools to attend. Illiteracy stands at 50 per cent and there is little opportunity or incentive for progress. Half the national territory has never been fully explored, so there is no way of knowing what resources it may hold.

Honduras has had a succession of military dictatorships for many decades, with very brief periods of democratic government. Two thirds of the population are impoverished subsistence farmers. The country's large northeast is so thinly populated that it is not effective national territory. Salvadorans, packed like sardines in their own overpopulated country, have for years illegally entered Honduras in waves, much as Mexicans have flocked into the United States. A total of 600,000 Salvadorans have found their way across the border in search of living room. The most recent border clash was in 1976, but there is no way that Honduras can put a stop to the pressure of incoming Salvadorans.

Inside Honduras the latifundia system still prevails, and landless poverty is the rule rather than the exception. Bananas, coffee, and cattle are the principal products, but there are few roads, few schools, fewer hospitals, and both business and government are shot through with corruption and inefficiency. Honduras has become the transshipment center for the drug traffic between Latin America and the United States. Drugs valued at $1 billion pass through Honduras every year on their way to the United States, often with governmental complicity.

Honduras was devastated by hurricane Fifi in 1974. There was property damage of $500 million and at least 5,000 persons were killed. In 1975 the government took over the properties of the U.S. banana companies (United Brands and Standard Fruit), but banana profits have had little effect on ameliorating the widespread misery of the masses. Economically Honduras is far behind its neighbors, and there is not much chance of its catching up. The rate of growth in the economy is low, and the country's national resources, which are considerable, have been squandered by corrupt and ineffective development. Conditions are ripe for a Nicaragua-type explosion.

Honduras is the only Central American country that still depends largely on bananas for its foreign exchange. Some commentators have facetiously referred to the country as the only remaining banana republic. The recent development of large banana plantations in Ecuador and on Taiwan, plus a pest that has attacked the fruit in Central America, account for the decrease in importance of bananas in this area.

The history of Honduras in this century is closely tied to that of the United Fruit Company (now Standard Brands) to which the Honduran government granted one million acres of land for banana plantations in the early 1900s. For years the company controlled both the economy and the government of Honduras, and whenever a challenge arose to this authority, the United States sent in marines to protect American interests. In 1942, in contrast, at the height of the Good Neighbor Policy, United Fruit established at Zamorano, near Tegucigalpa, the capital, an experimental agricultural school "in the service of the Americas." This school quickly became an outstanding center for agricultural teaching and development. At Zamorano plants and seed crops of various kinds are carefully studied. Selective seeds and scientific animal husbandry have greatly improved harvests and animal production in many neighboring nations. Zamorano owns twelve thousand acres of land where students from fifteen Latin American countries "learn by doing." There is an insatiable demand throughout the Southern Hemisphere for Zamorano graduates in all areas of specialization.

In the last two decades more than twelve thousand Palestinian Arabs have settled in Honduras, where they have become a very progressive element of the population. They are merchants, manufacturers, and business people who produce wearing apparel, sports goods, cigars, and hardwoods for export. Added to the Arabs are the droves of Salvadorans who have illegally entered Honduras, literally squeezed out of their own overpopulated country. The World Bank has lent Honduras $20 million to develop a touristic program and to help restore and make accessible its many Mayan ruins. Honduras is potentially a wealthy country, with large deposits of gold, copper, iron ore, and rich hardwood forests, but inaccessibility and the lack of a proper labor supply have left these resources largely unexploited. The country produces mainly bananas, coffee, and cattle.

With the election of Dr. Roberto Suárez Córdoba as president in 1982, Honduras definitely entered the U.S. camp. Suárez Córdoba's successor, José Azcona Hoyo, continued friendly relations with the United States. The Nicaraguan Contras were based in Honduras, where they were trained by U.S. advisers. In 1983 the United States established a large military base in Honduras, and in the past decade our country has also sent many thousands (the United Press estimates 80,000) troops of the U.S. National Guard to Honduras, ostensibly to build roads, bridges, airstrips, clinics, and to receive military training. These troops often go on joint maneuvers with Honduran soldiers. A considerable opposition has built up inside Honduras to this vast United States military presence on Honduran national soil. However, at least on one occasion the mere fact that so many U.S. soldiers were in Honduras probably prevented a military takeover of the government, and the economic as well as military advantages these soldiers give the country are obvious.

During the final years of the 1980s, Honduran resentment against the United States rose to fever pitch. The American flag was burned in the streets, hundreds marched protesting the U.S. and Contra presence in Honduras, anti-Yankee slogans were painted on walls, and it even became unwise for American military personnel to wander far from their barracks. One Honduran deputy remarked: "Maybe the President of the United States did us a favor by bringing all Hondurans together."

Growing economic distress and political uncertainty fed this resentment continuously. Unemployment was officially set at 40 per cent, per capita income was among the lowest in Latin America, the Contras occupied a large strip of Honduran territory, and the very visible North American soldiers became a thorn in the side of the Hondurans. The Contras, with their millions in U.S. aid, were better fed and better taken care of than many of the Honduran poor.[288]

In October 1989 President Azcona, who had frequently been accused of being too pro-United States as well as being a "do-nothing" executive, declared categorically that the Contras would have to leave Honduras. He made this clear at the summit in San José, Costa Rica. It was at this same summit that President Ortega of Nicaragua called off the cease-fire agreement he had made with the Contras.

A new president, Rafael Leonardo Callejas, former minister of agriculture, was elected in November 1989. Callejas was educated in the United States as an agroeconomist. He promised to reduce unemployment and to give more help to the poor as he pulled Honduras out of its critical economic decline. This is a task that will take a master hand, for 60 per cent of all rural Hondurans earn an average of only $250 a year—hardly a subsistence income. A program of strictest austerity and inspired political leadership is required, combined with considerable U.S. aid. Callejas, in his inaugural address given in January 1990, made an impassioned plea for the demilitarization of Central America. If this wise counsel were followed, not only would millions of dollars be saved that could be put to far better use in other sectors but also the ever threatening specter of military intervention in civil affairs would be removed. [289]

Callejas later pleaded with the people of Honduras to help him get the country back to solvency. "Honduras is bankrupt," he said. "For years we have been spending far more than we take in. Our treasury has been printing money without any backing. Our deficit is staggering and only the hard work and sacrifice of us all can save our country." Brave words, but the impoverished people of Honduras are tired of such rhetoric. Their politicians made stupid mistakes and the people are always asked to pay the piper.

On March 14, 1990, President Callejas, exasperated by the continued presence of the Contras in Honduras, took the bull by the horns and ordered them to turn in their arms and get out of the country. "The war is over," he said. "There is a popularly elected government in Nicaragua now, and it is time for you to go home." Shortly after this, the Contras took the long road back, and laid down their arms.

Honduras is not as thoroughly militarized as Nicaragua, Guatemala, or El Salvador, but its military establishment is still the most disciplined and best organized pressure group in the country. When political and economic conditions get out of hand, the military is invariably called on to restore order. Young men are regularly obligated to serve their stint in the armed forces, but thousands are reluctant to do so, and will use any stratagem to avoid being drafted. Reports from Honduras tell of the arrest and conscription of groups of students standing in line at bus stops on their way to class. Maintaining an army is the last thing that this poor country needs, but the military tradition is deeply rooted and overrides all reason.

PANAMA

Panama also has extensive banana plantations, but its oil refineries and the revenue the country receives from the operation of the Canal do not leave it dependent on this one product. The United States originally paid Panama $10 million in cash, and agreed to make additional yearly payments of $250,000 for canal rights in perpetuity in the ten-mile-wide Canal Zone strip. This annual payment was increased to $430,000 in 1933 when the dollar was devalued, and in the treaty of 1955 it was further increased to $1,930,000.

In December 1964, President Johnson announced that the United States would consult with Panama about a possible change in status of the canal strip, and would discuss with Panama and other interested Central American countries the planning of a new sealevel canal 1,000 feet wide and 250 feet deep, an unprecedented engineering project. Colombia, Costa Rica, Nicaragua, and Panama were all suggested as possible sites for the new canal. The president later proposed that the United States and Panama negotiate a new treaty that would recognize Panama's sovereignty over the canal strip, and would call for the administration of the Panama Canal by a joint U.S.–Panamanian committee, which Panama had long clamored for.

Unfortunately, settlement did not come until after there had been an explosion of resentment in Panama. During the 1960s Panamanian feelings toward the United States had risen to a fever pitch. Egypt's seizure of the Suez Canal had helped bring these feelings to a head, and both Nassar and Fidel Castro did all they could to fan the flames. In 1964 there was a full-scale anti-U.S. riot in the canal area. This was triggered by a bunch of American high school students in Balboa who had pulled down the Panamanian flag over their school and had hoisted the Stars and Stripes. In the ensuing violence twenty-four Panamanians and three U.S. soldiers were killed and hundreds were wounded before American troops brought the situation under control.

For years U.S. racial, political, and economic policies have been an irritant in Panama. There was not only the rankest kind of discrimination but U.S. employees were divided into two categories, called the "gold" and "silver" groups. Only U.S. citizens fell into the privileged "gold" category; they received twice as much pay for the same kind of work, and even had special windows in the post offices. Under President Johnson such problems were finally resolved, and Panama was exultant when the United States agreed in principal to share the canal with her.

Panama is not a self-sufficient republic; it imports five times as much as it exports. The gap was long closed by tourist spending, by canal payments, by income derived from allowing foreign ships to register under the Panamanian flag, and by Canal Zone jobs that poured $100 million a year into the economy. A thriving new shrimp industry has added millions to the national income, and "120 foreign banks keep roughly $40 billion in deposits registered here."[255] The practice of registering foreign vessels, which thus get by with lower safety standards and lower crew requirements, is a questionable one. Many such ships never enter a Panamanian port. The government of Panama had a fat treasury, but Panamanians were demanding control of the Canal itself.

In 1978 after more than thirteen years of negotiations, the United States and Panama signed two treaties in which the United States agreed to allow the Canal to be administered immediately by a binational committee, and to turn it over completely to Panama on December 31, 1999. The United States also agreed to pay Panama $10 million yearly out of the revenues of the canal (plus a percentage of the additional profits), and to give Panama $50 million a year in military aid for the next ten years. On October 1, 1979, the Canal Zone itself ceased to exist and officially became a part of the Republic of Panama. The canal continued to run smoothly, and after several years of deficits in the mid-1970s began to operate at a profit.

In the second treaty with Panama both countries agreed to maintain the neutrality of the canal after the year 2000, and the United States, much to the discomfiture of Panama, was conceded the right to intervene unilaterally should that neutrality ever appear to be threatened. This provision was added at the last minute in order to protect United States national interests, and to make possible Senate ratification of both Panama treaties, which were having very hard sledding. Ronald Reagan and other conservatives were dead set against accepting the treaties as they stood, and many senators fought vigorously against them. On April 18, 1979, the final vote was 68 to 32 in favor of the treaties.

General Omar Torrijos, who negotiated these treaties with President Carter, had seized control of the government of Panama in 1968 and abolished all political parties. The majority of the American people were opposed to turning the Canal over to him, but Washington realized: (1) the Canal was indefensible; (2) had the treaties been rejected, Torrijos, with the enthusiastic support of the people of Panama, would have assaulted the Canal, forcing the United States to take military action, thus alienating all of Latin America; (3) the United States *was* given the right to intervene unilaterally if the Canal is threatened.

Torrijos was killed in a plane crash in 1981 and General Manuel Noriega, who soon took his place as the dictator of Panama, was accused of arranging his death. There were also accusations of CIA complicity in this event. Noriega tightened his grip and became increasingly unpopular in Panama. His corruption, double-dealing, and suppression of human rights alienated thousands of his followers, and in 1987 there were mass demonstrations against his dictatorship. Free elections were called for, to no avail. The interests of the United States would be better served if elections were free and unrigged everywhere in Latin America. What our country needs in this area are governments that share our values, not governments we can control, which are inevitably doomed to fall.[255]

The Peruvian writer, Vargas Llosa, characterized Panama as a kind of pseudo democracy where "civilian authorities govern, but the National Guard rules." Noriega, as commander of the guard, was only one in a long line of military dictators who have held the real power behind the government in Panama. For many years the U.S. Department of State and the CIA were his staunch supporters and Noriega, in his turn, cooperated with them to the fullest. He was on the U.S. payroll for many years, and during this time he was involved in drug trafficking, gun running, money laundering, fraud, assassinations, and autocratic rule, but the United States turned the other way as long as he remained a key ally.[256]

Panama is of great importance to the United States, not only because of the Canal but because it is an ideal intelligence gathering and listening post for all Central America and much of northern South America. For a time Noriega lent his support to this surveillance and was well paid for it. At the opposite extreme, it should be mentioned that several hundred young Panamanians went to Moscow to study, and there began to be indications of a Marxist ideological buildup among the future intellectual and political leaders of the country.

In 1987, under increasing pressure from the United States, Noriega began to assert his independence of United States control, and he also backed away from the peace plan proposed by the other five Central American countries in the hope of achieving a negotiated settlement of the Nicaraguan conflict. Panama was not represented when this plan was drawn up in Guatemala City. In February 1988, Noriega was indicted for drug trafficking by a grand jury in Miami, and the United States began to expose his seamy side, already well known in Washington.

Noriega's growing anti-North American stand temporarily bolstered his popularity in Panama at the very time that Washington was calling for his downfall. His arbitrary rule, however, was so widely detested that some Panamanians were hoping for the Yankees to come in and help get rid of him. Noriega had made and unmade several puppet presidents of Panama, and in February 1988 when one of these, Eric Delvalle, fired him as commander of the National Guard, Noriega's friendly legislature deposed Delvalle. The entire Noriega episode is one of the most sordid ventures of U.S. Latin American policy which, on so many occasions, has supported venal and vicious military and political leaders in payment for their dubious cooperation. In so doing our country bypassed the needs of the people of those countries in whom lies our only real hope for democracy.

Throughout this stressful period Noriega stood firm against U.S. pressure for his resignation. In fact, the stronger the pressure the more support he had inside Panama where many enjoyed seeing him thumb his nose at Washington. When the Panamanian presidential elections took place in the spring of 1989, the opposition candidate, Guillermo Endara, who certainly had the moral support of the United States, was a certain loser. Noriega did not have wide enough support to win these elections honestly, but he controlled the ballot box and rigged the outcome heavily in his favor which gave him the victory. In May all ten of the country's Catholic bishops called on Noriega to resign, attacking him for massive electoral fraud and for violent assaults on his political opposition. They decried Noriega's "terrifying the hungry masses with a hateful and false nationalism that neither respects nor recognizes the rights and safety of the rest of the Panamanians." They demanded that he respect the will of the people as expressed in the recent elections which they all strongly felt had resulted in an overwhelming victory for his opponent.

The United States responded by sending additional troops to the Canal Zone, and by holding frequent and very visible maneuvers there. Noriega sat smugly tight, and in October 1989, when there was a poorly organized attempt at a coup to oust him, he turned it to his advantage. The leader of the attempted coup, who held Noriega a prisoner for three or four hours, instead of turning him over to the U.S. authorities, tried to persuade him to resign and leave the country. Noriega stalled for time, troops loyal to him moved in, the United States did nothing, and the attempted coup fell flat. It was reported that Noriega later personally held a pistol to the head of the rebellious leader and killed him.

Unable to overthrow Noriega by diplomatic pressure or intrigue, the United States on December 21, 1989, launched a full-scale military assault on Panama. This invasion and takeover was called, in Washington, Operation Just Cause. American troops and planes attacked the capital in full force and within a few hours had overcome all resistance. Several military experts called the operation "a brilliant success," much better planned and carried out than the previous invasion of the island of Grenada. Panamanians by and large looked favorably on the ousting of Noriega, who was taken into custody and flown back to the United States for trial. They did not regard the assault and invasion itself in such a kind light. After the takeover the duly elected Guillermo Endara was installed as president.[294]

This occupation of Panama must be judged as a blunder of the first magnitude. It was "an unprecedented use of American military power to overthrow and capture a single villain." Latin Americans had been brought to believe, after many decades of nonintervention, that such "big stick" diplomacy was a thing of the past. They were shocked at the invasion of a sovereign nation by American troops, remembering that the United States with great fanfare had in 1933 foresworn armed intervention in this hemisphere.

According to the official U.S. figures, the assault on Panama resulted in the death of at least 300 civilians and about the same number of Panamanian soldiers. Twenty-four American soldiers were killed, some of these by misdirected American fire. There was widespread destruction in parts of the city with damages amounting to at least a billion dollars, which left many hundreds homeless. American troops did almost nothing to prevent looters from breaking into and ransacking stores in the city. A spokesman for Panama's Chamber of Commerce said: "Our police force was nonexistent, and it was utter chaos for three days. A few American soldiers on guard at strategic points would have prevented this tragedy."

After the takeover many people were unable to verify the fate of friends and family members caught in the area, and in response to the pleas of some of these people the former attorney general of the United States, Ramsey Clark, flew to Panama to investigate personally. His report was appalling. He estimated that between 3,000 and 4,000 people had been killed, many thrown into mass graves before a proper tally could be taken. He received his information from the Red Cross, from hospitals, and from individuals who, in his judgment, were trustworthy personal observers. A few months later a television documentary on *Sixty Minutes* corroborated this mass destruction of life and property. Even if Ramsey Clark's estimate is disregarded entirely, the number of casualties given officially would be proportionately more than those suffered by the United States in the entire Vietnam War, which extended over many years. The assault on Panama has already been largely forgotten in the United States, but it will rankle in the memory of Latin Americans for decades to come.

President Endara took over the government of a country that was bankrupt and on the ropes. One-third of the labor force was unemployed, another third held government jobs in the grossly inefficient public sector; there were hundreds of homeless and thousands who were unemployed and underfed. Recovery is bound to be painfully slow, and widespread, perhaps violent, protests and impatience must be expected. All this while the government itself clearly operates as a U.S. protectorate.

Recent events in Panama have been well summarized by Stephen Van Evera, former editor of the journal *International Security*, and at present a professor at MIT. "The Bush Administration's invasion deposed the dictator Manuel Noriega and installed an elected government in his place. But the Administration also installed a sinister Noriega henchman, Colonel Eduardo Herrera Hassan, as the commander of the new Public Force, the successor to Noriega's Panamanian Defence Forces. Herrera staffed the PF with former PDF members, raising the risk that corrupt military cliques will continue to dominate the country's politics. Moreover, by invading, the United States merely sought to undo a mess of its own making. The United States created and trained the PDF; then, in 1968, the PDF destroyed Panamanian democracy, installing a junta that later gave rise to the Noriega dictatorship. Overall, U.S. policy toward Panama has not fostered democracy." [296]

As American control of the Canal is gradually being phased out, it might be well to recall that for many years the United States maintained a military school at Fort Gulick at the Atlantic end of the Canal which has given training to numerous Latin American military officers. Among these are Generals Torrijos of Panama, Pinochet of Chile, Hugo Bánzar of Bolivia, Carlos Romero of El Salvador, Romeo García of Guatemala. Since its founding in 1946 more than 36,000 Latin American military officers have attended the school at Fort Gulick. There were brief three-week seminars in administration and forty-two-week courses in military command, leadership, counterinsurgency, and *estado mayor*. North Americans generally refer to Fort Gulick as the "Army School of the Americas," but many Latin Americans have come to call it the "School for Dictators."

CUBA

The story of Cuba is unique in Latin America. It was the last Spanish colony to get its independence (1898); it granted all kinds of special privileges to the United States in the Platt Amendment, not abrogated until 1934; and it has, of course, the only Communist government in Latin America today. Cuba has never had a single efficient democratic administration since its independence. Since the first president, Estrada Palma, it has oscillated between dictatorship and civil government, with little to choose between them in the degree of corruption. The civil governments have been more tolerant, with civil liberties more secure, but politically and administratively they have all been deplorable. This is one of the primary reasons for the stunning success of Fidel Castro. Briefly, the background was as follows:

In 1933 Fulgencio Batista, a sergeant in the Cuban Army, headed a revolt of the non-commissioned officers and men in the army, and seized control of the government from dictator Machado, thus ending twelve years of brutal despotism. Batista ruled from behind the scenes until 1940, in which year he personally assumed the presidency. In 1944, partly in response to a request from Franklin Roosevelt, he allowed free elections to take place and Grau San Martín, a physician and college professor who had bravely opposed Machado, became president. Grau had the respect of all Cubans, and most especially of the intelligentsia, but his term was a complete fiasco. He was surrounded by corruption and inefficiency, and was able to do almost nothing to improve Cuba. In 1948 he was succeeded by Prío Socarrás, and again Batista, who was living like a millionaire in Miami, did not intervene. The government of Cuba went from bad to worse, and so when Batista came out of Florida in 1952 and again seized power nearly everyone in Cuba was glad.

Up to this time Batista, despite his personal plundering of the Cuban treasury, had given his country a fairly good government, some say the best the country ever had. But from 1952 to 1959, when Fidel Castro took over, his administration rapidly deteriorated, corruption grew, and Havana was turned into one vast brothel and gambling den for the entertainment of the North American tourists. There were pimps and prostitutes on every street, gambling houses were going full blast, and United States tourists were very much in evidence as participants in these activities.

Strangely, Batista allowed a considerable freedom of the press, and articles in the Cuban newspapers criticized his regime in the harshest terms. Criticism of the United States and its responsibility was also sharp. At this time United States investments in Cuba amounted to a billion dollars, covering everything from the sugarcane industry to petroleum. American enterprises paid out salaries which amounted to 71 per cent of the gross national product, and the United States bought 69 per cent of Cuba's exports, supplying 70 per cent of her imports. This imbalance of the economy naturally galled the citizens of Cuba who realized that they had won their independence but had lost their freedom to own and run their own country.

Batista was born on a poor Cuban farm and began working as a canecutter and banana picker. His older brother died of tuberculosis and malnutrition. Fulgencio himself did not own a pair of shoes and was an illiterate. In 1921 he entered the army, taught himself to read and write, and worked himself up to sergeant, winning great popularity among his men an fellow non-coms. He was only 32 when he first seized the government in 1933. His rags to riches story appealed to many Cubans, and Batista himself was a colorful mixture of all the races: Spanish, Indian, perhaps a bit of the Negro and of the Oriental.

Under him the Cuban wealthy and the Cuban middle class prospered as never before. So did the North American investors in the island. Batista built schools, roads, public works of all kinds, and both agriculture and industry flourished. But the Cuban workers did not flourish, and their discontent grew as time passed. Honesty, justice, and liberty died slow deaths. During the last years of his regime Batista alienated almost everybody. His police had begun to brutalize people, there was no justice in the courts, and there was a sickening corruption among the officials of the government. Pandering and prostitution made even a stroll down the streets a nauseating experience.

Enter Fidel Castro. Fidel, unlike Batista, was the son of a wealthy sugar planter, and held a college degree in law. He was also a perennial revolutionary. In 1953 he led a group of 165 men who tried to take the Moncada army barracks in the city of Santiago, Cuba. Many in the group were killed but Fidel and his brother Raul escaped. Months later, they came in and gave themselves up "in order to stop Batista's persecution" of other people in Santiago who were accused of having a part in the revolt. Fidel was sentenced to fifteen years in prison, but he served only eleven months and was granted amnesty.

He went to Mexico, assembled another band of followers, and in 1956 returned to Cuba, this time with 82 followers. Again, most of his men were slain, but Fidel and a handful of companions escaped to the Sierra Maestra mountains where they holed up and were never caught despite the all-out attempts of Batista's army and police. Admiration for this small, audacious band grew, country folk brought food, a few volunteers straggled in to swell their ranks, and patiently they awaited their chance.

They were wise, because all they had to do was wait. Opposition to Batista was mounting rapidly, and in January 1959 the little sergeant realized that the jig was up and fled to the Dominican Republic with his friends and his loot. Fidel Castro, now at the head of a sizable but motley militia, entered Havana and was cheered enthusiastically by the crowds. The regular Cuban army troops did not lift a finger to stop him; most of them had passed over to his side. He was their deliverer too. Batista's flight had left a political vacuum in Cuba which Fidel and his trustees very promptly filled.

Shortly afterward Fidel made a visit to the United States, where he spoke with the Secretary of State, but he was dissatisfied with his reception and returned to Cuba much affronted. He had expected the presidential red carpet. Up to this time he had been presented to the North American public as a kind of Robin Hood. The motion picture actor Errol Flynn, had visited him in his Sierra Maestra hideout, and Flynn then appeared on United States television where he stated that Fidel's revolution would give Cuba her first truly free, just, and democratic government. *The New Yorker* magazine had printed a long profile of Fidel and his activities, and he became a sort of folk hero in this country. Fidel himself, also on United States national television, had loudly denied that he was a Communist.

But after he returned to Cuba Fidel began his verbal assaults on the United

States and its imperialism. He was infuriated by what American newspapers had said about his highhanded methods and boorish manners. Then he began to take over United States-owned properties, and the United States stopped all sugar purchases from Cuba. This was a severe blow, because the United States had been paying Cuba $150,000,000 a year more for this sugar than she could have gotten in any other market. Fidel ordered that the American embassy staff be reduced to eleven, barely a sufficient janitorial force, and in January 1961, the United States broke off diplomatic relations with Cuba.

There have been no real elections in Cuba since Castro took over the government, nor will there be as long as he survives. His rule is personal. Whatever he says is the law of the land. Whatever he proclaims to be just is considered just. If he says that Cubans must work overtime for their country, they do so. If he says that a man must be executed or released that man is executed or released. If he announces a certain kind of economic or social reform, it is immediately and enthusiastically adopted.

The Cubans accept but do not originate the changes that Fidel so vociferously proclaims. There was and is no great popular demand for the particular things that he is doing. True, Castro has proclaimed himself as a Communist, but his regime is quite unlike that of Russia or China. Cuba is not ruled by a closely knit and well-trained Communist clique; it is ruled by Fidel Castro. And Castro would rule Cuba no matter what he called himself. When he dies no one can predict what the results may be.[190]

Castro fell into the vacuum that Batista had left behind. He had no real army, no organized labor support, no political party behind him, yet the immense majority of the Cuban people wanted him as their leader. Overnight he became personally responsible for everything. Fidel pointed out how corrupt all previous parties had been in Cuba, as he made a clean sweep of all officials replacing them with his own trusted followers. He did the same thing in the army. Army officers are now constantly moved about and their duties frequently altered in order not to allow them any chance to organize a resistance. And Castro today has at his *personal* command one of the most powerful military forces in Latin America.

Fidel had promised that he would put an end to *relajo* government. The word as used in Cuba synthesized the national pre-Castro character of the people; it means "slap-happy, hit or miss administration, shot through with inefficiency and graft." Before Castro appeared on the scene practically everything in Cuba was a *relajo*, a big fat joke.

At first Castro, prodded and persuaded by his right-hand man, the Argentine Che Guevara, had dreams of spreading his revolution all over Latin America, while the nerve center remained in Havana. The capture and death of Che Guevara, in Bolivia in 1967, made this impossible. Fidel and Che had hoped to plant a new *focus* of the Cuban revolution in Bolivia, in the very heart of South America. The Bolivian army, with some astute aid from the CIA, dramatically put an end to that plan. Che Guevara's death was a traumatic experience for Fidel and indeed for all Cuban revolutionaries, and forced them to become much more nationalistic. After Che's death there was an immediate surge of interest in Cuban history, the country's national heroes, its early struggle for independence and its search for self-identity.

Two Bolivian journalists, Luis J. González and Gustavo A. Sánchez, in their book *The Great Rebel*, give a detailed and relatively dispassionate account of Che's activities and violent death in Bolivia. He was captured alive but was executed in cold blood on direct orders from Bolivian President Barrientos. His small guerrilla band had been in desperate straits for months. They were all ill, they suffered terribly from lack of water, they were surrounded and isolated, and there was no hope of escape. Not one single Bolivian peasant had been converted to their cause. Che had broken every rule outlined in his own book on guerrilla warfare. There had been many defectors, who became informers, and Che never really had a chance. After his death, however, peasants began to come in from the remote corners of the province to buy his picture, taking it to the church to be blessed. They have an astounding reverence for the dead and believe that those who die tragically "have the power to answer requests for miracles."[191]

Fidel drew in his antennae and exalted the glory of Cuba, where conditions called for a further tightening of the belt. Many Cubans were in despair at the protracted deprivations. Lacking United States aid and having no way to obtain spare parts for his automobiles, tractors and machines of all kinds made Fidel dependent on Western Europe and on Russia, particularly on Russia, who has footed the bill for Cuba's deficit in her foreign exchange balance. The Soviet Union was pouring over a *billion dollars a year* into Cuba in order to sustain the economy. For this reason Russia was in no mood to give her support to Fidelista revolutions in other Latin American countries. Indeed, the Communists of Chile not only turned on the Chilean Fidelistas, but turned them in. With five or six Fidelista regimes to support in Latin America the Soviet Union would soon face bankruptcy.

Fidel is not a new phenomenon in Latin American life. He is merely the old *caudillo* brought sharply up to date. The coming decades will have many more caudillos like him. Fidel's significance lies in that he is the first truly twentieth-century leader. He uses the radio, television, the public rostrum, the political forum, the school auditorium, or indeed any stage or lectern to proclaim his beliefs and to pontificate his solutions. His harangues go on for hours and hours. He is without a doubt the longest-winded Latin American caudillo of history. But he possesses the charisma, the magic which has enabled him to gain power and enables him to hold onto power, and now that he has it in his hands he cannot divide it, delegate it, or pass it on to any successor. He is stuck with *la suma del poder*, absolute power, until he dies or until the Cuban people get tired of him and replace him. His enemies refer to him as *el caballo* (the horse) because his words come out kicking like a horse and because they believe he has no more ability to rule than a horse. Fidelistas say that he is "strong as a horse," and then retaliate by calling all who refuse enthusiastic cooperation with the regime *gusanos* (worms). It has been an effective epithet.

There is no doubt that Castro has achieved many things for Cuba. In the first place, he has built schools by the thousands, and it is now claimed, perhaps with truth, that illiteracy has been completely eliminated in the island. Many of the teachers are army officers or young folks under twenty with only a modicum of education themselves, but they know more than their pupils, and this is what they are able to pass on. Fidel also brought Cuba a relatively honest government. In the early years, his officials did not plunder the treasury. Bribery was not a way of life among them as it had been in the past. There was very little corruption but almost no freedom. Prostitution and public gambling had been pushed underground. The whole country was on a moralistic binge and the strong hand of the government reached into every activity. Fidel even closed down the bars and cabarets for a time, but workers who couldn't get a glass of beer complained, and the ban was lifted.

The once promised tens of thousands of small farms for rural Cuban families have not materialized, and instead there are now large government cooperatives. There is a shortage of many foods, of clothes, of drugs. About 30 per cent of the gross national product goes into developmental projects, which has meant a program of austerity for the average Cuban family with a sharp deterioration in living conditions for everybody. But the cry is that this is all for the country; sacrifice is necessary to make Cuba independent and productive, sacrifice is needed to make Cuba great.

Around Havana is a 100,000-acre "green belt," on which the city workers volunteer to labor at night, planting coffee, vegetables, and fruit, often spending four hours in the fields without pay after a long day's work in town. The revolution has clearly directed its main energy and resources into the countryside to the detriment of the city. Havana is an unimpressive capital. The state has taken over nearly all industries and businesses, even the barbers, jewelry shops, shoemakers, laundries, 55,000 small businesses in all. Services are often aggravatingly slow. Laundry may not be returned for a month or six weeks, whereas formerly it took less than a week.

The Cuban peso has maintained its value in the international market, but inside Cuba money is virtually worthless because there is so little to buy. Each individual is rationed to receive one shirt, one pair of pants or one dress, and two sets of underwear a year. Many stores are open only one morning in the week, so short is their supply. There are long lines in front of the grocery stores, the clothing shops, the restaurants, where an average meal can easily cost $20. A nine-year-old refrigerator will bring $1,000, a 1970 medium-priced car $10,000, a set of tires $1,000. Each Cuban is rationed to three fourths of a pound of meat a week, only children receive fresh milk, and chickens are almost unobtainable. The state economy, of course, is lacking in qualified personnel, and red tape bogs down everything. The more loyal invariably replace the more efficient.

Yet there are 150,000 young Cuban students on scholarships with free room, board, and tuition, and the younger generation is deeply indoctrinated in the ideals of the revolution. They proclaim passionately that they would gladly sacrifice their lives for it. Everywhere in Cuba the young have risen to positions of authority. Fidel has not spent lavishly on showy buildings, but he has done some very strange things, as for instance building an eight-lane highway half way across Cuba when there are scarcely enough cars for a two-way road. The justification given is: "We'll need it someday, perhaps sooner than you think."

Cuba, economically, still depends mainly on sugar, which accounts for 85 per cent of its export trade. Yearly production of this product averages six to eight million tons, but all this sugar plus all of the country's other exports still leave a large exchange deficit. Cuba has been extremely anxious to build up trade with Western Europe as well as with Russia, which means that Fidel's government absolutely must honor its export commitments, leaving many essential products in short supply on the island. They are made still shorter because there is in Cuba today so little that money can buy, and the small farmer refuses to plant or will not deliver any excess produce. Only the cooperative farms can deliver these goods.

While Fidel has been unable, even with a controlled economy, to produce all of the things Cuba needs, he was able to stamp out unemployment almost completely. A total of perhaps one million workers have been materially aided by the revolution, while the well-to-do and the Cuban middle class have been almost eliminated. Half a million of them have emigrated to the United States. By allowing these people to leave Cuba Castro rid himself of his principal enemies, and provided the United States with a sizeable refugee problem. But by 1969 this problem had been solved, for there was an unemployment rate of only 1 per cent among these exiles, who quickly adapted to their new way of life. The exodus continues, with additional emigrés leaving Cuba every month.

Fidel insists on giving his developmental goals first priority, and this inevitably means increased regimentation. As a result the national economy is becoming almost completely militarized. Many Cuban intellectuals have observed this process with diminishing hope and are now beginning to feel a strong sense of resentment against the regime.

In 1970 everything was sacrificed in order to meet Fidel's goal of ten million tons of sugar which was needed to build up the foreign exchange. Workers left other jobs to cut sugarcane, and the entire economy suffered a severe jolt. Only eight and a half million tons of sugar were produced, most of it bought by Russia at double the world market price. But overused and unrepaired trucks broke down, beef could not reach the cities, milk production decreased by 25 per cent, stores and markets were more empty than ever. Long lines and empty shelves took away the drive to work and there was much absenteeism and inefficiency among workers. The poor worker is almost never fired.

Cubans were allowed only two cigars and two packages of cigarettes a week;

the rest must be exported. For five months there was no beer because of a shortage of bottles. Beer is now rationed at two bottles a week. And yet the Communist elite have plenty of cigars and cigarettes, and two thousand Alfa Romeos were imported from Italy for their exclusive benefit. Castro himself went on the air and took the blame for most of Cuba's troubles. "It is easier to make a revolution than to make a revolution work," he said. So far the Cuban revolution has been a managerial disaster, as those with managerial skills left the country almost en masse. Cuba is still tied to a one-crop sugar economy. Industrial dreams have not materialized. Fidel's sister, Juana, now an exile in Miami, characterized the regime saying: "Cuba is a prison surrounded by water."

In the decade 1970–80 economic conditions improved considerably inside Cuba. The rate of growth averaged at least 7 per cent a year. Everything from food to clothing was still rationed, but there was now also a legal parallel market where for one-and-a-half times the rationed prices many goods could be bought freely. Outside the law there exists a flourishing black market where certain hard-to-get necessities like meat can be purchased. Each person is rationed one pound of meat every ten days and one ounce of coffee a week.

A few luxury items began to appear again in the windows: cameras, perfumes, toilet articles, and the like. Even automobiles became more plentiful, but the preferred mode of transportation is the motorcycle with sidecar attached. There are very few bicycles. There are long well-behaved lines before many of the stores, movie houses, and restaurants. Ice cream parlors are very popular, boys play baseball in almost every vacant lot, and old men play dominoes in lighted underground garages until one or two at night. Cubans have money, but there is very little to buy.

There are fewer soldiers on the streets than formerly, and although many armed men are on patrol or guard, especially in front of government buildings, there is no arrogance or swagger in evidence. Things are much more relaxed than they were in the 1960s. Few pictures or images of Fidel Castro are on public display, but busts of José Martí, Cuba's liberator, are visible everywhere. Women still do not walk the streets alone without hearing the proverbial *piropo*, sometimes a compliment, sometimes a proposition. The 40,000 or so Cuban soldiers who went to serve in Africa are regarded as heroes, and are often compared to the Poles and French who aided the United States in its struggle against British colonial rule. This African venture, however, was regarded as a mistake by a sizeable contingent, especially those who had lost sons or brothers in the conflict.

The Soviet Union poured an average of $2.8 million into Cuba every day during the decade 1980–90, and the total Cuban debt to Russia rose to something like $10 billion. It has been said that Cuban soldiers sent to Africa are in part a repayment for this vast Russian investment in the country. These troops have acquitted themselves well as fighters and technicians, but Cuba could not afford to indefinitely station in Africa the flower of its youth, its most competent managers, and its most skilled technicians.[224]

> Indeed, the armed forces—born of necessity in the 1960's, spectacularly successful abroad in the 1970's—may become Cuba's albatross in the 1980's. Wars without end are wars without purpose, and Cuba's African wars may be acquiring these features. The burden on Cuba—in lives, suffering, property and the lost opportunities for growth—is already quite high, and rising. Cuba soon may have to choose between costly honor and influence abroad and the mundane need to provide a safe and decent life for its citizenry at home.

Cuban troops abroad are sometimes called by natives of the countries they are supporting "Latin Legions" and "Prussians of Africa."[225]

The rationing system, originally the symbol of equality, may be becoming the new dispensary of privilege. Access to consumer goods, to vacation resorts, to trips abroad, are all rationed. Preference is always given to "good revolutionaries." Revolutionary virtue had once been its own reward, but this seems no longer to be the case. In the early Castro years

> the Cuban revolution's claim to legitimacy had not been that it was efficient; it had been that it was right. Now Cubans are being told that those in power shall have greater access to the good things of life as rewards for their burdens of leadership. As a clarion call for the 1980's, it sounds distinctly less rousing than earlier calls for egalitarianism.[226]

The church has never been a problem in Cuba, and under Castro a large degree of freedom of religion is practiced. One almost gets the feeling that the government encourages it. The numerically small group of Jehovah's Witnesses, who refuse to serve in the armed forces or to salute the flag, are the only religious minority that is not tolerated. The city of Havana is drab-looking, its streets are filled with potholes, and there is no feeling of brightness or prosperity. American blue jeans have become widely popular, and visiting Americans are offered incredible prices for their own. There are a few bright spots in the city: military installations, schools, hospitals, offices of the Communist party and its local committees are all marked with colorful and decorative signs that are lighted up like those advertising commercial establishments in the United States.

Censorship has relaxed, and writers who could not have been published ten or fifteen years ago now appear in print without difficulty. Many libraries have been established, and the publishing industry is very active. The National Dance Company, under the direction of the incomparable Alicia Alonso, has given many performances in the United States which were received with great enthusiasm. Cuba has also been eagerly training doctors, dentists, nurses, paramedics, and for this purpose medical texts were pirated out of the United States.

Agricultural cooperatives are strongly encouraged. Loans made to these groups are at a low 4 per cent, and many farmers living in the country just outside Havana who agreed to lease their lands to the state, leave their thatched huts, and join the collective farms, were given color television sets and refrigerators. All sports are encouraged, and outstanding athletes are subsidized by the government. In basketball, long distance running, and boxing, Cuban athletes have distinguished themselves in the Olympic Games.

Relations with the United States have greatly improved. In 1973 Cuba and the United States signed a hijacking agreement guaranteeing the extradition of all hijackers except valid political refugees. Between 1961 and 1973 eight-five airplanes of American and Canadian origin had been hijacked and flown to Cuba. Since the agreement there have been almost none. In 1975 the United States and fifteen Latin American countries voted to end the OAS sanctions against Cuba. In 1977 Castro stated publicly that he had released all but two or three thousand of the 15,000 admitted political prisoners. Remaining in prison were those guilty of hardened crimes against individuals. In September 1977 the United States and Cuba exchanged diplomatic representatives, calling them "counselors" rather than ambassadors. The U.S. contingent in Havana was affixed to the Swiss Embassy. Castro made strong overtures toward the United States for full diplomatic recognition and a lifting of the economic embargo imposed by this country. President Carter responded that until Cuba agreed to reimburse U.S. companies for the $1.8 billion of properties confiscated, and also withdrew its troops from Africa, full diplomatic recognition would be withheld.

Castro has allowed the Cubans living in the United States, nearly all of them exiles from his regime, to return to Cuba and visit their friends and families. Formerly referred to as "worms," these exiles are presently being called "overseas Cubans," and the red carpet is thrown out for them when they enter Cuba. Cubans who wish to leave the country for the United States are granted such permission with increasing readiness. Castro is obviously still anxious for recognition and a lifting of the embargo, hoping that another American president may see the light.

Already 35,000 Canadian tourists a year visit Cuba. U.S. tourist operators have begun to run package tours to Cuba, out of Miami. Varadero's harbor has been modernized at a cost of $500,000 and foreign yachts now anchor there frequently. Cyrus Eaton, Jr., son of the famous Eaton of the Eastern Europe trade agreements, is planning to build a $200 million tourist complex in Cuba, possibly in Cayo Sabinal island, off the coast of Camaguey, 350 miles from Havana. There are beautiful beaches here, and vast open spaces. This development would be the largest of its kind in the world. Cubans would own it, and would pay Eaton back for his investment out of the profits. Cuba desperately needs tourist money in order to decrease its foreign trade deficit.

Cuba is clearly a thorn in the side of the United States. U.S. actions helped to place Castro in power, U.S. criticisms and threats helped to entrench his position, and the United States is now paying the piper. All Cubans unite at the drop of a hat behind the cry of Yankee imperialism, and so will the citizenry of any other Latin American country. Knowing this, Cuba will play a very steady and a very stealthy hand in Nicaragua, in Salvador, in Guatemala, wherever the opportunity is afforded. In the meantime, Soviet pilots are manning the Russian-made MIGs that provide Cuba's air defense, and Soviet planners are helping to direct the economic and political policies of the Cuban government.

If there is a privileged class in Cuba today, aside from the ruling elite, it is the Cuban children. They are treated well and are given everything. There is medical service even in the remote rural areas among people who never had any before. Telephones are free. Most farms have electricity. These countryfolk live and eat better than they ever did before. We must learn from the Cuban experience that people who are hungry would rather have food than free speech; people who are sick would rather have medicine than fair elections.

The Cuban revolution, or as it probably should be called, Fidelismo, has already made many converts in other Latin American countries. Castro did not need any Che Guevara to achieve this. But with Che's death Fidelismo ceased to be a monolithic movement and is taking different forms in different countries, fashioning itself after such charismatic local leaders as may arise to lead the people. Great national leaders have not as yet arisen, but it is almost certain that sooner or later they will. The result will probably be a series of very nationalistic revolutions. All of these will most certainly be anti-United States. They will also be strongly anti-latifundia and anti-big business, especially if the business represents a foreign investment. These are the qualities of the Cuban revolution that Latin American liberals, especially young liberals, admire.

Young rebels in the other Latin American countries all stress the need, indeed the inevitability, of such revolutions in their own lands. This is bound to smack of communism to North Americans because of the Cuban experience, but it is not necessarily communism at all. It does signify a need for fundamental and drastic changes in the old stratified economic and social order. Communism is only the final desperate attempt to solve the problem. How the United States meets this challenge will determine future hemispheric relations.

Despite the positive achievements of the Castro regime, Fidel's popularity in Cuba began to wane in the 1980s. The economy was in a deplorable state, and in 1987 there was a 45 per cent decrease in the profits from export trade. The government reversed its policy of benevolent controls and imposed new restrictions. Castro tightened the belt in order to rescue the economy; there were cuts in electricity and in the rations of milk, rice, meat, and gasoline. Long lines of Cubans waited throughout the night in order to make sure of getting into Havana's largest department store (formerly Sears) where surplus government goods are sold. Shortages and high prices continue. A small bar of chocolate costs two dollars. A good steak or a leg of lamb are impossible to obtain. A stifling bureaucracy directs the daily lives of the people. Filling out government forms has proliferated to the point of insanity. Buying a few bricks, a pane of glass to fix a broken window, or a can of paint, requires filling out long permits and entails a long delay. The list of government ministries in the Havana telephone book takes up seventy-seven pages. Cubans restively read press reports of recent Soviet openness and flexibility, but find no evidence of such a change in Cuba.

Out of a total Cuban population of just over six million in 1959, one million Cubans have fled from the country since Castro's takeover in that year. One of these refugees, Alberto Montaner, now a syndicated columnist in Miami, wrote that this exodus has weakened Castro's international image, and has hindered the consolidation of the regime. The hope of someday being able to leave Cuba has caused many Cubans to resist making an accommodation with the government. Unable to oppose the regime directly, these discontented citizens take advantage of every opportunity not to cooperate. It has been reported that in several factories in the urban centers the rate of absenteeism is regularly around 20 per cent.[258]

Manufactured goods account for only 5 per cent of Cuban exports, the same as it was thirty years ago. Other Latin American countries have shown substantial increases in manufactured exports on which a progressive economy basically depends. Cuban agricultural production stands at only 20 per cent above the level of prerevolutionary days, even though the population is 66 per cent greater. Unemployment, almost nonexistent during the early years of the regime, has risen to almost 100,000 workers. Per capita income in 1990 was about $1,700, as compared with Canada's $15,000. More than 75 per cent of the island's trade is with Russia. Russia agreed to suspend repayment on Cuba's debt, now about $10 billion. Despite these weaknesses the regime itself is not about to collapse because of internal pressures, discontent, or economic difficulties. A well-organized, well-disciplined, and dedicated Communist government, with a large and well-paid army, plus the solid support of the Soviet Union, make this very unlikely.

In the summer of 1987 two of Castro's high-ranking supporters inside Cuba defected to the United States: Air Force general Rafael del Pino Díaz, and a much decorated major in Cuban intelligence, Florencio Aspillaga Lombard, who brought with him a complete list of the names and activities of Castro's foreign intelligence personnel. These defections were not in any way connected, as neither man knew about the other. Del Pino Díaz and Aspillaga both then broadcasted on Radio Martí, the U.S. radio channel beamed toward Cuba, and revealed many disillusioning details about Fidel's lavish life-style and the growing corruption of the regime. It was reported that Castro has a private fleet of yachts and keeps a luxury residence in each of Cuba's fourteen provinces. It was also reported that Fidel had stashed away several million dollars in a private Swiss bank account, and that he had set aside hundreds of dwellings in Havana for his security guards and aides—all this at a time of critical housing shortage on the island.[257]

Numerous housing units have been constructed since the Revolution began in 1959, but construction has not kept pace with population growth. Because of poor construction and inferior building materials these apartments are now dilapidated. No paint is available to brighten them up, no glass to repair their windows, no bricks to restore walkways or bolster falling walls. Electricity and water are turned on five or six hours a day, and sometimes less.

After more than thirty years of Castro rule the Cuban Revolution is deep in the red. The trade deficit is estimated to be $20 billion, now listed as a debt to the Soviet Union. By longstanding agreement Russia subsidizes Cuba's sugar production by paying as much as four times the market price for this product, a total of more than $2 billion a year. Each year the Soviet Union has been giving Cuba approximately $1 billion in economic aid and over half a billion in military aid. There are about 3,500 Soviet troops in Cuba and some 10,000 Soviet civilian technicians.

Gorbachev visited Cuba in 1989 and asked Castro to use this Soviet aid more effectively, to cut down on the overweighted Cuban bureaucracy, and to do some restructuring in the economy and in the government. Castro turned a cold shoulder to all of these proposals. He bristled at the implication that Cuba might be regarded elsewhere in the world as a Soviet colony. Castro is a dyed-in-the-wool Communist, completely dedicated and self-assured, who insists on following a very orthodox line. He does not like what has happened in Poland, East Germany, the Balkans, and inside Russia itself.

Cuba is suffering from all of the ills to which Russians themselves have become so accustomed: very little to buy, long waiting lines, a dire shortage in housing, not much to eat, discontented workers. Castro is aware of these insufficiencies, but has been unable to do much about them. On the contrary, he points with pride to Cuba's notable strides in public health, education, and in clean and "honest" government. He is proud that literacy in Cuba now stands at 96 per cent. He boasts that he has eradicated prostitution and political corruption, and is carrying on the most vigorous and most successful antidrug campaign of any country in the hemisphere. He will go to almost any extreme to protect his image. In mid-1989, when a handful of highly placed Cuban military officers were caught drug trafficking, four of them were summarily executed after highly publicized televised trials. There is considerable evidence that these trials and executions were a cynical charade to bolster Castro's image as "Mr. Clean," and to tighten his grip on the country. Juan Antonio Rodríguez, a longtime Cuban intelligence officer who defected to the United States, testified that Castro himself was surreptitiously involved in the drug traffic which, he said, brings into Cuba millions of dollars of desperately needed hard cash each year.

Cuba's depressed and deteriorating economy is making life increasingly difficult and unpleasant for the people at large. A recent British visitor, Carlo Gebler, in his book, Riding through Cuba, noted that the Cubans he saw no longer felt that their island radiated revolutionary fervor and reform, but that on the contrary, it was "a sullen, miserable place, full of police spies and resignation." Many of Castro's schemes for improving things have been harebrained and totally unworkable. For example, years ago he took over hundreds of acres of land in fruit and vegetable farms in order to plant coffee trees, the produce of which could be exported. But coffee trees would not grow on this terrain, and today Cubans cannot find sufficient fruit or even beans in their markets.

The Soviet Union's reduction of aid to the economy has also resulted in severe shortages of flour, bread, machine parts, razor blades, appliances, television sets, and many other items. In Cuba today almost everything is rationed. This means that while everybody does get something, nobody gets enough. Cuba has relied on the East bloc for nearly 90 per cent of its imports and exports. Aside from her artificially pumped-up sugar profits, Cuba also generates foreign exchange by reselling oil that Russia supplies in large quantities at cut-rate prices. The recent decline in the price of petroleum was the *coup de grace* for this bonanza. The U.S. trade embargo further depresses the supply of many necessary goods.

Despite all these things, Castro personally has been able to maintain an impressive level of popularity. He has not alienated himself from the masses like Ceaucescu in Romania. He still mingles freely among the crowds, hears their complaints, promises to improve things, gives an encouraging slap on the back. But his support has clearly waned, and the dramatic changes in Eastern Europe and Nicaragua are making Cubans question their future as never before. Transmissions from U.S. Radio Martí and Television Martí keep the people well informed.

In spite of the gradual relaxing of governmental inhibitions, Cuba today is still very much a police state. It stands alone with China in the scope of its repression. Everyone in Cuba spies on everyone else. The people in general live in a kind of resigned, passive state that is both omnipresent and terribly depressing. Spying is the cruelest evil of the Castro regime, for its pervades every place and every human activity. Cubans are routinely given *Opinion Collection Forms* that they pass on to the police after listing all critical comments on Cuba overheard anywhere. The good revolutionary takes notes on the daughter's boyfriend, the wife or husband's cousins, the brother-in-law, neighbors, working companions, conversations with strangers made while standing in one of those endless Cuban lines, even something overheard in the darkness of a theater. Carefully noted also is the place the comment was made, the identity of the speaker, and the reactions of the nearby listeners. By definition every Cuban is either a good revolutionary, or an enemy of the revolution, and spying reports often determine in which category one is placed.[295]

Censorship is not as rigorous as it once was, but the press is 100 per cent official, contrary viewpoints are not permitted, and what is going on to democratize Europe and Russia is not fully reported. The Colombian Nobel Laureate, García Márquez, who is perhaps Castro's closest foreign friend, is the one notable author whose works do not even go to the censor, but when he recently interviewed Gorbachev on Soviet peristroika, which García Márquez enthusiastically endorses, the interview was not permitted to be reported inside Cuba. García Márquez has frequently praised Castro, making him out to be an almost mythological hero, capable of the most incredible feats. He reported that Fidel sleeps only five or six hours a night, but regularly reads 200 pages of news reports while eating breakfast, and during the rest of the day peruses and digests at least fifty documents, with time left over for his verbose speeches. Also, Fidel has an extremely wide range of knowledge, says García Márquez. Once a doctor friend gave him a scholarly article on orthopedic procedures, and Castro not only read the report but returned it with detailed marginal comments.

Quite another opinion of Castro was given by Jacobo Timerman, a well-known Argentine author, who has written important books on both Argentina and Chile. He recently traveled across Cuba in an automobile and came into contact with a large cross section of the population. To Timerman García Márquez's remarks on Castro were unbelievable. In his own report on Cuba, after summarizing the Colombian's panegyric, he ironically concludes: "Fidel Castro, thus, has a secret method, unknown to the rest of mankind, for sleeping only briefly, for reading quickly, and he has a great knowledge about orthopedics, yet thirty years after the revolution he has not managed to organize a system for making and distributing bread." [295]

It is hard to understand why Castro still insists that he has wiped out prostitution in Cuba, whereas this is obviously not so. Prostitution is not as blatant as it was in pre-Castro days, but it is widely in evidence, especially where foreigners congregate. Many prostitutes are young college girls out on the town. They usually do not ask money for their services, much preferring to spend a couple of nights with their pickup at a nice hotel or on Varadero beach, where they can enjoy comforts and good food not available to ordinary Cubans, and at the same time have access to hotel specialty shops where they can load up on lipstick, makeup cream, mascara, and other items dear to a young girl's heart. Tourists are not rationed and buy whatever they want.

A few final comments on Castro, the man, and Castro the Comandante. Official mail is addressed to him as follows: *Comandante Fidel Castro Ruz, Commander-in-Chief, First Secretary of the Cuban Communist Party, President of the State Council, President of the Council of Ministers.* In conversation he is generally referred to simply as El Comandante. For years his long-winded speeches were not only listened to but praised, for Castro was both a teacher and a hero to his people. Thus it was incumbent on them to listen and for him to repeat ad infinitum those things that his people must learn about the Revolution. Now at last the Comandante's omniscience is beginning to be questioned and his rhetoric is beginning to sound a little thin. The Cuban spirit, at first impassioned by his words, is now frustrated and benumbed by the country's endless shortages and the suppression of freedom and human rights. It is probably true that Castro did more for Cuba than any other Latin American dictator was able to achieve for his own country, but he has led all Cubans down a dead-end street. He has become for his people the epitome of a broken dream.

The end result of all this is that now there is a real possibility that Castro may lose his position as the number one man in Cuba. Unfortunately, riddance of Castro would be no assurance of an improvement in the Cuban government, for if Fidel's younger brother, Raúl, should take over—he is the logical successor—conditions would almost certainly become much worse. Castro is still a hero and a beacon for the revolutionaries of the other Latin American nations who applaud his having kicked the United States out of Cuba and gotten away with it.

VENEZUELA

Venezuela has made incredible progress since the end of World War II, politically, economically, culturally. Her government has straightened out and become one of the most democratic and honest in Latin America, oil has continued to provide an enormous income for the state thus facilitating social progress, and 800,000 European immigrants have entered the country since 1946 thus swelling the ranks of the middle class. Most of these immigrants arrived at the peak of their productive power, their education already paid for by their native lands. Venezuela was catapulted into the twentieth century.

This was not achieved without passing through a period of trial which would vex the most optimistic. In the first decade after the death of Gómez (1935–45) there were brave attempts at democratic government, but the military was always in the wings and often in the palace. Not until 1945 when Rómulo Betancourt became provisional president did things level off. He governed wisely and well for three years, wiped out malaria in a dramatic health campaign, and prepared the way for the country's first honest elections which took place in 1947. Venezuela's most honored writer, Rómulo Gallegos, was elected president by an overwhelming vote.

Gallegos was the author of several novels and short stories dealing with Venezuelan life. In his most famous novel, *Doña Bárbara*, 1929, he had delineated clearly the crucial problem of his country: the struggle between civilization and barbarism. His Caracas-educated hero, Santos Luzardo, returned to his rundown country estate inspired with the desire to bring law to the barbaric hinterland. Unwilling to use force, Santos Luzardo strives for justice in the courts. In encounter after dramatic encounter he wins out over the forces of evil and darkness, represented by Doña Bárbara, and the novel closes with his marriage to Doña Bárbara's illegitimate daughter, thus symbolically marking the end of an epoch.

Gallegos wrote this novel in exile from the Gómez dictatorship. It was the fictional expression of a beautiful dream, but it did not represent the Venezuelan social reality. The novelist was indulging himself in wishful thinking: let the faith be strong enough and the reality will follow. When Gallegos assumed the presidency, his supporters were also inspired with that belief. Before the year was out they witnessed his defeat by the harsh and ugly hand of venal politics. Gallegos' program, from which he would not budge, was considered too liberal by the military, and the president was too trusting and too idealistic for his own good. Scarcely ten months after he had been sworn in, a military escort accompanied Gallegos from the palace to the airport where he was put on a plane for Havana and another long period of exile. In Havana he spoke before a gathering which this writer attended, and gave the impression of a frustrated and broken man. He later came to the United States, where his son was educated at the University of Oklahoma, and then he departed for Mexico.

The junta that displaced Gallegos was followed by Pérez Jiménez, who was another Gómez insofar as his political machinations were concerned, but he was a Gómez brought up to date. He crushed all "Communists" and dissidents with an iron hand, and turned his capital into a modern city. A seventy-million-dollar four-lane highway was constructed to connect Caracas to the sea, and skyscrapers rose suddenly in the heart of town where colonial buildings had stood before. But Pérez Jiménez acted as if the Venezuelan countryside did not exist. He exploited its colonial economy for his plush capital but did not lift a finger to alleviate its age-old destitution.

The foreign club set did well under the government of Pérez Jiménez, but the country staggered. The medieval torture chamber returned to daily life, the filthy jails were filled with political prisoners, as the president quickly built up his private bank account. He visited the United States under Eisenhower and Dulles and was warmly greeted and honored with the Order of Merit. Decent Latin Americans shuddered. In 1958, with the mob at his heels, he fled from Caracas to Miami. According to the New York *Times* his fortune amounted to something like half a *billion* dollars. He promptly bought a sumptuous $300,000 home, and provided himself with a yacht, five automobiles, and a retinue of bodyguards and numerous servants. His bodyguards were ex-Miami policemen to whom he paid salaries of $1,000 a month. Rómulo Betancourt again assumed the presidency, and with his sure hand soon returned the country to solvency and honor.

The Betancourt government asked for the extradition of Pérez Jiménez, and after several legal delays this was finally granted. It was the first time that a head of state had been extradited from the United States. Pérez Jiménez blamed Robert Kennedy, then Attorney General, for the whole thing, crying that he was innocent of the charges against him. When he got back to Venezuela he was incarcerated in a comfortable suite in the country's most modern jail.

Betancourt was the first honestly elected president of Venezuela who was able to serve out his full term and then peacefully pass the office on to his successor. He was followed by a long line of democratically elected presidents. Betancourt's wise leadership and steady judgment made this possible. At first it was very hard sledding. Immediately after his inauguration Betancourt was attacked by both the right and the left. Leftist sentiment was running high after Fidel Castro's triumph in Cuba.

Betancourt had supported Castro in his struggle against Batista, but when Fidel announced his communism, the two men parted company. Castro sympathizers and other leftists in Venezuela turned on Betancourt with a vengeance. There were two serious mutinies at Venezuelan naval bases which were suppressed with considerable bloodshed. In 1962 leftists and rightists ganged together to foment widespread disorders and acts of terrorism in an attempt to discredit the Betancourt government. The president, realizing that democracy itself was at stake, clamped down with full force. The discovery of a large cache of weapons, supplied by Castro (September 1963), helped to turn the tide in Betancourt's favor. Betancourt appealed to the OAS, which had already expelled Castro from that organization, to apply sanctions against Cuba, and this action was approved.

The overall evaluation of Betancourt's presidency is extremely positive. Not only did he show a wise hand politically but under Betancourt's administration Venezuela began to make progress in every aspect of the national life. Schools and industries arose in the hinterland and a nationwide sanitation drive soon gave the country the lowest infant mortality rate in South America. Betancourt was succeeded by his labor minister, Raúl Leoni, a worthy lawyer, who continued the policies of his predecessor. Land distribution to small farmers was increased and the country's mineral resources became the focus of an all-out development program.

Capitalist oil has made much of this progress possible; the rest has been accomplished by the hard work and the alert government of the Venezuelan people. The country's petroleum deposits, discovered in 1917, are among the richest in the world, and provided between 60 and 70 per cent of the national revenue. In fact, oil profits for years emptied into the national treasury between three and four million dollars *every single day* of the year. Oil still provides about 70 per cent of Venezuela's foreign exchange, and helps to give it the highest per capita income of any Latin American country, almost $3,000. For many years foreign companies took 34 per cent of the profits, while the government received 66 per cent. A generation ago foreign interests got 80 per cent of the revenues. All foreign concessions terminated in 1976, but geologists believe that the fields themselves will play out by 2000, so Venezuela does not have much time to get her economic house in order.

Education has surged ahead in the past decade, and hundreds of new schools have been provided for the remote areas where none existed before. The rate of illiteracy has decreased dramatically. Improved nutrition, better medical care, and a well-organized program of hygiene have increased the life span to sixty-six years. The agrarian reform agency has distributed over seven million acres of land since 1960, and 200,000 additional families will receive small farms in the next five years. Only those portions of the large estates that are not productive are expropriated and distributed. In order to make these new farms more appealing the government has built 5,000 miles of roads so that the produce can get to the markets, and has also established schools, clinics, credit, and agricultural specialists to help the small farmer. Farm produce has increased at a rapid rate. Only recently has Venezuela become self-sufficient in eggs, poultry, and beef. A system of levees has been built across the Orinoco delta which will bring 500,000 additional acres of land under cultivation.

Every attempt has been made to diversify the economy. A whole new city was built from scratch at Santo Tomé 350 miles out in the bush, and about 67 miles downriver from Ciudad Bolívar, near the site of huge iron and aluminum deposits. Not far upriver is one of the largest hydroelectric dams in the world; it produces twice the power of the largest United States dam, Grand Coulee. Santo Tomé already has a population of over 200,000, and is growing rapidly. Access to Caracas is by air, but the Orinoco is navigable to the sea for freight. Santo Tomé may become a metropolis of one million before many years have passed. A $350 million steel plant has already been constructed here, which now produced 3,750,000 tons of steel a year and by 1995 will produce 8 million tons; new shops and homes have risen, and the whole country points to the booming project with justifiable pride.

This is the part of Venezuela known as the Guiana Highlands, which constitutes half the national territory but so far contains but a fraction of the population. Further southward toward Brazil the Highlands soar to majestic heights and much of this area is unexplored. Conan Doyle made it the scene of his fabulous *Lost World* teeming with strange prehistoric animals, and William Henry Hudson used it as the scene of his *Green Mansions* in which Rima, the birdlike girl of the jungle, lived and met her tragic fate. James Angel, a North American bush pilot, once discovered in this part of Venezuela a mountaintop covered with nuggets of gold; he took some home with him but has never been able to locate the place again. He did give his name to Angel Falls, which he was the first white man to see, the highest unbroken falls in the world which drop 3,212 feet in a virgin wilderness. The Guiana Highlands are one of the few still unknown regions left in the world today. Who can say what hidden wealth may lie in their midst?

In December 1968 Rafael Caldera, who had four times unsuccessfully tried for the presidency, was elected over the candidate of the old-line Democratic Action Party. His margin of victory was a small fraction of the total vote, and he occupied the presidential chair with no strong party majority supporting him. But Caldera and his COPEI, Christian Democrats, made a good beginning. In his campaign the president had used the slogan "time for change" with far more appeal than Thomas Dewey, and after his inauguration he promptly set about to make this change mean something. His first important act was to offer amnesty to all guerrilla fighters in the hills and to legalize the Communist party in order to give these dissidents a lawful platform. He emptied the jails of political prisoners, and appointed good men to key government posts.

The leftist opposition responded favorably to these overtures, and one of the guerrilla leaders proclaimed: "The mountain roads are open to President Caldera and even to Nixon." They were apparently not open to Nelson Rockefeller, who had to cancel his visit to that country. Caldera was obviously up against a very tough situation, but he did manage to control the leftists as well as the Venezuelan military establishment. He was able even to placate the large Democratic Action opposition party, thus achieving a minor miracle in political strategy.

U.S. companies poured millions of dollars into Venezuela to exploit and market that country's vast oil deposits, but ineptness in Washington caused them to lose their investment. Back in the early 1950s when Venezuela was the only Latin American exporter of petroleum the U.S. Congress imposed mandatory control on Venezuelan oil. Canada and Mexico, however, were exempt from these restrictions. Venezuela asked for the same treatment, pointing out that it had kept its oil flowing to this country during World War II despite the hazards of submarine attack. Venezuela also argued that it was one of the world's leading customers for U.S. goods and services. But oil was now flowing in from the Mideast in ever increasing quantities, and Congress refused to grant Venezuela's request. The world oil market was soon flooded and prices went down. Opening of the Suez Canal in 1959 hastened the founding of the oil cartel. Venezuela then became one of the prime movers in the organization of OPEC (Organization of Petroleum Exporting Countries), which now fixes world petroleum prices.

But this was not the end of the story. In 1970 President Rafael Caldera of Venezuela went to Washington personally in order to plead with President Nixon for hemispheric preferential treatment in the importation of the product on which his nation's economy was so dependent. Caldera returned to Caracas empty-handed, and soon thereafter signed the decree canceling Venezuela's longtime trade agreement with the United States. Other partly retaliatory events followed during the presidency of Caldera's successor, Andrés Pérez (1974–79). On January 1, 1975, Venezuela nationalized the U.S.-owned iron mines in that country, and one year later, January 1, 1976, all foreign-owned oil fields were also nationalized. Twenty-one American companies were involved, and were offered compensation of $1.28 billion. Exploration and production of oil in Venezuela was placed in the hands of the national oil company. Petróleos Venezolanos (Petrovén) which kept production moving efficiently. In 1980 regular gasoline sold for fifteen cents a gallon in Venezuela and super (alta) for thirty-five cents a gallon.

In the 1970s, as the price of oil skyrocketed, serious attention began to be paid to Venezuela's Orinoco Tar Belt, reported to contain more than a trillion barrels of heavy oil, 200 billion barrels of this recoverable. Development of these fields would cost at least $30 billion, and new technologies would be needed to make extraction profitable. When oil prices began to fall in the 1980s the exploitation of the Tar Belt was put off for a better day. However, these vast reserves, reported to be larger than those of Saudi Arabia, represent an untapped potential.

Nationalization brought Venezuela more income from her petroleum, and the country embarked on a four-year development plan (1976–80) costing $52 billion. The purpose was to diversify the economy and increase farm production, but the effect was marginal. The $4 billion invested in the construction of a huge industrial complex at Ciudad Guayana met with more success and has made Venezuela into a real industrial power. However, many basic necessities must still be imported, and prices are high.

Since 1958 Venezuela has had six consecutive free elections. Luis Herrera Campins, who was inaugurated president in 1978, initially supported the policy of the United States in Central America, but he later lined up with the majority of the other Latin American nations in demanding a negotiated settlement to the conflict with Nicaragua. He was disillusioned by the Reagan policy of seeking the forceful ousting of the Nicaraguan Sandinistas. When the United States decided to back Great Britain in the Falklands War, Venezuela was one of the most vociferous advocates of the Argentine cause. In March 1984, Jaime Lusinchi succeeded Herrera Campins as president, and Venezuela, along with Mexico, Peru, Panama, and Colombia helped to organize and put all its influence behind the Contadora Group which continued to seek a peaceful resolution to the Central American problem.

Caracas, one of the fastest growing cities in South America, now has a population of more than four million. The city boasts a new $2 billion air-conditioned subway system that has greatly relieved the terrible congestion on the streets above. Caracas is a bustling mixture of the old and the very modern. Its wealthy suburbs are beautiful, but nearly a third of the city's inhabitants live in makeshift houses in slum areas on the hillsides of the capital. Police carrying automatic weapons patrol the narrow streets and alleys constantly. Caracas is a city of conspicuous consumption, and produces fifteen to twenty million tons of garbage a year. The government has estimated that it will cost nearly $200 million to hygienically solve the problem. In the meantime, the city is host to more than six million rats that are very much in evidence in the slum areas. There are plans to replace the slum hovels with low-cost multiple housing units, but this will take time. Inflation in Venezuela has risen to about 40 per cent a year, painfully high but considerably less than that of most Latin American countries. Following the devaluation of the currency prices have declined on some items, but there is at least 12 per cent unemployment and the economy in general is in a period of stagnation. Agricultural production is sagging as country folk continue to pour into the cities in search of a more stable life. Despite these difficulties Venezuela is the only South American country, besides its neighbor Colombia, that can claim a democratically run civilian government for a period of more than thirty years.

A journey up the Orinoco River made in the 1950s produced one of the finest Latin American novels, *The Lost Steps*. The author, Alejo Carpentier, is a Cuban musicologist and writer who went to Venezuela to arrange for a series of radio broadcasts. While there he traveled up to the headwaters of the Orinoco. In his novel the unnamed protagonist is sent into the jungles of Venezuela by the museum that employs him in New York in order to collect primitive musical instruments. This is only the pretext for a fabulous Odyssey, paralleling that of Homer, which takes him back to the roots of civilization. As calendar time actually moves forward, the traveler moves backward in the chronology of human history, passing through the colonial epoch, the period of conquest and colonization, then into a stone-age village where time has stopped. He sees the birth of music, of religion, of the dance, of poetry, and he recaptures the values that man has lost: authentic love, loyalty, the pledged word, honor, human understanding, acceptance, complete dedication. But he is a man of the twentieth century, and is outside his time frame. He returns to civilization for a few necessities (one of them is paper on which to write), and cannot find his way back into that sylvan paradise, that lost Eden. The Orinoco has flooded and all traces of the path are gone. The novel poses many fundamental questions: What is the meaning of civilization, of human society, and what, stripped of his conceits and garments, is man?

The Lost Steps can take its honored place alongside *The Lost World* and *Green Mansions* as the most recent in a trio of excellent novels laid in Venezuela. Strangely, not one of these books is by a Venezuelan. Why is the locale so irresistible? Perhaps it may be because Venezuela is a kind of microcosm of the entire continent. Here in a relatively compact area flows a mighty river, here also are towering mountains, fruitful plains, impenetrable jungles, and the open sea. Here twentieth-century man can travel but a few miles and shake hands with stone-age man. Venezuela is the capsule and the epitome of Latin American geography and history. Viewed in this light it is no wonder that the imagination of so many creative minds has been sparked by this beautiful land.

The Orinoco today is a river of commerce: oil, steel, machinery, and produce more daily along its picturesque course. Venezuela has the highest per capita income in Latin America: one million television sets, nearly as many automobiles, the largest number of telephones per capita, the greatest per head consumption of electricity, and a manageable inflation. The country consumes more than twice as much energy per person (oil, gas, electricity) as Argentina. It has one of the best network of highways on the continent, and a growing industrial complex. But, as the Venezuelan writer Carlos Rangel comments: "The curse of Venezuela is the big state, the bloated government. The portion of our economy in the hands of the state rose from 15 per cent in 1914 to 50 per cent in 1920, to 65 per cent today. This is a recipe for disaster. I do not believe that the process can be reversed without a revolution. Even our non-Marxist leaders have opted for state controlled industrialization. Both the private and state sectors have assumed loans, thus building up a huge debt of $34 billion that the country cannot pay. In the 1980s the entire structure collapsed with the fall of the price of oil on which 90 per cent of our national economy still depends." It is apparent that the moment of truth is near at hand for Venezuela.

Andrés Pérez took over as president of Venezuela early in 1989, and was confronted by a situation of serious economic deterioration. In 1988 inflation had risen to 35 per cent, oil income had been cut in half, and oil accounts for 90 per cent of the country's export total. The president was a pragmatist, so he raised taxes and lifted price controls; there was an 89 per cent hike in gasoline prices and bus fares, and other prices rose accordingly. There were widespread protests and in March the country exploded. Mobs took to the streets and looted everything they could lay their hands on from food to furniture. The troops were called out and before the tumult was under control there were at least 300 deaths and many hundreds wounded. This widespread revolt was not against the rich and not against any particular political party but was directed against the government in general and its team of big technocrats who had borrowed recklessly from foreign creditors while doing next to nothing to aid the impoverished masses.

Following the riots Andrés Pérez froze prices on many consumer goods, and suspended all payments on the country's foreign debt. To continue these payments would inevitably result in lowering the living standards of the Venezuelan people. During the previous administration Venezuela had already paid out $25 billion in interest alone of its foreign debt, without decreasing by one iota the debt itself. Hungry Venezuelans were incensed at seeing this money go. All over Latin America the burden of the foreign debt at high rates of interest is creating conditions of political unrest and violence, and until this problem is resolved there will be additional and more frequent explosions throughout the region.

COLOMBIA

When the depression hit Colombia an admirable thing took place. The elections of 1930 were held in an atmosphere of honesty and tranquility, and the Conservatives, who had been in power for over twenty years, yielded gracefully to the Liberals. This peaceful transition was a source of great pride to all Colombians, and caused many specialists in the Latin American field to announce that Colombia had thus proved her political maturity. They spoke too soon! The Liberals began their presidential stint with wisdom and restraint, but by the time World War II came to an end their administration was beginning to lose steam. Eduardo Santos, of an old distinguished family and publisher of the country's best newspaper *El Tiempo*, who served as president between 1938–42, was perhaps the most notable of the Liberal presidents, but when he was followed by Alfonso López Pumarejo, who was elected for his second term in 1942 (he had previously served in 1934–38), the breaking point was reached.

Exacerbated Conservatives, and equally exacerbated extremists of the left, made the continuance of constitutional government almost impossible, and inflation was hurting the people at large. The fanatical Colombian Catholic party, a very large and very powerful group, hated López because he had rigorously attempted to separate church and state. As a result of all these pressures López resigned in 1945. Alberto Lleras Camargo took his place provisionally. He tried hard, but was unable to restore unity either to the country or to his Liberal party, which had split into two segments, the leftist group headed by the charismatic Jorge Eliécer Gaitán, who had made a good name for himself as mayor of Bogotá. This split made possible the election of a Conservative, Mariano Ospina Pérez, in 1946. When the Ninth Conference of the Pan American Union (now called Organization of American States) met in Bogotá in April 1948, emotions exploded.

Gaitán, the leftist demagogue, was assassinated on April 9, and sympathetic mobs beat and burned the capital into a shambles. There were at least 2,000 killed, with property damage running into the millions. Thus began "la violencia" or "the violence," as the Colombians call it, a period of many years of lawless government, banditry, guerrilla warfare, pillaging, and widespread unrest during which Liberals and Conservatives all over the country kept trying to get even. Laureano Gómez, an extreme Conservative, was elected president in 1950. He was a warm admirer of General Franco and wanted to move Colombia back to the sixteenth century. His administration staggered under the "violence" and every vestige of civil liberties disappeared. Colombia's few Protestants, about 25,000, were viciously attacked and their churches vandalized.

In the countryside, fighting was on such a large scale that thousands of rural dwellers deserted their farms and villages to take refuge in the cities. Tens of thousands were slain by the senseless banditry which often verged on civil war. Gomez was overthrown by the military in 1953, and replaced by General Gustavo Rojas Pinilla, who was president for four years 1953–57. The people heaved a sign of relief hoping that the general could at least restore law and order, but Rojas Pinilla had been in power only a short time when everyone realized that the country had jumped from the frying pan into the fire.

The dictator made himself rich, bought vast tracts of lands, filled them with herds of prize cattle, and administered the law, his law, with a mailed fist. The citizens of Bogotá, better educated and more astute politically than the country dwellers, seized the right moment to turn the tide irrevocably against Rojas Pinilla, and in May 1957 stormed into the streets and marched to the presidential palace shouting: "Get out, Rojas Pinilla! We don't want this government any longer!" The massive antigovernment demonstration so obviously represented the majority sentiment that the dictator resigned his office.

In exile in Spain, Lleras Camargo, leader of the Liberals, and Laureano Gómez, Conservative ex-President, met in conference to find some way to restore sanity to Colombia. They agreed upon a plan known as "The National

Front," later approved in a national plebiscite, by which for the next sixteen years (1958–74) the presidency would alternate between a Conservative and a Liberal. Both parties would be equally represented in the cabinet and in the Congress. Congressional bills would require a two-thirds majority for passage.

To the amazement of most observers the plan was actually put into effect, and Lleras Camargo, the Liberal, became the first National Front president, 1958–62. Under his intelligent and conciliatory administration Colombia began her tortuous return to the rule of law. In 1959 Rojas Pinilla, the ex-dictator, was brought to trial for having fomented rebellion and subverted the office of the president for his own private gain. By a vote of 65 to 1 he was stripped of his civil rights, his military rank, his army pension, and even his decorations.

In 1962 Guillermo León Valencia, son of one of Colombia's most famous poets, was elected as the Conservative president to replace Lleras Camargo, who had done a bang-up job of financial and land reform. Lleras and Valencia both hit a snag, however, when it came to resettling farm families in the thinly populated regions of Colombia. The "violence" frightened even the old settlers away from their farms.

Valencia was enthusiastically welcomed when he was inaugurated, but his administration was certainly not very spectacular. He belonged to the old school, and strongly recalled the thinking of his father, Guillermo Valencia, a poet whose profound classical interests had enabled him to live and write so well in his ivory tower. His father, for example, in a poem on Popayán, the traditional family dwelling place, referred to it (and we might extend the comparison to include all of Colombia) as "a nostalgic well of oblivion," a town that "is living on silence, past glories, precious gifts, impossible dreams, martyrdom, and pride." Of such elements success in contemporary government is not made, however great the poetry.

The violence continued. Colombia has lost perhaps 200,000 dead during the past four decades through this senseless but compulsive rule of the gun. There have even been several local "peasant republics" proclaimed in the hinterland. The federal army has found it extremely difficult to deal with them, and in 1964 when the armed forces finally crushed the independent republic of Marquetalia the Colombian minister of war found it expedient to travel to the area and hoist the national flag in a symbolic gesture over the territory. These independent peasant republics indicate the degree to which the frustration of the countryside had grown.

A land reform program was worked out as the answer to this malaise. The traditional parties have little real feeling for fundamental land reform, but they agreed to it in public (although many opposed it in private), because they are sufficiently enlightened to realize that they must either introduce reforms of their own making or have other more drastic reforms thrust upon them by an enraged peasant population. At present there is a shortage of peasants capable of running small farms in Colombia. Most peasants simply do not know how to cultivate a small farm in order to raise what their family needs and at the same time have a surplus to sell in the market. And indeed many of the farms are so small that they make the solution to this problem impossible, even if there were proper agricultural training, willingness, and energy.

For example, in the fertile Cauca Valley 70 per cent of the farmers own plots of less than twenty-five acres in size. These *minifundia* are really too small to support a family and produce a marketable excess. On the other hand, about 70 per cent of the land in the Cauca Valley is held in large plots which the owners are disinclined to work efficiently. Thus at both ends of the spectrum the country finds its land distribution in a wasteful and unmanageable disequilibrium. To alter this would require an almost incredible change of heart in the citizenry as a whole.

In 1966 a Liberal, Carlos Lleras Restrepo, took the place of Valencia. In spite of past experiences the groundswell for land reform gathered momentum, and two million acres of land have been made available in farms of forty acres each for the country's landless rural families. Possibly 75,000 families in all have received their lands. New villages have been established, credit and agricultural aid have been extended, and 1,500 miles of roads have been constructed to provide access to markets. Perhaps at last the eastern two thirds of Colombia where almost no one lived before will slowly begin to move forward. Up to the present this vast region has not really been effective national territory.

Colombia's economic future depends not only on a better land distribution, elimination of the *latifundia* and *minifundia*, but also on a more diversified development, with particular emphasis on cattle and petroleum. At present one worker out of four is connected with the coffee industry. Every one cent change in the price of a pound of coffee in New York means an increase or decrease of between seven and eight million dollars of annual income in Colombia.

Another almost untouched potential in Colombia is the immense forests which cover a large portion of the republic. Geography and tradition handicap both industrial and agricultural expansion. Per capita income stands at $1,475 a year; poverty and the somber bleakness of village life, interrupted by fits of violence that replace the fiestas and folk rituals of a happier day, make Colombia one of the critical areas of Latin America today.

Colombia still has about 500,000 families without land, and this number is increasing at the rate of 10 per cent a year. The people are apathetic about their government and distrustful of its ability to help them; in the 1966 elections fewer than 30 per cent went to the polls. The National Front, necessary as it was, has greatly lessened interest in political affairs. United States aid has been abundant, and it was hoped that Colombia might become the showcase of the Alliance for Progress, but although $732 millions in aid were received between 1962–68, the country's per capita gross national product increased only from $276 to $296, an annual average increase of 1.2 per cent, while the Alliance for Progress goal was 2.5 per cent.

Colombia has barely begun to tackle the problems of a more equitable distribution of income, and the national social structure remains basically unchanged. Two thirds of the population are on the margin of the national economy, scarcely participating in any way whatsoever. One product, coffee, still brings in over 40 per cent of the foreign exchange. The number of functional illiterates has increased from approximately five million to six million in the past ten years, because it has been impossible for the very primitive school system to keep up with the increase in population.

Between 1970 and 1980 Colombia improved economically and industrially, but her internal violence continued. President Pastrana-Borrero (1970–74) was barely able to keep things from exploding, and his successor, Alfonso López Michaelson (1974–78), formed a coalition cabinet and strove desperately to restore stability. He had won a landslide victory over his conservative opponent and had the support of the people. In 1975 his government faced widespread guerrilla uprisings and the threat of a general strike called by 100 labor unions representing 100,000 workers demanding a boost in wages. Inflation and low wages continued to gnaw at the best hopes of all Colombians; farm families, unable to eke out a living in the rural areas, poured into the cities in an ever-increasing flood, dumping their children into the city streets to shift for themselves. Teenage thefts and muggings, usually in groups of two or three, made, and still make, the streets unsafe for citizens and tourists alike.

To many rural Colombians a "small" family consists of six children, a medium-sized family of eight to ten, and a large family of twenty. Hundreds of these farm children become street urchins and make life miserable for the city dwellers. Tourists often find themselves being unobtrusively escorted along the streets and in the parks by total strangers of the middle or upper class who are doing their best to protect the foreign visitor. Pickpockets and purse-snatchers operate in the midst of crowds, and frequently thieves present themselves as plainclothesmen offering "protection."

The decade of the 1980s was a very trying period for Colombia. Good men were elected as presidents, but they were unable to control the wave of senseless violence that gripped the country. Julio César Turbay, a Liberal, was inaugurated in 1978, and he was followed by Belisario Betancur, a Conservative, who became president in 1982. Betancur, in his turn, was succeeded by Virgilio Barco who assumed the presidency in 1986. In an effort to curb the violence, Betancur offered amnesty to the guerrillas, but the gesture was futile. Barco, in his turn, also attempted unsuccessfully to restore law and order to a society ruled by unbridled hatreds, frustration, and distrust. In 1987, within a period of only three days, a Bogotá newspaper reported that "43 people were killed on the streets of Bogotá, Cali and Medellín, the three largest cities, assassinated by armed hoodlums who indiscriminately gunned down women, children, beggars, and garbage collectors for fun and target practice." The highly respected news sheet, *El Tiempo*, estimated that in this recent wave of violence at least

850 persons "disappeared." Vigilantes and paramilitaries operate freely, "and not a single person, least of all those in the armed forces, has been prosecuted, let alone convicted."

The original root of this violence was rabid political polarization, but during the 1980s the illicit drug traffic became Colombia's number one problem, affecting all aspects of the national life.[284] The courts have broken down completely, one of the main reasons being the assassination of forty-seven judges who had given some indication of prosecuting the accused drug dealers. The ex-minister of justice, Enrique Parejo González, put it bluntly: "We now have a war to the final extremity. It is a war that we know will be costly in lives and in suffering, but it is a war that we must wage in order to rescue ourselves from those who would turn our nation into a vicious den of cocaine traffickers, of evil men without conscience and with immense power and wealth. The illicit drug traffic in Colombia brings in $3 billion a year, and has branched out to new markets from Austria to Australia, its profits already surpassing those of our traditional export products, like coffee and oil."*

Coffee is still the major legal product of Colombia, but oil and gas have recently been discovered in great quantities. In 1987 Colombia produced 380,000 barrels of oil a day, and by 1995 the total is calculated to reach 500,000 barrels daily. Natural gas is even more plentiful. Texaco has discovered a huge gas field offshore and onshore in the Guajira Peninsula, with reserves of three-and-a-half *trillion* cubic feet. Gas production for 1987 was over 500 million cubic feet a day. Colombia also has huge coal and iron deposits. Potential coal reserves are estimated at 20 *trillion* metric tons, the highest in Latin America.

Colombian coffee is of the finest quality and sells at a premium in the world market. It is planted in the shade, where there is a steady temperature of close to 70 degrees, beneath orange and banana trees. It has a mild, fragrant, but very full flavor. Recently Colombia has also developed a large export trade in fresh flowers, mainly orchids, that bring in millions of dollars a year. And since 1983 Colombia has been the largest exporter of publications in Latin America, over 20 per cent of which are sold in the United States. In a recent first-run edition of a novel by García Márquez, *Love in the Times of Cholera,* 750,000 hardback copies were printed. Spain and other countries are now sending materials to Colombian publishing houses.[261]

Two other Colombian operations, strictly outside the law, are printing counterfeit United States currency, and processing coca leaves in widespread clandestine laboratories. Approximately 65 per cent of all U.S. counterfeit currency printed abroad comes from Colombia. The national government, with U.S. help, is making heroic efforts to combat the cocaine trade, of which Colombia is the nexus, but many Colombians blame the United States for this drug traffic,

---

* In January 1988 the kingpin of the drug cartel, Jorge Ochoa Vásquez, was suspiciously released from jail, and Colombia's attorney general, Carlos Mauro Hoyos, was gunned down by the cartel because of his antidrug stand. This cartel supplies 80 per cent of the cocaine imported into the United States.[259]

because without the wide market that exists in this country, which our own government has been powerless to control, there would be no problem for Colombia.

Colombia has one of the highest population growth rates in the world. This is coupled with 100 per cent inflation, huge depressed rural areas with polluted drinking water, and a languishing agriculture. Deplorable shantytowns with no sewers and no electricity surround the largest cities and as a result of these unsanitary conditions there is widespread goiter, venereal disease, intestinal parasites, hepatitis, anemia, scurvy, and pellagra. The eastern half of the country, however, comprising an area more than five times the size of New York state, is almost unpopulated.

Colombia has common frontiers with five Latin American nations: Brazil, Ecuador, Panama, Peru, and Venezuela, for a total of 3,805 miles. Over 60 per cent of these boundary areas is covered by dense tropical jungles. The 1,277-mile border with Venezuela is the hub of an active border trade. There are good highways leading into the interior of both countries, and goods are exchanged freely. The 352-mile Ecuadorean border is rich in timber and oil. Near the Brazilian border other oil fields have been discovered.

In spite of their critical problems the bustling cities of Colombia are among the largest, most modern, and most beautiful in Latin America. Bogotá, Cali, Medellin, Barranquilla, and Cartagena are all impressive cities, despite their shantytowns. The "Unicentro" shopping center in Bogotá contains 365 stores, and is one of Latin America's most modern retail malls. Sears Roebuck and jewelry shops selling fine emeralds stand side by side with "Whopper Drive-in Hamburgers." Bogotá also holds an international trade fair every two years, which draws over a million visitors, and has sales of $500 million. It is a temporary "free trade zone": allowing duty-free entry of goods. About 70 per cent of the fairgrounds space is occupied by foreign exhibitors. The grounds are only a ten-minute taxi ride from the airport. In spite of all this admirable modernity, however, unless Colombia can find some way to control its violent political polarization and drug production, it may all go down the drain.

Colombia was the only Latin American country to maintain positive economic growth every year during the decade 1980–1990. Over 700 international companies do business in Colombia, with the United States in first place. Chemicals are the largest single area. There is a very strong urban structure in the country despite its relatively small population. Foreign investment is encouraged, and Colombia is no longer a one-crop country. Besides coffee, exports in other areas have grown rapidly: cotton, sugar, bananas, flowers, cacao, fish and crustaceans, textiles, garments, oil, natural gas, chemicals, precious stones, coal, gold, books, and a huge black market in drugs.

Drug barons have become a law unto themselves in Colombia. The Medellín Cartel, centered in the country's large industrial metropolis, has been responsible for the assassination of so many judges that persons of probity are now reluctant to accept that position. In August 1989 the highly regarded presidential candidate, Luis Carlos Galán, was shot to death in front of a large crowd before which he was to give a speech. It was reported that the cartel had offered $500,000 to have a "hit" put on this much admired political leader who had spoken out strongly against the drug traffickers. Journalists who took on the cartel were also threatened daily—newspaper offices were blown up, bombings and killings became a daily occurrence.[285] President Barco asked for U.S. help in combatting the well-organized and heavily financed cartel, and helicopters were sent to Colombia for this purpose. It was a drop in the bucket.

Colombia began to allow some of drug traffickers who had been caught to be extradited to the United States, and this did have an effect. The drug barons are deathly afraid of the U.S. courts. The Medellín Cartel had the affrontery to offer to pay off Colombia's entire foreign debt if the government would ease up on them. This offer had many supporters. Not all Colombians hate the drug dealers, because the cartel has doled out millions of dollars to buy and equip children's playgrounds in many poor areas, to provide food and clothing, and in other ways to create good will among the masses.

What most citizens of the United States fail to realize is that the drug problem is clearly a two-way street. Colombians strongly hold to the view that if we in this country would put an end to the selling and buying of drugs, there would be no reason for drug production in Latin America. The drug lords everywhere are well organized and wealthy. Their opposition is sporadic and ineffective. As the decade of the 1990s began, there was little reason to believe that any antidrug program in the United States or Latin America would soon put an end to the drug traffic.

In the presidential elections of 1990 in Colombia, the Liberal candidate, César Gaviria, was chosen to take Virgilio Barco's place as president. Gaviria strongly supported continuing the policy of extraditing drug criminals to the United States, and he was totally opposed to any kind of negotiations or deals with those engaged in the drug traffic. This gave him the dubious distinction of becoming number one on the Medellín Cartel's hit list. He took over the presidential office at perhaps the worst time in Colombian history. During the twelve months prior to his inauguration there had been in Medellín at least 3,000 killings, among them 155 policemen. No one's life was any longer safe. A reign of terror gripped the country in spite of the government's courageous effort to maintain order.

ECUADOR

The imprint of García Moreno and his theocracy still lies on Ecuador despite many intervening years of "anticlerical" government. In Quito, perhaps the most picturesque city in Latin America, the churches are still bright with hundreds of burning candles, services seem continuously in progress, and rapt crowds of worshipers, mostly Indianist, sit or kneel in fixed attention until the mass has ended. On the street corner outside an Indian will be playing a strange and haunting melody on his Panpies (*rondador*), and in the market, a real Indian market, produce and bright-colored fabrics are bulging in the stalls.

"The city of churches" has not changed greatly since colonial days, except that now many of her churches are in disrepair and even while the mass goes on, the roof may be leaking as the rain pours down, some of it running along roof and wall to stain the lovely baroque decorations and polychrome statues. This is indeed the land that time forgot, a beautiful and, but one suffused with a great inertia and a great sadness.

Ecuador is South America's most thickly populated country. Only one fourth the size of Bolivia, Ecuador has three and a half million more people. Quito, the old colonial capital, 9,000 feet above sea level, a city "of perpetual spring," prides itself on its glorious past and its lack of insects, while Guayaquil, the country's bustling port, sultry and teeming with bugs throughout the year, with equal pride proclaims its extra quotient of modernity and its receptivity to new ideas. The half-hour trip by air which separates these two leading cities transports a person with starting rapidity between two completely different worlds.

After García Moreno's death in 1875 Ecuador went through twenty years of political turmoil during which effective government ceased to exist. In 1895 Eloy Alfaro, first of a long line of liberal presidents, came to power, and he was the country's strong man until 1912, when he attempted to seize control of the government for a third term unconstitutionally. The army slapped him in prison from which an infuriated mob hauled him and lynched him.

Several other liberal presidents have occupied the presidency during the twentieth century, some good, some bad, and there were also numerous takeovers by the military. In summary and in general one can say that Ecuador's national government has been deplorable. But there have been a few bright spots: Leonidas Plaza Gutiérrez served honorably and well between 1901–5, and was elected to a second term in 1912. His son, Galo Plaza Lasso, who was born and educated in the United States, served an equally honorable and admirable term during the years 1948–52.

During his four years in office Galo Plaza did all that one man possibly could to build up the economy of his country and to modernize its primitive agriculture. The monoculture of cacao, which had been deadly for centuries, was at last abandoned and large areas were planted in bananas and coffee in order to diversify the economy. Each of these two products now brings in more revenue than does cacao. But Galo was always suspect in some quarters of his own country because of his open admiration for the United States.

Galo Plaza was followed by José María Velasco Ibarra, a man who had twice before come to power and had twice been thrown out by the military. Galo's steadying hand had so improved conditions that this time Velasco Ibarra, a real demagogue, served out his four-year term. He had made every kind of promise under the sun, but he did little to help the country. He was an Ecuadorian Huey Long without Long's material accomplishments. The elections of 1956, however, were apparently honest, and Camilo Ponce Enríquez, a Conservative, became president.

Velasco Ibarra bided his time, and after Ponce Enríquez's term was up in 1960, the old-timer, then sixty-seven, was reelected to a fourth term. The Ecuadorian electorate responded to his trumpetings with enthusiasm, and Velasco Ibarra, Ecuadorian to the core, became widely known as "the National Personification." He did, indeed, personify torrid rhetoric, irrational patriotism, and poor administration. He plundered and deceived the country, and by 1961 things were so bad that the military again took over and Velasco Ibarra fled to Argentina.

His vice-president, Carlos Julio Arosemena, who had often spoken admiringly of Russia, took over the government. Arosemena was an inveterate drunkard, and his administration was a disgrace to the country. In 1962 he visited the United States in order to ask for aid and made a spectacle of himself by appearing drunk before President Kennedy. The inevitable military ousted him in 1963, and for the next five years Ecuador was under military control, but even that control was not stable for the junta itself was overturned by the air force in 1966 after violent student and labor union demonstrations against the government.

Little headway had been made in resolving the critical problems of the country. The treasury was bankrupt, there were endless lists of delinquent taxpayers, state officials operated from cubbyholes piled high with junk and disorderly files, the Indian citizens of the country, constituting about half the total population, were just as impoverished and unproductive as they had been for centuries, and the land problem had scarcely been scratched. This was the situation when the elections of 1968 took place. The nation was unhinged and the people were ready to vote for anybody who would promise to pull them out of the mess.

"The National Personification" was ready to do just that, and so in 1968 Velasco Ibarra, at the age of seventy-five, was elected to his fifth term as president of Ecuador. His promises were golden but undeliverable. He continued to proclaim that Peru had stolen a hunk of the national territory, abetted by the United States, and on occasion he insisted on Ecuador's right to a 200-mile limit when United States fishing ships got too close. By focusing attention on outside "imperialism," Velasco Ibarra reduced the pressure against him inside Ecuador. But it was only a temporary respite, for the old man was undoubtedly the worst administrator in modern Ecuadorian history, and in the summer of 1970 as he faced overwhelming problems with a huge deficit in his budget the army "requested" him to assume dictatorial power. He did.

Velasco Ibarra was probably the last of the old line dictators whose principal appeal was their *personalismo*, their personal magnetism. Velasco Ibarra used to exclaim: "*Give me a balcony, and Ecuador is mine!*" He could talk his people into anything. But his day finally came when he was deposed for the fifth time by a bloodless military coup on February 15, 1972. The old man lived for another seven years, and when he died in 1979 his funeral attracted one of the largest turnouts in Ecuador's history.

Ecuador continued under military rule until the elections of 1978 when Jaime Roldós Aguilera, Latin America's youngest head-of-state, became president. This was Ecuador's first democratically elected government in many years. Roldós was not a military man, and he won a landslide victory by running on a platform of reform with mild leftist tendencies. He was, however, running against six other candidates, and initially received only 32 per cent of the total vote. In the runoff election that followed he won easily with over 80 per cent of the votes. The most popular candidate would have been Assad Bucaram, the former populist mayor of Guayaquil, but the army would not allow him to run because he was born in Lebanon. It was his nephew-in-law, Roldós, who ran instead and achieved the victory, thus giving Ecuador a long-denied civilian government.

During the decade 1970–80 the Ecuadorean economy continued to grow at a rapid pace, an average of 10 per cent a year. Until 1972 the main source of wealth was agriculture—sugar, bananas, coffee, and cocoa. The discovery of oil in the Oriente selva near the Colombian border changed this almost overnight. A 504 kilometer pipeline was built from this jungle area to Esmeraldas on the northern coast, and by 1973 Ecuador was exporting 250,000 barrels of oil a day. This made it the second largest petroleum exporting country of South America, outranked only by Venezuela. The biggest operator in the development of these oil resources was the Texaco-Gulf combine, but in 1973 the state oil company, Cepe, took a 25 per cent share of this consortium; later on, it bought out Gulf and now owns 62.5 per cent of the nation's petroleum industry. Large deposits of natural gas have also been found in Oriente and in the Gulf of Guayaquil.

This sudden wealth brought with it a rapid rise in the rate of inflation. Agriculture was neglected, and prices rose alarmingly. In 1978, when Jaime Roldós became president, oil exports had declined to 220,000 barrels a day, and many experts were predicting an end to the oil bonanza within the next six or seven years. There was little further exploration, much of which had to be carried on by helicopters, there were several breaks in the pipeline, and there were frequent tensions between the Texaco-Gulf consortium and Cepe. All these things caused a further weakening of the basic economic progress of the country, despite its impressive annual growth.

Ecuador's agriculture, which for many years accounted for 90 per cent of the export trade, is largely underdeveloped. Only 5 per cent of the land is under cultivation, and outmoded methods prevail. Approximately 74 per cent of the country is covered with forest. Landownership is concentrated in relatively few hands, and the masses of people, mostly Indians, still live at the poverty level. The "huasipungo" system, under which the Indians lived and worked as slaves, is gradually disappearing, and cooperatives are expanding. Serious attempts are being made to improve the conditions of the Indians without destroying their ancient cultural values, but the process is hard and long. Only half of Ecuador's children attend school, and more than 30 per cent of the total adult population is illiterate.

Aside from the lovely colonial churches and convents of Quito, Ecuador's Indian markets are equally great tourist attractions. The small town of Otavalo, 121 kilometers north of Quito, is noted for its picturesque Indian fair which is held every Saturday. Indian woven goods of wool with beautiful colors and designs have long been an appealing buy at this fair. But even in Otavalo things have changed. Under the pressure of tourist purchases prices are no longer low, the weaving is not particularly good, and many ponchos are now being made of orlon instead of wool.

Ecuador is a magnificent country geographically. In the southern sierra the Pan American Highway climbs to a height of 10,500 feet at Tinajillas Pass. From the summit there are magnificent views to the west and east, where towering mountains are marked by huge cloud banks. The road then descends sharply into a warm valley past cane fields before rising again on the other side. Here live some of the most interesting Indians of the country, dressed all in black. The women wear necklaces of colored beads and silver *topos*, ornate pins fastening their shawls.

Two outlying regions of Ecuador are of special interest, the tropical jungles near the border of Brazil, and the Galápagos Islands, several hundred miles off the western coast. In the Amazonian selva there are regular excursions on a "Flotel," which sails down the Napo River. This small ship bears the same *Orellana*, after the first explorer of the area. In this small area there are nearly 500 kinds of trees, teeming wildlife, brilliantly colored giant butterflies, and exotic tropical flowers. Francisco Orellana was the first Spaniard who came to this region in 1541 in search of gold. He and his men made a boat of logs and sailed all the way down the Napo into the Amazon and to the Atlantic, a distance of over 3,000 miles. En route they were attacked by an Indian tribe whose women did most of the fighting. Orellana, recalling the Amazons of ancient Greek tradition, referred to them with this word, and thus he also gave the river its name.

The Galápagos Islands are unique in this world. It is possible that they were never connected with the mainland, for half the plants and almost all the reptiles are found nowhere else on earth. When Charles Darwin arrived here in 1835 he was fascinated by the flora and fauna of the islands, and his studies of them helped to confirm his theory of evolution. The animals show little instinctive fear of man. Giant tortoises weighing 200 pounds with a life span of 200 years may be seen side by side with huge lizards that are close relatives of the ancient dinosaurs. Many strange and beautifully colored birds also live on the Galápagos. There are regular excursions from the mainland, and Pacific steamers often stop at the islands allowing tourists to have a short visit.

President Roldós was killed in an airplane accident in 1981 and was succeeded by his vice-president, Osvaldo Hurtado Larrea. When Larrea's term was completed in 1984, he turned the office over to León Febres Cordero, his political adversary, a conservative, who had defeated him at the polls. In the congressional elections a few months later the opposition party won control of the Ecuadorean parliament, and Febres Cordero's administration reached a stalemate. Febres did affirm his friendship with the United States, and broke off diplomatic relations with Nicaragua, accusing that country of subversive actions in Ecuador.

Febres was hamstrung throughout the last years of his presidency. Under him oil prices collapsed and the country went from boom to bust almost overnight.

In the fall of 1988 Rodrigo Borja, of the Democratic Liberal party, was elected president, and Ecuador took a dramatic turn to the left. Borja asked his countrymen to tighten their belts; he increased gasoline prices 100 per cent and devaluated the currency 35 per cent in order to curb the inflation which had risen to 60 per cent a year. "We all have to endure a time of sacrifice," he said. "Our country faces a formidable crisis." He had a hard task before him: Ecuador was on the verge of bankruptcy. Prices had risen sky high and the masses were destitute. A severe earthquake in 1987 had wrecked thirty miles of oil pipeline, and oil profits had temporarily sunk to almost zero, leaving an empty treasury. The president's program of austerity, however, did begin to pay off, and gradually Ecuador showed signs of improvement. But things did not improve fast enough for the Ecuadoreans, and popular sentiment soon turned against the government.

Economic conditions in Ecuador have always swung wildly up and down because of the country's excessive dependence on the main crops of bananas, cacao, rice, tagua, oil, coffee. In the 1980s a new industry, shrimp raising, took root and grew by leaps and bounds. Shrimp is now the second largest export product. Inflation and the cost of living are high and the overall future of Ecuador is precarious and unpredictable. The wealthy land barons and the military still hold onto a benighted concept of government, and are always waiting for an opportunity to take control. In reality, the staggering problems that Ecuador faces at the present juncture make the burden of Sisyphus look like a bag of feathers.

PERU

The face of Peru has changed visibly since World War II. Between 1950 and 1980 her population increased by over 100 per cent. There was a sizable influx of immigrants from Europe, adding considerably to Lima's cosmopolitan flavor. The land problem remains acute, as Peru's "forty families" still own most of the good arable land. Industries have expanded, roads and schools have been built, and in recent years the massive problems of the slums and of the Indians have begun to attract national attention. Politically Peru has struck a precarious balance between military dictatorship and constitutional government, never staying for long on any one course. Leadership has been inept and erratic, and the cleavage between classes is still abysmal.

Geographically the country is a far cry from a cohesive economic unit. The narrow coastal strip 1,400 miles long contains only one ninth of the national territory, but holds 35 per cent of the population. This area is natural desert, but irrigation has turned it into productive farmland. Over a million acres are watered from the flow of the fifty rivers that come down from the mountains to the Pacific.

The Sierra (average elevation over 12,000 feet) contains 26 per cent of the land and 55 per cent of the people. This is Indian Peru, enigmatic, unproductive, hostile, cold. Lands on the other side of the Sierra, the Selva, the forested eastern slopes of the Andes, and the tropical jungle lands beyond, make up 62 per cent of Peru's national territory, and hold only 10 per cent of the population. This area is not yet an effective part of the nation. Isolated, unpopulated, but rich in natural resources, the Selva's potential is enormous. It contains great reserves of timber, much potentially productive farm and cattle land, and very probably mineral and oil deposits of incalculable value. Roads and airlines are at last beginning to penetrate this hitherto inaccessible and untapped reservoir on which so much of the nation's future depends.

Peru has the potential of becoming a great nation. It is twice the size of France, and properly developed could support twice the population, close to a hundred million. But so far the lack of population, and especially the lack of an integrated population and of an effective political and economic development, have kept the country in its colonial straitjacket. Peruvian politics have been anything but serene during the recent decades, and on the several occasions that a brave try was made at constitutional government every effort to broaden the political base was met with violent action on the part of the ruling caste and the military.

Since World War II Peru has had some brilliant and some mediocre presidents, but only those who walked the tightrope have been permitted to serve out their terms, for the army sits restively in the wings. Manuel Prado, Peru's first civilian president, occupied the office during the crucial World War II years (1939–45). He guided his country toward financial solvency and civilian rule, moved into alignment with the Allies in the war, visited the United States where he was honored, feted, and given an honorary university degree, received large-scale United States financial aid to build up his country and to improve its military establishment, and in general did a creditable job of holding Peru together in the face of the European threat, without, however, attacking any of its fundamental problems.

Prado allowed Haya de la Torre, famous Aprista leader, to return to Peru, where he lived more or less under house arrest. Nevertheless, Haya's party increased its popularity among the people and, in view of world conditions, revised its ideological position. Under Haya's coaxing it changed from a strongly anti-United States party to one which saw in hemispheric cooperation and massive development the solution to most Latin American problems. APRA now admitted the need for United States capital to develop the untapped natural resources and semicolonial economies of the area.

Peru's next President was José Luis Bustamente, who was elected with strong APRA support in 1945. Haya was not allowed to become an official candidate, but after the elections he was in fact the power behind the presidential chair. Apristas occupied important cabinet and other influential posts, while Bustamente assumed the presidency. This strange alliance was ineffectual, not only because of its unnatural quality, but because the edgy military observed every political move with a jaundiced eye and stood absolutely opposed to any drastic reform.

Bustamente's government hardly had a chance. An anti-Aprista editor was slain, there were flurries of rebellion in Callao, APRA was blamed for it all, and the forty families became anxious. Their answer, as usual, was to clamp down. In 1948 General Odría headed an army coup and seized control. Odría ruled for two years as dictator, and then in 1950 he was duly elected to serve another six years. His eight years in power signified the return of Peru to the establishment. Apristas were arrested wholesale and thrown into prison. Haya took refuge in the Colombian embassy in Lima and remained there for five years, 1949–54.

Odría had the case taken before the International Tribunal in an attempt to extradite him, but the attempt was ineffectual; finally an agreement between Colombia and Peru was reached and Haya was permitted to leave for Mexico. He also visited and lectured in the United States, and on one occasion I spent a fascinating afternoon and evening in conversation with him. The gist of his thoughts might be telescoped in two or three sentences: his primary objective was no longer to take from the "haves," but was to increase production by continuous effort. Then there would be plenty for all. He called for unstinting work, not violence. Peru's untold and untapped potential could only be developed and put to use through foreign (that is, United States) aid, and his country desperately needed land reform so that the landless Indians might at least be able to live as human beings.

Peru also desperately needed constitutional government, without which progress would be unnecessarily painful and erratic. Haya swore that his own party, APRA, which he was firmly convinced enjoyed majority support in Peru, would never take control of the country via a coup, for such an act would be both self-indicting and self-defeating. APRA had always stood for ballots and not bullets. Men of good will could solve any problem if they would only work together. Haya called for a concerted effort in the Americas, and he hoped that ARPA would be the mainspring of this new turn of events. He was a man born before his time.

Haya spoke modestly and sincerely, his optimism was almost romantic, but there were some who called him an opportunist because of his about-face in regard to economic imperialism. Be it said in passing that Haya thrice had the government of Peru in his hands, and three times he let it slip away rather than call on the populace for armed support. Political fraud and the army defeated him, but he believed that those who live by the sword die by the sword, and Haya saw no future in that way of life. However, if Haya's personal political philosophy was intelligent and idealistic, the political behavior of the Aprista deputies and cabinet ministers during the periods they have held positions of power was anything but intelligent. Their political know-how was close to zero.

Another nostalgic recollection comes to mind concerning ex-President Bustamente, who lost his office as a result of General Odría's coup in 1948. Bustamente fled to Spain, where he lived in a state of poverty and desperation. At the time, I was Chairman of the Department of Spanish at the University of California, Los Angeles, and I received a pathethic letter from Bustamente in which he said that a graduate student of ours, a lady from Peru, had told him that we might need a professor of Spanish, and that he would be eager to accept the position, at whatever salary. He pointed out that he was still the "constitutional president of Peru." There was no position available even for Bustamente. How quickly the gods can fall! One moment the president of Peru, and the next seeking a job as a teacher of Spanish.

General Odría ran Peru until 1956. His motto was "Order and Progress," and he did deliver a modicum of both, but the source of Peru's indescribable poverty and ineradicable desperation was not even touched. The facade went higher, wider in order to conceal the national affliction. In 1956 Manuel Prado was again elected president, and this time APRA supported him with many votes, because the opposing candidate, Belaunde Terry refused to make any deal with the Apristas. Inflation set in, and prices soared.

In 1958 Vice-President Nixon, on a Latin American tour for President Eisenhower, was loudly booed at the University of San Marcos in Lima. Anti-United States animus was beginning to focus on our "official" representatives. Later, in Venezuela, Nixon and his wife were spat upon as an angry mob followed his car down the street hurling insults, and wielding rocks and clubs despite the heavily armed military escort. Pérez Jiménez, dictator of Venezuela, had just been ousted by a military coup, and many Venezuelans were incensed on recalling his warm treatment by United States officialdom. Venezuelan Communists found in the nation's misery a flame easy to focus on Yankee imperialism.

In 1962 there were three principal candidates for the presidency of Peru: Haya, Belaunde Terry, and Odría. They came in in that order, but none of them received over one third of the votes, which was necessary for election. Haya made a deal with his archenemy, Odría, when Belaunde again refused to come to terms with him. Odría was to become president while the Apristas were to control the cabinet. According to Peruvian law, Congress should have chosen which man was to be president, and Haya, who had received a larger percentage of votes than either of the other two candidates, was the logical choice. But the military, as everyone knew, was adamantly opposed. Hence these devious dealings, which did not fool the generals for one moment. An army contingent marched on the palace, arrested seventy-three-year-old President Prado (who was *not* their real target), and took over the government. Haya, clearly, was not to be permitted to get his hands on the reins of power.

This time conditions deteriorated rapidly and the army government soon fell apart. Between two and three thousand opponents were jailed and held for months without trial, but the general unrest continued unabated. The junta even tried to work temporarily with the Communists who, like they, were eager to crack down on the Apristas. As usual the Communists took every advantage of this opportunity and infiltrated the Peruvian labor unions, occupying many key positions.

The junta did make good on one of its promises: elections were actually held in June 1963, as scheduled, and this time the three-way race came out as follows: Belaunde Terry 39 per cent of the votes, Haya 34 per cent, and General Odría 26 per cent. Belaunde Terry was duly installed in office, and despite an unnatural alliance between Odría and Haya, who appeared driven together by circumstances, the new president ensconced himself precariously in the driver's seat and began to guide his cumbersome coach-and-four straight down the road, a cautious fraction left of center. In Peru even this was revolutionary. In the United States it would be regarded as middle-of-the-road politics. We have long had government participation in the social and economic order at a level that would make Peru's forty families shudder.

Belaunde made a courageous attempt to understand and to help the impoverished and depressed Indian half of Peru. He visited the native villages, saw at firsthand their problems, and began a poverty aid program which might have worked if he had had the support of two essential elements: (1) the United States foreign-aid program, and (2) the backing of the Peruvian military, which had helped put him in office. Unfortunately, he had neither, and herein lies a great tragedy both for Peru and for the United States.

The most obvious, but certainly not the only cause of Belaunde's failure, was his unsuccessful attempt to resolve the long-standing dispute between the Peruvian government and the International Petroleum Company, a subsidiary of Standard Oil of New Jersey, an old Rockefeller interest. Before his election Belaunde had promised to settle the problem within ninety days. He was unable to do so within five years, but not all of the blame was his.

The dispute centered on the La Brea oil field near Talara in northern Peru, and did not concern the other interests of I.P.C. The La Brea field, indeed, was producing only about half as well as it had in its peak years, and its yield was steadily decreasing. I.P.C. owned half interest in the more productive Lobitos field, had a large refinery at Talara, and controlled the sale of 55 per cent of the gasoline sold in Peru. It also had excellent prospects of getting concessions to drill in the jungle lands east of the Andes, where Mobil Oil has already invested twenty million dollars. Now that things have gone sour the I.P.C. will be lucky to hold onto anything of value in Peru.

The trouble began almost half a century ago. The International Petroleum Company had bought the disputed La Brea field in 1924 from a British oil company under circumstances which Peruvians have never considered legal. The area in question had been under litigation for some time when British and Peruvian representatives met with the president of the Swiss Federal Court and reached an agreement giving the British ownership.

This arbitration granted the owners a privileged tax status and took place under the Augusto Leguía dictatorship. It also happened to be at the time Harding was President of the United States and the Teapot Dome Oil scandal was shaking this country. The Peruvian government has never considered the arbitration agreement as binding, and the I.P.C.'s operations at the La Brea field have been a bone of contention between Peru and the American company ever since.

When Belaunde became president in 1963 he made every effort to resolve the problem. He offered I.P.C. concessions to expand its interests in other areas in return for a settlement concerning La Brea. The oil company, being a business and not a government agency, took a hard legalistic line in order to protect its interests. For years it had been paying the highest wages in Peru and its housing facilities for workers had evoked from Belaunde himself before he became president this injudicious remark: "If this is imperialism we need not less but more of it." But on the other hand, the I.P.C. had constantly applied its considerable weight to various Peruvian governments to improve its corporate position. Peruvians claim that it also "bribed ministers, corrupted governments, and promoted revolutions." At the very least the I.P.C.'s public relations left much to be desired, while Belaunde's continuing delay in reaching a settlement was rapidly raising the dander of his supporters.

The government of the United States, which should have used its formidable influence to bring the two divergent points of view together, chose instead to cut off practically all aid to Peru in an effort to pressure that country into a settlement favorable to I.P.C. This policy continued for five years. It was never announced officially but was the result of a deliberate standstill in all aid ventures in Peru. Schools, roads, water supply systems, and countless other projects receiving United States aid were stopped dead in their tracks. Peru's poor masses, who had never even heard of I.P.C., were the ones who suffered. Meanwhile, passions mounted among the Peruvian ruling caste, and when finally the two sides did come to terms it was too late. Both Belaunde and the United States Department of State had lost their chance. Peruvians regarded the final agreement as a sellout and were deeply frustrated.[194]

A military coup, headed by General Juan Velasco Alvarado, October 3, 1968, ousted Belaunde, he was put on a plane bound for Buenos Aires, and the La Brea field was expropriated by the junta. By this time anti-Yankee sentiment was so strong that General Velasco had the support of the great majority of all Peruvians in the action he had taken. The left as well as the right hailed the expropriation. No one knows what would have happened had the oil dispute been settled earlier. Perhaps APRA was rapidly gaining strength and looked like a sure winner in the forthcoming 1969 elections. This was the one thing neither the generals nor the forty families would permit under any circumstances. On the other hand, it was Belaunde's failure as president which caused APRA to win increasing support among the people.

I.P.C. then demanded compensation for the property taken over and General Velasco responded that Peru would gladly pay compensation if first the I.P.C. handed over to his government the $690 million of profits made during their forty-four years of illegal operations in the La Brea field. The United States and Peru then squared off. Peru seized fishing boats which came within the two hundred-mile limit (the United States recognized a twelve-mile limit), and the Hickenlooper Amendment required that the United States automatically cut off all aid to a country expropriating United States-owned property without prompt and adequate compensation. In retaliation Peru recognized the Soviet Union and entered into a trade agreement with that country.

This dispute between Peru, long one of the best friends of the United States in South America, and the International Petroleum Company, at once had the gravest international consequences. It helped to unseat a constitutional government, united Peruvians behind a junta regime, increased anti-United States feeling all over Latin America, placed the United States Department of State in the very bad light of attempting to compel a sovereign and constitutionally elected Latin American government to come to favorable terms with a private North American corporation. Net result: the good intentions of both the Good Neighbor Policy and the Alliance for Progress were suddenly brought into question. In a word, all this "is the result of the American corporate presence, which operates independently of American foreign policy, but has more to do with Latin American attitudes than any speech by the President, or any white paper or soothing statement from the Department of State." [193]

An American analyst who has probably probed more objectively into the I.P.C. problem than anyone else in this country stated that the episode fortified

> . . . those who claim that the United States is more concerned with its business interests than with the welfare and freedom of its sister republics. Many events and forces have contributed to these results, but our policy toward Peru was among them. It was, therefore, a policy damaging to our self-interest and harmful even to American investments.
>
> It didn't work, and if it had succeeded the price would have been high. For we have interests in Peru far more significant than protection of the relatively small investments of Standard Oil. Among them are the social and economic progress of the Peruvian people, the strengthening of democracy, and the encouragement of political forces congenial—but not submissive—to the United States. [194]

Another North American analyst of the situation concluded that "Velasco's was a dazzling performance, a policy run on little more than opposition to the

United States." To the extent that this is true it represents the failure of our Department of State to fulfill its primary mission, which is to maintain the good will of foreign peoples, to aid the forces of democracy when it is able to do so, to improve the lot of those who are less fortunate than we, most particularly in our own hemisphere, and especially to follow the course which will best serve the long-term interests of the United States. It achieved none of these things.*

If the International Petroleum Company represents one of the more unhappy North American ventures in Latin America, the Vicos community experiment symbolizes one of the most promising. Vicos probably represents the greatest return on any investment ever made by the United States in Peru, not a return in money, to be sure, but a return in human redemption and good will, an even greater reward.

The Vicos Indian community is situated in the Andean Highlands of northern Peru. Its 37,000 acres of land extend from an elevation of about 9,000 feet to an elevation of some 14,000 feet. The pass eastward leads to the lower hills that are dotted with mines; the way out westward is frequented by mule trains bearing silver and lead. Vicos itself, however, is an agricultural community. In 1594 the Viceroy of Peru sold "the land of Vicos and all the Indians on it" to a Don Fernando de Colonia for 300 pesos and 9 reales. From that year to 1952 the Vicos domain passed from owner to owner and from owner to renter. In 1952 an American, Allan R. Holmberg, professor of Anthropology at Cornell University, rented the parcel and its inhabitants for a five-year period.

Vicos was owned by the Public Benefit Society of Peru, which owns over three thousand similar communities in the Andean Highlands. The Public Benefit Societies are responsible for running the local hospitals. They lease out Benefit properties in order to obtain necessary operating funds. The renters or leaseholders are free to make as much for themselves as they can, but Vicos had never been a very profitable community. The renter just before Holmberg had gone bankrupt trying to grow flax and weave linen cloth in a nearby textile mill.

Holmberg had a $100,000 grant from the Carnegie Corporation to study life in these highland communities, and when he learned that Vicos was up for rent, the opportunity seemed too good to pass by. However, he was reluctant to become the sole leaseholder, for he knew that a gringo landlord might arouse all kinds of Peruvian antipathies, so he persuaded Dr. Carlos Monge Medrano, President of the Institute of Indian Affairs in Lima, to come in with him and act as front man. Monge Medrano was a specialist in the biology of the Andean Indian, and was also one of the most distinguished physicians in Peru. Monge

---

* In June 1970 the highlands of Peru were hit with a violent earthquake which toppled whole villages, destroyed dams, inundated the countryside and resulted in 60,000 dead and incalculable economic loss. U.S. planes and helicopters immediately helped to bring food and medicine and Mrs. Nixon visited the stricken area. An estimated 800,000 were left homeless by the quake. Tons of Soviet supplies were also sent to Peru.

Medrano took care of the legal and political details of the arrangement, while Holmberg, with his wife and three children, established themselves in a run-down adobe house on the Vicos hacienda plaza. The place had no plumbing, drinking water was drawn from a nearby irrigation ditch, and everything else was equally primitive. In this adobe hut Holmberg became the absolute boss of 380 Indian families, consisting of about 1,700 persons.

The head of each family owed him three days of work each week, doing whatever he told them to do. The wives and children also owed him personal services as cooks, maids, grooms, repairmen, shepherds, and the like. The best fields of the community, along the Santa River, were his, and all produce from them went to him. The Indians on their free days would be allowed to cultivate the less productive rocky soil at higher altitudes. Tradition decreed that the owner or renter of the domain seldom appeared in person among his Indians, but when he did he was privileged to be carried around on their backs. In fact, it was customary for upper-class Peruvians to refer contemptuously to the native Indian as "the animal that resembles man."

The natives of Vicos held no secular or political power whatsoever. For centuries the only collective aspect of their lives under their own control were the religious celebrations, and as a result they had become utterly inept in social organization or action. Their lives were poor, static, hopeless, and they distrusted their landlord absolutely. Holmberg obtained the aid of Peruvian anthropologist Mario Vásquez to break through this wall. With Vásquez as speaker at the weekly meetings which Holmberg held with the heads of families, meetings held formerly only to tell the workers where to go and what to do, they began to discuss the real problems of Vicos. As evidence of his good faith Holmberg publicly gave up his right to personal services and further decreed that all profits from his own river fields as landlord would become the community's cash balance, which he hoped would someday be enough to help Vicos buy itself back from the Public Benefit Society.

Slowly the Indians came out of their shells and began to take an interest in tilling Holmberg's fields. The professor taught them how to produce more and better potatoes at less cost by using superior seed potatoes, more efficient planting methods, fertilizer and spraying. After seeing the increased harvest the Indians began to use these improvements on their own lands, and output jumped so dramatically that Vicos not only was able to feed itself better than ever before but had a large surplus of potatoes to sell in the urban market. Cash began to accumulate. Profits from Holmberg's fields were used to build a new school, the best rural school in Peru. The Indians of the community made up a slogan, Se cambiará, "things will be changed," and the spirit of the village began to improve.

Filled with a new sense of pride and accomplishment they elected a council of ten to organize and govern their community. By 1962 Vicos had enough money saved up to negotiate buying its independence, but by this time things were going so well that the Public Benefit Society was reluctant to close the deal. It happened that Edward Kennedy was in Peru at this juncture, and after a visit to Vicos he was so deeply impressed by what had already been accomplished that he spoke warmly in the community's behalf to government representatives in Lima. These people put pressure on the Benefit Society and negotiations were favorably concluded. Vicos had at last purchased its own independence. Indians in the surrounding area had watched the whole drama unfold with mounting enthusiasm, and the Vicos community development program quickly spread to nine adjacent communities, while the idea itself has sent arrows of hope out into all corners of Peru.

One interesting aspect of the Vicos development was that when it began to make real progress all of those connected with it were called "Communists" by the big landowners nearby. On the other hand, the Communist party in Peru not only showed no sympathy with the project but actually denounced the whole idea as just another capitalist deceit. Evidently, the Peruvian Communists realized that every such success would diminish by just that much their own chances of stirring up trouble.

Total cost of the Vicos project in United States dollars was small. The $100,000 provided by the Carnegie Corporation provided salary for a Cornell professor for five years, enabled seventeen hundred Peruvians to move out of slavery into independence, and immediately affected at least five to ten thousand additional Peruvians in adjacent communities. Subtracting a nominal salary for Holmberg for five years we might conclude that $50,000 made possible the means of freedom for at least five thousand people, which would be at a cost of ten dollars per head. Such people-to-people projects are the cheapest, the best, the most certain way to help those who live in the poverty-stricken areas of Latin America.

In the long run, this is the only kind of improvement that will endure, because it strengthens the character of the people themselves. It would not be difficult to imagine what such a program might achieve were it applied to all of the enslaved communities in the Peruvian Highlands, then to Bolivia, and finally to Northeast Brazil. If fifty million of the poorest and most desperate people were helped in this way the total cost would approximate one billion dollars, or one fifth the amount of United States aid to the small island of Taiwan (Nationalist China), and of course a much smaller fraction of the many billions representing the cost of the war in Vietnam.

Velasco's military government had strong socialistic overtones. It took a cue from Vicos and another from Cuba and tried to radically restructure the Peruvian economy. Seventeen million acres of lands were expropriated and distributed among 300,000 peasants. Fidel Castro looked on from the sidelines and gave General Velasco his warmest endorsement. Up to this time Castro had abhorred all Latin American military governments, and they abhorred him. But now that the Peruvian generals were nationalizing the big estates, expropriating foreign industries, and destroying the local oligarchy, they got his enthusiastic approval. Of course, he viewed them as only a transition step on the road to total socialism.

For a few years Velasco and his supporters enjoyed a burst of economic activity and a great building boom. Oil profits and the ego surge touched off by the land takeover stimulated a wide range of public works, including a transandean pipeline, the construction of many public buildings, roads, schools, clinics, a broad welfare program, and so on. A great amount of military equipment was also purchased. Peru borrowed heavily in order to pay for this expansion and modernization, and the cost was great. A vast government bureaucracy sprang up, the builders had soon overextended themselves, and the national finances began to be very shaky indeed. There was already a debt of $5 billion on loans which the government had received, and Peru was on the verge of having to default on her payments.

Inflation increased rapidly, and prices skyrocketed. The cost of food went up 30 per cent, gasoline 50 per cent, and there were repeated riots and strikes in protest. The government imposed a state of siege, and decreed an austerity program for the country. In 1975 General Francisco Morales Bermúdez, who was more conservative in his social and political philosophy, seized power in a bloodless coup. There was no resistance because Velasco had gotten himself into a quagmire and had lost all public support. One of the first acts of General Bermúdez was to drop all the Marxists from his cabinet, and then to seek ways to make the government more solvent.

Nearly one half of the national labor force was unemployed or underemployed. A gallon of gasoline now cost ten times as much as it had five years previously, a cup of coffee six times as much, a bus ride five times as much, electricity four times as much, and the cost of clothes had more than doubled. Approximately 85 per cent of the population was classified as poor. The more fortunate lived on a diet of soup, beans, peas, fish, potatoes, rice, bananas, and wheat.

The huge shantytown of El Salvador (The Savior) on the outskirts of Lima gives some indication of how bad conditions still are. Here on a plot of arid land 300,000 people live in 30,000 tiny huts made of adobe, stucco, scrap lumber, tin sheets, and oil cans. The leftist government of General Velasco gave the first settlers of this colony water, electricity, and a clinic, but when the welfare and slum modernization programs were cut this barely made a dent in the needs of the impoverished and rapidly growing community. The austerity program also threw 65 per cent of the workers of El Salvador out of their jobs. Many of the women earn a pittance by cooking, washing, and selling things in the market, but most of the men are not working. Malnutrition and disease are rampant, and over 50 per cent of the people have tuberculosis. The average income per month for each family is about $35.

In 1980, in the first free elections in fifteen years, Belaunde Terry was elected president for a second time. Educated in the United States, this intelligent and compassionate leader made every attempt to carry out a program of agricultural reforms and public works, but only a few months after his inauguration there was a severe drop in the price of oil, copper, and silver, three of Peru's principal exports, and these reforms had to be curtailed. Another obstacle to progress was the emergence in Peru of a Maoist terrorist group, the Shining Path, which launched, and has continued, a witless campaign of destruction and assassinations throughout the country.[260] One night in Lima (the city's Black Night) members of this group assaulted public and private buildings in the capital with gunfire and incendiary bombs. Losses in property were calculated to be $250 million. Several thousand people were arrested, but terrorism still continues in Peru at a frightening pace.

In 1986 Belaunde Terry was succeeded by Alan García, a young charismatic APRA leader whose popularity at last brought that party into power with a smashing victory at the polls. Alan García faced widespread terrorism and almost insurmountable economic problems. First of all, under Peru's depressed economic conditions the nation's foreign debt of $14.7 billion became an unmanageable burden. Alan García attempted to meet the crisis by limiting repayment of this debt to 10 per cent of the annual profits from Peru's foreign trade, and by making some payments in goods rather than in cash. But there was another problem of even more grave proportions: both internal and foreign capital, fearing the risk of investments in Peru, fled the country in steadily increasing numbers. The president, confronting this situation, decided to nationalize all banks and savings-and-loan companies, thus at least making it impossible for further internal capital to escape. This infuriated Peruvian financial circles, and the two sides squared off for a fight to the finish.

Strangely, the leader of the opposition was Peru's most famous living writer and internationally famed novelist, Mario Vargas Llosa, who called the proposed nationalization a harebrained scheme of the first water. Vargas Llosa pointed out that if the programs were carried out it would create a bloated, corrupt, and powerful federal bureaucracy "undermining our fragile democracy to such a degree that it would surely crumble. A totalitarian threat is hovering over our country."

Vargas Llosa was telling the sad truth about his country's predicament. Alan García had been inaugurated president with jubilation, and a surge of idealism and hope was felt throughout Peru, but as his term neared its end the president faced a nation that had literally fallen to pieces. The economy was paralyzed; the terrorists, who had killed at least 12,000 people, controlled one third of the national territory, and were making serious plans to close in on Lima itself. Inflation rose to a catastrophic 2,000 per cent, real income declined by 50 per cent, and in 1988 alone an estimated 150,000 despairing Peruvians left the country. Paramilitary groups added to the general breakdown of authority, and in many parts of Peru unemployment reached 40 per cent. Violence and instability became a way of life. A real crackdown on terrorism never got under way. The Shining Path was not actually winning this war, the government of

Alan García was losing it. The mystique of a compact, well-organized minority enabled this small, dedicated group to terrorize a much more numerous majority.

As the elections of 1990 approached, Mario Vargas Llosa threw his hat into the presidential ring, and at first most Peruvians thought his election was a sure thing. Vargas Llosa had pinpointed and called public attention to his country's insufficiencies and to the government's inability to deal with them. He is an extremely intelligent person, who has swung from a youthful far-left position to a pragmatic, middle-of-the-road today, with most of his support coming from centrist, rightist, intellectual, and aristocratic groups. But he was a candidate inexperienced in politics, and if elected president he would have faced a divided nation, a bankrupt economy, a huge foreign debt, an empty treasury, a well-entrenched terrorist opposition, and a lackadaisical support from those who voted for him. The only well-organized elements in Peru which might be on his side were the military and perhaps the Catholic church.

Then, unexpectedly, three or four months before the elections, a new and unknown dark-horse candidate burst suddenly on the scene—Alberto Fugimori, an agricultural engineer and university president. Fugimori had a down-to-earth quality as a speaker and he persuasively espoused the causes of the underdogs. Not being very well known helped him, for the masses distrusted all well-known politicians. The son of hard-working Japanese immigrants, Fugimori was born and educated in Peru and was well acquainted with the country's strong caste system. In the campaign he very effectively emphasized Vargas Llosa's élitist connections, and his own humble beginnings. The opposition often referred to him as *el chinito*, "the little Chink," which boomeranged and helped his case with Peru's similarly derided urban poor.

As a candidate Fugimori also gained immediate popularity among the Indianist country masses, and he was warmly supported by Peru's powerful and growing evangelical Protestant groups. In June 1990 he won an impressive electoral victory over Vargas Llosa. With his Japanese background it was widely hoped that he would be able to obtain substantial financial aid for Peru from Japan. The country desperately needed an infusion of foreign capital, which did not seem forthcoming from the United States. Fugimori's first pronouncement was to propose a Latin American common market, much like the European common market, which has worked so well as a large-scale economic unit combining the strengths of several nations. Being a dynamic technocrat as well as a popular figure, Fugimori might just possibly be the man to get this good idea off the ground.

BOLIVIA

The puna or altiplano, that cold and barren region which forms a high tableland in the heart of South America at an average elevation of 12,500 feet, is one of Latin America's two permanent disaster areas. The other is Brazil's equally unproductive Northeast. The altiplano takes in a part of Peru, and most of inhabited Bolivia. Fifty-five per cent of Peru's population lives in the Sierra or on the altiplano, as do over 80 per cent of all Bolivians. It is a region of windswept steppes, and resembles an ancient seabed without the sea. The puny plant life bends in the wind as sea plants bend in the undersea currents of water.

The Indians of the altiplano, who once formed part of the "empire" of the proud Incas, lead a life of hopelessness and hate. True, they do not live in crowded urban slums, whose filth and poverty contrasts horribly with the nearby rich suburbs, for there is no real city on the altiplano, if we except La Paz, Bolivia's cold, gray capital. But the Indians of the altiplano live on land which does not produce enough to sustain life decently. They live like their animals, huddled together in the same bleak shelter. An Indian family will often raise a pet llama in this fashion in order to sell it at the end of the year for perhaps $75 or $100, the greater part of their annual income. These Indians are eternally hungry. They chew coca leaves in order to deaden the constant pangs of hunger, and by age thirty often look seventy.

They are nominal Christians, but it is a Christianity mixed with paganism whose main significance is to supply the reasons for their many brilliant religious celebrations, the only collective part of their lives that they control. But the religion of love is unknown to them, for all they have learned is suffering and hate, and none would wish to prolong such feelings beyond this life. Hunger is mortal and takes humanity away from man. The faces of these Indians are impassive, expressionless, deadpan, dead. They are walking corpses. Their feelings have been so long repressed that they appear nonexistent. They walk like cowed animals, shying away from the white man. The women carry their children or a load of wood as they trot along, somewhat as Jesus must have borne His cross.

Bolivia is not only a country of "sick people" but also holds the dubious distinction of having undergone more revolutions than any other Latin American nation. Some historians, perhaps with a penchant for colorful detail, have placed the figure as high as 180. In any case, Bolivia has seldom been governed well; indeed, it has seldom been governed at all. Until recently the tin and land barons combined with a few foreign investors ran the country like a private estate. The poverty of the masses was (and is) unbelievable.

I remember vividly a few days (back in 1942) spent in the town of Santa Cruz, 300 airline miles east of La Paz in Bolivia's thinly populated tropical lowlands. The general impression was of a squalid cluster of mud houses in the middle of nowhere whose sole connection with the outside world was the airplane. Yet strangely there in the center of the town plaza was the proverbial and anomalous Englishman with his lost blue eyes and his tobacco stand. He gave us a nostalgic look, and made us a gift of cigars.

The town radiated like a squat and filthy line of barnyards from that central axis. Pigs and chickens scrounged in the dirt streets, and the smell of outdoor toilet facilities permeated the air. Santa Cruz, occasionally called "queen of the tropics," was and is clearly a transition town, for recently people have begun to settle in this lower region of Bolivia, linking it to the national life. Today booming Santa Cruz has a population of 425,000 and is connected by rail or highway to Brazil, Argentina, and to Cochabamba and the altiplano.

Like Santa Cruz Bolivia is a country in transition, but it is still not certain in transition toward what. Within the past two decades, however, the country has suddenly broken loose from the chains of serfdom and made a revolution, the only real revolution in any South American country. The Bolivian revolutionaries demanded "land, control of their tin, food, and justice." Author and pilot of the revolution, and prime activator of the party which carried it out, the MNR (National Revolutionary Movement), was well-educated Victor Paz Estenssoro, formerly a professor of economics.

. He is a slight man, of unimposing mien, but when he speaks it is clear that he has all the essential charisma. His appeal, however, is not only to the emotions for he speaks with authority and confidence, facts and statistics rolling off his tongue as if he knows exactly what he is talking about. I once heard him deliver a lecture before a large group of sophisticated students at UCLA, and before he had stopped talking he had them all with him. On the following day many admitted with some chagrin that they were not quite sure whether or not they had been "taken." After a few years of Paz Estenssoro as president of Bolivia, many Bolivians had similar reservations. But for twelve years he was either president or head man (1952–64) in his country before he was ousted by the inevitable military coup. Yet Paz is undoubtedly a leader of exceptional qualifications, and it must be stated that there can be no turning back from the revolution that he made in Bolivia.

The MNR was organized in 1941 by Paz Estenssoro and other Bolivian intellectuals, some with strong leftist leanings, others with Nazi and Peronist sympathies. They were all united through their hatred of the Bolivian tin tycoons, the big landlords, and the foreign capitalists. In 1943 the MNR group overthrew General Peñaranda, an uneducated ally of the tin interests and an outspoken friend of the United States. Peñaranda's army crushed strikes while his government did nothing to help the masses. The United States gave him extensive financial aid. Hubert Herring tells the story that when news of Peñaranda's election reached his mother, the old lady said: "If I had known Enrique would be president, I would have sent him to school." The remark was superfluous, for in 1943 when he was in the United States on a goodwill and fund-seeking mission, Columbia University granted him an honorary Doctorate of Laws degree. This was the man deposed by Paz and his MNR.

Major Gualberto Villaroel, a hero of the Chaco War, became MNR's first president in that same year, 1943. His administrative capacity was not the most enlightened, and his purported friendship with Perón made Washington very wary of him. Villaroel stumbled along in a political morass for two and a half years after which he was hanged from a lamppost by an uncontrollable mob.

Villaroel was followed by six years of conservative rule (1946–52) during which inflation and continued poverty further inflamed the Bolivian masses. Europe and Japan rose from the ashes but Bolivia remained inert and prostrate.

In the elections of 1951 Paz Estenssoro was MNR's presidential candidate. He had been living in exile in Argentina for six years. Paz did not win the elections, but despite the probably rigged returns he polled a stunning number of votes, so once again the military seized control. A few months later there was a massed uprising in La Paz, the junta was tossed out, and the MNR called Paz back from Buenos Aires to take over the government in 1952. Thus began his twelve-year stint.

Paz did fulfill his campaign pledges. He expropriated vast tracts of land, nationalized the tin mines, raised the miners' wages, strove to diversify the economy, opened up oil fields for which he was forced to seek foreign capital, and built up the school system. Paz also liquidated the landholding class and distributed thousands of acres to landless Indians; he even moved 50,000 farmers into the lowlands of Bolivia's underpopulated tropical eastern territories giving each family 123 acres. But his revolution was largely a makeshift affair. The administration lacked properly trained personnel, the country's population was undisciplined and lacked the training, equipment, and intelligent willpower to make a concerted effort for the national good.

The most immediately evident weakness of the Bolivian revolution was the decrease in the country's food productivity. The newly created small farmers worked only enough to supply their own needs; having no experience in the marketplace and not understanding the need for accumulating capital, they balked at producing more. The cities soon began to find the most essential foods in short supply, and prices soared. The national currency, the boliviano which was 60 to the dollar in 1950, dropped sharply and in 1957 the rate was 12,000 to the dollar. Not until 1960 with aid from the International Monetary Fund, was the government finally able to get the currency under control.

Another weakness of the revolution was Paz's high-handed treatment of the opposition. He openly admits that many landowners and rich landowners were put in jail, but he insists that this was because they refused to cooperate with the policies of the federal government. He does not admit that there was widespread torture and starvation of these prisoners, that political bosses replaced landlords in many regions, that corruption was almost endemic in his government. In 1964, Paz even rigged the constitution so that he might run again for president, but the opposition abstained, so his election carried no weight and the country soon became unmanageable. The well-organized tin miners were on the verge of open revolt.

In November of that year General Ovando, commander-in-chief of the armed services, confronted Paz and told him summarily: "I am taking you either to the airport or to the cemetery. Which do you choose?" Paz took the airport and exile in Lima. The military returned to the presidential palace, the armed forces received a 40 per cent increase in salary while the wages of miners were reduced and their objections stifled with bullets.

Bolivia got set for the elections of 1966 in which General Barrientos, who campaigned in the remote villages, wearing an Indian costume and speaking in Quechua, was enthusiastically elected president. Barrientos tried to get along with everybody, but his administration was visibly shaken in 1968 when it was revealed that his right-hand man, Minister of Government Antonio Arguedas, had shipped Che Guevara's diary off to Fidel Castro via Paris, so that Fidel might first publish it. Arguedas then fled to Chile and announced that he was a Marxist. The entire Bolivian cabinet resigned in protest.

Paz Estenssoro, in exile was still one of Latin America's most adroit leaders. When he first arrived in Peru it was under the rule of Belaunde Terry, but later he found no difficulty in adjusting to the junta takeover in that country. He said that the military leaders of Peru treated him well. Perhaps, too, they may have listened to some of his persuasive arguments for the nationalization of foreign interests in Peru and for the expropriation of the country's great estates. After all, it was somewhat demeaning that Bolivia, one of the most backward countries in Latin America, should in economic reform get the jump on Peru, center of the ancient Inca empire, heart of the Spanish colonial regime, and birthplace of more recent APRA revolutionary theorists who were never quite able to gain control of the government.

Paz explained that he and his friends who organized the Bolivian MNR had read everything they could find on the Mexican Revolution, the impassioned *Seven Essays* of the Peruvian Communist Mariátegui, and Nehru's *Discovery of India*. They fused what was gleaned from these sources into their own revolutionary theory. Paz points out that revolution and nationalism go hand in hand in Latin America today. In the undeveloped countries the process is necessarily very different from what it is in the more developed nations, because in the former the state itself is the only possible means of change. No other element in the national life is strong enough to effect a radical transformation in the national life. The state must break the age-old stratification and must then introduce the masses to a money economy. In this way they will eventually become incorporated into the nationhood.

In Bolivia today, Paz claims, 200,000 families who worked as serfs before the revolution, now own farms of their own, and 500,000 citizens now have social security. But the greatest success of the revolution, he says, is that "the Indian no longer bows down when he greets a white man." Paz is enlightened enough to recognize and also to point out the endemic weaknesses with which any revolution must cope: the overall backwardness of his and of similar undeveloped countries, the lack of any understanding of social and political duties among the masses, among the leaders a bogging down of responsibility which results in splintered political factions, and among the labor unions an overriding self-interest, as if they alone should be the recipients of the state's broadened control of the national productivity. The abyss between the leaders and the led is still the great peril of the underdeveloped Latin American nations. How can these two extremes be integrated in the midst of poverty, ignorance, and venal politicians?

Colorful President Barrientos, elected in 1966, enjoyed hopping about Bolivia visiting the remote villages, especially when some project financed or subsidized by his administration was inaugurated. An avid air traveler (he was an ex-air force officer) he spent more time in the cockpit than he did in his presidential office. He even boasted that he had walked away from twenty-five air crashes large and small. He did not walk away from crash number twenty-six.

In May 1969 he visited by helicopter the small Andean village of Arque in order to dedicate a school honoring John F. Kennedy and to inaugurate a new public health dispensary. He also turned over to the municipality a sum of money which would make possible the village water supply. When the ceremonies were concluded his helicopter rose from the ground on a placid afternoon, struck some telephone and telegraph wires, and fell into a riverbed. When the villagers reached the wreckage all three occupants were dead. Vice-President Adolfo Siles Salinas took over for the remaining fifteen months of Barrientos' term. The peasants immediately began to grumble that the city folks and their oligarchy were again in control of Bolivia. September 26, 1969, General Alfredo Ovando, commander of the Bolivian military forces, ousted Siles Salinas and established junta control. Bolivia was back where it had started from.

Things did not improve greatly for Bolivia during the 1970s. In many ways they became worse. Colonel Hugo Bánzer Suárez seized power in August 1971 and ruled the country with an iron hand for seven years, almost a record for continuous rule in Bolivia. After many leftist governments, he turned Bolivia to the right, banning political parties and labor unions. When the miners declared a strike, troops occupied the mines. There was a modicum of stability in the political sphere, but civil rights were violated right and left, and in 1977 the United States officially called this to the attention of the Bolivian government. Financial aid was denied for a brief period, supposedly during which civil rights were restored. But this was like a tap on the hand, meaning nothing, for almost immediately further U.S. millions were forthcoming. United States financial aid to Bolivia totals approximately $100 million annually, while private investment banks extend another $200 million.

In the meantime, Bolivia continued to be the source of a great portion of the drugs which illegally find their way into the United States, via Colombia and Honduras. Bolivian officialdom has long abetted the drug traffic. Another side to the picture is that some Americans visiting Bolivia have been arrested by the police who find drugs that have been "planted" on them. They are then slapped in jail without due process, and may spend weeks or months in a filthy cell before being released. During this experience every Bolivian policeman, soldier, or official with whom they come in contact expects a bribe for his "help." In some instances thousands of dollars are paid before the prisoner is finally freed and allowed to leave the country.

The Bolivian economy has never been well managed or properly diversified. The country, however, is rich in natural resources, mostly undeveloped because of the lack of capital, technical experts, and roads. The country has vast deposits of tin, lead, zinc, copper, oil, tungsten, bismuth, antimony, gold, sulfur, silver, iron ore; it has great stands of timber and fertile soil. Tin, which has been the source of greatest wealth in recent years, is reaching the point of depletion and may run out completely by the end of this century.

Bolivia has been singularly unfortunate in the outcome of her wars, each of which has further depleted the national territory. In 1870 she lost 55,000 square miles to Argentina, Brazil, and Uruguay. In 1879 Chile took her only port and corridor to the Pacific, in 1903 Brazil took her rubber producing area, and in 1935, after the Chaco War, Paraguay seized 100,000 square miles of her tropical lowlands, thought to contain petroleum. U.S. companies drilled for oil all over the Paraguayan Chaco under generous forty-year contracts, but no oil was found. Rich deposits of petroleum were discovered in Bolivia's remaining narrow slice of this region, and she is now oil sufficient and even exports sizeable quantities of this product.

The cost of living in Bolivia has been steadily rising, and unofficially the increase during the 1970s is placed at 350 per cent. The tin miners, whose leftist labor union is very strong, declared a wages war against the Bolivian government which was trying to keep inflation from getting out of control. They demanded wage increases amounting to more than 30 per cent. Their level of pay in 1978 was approximately $4.80 a day.

Since the beginning of the century, tin has been Bolivia's principal product. It is the country's greatest boon as well as its greatest bane, for it caused great distortion in the economy, which came to depend almost solely on that one product for its export trade. The discovery and development of the tin mines is one of the most unusual rags to riches stories of all time. A young Indian named Simón Patiño worked as a clerk in a store in Cochabamba where he received miserable wages but did his work well and made many friends. Customers were frequently overdue in paying their bills, and some never paid at all. One particular customer, an impoverished Portuguese prospector, was many months behind in his payment. As he was a good friend of Simón's, the proprietor of the store sent Simón to collect the bill, telling him in no uncertain terms that if he did not come back with the money he would be fired.

Simón traveled the thirty miles into the mountains where the Portuguese lived in a mud hut near his "mines." Simón asked for the money, but his friend swore that he had not a penny. Simón explained that he would lose his job unless he returned with the payment, and the Portuguese then offered to pay his debt by passing over to Simón's boss ownership of his tin mine, which he insisted was very rich. Reluctantly, Simón took the papers of ownership and gave them to his boss, who in a fit of fury fired him on the spot. He had not paid Simón his last month's wages and shouted: "You take the papers. They will be your wages for last month!"

Simón and his young wife left Cochabamba to occupy a hut near the mine. For many months they worked it with pick and shovel, grinding the ore by hand in order to extract the small amounts of tin inside. Then a child was born, and they felt trapped at the site. Another baby made it impossible for them to even think of getting away. There was no work in Bolivia. The family all suffered from malnutrition and from the extreme cold of the altiplano. Simón's hands were constantly swollen and lacerated from the arduous labor. Then one day he hit a vein of pure tin, and soon he discovered another, and another. He took some of his samples to Oruro and sold them at a good price. He was told that he had made a bonanza strike, and news of the discovery soon traveled far and wide. A foreign mining company sent representatives to examine the site and offered Simón a million dollars for ownership. He was eager to accept, but his wife refused insisting that the mine was worth much more than that.

She was right, for the family soon prospered beyond their wildest dreams. Simón soon had a couple of dozen Indians working for him, then a hundred, and finally two or three thousand. In 1920 when he decided to leave Bolivia, his fortune was estimated at $500,000,000. The family traveled to Paris, London, New York. While in New York they occupied an entire floor of the Waldorf Astoria Hotel, where they were visited by many of the richest and best-known North American tycoons. Bolivia called Simón back to appoint him as her ambassador to Spain, and then to France. In 1940 he left his country for good and established residence in New York. His two daughters married into the wealthy aristocracy, and his son took as his wife a Bourbon princess. The Patiño family was unquestionably the wealthiest in Latin America.

Tin is still the most important *legal* export of Bolivia, but in recent years cocaine has surpassed in value all other exports combined. As drug demand grew throughout the world, Bolivians began to plant coca bushes in large areas where they had never been grown before, neglecting basic food crops whose prices then rose astronomically. While the masses starved, big money was made on cocaine. Several high-ranking officials and military officers were implicated in the illegal drug traffic, including one president and a minister of the interior. Political and economic conditions inside Bolivia rapidly disintegrated. Within a period of three years (1980–83) there were seven different governments, and inflation skyrocketed.

In 1985 Paz Estenssoro was reelected president. He saw clearly that cocaine was destroying Bolivia and asked the United States for help. This country sent several helicopters and a couple of hundred men to aid Bolivian police to seek out and destroy the new coca farms, sparing fields where the plant had been grown for centuries "for traditional uses." In the Andean area *chewing* coca leaves is regarded as on a par with drinking alcohol or smoking tobacco. This combined U.S.–Bolivian assault on cocaine had only a marginal effect. When the helicopters appeared over a village, church bells began to ring and the coca dealers all cleared out.

Paz stabilized Bolivia's finances without price controls by selling outright or closing down many state-owned mines and enterprises, then devaluating the currency, firing thousands of state workers, and drastically reducing spending. The inflation rate, which had risen to 10,000 per cent a year, decreased to approximately 15 per cent. Paz used the funds he had thus accumulated, and what he could borrow, to develop agriculture and cattle raising, especially in the province of Santa Cruz, which lies between the mountains and the plains in a fertile area of tremendous potential. Whatever criticisms may be leveled at Paz, this 75-year-old political veteran showed the more advanced Latin American nations what can be achieved when there is a strong and intelligent leader at the helm.

President Paz Estenssoro had pulled Bolivia back from the brink of the abyss, and given her a new lease on life. Faith in democratic government was restored, inflation brought under control, and there was at last a firm basis for economic stability and growth. Such an achievement in South America's poorest country was nothing less than monumental, and indeed it was something unique in Latin America. The difficulty lay in the succession. In the elections of 1989 there was no clear winner to succeed Paz, and no one of his caliber among the candidates. When the balloting produced inconclusive results, the Congress chose Jaime Paz Zamora as the next president.

Paz Zamora had studied for the priesthood earlier in his life, but dropped out of the seminary before being ordained. Later he attended the University of Louvain in Belgium where he received a degree in the social sciences. He became a Marxist radical and served as the vice president in the highly unsuccessful left-wing Bolivian coalition government of 1982–84. His political views changed when he had to confront the Bolivian reality, and as a candidate for the presidency in 1989 he ran as a moderate leftist. He received only 20 per cent of the votes initially, but he was able to form an alliance with Hugh Banzer and his Conservative party, thus broadening his base. Banzer was assured of at least half of the cabinet posts in the Paz Zamora government. This fragile coalition hamstrung the new administration even before Paz Zamora had assumed the presidency. It was not an auspicious beginning for the decade of the 1990s in Bolivia.

CHILE

Chile has not been subject to the series of coups and political upheavals which have plagued her neighbors—Argentina, Peru, and Bolivia. With the exception of one experiment in dictatorship under Carlos Ibáñez in 1925–31 and its feverish, soul-searching aftermath, Chile was an exemplary democracy until the tragic 1970s. Charles de Gaulle called her "the pilot country of Latin

America." Chile has a large, well-organized working class, an intelligent electorate, even her women voters are politically sophisticated and very articulate. Until 1973 there was a very powerful Communist party, whose leftist front won control of the country in the 1970 elections, and there is, of course, a wealthy landed class supported by a body of dirt-poor farm laborers. Last of all there are some large and very deplorable city slums called *callampas* or mushrooms.

But with a population of only thirteen million, Chile has produced an outstanding culture, a virile literature and art, a singularly beautiful music, a large and strong middle class, while her capital, Santiago, a city of four million, is considered by many foreigners as the most attractive and most intellectually stimulating city in which to live in South America. Chile has not received great numbers of immigrants like Argentina, and she does not have a huge depressed Indian population like Peru and Bolivia. In her racial makeup there is only a small proportion of Indian blood.

There is an upper crust of people of European stock in the central valleys, and there are colonies of Germanic and Yugoslav settlers in the south. The overall homogeneity of the country is exceeded only by that of tiny Uruguay, with which Chile long vied for first place in Latin America in the matter of an enlightened public opinion, political stability and democratic government. Chile was ahead of Uruguay in the honesty of her public servants and in her less omnipresent and less omnivorous bureaucracy. She was behind largely middle-class Uruguay in her land distribution and in her extremes of rich and poor.

The visitor has but to make a train or a bus trip in Chile to see at once that the large mass of Chileans take a great personal pride in keeping themselves neat and clean. They are a confident and hard-working lot. They have made a success of their small nation against considerable odds, and they know it. In recent years Chileans have by choice limited their increase in population. Contraceptives are widely employed; an abortion (not always surgically antiseptic) can be had for a pittance; out of 380,000 pregnancies a year approximately 140,000 are aborted. Unfortunately, the birth rate still remains higher than they would like and infant mortality is excessive.

A well-known Chilean writer, Benjamín Subercaseaux, has probed into this problem and come up with the following conclusion. The Chilean woman, he says, suffers from a lack of femininity. She is neither soft, nor tender, nor sweet. When she pursues a man she bumps into him or takes a personal object from him, daring him to get it back. The woman without femininity "little understands the tender relationship which should exist between mother and child. Among us the infants are treated so roughly, abortions are frequent and voluntary; and among the common people the mother looks upon the appearance of offspring as a misfortune."

Subercaseaux admits that the miserable conditions under which the proletarian family exists account in part for this lack of a maternal instinct, but he points out that in his generation, 1920–40,

. . . in China, where conditions are even worse, the families are numerous and the mothers solicitous. Here in Chile the children die almost intentionally. . . . The terrible infant-mortality rate which besets Chile is due, in large part, to the absence of maternal instinct and, to a far lesser degree, to the wretchedness and the pretended physiological poverty of our race.[195]

Chile's rate of population growth is moderate, about 1.8 per cent a year, and this plus her small total population necessarily results in a very severely restricted national market. Land distribution has only begun within the past few years, and has not yet proceeded very far. Farmlands are improperly used, and even foodstuffs have had to be imported in increasing quantities. As a consequence almost 50 per cent of the population suffers from malnutrition: 12 per cent from slight deficiencies, 27 per cent from serious malnutrition, and 11 per cent from desperate malnutrition. A very small percentage of the people own most of the land. In recent years the mass of Chile's population has shifted toward the cities, and is now nearly 70 per cent urban. Santiago contains nearly 25 per cent of the total population.

The extreme political left is numerically small in Chile but for several decades this group has exercised an influence far beyond its relative size. Under President Aguirre Cerda 1938–41 there was a brief "popular front" government in which the Communists participated, but Communist obstruction tactics prevented effective government and the popular front did not long endure.

After World War II President González Videla 1946–52, who had received Communist support in the elections, actually appointed three Communists to cabinet posts. Their actions, like those of their predecessors in the government of Aguirre Cerda, became so intolerable that the president soon threw them out of the cabinet, broke off diplomatic relations with Russia because of that country's interference in Chilean affairs, and even expelled Communist deputies from the national Congress. Among those so expelled was the world-famous poet, Pablo Neruda, perhaps the best poet writing in the Spanish language at that time. In 1948 the Communist party was made illegal in Chile, but this did not diminish its influence by very much.

Under González Videla, Chile built up her industries. New hydroelectric plants and copper refineries were constructed, and a steel plant was built to relieve the country of foreign dependence on this basic commodity. In the elections of 1952 Chile's ex-dictator, Carlos Ibáñez, then aged seventy-five, was voted into the presidency with the support of the still-furious Communists. Ibáñez was a friend of Perón and an admirer of Mussolini, but during his term in office he did not revert to the dictatorial tactics of his previous administration. Perhaps he recognized that there was no turning back the clock. Chile had outgrown her political immaturity of the 1920s and would no longer permit the military to control the state. Carlos Ibáñez was eighty-one when Jorge Alessandri, son of a famous former president of Chile, was voted into office.

Alessandri stabilized the currency and established a new monetary unit, the escudo, worth 1,000 Chilean pesos. For about three years, under rigid currency controls, the escudo was equal to approximately one United States dollar, but after this the lid blew off and inflation ran the cost of living up 532 per cent. Wages in the urban centers, low as they were, attracted rural laborers who worked for almost nothing, and Santiago entered a period of rampant growth while fertile agricultural lands were left uncultivated and more and more food had to be imported to feed the people. Extensive new slum areas sprang up suddenly around Santiago; no wonder they were called "mushrooms." In 1960, to make matters worse, a devastating earthquake hit Chile, killing many thousands of people and causing untold property damage. (Government officials estimated 5000 dead, half a billion dollars of property damage, and 350,000 left homeless.)

The country staggered under these blows, but somehow the strength of the people pulled it back on the right track again. However, the clamor for drastic economic, political and social reforms was becoming louder and louder, and in the elections of 1964 Chile faced its most crucial decision of many decades: would the people elect an out-and-out far leftist, Salvador Allende, an official Socialist whose strong Communist leanings would doubtless allow that group to control the government, or would they elect instead Eduardo Frei, a Christian Democrat, whose campaign cry of "revolution with freedom" aptly characterized his more humanistic point of view.

As the elections drew near the world tensed with anxious and watchful waiting. A real shudder ran through the United States Department of State. What would our foreign policy be if a clearly socialistic regime were voted into power in Chile as a result of honest elections? The time was not yet ripe for it. Frei's party received 1,410,000 votes to 980,000 for Allende, and there was a sigh of relief in Washington. One of the main causes for Frei's success at the polls was the feminine vote, which is tallied separately in Chile. Women have been voting since 1949, and with increasing political astuteness. They voted for Frei in considerably larger numbers than their brothers and husbands. Allende's appeal had been an impassioned and demagogic call for state ownership of the nations's sources of wealth. Frei was more restrained, his approach more moderate, but he also recognized the inevitability of change in Chile and demanded only that it be effected within liberty, without violence, and with justice and proper compensation for all, even for the large landowners and copper barons whose properties would have to be taken over by the state.

In July 1967, after two and a half years of debate and bickering, Congress finally passed a basic agrarian reform bill which empowered the state ultimately to take over fifteen million acres of land to be distributed to small farmers. The Chilean copper industry, which provided the country with 80 per cent of its foreign trade, was also brought under more effective state control and partial state ownership, and in October 1966 the New York *Times* reported that final success of the plan was only a matter of ironing out details, and that this was "all negotiated on a voluntary basis." The report continues:

The political importance of the Chileanization plan is that it provides a new method for meeting and perhaps overcoming one of the most vexing problems in United States–Latin American relations. This is the invariably disturbing effect of American ownership of a nation's natural resources.

One of the most pressing problems Chile faced was how to feed itself. In the last few decades population had grown faster than the productivity of foodstuff, and Chile spent one quarter of her foreign exchange earnings to import food: beef, sugar, milk products, edible oils, wheat, coffee, tea. Almost 40 per cent of the national territory could be cultivated, but only 8 per cent was under actual cultivation. Chile then had about 2.8 million head of cattle, fewer than she had in the year 1910. The basic weakness of the Chilean economy was too few people improperly using or not using at all too much land.

The government of Eduardo Frei did try desperately to set this right. Approximately 700,000 acres of land in big *fundos* were expropriated, but this was clearly only a beginning. The problem still remained how to get the right people back on the right land with sufficient equipment and sufficient incentive to expand agricultural productivity. It was not only an economic and agrarian problem but also a psychological problem. The ordinary Chilean citizen would rather be a moderately paid urban worker than a dubiously rewarded farmer. Few Chilean workers are willing to till the soil "like a peasant." Instead, they live and wait in the filthy, makeshift hovels of those dank and ugly mushrooms that have arisen beside the glittering city.

In June 1969 Chile announced the nationalization of Anaconda Copper, which separates the company from more than 70 per cent of its copper supply and an estimated two-thirds of its earning power. The giant company's stock immediately plummeted on the New York Stock Exchange, and tens of thousands of Americans who owned the stock lost heavily. Chile promised to pay for the Anaconda properties in installments during the next twelve years. Significant in itself, this action of Chile was representative of a broad trend in Latin America's "new look" at the United States, and shows how closely intertwined are the destinies of the two portions of the hemisphere.

In the presidential elections of September 1970 Chile reversed her moderate stand of 1964 and elected a Marxist president, the thrice defeated Dr. Salvador Allende. Dr. Allende, a charming man personally, had Fidel Castro's eager backing and was also supported by many Catholic voters in Chile. The United States, now anxious over the Near East and Vietnam, took little notice. A split in the opposing forces this time made Allende's election possible. Frei, who could have won hands down, was prevented by law from running again, and Allende, backed by the Socialist-Communist alliance, was faced with two weaker opponents in a three-way race: seventy-four-year-old Jorge Alessandri, candidate of the old right and the Christian Democratic choice, and Radomiro Tomic, who had Frei's support. Final official votes were: Allende, 1,075,615, or 36.3 per cent of the popular vote; Alessandri, 1,036,278, or 34 per cent;

and Tomic, 824,849, or 27.8 per cent. Allende's lack of a majority made his position extremely precarious, and the Chilean Congress had to offically "elect" him before he was installed in power. A military coup was very clearly hovering over Allende's head.

Just prior to his election Allende stated that "We are not going to implant a Socialist state by decree. We are going to have a government of six parties and start down the road to Socialism." He planned to begin by completely nationalizing the copper industry and by expropriating almost all rural lands for redistribution in peasant cooperatives.

Allende's election was a bonanza for world Communism, and Allende knew that even if he were ousted by force the contention could then be made that free elections in democratic countries are useless and meaningless. Allende himself pointed out that with Cuba at one end of the hemisphere and with Chile at the other, these two countries, aided by broad leftist forces throughout the Americas, would be able to create "the beginning of the Latin-American revolution." He also stated that he would now see to it that Chile's most distinguished newspaper, *El Mercurio*, would either begin to reflect the true feelings of the masses and the true conditions inside Chile, or face being closed down.

Dr. Allende's election at this critical juncture in one of Latin America's few remaining democracies indicated the depth of the need for radical social and economic reforms. As G. A. Geyer wrote in the Chicago *Daily News*: "Four or five years ago, the ways that Latin America might go were perfectly clear. It was either going to be democracy or Marxism, and there was very little ideological ad libbing in between.

"Today, after some psychedelic political transmutations, Latin America is in the midst of a process of convergence of ideologies that is ultimately far more important to us than anything happening in Vietnam. Old distinctions are disturbingly blurred. Marxists are working with leftist Catholics, who are working with military statists, and nobody thinks twice about it.

"Slowly but steadily, Cuban premier Fidel Castro is using the new mood to edge his way back into hemispheric affairs; and slowly but steadily, the United States is being edged out. . . ."

Eduardo Hamuy, a well-known Chilean sociologist, put it this way: "A process is going on that nobody can stop. The term *nationalism* is over-used; *statism* is better. The state is being converted into something more powerful, and the private sector is losing."

The hardness of old beliefs has softened, and political parties do not mean as much as they used to mean. What more and more Latin Americans want is not pure "democracy" or "Marxism" or "military statism," or whatever the term might be, but what will bring them more of the good things in life. They are tired of being told to wait and are willing to take very extreme risks in the hope of achieving a little more of their share in the pie. The election of Allende temporarily gave many Chileans the feeling that they were soon to get that share.

Allende was the first Marxist to be elected head-of-state in free democratic elections, and there were all kinds of expectations attached to his election, none of them very realistic. Viewed objectively he never had a chance. President Nixon admitted that he had charged the CIA with trying to instigate a military coup that would prevent Allende from assuming the presidency and, although this did not work, the United States continued to use its very strong influence to unseat him. When the Chilean national elections of March 4, 1973, gave Allende's opposition a majority in both the Senate and Chamber of Deputies, it became a foregone conclusion that he was carrying on a losing fight.

During his brief stay in power, however, Allende attempted to impose a frantic program of socialist reforms. He began by breaking up the big estates, then he nationalized the banks and expropriated the foreign-owned companies: Kennecot Copper, Anaconda, Cerro, International Telephone and Telegraph, and many others. Rural workers took possession of lands without waiting for legal distribution, and there was a euphoric "high" among the masses. Wages shot up, but there were no consumer goods to buy because curbs on profits had reduced output. Inflation hit with a vengeance. In 1973 it rose to 508 per cent, in 1974 it stood at 376 per cent, in 1975 it was still at 340 per cent, and then it began to decline. In 1978–80 it was about 70 per cent.

Allende's socialistic program and his closeness with Cuba and the Soviet Union infuriated many Chileans, who began to have real fears that communism would take permanent control of their country as it had in Cuba under Fidel Castro. The Chilean armed services were the most restive group. In September 1973, no doubt given every encouragement by the United States, military forces surrounded the presidential palace, bombarded it, and in the ensuing battle Allende was killed. There are many who say that the blame for his death should be laid squarely at the doors of the CIA. Be that as it may, the commander-in-chief of the Chilean army, General Augusto Pinochet Ugarte, seized control of the government, disbanded congress, and ruled through a military junta, which bloodily suppressed all opposition. The United States gave immediate recognition to the military regime and showered it with economic and military assistance.

The new government promptly reached a settlement with the U.S. companies whose properties had been expropriated, and they were invited back into the country. In fact, the junta made every possible effort to attract additional foreign investments. Import tariffs, established by Allende in order to encourage small businesses in Chile, were lifted by the junta in order to stimulate trade. Many small businesses went bankrupt as a result, but the economy as a whole began to burgeon. National productivity expanded an average of 7 per cent a year in the late 1970s, whereas in the period 1973–74 it had actually declined 7 per cent a year. Unemployment, however, was high, averaging 15 per cent in 1976–79; it was 17 per cent for female unemployment.

The government made gargantuan efforts to diversify the economy in order to free the country from its dependence on a few traditional products, primarily copper. The State Development Corporation (CORFO) was the main impetus in this diversification. The number of new nontraditional products shot up from about 400 in 1973 to more than 1,000 in 1977. The value of these exports rose 550 per cent during the same period. Industrial products made the biggest gain by growing over 600 per cent in value, but agricultural produce, formerly the bane of the national economy, increased 400 per cent during the same period, and Chile's dependence on imported foods greatly declined. Prior to 1973 the country had to import nearly 66 per cent of its foodstuffs, but by 1980 this had decreased to approximately 30 per cent. In 1978 and 1979, however, Chile imported over 900,000 tons of wheat each year, most of it from the United States. In search of new markets the government's economic team made promotional trips to Japan, South Korea, the Middle East, and Africa.

In the area of land distribution, Chile has undergone a radical restructuring since the presidency of Eduardo Frei who had emphasized a "revolution in freedom." Allende took up where Frei left off, and the large estates were broken up and given into the hands of their workers. Since General Pinochet assumed control this process has been cautiously reversed, and a few of these estates have been sold back to their former owners. These are the exceptions, however. Most of the lands that formerly belonged to the old estates have been put under the control of the Agrarian Reform Corporation (CORA) and are being worked as cooperatives. There are few small independently owned farms.

General Pinochet and the junta have an abysmal record in the area of human rights. On assuming power at least 2,500 Allende supporters were summarily executed, and from ten to fifty thousand others were imprisoned incommunicado. Chile's foreign image took on a repugnant hue. In 1977 Pinochet said that all political prisoners had been set free, but the Inter-American Human Rights Commission reported that several hundreds had simply "disappeared" with no trace. An editorial in the *Christian Science Monitor* says it very well: "The tragedy of the Pinochet government has been its failure to observe the codes of normal conduct in the Western world. The extensive use of torture, the repression of traditional constitutional guarantees, and a tough, almost belligerent stand against its longtime friends became the hallmarks of the Pinochet government." [262]

The secret police organization, DINA, consisting of 20,000 trained men, was abolished in 1977, and Pinochet allowed the election of a unicameral assembly in 1980, giving it the task of eventually electing a president. Conditions became more relaxed in Chile, and many exiles returned. There was an implicit agreement that they would not be molested unless they deliberately challenged the government. In the economic sphere there also began to be improvement. Higher copper prices had given Chile a better trade balance. Foreign capital began to feel safe in Chile and was carefully encouraged. Exxon paid $111 million for La Disputada copper mine, Goodyear bought a tire plant for $34 million, and ARCO was given the right to explore oil and gas tracts.

Overall some 300 companies signed contracts with the government, and foreign investments totaling $3 billion were approved by the junta.

Chile is one of the most homogeneous countries of Latin America; the few Indians live in a small corner of the country, and there are no blacks. It is a white country. Nothing infuriates a Chilean more than to be considered or referred to as an "Indian." This homogeneity is a rich blend of many diverse European stocks. The George Washington of Chile, Bernardo O'Higgins, was the son of an Irishman. Auturo Alessandri, a well-known president of the 1920s, was of Italian background. Eduardo Frei Montalva, former liberal president and leader of the Christian Democrat party, is from a Swiss-Spanish bloodline. Salvador Allende Gossens had Germanic forebears; and Augusto Pinochet is partly French. English influence is also very strong. Afternoon tea is an institution in Chile much as it is in England. The English also helped Chile to organize her excellent navy, once the biggest and best in Latin America. Chilean warships easily destroyed or captured the entire Peruvian navy in the War of the Pacific. Chilean soldiers also marched 1,000 miles overland and captured Lima, which they occupied for more than two years. Former President Odría of Peru once commented: "Let the soldiers march and the tanks rattle through the streets of Santiago in an armed forces parade, and in Lima the ground shudders." Chile still maintains an excellent army, navy, and air force.

Pablo Neruda, the great Chilean poet who was awarded the Nobel Prize in 1971, characterized his country thus: "We are a melting-pot of peoples grafted into the Spanish root stock." This homogeneity has produced one of the toughest and most flexible peoples of Latin America. Chile's rate of literacy is among the highest, her cultural life is fertile, her literature is first rate, and her willingness to self-criticize is admirable in the extreme. A sense of responsibility and self-discipline is strongly developed in Chilean family and school life.

The country is a geographical oddity. It is 2,650 miles long, and averages only 110 miles in width. It is more like an eel or a ribbon than a country, yet Chile contains 286,000 square miles of territory, which makes her larger than any West European nation. The rich central valley is about 600 miles long and 40 to 50 miles wide. The north of Chile is a vast desert where no rain ever falls and water has to be piped in for over two hundred miles. There is no green growth in this part of Chile and the inhabitants paint their houses green in order to be able to enjoy that color. In the south there are magnificent lakes and forests. All along the eastern frontier rise the towering Andes, and one is never out of sight of this formidable mountain barrier. But if Chile is a mountainous country, it is even more a nation of the sea. Until the advent of the airplane everything entered and left the country by sea, and every major city is on or near the coast.

The population of Chile is about 13 million, and this population has almost reached a point of stability. In some years the total population has actually diminished. Birth control education is widely fostered by the government, and even the church tends to look the other way. Uruguay is the only other Latin American country where population control is so deeply rooted in the daily life.

General Pinochet's regime, despite its harsh treatment of political dissidents, provided a favorable climate for foreign investments. In Chile production costs are 25 per cent lower than the world average, the government has been cooperative, and the country has modern ports, highways, rail, air, and steamship lines. The rate of inflation is low, and 90 per cent of the people have electricity. There is a high rate of literacy. Since the military takeover in 1973 economic progress of the big industries has continued unabated, and Chile has built up well over $1 billion of surplus in foreign trade. The country is the world's largest producer of copper, molybdenum, and fish meal. One million cases of wine are exported annually by fifty-one wineries, also nearly six million tons of fish, and $1 billion worth of forest products. Pine matures in twenty years on the two-and-a-half-million acres of Chile's timber plantations. There is a thriving furniture industry, and large amounts of pulp and newsprint are exported. Chile is also manufacturing and exporting arms of a very sophisticated kind.[263]

The other side of the coin, however, reveals quite a different picture. Under the military dictatorship total national income declined 15 per cent, but at the same time there was a steady growth in the income of the rich. The military establishment became a separate privileged society. Nevertheless, Chile's economy expanded dramatically in the late 1980s. The military dictatorship relaxed somewhat its repression of human rights, and provided a secure, stable, and profitable climate for both foreign and domestic capital. The regime gave Chile six straight years of economic growth and a declining foreign debt. It kept unemployment and inflation low, encouraged industry and foreign investment, rewarded hard work, and opened up new frontiers. The general built a road several hundred miles long that reached down into the southernmost part of Chile, a sparsely inhabited area rich in natural resources.

In spite of this material progress, Chileans did not forget the hundreds of people killed by Pinochet during the early months of his tenure, nor the hundreds persecuted, imprisoned, and tortured under his oppressive government. The result was that in October 1988, when a plebiscite was finally allowed concerning the presidency of the country, a large majority voted against a continuance of the Pinochet government, and demanded free elections to determine who would be his successor. At this point Pinochet capitulated and agreed to a vote, but he had already so solidified his position that he would be a senator for life, would continue as commander-in-chief of the armed forces until 1994, and would continue to be a member of the National Security Council. Most Chilean mayors and regional governors and many judges were appointed by Pinochet, and many of these remained in their posts. Pinochet himself stated bluntly: "Our mission does not end with a change in government, because the Chilean Armed Forces are above all governments, all groups and all opinions." His position with the military could assure him of control of any civilian president for years to come, but there is always the possibility that an opposition government, if it is strong enough, may take many of these perquisites away.

As elections approached in late 1989, the various opposition parties, having learned their lesson in 1970 when they split into several groups and so assured the election of the Socialist Salvador Allende, now got together and put up a single candidate, Patricio Aylwin. With the support of that seventeen-party, center-left coalition, he was elected president by a landslide. Aylwin stated clearly that under his presidency the Chilean military would be subordinate to the civil authority, and in this he had the support of the majority of all Chileans. However, the deeply entrenched military bitterly opposes subordinate status and is working for a constitutional amendment that would guarantee its immunity from civil control.

ARGENTINA

During the two decades prior to World War II Argentina had begun to fall apart. Irigoyen's second term was even more arbitrary, chaotic, wasteful and corrupt than his first, and when he left office in 1930, after serving only two frenzied years, the hopes of the Argentine people had turned to gall. The senile Radical octogenarian president had embodied and then destroyed their humble dream. Argentine writers, in a pathetic effort to recapture the old faith, spoke of an "invisible Argentina" of sleeping promise and hidden strength, but the majority of the people were not even aware of these tenous sentiments.

Argentine pride was still alive, but it was the pride of hollow men. The last chance came when Roberto Ortiz, a wealthy corporation lawyer, was elected president in 1938. He was already a sick man, but he did his best to restore integrity to the government and honest secret balloting at the polls. When World War II broke out he immediately made known his sympathies with the allies. His own class turned against him because of both these stands.

In 1940 his vice-president, Ramón Castillo, had to take over the presidency. Ortiz was suffering from severe diabetes, exhaustion, near blindness, and could no longer perform the duties of his office. Castillo reversed all the efforts Ortiz had made to restore democratic government, and announced his own pro-Axis feelings. Argentina now became a hotbed of Axis activities. Axis sympathizers penetrated and at times dominated the government, while Axis propaganda flooded the country and flowed out into the rest of South America by the tons. Castillo's government was so inept and so corrupt that even the military clique could not stand it, and in June 1943 he was overthrown by a military coup. General Pedro Ramírez became president, but nothing was done to control Axis activities.

Argentine fascists got government jobs, and the Argentine Jewish press was suppressed as official anti-Semitism continued unabated. The popular novelist

Hugo Wast, author of many tawdry romances (*Peach Blossom, Stone Desert,* etc.), and a well-known anti-Semite, was made Minister of Education. He promptly fired all university professors who opposed the military regime, which meant the most and the best of them. Then he filled the vacant chairs with his third-rate yes-men. One distinguished professor, Bernard Houssay, a Nobel Prize winner, said good-bye to his class in these dramatic words: "This will be my last lecture. The next one will be given by a colonel."[202]

Hugo Wast put religion back into the curriculum of the public schools, and stirred up as much anti-Jewish and anti-United States sentiment as he could manage. In February 1944 the United States and Britain were able to present indisputable proof that foreign Axis agents were operating under Argentine diplomatic immunity, and the government finally had a change of heart. General Ramírez was obliged to resign and turn over the presidency to his vice president, Edelmiro Farrell, called by one historian "a blundering nonentity." Throughout these trying months the majority of the Argentine people had supported the allied powers, and in 1945 Argentina finally declared war on the Axis.

The real leader of Argentina now was Juan Domingo Perón, head of the Group of United Officers (the G.O.U.), the armed services élite which controlled the country. Perón was one of those very *macho* leaders, proudly virile, a fine physical specimen, good at sports, an expert fencer, a respected officer, in a word, a real he-man. He had served as Argentina's military attaché in Italy during the heyday of Mussolini, and the idea of the corporate state intrigued him. Perón judiciously decided to move into power obliquely, and first took the not very popular position of Labor Minister. He had already courted the middle class, but found it too disorganized and too independent for his liking. Now as labor minister he made common cause with Argentina's underpaid urban workers and the even more underpaid farm hands. He fondly called these workers "*los descamisados,*" the shirtless ones.

Perón promised not only to put shirts on their backs, but to give them stronger labor unions, a bargaining power undreamed of in Argentina before, and all kinds of fringe benefits: better working conditions, bonuses, expanded social security, tenure, and pensions. It was with labor support almost 100 per cent behind him that Perón became president and dictator of Argentina, moving from labor minister to minister of war, then to the vice-presidency, until in 1946 he was elected president. His opposition, mainly upper class, tried to get rid of him in 1945 by suddenly arresting him and shipping him off to an island in the Plata, but the masses raised such a hue and cry that they had to turn him loose before the national elections, which he won handily.

Once in the presidency Perón did not waste any time. In 1949 he replaced the 1853 constitution, under which the country had been governed since the time of Rosas, and with which it had risen to greatness among the states of Latin America. Perón, incidentally, has often been compared with Rosas, who was put into power by his gauchos and kept there by them and by the Argentine servant class and urban masses. Both men alienated the intellectuals of their country, who went into exile by the hundreds.

The constitution of 1949 gave the federal government control of the national economy and financial structure, and in order to make this pill less bitter, Perón kept shouting that he was "emancipating" Argentina from foreign domination. This battle cry is almost sure-fire in any Latin American country. Perón did indeed expropriate the British railways, paying £150,000,000 for them, and he bought the American Telephone Company of Argentina for $100,000,000. He also nationalized the airlines and the shipping. He gave to women the right to vote, and granted legal status to illegitimate children. He increased the salaries of the army and navy officers to such a degree that by 1950 these were receiving more than their counterparts in the United States.

With the army and the masses behind him Perón then proceeded to destroy Argentine business, banking, the national press, the universities, and eventually even the farmer. Those who had money would no longer invest it in Argentina, and the flow of Argentine capital to Switzerland, the United States, and other foreign countries became a flood. Wages for urban workers kept going up as the labor unions strengthened their grip on the economy, but farm wages did not keep pace and production soon began to decline as rural workers poured into the cities, the new promised land. Between 1940 and 1950 the production of wheat decreased from over eight million tons to about two and one-half million tons, while the rate of capital investment in the nation declined by 70 per cent. By 1950 the Perón regime was staggering but the United States came to its rescue with a loan of $125,000,000 which helped pull it off the ropes.

While Perón was destroying Argentine farms and strangling the financial system and the press he made a big show of building up industry. It was a hollow victory, for while new power plants, public works, hydro-electric projects, ordnance factories, and even steel plants were planned on a good scale, this was mostly window dressing, because the country was slowly going bankrupt as a result of both fiscal and political ineptitude. Wages in the cities continued to rise, but inflation wiped out nearly all labor gains, except the cherished and unassailable gain of organized labor power.

Argentina's great *La Nación* and *La Prensa*, two of the best newspapers in the Hispanic world, were ignominiously muzzled, and free speech was stifled. The Supreme Court was packed and lost its integrity. University professors, writers, scientists, and intellectuals of all classes fled the country if they could find the means of doing so. Many of them came to the United States, where they still occupy positions of prominence in our educational system and intellectual life. But in Argentina the shirtless ones and even the servants were dedicated supporters of the dictatorship and especially of the person of the dictator.

As Perón tightened his stranglehold on Argentina, he pointed with pride to what he was doing, calling it a middle road between capitalism and socialism.

Perón himself, of course, was the messiah of the new movement of national emancipation, and "messiah" is not too strong a term, for the cult of Peronism soon became (and still is) the most powerful single force in the national life.

Perón ran the country *personally*, in the old Hispanic tradition. He had no right-hand man, but he did have a right-hand woman, Eva Duarte, who was first his mistress and then his wife. Eva gave Perón glitter among the poor, of whom she had been one; she knew how to do just the right thing to ingratiate herself and the regime in the hearts of the shirtless ones of Argentina.

Eva herself was of illegitimate birth, and when Perón first appeared on the horizon she was working in a radio station at a salary of about a dollar a day. After the military coup of 1943 had seized power from Vice-President Castillo, she made friends among the new leaders, and toward the end of that year she became Perón's mistress. In 1945 when the upper classes temporarily deprived Perón of his ministries and exiled him, it was Eva who steamed up the populace to take to the streets and put on a tumultuous demonstration insisting on his freedom, which was followed by his election to the presidency. Shortly after this Perón and Eva were married and Eva moved into the fabulous Pink House (Casa Rosada), which, one noted writer says, makes our White House look like a chicken coop.

Eva worked among the poor with an astute instinct for arousing love and loyalty, and with a diligence and an organizational capacity which were truly amazing. She doled out relief to those who were unemployed or ill, she built hospitals and clinics, established free blood banks, helped pay funeral expenses, put up child-care centers, played the role of the good Samaritan generally. Illegitimate, with little education and reared in poverty she sensed how these people felt, and knew what to do to alleviate their frustrations and their suffering. The fact that she was scorned by the Argentine upper classes added a cubit to her height.

Where did all the money come from? The well-born ladies of Argentina had for years controlled the Society of Beneficence, Argentina's associated charities, and had made the collection of funds one of their principal social as well as eleemosynary activities. When Eva became the first lady these great dames coldly shut her out of any participation in their affairs. The Perón government retaliated by taking over the control of all charities, and by making Eva the head of that control. The society ladies were thus forced to withdraw from the arena, and Eva's fund-gathering ability, aided by considerable governmental pressure on the enterprises from which contributions were requested, soon enabled her to collect immense sums of money.

These funds were immediately available for Eva's charitable work. There was no accounting. The suggestion that an audit be made met with an indignant response on the part of the masses, and Eva continued her good work unmolested. She also began to accumulate a costly wardrobe, lavish jewelry, expensive foreign automobiles, everything to permit her to live like a millionairess, which indeed she was. The poor saw in her an idealized image of themselves occupying the throne, dispensing largesse, snubbing the great families, moving like a Florence Nightingale among the ill, holding them all together, giving them faith and dignity.

Perón, now at the peak of his power, was elected to a second term in 1951. He received twice as many votes as his opponent. One thing only marred his good fortune: Eva was critically ill. The best doctors were called but there was no hope. In 1952, at the age of thirty-three, Eva Perón died of cancer. An uncontrollable mob attended her funeral and eight people were trampled to death, while hundreds were injured. Many Argentines wanted to make her a saint, but the Church turned a deaf ear.

Perón now slowly began to lose power. In 1951 he had closed down *La Prensa*, and all semblance of criticism of the regime vanished. A few months later he turned the paper over to the Argentine labor unions. It was an affront to fair-minded men all over the world. In 1953 a meeting of Perón's followers was bombed, and the Peronistas retaliated by burning the Jockey Club, center of Argentine high society, based on the horse, as one might suspect.

Perón compounded his mistakes by affronting the Catholic church; he legalized divorce, prostitution, moved to tax church properties, and to take away all church participation in the schools. In June 1955 an attempted military coup against him failed, but over three hundred persons were killed. Peronist mobs flooded the streets that night and looted and burned many churches destroying priceless art objects and gutting buildings. Two bishops protested vigorously and were bustled off to Rome, the Vatican excommunicated Perón, who was now on his last legs.

In September 1955 the military again closed in on him, this time for certain. A naval contingent came down the river, the army and air force joined in, and Perón took refuge on a Paraguayan gunboat anchored in the river. He was so nervous that he slipped and fell into the muddy water and had to be fished out and put on board. His treasure cellars in Buenos Aires were quickly entered, $25,000,000 in gold was found, several foreign cars, and much other loot. Perón did not flee alone. He took along with him his newest mistress, a girl of barely thirteen. Eva's devotees were scandalized, but most of them later forgave him. Three years had passed since Eva's death, and was not Perón a man?

Since the overthrow of Perón, Argentina has vacillated between military dictatorship and civilian rule, without ever being fully able to reestablish a democratic republic with a duly elected government and a duly observed constitution. The easy explanation of this flaw in a nation whose relatively well-educated electorate should make it Latin America's most successful democracy is to point to Perón himself who had cast such a spell on Argentina. Even in exile he continued to be a powerful influence in the national life.

The Argentine masses still remembered him with admiration verging on idolatry. Had he not given them well-organized and powerful labor unions, had he not increased their wages regularly, had he not given them extra bonuses for each additional child, had he not provided for their social security, their retirement, even for their various physical ills, had he not obliged the state to purchase at set prices all they could produce on the farms? The masses remembered these things, and wanted them all back again. And so with Perón gone Peronismo continued as strong as ever. But a lack of homogeneity, deep class hatreds, political charlantanism, the absentee landlords, and the division of land into vast feudal type estates also contribute to this fatal flaw in the Argentine body politic.

The generals who took over the Argentine government in 1955 had no wish to control it permanently. They simply wanted to oust Perón and then to restore the nation to regular elections and to civilian rule. But on one point they would not budge: Perón and his followers must not be allowed to get back into positions of power, for this, they were convinced, would be ruinous to Argentina. The military held on to the reins until 1958 when national elections were held. During the two and a half intervening years General Aramburu was the head of state, but he was clearly anxious to reestablish a civilian government. He restored the constitution of 1853, gave *La Prensa* back to its owners, made the Central Bank autonomous again, and made the Peronista party illegal. He could not, however, wish the Peronistas into extinction.

In the 1958 elections, unable to vote for a candidate of their own, the Peronistas cast their ballots for Arturo Frondizi, following Perón's direct orders from Madrid. Frondizi, an able professor of law, in preelection campaigning had promised to restore political power to them. But after his election the new president refused to make good this promise. In the first place, had he done so the military would have overthrown him at once. Many Argentines believed he had made such a promise merely to get elected, while others thought that he truly favored Peronismo without Perón, a kind of corporate state.

In any case, Frondizi very quickly saw that the main problem of his administration was the terrible economic depression that gripped the country. His government would have to find a way to keep Argentina from destroying itself through inflation and curtailed productivity. Inflation had already struck the economy a devastating blow. In 1946 the international rate of exchange stood at five Argentine pesos to the dollar. When Frondizi took over as president he was confronted with an absolutely incredible soaring of prices. In 1959 alone prices went up 114 per cent.

The president announced an austerity program which called for sacrifices from every citizen. He invited foreign investors and specialists into the country in order to increase production, especially of petroleum, which had always been in short supply. He carried out stringent fiscal and economic reforms, streamlined the government, courted capital investment, tightened the tax structure, restricted credit, and got the country moving again. His plan paid off, for in 1961 inflation had been slowed down to a mere 14 per cent. But Frondizi was now getting it from both extremes. The Peronistas were pressuring him from one side, and the military, without whose support no Argentine president can rule, from the other.

By the time the Punta del Este Conference of American states was held in January 1962 his situation was critical. The Peronistas did not want him to align himself with the United States in a strong stand against Castro's Cuba, while the military wanted him to go all the way. Frondizi did as nimble a job of double talk and tightrope walking as was possible, but he satisfied no one. When the national elections of 1962 were held a few months later, he made the fatal decision to allow the Peronistas to run their own slate. The result was a stunning victory for the Peronista candidates who received 35 per cent of all votes cast winning 45 out of 86 vacancies in the Chamber of Deputies, and 9 out of 14 governorships, including that of the province of Buenos Aires.

The military, which had vainly hoped that the Peronistas would meet with a convincing defeat at the polls, saw national disaster in their political victory. They refused to allow the duly elected Peronistas to take their seats. The latter retaliated with a general strike, the result was national chaos, and Frondizi found himself in an untenable position. When he refused to resign, the army picked him up bodily in the Casa Rosada and hustled him out of the country. There was another period of military government, which lasted until the elections of 1963.

During this period there was a split in the military, a brief skirmish in the streets, and General Onganía won out over his more demanding colleagues who were insisting on a long-term junta government to rid Argentina once and for all of Peronismo. Onganía would not go that far, but under pressure he did refuse to allow Perón's supporters to vote in the 1963 elections, so they cast blank ballots in protest. Arturo Illia was elected president and another period of civilian government ensued which lasted until 1966.

Illia, like Frondizi, was an Italian-Argentine. He was a relatively unknown figure before his election, and his physical mannerisms and slow movements resembled those of a tortoise, so to the Argentines he was soon widely known by that name, *la tortuga.* Illia fulfilled his promise to nationalize the Argentine oil industry by canceling contracts with all foreign companies and production began to decline immediately. He also broke with the World Bank and the International Monetary Fund, in two swift strokes thus slowing down the country's production of oil and obstructing the progress of direly needed industrial improvments. Instead, the new president chose the path of printing more paper money, which increased the rate of inflation alarmingly.

After these initial moves Illia adopted a tortoiselike policy of slow drift. He even drifted amiably along with the Peronistas, hoping perhaps to turn them into a respectable opposition party. But in the elections of 1965 the Peronistas received 37 per cent of the total vote, and the military again became alarmed. They allowed things to simmer for a few months, then in June 1966 a junta again took over the government, with General Onganía at its head. With their penchant for insulting nicknames the Argentines were soon referring to the general *la tortuga blindada*, "the armored tortoise."

Formerly one of the military's most ardent proponents of civilian rule, Onganía now held firmly in his hands the reins of power. Congress was dismissed and the Supreme Court became a rubber stamp. Onganía, a conservative and a good Catholic, was like an Argentine Francisco Franco, except that he had come to power via a successful coup rather than as a result of victory in a civil war. So in Argentina the people were not even violently pro or violently con; they were merely indifferent.

With "the armored tortoise" in control, Argentina continued its long period of economic and political stagnation. During the twenty years between 1946 and 1966 per capita productivity had increased at the incredibly low rate of less than one half of one per cent per year, and Onganía did little to improve the situation. He put forth his strongest effort in clamping down the lid. The police were given the right to search and seizure without warrants.

He also sent the police into the universities, which he regarded as hotbeds of communism, and they clubbed the students and faculty into submission. Onganía then fired obstreperous professors, stationed a policeman at every classroom door, and proceeded to reward the professors who had not given him any trouble with better salaries than they had ever enjoyed before. The students, after a few noisy whimpers, settled down to the serious work of passing their courses and getting their degrees.

Similar hard-nosed tactics were applied in other areas of dissent. The powerful credit union cooperatives were squelched, banks were thus given a boost, and labor got a 35 per cent increase in wages. Argentina entered a sea of tranquility, conservative vintage. The Catholic church became very important in the economy and in the government, a deceptive prosperity took hold of those whom the government favored, opposition quieted down to a whisper, and the people generally decided that peace at the price of liberty had much to be said for it. Onganía, for his part, had veered to the right, he was strongly anti-Communist, strongly pro-United States, and thus respresented an about face from the anti-North American program of his predecessor, Arturo Illia. Again the United States was obliged to maintain amicable relations with a regime that did not represent the people.

Onganía lasted until June 1970, when he was deposed by a military coup representing the army, the navy, and the air force. It was thought that the general was trying to pave the way for perpetuating himself in power. Onganía was never well liked, and the Argentines said that he was able to stay in office because he was in a vacuum like the astronauts, and so was weightless. Nobody wanted to rock the boat until other generals got scared and carried out the fifth military coup in fifteen years. Business was again humming. People thought only of getting a new car, a new apartment, a vacation, an expensive mistress. Inflation was temporarily controlled. No one dared to discuss politics. General Aramburu, a popular ex-head of state, was kidnaped and brutally murdered by a bunch of hoodlums who called themselves Peronistas. Perón vigorously denied any approval of the deed.

Conditions in Argentina went from bad to worse during the 1970s. In 1971 General Alejandro Augustín Lanusse became president and legalized political activities after five years of suppression. The country breathed a sigh of relief and readied itself for free elections, but when these were held Argentina jumped from the frying pan into the fire. In 1973 the seventy-seven-year-old Perón returned from eighteen years of exile and was elected president; his forty-three-year-old third wife, Isabel Martínez de Perón, was elected vice-president. Perón died the following year, and on July 1, 1974, his wife succeeded him in the presidency, thus becoming the first woman to serve as head-of-state in the Western Hemisphere. Economic conditions were growing worse daily, inflation increased at an astronomical rate, terrorist activities were a constant threat to safety, there were hundreds of political kidnappings and murders. On March 24, 1976, the military overthrew Isabel Perón, disbanded congress, and declared martial law. The commander-in-chief of the army, General Rafael Videla, assumed the presidency. He promptly applied full military force to stamp out terrorism and restore order. In the beginning Videla had the support of the majority of the Argentine people, but his antiterrorist campaign soon got out of hand and became brutal, indiscriminate, anti-Semitic, anti-intellectual, antihuman. In the economic area, however, there was some improvement. Inflation was reduced from 750 per cent a year to 160 per cent, and to sustain purchasing power wages were officially linked with the rate of inflation by "indexing." Austerity was called for and solvency was restored to the treasury.[265]

In spite of these measures salaries and wages did not keep up with the rise in prices. Many workers were forced to hold two jobs in order to make ends meet. The price of a kilo of bread jumped from 60 to 350 pesos, a dozen eggs from 60 to 600 pesos, a kilo of the cheapest beef from 30 to 700 pesos, and a pair of men's shoes from 1,350 to 25,000 pesos. The cost of an automobile was at least six or seven times the price of the same car in the United States.

The *guerra sucia* (dirty war) against all who opposed the military government continued with a kind of blind and compulsive fury. Assassinations, imprisonments, torture, disappearances were an everyday occurrence. Thousands of Jews fled from the country, and at least 10,000 people simply "disappeared." The total killed was three times that. The economy began to fall apart and inflation again soared. In March 1981 Videla was ousted and replaced by General Roberto Eduardo Viola, former Army Chief-of-Staff. He lasted only a few months, and in December 1981 Leopoldo Galtieri, Commander of the Army, took over as president. His administration was no improvement over those of his predecessors. The streets of Buenos Aires were flooded with thousands of citizens screaming for an end to military rule. These cries of hatred turned suddenly to cheers on April 2 when Galtieri announced that he had sent Argentine troops to invade and take over the Falkland Islands. The 84 British marines and 2,000 British colonists on the islands were easily overpowered. A wave of unfounded pride swept over Argentina.

The Falkland Islands (*Las Malvinas* in Spanish) are only 250 miles off the Argentine coast. They were discovered by the British in 1592 and named Falkland. The French later founded a colony there and called the islands Les Iles Malouines, whence the name Malvinas. In 1766 France signed these islands over to Spain, and when Argentina won its independence from Spain in 1816 she claimed sovereignty; but in 1833 the British drove the Argentines out and have occupied the islands since that time. However, Las Malvinas appear on all Argentine maps as Argentine territory. Britain responded to the invasion with full force, the Argentines were forced to surrender, and in June 1982 Galtieri resigned in disgrace. For a few months Reynaldo Bignone headed the government, but the people were fed up with army rule and when free elections were held at last in October 1983, Raúl Alfonsín, of the Radical Civic Union party, won a smashing victory over his Peronist opposition and became the first civilian president of Argentina in many years.

There was great jubilation and pride in Argentina after Alfonsín's election. But the new president faced staggering problems: the economy was prostrate, Argentina's foreign debt of $50 billion could not possibly be honored—indeed, arrears on the debt were accumulating at the rate of $150 million a month— and to top it all, inflation was completely out of hand at more than 1,000 per cent annually. Obtaining further loans under these conditions was out of the question. Alfonsín immediately adopted a policy of extreme austerity called the Austral Plan. The national currency was abandoned, there was a bank holiday, the austral replaced the peso, wage and price controls were enacted, deficit government spending was stopped, and the national treasury was prohibited from printing additional currency. Argentina was then able to borrow enough to tide her over, but the drastic belt-tightening had a brutal effect on the standard of living, and Argentines complained bitterly.

The United States made the situation worse by signing an agreement to sell four million tons of wheat annually to the Soviet Union at less than the market price. This pulled the rug right out from under Argentina.[266] How could that country be expected to repay its debt if it could not sell its principal export at a profit? Alfonsín complained that the debt had now become political. His country could hardly be expected to further tighten the belt in order to honor its financial obligations if it received neither cooperation nor understanding from its foreign friends.[267]

In the following months things did not improve greatly inside Argentina, and when parliamentary elections were held in September 1987, the opposition Peronist party triumphed at the polls. Alfonsín's administration began to fight a losing battle. The national economy and finances were in total disarray. In retrospect, perhaps Alfonsín's brightest star was his effort to make the military accountable. One of his first official acts as president was to put on trial those accused of terrorist killings in Argentina's dirty war, many of whom were high-ranking military officers. In the trials junta generals admitted to having killed 30,000 persons. Alfonsín pursued the prosecution of these criminals with courage and vigor. The sentences imposed, alas, hardly fit the crimes.[264]

A second accomplishment of Alfonsín's administration was the decision to move Argentina's capital from Buenos Aires to a site in Patagonia, 600 miles to the south. This move would not only encourage development of one of the great wilderness areas of the world but would also reduce the bloated, corrupt, and entrenched federal bureaucracy living in Buenos Aires. These political fat cats would never be willing to leave the opulent and glittering city for the unpopulated hinterland. Unfortunately, with the decline in Alfonsín's popularity this move was indefinitely postponed.

During the final months of Alfonsín's presidency Argentine economic and political conditions became explosive. Inflation was uncontrollable and the ordinary daily operation of business had become unmanageable. The cash flow was so erratic that no businessman could tell from one day to the next what the cost of any item might be. Many businesses simply had to shut down. Elections took place in May 1989 and Carlos Saul Menem, a Peronist, was chosen as president. Facing a situation that was chaotic, Alfonsín turned the government over to Menem five months earlier than the usual date for the assumption of power.

Menem was the son of Islamic Syrian immigrants, but he himself had converted to Roman Catholicism. His father had prospered in business, and Menem, well liked and persuasive, had risen in the political arena to become governor of the northern province of La Rioja. His administration gave the outward appearance of success, particularly as compared with the rest of Argentina, but this was not based on solid financial or economic principles. Menem was a free spender who did not seem to care how or where he got the money to run his government or to provide aid for his constituents. Nevertheless, he promised solemnly that as president he would place Argentina on a firm financial and economic footing, but with the proviso that this could not be achieved overnight. Argentina, he said, was in for a considerable period of sacrifice. The people believed him and things quieted down; utter chaos and helplessness turned into muted expectation.

The entire country was in a state of collapse. The foreign debt stood at $70 billion, and Argentina was already $2 billion in arrears on interest payments on this debt. Countless billions in private capital had been sent out of the country and deposited in foreign banks. The national treasury was empty. Menem faced a task of monumental proportions, and the only possible solution lay in effecting a change in the psychology and habits of the Argentine people, who had become accustomed to living under a "free ride" economy.[282]

One example will suffice to explain what was taking place. The head of the Argentine railway system, on a trip from Buenos Aires to Bahía Blanca, asked the conductors on his train to find out how many passengers were traveling on passes. The answer was: over 40 per cent. The same man later checked out the entire rail system and found out that this was what was happening all over the country, and not only on the rails.

Millions of people were getting free electricity, free telephone service, free air travel, government subsidies, freedom from taxes, and so on ad infinitum. State-owned enterprises were corrupt and notoriously inefficient. Bureaucracy was completely out of hand. Argentina was trying to make a go of it with this "free ride economy." Only one person out of 31,000 pays any federal income tax, and untold thousands cheat on their returns without being called to account. No country and no business can long operate under these conditions. Argentines themselves see this clearly. In August 1991 *La Nación* reported that between 70 and 80 billion dollars of their money was deposited in foreign banks, a sum greater than the nation's entire foreign debt.

On the positive side, Menem did have some noteworthy initial successes. He was able to cut government subsidies; he even reduced the budget deficit temporarily, he raised hard currency reserves, and he began the process of privatizing the nation's economy. In his first year, inflation decreased from 196 per cent in July to only 6 per cent in November. However, he was not able to control the value of Argentina's currency, the austral, which became steadily weaker when exchanged for the U.S. dollar, and inflation returned with a vengeance. Menem's initial victories suddenly became hollow.

Argentines were desperate when the prices of necessities rose as much as 200 per cent in a few days. In 1990, inflation reached 8,000 per cent annually. It was impossible to operate a business, make necessary purchases, pay debts, set aside savings, or run a bank. Confronted by that instability and an ever-rising rate of inflation, Argentines came to rely on seven-day time deposits that paid enormous interest rates of up to 600 per cent a month. It was a way to protect income in spite of the national depreciating currency. Banks were required to lend more than half of the value of these short-term deposits to the central bank, which used them to cover the deficit. To pay the exorbitant interest on these loans the government mints worked day and night cranking out more and more australes, thus aggravating inflation.

Menem, in a bold move, seized these short-term time deposits, and gave the investors ten-year dollar bonds in their place. People were suddenly told that they would have to wait ten years to get their money back. The shock of this move temporarily steadied the country's chaotic financial gyrations, but its effect was short lived because the basic problems of the economy had scarcely been touched. Privatization of the nation's industries was essential. The big, unwieldly, inefficient, bureaucratic state had passed its limits. The ruinous "free ride" would have to be abolished. Austerity measures were mandatory, but to work fairly these would have to begin at the top, and there was little to indicate that such would be the case. People began to long for the days of military rule when the generals, by fiat, could set productive quotas, control prices, curb inflation, maintain order, and provide a favorable atmosphere in which business might operate. Argentina did not seem to be ready yet for a free-market economy. In one way it resembled the countries of Eastern Europe which did not know how to use their suddenly gained freedom. A healthy and successful free-market economy demands competition, hard work, increased production, investment capital, control of federal spending, severe cuts in the bloated governmental bureaucracy, and intelligence and sacrifice on the part of all citizens. These things are alien to the present Argentine reality, character, and frame of mind.

Menem was hardly the moral leader to guide his people in the right direction. In addition to his official problems as president, his stormy domestic life got entirely out of hand, and after many violent disputes with his wife, all widely publicized, he ordered the lady to leave the presidential palace, Argentina's famous "Pink House." People were disillusioned and stunned by this scandalous affair, which made their country appear ridiculous before the world.

But when all is said and done perhaps the most disturbing thing in Argentina today is the rapidly shrinking middle class. Once vigorous and expanding, it distinguished Argentina from the other Latin American nations. In the ten years 1980–1990 the national economy has shrunk by 10 per cent, salaries have dropped 15 per cent, and inflation averaged 400 per cent annually. In 1973 Argentina produced 300,000 automobiles; in 1990 fewer than 100,000 were produced. In Buenos Aires construction declined to one third the level of the 1970s. Mortgage rates rose to over 20 per cent. The gap has widened precipitously between the rich and the poor and, caught in this squeeze, the middle class is slowly being choked to death. The years 1980–1990 were truly "a lost decade" for Argentina, and conditions now are ripe for another military takeover, characterized perhaps by odious fascist principles.

In spite of its unfortunate series of inept governments Argentina has maintained a thriving cultural life. There has been a tremendous cultural explosion in Argentina during the past two decades. There are fifty-five legitimate theaters in Buenos Aires and at least seventy-five art galleries, with frequently changing dramas and exhibits. Argentine writers, painters, composers, and architects are all making huge amounts of money. On the other side of the picture, hot-rodders (*tuercas*) are almost a national sport in Argentina, automobile races bring out 200,000 spectators, and soccer games stir other hundreds of thousands to a frenzy. There is much of Sweden and much of the United States in this cult of the flesh in Argentina today. The good things of Sweden and of the United States are not so zealously observed. Anti-U.S. sentiment is voluble. Argentina's writers are among the best in Latin America, and its musical performances are outstanding in the world. The Argentine national orchestra is one of the truly fine musical bodies of our generation. Musical activities take place mainly in the Colón Theater, one of the world's most famous opera houses. It has its own orchestra, opera, and ballet, and the performances given here rival those of Milan's La Scala or New York's Metropolitan. "Like a huge jewel box, the Colón's interior is resplendent with red plush and gilt; its vast stage is almost a block long. Salons, dressing rooms and banquet halls are equally sumptuous."[241]

Buenos Aires itself is a city of an extraordinary vitality. Its inhabitants "presume to have the longest and the widest avenues in the world. Rivadavia is 35 kilometers in length, and the width of the Avenida 9 de Julio is approximately half a kilometer. In order to open this street it was necessary to demolish entire blocks of houses. Its aspect by day or night, with an incessant flow of automobiles, is truly amazing."[236] Buenos Aires is a spectacular city in every respect, one of the world's great capitals, which bears comparison with the most beautiful capitals of Europe. There is tremendous wealth centered here, but it is not primarily new wealth, so the city has a settled and aristocratic appearance that is lacking in most other Latin American capitals. Buenos Aires reminds the traveler most of Paris. Beside it Santiago would seem quite poor indeed and São Paulo would give the impression of a gigantic beehive. But in this magnificent city, as in the country at large, the government is uneasy and unsettled, a huge, costly, and inept bureaucracy runs the state, and democracy itself rests on a fragile base, its continuance uncertain.

Has the clock stopped in Argentina? Here is a country blessed with a well-educated citizenry, a vast stretch of the most fertile land on earth, a fabulous capital city, and the possibility for rapid and efficient industrialization. As Lord Bryce pointed out in 1912, Argentina is still a nation in the making, but as yet unmade. The immigrant millions have not been fused to provide a homogeneous electorate with democratic ideals.

The farm workers have in recent years been coming to the cities in a great tide so that today 75 per cent of all Argentines, many of them rootless folk, live in urban centers. Buenos Aires itself is now a metropolitan area of nine million, nearly one third of the national population. It is a Goliath's head, as one pungent Argentine essayist called it. New York would have to contain a population of over seventy million if an analogous situation prevailed in the United States.

The imbalance of this population distribution is obvious. By all logical standards Argentina would have to contain eighty to ninety million people in order to sustain such an enormous city, the Goliath's head which deprives the whole body of its blood and its nutriment. One well-known Argentine writer put it this way:

> The geographic and historic situation of Buenos Aires and the primitiveness of the undeveloped neighboring countries gave the city its greatness. But the hinterland has remained withered, anemic, stretched out endlessly in its solitude. Buenos Aires has the responsibility for the progress of several nations, as it had in the struggle for independence. Therefore, it represents a South American rather than merely a national problem.[196]

The head that played a giant's role had plenty of wealth and plenty of big ideas, but lacked the intelligence to carry them out with a concerted effort. Meanwhile, the hinterland with its great estates is dying, and its sense of solitude and desperation have penetrated the big city and pierced its heart.

Argentine labor gave up its democratic birthright by becoming with blind enthusiasm a part of Perón's corporate state. Native capital fled to other and safer countries. The country has gone through forty years of political ups and downs, and as a result no one in Argentina today has much faith in any political party, in any political dogma, or in any economic creed. The national motto is Horace's *Carpe diem* (Let us live for this day). Or perhaps the same poet's: "Get money first, virtue comes later." In any case, the once great nation has bowed its head like all of the less fortunate nations of Latin America and has allowed, even encouraged, the military to take control. Saddest of all, conditions will probably get a lot worse in Argentina before they get any better.

The great city of Buenos Aires with all its power, wealth, beauty, and magic is not enough to give a real spirit to these people, who have flowed into it from the countryside. As Martínez Estrada, the country's most famous essayist, has so cogently pointed out, while they lived in the country in their solitude these Argentines formed a system with their environment, because there was no connection with anything better. Distance then kept them separated from urban civilization, and all the points of reference to which the threads of their lives were linked were right at hand: the farmhouse, the tree, the well, the dog, the horse, and their family. But once the interior village and along with it their farm, their tree, their dog, their horse, and their family were joined with the big city, either from a distance or closer at hand in the shantytown, they were obliged to become part of a larger system. Everything around them was put into motion while their own stillness took on the rigidities of a cadaver. This sickness of the soul is what Argentina is suffering from today.

PARAGUAY AND URUGUAY

Those untutored in Latin American affairs frequently confuse Uruguay and Paraguay because the names have a similar sound and because of the two countries' geographic proximity. Two more dissimilar nations, however, could not be found. Landlocked Paraguay is still Indian country; half the population is bilingual and speaks Guaraní as well as Spanish; there is even a literature in the language, and newspapers print a portion of their news in it. The people of Paraguay are poor in a land of potential wealth; the women still far outnumber the men; about 500,000 Paraguayans live in exile because of the unpleasant political and economic conditions in the country, for General Alfredo Stroessner, who was in power from 1954 to 1989, maintained the ancient tradition of Francia and López, and ruled the nation with a stern hand. Asunción, the capital, is a picturesque city of about 500,000, but it is a far cry from Uruguay's bustling Montevideo. There are no other cities of consequence in Paraguay.

Uruguay, in contrast, is one of the most literate, intelligent, and homogeneous countries in Latin America. Its population is almost entirely Spanish and Italian, the Indian influence is practically nil, and it has the one large capital in Latin America with no sprawling slums. The extremes of rich and poor are not obvious in Uruguay; the middle class predominates in the national life.

The only real similarities between Uruguay and Paraguay are in that (a) the population of each country is under five million, less than the city of Buenos Aires; (b) the area of each country is relatively small; Paraguay is about the size of California, and Uruguay approximates the area of Nebraska; and (c) the two nations do lie almost side by side geographically, but they have no common border because a finger of Argentina separates them. Above the extended finger of Argentina, Paraguay reaches northward, which means that a considerable part of it lies within the torrid zone. Actually, Paraguay is more than twice as large as Uruguay in area, but much of its territory is totally undeveloped, while primitive methods of agriculture prevail in the remainder.

Paraguay's needless war with Bolivia over the Chaco (1932–35) ended in a stalemate, but the more poorly equipped Paraguayan soldiers, many of them barefooted and without proper rifles or ammunition, fought bravely for their "homeland" and captured all the equipment they needed, while the Bolivian Indians, accustomed to living at very high elevations where the air is cold and rare, died like flies in the tropical lowlands for which they felt no patriotic attachment. At the war's end Paraguayans occupied all of the disputed territory. The final peace granted Bolivia rights to send goods down the river, but Paraguay held onto the Chaco territory.

A whole literature grew up around this conflict, of which Bolivians created the better part. A group of short stories by Augusto Céspedes called *Sangre de mestizos* (*The Blood of Mestizos*), 1936, is perhaps the best-known book about the Chaco War. One story in particular, called "The Well," has become a classic. It is a day-by-day account of Bolivian soldiers digging a well in the dry and blistering Chaco in order to locate water, which otherwise trucks must haul from a great distance. Driven by their officers they laboriously burrow over two hundred feet down, but find no water. One day they are attacked and they defend the well as if it were filled with water. The attacking Paraguayans are similarly inspired. Many soldiers are killed; their bodies are thrown into the well (for which a use has now been found) and covered with dirt, but the abandoned well is still the deepest in the Chaco. The war's futility was never more dramatically stated.

Scenically, parts of Paraguay are very beautiful; giant trees, ancient Jesuit missions, rolling fields, and sounding rivers. Approximately 54 per cent of the land is covered with forests, 40 per cent is grassland and meadows, and only one per cent is cultivated. There are large Mennonite colonies in the north, whose model settlements may someday bring civilization to the surrounding wilderness. The country's isolation no longer exists because of air communications, but transportation by land or water is very slow. It takes four days by river to reach Asunción from Buenos Aires, and at least fifty-four hours by the fastest train, but less than two hours by air. The circuitous rail line to La Paz, Bolivia, requires six days, while the flight by air is about three hours. With additional population and a better system of highways and rail lines Paraguay could become a prosperous country.

Paraguay remained under the iron grip of General Stroessner who purged the country of its most able leadership at all levels, characterizing as "leftists" those who opposed his policies. His was the only OAS country not to vote in favor of condemning the Somoza regime in Nicaragua, because Stroessner and Somoza were old friends, but this action made Paraguay a political outcast in the hemisphere. When Somoza found himself to be a persona non grata in the United States and facing extradition, he decided to seek asylum in Paraguay where he was assassinated.

Stroessner tried to build up his economy by inviting U.S. oil companies to drill in the Chaco, but no oil was found. Ironically, in the small slice of that area which Bolivia retained thousands of barrels are being pumped daily. In 1973 Paraguay and Brazil signed an agreement to construct a $9 billion dam and hydroelectric power plant at Itaipú on the Paraná River. Stroessner and President Figueiredo of Brazil inaugurated this dam, the largest in the world, in 1982. It is 750 feet high with a reservoir of 500 square miles. Paraguay's share of the electricity will not only meet domestic requirements, but will provide a large surplus that will be sold for $300 million a year. This is three times the total value of Paraguay's exports in 1972. A similar binational agreement was made with Argentina to build two additional dams at a cost of $10 billion. These dams will alter radically the traditional picture of Paraguay's economy. They have already given employment to many thousands of workers, have spurred a small building boom, and have attracted considerable foreign capital to the country. The Yacyreta dam being built by Paraguay and Argentina will stretch 47 miles, making it the Western Hemisphere's longest dam. Electricity will be provided for many poor people of both countries, and cheap energy will stimulate further industrialization and modernization in Paraguay. For Argentina, the project will provide a great source of energy to replace expensive thermal generation and will help meet the country's growing demand for electricity.

Paraguay's economy is seriously strained by widespread contraband trade (coffee, shoes, soya products, motor vehicles, machinery) which can neither be taxed nor regulated. Contraband shoes have almost wiped out the domestic shoe industry. Paraguay is still essentially an agricultural and cattle country. There are many estates of enormous size, but more than 100,000 small farmers work land to which they hold no title. The principal products are meat, leather, sugar, yerba mate, tobacco, soybeans, timber, coffee, and cotton, but the new hydroelectric plants have encouraged steel, aluminum, textile, and metal industries. Nevertheless, Paraguay is still one of the most underdeveloped Latin American countries.

In the late 1980s in order to strengthen his hand Stroessner sent a large military force into the Chaco on the pretext that Bolivia had plans to reclaim the territory lost in the Chaco War fifty years previously. This military-political fiction stimulated the Paraguayan martial spirit by stirring up fear of a former enemy, and it reinforced the position of the army as the most decisive element in the national life. To finance this venture Stroessner increased his military budget by 30 per cent. The army clearly remained the key to the political future of Paraguay.

In February 1989, Alfredo Stroessner's 35 years of dictatorial rule came to a sudden and inglorious end. A senior army general, Andrés Rodríguez, ousted the seventy-four-year-old president in a coup that left some 300 dead. Stroessner was ordered to leave the country, and fled to Brazil. At the moment of the coup the aged president was keeping his weekly tryst at the home of his longtime mistress, Estela Legal, where he was taken completely by surprise.

Andrés Rodríguez had been close to Stroessner for many years, and one of his daughters was married to Stroessner's younger son, Alfredo Junior. Although Rodríguez solemnly promised a democratic government, and a complete restoration of human rights to all citizens, he has since done little to achieve these worthy goals. Paraguay, long a haven for Nazi criminals and drug traffickers, is a country where things change so that they can remain the same, as an old Italian proverb puts it. Its economy continues to sputter, and its future is still questionable and murky.

Uruguay is everything Paraguay is not. From 1903 to 1973 it had an almost unbroken record of constitutional governments, owing in great part to its most famous president, Batlle y Ordóñez. Batlle served two terms as president between 1903–15 and was the originator of his country's progressive social program. In 1967 Uruguay's cumbersome nine-man council, which had run the country since 1952 was abolished, and Uruguay adopted the presidential form of government with a bicameral Congress. Uruguay's social reforms have made many observers refer to her as a "welfare state" or as "the Denmark of South America." The accuracy of such comparisons is dubious.

In any case, Uruguay nationalized its electrical output, its rail lines, buses, streetcars, and waterworks. The state also controls the production and distribution of gasoline and chemicals; handles insurance; has its own banks, casinos, hotels, theaters, and telephone system; subsidizes music and broadcasting. Its labor regulations provide for a short work week, a minimum wage, holidays and vacations with pay, liability insurance, free medical care, unemployment compensation, and generous retirement pensions. A person can earn a pension in one branch of work and then pick up a second pension in another. The per capita income was for years second in Latin America, surpassed only by that of Venezuela. Divorce is not only legal, but a woman need give no cause whatsoever if she wishes to divorce her husband. The man enjoys no such freedom.

All of this sounds utopian in the extreme, and indeed it was as long as it lasted. But the optimistic Uruguayans overdid things and as a result the state almost went bankrupt. Out of a total labor force of approximately one million, 250,000, or one person out of every four, worked for some government agency. Red tape prevented the quick settlement of many social security claims. In 1964 this swollen bureaucracy, plus a rampant inflation and an overdose of credit, sent the national finances into a tailspin from which Uruguay has not yet recovered.

A worker who earned a salary of 4,000 pesos a month, in the 1960s received the equivalent of $450 in purchasing power. An inflation of over 1,100 per cent made his pesos worth only a fraction of that a few years later. Rising wages barely gave him enough to scrimp by on as his standard of living steadily deteriorated. A crazy tax structure has further weakened the state; no one earning less than $4,000 a year (i.e., about 95 per cent of all workers) pays any income tax. A short work day and an average retirement age of fifty decreased productivity.

In 1967 when President Pacheco Areco took office he remarked that his country needed "a little help from heaven." Help did come in the form of rains to put an end to a prolonged drought, and Uruguayan citizens, realizing the seriousness of the situation, tightened their belts. This austerity program soon paid off, and inflation was temporarily brought under control.

Another imbalance in the national economy is the fact that the capital city contains almost half the total population of the nation. The relatively underdeveloped countryside could not long sustain this superstructure. The *South American Handbook* points out that

> . . . the long continued economic distress of Uruguay has its roots in a lack of balance between industry, actively fostered in a country which has few natural advantages for it, and farming, for which it is magnificently endowed, but which has been neglected; the town, in fact, has dominated the countryside, to the undoing of both.[197]

It might be added that sheep, cattle, and wheat make up most of the farm produce. Improved methods of farming or animal husbandry are not widely employed, for a Uruguayan rancher prefers simply to buy more land rather than to spend his capital making these improvements. Land ownership is a status symbol even in enlightened Uruguay. Uruguayans are able to boast of one world first place: they eat more meat per capita than any other country in the world, 227 pounds a year. The United States comes in fifth place, after Uruguay, New Zealand, Argentina, and Australia.

William Henry Hudson, the British-Argentine naturalist, in one of his best-known books referred to Uruguay as "The purple land that England lost," because of the great stretches of purple sage which cover the rolling earth. The beautifully written and nostalgic works of this author, who was born in Argentina and spent his first thirty-three years in that region before going to England, give such a strong feeling of the land that Argentines and Uruguayans still consider him as an integral part of their literature. In *The Purple Land* Hudson characterizes the unique quality of the Uruguayan people in this striking paragraph:

> The unwritten constitution, mightier than the written one, is in the heart of every man to make him still a republican and free with a freedom it would be hard to match anywhere else on the globe. Here the lord of many leagues of land and of herds unnumbered sits down to talk with the hired shepherd, a poor, barefooted fellow in his smoky rancho, and no class or caste difference divides them, no consciousness of their widely different positions chills the warm current of sympathy between two human hearts. How refreshing it is to meet with this perfect freedom of intercourse, tempered only by that innate courtesy and native grace of manner peculiar to Spanish America.

The visitor in Uruguay today might wonder if he was in the same country as that described in this idyllic picture. While the essential warmth of the Uruguayan people has not changed, the country is experiencing the deep social cleavages so rampant throughout the world in this generation. Inflation has grown at a fantastic rate, totaling 1,200 per cent between 1968–78. People were thrown out of work; there was profound demoralization and great political unrest.

A band of leftist radicals who called themselves Tupamaros, after the Indian hero of Colonial days, Tupac Amaru, organized themselves into guerrilla bands and began a widespread campaign of terrorism against the government. Many of the young Tupamaros belonged to upper- and middle-class Uruguayan families, but they had become dedicated revolutionaries and were intent on destroying the government by undermining its control over law and order. Political extremists, whose sole inspiration was violence, and a few out-and-out criminals, joined the organization and made peaceful life impossible in Uruguay. The Tupamaros were spawned during the country's most desperate economic upheaval in the late 1960s, but when conditions improved they did not die away but actually increased their terrorist activities.

In August 1970 they kidnapped a U.S. AID official, Daniel Mitrione, who was in Uruguay to help the police, and when the government refused to release Tupamaro prisoners in return for Mitrione's safety, he was killed. President Pacheco not only refused to bargain with the Tupamaros but asked for special powers to combat them, and the Uruguayan police began a house-to-house search which netted them several Tupamaros, including the movement's leader, Raul Sendic. Shortly afterward, however, the British ambassador was kidnapped and held for ransom for several months before he was finally freed. Kidnappings and assassinations became a daily occurrence, and law-abiding citizens began to be afraid of appearing on the streets.

The *New York Times* summarized conditions as follows:

> In their intensified harassment of the government, Tupamaros have forced a series of cabinet crises. They have caused a partial suspension of the national constitution, the long-term closing of secondary schools throughout the country, and

the closing of scores of bank branches deemed incapable of defending themselves against robbery. The Tupamaros have kidnapped half a dozen prominent persons, demanding either ransom or propaganda benefits each time. The guerrillas have robbed the banks and casinos of well over $1 million, and have accumulated a substantial arsenal of arms, ammunition and explosives.

Under these intolerable conditions Pacheco was impeached, and in 1971 his handpicked successor, Juan M. Bordaberry, was elected president. He devalued the peso thirty-two times in his first three years in office, but was unable to control either the Tupamaros or the economic chaos. Finally, realizing that the government was paralyzed, Bordaberry in 1973 handed control over to the military, thus putting an end to forty years of constitutional rule in Uruguay. The military wasted no time in cracking down hard on the terrorists. The legislature was dissolved and a state of emergency was declared. When the labor unions protested and called for a general strike, troops and tanks moved in and brutally suppressed all labor opposition. Several union leaders were imprisoned, and many others fled. A rigid censorship was imposed and all political activities were banned.

The government itself now began a campaign of terror against the Tupamaros, and during the next few months more than 3,500 persons were arrested on terrorist and political charges. Many of these later "disappeared." There was no longer any such thing as civil rights or a fair trial. In 1977 the United States Congress cut off further economic aid to Uruguay because of this repression, and Uruguay retaliated by refusing all military aid as well. In 1979 Amnesty International reported that 5,000 political prisoners still remained in Uruguayan jails.

The government's campaign to stamp out the Tupamaros, however, was eminently successful, and by 1978 they had been liquidated completely. Many had been imprisoned or killed, and others had fled the country. Uruguay then began the long, hard task of starting out all over again. Behind the mask of a civilian presidency, the military kept a tight grip on the reins, but as a modicum of tranquility was restored to the country, free elections and a return to constitutional government took place in 1985.

The new, and fairly elected, president was Julio María Sanguinetti of the Colorado party, the first civilian to occupy that office in twelve years. He proposed giving amnesty to the military personnel, police, and their accomplices who had carried out the terrorist repressions of the decade 1970–80. The president was eager to bury the hatchet and use all hands to move the country forward. There was definite economic improvement in Uruguay in 1986–87, with the gross national product growing by 5 per cent. However, in actual buying power the average worker's income is worth only one half of what it was in 1968. The net result has been a growing disillusion among the young people, and a growing emigration problem.

During the last ten years Uruguay has lost 25 per cent of her skilled technicians, 10 per cent of her doctors, 15 per cent of her architects, and 9 per cent of her engineers. Great numbers of young workers leave the country every year. The total of these emigrants during the period 1968–88, just twenty years, was greater than the total of all European immigrants entering Uruguay since 1900. One newspaper in Montevideo recently ran a headline A COUNTRY OF OLD PEOPLE?

Uruguay's social idealism was carried too far. Gross overspending and a credit card philosophy of spend now, pay later, plus a huge governmental bureaucracy, brought this once prosperous and progressive country to the brink of ruin. Uruguayans now know that welfare and social reforms in a poor country bear a higher price than nearly any other enterprise on which a government may embark, because their cost continues and decreases the country's total wealth. A very long period of austerity is certainly in store for the next several years.

The Sanguinetti administration did struggle courageously to restore some sanity to the country's economy, but an inflation rate of 75 per cent made this a losing battle. The chaotic situation in Argentina and Brazil had an increasingly negative effect on Uruguay. In order to hold his ground Sanguinetti began to borrow heavily, and by the end of his term Uruguay's foreign debt had risen 36 per cent to approximately $7 billion, which made it the highest foreign debt of any Latin American country on a per-capita basis. Interest payments amounted to approximately 30 per cent of the total export trade. Things had reached this stage when elections took place in November 1989, and for the first time since 1971, they were truly open and free, with no proscribed political parties. Luis Alberto Lacalle, a neoliberal lawyer, was elected president. He promised to govern on a bipartisan base and to strive for "the well-being of all Uruguayans."

Uruguay's fundamental economic problem is its lack of investment capital. Uruguayans are simply not earning enough to build up much of an investment nest egg, and borrowing is at best a stopgap solution. In addition to this, until such time as Brazil and Argentina can attain a reasonable stability, Uruguay is caught between these two giants and squeezed by ever-tightening pincers. The future of Uruguay, once bright and promising, has become a tragic question mark in Latin America today.

BRAZIL

Brazil is a country of colossal size. Her vast territories comprise an area approximately the size of that occupied by all nine Spanish-speaking countries of South America. She has the biggest river, the largest tropical jungle, and one of the fastest growing populations in the world. Her Atlantic coastline is 4,579 miles in length, and her meandering land frontier extends for 14,000 miles. Brazil is more than fifteen times as large as France, and more than thirty times the size of West Germany. São Paulo, her great industrial center of fourteen million inhabitants, is the fastest-growing city in South America.

Historically the Brazilian has tended to seek a quick way to wealth, moving abruptly from one Midas dream to another. As the Brazilian writer Holanda put it, he has the desire "of collecting the fruit without planting the tree." This has held back the economic growth of the country, and has kept it subject to the caprices of the world market. Brazil, despite her tremendous size, has never controlled her own destiny. She is a beggar sitting on a bag of gold. Her vast interior hinterland is still largely uninhabited. Her present economic resources are limited, and so is her know-how in the ways of this highly technical century. Her educational system is insufficient and spotty. Since the days of the emperors she has never had a truly efficient and enlightened government. Her future is at the mercy of a constrictive and costly military machine and a very poor, deeply frustrated, and illiterate populace.

Brazil, like Argentina, was hard hit by the worldwide economic depression of 1929–32. Her foreign coffee markets skidded, and tons of Brazilian coffee had to be piled up and burned. As her one-crop colonial economy shuddered, the coffee barons of São Paulo lost their grip on the national government. Getulio Vargas, a rancher, supported by the landowners and cattlemen of Rio Grande do Sur, was defeated at the polls in 1930 but he cried "fraud," and headed an easily successful coup. He represented a new direction in the national life. His opposition to the great coffee interests and his statements on social reform brought him widespread support among the middle class and the masses, as was the case with Perón in Argentina. Younger Brazilian officers took over control of the army and converted it into an instrument supporting the Vargas "revolution."

Under Getulio Vargas the Brazilian urban masses and bourgeoisie began for the first time to participate widely in the government. Psychologically, this gave them a new feeling of dignity and pride. When the depression was overcome their miserable economic state was also somewhat improved. Public works and urban improvements gave the heavily populated Brazilian seaboard the "look" of modernity. In this process United States financial help was of key importance. The Good Neighbor Policy was in full swing, and there was little talk of scrimping on hemispheric aid. Uncle Sam was amiable, generous, deferential. It was a new wrinkle in hemispheric relations.

Vargas served as "president" of Brazil for almost eighteen years, from 1930 to 1945, and again from 1951 to 1954. He was a reformist president until 1937 in which year he announced that there was a Communist plot to unseat him and that he was seizing *personal* control of the state. The real danger in Brazil was from quite another direction in the form of the immensely popular "green shirts" or integralista rightists.

It was under Vargas that Brazil came in on the side of the West during World War II, and permitted the United States to construct air and naval bases in Brazilian territory and waters. Vargas himself, an admirer of the corporate states of Europe (Portugal, Italy, Germany) was lukewarm about the war, but the majority of the Brazilian people were pro-Western, and Getulio went along. His personal dictatorship (known as "the New State") did put an end to the fascist green shirts' hopes of taking over the government.

After serving as president of Brazil from 1930 to 1945 Vargas lost power for one term but was easily reelected in the elections of 1950. But he had shot his bolt. After a few months his regime began to stagger under widespread corruption and nepotism. When an opposition newspaper owner was attacked by assassins, Vargas was accused of the plot (he was not guilty), and officers went to the palace to arrest the head of the presidential guard, who was the alleged chief assassin. A group of higher officers pushed into Vargas's presidential quarters, demanding his resignation. The president shot himself rather than relinquish his office. The date was August 24, 1954. The suicide note read: "To the hatred of my enemies I leave the legacy of my death."

Under Vargas, Brazil had moved ponderously forward in her attempt to become a modern nation; with his death it was plain that while the nation had put on a new set of clothes the body beneath was still weak, poor, and afflicted. But even the unfortunate and the dispossessed can have their dream, and the people of Brazil were already thinking of themselves as a great nation. Their vast potential in land and untapped resources, their great unpopulated territories, their population explosion that gave the country over fifty million inhabitants by 1950, and their new political vitality were more than sufficient cause for this articulation of the national consciousness.

Getulio Vargas was a supremely Brazilian figure. According to Brazilian custom he was "Getulio" to everyone in Brazil, even to his enemies, and for many years nearly all liked him. This intimacy often echoed a mixture of admiration, envy, and fear, but Getulio was always "one of our own. That's what we Brazilians are really like." He was a man of exceptional shrewdness, charm, and sophistry. Getulio did accomplish much for the forgotten man of Brazil, and so it might be said that he made Brazil take the first long step into the twentieth century, for once recognized the forgotten man in Brazil, as elsewhere in the world, became extremely vocal and intensely aware of his condition and of the possibility of bettering it through political action.

Getulio gave the voiceless Brazilians a voice, and he also improved wages and working conditions for the urban workers, but this improvement was only the equivalent of attaining what in the more progressive countries would be considered as the lowest possible standard of living. Brazil was and is a terribly poor country, even by South American standards. In 1937 when Getulio became dictator the average *monthly* wage of the Brazilian worker in all fields was less than twelve dollars. Argentina was selling more than five times as much per capita in foreign markets, and the entire Brazilian national budget (1938) was approximately that of the *annual municipal* budgets of Baltimore or of San Francisco, cities with less than one fiftieth the population.

World War II quickened the pace of industrialization in Brazil. By the end of the war (1946) the industrial product was fifty times greater than it had been forty years previously. Even so, it amounted to less than $2 billion. By 1970 the industrial product totaled about $7 billion, and per capita income reached $1,300 a year, but half of the people were still wretchedly poor and illiterate, lived at a bare subsistence level, were not allowed to vote *because* of being illiterate.

After the suicide of Vargas, Brazil had three "constitutional" presidents, only one of whom served out his term; while another, Jânio Quadros, lasted only seven months and then resigned in a neurotic huff. The full-term president was a brilliant Brazilian of Czechoslovak background, Juscelino de Oliveira Kubitschek, who was chief of state during the period 1956–61. Kubitschek gave symbolic fulfillment to the Brazilian dream of moving out into the hinterland by establishing a new national capital six hundred miles in the interior at Brasília. He almost bankrupted the state by having crews of laborers work around the clock so that the city would be so far along when he was retired from office that there could be no retreat from accepting it.

This project, plus Kubitschek's emphasis on the further industrialization of São Paulo, Latin America's greatest industrial center, and now also her most populous city, gave Brazil a new dimension. But there was one fly in the ointment. The cost of Kubitschek's grandiose schemes was exorbitant and he printed money to defray a portion of the expense. The cost of living rose to unprecedented heights. According to one astute critic, Kubitschek's promise to "achieve 50 years' progress in five" had resolved itself by his having "achieved 40 years' inflation in four."

Only the future will tell whether Kubitschek's new capital with all its attendant growing pains and heavy costs was worth the price. In any event, Brasília now stands out there in the beckoning interior as a monument to the president who sacrificed everything in order to make it a reality. By any standards Brasília is an incomparably magnificent capital, worthy of any nation. Perhaps the ungainly, incohesive, heterogeneous, disjointed nation will someday grow up to it, and when that day comes Brazil will have achieved her destiny.

There is no doubt that by the mid-twentieth century some such symbolic act was needed to start once again a westward migration of the Brazilians. Eighty per cent of the nation's people still lived crowded together on a narrow strip one or two hundred miles wide along the Atlantic coast, hundreds of thousands of them in shantytown hovels made of tin cans and other debris of the big cities. To make the problem worse, a population explosion literally burst all these cities at the seams. In 1900 the total population of Brazil was 17,300,000; by 1950 that figure had risen to 51,000,000, by 1960 it stood at 71,000,000, and in 1970 the figure was 90,000,000. In the interior of the gigantic country lay tremendous extensions of unpopulated and undeveloped lands, for the total area of Brazil is considerably larger than that of the United States before the addition of Alaska.

The South American Handbook, published yearly by a group of British businessmen interested in the area, a group hardly given to overstatement, refers to the founding of Brasília in these words:

> On April 21, 1960, Rio de Janeiro ceased to be the Federal Capital of Brazil; it had outrun its water supply and power supply and had not another foot of soil to build upon. It was replaced by Brasília, 600 miles away in the impoverished uplands of Goias, deep in the heart of the undeveloped *sertão*. Such a superbly act of faith has few precedents in history; it is not in the nature of governments to turn their backs on luxury and make for the wilderness.

All government agencies are now firmly ensconced in Brasília. If the original plan had been followed population would have been limited to half a million, but that figure has already been passed as the exodus of those moving west has swollen. Only light industries are permitted. Brasília is located at an elevation of 3,000 feet on an undulating plain. The year round climate is mild with a very low humidity. There are frequent summer rains to cool the night air. There is a fine airport and two excellent paved roads connect the city with the coast, one through Belo Horizonte, the other through Anápolis to São Paulo. From the fork at Anápolis a secondary road heads north for 1,350 miles to Belém, the last fourth of its length through tropical jungle.

The city was planned from scratch after a nationwide competition. Professor Lucio Costa won first-place honors and headed the designing crew. Brasília is laid out in the shape of a bent bow and arrow, the bent bow following the lakeshore, while along its curve are the residential areas, schools, and a few small shops. The main shopping area is in the heart of the city. At right angles to these residential areas flows the five-mile long, 820-foot wide Avenida Monumental. At the tip of the arrow on somewhat higher ground are the government buildings. Recreational and cultural areas are being developed where the bow and arrow intersect. A new university occupies a 625-acre campus next to the lake. It already has one of the best science departments in the country, and an enrollment of several hundred students.

Oscar Niemeyer, Brazil's gifted architect, is responsible for the most impressive buildings in Brasília, which are in the modern style. The city also boasts of many statues in the same style. Motor and pedestrian traffic are carefully separated, and motor vehicles can move freely without interruption to almost any point in town. There is a series of zones along the shaft of the arrow: a hotel complex, a radio and television city, an area for fairs and circuses, a sports center, a municipal square, and a railway station. Two yacht clubs occupy choice spots on the lakeshore. Foreign embassies give the new capital a cosmopolitan accent.

Unfortunately, at one end of the city at least 50,000 workers live in extremely poor quarters, and the larger apartment buildings which house the minor government officers and clerks have a blocklike sameness and angularity to them which is distressing. In spite of these drawbacks Brasília has already begun to fulfill its purpose. Kubitschek's folly is now being called a miracle. The population of the surrounding area has more than doubled, and in another ten years will at least quadruple. After four centuries Brazilian hinterland is being opened up. People are on the march westward, hopes are rising, and the fire is bright.

After Kubitschek's term ended, Brazil had two more civilian presidents, the first of whom, Jânio da Silva Quadros, lasted less than a year (January–August 1961). His vice-president, João Belchior Marques Goulart, then took over. Goulart was noted for his "leftist" sympathies, and the conservative oligarchy, allied with the middle-class military establishment, eyed his regime with suspicion from the beginning. As events would have it Goulart was in China when Quadros abruptly resigned from the presidency. He had rubbed elbows with Mao Tse-tung and the Communist mayor of Shanghai, praising both for what they had accomplished in China.

When Goulart returned to Brazil the military leaders kept him waiting for several days before they would allow him to assume office, and in the interim, under military pressure, Congress quickly passed a constitutional amendment reorganizing itself along European parliamentary lines, thus greatly reducing the power of the president. Goulart took office with two strikes already against him. Communists were allowed to infiltrate the government, although none held a high public office. Carlos Prestes, the Communist leader, brashly declared on a European trip that there was no longer any need for a Communist takeover in Brazil because his party already controlled the government. The statement was not only injudicious, it was not true. But Preste's wishful thinking caused shivers of fear among the military.

In the economic sphere things were going rapidly from bad to worse. The cost of living had tripled within a couple of years, and wealthy Brazilians hastily sent their capital to Swiss and American banks, fearing that the inflation would wipe them out financially. Workers pressed for higher wages, and the country's financial state became chaotic. Student rebellions and labor agitation kept the cities in an uproar. The president's left-wing supporters demanded a quickening of Goulart's liberal reforms, but there were no funds to carry out any reforms whatever. The treasury was empty; the country was at a standstill. There was neither order nor progress. The military, promising both, took over the government. The streets teemed with hundreds of thousands rejoicing at the coup. General Castelo Branco, elected by the Congress, became the military "president" of Brazil (1964). In 1967 he was replaced by Artur da Costa e Silva, who was also elected by Congress. He promised to humanize the government and to cut inflation. The military kept a wary eye on every political and economic move made by Costa e Silva, often calling the play. The president himself— Brazilians refer to him as "the big shadow"—was simply the prisoner of his office.

The military proclaimed that it was carrying out the will of the people by making a popular revolution, but this was clearly a charade. Costa e Silva was a good general but he was neither a good nor a popular president. His brief term was "marked by a paralysis of leadership, a carnival of blunders, and a lack of cohesion within the government." On one occasion three ministries released three different versions of the government's new minimum wage law. As a respected Brazilian neewspaper put it: "No previous government was ever endowed with so many powers to tackle questions, but no other previous government ever showed such a lack of decision and initiative."

In late 1969 Brazil was declared under a state of siege (martial law), Congress was closed, a rigid censorship was imposed on the press, due process and habeas corpus were suspended, and two hundred oppositions and journalists were imprisoned. Even the Supreme Court was muzzled, an unprecedented act. Former President Kubitschek was also arrested, but he was still one of the country's most popular political figures. On October 25, 1969, General Emilio Garrastazu Medici took over the presidency. He promised many fundamental social, economic, and agrarian reforms, but no sooner had the military committee chosen him as Brazil's next president, than urban guerrillas launched a campaign of terror in order to harass the dictatorship. There were bombings, bank robberies, the seizure of radio stations, and kidnappings of foreign diplomats who were held for ransom. The first kidnap victim was U.S. Ambassador C. Burke Elbrick. He was held for some time and finally released in return for the freedom of fifteen political prisoners. Soon after Elbrick's capture the German ambassador, and then the Japanese consul general in São Paulo, were kidnapped. There were many other victims. At first the police seemed powerless to control this wave of terrorism, but once they countered with a policy of ruthless extermination unincumbered by legal restrictions, the terrorist campaign was quickly ended. There is no doubt that many innocent persons were killed in this process of "liquidating the leftists," as the government put it. In any event, Brazil was soon back on the path of economic and geographic expansion.

The twelve years 1968–80 were for Brazil a period of astounding growth and incredible blunders. Perhaps the two must always go hand in hand in order to attest to the imperfection of humankind. The annual growth rate between 1968–72 was over 10 per cent, then in 1973, when world oil prices quadrupled, the economy was dealt a devastating blow. Brazil produces very little petroleum and must pay an immense import bill for this product, so necessary in an industrialized nation. Inflation hit Brazil with a vengeance, averaging 40 per cent a year and, in an effort to control the economy, government spending was sharply curtailed. General Ernesto Geisel, who in 1974 succeeded General Medici as president, took over a country that was on the ropes. Brazilians were tired of being ruled by generals and made no bones about saying so at the polls. After the elections of 1974 freedom of the press was restored, and there was a decrease in police brutality. Television and radio were still subject to strict government censorship: and human rights again became a public issue. Up to this time, off-duty policemen, using vigilante methods, had simply wiped out hundreds of people thought to be political troublemakers while the authorities looked on.

High world coffee prices in 1977 helped to turn the economy around, and initiated another period of expansion, perhaps not as dramatic as that of the late 1960s, but financially and economically more responsible. Gross National Productivity averaged 7 per cent a year during 1977–80, and signs bearing the words: WATCH OUT! THE BRAZILIANS ARE COMING! began to appear frequently reflecting the national optimism. In order to prevent serious financial distress in the wake of a continuing high rate of inflation, Brazil worked out an ingenious system of indexing in which wages were automatically increased by law in order to keep pace with the inflation spiral.

The population explosion continued; by 1990 Brazil had 159,000,000 inhabitants, and was growing faster than all the Spanish-speaking countries of South America combined. São Paulo was one of the most rapidly growing cities in the world, with an increase of nearly half a million persons a year, two thirds of which was internal growth. In 1990 the metropolitan area of São Paulo had well over fourteen million people.[238]

It is a dynamic city of towering, bright skyscrapers, wide boulevards, thriving banks, and industries. It is also a city of slums. Half the families of São Paulo receive less than $2,500 a year, only half the homes have running water, and scarcely a third have indoor plumbing connected to sewer lines. There is a new subway system to help take traffic off the already overcrowded streets, and there is a growing pollution in the air.

Brazil's population explosion would be more than doubled each year if it were not for the 3.4 million abortions carried out annually. A São Paulo doctor, Nelson Luiz de Araujo Morais, reported in 1979 that about a quarter of Brazilian women of fertile age become pregnant yearly, and about half of these decide to have abortions, the most damaging form of birth control. Abortions are illegal, so many are performed under less than hygienic conditions, and more than 20 per cent of the women suffer postoperative infections, 600,000 of them requiring hospitalization. The price paid for an abortion varies from U.S. $13 to as much as U.S. $500, depending on the social class of the woman involved.

After the success of Brasília, the government embarked on a long range plan for western expansion. At tremendous cost 14,000 miles of highways were pushed into the interior, and people living along the seaboard were urged to move into the western territories by grants of land and interest-free loans. In its exuberance to expand the western frontier the government built some highways that really went nowhere. Boom towns that were expected to spring up along these roads did not materialize, and many highways were then allowed to fall into disrepair because of lack of funds for upkeep. The government had shot its bolt with the many millions appropriated as an initial outlay for this development and was unable to follow up.

The most famous of these roads, the Trans-Amazon Highway, was opened in 1974, and large portions of it have already been all but abandoned. One Brazilian newspaper called it "the longest, poorest, and most useless highway on earth."[230] Nevertheless, the Amazon basin, which occupies 60 per cent of Brazil's area, and contains only 8 per cent of the population, is still one of the world's richest areas. Eric Echolm, principal investigator for the Worldwatch Institute, a group that studies the quality of human life in various parts of the planet, stated that Amazonia is the richest area on earth in a biological sense, having a million species of animal and plant life, many of which are unique here. The Amazon basin also contains one trillion dollars worth of forest products. Since colonial times it has been considered as Brazil's security blanket.[231]

This unique rain forest is today in the process of being destroyed by man's encroachment. An Englishman who recently flew over the area was appalled to see miles of forest going up in smoke to make way for pasture lands and farms. Knowing the territory well he exclaimed: "My God, they are burning mahogany down there!" Perhaps as much as 20 per cent of the Amazon rain forest has already succumbed to cutting and burning, and once gone it can never be replaced.[230] Small plane pilots frequently complain that they cannot see landmarks below because of the extensive layer of smoke.

The Amazon rain forest is not good farm land except for a stretch of alluvial plains along the banks of the great river that overflows and leaves its deposit of silt behind. This constitutes about 20 per cent of the total area.[232] The rest of the selva has only a thin layer of topsoil that is quickly leached of nutrients by the tropical rains once the growth is cut or burned down. Exposed to the baking rays of the sun this laterite becomes hard as brick, and the entire denuded area then becomes a desert wasteland. The fragile ecological balance of the rain forest is already being seriously disturbed. Laterite soil may produce a crop for two or three years before its nutrients are gone, and this has led thousands of itinerant farmers to move into the selva, burn it down, plant their crops for two or three years, and then move on to another area to do the same thing all over again.

Brazilians are still referring to the selva as their Amazon bonanza. Many are convinced that vast deposits of oil lie underneath, although there is no justification for such a belief. Others, overcome by the fever to participate in the westward expansion and to settle and make money quickly, have little concern for the long-term consequences. Brazil's new timber program, for example, entails the deforestation of 100,000,000 acres of selva. That much is now leased to lumber companies. If cutting proceeds on schedule, by the year 2000 only one third of the selva will remain, and there is no surety that this can survive. The ecological and climatic results for Brazil are unpredictable, but they will clearly be unfavorable.

In 1967 Daniel K. Ludwig, a New York shipbuilder, bought four million acres of selva along the Jari River to the south of Surinam, to cut timber, use as grazing land, replant portions in quickly growing trees to use in the manufacture of paper and cellulose, and to grow rice. Another U.S. concern, Georgia Pacific, owns 575,000 acres of the selva, and the King Ranch of Texas has 180,000 acres in the state of Pará on which to raise cattle. There are also Japanese and German companies that have land in this area, and Volkswagon owns a 300,000 acre cattle ranch.

Ludwig, however, was by far the biggest operator. He initially spent $750 million here, and planned to spend an additional $800 million in the next few years. In 1978 two enormous barges were towed all the way from Japan then up the Amazon and Jari rivers with heavy equipment. One contained a wood-burning power plant, the other a huge paper pulp mill that was soon in operation producing 750 *tons* of paper daily. In order to produce pulp Ludwig replaced 225,000 acres of virgin forest with pines (*pinus caribae* imported from Honduras) and *gmelina*, an Asiatic tree that grows easily in this area. His rice farms planted on the reclaimed floodplains of the Jari had the potential of producing four tons of rice per acre for a world faced with the growing specter of famine.[233]

The project was initially greeted with enthusiasm by the Brazilian government which granted Ludwig ten years tax exemption from Brazil's value-added tax. The government also acted as guarantor of a $200 million U.S. loan. In the twelve years that have passed since the Jari enterprise began, criticism of it has mounted. Brazilians, like peoples of many other nations, have become more ecology minded, and the entire project soon became highly controversial. The Brazilian government supported Ludwig, but many voices were raised against him in the congress. One federal deputy rose to his feet and raged: "To allow a transnational into the Amazon region is the same as letting a goat into an orchard!" Other deputies were no less violent in their criticism. One thing that infuriated the deputies was that the actual acreage was never clearly delineated. Francisco Andrade, director of Jari, testified before the Chamber of Deputies that it contained 1,632,121 hectares (4,080,000 acres). But upon further questioning he admitted that the project was in fact claiming possession of 3,600,000 hectares (9,000,000 acres). In any event, Ludwig finally won out, and Jari got started with great fanfare. It was one of the biggest dreams in the history of any South American country.

The Jari project opened up a wild and almost unpopulated stretch of virgin rain forest. The headquarters, growing out of nowhere, soon became a town of 9,000 inhabitants. Airports were opened up in the area, roads were constructed; barges, ferries, and river boats began to ply the waters. Employment was given to 30,000 workers. Thousands of tons of timber, paper pulp, and rice were produced. For a time things looked very promising for the success of the project, but before long disease and insects hit the gmelina trees that Ludwig had planted, and half of them died. The Brazilian government stopped the cutting of timber to be used for fuel in the manufacture of paper pulp and this work came to a standstill. The workers who had been hired with such high expectations turned into squatters, the rice planting part of the project was abandoned, and the whole Jari dream disintegrated. The Brazilian government finally took control of what was left.

Ludwig was by no means the only foreigner operating in the Amazon area. A total of at least sixty foreign firms hold investments there, including Alcoa, Reynolds Aluminum, Bethlehem Steel, and U.S. Steel, until it recently pulled out. The cost of starting productive operations is astronomical, because every pound of cement and piping has to be flown in or roads have to be opened so that it may be hauled in. U.S. Steel, after investing several millions of dollars in the Carajás project in the hope of producing iron ore, finally gave the whole thing up before processing a single pound of ore. The largest mining operation now functioning in Amazonia is the Trombetas bauxite project, which is being financed by the Brazilian government, Reynolds Aluminum, and firms from Canada, the Netherlands, Spain, and Norway. Trombetas expects to produce 4.5 million tons of bauxite in 1992, with an eventual target of 8 million tons a year.

In a totally different area the Brazilian government is participating heavily in a binational hydroelectric dam and power plant on the upper Paraná. Brazil is feverishly doing everything it can in order to offset the nation's unfavorable trade balance and foreign debt. Industrialization, building, exploration, westward expansion, and the intensive exploitation of her vast natural resources all form a part of the picture.

President Carter's human rights program infuriated many members of the ruling military caste, and in 1979 they became so angry that Brazil's twenty-five-year-old military pact with the United States was canceled, and all further U.S. military aid rejected. Brazil began to import her arms from other countries or to manufacture them herself. But if Carter's criticism of human rights violations in Brazil angered the rulers of that country, it made us many friends among the people, and one well-known and highly respected periodical reported that this may indeed make Carter more popular in Brazil than John F. Kennedy.

The Brazilian parliament has recently legalized divorce, despite the opposition of the church, and labor unions are now allowed to go on strike, a freedom unthinkable a decade or so ago. In view of its fuel shortage Brazil has embarked on the widespread construction of nuclear reactors. A multibillion dollar deal was signed with West Germany in 1978 to provide for at least eight reactors, and the United States (Westinghouse) has provided one. Brazil will import her uranium from West Germany, an arrangement that caused great concern in Washington, because out of this uranium Brazil could, if she wished, also make nuclear weapons. West Germany is Brazil's number one foreign customer.

Brazil already assembles and manufactures hundreds of thousands of motor vehicles and a wide range of machinery and military equipment. She manufactures one jet bomber, the Xavante, for her own use, and also makes a large transport-reconnaissance plane that is being sold to countries with human rights violations so flagrant that most Western nations will not sell them weapons.

In 1979 stern-mannered General Geisel was succeeded in the presidency by João Baptista Figueiredo, who was arrogantly optimistic about his country's progress. He took the stance that Brazil was already a world power of the first magnitude: "We are no longer little boys to have our ears pulled," he said, "today we create our own alternatives." If Figueiredo was referring to Brazil's potential, he was right. The country occupies half of the South American continent, and its population is greater than that of all the Spanish-speaking countries of South America combined. Brazil's potential is inestimable. However, Brazil's history of swinging wildly between periods of boom and bust has never created either economic or political stability. Democratic regimes of political uncertainty, followed by rigid military governments, have repeatedly eroded public confidence and made progress erratic. Brazil is an amorphous giant. Finally, in 1985, after twenty-one years of increasingly unpopular military rule, the generals allowed the national electoral college to choose a nonmilitary candidate for president. Tancredo Neves was chosen and then approved in a national plebiscite, but he died after a few months in office and was succeeded by his vice-president, Jose Sarney.

There was a period of aimless government until Sarney announced his bold Cruzado Plan: a new currency, a freeze on prices and wages, a broad program of social welfare, and widespread land reform. The public enthusiastically supported the plan, inflation was cut dramatically, and all economic indexes soared. Sarney became a hero' overnight. But because of erratic implementation and overspending by both the public and private sectors, shortages developed, the government began to print money to finance its expenditures, inflation returned with a vengeance, prices and wages then rose, and the bubble burst. Sarney called for a nationwide austerity program which did steady the economy, but inflation for 1987 was still 338 per cent. One good sign: for the year 1987 Brazil had a favorable trade balance of $8.6 billion; exports totaled $23.1 billion while imports were only $14.5 billion; but this favorable balance evaporated quickly when the country came to grips with its foreign debt which required $12.4 billion a year merely to service.[268]

Brazil's foreign debt in early 1987 stood at $114 billion, and in February when the economy plummeted the government suspended payments on $78 billion of this, and asked for a 30 per cent reduction in the remainder.[269] One U.S. bank wrote off its Brazilian loan as a total loss. Nick Eberstadt of the Harvard Center for Population Studies made the following statement about how Brazilians regard this debt: "Their economic attitudes were shaped by the perception that this was gift money. Needless to say, when you make unlimited amounts of capital available directly to governments, it changes the balance of power rather dramatically between the public and private sectors." But the Brazilians say that paying the debt at this time would cause them financial disaster, and they refuse to make any concrete commitment until the economy reaches a 6 to 7 per cent annual growth rate and remains there for some time. Eberstadt continues: "What is dramatically unconvincing is the notion that

Brazil is unable to pay its debt. You need only look at the government owner-ship of industry and land to realize how preposterous it is. What we are dealing with is patent unwillingness to honor obligations that they contracted for."[270]

Brazil's President Sarney, unable to handle his apparently insurmountable problems at home, like many Latin American heads-of-state, let off steam by lambasting the United States, always the convenient goat in such predicaments. However, his bitter words do indicate the depth of the growing anti-U.S. sentiment in Latin America today: "I do not believe there is a greater error on the part of the United States in its relations with Latin America than the third-class treatment it has given to our countries. Latin America has been a friend whose loyalty the United States has too long taken for granted, but the idea that we are the backyard of the hemisphere, a kind of vacant lot, naturally wounds and troubles us. Reacting to this attitude Latin America is beginning to nurture anti-North American feelings that did not exist in the past. When problems arise, Washington's preoccupation is security, its solution, military. This complicates matters; it does not solve them. What we need in our relations today is more cooperation, and less belligerence."

In spite of his aptitude for turning a neat phrase, the objective appraisal of Jose Sarney must be that he was not an inspiring or successful leader of his own country. Inflation soared during his term in office, the economy began to stagger, and the people lost confidence in their government. Brazil has lived so long with high inflation that this has come to be accepted almost as normal. A São Paulo economist, Luis Carlos Mendoca, said that his country has created "an inflationary culture," in which rapidly rising inflation is routine. Salaries are raised every month in order to keep pace with prices.

Rents, loan installments, and other contracted debts are indexed by governmental decree, pegged to a constantly adjusted index that reflects inflation. On the other side of the ledger, investors are not inclined to put their money into such an unpredictable economy. They send it out of the country, and as a consequence business languishes. The result is that the government has no money and spins its wheels; unless the trend is reversed the economy will collapse. With such a collapse there would come a critical loss of confidence in the democratic process. And many Brazilians remember, nostalgically, that military regimes would not allow such chaos under their rule.

At the end of his term Sarney was no longer in control of the government. Brazil had become strongly polarized politically and was floundering. There was a desperate need for new leadership, but when elections were held in December 1989, giving Brazilians the opportunity of choosing their first popularly elected president in twenty-nine years, the winner was young, popular, conservative, and inexperienced Fernando Collor de Mello, son of a wealthy landowner. He was forty years old, the youngest chief executive in Brazil's history. Collor had previously served as governor of one of the country's smallest and least populous states. He was elected president by a narrow margin of 5 per cent of the votes, and only 25 deputies of his National Reconstruction

Party won seats in the 559-member congress. Consequently, the new president faced major difficulties in finding legislative support for his program.

Collor's primary source of popularity had come from his dramatic fight against the "maharajahs" of Brazil—elite government bureaucrats who receive exorbitant salaries for doing nothing. His achievements as governor of the small northeastern state of Alagoas had not been outstanding. On taking office in March 1990 Collor was confronted by an annual inflation rate of 5,000 per cent and the almost total collapse of his nation's economy. One of his first moves was to promise that he would fire 300,000 useless government workers which, of course, brought forth a hue and cry from those affected and their families. Then he froze a large part of the bank deposits in order to curb inflation. But Brazil and Collor needed a real miracle to pull themselves out of the morass. An energetic and growing leftist opposition readied itself to skewer the new administration, while the military, not at all eager to take over a nation already hanging on the ropes, reluctantly prepared to act "in case of necessity."

Brazil is now the eighth most productive Western country, as many of the more optimistic reports are pointing out. But viewed in a more reasonable light this means little, for Canada, with only one fifth as large a population produces $40 billion more annually, or approximately seven times as much per inhabitant. Japan, with less population than Brazil, has a GNP five times as high. Brazil still has a long way to go before her economy can reasonably be called properly diversified and decently distributed.

Brazil is more of a melting pot than any other Latin American country. There are millions of Brazilians whose ancestral home was Italy, Portugal, Germany, or Spain. Almost 60 per cent of the total population is white, of European extraction. There are 950,000 Japanese in Brazil today, 250,000 of them native born. They have achieved considerable prominence in Brazil's economy and culture because of their tenacity, capacity of tireless work, and the high degree of literacy of the immigrants. Ethnic Japanese constitute only 2 per cent of the population of the state of São Paulo, for example, but more than 13 per cent of the students at the 30,000 student body University of São Paulo are Japanese. Though relatively few in number, the Japanese produce one fifth of Brazil's coffee, 30 per cent of her cotton, all of the tea, and a high percentage of the truck garden produce. Japanese are also extremely prominent in business, industry, and art.

Brazil spends over $8 billion a year to pay for imported oil, which the country produces in very small quantity. Gasoline costs twice as much as it does in the United States, and this is catastrophic in a country where 75 per cent of the freight is carried over roads. Any hike in the price of oil sends shudders throughout the Brazilian economy. Brazil, however, is far ahead of the United States in producing alternate fuels. Alcohol made from manioc, sugar beets, and sugarcane is at present the main synthetic fuel, but serious work is being done to convert coal. In Brazil's largest cities gasohol is already the principal fuel for cars.

At this point a personal reflection may be appropriate. I remember well that when I was in Brazil during World War II there was hardly a gasoline motor car on the streets, yet the streets were teeming with automobiles. In those days, in the 1940s, each car had a stovelike contraption attached to its rear in which was burned a kind of charcoal. These cars and motors were then called *gasogenios*, and they ran perfectly. Man's ingenuity has always been able to find an alternate source of energy when his accustomed source became too scarce. Brazil already has the capacity to produce more alcohol than can be stored.

Ninety per cent of the automobiles produced in Brazil run on 185 proof alcohol, which is almost smog free, and the country thus saves 200,000 barrels of gasoline a day. On the adverse side, government subsidies to encourage the production of this expensive fuel have severely drained federal resources at a time of economic crisis. There is now a crunch in the supply because Brazilian sugarcane refineries earn more producing sugar than they do alcohol. But the use of alcohol as an automobile fuel is clearly set to stay. Half a million new jobs have been created, at great government expense, and these cannot be taken away. Besides, Brazil's supply of petroleum-based gasoline is limited and meets only 10 per cent of the country's needs. As one big automobile manufacturer commented: "Alcohol is the AIDS of Brazil, and we don't know how to cure it!"

Another Brazilian problem of mammoth proportions is the rapid increase in population. Each year the country adds more people than the total population of Uruguay. Well over one million new applicants enter the job market every year, and there is not enough work to go around. This has placed a high priority on westward expansion, where the frontier beckons and the people follow. World Bank loans since 1982 to help Brazil build a 1,100-mile road into the Amazon selva have opened up a forested area the size of West Germany. The road has encouraged half a million land-hungry laborers displaced by mechanization elsewhere in Brazil to stream into the forest to scratch a living from fragile soils unsuitable for either farming or grazing. They soon move on, leaving a desert behind. Each year Brazil loses 3,650,000 acres of selva in this way, which amounts to the destruction of ten thousand acres of tropical forest *every day*.

A precious and irreplaceable resource is being squandered. The tropical forest helps to keep the earth's air clean, and "it is not surprising that one out of four pharmaceuticals comes from these forests. Or that an estimated 1,400 tropical plants, like the rosy periwinkle, have promising anti-cancer properties. As home to half the world's plant and animal species, these forests are a vast biochemical warehouse. The future of medicine and agriculture, the existence of thousands of wildlife species, and the survival of hundreds of millions of people all over the world depends on what we do now to keep the tropical forests alive."[271] As one observer noted, "the senseless destruction of Brazil's rain forest is like buring the paintings of Rembrandt in order to cook a meal."

The Amazon is by far the largest river in the world. It is 4,000 miles long, with nearly one thousand tributaries, and by the time the majestic river reaches the Atlantic it is flowing with such force that fresh water can be dipped up 200 miles out to sea. The mouth of the river is 200 miles wide. Its total flow is 60 times that of the Nile, and in a single hour the Amazon empties enough fresh water into the ocean to supply the needs of New York City for seven years. It drains one fifth of the world's fresh water into the sea. The Amazon and its tributaries contain more species of fish than the Atlantic Ocean, and in the Amazon rain forest live more than one half of all known species of flora and fauna in the world. This vast forest replenishes one half of the earth's oxygen, and its great river basin is the source of one fifth of the earth's fresh water.

One thousand miles up the Amazon lies the fabulous city of Manaos of nearly one million inhabitants, a tribute to man's ability to live in the tropics. In its famed opera house, built many years ago by the wealthy rubber barons, were once presented concerts and operas featuring the greatest singers of the world. Caruso and Adelina Patti sang here, as did many others of that golden age of opera. This once beautiful auditorium, now somewhat ravaged by time, sadly reflects the devastation of the rain forest that surrounds it.

During the early years of this century wild rubber collected in the Amazon rain forest brought in millions of dollars. In order to increase production, rubber trees were planted on several large plantations, but these trees became infested and were unprofitable. Isolated trees in the selva did not suffer from this blight. The plantations had been laid out on a terrain of too much humidity and heat. In recent years domestic plantings have been made in drier, cooler areas and have thrived.

Michelin has an exemplary plantation of one-and-one-half-million trees on 5,500 hectares among rolling hills near the coast between Rio and the mouth of the Amazon. Here they employ 800 bleeders and 700 support workers to produce 3,000 tons of rubber a year. To collect this much rubber from the forest would require the labor of at least 6,000 rubber tappers, and this wild rubber would be dirty and filled with debris. Michelin has provided each worker with a free house with running water and electricity, and has set up a twenty-bed hospital to take care of the ill.

Brazil today is a big question mark among the great nations of the world. No one knows where it is heading. It has neither a homogeneous population, nor an orderly and intelligently run government, nor an efficiently organized economy, nor indeed any well-defined program for future development, but it is, quite simply, the most dynamic large country in the world, unique in its diversity, magnificent in its unfulfilled promise.

GENERAL CONCLUSIONS

A Hemispheric Guessing Game

Almost any general conclusion concerning Latin America is bound to be problematical or downright deceiving. The public view is to lump all the southern countries together in a great mass known as *Latin America*. Many scholars fall into the same trap, despite the well-known fact that differences far outweigh similarities. Nevertheless, it is occasionally interesting to play at this hemispheric guessing game.

For example, in July 1979 there appeared a scholarly study called *Interfutures*, sponsored by OECD, and directed by the French professor, Jacques Lesorne. This report predicts that by the year 2000 Latin America's share of the world productivity is likely to increase by more than 60 per cent, a rate of growth exceeding that of any other area of the world. The report states: "In many respects, Latin America seems closer to the advanced industrial countries than to the developing world." The report predicts that per capita income in Latin America by the year 2000 will rise to between U.S. $2,600 and U.S. $3,200 (in 1979 dollars), approximately the same as in Italy today. Mexico City and São Paulo will be the two largest cities in the world, with populations of over thirty and twenty-six million respectively.

The report predicts that the annual rate of growth in productivity will average from 7 to 8 per cent between 1980 and 2000, because of the strong resource base and the rising level of industrialization. Approximately two thirds of the production and population will then be (as they are now) concentrated in three countries: Brazil, Mexico, and Argentina. The report points out that the economies of these countries are export-oriented because of the larger foreign market and more remunerative return. This has the effect of restricting the domestic market, which is at present confined to the upper income brackets, and it also gives very little support to internal employment. Of the three leading countries, only Argentina is able to maintain self-supporting agriculture. In Mexico and Brazil agriculture is languishing under the glitter of export profits. In the late 1970s and throughout the 1980s Latin America had to import 15 million tons of food, mostly grains, each year. Foreign indebtedness is increasing at a more rapid rate than economic growth. [240]

After pointing out these weaknesses the report warns that the predicted phenomenal growth will be achieved only if there is: political and social stability, a less inegalitarian social and economic structure, increased efficiency of the productive system, and control of population growth. The report indicates what the total productivity of Latin America may become by the year 2000, and by studying the graphs the conclusion is inevitable that even in the year 2000 Latin America, with double the population of the United States, will be producing only one half as much. In brief, per capita productivity will be only one fourth the U.S. average. This sounds terribly depressing unless we emphasize that at present it is only one eighth as much.

A considerably darker picture is painted by the Inter-American Development Bank, in its most recent annual reports on Latin America. Here the emphasis is on the recent decline in productivity, which expanded so rapidly from 1968 to 1974, when a growth rate of 7.2 per cent a year was maintained. In 1977–79, however, the annual rate of growth was only 4.5 per cent, and in the 1980s it was less than 2 per cent. The reasons for this decline were: a continuing inflation, an exploding population, social and political unrest, and the failure of the region to adjust to the higher costs of energy.[243] If a single one of these four weaknesses continues, it will subvert the possibility of rapid future growth. What is the reader to conclude? You pay your money and you take your choice. After all, it is only a guessing game.

During the 1980s there arose a new problem for Latin America: the foreign debt crisis. The overwhelming size of this debt, totaling $410 billion, still hangs like a great storm cloud over the entire area. In 1990 Brazil owed $117 billion, Mexico $114 billion, Argentina $60 billion, Venezuela $34 billion, Peru $25 billion. These countries are finding it intolerable to pay even the interest on these huge sums, let alone any part of the principal. They say that the debt is paralyzing their countries, making economic growth impossible, threatening the very survival of fragile democratic regimes. Big debt obligations also increase fiscal deficits, a major cause of inflation, which in 1987 was a staggering 187 per cent annually as an overall average, compared to 65 per cent for 1986. Nicaragua had the highest inflation at 1,226 per cent, Brazil 338 per cent, Argentina 178 per cent, Mexico 144 per cent, Peru 105 per cent.[272] There was only moderate improvement in the succeeding years 1988–92.

All the national economies continued to lose momentum. There was a decrease in productivity, in employment, per capita income, the standard of living, the influx of foreign capital, internal investment, the quality of work, and the quality of education. Furthermore, because of growing poverty and malnutrition, several diseases, once thought to be eradicated, reappeared in epidemic proportions: malaria, yellow fever, Chagas disease, and other parasitic infections.[273] A serious cholera epidemic broke out in 1991.

It is a Catch-22 situation: if the Latin Americans pay the debt their economies and very well-being are strangled; if they do not, it may become impossible to obtain the additional capital so desperately needed for their development. The foreign debt, therefore, has become for them a political and humanitarian rather than a financial problem. But in seeking a way out of this predicament Latin Americans are already asking for more money, for some kind of long-range Marshall Plan, for an outright cancellation of a considerable portion of the debt. Once off the hook, they think, some way will be found to resolve the basic problem. There is an unwillingness among the Latin American nations to tackle their insolvency with drastic cuts in their governmental bureaucracies and federal spending, with heavier taxes on the well-to-do, with more efficient economic programs, with better organized, more dedicated workers and fewer holidays in order to increase productivity and export profits. South Koreans, left in a shambles by war and with a debt equally onerous, worked around the clock for a pittance in order to build up their productive capacity for exports, and are now prospering. But such a course in Latin America is not conceivable.

We will take a guess at what may happen. The United States will probably respond to Latin America's request for further loans by throwing good money after bad, only to see this, too, evaporate under corrupt and inept governments. The politicians, as always, will feather their own nests rather than invest in productive enterprises which would benefit all the people.

The Colombian Nobel Laureate, García Márquez, made this comment on the problem: "Latin American unity is being achieved by the foreign debt. This unity," he continues, "will ultimately not be *against* but in *collaboration* with the United States. It will make us allies in a world of peace and creativity."[274]

Latin America's foreign debt could be turned to immediate advantage if used in part to provide exchange fellowships in our hemisphere. Similarly endowed Fulbright fellowships for other areas have been highly successful. In such an exchange Latin American host countries would cancel a portion of their debt by providing transportation, housing, food, medical care, tuition, etc., for visiting fellows. Theoretically, Argentina's debt alone ($60 billion), if all used for this purpose, could give the equivalent of $20,000 a year to each of 5,000 fellows for a period of *six hundred years*.

It is pertinent at this point to emphasize that U.S. policy toward Latin America, often excoriated in previous chapters, does have a bright side which calls urgently for attention and for expansion. The U.S. Department of State operates popular binational cultural centers in many of the larger Latin American cities. These centers are gathering places where students and citizens learn English and study a variety of other subjects absolutely free. Each center has a library, offers lectures by outstanding specialists, and has an area for exhibits. The centers have created incalculable good will.

Another strong but unheralded arm of our Latin American policy is the U.S. Peace Corps, whose dedicated workers have achieved phenomenal results in many primitive rural areas. A third inexpensive way to give productive and direct aid would be to set up several Vicos-type projects (see pages 818–820), in which residents participate actively in community reform. Millions of rural families desperately need clean drinking water, more hygienic living conditions, improved seed crops, more expertise in farming and animal husbandry, traveling clinics offering dental and medical care, and consolidated schools. The primary thrust of our Latin American policy should always be to provide aid directly to those in need, not to wasteful governmental agencies.

In the concluding chapters an attempt will be made to specify in more detail some of the realities with which the various countries of Latin America must grapple before there can be a truly dramatic change. Perhaps the greatest obstacle of all is the restriction of human freedom: in speech, in education, in the distribution of wealth, and of political power. The military clique invariably justifies its repression of these liberties with the cry of need. William Pitt put it well many years ago: "*Necessity is the plea for every infringement of human freedom. It is the argument of tyrants, it is the creed of slaves.*"

55

THE CONTEMPORARY SCENE

The most formidable question concerning Latin America today is not will there be revolution, but rather what form will this revolution take? For revolution with a capital "R" is inevitable. This does not mean that the revolution will be violent and bloody; it does mean that it must bring about fundamental changes in the national economy, land distribution, political and social life of the peoples. Gerald Clark, a very perceptive Canadian, put it well when he decided to entitle his book on the area *The Coming Explosion in Latin America.*

The key word in the title is, of course, "explosion." When we consider the problem dispassionately we soon realize there are several kinds of pressures accumulating which will result in several kinds of explosions. The most obvious is the population explosion. In recent decades no matter how fast the gross national product increased in Latin American countries it amounted to very little if any increase in the standard of living for the people at large because the increase in productivity could scarcely keep up with the increase in population. Almost half of the present population of the area is under eighteen, hence is consuming but nonproductive. Also "by 1995 there will be 50–60 per cent more women in the child-bearing ages than in 1960 so that unless social patterns change significantly by that time the absolute population growth will be prodigious."[199]

The total population of Latin America in 1970 reached approximately 250,000,000, but by 1990 it grew to 450,000,000, and by the year 2000, only ten years later, it will reach beyond 500,000,000, if present rates of growth continue. In that same year, 2000, the United States will have an estimated population of about 272,000,000, not much more than half that of Latin America. The entire Latin American area has one of the highest rates of population growth of any major region of the world, an average of more than 2 per cent a year. In the United States the rate of annual increase is less than 1.2 per cent, only half as much.

There are, of course, wide variations within Latin America itself. The larger countries, with a rate of growth higher than 2 per cent, are Brazil, which has a larger population than all of the Spanish-speaking countries of South America put together; Mexico, the next most populous country; Ecuador, Colombia, and Venezuela. Countries with a relatively low rate of growth are Argentina, Uruguay, Chile, and Bolivia. With the exception of Bolivia, where this low rate reflects an extremely high death rate because of poverty and disease, the other low increase countries represent the most progressive and best educated portion of South America, the very part which should be expanding in order to lead the rest.

In Spanish America the areas of greatest increase are those where there were great concentrations of Indians in pre-Columbian days, and where the Indian or Indianist element in the present population constitutes a drag on the national organism today because of the vast chasm which separates it from the remainder of the population.

The only exception to this is Venezuela, which is a unique case. Venezuela has received approximately 800,000 European immigrants since the end of World War II, most of them adults at the peak of their productive powers. In the country's relatively small population of 22,000,000, this represented a powerful influence on the national life. Oil has done the rest. The present rate of increase will almost surely not continue to the danger point in Venezuela, because the Venezuelans are a cosmopolitan and relatively nonorthodox people who will practice birth control on a wide basis when the necessity for it becomes apparent.

In the other regions of Latin America immigration in recent years has been at a minimum, and has not appreciably changed the make-up of the total population or added greatly to the culture. The only exception here was the entrance of a few thousand exiles from Spain after the defeat of the Spanish Republic by General Franco in 1939. These exiles were concentrated mainly in Buenos Aires and Mexico City, and while their numbers were relatively small their cultural impact was very great. They made these two cities the greatest publication centers for works in the Spanish language, taking the leadership away from Spain in this regard, and they also became a dynamic increment in the cultural life of Argentina and Mexico, many of them continuing their productive lives as professors, writers, architects, engineers, artists, doctors, lawyers in their new homes. Their distinction as a group plus the fact that their native language was Spanish made their contribution both exceptional and immediate.

Not only has the population explosion hit mainly the Indianist regions of Spanish America but families are largest among the poorest elements in those regions—the Indians and mestizos of the Andean and Mexican highlands, and the filthy crowded shantytowns of the great urban centers. Theoretically, it is not a question of space. In England and Wales 827 people live in a square mile, in the United States about 60, but in South America only 30. Nevertheless, there is a terrible land hunger among the rural masses.

The civilization of Spain was an urban thing, and building cities was one of the greatest talents of the Spanish colonizers. This talent has placed an increasing burden on the national economies of the various republics. In recent decades the exodus from the rural interior to the cities has turned into a flood. As Betancourt, president of Venezuela, pointed out, the poor country peasant would rather come to the city and try to make a living selling lottery tickets than remain in the hinterland where he has absolutely nothing.[204]

Thus the urbanization of Latin America has grown at a much too rapid rate and constitutes a drain on the nations as a whole. As the Argentine essayist Martínez Estrada has pointed out, the hinterland is like a dead satellite revolving around the great urban center, a veritable Goliath's head. Almost one third of all Argentines live in metropolitan Buenos Aires, one half of all Uruguayans reside in Montevideo, nearly one fourth of all Chileans live in Santiago, and a fifth of all Venezuelans live in Caracas. A similar disequilibrium prevails over all Latin America. Metropolitan São Paulo in Brazil has a population of 15,000,000, Mexico City 18,000,000, Rio over 8,000,000. Santiago, Lima, Caracas, and Bogotá have already passed, or within a few months will pass, the 4,000,000 mark.

All of these cities are fringed with the shanty *barriadas* of the miserable proletarian masses. In Caracas and Buenos Aires some of the hovels are topped with television antennas, but few have running water or sanitary facilities. In Buenos Aires the average worker in these slums makes eighty to ninety dollars a month as an unskilled laborer. These masses are slowly gaining a comprehension of the fact that there is strength in organization, and so they apply organized pressure to obtain a few public water faucets, electric lighting, perhaps a school or park near enough to use. Sometimes they win, sometimes they lose. But those who win inspire the others, and there is no end to what they may demand with increasing intensity in the coming decade.

A whole new vocabulary has grown up concerning these shantytowns and their inhabitants. The Spanish phrase *barrios bajos* (low districts) was originally used to indicate all slum areas, but such has been the growth of these Latin American slums in recent years that they have acquired new names in keeping with their character. In Chile the shantytowns are called *callampas* (mushrooms), in Venezuela the name is *ranchos* (country hovels), in Bogotá it is *tugurios* or *barrios clandestinos*, in Brazil it is *favelas*, in Lima *barriadas*, and in Buenos Aires *villas miserias*.

The mushrooming of these shantytowns is not due to any unwillingness to work; Latin Americans are not lazy. The traditional North American view of the Mexican asleep under his sombrero has never been accurate. The citizens of this part of the world are hard workers in a society which cannot provide them with decent jobs. The society itself, however, is guilty of perpetuating wasteful working habits which immediately irritate the foreign visitor. The worker in Germany or Japan, by comparison, would regard such habitual waste of man-power as ridiculous and inexcusable. The sad truth is that while Latin Americans are hard workers individually, there is no organized collective effort to strive together for a common goal, and there is almost universal inefficiency.

Item: In Paraguay the banks are open only from 7 to 10 or 11 A.M., and are closed for the rest of the day. The government agencies observe only a slightly more rigorous schedule.

Item: In Argentina there are 1.3 million government and state employees (in 1958 there were 500,000 more), while in Canada, which has about the same population but a lot more productivity, there are only 440,000, or one third as many, who are able to handle their work even more effectively.

Item: Again in Argentina the railways employ 8,755 railwaymen for every million tons of freight hauled, while in Canada the number is 1270 men.

Item: In Uruguay the small national economy has 250,000 public workers to support, or about one fourth of the total labor force.

Item: In Colombia a secretary would rather be caught dead than pick up a file and carry it across the office. The same feeling prevails in many other regions. Such chores are for menials only, and so a special corps of flunkies must be hired to do this work.

The bribe, or as they say in Mexico "mordida," is in evidence in all of the poorer countries. Officials and other employees seldom come out with an absolute refusal to do what is obviously their duty, they simply go into a very aggravating slowdown until that *mordida* has passed hands. This, of course, is in response to poverty, and may be overlooked, but the corruption at the top which drains off the lifeblood of the nation has no excuse: the multimillions of President Alemán of Mexico, Perón in Argentina, Pérez Jiménez or Vicente Gómez in Venezuela, Rojas Pinilla in Colombia, Leguía in Peru, Batista in Cuba, etc., etc.

Another fundamental flaw in the Latin American social structure is widespread tax evasion among those with the greatest ability to pay. Nowhere in Latin America is it considered a crime to evade taxes, and almost everyone does so. As ex-President Lleras Camargo of Colombia wrote in a recent issue of *Foreign Affairs*:

> To indicate how outlandish this situation is, it is enough to say that not a single Latin American, whether of high standing or of the underworld, has ever been imprisoned for not paying his taxes or for sending in a fraudulent income tax report.

In a recent year in Brazil, Peru, and Ecuador, less than half of the eligible taxpayers filed returns. Guatemala and Paraguay have no income tax at all.

In the second place, income taxes are unreasonably low, perhaps in part because there is no hope of ever collecting them. In relatively wealthy Venezuela a man making $100,000 a year in taxable income owes an income tax of approximately eight thousand dollars, while in the United States or Canada the amount due would be four times as much. With such a tax structure and such an attitude among the wealthy citizens, financial solvency at the federal level is difficult to come by, and there is never enough money in the federal treasury to carry out the fundamental economic reforms which are becoming increasingly urgent.

Moreover, wealthy Latin Americans are reluctant to invest their capital in their own countries because of unsettled political conditions and because in most countries a rampant inflation has greatly decreased the value of such investments. Many North American and Canadian critics have expressed the opinion that more native capital had fled from Latin American to Swiss and North American banks than the total of United States aid extended to that area. This opinion is correct, lamentable, but perhaps irrelevant, for nobody anywhere wants to see his money become worthless.

There are, however, some notable exceptions to the rule. In Mexico in the past decade 85 per cent of all capital invested in the country was Mexican capital. In Venezuela a similar situation prevails. This is one reason these two countries have been able to progress so rapidly in their industrial expansion, agrarian reform, education programs, and other social improvements. However, Mexico and Venezuela have been unable to maintain stability in their currencies and in the cost of living. Inflation has soared in every country of Latin America, often well over 100 per cent a year, because of the mounting foreign debt, low productivity, overall political and economic ineptitude. Excessive government spending on borrowed funds helped send prices up, and the population explosion which each year added millions of new buyers to a limited market kept the spiral soaring. Some countries tried to solve the problem by printing more money, which, as any economist knows, is the kiss of death to a stable currency.

An austerity program for government spending and a clampdown on wealthy citizens would help the situation. It would also be a symbolic gesture to the masses and would give a sense of sharing the sacrifices of a common destiny. In the 1990s such measures are at last being attempted. This will make the totality of the population more productive, but it almost certainly will not be achieved without the very strongest mass political pressure.

After World War II both Germany and Japan were devastated and their economies were prostrate. Within twenty years both countries were booming, their productivity and standard of living higher than before the war. What were the magic ingredients of the remarkable recovery of these two countries? United States aid was one thing but it would have achieved nothing had it not been for two other indispensable elements: German and Japanese know-how and the will and hard work of the German and Japanese people. The inhabitants of Latin America have neither the know-how nor the will to work for the common destiny. Great masses of their population are not effective citizens.

If we contrast the two areas objectively some of the deep flaws in Latin American life begin to stand out: the lack of a homogeneous population, a lopsided land distribution, a lack of industrial know-how, lack of education, inefficient methods and habits of work, lack of a feeling of dedication or nationhood, a wealthy oligarchy unwilling to sacrifice for the common good, the absence of efficient public servants and honest governments.

All of which takes us straight to the problem of education, for it is only through education that Latin Americans can achieve the things which their society now lacks. But North Americans make a great mistake by equating Latin American educational problems and systems with our own. The attitude "if we did it, so can you," puts all the emphasis in the wrong place, for things are not the same now as they were when our own public schools began to grow.

In the middle of the last century if a man went through the sixth grade he often became educationally superior to his boss. He also rose in the social scale, because the little red schoolhouse brought the extremes together. Only a very rudimentary education was needed to achieve success. The incredibly rapid advance of knowledge and technology has changed all this.

> Today in Latin America, in the midst of modern technology, three times as many years of schooling and twenty times as much money as was then spent on grammar schools will not produce the same social result. The dropout of the sixth grade is unable to find a job even as a punchcard operator. . . .[200]

Schools in the United States grew in answer to the demand for skills essential to an industrial society in the making. Massive education realized this potential. At the present moment in history the United States, because of its earlier industrialization and immensely greater wealth, can afford all the schools it needs and at the same time pay for moon explorations, anti-ballistic missiles, public works of all kinds, poverty programs, a thousand universities, and a widespread system of social security and social welfare.

No Latin American nation remotely approaches this potential. Even a high school education is beyond the reach of 85 per cent of all persons of our epoch unless they are fortunate enough to live in one of those relatively small islands where capital accumulates. "Nowhere in Latin America do 27 per cent of any age group get beyond the sixth grade, nor do more than 1 per cent graduate from a university." Yet no country spends less than 18 per cent of its income on schools, if we include local expenditures, and many spend more than 30 per cent. Universal schooling is beyond their means. "The *annual* cost of schooling a United States citizen between the ages of 12 and 24 costs as much as most Latin Americans earn in two or three years."[200]

Thus, the same school which in the nineteenth century helped the United States to become an economically homogeneous industrial society, in Latin America today has become "an oppressive idol which protects those who are already schooled." Schools have created a new elite, and have forced the masses who are unschooled to accept their secondary status. Schools in poor countries like Paraguay, Bolivia, Ecuador, Guatemala, Peru, many parts of Brazil, simply provide a privilege for the few which must be paid for in one way or another by all the rest.

Yet universal schooling has become such a strong political ideal that no government and no citizen would dare speak out against it. Indeed, schools have replaced the church as the great religion. This ideal has been incorporated in national constitutions and in many statutes. And as the new elite raises itself the unlettered masses feel even more strongly the burden of discrimination against them. This intensifies their feelings of lesser value, frustration, hostility, and degradation.

If universal education as we know it is beyond the means of developing nations, a great improvement in the schooling that already exists and which is bound to expand is a matter of highest priority. It is the focus that has to be changed. The urbanization of Latin American society has already taken away the numerical importance of the landless rural masses. The big-city shantytowns have grown at several times the rate of the traditional rural population. This has increased the imminence of massed political and economic pressures, but it has also increased the viability of the new methods of education at the disposal of contemporary society: the radio, television, adult education classes, education classes run by factories, labor unions or political groups, trade-school training at all age levels, new ways of teaching skills in reading, writing, and arithmetic—all with the masses of potential students concentrated in an area of easy accessibility. Yet, until the very late 1970s, no shantytown had its own schools, its own adult training programs, its own recreation or health care centers, and so on.

University education presents a very different kind of problem. We who live in the United States are likely to regard the student unrest which occasionally reached the boiling point on some of our university campuses as a purely North American phenomenon. This is far from the truth. In Latin America this same student unrest exploded in the year 1918 at the University of Córdoba, Argentina, and soon spread to universities in other parts of Argentina, then to Uruguay, Peru, and finally, to the rest of Latin America. The movement was known as the Reforma Universitaria, the University Reform.

Up to 1918 Latin American universities had been clinging doggedly to a rigid and outworn curriculum which strongly reflected the old colonial theocratic, philosophical, and classical education. All courses were prescribed, there were no electives, the subject matter was highly irrelevant in most students' lives, the professors were politically appointed and many were very incompetent, because knowing someone in power could mean a position for life. Professors demanded the strictest discipline and class attendance and were often accused of failing a student because of the latter's political ideas. The universities were controlled by the federal governments and were open to only a very few students of upper-class families.

The 1918 Reform movement was directed against all these things. The University of Córdoba in that year was host to the first National Congress of University Students at whose meetings the protests began to boil. The students at Córdoba then went on strike against the educational system and the political establishments. One day a group of photographers went to the office of the rector (president) and told him that the students were on the warpath and wanted his scalp. They advised the rector to slip out of a window while there was still time. The poor man, deceived and frightened, listened to this advice and put one leg over the window sill. At that moment a battery of cameras clicked and the next day every news sheet in the country displayed the rector in this ignominious pose. Inevitably and in disgrace he lost his job.

This was the beginning of the end of the old university, but it was not until after ten years of unrest that the following necessary reforms were adopted. The professors had to take competitive examinations before appointment, students were given a share in university government, the curriculum was altered to include more modern fields, such as engineering, physics, chemistry, foreign languages and literatures, social sciences, etc. Students were also given the right to attend or not attend classes, everything depending on their examinations. The universities also made it possible for a much larger percentage of middle-class students to gain entrance to their sacrosanct halls.

Since that day these have been the rules of Latin American university life. But unfortunately the unrest never ended, and the universities also became a miniature battleground of national politics. "Students strike, riot, and stage political demonstrations on the slightest provocation. They picket their professors, barricade themselves in the buildings, throw bombs at the police, print partisan handbills." This statement appears in a book on Argentina which came out in 1945. For the next several years student unrest was high until the military clamped down, sent a policeman to every classroom, and forced the students either to keep quiet and study, or get out and so sacrifice their careers.

For decades student strikes and demonstrations seriously interfered with the quality and continuity of higher education. Sometimes months passed without classes ever meeting. Peru, Argentina, and Venezuela were the most notable examples, but Mexico, Bolivia, and Chile had serious troubles. Students at the University of San Marcos in Lima were the ones who demonstrated so violently against Vice-President Nixon in 1958; in 1968 students went on a rampage in Mexico City; and students made it impossible for Rockefeller to visit Venezuela, Chile, and Bolivia in 1969. Student political thinking has veered far to the left in recent years, and now smacks strongly of Fidelismo, even of Mao, and of the already outmoded Soviet ideology. Most organized student groups are violently anti-United States, even if they are not leftist-oriented. Everywhere they are feeling their oats, and it is going to be very difficult to deal with them on a reasonable basis, because they are no longer amenable to reason.

In spite of this student rebellion, Latin American universities, like their counterparts in the United States, continue to produce many high-quality graduates. There is one great difference: Latin America is suffering acutely from the brain drain. Advanced students are coming from the southern republics to the United States in increasing numbers to finish their education or to take graduate degrees from American universities. Hundreds of these choose to remain in the United States. They are joined by hundreds of others who come to the United States (or go to some other foreign country) after taking their professional degrees in their homelands. These emigrants, it must be remembered, all come from that highly privileged one per cent of Latin Americans who do graduate from college. The cost of giving a student that kind of education is many thousands of dollars. Add to this the total loss of these graduates' years of productivity, and the significance of this brain drain assumes mammoth proportions.

"Can Latin America with her incalculably rich but unexploited resources hope to step up into the industrial age if 20 per cent of her engineers and 15 per cent of her doctors leave to work abroad? Between 1962–66 Chile lost 30.3 per cent, Ecuador 32 per cent, Paraguay 23.3 per cent of their engineers."[213] The percentage who become college professors in the various fields in the United States includes some of the most brilliant Latin American minds. Money is not the only attraction that draws these people away. A way of life which does not glorify and exalt the political boss appeals greatly to those in the professions.

In Latin America today both at the bottom and at the top the established structure is beginning to let the people down. Waves of discontent, signals of distress, now only indications of the gathering storm, are clearly visible but are grudgingly acknowledged. The cities burgeon, the culture flowers, money pours into the urban till and into the pockets of a favored few, while half of the people continue to live at the subsistence level, scarcely one jump ahead of starvation. Let a man come along who will promise to change all that, and the people may listen. They are not trained or educated to see beyond the pressing needs of the moment. In a society where poverty is almost king the long-range view is impossible. Have not the people been hearing of long-range goals throughout the centuries?

Many Latin American writers and a few foreigners have commented on one intriguing psychological aspect of character and culture in the southern countries: *machismo*. The word actually means "maleness," and has all the obvious connotations of virility, aggressive masculinity, intransigeance, arrogant self-confidence in the face of the adversary, and, if necessary, violence. The Latin American man regards himself first, last and always as *muy macho*, very much of a male. If he is not this he is nothing. This element of maleness implies that the Latin American man, and most especially the leader, must constantly prove his aggressive masculinity. Rosas and Perón in Argentina were ragarded as *muy machos*, so was Simón Bolívar, so was President Alemán of Mexico. Pancho Villa, another very *macho* Mexican hero, said to idealistic Madero, as Sancho might have said to Don Quixote, "All you have to do is hitch up your pants and be a man!"[201] Little wonder that Don Juan was a creation of the Spanish literary genius. He has always been more important than Don Quixote in the national life of the Hispanic countries, but he is always a Don Juan with a twist or two of the Quixote thrown in.

Octavio Paz, the distinguished Mexican poet and essayist, comments on this *machismo* at length in his *The Labyrinth of Solitude*. "The primary element of our "maleness' consists," he said, "of never giving in to anything outside. A man may have to bend, to bow down, to lie, to humiliate himself, but he must never 'give in,' that is allow the exterior world to penetrate his interior self, his interior maleness." Paz goes on: "We instinctively consider the environment that surrounds us as dangerous. This reaction is justified if one will only consider what our history has been like and what the character and society that we have created have become."[211]

The cult of *machismo* demands that the Latin American male be a real he-man, sexually very potent, a good fighter, stubborn, brave, and strong. He will readily fight and die for what he believes in, making a great gesture as he does so. He believes absolutely that when there is any conflict—social, political, economic, or individual—if he does not come out on top he comes out on the bottom. A man must get his way, and he must *not* share his power. The truce, the compromise, the middle ground do not exist for him. "The outcome of defeat is bondage or death." And if he is too kindly or too gentle or too tender in his attitudes, or too timid or too moderate in his actions, then he may be accused of femininity, the one insult that destroys absolutely.

The historian might view the Mexican Revolution itself, and the many novels that deal with it, as machismo operating on a grand scale. He might even carry the parallel farther and find in the continuously violent and aggressive eruptions of Latin American politics everywhere (and in the unending military takeovers of civilian governments) further evidence of this same machismo. Certainly he may assume that machismo accounts for the widespread, and to the foreigner incomprehensible, lack of charity or human compassion so prevalent in Latin American life.

Machismo implies a strong self-centered dominance on the one hand, and an almost total indifference on the other. Well-to-do and well-educated Latin Americans, men and women, will pass along a street while a child is sobbing disconsolately in the gutter, and scarcely turn to find out what is the matter. Since the child is inevitably filthy, in poor health, probably with sores on his skin, and obviously belonging to the lowest class, this suffering is regarded as his natural human condition. Neither individual nor collective charity in Latin America go very far toward alleviating this condition. At the upper end of the social scale the disease is endemic. Poor citizens, who have almost nothing, are far more willing to share the very little that they do possess.

In Mexico, and the same would be true of any Indianist country, this machismo results in part from pre-Columbian Indian cruelty, in part from the

Don Juan attitude of the Spaniard, and in part from the trauma of the Conquest itself and the resultant class cleavage. Dona Marina (Malinche, the Indian princess), who became the mistress of Cortes and later married another Spaniard when Cortes grew tired of her, symbolizes what the mestizo race of these countries hate most, "the violated one." In this case, of course, the violated one is their direct ancestor, the beginning of their race and of their secondary social status. Machismo is the obvious defense against further violations. Thus, when Mexicans are furious at an adversary, they will shout: "*Hijos de la chingada* [Sons of the violated woman]." It is an overcompensation for their own inadequacies, their own deeply rooted feeling of lesser value.[211]

Some of this same feeling is found in the "Chicano" movement of the American Southwest. Rodolfo "Corky" Gonzalez, mainspring of the movement in the Denver area, puts it this way: "We don't need any more Anglo hypocrisy. We need people who have *machismo*, who have beautiful hearts, who have free Chicano minds." The group headed by Gonzalez has put forth the "Plan of Aztlan," which proposes the restoration of the U.S. Southwest to the Chicanos. "Chicanos are already a nation," was one policy statement endorsed by a conference of this group, which asks for an "independent Chicano school system" in the "independent nation of Aztlan." Aztlan was the Aztec name for this territory. Gonzalez and his supporters urge that a plebiscite be held in the Southwest in the hope that this area will be restored to the Chicanos as Israel was restored to the Jews.

Whether or not the connection is a direct one it is but a short step from machismo to the military coup and the military junta. One of the manifestations of the law of social control is that in those countries where individualism is the strongest we have also found in history some of the strongest centralized controls. Obviously this is because a stubborn individualism will not submit to any other kind of discipline. Self-discipline and self-government are beyond its ken. Hence, in Italy we find the Mafia and Mussolini, in Spain the Jesuit Society, the Inquisition, and absolutism in government, and in Latin America a series of stern military regimes.

The number of military coups in Latin America in recent years is staggering and must indicate a fundamental flaw in the national life. Since the year 1930 the record is as follows: in Argentina there have been nine military coups, in Cuba four, in Venezuela four, in Colombia nine, in Brazil five, in Bolivia eleven, in Peru six, in Paraguay seven, in El Salvador six, in Guatemala six, and in the Dominican Republic four. This list records only the most flagrant and most often repeated examples; not a country has been completely immune from military intervention in its government except Costa Rica. The best that can be said for these repeated coups is that they brought "law and order" out of political chaos. But seldom indeed did they work out any succession, so the process had to be repeated again and again. This is the great tragedy of Latin American life.

However, during the last twenty to thirty years both the character and method of operation of these military takeovers have changed. What has emerged is the middle-class military coup, with very definite characteristics of its own. The middle class and the urban working classes have both been growing very rapidly in recent years, and the process of industrialization which has strengthened the one has also given strength to the other. The working class, with its well-organized labor unions, has a greater feeling of solidarity economically and politically. It can mobilize its resources for economic or political purposes better than the middle class.

When a worker makes a demand or goes on strike for more wages he has the support of his union. He does not ask for himself alone, but for all the members of his union. The middle-class employee, on the other hand, speaks only for himself. This is the basic weakness of the middle class, as Argentine President Perón pointed out many years ago. But the middle class is no longer impotent, for it has created a new and very effective weapon in the middle-class army.

As Aristotle said in the days of classic Athens: "Those who are unequals revolt in order to become equals, and those who are equals because they want to become superior. Such is the state of mind which creates revolutions." Thus, the middle class refuses to stay in the middle; it is always a group in transition. Furthermore, the middle class is composed of many shades of political and economic opinion. It does not function effectively in free elections because it is split into many diverse groups. But it does demand with something like unanimity "law and order," for without a stable political base its economic position is placed in jeopardy, and all of its members, of whatever opinion, are bound to lose.

The middle-class army is made up of deprived rural and urban workers, who thus become less deprived middle-class soldiers. They are no longer at the mercy of the weather, the landlord, or the market place. Their income is assured, they have security and health benefits, they may even receive an education, and they have a new sense of dignity and of power. The entire middle class does not always endorse the military when it intervenes in politics, although this is generally the case, but the military establishment itself has become the only middle-class institution capable of effective political action.

Middle-class soldiers learn discipline first, last and always. This is the basis of their being and of their effectiveness. Discipline is the one quality which no Latin American political party has developed to a very high degree, excepting only the Communists, and so the army supplies what political parties lack. In the army discipline means respect for authority, and authority resides in the officers. The officer is thus regarded as the upholder of the right values, the values which should be defended, he is the protector of the nation's glory and of its history, its laws, and its institutions. The nation's progress depends on him.

The more professionalized the army and the better educated it becomes, the more aware it is politically, and thus the more identified with the rest of society.

When there is a national crisis of any kind the army instantly senses what has taken place and responds as a body. If it is violence in the streets, or political chaos, its power is mobilized immediately to take care of this "threat to the nation," which is thus aroused to follow. If it is the unpalatable action of some United States corporation, the same response is often made, and again the whole nation follows.

The middle-class army usually counts on the Right for support, as well as on large segments of the middle class, but the far Left is always its enemy. The Left's violent unrest, demonstrations, strikes and protests are the one thing that the military cannot tolerate. Thus any severe crisis may bring about a coup. The lower class wants to destroy privilege, the upper class wants to preserve privilege, and the middle class wants to acquire privilege. When political or economic stability begin to break down the salaried middle class is the first to lose, and the army feels uneasy and readies itself for action.

Disorder is not to be tolerated, and revolution implies disorder. But the middle-class military establishment is sufficiently astute to realize that changes must be made, so it seizes power in order to keep these changes under tight control, its own middle-class control. The result, unfortunately, is that no valid succession is ever worked out, for while the military can control a regimented government it cannot control open and honest elections.

The middle-class military coup, invariably, is a move to protect the emerging importance of the middle-class value system. The middle-class army would find intolerable a leftist revolution which would destroy all of the nation's old values, and it would find equally intolerable a rightist dictatorship of the Porfirio Díaz, Vicente Gómez, Gerardo Machado, or Juan Domingo Perón type. Either of these extremes would disrupt the national economy, injure the national image, and hurt the middle class itself. On the other hand, the middle-class army may take a strongly pro- or anti-United States stand depending on the exigencies of the moment. It might even regard with sympathy many of the accomplishments and ideals which it believes are embodied in Fidelismo, although it would continue to look askance on the figure of Fidel himself, his Communist affliction, and a good many of his particular actions.

The amounts spent on maintaining the armed forces of the Latin American republics have been overwhelming. The only bright spots here are Costa Rica, which abolished its army more than twenty years ago, Mexico, which now spends only 10 per cent of its budget on the military, and perhaps Uruguay, which has only a small defense establishment. But in Argentina there have been many recent years in which the federal government has spent nearly one half its total budget on the armed forces, Chile was not far behind, Peru's military expenditures often come to 25 per cent of the budget, Venezuela under Pérez Jiménez spent nearly 50 per cent, Brazil has spent as much as 30 per cent, Colombia up to 23 per cent, even poor Ecuador as much as 22 per cent. Some specifics of these expenditures are shocking: Brazil has thirty-eight officers at the rank of "Marshal of the Army," more men of that rank than all the other countries of the world combined, and not long since a Chilean congressman arose to denounce the absurdity that his country should have as many generals as Canada, when that nation had 500,000 men under arms in the Second World War.

The Latin American Armed Services insist on buying airplane carriers, submarines, jet planes, tanks, all the implements of modern warfare. Yet they are able to obtain only outdated versions of these items, and their ability to hold off any first-rate outside aggressor who might attack them would be almost nil. Their only realistic protection against an outside invader is the United States, a fact too seldom mentioned and too little appreciated in Latin America. A Brazilian congressman recently pointed out that the cost of an airplane carrier that his country wished to buy would provide free lunches for two million Brazilian school children until the year 2000. Or, it would pay for the construction of nearly 5,000 miles of roads in a land where people are starving because foodstuffs cannot reach the marketplace.[203]

A Chilean writer, Alejandro Magnet, in an essay lamenting the intolerable financial burden of military expenditures, pointed out that

> . . . in the countries of Latin America, brief and incomplete in their evolution, with the great masses of their citizenry unaware of any sense of nationhood or cultural destiny, military glory is the only kind of glory that can truly move the tenuous collective soul. The military establishment thus, first before its own members and then before the citizenry as a whole, appears as the veritable incarnation of the Fatherland itself.[203]

Any government, therefore, that strove toward a real disarmament, would be toppled overnight. And in the United States our officialdom says: "If we did not sell Latin America arms some other country would!" The dilemma is painfully complete.

But even this is not the worst side of the picture. The present armed forces of Latin America really exist in order to protect the oligarchy from the people at large, and the middle class is now a part of that oligarchy. A war between two Latin American nations would be utterly senseless. In this one regard the Organization of American States has proved to be an excellent substitute for violent conflict. Yet the military expenditures continue, and so do the military coups. The governments they produce, with their disdain for democracy, provide a fertile ground for the growth of Communism or some other form of state socialism.

President Jorge Alessandri of Chile told a correspondent of the New York *Times* that while the countries of Latin America and the United States engaged in pacific and long-winded discourses, those countries were spending on military equipment the money that they all desperately needed for their economic development. "It is high time," he went on, "to reduce and equalize these expenditures before we continue any other kind of discussion, because until this is done all other discussions are merely academic."

President Eduardo Santos of Colombia went even further. "We don't want to be skeletons in armor," he said. Then he added:

> Against whom are we Latin Americans arming ourselves? Why are our countries ruining themselves buying arms they will never use? Because the crime of an American international war, of one group of nations against the others, would be the unforgiveable sin against the Holy Spirit. That would be a crime which nothing could explain, nothing justify. . . . We have no reason to fight one another; we have only reasons to live together in peace and harmony. . . .
>
> Then, what we are doing is building up armies which weigh nothing in the international scale but which are Juggernauts for the internal life of each country. Quixotic to the end, I have fought against this for twenty-five years. When I was about to be inaugurated president of Colombia I said to Sumner Welles . . . , "*My dear friend, do not arm us because that is like giving a child morphine; it is the most habit-forming of drugs.*" Later, at a meeting of certain historic import with President Franklin D. Roosevelt in 1945 I repeated this same plea in the presence of Nelson Rockefeller. . . .
>
> And yet, every day, all the countries are buying more armaments, ridiculous armaments which arouse jealousy in some of our neighbors and fear in others. This, in my opinion, is the greatest mistake that could be made with Latin America, the greatest sin. The United States has pushed us along this road, and has deflected us from our historic destiny, and may jeopardize the future of the entire continent, uselessly, stupidly, inexplicably.

Santos then goes on to explain why all this is so closely connected with the problem of freedom, and why it represents the strongest threat to freedom in the Americas. "The problem in Latin America," he says, "is for us to bear with one another. Our difficulty lies in achieving that noble Anglo-Saxon tolerance out of which the greatness of your land has grown. And to arm our intolerance is sheer madness. If we are unarmed, we will, at least, continue to be relatively inoffensive. But there is no greater danger than an armed intolerant."[205]

In theory, if all of the money expended on arms in Latin America during the last five or six years had been invested instead in the national welfare, it might have wiped out all of the shantytowns which now fringe the great urban centers. It might have saved countless lives from death or permanent disability because of malnutrition and disease. It might have provided homes, jobs, water, medical care, electricity, food, and clothing for those who have none of these things. It might have given hope to the hopeless, strength to the weak, and spirit to the depressed and disenchanted.

The same statements, of course, are applicable to the United States, where 40 per cent of our own national budget is spent on the armed services. These military funds, for even one or two years, could wipe out the filth of our ghettos, give sustenance and spirit to our depressed, and make the American dream come true. It is something to think about. It is something which makes the mind turn cold with the agony of its human condition. It is something that we will never do. Man is too proud and too fearful a beast ever to allow reason or love to dominate his actions completely. War is seldom logical or inevitable. "The main characteristic of war is the abandonment of logic and reason by those who embark upon it." It is sad to relate that the only lesson learned from history is that nations never really learn anything from history. Perhaps the explanation is that nations invariably predicate present dicisions on past experiences which are no longer applicable.

However, men who have suffered and seen the mistakes of the history that they themselves helped to make are sometimes able to pinpoint what went wrong. Major General Smedley D. Butler of the U.S. Marine Corps, who twice won the Congressional Medal of Honor, and who fought in every Marine Corps campaign from the Spanish-American War to World War I, after his retirement in 1931 expressed his views in an autobiography called, *War Is a Racket*. Among his statements was the following:

> I spent 33 years and 4 months in active service as a member of our country's most agile military force—the Marine Corps . . . I helped make Mexico and especially Tampico safe for American oil interests in 1914. I helped make Haiti and Cuba a decent place for the National City bank boys to collect revenues in . . . I helped purify Nicaragua for the international banking house of Brown Brothers in 1909–12. I brought light to the Dominican Republic for American sugar interests in 1916. I helped make Honduras *right* for American fruit companies in 1903 . . . Looking back on it, I feel I might have given Al Capone a few hints.

Is it any wonder that the United States now faces the most serious crisis which Washington has ever confronted in its own hemisphere? Our national leaders appear to have insight and wisdom only in hindsight. The brilliant British historian, Lord Acton, concluded his provocative essay on "The New World" with these disturbing words, which further increase one's doubt: *History is often made by energetic men, steadfastly following ideas, mostly wrong, that determine events.*

During the past few years energetic men in Latin America have given history an unexpected twist in more ways than one; first of all, in the dramatic changes that are taking place in the national economies. It has often been noted that one of the glaring weaknesses in the economy of many Latin American countries (Argentina, Venezuela, Brazil, and Mexico are prime examples) is the big state, the state as owner of big companies and of vast amounts of land. This concentration of economic power in the hands of the state resulted in padded payrolls and overstuffed, inefficient bureaucracies that are seldom cost effective. State-owned firms drain $4 billion yearly from Argentina's federal budget, they account for one third of Brazil's yearly expenditures, while Mexico shells out $7.7 billion in subsidies to inefficient state-run concerns.[300]

Goaded on by the recent changes in Eastern Europe, Latin America has now begun to turn toward privatization of these companies. Anything that would encourage, rather than stifle, competition would be helpful; but privatization is just the beginning, not the solution to the problem. It is a buzzword that has caught on, as the state, strapped for cash, bolsters itself by selling these companies to private investors. Mexico alone has divested itself of more than 700 enterprises in the past decade. Such sales give the state a much needed balance of cash and rid it of having to continue the operation of unprofitable companies. However, this is much like a poor man selling his house in order to get money. It is only a stopgap to tide him over a rough period. Unfortunately, concerns that lost money under state ownership will probably continue to lose money under private ownership. What is needed is a complete change in the way of doing business, a rigorous pruning of unnecessary employees and expenses, updated equipment, the development of corps of loyal workers, more technical knowhow, and company management that is well trained, well organized, dedicated, and competitive. In the final analysis, competition is the key ingredient of economic growth, as Adam Smith pointed out two centuries ago.

A second, very dynamic aspect of twentieth-century Latin American life is the rapid expansion of an underground economy, a widespread black market kept going by ingenious and energetic participants. In some countries the underground economy accounts for as much productivity as the legal economy, and operates far more democratically. An underground economy bypasses the red tape tied to establishing and running a business via official channels, which can take an inordinate amount of time and cost a considerable amount of money, money that could be better spent if invested directly in the new business. Several test cases were researched in Peru that proved the point. A typical business required the applicant to obtain eleven official permits or approvals and took a total of 289 days, at a cost of $1,231, which is 31 times the monthly minimum living wage. Underground businesses get around all this delay and expense by operating illegally.

Much the same avoidance of officialdom applies to the group occupation of unused land. "Once the land has been chosen, the original group tries to show other interested parties that they stand to gain more by joining an invasion than by acting on their own. In this way it begins to assemble the critical mass essential to reducing the possibility of police repression or reinvasion of the settlement by new individuals." Then, with the help of engineers or engineering students, a municipal plan is drawn up and individual lots are chalked off and distributed. Areas to be occupied by schools, public buildings, and parks are also clearly marked. At an agreed hour the invaders arrive in rented trucks and minibuses bringing poles, matting, and straw for the roofs of rapidly raised tents.[292]

After the invasion a communal kitchen is set up to feed the invaders during the first hectic days of the new settlement. A childcare center is also set up and vendors begin to ply the streets selling the things needed by the new colonists. Nothing is left to chance; everything is carefully planned. A widely observed national holiday is usually chosen for the invasion, as this makes police intervention less likely. Numerous flags are displayed to prove the patriotism of the invaders and as a symbolic gesture for official cooperation. Once the settlement is occupied it is very difficult, almost impossible, to drive the occupants out. The entire process is made more acceptable because 90 per cent of all settlements are established on municipal or state-owned land which has long lain unused and fallow. The new colony quickly becomes an integral functioning unit. This practice of operating in competition with the official economy has become so widespread that it is the subject of the bestselling book in Latin America today, *The Other Path*, by the well-known Peruvian author, Hernando de Soto.

Even religion is changing in Latin America today with the rapid growth of evangelical Protestantism. For many years the Mormon church, the Seventh Day Adventists, and Jehovah's Witnesses have operated on a limited scale in the area, but at the beginning of this century there were fewer than 200,000 Protestants in all Latin America. Today there are about 50 million, and the average rate of conversion is estimated to be close to 400 per hour. These new Protestants are fundamentalists in their beliefs and Pentecostal in their practice; that is, in their services they strive to be filled with the spirit of the Holy Ghost. They accept Jesus Christ as their personal savior, the central tenet of their faith is that of the individual standing alone before God, and they need no central authority to tell them how to interpret the Bible, which is God's literal and authentic word.[302]

Among these new Protestants are numerous sects, but all are alike in their emotional approach to religion. They are not allied with any specific political party, but the majority are conservatives, just as they are in the United States. As a body, therefore, they represent a new and well-organized force on the right side of the political spectrum. And this at the very time in history that the Catholic church has moved toward the Left in its zeal to protect the poor, distribute wealth more equitably, and support governments working for social reform and human rights. It is still too early to tell whether this new movement away from the Catholic church is a flash in the pan, or a more permanent rift with the traditional Catholic past. In any event, evangelical Protestantism is a very dynamic movement in Latin America today, responsive to the fiery word, dedicated to the principles of a very personal religion, anti-Catholic in attitude and in belief.

But 2,000 years of history and tradition will not disappear overnight. The Catholic church in Latin America represents not only a religion, it embodies a whole culture and a way of life. On more than one occasion, and before many challenges, it has, like the soft grasses, been bent but not broken by winds of change, and it is adapting itself today to meet the needs of a much disturbed social order. Utopia is still a long way off, and there are many obstacles along the road; as the old Spanish proverb says, it is wise to have patience in times of stress: *Paciencia, y barajar,* "Patience and shuffle the cards!"

Another idea that has caught fire in Latin America today is that of the common market. Brazil and Argentina already have definite plans for establishing a Common Market in 1995. The Andean countries are working on a regional Common Market of their own, and other areas have similar plans. President Bush has proposed a Free Market between the United States and Mexico and has suggested that this be extended to include the entire hemisphere. The proposal has been favorably received in Latin America.[297]

Pooling regional resources and expertise in mutually beneficial projects is the quickest way to bypass the limited potential of individual countries. In this regard, Brazil and Argentina, the two largest South American nations, have taken the lead. In addition to cooperating on the construction of powerful dams in Paraguay, these countries have recently become partners in the manufacture of a state-of-the-art medium-range passenger aircraft, the CBA-123. In July 1990 presidents Menem and Collor de Mello met in Sao Jose dos Campos, 100 kilometers from São Paulo, to witness the inaugural flight of the new plane. On this occasion the president of Brazil said: "We are going to integrate our efforts here in South America. We will combine our resources in order to manufacture products that are more modern, more sophisticated, and above all, more competitive in the world market. This is a pioneering venture that marks the beginning of a new era in the relations between Brazil and Argentina, and it projects a future of our two nations continuing to work together on the international scene." President Menem of Argentina added: "This CBA plane is the final result of pooling the economic, political, and technical resources of our two nations. It is proof of what cooperation between us can achieve." The new aircraft incorporates the latest concepts in aeronautical engineering, and is constructed of materials more resistant to metal fatigue than steel, and of less weight than aluminum. The newest generation of computers for navigation and automatic flight were installed. In other areas any move toward cooperation and the pooling of resources would certainly be a step forward in political progress and economic productivity.

On the other side of the ledger, Latin American military establishments in many countries still jeopardize self-government. Any army, in order to function effectively, requires discipline, more discipline than the society at large. Therefore, in periods of great stress, fear, or uncertainty there always exists the illusion that the military can take over and control everything, restore order, bring back "business as usual," repair the disruptions caused by social or political upheaval. The military can pull together a society that is falling apart, and get things going again. The fact is that this restoration of order exacts a tremendous toll, and after a brief period of stability that toll quickly becomes apparent.

Elio Gaspari, New York correspondent of the Brazilian newsmagazine *Veja*, is more specific: a military government of leftist leanings bankrupted Peru. In Argentina a rightist slanted military establishment "slaughtered tens of thousands, wrought economic chaos and dragged the nation into an ill-advised war with Britain over the Falkland Islands. In Brazil, after assassinating hundreds of people and torturing thousands more, the generals bequeathed a foreign debt of one hundred billion dollars to their civilian successors." And in Chile, a military government executed thousands and became a police state that suppressed all human rights. The bottom line is that military control, however beneficial temporarily, is never a solution to deepset economic and social problems.

56
INTER-AMERICAN RELATIONS TODAY

The acute problem in inter-American relations at this juncture is U.S. apathy and the very strong anti-Yankee sentiment in the southern countries, aroused mainly by the corporate presence of United States interests, but strongly abetted by the unhappy interventions recently engineered by the United States Department of State. These two things constitute the outward and visible sign of that inner and very nonspiritual odium now being so widely directed against us. José Martí of Cuba, one of the most astute Latin American critics of this country because of his own incomparable intellect and sense of humanity, and also because of his long residence (eighteen years) in the United States, prophetically foretold the whole sad and ugly story in an article entitled "Our America," published in *El Partido Liberal* of Mexico, in the year 1889. The Spanish-American War was still ten years away, and the many United States interventions in Latin America had not yet begun.

Martí spoke of the Latin penchant for elevating the virile character of the race, of the early wars of neighbor against neighbor and of the emergence of great bands of undisciplined troops which controlled destiny, and then he went on:

> But our America perhaps runs another danger, which does not come from within, but which arises from a difference in origin, character and interests between the two segments of our hemisphere. Very soon indeed the enterprising and aggressive neighbor who does not know us and who disdains us will be demanding closer relations with us. . . . The disdain of this formidable neighbor, who is ignorant of what we really are, is the greatest danger of our America. It is urgent that this neighbor get to know us soon so that it will not look down on us. Through ignorance, perhaps, it might through greed be brought to lay hands upon us.

Manuel Ugarte of Argentina writing much later (1923), when the United States interventions were at their peak, made the charge much more specific.

His *Destiny of a Continent,* a classic indictment of inter-American relations, is a very objective analysis of United States penetration. In the chapter entitled "The New Rome" he writes as follows concerning the historic process of imperialism:

> The first conquerors in world history, of primitive mentalities, annexed the inhabitants of a country as slaves. Those who came next annexed the territories without the inhabitants. The United States has inaugurated the system of annexing the wealth without either the inhabitants or the territories, disdaining appearances to get right at the bone of domination without all the deadweight. . . .

Ugarte suggests that "the ideal of imperialism consists of governing through alien hands," that is, through puppets or at the very least rulers who are favorable to the outsider.

Strangely, Ugarte evoked very little response in Latin America, where he stumped the university and public rostrums in an attempt to awaken his compatriots. He wrote that his biggest and most intelligent reception was at Columbia University in New York City. Ugarte did not blame the United States for its imperialism. He laid the blame on the chaotic political and economic conditions among the Latin Americans themselves which encouraged this imperialism in the first place and then sustained it as one Latin American faction was pitted against another. "The United States will support a tyrant here, back a revolutionary regime there, anything to gain the upper hand . . . ," explains Ugarte. "And no use screaming that we are innocent victims," he concludes, "because for a nation to invoke ethical principles is already a confession of defeat."

Ugarte was not really saying anything new. Robert Lansing, who was President Wilson's Secretary of State, as early as 1914 had said the same thing:

> A power whose subjects own the public debt of an American state and have invested there large amounts of capital may control the government of the state as completely as if it had acquired sovereign rights over the territory through occupation, conquest, or concession.

Such was the case in Mexico during the early decades of this century, and such is still the case in far away Peru at the present moment, in the 1990s. In Peru, United States interests own almost all the copper, perhaps that republic's most valuable resource, nearly all of the shipping, a fourth of the sugar and fishing industries, most of the oil resources (at least until the I.P.C. properties were expropriated), the telephone company, and many major businesses. "Peru is almost totally dependent on the American government and private banks for the refinancing of its large external debt and for the funds necessary to expand its mining." Little wonder, then, that the cry is so loud when Peruvians conclude that American corporations actually hold more power than their own sovereign government.

The United States now finds itself in the unfortunate position of defending

United States investments and unpopular governments which favor these interests instead of making itself the ally of the people. The cases are legion: Argentina, Brazil, Paraguay, Guatemala, Dominican Republic, Spain, Greece, et cetera. It would be far wiser to keep the United States government and the United States corporate presence separated, and to use all of the influence of the first to keep the second in line with national sentiments within foreign states. This is the only honest way to operate. We either learn how to go directly to the people, or we fail in our mission as a world power.

The whole thing's going to be won or lost, right here in Latin America. These words of John F. Kennedy set the stage in our hemisphere at the beginning of the 1960s. Latin Americans responded almost en masse to the President's personal charm, and they believed in the sincerity of his public statements. Not since Franklin Roosevelt had an American president evoked such enthusiastic admirers in a foreign land. Despite President Eisenhower's good intentions, his brother Milton's good-will trip through Latin America and his extremely perceptive report on his return, despite Vice-President Nixon's visit, and a growing liberalism within the United States, the Eisenhower administration had never stirred up much response in the southern republics. The Guatemalan episode of 1954 in which the CIA displaced a sovereign government with its own man gave all the soft words a deceptive ring. United States quotas placed on key products, its cotton dumping, the wild gyrations of coffee prices and a full-blown storm of inflation within, all rightly or wrongly aroused further enmity against the United States.

Kennedy was a younger man, he had fought bravely in the war, he was an intellectual of some repute, and he belonged to the younger generation of national leaders who knew that there must be far-going changes in the hemisphere if disaster was to be avoided. President Kennedy did not believe that "revolution" was a dirty word. He used it repeatedly and he aligned himself with those who wanted to make the revolution. "If we cannot help the many who are poor, we cannot save the few who are rich," he said, warming the cockles of many a Latin American heart. Then came his real clarion cry: *"Those who make peaceful revolution impossible make violent revolution inevitable!"*

The Alliance for Progress, President Kennedy's dramatic proposal for a hemispheric, indeed a world-wide attack on the critical underdevelopment of Latin America, was born on March 31, 1961. The President spoke of his proposal as being "staggering in its dimensions," and called it "a vast cooperative effort, unparalleled in magnitude and nobility of purpose," to provide for Latin Americans the basic needs which so many millions of them lacked: "homes, work and land, health and schools." With massive capital investment, plus basic land and tax reform, these problems could be solved, the standard of living could be raised for all, and then "all men can live out their lives in dignity and freedom."

The Alliance called for the investment of one hundred *billion* dollars in Latin America by 1970, eighty per cent to come from Latin America itself, twenty per cent from other sources. Eleven billion dollars would come from the United States, and of this sum $300,000,000 a year would represent United States private capital. (Total U.S. investments in Latin America were four billion dollars in 1924 and fourteen billion dollars in 1970.) The Alliance got off with a big verbal bang, but Latin Americans had heard great promises before, and many of them adopted a "wait and see" attitude despite their personal admiration for President Kennedy. When the President was assassinated, the whole bright dream came to an abrupt end. Indeed, for the first two or three years of the Alliance for every United States dollar that went into Latin America, a dollar and a half came out, most of it native capital in flight. And as for the $300,000,000 a year which United States capitalists were supposed to invest in Latin America, the annual sum was somewhat less than a third as much. Conclusion, the Alliance was a great idea, but it did not work out as planned. It was again a matter of too little and too late.

Kennedy's Bay of Pigs invasion of Cuba from bases in Guatemala (without OAS consultation) was the young president's greatest defeat, while his ultimatum to the Soviet Union to get its missiles out of Cuba (after OAS consultation), represented his finest hour. Under the tensions of these trying months he once gave the Latin Americans a jolt by coming out flat-footed and saying that if the United States ever felt that it had to intervene in Latin America in order to protect its own security, it would first try to get OAS approval if there was time, but the intervention would take place, with or without that approval. On hearing these words the Latin Americans muttered to each other: "I told you so."

President Johnson's Vietnam buildup and his Dominican venture in 1965 were widely opposed in Latin America, but when he gave the Chamisal strip back to Mexico it put an end to a long standing sore spot in the United States-Mexican relations. His Punta del Este appearance in 1967, however, was somewhat anticlimactic. His "Decade of Urgency" was the hollow repetition of the already overpromised Alliance for Progress.

President Nixon, in the spring of 1969 sent Governor Nelson Rockefeller to Latin America (accompanied by at least three dozen specialists in the area) to find out why hemispheric relations had gone sour, and to report on what might be done to improve them. Rockefeller, former head of the Division of Latin American Affairs in the United States Department of State, and twice governor of New York state, was himself very knowledgeable in the problems of this area. If he had gone to Latin America as an individual, he would probably have been welcomed, for personally he was well liked and widely respected in the southern republics.

As the official representative of the Nixon administration he was met with widespread abuse, and the governments of Bolivia and Guatemala so feared for his personal safety that they allowed him only a couple of hours in their countries, under the heaviest guard. Indeed, he was kept bottled up at the airports in each place until his brief meetings with the respective heads of state were concluded. Rockefeller was invited not to enter Venezuela and Chile at all, and of course he did not seriously consider going to Peru. Even in Uruguay there were violent demonstrations against his mission, and in Brazil the government would not allow news of any anti-United States demonstrations to be printed. Paraguay, as one might expect, threw out the red carpet for him. Rockefeller did not get even a glance at the two disaster areas of Latin America, the altiplano-Andean region of Bolivia and Peru, and Brazil's poverty-stricken Northeast. Here, where the life expectancy is about thirty-two years, only a few months more than it was in Roman days, are the two big powder kegs in Latin America, the rotten roots that spread their diseased branches so far and wide.

Rockefeller's visit called for a much greater show of local security forces than that of Vice-President Nixon in 1958, and worst of all even the democracies: Chile, Venezuela, Uruguay did not want to receive him. Obviously things had gotten much worse than they were a decade earlier, despite the Alliance for Progress and the Decade of Urgency. The Vietnam War, which was very unpopular in Latin America, was one cause of this increased animosity, disillusionment with United States aid was another, and still a third was the worldwide student rebellion against established values.

In Latin America even more than in the United States students carry the banners of protest and shout anti-establishment battle cries. David Belnap, former Latin American correspondent for the *Los Angeles Times*, mentions two other factors:

> The tremendous gap between the basic power and wealth of the United States and Latin America causes jealousies and fears which feed a rising tide of nationalism. Nationalistic extremism is generated by the over-reaction of most Latin Americans to vague uncertainties they feel about their own national identities. The Mexicans among all Latin Americans are perhaps the only ones who have overcome these uncertainties. Nationalism is the sentiment most easily exploited by extremists working to diminish the influence of the United States in Latin America.[214]

Rockefeller himself, after his return to the United States, referred to the "magnificent objectives of the Alliance for Progress," but he also called it "over-promised and underdelivered." He made a special point of highlighting some of the stupidities and inequities of the United States commitments, as for example, the written-in requirement that a certain project utilize United States engineers who would be paid $3,000 a month alongside native engineers who would be receiving about $150 a month. But Rockefeller, in a burst of unwarranted optimism, said that on the whole he considered his visit very worthwhile. It would have appeared the wiser move to send Latin America representatives not as well known officially, if the real problems were to be dug out and laid in the sun.

The Mexico City newspaper *Excelsior* pointed out that Rockefeller's visit was met not only with mounting tensions, but actually caused several deaths in

Latin America. "The necessity for a complete overhaul of United States–Latin American relations is urgent, but the fundamental problem," continued *Excelsior*, "has nothing to do with philanthropy or the price of raw materials. It seems paradoxical that this must be proclaimed so energetically at a time when the communications media are so prodigiously developed. But the fact is that we just don't know each other, and in this ignorance we accumulate resentments which can explode at any moment."

Nelson Rockefeller beyond any doubt was an astute and well-meaning man who truly loved Latin America. The report that he turned in to President Nixon was a good one, but it unfortunately had very little effect on the foreign policy of the United States. Nor did the Kissinger report made years later. North Americans by and large simply do not know or care much about Latin America until the shoe really pinches. Then it is too late. Washington never moves until public opinion (or the CIA, or the Armed Services, or the Dept. of State) applies unrelenting pressure.

Some of the facts presented by Rockefeller are sobering: one half of Latin America is forested, one quarter consists of barren mountains, deserts, and other wild lands, 20 per cent is in grazing lands, and only 5 per cent is planted in crops, compared with 20 per cent in cultivated land in the United States. Latin American farmers utilize mainly the "fire and hoe" method of agriculture. Very little conservation is practiced anywhere. While overall food production is going up, food production per person, due to the population explosion, is estimated at *10 per cent less* than it was at the end of World War II. And each year there are eight to ten million more mouths to feed.

There is a great increase in the gulf between the advantaged and the disadvantaged. People are now aware of this gulf and of the fact that it need not exist if technology and government and economics were dedicated to solve the problem. Over and above all this there is an uneasy nationalism, striving for self-identification. We stand at the crossroads, and our very way of life is being challenged.[216]

The Latin American policy of the United States during the past few decades has shown a surprising lack of correlation between words and actions. Interventions in Guatemala, Cuba, the Dominican Republic, and more recently, Panama, belied our promises. Uprooting the Arbenz regime in Guatemala in 1954 when Castillo Armas invaded that country from Honduras with United States support (strictly contrary to the OAS charter) ruffled millions of Latin American liberals but caused a pleasant sensation among those on the far right.

President Kennedy himself referred to the Cuban Bay of Pigs episode of 1961 as "a colossal mistake." The whole cloak-and-dagger nature of the operation, the training of the invaders on Guatemalan soil, their takeoff from bases in that country, their clear-cut United States backing, the presence of several Batista men among them, and the sad bloody defeat of the invading band within a few hours—all these things brought forth a great hue and cry from Latin America.

President Johnson's unilateral invasion of the Dominican Republic in 1965 (again without prior OAS consultation) evoked an equally loud wail of protest from the South. Later OAS approval, and the presence of a few token Latin American troops in Santo Domingo, was gratuitous but unreal. Chile, Uruguay, Mexico, Ecuador, and Peru voted against this occupation, and Venezuela abstained.

Despite President Kennedy's high-sounding words there is a widespread feeling in Latin America today that the United States simply will not allow a real revolution against vested interests in any of the southern republics. President Reagan's Latin American policy, with his insistent demand for aid to the Contras, to whom he invariably referred as "freedom fighters," only served to increase this uneasiness. Latin Americans generally opposed Contra aid, and were particularly upset by President Reagan's unwillingness to work more closely with the Contadora Group, the Organization of American States, and the Committee of Presidents, headed by Oscar Arias of Costa Rica. All these groups sought a nonmilitary solution to the Central American problem. As a result, Latin Americans by and large enjoyed the Reagan administration's discomfiture during the Iran-Contra scam of 1987, but at the same time they admired the deeply rooted democratic tradition that could produce a congressional investigation of this issue. In 1989 one of the first acts of the Bush administration was the assault on Panama which was a bitter pill for Latin Americans to swallow.

The United States finds itself between the horns of a dilemma when a violently anti-U.S. regime or a strong leftist government comes into power in Latin America, but the only honest course is to walk the tightrope, consult with the other American states, then act with wisdom, firmness, and restraint. Consultation is mandatory. The OAS has been able to stop more incipient wars in this hemisphere than the United States. Distinguished Latin American leaders like Lleras Camargo (once president of Colombia) and Galo Plaza (once president of Ecuador) have served as Secretary General of this organization. The United States should share more of its sovereignty with this tribunal.

Inside Latin America there is a desperate need for radical change in the social order. If revolutionary efforts are aborted, or if reformers move too slowly, or if the revolutionaries themselves are so inept politically that they fall into unmitigated chaos, things will be much worse. An interregnum of inevitable turmoil confronts us in this hemisphere.

"Everything and anything can happen in Latin America," writes Mexico's distinguished historian, Cossío Villegas. "Or, to put it another way, in Latin America nothing is firm and stable, nothing is based on solid rock, but everything seems to rest lightly on a powder keg that may explode at any moment. The second lesson which is the reverse of the first—is the incredible power of the fiery word, a power all the greater in proportion to its recklessness. This leads us to the sad conclusion that man in the mass loses much of his individual reasoning and judgment, which give way in him to violent emotion."[189]

Whatever the passions aroused in Latin America the influence of the United States should always be toward bringing a greater freedom and a greater justice to all. As Eduardo Santos, President of Colombia, has said: "*Divide up property as seems best, but let everyone speak freely, express himself freely, defend his ideas freely—live free. And this is what Communism will tolerate nowhere.*"[205] The United States should never underestimate its power for freedom, a freedom which does not depend on force, but which arises from the people. This is what all intelligent Latin Americans really want, along with fundamental economic and political reforms.

Despite its overall wake of frustrations United States aid to Latin America has been continuous, life-saving, extensive. What Latin Americans resent is their downgrading in the world picture as a whole. Since the end of World War II, in which they were our allies, limited U.S. aid to their part of the world has kept them at the bottom end of the totem pole. The United States, they feel, has treated its European enemies, Japan, and even the smaller Asian countries, far better than it has its own sister nations. From 1945 to 1979 the total of all United States governmental aid to every Latin American country (population well over 350 million) was $5 *billion* less than the amount of such aid received by Taiwan (population 14 million) and South Korea (population 30 million),* and $8 billion less than the aid to South Vietnam alone.

The Alliance for Progress stepped up the pace and altered the focus of United States aid to Latin America, but it is a great mistake for North Americans to regard this as one-sided generosity. Up to the end of 1978 the United States had extended a total of $15.7 billion to Latin America, but of this total over $10 billion was in loans, on which over $1 billion interest has already been paid. Latin Americans themselves have invested in their own countries over fifty billion dollars. These amounts are large, but do not come anywhere near meeting the original goals set for the program. This is not to deny that many admirable things have been accomplished. There have been roads, hospitals, dams, power plants, colleges, irrigation projects, homes, business expansion, mobile health units and foods provided in nearly every country.

The "Operation Children" (Operación Niños) of the Food for Peace Program has provided school lunches for 15,000,000 Latin American children in eighteen countries. Water systems have been installed in parts of Brazil's miserable Northeast, and in a hundred rural communities in Peru. Several million

---

* Gerald Clark reports as follows: "From 1945 to 1960, of the billions in loans and grants the United States delivered to the world, scarcely 2 per cent of the total went to Latin America, less even than to the Philippines. And then one day Washington, to its horror, awoke to discover there were masses of people next door who were discontented and restless and volatile." In the 1980s the situation was infinitely worse.

textbooks have been made available for use in the elementary schools. New schoolrooms have been constructed for over a million school children, and more than 300,000 homes have been built. But over three million homes *a year* are needed over the next thirty years in order to catch up with the housing shortage and the population explosion.

The record is not one to be ashamed of, but it is simply a matter of not keeping pace with the rapidly increasing demands of our time. Another source of frustration in the program has been that funds disbursed and funds received by governmental agencies inevitably create bureaucracies at both ends of the line and not enough reaches those for whom the aid was intended. The Peace Corps, which has cost a bare $10,000,000 a year, has been more effective on a return per each dollar expended than the much larger government or corporation investment.

The goal of the Alliance for Progress was a yearly per capita economic growth in Latin America of 2.5 per cent. From the program's beginning up through 1988 the actual percentage of growth was about 1.8 per cent, less than the average 2.2 per cent a year during the decade of 1950–60. But these statistics fail to reveal one of the most successful aspects of the Alliance: the saving of human lives. Indeed, it is this very increase in life expectancy which has led to the present population explosion and made all previous yardsticks irrelevant. During the 1980s U.S. banks did indeed unwisely *lend* enormous sums to Latin America, most of which unfortunately went down the drain.

However much the planners may wish, the problems of the future will not be solved by applying equations which might have worked ten years ago. This is the crux of the matter. We have learned that no amount of conventional sweetness will eradicate acute social problems. Our hemisphere is faced with a complete blowup unless the combined imagination and intelligence of our peoples can devise and implement a better inter-American program than any we have ever had before.

Another source of irritation to Latin Americans is that so few of our diplomatic representatives, and almost none of our ambassadors, speak the language of the country, while Latin American representatives in this country, almost without exception, speak English fluently. The same can be said for the Latin American heads of state, most of whom know English well, whereas the presidents of the United States have been notably lacking in their ability in any foreign language. It is difficult for Latin Americans (and for Europeans as well) to reconcile this linguistic narrowness with cultural leadership. United States diplomats and presidents, therefore, are widely regarded as successful and well-to-do executives, not cultural leaders.

Américo Castro, a Brazilian-born, Spanish-educated writer and professor who lived and taught for many years in the United States, once commented that the cultural ideal of the Latin American is to achieve all that he can without the necessity of going beyond himself. Therefore, his culture is "rich in such values as literature, art, personal dignity, heroism, religious feeling, richness of interior life expressed with beauty, distinction or grace." His primary goal is always an idealized cultural image.

While the North American, says Castro, lives primarily for, in and through things, tangible things, and his sense of values is molded by the collectivity. Therefore, Latin American intellectuals and writers become diplomats and presidents, for they are exalted by the state, which regards them as its own highest achievement. The best-known poets, novelists and essayists in Latin America have frequently occupied diplomatic posts, and this included three Nobel Prize winners in literature.

Castro considers this difference in our value systems at the root of all our misunderstanding of each other.

> When I witness the noble and laudable efforts of some United States groups in-
> tent upon attracting the sympathy of their neighbors, I am reminded of the error
> committed by someone who tried to hammer a nail by striking it with a few tons
> of some valuable but emollient stuff-wool, for instance. All of it comes from the
> idea, igenuous at bottom, that Latin America is like the United States, and that
> what succeeds in the United States—collective movements which swallow up the
> individual—will also succeed in nations where the masses are more indifferent,
> where only individuals are reckoned with, who, while contradicting the crowd,
> tower above it. [210]

Then Castro concludes that half a dozen American visitors noted in the field of literature or the arts would leave a more profound imprint in Latin America than twenty good-will tours.

"The English language itself," he adds sadly, "is being impoverished in the cultural circles of the United States, because the university man, caught by the spirit of the masses, does not dare avoid triviality." He might have added that widespread radio and television broadcasts and high pressured business dealings have lowered considerably the level of American speech because the best examples are no longer held up before us, and because a correct knowledge of the language is no longer considered necessary for success. The burden of all this is that the Latin American still regards the North American as a some-what callow businessman without profound intellectual interests. The fact that presidents Kennedy and Roosevelt were able to speak a few words of French impressed Latin American leaders more deeply than did their wealth or their position as heads of a great government.

Latin Americans are their own severest critics, and if we are interested in knowing what is wrong with them we should consult their best writers. Gone are the days when a universal chauvinism beclouded the reality of self-analysis in the southern republics. The Mexican essayist Francisco Bulnes, wrote these pungent and reproaching lines:

> The great Latin delusion is the belief that art is the highest, almost the only
> object of national life. Latins bend every effort to being artists in religion and turn

out to be idolators; they strive to be artists in industry, and impoverish themselves; even in science they want to be artists, and they fail to understand scientific method. . . . Latins set themselves to be the great artists in politics, and the result is that a republic becomes for them a perfectly impossible system of government.

Culture and art have always been aristocratic unless one is speaking of the folk arts and oral tradition which do not depend on literacy for their expression. People who cannot read or write have a language of their own which embraces everything and everybody, but obviously a modern state cannot sustain itself on such a primitive base, however beautiful. Technocracy has created a psychology which demands an integrated society if that society is to function smoothly. Plato's *Republic* was supremely aristocratic, and Latin Americans regard themselves as the perpetuators of the Hellenic tradition. "Democracy," Plato wrote, "is a charming form of government, full of variety and disorder, dispensing a sort of equality to equals and unequals alike." No wonder that it has had such rough sailing in Latin American waters.

The years since World War II have seen a great flowering in Latin American literature. The gossamers of modernism have been pulled down in order to get a clearer view of man and of the world today. Five writers have won the Nobel Prize, and many Latin American works have been widely translated into foreign languages, particularly English. These much admired translations have added a new dimension to inter-American relations. For us to exalt *their writers* is quite a change.

In the previous generation poetry was the strongest genre in the southern republics, but after the war prose fiction, the novel and the short story came into their own. Not on that account did poetry languish. Gabriela Mistral of Chile, a poet, was awarded the Nobel Prize in 1945, and in 1967, Miguel Angel Asturias of Guatemala, who is essentially a poet in all of his prose fiction, was similarly honored. Juan Ramón Jiménez, a Spanish poet who had lived for years in the United States and Puerto Rico, an exile from his own country after the cruel Spanish Civil War, was the third writer living in Latin America to gain this international honor (1956). Another superb poet, Pablo Neruda of Chile, was awarded the prize in 1971. The Colombian novelist, Gabriel García Márquez, became a Nobel Laureate in 1982. He has enjoyed great acclaim in the United States. In 1990 Octavio Paz, Mexico's fine poet and essayist, was the fifth Latin American writer to win the prize.

In the field of prose fiction, to this historian's mind, there were many writers more worthy than Miguel Angel Asturias, the 1967 Laureate, whose best novel is one of his earliest, *El señor presidente*, and whose later works have much less appeal. Superior contenders were Jorge Luis Borges and Eduardo Mallea of Argentina, Octavio Paz, Carlos Fuentes, Agustín Yáñez of Mexico, and Alejo Carpentier of Cuba. Why the committee chose Asturias instead of any of these writers is a mystery.

García Márquez has opened up an entirely new vista on Latin American life with his uniquely imaginative fiction. His personal life is quite another matter. He is a good friend of Fidel Castro, and spends much time in Havana in a Mediterranean-style villa with a large swimming pool that Castro provides for him when he visits Cuba. García Márquez says that he and Castro are friends because they share a profound solitude—Fidel the solitude of power, García Márquez the solitude of fame. García Márquez, although a vigorous socialist, owns plush homes in Mexico City, Cuernavaca, Paris, Barcelona, and Barranquilla. The Peruvian novelist, Vargas Llosa, who wrote an excellent book on García Márquez, excoriates him for his friendship with Castro, who has ruthlessly censored and exiled so many Cuban writers.[301]

Agustín Yáñez in his *Al filo del agua* (called *The Edge of the Storm* in English), 1947, was the first postwar novelist to make full use of Freudian impulses and the fragmented poetic imagery floating on the waters of that epoch. James Joyce, John Dos Passos, and William Faulkner are obvious influences on this fine work, which traces the life and death of a small isolated Mexican village in Jalisco just prior to the Revolution, which is the storm that will destroy the old social order. But Yáñez does not concern himself with that social order. His primary interest is the psychological state of mind of his characters, prison pent in the chains of their fanatical Catholic tradition which produces repressions, sex fantasies, intolerance, guilt, violence. His is the universal composite Hispanic village. Yáñez was followed in his country by Juan Rulfo and Carlos Fuentes. Regionalism is present in all of these writers, but no longer as a confining geography.

> There is a region, but hardly regionalism any more, in Colombia's García Márquez (*A hundred years of solitude*), in whom we detect the influx of Faulkner, Hemingway, and Camus. Shadows of Faulkner again inhabit the regions of Vargas Llosa (of Peru) (*Time of the hero* and *The green house*). In fact, Faulkner has been the single greatest influence on our literature in the past twenty years or so.[206]

Borges of Argentina (1899–1986), a professor of English literature at the University of Buenos Aires, was a unique figure in Latin American and world letters. There is no one else even remotely like him. He has written only three or four collections of short stories, a few essays, and a few poems, but he writes so well and in a manner so completely his own that he has no peers. "I could never write a novel," he has said, "because my wish is to condense it all into ten or twelve pages." His stories, as a result, are so telescoped and on occasion so erudite that they almost become intellectual puzzles.[208]

Among the moderns his own favorite writers have been H. G. Wells, G. K. Chesterton, Nathaniel Hawthorne, Joseph Conrad, Charles Dickens, Robert Louis Stevenson, and Henry James. He prefers James to Kafka, and English and North American literature to French or Spanish. The two writers he most reveres in history are Shakespeare and Cervantes. In a recent interview Borges remarked:

> Cervantes is one of the few Spanish authors I can imagine. I know, more or less, what a chat with him would be. I know, for example, how he might apologize for

some of the things he's written. How he wouldn't take himself too seriously. . . . I hardly ever get that feeling with Spanish books, or with Italian books. But I get that feeling all the time when I'm reading American or English literature.[207]

Borges deliberately confuses the dream and the reality. He is haunted by the labyrinths of life and history, by man's external return, by the universal present and by the microcosms of human knowledge and human experience, and by the constant blending of individual man with all mankind. His stories have opened a new corridor along which the reader may relentlessly pursue the search for his own identity.

Borges has spoken passionately of the deep sense of guilt that all Argentine intellectuals feel because they allowed the authoritarian Perón regime to become rooted in their country. Significantly, when the chips were down it was Borges' mother, and not Borges, who was put in jail for protesting against Perón in a street demonstration. Borges dedicated himself to producing fine literature, but it was a literature of escape. Gone was his early patriotic zeal expressed so well in a book of poetry written in 1923:

> I saw the pampas
> The only place on earth
> Where God can walk
> Without bending over.

Borges' stories have a tight metaphysical tone to them which engages both the intellect and the emotions. His central thesis is that since man is incapable of understanding the infinite labyrinth of the universe, he must spend his time fabricating labyrinths (and solutions) of his own. Each life, each work of literature or art is such an invention. Commenting on one of his books, *The Maker*, Borges wrote: "On the closing page of that book I told of a man who sets out to make a picture of the universe. After many years he has covered a blank wall with images of ships, towers, horses, weapons, and men, only to find out at the moment of his death that he has drawn a likeness of his own face."

In 1961 Borges paid his first visit to the United States, where he visited several universities, giving lectures and seminars. His comments on that visit are memorable: "I found America the friendliest, most forgiving, and most generous nation I have ever visited. We South Americans tend to think in terms of convenience, whereas people in the United States approach things ethically. This—amateur Protestant that I am—I admired above all. It even helped me overlook skyscrapers, paper bags, television, plastics, and the unholy jungle of gadgets."[218]

Second in the list of outstanding Argentine writers today is Eduardo Mallea (born in 1903). He began to write back in the 1920s, but it was not until his novellas *Fiesta in November* (1938) and *All Green Shall Perish* (1941) came out that he stepped into the front rank of contemporary novelists. Mallea's preoccupation is with the alienation of man, his inability to find any language but a cry, his singular feeling of emptiness in a world without faith. Mallea describes the agony of man's inward journey toward his abyss, "toward the almost inhuman source of his being, that return journey to the original solitude from which we all spring. . . ."[212] Suffering and authenticity are one, and Mallea's characters are alive to the extent that they are capable of suffering. The defeat of the tragic hero, of course, from the earliest days of Greek drama to the contemporary epoch, has always underlined the triumph of man, who looks death in the face and denies it all the way. Mallea writes with a concinnity and emotional intensity unequalled among contemporary authors. Here is a writer of world-wide significance who has never received proper recognition in the United States.

A third and younger Argentine writer of fiction, Julio Cortázar (born in 1914), long a resident of Paris, gained great praise from critics in the United States with his novels *The Winners* (1960), *Hopscotch* (1963), and his collections of short stories. Borges and Cortázar represent a sort of master and disciple relationship, with Cortázar taking a cue from the master and then striking out in all the new directions which are his especial bag. His novels do not make easy reading; Cortázar creates a world in which sexual episodes, drunken bouts, the drive to create, hallucinations, dreams, and loss intermingle dramatically as man, from his precarious brink, searches for the meaning of life and love, and for his authenticity.

Cortázar confuses and intrigues the reader by not observing either the canons of historical time or the limitations of physical reality. Individual human beings like individual stars have no idea that they are forming a constellation, but the constellations are obvious to the creative artist, and Cortázar seeks to give them a structure and a center of existence. The recent motion picture *Blow-Up* was based on one of Cortázar's short stories.

The Cuban novelist Alejo Carpentier (actually he was the son of a French architect and a Russian professor) was born in Havana in 1904. He died recently in France. Carpentier has written several outstanding novels, *The Lost Steps* (1953), *Manhunt* (1956), *Explosion in a Cathedral* (1962), and several incomparable short stories. *The Lost Steps* tells of a musicologist's journey to a primitive valley in the upper reaches of the Orinoco, where he finds a group of forest people living in the Stone Age. Here is sees religion, music, and dance all born again as he witnesses the original explosion of life into art. There are certain basic values rooted in the past which modern man has lost: authentic love, tolerance, honesty, understanding. The hero's life had become absurd without these values. This insight inspires him to a state of feverish creativity; he learns to love with complete abandon, finding in that love the dark roots of his own being. But after returning to civilization he tries to go back and is unable to find his lost paradise again, for all landmarks have vanished.

Man cannot repeat himself, he can never relive the same miracle, or recapture the lost dream. He belongs to his epoch and cannot escape it; only lost steps lead him back toward the mythological sources of human culture and art.

Explosion in a Cathedral (called *El siglo de las luces*, *The Century of En-*

lightenment, in its original Spanish version) is about the French Revolution, and Carpentier holds that all revolutions are chaotic and bloody, and those who lead them and believe in them inevitably are defeated, that old victims become new executioners, and that mankind makes a slow and precarious advance along the road of broken dreams, suffering, and death. When Carpentier's protagonist cries out that he had dreamed of something very different, he is answered: "Who asked you to believe in something that doesn't exist? One doesn't discuss a revolution, one makes it." Even the short-term defeat may thus become an eventual victory for those who are to follow.

An existential anguish permeates the contemporary literature of Latin America. The first step was a preoccupation with the alienation of man. Writers felt that fictional man, reflecting the malaise of his creators, did not know where he belonged. He was alone and lost; he could not communicate. The city separated him from nature, technocracy separated him from creativity, science separated him from God. Even the surrounding community was alien to him. Then, as if alienation were not enough, Latin American writers proceeded on to the fragmentation of man. The individual was torn apart; his little fragments were mercilessly disunited.

We begin to see both of these tendencies in Mallea, *All Green Shall Perish,* and in Yáñez, *The Edge of the Storm,* but we find them ominously present in Juan Rulfo, *Pedro Páramo,* and in Carlos Fuentes. Guatemala's Asturias, *Mulata* and *Men of Corn,* drinks at the same spring, but fabricates a contorted mythology of his own. Argentina's Cortázar makes a great ploy with the whole mad scene, and García Márquez of Colombia enjoys himself immensely ribbing those who take it all too much to heart. His A *Hundred Years of Solitude* may well become a world classic. Certainly, it is unique. There will never be another novel like it.

García Márquez creates an imaginary town which he calls Macondo in some far corner of Colombia. We see the town born, we see it live and repeat itself for six generations, then we see it die. Macondo is a microcosm of Latin American history, perhaps of human history. It represents the mythology of human experience, which repeats itself *ad infinitum,* outside the chronology of ordinary time. The inhabitants of Macondo have their own childish dream of life, miracles are an everyday occurrence in their experience. Flying carpets, a rainfall of birds, a girl assumed into heaven along with the sheets she is folding, and many other similar things.

A plague of insomnia hits the town and while the people do not suffer from their loss of sleep, they forget everything, even the names of the most common objects. They go about pasting names on these objects, again recreating their past out of pure invention. Does not every historian do the same? The author dramatizes the anguish and fear of losing the self. The human desire that things endure is pitted against the realization that they cannot last. Nature creates only in order to destroy her creatures, but people repeat themselves in their children.

The cyclic character of the universe and of man's history is basic in this novel which is a kind of parallel with the Bible: Genesis and the Apocalypse. Being mythic rather than realistic the novel embraces the universal experience of being human. It also embodies the spirit of poetry: where are the snows of yesteryear? And lastly, it dramatically states the dilemma of mankind who always forgets, rejects, or attempts to remake history.

Brazil also has produced much fine contemporary literature. João Guimarães Rosa (*Grande sertão*, 1956) rediscovers in the vastness of the *sertão* a symbolic land where all paths go and all paths converge, "the land of the soul." This book is called in English, *The Devil to Pay in the Backlands*. The private road of every man is there, but it is difficult for him to find it. All the same it is there. Otherwise life would be only a stupid mess. Every day, every moment, "there is only one act for us that's right and proper." It's hidden, but it's there. If it were not so, everything else would be false. Man dreams, and it's over, but he leaves an indelible stamp on the shapeless world before he has departed.[206]

The alienation and fragmentation of man is not limited to Latin America. The atom bomb has already exploded in man's soul. Günter Grass, *The Tin Drum*, in Germany, John Barth and John Updike in the United States, and the contemporary French novelists all show that the psychosis is world-wide. Marcel Proust, James Joyce, and John Dos Passos (the name is Portuguese) could not have known what kind of sickness they were stirring up only a few decades ago. No one has yet appeared to tell us if there is a cure.

In the Latin American scale of values creativity is more highly regarded than cash. For persons of humble origin it is often the only possible means of crossing the rigid caste barriers. When *Life in Spanish* held its short story contest in Latin America in 1960, more than three thousand manuscripts were received, and not one of these was by a professional writer, if by professional we mean a person who earns his living with his pen. The contestants were doctors, lawyers, teachers, clerks, journalists, politicians, dentists, social critics—always anything and everything but professional writers. The simple fact is that the market in Latin America seldom allows a professional to earn his living by writing alone, so he is obliged to undertake one, and often two or three, additional jobs.

This often gives to Latin American literature a certain lack of architectural tightness, because there is insufficient time for a scrupulous polishing and rewriting. But if tightness is sometimes lacking, vitality, a very down-to-earth vitality, is always present. The individual is placed in a position of perpetual tension against the backdrop of his epoch. The best writers have probed deeply into the heart of man and illuminate what is paramount and universal in human relationships. Today's author has come to realize the great truth of literature and of life: it is not the particular emotion or tragedy that is important to man, but emotion and tragedy itself, which twists and molds his being, whatever his social state. The attempt to universalize this anguish and this longing is the heart of all great literature.

Many persons have spoken of Latin America as a "last frontier." In a world of industrialized might it is indeed a last great reservoir of unexploited wealth. Arturo Frondizi, president of Argentina in 1958–62, put it this way: "The enormous potential of Latin America is dormant, while its people stumble in the crisis characteristic of countries which have not yet reached their full national development." But citizens of the southern countries resent more than anything else in the world the inference that their territories constitute a last frontier calling for some outsider to come and milk away its profits. They feel very strongly that it is first of all their frontier, and that the real future of any region lies not only in its undeveloped resources but in the growth of its people.

Latin America's last frontier is thus one of untapped resources, of unused man power, of undeveloped purchasing power, of untrained minds and hands. It is a frontier behind which the old colonial economy persists, where in every region the mountain of tradition obstructs the march toward a new horizon. It is an American frontier whose development is a responsibility to be shared by all the citizens of the hemisphere, for all shall profit when it has pushed beyond the pale of economic misery and political exploitation.

"We have more land than space for stars in the sky," wrote an Argentine poet a hundred years ago. Those words are as true today as when they were written. * But land, which is the nutriment of things that grow and the covering place upon all precious stores within the earth, chained man to its surface until the machine was discovered to set him free. Latin America is a land of men with few machines competing in a world where industry is king. She is a land where the vocal few have profited from the voiceless many.

In art, in literature, in music, in all of the spiritual values she has found her way. Sometimes these values speak with a strong folk voice which springs constantly and forever from the genius of a great people. Sometimes they are embodied in the works of gifted men who have reached out and touched the magic spring. But the body of Latin America is weak. In the bone and sinews of life, in cold economy and just government, she is still a land of unfulfilled promise.

Her great cities, as in the days of Alberdi, fringe upon the wilderness. Yet already the shadows of endless wings darken her skyways over deserts and mountain crags and trackless jungle. Their further concourse will surely bring into the orbit of modern life great new regions, peoples, and products. It may be in an expansion comparable to the opening of our West; it may be that a great part of two continents will be catapulted by air over the slow, earthbound growing pains of the nineteenth century into the air age of tomorrow.

---

* The Rockefeller report comments on the potential of Latin America as follows: "The grasslands of South America are one of the greatest sources of animal protein in the world. The tropical forests of the hemisphere represent one of the world's largest reamining timber reserves. A vast expanse of the richest land in all the world lies in a broad belt on the eastern slopes of the Andes . . . With existing modern scientific and technical knowledge, the other American nations *could* become one of the great food baskets of the world."[216]

There is no reason to say that the civilizations of the Old World are being eclipsed and may never again reach a new zenith, but there is every reason to believe that American civilization, North and South, stands upon the threshold of a new and magnificent achievement. Whatever fate willed it, geography has linked our Americas together for this flight of the future. An understanding of differences is the true beginning of every great co-operative endeavor, whether of friendship, marriage, or of the community of nations.

Americans of the North, though of many races, speak English, bear the imprint of Puritan stock, came to these shores willing to mold with the hands their measure of liberty. Our ancestors sought new homes and brought their wives and lived meagerly in the hope of their children. They worked hard, fought the Indians, swore by the Bible, built churches as new and shiny as their homes, but far less comfortable, and, on the whole, far less lovely. They had no cult of beauty; their lives were grim, so was their religion. A man in this world became what he made himself, with his own hands, his own mind, his own dreaming. It was a hard world which for many long years did not feel the divine frenzy of poem or picture. It was a world of slow birth, but of quick growing, of gigantic conception. It was a world which, as the Uruguayan Rodó said, might well have wished to see the Bible rewritten in order to place itself with Genesis on the front page. It was also a world of immense strength, a world in the making which has never yet been wholly wrought—a world of political oneness and liberty where material achievement, not culture, still marks the path of progress and measures the value of man.

Down south there was another world overcome by small bands of zealous conquistadores and proselyting friars. The epic of that conquest is one of the marvels of history. It was a world of no cleavage from Mother Iberia, no new homeseeking for self-rule or for personal liberty. It was an epic of expansion as only the amoeba and fire and man can expand by overflowing. It was a world of fusion, of slow growing, of slow attainment. But Iberia's overflowing was itself a fulfillment of her belief in God and glory, and her sons marched the length and breadth of two continents strewing monuments to His name. If that name was sometimes taken in vain, it was incidental to the process, not intrinsic. For the Spaniard and Portuguese believed that there are values above man's striving which form and lead him, and against which he is pitifully inadequate. This became on occasion a fit dodge for economic backwardness and for intolerance. It was also an expression of the light as he saw it, and he saw it lovely.

In this world of the priest and soldier, of the landholder and government official, of Indian and Negro mistress and slave, a man's worth came from his Church and his family, from without and beyond him, from the unalterable. He might sway or joggle the scales, but he could seldom change them for a weighing more to his own choosing. Caste was intrinsic to this process, and so was culture, which from the beginning thrived in those regions fertilized by the millions.

Then came the days of conflict with the old regime and the slow struggle toward the achievement of material growth and democratic liberties. In this struggle the United States lighted the way for the nations of the south. There was a real communion of spirit during those years of the New World's long and faltering childhood. It was followed, unfortunately, by separation, distrust, and the violences of immature actions. Now again by that dark miracle of chance which sometimes alters the destiny of men and of nations both Americas stand once more on the threshold together.

There is a legend that the path of civilization, our civilization, has been ever westward. Originating in the fabulous garden of the East, it has touched in turn Babylonia, Greece, Rome, western Europe, and last America. Even in the beginning America was a land of promise, and in this land the civilization and history of the South, the trials and aspirations of its governments, the visions of its artists, and the voices of its people speak out today louder than ever with the concord of their strength, with their immensity of hope, their colossus of promise.

References

1. Ríos, Fernando de los, *Iglesia y estado en la España del siglo XVI*, New York, 1927.
2. Morison, Samuel Eliot, *Admiral of the Ocean Sea*, Boston, 1942.
3. Hildebrand, J. R., "The Pathfinder of the East," article in *The National Geographic Magazine*, November 1927.
4. Ríos, Fernando de los, "Spain in the Epoch of American Colonization," article in *Concerning Latin American Culture*, New York, 1940.
5. Prescott, William H., *History of the Reign of Ferdinand and Isabella*, Philadelphia, 1874.
6. Machiavelli, Niccolo, *The Prince*, Oxford University Press, London.
7. Vaillant, George C., *Aztecs of Mexico*, rev. edition, New York, 1962.
8. Hewett, Edgar L., *Ancient Andean Life*, Indianapolis, 1939.
9. Morley, S. G., "Unearthing America's Ancient History," in *The National Geographic Magazine*, July 1931.
10. Cortés, Hernán, *Cartas de relación de la conquista de Méjico*, Madrid, 1922. (Translated in L. B. Simpson, page 26. See reference number 45.)
11. Morley, S. G., "The Foremost Intellectual Achievement of Ancient America," article in *The National Geographic Magazine*, February 1922.
12. Spinden, Herbert J., *Ancient Civilizations of Mexico and Central America*, New York, 1922.
13. Hewett, Edgar L., *Ancient Life in Mexico and Central America*, Indianapolis, 1936.
14. Verrill, A. Hyatt, *Old Civilizations of the New World*, New York, 1929.
15. Spinden, Herbert J., "Primitive Arts of the Old and New Worlds," article in *The Brooklyn Museum Quarterly*, October 1935.
16. Garcilaso de la Vega, Inca, *Comentarios reales*, edition of García Calderón and the Madrid edition of 1723.
17. Prescott, William H., *The Conquest of Peru*, Modern Library edition which appears in same volume with *Conquest of Mexico*, New York.
18. Squier, E. George, *Incidents of Travel and Exploration in the Land of the Incas*, New York, 1877.

19. Cook, O. F., "Staircase Farms of the Ancients," article in *The National Geographic Magazine*, May 1916.
20. Díaz del Castillo, Bernal, *Verdadera historia de la conquista de la Nueva España*, edition of Ramírez Cabañas. English translation of this work by Alfred P. Maudslay.
21. Prescott, William H., *The Conquest of Mexico*, edited by T. A. Joyce and illustrated by Keith Henderson, 2 vols., New York, 1922.
22. Levene, Ricardo, and Gandía, Enrique de, *Historia de América*, Vol. III, Buenos Aires, 1940.
23. Blanco Fombona, Rufino, *El conquistador español del siglo XVI*, Madrid, 1922.
24. Madariaga, Salvador, *Hernán Cortés*, Buenos Aires, 1941.
25. Bancroft, Hubert Howe, *A History of the Mexican People*, San Francisco, 1887.
26. Vasconcelos, José, *Breve historia de México*, Mexico City, 1937.
27. Chase, Stuart, *Mexico*, New York, 1935.
28. Carrión, Benjamín, *Atahuallpa*, Guayaquil, Ecuador, 1939.
29. Kirkpatrick, F. A., *The Spanish Conquistadores*, London, 1934.
30. Mitre, Bartolomé, *Historia de San Martín y de la emancipación sudamericana*, 6 vols., Buenos Aires, 1903–07.
31. Valdivia, Pedro, *Cartas de Don Pedro de Valdivia al emperador Carlos V*, from "Colección de documentos de historiadores de Chile," Santiago, 1861. Letters translated into English in *Pedro de Valdivia*, by R. B. Cunningham Graham, London, 1926.
32. Hayley, William, *Poems and Plays*, Vol. IV, London, 1785.
33. Díaz Meza, Aurelio, *Crónicas de la conquista*, II, Santiago, 1929.
34. Pereyra, Carlos, *Historia de la América española*, VIII, *Chile*, Madrid, 1925.
35. Arciniegas, Germán, *El caballero de El Dorado*, translated into English under title *The Knight of El Dorado*, New York, 1942.
36. Gil Fortoul, José, *Historia constitucional de Venezuela*, 3 vols., Caracas, 1930–32.
37. Graham, R. B. Cunningham, *The Conquest of New Granada*, New York, 1922.
38. Pereyra, Carlos, *Historia de la América española*, Vol. 6, Madrid, 1925.
39. Castellanos, Juan de, *Elegías de varones ilustres de Indias*, from Germán Arciniegas, *El caballero de El Dorado*, Buenos Aires, 1942.
40. Schmidl, Ulrico, *Derrotero y viaje a España y las Indias, traducido y comentado por Edmundo Wernicke*, Santa Fe, Argentina, 1938.
41. Graham, R. B. Cunningham, *Conquest of the River Plate*, New York, 1924.
42. Levene, Ricardo, *A History of Argentina*, English translation of *Lecciones de historia Argentina*, made by William Spence Robertson, Chapel Hill, North Carolina, 1937.
43. Galdames, Luis, *A History of Chile*, English translation of *Estudio de historia de Chile*, made by Isaac J. Cox, Chapel Hill, North Carolina, 1941.
44. Bourne, Edward Gaylord, *Spain in America*, New York, 1904.
45. Simpson, Lesley Byrd, *Many Mexicos*, New York, 1941.
46. Moses, Bernard, *Spain Overseas*, New York, 1929.
47. Means, Philip Ainsworth, *Fall of the Inca Empire, and the Spanish Rule in Peru*, New York, 1932.
48. Levillier, Roberto, *Don Francisco de Toledo*, Madrid, 1935.
49. Sánchez, Luis Alberto, *Historia de América*, Santiago, 1942.
50. Altamira y Crevea, Rafael, *Historia de España y de la civilización española*, Vol. 3, Barcelona, 1913–30.
51. Steinbeck, John, *Cup of Gold*, New York, 1939.
52. Graham, R. B. Cunningham, *A Vanished Arcadia*, New York, 1924.

53. Southey, Robert, *History of Brazil*, 3 vols., London, 1819–22.
54. *Cartas del Amazonas escritas por los misioneros de la Compañía de Jesús*, Bogotá, 1942.
55. Lea, H. C., *The Inquisition in the Spanish Dependencies*, New York, 1922.
56. Quevedo Villegas, Francisco de, *Pablo de Segovia*, introduction to English translation of same by H. E. Watts, New York, 1926.
57. Calogeras, João Pandiá, *A History of Brazil*, English translation of A *Formação historica do Brasil*, made by Percy Alvin Martin, Chapel Hill, North Carolina, 1939.
58. Schurz, William Lytle, *Latin America*, New York, 1942.
59. Verrill, A. Hyatt, *The American Indian*, New York, 1927.
60. Elliott, L. E., *Brazil Today and Tomorrow*, New York, 1917.
61. Oliveira Lima, Manoel de, *The Evolution of Brazil Compared with that of Spanish and Anglo-Saxon America*, Stanford University Press, 1914.
62. Priestley, Herbert I., *The Coming of the White Man*, New York, 1927.
63. Moses, Bernard, "Flush Times at Potosí," article in University of California *Chronicle*, July 1909.
64. Acarette du Biscay, *Relación de un viaje al Río de la Plata y de allí por tierra al Perú*, Spanish translation by Francisco Fernández Wallace, Buenos Aires, 1943; book appeared originally in French in 1672.
65. Lanning, John Tate, *Academic Culture in the Spanish Colonies*, New York, 1940.
66. Juan, Jorge, and Ulloa, Antonio de, A Voyage to South America, London, 1806.
67. Webster, Hutton, *History of Mankind*, Boston, 1928.
68. González, Peña, Carlos, *Historia de la literatura mexicana*, Mexico City, 1940.
69. Lorente, Sabastián, *Historia del Perú*, Lima, 1863.
70. Kirstein, Lincoln, *The Latin American Collection of the Museum of Modern Art*, including an essay on Latin-American art, New York, 1943.
71. Frank, Waldo, *South American Journey*, New York, 1943.
72. Valle-Arizpe, Artemio de, *Virreyes y virreinas de la Nueva España*, Madrid, 1933.
73. Phipps, Helen, *Some Aspects of the Agrarian Question in Mexico*, Austin, Texas, 1925.
74. Simpson, Eyler N., *The Ejido, Mexico's Way Out*, Chapel Hill, North Carolina, 1937.
75. Solar Correa, Eduardo, *Las tres colonias*, Santiago, 1943.
76. Amunátegui Solar, Domingo, *Formación de la nacionalidad chilena*, Santiago, 1943.
77. Díaz Meza, Aurelio, *En plena colonia*, Vol. 3, Santiago, 1930.
78. Priestley, Herbert I., *José de Gálvez*, Berkeley, California, 1916.
79. Mitre, Bartolomé, *Historia de Belgrano y de la independencia argentina*, Buenos Aires, 1913.
80. Gandía, Enrique de, *Francisco de Alfaro y la condición social de los indios, Río de la Plata, Paraguay, Tucumán y Perú*, Buenos Aires, 1939.
81. Freyre, Ricardo Jaimes, *El Tucumán del siglo XVI*, Buenos Aires, 1914.
82. Domínguez, Manuel Augusto, *Buenos Aires colonial*, Buenos Aires, 1943.
83. Concolorcorvo, *El lazarillo de ciegos caminantes desde Buenos Aires hasta Lima 1773*, Buenos Aires, 1942.
84. Freyre, Gilberto, *Casa-Grande e senzala*, fourth definitive edition, Rio de Janeiro, 1943.
85. Freyre, Gilberto, "Portuguese America," essay in *Concerning Latin American Culture*, New York, 1940.
86. Juan, Jorge, and Ulloa, Antonio, *Noticias secretas de América*, London, 1826.
87. Wiesse, Carlos, *Historia del Perú colonial*, Lima, 1927.

88. Arciniegas, Germán, *Los comuneros*, Bogotá, 1939.
89. Moses, Bernard, *South America on the Eve of Emancipation*, New York, 1908.
90. Henao, Jesús María, and Arrubla, Gerardo, *Compendio de la historia de Colombia*, Bogotá, 1943.
91. Robertson, William Spence, *Rise of the Spanish American Republics*, New York, 1918. (Quotations by permission of publisher.)
92. García Calderón, Francisco, *Latin America: Its Rise and Progress*, London, 1913.
93. Navarro Lamarca, Carlos, *Compendio de la historia general de América*, 2 vols., Buenos Aires, 1910.
94. Blanco Fombona, Rufino, *La evolución política y social de Hispano-América*, Madrid, 1911.
95. Pereyra, Carlos, *Historia de la América española*, Vol. 6, Madrid, 1925.
96. Bolívar, Simón, *Doctrina política: carta de Jamaica, discurso de Angostura, la constitución vitalicia*, Santiago, 1941.
97. Manchester, Alan K., *British Preeminence in Brazil*, Chapel Hill, North Carolina, 1933.
98. Oliveira Martins, J. P., *O Brazil e as colonias portuguezas*, Lisbon, 1920.
99. Williams, Mary Wilhelmine, *Dom Pedro the Magnanimous*, Chapel Hill, North Carolina, 1937.
100. Normano, J. F., *Brazil, a Study of Economic Types*, Chapel Hill, North Carolina, 1935.
101. Bezerra Cavalcanti, J. A., *Infancia e adolescencia de D. Pedro II*, Rio de Janeiro, 1925.
102. Harding, Bertita, *Amazon Throne, The Story of the Braganzas of Brazil*, Indianapolis and New York, 1941.
103. Carlyle, Thomas, *Critical and Miscellaneous Essays*, Vol. II, London, 1888.
104. Head, Captain F. B., *Rough Notes Taken During Some Rapid Journeys Across the Pampas*, London, 1826.
105. Azara, Félix de, *Viajes por la América meridional*, 2 vols., Madrid, 1923.
106. González, Manuel Pedro, *Trayectoria del gaucho y su cultura*, Havana, 1943.
107. Morales, Ernesto, *Lírica popular rioplatense, antología gaucha*, Buenos Aires, 1927.
108. Scarone, Arturo, *El Gaucho*, Montevideo, 1922.
109. Furt, Jorge M., *Cancionero popular rioplatense. Lírica gauchesca*, Vol. I, Buenos Aires.
110. Sarmiento, Domingo Faustino. *Facundo, Civilización y barbarie en la República Argentina*, Buenos Aires, 1938.
111. Tiscornia, E. F., edition of *Martin Fierro*, Buenos Aires, 1925.
112. Bunge, Carlos Octavio, *Nuestra América*, Buenos Aires, 1918.
113. Alberdi, Juan Bautista, *Bases para la organización política de la República Argentina*, Buenos Aires, 1910.
114. Palcos, Alberto, *Sarmiento. La vida, la obra, las ideas, el genio*, Buenos Aires, 1938.
115. Nichols, Madaline, *Sarmiento. A Chronicle of Inter-American Friendship*, Washington, 1940.
116. Ingenieros, José, *El hombre mediocre*, which includes an essay on Sarmiento, Buenos Aires, 1917.
117. García Prada, Carlos, *La personalidad histórica de Colombia*, Bucaramanga, 1936.
118. Uzcategui, Emilio, *Historia del Ecuador*, Quito, 1943.
119. Berthe, Father A., *García Moreno, President de l'Equateur*, Paris, 1888.
120. Barrera, Isaac, *Historia de la literatura hispanoamericana*, Quito, 1935.

121. Franklin, Albert, *Ecuador*, New York, 1943.
122. García Prada, Carlos, introduction to *González Prada, antología poética*, Mexico City, 1940.
123. Melfi, Domingo, *Dos hombres, Portales y Lastarria*, Santiago, 1937.
124. Crawford, William Rex, *A Century of Latin American Thought*, Cambridge, Massachusetts, 1961.
125. Woodward, W. E., *A New American History*, New York, 1938.
126. Adams, James Truslow, *The Epic of America*, New York, 1931.
127. Beals, Carleton, *Porfirio Díaz*, Philadelphia, 1932.
128. Robles, Fernando, *El santo que asesinó*, Mexico, 1936.
129. McBride, George M., *The Land Systems of Mexico*, New York, 1923.
130. Nerval, Gaston, *Autopsy of the Monroe Doctrine*, New York, 1934.
131. Pringle, Henry F., *Theodore Roosevelt, A Biography*, New York, 1931.
132. Nearing, Scott, and Freeman, Joseph, *Dollar Diplomacy*, New York, 1925.
133. O'Shaughnessy, Edith, *A Diplomat's Wife in Mexico*, New York, 1916.
134. Darío, Rubén, *Cantos de vida y esperanza*, 1905.
135. Aikman, Duncan, *The All-American Front*, New York, 1938.
136. Weil, Felix J., *Argentine Riddle*, New York, 1944.
137. Bureau of Labor Statistics, U.S. Dept. of Labor, and *South American Handbook*, 1969 issues.
138. Silva Herzog, Jesús, "La Revolución Mexicana en Crisis," article in *Cuadernos Americanos*, Mexico City, Sept.–Oct. 1943.
139. Azuela, Mariano, *The Underdogs*, English translation of *Los de abajo*, New York, 1929.
140. Guerrero Galván, Jesús, "A Mexican Painter Views Modern Mexican Painting," a pamphlet printed by the University of New Mexico Press, 1942.
141. Beals, Carleton, *Fire on the Andes*, Philadelphia, 1934.
142. Sanín Cano, Baldomero, introduction to *José Asunción Silva, Poesías*, Santiago, Chile, 1923.
143. Samper Ortega, Daniel, *Bogotá 1538–1938*, profusely illustrated, Bogotá, 1938.
144. Mecham, J. Lloyd, *Church and State in Latin America*, Chapel Hill, North Carolina, 1934.
145. Bunge, Alejandro E., *Una nueva Argentina*, Buenos Aires, 1940.
146. Welles, Sumner, *The Time for Decision*, New York, 1944.
147. Calmon, Pedro, *Historia social do Brasil*, II, Rio de Janeiro, 1940.
148. James, Preston, *Introduction to Latin America*, New York, 1964.
149. Lyra, Heitor, *Historia de Dom Pedro II*, Rio de Janeiro, 1938.
150. Creelman, James, *Díaz, Master of Mexico*, New York, 1911.
151. Magalhães, Basilio de, *Historia do Brasil*, Rio de Janeiro, 1942.
152. Orico, Osvaldo, *Hombres, de América*, Buenos Aires, 1943.
153. Ibarguren, Carlos, *Juan Manuel Rosas, su vida, su tiempo, su drama*, Buenos Aires, 1935.
154. John Gunther in *Inside Latin America*, and Katherine Carr in her *South American Primer*, both report this incident.
155. From *The Green Continent*, edited by Germán Arciniegas, which is a symposium of selections from Latin-American authors translated by Harriet de Onís and others, New York, 1944.
156. Ríos, Fernando de los, article entitled "The Action of Spain in America" in the book *Concerning Latin American Culture*, New York, 1940.
157. Arguedas, Alcides, *Pueblo enfermo*, Santiago de Chile, 1937.
158. Salas, Samuel J. A., Pauletto, Pedro I., and Salas, Pedro J. S., *Historia de la música América Latina*, Buenos Aires, 1938.

159. Cardeza, María Elena, *Historia de la música americana*, Buenos Aires, 1938.
160. Uribe White, Enrique, *Informe que el Director de la Biblioteca Nacional presenta a los miembros de la Comisión de Presupuesto de la H. Cámara de Representantes*, Bogotá, October 1942.
161. From Rippy, J. Fred, *Historical Evolution of Hispanic America*, New York, 1940.
162. Watters, Mary, *A History of the Church in Venezuela 1810–1930*, Chapel Hill, North Carolina, 1933.
163. Graham, R. B. Cunningham, *José Antonio Páez*, London, 1929.
164. *New York Herald*, April 17, 1876. See *Dom Pedro II in the United States*, scrapbook of clippings, Catholic University of America.
165. Sánchez Gómez, Gregorio, *Sociología política colombiana*, Cali, n.d.
166. Jones, Clarence F., *South America*, New York, 1930.
167. Milano, Miguel, *Heróis brasileiros*, Porto Alegre, 1943.
168. Buschiazzo, Mario J., "Indigenous Influences on the Colonial Architecture of Latin America," in *The Art of Latin America*, Pan American Union, Washington, D.C., 1942.
169. "Work of the South American Silversmith," in *The Art of Latin America*, Pan American Union, Washington, D.C., 1942.
170. "Latin American Painting Comes into its Own," article by Robert G. Smith, in *The Art of Latin America*, Pan American Union, Washington, D.C., 1942.
171. Henríquez-Ureña, Pedro, *Literary Currents in Hispanic America*, Cambridge, Massachusetts, 1945. (See number 176.)
172. Lugones, Leopoldo, *El imperio jesuítico*, Buenos Aires, 1904.
173. Menéndez, Oriel, *Bernardo Monteagudo*, Buenos Aires, 1943.
174. Henao, J. M., and Arrubla, Gerardo, *History of Colombia*, translated into English by J. Fred Rippy, Chapel Hill, North Carolina, 1938.
175. Quintanilla, Luis, *A Latin American Speaks*, New York, 1943.
176. Cunha, Euclides da, *Rebellion in the Backlands*, translation of *Os Sertões* by Samuel Putnam, Chicago, 1944.
177. Vargas, Fray José María, *Arte quiteño colonial*, Quito, 1945.
178. Soule, Efron, and Ness, *Latin America in the Future World*, New York, 1945.
179. Morley, S. G., and Brainerd, George, *The Ancient Maya*, Stanford University, 1956.
180. McDowell, Bart, and Stewart, B. Anthony, "Mexico's Window on the Past," *The National Geographic*, October 1968. Map of ancient Indian civilizations by George Stewart and Ignacio Bernal, Director of Museum of Anthropology, Mexico.
181. Gamboa, Fernando, various articles in *Master Works of Mexican Art*, pub. of Los Angeles County Museum of Art, January 1964.
182. Paz, Octavio, "El partido gubernamental es un obstáculo para el desarrollo del país," originally appeared in *Le Monde*, Paris, November 13, 1968.
183. Botsford, Keith, "Mexico follows solo camino," in the New York *Times*, April 26, 1964.
184. Ramos, Samuel, *Profile of Man and Culture in Mexico*, Austin, Texas, 1962.
185. Lewis, Oscar, *The Children of Sanchez*, New York, 1961.
186. Reyes, Alfonso, *Mexico in a Nutshell*, Berkeley, California, 1964.
187. New York *Times*, June 16, 1968, article by Henry Giniger, "Guatemala is a battleground."
188. Galeano, Eduardo, "With the Guerillas in Guatemala," article in *Latin America: Reform or Revolution*, ed. by James Petras and Maurice Zeitlin, Greenwich, Connecticut, 1968.

189. Cosío Villegas, Daniel, *American Extremes* (*Extremos de América*), Austin, Texas, 1964.
190. Tannenbaum, Frank, "Fidel Castro," essay in *Latin American Panorama*, ed. by Paul Kramer and Robert McNicoll, New York, 1968.
191. González, Luis J. and Sánchez, Gustavo A., *The Great Rebel*, New York, 1968.
192. Kidd, Paul, "The Price of Achievement under Castro," article in *The Saturday Review*, May 3, 1969.
193. "Report on Peru," article in *The Atlantic*, May 1969, by Ward S. Just.
194. "Letter from Peru," article in *The New Yorker*, May 17, 1969, by Richard N. Goodwin, one of the originators of the Alliance for Progress. It was Goodwin who conceived the phrase. He was a leading member of the White House staff under President Kennedy.
195. Subercaseaux, Benjamín, *Chile: a Geographic Extravaganza*, New York, 1943.
196. Martínez Estrada, Ezequiel, *Radiografía de la pampa*, Buenos Aires, 1933.
197. *The South American Handbook*, forty-fifth annual edition, 1969, published by Trade and Travel Publications, Ltd., London.
198. Clark, Gerald, *The Coming Explosion in Latin America*, New York, 1962.
199. González, Alfonso, "Some effects of population growth," article in *Latin American Panorama*, ed. by Paul Kramer and Robert McNicoll, New York, 1968.
200. Illich, Ivan, "The Futility of Schooling in Latin America," *The Saturday Review*, April 20, 1968. Illich, who now works in Cuernavaca, was formerly vice-president of the Catholic University of Puerto Rico.
201. Stevens, Evelyn F., "Mexican Machismo: Politics and Value Orientations," chapter in *Latin American Panorama*, ed. by Paul Kramer and Robert McNicoll, New York, 1968.
202. Herring, Hubert, *A History of Latin America*, New York, 1968.
203. Magnet, Alejandro, "Armamentismo y desarme en América Latina," in *Política*, Caracas, Venezuela, February 1960.
204. Betancourt, Rómulo, *Posición y doctrina*, Caracas, 1959.
205. Santos, Eduardo, "The Defense of Freedom in Latin America," essay in *Responsible Freedom in Latin America*, ed. by Angel del Río, New York, 1955.
206. Harss, Luis, and Dohmann, Barbara, *Into the Mainstream* (Conversations with Latin-American Writers), New York, 1966.
207. Burgin, Richard, *Conversations with Jorge Luis Borges*, New York, 1969.
208. Borges, Jorge Luis, *Labyrinths, Selected Stories and Other Writings*, preface by André Maurois, New York, 1964.
209. Gunther, John, *Inside South America*, New York, 1967.
210. Castro, Américo, *On the Relations Between the Americas*, Pan American Union, Washington, D.C., bound pamphlet, n.d.
211. Paz, Octavio, *El laberinto de la soledad*, Mexico, 1950.
212. Mallea, Eduardo, *All Green Shall Perish*, New York, 1966.
213. "Supply, Demand, and the Brain Drain," by Nuri Eren, *The Saturday Review*, August 2, 1969.
214. Los Angeles *Times*, June 8, 1969, David Belnap.
215. Sommers, Joseph, *After the Storm*, Albuquerque, 1968. The Passage quoted was translated by Sommers.
216. Rockefeller, Nelson A., *The Rockefeller Report on the Americas*, Chicago, 1969.
217. Crow, John A., *Mexico Today*, New York, 1971.
218. "Profiles (Jorge Luis Borges)," in *The New Yorker*, September 19, 1970.
219. "Mexico's Oil Bonanza," in *Newsweek*, August 14, 1978.
220. "Mexico: New Era of Challenge," in *National Geographic*, May 1978.

221. "Mexico's Squatters Hoist Maoist Banner," in Los Angeles *Times*, August 30, 1978.
222. "Mexico's Oil Bonanza," in *Newsweek*, February 19, 1979.
223. "Nicaragua: the Latin American Dimension," in *Latin America, Political Report*, London, July 27, 1979.
224. "Castro's Cuba and the Romantic Left," by Steve Wasserman, in Los Angeles *Times*, September 17, 1978.
225. "Cuba's Lean Revolution Puts on Weight," by Mark Pinsky, *Christian Science Monitor*, June 1, 1979.
226. "Castro's Revolution is Secure With Help From a Friendly Russian Bear," by Jorge I. Domínguez, in Los Angeles *Times*, January 7, 1979.
227. "Petroleum and Natural Gas," in *Colombia Today*, Colombian Information Service, New York, Vol. 14, no. 2, 1979.
228. "Smuggling Out the Truth on Paraguay's Economy," in *Latin America, Economic Report*, London, June 2, 1978.
229. "Uruguayan Farmers Denounce Agricultural Stagnation," in *Latin America, Economic Report*, London, June 2, 1978.
230. "The Amazon Bonanza," in *Newsweek*, January 15, 1979.
231. "Tropical Rain Forests," by Robert A. Jones, in Los Angeles *Times*, May 7, 8, 9, 1979.
232. Robert A. Jones, in a personal letter to the author.
233. "Jari: poison or healthy medicine," in *Latin America, Economic Report*, London, July 13, 1979.
234. *Christian Science Monitor*, August 28, 1979.
235. Los Angeles *Times*, February 18, 1979.
236. From the book *Buenos Aires*, ed. H. Ernest Lewald, Houghton Mifflin, Boston, 1968.
237. James Nelson Goodsell, on "Argentina," in *Christian Science Monitor*, October 13, 1978.
238. "Brazil's Golden Beachhead," in *National Geographic*, February 1978.
239. "The Newest Superstate," in *Newsweek*, April 10, 1978.
240. "Latin America To Be World's Fastest Growing Area," in *Latin America, Economic Report*, July 27, 1979.
241. *South American Handbook*, 1979 edition, (55th annual edition), edited by John Brooks and Joyce Candy, Trade and Travel Publications, Bath, England.
242. "Un nuevo plan para América: Latinoamérica más allá del despegue," by Walt W. Rostow, in *Américas*, February 1979.
243. "Energy Costs Still Slow Latin American Growth," by James Nelson Goodsell, in the *Christian Science Monitor*, September 12, 1978.
244. "MEXICO: Crisis of Poverty, Crisis of Wealth." This is a 32 page special supplement on Mexico, by several authors, in the Los Angeles *Times*, July 15, 1979.
245. Riding, Alan, *Distant Neighbors*, New York, 1986.
246. *El Excelsior*, Mexico City, January 19, 1988.
247. *El Excelsior*, Mexico City, January 2, 1988.
248. *La Opinión*, Los Angeles, September 9, 1987.
249. *New York Times*, "Will debt plan for Mexico work?," January 10, 1988.
250. *Insight*, "Clinging to power in moral morass," October 5, 1987.
251. *Wall Street Journal*, "Mexico's capital reserves," September 10, 1987.
252. *New York Review of Books*, "Nicaragua," October 8, 1987.
253. Simon, Jean Marie, *Guatemala*, New York, 1988.
254. *New York Times*, "Oscar Arias," magazine section, January 10, 1988.

255. *Insight*, "Unrest jars Noriega's military rule," July 13, 1987. Also, *Newsweek*, August 24, 1987.
256. *Amnesty Action*, "Repression in Panama," January-February 1988.
257. *Time*, "Cuban defectors," September 21, 1987.
258. Brock, David, "Semper Fidel The Cuban ruler's bitter legacy," in *Insight*, February 29, 1988.
259. *Newsweek*, "Assassination of Hoyos," February 8, 1988.
260. Bonner, Raymond, "Peru," long article on the *Shining Path*, in *The New Yorker*, January 4, 1988.
261. *Colombia Today*, vol. 22, no. 3, 1987.
262. Timerman, Jacobo, *Chile: death in the south*, New York, 1987.
263. *Insight*, "What about Chile?" August 24, 1987.
264. *La Nación*, Buenos Aires, "La crisis militar," January 5, 1988.
265. Timerman, Jacobo, *Prisoner without a name*, New York, 1981.
266. *La Nación*, Buenos Aires, August 2, 1986.
267. *La Nación*, Buenos Aires, "La deuda no es negociable," September 1, 1986.
268. *Insight*, "Brazil on Hold," August 17, 1987.
269. Kissinger, Henry, "Brazil's Crisis," *Los Angeles Times*, May 24, 1987.
270. *Insight*, "Third World Loans," August 31, 1987.
271. "La selva," Tropical Forest Project, World Resources International, *National Geographic*, May 1986.
272. *Los Angeles Times*, "Latin American Debt," December 23, 1987.
273. *La Opinión*, Los Angeles, "Nuevas epidemias," September 19, 1987.
274. Hamill, Peter, "Love and Solitude," an interview with García Márquez, in *Vanity Fair*, March 1988.
275. Schoultz, Lars, *National Security and the United States Policy Toward Latin America*, Princeton, 1987.
276. Harvey, Robert, *Fire Down Below*, New York, 1989.
277. Black, George, *How the United States Wrote the History of Central America and the Caribbean*, New York, 1989.
278. Meyer, Doris, ed., *Lives on the Line*, the testimony of Latin American authors, Berkeley, Los Angeles, London, 1989.
280. Booth, John A., and Thomas Walker, *Understanding Central America*, Boulder, Colo., 1989.
281. Pastor, Robert A., *Condemned to Repetition: the United States and Nicaragua*, Princeton, 1988.
282. Lewis, Paul H., *The Crisis of Argentine Capitalism*, Chapel Hill, N.C., 1989.
283. Lang, James, *Inside Development in Latin America*, Chapel Hill, N.C., 1989.
284. Eddy, Paul, *The Cocaine Wars*, with Hugo Sabogal and Sara Walden, New York, 1989.
285. Gugliotti, Guy, and Jeff Leen, *Kings of Cocaine*, inside the Medellín Cartel, New York, 1989.
286. Shannon, Elaine, *Desperadoes: Latin American Drug Lords*, New York, 1989.
287. Sklar, Holly, *Washington's War on Nicaragua*, Boston, 1988.
288. Eich, Dieter, and Carlos Rincon, *The Contras*, San Francisco, 1985.
289. Acker, Alison, *Honduras*, Boston, 1988.
290. Davis, Peter, *Where is Nicaragua*, New York, 1987.
291. Edmisten, Patricia Taylor, *Nicaragua Divided*, Gainesville, Fla., 1990.
292. de Soto, Hernando, *The Other Path*, Harper and Row, 1989.
293. Kandell, Jonathan, *La Capital*, the biography of Mexico City, New York, 1988.
294. "Noriega on Ice," *Time*, January 15, 1990.

295. Timerman, Jacobo, "Reflections on Cuba," *The New Yorker*, August 13, 1990.
296. Van Evera, Stephen, "The Case Against Intervention," *The Atlantic*, July 1990.
297. "Economic Integration in Latin America," *Los Angeles Times*, October 8, 1989.
298. Kissinger, Henry A., "Latin America: Growing Debt, Growing Pains," *Los Angeles Times*, January 8, 1989.
299. Rodríguez, Richard, "A Continental Shift, Latin Americans Convert to Protestantism," *Los Angeles Times*, August 13, 1989.
300. "Big State Owned Companies for Sale," *Time*, June 18, 1990.
301. Adams, Robert M., "Liberators," an essay on several novels by García Márquez and Vargas Llosa, *New York Review of Books*, October 11, 1990.
302. Stoll, David, *Is Latin America Turning Protestant*, Berkeley, Los Angeles, Oxford, 1990.
303. Eckstein, Susan, *Power and Popular Protest*, Latin American Social Movements, Berkeley, Los Angeles, Oxford, 1990.

BIBLIOGRAPHICAL ESSAY

For those who have a general interest in Latin America and would like further references in this area the annual *Handbook of Latin American Studies*, compiled by leading scholars in the field and published by the University of Florida Press, gives a selective bibliography of current works in each of the pertinent categories of Latin American life: literature, art, political science, economics, geography, history, folklore, and so on. Each title listed in the bibliographies is critically evaluated by a specialist. Another annual publication is the excellent *South American Handbook*, now in its 68th year, edited by John Brooks and Joyce Candy, which is published in England. This handbook also includes Mexico and Central America. The editors make every attempt to keep their reports accurate and current, and for updated information rely heavily on well-established residents in each country. This book includes information on sight-seeing, hotels, highways, travel, restaurants, museums, and the like. The most detailed and objective report on what is happening in Latin America today is found in the weekly *Latin American Newsletters*, published in London. These reports include the most recent data available on politics, economics, and commodities. The newsletters appear in three separate bulletins which carry the subtitles: *Political Report, Economic Report, Commodities Report*.

Additional information may be found in the following: *Statistical Abstract of Latin America*, ed. James W. Wilkie, SALA, vol. 25, 1988, University of California, Los Angeles; *The Cambridge History of Latin America*, ed. Leslie Bethell, 5 vols., Cambridge University Press; *The Times of the Americas*, published fortnightly in Washington; *Americas*, a monthly journal published by The Organization of American States, Washington; the annual published reports of the Inter-American Development Bank, Washington; *Inter-American Affairs*, Washington; *Latin American Perspectives*, published four times a year in Riverside, California; *Latin American Research Review*, issued three times yearly, by the University of North Carolina, Chapel Hill; *The Hispanic American Historical Review*, a scholarly journal, published by Duke University,

Durham, N.C. Among the daily newspapers published in the United States, *La Opinión*, the Spanish language daily of Los Angeles, gives very broad and objective coverage on all of Latin America, as does *La Prensa* of New York. Some individual countries maintain information centers that periodically distribute reports on recent developments. *Colombia Today* and *Brazil Today* are two of the best. Among the English language dailies the *New York Times*, the *Los Angeles Times*, and *The Christian Science Monitor*, Boston, have special reporters in the Latin American field. The University of California Press is in the process of publishing a major new series on "Latinos in American Society and Culture." Three volumes have already been submitted for publication.

Acknowledgments

Special gratitude is due to Germán Arciniegas, Gilberto Freyre, Fernando de los Ríos, Waldo Frank, John Tate Lanning, Samuel Eliot Morison, Lesley Byrd Simpson, and to W. T. Couch for permission to quote from copyrighted works whose titles appear in full in the bibliography which follows. Several publishing companies, also listed, kindly granted the same permission. I also wish to express here, for I do not know of a better place, my deepest gratefulness to my father, George Davis Crow, who read this entire manuscript with loving care.

While the greater part of the reading and research done in preparation for this book was necessarily carried out in Spanish and Portuguese, there are also available in English several outstanding works on particular Latin-American countries or subjects which might be of interest to the general reader. The University of North Carolina Press, Chapel Hill, has published in English histories of several Latin American countries by leading scholars of those countries. The University of Texas Press, Austin, has published Agustín Yáñez, *The Edge of the Storm*; Samuel Ramos, *Profile of Man and Culture in Mexico*; Daniel Cosío Villegas, *American Extremes*. The University of Oklahoma Press has put out Alfonso Caso, *The Aztecs*, 1958; B. C. Brundage, *Empire of the Inca*, 1963; Leopoldo Zea, *The Latin American Mind*, 1963. The University of California Press has J. Cruz Costa, *A History of Ideas in Brazil*, 1964; F. P. Ellison, *Brazil's New Novel*, 1962; Mariano Picón Salas, *A Cultural History of Spanish America*, 1963.

By far the most complete bibliography in the Latin American field is that published yearly in *The Handbook of Latin American Studies*, University of Florida Press. Other works of special interest are: Américo Castro, *The Structure of Spanish History*, 1954; Ignacio Bernal, *Mexico Before Cortés*, 1963; Hubert Herring, *A History of Latin America*, 1968; Germán Arciniegas, *Latin Amer-*

ica: A Cultural History, 1966; W. L. Schurz, *Latin America: A Descriptive Survey,* 1963; *Latin American Politics,* a bibliography, ABC-CLIO Information Services, 1986; *Labor in Latin America,* Charles Bergquist, 1986; *Latin America and the World Recession,* ed. Esperanza Durán, 1986.

Works quoted, whose titles the publishers wished to appear in a particular form, are listed herewith as well as in the references:

4. Reprinted from Griffin, *Concerning Latin American Culture,* by permission of Columbia University Press.

8. From *Ancient Andean Life,* by Edgar L. Hewett, copyright 1939. Used by special permission of the publishers, The Bobbs-Merrill Company.

13. From *Ancient Life in Mexico and Central America,* by Edgar L. Hewett, copyright 1936. Used by special permission of the publishers, The Bobbs-Merrill Company.

85. and 156. Same as number 4 above; see References for specific essays cited.

184. Ramos, Samuel, *Profile of Man and Culture in Mexico,* Austin, 1962. Permission to quote given by University of Texas Press.

185. Lewis, Oscar, *The Children of Sanchez,* New York, 1961. Permission to quote given by Random House, Inc. Copyright 1961 by Oscar Lewis.

186. Reyes, Alfonso, *Mexico in a Nutshell,* Berkeley, 1964. Quotation reprinted by permission of The Regents of the University of California.

189. Cosío Villegas, Daniel, *American Extremes,* Austin, 1964. Permission to quote given by University of Texas Press.

Index